Oriental Despotism

A COMPARATIVE STUDY OF TOTAL POWER

Oriental Despotism

A COMPARATIVE STUDY OF TOTAL POWER

by Karl A. Wittfogel

10489

New Haven: YALE UNIVERSITY PRESS, 1957

NOTE

For permission to quote from the following works the author is very
grateful: H. Idris Bell, *Egypt from Alexander the Great to the Arab
Conquest*, Oxford, Oxford University Press, 1948; J. A. Dubois, *Hindu
Manners, Customs and Ceremonies*, tr. and ed. Henry K. Beauchamp,
Oxford, the Clarendon Press, 1943; Dwight D. Eisenhower, *Crusade
in Europe*, Garden City, Long Island, Doubleday, 1948; *Kauṭilya's
Arthāśāstra*, tr. R. Shamasastry, 2d ed. Mysore, Wesleyan Mission
Press, 1923; S. N. Miller, "The Army and the Imperial House," in
Cambridge Ancient History, Cambridge, England, Cambridge Uni-
versity Press, 1939; Vincent A. Smith, *Oxford History of India*, Ox-
ford, the Clarendon Press, 1928; W. W. Tarn, *Hellenistic Civilization*,
London, Edward Arnold, 1927; Alfred M. Tozzer, *Landa's Relacion
de las Cosas de Yucatan*, Papers of the Peabody Museum of American
Archaeology and Ethnology, Cambridge, Harvard University, 1941;
John A. Wilson, "Proverbs and Precepts: Egyptian Instructions," in
Ancient Near Eastern Texts, ed. James B. Pritchard, Princeton,
Princeton University Press, 1950.

ACKNOWLEDGMENTS

A COMPARATIVE STUDY of total power, when it is based on documentary evidence for the institutional peculiarities of the East and the West, requires time, patience, and much friendly help. I am profoundly indebted to the Far Eastern and Russian Institute of the University of Washington for enabling me to engage in the diverse research that constitutes the factual basis of the present book. As co-sponsor of the Chinese History Project, New York, Columbia University provided facilities of office and library. For a number of years the Rockefeller Foundation supported the over-all project of which this study was an integral part. Grants given by the American Philosophical Society and the Wenner-Gren Foundation for Anthropological Research made possible the investigation of special aspects of Oriental despotism.

Scholars from various disciplines have encouraged my efforts. Without attempting to list them all, I mention in gratitude Pedro Armillas, Pedro Carrasco, Chang Chung-li, Nathan Glazer, Waldemar Gurian, Hsiao Kung-chuan, Marius B. Jansen, Isaac Mendelsohn, Karl Menges, Franz Michael, George P. Murdock, Angel Palerm, Julian H. Steward, Donald W. Treadgold, Hellmut Wilhelm, and C. K. Yang. I have been privileged to discuss crucial problems with two outstanding students of modern totalitarianism: Bertram D. Wolfe and Peter Meyer.

In the field of the Muslim and pre-Muslim Near East I was particularly aided in my researches by Gerard Salinger. In the realm of Chinese studies I drew upon the knowledge of Chaoying Fang, Lienche Tu Fang, Lea Kisselgoff, and Tung-tsu Chu, all of whom were, at the time of writing, on the staff of the Chinese History Project. Bertha Gruner carefully typed and checked the first draft of an analysis of Russian society and the Marxist-Leninist attitude toward Oriental despotism, intended originally as a separate publication but eventually included in significant part in the present volume. Ruth Ricard was indefatigable in preparing the manuscript, which offered many problems of form, source material, and bibliography.

An inquiry into the nature of bureaucratic totalitarianism is bound to encounter serious obstacles. Among those who helped in overcoming them, two persons must be mentioned particularly. George E. Taylor, director of the Far Eastern and Russian Institute of the University of Washington, never wavered in his understanding of my endeavors and in his support for what seemed at times beyond hope of completion. My wife and closest collaborator, Esther S. Goldfrank, shared every step in the struggle for the clarification of basic scientific truths and human values.

It was my belief in these values that put me behind the barbed wire of Hitler's concentration camps. My final thoughts go to those who, like myself, were passing through that inferno of total terror. Among them, some hoped for a great turning of the tables which would make them guards and masters where formerly they had been inmates and victims. They objected, not to the totalitarian means, but to the ends for which they were being used.

Others responded differently. They asked me, if ever opportunity offered, to explain to all who would listen the inhumanity of totalitarian rule in any form. Over the years and more than I can express, these men have inspired my search for a deeper understanding of the nature of total power.

KARL A. WITTFOGEL
University of Washington, Seattle

New York, July 1955

CONTENTS

INTRODUCTION

1.

WHEN in the 16th and 17th centuries, in consequence of the commercial and industrial revolution, Europe's trade and power spread to the far corners of the earth, a number of keen-minded Western travelers and scholars made an intellectual discovery comparable to the great geographical exploits of the period. Contemplating the civilizations of the Near East, India, and China, they found significant in all of them a combination of institutional features which existed neither in classical antiquity nor in medieval and modern Europe. The classical economists eventually conceptualized this discovery by speaking of a specific "Oriental" or "Asiatic" society.

The common substance in the various Oriental societies appeared most conspicuously in the despotic strength of their political authority. Of course, tyrannical governments were not unknown in Europe: the rise of the capitalist order coincided with the rise of absolutist states. But critical observers saw that Eastern absolutism was definitely more comprehensive and more oppressive than its Western counterpart. To them "Oriental" despotism presented the harshest form of total power.

Students of government, such as Montesquieu, were primarily concerned with the distressing personal effects of Oriental despotism, students of economy with its managerial and proprietary range. The classical economists particularly were impressed by the large water works maintained for purposes of irrigation and communication. And they noted that virtually everywhere in the Orient the government was the biggest landowner.[1]

These were extraordinary insights. They were, in fact, the starting point for a systematic and comparative study of total power. But no such study was undertaken. Why? Viewed alone, the social scientists' withdrawal from the problem of Oriental despotism is puzzling. But it is readily understandable when we consider the changes that occurred in the 19th century in the general circumstances of Western life. Absolutism prevailed in Europe when Bernier described his experiences in the Near East and Mogul India and when Montesquieu wrote *The Spirit of the Laws*. But by the middle of the 19th century representative governments were established in almost all industrially advanced countries. It was then that social science turned to what seemed to be more pressing problems.

1

2.

FORTUNATE AGE. Fortunate, despite the sufferings that an expanding industrial order imposed on masses of underprivileged men and
women. Appalled by their lot, John Stuart Mill claimed in 1852
that "the restraints of Communism would be freedom in comparison
with the present situation of the majority of the human race." [2]
But he also declared that the modern property-based system of
industry, outgrowing its dismal childhood, might well satisfy man's
needs without grinding him down into "a tame uniformity of
thoughts, feelings, and actions." [3]

Fortunate age. Its ever-critical children could combat the fragmented despotism of privilege and power, because they did not live
under a system of "general slavery." [a] Indeed they were so far removed from the image of absolutist power that they felt no urge to
study its substance. Some, such as Max Weber, did examine illuminatingly, if not too systematically, certain aspects of Oriental statecraft and bureaucracy. But by and large, what Bury said at the close
of the period of liberalism was true: little effort was made to determine the peculiarities of absolutism through detailed comparative
study. [4]

Fortunate age. Optimistic age. It confidently expected the rising
sun of civilization to dispel the last vestiges of despotism that beclouded the path of progress.

3.

BUT the high noon has failed to fulfill the promises of the dawn.
Political and social earthquakes more terrifying than any that
previously shook the homelands of modern science make it painfully
clear that what has been won so far is neither safe nor certain. Total
power, far from meekly withering away, is spreading like a virulent
and aggressive disease. It is this condition that recalls man's previous
experience with extreme forms of despotic rule. It is this condition
that suggests a new and deepened analysis of Oriental—or as I now
prefer to call it, hydraulic—society.

4.

FOR three decades I studied the institutional settings of Oriental
despotism; and for a considerable part of this time I was content
to designate it "Oriental society." But the more my research ad-

a. Marx (1939: 395) applied this term to Oriental despotism without realizing that
more comprehensive forms of state slavery might emerge under conditions of industry.

vanced, the more I felt the need for a new nomenclature. Distinguishing as I do between a farming economy that involves small-scale
irrigation (hydroagriculture) and one that involves large-scale and
government-managed works of irrigation and flood control (hydraulic agriculture), I came to believe that the designations "hydraulic
society" and "hydraulic civilization" express more appropriately
than the traditional terms the peculiarities of the order under discussion. The new nomenclature, which stresses institutions rather
than geography, facilitates comparison with "industrial society" and
"feudal society." And it permits us, without circumstantial reasoning,
to include in our investigation the higher agrarian civilizations of
pre-Spanish America as well as certain hydraulic parallels in East
Africa and the Pacific areas, especially in Hawaii. By underlining
the prominent role of the government, the term "hydraulic," as I define it, draws attention to the agromanagerial and agrobureaucratic
character of these civilizations.

5.

THE present inquiry goes considerably beyond the findings of the
early students of Oriental society. In the following pages I endeavor
to describe systematically man's hydraulic response to arid, semi-
arid, and particular humid environments. I also indicate how the
major aspects of hydraulic society interlock in a vigorously functioning institutional going concern.

This going concern constitutes a geo-institutional nexus which
resembles industrial society in that a limited core area decisively
affects conditions in large interstitial and peripheral areas. In many
cases these marginal areas are politically connected with hydraulic
core areas; but they also exist independently. Manifestly, the
organizational and acquisitive institutions of the agrodespotic state
can spread without the hydraulic institutions which, to judge from
the available data, account for the genesis of all historically significant
zones of agrarian despotism. An understanding of the relations
between the core and the margin of hydraulic society—a phenomenon barely noted by the pioneer analysts—is crucially important for an understanding of Western Rome, later Byzantium,
Maya civilization, and post-Mongol (Tsarist) Russia.

In the matter of private property the early institutionalists were
satisfied to indicate that the Oriental state controlled the strategic
means of production, and most importantly the cultivable land. The
real situation is much more complicated and, from the standpoint
of societal leadership, much more disturbing. History shows that in

many hydraulic societies there existed very considerable active (productive) private property; but it also shows that this development did not threaten the despotic regimes, since the property holders, as property holders, were kept disorganized and politically impotent.

Obviously, too much has been said about private property generally and too little about strong and weak property and about the conditions which promote these forms. The analysis of the varieties of private property in hydraulic society determines the limitations of nonbureaucratic (and of bureaucratic) private property under Oriental despotism. Its results contradict the belief that practically any form of avowedly benevolent state planning is preferable to the predominance of private property, a condition which modern sociological folklore deems most abhorrent.

And then there is the problem of class. Richard Jones and John Stuart Mill indicated that in Oriental society the officials enjoyed advantages of income which in the West accrued to the private owners of land and capital. Jones and Mill expressed a significant truth. But they did so only in passing and without stating clearly that under agrodespotic conditions the managerial bureaucracy was the ruling class. They therefore did not challenge the widely accepted concept of class which takes as its main criterion diversities in (active) private property.

The present inquiry analyzes the patterns of class in a society whose leaders are the holders of despotic state power and not private owners and entrepreneurs. This procedure, in addition to modifying the notion of what constitutes a ruling class, leads to a new evaluation of such phenomena as landlordism, capitalism, gentry, and guild. It explains why, in hydraulic society, there exists a *bureaucratic* landlordism, a *bureaucratic* capitalism, and a *bureaucratic* gentry. It explains why in such a society the professional organizations, although sharing certain features with the guilds of Medieval Europe, were societally quite unlike them. It also explains why in such a society supreme autocratic leadership is the rule.[5] While the law of diminishing administrative returns determines the lower limit of the bureaucratic pyramid, the cumulative tendency of unchecked power [6] determines the character of its top.

6.

THE PROPONENT of new scientific ideas unavoidably discards old ideas. Almost as unavoidably he will be criticized by those who defend the old position. Not infrequently such a controversy throws new light on the entire issue. This has certainly been the case with the theory of Oriental (or hydraulic) society.

The reader will not be surprised to learn that this theory has aroused the passionate hostility of the new total managerial bureaucracy that, in the name of Communism, today controls a large part of the world's population. The Soviet ideologists, who in 1931 declared the concept of Oriental society and a "functional" ruling bureaucracy politically impermissible, no matter what the "pure truth" might be,[7] cynically admitted that their objections were inspired by political interests and not by scientific considerations. In 1950 the leaders of Soviet Oriental studies designated as their most important accomplishment "the rout of the notorious theory of the 'Asiatic mode of production.' "[8]

The reference to the "Asiatic mode of production" is indicative of the kinds of difficulties that confront the Communist attack on the theory of Oriental society. To understand them, it must be remembered that Marx accepted many values of the Western world, whose modern private-property-based institutions he wished to see destroyed. In contrast to the Soviet conception of partisanship in art and science, Marx rejected as "shabby" and "a sin against science" any method that subordinated scientific objectivity to an outside interest, that of the workers included.[9] And following Richard Jones and John Stuart Mill, he began, in the early 1850's, to use the concept of a specific Asiatic or Oriental society. Stressing particularly the Asiatic system of economy, which he designated as the "Asiatic mode of production," Marx upheld the "Asiatic" concept until his death, that is, for the greater part of his adult life. Engels, despite some temporary inconsistencies, also upheld to the end Marx' version of the Asiatic concept. Neither Marx nor Engels clearly defined the phenomenon of a marginal Oriental society; but from 1853 on, they both emphasized the "semi-Asiatic" quality of Tsarist society and the Orientally despotic character of its government.

Lenin spoke approvingly of Marx' concept of a specific Asiatic mode of production, first in 1894 and last in 1914. Following Marx and Engels, he recognized the significance of "Asiatic" institutions for Tsarist Russia, whose society he viewed as "semi-Asiatic" and whose government he considered to be despotic.[10]

7.

I WAS UNAWARE of the political implications of a comparative study of total power when in the winter of 1922–23 and under the influence of Max Weber I began to investigate the peculiarities of hydraulic society and statecraft. I was unaware of it when, in 1924 and now with reference to Marx as well as Weber, I pointed to "Asiatic" society [11] as dominated by a bureaucratically despotic state.[12] I was unaware of having drawn conclusions from Marx' version of the Asiatic concept, which Marx himself had avoided, when in 1926 and employing Marx' own socio-economic criteria, I wrote that Chinese developments in the second half of the first millennium B.C. made "the administrative officialdom—headed by the absolutist emperor—the ruling class" [13] and that this ruling class, in China as in Egypt and India, was a "mighty hydraulic [*Wasserbau*] bureaucracy." [14] I elaborated this thesis in 1926,[15] 1927,[16] 1929,[17] and 1931,[18] impressed by Marx' insistence on an unbiased pursuit of truth.[b] In 1932, a Soviet critic of my *Wirtschaft und Gesellschaft Chinas* denounced my belief in the objectivity of science.[19] It was at this time that the Soviet publishers ceased to print my analyses of Asiatic society in general and of Chinese society in particular.[c]

In the 1930's I gradually abandoned the hope that in the USSR the nationalization of all major means of production might initiate popular control over the government and the rise of a classless society. Deepened understanding of the character of Soviet society paved the way to further insights into the structure and ideology of bureaucratic despotism. Re-examination of the Marxist-Leninist view of Oriental society made it clear that Marx, far from originating the "Asiatic" concept, had found it ready-made in the writings of the classical economists. I further realized that although Marx accepted the classical view in many important essentials, he failed to draw a conclusion, which from the standpoint of his own theory seemed inescapable—namely, that under the conditions of the Asiatic mode of production the agromanagerial bureaucracy constituted the ruling class.

Lenin's ambivalence toward the "Asiatic system" is perhaps even more revealing. In 1906–07 Lenin admitted that the next Russian revolution, instead of initiating a socialist society, might lead to an

b. I cited Marx' statements on this point in 1927 (Wittfogel, 1927: 296) and again in 1929 (*ibid.*, 1929a: 581 and n. 60; see also 585).

c. My article, "Geopolitik, geographischer Materialismus und Marxismus," which argued the importance of the natural factor for societal growth in general and for Asiatic society in particular (see Wittfogel, 1929: 725–8) was published in *Unter dem Banner des Marxismus* without editorial comment, whereas in the Russian version of the same journal (*Pod znamenem marxizma*, 1929, Nos. 2/3, 6, 7/8) the editor indicated his disagreement with some of the author's views. In 1930, the journal refused to publish the continuation of my article, which carried farther the analysis of the natural foundations of Asiatic society (see Wittfogel, 1932: 593 ff., 597–608). For corrections of certain of my early views on the man-nature relationship see below, Chap. 1; cf. Chap. 9). My book *Wirtschaft und Gesellschaft Chinas* was translated into Russian, and the typewritten translation was circulated among a number of Soviet experts, who were asked to write a critical introduction. To my knowledge, such an introduction was never written. The translation was never published.

"Asiatic restoration." But when World War I opened up new possibilities for a revolutionary seizure of power, he completely dropped the Asiatic concept, which, with oscillations, he had upheld for twenty years. By discussing Marx' views of the state without reproducing Marx' ideas of the Asiatic state and the Oriental despotism of Tsarist Russia, Lenin wrote what probably is the most dishonest book of his political career: *State and Revolution*. The gradual rejection of the Asiatic concept in the USSR, which in 1938 was climaxed by Stalin's re-editing of Marx' outstanding reference to the Asiatic mode of production, logically followed Lenin's abandonment of the Asiatic concept on the eve of the Bolshevik revolution.

8.

THE CAMPAIGN against the Asiatic concept shows the master minds of the Communist camp unable to bolster their rejection with rational arguments. This in turn explains the oblique and primarily negative methods with which the friends of Communist totalitarianism in the non-Communist world oppose the outlawed concept. To the uninitiated these methods, which use distortion and de-emphasis rather than open discussion, are confusing. To the initiated they disclose once more the scientific weakness of the most powerful attack against the theory of Oriental (hydraulic) society.

9.

THE PICTURE of hydraulic society given in this inquiry implies definite concepts of societal type and development. No doubt there is structure and cohesion in man's personal history. All individuals base their behavior on the conviction that the regularities of yesterday are necessarily linked to the regularities of today and tomorrow. And there is structure and cohesion in the history of mankind. Individuals and groups of individuals like to speak of institutional units which they see operating in the present and which they expect to operate, or to change recognizably, in the future. Agnostic withdrawal from the problem of development therefore ceases to be plausible as soon as it is clearly defined.

However, the absurdity of developmental agnosticism provides no excuse for a scheme of historical change that insists on a unilinear, irresistible, and necessarily progressive development of society. Marx' and Engels' acceptance of Asiatic society as a separate and stationary conformation shows the doctrinal insincerity of those who, in the name of Marx, peddle the unilinear construct. And the comparative study of societal conformations demonstrates the empirical untenability of their position. Such a study brings to light a complex sociohistorical pattern, which includes stagnation as well as development and diverse change and regression as well as progress. By revealing the opportunities, and the pitfalls, of open historical situations, this concept assigns to man a profound moral responsibility, for which the unilinear scheme, with its ultimate fatalism, has no place.

10.

CONGRUENT with the arguments given above, I have started my inquiry with the societal order of which agromanagerial despotism is a part; and I have stressed the peculiarity of this order by calling it "hydraulic society." But I have no hesitancy in employing the traditional designations "Oriental society" and "Asiatic society" as synonyms for "hydraulic society" and "agromanagerial society"; and while using the terms "hydraulic," "agrobureaucratic," and "Oriental despotism" interchangeably, I have given preference to the older formulation, "Oriental despotism" in my title, partly to emphasize the historical depth of my central concept and partly because the majority of all great hydraulic civilizations existed in what is customarily called the Orient. Originally I had planned to publish this study under the title *Oriental Society*.

The preservation of the old nomenclature stands us in good stead when we examine recent developments. For while there are some traces of hydraulic society left in certain regions of Latin America, the heritage of the old order is still very conspicuous in many countries of the Orient proper. The problem of hydraulic society in transition is therefore primarily the problem of this area.

Under what influences and in what ways are the people of the East throwing off the conditions of hydraulic society which they maintained for millennia? The significance of this question becomes fully apparent only when we understand that Oriental despotism atomized those nonbureaucratic groups and strata which, in feudal Europe and Japan, spearheaded the rise of a commercial and industrial society. Nowhere, it seems, did hydraulic society, without outside aid, make a similar advance. It was for this reason that Marx called Asiatic society stationary and expected British rule in India to accomplish "the only *social* revolution ever heard of in Asia" by establishing there a property-based non-Asiatic society.[20]

Subsequent events indicate that Marx seriously overrated the transformative strength of capitalist economy. To be sure, Western rule in India and other Oriental countries provided new possibilities for a nontotalitarian development; but at the end of the era of Western colonialism and despite the introduction of parliamentary governments of various kinds, the political leaders of the Orient are still greatly attracted by a bureaucratic-managerial policy which keeps the state supremely strong and the nonbureaucratic and private sector of society supremely weak.

11.

IN THIS CONTEXT, certain aspects of Russia's recent development deserve the most careful scrutiny. The marginally Oriental civilization of Tsarist Russia was greatly influenced by the West, though Russia did not become a Western colony or semi-colony. Russia's Westernization radically changed the country's political and economic climate, and in the spring of 1917 its antitotalitarian forces had a genuine opportunity to accomplish the anti-Asiatic social revolution which Marx, in 1853, had envisaged for India. But in the fall of 1917 these antitotalitarian forces were defeated by the Bolshevik champions of a new totalitarian order. They were defeated because they failed to utilize the democratic potential in a historical situation that was temporarily open. From the standpoint of individual freedom and social justice, 1917 is probably the most fateful year in modern history.

The intellectual and political leaders of non-Communist Asia, who profess to believe in democracy and who in their majority speak deferentially of Marx, will fulfill their historical responsibility only if they face the despotic heritage of the Oriental world not less but more clearly than did Marx. In the light of the Russian experience of 1917 they should be willing to consider the issue of an "Asiatic restoration" not only in relation to Russia but also to present-day Asia.

12.

THE MASTERS of the modern totalitarian superstate build big and integrated institutions, which, they say, we cannot emulate. And they display big and integrated ideas, which, they say, we cannot match. They are right in one respect. We do not maintain totalitarian systems of integrated power and ideology. Favorable constellations of historical events have permitted us to avoid these monstrous developments that paralyze the search for scientific truth and social improvement. But our opponents are wrong when they hold us incapable of voluntary association because we reject the disciplines of general (state) slavery. They are wrong when they hold us incapable of producing big and structured ideas because we reject state-imposed dogma.

Political freedom is not identical with the absence of organized action, though our enemies would be happy if this were so. And intellectual freedom is not identical with the absence of integrated thought. It is only under the conditions of free discussion that comprehensive sets of ideas can be genuinely tested.

In the recent past, scholars often gave themselves to the study of details because they took the broad principles of life and thought for granted. Seeing these principles threatened, they today begin to recall that the trail blazers of modern thought viewed nature and society as integrated orders whose architecture they explored. The Newtons, Montesquieus, Adam Smiths, and Darwins provided new interpretations of the world that were as spontaneous as they were coherent, and as bold as they were competent.

You cannot fight something with nothing. In a crisis situation, any theoretical vacuum, like any power vacuum, invites disaster. There is no excuse for letting the enemy have things his way when our side possesses infinite reserves of superior strength. There is no excuse for letting the totalitarian strategists parade their contrived doctrines on ground that is legitimately ours. There is no excuse for letting them win the battle of ideas by default.

Scientific inquiry has its inner laws. But it earns the privilege of freedom only when, rooted in the heritage of the past, it alertly faces the threats of a conflict-torn present and boldly exhausts the possibilities of an open future.

CHAPTER 1

$\mathcal{T}$he natural setting of hydraulic society

A. CHANGING MAN IN CHANGING NATURE

CONTRARY to the popular belief that nature always remains the same—a belief that has led to static theories of environmentalism and to their equally static rejections—nature changes profoundly whenever man, in response to simple or complex historical causes, profoundly changes his technical equipment, his social organization, and his world outlook. Man never stops affecting his natural environment. He constantly *transforms* it; and he *actualizes*[a] new forces whenever his efforts carry him to a new level of operation. Whether a new level can be attained at all, or once attained, where it will lead, depends first on the institutional order[b] and second on the ultimate target of man's activity: the physical, chemical, and biological world accessible to him. Institutional conditions being equal, it is the difference in the natural setting that suggests and permits—or precludes—the development of new forms of technology, subsistence, and social control.

A waterfall interested primitive man little except as a landmark or an object of veneration. When sedentary man developed industry on a sophisticated mechanical level, he actualized the motive energy of water; and many new enterprises (mills) arose on the banks of rushing streams. The discovery of the technical potential inherent in coal made man geology conscious as never before, and the water mill became a romantic survival in the revolutionized industrial landscape dominated by the steam engine.

a. For the terms "transformation" and "actualization," as used here, see Wittfogel, 1932: 482.

b. This formulation differs from my earlier concept of the relation between man and nature (Wittfogel, 1932: 483 ff., 712 ff.) in its emphasis on the primary importance of institutional (and cultural) factors. From this premise follows the recognition of man's freedom to make a genuine choice in historically open situations, a point developed in the later part of the present chapter. Except for these corrections—which are essential also for my criticism of certain ideas of Marx that I had previously accepted—I am upholding the substance of my earlier views (see Wittfogel, 1931: 21 ff.; *ibid.*, 1932: 486 ff.).

In recent years man has uncovered the productive energies of electricity. Again he is turning his attention to falling water. But even when the engineer of the 20th century erects his power plant on the very spot that previously supported a textile mill, he actualizes new forces in the old setting. Nature acquires a new function; and gradually it also assumes a new appearance.

B. THE HISTORICAL PLACE OF HYDRAULIC SOCIETY

WHAT is true for the industrial scene is equally true for the agricultural landscape. The hydraulic potential of the earth's water-deficient regions is actualized only under specific historical circumstances. Primitive man has known water-deficient regions since time immemorial; but while he depended on gathering, hunting, and fishing, he had little need for planned water control. Only after he learned to utilize the reproductive processes of plant life did he begin to appreciate the agricultural possibilities of dry areas, which contained sources of water supply other than on-the-spot rainfall. Only then did he begin to manipulate the newly discovered qualities of the old setting through small-scale irrigation farming (hydroagriculture) and/or large-scale and government-directed farming (hydraulic agriculture). Only then did the opportunity arise for despotic patterns of government and society.

The opportunity, not the necessity. Large enterprises of water control will create no hydraulic order, if they are part of a wider nonhydraulic nexus. The water works of the Po Plain, of Venice, and of the Netherlands modified regional conditions; but neither Northern Italy nor Holland developed a hydraulic system of government and property. Even the Mormons, who established a flourishing hydraulic agriculture in the heart of arid North America, never succeeded in completely eliminating the political and cultural influence of their wider industrial environment. The history of the Latter-Day Saints illustrates both the organizational potential of large-scale irrigation and the limitations imposed on the development of hydraulic institutions by a dominant Western society.

Thus, too little or too much water does not necessarily lead to governmental water control; nor does governmental water control necessarily imply despotic methods of statecraft. It is only above the level of an extractive subsistence economy, beyond the influence of strong centers of rainfall agriculture, and below the level of a property-based industrial civilization that man, reacting specifically to the water-deficient landscape, moves toward a specific hydraulic order of life.

C. THE NATURAL SETTING

1. HISTORICAL CONDITIONS BEING EQUAL, A MAJOR NATURAL DIFFERENCE THE POSSIBLE CAUSE OF DECISIVE INSTITUTIONAL DIFFERENCES

MANY factors differentiated agrarian life prior to the industrial age, but none equaled in institutional significance the stimulating contradictions offered by arid areas possessing accessible sources of water supply other than on-the-spot rainfall. Under the just-defined conditions of preindustrial agriculture, this natural configuration decisively affected man's behavior as a provider of food and organizer of human relations. If he wanted to cultivate dry but potentially fertile lands permanently and rewardingly, he had to secure a reliable flow of moisture. Of all tasks imposed by the natural environment, it was the task imposed by a precarious water situation that stimulated man to develop hydraulic methods of social control.

2. SEVERAL NATURAL FACTORS ESSENTIAL TO FARMING

WATER is not the only natural factor essential for successful crop raising. Anyone wishing to farm must have at his disposal useful plants, an arable soil, adequate humidity, appropriate temperature (sufficient sun and a proper growing season), and a suitable lay of the land (relief, surface).[a]

All these elements are equally essential. The lack of any one of them destroys the agronomic value of all the others. Cultivation remains impossible unless human action can compensate for the total deficiency of any essential factor.

3. SOME ESSENTIAL FACTORS DEFY COMPENSATING ACTION; OTHERS RESPOND MORE READILY

THE effectiveness of man's compensating action depends on the ease with which a lacking natural factor can be replaced. Some factors must be considered constants because, under existing technological conditions, they are for all practical purposes beyond man's control. Others are more pliable. Man may manipulate or, if necessary, change them.

Temperature and surface are the outstanding constant elements of the agricultural landscape. This was true for the premachine age; and it is still essentially true today. Pre-industrial attempts to change

a. For similar attempts at defining the natural factors basic to agriculture see CM: 125; SM: 753; Widtsoe, 1928: 19 ff.; Buck, 1937: 101.

the temperature of farming areas have, for obvious reasons, met with no success; and even such achievements as central heating and air conditioning have wrought no major change. Still less has man succeeded in altering the cosmic circumstances which ultimately determine the temperature of the earth.

The lay of the land has equally defied human effort. Man has made many minor adjustments such as leveling or terracing—most frequently, it would seem, in connection with operations of hydro-agriculture. But before modern power machines and high explosives were invented, the globe's relief remained fundamentally unaltered. Even machine-promoted agriculture, like the technically less advanced forms of farming, prospers on the even surfaces of lowlands and high plateaus or on gently graded slopes and hills, and not in rugged mountainous terrain.

Vegetation and soil do not resist human action to any comparable degree. The farmer professionally manipulates plants and soils. He may transfer useful plants to regions lacking them, and he frequently does so. However, such action is sporadic and temporary; it ceases when the limited objective is achieved. In a given agricultural area the operations of crop breeding are repeated again and again; but the plants cover the ground discontinuously, and although under certain circumstances farm labor may be coordinated in work teams, there is nothing in the nature of the individual plants or plant aggregates which necessitates large-scale cooperation as a prerequisite for successful cultivation. Before the machine age the greater part of all agriculture proceeded most effectively when individual husbandmen or small groups of husbandmen attended to the crops.

The second variable factor, soil, follows a similar pattern, with special limitations dictated by the relative heaviness of pulverized mineral substance. While seeds or plants have frequently been transferred to deficient areas, soil has rarely been moved to barren regions. No doubt, poor or useless fields have been improved by bringing better soil from a distance. But such action is of little consequence for the character of any major farming area.[1] Man's efforts seek primarily to adjust the existing soil to the needs of the crops by hoeing, digging, or plowing, and on occasion by improving its chemical composition through the application of fertilizers.

Thus soil is susceptible to manipulation, but to a type of manipulation that requires work groups no larger than are necessary for the cultivation of the plants. Even when, under primitive conditions, the clearing of the ground and the gathering of the harvest are undertaken by large teams, the actual task of tilling the fields is usually left to one or a few individuals.

4. The Specific Qualities of Water

COMPARED with all other essential natural prerequisites of agriculture, water is *specific*. Temperature and surface, because of their respective cosmic and geological dimensions, have completely precluded or strikingly limited human action throughout the preindustrial era and afterward. In contrast, water is neither too remote nor too massive to permit manipulation by man. In this regard it resembles two other variables, vegetation and soil. But it differs greatly from both in its susceptibility to movement and in the techniques required to handle it.

Water is heavier than most plants. It can nevertheless be much more conveniently managed. Unhampered by the cohesiveness of solid matter and following the law of gravity, water flows automatically to the lowest accessible point in its environment. Within a given agricultural landscape, water is the natural variable *par excellence*.

And this is not all. Flowing automatically, water appears unevenly in the landscape, gathering either below the surface as ground water, or above the surface in separate cavities (holes, ponds, lakes), or continuous beds (streams, rivers). Such formations are of minor significance in an agricultural area enjoying ample precipitation, but they become immensely important in the water-deficient landscape. The human operator who has to handle water deals with a substance that is not only more mobile than other agronomic variables, but also more bulky.

This last quality presents special difficulties whenever man tries to utilize large agglomerations of moisture; and this he is prone to do whenever natural and technological conditions permit. No operational necessity compels him to manipulate either soil or plants in cooperation with many others. But the bulkiness of all except the smallest sources of water supply creates a technical task which is solved either by mass labor or not at all.

D. MUST THE HYDRAULIC POTENTIAL BE ACTUALIZED?

1. An Open Historical Situation—but Recognizable Patterns of Response

THE stimulating contradiction inherent in a potentially hydraulic landscape is manifest. Such a landscape has an insufficient rainfall or none at all; but it possesses other accessible sources of water supply. If man decides to utilize them, he may transform dry lands into fertile fields and gardens. He may, but will he? What makes him engage in a venture which involves great effort and which is fraught with highly problematic institutional consequences?

Historical evidence reveals that numerous groups of persons have made this decision. Yet it also reveals that many others have failed to do so. Over millennia, tribal gatherers, hunters, fishermen, and pastoralists inhabited potentially hydraulic regions, often in close proximity to irrigation farmers, but few abandoned their traditional occupations for a hydroagricultural way of life.

Manifestly, no irresistible necessity compelled man to utilize the new natural opportunities. The situation was open, and the hydro-agricultural course was only one of several possible choices. Nevertheless, man took this course so frequently and in so many separate areas that we may assume regularity in evaluation as well as in procedure.

Man pursues recognized advantage. Whenever internal or external causes suggest a change in technology, material production, or social relations, he compares the merits of the existing situation with the advantages—and disadvantages—that may accrue from the contemplated change. Special effort is required to attain the new objective; and this effort may involve not only increased work and a shift from pleasant to unpleasant operations, but also social and cultural adjustments, including a more or less serious loss of personal and political independence.

When the sum total of the accruing benefits clearly and convincingly exceeds the required sacrifices, man is willing to make the change; but problematic advantage usually leaves him cool. Here, as elsewhere, the human budget is compounded of material and non-material items; any attempt to formulate it exclusively in terms of smaller or larger quantities of things (goods) will prove unsatisfactory. To be sure, the material factor weighs heavily, but its relative importance can be reasonably defined only when full recognition is given to such other values as personal safety, absence of oppression, and time-honored patterns of thought and action.

Culture historians have made much of the fact that during the "recent" epoch of geozoology [1] clusters of persons adopted agriculture, either as a supplementary occupation or, and increasingly, as their main subsistence economy. No doubt this transition profoundly affected the fate of mankind; but any reference to the law of recognized advantage must take into account the many primitive groups that did not turn to crop-raising either during the days of incipient agriculture or after the rise of powerful and stratified agrarian civilizations.

The agrarian alternative had a limited—and very diverse—appeal to nonfarming groups when cultivation was primitive and leadership not overly demanding. After the emergence of stratified agricultural societies, choice became even more serious. The authority wielded by the governments and wealthy landowners of nearby agrarian states acted as a deterrent, for under these conditions a shift might involve submission to distasteful methods of political and proprietary control. Often women, children, and war captives tilled some few fields close to a camp site; but the dominant members of the tribe, the adult males, stubbornly refused to abandon their hunting, fishing, or herding activities. The many primitive peoples who endured lean years and even long periods of famine without making the crucial changeover to agriculture demonstrate the immense attraction of nonmaterial values, when increased material security can be attained only at the price of political, economic, and cultural submission.

2. THE RECOGNIZED ADVANTAGES OF IRRIGATION AGRICULTURE

THE transition to irrigation farming poses the problem of choice in a still more complex form. The primary choice—whether or not to start hydroagriculture where it had not been known previously—was generally, though perhaps not exclusively, made by groups familiar with the techniques of primitive rainfall farming.

The secondary (derivative) choice—whether or not to emulate an established irrigation economy—confronts the traditional rainfall farmer as well as the nonagricultural tribesman. But the nonagriculturist is much less prepared technically and culturally to make this shift; and in both cases decision becomes more precarious when acceptance of a materially attractive irrigation economy involves reduction to an abjectly low social and political status.

It is obviously for this reason that a number of communities practicing rainfall farming in Southwest China, India, and Meso-America as well as many tribal hunters, fishermen, and herders on the fringe of the hydroagricultural world failed to make the change. The fate of those who rejected the ambivalent opportunity varied greatly; but whatever their subsequent fortunes, history offered most of them a genuine choice, and man proceeded not as the passive instrument of an irresistible and unilinear developmental force but as a discriminating being, actively participating in shaping his future.

a. If . . . , then . . .

IRRIGATION farming always requires more physical effort than rainfall farming performed under comparable conditions. But it requires radical social and political adjustments only in a special geohistorical setting. Strictly local tasks of digging, damming, and water distribution can be performed by a single husbandman, a single family, or a small group of neighbors, and in this case no far-reaching organizational steps are necessary. Hydroagriculture, farming based on small-scale irrigation, increases the food supply, but it does not involve the patterns of organization and social control that characterize hydraulic agriculture and Oriental despotism.

These patterns come into being when an experimenting community of farmers or protofarmers finds large sources of moisture in a dry but potentially fertile area. If irrigation farming depends on the effective handling of a major supply of water, the distinctive quality of water—its tendency to gather in bulk—becomes institutionally decisive. A large quantity of water can be channeled and kept within bounds only by the use of mass labor; and this mass labor must be coordinated, disciplined, and led. Thus a number of farmers eager to conquer arid lowlands and plains are forced to invoke the organizational devices which—on the basis of premachine technology—offer the one chance of success: they must work in cooperation with their fellows and subordinate themselves to a directing authority.

Again history followed no unilinear course dictated by unavoidable necessity. There were recognized alternatives; and those who were faced with them were able to make a genuine choice. But whatever their decisions, they were made within a framework that offered only a limited number of workable possibilities.

Thus the changeover to hydraulic agriculture, or its rejection, was not without order or direction. The various decisions displayed regularities in conditioning and motivation. But the relative equality of the original choices did not imply a relative equality in the final results. The majority of all hunters, fishermen, and rainfall farmers who preserved their traditional way of life were reduced to insignificance, if they were not completely annihilated. Some groups, practicing a mixed economy with little or no hydroagriculture, were strong enough to impose their will on adjacent hydraulic civilizations.

The herders came into their own at a relatively late time and in a special geohistorical setting. Often they maintained themselves against all manner of agriculturists, and in a number of instances they engaged in sweeping offensives, accomplishing conquests that profoundly modified the political and social structure of the subdued agrarian civilizations.

The representatives of rainfall farming made history in certain areas of the West, which was uniquely suited to this type of economy.

But the hydraulic agriculturists outgrew and outfought the majority of all neighboring peoples wherever local conditions and international circumstances one-sidedly favored an agromanagerial economy and statecraft.

The pioneers of hydraulic agriculture, like the pioneers of rainfall farming, were unaware of the ultimate consequences of their choice. Pursuing recognized advantage, they initiated an institutional development which led far beyond the starting point. Their heirs and successors built colossal political and social structures; but they did so at the cost of many of those freedoms which the conservative dissenters endeavored and, in part, were able to preserve.

b. Arid, Semi-arid, and Humid Areas: Hypothetical Patterns of Interaction and Growth

IN THEIR PURSUIT of recognized advantage, rainfall farmers experimented with hydroagriculture not only in desert-like areas of full aridity and steppe-like areas of semi-aridity, but also in humid areas suitable to the cultivation of useful aquatic plants, above all rice.

The first two types of landscapes, taken together, cover almost three-fifths [2]—and all three possibly something like two-thirds—of the globe's surface. Within this area each of the three types of potentially hydraulic landscapes may have played a specific role, particularly in the formative period of a hydraulic economy. In a major sector comprising all three types, the semi-arid regions are highly suitable to small and gradually growing enterprises of water control. The arid regions provide an ultimate testing ground for the new techniques. And the semi-arid and humid regions profit further from the technical and organizational experience gained in man's victory over the desert.

This may well have been the sequence in the spread of hydraulic agriculture in such widely separated areas as ancient Mesopotamia, India, and the western zone of South America. A different order of development is probable for landscapes that are homogeneously arid, and still another for those that are predominantly semi-arid.

In each case, the presence or absence of adjacent humid regions complicated the pattern of growth. In Egypt, gatherers, hunters, and fishermen seem to have practiced agriculture as a subsidiary occupation on the naturally flooded banks of the Nile long before farming became the primary pursuit. In Meso-America [a] and in

a. Some twenty years ago I considered Aztec Mexico, like pre-Tokugawa Japan, a feudal society with small-scale irrigation (Wittfogel, 1932: 587 ff.). On the basis of a

China diffusion (from South America and Inner or South Asia respectively) cannot be excluded. But such external stimulation need not have occurred; if it did, it was effective only because the rainfall farmers in the "stimulated" areas were ready to recognize the advantages of the new technique.

In ancient China the semi-arid North and the rice-growing South established noteworthy forms of interaction. The ancient Yangtze states developed early and perhaps under the influence of the rice culture of Southeast Asia; but it was the semi-arid North which,

---

growing familiarity with the early sources I came to recognize the hydraulic character of the core areas of pre-Spanish Mexico; and the recent work of Mexican archaeologists and historians fortifies me in my conclusion (see Armillas, 1948: 109; *ibid.*, 1951: 24 ff.; Palerm, 1952: 184 ff.). I quote particularly from a study by Palerm which provides a wealth of historical data on irrigation in both pre-Spanish and early Spanish Meso-America:

> 4. The majority of the irrigation systems seem to have been only of local importance and did not require large hydraulic undertakings. Nevertheless, important works were undertaken in the Valley of Mexico, and irrigation appears in concentrated form in the headwaters of the rivers Tula, Lerma and Atlixco, and in the contiguous area of Colima-Jalisco.
>
> 5. The largest concentrations and most important works of irrigation coincide, generally, with the greatest density of population, with the distribution of the most important urban centers, and with the nuclei of political power and military expansion [Palerm, 1954: 71].

How far back can we trace hydraulic activities in Meso-America? Armillas believes that the great cultural advance in the Hohokam civilization of Arizona (A.D. 500–900) was probably due to the construction of irrigation canals, a fact which is archaeologically established. And since the remains point to relations between Hohokam and Meso-America, he believes that "the same factor may underlie the cultural development in certain areas of western Meso-America during this period" (Armillas, 1948: 107). The Hohokam data tie in with the "classical" period of Meso-American history, which, in the Mexican lake area, probably began in the early centuries of the first millennium A.D. Armillas' assumption is reinforced by a recent pollen analysis, which suggests that aridity increased during the late "archaic" period (Sears, 1951: 59 ff.). Palerm has stated that this climatic change may have caused "the emergence or extension of irrigation" in Meso-America (1955: 35). Such a hypothesis, and it seems an eminently plausible one, would go far to explain the beginnings of a "classical" period of concentrated populations and monumental building, not only in the highlands but also in the marginal hydraulic Maya civilization.

If a vigorous hydraulic development occurred in Meso-America at the end of the first millennium B.C. or shortly thereafter, subsequent oscillations in hydraulic operation present no basic theoretical difficulties. Recent investigations by Palerm and Wolf indicate a rather late date for the comprehensive waterworks undertaken by the territorial state of Texcoco, which, when the Spaniards arrived, was second only to Mexico. The relative lateness of this development does not necessarily indicate that originally Texcoco was outside the hydraulic pale. More likely, the Texcocan government moved gradually from marginal to more central hydraulic conditions. (For the problem of changing hydraulic density, see below, Chap. 6.)

over a long period of time, constituted the dominant center of power and cultural advance in Eastern Asia. In India the arid, semi-arid, and humid regions of the North became historically prominent before the excessively humid area of Bengal.

These developmental sequences are presented as hypotheses. Their validity, or lack of validity, is of no consequence to our analysis of societal structure. They are worth noting, in the main, because on the basis of our present archaeological and prehistorical knowledge they suggest a highly dynamic interplay between the various types of landscapes which combine to form the larger areas of hydraulic civilization.

CHAPTER 2

Hydraulic economy—a managerial and genuinely political economy

THE CHARACTERISTICS of hydraulic economy are many, but three are paramount. Hydraulic agriculture involves a specific type of division of labor. It intensifies cultivation. And it necessitates cooperation on a large scale. The third characteristic has been described by a number of students of Oriental farming. The second has been frequently noted, but rarely analyzed. The first has been given practically no attention. This neglect is particularly unfortunate, since the hydraulic patterns of organization and operation have decisively affected the managerial role of the hydraulic state.

Economists generally consider the division of labor and cooperation key prerequisites of modern industry, but they find them almost completely lacking in farming.[a] Their claim reflects the conditions of Western rainfall agriculture. For this type of agriculture it is indeed by and large correct.

However, the economists do not as a rule so limit themselves. Speaking of agriculture without any geographical or institutional qualification, they give the impression that their thesis, being universally valid, applies to hydraulic as well as to hydroagriculture and rainfall farming. Comparative examination of the facts quickly discloses the fallacy of this contention.

---

a. For early formulations of this view see Smith, 1937: 6; Mill, 1909: 131, 144; Marx, DK, I: 300, 322 ff. Modern economists have perpetuated and even sharpened them. Writes Seligman (1914: 350): "In the immense domain of agricultural production the possibility of combination is almost entirely eliminated." And Marshall (1946: 290): "In agriculture there is not much division of labour, and there is no production on a very large scale."

A. DIVISION OF LABOR IN HYDRAULIC AGRICULTURE

1. PREPARATORY AND PROTECTIVE OPERATIONS SEPARATED FROM FARMING PROPER

WHAT is true for modern industry—that production proper depends on a variety of preparatory and protective operations [b]—has been true for hydraulic agriculture since its beginnings. The peculiarity of the preparatory and protective hydraulic operations is an essential aspect of the peculiarity of hydraulic agriculture.

a. Large-scale Preparatory Operations (Purpose: Irrigation)

THE combined agricultural activities of an irrigation farmer are comparable to the combined agricultural activities of a rainfall farmer. But the operations of the former include types of labor (on-the-spot ditching, damming, and watering) that are absent in the operations of the latter. The magnitude of this special type of labor can be judged from the fact that in a Chinese village a peasant may spend from 20 to over 50 per cent of his work time irrigating, and that in many Indian villages irrigation is the most time-consuming single item in the farmer's budget.[1]

Hydroagriculture (small-scale irrigation farming) involves a high intensity of cultivation on irrigated fields—and often also on non-irrigated fields.[2] But it does not involve a division of labor on a communal, territorial, or national level. Such a work pattern occurs only when large quantities of water have to be manipulated. Wherever, in pre-industrial civilizations, man gathered, stored, and conducted water on a large scale, we find the conspicuous division between preparatory (feeding) and ultimate labor characteristic of all hydraulic agriculture.

b. Large-scale Protective Operations (Purpose: Flood Control)

BUT the fight against the disastrous consequences of too little water may involve a fight against the disastrous consequences of too much water. The potentially most rewarding areas of hydraulic farming

b. For the concept of "previous or preparatory labor" see Mill 1909: 29, 31. The general principle was already indicated by Smith (1937), who, when discussing the division of operations in industry, pointed to the "growers of the flax and the wool" and the miners as providers of raw material (5 ff., 11), to the spinners and weavers as engaged in special processing operations (6), and to the makers of tools as combining elements of both procedures (11). Mill (1909: 36 ff.) also includes, in the category of previous labor, activities aimed at protecting industrial production proper.

are arid and semi-arid plains and humid regions suitable for aquatic crops, such as rice, that are sufficiently low-lying to permit watering from nearby rivers. These rivers usually have their sources in remote mountains, and they rise substantially as the summer sun melts part of the snow accumulated there.

Upstream developments of this kind cause annual inundations in Egypt, Mesopotamia, Turkestan, India, China, and in the Andean and Mexican zones of America. In semi-arid areas on-the-spot rains create additional dangers when they are overconcentrated (convectional) or irregular. This condition prevails in North China, northern Mesopotamia (Assyria), and the Mexican lake region. Thus a hydraulic community that resorts to preparatory labor to safeguard the productive use of water may also have to resort to protective labor to safeguard its crops from periodic and excessive inundations.

When, in protohistorical times, the Chinese began to cultivate the great plains of North China, they quickly recognized that the centers of greatest potential fertility were also the centers of greatest potential destruction. To quote John Lossing Buck: "Geologically speaking, man has settled these plains thousands of years before they were ready for occupation. . . ."[3] The Chinese built huge embankments which, although unable to remove entirely the risk inhering in the ambivalent situation, matched and even surpassed in magnitude the area's preparatory (feeding) works.[4]

In India enormous problems of flood control are posed by the Indus River[5] and, in a particularly one-sided way, by the Ganges and Brahmaputra Rivers, which in Bengal create optimal conditions for the cultivation of rice and maximal dangers from floods. By 1900 Bengal boasted ninety-seven miles of larger irrigation canals and 1,298 miles of embankments.[6]

In ancient Mesopotamia even watchful rulers could not completely prevent the inundations from damaging the densely settled plains.[7] In Turkestan excessive floods periodically threatened the Zarafshan River Valley.[8] In Upper Egypt the Nile, in very high flood, rises one meter above the level of the settled countryside, in Middle Egypt two meters, and in the Delta area up to three and a half meters.[9] The inhabitants of the lake area of Mexico could benefit from its fertility only if they accepted the periodic overflow of its short, irregular, narrow streams,[10] which they sought to control through a variety of protective works. Thus in virtually all major hydraulic civilizations, preparatory (feeding) works for the purpose of irrigation are supplemented by and interlocked with protective works for the purpose of flood control.

2. COOPERATION

A STUDY of the hydraulic patterns of China (especially North China), India, Turkestan, Mesopotamia (especially Assyria), Egypt, or Meso-America (especially the Mexican lake region) must therefore consider both forms of agrohydraulic activities. Only by proceeding in such a way can we hope to determine realistically the dimension and character of their organizational key device: cooperation.

a. Dimension

WHEN a hydraulic society covers only a single locality, all adult males may be assigned to one or a few communal work teams. Varying needs and circumstances modify the size of the mobilized labor force. In hydraulic countries having several independent sources of water supply, the task of controlling the moisture is performed by a number of separated work teams.

Among the Suk of Northeastern Africa, "every male must assist in making the ditches." [11] In almost all Pueblos "irrigation or cleaning a spring is work for all." [12] Among the Chagga, the maintenance of a relatively elaborate irrigation system is assured by "the participation of the entire people." [13] In Bali the peasants are obliged to render labor service for the hydraulic regional unit, the *subak*, to which they belong.[14] The masters of the Sumerian temple economy expected every adult male within their jurisdiction "to participate in the digging and cleaning of the canals." [15] Most inscriptions of Pharaonic Egypt take this work pattern for granted. Only occasionally does a text specify the character of the universally demanded activities, among which lifting and digging are outstanding.[16]

In imperial China every commoner family was expected on demand to provide labor for hydraulic and other public services. The political and legal writings of India indicate a similar claim on corviable labor.[17] The laws of Inca Peru obliged all able-bodied men to render *corvée* service.[18] In ancient Mexico both commoner and upper-class adolescents were instructed in the techniques of digging and damming.[19] At times the masters of this hydraulic area levied the manpower of several territorial states for their gigantic hydraulic enterprises.[20]

In 19th-century Egypt "the whole corviable population" worked in four huge shifts on Mehmed Ali's hydraulic installations. Each group labored on the canals for forty-five days until, after 180 days, the job was completed.[21] From 1881 on, at a time of decay and disintegration, "the *whole* of the corvée fell on the poorest classes," [22] the smaller number being compensated for by an increase in the labor-time to ninety days. In some regions the conscripts were kept busy "for 180 days." [23]

b. Integration

ORDERLY cooperation involves planned integration. Such integration is especially necessary when the objectives are elaborate and the cooperating teams large.

Above the tribal level, hydraulic activities are usually comprehensive. Most writers who mention the cooperative aspect of hydraulic agriculture think in the main of digging, dredging, and damming; and the organizational tasks involved in these labors is certainly considerable. But the planners of a major hydraulic enterprise are confronted with problems of a much more complex kind. How many persons are needed? And where can such persons be found? On the basis of previously made registers, the planners must determine the quota and criteria of selection. Notification follows selection, and mobilization notification. The assembled groups frequently proceed in quasimilitary columns. Having reached their destination, the buck privates of the hydraulic army must be distributed in proper numbers and according to whatever division of operations (spading, carrying of mud, etc.) is customary. If raw materials such as straw, fagots, lumber, or stone have to be procured, auxiliary operations are organized; and if the work teams—*in toto* or in part—must be provided with food and drink, still other ways of appropriation, transport, and distribution have to be developed. Even in its simplest form, agrohydraulic operations necessitate substantial integrative action. In their more elaborate variations, they involve extensive and complex organizational planning.

c. Leadership

ALL TEAMWORK requires team leaders; and the work of large integrated teams requires on-the-spot leaders and disciplinarians as well as over-all organizers and planners. The great enterprises of hydraulic agriculture involve both types of direction. The foreman usually performs no menial work at all; and except for a few engineering specialists the sergeants and officers of the labor force are essentially organizers.

To be sure, the physical element—including threats of punishment and actual coercion—is never absent. But here, if anywhere, recorded experience and calculated foresight are crucial. It is the circumspection, resourcefulness, and integrative skill of the supreme leader and his aides which play the decisive role in initiating, accomplishing, and perpetuating the major works of hydraulic economy.

d. Hydraulic Leadership—Political Leadership

THE effective management of these works involves an organizational web which covers either the whole, or at least the dynamic core, of the country's population. In consequence, those who control this network are uniquely prepared to wield supreme political power.

From the standpoint of the historical effect, it makes no difference whether the heads of a hydraulic government were originally peace chiefs, war leaders, priests, priest-chiefs, or hydraulic officials *sans phrase*. Among the Chagga, the hydraulic corvée is called into action by the same horn that traditionally rallied the tribesmen for war.[24] Among the Pueblo Indians the war chiefs (or priests), although subordinated to the *cacique* (the supreme chief), direct and supervise the communal activities.[25] The early hydraulic city states of Mesopotamia seem to have been for the most part ruled by priest-kings. In China the legendary trail blazer of governmental water control, the Great Yü, is said to have risen from the rank of a supreme hydraulic functionary to that of king, becoming, according to protohistorical records, the founder of the first hereditary dynasty, Hsia.

No matter whether traditionally nonhydraulic leaders initiated or seized the incipient hydraulic "apparatus," or whether the masters of this apparatus became the motive force behind all important public functions,[c] there can be no doubt that in all these cases the resulting regime was decisively shaped by the leadership and social control required by hydraulic agriculture.

B. HEAVY WATER WORKS AND HEAVY INDUSTRY

WITH regard to operational form, hydraulic agriculture exhibits important similarities to heavy industry. Both types of economic activities are preparatory to the ultimate processes of production. Both

c. Rüstow, who in general accepts Kern's view concerning the correlation between large-scale and government-directed water control and the centralized and despotic character of the state in ancient Egypt and Mesopotamia, assumes that in these areas nomadic conquerors developed the hydraulic works *after* establishing conquest empires (Rüstow, OG, I: 306).

Patterns of leadership and discipline traditional to conquering groups could be, and probably were, invoked in establishing certain hydraulic governments; but Pueblo, Chagga, and Hawaiian society show that such formative patterns could also be endogenous. In any case, the ethnographic and historical facts point to a multiple rather than a single origin for hydraulic societies.

provide the workers with essential material for these ultimate processes. And both tend to be comprehensive, "heavy." For these reasons the large enterprises of hydraulic agriculture may be designated as "heavy water works."

But the dissimilarities are as illuminating as the similarities. The heavy water works of hydraulic agriculture and the heavy industry of modern economy are distinguished by a number of basic differences, which, properly defined, may aid us in more clearly recognizing the peculiarities of hydraulic society.

Heavy water works feed the ultimate agrarian producer one crucial auxiliary material: water; heavy industry provides auxiliary and raw materials of various kinds, including tools for finishing and heavy industry. Heavy water works fulfill important protective functions for the country at large; the protective installations (buildings, etc.) of industry do not. Heavy water works cover at their inception a relatively large area; and with the development of the hydraulic order they are usually spread still further. The operations of heavy industry are spatially much more restricted. At first, and for a number of preliminary processes, they may depend on small and dispersed shops; with the growth of the industrial order they tend to merge into one, or a few, major establishments.

The character of the labor force varies with these spatial and operational differences. Heavy water works are best served by a widely distributed personnel, whereas heavy industry requires the workers to reside near the locally restricted "big" enterprises which employ them. The hydraulic demand is satisfied by adult peasant males, who continue to reside in their respective villages; whereas the industrial demand is satisfied by a geographically concentrated labor force.

The bulk of the hydraulic workers are expected to remain peasants, and in most cases they are mobilized for a relatively short period only—at best for a few days, at worst for any time that will not destroy their agricultural usefulness. Thus division of agrohydraulic labor is not accompanied by a corresponding division of laborers.

The contrast to the labor policy of heavy industry is manifest. Different from heavy water works, which may be created and maintained during a fraction of the year, heavy industry operates most effectively when it operates continuously. The industrial employers prefer to occupy their personnel throughout the year; and with the growth of the industrial system full-time labor became the rule. Thus division of industrial labor moves toward a more or less complete division of laborers.

The two sectors are also differently administered. In the main, modern heavy industry is directed by private owners or managers. The heavy water works of hydraulic agriculture are directed essentially by the government. The government also engages in certain other large enterprises, which, in varying combinations, supplement the agrohydraulic economy proper.

C. CALENDAR MAKING AND ASTRONOMY—IMPORTANT FUNCTIONS OF THE HYDRAULIC REGIME

AMONG the intellectual functions fulfilled by the leaders of agro-hydraulic activities, some are only indirectly connected with the organization of men and material; but the relation is highly significant nevertheless. Time keeping and calendar making are essential for the success of all hydraulic economies; and under special conditions special operations of measuring and calculating may be urgently needed.[1] The way in which these tasks are executed affect both the political and the cultural development of hydraulic society.

To be sure, man is deeply concerned about the swing of the seasons under all forms of extractive economy and throughout the agrarian world. But in most cases he is content to determine in a general way when spring or summer begin, when cold will set in, when rain or snow will fall. In hydraulic civilizations such general knowledge is insufficient. In areas of full aridity it is crucial to be prepared for the rise of the rivers whose overflow, properly handled, brings fertility and life and whose unchecked waters leave death and devastation in their wake. The dikes have to be repaired in the proper season so that they will hold in times of inundation; and the canals have to be cleaned so that the moisture will be satisfactorily distributed. In semi-arid areas receiving a limited or uneven rainfall an accurate calendar is similarly important. Only when the embankments, canals, and reservoirs are ready and in good condition can the scanty precipitation be fully utilized.

The need for reallocating the periodically flooded fields and determining the dimension and bulk of hydraulic and other structures provide continual stimulation for developments in geometry and arithmetic. Herodotus ascribes the beginnings of geometry in Egypt to the need for annually remeasuring the inundated land.[2]

No matter whether the earliest scientific steps in this direction were made in the Nile Valley or in Mesopotamia, the basic correlation is eminently plausible. Obviously the pioneers and masters of hydraulic civilization were singularly well equipped to lay the foundations for two major and interrelated sciences: astronomy and mathematics.

As a rule, the operations of time keeping and scientific measuring and counting were performed by official dignitaries or by priestly (or secular) specialists attached to the hydraulic regime. Wrapped in a cloak of magic and astrology and hedged with profound secrecy, these mathematical and astronomical operations became the means both for improving hydraulic production and bulwarking the superior power of the hydraulic leaders.

D. FURTHER CONSTRUCTION ACTIVITIES CUSTOMARY IN HYDRAULIC SOCIETIES

THE masters of the hydraulic state did not confine their activities to matters immediately connected with agriculture. The methods of cooperation which were so effective in the sphere of crop-raising were easily applied to a variety of other large tasks.

Certain types of works are likely to precede others. Generally speaking, the irrigation canal is older than the navigation canal; and hydraulic digging and damming occurred prior to the building of highways. But often derivative steps were taken before the original activities had progressed far, and different regional conditions favored different evolutionary sequences. Thus the divergencies of inter-action and growth are great. They include many constructional activities above and beyond the sphere of hydraulic agriculture.[a]

1. NONAGRARIAN HYDRAULIC WORKS

a. Aqueducts and Reservoirs Providing Drinking Water

A COMMONWEALTH able to transfer water for purposes of irriga-tion readily applies its hydraulic know-how to the providing of drinking water. The need for such action was slight in the greater part of Medieval Europe, where the annual precipitation furnished sufficient ground water for the wells on which most towns depended for their water supply.[1]

Even in the hydraulic world, drinking water is not necessarily an issue. Wherever rivers, streams, or springs carry enough moisture

a. Anyone interested in studying the technical and organizational details of a major hydraulic order may consult Willcocks' admirable description of irrigation and flood control in 19th-century Egypt (Willcocks, 1889: *passim*). A comprehensive survey of the hydraulic conditions in India at the close of the 19th century has been made by the Indian Irrigation Commission (RRCAI). In my study of Chinese economics and society I have systematically analyzed the ecological foundations and the various aspects of China's traditional hydraulic order (Wittfogel, 1931: 61–93, 188–300, and 410–56). Today we also have an archaeological account of the growth of hydraulic and other construc-tions over time and for a limited, but evidently, representative area: the Virú Valley in Peru (see Willey, 1953: 344–89).

to satisfy the drinking needs of the population throughout the year, no major problem arises. The inhabitants of the Nile and Ganges Valleys and of many similar areas did not have to construct elaborate aqueducts for this purpose.

The irregular flow of rivers or streams or the relatively easy access to fresh and clear mountain water has stimulated in many hydraulic landscapes the construction of comprehensive installations for the storage and distribution of drinking water. In America great aqueducts were built by the hydraulic civilizations of the Andean zone and Meso-America.[2] The many reservoirs (tanks) of Southern India frequently serve several uses; but near the large residential centers the providing of drinking water is usually paramount. In certain areas of the Near East, such as Syria and Assyria, brilliantly designed aqueducts have satisfied the water needs of many famous cities, Tyre,[3] Antioch,[4] and Nineveh[5] among them. In the Western world of rainfall agriculture, aqueducts were built primarily by such Mediterranean peoples as the Greeks and the Romans, who since the dawn of history maintained contact with—and learned from— the technically advanced countries of Western Asia and North Africa. No doubt the Greeks and Romans would have been able to solve their drinking-water problem without inspiration from the outside; but the form of their answer strongly suggests the influence of Oriental engineering.[6]

b. Navigation Canals

AMONG the great agrarian conformations of history, only hydraulic society has constructed navigation canals of any major size. The seafaring Greeks, making the Mediterranean their highway, avoided an issue which the ancient city states were poorly equipped to handle. The not-too-numerous Roman canals were apparently all dug at a time when the growing Orientalization of the governmental apparatus stimulated, among other things, a growing interest in all kinds of public works.[7]

The rainfall farmers of Medieval Europe, like their counterparts elsewhere, shunned rather than sought the marshy river lowlands. And their feudal masters paid little attention to the condition of the watercourses, for which they had no use. Still less did they feel obliged to construct additional and artificial rivers—canals. Few if any important canals were built during the Middle Ages,[8] and medieval trade and transport were seriously handicapped by the state of the navigable rivers.[9]

It was in connection with the rise of a governmentally encouraged commercial and industrial capitalism that the West began to build canals on a conspicuous scale. The "pioneer of the canals of modern Europe," the French Canal du Midi, was completed only in the second half of the 17th century, in 1681,[10] that is, little more than a century before the end of the absolutist regime. And in the classical country of inland navigation, England,[11] "little . . . was done in making canals . . . until the middle of the eighteenth century" [12]— that is, until a time well after the close of England's absolutist period and immediately prior to the beginning of the machine age.

As stated above, the members of a hydraulic commonwealth felt quite differently about the management of natural and artificial watercourses. They approached the fertility-bearing rivers as closely as possible, and in doing so they had to find ways of draining the lowland marshes and strengthening and reshaping the river banks. Naturally the question of inland navigation did not arise everywhere. Existing rivers and streams might be suitable for irrigation, but not for shipping (Pueblos, Chagga, Highland Peru); or the ocean might prove an ideal means of transportation (Hawaii, Coastal Peru). In certain localities inland navigation was satisfactorily served by man-managed rivers (Egypt, India) and lakes (Mexico) plus whatever irrigation canals were large enough to accommodate boats (Mesopotamia).

But when supplementary watercourses were not only possible but desirable, the organizers of agrohydraulic works had little difficulty in utilizing their cooperative "apparatus" to make them available. The new canals might be only minor additions to the existing watercourses. The ancient Egyptians constructed canals in order to circumnavigate impassable cataracts, and they temporarily connected the Nile and the Red Sea; [13] but these enterprises had little effect on the over-all pattern of the country's hydraulic economy. In other instances, navigation canals assumed great importance. They satisfied the needs of the masters of the hydraulic state: the transfer of parts of the agrarian surplus to the administrative centers and the transport of messengers and troops.

In Thailand (Siam) the different hydraulic tasks overlapped. In addition to the various types of productive and protective hydraulic installations, the government constructed in the centers of rice production and state power a number of canals, which essentially served as "waterways," that is, as a means for transporting the rice surplus to the capital.[14]

The corresponding development in China is particularly well documented. In the large plains of North China the beginnings of navigation canals go back to the days of the territorial states—that is, to the period prior to 221 B.C., when the various regional governments were still administered by officials who were given office lands in payment for their services. The difference between the state-centered system of land grants as it prevailed in early China and the knighthood feudalism of Medieval Europe is spectacularly demonstrated by the almost complete absence of public works in feudal Europe and the enormous development of such works—hydraulic and otherwise—in the territorial states of China.[b]

The geographical and administrative unification of China which vastly increased the political need for navigation canals also increased the state's organizational power to build them. The first centuries of the empire saw a great advance not only in the construction of irrigation canals,[15] reservoirs, and protective river dikes but also in the digging of long canals for administrative and fiscal purposes.[16]

When, after several centuries of political fragmentation, the Sui rulers at the end of the 6th century again unified "all-under-heaven," they bulwarked the new political structure by creating out of earlier and substantial beginnings the gigantic Imperial Canal, significantly known in China as Yün Ho, "the Transport Canal." This canal extends today for about 800 miles, its length equaling the distance from the American-Canadian Great Lakes to the Gulf of Mexico or

b. Previously I viewed Chou China as a feudal society exhibiting Oriental features, which appeared early and became increasingly conspicuous until, at the close of the period, they prevailed completely (Wittfogel, 1931: 278 ff.; ibid., 1935: 40 ff.). The idea of a society that crosses the institutional divide is entirely compatible with the findings of the present inquiry (see below, Chap. 6); and by interpreting Chou society in this way, I would not have had to change a long-held position. But intensified comparative studies compel me to change. The arid and semi-arid settings of North China (17 inches annual rainfall in the old Chou domain and 24 inches in the domain of the pre-Chou dynasty, Shang) suggest hydraulic agriculture for the ancient core areas. The lay of the land, the summer floods, and the periodic silting-up of the rivers necessitated comprehensive measures of flood control especially in the heartland of Shang power. A realistic interpretation of legends and protohistorical sources (cf. Wittfogel and Goldfrank, 1943: passim) points to the rise of a hydraulic way of life long before the Shang dynasty, whose artifacts (bronzes) and inscriptions reflect a highly developed agrarian civilization with refined techniques of record keeping, calculations, and astronomy. The recognizable institutions of early Chou are those of a hydraulic society, which gradually intensified its managerial and bureaucratic "density" (for this concept see below, Chap. 6). The Chou sovereigns behaved toward the territorial rulers not as the first among equals but as supreme masters responsible only to Heaven. It was not their fault that their despotic claims, which possibly imitated Shang precedents, were realized imperfectly and with decreasing effect. In contrast, the rulers of the territorial states were strong enough to proceed absolutistically within their respective realms. The lands that they assigned were given not in a contractual way and to independently organized (corporated) knights and barons, but to office holders and persons permitted to enjoy sinecures. They were not fiefs but office lands (see below, Chaps. 6-8).

—in European terms—the distance from Berlin to Bordeaux or from Hamburg to Rome. For labor on part of this gigantic water work the Sui government mobilized in the regions north of the Yellow River alone "more than a million of men and women," [17] that is, almost one-half of the total population which England is said to have had from the 14th to the 16th century.[18]

The gigantic effort involved in banking the rivers and building the canals of China is indicated by the American agronomist, F. H. King, who conservatively estimates the combined lengths of the man-managed watercourses of China, Korea, and Japan at some 200,000 miles. "Forty canals across the United States from east to west and sixty from north to south would not equal in number of miles those in these three countries today. Indeed, it is probable that this estimate is not too large for China alone." [19]

2. LARGE NONHYDRAULIC CONSTRUCTIONS

a. Huge Defense Structures

THE need for comprehensive works of defense arises almost as soon as hydraulic agriculture is practiced. Contrary to the rainfall farmer, who may shift his fields with relative ease, the irrigation farmer finds himself depending on an unmovable, if highly rewarding, source of fertility. In the early days of hydraulic cultivation reliance on a fixed system of water supply must in many cases have driven the agrarian community to build strong defenses around its homes and fields.

For this purpose hydraulic agriculture proved suggestive in two ways: it taught man how to handle all kinds of building materials, earth, stone, timber, etc., and it trained him to manipulate these materials in an organized way. The builders of canals and dams easily became the builders of trenches, towers, palisades, and extended defense walls.

In this, as in all corresponding cases, the character and magnitude of the operations were determined by internal and external circumstances. Surrounded by aggressive neighbors, the Pueblo Indians ingeniously utilized whatever building material was at hand to protect their settlements, which rarely comprised more than a few hundred inhabitants.[c] The fortress-like quality of their villages is manifest to the present-day anthropologist; it struck the Spanish

---

[c]. Castañeda, 1896: 512. Bandelier upholds Castañeda's figures against divergent statements made in other early Spanish sources (Bandelier, FR, I: 120 ff. and nn.; cf. *ibid.*, DH: 312, 46 ff., 171–3).

conquistadores, who were forced at times to besiege a single settlement for days and weeks before they could take it.[d] Rigid cooperation assured security of residence, just as it assured success in farming. An early observer stresses this aspect of Pueblo life: "They all work together to build the villages." [e]

d. Castañeda, who was the official chronicler of the first Spanish expedition, notes (1896: 494) that the defense towers of a large Zuni settlement were equipped with "embrassures and loopholes . . . for defending the roofs of the different stories." He adds, "The roofs have to be reached first, and these upper houses are the means of defending them." The experiences of the second expedition confirmed and supplemented the initial observations. Gallegos concludes his remarks concerning Pueblo building by referring to the movable wooden ladders "by means of which they climb to their quarters." At night "they lift them up since they wage war with one another" (Gallegos, 1927: 265). Obregon also stresses the military value of the ladders; in addition, he explains how the edifices themselves served to protect the community: "These houses have walls and loopholes from which they defend themselves and attack their enemies in their battles" (Obregon, 1928: 293).

One of Coronado's lieutenants, approaching certain Tigua settlements, "found the villages closed by palisades." The Pueblos, whose inhabitants had been subjected to various forms of extortion and insult "were all ready for fighting. Nothing could be done, because they would not come down onto the plain and the villages are so strong that the Spaniards could not dislodge them." Attacking a hostile village, the Spanish soldiers reached the upper story by surprise tactics. They remained in this dangerous position for a whole day, unable to prevail until the Mexican Indians, who accompanied them, approached the Pueblo from below, digging their way in and smoking out the defenders (Castañeda, 1896: 496). For a discussion of Castañeda's report see Bandelier, DH: 38 ff.)

Besieging a large Tigua settlement, Coronado's men had an opportunity to test thoroughly the defense potential of a Pueblo which was not taken by surprise: "As the enemy had had several days to provide themselves with stores, they threw down such quantities of rocks upon our men that many of them were laid down, and they wounded nearly a hundred with arrows." The siege lasted for seven weeks. During this time, the Spaniards made several assaults; but they were unable to take the Pueblo. The villagers eventually abandoned their fortress-like bulwark, not because the aggressors had penetrated their defenses, but because of lack of water (Castañeda, 1896: 498 ff.; cf. RDS: 576). Bandelier supplements Castañeda's report of this significant event by an account given by Mota Padilla, an 18th-century author, who claims to have had access to the original writings of still another member of Coronado's staff (Bandelier, DH: 323). Mota Padilla's version contains a number of details which reveal the techniques of attack as well as the strength and ingenuity of the defense. Some of the Spaniards "reached the top of the wall, but there they found that the natives had removed the roofs of many (upper) rooms, so that there was no communication between them, and as there were little towers at short distances from each other, from which missiles were showered upon the assailants on the top, the Spaniards had more than sixty of their number hurt, three of whom died of their wounds" (*ibid.,* 48).

e. Castañeda (1896: 520) qualifies this general statement by saying that the women were "engaged in making the [adobe] mixture and the walls, while the men bring the wood and put it in place." Modern reports assign the above duties to the men and credit them in addition with erecting the walls, the construction labors of the women being confined to plastering (White, 1932: 33; cf. Parsons, 1932: 212). The

The Chagga were equally effective in the transfer of their hydraulic work patterns to military constructions. Their great chieftain, Horombo (*fl.* 1830), used "thousands of people" to build great fortifications, which in part still stand today.[20] "The walls of these fortifications are some six feet high, and in length 305 yards on the south side, 443 yards on the north, 277 yards on the east side, and 137 yards on the west side."[21] Tunnels, extended trenches, and dugouts added to the defense of the walled settlements, which appeared early in the history of the Chagga.[22] "Deep dugouts excavated under the huts and often leading into underground passages with outlets at some distance, were used for refuge. Almost every country was secured with great war trenches, which are everywhere to be seen at the present day and are often still of great depth."[23]

These instances show what even primitive hydraulic societies could achieve in the field of defense construction, when they strained their cooperative resources to the full. Higher hydraulic societies employed and varied the basic principle in accordance with technical and institutional circumstances.

In pre-Columbian Mexico the absence of suitable labor animals placed a limitation on transport, and while this restricted siege craft, it did not preclude the struggle for or the defense of the cities. In emergencies many government-built hydraulic works in the main lake area fulfilled military functions, just as the monster palaces and temples served as bastions against an invading enemy.[24] Recent research draws attention to various types of Mexican forts and defense walls.[25] Because of their size and importance, they may safely be adjudged as state-directed enterprises. The colossal fortresses and walls of pre-Inca Peru, which astonished early and recent observers,[26] are known to have been built at the order of the government and by "incredibly" large teams of corvée laborers.[27]

Many texts and pictorial representations have portrayed the walls, gates, and towers of ancient Egypt, Sumer, Babylonia, Assyria, and Syria. The *Arthashāstra* indicates the systematic manner in which the rulers of the first great Indian empire treated problems of fortification and defense.[28] At the dawn of Chinese history new capitals were created at the ruler's command, and during the last centuries of the Chou period the territorial states used their corviable manpower to wall entire frontier regions, not only against the tribal barbarians but also against each other. In the 3d century B.C. the unifier of

---

divergence between the early and recent descriptions may reflect an actual institutional change or merely a difference in the accuracy of observation. While interesting to the anthropologist, this discrepancy does not affect our basic conclusions regarding the communal character of large-scale building in the American Pueblos.

China, Ch'in Shih Huang-ti, linked together and elaborated older territorial structures to form the longest unbroken defense installation ever made by man.[29] The periodic reconstruction of the Chinese Great Wall expresses the continued effectiveness of hydraulic economy and government-directed mass labor.

b. Roads

THE existence of government-made highways is suggested for the Babylonian period;[30] it is documented for Assyria.[31] And the relationship between these early constructions and the roads of Persia, the Hellenistic states, and Rome seems "beyond doubt."[f] The great Persian "royal road" deeply impressed the contemporary Greeks;[32] it served as a model for the Hellenistic rulers,[33] whose efforts in turn inspired the official road builders of the Roman empire.[34] According to Mez, the Arabs inherited "the type of 'governmental road,' like its name, from the Persian 'Royal Road.' "[35] Beyond this, however, they showed little interest in maintaining good roads, probably because they continued to rely in the main on camel caravans for purposes of transport. The later Muslim regimes of the Near East used highways, but they never restored them to the state of technical perfection which characterized the pre-Arab period.[36]

Roads were a serious concern of India's vigorous Maurya kings.[37] A "royal road" of 10,000 *stadia,* which is said to have led from the capital to the northwestern border, had a system of marking distances which, in a modified form, was again employed by the Mogul emperors.[38] In Southern India, where Hindu civilization was perpetuated for centuries after the north had been conquered, government-made roads are mentioned in the inscriptions; and "some of them are called king's highways."[39] The Muslim rulers of India continued the Indian rather than the West Asian pattern in their effort to maintain a network of state roads.[40] Sher Shāh (*d.* 1545) built four great roads, one of which ran from Bengal to Agra, Delhi, and Lahore.[41] Akbar is said to have been inspired by Sher Shāh when he built a new "king's highway," called the Long Walk, which for four hundred miles was "shaded by great trees on both sides."[42]

In China, a gigantic network of highways was constructed immediately after the establishment of the empire in 221 B.C. But in this case, as in the cases of the irrigation and navigation canals or

f. Meissner, BA, I: 341. The term "royal road" was used in an Assyrian inscription (Olmstead, 1923: 334). The operational pattern of the Roman state post, the *cursus publicus,* can be traced back through the Hellenistic period to Persia and perhaps even to Babylonia (Wilcken, 1912: 372 and n. 2).

the long defense walls, the imperial engineers systematized and elaborated only what their territorial predecessors had initiated. Long before the 3d century B.C. an efficient territorial state was expected to have well kept overland highways, supervised by central and local officials, lined with trees, and provided with stations and guest houses.[43] Under the empire, great state roads connected all the important centers of the northern core area with the capital. According to the official *History of the Han Dynasty*, the First Emperor

> built the Imperial Road throughout the empire. To the east it stretched to Yen and Ch'i and to the south it reached Wu and Ch'u. The banks and the shore of the Chiang [the Yangtze River] and the lakes and the littoral along the sea coast were all made accessible. The highway was fifty paces wide. A space three *chang* [approximately twenty-two feet] wide in the center was set apart by trees. The two sides were firmly built, and metal bars were used to reinforce them. Green pine trees were planted along it. He constructed the Imperial Highway with such a degree of elegance that later generations were even unable to find a crooked path upon which to place their feet.[44]

In the subsequent dynasties the building and maintenance of the great trunk roads and their many regional branches remained a standard task of China's central and local administration.

The rugged terrain of Meso-America and the absence of fully coordinated empires seems to have discouraged the construction of highways during the pre-Columbian period, at least on the high plateau. But the Andean area was the scene of extraordinary road building. The Spanish conquerors described in detail the fine highways which crossed both the coastal plain and the highlands and which formed connecting links between them.[45] Commenting on the Andean roads, Hernando Pizarro writes he never saw their like in similar terrain "within the entire Christian world." [46] In fact the only parallel he could think of was the system of highways built by the Romans. The similarity is telling. As we shall discuss below, the extensive Roman roads were the fruits of a fateful transformation that made the Roman Empire a Hellenistically (Orientally) despotic state.

The efforts required to build all these great highways have attracted much less attention than the finished products. But what evidence we have indicates that like most other major government enterprises, they were mainly executed through the cooperative effort of state-levied corvée laborers. Under the Inca empire supervisory officials marked off the land and informed the local inhabitants "that they should make these roads." And this was done with little cost to the government. The commandeered men "come with their food and tools to make them." [g]

The highways of imperial China required an enormous labor force for their construction and a very sizable one for their maintenance. A Han inscription notes that the construction of a certain highway in the years A.D. 63–66 occupied 766,800 men. Of this great number only 2,690 were convicts.[47]

c. Palaces, Capital Cities, and Tombs

A GOVERNMENTAL apparatus capable of executing all these hydraulic and nonhydraulic works could easily be used in building palaces and pleasure grounds for the ruler and his court, palace-like government edifices for his aides, and monuments and tombs for the distinguished dead. It could be used wherever the equalitarian conditions of a primitive tribal society yielded to tribal or no-longer tribal forms of autocracy.

The head chief of a Pueblo community had his fields worked for him by the villagers. But apparently his dwelling did not differ from the houses of other tribesmen, except perhaps that it was better and more securely located. The Chagga chieftains had veritable palaces erected for their personal use; and the corvée labor involved in their construction was substantial.[48]

The colossal palaces of the rulers of ancient Peru were erected by the integrated manpower of many laborers. In pre-Columbian Mexico, Nezahualcoyotzin, the king of Tezcuco, the second largest country in the Aztec Federation, is said to have employed more than 200,000 workers each day for the building of his magnificent palace and park.[49]

Unlimited control over the labor power of their subjects enabled the rulers of Sumer, Babylon, and Egypt to build their spectacular palaces, gardens, and tombs. The same work pattern prevailed in the many smaller states that shaped their government on the Mesopotamian or Egyptian model. According to the biblical records, King Solomon built his beautiful temple with labor teams that, like those of Babylonia, were kept at work for four months of the year.[50]

g. Cieza, 1943: 95. The regional organization and the repair work on the roads had already been noted by a member of the conquering army (Estete, 1938: 246). The lack of payment for services rendered in the road corvée is also recorded by Blas Valeras, who states that similar conditions prevailed with regard to work on the bridges and irrigation canals (Garcilaso, 1945, I: 258).

The great edifices of Mogul India have been frequently described. Less known but equally worthy of mention are the constructions of the earlier periods. The third ruler of the Tughluq, Fīrūs Shāh (ca. 1308–88), dug several important irrigation canals, the famous "Old Jumna Canal" among them. He built forts, palaces, and palace-cities, mosques, and tombs. The palace-fort of Koṭla Fīrūs Shāh, which rose in his new capital of Fīrūsābād (Delhi), faithfully preserved the grand style of pre-Islamic Indian and Eastern architecture.[51]

The Chinese variant of the general agromanagerial building trend is revealed in many elaborate works. The First Emperor of China, Ch'in Shih Huang-ti, began to build great hydraulic works in the early days of his power; and in the course of his reign he completed colossal works of the nonhydraulic public and semiprivate types. Having destroyed all his territorial rivals, he constructed the previously mentioned network of highways which gave his officials, messengers, and troops easy access to all regions of his far-flung empire. Later he defended himself against the northern pastoralists by consolidating the Great Wall. Palaces for his personal use had been built in the early days of his reign; but it was only in 213 B.C. that work was begun on his superpalace. This monster project, together with the construction of his enormous tomb,[52] is said to have occupied work teams numbering over 700,000 persons.[53]

Eight hundred years later the second monarch of a reunified China, Emperor Yang (604–17) of the Sui Dynasty, mobilized a still larger labor force for the execution of similar monster enterprises. In addition to the more than one million persons—men and women —levied for the making of the Grand Canal,[54] he dispatched huge corvée teams to extend the imperial roads [55] and to work on the Great Wall. According to the *History of the Sui Dynasty,* over a million persons toiled at the Great Wall.[h] According to the same official source, the construction of the new eastern capital, which included a gigantic new imperial palace, involved no less than two million people "every month." [56]

d. Temples

THE position, fate, and prestige of the secular masters of hydraulic society were closely interlinked with that of their divine protectors. Without exception, the political rulers were eager to confirm and bulwark their own legitimacy and majesty by underlining the greatness of their supernatural supporters. Whether the government was

h. Over a million in 607; an additional 200,000 persons were employed in 608 (*Sui Shu* 3. 10b, 12a).

headed by secular monarchs or priest-kings, the commanding center made every effort to provide the supreme gods and their earthly functionaries with adequate surroundings for worship and residence.

Government-directed work teams, which erected gigantic palaces, were equally fitted to erect gigantic temples. Ancient inscriptions note the many temples built by the Mesopotamian rulers.[57] Usually the sovereign speaks as if these achievements resulted solely from his personal efforts. But occasional remarks indicate the presence of "the people" who toiled "according to the established plan." [i] Similarly, most Pharaonic texts refer to the final achievement [j] or to the greatness of the directing sovereign; [58] but again a number of texts refer to the government-led labor forces, "the people." [k]

In the agromanagerial cultures of pre-Columbian America, buildings for religious purposes were particularly conspicuous. Native tradition as well as the early Spanish accounts emphasize the tremendous labor required to construct and maintain the sacred houses and pyramids. The Mexicans coordinated their communal energies to erect the first temple for the newly established island city, the later Aztec capital; [59] and their increasingly powerful descendants mobilized the manpower of many subjugated countries for the construction of increasingly huge temples.[m] The city-like palace of the famous King of Tezcuco, Nezahualcoyotzin, contained no less than forty temples.[60] The great number of laborers engaged in building this palace- and temple-city has already been cited. Like the monster work teams of Mexico, those of Tezcuco could draw upon the entire corviable population.[n] In another country of the main lake region, Cuauhtitlan, the construction of large-scale hydraulic works [61] was followed by the building of a great temple. It took thirteen years to complete the second task.[62]

In the Andean zone, as in most other areas of the hydraulic world, the attachment of the priesthood to the government is beyond doubt. The Incas made heavy levies on their empire's material wealth in

i. Price, 1927: 24; cf. Thureau-Dangin, 1907: 111, and Barton, 1929: 225. Schneider (1920: 46) and Deimel (1931: 101 ff.) deplore the scarcity of concrete data concerning the Sumerian construction industry.

j. Thus in one of the oldest inscriptions of Egypt extant, the Palermo Stone (Breasted, 1927, I: 64).

k. "I have commanded those who work, to do according as thou shalt exact" (Breasted, 1927, I: 245). The "people" bring the stone for the Amon Temple; and the "people" also do the building. Among the workmen are several types of artisans (ibid., II: 294, 293).

m. Tezozomoc, 1944: 79 (the Temple of Huitzilopochtli) and 157 (the great Cu edifice of the same god).

n. Ixtlilxochitl, OH, II: 173 ff. The Annals of Cuauhtitlan also refer to this construction (Chimalpópoca, 1945: 52), without, however, discussing the labor aspect.

order to beautify their temples and pyramids.[63] They called up whatever manpower was needed to collect the raw material, transport it, and do the actual work of construction.[64]

E. THE MASTERS OF HYDRAULIC SOCIETY— GREAT BUILDERS

EVIDENTLY the masters of hydraulic society, whether they ruled in the Near East, India, China, or pre-Conquest America, were great builders. The formula is usually invoked for both the aesthetic and the technical aspect of the matter; and these two aspects are indeed closely interrelated. We shall briefly discuss both of them with regard to the following types of hydraulic and nonhydraulic construction works:

I. Hydraulic works
   A. Productive installations
      (Canals, aqueducts, reservoirs, sluices, and dikes for the purpose of irrigation)
   B. Protective installations
      (Drainage canals and dikes for flood control)
   C. Aqueducts providing drinking water
   D. Navigation canals

II. Nonhydraulic works
   A. Works of defense and communication
      1. Walls and other structures of defense
      2. Highways
   B. Edifices serving the public and personal needs of the secular and religious masters of hydraulic society
      1. Palaces and capital cities
      2. Tombs
      3. Temples

1. THE AESTHETIC ASPECT

a. Uneven Conspicuousness

THE majority of persons who have commented on the great builders of Asia and ancient America are far more articulate on the nonhydraulic than on the hydraulic achievements. Within the hydraulic sphere more attention is again given to the aqueducts for drinking water and the navigation canals than to the productive and protective installations of hydraulic agriculture. In fact, these last are frequently overlooked altogether. Among the nonhydraulic works, the "big houses" of power and worship and the tombs of the great are much more carefully investigated than are the large installations of communication and defense.

This uneven treatment of the monster constructions of hydraulic society is no accident. For functional, aesthetic, and social reasons the hydraulic works are usually less impressive than the nonhydraulic constructions. And similar reasons encourage uneven treatment also within each of the two main categories.

Functionally speaking, irrigation canals and protective embankments are widely and monotonously spread over the landscape, whereas the palaces, tombs, and temples are spatially concentrated. Aesthetically speaking, most of the hydraulic works are undertaken primarily for utilitarian purposes, whereas the residences of the rulers and priests, the houses of worship, and the tombs of the great are meant to be beautiful. Socially speaking, those who organize the distribution of manpower and material are the same persons who particularly and directly enjoy the benefits of many nonhydraulic structures. In consequence they are eager to invest a maximum of aesthetic effort in these structures (palaces, temples, and capital cities) and a minimum of such effort in all other works.

Of course, the contrast is not absolute. Some irrigation works, dikes, aqueducts, navigation canals, highways, and defense walls do achieve considerable functional beauty. And closeness to the centers of power may lead the officials in charge to construct embankments, aqueducts, highways, bridges, walls, gates, and towers with as much care for aesthetic detail as material and labor permit.

But these secondary tendencies do not alter the two basic facts that the majority of all hydraulic and nonhydraulic public works are aesthetically less conspicuous than the royal and official palaces, temples, and tombs, and that the most important of all hydraulic works—the canals and dikes—from the standpoint of art and artistry are the least spectacular of all.

b. The Monumental Style

SUCH discrepancies notwithstanding, the palaces, government buildings, temples, and tombs share one feature with the "public" works proper: they, too, tend to be large. The architectural style of hydraulic society is monumental.

This style is apparent in the fortress-like settlements of the Pueblo Indians. It is conspicuous in the palaces, temple cities, and fortresses of ancient Middle and South America. It characterizes the tombs, palace-cities, temples, and royal monuments of Pharaonic Egypt and ancient Mesopotamia. No one who has ever observed the city gates and walls of a Chinese capital, such as Peking, or who has walked through the immense palace gates and squares of the Forbidden City to enter its equally immense court buildings, ancestral temples, and private residences can fail to be awed by their monumental design.

Pyramids and dome-shaped tombs manifest most consistently the monumental style of hydraulic building. They achieve their aesthetic effect with a minimum of ideas and a maximum of material. The pyramid is little more than a huge pile of symmetrically arranged stones.

The property-based and increasingly individualistic society of ancient Greece loosened up the massive architecture, which had emerged in the quasihydraulic Mycenaean period.[1] During the later part of the first millennium B.C., when Alexander and his successors ruled the entire Near East, the architectural concepts of Hellas transformed and refined the hydraulic style without, however, destroying its monumental quality.

In Islamic architecture the two styles blended to create a third. The products of this development were as spectacular in the westernmost outpost of Islamic culture—Moorish Spain—as they were in the great eastern centers: Cairo, Baghdad, Bukhara, Samarkand, and Istanbul. The Taj Mahal of Agra and kindred buildings show the same forces at work in India, a subcontinent which, before the Islamic invasion, had evolved a rich monumental architecture of its own.

c. The Institutional Meaning

IT hardly needs to be said that other agrarian civilizations also combined architectural beauty with magnitude. But the hydraulic rulers differed from the secular and priestly lords of the ancient and medieval West, first because their constructional operations penetrated more spheres of life, and second because control over the entire country's labor power and material enabled them to attain much more monumental results.

The scattered operations of rainfall farming did not involve the establishment of national patterns of cooperation, as did hydraulic agriculture. The many manorial centers of Europe's knighthood society gave rise to as many fortified residences (castles); and their size was limited by the number of the attached serfs. The king, being little more than the most important feudal lord, had to build his castles with whatever labor force his personal domain provided.

The concentration of revenue in the regional or territorial centers

of ecclesiastical authority permitted the creation of the largest individual medieval edifices: churches, abbeys, and cathedrals. It may
be noted that these buildings were erected by an institution which,
in contrast to all other prominent Western bodies, combined feudal
with quasihydraulic patterns of organization and acquisition.

With regard to social control and natural resources, however, the
master builders of the hydraulic state had no equal in the nonhydraulic world. The modest Tower of London and the dispersed
castles of Medieval Europe express the balanced baronial society of
the Magna Carta as clearly as the huge administrative cities and
colossal palaces, temples, and tombs of Asia, Egypt, and ancient
America express the organizational coordination and the mobilization potential of hydraulic economy and statecraft.[a]

F. THE BULK OF ALL LARGE NONCONSTRUCTIONAL INDUSTRIAL ENTERPRISES MANAGED ALSO BY THE HYDRAULIC GOVERNMENT

1. A Comparative View

A GOVERNMENT capable of handling all major hydraulic and nonhydraulic construction may, if it desires, play a leading role also in
the nonconstructional branches of industry. There are "feeding" industries, such as mining, quarrying, salt gathering, etc.; and there are
finishing industries, such as the manufacture of weapons, textiles,
chariots, furniture, etc. Insofar as the activities in these two spheres
proceeded on a large scale, they were for the most part either directly
managed or monopolistically controlled by the hydraulic governments. Under the conditions of Pharaonic Egypt and Inca Peru, direct management prevailed. Under more differentiated social conditions, the government tended to leave part of mining, salt gathering, etc. to heavily taxed and carefully supervised entrepreneurs,
while it continued to manage directly most of the large manufacturing workshops.

By combining these facts with what we know of the hydraulic and
nonhydraulic constructional operations of the state, we may in the
following table indicate the managerial position of the hydraulic
state both in agriculture and industry. For purposes of comparison,
we include corresponding data from two other agrarian societies and
from mercantilist Europe.

a. For another peculiarity of hydraulic architecture, the "introvert" character of
most of the residential buildings, with the exception of those of the ruler, see below,
p. 86, n. b.

TABLE 1. *Government Management in the Spheres of Agriculture and Industry*

| INSTITUTIONAL CONFORMATIONS | AGRICULTURE | | INDUSTRY | | Manufacturing | |
	Heavy Waterworks	Farming	Mining, etc.	Construction Industry	Large Shops	Small Shops
Hydraulic society	**+**	−	(+)[1]	**+**[2]	+	−
Coastal city states of classical Greece	−	−	−	−	−	−
Medieval Europe	−	(+)[3]	−	(+)[3]	(+)[3]	−
Mercantilist Europe	−	−	(−)	−	−	−

Key
+ Predominant
+ Outstandingly significant
− Irrelevant or absent
( ) Trend limited or modified by factors indicated in the text

1. Simpler conditions.
2. On a national scale.
3. On a manorial scale.

In ancient Greece, mining was mainly in the hands of licensed businessmen. As long as the concessionaire delivered a fixed part of his output to the state, he enjoyed "very extensive" rights; he "was said to 'buy' the mine, he organized the working as he pleased, the ore was his, and he could cede his concession to a third party." [1] In Medieval Europe mining was also essentially left to private entrepreneurs, who, having obtained a concession from the royal or territorial authorities, proceeded independently and mostly through craft cooperatives.[2] The mercantilist governments of Europe operated some mines directly; but the majority was managed by strictly supervised private owners.[3]

All these arrangements differ profoundly from the system of government mining prevailing in Pharaonic Egypt and Inca Peru. Mercantilist usage resembles in form, but not in institutional substance, the policy pursued in certain of the more differentiated hydraulic societies, where government operation of some mines was combined with private, but government-licensed, handling of others.[4]

Except for mining, Oriental and Occidental absolutism are less similar in the industrial sphere than has been claimed, whereas a resemblance of sorts does exist between hydraulic society and feudal Europe. In hydraulic society, the majority of the not-too-many larger industrial workshops was government managed. In the mercantilist Occident they were, under varying forms of state supervision, predominantly owned and run by private entrepreneurs. In the coastal city-states of classical Greece the government was neither equipped nor inclined to engage in industrial activities. The rulers of Medieval Europe, faced with a different situation, proceeded differently. In their manorial workshops they employed a number of serf-artisans, who were kept busy satisfying the needs of their masters. The feudal lords also summoned serf labor for the construction of "big houses" —castles. The similarity between this manorial system of cooperative work and the hydraulic pattern is evident. But again the functional similarity is limited by the differences in the societal setting. The medieval kings and barons could dispose only over the labor force of their own domains and estates, while the hydraulic rulers could draw on the unskilled and skilled labor of large territories, and ultimately on that of the whole country.

The decisive difference, however, between hydraulic society and the three civilizations with which we compare it lies, insofar as industry is concerned, in the sphere of construction. It is this sphere which more than any other sector of industry demonstrates the organizational power of hydraulic society. And it is this sphere which achieved results never attained by any other agrarian or mercantilist society.

The full institutional significance of this fact becomes apparent as soon as we connect it with the corresponding agrarian development. Government-managed heavy water works place the large-scale feeding apparatus of agriculture in the hands of the state. Government-managed construction works make the state the undisputed master of the most comprehensive sector of large-scale industry. In the two main spheres of production the state occupied an unrivaled position of operational leadership and organizational control.

2. THE POWER OF THE HYDRAULIC STATE OVER LABOR
GREATER THAN THAT OF CAPITALIST ENTERPRISES

In both spheres the hydraulic state levied and controlled the needed labor forces by coercive methods that were invocable by a feudal lord only within a restricted area, and that were altogether different from the methods customary under capitalist conditions. The hydraulic rulers were sufficiently strong to do on a national scale what a feudal sovereign or lord could accomplish only within the borders of his domain. They compelled able-bodied commoners to work for them through the agency of the corvée.

Corvée labor is forced labor. But unlike slave labor, which is demanded permanently, corvée labor is conscripted on a temporary, although recurring, basis. After the corvée service is completed, the worker is expected to go home and continue with his own business.

Thus the corvée laborer is freer than the slave. But he is less free than a wage laborer. He does not enjoy the bargaining advantages of the labor market, and this is the case even if the state gives him food (in the ancient Near East often "bread and beer") or some cash. In areas with a highly developed money economy the hydraulic government may levy a corvée tax and hire rather than conscript the needed labor. This was done largely in China at the close of the Ming dynasty and during the greater part of Ch'ing rule.

But there as elsewhere the government arbitrarily fixed the wage. And it always kept the workers under quasimilitary discipline.[5] Except in times of open political crisis, the hydraulic state could always muster the labor forces it required; and this whether the workers were levied or hired. It has been said that the Mogul ruler Akbar, "by his *firmān* (order) could collect any number of men he liked. There was no limit to his massing of labourers, save the number of people in his Empire." [6] *Mutatis mutandis,* this statement is valid for all hydraulic civilizations.

G. A GENUINE AND SPECIFIC TYPE OF MANAGERIAL REGIME

THUS the hydraulic state fulfilled a variety of important managerial functions.[a] In most instances it maintained crucial hydraulic works, appearing in the agrarian sphere as the sole operator of large preparatory and protective enterprises. And usually it also controlled the major nonhydraulic industrial enterprises, especially large constructions. This was the case even in certain "marginal" areas,[1] where the hydraulic works were insignificant.

The hydraulic state differs from the modern total managerial states in that it is based on agriculture and operates only part of the country's economy. It differs from the laissez-faire states of a private-property-based industrial society in that, in its core form, it fulfills crucial economic functions by means of commandeered (forced) labor.

---

a. Social science is indebted to James Burnham for pointing to the power potential inherent in managerial control. The present inquiry stresses the importance of the general (political) organizer as compared not only to the technical specialist (see Veblen, 1945: 441 ff.), but also to the economic manager. This, however, does not diminish the author's appreciation of the contribution made by Burnham through his concept of managerial leadership.

CHAPTER 3

A state stronger than society

A. NONGOVERNMENTAL FORCES COMPETING WITH THE STATE FOR SOCIETAL LEADERSHIP

THE hydraulic state is a genuinely managerial state. This fact has far-reaching societal implications. As manager of hydraulic and other mammoth constructions, the hydraulic state prevents the nongovernmental forces of society from crystallizing into independent bodies strong enough to counterbalance and control the political machine.

The relations between the governmental and nongovernmental forces of society are as manifold as the patterns of society itself. All governments are concerned with the protection of the commonwealth against external enemies (through the organization of military action) and with the maintenance of internal order (through jurisdiction and policing methods of one kind or another). The extent to which a government executes these and other tasks depends on the way in which the societal order encourages, or restricts, governmental activities on the one hand and the development of rival nongovernmental forces on the other.

The nongovernmental forces aiming at social and political leadership include kin groups (particularly under primitive conditions); representatives of autonomous religious organizations (customary in certain primitive civilizations but, as the history of the Christian Church shows, by no means confined to them); independent or semi-independent leaders of military groups (such as tribal bands, armies of feudal lords); and owners of various forms of property (such as money, land, industrial equipment, and capacity to work).

In some cases the rise of hydraulic despotism was probably contested by the heads of powerful clans or by religious groups eager to preserve their traditional autonomy. In others, semi-independent military leaders may have tried to prevent the masters of the hydraulic apparatus from attaining total control. But the rival forces lacked the proprietary and organizational strength that in Greek and Roman antiquity, as well as in Medieval Europe, bulwarked the nongovernmental forces of society. In hydraulic civilizations the men of the

49

government prevented the organizational consolidation of all non-governmental groups. Their state became "stronger than society." [1] Any organization that gives its representatives unchecked power over its subjects may be considered an "apparatus." In contrast to the controlled state of multicentered societies, the state of the single-centered hydraulic society was a veritable apparatus state.

B. THE ORGANIZATIONAL POWER OF THE HYDRAULIC STATE

1. THE GREAT BUILDERS OF HYDRAULIC SOCIETY— GREAT ORGANIZERS

SUPERIOR organizational power may have different roots. In a hydraulic setting the need for comprehensive organization is inherent in the comprehensive constructions necessitated or suggested by the peculiarities of the agrarian order.

These constructions pose numerous technical problems and they always require large-scale organization. To say that the masters of hydraulic society are great builders is only another way of saying they are great organizers.

2. FUNDAMENTALS OF EFFECTIVE ORGANIZATION: COUNTING AND RECORD KEEPING

AN organizer combines disparate elements into an integrated whole. He may do this *ex tempore* if his aim is simple or passing. He must make more elaborate preparations if he is confronted with a permanent and difficult task. Dealing with human beings—their labor power, their military potential, and their capacity to pay taxes—he must know their number and condition. To this end he must count the people. And whenever he expects to draw from them frequently and regularly, he must preserve the results of his count either by memorizing them or, above the most primitive level, by utilizing preliterary or literary symbols.

It is no accident that among all sedentary peoples the pioneers of hydraulic agriculture and statecraft were the first to develop rational systems of counting and writing. It is no accident either that the records of hydraulic society covered not only the limited areas of single cities or city states, of royal domains or feudal manors, but the towns and villages of entire nations and empires. The masters of hydraulic society were great builders because they were great organizers; and they were great organizers because they were great record keepers.

The colored and knotted strings (*quipus*) by which the Incas preserved the results of their frequent countings [1] show that the lack of a script constitutes no insurmountable barrier to numbering and registering the population. In pre-Conquest Mexico the various forms of land and the obligations attached were carefully depicted in codices; and the procedures of local administrators were apparently based on these all-important documents.[2]

In China an elaborate system of writing and counting existed as early as the Yin (Shang) dynasty, that is, in the second millennium B.C. Under the subsequent Chou dynasty census lists were used for determining potential fighters and laborers and for estimating revenue and expenditures. Specific evidence testifies to a detailed system of counting and registering in the ruling state of Chou,[3] and we know that at the close of the Chou period the people were registered in the great northwestern country of Ch'in,[4] and also in Ch'i. In Ch'i the census is said to have been taken every year in the autumn.[5] It was in this season that people were also counted under the first long-lived imperial dynasty, Han.[6] Preserved bamboo records indicate that the Han registers follow a regular pattern.[7] The two sets of Han census figures contained in the official history of the period [8] are the most comprehensive population data to come down to us from any major contemporary civilization, including the Roman Empire.

The later history of the Chinese census presents many problems which are far from solved. The methods and the accuracy of procedures changed greatly with time, but the government's role in the handling of these matters cannot be doubted. In one way or another, the imperial bureaucracy succeeded in keeping track of its human and material resources.

The same holds true for India. The *Arthashāstra* [9] and the Islamic sources [10] reveal the interest which both native and foreign rulers took in counting their subjects and estimating their revenues. And this interest was by no means academic. Megasthenes found various groups of officials in the Maurya empire charged with such tasks as measuring the fields and counting the people.[11] Numerous inscriptions throw light on surveys made during the last period of Hindu India.[12]

After China, we are probably best informed on the Near Eastern development of governmental counting and registering. The oldest deciphered inscriptions dealing with the economy of a Mesopotamian temple city contain many numerical data on land, people, agriculture, and public services.[13] In Pharaonic Egypt the people were counted regularly from the time of the Old Kingdom.[14] Documentary evidence for the connection between the census and fiscal and personal obligations exist only for the Middle and New Kingdoms, but the absence of still earlier data on this point is certainly accidental.[15] On the eve of the Hellenistic period persons and property seem to have been listed annually; [16] and the Ptolemies probably perpetuated the ancient system. The papyri suggest that there were two cadasters used for mutual checking, one in the individual villages and one in the metropolis.[17]

Under the succeeding regimes the methods of counting people and property, particularly land, underwent many modifications; but as in India and China the underlying principle continued to receive recognition. The Romans inherited the Hellenistic pattern [18] and the Arabs based their system on that of Eastern Rome.[19] The Mamluks upheld the time-honored system of record keeping,[20] as did the Ottoman Turks, who during the heyday of their power insisted that "every thirty years a census must be taken, the dead and the ill must be separated off, and those not on the rolls must be newly recorded." [21]

3. Organizational and Hydraulic Management

A GLANCE at the metropolitan and local centers of hydraulic record keeping recalls the original meaning of the term "bureau-cracy": "rule through bureaus." The power of the agromanagerial regime was indeed closely interlinked with the "bureaucratic" control which the government exerted over its subjects.

a. The Organizational Task Inherent in Large Constructions, Hydraulic and Otherwise

As stated above, enormous organizational tasks are inherent in the large constructions which the agrarian apparatus state accomplishes and which, particularly in their hydraulic form, play a decisive role in crystallizing the over-all conformation. Having, in the preceding chapter, dealt at some length with the constructional developments of hydraulic society, we shall confine ourselves here to re-emphasizing once more the cardinal importance of organization in this field.

b. Hydraulic Management

THE outstanding forms of hydraulic management (as juxtaposed to construction) are the distribution of irrigation water and flood watching. In general, these two operations require much less manpower than does the work of construction and repair, but those engaged in the former must cooperate very precisely.

Megasthenes describes the care with which officials of the Maurya empire opened and closed the canals and conduits to regulate the distribution of the irrigation water.[a] The highly systematized handbook of Chinese statecraft, the *Chou Li*, speaks of special officials who conducted the irrigation water from the reservoirs and larger canals to the smaller canals and ditches.[22] Herodotus, in a frequently quoted passage, tells how in Achaemenian Persia the sovereign himself supervised the major hydraulic operations: "The king orders the floodgates to be opened toward the country whose need is greatest, and lets the soil drink until it has had enough; after which the gates on this side are shut, and others are unclosed for the nation which, of the remainder, needs it most."[23]

Megasthenes and Herodotus make it very clear that the government was the distributing agent of the irrigation water; but they do not furnish organizational details. Such data are buried in administrative manuals and regulations which, because of their predominantly technical nature, have received little scholarly attention. Among the exceptions are some accounts of 10th- and 16th- (or 17th-) century Persia and several irrigation codes discovered in Bali.

The documents dealing with Persian conditions show the care with which the available water was assigned. They indicate also the clocklike cooperation between the "water master" (*mīrāb*), his subordinate officials and aides, and the village heads.[b] The Bali data familiarize us with the workings of a well-integrated hydraulic order. Here the ruler and the minister of revenues (*sedahan agong*) make the key decisions as to when and how to flood the various local hydraulic units, the *subak*.[24] The official head of a cluster of such units supervises the supply for each *subak*;[25] and the chief of the local unit, the *klian subak*, coordinates the individual peasants, who swear a solemn oath to submit to regulations while the rice fields, *sawah*, are being flooded.[26] "Thus the orderly distribution of the water among the various *sawah*-holders is accomplished with extreme care, and also with well-based reasons. The *sawah*-holder cannot at any time dispose over his share of the water supply where the water is scarce. The

---

a. Strabo 15. 1. 50. Smith, 1914: 132. Buddha himself is said to have settled a conflict between two city states over their rights to use the waters of a nearby river (*Jātakam*, V: 219).

b. Lambton, 1948: 589 ff. *Ibid.*, 1938: 665 ff. The organization of the irrigation system in East Persia at the time of the Abbassid caliphate is described in Arab sources. The head of the water office in Merv had at his disposal ten thousand hands, and his power surpassed that of the district police chief. The storage dam below the city was operated by four hundred guards; and the technique of measuring and distributing the water was minutely regulated (Mez, 1922: 423 ff.). For the institution of the water master in ancient and modern South Arabia see Grohmann, 1933: 31.

various *sawah*-holders, even if they belong to the same *subak,* must share the available water and must have their *sawah* flooded in sequence." [27]

The organizational operations involved in the distribution of the irrigation water are remarkable for their subtlety and for their centralization of leadership. Conflicts are frequent between cultivator and cultivator and between *subak* and *subak.* "If each *sawah*-holder could do as he pleases, there would soon arise the greatest disorder and the lower *subak* would probably never get their water." All these problems are successfully resolved because essentially "the distribution of the water as well as the water law lies in the hands of a single person." [28]

The control of flood water necessitates greater organizational effort only under special circumstances. An operational problem arises primarily where the seasonal overflow of an extended source of water threatens the irrigation system and the safety of those depending on it. In Bali the upper courses of the river have to be watched; and especially assigned men fulfill this function as a regular part of their hydraulic corvée.[29] In imperial China, even in times of decay, the government placed thousands of persons along their extended embankments in the battle against potential floods.[30] Between 1883 and 1888 the Egyptian government levied about one hundred thousand corviable persons annually to watch and fight the flood.[31]

4. The Organization of Quick Locomotion and Intelligence

UNDER hydraulic conditions of agriculture, certain large operations of construction and management must be organized. Other organizational activities are not imperative, but they are made possible by a political economy which compels the government to maintain centers of direction and coordination in all major regions of production. Being able to establish its authority not only over a limited "royal domain" and a number of royal towns—as does the typical feudal state—the hydraulic regime places its administrators and officers in all major settlements, which virtually everywhere assume the character of government-controlled administrative and garrison towns.

Effective governmental control involves first the political and fiscal superiority of the directing agency and second the means for conveying commands and commanders to the subcenters of control. The desire to exert power through the control of communications characterizes all political hierarchies; but circumstances determine the extent to which this desire will be satisfied. The overlord of a feudal society valued fast communications as much as any Oriental despot; but the spotty distribution of his administrative centers and the politically conditioned lack of good roads prevented his messages from traveling as quickly or as safely as did the messages of the hydraulic sovereign.

The development of long highways and navigation canals is only another manifestation of the extraordinary construction potential of hydraulic society. Similarly the development of effective systems of communication is only another manifestation of its extraordinary organizational potential. Almost all hydraulic states bulwarked their power by elaborate systems of "postal" communication and intelligence.

The terms "post" or "postal service" express the fact that persons are "posted" at intervals along the road; the formula "relay system" points to the regulated interaction between the persons so posted. The terms will be used interchangeably and with the understanding that, within our context, they refer to an organization maintained by the state for the purposes of the state. On occasion the post handled rare and perishable goods (fruit and fish for the court, etc.). But its primary aim was the movement of persons of privilege (envoys, officials, foreign diplomats), messengers, and messages—these latter including intelligence of the most confidential, important, and delicate nature.

In the decentralized society of Medieval Europe individuals or groups of individuals (merchants, butchers, towns) established overland communications long before the government undertook the organization of a systematic postal service.[32] In the hydraulic world, private communications were not lacking,[33] but they never competed with the far-flung and effective relay system of the state. By running the post as a political institution, the representatives of Oriental government maintained a monopoly over fast locomotion, which— interlocked with an elaborate system of intelligence—became a formidable weapon of social control.

The hydraulic countries of ancient America present the relay system in a simple but highly effective form. In the absence of suitable transport animals, messages were carried by runners, who in the Mexican area proceeded along more or less informal routes and in the Andean area, along excellent state highways. The Mexican relay stations are said to have been set something like two leagues (ca. 6 miles) apart;[34] and, according to Torquemada, the speed with which messages could be delivered exceeded one hundred leagues (300 miles) per day.[35] The stations along the Inca road were closer to each other, at times no more than three-quarters of a mile separating them. The runners could move at a speed of one hundred and fifty miles per day. According to Cobo, one message was carried from the coastal town of Lima to Cuzco, the capital of the *altiplano,* over approximately four hundred miles of difficult and often steep terrain, in something like three days. A hundred years after the conquest it took the Spanish horse-mail twelve to thirteen days to cover the same ground.ᶜ While on service, the runners had to be fed; and this was the responsibility of the settlements through which the relay routes passed.³⁶ As a matter of fact, in all parts of the hydraulic world those who lived along the post roads were generally compelled to provision the stations, furnish auxiliary labor, and supply the draft and transport animals, carriages, sedan chairs or boats demanded by the relay officials.

The Incas are said to have been extremely well informed about the remotest regions of their empire.³⁷ The far-flung organization of the postal system of Achaemenian Persia greatly impressed Herodotus.³⁸ Private letters might also be carried, but for security reasons they were read by the postal officials.³⁹ Xenophon stressed the intelligence angle. Through the royal post the Achaemenian kings were able "to learn with great celerity the state of affairs at any distance." ⁴⁰

The technical peculiarities of the Roman state post have been frequently described. The layout of its larger and smaller stations (*mansiones* and *mutationes*) and the organizational pattern of the institution are indeed remarkable.⁴¹ But it is important to remember that from the very beginning the *cursus publicus* was primarily aimed at providing the imperial center with information.⁴² By establishing the post, Augustus laid the foundations for a comprehensive intelligence system. Special officials, first called *frumentarii* and from Diocletian on *agentes in rebus,* operated in conjunction with the technical staff. Their activities enormously strengthened the hold of the autocracy over its subjects.⁴³

At the beginning of the Byzantine period the postal system is said to have been excellent.⁴⁴ According to Procopius, it enabled the couriers to cover in one day a distance otherwise requiring ten days.⁴⁵ The Sassanid rulers of Persia followed the Achaemenian tradition both in maintaining an effective postal service and in using it essentially for the purposes of the state.⁴⁶

It is generally claimed that the caliphs shaped their postal system after the Persian model.⁴⁷ This seems to be true with one important qualification. The Arabs, who carried with them the tradition of the steppe and the desert, moved on horseback or by means of camel

c. Cobo, HNM, III: 269; Rowe, 1946: 231 ff. According to Cieza (1945: 137), a message was carried this distance in eight days.

caravans. Consequently they paid little attention [48] to the well-kept highways, which had been the glory of the Near Eastern postal service until the days of the Sassanids. Otherwise they were indeed eager to keep the state post in good condition. In the 9th century the caliphate is said to have maintained over 900 relay stations.[49]

Under the caliphs the postmaster-general was often at the same time the head of the intelligence service.[50] An appointment decree of the year A.H. 315 (A.D. 927–28) states clearly that the caliph expected the head of the postal service to observe in detail the state of farming, the condition of the population, the behavior of the official judges, the mint, and other relevant matters. The secret reports were to deal separately with the various classes of functionaries, judges, police officials, persons in charge of the taxes, etc.[51] The directives imply elaborate methods of gathering and tabulating information.

The Fatimids perpetuated the postal tradition of their Arab predecessors; [52] and the Mamluks were at least as eager to maintain the state post, which during the period of their prosperity connected the Egyptian metropolis with the various regions of Syria.[53] Qalqashandi notes the connection between the regular postal system and the organization of intelligence and espionage. Government offices dealing with these matters were under the same ministry, the *Diwan* of Correspondence.[54] The dispatch-bearers of the Ottoman government carried the regime's political and administrative correspondence "through the length and breadth of the Ottoman Empire." [55]

Megasthenes mentions the activities of intelligence officials in Maurya India; [56] and the *Arthashāstra* and the *Book of Manu* discuss in some detail the methods to be employed by spies.[57] The relation between the government-maintained courier system and secret intelligence becomes clearly apparent in texts dealing with the Gupta period (3d–8th century A.D.); [58] and it can also be documented for the Muslim period.[59] In Mogul times local intelligence was bureaucratically organized under an official designated as *kotwāl*.[60] It seems legitimate to assume that the national intelligence service was interlinked with the road system, whose public inns (*sarāis*) and other conveniences were organized "in accordance with the practice of the best Hindu kings in ancient times." [61]

In China the relay system developed together with state roads and man-made waterways. Perpetuating and elaborating earlier patterns,[62] the masters of the empire established a postal service which, with numerous disruptions and modifications, lasted for more than two thousand years. The imperial post provided the government with quick and confidential information on all parts of the country. During the Han period, rebellious barbarians not infrequently burned the postal stations.[63] A high dignitary, titled King of Yen, who conspired to become emperor, set up a relay system of his own for the speedy transmission of messages.[64] A former official, wanted by the government, stated in a plaintive memorandum that the government began its search for him by dispatching "messages by the post service and the post-horse system to make a proclamation near and far." His pursuers "examined every footprint of man" and "followed every rut of the carriage." Eventually the net that was "spread all over the empire" closed in upon the fugitive; he was caught and delivered to his death.[65]

The relay system of the T'ang government (618–907) operated through more than 1,500 stations, of which nearly 1,300 served overland communications, 260 functioned as "water posts," and 86 as both.[66] The Liao post was also exclusively reserved for the use of the state; its support remained the burden of the people. "Every county was supposed to have its own relay stations for which the local population had to provide the necessary horses and oxen." [67]

Viewed against such historical precedents, Marco Polo's report of the postal system of Mongol China does not seem unreasonable, particularly if we remember that the Great Khan's empire included many a "roadless tract." [68] The Mongol rulers of China kept an unusually large number of horses. But it is noteworthy that in addition to maintaining many major "horse post houses," even these mounted conquerors had many smaller stations for the use of foot runners. Through the runners, whose number was "immense," the Mongol Empire received "despatches with news from places ten days' journey off in one day and night." [69]

The use of foot runners—as a supplement to the horse- and boat-post—continued until the last imperial dynasty, Ch'ing (1616–1912). In 1825 the postal service operated an elaborate network of trunk and branch roads with more than 2,000 express stations and almost 15,000 stations for foot messengers. For the former the administration budgeted 30,526 horses and 71,279 service men and for the latter, 47,435 foot messengers. These figures cover only the technical personnel. Official information and secret intelligence were handled by regional and local officials, whose vigilance was sharpened by threats of severe punishment.

The organizational effort involved in maintaining this gigantic network is obvious. The extraordinary opportunities for speedy and confidential information are no less striking. The metropolitan province, Chihli, alone had 185 express stations and 923 foot dispatch posts. Corresponding figures for Shantung are 139 and 1,062; for Shansi, 127 and 988; for Shensi, 148 and 534; for Szechwan, 66 and

1,409; for Yunnan, 76 and 425. During the 17th and 18th centuries the Ch'ing government allocated as much as 10 per cent of its total expenditures for the maintenance of its postal system.[70]

5. The Organizational Pattern of Warfare in Hydraulic Society

ORGANIZED control over the bulk of the population in times of peace gives the government extraordinary opportunities for coordinated mass action also in times of war. This becomes manifest as soon as we contemplate such crucial aspects of defense as the monopolization and coordination of military operations, organization of supplies, military theory, and potential size of the armed forces. A comparative view of these and related features reveals the institutional peculiarities of hydraulic society in this field as in others.

a. Monopolization and Coordination

THE sovereign of a feudal country did not possess a monopoly of military action. As a rule, he could mobilize his vassals for a limited period only, at first perhaps for three months and later for forty days, the holders of small fiefs often serving only for twenty or ten days, or even less.[71] This temporary levy tended to affect only part of the vassals' military strength, perhaps a third or a fourth, or a still smaller fraction.[72] And frequently even this fraction was not obliged to follow the sovereign, if he campaigned abroad.[73]

The national sovereign had full control only over his own troops, which in accordance with the decentralized character of society constituted only a part—and often a not very large part—of the temporarily assembled national armies. In England the Norman Conquest accelerated the growth of governmental power; but even here the royal core was slow in prevailing. In 1300 during the Carlaverock campaign, the king accomplished what Tout considers a maximal mobilization of "horse guards of the crown." At this time the "household" element was "roughly about a quarter of the whole number of men-at-arms"; at best it was "nearer a third than a quarter." [74] In 1467 the German emperor tried to gather an army of 5,217 horsemen and 13,285 foot soldiers for fighting against the Turks. Out of the aimed-at total, the emperor's own contingent was expected to comprise 300 horsemen and 700 foot soldiers, while six electors were expected to contribute 320 and 740 respectively; forty-seven archbishops and bishops 721 and 1,813; twenty-one princes 735 and 1,730; various counts and seigneurs 679 and 1,383; and seventy-nine towns 1,059 and 2,926.[75]

In all these respects the armies of the hydraulic state proceeded on an entirely different level. The soldiers were not protected by democratic checks or feudal contracts. No matter whether they held office land or not, they came when they were summoned; they marched where they were told; they fought as long as their ruler wanted them to fight; and there was no question as to who gave the orders or who obeyed.

The constant rotation of the many armed contingents that in accordance with the feudal contract served only for a short period constituted a major reason for the restlessness that characterized virtually all compound feudal armies. Another reason was the lack of a definite authority. Where the sovereign was little more than the first among equals, and where the many lords proudly insisted on the privileges of their position, argument easily replaced obedience. Consequently military action was marked as much by the lack of discipline as by individual valor.[76]

b. Training and Morale

THE army of a hydraulic state might include among those it drafted many persons of poor training and little fighting spirit. With regard to skill these men might compare unfavorably with a feudal host, whose members were carefully trained, and with regard to morale they might be inferior to the warriors of both ancient Greece and feudal Europe. But in planned coordination they approached the ancient Greeks; and they far surpassed the European chevaliers.

TABLE 2. *Types of Societies and Types of Fighters*

	ARMIES OF			
QUALIFICATIONS	*Hydraulic Society*		*Classical Greece*	*Feudal Europe*
	Professional troops	Drafted men: "militia"		
Training	+	−	+	+
Spirit	+	−	+	+
Coordination	+	+	+	−

Key
+ Feature developed
− Feature weak or absent

The Greeks, who recognized the high quality of the Oriental elite warriors,[d] commented contemptuously on the poorly trained mass of auxiliary soldiers,[77] who obviously were draftees. Most of them did indeed lack the spirited integration which was the pride of the

d. See Herodotus' account of the conversation between the exiled Spartan king, Demaratus, and Xerxes (Herodotus 7. 103 f.).

Greek citizen armies.[78] But opposed to the disorderly hosts of Medieval Europe the well-coordinated troops of the Eastern monarchies made formidable enemies. About A.D. 900 the author of the *Tactica,* Emperor Leo VI,[e] advised his generals to "take advantage of their [the Franks' and Lombards'] indiscipline and disorder." "They have neither organisation nor drill" and therefore, "whether fighting on foot or on horseback, they charge in dense, unwieldy masses, which cannot manoeuvre." [79] In the organization of the Western armies "there is nothing to compare to our own orderly division into batallions and brigades." Their camping is poor, so they can be easily attacked during the night. "They take no care about their commissariat." Under privation, their ranks tend to disintegrate "for they are destitute of all respect for their commanders,—one noble thinks himself as good as another,—and they will deliberately disobey orders when they grow discontented." [80]

This picture of "a Western army of the ninth or tenth century, the exact period of the development of feudal cavalry," [81] remains valid, with certain modifications, for the entire age of European feudalism. Oman describes the hosts of the Crusades as "a mixed multitude, with little or no organisation." [82] "Their want of discipline was as well marked as their proneness to plunder; deliberate disobedience on the part of officers was as common as carelessness and recklessness on the part of the rank and file. This was always the case in feudal armies." [83]

The modern Egyptian historian, Atiya, ascribes the victory of the Turks in the last major crusade to the Christians' lack of "unity of arms and companies" and of "common tactics." Conversely, the "Turkish army was . . . a perfect example of the most stringent discipline, of a rigorous and even fanatic unity of purpose, of the concentration of supreme tactical power in the sole person of the Sultan." [84]

c. Organization of Supplies

THE masters of hydraulic society applied the same organizational devices in the military sphere that they employed with such success in construction and communication. In many cases, the recruits for war could be as comprehensively mobilized as the recruits for toil. The assembled armies moved in orderly fashion, and camping

---

e. For reasons indicated in the Introduction, above, our presentation includes references to Byzantium after the Arab conquests, to the Liao empire, to Maya society, and to other marginal hydraulic civilizations. The marginal areas of the hydraulic world are more fully discussed in Chap. 6, below.

and scouting were often highly developed. Whenever feasible, the armies lived off the land; but numerous means were invoked to cope with possible shortages.

The Incas had a "superb supply system." [85] The Persian king, Xerxes, in preparation for his invasion of Greece "laid up stores of provisions in many places. . . . He inquired carefully about all the sites, and had the stores laid up in such as were most convenient, causing them to be brought across from various parts of Asia and in various ways, some in transports and others in merchantmen." [86] The Byzantine generals were definitely concerned with the "commissariat" of their troops. [87] The Arabs and Turks, at the peak of their power, paid considerable attention to the supply problem, which was handled by methods suited to their special form of warfare. [88] The history of Chinese warfare is filled with references to precisely this matter. [89]

d. Planned Warfare and Military Theory

FEUDAL warfare, being unfavorable to the development of tactics and strategy in the proper sense of these terms, [90] also failed to develop military theory. Medieval chronicles contain innumerable references to battles, and the epics of knighthood never tire of describing military adventures. But they are concerned essentially with the prowess of individual fighters. Tactical considerations remain as irrelevant in literature as in reality.

In the hydraulic world the organization of warfare was elaborately discussed. Military experts liked to evaluate their experiences in treatises on tactics and strategy.[f] The *Arthashāstra* shows Maurya India well aware of the problems of aggression and defense. [91] The comprehensive Byzantine literature on warfare indicates the many problems posed by the empire's defense strategy. [92]

The organizational trends of Islamic warfare are significantly foreshadowed in a passage of the Koran which assures the love of Allah to those who fight for him "in ranks as though they were a compact building." [93] Later many Muslim writers discussed military questions. [94]

Yet probably no great hydraulic civilization produced a more extensive military literature than China. Contrary to the prevailing notion, Chinese statesmen paid much attention to military problems; they already did so during the period of the territorial states, which in this respect as in so many others followed hydraulic rather

f. The military writings of ancient Greece reflect a similar, though differently rooted, interest in organized warfare.

than feudal patterns. The author of *The Art of War,* Sun Tzŭ,[95] however brilliant, was not the sole great military theoretician in this period—Sun Ping and Wu Ch'i rate as high,[96] and many of the ideas Sun Tzŭ put forth are acknowledged to have been based on earlier writings.[97]

Almost every major territorial state had its own school of military thought.[98] But no matter how early the various concepts were first formulated, it was in the period of the territorial states that they assumed their classical shape. For very pragmatic reasons the empire maintained a lively interest in the problems of warfare. To mention but one piece of evidence, all major official histories from the T'ang dynasty (618–907) on included special, and often large, sections on military affairs.

e. Numbers

THE masters of the hydraulic state, who monopolized coordinated military action, could—if they so wished—raise large armies. Their mobilization potential was entirely different from, and greatly superior to, that of feudal Europe.

In Medieval England the Normans inherited a military order which, in addition to a feudal elite, contained elements of an older tribal levy. The conquerors succeeded in preserving and developing these rudiments of a national army; but even in England the feudal state could draw on only a part of the population.

The armies of hydraulic civilizations were not so limited. Their numerical strength varied with such factors as military techniques (infantry warfare, chariots, and light or heavy cavalry), economic conditions (a natural or a money economy), and national composition (indigenous rule or submission under a conquering people). But potentially it was large.

Where all soldiers fight on foot—either because suitable animals are lacking or because charioteering or riding are unknown skills—numbers tend to be important, even when different parts of the army are differently armed and trained. In ancient Mexico,[99] as well as in Inca Peru,[100] the government levied large infantry armies. Where charioteering or riding are practiced, foot soldiers may count for less and their number may decrease substantially. The rise of a money economy favors the recruiting of mercenaries, who may constitute the only major standing (cadre) army or who may serve along with a "noble" elite.

And then there is conquest. Often, and especially at the beginning of a conquest dynasty, the alien ruler will depend on his own nationals to keep his power secure; and he will give little special training to his newly acquired subjects.[101]

But no matter how the armies of agrarian despotism are conditioned, the advantages of size rarely disappear altogether. The best armies of the advanced type are usually composite bodies.[102]

As noted above, the feudal armies of Medieval Europe were small units of mounted elite fighters. An army dispatched by Charles the Bald numbered less than five thousand warriors; and on several later occasions the records speak only of a couple of hundred horsemen.[103] The international armies of the crusades were usually composed of a few thousand to no more than ten thousand men.[g] The Arabs had brilliant cadre armies of mounted fighters, which were supplemented by sizable units of auxiliary troops.[104] The standing armies of the first Umayyad caliphs are said to have numbered about sixty thousand men; and the last ruler of this dynasty is credited by Ibn al-Athīr with a host of 120,000 soldiers.[105] Harun al-Rashīd once undertook a summer campaign with 135,000 regular soldiers and an unspecified number of volunteers.[106]

Similarly illuminating is a comparison of the armies of feudal Europe with those of the "Western Caliphate" of Cordoba. According to Islamic sources, Moorish Spain in the 10th century dispatched twenty thousand horsemen on a northern campaign. Lot doubts this figure because, in the contemporary European context, it seems unbelievably large. Says he: "The whole of Europe was unable to levy at this epoch such a number."[107] His comment is as correct as it is inconclusive. The distinguished historian himself notes the enormous revenues collected by the Cordoban caliphate: "What a contrast to the Carolingian Empire or the Ottoman Empire, states without finance! Only the emperor of Eastern Rome, the Byzantine *basileus,* had perhaps equivalent resources."[108] In another part of his study he credits the early Byzantine Empire with two armies of eighteen thousand men each, plus an unknown number of occupation troops in Africa and Italy[109]—that is, with a force of more, perhaps considerably more, than 40,000 men. In view of these facts there is no reason to doubt that Moorish Spain, a hydraulic country with a very dense population and a revenue far in excess of any of its European contemporaries, could put into the field a host half

g. Lot, 1946, I: 130, 175, 201. Even at the close of the Crusades, the international European army that fought in 1396 at Nicopolis against the invading Turks had no national contingent comprising more than ten thousand warriors, except that of the immediately threatened Hungarians. The Hungarians are said to have levied some 60,000 men (Atiya, 1934: 67), which would indeed have been something like a *levée en masse.*

as large as the army of the Byzantine Empire, whose revenues, according to Lot's own statement, it easily matched.

At the time of Achaemenian Persia, foot soldiers still constituted the bulk of all fighting men. Herodotus estimates that the Persian Great King mobilized against the Greeks about two million men,[110] including his elite fighters, the ten thousand "Immortals."[111] Delbrück is certainly justified in doubting that any such large force was actually sent to Europe, but his argument becomes problematic to the extreme when he suggests that the invasion army numbered only some five or six thousand armed men.[112] Nor is there any reason to reject the possibility that, within its confines, the Persian empire was able to raise armies of several hundred thousand men. Munro suggests that Herodotus misinterpreted an official Persian source when he estimated Persia's total armed strength at 1,800,000 men. Munro himself assumes that Xerxes could muster 360,000 men and that the expeditionary force against Greece might have numbered 180,000.[h]

The size of India's earlier armies, which appears "incredible at first sight," [113] becomes plausible through comparison with the figures we have for the later phase of Muslim India. According to Greek sources, on the eve of the Maurya empire King Mahapādma Nanda is said to have had 80,000 horsemen, 200,000 foot soldiers, 8,000 chariots, and 6,000 fighting elephants; [114] and the figures given for Chandragupta's host are, with the exception of the cavalry, much larger, totaling "690,000 in all, excluding followers and attendants." [115] Data for later periods claim armies of 100,000 foot soldiers in the Āndhra kingdom and hundreds of thousands to several million soldiers under the last Southern Hindu kings [116] and the great Muslim rulers.[117]

In ancient China elite units of charioteers fought alongside large detachments of foot soldiers. During the later part of the Chou dynasty cavalry began to supplement the chariots, but apparently the new composite armies were more rather than less numerous. On the eve of the imperial period the leading territorial states are said to have mobilized three and a half million foot soldiers, plus an undefined number of charioteers and over thirty thousand horsemen.[118]

The Liao empire had, in the *ordus*, a cadre cavalry of about fifty

---

h. See Munro, 1939: 271–3. Eduard Meyer (GA, IV, Pt. 1: 5) states that Herodotus' description of Xerxes' army, like the list of Darius' tributes and other specific pieces of information, was based on authentic Persian sources. Munro (*ibid.*, 271) feels certain that Herodotus' list of Xerxes' army was substantially the reproduction of "an official document."

to sixty thousand fighters; and its records boast a militia of a million men.[119] Under the Sung dynasty (960–1269) the Chinese government is said to have trained—poorly, but nevertheless trained—a standing army of more than one million soldiers.[120] The Banners of the Manchu dynasty were a standing army that at least during the first phase constituted a highly qualified cavalry elite. At the end of the 19th century these armies, which included Manchu, Mongol, and Chinese Bannermen, totaled 120,000 soldiers. In addition, the government also had an essentially Chinese "Green" Army, which numbered some five to six hundred thousand men.[121]

f. Percentages

WHILE noting this, we have to remember that the hydraulic civilizations that maintained large armies generally also had large populations. Yet different external and internal conditions made for a wide range in the percentages of the total population included in the fighting forces.

The army of late Ch'ing probably constituted less than 0.2 per cent of the total population. In the Han empire every able-bodied peasant was obliged to render both labor and defense service. Theoretically this affected 40 per cent of the rural population [122] or something like 32 per cent of the entire population. The cadre army of the Liao dynasty amounted to about one per cent of the population. The peasant militia comprised, on paper, about 20 per cent. Herodotus' data, as interpreted by Munro, suggest that in Achaemenian Persia out of a population of less than twenty millions [123] about 1.8 per cent could be mobilized. Assuming that the population of late Chou China was as large as that of the Han empire at its best, namely about sixty millions (which probably it was not), the average mobilization potential of the great absolutist territorial states would have been almost 6 per cent.

Of course, there is no evidence that in any of these cases an attempt was made to realize the full mobilization potential. The Sung government, which in the 11th century levied a million soldiers from almost twenty million families, that is, from almost one hundred million people, was actually drafting slightly more than one per cent of its population.

Comparison with ancient Greece and feudal Europe is instructive. In an emergency all able-bodied free men of a Greek city state could be mobilized. During the 5th century B.C., Athens may temporarily have had under arms over 12 per cent of the total population, and something like 20 per cent of all free persons.[124]

The army that the German emperor raised in 1467 may have represented 0.15 per cent of the total population of twelve millions, and
Charles the Bald's above-mentioned army about 0.05 per cent of
what is estimated to have been the population of France.[125] Thus
the extremely low percentage for the late Ch'ing period still is
higher than the German figure for 1467, and it is almost four times
higher than the figure for 9th-century France. The difference between the feudal ratio and our other hydraulic percentages is
enormous.

To be sure, in Medieval Europe the feudal lords, monasteries, and
burgher towns had many more soldiers; but these soldiers, being
in excess of the agreed-upon service quota, were not obliged to
fight in the armies of their supreme overlord. The feudal government was too weak to mobilize more than a fraction of the nation's
able-bodied men; the agrodespotic regimes, like the ancient city
states, were not so handicapped. Technical and political considerations might induce them to employ only a small percentage of
their subjects for military purposes. But compared to feudal conditions, even relatively small armies of hydraulic states tended to be
quantitatively impressive; and the mass armies of agromanagerial
regimes completely exceeded both in absolute and relative terms
the armies of comparable feudal governments.

C. THE ACQUISITIVE POWER OF THE HYDRAULIC STATE

1. ORGANIZATIONAL AND BUREAUCRATIC PREREQUISITES

THE men who direct the constructional and organizational enterprises of hydraulic society can do so only on the basis of an appropriately regulated income. Special modes of acquisition emerge
therefore, together with special modes of construction and organization.

The acquisition of a steady and ample governmental revenue involves a variety of organizational and bureaucratic operations as
soon as the hydraulic commonwealth outgrows local dimensions;
and the need for such devices becomes particularly great when the
administrative and managerial functions are fulfilled by numerous
full-time officials. Gradually the masters of the hydraulic state
become as much concerned with acquisitive operations as with their
hydraulic, communicational, and defense tasks. As will be shown
below, under certain conditions taxation and related methods of
proprietary control may flourish together with an integrated army
and a state post without any relevant hydraulic enterprises.

2. LABOR ON THE PUBLIC FIELDS AND/OR THE
LAND TAX

THE incipient hydraulic community may make no special arrangements for the support of its leadership. However, the consolidation of hydraulic conditions is generally accompanied by a tendency to free the chief from agricultural work in order that he may devote himself completely to his communal secular or religious functions. To this end the tribesmen cooperate on the chief's land, as they do on the irrigation ditches, defense works, and other communal enterprises.

The Suk, who give only a fraction of their economic effort to hydraulic agriculture, have no public land; but in the Pueblos the commoners are rallied for work on the *cacique*'s fields.[1] This is done largely by persuasion; but coercion is not shunned when the situation requires it.[a] In the larger communities of the Chagga the ruler wields more power and disposes over much land. The communal work involved in its cultivation is by no means light, but the tribesmen receive little or no compensation for doing it— at most some meat and a few swallows of beer at the conclusion of their tasks. Thus the Chagga commoner who tells his white friend, "For you we are working, not as in the corvée, but as on our own fields," [2] manifestly performs his agricultural corvée duty without enthusiasm.

The masters of a developed hydraulic state depend for their maintenance on the population's surplus labor or surplus produce, on the cash equivalent of such produce, or on a combination of all, or some, of these sources. Work on government (and temple) fields was regular practice in Inca Peru, Aztec Mexico,[b] and throughout the greater part of Chou China. The extensive temple lands of the Sumerian temple cities were cultivated in the main by soldier-peasants, who constituted the bulk of the temple personnel; but the communal farmers apparently delivered only a fixed part of their crop to the storehouses, and this they did personally and directly.[3]

a. Aitken (1930: 385) juxtaposes "the gay working parties of the Hopi" to the "compulsory work for the priest-chief and on the communal irrigation ditches" in the Rio Grande Pueblos. Significantly, the work on the chief's field was directed by the war chief, the chief disciplinary agent in the Pueblos (see White, 1932: 42, 45; *ibid.*, 1942: 97 ff. and 98, n. 10; also Parsons, 1939, II: 884, 889), and this was the case not only in the hydraulically more compact eastern Pueblos but in the western Pueblos as well.

b. Maya commoners, like the members of the Mexican *calpulli*, cultivated special land for the "lords," the representatives of the local and central government (see Landa, 1938: 104).

The Sumerian arrangement contrasts sharply with the coordinated work teams of the Inca villages [4] and the "thousands of pairs" that, according to an old Chinese ode, jointly tilled the public fields in early Chou times.[5] In Pharaonic Egypt the bulk of all arable land seems to have been assigned to individual peasants, who, after the harvest had been gathered, delivered part of their crop to the appropriate officials.[6]

State farms ("domains"),[c] on which special groups of serving men were employed, occurred in a number of hydraulic civilizations; but except for pre-Conquest America and Chou China, the majority of all hydraulic states [d] seem to have preferred the land tax to corvée labor on large government fields. Why?

There is no consistent correlation between the predominance of a natural economy and the predominance of the public land system. International trade and money-like means of exchange were more developed in Aztec Mexico than in the Old and Middle Kingdoms of Egypt. Possibly the absence—or presence—of agricultural labor animals exerted a more basic influence. Peasants who, without benefit of such animals, tilled the land with a digging stick (as they did in ancient Peru and Meso-America) or with a hoe (as they did in the greater part of Chou China), may be effectively coordinated in semimilitary teams, even when they work irrigated fields, whereas plowing teams function more effectively when permitted to operate as separate units on separate fields.

Significantly, plowing with oxen spread in China during the final phase of the Chou dynasty [7] that witnessed the gradual abolition of the public field system. The peasants of Lagash, who for the most part seem to have worked the temple land individually, were entirely familiar with the use of agricultural labor animals. So were the peasants of Pharaonic Egypt and of Hindu and Muslim India. Thus most of the hydraulic states, in which work animals were used in cultivation, were maintained by the production of individual farmers and not by the joint effort of an agricultural corvée.

c. State farms, *sita*, flourished in India during the later part of the first millennium B.C. (*Arthaçāstra*, 1926: 177 ff.). These farms, however, must be distinguished from the Mogul *khālsa*, which is often referred to as the rajah's "domain." Unfortunately, the term "domain" has been applied both to large sectors of public land ("the king's land") and to limited farmlike estates. The Mogul *khālsa* certainly falls within the first category. According to Baden-Powell (1896: 198), the Mogul rulers used the term *khālsa* to designate "the whole of the lands paying revenue direct to the Treasury."

d. Traces of public fields are reported for certain regions of India. Whether they reflect primitive tribal institutions, possibly of Dravidian or pre-Dravidian origin, is an open question (see Baden-Powell, 1896: 179, 180; *ibid.*, 1892, I: 576 ff.; Hewitt, 1887: 622 ff.).

The following table indicates different forms in which a number of representative hydraulic governments obtained their rural revenues.

TABLE 3. *Rural Revenue of Hydraulic Governments*

REPRESENTATIVES	SOURCE OF REVENUE		
	"Public" Land	Taxes	
		Essentially in Kind	Partly in Kind, Partly in Cash
Tribal societies:			
Suk	—		
Pueblos	+		
Chagga	+		
Hawaii	(+)¹	+	
Ancient America:			
Inca Peru	+		
Mexico	+	(+)¹	
The Near East:			
Sumerian temple cities (Lagash)	+²		
Babylonia		+	
Pharaonic Egypt		+	
Hellenistic and Roman period			+
Early Byzantium			+
The Arab caliphates			+
Ottoman Turkey			+
India	traces	+	
China:			
Early Chou	+		
Late Chou	Documented Transition		
The Imperial period (roughly)			+

Key
+ Feature developed
— Feature undeveloped or absent

1. Some.
2. Individual responsibility.

3. UNIVERSALITY AND WEIGHT OF THE HYDRAULIC TAX CLAIM

THE fact that work on the public fields was usually shared by all corviable adult males indicates the power of the hydraulic leadership to make everyone contribute to its support. The establishment of a money economy goes hand in hand with greater differentiations in property, class structure, and national revenue. But the hydraulic state, as the master of a huge organizational apparatus, continues to impose it fiscal demands on the mass of all commoners. Comparison shows that in this respect it was much stronger than the governments of other agrarian societies.

In classical Athens "the dignity of the citizen could not submit to personal taxes."[8] When the famous city "already held the hegemony in Greece, she had neither regular taxes nor a treasury";[9] and her national support came essentially from customs and oversea revenues. In republican Rome the free citizens were equally eager to keep public expenses low. The only major direct tax, the *tributum,* amounted to 0.1–0.3 per cent of the taxed person's property.[e] In both cases the nongovernmental forces of society kept the administrative apparatus small in both personnel and budget, distinguished office holders receiving only an insignificant salary or none.

The rulers of Medieval Europe supported themselves essentially from their personal domains, which comprised only a fraction of the nation's territory. The occasional or regulai fees which they collected in their wider territory were so limited that they demonstrate the weakness rather than the strength of the sovereign's fiscal power. The Norman conquerors pioneered in establishing a stronger state; but for reasons discussed below even they were able to impose taxes on all their subjects only intermittently.[10] After a century of struggle a mighty knighthood restricted the king's right to levy taxes without the consent of the "common council" to the three "aids," as was the custom in almost every feudal country on the continent.

It is with these agrarian societies, and not with the proto-industrial and industrial West, that the great societies of the East must be compared. The masters of hydraulic agriculture spread their tax-collecting offices as widely as their registering and mobilizing agencies. All adult males were expected to toil, fight, and pay whenever the state willed it. This was the rule. Exemptions had to be especially granted, and even when granted, they were often canceled either after a prescribed period or when the grantor's reign ended.

Rural revenue was calculated in varying ways. Sometimes adult males, sometimes family "heads," and sometimes land units formed the basis for assessment. In Babylonia the land tax was collected even from soldiers who held service fields.[11] The government might demand as a general land tax 20 per cent of the annual crop. The same official rate is suggested also for the New Kingdom of Pharaonic Egypt.[12] In India during the later part of the first millennium B.C. it was one-twelfth, one-sixth, or one-fourth of the crop. The *Arthashāstra* permits the king, in an emergency, to take up to one-third (instead of one-fourth) of the crop of the cultivator of good irrigated land.[13] Many different rate-scales are recorded for late Chou and imperial China. Originally the Islamic regulations made

e. Originally taxable property was confined to land, slaves, and animals; later it included property of all kinds (Schiller, 1893: 196; cf. Homo, 1927: 237).

distinctions mainly in accordance with creed; but gradually conditions became much more involved; and, of course, they differed
widely in time and space. The many arguments about heavy taxation
show that, under Islamic rule, the land tax was as burdensome, and
tended to become as universal, as in other parts of the hydraulic
world.

A government that keeps to the official rates is considered just;
but most governments preferred material to moral satisfaction.
Many a sovereign went beyond the letter of the law. The clay tablets
of Babylonia indicate that the state, which theoretically was content
with about 10 per cent, occasionally raised the tax "to 1/5, 1/4, 1/3,
and even one half" of the crop.[14]

Nor is this all. The payments, which appear in official lists, are in
most cases below, and often far below, the payments which the
tax gatherers actually extracted. Even in the most rational of all
hydraulic states the higher echelons of the bureaucracy found it
difficult to exert full control over their subordinates. Often the very
effort to compel complete delivery was lacking.

The distribution of the total tax income among the various strata
and categories of the officialdom varied greatly. The divergencies
are highly significant for the distribution of power within the
bureaucracy; but they are irrelevant from the point of view of the
state as a whole. The fiscal power of the hydraulic apparatus state
must be measured by the total tax that the bureaucracy in its
entirety is able to extract from the nongovernmental population in
its entirety. Contrasted with the almost complete absence of universal and direct taxation in the city states of ancient Greece and
in Rome, and compared with the pathetically feeble fiscal policy
of feudal Europe, the scope and strength of the hydraulic system
of taxation is striking.

4. CONFISCATION

THE hydraulic state, which asserts its fiscal power so effectively in
the countryside, pursues a similar policy also toward artisans, merchants, and other owners of mobile property not protected by
special prerogatives. The fact is so obvious that in the present
context we shall refrain from discussing the methods invoked for
taxing handicraft and commerce. However, another acquisitive feature of hydraulic statecraft does deserve comment: the seizure of
conspicuous property by outright confiscation.

An association of free men may ask of itself whatever sacrifices
it holds necessary for the common weal; and occasionally it may

employ the weapon of confiscation against criminals or excessively powerful men.[f] But arbitrary confiscation as a general policy is characteristic of a genuinely absolutist regime. Having established unrestricted fiscal claims, such a regime can modify them at will. In addition, it can encroach on private property even after all regular and irregular taxes have been paid.

Under simpler conditions of power and class, there is little or no large independent business property; and whatever confiscation occurs essentially hits members of the ruling group. Under more differentiated conditions, business wealth becomes a favorite target, but attacks on the property of officials do not cease.

Large landed property is by no means immune to confiscation. But it is more readily accessible to taxation than are precious metals, jewels, or money, which can be hidden with relative ease and which are indeed carefully hidden by all except the most powerful members of the apparatus government. The confiscatory measures of the hydraulic state therefore hit with particular harshness the owners of mobile—and concealed—property.

The declared reasons for confiscating the property of officials and other members of the ruling class are almost invariably political or administrative. The political reasons include diplomatic blunders, conspiracy, and treason; the administrative, mismanagement and fiscal irregularities. Serious crimes frequently lead to the wrongdoer's complete political and economic ruin; lesser ones to temporary or permanent demotion and total or partial confiscation. Businessmen are primarily prosecuted for tax evasion, but they too may become involved in a political intrigue. In the first instance they may be partially expropriated; in the second, they may pay with their entire fortune and with their life.

Within the ruling class, conspiracies to replace the ruler or an important dignitary occur periodically, and particularly during times of insecurity and crisis. Wanton persecutions are equally frequent. A power center which is both accuser and judge may declare any activity criminal, whatever the facts. Manufactured evidence appears with great regularity; and legally disguised political purges are undertaken whenever the masters of the state apparatus deem them expedient.

The danger of being persecuted is augmented by the fact that under conditions of autocratic power the majority of all officials and the bulk of all wealthy businessmen tend to commit acts that,

f. For confiscation in ancient Greece, see Busolt, GS, II: 1109 ff. The confiscations during the last phase of republican Rome reflect the rise of uncontrolled Orientally despotic power (see below, Chap. 6).

legally speaking, are crimes, or may be so interpreted. At the court and/or in the administration there are always individuals or groups that try to promote their own interests by winning the favor of the ruler or other persons of high rank. The sovereign and his close relatives or friends, the chancellor (vizier) or other prominent members of the bureaucracy are all potential targets of political intrigues. And in an atmosphere of absolutist power, secrecy and quasiconspiratorial methods appear perfectly normal. This being the case, the dominant center has little difficulty in pinning the label of conspiracy on whomever it wishes to destroy.

To be sure, many persons who engage in such intrigues are never brought to book; and many others escape with minor bruises. In periods of prosperity and calm this is by no means rare. But politically phrased accusations are an essential feature of the absolutist order; and any unusual tension may spell the doom of many individuals or groups.

In the administrative sphere the borderline is similarly fluid, and the possibilities of disaster are similarly great. Many officials have to make decisions regarding goods or money; and in the absence of rational methods of procedure and supervision, deviations from prescribed standards are as usual as the attempts to increase personal income are alluring. The classic of Hindu statecraft describes the almost unlimited opportunities for embezzlement offered by such conditions. In what amounts to a veritable catalogue, the *Arthashāstra* mentions some forty ways in which government funds may be diverted.[15] The author of the *Arthashāstra* doubts whether any person can resist so many tempting opportunities. "Just as it is impossible not to taste the honey or the poison that finds itself at the tip of the tongue, so it is impossible for a government servant not to eat up, at least, a bit of the king's revenue." [16]

The wealthy businessman is equally vulnerable. Taxation being the prerogative of a government whose declared demands are heavy and whose agents tend to go beyond the official demands, the private men of property seek to protect themselves as best they can. They hide their treasure in the ground. They entrust it to friends. They send it abroad.[g] In brief, they are driven to commit acts which make most of them potential fiscal criminals.

In many instances their efforts are successful, particularly when they are buttressed by well-placed bribes. But a technical error or a

g. In classical India "capital wealth was hoarded, either in the house—in large mansions over the entrance passage . . . under the ground, in brazen jars under the river bank, or deposited with a friend" (C. A. F. Rhys-Davids, 1922: 219).

change in the bureaucratic personnel may shatter the uneasy balance; and warranted accusations combined with trumped-up charges will initiate actions that may ruin the accused businessman economically, and perhaps also physically.

In Pharaonic Egypt officials were the essential targets of confiscatory actions. Members of the bureaucracy who were found guilty of a major crime were severely punished. A demotion usually involved the loss of revenue and property, including whatever fields the culprit possessed either in the form of office land or as a sinecure.[17] At the beginning of a new dynasty the new ruler resorted to such measures to consolidate his position.[18]

Disobedience to the Pharaoh, even when conspiracy was not involved, might be severely punished. A decree of the Fifth Dynasty threatened "any official or royal intimate or agricultural officer," who disregarded a certain royal order, with the confiscation of his "house, fields, people, and everything in his possession." The culprit himself was to be reduced to the status of a corvée laborer.[19]

The history of Chinese bureaucracy abounds with incidents of demotion and confiscation. When the Ch'ing emperor, Kao-tsung (reign-title Ch'ien-lung) died, his all-powerful minister, Ho Shên, was immediately arrested and "although out of respect to the memory of his master he was permitted to take his own life, his huge accumulation of silver, gold, precious stones, and other forms of wealth, was confiscated." [20]

The expropriation of officials for administrative and fiscal offenses demonstrates the vulnerability of almost all officials. Again the *Arthashāstra* neatly formulates the crux of the matter. Since every official who deals with the king's revenue is inevitably tempted to embezzle, the government must use skilled spies [21] and informers [22] to aid in the recovery of the state's property. Crude criteria determine whether an official is guilty or not. Whoever causes a reduction of the revenue "eats the king's wealth." [23] Whoever is seen enjoying the king's possessions is guilty.[24] Whoever lives in a miserly way while accumulating and hoarding wealth is guilty.[25] The king may "squeeze them after they have drunk themselves fat, he may transfer them from one job to another so that they do not devour his property or that they may vomit up what they devoured." [26]

Of course, in all these matters discrimination is of the essence. The king should treat petty crimes indulgently.[27] And he should also be lenient when circumstances permit. Do not prosecute even for a serious crime, if the offender "has the support of a strong party"; but "he who has no such support shall be caught hold

of" and, the commentary adds, "be deprived of his property." [28]
These bald maxims do not even bother with an appearance of
justice.

Confiscation may be partial or total; and it may be invoked during
the victim's lifetime or after his death. Post-mortem expropriation
is frequently made easy by the fact that the deceased's family is no
longer influential. In 934 the Abbassid caliph seized the entire
property of his deceased vizier, al-Muhallabī, squeezing money even
from his servants, grooms, and sailors.[29] After the death of the
mighty North Persian vizier, the aṣ-Ṣāḥib, "his house was surrounded
at once; the ruler searched it, found a bag with receipts for over
150,000 dinars, which had been deposited out of town. They were
cashed without delay, and everything contained in the house and
treasure room was brought into the palace." [30] After the death of
the great general, Bejkem, in 941, the caliph "sent immediately to
the house, dug everywhere, and gathered two millions of gold and
silver. Eventually he ordered the earth in the house to be washed,
and this yielded a further 35,000 dirhem," but it is doubtful whether
he found the chests of money that Bejkem had buried in the desert.[31]

Persons suspected of having defrauded the government suffered
all manner of mistreatment. The caliph al-Qādir (991–1031) had his
predecessor's mother severely tortured. After her resistance was
broken, she handed over her ready cash as well as the proceeds from
the sale of her land.[32]

The confiscation of business fortunes follows a similar pattern. As
stated above, any prosecution could be justified politically; and
the international connections of the big merchants made political
accusation easy. But in the majority of cases the offense was openly
declared to be fiscal in nature. Frequently the line between a special
tax (for a military campaign or other emergencies) and partial confiscation is hard to draw; but whatever the pretext, the consequences
for the victim could be grim. The *Arthashāstra* encourages the king
to enlarge his treasure by demanding money from rich persons
according to the amount of their property.[33] He may squeeze such
persons "vigorously, giving them no chance to slip away. For they
may bring forth what others hold (for them), and sell it." [34]

In the case of political accusation, spies and agents could be depended upon to supply the required evidence. A middle-class
"traitor" might be framed in several ways. An agent could commit
a murder on a businessman's doorstep. The owner could then be
arrested and his goods and money appropriated.[35] Or an agent could
smuggle counterfeit money, tools for counterfeiting, or poison into

the house of the potential victim, or plant a sign of allegiance to some other king on his property, or produce a "letter" from an enemy of the state.[36] Theoretically these measures were only to be invoked when the victim was known to be wicked; [37] but along with other devices they are recommended in a chapter discussing ways for replenishing the treasury. History shows how ready the average despot was to use them for precisely this purpose. "Just as fruits are gathered from a garden as often as they become ripe, so revenue shall be collected as often as it becomes ripe. Collection of revenue or of fruits, when unripe, shall never be carried on, lest their source may be injured, causing immense trouble." [38]

In the Islamic world the death of a wealthy man provided the government with untold opportunities for decimating or liquidating his possessions. "Woe to him," wails an Arab text of the 9th century, "whose father died rich! For a long time he was kept a prisoner in the house of misfortune, and he [the unjust official] said [to the son]: 'Who knows that you are his son?' And if he said: 'My neighbor and whoever knows me,' then they tore his mustache until he grew weak. And they beat and kicked him generously. And he stayed in closest captivity until he threw the purse before them." [39] During certain periods of the Abassid caliphate, "the death of a rich private person was a catastrophe for his whole circle, his bankers and friends went into hiding, objection was raised against the government's inspecting the testament . . . and eventually the family bought itself off with a major payment." [40]

To be sure, violence and plunder are not the monopoly of any society. But the hydraulic mode of confiscation differs in quality and dimension from the acts of arbitrary violence committed in other higher agrarian civilizations. In classical Greece it was not an overwhelmingly strong government but the community of propertied and (later also) propertyless citizens who checked a potentially over-powerful leader by sending him into exile and seizing his wealth. In Medieval Europe the rulers had only a small staff of officials, so small a staff indeed that intrabureaucratic struggles of the Oriental kind had little chance to develop. The conflicts between the feudal centers of power were many and often violent; but the rival forces fought it out more often on the battlefield than *in camera*. And those who wished to destroy their enemies by tricks preferred the ambush to the legal frame-up. The opportunities for using the first device were as numerous as those for using the second were rare.

As to the fate of businessmen, men of property in classical Greece were not plagued by heavy direct taxes; and their medieval counter-parts were extremely well protected against the fiscal claims of territorial or national overlords. Like the former, the burghers of the semi-independent guild cities were in no permanent danger of being arrested, questioned, tortured, or expropriated by the officials of a centralized autocracy. True, medieval trade caravans were held up and robbed as they moved from town to town. But within the confines of their walled cities the artisans and merchants enjoyed reasonable safety of person and possession.

The rulers of European absolutism schemed as ruthlessly and killed as mercilessly as did their Eastern confrères. However, their power to persecute and appropriate was limited by the landed nobles, the Church, and the cities, whose autonomy the autocratic overlords could restrict, but not destroy. In addition to this, the representatives of the new central governments saw definite advantages in developing the newly rising capitalistic forms of mobile property. Emerging from an agrarian order, which they had never controlled or exploited in the hydraulic way, the Western autocrats readily protected the incipient commercial and industrial capitalists, whose increasing prosperity increasingly benefited their protectors.

In contrast, the masters of hydraulic society spun their fiscal web firmly over their country's agrarian economy. And they were under no pressure to favor the urban capitalists as did the postfeudal Western rulers. At best, they treated what capitalist enterprise there was like a useful garden. At worst, they clipped and stripped the bushes of capital-based business to the stalk.

D. HYDRAULIC PROPERTY—WEAK PROPERTY

1. FOUR WAYS OF WEAKENING PRIVATE PROPERTY

IN a number of stratified civilizations the representatives of private property and enterprise were sufficiently strong to check the power of the state. Under hydraulic conditions the state restricted the development of private property through fiscal, judicial, legal, and political measures.

In the preceding pages we have discussed the pertinent fiscal and judicial methods (taxes, frame-ups, and confiscations). Before turning to the political aspect of the matter we must first deal with a legal institution which, perhaps more than any other, has caused the periodic fragmentation of private property: the hydraulic (Oriental) laws of inheritance.

2. HYDRAULIC LAWS OF INHERITANCE: THE PRINCIPLE

THROUGHOUT the hydraulic world the bulk of a deceased person's property is transferred not in accordance with his will but in accordance with customary or written laws. These laws prescribe an equal, or approximately equal, division of property among the heirs, most frequently the sons and other close male relatives. Among the sons, the eldest often has special duties to fulfill. He must care for his mother and his younger siblings; and he may be primarily responsible for the religious obligations of the family. The laws take all this into account. But their modification does not upset the basic effect: the parceling out of a deceased person's estate among his heirs.

3. THE APPLICATION

IN Pharaonic Egypt the eldest son, who had important ceremonial tasks, received a larger share of his father's estate. But the remaining children also could claim a legally prescribed share of the total.[1]

The principle of more or less even division is clearly stated in the Babylonian code. A present made by a father during his lifetime to the first-born is not included in the final settlement, but "otherwise they [the sons] shall share equally in the goods of the paternal estate."[2] Assyrian law is more complicated. Again the eldest son has an advantage, but all other brothers are entitled to their share.[3]

In India the eldest son's originally privileged position was gradually reduced, until the difference between him and other heirs virtually disappeared.[4] In the Islamic world inheritance was complicated by a number of factors, among them the freedom to will up to one-third of an estate.[a] But the system of "Koranic heirs" is definitely fragmenting: it strictly prescribes division among several persons.[5] The last imperial code of China reasserts what seems to have been regular practice during the whole period of "developed" private property. A family's possessions must be divided equally among all sons. Failure to comply was punishable by up to one hundred blows with a heavy stick.[6]

In Inca Peru the bulk of all land was regulated by the state and its local agencies. Some grants made to relatives of the ruler or meritorious military or civil officials might be transferred hereditarily; but the usufruct from the inherited land was subject to equal

a. The Koran prescribes a highly intricate division of heritable property (Koran 4. 7–14).

division.[7] In Aztec Mexico the bulk of all land was occupied by village communities and thus barred from full transfer at the will of the possessor. Some land, privately held by members of the ruling group, was after the holder's death divided among his heirs.[8]

4. THE EFFECT

a. On Regulated Villages

A LAW of inheritance which prescribes a periodic division of private property affects different groups in hydraulic society differently. Peasants who live in regulated village communities may divide the movable property of a deceased family head, but not his fields. These must be kept intact or, from time to time, reassigned according to the recognized prerogatives or needs of the members of the community.

b. On Holders of Small Private Property

ENTIRELY new problems arise when the peasants own their land privately and freely. Scarcity of food may reduce the number of potential heirs, and this is an important demographic factor in all hydraulic societies. However, the will to live often outwits want; and despite periodic or perpetual shortages, the population tends to increase. This inevitably means smaller farms, more toil, more hardship, and, frequently, flight, banditry, and rebellion.

Demographic pressures are certainly not lacking in regulated villages. But they are particularly serious where private landed property is the rule. For in such areas the impoverishment of the economically weaker elements is not counterbalanced, or retarded, by the corporate economy of the village, which prevents both individual economic advance and collapse.

c. On Holders of Large Private Property

AMONG the wealthy property owners another factor of hydraulic demography becomes important: polygamy. In hydraulic civilizations rich persons usually have several wives; and the greater their fortune, the larger their harem is apt to be. The possibility of having several sons increases proportionately. But several sons mean several heirs; and several heirs mean a quicker reduction of the original property through equal inheritance.

Commenting on the dynamics of Chinese traditional society, two modern social scientists, Fei and Chang, find it "all too true" that

in this society "land breeds no land." Why? "The basic truth is that
enrichment through exploitation of land, using the traditional
technology, is not a practical method of accumulating wealth."
Landed wealth tends to shrink rather than to grow; and this essentially because of the law of inheritance; "so long as the customary
principle of equal inheritance among siblings exists, time is a strong
disintegrative force in landholding." [9]

The Islamic law of inheritance has a similarly disintegrative effect.
Wherever it prevails, it "must in the long run lead to the inevitable
parceling out even of the largest property. . . ." [10] The land grants
in the Inca empire apparently fared no better. After a few generations the revenue received by individual heirs might shrink to insignificance. [11]

5. PERTINENT WESTERN DEVELOPMENTS

a. The Democratic City States of Ancient Greece

THE fragmentation of landed property through more or less equal
inheritance is certainly a significant institution. But are we justified
in considering it characteristic primarily for hydraulic civilizations?
"The rule of dividing up an estate on succession" also operated in
the city states of classical Greece. Consistently applied, it "split up
the land without ceasing." [12] In the 4th century "apart from one
exceptional case, the largest property which Attica could show . . .
measured 300 *plethra* or 64 acres." Glotz adds: "This state of things
was common to the democratic cities." [13]

b. The United States after the War of Independence

AND then there is the fight against entail and primogeniture in the
early days of the United States. During and immediately after the
American Revolution the spokesmen of the young republic vigorously attacked the perpetuities, which were correctly described as
remnants of Europe's feudal tradition. Once the law of entail was
abolished, the colossal aristocratic landholdings quickly dissolved.
"By about the year 1830 most of the great estates of America had
vanished." [14]

c. A Spectacular Contrast: the Strength of Landed Property in Late Feudal and Postfeudal Europe

SIMILAR attempts at breaking the power of large landed property
were made in Europe after the close of the feudal period. The

governments of the new territorial and national states attacked entail and primogeniture through a variety of measures, statutory enactments prevailing on the continent and judicial reforms in England.[15] Resourceful protagonists of absolutism lent the struggle impetus and color. But in the leading countries of Western and Central Europe the governments were unable for a long time to abolish the perpetuation of big property. In France this institution persisted intact until the Revolution, and in a modified form until 1849. In England and Germany it was discarded only in the 20th century.[16]

6. DIFFERENT SOCIAL FORCES OPPOSED TO PROPRIETARY PERPETUITIES

a. Small and Mobile Property

MANIFESTLY, the perpetuation of large landed property may be opposed by different social forces. The Greek legislators, who, according to Aristotle,[17] recognized the influence of the equalization of property on political society, very possibly did not identify themselves with one particular social group or class. But their efforts benefited smaller rural property [18] as well as the new forms of mobile (urban) property and enterprise. It stands to reason that the groups which profited from a weakening of big landed property accomplished this result through methods that became increasingly effective as the city states became increasingly democratized.

In the young United States Jefferson fought for the abolishment of entail and primogeniture as a necessary step toward the elimination of "feudal and unnatural distinctions." [19] And he based his policy on a philosophy which distrusted commerce and industry as much as it trusted the independent landowning farmers. Middle and small rural property may not have been directly represented among those who wrote the Constitution; [20] but its influence was nevertheless great. The Revolution, which "was started by protesting merchants and rioting mechanics," was actually "carried to its bitter end by the bayonets of fighting farmers." [21]

And not only this. A few decades after the Revolution the agricultural frontier prevailed so effectively over the commercial and banking interests of the coastal towns that it "brought about the declaration of hostilities against England in 1812." [22] It therefore seems legitimate to claim that it was a combination of independent rural (farming) and mobile urban property that brought about the downfall of the feudal system of entail and primogeniture in the United States.

b. The States of Feudal and Postfeudal Europe

THE consolidation of feudal and postfeudal landed property in Europe was challenged by a very different force. At the height of the conflict the attack was conducted by the representatives of the absolutist state; and the external resemblance to the Oriental version of the struggle makes it all the more necessary to understand the exact nature of what happened in the West.

Why were the feudal lords of Europe able to buttress their landed property to such an extraordinary degree? Because, as indicated above, in the fragmented society of Medieval Europe the national and territorial rulers lacked the means to prevent it. Of course, the sovereign, the most powerful master of land and men, did exercise a certain public authority.[23] He claimed certain military services from his seigneurs, vassals, or lords; he had certain supreme judicial functions; he was expected to handle the foreign relations of his country; and his authority was strengthened by the fact that the bulk of his vassals held their fiefs only as long as they fulfilled the obligations mentioned in the investiture. Thus the lords were originally possessors rather than owners of their lands; and they remained so, at least theoretically, even after tenure became hereditary.

This state of affairs has been frequently described. With certain differences—which became especially important in such countries as post-Conquest England—it prevailed in the greater part of Western and Central Europe during the formative period of feudalism. However, the conventional picture stresses much more strongly the relation between the feudal lord and his ruler than the relation between the various lords. From the point of view of proprietary development, the second is pivotal.

No matter whether the baron held his fief temporarily or hereditarily, his life was centered in his own castle and not at the royal court; it was his detached position that determined his personal and social contacts. The king might claim the military services of his vassal for some few weeks; but beyond this contractually limited period —which might be extended if proper payments were offered[24]—he was unable to control his movements. The baron or knight was free to use his soldiers for private feuds. He was free to engage in the chase, in tournaments, and in expeditions of various kinds. And most important, he was free to meet with lordly neighbors who, like himself, were eager to promote their joint interests.

The atomized character of the political order stimulated the association of the local and regional vassals, who singly were no match for the sovereign but who together might successfully oppose him. In the race between the growth of lordly (and burgher) power on the one hand and royal power on the other, the rising central governments found themselves confronted not by the scattered feudal and urban forces of the early days but by organized estates capable of defending their economic as well as their social rights.

In England as early as the 11th century the king's tenants-in-chief were known as *barones;* originally the term connoted a group rather than an individual: "that word is not found in the singular." [25] But it was only when the government tried to check their independence that the barons felt the need for united action. The final section of the Magna Carta has been correctly called "the first royal recognition of the baronial right collectively to coerce the king by force." [26] Shortly afterward, *"totius Angliae nobilitas . . .* took an oath each to the other that they would give the king no answer except a *communis responsio."* [27] It was in the very century in which the English lords incorporated themselves as an estate that they laid the foundations for the perpetuation of their lands by entail and primogeniture.[28]

On the continent the timetable and many other details differed. But the over-all trend was the same. Applying to their fiefs the principle of indivisibility—which, with the abandonment of the feudal form of military service, had lost its original meaning—the noble landholders consolidated their property in Spain, Italy, France, and Germany.[29]

It is worth noting that the nobles, who kept the late feudal and postfeudal societies balanced, owed their proprietary success partly to the attitude of the absolutist bureaucracy. Among the aristocratic members of this bureaucracy not a few felt a deep affinity for the landed gentry, to which they were linked by many ties. Torn by conflicting proprietary and bureaucratic interests, the representatives of Western absolutism did not press to the extreme their organized resistance against the privileged big landowners. In consequence, there emerged out of the womb of feudal society one of the strongest forms of private property known to mankind.

c. Hydraulic Absolutism Succeeded Where the States of Occidental Feudalism and Absolutism Failed

IN late feudal and postfeudal Europe the state recognized a system of inheritance for the landed nobles which favored one son at the expense of all others. And in the modern Western world the state by and large permitted the individual to dispose over his property at will. The hydraulic state gave no equivalent freedom of decision either to holders of mobile property or to the landowners. Its laws of inheritance insisted upon a more or less equal division of the deceased's estate, and thereby upon a periodic fragmentation of property.

Among primitive peoples living on an extractive economy or on crude agriculture, the pattern of inheritance apparently varied greatly; [30] thus it is unlikely that the predecessors of hydraulic society in their majority maintained a one-heir system of inheritance which the hydraulic development had to destroy. In some cases, the germs of a single-heir system may have had to be eradicated. Where no such germs existed, the hydraulic rulers made sure that efforts to undermine the traditional distributive pattern could get nowhere. They achieved their aim by a multiplicity of methods, among which the standardization of the fragmenting law of inheritance was only the most prominent one.

In the later feudal and postfeudal societies of the West the landed nobles were able to create the one-sided system of inheritance called entail and primogeniture primarily because they were armed and because they were nationally and politically organized. In hydraulic society the representatives of private property lacked the strength to establish similarly consolidated and strong forms of property, first because the governmental monopoly of armed action prevented the property holders from maintaining independent military forces, and second because the governmental network of organization (corvée, state post and intelligence, integrated army, and universal taxation) prevented the property holders from protecting their interests by means of an effective national organization.

In this setting the struggle for or against the divisibility of property did not become a clear-cut political issue as it did in ancient Greece, absolutist Europe, or the United States. And in contrast to the areas of open conflict the hydraulic world did not favor political arguments which justified—or challenged—the fragmenting law of inheritance.

7. THE ORGANIZATIONAL IMPOTENCE OF HYDRAULIC PROPERTY HOLDERS

As an armed and ubiquitously organized force, the hydraulic regime prevailed in the strategic seats of mobile property, the cities, as well as in the main sphere of immobile property, the countryside. Its cities were administrative and military footholds of the government; and the artisans and merchants had no opportunity to become serious political rivals. Their professional associations need not have been directly attached to the state, but they certainly failed to create strong and independent centers of corporate burgher power such as arose in many parts of Medieval Europe.

The countryside fared no better. The owners of land were either wealthy businessmen and as limited in the scope of their organization as were the representatives of mobile property, or—and more often—they were officials or priests, and a part of—or in association with—the nationally organized bureaucracy. This bureaucracy might permit its property-holding members or associates to establish local organizations, such as the Chinese "sash-bearers" (inadequately translated as "gentry") and as the priests of various temples or creeds. But it discouraged any attempt to coordinate landed property on a national scale and in the form of independent corporations or estates.

The holders of family endowments (*waqfs*) in the Islamic Near East kept their land undivided, because these lands were destined ultimately to serve religious and charitable purposes. But while the family *waqf* temporarily benefited the grantee and his descendants, it represented neither a secure nor a free and strong form of property. Although less frequently singled out for confiscation, the family *waqfs*, like the other *waqfs*, might be seized if the state wished it. They were taxed; and their beneficiaries never consolidated their power through a nationwide political organization.

The family *waqf* resembles in its announced purpose, though frequently not in its immediate functions, the lands held by temples and priests. But contrary to the religious functionaries, the holders of these endowments are conspicuous not for any active participation in public life but for their rentier-like position. Temple land, like secular office land, was undivided; but it is indicative of the relation between the hydraulic state and the dominant religions that the landholding priests or temples did not engage in any effective struggle to limit the absolutist state by constitutional checks.

Nor did the landowning members of the bureaucracy—those in office as well as the nonofficiating "gentry"—organize themselves into a national body capable of upholding their proprietary rights against the acquisitive and legal pressures of the state apparatus. They were content to use their land as a means for comfortable living, leaving it to those in office to organize and operate a nationally integrated system of political power. The Chinese general who demonstrated his political harmlessness by pretending to be exclusively interested in acquiring land [31] strikingly illustrates the political impotence of Oriental property, even when it is held by men of the apparatus itself.[b]

---

b. These conditions favored what may be called the introvert character of most residential architecture in agrobureaucratic society, as juxtaposed to the extrovert architecture of the corresponding type of buildings in the West. The tendency to hide luxurious courtyards and dwellings behind a noncommittal facade was not

E. THE HYDRAULIC REGIME ATTACHES TO ITSELF
THE COUNTRY'S DOMINANT RELIGION

SIMILAR causes led to similar results also in the field of religion. The hydraulic state, which permitted neither relevant independent military nor proprietary leadership, did not favor the rise of independent religious power either. Nowhere in hydraulic society did the dominant religion place itself outside the authority of the state as a nationally (or internationally) integrated autonomous church.

1. SOLE, DOMINANT, AND SECONDARY RELIGIONS

A DOMINANT religion may have no conspicuous competitors. This is often the case in simpler cultures, where the only relevant representatives of heterodox ideas and practices are sorcerers and witches. Here the very problem of choice is lacking; and the hydraulic leaders readily identify themselves with the dominant religion.

Secondary religions usually originate and spread under relatively differentiated institutional conditions. Wherever such beliefs are given a chance to persist (non-Hindu creeds in India; Taoism and Buddhism in Confucian China; Christianity and Judaism under Islam), the rulers tend with time to identify themselves with the dominant doctrine. It need scarcely be asserted that in the present context the word "dominant" merely refers to the social and political aspects of the matter. It implies no religious value judgment. Whether the societally dominant religion is also superior in terms of its religious tenets is an entirely different (and legitimate) question, but one which does not come within the scope of the present study.

2. RELIGIOUS AUTHORITY ATTACHED TO THE HYDRAULIC STATE

a. The Hydraulic Regime—Occasionally (quasi-) Hierocratic

IN seeking to determine the relation between hydraulic power and the dominant religion, we must first discard a widespread misconception. In the hydraulic world, as in other agrarian societies, religion plays an enormous role; and the representatives of religion tend to be numerous. However, the importance of an institution does not necessarily imply its autonomy. As explained above, the government-supported armies of hydraulic civilizations are usually large, but the same factors which make them large keep them dependent.

---

confined to wealthy commoners. It also dominated the men of the apparatus—but, of course, not their supreme master.

Of course, the patterns of religion cannot be equated with the patterns of defense. But in both cases size results essentially from closeness to a governmental machine, which is capable of mobilizing huge resources of income.

The majority of all hydraulic civilizations are characterized by large and influential priesthoods. Yet it would be wrong to designate them as hierocratic, "ruled by priests." Many attempts have been made to determine the meaning of the word "priest"; and outstanding comparative sociologists, such as Max Weber,[1] have provided us with a wide choice of definitions for a phenomenon whose institutional borders are not easily established.

Obviously the priest has to be qualified to carry out his religious tasks, which generally include the offering of sacrifices as well as prayers. A qualified priest may give only a fraction of his time to his religious duties, the greater part of it being spent to insure his livelihood, or he may serve professionally, that is, full time.

If we define priestly rule as government rule by professional priests, then few if any of the major hydraulic states can be so characterized. In a number of cases the officialdom included many persons who were trained as priests and who, before assuming a government position, acted as priests. It is important to note such a background, because it illuminates the role of the temples in the ruling complex. But it is equally important to note that when persons with a priestly background become prominent in the government, they do not, as a rule, continue to spend most of their time fulfilling religious duties. Thus their regimes are not hierocratic in the narrow sense of the term, but quasihierocratic. The few hydraulic governments headed by qualified priests are almost all of them of this latter type.

The hydraulic tribes of the Pueblo Indians are ruled by chiefs who play a leading part in many religious ceremonies. However, except for one or a few among them—often only the *cacique*—these priest-chiefs spend the bulk of their time in farming. The Pueblo government is therefore represented by a hierarchy of men who, though qualified to hold ceremonial offices, are not in their great majority full-time priests.

The city states of ancient Sumer are said to have been usually ruled by the head priests of the leading city temples,[2] and the prominent courtiers and government officials, who had an important role in the administration of the temple estates,[3] were quite possibly also qualified priests.[a] But did these men, who were theologically

a. In the history of Sumer, professional priests appear early (Deimel, 1924: 6 ff.; Falkenstein, 1936: 58; Meissner, BA, II: 52). The ancient inscriptions mention priests

trained, still have time to fulfill the many religious functions of a professional priest? Deimel assumes that the priest-kings officiated in the temples only on particularly solemn occasions.[4] Their subordinates were kept equally busy by their secular duties—and equally restricted in their religious activities.

The ruler's top-ranking aides, and also no doubt many of his lower officials, entered the political arena because they were members of the country's most powerful economic and military sub-units, the temples. The governments of the Sumerian temple cities were therefore quasihierocratic. But even in Sumer the power of the temples seems to have decreased. The reform of the priest-king, Urukagina, of Lagash indicates that as early as the third millennium B.C. leading priestly families tried to secularize the temple land;[5] and soon after Urukagina, the great kings of Akkad and Ur succeeded in transferring some temple lands to the royal domains.[6] During the subsequent Babylonian period the temples ceased to be the outstanding economic sector of the society, and the bulk of the high officials were no longer necessarily connected with the priesthood.

The Babylonian pattern is much more frequent than the Sumerian. As a rule, the hydraulic governments were administered by professional officials who, though perhaps educated by priests, were not trained to be priests. The majority of all qualified and professional priests remained occupied with their religious tasks, and the employment of individual priests in the service of the state did not make the government a hierocracy.

Among the few attempts at priestly rule in a hydraulic country [b] the Twenty-first Dynasty of Pharaonic Egypt seems particularly worthy of note. But the usurper-founder of this dynasty, Herihor, who started out as a priest, held a secular government position before the Pharaoh made him high priest; and he was given this position not to strengthen but to weaken the power of the leading priesthood, that of Amon.[c] Like the priest-kings of Sumer, the rulers of Pharaonic Egypt—Herihor included—obviously spent the greater part of their time in carrying out their governmental tasks. From the standpoint of ancient Egyptian history, it is significant that out

as well as representatives of secular occupations (Schneider, 1920: 107 ff.; Deimel, 1924: 5 ff.; Falkenstein, 1936: 58 ff.; Deimel, 1932: 444 ff.).

b. Tibet is discussed as a marginal hydraulic society in Chap. 6, below.

c. Kees, 1938: 10 ff., 14, 16; cf. Wilson, 1951: 288 ff. Even E. Meyer (GA, II, Pt. 2: 10 ff.), who strongly, and probably unduly, stresses the priestly background of Herihor's rise to power, feels that the Twenty-first Dynasty did not succeed in establishing "a real theocracy."

of the twenty-six dynasties of the Pharaonic period at best only one can be classed as quasihierocratic.

b. The Hydraulic Regime—Frequently Theocratic

THE constructional, organizational, and acquisitive activities of hydraulic society tend to concentrate all authority in a directing center: the central government and ultimately the head of this government, the ruler. From the dawn of hydraulic civilization it was upon this center that the magic powers of the commonwealth tended to converge. The bulk of all religious ceremonies may be performed by a specialized priesthood, which frequently enjoys considerable freedom. But in many hydraulic societies the supreme representative of secular authority is also the embodiment of supreme religious authority.

Appearing as either a god or a descendant of a god, or as high priest, such a person is indeed a theocratic (divine) or quasitheocratic (pontifical) ruler. Obviously, the theocratic regime need be neither hierocratic nor quasihierocratic. Even if the divine or pontifical sovereign was trained as a priest, the majority of his officials would not necessarily have to be so qualified.

The chieftains of the Pueblo Indians and the Chagga, who are the high priests of their respective communities, occupy a theocratic position; and the divine quality of the Hawaiian kings is beyond doubt. However, under primitive agrarian conditions religious and secular authority are often closely combined, whether cultivation is carried out by means of irrigation or not.

In contrast to the wide distribution of theocratic institutions among primitive agrarian peoples, theocracy developed unevenly in the higher agrarian civilizations. Theocratic or quasitheocratic trends prevailed in many state-centered hydraulic societies, whereas they came to nothing in ancient Greece and Medieval Europe.

In Homeric Greece the king was of divine origin,[7] and his preeminence in religious matters was so strong that he has been called the "chief priest." [8] Subsequent democratic developments did not destroy the relation between state and religion; but they placed the control of both types of activities in the hands of the citizens. Strictly supervised by the citizen community, the state religion of ancient Greece developed neither a clerical hierarchy [9] nor a closed priestly order.[10] As a rule, those destined to officiate as priests were chosen by either lot or election.[11] Hence they lacked the training which plays so great a role in professional and self-perpetuating priesthoods. The finances of the temples were strictly controlled by political authorities, who in their majority were similarly chosen. More-over, governmental leaders were not considered divine, nor did they act as high priests or heads of any coordinated religious order. The designation "theocracy," which may be applied to the primitive con-ditions of early Greece, therefore hardly fits the "serving" citizen state of the democratic period.

In the great agrarian civilizations of Medieval Europe, nontheo-cratic development went still further. Attempts by Pepin and Char-lemagne to establish theocratic authority [12] were unable to reverse the trend toward feudal decentralization. Among the many secondary centers of proprietary, military, and political power, which restricted the authority of the national and territorial rulers, the Church proved eminently effective, since a unified doctrine and an increasingly unified leadership endowed its quasifeudal local units with quasi-Oriental organizational strength. After a prolonged period of intense conflict, the Church gained full autonomy. In the 11th century the French crown "had given way to the Holy See," [13] and the German Emperor Henry IV humiliated himself before Pope Gregory VII. For some time the struggle between secular and eccle-siastical power continued inconclusively, until Innocent III (1198–1216) raised papal authority to such a peak that he could try, al-though without success, to subordinate the state to the leadership of the Church.

Among the many manifestations of autonomous ecclesiastical be-havior the English instance is particularly instructive. In 1215 the English bishops together with the feudal lords forced King John to recognize, in the Magna Carta, the legitimacy of a balanced con-stitutional government. The Carta was " 'primarily' a concession made 'to God' in favour of the Anglican Church. . . . By the first article the king granted 'the English Church should be free, enjoy its full rights and its liberties inviolate' and, in particular 'that liberty which is considered the greatest and the most necessary for the English Church, freedom of elections.' Article 42 concerning freedom to leave the kingdom involved for the clergy the extremely important right to go to Rome without the king's permission." [14]

The Church under the Carta was not just one of several groups of effectively organized feudal landowners. In its national as well as in its international organization it was different from, and in a way superior to, the corporations of the secular nobility. Further-more, it struggled for autonomy as a religious body with specific religious objectives and claims. But however crucial these peculi-arities were, the Church could not have checked the power of the political regime if it had not, at the same time, strengthened the proprietary and organizational forces of the secular nobility. As the religious sector of these forces, the Church in the agrarian society of Medieval Europe became an essentially independent entity.[15] In achieving this goal, it fatefully supported the growth of the balanced late feudal order, which eventually gave birth to modern Western society.

Thus whether originally they were theocratically ruled or not, the higher agrarian civilizations of the West did not evolve massive theocratic power structures. The city states of classical Greece presented a nontheocratic combination of government and religion; and in Medieval Europe the secular and religious authorities, far from establishing an integrated system of Caesaro-Papism, crystallized into two spectacularly separate bodies.

Hydraulic civilization moved in a radically different direction. Where tribal hydraulic governments were theocratically shaped, the original pattern usually persisted even under more complex institutional conditions. And where theocracy was lacking in prehydraulic times, it frequently emerged as part of the hydraulic development.

A society which provided unique opportunities for the growth of the governmental machine left no room for the growth of a politically and economically independent dominant religion. The agro-managerial sovereign cemented his secular position by attaching to himself in one form or another the symbols of supreme religious authority. In some instances his position is not conclusively theocratic, but this is more the exception than the rule. In the majority of all cases hydraulic regimes seem to have been either theocratic or quasitheocratic.

The institutional diversity of the hydraulic world precludes a rigid correlation. But it seems that divine sovereigns appear primarily under less differentiated societal conditions. On a neolithic level of technology the Incas ruled theocratically over a simple hydraulic society. The supreme ("Unique," *Sapa*) Inca was a descendant of the Sun, and thus divine; [16] and in varying degrees his relatives shared this status.[17] The Sapa Inca performed the most solemn sacrifices,[18] ranking ceremonially above the professional high priests, who were usually chosen from among his uncles or brothers.[19] His officials managed the distribution and cultivation of the temple land,[20] and they administered the storehouses of the temples as well as those of the secular government.[21] Thus the government, headed by a divine ruler, controlled both the country's secular affairs and the priesthood of its dominant religion.

The theocratic development of the Near East is evidenced by many literary and pictorial records. Arising without any conspicuous

institutional attachment to—though not without cultural connections with—Mesopotamia,[d] the state of ancient Egypt demonstrates
the power potential of a highly concentrated and relatively simple
hydraulic order. The Pharaoh is a god or the son of a god,[22] a great
and good god.[23] He is the god, Horus,[24] a scion of the Sun god, Re.[25]
He derives "bodily" from his divine parent.[26] Being thus distinguished, he is the given middleman between the gods and mankind.
Lack of time prevents him from personally attending to most of his
religious duties; [27] but he is a high priest,[28] and the priest of all
gods.[29] About the exaltedness of his position there can be no doubt.

Originally the temple services were performed in considerable
part by royal officials,[30] and the temple administration was managed
by the king's men.[31] But even after the crystallization of a substantial professional priesthood, the state continued to have jurisdiction over the temple revenues; and the Pharaohs appointed the
individual priests.[32] This system of control prevailed throughout
the Old and Middle Kingdoms, and even at the beginning of the
New Kingdom. It disintegrated during the period of crisis and unrest, which at the end of the Twentieth Dynasty [e] enabled a high
priest to ascend the throne.[33] From the Twenty-second to the
Twenty-fifth Dynasty, Egypt was ruled by Libyan and Nubian conquerors, but the Pharaohs' divine position persisted despite all
political changes down to the Twenty-sixth and last dynasty.[34]

In ancient Mesopotamia society was from the dawn of written
history more differentiated than in early Egypt. This may be the
reason—or one of the reasons—why the divinity of the Sumerian
kings is formulated in a relatively complicated way. In contrast to
the Pharaoh who was "begotten by the god—corporealized in the
king—and the queen," [35] the Sumerian king is in his mother's womb
"endowed with divine qualities, first of all strength and wisdom." [36]
After his birth he is nurtured by the gods; and enthronement and
coronation confirm his divinization.[37] If, as Labat suggests, the
deities recognize the king as divine only after his birth, he is not
the divine offspring of divine parents, but rather their adopted
son.[38]

The controversy concerning the exact nature of the king's divinity
in ancient Mesopotamia [39] indicates the complexity of the early
Mesopotamian pattern, but it cannot hide the fact that the Sumerian
king, in one way or another, represented supreme divine authority

d. Contact between the two civilizations probably began long before the dawn
of written history (cf. Kees, 1933: 7 ff.).

e. For the establishment of an independent temple economy during the Twentieth
Dynasty see Breasted, 1927, IV: 242 ff.; cf. Rostovtzeff, 1941, I: 281 ff.

on earth.[40] He held the position of high priest.[41] In principle he was "the only sustainer of the high priest's office." [42] His administrative control over the temples was easily maintained, since in the Sumerian city states all major temples were headed by the priest-king, his wife, or some other member of his family.[43]

From the end of the Sumerian period on, the relations between the governments of Mesopotamia and the temples grew less close, but the temples were unable to free themselves from the control of the secular ruler. The king continued to occupy a quasidivine position, similar to that held by his Sumerian predecessors. As of old, he had the right to perform the highest religious functions. In Assyria he did so personally,[44] whereas in Babylonia these tasks were usually delegated to a representative.[45] Usually, not always. In the great "creation" rites at the New Year he played so important a religious role [46] that "during these ceremonies the sovereign was for his people really the very incarnation of the gods." [47]

In Assyria the government maintained strict administrative and judicial control over the dominant religion; [48] in Babylonia control was much less rigid. But here, too, the kings successfully upheld their right to appoint the high-ranking priests,[49] and having been appointed by the sovereign, "the priest had to swear an oath [of allegiance] like all other officials." [50]

The Achaemenian kings, who through conquest made themselves masters of the entire Near East, are said to have lacked divinity. Did they retain in their Persian homeland certain of their earlier non-theocratic concepts? Or were they worshiped as divine beings by their Persian subjects, because they were imbued with a divine substance? [51] Whatever the answer to these questions may be, the victorious Cyrus adopted in Babylonia "all the elements of Chaldean monarchy," [52] including royal divinity; and his successors acted similarly in Egypt. Like all earlier Egyptian rulers known to us, Darius was called divine: "Horus" and the "good god." [53]

The Hellenistic sovereigns of the Ptolemaic and Seleucid empires quickly learned to combine religious and secular authority.[54] Significantly the worship of the king was less fully developed at the institutional fringe of the hydraulic world, in Anatolia. But here, too, the Hellenistic rulers definitely, if cautiously, sought theocratic status.[55]

The Romans adopted many of the institutions of their new Oriental possessions. Acceptance of the emperor's divinity was gradual; but the beginnings of emperor worship go back to the early days of the empire. The cult, which had already been proposed by Caesar,[56] was officially established by the first emperor, Augustus.[57]

In Early Byzantium, Christianity adjusted itself to an autocratic regime that felt "completely competent to legislate in all religious as in all secular affairs"; [58] but it proved incompatible with the concept of a divine ruler. Despite significant efforts to assert the quasi-divine quality of the emperor,[59] the Byzantine government was, according to our criteria, at best marginally theocratic.

Islam objects to the divinization of the ruler for reasons of its own: Mohammad was Allah's prophet, not his son; and the caliph, who inherited the prophet's authority, had no divine status. Although he was in charge of important religious matters,[60] he cannot well be called a high priest either. Measuring the position of the caliph by our criteria, we therefore, and in conformity with expert opinion, consider it neither theocratic nor hierocratic.[f]

In China the ruler emerges in the light of history as the supreme authority both in secular and religious matters. Whether the traditional designation, "Son of Heaven," reflects an earlier belief in the sovereign's divinity, we do not know. The overlords of the Chou empire and of the subsequent imperial dynasties, who all used this appellation, were considered humans, yet they occupied a quasi-theocratic position. Entrusted with the Mandate of Heaven, they controlled the magic relations with the forces of nature by elaborate sacrifices. In the great religious ceremonies the ruler and his central and local officials assumed the leading roles, leaving only secondary functions to the professional sacerdotalists and their aides. The emperor was the chief performer in the most sacred of all ceremonies, the sacrifice to Heaven; [61] and he was the chief performer also in the sacrifices to Earth, for the prospering of the crop,[62] for the early summer rains,[63] and for the national deities of Soil and Millet.[64] Some of these rites were confined to the national capital. Others were also enacted in the many regional and local subcenters of state power by distinguished provincial, district, or community officials: the great rain sacrifice,[65] the ceremonial plowing,[66] the sacrifices to Confucius [67] and to the patron of agriculture,[68] etc.[g]

To sum up: in the Chinese state religion, the ruler and a hierarchy of high officials fulfilled crucial priestly functions, although in their

f. See Arnold, 1924: 189 ff., 198 n.; *ibid.*, 1941: 294. All this is true essentially for the Sunnite sector of the Islamic world. In the Shi'ite sector the theocratic tendencies occasionally became very strong. For instance, Shah Ismā'īl of the Safawid Dynasty apparently "considered himself as God incarnate" (Minorsky, 1943: 12 n.).

g. Thus in the political order of traditional China religious ideas and practices played a significant role, and certain of the latter were as comprehensive as they were awe-inspiring. The outstanding European expert on Chinese religion, De Groot, calls the great sacrifice to Heaven "perhaps the most impressive ceremony ever performed on earth by man" (De Groot, 1918: 180).

vast majority these officials and the emperor himself were primarily occupied with secular matters. The government of traditional China therefore presents a consistent—and unusual—variant of theocracy.

c. Agrarian Despotism Always Keeps the Dominant Religion Integrated in Its Power System

THUS within the hydraulic world some countries were ruled quasi-hierocratically by qualified priests who, however, no longer engaged professionally in their vocation; and many were ruled theocratically, or quasitheocratically, by divine or pontifical sovereigns. Of the remainder some were borderline cases; and others were probably neither hierocratic nor theocratic. But even among the latter the dominant religion was unable to establish itself as an independent church vis-à-vis the government. In one form or another, it became integrated in the power system of the hydraulic regime.

In certain regions of pre-Conquest Mexico the political ruler was originally also the supreme priest,[69] and in Michoacán this pattern persisted until the arrival of the Spaniards.[70] In the territorial states on the Lake of Mexico the two functions were manifestly separated long before the conquest, but the king continued to fulfill certain religious tasks, and the temples and their personnel were under his authority. On occasion the sovereign, alone or together with his top-ranking aides, might don priestly attire;[71] and he personally performed certain sacrifices.[72] Furthermore, and perhaps most important, the king and his top-ranking aides appointed the Great Priests;[73] and temple land was apparently administered together with government land.[74]

Should we for this reason call pre-Conquest Mexico quasitheocratic? Perhaps. The Mexican constellation defies simple classification, but this much is certain: The priests of the various temples who assembled for ceremonial purposes had no independent nationwide organization of their own. Cooperating closely with the secular leaders, whose offspring they educated and in whose armies they served,[75] they were no counterweight to, but an integral part of, the despotic regime.

The borderline cases of early Achaemenian Persia and of Byzantine and Islamic society have already been touched upon. But even when in these cases the government was only peripherally theocratic, the dominant religion was everywhere firmly enmeshed in the secular system of authority. The Achaemenian king, who in secular matters ruled absolutely, in theory also had the final say in religious matters. And not only in theory. The case of Artaxerxes II shows that the Achaemenian king could change the religious cult in significant ways.[76] The dominant priests, the *magi,* constituted a privileged group,[77] but they did not establish a national and autonomous Church.

Early Byzantium is among the very few hydraulic civilizations that permitted the dominant religion to function as a Church. But while this Church was well organized, it did not evolve into an independent entity, as did the Roman branch after the collapse of the Western half of the empire. During the early period of Byzantine history—that is, from the 4th to the 7th century—the "saintly," [78] if not divine, emperor followed Roman tradition which held that the religion of his subjects was part of the *jus publicum;* he consequently exerted "an almost unlimited control over the life of the Church." [79]

Under Islam, political and religious leadership was originally one, and traces of this arrangement survived throughout the history of the creed. The position of the Islamic sovereign (the caliphs and sultans) underwent many transformations, but it never lost its religious quality.[80] Originally the caliphs directed the great communal prayer. Within their jurisdictions, the provincial governors led the ritual prayer, particularly on Fridays, and they also delivered the sermon, the *khutba.* The caliphs appointed the official interpreter of the Sacred Law, the *mufti.*[81] The centers of Muslim worship, the mosques, were essentially administered by persons directly dependent upon the sovereign, such as the *kadis;* and the religious endowments, the *waqfs,* which provided the main support for the mosques, were often, though not always, administered by the government. Throughout the history of Islam the ruler remained the top-ranking authority for the affairs of the mosque. "He interfered in the administration and shaped it according to his will," and he "could also interfere in the inner affairs of the mosques, perhaps through his regular agencies." [82] All this did not make the caliphate a theocracy, but it indicates a governmental authority strong enough to prevent the establishment of an Islamic Church that was independent of the state.

In India the relation between secular and religious authority underwent considerable transformation, but certain basic features persisted throughout and even after the close of the Hindu period. Available evidence suggests that in the early days of Hindu history the government depended less on priestly participation than it has since the later part of the first millennium B.C.[83] But whatever changes have occurred in this respect, secular and religious authority remained closely integrated.

Were the Brahmins disinclined, or unable, to create an autonomous position similar to that of the Church in feudal Europe? Did they live by gifts and government grants because they wanted to or because they had no choice? Everything we know about the attitudes of the Brahmins shows that they, like other priestly groups, preferred a strong and secure position over one that was weak and insecure. However, the Hindu sovereigns willed it otherwise. Like their hydraulic fellow monarchs, they favored regulated and weak forms of property for their subjects. They paid their secular aides in money, consumable goods, and the usufruct of land ("villages"); and they remunerated the representatives of the dominant religion in exactly the same way. In India this was still the policy at the end of the Hindu period, when an increase in private landownership failed to consolidate proprietary power in any way comparable to that of late feudal or postfeudal Europe.

To say this does not mean to deny the extraordinary role of Brahminism—and of the Brahmins—in the governments of Hindu and Muslim India. All four castes are said to have been made from parts of Brahma's body, and the Brahmin caste from a particularly noble part, the mouth.[84] But the great Law Book ascribed to Manu especially stresses the divinity of the king.[85] It thus credits his rule with a definitely theocratic quality.

Hindu government also had significant quasihierocratic features. From Vedic times the king had had a priest attached to his person, the *purohita;*[86] and this dignitary soon became his advisor in all matters of importance.[87] The Law Books, which were written by Brahmins and accepted by the government as guides for action, require the king to have a *purohita*[88] "(who shall be) foremost in all (transactions). Let him act according to his instructions."[89]

A priest advised the king; and a priest aided him in administering the priest-formulated laws. The Book of Manu insists that "a learned Brâhmana must carefully study them, and he must duly instruct his pupils in them, but nobody else (shall do it)."[90] In doubtful cases well-instructed Brahmins were to decide what was right,[91] and in the courts the priests, either with the king and his aides or alone, were to act as judges.[92]

Well educated and politically influential, the priests had unique opportunities for handling administrative tasks. The *purohita* might become the king's top-ranking minister.[93] In a similar way, priests might be entrusted with all manner of fiscal tasks. This was so during the classical days of Hindu culture,[94] and it continued to be a major trend until the end of the Muslim period. Du Bois states that "Brahmins become necessary even to the Mussulman princes

themselves, who cannot govern without their assistance. The Mo-
hamedan rulers generally make a Brahmin their secretary of state,
through whose hands all the state correspondence must pass. Brahmins also frequently fill the positions of secretaries and writers to
the governors of provinces and districts." [95]

The English did little to change this age-old pattern. The Brahmins

> occupy the highest and most lucrative posts in the different
> administrative boards and Government offices, as well as in the
> judicial courts of the various districts. In fact there is no branch
> of public administration in which they have not made them-
> selves indispensable. Thus it is nearly always Brahmins who
> hold the posts of sub-collectors of revenue, writers, copyists,
> translators, treasurers, book-keepers, etc. It is especially diffi-
> cult to do without their assistance in all matters connected
> with accounts, as they have a remarkable talent for arithmetic.
> I have seen some men in the course of a few minutes work out,
> to the last fraction, long and complicated calculations, which
> would have taken the best accountants in Europe hours to get
> through.[96]

During the Hindu period and after, many trained and qualified
priests indeed fulfilled important government functions. But except
for the *purohita* and perhaps certain others who temporarily acted
as judges, the priests became full-time officials. As in other hydraulic
civilizations, they preserved their religious quality, but they ceased
to be professional priests. In all probability, they did not constitute
the majority of all officials, for there already existed a numerous
"ruling" caste,[97] the Kshatriya, who were specialists in administrative
and, particularly, military matters.

d. The Changing Position of the Dominant Priesthood in Hydraulic Society

THESE observations protect us against assuming that, during an
early phase, hydraulic civilization was ruled by priests and that, later
on, it was dominated by a secular group, preferably warriors.

To repeat: hierocracy, the rule of priests who remained officiating
priests while they governed, was rare; and rule by trained priests was
far from being a general feature of early hydraulic civilizations.
Theocracy characterized many hydraulic civilizations, both late and
early; but it did not necessarily involve priest rule.

True, in the early days of Mesopotamia and of many (most?)

hydraulic areas of the Western hemisphere, the temples apparently played a dominant role in the choice of sovereigns and officials; but in several major hydraulic centers of the Old World this was not the case. In China no conspicuous body of professional priests represented the dominant religion. In Pharaonic Egypt a professional priesthood was not lacking; but in the Old Kingdom many important religious functions were fulfilled by the ruler and certain ranking officials. In the early days of Aryan India the government was run by secular "warriors" (Kshatriyas). Only later and gradually did the priests, directly or indirectly, participate in the government.

Nor can it be said that later and larger hydraulic societies were generally ruled by military men. As will be explained more fully in subsequent chapters, military officials and "the army" might indeed prevail over the civil bureaucracy. But this development was by no means confined to later and more complex hydraulic societies. Moreover, for obvious reasons, it was the exception rather than the rule, since in an agromanagerial state the political organizer (the "pen") tends to be more powerful than the military leader (the "sword").

F. THREE FUNCTIONAL ASPECTS, BUT A SINGLE SYSTEM OF TOTAL POWER

BUT whatever the deficiencies of this assumption of a development from priest rule to warrior rule, it has the merit of drawing attention to the multiple functions of the hydraulic regime. Different from the society of feudal Europe, in which the majority of all military leaders (the feudal barons) were but loosely and conditionally linked to their sovereigns, and in which the dominant religion was independent of the secular government, the army of hydraulic society was an integral part of the agromanagerial bureaucracy, and the dominant religion was closely attached to the state. It was this formidable concentration of vital functions which gave the hydraulic government its genuinely despotic (total) power.

$\mathcal{D}$espotic power—total and not benevolent

THE despotic character of hydraulic government is not seriously contested. The term "Oriental despotism," which is generally used for the Old World variants of this phenomenon, connotes an extremely harsh form of absolutist power.

But those who admit the ruthlessness of Oriental despotism often insist that regimes of this type were limited by institutional and moral checks which made them bearable and at times even benevolent. How bearable and how benevolent was hydraulic despotism? Obviously this question can be answered only by a comparative and reasoned examination of the pertinent facts.

A. TOTAL POWER

1. ABSENCE OF EFFECTIVE CONSTITUTIONAL CHECKS

THE existence of constitutional regulations does not necessarily involve the existence of a constitutionally restricted government. All governments that persist over time—and many others as well—have a certain pattern (constitution). This pattern may be expressed in written form. Under advanced cultural conditions, this is usually done, and at times in an orderly collection, a code.

The development of a written constitution is by no means identical with the development of a "constitutionally" restricted government. Just as a law may be imposed by the government (*lex data*) or agreed upon both by governmental authority and independent nongovernmental forces (*lex rogata*), so a constitution may also be imposed or agreed upon. The term *constitutiones* originally referred to edicts, rescripts, and mandates that were one-sidedly and autocratically issued by the Roman emperors.

Even a highly systematized law code does not bind the autocratic lawgivers by restrictions other than those inherent in all self-imposed norms. The ruler who exercises complete administrative, managerial, judicial, military, and fiscal authority may use his power to make whatever laws he and his aides deem fit. Expediency and inertia favor the perpetuation of most of these laws, but the absolutist regime is free to alter its norms at any time; and the history of hydraulic civilizations testifies to the periodic promulgation of new laws and new codes. The "Collected Regulations" (hui yao) of imperial China,[1] the Law Books (dharma shāstra) of India,[2] and the administrative and judicial writings of the Byzantine and Islamic East are all cases in point.

Having been imposed one-sidedly, constitutional regulations are also changed one-sidedly. In China "all legislative, executive and judicial powers belonged to him [the emperor]."[3] In Hindu India "constitutionally the king was in a position to accept or repudiate the laws accepted by his predecessor."[4] In Byzantium "there was no organ in the state that had a right to control him [the emperor]." Or, more specifically: "For his legislative and administrative acts, the monarch was responsible to none, except to Heaven."[5]

In Islamic society the caliph, like all other believers, was expected to submit to the Sacred Law,[6] and generally he was quite ready to uphold it as part of the dominant religious order. But he asserted his power whenever he thought it desirable by establishing (administrative) secular courts and by directing them through special decrees (qānūn or siyāsa).[7] And the religious judges, the kadis, were eager to support a government that appointed and deposed them at will.[a] Thus the theoretical absence of a legislature modified the appearance but not the substance of Islamic absolutism. "The Caliphate . . . was a despotism which placed unrestricted power in the hands of the ruler."[8]

In these and other comparable instances the regime represents a definite structural and operational pattern, a "constitution." But this pattern is not agreed upon. It is given from above, and the rulers of hydraulic society create, maintain, and modify it, not as the controlled agents of society but as its masters.

2. ABSENCE OF EFFECTIVE SOCIETAL CHECKS

a. No Independent Centers of Authority Capable of Checking the Power of the Hydraulic Regime

OF COURSE, the absence of formal constitutional checks does not necessarily imply the absence of societal forces whose interests and

a. Schacht, 1941: 677. The Sacred Law, the Islamic law proper, was in time confined essentially to personal matters, such as marriage, family, and inheritance, while secular law dealt primarily with criminal cases, taxation, and land problems. This was so not only under the Arab caliphs, but also under the Turkish sultans.

intentions the government must respect. In most countries of post-feudal Europe the absolutist regimes were restricted not so much by official constitutions as by the actual strength of the landed nobility, the Church, and the towns. In absolutist Europe all these nongovernmental forces were politically organized and articulate. They thus differed profoundly from the representatives of landed property, religion, or urban professions in hydraulic society.

Some of these groups were poorly developed in the Orient, and none of them congealed into political bodies capable of restricting the hydraulic regime. The Indian scholar, K. V. Rangaswami, correctly describes the situation when, in his discussion of Hindu absolutism, he defines genuine absolutism as "a form of government in which all the powers *must* be vested in the hands of the Ruler, there being *no other concurrent and independent authority,* habitually obeyed by the people as much as he is obeyed, and which lawfully resist him or call him to account." [9]

b. The So-called Right of Rebellion

THE lack of lawful means for resisting the government is indeed a significant feature of despotism. When such means are not available, discontented and desperate men have time and again taken up arms against their government, and under extreme conditions they have succeeded in overthrowing it altogether. Subsequently the new rulers justified their procedure by juxtaposing the worthiness of their cause to the unworthiness of the former regime; and the historians and philosophers have in the same manner explained periodic dynastic changes. It is from events and ideas of this kind that the so-called right of rebellion has been derived.

The term "right of rebellion" is unfortunate in that it confuses a legal and a moral issue. The official discussions on the rise and fall of dynastic power were presented as warnings against rebellious action rather than as guides for it; and they were certainly not incorporated into any official constitutional regulations or laws. The right of rebellion could be exercised only when the existing laws were violated and at the risk of total destruction for whoever asserted it.

Traces of the so-called right of rebellion can be found in virtually all hydraulic societies. Pueblo folklore proudly relates successful action against unworthy *caciques*,[10] and revolutions in Bali have been so justified.[11] Hindu and Muslim rulers have been similarly warned—and similarly challenged.[12] The fact that in China the right of rebellion was formulated in the Confucian classics did as little to check total power [13] as does the presence in the USSR of Marx' and Lenin's writings, which postulate revolutionary action against oppression.

c. Election of the Despot—No Remedy

NOR does the regime become less despotic because the ruler attains his position through election rather than through inheritance. The transfer of title and authority to a close relative of the deceased sovereign, preferably to the oldest son, favors political stability, while election favors gifted leadership. The first principle prevails among the indigenous rulers of hydraulic societies, the second among pastoral or other peoples who, as conquerors of such societies, frequently perpetuated their original patterns of succession.[14]

The Byzantine custom of determining the emperor through election goes back to republican Rome. It suited the conditions of the early empire, which, being largely controlled by military officials, chose its sovereigns more often through "the army" [15] than through the top-ranking body of civil officials. When, from Diocletian on, the Senate took a more prominent part in the election of the emperor, the political center of gravity shifted from the military to the civil branch of the officialdom.[b] Election was not the best method by which to establish a new emperor, but wrapped in the cloak of tradition and legitimacy it proved definitely compatible with the requirements of bureaucratic absolutism.[c] And the frequent changes in the person of the supreme leader deprived neither his position nor the bureaucratic hierarchy, which he headed, of its despotic character.

In ancient Mexico and in most Chinese dynasties of conquest the new ruler was elected from members of the ruling kin group. The procedure combined the principle of inheritance with the principle of limited choice; and, as in the case of Byzantium, those who made the choice were top-ranking members of the political hierarchy. This arrangement increased the political opportunities among the masters of the apparatus, but it did not increase the authority of the nongovernmental forces of society.

Two nonhydraulic parallels may aid in dispelling the misconception that despotic power is democratized by an elective system of succession. The regime of Chingis Khan, which was perpetuated

b. The Byzantine Senate was nothing but "the rallying-point of the administrative aristocracy" (Diehl, 1936: 729).

c. Dynastic forms of government crystallized only after the Byzantine state had lost its hydraulic provinces.

through limited election, remains one of the most terrifying examples of total power. And the transfer of leadership from one member of the Bolshevik Politburo to another makes the Soviet government temporarily less stable but certainly not more democratic.

Mommsen called the state of Eastern Rome "an autocracy tempered by a revolution which is legally recognized as permanent." [16] Bury translates Mommsen's unwieldy formulation as "an autocracy tempered by the legal right of revolution." [17] Both phrasings are problematic because they imply that the subjects were legally entitled to replace one emperor by another. Actually no such right existed. Diehl recognizes this by speaking of "an autocracy tempered by revolution and assassination"; [18] and Bury admits that "there was no formal process of deposing a sovran." But he adds, "the members of the community had the means of dethroning him, if the government failed to give satisfaction, by proclaiming a new emperor." [19]

This was indeed the pattern established by the military officials of Eastern Rome; and congruent with it, usurpation was considered legitimate if and when it was successful. That is, rebellion becomes legal—*post festum*. Says Bury: "If he [the pretender] had not a sufficient following to render the proclamation effective and was suppressed, *he was treated as a rebel.*" [20]

Thus, in Byzantium as in other states of the hydraulic world, anyone might try to usurp power; and the elective nature of sovereignty combined with the temporary dominance of military leadership inspired frequent attempts of this kind. But no law protected such actions while they were being undertaken. In Byzantium persons attacking the existing government were punished with barbarous brutality. [21] In China persons caught while trying to exercise the right of rebellion were executed. Under the last three dynasties they were cut to pieces. [22]

If armed conflict, rebellion, and the assassination of weak rulers do not make Oriental despotism more democratic, do they not at least give the populace some relief from oppression? The argument has less validity than may appear at first glance. Such diversions rarely reduce in any decisive way the traditional administrative and judicial pressures; and the inclination to assert supreme leadership through open violence is more than likely to intensify the tendency to brutality among those in power. Furthermore, the devastations of any major civil war generally lay increased economic burdens on the commoners. The frequent occurrence of violence within the ruling circles, far from tempering despotism, tends to make it more oppressive.

d. Intragovernmental Influences: Absolutism and Autocracy

BUT are there perhaps forces inside the government that mitigate the ruthlessness of agromanagerial despotism? This question focuses attention on the relation between absolutism and autocracy. Absolutism and autocracy are not identical, but they interlock closely. A government is absolutist when its rule is not effectively checked by nongovernmental forces. The ruler of an absolutist regime is an autocrat when his decisions are not effectively checked by intragovernmental forces.

The absolutist regimes of hydraulic society are usually[d] headed by a single individual in whose person is concentrated all the power over major decisions. Why is this so? Do the great water works, which characterize the core areas of the hydraulic world and which indeed require centralized direction, necessitate autocratic leadership? After all, controlled (democratic or aristocratic) governments also initiate and maintain huge public enterprises. They muster large and disciplined armies and/or fleets; and they operate thus, for substantial periods of time, without developing autocratic patterns of rulership.

Manifestly, the rise of autocratic power depends on more than the existence of large state enterprises. In all hydraulic societies proper such enterprises play a considerable role; and there, as well as in the institutional margin, we always find disciplined armies and almost always, also, comprehensive organizations of communication and intelligence. But there is no technical reason why these various enterprises could not be headed by several leading officials. This is indeed the case in controlled governments, whose department chiefs are carefully separated from, and balanced against, one another.

However, despotic states lack appropriate mechanics of outside control and internal balance. And under such conditions there develops what may be called a *cumulative tendency of unchecked power*. This tendency could be countered if all major subsections of authority were more or less equally powerful. It could be countered if the chiefs of the public works, of the army, of the intelligence service, and of the revenue system were more or less equally strong in terms of organizational, communicational, and coercive power. In such a case, the absolutist regime might be headed by a balanced oligarchy, a "politburo," whose members would actually, and more or less equally, participate in the exercise of supreme authority. However, the organizational, communicational, and coercive power of the major sectors of any government is rarely, if ever, so balanced; and under absolutist conditions the holder of the strongest position, ben-

---

d. For a few temporary exceptions, like early India, see below, Chap. 8.

efiting from the cumulative tendency of unchecked power, tends to expand his authority through alliances, maneuvers, and ruthless schemes until, having conquered all other centers of supreme decision, he alone prevails.

The point at which the growth of government functions precludes effective outside control differs in different institutional configurations. But it may safely be said that whenever this critical point is passed, the cumulative strength of superior power tends to result in a single autocratic center of organization and decision making.

The crucial importance of this center is not negated by the fact that the supreme power-holder may delegate the handling of his affairs to a top-ranking assistant, a vizier, chancellor, or prime minister. Nor is it negated by the fact that he and/or his aide may lean heavily for advice and speedy action on selected groups of strategically placed and carefully tested officials. The governmental apparatus as a whole does not cease to be absolutist because the actual center of decision making temporarily, and often in a veiled manner, shifts to persons or groups below the ruler.

The sovereign of an agrobureaucratic state may be completely under the influence of his courtiers or administrators; but such influence differs qualitatively from the institutional checks of balanced power. In the long run the head of a controlled government must adjust to the effective nongovernmental forces of society, while the head of an absolutist regime is not similarly restricted. Simple self-interest urges any intelligent despot to listen to experienced persons. Councillors have existed in most agromanagerial civilizations, and not infrequently councils were a standard feature of government. But the ruler was under no compulsion to accept their suggestions.[23]

Whether the sovereign was his own chief executive, whether he delegated many of his functions to a vizier, or whether he or his vizier largely followed the advice of official and nonofficial advisors depended, in addition to custom and circumstance, on the personalities of the ruler and his aides. But despite significant bureaucratic attempts to subordinate the absolutist sovereign to the control of his officialdom, the ruler could always *rule*, if he was determined to do so. The great monarchs of the Oriental world were almost without exception "self-rulers"—autocrats.

3. Laws of Nature and Patterns of Culture—No Effective Checks Either

SERIOUS observers do not generally contest these facts. However, not a few among them seek to minimize their significance by reference to mores and beliefs, which are assumed to restrict even the most tyrannical regime.

Mores and beliefs do indeed play a role; and so, for that matter, do the laws of nature. However, the potential victims of despotic power seem to find little consolation in either fact. They know that their masters' behavior, like their own, is affected by the laws of nature and by more or less firmly established cultural circumstances. But they know also that, nevertheless and in the last analysis, their fate will be determined by the will of those who wield total power.

The mechanics of administration and coercion depend on man's insight into the laws of nature and his ability to use them. A despotic regime will proceed in one way in the neolithic period, in another in the iron age, and in still another in our own time. But in each case the ruling group asserts its total superiority under the then actual natural conditions and by means of the then available technology. The victim of a crude form of despotism does not consider his persecutors less powerful because, under more advanced technical conditions, they may catch and destroy him by different methods or with greater speed.

Nor does he doubt their absolute superiority because they act in conformity with prevailing cultural patterns. Such patterns always shape the manner in which the ruler (and his subjects) act; and occasionally they mitigate or prolong governmental procedures at particular stages. But they do not prevent the government from ultimately achieving its goal. The fact that in many countries persons under sentence of death are normally not executed in certain seasons or on certain days [24] does not mean that they escape their doom. And the fact that a dominant religion praises acts of mercy does not mean that it refrains from invoking measures of extreme harshness.

The potential victim of despotic persecution knows full well that the natural and cultural settings, whatever temporary respites they may provide, do not prevent his final destruction. The despotic ruler's power over his subjects is no less total because it is limited by factors that mold human life in every type of society.

B. THE BEGGARS' DEMOCRACY

THE power of hydraulic despotism is unchecked ("total"), but it does not operate everywhere. The life of most individuals is far from being completely controlled by the state; and there are many villages and other corporate units that are not totally controlled either.

What keeps despotic power from asserting its authority in all spheres of life? Modifying a key formula of classical economics, we may say that the representatives of the hydraulic regime act (or refrain from acting) in response to the *law of diminishing administrative returns*.

1. THE MANAGERIAL VARIANT OF THE LAW OF CHANGING ADMINISTRATIVE RETURNS

THE *law of diminishing administrative returns* is one aspect of what may be called the *law of changing administrative returns*.[1] Varying efforts produce varying results not only in a property-based business economy [a] but also in governmental enterprise. This fact affects decisively both the political economy and the range of state control in hydraulic society.

a. Hydraulic Agriculture: the Law of Increasing Administrative Returns

IN a landscape characterized by full aridity permanent agriculture becomes possible only if and when coordinated human action transfers a plentiful and accessible water supply from its original location to a potentially fertile soil. When this is done, government-led hydraulic enterprise is identical with the creation of agricultural life. This first and crucial moment may therefore be designated as the "administrative creation point."

Having access to sufficient arable land and irrigation water, the hydraulic pioneer society tends to establish statelike forms of public control. Now economic budgeting becomes one-sided and planning bold. New projects are undertaken on an increasingly large scale, and if necessary without concessions to the commoners. The men whom the government mobilized for corvée service may see no reason for a further expansion of the hydraulic system; but the directing group, confident of further advantage, goes ahead nevertheless. Intelligently carried out, the new enterprises may involve a relatively small additional expense, but they may yield a conspicuously swelling return. Such an encouraging discrepancy obviously provides a great stimulus for further governmental action.

b. The Law of Balanced Administrative Returns

THE expansion of government-directed hydraulic enterprise usually slows down when administrative costs approach administrative

a. Significantly, the law of diminishing returns has so far been studied primarily in connection with private economy (see Clark, 1937: 145 ff.).

benefits. The upward movement has then reached "Saturation Point 'A' (Ascent)." Beyond this point further expansion may yield additional rewards more or less in proportion to additional administrative effort; but when the major potentials of water supply, soil, and location are exhausted, the curve reaches "Saturation point 'D' (Descent)." The zone between Points "A" and "D" is characterized by what may be called the *law of balanced administrative returns*.

c. The Law of Diminishing Administrative Returns

WHETHER Saturation Points "A" and "D" are close together or far apart, or whether they coincide, any move beyond this zone of balanced returns carries man's action into an area of discouraging discrepancy. Here similar, and even increased, administrative endeavors cost more than they yield. It is under these conditions that we observe the workings of the *law of diminishing administrative returns*. The downward movement is completed when additional outlay yields no additional reward whatsoever. We have then reached the absolute administrative frustration point.

d. Ideal Curve and Reality of Changing Returns

THIS ideal curve does not describe the development of any specific government-directed system of water works in any specific hydraulic society. It indicates in a schematic way the critical points through which any hydraulic enterprise passes, if it moves steadily through all zones of growing and shrinking returns.

Rarely, if ever, do the actual and the ideal curves coincide. Geology, meteorology, potamology, and historical circumstance make for countless variations. Progress toward saturation and beyond may be interrupted by longer or shorter countermovements. But every section of the curve reflects a genuine trend; and the entire curve combines these trends to indicate all possible major phases of creation and frustration in hydraulic enterprise.

e. Nonhydraulic Spheres of Political Economy

IN the sphere of agricultural production itself, coordinated and government-directed action yields increasing administrative returns only under primitive and special conditions. It is only in technologically crude hydraulic societies that mass labor on "public" fields prevails. And even in these societies the government does not try to assume managerial direction over the fields which have been set aside for the support of the individual farmer. In a technically more advanced setting, the administrative creation point and the administrative frustration point tend to coincide. For there the hydraulic regime prefers to refrain altogether from agricultural production, which from the standpoint of administrative returns is more reasonably handled by many small individual farming units.

Of course, political needs take precedence over economic considerations. The great agromanagerial enterprises of communication and defense are cases in point, as are certain government-run workshops (arsenals, shipyards). However, the hydraulic regime's reluctance to assume direct control over the finishing industries derives from the realization that in this field state management would involve deficits rather than gains. In hydraulic as well as in other agrarian societies the government is therefore satisfied to leave the bulk of all handicraft to small individual producers.

2. The Power Variant of the Law of Changing Administrative Returns

a. *Imperative and Worth-while Efforts*

It is easy to recognize the workings of the law of changing administrative returns also in the sphere of political power. The efforts of the hydraulic regime to maintain uncontested military and police control over the population prove increasingly rewarding until all independent centers of coercion are destroyed. The expenses incurred in supporting speedy communications and intelligence follow a similar pattern; and the expansion of fiscal and judicial action appears reasonable as long as it satisfies the rulers' desire for uncontested political and social hegemony.

Some of these operations are imperative, others at least worth while. But carried beyond Saturation Point "D", they all become problematic. The discouraging discrepancy between continued endeavor and decreasing political rewards makes the government reluctant to use its apparatus much below this point.

b. *The Forbidding Cost of Total Social Control in a Semimanagerial Society*

The developed industrial apparatus state of the USSR has crushed all independent nationwide organizations (military, political, proprietary, religious); and its total managerial economy permits the establishment of innumerable bureaucratic bases for controlling all secondary (local) professional groupings and even the thought and behavior of individuals. The hydraulic apparatus state does not have equal facilities. It is strong enough to prevent the growth of effective primary organizations; and in doing so, it brings about that one-sided concentration of power which distinguishes it from the ancient and medieval agrarian societies of the West. But being only semimanagerial, it lacks the ubiquitous bases which enable the men of the apparatus to extend their total control over secondary organizations and individual subjects. In the USSR such total control was initiated through the nationalization of agriculture (the "collectivization" of the villages); and it was accomplished through the pulverization of all nongovernmental human relations. Hydraulic society never made the first step, and it therefore never laid the foundations for the second.

To be sure, the notion of a ubiquitous control also attracted the master minds of hydraulic despotism. Garcilaso de la Vega, a scion of native royalty, claimed that under Inca rule special officials went from house to house to make sure that everybody was kept busy. Idlers were punished by blows on the arms and legs "and other penalties prescribed by the law." [2] The great Chinese "Utopia" of bureaucratic government, the *Chou Li,* lists several officials who, in a well-managed state, should regulate the people's life in village and town.

There is no reason to doubt that the Incas wanted their subjects to work as much as possible; but any effective inspection of the commoners' domestic life would have required an army of officials, which would have eaten up a great part of the public revenue without providing a compensatory increase in income. It is therefore hard to believe that the "laws" mentioned by Garcilaso went far beyond a general—and therefore not too costly—supervision. The same may be said for the classic book of Chinese bureaucracy. All educated Chinese officials studied the *Chou Li;* but once in office, they soon learned to distinguish between the sweet dream of total social control and the sober administrative reality. Except for some short-lived attempts at extreme interference, they were content to maintain firm control over the strategically important spheres of their society.

c. Total Social Control Not Necessary for the Perpetuation of Agromanagerial Despotism

To say that the law of diminishing administrative returns discourages the hydraulic state from attempting to control individuals and secondary organizations totally is only another way of saying that the government feels no fundamental need to do so. If it were otherwise—that is, if total control were imperative for the perpetuation of the despotic regime—the rulers might have to spend all their income to be safe. Obviously, such a power system would be unworkable.

Historical experience shows that during long periods of "peace and order" the hydraulic rulers can maintain themselves without resorting to excessively costly measures. It also shows that under "normal" conditions they need not make severe material sacrifices. Except in times of unrest, they are adequately protected by their wide-flung network of intelligence and coercion, which successfully blocks the rise of independent nationwide primary organizations and prevents discontented individuals or secondary organizations from gaining prominence.

The political crises that develop periodically may be caused in part by the dissatisfaction of such individuals and organizations.[3] But serious unrest, whatever its origin, soon assumes a military form, and it is combated by outright military measures. Responding to the law of diminishing administrative returns, the masters of the agrarian apparatus state run the risk of occasional uprisings and do what their modern industrial successors do not have to do: they grant a certain amount of freedom to most individuals and to certain secondary organizations.

3. Sectors of Individual Freedom in Hydraulic Society

a. Limitations of Managerial Control

THE duration of the state corvée determines the period during which a member of hydraulic society is deprived of his freedom of action. The corvée may have many objectives, but it must allow the mass of the laborers—the peasants—sufficient time to attend to their own economic affairs. Of course, even in the villages the peasants may have to submit to a policy of economic planning, but at most this policy involves only a few major tasks, such as plowing, sowing, harvesting, and perhaps the choice of the main crop. Often it does not go this far; and at times it may be altogether absent.

Under conditions of advanced technology the corvée also tends to change and shrink. Work on the public fields may be replaced by a tax; and larger or smaller segments of the nonagricultural corvée may be similarly commuted.

But whatever the character of the rural communities and whatever the duration of the public labor service may be, there are definite and at times considerable periods in the peasant's life during which he proceeds at his own discretion. This is still more true for the nonagrarian commoners. Artisans and traders who, in a differentiated societal setting, pursue their occupations professionally and privately [4] may become more valuable as taxpayers than as corvée laborers. Their freedom of movement will increase correspondingly.

Marx speaks of the "general slavery" of the Orient. According to him, this type of slavery, which is inherent in man's attachment to the hydraulic commonwealth and state,[5] differs essentially from Western slavery and serfdom.[b] The merit of Marx' formula lies in the problem it raises rather than in the answer it gives. A person commandeered to toil for an "Asiatic" state is a slave of the state as long as he is so occupied. He is perfectly aware of the lack of freedom, which this condition involves, and he is equally aware of the pleasure of working for himself. Compared with the total state slavery of the total managerial industrial society, the partial state slavery of the partial managerial hydraulic society makes indeed considerable concessions to human freedom.

b. Limitations of Thought Control

A COMPARABLE tendency to make concessions arises also in the sphere of thought control. To appreciate fully what this means, we must understand the enormous stress that the masters of the hydraulic state place on the society's dominant ideas. The close coordination of secular and religious authority makes it easy to apply this stress to both the higher and the lower strata of society. The sons of the dominant elite are generally educated by representatives of the dominant creed; and the whole population is in continued and government-promoted contact with the state-attached temples and their priesthoods.

Education usually is a long process, and its influence is profound. In India the young Brahmin who prepared himself for priestly office had to study one, two, or all three Vedas, applying himself to each one of them for twelve long years. And the members of the "protecting" Kshatriya caste, and even those of the next lower caste, the Vaisya, were also advised to study the Sacred Books.[6] In China "learning"—the study of the canonical (classical) writings—was already considered a basic prerequisite for administrative office in Confucius' time.[7] Increasing systematization led to the holding of

---

b. Marx assumed that from the European point of view, in this general Asiatic slavery, the laborer seems to be a natural condition of production for a third person or a community, as under [private-property-based] slavery and serfdom, but that actually "this is not the case" (Marx, 1939: 395).

elaborate and graded examinations, which fostered perpetual ideological alertness in all energetic and ambitious young, and in many middle-aged and even elderly, members of the ruling class.

But the same societal forces that led to the systematic perpetuation of the dominant ideas also encouraged a variety of secondary religions. Many simple hydraulic civilizations tolerated independent diviners and sorcerers,[8] whose artisan-like small-scale activities modestly supplemented the coordinated operations of the leading tribal or national creed. Under more complex conditions, ideological divergence tended to increase. Often the subject of a hydraulic state might adhere to a secondary religion without endangering his life. Non-Brahministic creeds, such as Jainism or Buddhism, are documented for India from the first millennium B.C. Buddhism persisted in traditional China, despite temporary persecutions, for almost two thousand years. And the Islamic Near East, India, and Central Asia were similarly indulgent.

In the ideological as in the managerial sphere, the policies of the agrarian apparatus state contrast strikingly with policies of the modern industrial apparatus states, which, while feigning respect for traditional ("national") culture and religion, spread the Marxist-Leninist doctrine with the avowed aim of eventually annihilating all other ideologies. Again, the difference between their policies is not due to any innate tolerance on the part of the agrobureaucratic rulers, whose insistence on the unique position of the dominant religion is always uncompromising and frequently ruthless. But the law of diminishing administrative returns places an exorbitant price on the attempt to maintain total ideological control in a differentiated semimanagerial society. And here, as in the operational sector, experience shows that the absolutist regime can perpetuate itself without making so costly an effort.

4. GROUPS ENJOYING VARYING DEGREES OF AUTONOMY

EXPERIENCE shows still more. It assures the hydraulic rulers that they may—for the same reasons—permit some autonomy not only to their individual subjects but to certain secondary groups as well. In referring to heterodox creeds, we are aware that their adherents are usually permitted to establish congregations, which support either individual priests or larger or smaller priesthoods. Since the early days of written history, the artisans and traders of hydraulic civilizations have formed professional organizations (guilds). More ancient still are the village communities, which have probably existed as long as hydraulic civilization itself. Kin groups are institutionally older than agriculture; and like the village community, they are present everywhere in the hydraulic world.

These types of associations differ greatly in distribution, composition, quality, and purpose. But they have one thing in common. All of them are tolerated by the despotic regime. Many supervisory measures notwithstanding, they are not subjected to total control.

a. Less Independence than Frequently Assumed

ROMANTIC observers have taken the absence of such control as evidence for the existence of genuine democratic institutions in the lower echelons of hydraulic society. In this form, the claim cannot be accepted. Throughout the hydraulic world, government authority and family authority are interlinked; and measures of political control affect the majority of all villages, guilds, and secondary religious organizations.

Parallels can be found in other agrarian societies for most of these restrictive trends. (The free guilds of feudal Europe are as exceptional as they are significant.) This, however, is not the issue here. What we are concerned with is whether, in contrast to corresponding developments in other despotic states—and also in contrast to restrictive developments in other agrarian civilizations—the secondary organizations of hydraulic society were genuinely autonomous. The answer to the question is "No."

i. THE FAMILY

THE family of traditional China has often been said to be the institution that gave Chinese society its peculiar character and strength. This thesis is correct insofar as it stresses the family as a basic component of society; but it is misleading insofar as it implies that the family determined the quality and power of the institutional setting of which it was a part.

The authority of the Chinese *pater familias* was much stronger than intrafamilial leadership required; [c] and he owed his extraordinary power essentially to the backing of the despotic state. Disobedience to his orders was punished by the government.[9] On the other hand, the local officials could have him beaten and imprisoned, if he was unable to keep the members of his family from violating the law.[10] Acting as a liturgical (semi-official) policeman of his kin group, he can scarcely be considered the autonomous leader of an autonomous unit.

c. For the nongovernmental roots of paternal authority in the Chinese family see Wittfogel, 1935: 49; *ibid.,* 1936: 506 ff.

The Babylonian father, who could place his wife, son, or daughter in the service of a third person for several years,[11] also owed his power to the government which backed him up in his decision. Whether he was legally responsible for the behavior of the family members is not clear.

The *patria potestas* of ancient Egypt has been compared with that of Rome. The strongly militarized society of republican Rome did indeed encourage the development of highly authoritarian family relations; but the Egyptian father seems to have had still greater power than his Roman counterpart.[d]

In the Islamic world, respect for the parents is prescribed by the Sacred Law; [12] and the degree to which paternal authority operated, particularly in the villages, may be judged from the fact that in such countries as Syria the father customarily was the master over his family until his death.[13]

The Law Books of India give the father an almost kinglike power over members of his kin group.[14] Despite several restrictions,[15] his authority over his wife and children seems to have been extremely great.[e]

Evidently the father's power varied notably in different hydraulic civilizations. But almost everywhere the government was inclined to raise it above the level suggested by his leadership functions in the family.

ii. THE VILLAGE

GENERALLY the villages of hydraulic civilizations are under the jurisdiction of headmen who are either government-appointed or elected by their fellow villagers. Appointment seems to be frequent in the regulated rural communities of compactly hydraulic civilizations, whereas free choice is more apt to be permitted in less compactly hydraulic societies. In Inca Peru the local officials down to the lowest functionary—the head of ten families—was appointed.[16] In pre-Conquest Mexico, too, the village land was communally regulated. But its agrarian economy was much less bureaucratized

---

d. Dr. Taubenschlag's assertion that the Egyptian father's right to sell his child has a Roman precedent is documented only for "the fourth century" (Taubenschlag, 1944: 103 ff.).

e. Jolly, 1896: 78. At the beginning of the 19th century, Dubois (1943: 307 ff.) found the authority of the Brahmins enormous, whereas paternal authority was weak. The author lived in India from 1792 to 1823. Assuming that he observed the phenomenon correctly, we are at a loss to explain it. Was it, at least in part, due to the turmoil of the time?

than that of the Inca empire. The heads of the Mexican local administrative units, the *calpulli*, were elected.[17]

However, this correlation does not prevail generally, perhaps because appointment is only one among several ways of controlling a
local functionary. Almost everywhere the hydraulic government
holds the headman responsible for the obligations of his co-villagers.
It thus places him in a position of state dependency. Where land is
communally held and where taxes are communally paid, the village
headman is likely to wield considerable power. Assisted by a scribe
and one or several policemen, he may become something of a local
despot.

The inscriptions of the early Near East show the regional officials
actively concerned with plowing and the collection of the revenue; [18] but we are unable to get a clear picture of how the village
functionaries fitted into the administrative nexus.[19] As in other
spheres of life, the Persians and their Hellenistic and Roman successors may well have perpetuated an earlier village pattern. In
Ptolemaic and Roman Egypt the leading village official, the scribe,
assisted by the elders, executed his government-imposed tasks.[20]
These men, no matter whether they were appointed [21] or elected
like the elders,[22] were all "directly dependent on the central government . . . they all especially obeyed the *strategos* of the district." [23]

The data for Roman Syria seem to suggest considerable popular
participation in village affairs,[24] whereas the Egyptian village officials
probably acted in a very authoritarian manner. But this divergence
must not make us overlook the basic similarities that existed throughout the ancient Near East in village organization and government
dependency.[25] In Hellenistic times,[26] as previously, the "royal"
villagers were attached to the land they cultivated.[27] It therefore
seems safe to conclude that in the pre-Roman as well as in the Roman
period the peasants of Syria and Asia Minor did not administer their
villages autonomously.

In Arab Egypt, as in Byzantine Egypt,[28] the village administration
was in the hands of a headman and the elders. Under the Arabs
the headman, who possibly was nominated by the peasants and confirmed by the government,[29] seems to have apportioned and collected
the tax.[30] He designated the corvée laborers and exercised police and
judicial functions.[31]

In the Arab provinces of the Turkish Near East the village headman (*sheikh*) assisted the official and semi-official representatives of
the government in allocating the tax.[32] He "policed the *fellāhs* who
cultivated the lands under his charge, and the principal *seyh* acted
as magistrate and arbitrator, with authority not only over the culti-

vators but over all the inhabitants." [33] Controlling "his" peasants in an arbitrary way and being in turn controlled with equal severity by the state bureaucracy,[34] he certainly was not the representative of a free rural village community.

In India the village headman may have been elected originally; [35] but from the time of the later Law Books on—that is, from the end of the first millennium B.C.—his appointment is documented.[36] As the king's representative in the villages, who "collected taxes for him" [37] and who also fulfilled policing and judicial functions,[38] the headman held a position of authority not dissimilar to that enjoyed by his Near Eastern counterpart. Muslim rule did not fundamentally change this administratively convenient arrangement, which in fact persisted in the majority of all Indian villages up to modern times.[39]

In China the regulated village yielded to a property-based pattern more than two thousand years ago. The duties of the village officials shrank correspondingly, but they did not disappear altogether. At the close of the imperial period most sizable villages had at least two functionaries, a headman, *chuang chang,* and a local constable, *ti fang* or *ti pao.*[40] The headman, who was usually chosen by the villagers, executed the directing, and the constable, who usually was government appointed,[f] the coercive, functions of the village government. They cooperated in their official tasks: the collection of taxes and materials for public constructions, the organizing and directing of corvée services ("government transportation . . . work on river-banks, patrols for the Imperial roads" etc.),[41] and the making of intelligence reports.[42]

All these activities linked the headman to the central government, although he was not part of its bureaucracy.[g] The villagers found it hard to bring a complaint against him, even if their case was good, for he monopolized communication with the district magistracy.[43] The constable was controlled by the county officials. They could

f. According to Smith (1899: 227), the candidates for this position were "not formally chosen, nor formally deposed." Instead they used to "drop into their places" as the result of what Smith calls "a kind of natural selection."

It would probably be better to speak of an informal election based on an understanding between all family heads of some standing. Dr. K. C. Hsiao, who has almost completed his comprehensive study, *Rural China, Imperial Control in the Nineteenth Century,* ascribes "a certain amount of informal local influence on village leadership," especially that of "wealthy or gentry families." But he finds it impossible to give quantitative data about "the proportion of government-appointed village headmen (pao-chang, chia-chang, etc.; and later, chuung-chang, ti-pao, ti-fang, etc.)." He adds: "The official scheme called for universal institution of such headmen, wherever rural communities existed" (letter of January 15, 1954).

g. Usually the village paid him a salary (Werner, 1910: 106 ff.). In addition there were the usual material advantages inherent in the handling of public money.

have him "beaten to a jelly" for neglecting his duty as a local intelligence agent.[44]

The villages of imperial China were less strictly controlled than
those of pre-Conquest Peru, India, and most Near Eastern civilizations, but even they did not govern themselves. Their main functionaries, who were either appointed or confirmed by the government, were inescapably tied to an operational system that served
the interests of the government rather than the interests of the
villagers.

iii. THE GUILDS

THE professional corporations of the artisans and traders in hydraulic civilizations were similarly conditioned. Again the appointment
of the leading official is significant; but again it is only one of several
ways in which the despotic state assures its unchecked superiority
and the weakness of the tolerated organization.

Hellenistic Egypt seems to have followed ancient usage in having
persons "working for the State in industry, transport, mining, building, hunting, etc." gathered into professional groups that were
"organized and closely supervised by the economic and financial administration of the king."[45]

In the later part of the Roman empire and in Byzantium, the
government "strictly regulated" the activities of the guilds.[h] Until
the third century the members elected their own headmen; but from
that time on the government made the final decision on guild-
nominated headmen, who, after installation, were supervised and
disciplined by the state.[46]

In Ottoman Turkey officials inspected the markets [47] and controlled the prices, weights, and measurements,[i] thus fulfilling functions which in the burgher-controlled towns of Medieval Europe
were usually the responsibility of the urban authorities.[48] Furthermore, the state, which in most countries of feudal Europe collected
few if any regular taxes from the urban centers of strongly developed
guild power, was able in Turkey to tax the guilds and, as elsewhere
in the Orient, to employ as its fiscal agents the headmen of these
corporations, who "distributed the tax-quotas of their members" and
who were "personally responsible for their payment."[49]

In Hindu India, the *setthi,* the head of the merchant guild, was
a semi-official closely attached to the ruler's fiscal administration.[50]

h. Stöckle, 1911: 11. For reference to guild heads as tax collectors in Byzantine and
Arab Egypt, see Grohmann, PAP: 279 and n. 8. For conditions at the beginning of
Arab rule, see *ibid.:* 131, n. 3, and Crum, 1925: 103-11.

i. Specifically this was done by agents of the *kadi* (Gibb and Bowen, 1950: 287).

The merchants represented considerable wealth, and their corporations seem to have been more highly respected than those of the artisans.[51] But this did not make the merchant guild a significant political entity.

It has been said that the Indian guilds came into prominence in early Buddhist days.[52] In agreeing with this observation, however, we must be careful not to exaggerate its political significance. According to Fick, "the corporations of the manufacturers fall—partly at any rate—undoubtedly under the category of the despised castes"; [53] and Dr. Rhys-Davids insists that there is "no instance as yet produced from early Buddhist documents pointing to any corporate organisation of the nature of a gild or Hansa league." [54] A legend of the 3d or 4th century, which is supposed to show that the town of Thana [j] was "ruled by a strong merchant guild" actually describes the unsuccessful attempt of a group of merchants to combat a competitor by cornering the market.[k]

In China the existence of guilds is reliably documented only since the second half of the first millennium A.D. Under the T'ang and Sung dynasties the guild heads could be held responsible for the improper professional behavior of their members, such as violations of the currency regulations,[55] theft, and other misdeeds. And in many cases membership was compulsory.[56] The guilds as a unit also had to render special services to the state.[57] In recent centuries the government seems to have left the less significant craft and trade guilds largely to their own devices; [m] but the corporations of such important groups as the salt merchants [n] and a number of Cantonese firms dealing in foreign trade [o] were strictly supervised.

iv. SECONDARY RELIGIONS

OUR information on secondary religions is particularly plentiful for Islamic society and traditional China. Muslim rulers tolerated Christianity, Judaism, and Zoroastrianism.[p] But followers of these creeds had to accept an inferior status both politically and socially, and

j. Poona, south of modern Bombay.

k. Hopkins, 1902: 175. Hopkins' erroneous thesis is taken up by Max Weber in an argument stressing the temporary political prominence of the Hindu guilds (Weber, RS, II: 86 ff.). See below, p. 266.

m. Wittfogel, 1931: 580 ff., 714 ff. My 1931 analysis overlooked the state-controlled guilds of important trades, such as the salt business.

n. The guild heads collect the tax from the "small merchants" (*Ch'ing Shih Kao* 129. 1b).

o. The headmen were appointed by the government (*Yüeh Hai Küan Chih* 25. 2a).

p. Macdonald, 1941: 96; Grunebaum, 1946: 117. Zoroastrians were tolerated originally (Mez, 1922: 30); later they were more harshly treated (Büchner, 1941: 381).

they were prevented from spreading their ideas. The laws forbade conversion from Christianity to Judaism or vice versa; and penalties for apostasy from Islam were severe. Christians were not permitted to beat their wooden boards loudly,[q] or sing in their churches with raised voices, or assemble in the presence of Muslims, or display their "idolatry," "nor invite to it, nor show a cross" on their churches.[58] No wonder that the religious minorities—who during the Turkish period were set apart in organizations called *millet*[59]— vegetated rather than throve. The head of the *millet* was nominated by the *millet*[r] but appointed by the sultan;[60] once in office he was given "just enough executive power . . . to enable him to collect the taxes imposed on his community by the state."[61]

In traditional China, Buddhism was the most important secondary religion. It reached its greatest prominence in the barbarian dynasties of infiltration and conquest which ruled over the old northern centers of Chinese culture during the middle period of the first millennium A.D.[62] The harsh persecutions of 845 initiated a policy which over time reduced it to a carefully restricted secondary religion.

Specially designated officials supervised Buddhism and other problematic creeds.[63] The government limited the erection of monasteries and temples;[64] it licensed the number of priests and monks;[65] it forbade certain religious activities which in other countries went unrestricted; and it prescribed that "the Buddhist and Taoist clergy shall not hold sutra-readings in market-squares, nor go about with alms-bowls, nor explain the fruits of salvation, nor collect moneys."[66] Concluding his classical survey of what others have hailed as the elements of religious liberty, De Groot asks: "What is the good of this liberty where the State has cast its system of certification of clergy within such strict bounds, and has made the admission of male disciples extremely difficult, of females almost impossible, so that the number of those who could avail themselves of such liberty, is reduced to a miserably small percentage of the population? It makes this vaunted liberty into a farce."[67]

b. Genuine Elements of Freedom Nevertheless Present

THUS the hydraulic state restrictively affects practically all secondary groups and organizations, but it does not integrate them completely into its power system.

The traditional Chinese family, whose head enjoyed a particularly

q. These boards were used as bells (Grunebaum, 1946: 179).
r. Or its clergy?

distinguished position legally, was not forced by political and police pressure to set one family member against another, as is the case in modern apparatus states. In China and in India the government permitted the kin groups to settle their internal affairs in accordance with their own family "laws." [68] In other hydraulic civilizations the families enjoyed a less formal, but equally effective, quasi-autonomy.

Government control over the villages, although very specific, is also definitely limited. Even where village officials wield much power, the peasants who live alongside them have many opportunities to make their opinions on the day-to-day affairs of the community felt. And once the demands of the government are satisfied, the headman and his aides usually settle the affairs of their village with little, if any, interference from above.

Certain opportunities for self-government seem to have existed in the villages of Roman Syria [69] and in the Egyptian villages of the Roman and Byzantine period.[70] The village chief of Ottoman Turkey, like his counterparts in other Oriental civilizations, acted with great independence as far as the internal affairs of the rural community were concerned.[71]

The headman of an Indian village could fulfill his functions successfully only by trying "to conciliate the villagers." [72] He could not be "proud, intolerant, and haughty like the Brahmins"; instead he had to be "polite and complaisant" toward his equals and "affable and condescending" toward his inferiors.[73] Full-fledged committee organizations were probably confined to the small minority of rural settlements dominated by landholding groups, primarily Brahmins.[74] But the informal assembly (*panchāyat*) of village elders or all villagers is said to have been a general institution; [75] and its meetings apparently softened the authority of the headman. Since the villages, except for official demands, remained more or less in the charge of the headmen and their aides, they were indeed rural islands, enjoying partial autonomy.[76]

In the traditional Chinese village the local officials were still closer to the nonofficiating co-villagers, who, particularly when they belonged to wealthy or gentry families, might exert great influence in local affairs.[77] Criticism from an "out" group of fellow villagers might compel the headman and his supporters to resign. Under such pressure, a "band of men" who had been in power for a long time might withdraw "from their places, leaving them to those who offered the criticisms." [78]

Such behavior does not imply a formal democratic pattern; but it has a democratic flavor. Of course, there are various kinds of official requests; and there is always the constable, and often a tax collector, both government appointed and both spectacularly representing the interests of the bureaucratic apparatus. But here outside control usually ends. The government "places no practical restrictions upon the right of free assemblage by the people for the consideration of their own affairs. The people of any village can if they choose meet every day in the year. There is no government censor present, and no restriction upon liberty of debate. The people can say what they like, and the local Magistrate neither knows nor cares what is said." [79]

In many hydraulic civilizations the government was as little concerned about the internal affairs of the guilds. The Indian Law Books advised the king to recognize the statutes (laws) of the guilds.[80] And similar statutes existed elsewhere.[81] The Turkish guilds were subject to "the overriding authority of the temporal and spiritual powers, represented by governors, police officers, and *ķâḍîs*"; [82] and their headmen were held responsible by the government for the execution of its fiscal tasks. However, otherwise and "within the limits imposed by religion, tradition, and 'usage,' . . . the corporations were relatively free and autonomous." [83] Gibb and Bowen therefore list them among "the *almost* self-governing groups." [84]

Gibb's and Bowen's formula is valid also for the secondary religions. All external restrictions notwithstanding, these religions did enjoy "some fragments of religious liberty." In traditional China the priests of the secondary religions, "seeking their own and other people's salvation, are not forbidden to preach, recite sutras, and perform ceremonies within doors." [85] And under Islam, "each non-Moslem congregation administers its own affairs under its responsible head, a rabbi, bishop, etc." [86] As long as their worship disturbed no "true believers," and as long as their organization presented no security threat, the government usually permitted the religious minorities to live, within their congregations, a more or less autonomous life.

5. Conclusion

a. Politically Irrelevant Freedoms

These are indeed modest freedoms! They occur in varying combinations in several spheres of life. And by now we should be able to understand why they do occur, and why they are so limited.

Hydraulic society is certainly not immune to rebellious movements, but kin organizations even in their extended forms are no political threat to a normally functioning agrobureaucratic despotism. Nor are the villages a serious threat. The relatively far-reaching autonomy of the traditional Chinese village could, in case of an insurrection, "be extinguished in a moment, a fact of which all the people are perfectly well aware." [87] Secondary religious groups might be a danger in times of great unrest. And this is probably why the government of imperial China never relaxed its control over the tolerated creeds and was so ready to suppress certain sects.[88] The rebellious potential inherent in the guilds was perhaps never completely eliminated, but the hydraulic government was able to paralyze it without exhausting its revenues.

Grunebaum finds it "remarkable to observe how little the Muslim state was really hampered in its operation by the dead weight of these semi-foreign organizations within its structure." [89] And others have commented in the same vein on the political effect of guilds in hydraulic civilizations. The early Byzantine state had no need to liquidate the still-existing Roman guilds, "since they were not at all dangerous politically, and since they could exert no pressure whatsoever on the government and administration, as did, for instance, the German guilds of the Middle Ages." [90] Massignon, who more than most of his colleagues considers the Muslim guilds at least temporarily a political factor, is nevertheless aware that they "never attained a political influence comparable to that of the medieval European guilds." [91] Gibb and Bowen consider the powers of the medieval guilds in Europe so much broader than those of the Islamic corporations that they doubt the suitability of the very term "guild" for the latter.[92] An equation between the guilds of the Medieval West and the guilds of India [93] or of China [94] has been rejected for similar reasons.

To be sure, there existed many resemblances between the two types of corporations, resemblances created by the peculiarities and needs of the organized professions; [95] but the profoundly different societal settings in which they operated gave them profoundly different political and social qualities. The guildsmen of the later European Middle Ages frequently became the masters of their towns; and as such they might play an active part in the power struggles of their time. The guildsmen of the hydraulic world were permitted a certain autonomy, not because, politically speaking, they were so strong, but because they were so irrelevant.

b. A Beggars' Democracy

IN modern totalitarian states the inmates of concentration and forced labor camps are permitted at times to gather in groups and talk at will; and not infrequently certain among them are given minor supervisory jobs. In terms of the law of diminishing administrative returns such "freedoms" pay well. While saving personnel, they in no way threaten the power of the commandant and his guards.

The villages, guilds, and secondary religious organizations of agro-managerial society were no terror camps. But like them they enjoyed certain politically irrelevant freedoms. These freedoms—which in some instances were considerable—did not result in full autonomy. At best they established a kind of Beggars' Democracy.

C. HYDRAULIC DESPOTISM—BENEVOLENT DESPOTISM?

1. TOTAL POWER—FOR THE BENEFIT OF THE PEOPLE?

THE hydraulic state is not checked by a Beggars' Democracy. Nor is it checked by any other effective constitutional, societal, or cultural counterweights. Clearly it is despotic. But does it not at the same time benefit the people?

2. THE CLAIM AND THE REALITY

a. Operational Necessity Not to Be Confused with Benevolence

THE hydraulic state is a managerial state, and certain of its operations do indeed benefit the people. But since the rulers depend on these operations for their own maintenance and prosperity, their policies can hardly be considered benevolent. A pirate does not act benevolently when he keeps his ship afloat or feeds the slaves he plans to sell. Capable of recognizing his future as well as his present advantages, he is rational but not benevolent. His behavior may temporarily benefit the persons in his power; but this is not its primary purpose. Given a choice, he will further his own interests, and not the interests of others.

b. The Rationality Coefficient of Hydraulic Society

ON the level of total power, the representatives of hydraulic regimes proceed in a similar way. Their behavior may to some degree benefit the persons in their power, and far-sighted advisors and statesmen may stress the importance of satisfying the people; [a] but taken as a group they consider the needs of their subjects in the light of their own needs and advantages. For this purpose they must (1) keep the agrarian economy going; (2) not increase corvée labor and taxes to a

a. For India see Bhagavadgītā, *passim*, and Manu, 1886: 229, 396 ff. For China: the sayings of Confucius and still more important, those of Mencius.

point where the discouraged peasants stop producing; and (3) not permit internal and external strife to disrupt the life of the population.

The third task—the maintenance of peace and order—confronts the governments of all societies. The first and second tasks distinguish hydraulic from other agrarian civilizations. The continued existence of agrarian despotism depends on the satisfactory execution of these three functions. They constitute what may be called the regime's rationality minimum.

Conquest societies, whose rulers are steeped in nonhydraulic traditions, often proceed along or near the lowest hydraulic rationality level. And endogenous masters frequently sink to this level during periods of decay and disintegration. Strong moves toward a higher rationality coefficient occur particularly during the earlier phases of endogenous rule, but they may also occur during later periods of growth or consolidation.

The formative phase of a conquest society is largely determined by the conquerors' ability to identify themselves with their new institutional environment. The Mongols were completely alien to the traditions and mores of the hydraulic civilizations they overran. Chingis Khan's son, Ogotai, is said to have planned to convert the cultivated fields of China into pastures; and he refrained from doing so only because Yeh-lü Ch'u-tsai convincingly explained to him the superior tax potential of the agrarian order.[1] But although the Mongols maintained the hydraulic economy of their new realm, they remained indifferent to its subtler needs. Virtually everywhere they stayed close to the rationality minimum of hydraulic society.

Mohammed, who lived in arid Arabia, certainly understood the importance of irrigation for successful crop-raising, although in his official utterances he rarely refers to the problem, and then essentially to small-scale (well) irrigation.[2] His followers preserved, restored, and even created vigorous hydraulic economies in Syria, Egypt, Iraq, Northwest Africa, Spain, and briefly also in Sicily. The Manchus were familiar with irrigation agriculture before they moved southward across the Great Wall to conquer China.[3] In this respect they were not unlike the Incas, who practiced irrigation in the Andean highlands before they established their hydraulic empire.[4] When they were overrun by the Spaniards, they were probably operating close to their rationality maximum.

c. Whose Rationality Coefficient?

BUT no matter whether a hydraulic society is operated crudely or subtly, the claim of benevolence compels us to ask: *cui bono?* Evidently operational tasks may be handled in a way that satisfies the interests of the rulers at the expense of the nongovernmental forces of society. Or they may be handled in a way that satisfies the needs of the people and gives few, if any, advantages to the government. Intermediate solutions compromise between the two extremes.

As a rule, the three alternatives are seriously considered only if the actual circumstances permit genuine choice. In the managerial, the consumptive, and the judicial spheres of hydraulic life this is indeed the case. But in all these spheres we find the people's interests sacrificed to the rulers' rationality optimum.

3. The Rulers' Rationality Optimum Prevails

a. Necessity and Choice in the Policy of the Hydraulic Regime

In the territorial states of ancient China, as in other hydraulic civilizations, philosophers discussed the alternatives of altruistic, balanced, or crudely selfish rule before the representatives of absolutist power. Confucius pointed out that Yü, the legendary founder of the protohistorical Hsia dynasty, ate coarse foods, dressed poorly, dwelt in a modest house, and concentrated his energies on the irrigation canals. This great culture hero, whom Confucius considered flawless,[5] combined a minimum of personal demand with a maximum of public devotion.

In the later period of China's early history the kings lived very comfortably; but the best among them are said to have sought a balance between their own and their subjects' interests. The philosopher Mencius, who discussed this point, did not challenge the rulers' right to build lofty edifices, parks, and ponds by corvée labor; but he asked that the people be permitted to share these enterprises with their king.[6]

Thus the philosophers of ancient China assumed that within the framework of governmental needs there existed genuine alternatives for action. Without exception, however, the masters of the agrarian apparatus state satisfied the constructional, organizational, and acquisitive needs of their realm with a maximum stress on their own advantage and a minimum stress on the requirements of their subjects.

b. The Rulers' Managerial Optimum

In its early phase the hydraulic regime becomes stronger and wealthier with the growth of its hydraulic economy. But at a certain point the government can obtain additional revenue by intensifying its acquisitive rather than its productive operations. It is at this point that different power constellations lead to a different managerial optimum.

The rulers' managerial optimum is maintained whenever the government collects a maximum revenue with a minimum hydraulic effort. The people's managerial optimum is maintained whenever a maximum hydraulic achievement is accomplished with minimum administrative expense. Intermediate arrangements involve the collection of a large but not maximum revenue, a good part of which is used to produce sizable but not maximum hydraulic works.

The rulers' responses to these alternatives show clearly the effect of total power on those who wield it. Beyond the zone of stimulating discrepancy, they generally push only those hydraulic enterprises that improve their own well-being; and they are most ingenious in developing new methods of fiscal exploitation. In short, they aim at the rulers', and not at the people's, managerial optimum.

c. The Rulers' Consumptive Optimum

THREE major alternatives may also be distinguished in the sphere of consumption. The rulers' consumptive optimum is maintained whenever the masters of the hydraulic state arrogate to themselves a maximum of goods, which they may consume with a maximum of conspicuousness ("splendor"). The people's consumptive optimum is maintained whenever the nongovernmental members of society receive a maximum of goods, which they may consume as conspicuously as they please. Intermediate arrangements to some degree favor the representatives of the government without, however, seriously restricting the quality or conspicuousness of popular consumption.

Again the responses to these alternatives show the effect of total power on those who wield it. The proverbial splendor of Oriental despotism as well as the proverbial misery of its subjects have their roots in a policy that is directed toward the rulers', and not the people's, consumptive optimum.

This optimum has both an economic and a legal aspect. By concentrating the national surplus in their own hands, the rulers restrict the amount of goods physically available to nongovernmental consumers. By legally forbidding the general use of prestige-giving objects, they reserve to themselves conspicuous consumption. In simpler hydraulic civilizations both aims can be achieved without much difficulty. Increasing social differentiations complicate matters, but they do not preclude a situation that, for all practical purposes, realizes the rulers' optimum.

In the Inca empire the common people ate poorly and had little opportunity to drink heavily.[7] Their rulers ate extremely well, and they imbibed to excess.[8] Moreover, the gulf between the two groups was widened by laws which reserved the use of gold, silver, precious stones, colored feathers, and vicuña wool to the rulers. The commoners were permitted some modest ornaments, but even these could be worn only on special occasions.[9]

Arrangements of this kind are most easily enforced when the great majority of the commoners are peasants living in government-controlled and more or less equalitarian villages. The emergence of many property-based enterprises involves the growth of nonbureaucratic forms of wealth, both mobile and immobile; and such a development inevitably affects the pattern of consumption.

Even under these circumstances the bulk of the rural and urban population continues to live poorly; and the small stratum of nonbureaucratic property-holders sees their fortunes constantly threatened by taxation and confiscation (and in time split up through the laws of inheritance). But wherever large property-based business became essential, private wealth could not be eradicated, and those possessing it could not be prevented from enjoying at least some part of it.

Thus the laws which reserved certain types of dress or other conspicuous goods to the ruling class became a crucial means for placing the men of the governmental machine and the priests of the dominant religion above the mass of the commoners. In traditional China the officials and their nonofficiating relatives were distinguished by their houses, furniture, clothes, and vehicles.[10] The Indian Law Books prescribe very precisely the garments, girdles, staffs, etc. to be used by Brahmins, Kshatriyas, and Vaisyas.[11] In the Near East distinct bureaucratic features of dress are documented for Pharaonic Egypt,[12] Assyria,[13] Byzantium,[14] the Arab caliphate,[15] the Mamluks,[16] and Ottoman Turkey.[17]

Within the limits of these regulations the commoners might—theoretically speaking—enjoy their wealth. But they always hid their most precious possessions, and frequently their fear of confiscatory action was so great that they avoided all ostentation. The sweeping persecution of the merchants under the Earlier Han dynasty was provoked by the blatant show which the rich businessmen had made of their wealth.[18] Under a government which makes no effort to approach the rationality maximum, potential victims of confiscation may act with extreme caution. The French physician, Bernier, who from 1655 to 1658 lived in the Near East and afterward spent almost ten years in Mogul India, was struck by the frustrating atmosphere in which the businessmen of Asia operated. Enterprise found "little encouragement to engage in commercial pursuits," because greedy tyrants possessed "both power and inclination to deprive any man of the fruits of his industry." And "when wealth is acquired, as must sometimes be the case, the possessor, so far from living with increased comfort and assuming an air of independence, studies the means by which he may appear indigent: his dress, lodging, and furniture continue to be mean, and he is careful, above all things, never to indulge in the pleasures of the table." [19]

Bernier's observations must not be pressed. Under more far-sighted rulers the wealthy merchants of Asia lived luxuriously as long as their behavior did not invite disaster. And even in the India of Aurangzeb some few government-protected persons of wealth, Bernier tells us, "are at no pains to counterfeit poverty, but partake of the comforts and luxuries of life." [20]

But such exceptions do not negate the basic trend. In hydraulic civilizations wealthy commoners were denied the proprietary security which the burghers of the later Middle Ages enjoyed; and they did not dare to engage in the conspicuous consumption which the medieval businessmen practiced, despite the many sumptuary laws to which they too had to submit. The lavish display by the representatives of the state on the one side and the predominance of genuine and feigned poverty on the other spectacularly show the effect of total power on the consumptive optimum of hydraulic society.

d. The Rulers' Judicial Optimum

SIMILARLY one-sided decisions characterize the judicial field. As explained above, no society is without standardized norms; and few advanced agrarian civilizations are without written or codified laws. Thus it is the special setting and intent that separate the laws of hydraulic despotism from those of pluralistically controlled states.

The rulers' judicial optimum is maintained whenever the representatives of government exert a maximum influence on the formulation and application of their country's laws. The people's judicial optimum is maintained whenever the nongovernmental elements of society are decisive. In democratic commonwealths the constitutionally qualified citizen may participate in the formulation of the laws. He may exercise the functions of a judge, as he did in democratic Athens, or he may, as a lay juror, cooperate with professionally trained, but elected judges. In both cases the nongovernmental forces of society, and not a despotic state, are charged with the application of the law. Intermediate variants are characterized by an increased, but not absolute, governmental power and by a proportionately decreased popular control over the legislature and judiciary.

It is obvious that the first type of judicial optimum prevails in hydraulic society. And it is equally obvious that in the judicial sphere, as in others, the masters of the hydraulic state seek a maximum of results (internal order) with a minimum of governmental effort and expense. This they accomplish not by yielding important judicial functions to quasi-independent secondary centers of power, as did the sovereigns of feudal Europe,[b] but by permitting politically irrelevant groups to handle certain of their own legal affairs, or by permitting magistrates to handle legal matters along with their other duties, or, where professional judges are the rule, by having as few full-time judges as possible.

Such conditions preclude the development of independent juries. They discourage elaborate judicial procedures. And they leave little room for the functioning of independent professional lawyers. With these limitations the judges of a hydraulic society settle legal cases —many of which arise from clashes of proprietary interests, and in countries with a highly commercialized urban life this field of action may become very important indeed.[21]

However, even at their rational best, the laws of such countries express a fundamentally unbalanced societal situation. Even if they protect one commoner against the other, they do not protect the commoners—as individuals or as a group—against the absolutist state. Shortly after Bernier had commented on this phenomenon, John Locke did likewise; and his references to Ottoman Turkey, Ceylon, and Tsarist Russia show him aware that the tyrannical variant of judicial procedure, which English autocracy failed to develop fully, flourished unhampered under Oriental despotism.

Locke insists that the presence of laws in a despotic regime proves nothing as to their justness:

> "if it be asked what security, what fence is there in such a state against the violence and oppression of this absolute ruler, the very question can scarce be borne. They are ready to tell you that it deserves death only to ask after safety. Betwixt subject and subject, they will grant, there must be measures, laws, and judges for their mutual peace and security. But as for the ruler, he ought to be absolute, and is above all such circumstances; because he has a power to do more hurt and wrong, it is right

b. The holders of office land and the tax collectors who occasionally act as judges are, either fully or partially, integrated in the bureaucratic apparatus. See below, Chap. 8.

when he does it. To ask how you may be guarded from harm or injury on that side, where the strongest hand is to do it, is presently the voice of faction and rebellion. As if when men, quitting the state of nature, entered into society, they agreed that all of them but one should be under the restraint of laws; but that he should still retain all the liberty of the state of Nature, increased with power, and made licentious by impunity. This is to think that men are so foolish that they take care to avoid what mischiefs may be done them by polecats or foxes, but are content, nay, think it safety, to be devoured by lions.[22]

4. "Absolute Power Corrupts Absolutely"

This is a bitter indictment. Contrary to modern apologists for totalitarian laws and constitutions, Locke refuses to put any trust in the autocrat's potential benevolence: "he that thinks absolute power purifies men's blood, and corrects the baseness of human nature, need read but the history of this, or any other age, to be convinced to the contrary." [23] Lord Acton's affirmative version of Locke's thesis is well known: "Power tends to corrupt and absolute power corrupts absolutely." [24]

Acceptance of this idea need not include an acceptance of Locke's pessimistic views on "the baseness of human nature." Man acts from many motives, which under different circumstances operate with different strengths. Both self-centeredness and community-centeredness seek expression; and it depends on the cultural heritage and the over-all setting whether one or the other of them will prevail. A governmental—or proprietary—order leading to the emergence of absolute power encourages and enables the holders of this power to satisfy their own interests absolutely. It is for this reason that agrarian despotism, like industrial despotism, corrupts absolutely those who bask in the sun of total power.

5. The Rulers' Publicity Optimum

The corrupting influence is further consolidated by a one-sidedly manipulated public opinion. Public opinion may be shaped in a number of ways; and here, as elsewhere, the rulers' and the people's interests diverge sharply. This becomes clear as soon as the major alternatives are outlined.

The rulers' publicity optimum is maintained whenever the government's real or alleged achievements are given a maximum of uncritical publicity, while the people's experiences, sufferings, and views receive a minimum of notice. The people's publicity optimum combines a full presentation of the government's achievements and shortcomings. Intermediate arrangements favor the government without keeping the nongovernmental forces of society from stating their own case.

Independent popular criticism differs both in quality and intent from the many and continued criticisms made by leading members of the officialdom. Bureaucratic criticism is vital to the proper functioning of complex administration, but it is voiced either behind closed doors or in publications accessible only to a limited number of educated persons, who are usually members of the ruling group. In both cases, the people's problems are viewed essentially from the standpoint of a more or less rationally conceived government interest.[c]

Wielding total power, the masters of the hydraulic state can readily maintain the rulers' publicity optimum. Under socially undifferentiated conditions, the government's (frequently the sovereign's) voice drowns out all criticism except as it may appear in such inconsequential media as popular tales and songs. More differentiated conditions provide additional outlets in secondary religions and philosophies, in popular short stories, novels, and plays. But even these media remain significantly feeble. In contrast to the independent writers who, under Western absolutism, challenged not only the excesses but the foundations of the despotic order, the critics of hydraulic society have in almost every case complained only of the misdeeds of individual officials or of the evils of specific governmental acts.[d] Apart from mystics who teach total withdrawal from the world, these critics aim ultimately at regenerating a system of total power, whose fundamental desirability they do not doubt.

6. The Two-fold Function of the Benevolence Myth

a. It Stresses the Long-range Interest of the Despotic Regime

THE advantages of the benevolence myth for the despotism which it glorifies are twofold. By presenting the ruler and his aides as

c. In the total managerial societies of today, state-directed popular criticism is used to supplement and dramatize the government's criticism of problematic elements, particularly in the middle and lower echelons of the bureaucracy. Criticism of this kind has been encouraged in many hydraulic societies. The letters to Stalin differ technically, but not institutionally, from the letters and petitions addressed in the past to Oriental despots.

d. Often government functionaries indict blundering fellow functionaries or harmful administrative procedures more sharply than do persons who are not part of the regime.

eager to achieve the people's rationality optimum, they enable the official spokesmen to educate and discipline the members of their own group. The holder of power, who operates below the rulers' rationality minimum, endangers the safety of the governmental apparatus, whereas one who operates above this level enhances the stability of the regime. He exploits his orchard as an intelligent gardener should.[25] Moreover, the ruler and his men must not weaken their position by crude managerial neglect, excessive taxation, or provocative injustice. The myth of an unselfish (benevolent) despotism dramatizes these desiderata which, consciously or unconsciously, are underwritten by all thoughtful members of the ruling class.

b. It Weakens Potential Opposition

MORE important still than the impact of the benevolence myth on the holders of power is its effect on the nongovernmental forces of society. The myth admits that individual sovereigns and officials may be unworthy, but it depicts the despotic order as fundamentally good—in fact, as the only reasonable and commendable system of government.

Thus the embittered subject, who is permanently exposed to such propaganda, cannot well strive for the creation of a new and less despotic order. He and others who feel as he does may withdraw to the mountains. They may kill some local officials. They may defeat the government's men in arms. They may even overthrow a tottering dynasty. But eventually they will only revive—and rejuvenate—the agromanagerial despotism whose incompetent representatives they eliminated. The heroes of China's famous bandit novel, the *Shui-hu Ch'uan,* could think of nothing better to do than to set up on their rebel island a miniature version of the very bureaucratic hierarchy which they were so fiercely combating.

c. The Presence of Good Sovereigns and Just Officials Fails to Upset the Prevailing Trend

IF man were exclusively self-centered, the result of all this would be very simple indeed. And very sad. But man is also community-centered. And this side of his character finds expression also in hydraulic society. To be sure, under the conditions of agrarian despotism, it is difficult to be a good sovereign or a just official. But it is not impossible. Throughout the hydraulic world serious-minded rulers attended to their managerial and judicial duties conscientiously, and honest officials strove to prevent fiscal and judicial oppression. Courageous functionaries insisted on what they considered proper policies, although by doing so they opposed the wishes of powerful superiors, and occasionally even of the sovereign himself.

But those who pursue such a course clash with the interest of the vast self-indulgent and scheming ruling group; and history shows that only a handful of unusually community-minded (ethically "possessed") persons was so disposed. Furthermore, even this pathetically small number of "good" men was not completely aware of how slanted the rulers' optimum was, which they recommended. Confucius' gentleman bureaucrat, the ideal ruler of the *Bhagavadgītā,* and the "just" statesmen of the ancient Roman or Islamic Near East all try to be fair within the framework of a society which takes the patterns of despotic power, revenue, and prestige for granted.

7. HYDRAULIC DESPOTISM: BENEVOLENT IN FORM, OPPRESSIVE IN CONTENT

THUS agromanagerial despots may present their regimes as benevolent; actually, however, and even under the most favorable circumstances, they strive for their own, and not for the people's, rationality optimum. They plan their hydraulic enterprises according to what benefits their might and wealth. And they write their own ticket as fiscal masters of the national surplus and as conspicuous consumers.

Stalin claims that in a modern industrial apparatus state the culture of a national minority is national in form and socialist in content.[26] Experience shows that the "socialist" (read: *apparatchik*) substance quickly wipes out all but the most insignificant national elements. A similar mechanism is at work in the agrarian apparatus state. Paraphrasing Stalin's formula and replacing myth by reality, we may truthfully say that hydraulic despotism is benevolent in form and oppressive in content.

CHAPTER 5

Total terror—total submission
—total loneliness

A. AUTONOMOUS MAN UNDER TOTAL POWER

MAN is no ant. His efforts to escape from freedom [1] show him ambivalently attracted by what he ambivalently abandons. The urge to act independently is an essential attribute of *homo sapiens,* and a highly complex one. Not all of its components are socially valuable; but among them is man's most precious motivating force: the urge to obey his conscience, all external disadvantages notwithstanding.

What happens to man's desire for autonomy under the conditions of total power? One variant of total power, hydraulic despotism, tolerates no relevant political forces besides itself. In this respect it succeeds on the institutional level because it blocks the development of such forces; and it succeeds on the psychological level, because it discourages man's desire for independent political action. In the last analysis, hydraulic government is government by intimidation.

B. TERROR ESSENTIAL FOR MAINTAINING THE RULERS' RATIONALITY OPTIMUM

1. THE NEED

MAN is no ant. But neither is he a stone. A policy that upholds the rulers' publicity optimum confuses the people's mind, without however eliminating their feelings of frustration and unhappiness. Unchecked, these feelings may lead to rebellious action. To counter this dangerous trend the hydraulic regime resorts to intimidation. Terror is the inevitable consequence of the rulers' resolve to uphold their own and not the people's rationality optimum.

2. ITS OFFICIAL RECOGNITION:
"PUNISHMENT IS THE KING!"

MANY spokesmen of hydraulic despotism have emphasized the need for rule by punishment. Such a policy may be justified by the argument that guiltless people are few.[1] Confucius preferred education to punishment; yet he, too, believed that it would take a hundred years of good government "to transform the violently bad and to dispense with capital punishment." [2]

Thus with varying arguments, punishment has been viewed as an essential tool of successful statecraft. The Hindu law book of Manu establishes fear-inspiring punishment as the foundation of internal peace and order. Punishment, which—of course—must be just, makes everyone behave properly.[3] Without it caste barriers would be crossed; and all men would turn against their fellows. "Where Punishment with a black hue and red eye stalks about," [4] subjects live at peace. *"The whole world is kept in order by punishment."* [5]

By punishment the ruler protects the weak against the strong, sacrifice against animal violation, property against its (nongovernmental) enemies and social superiority against assaults from below. "If the king did not, without tiring, inflict punishment on those worthy to be punished, the stronger would roast the weaker, like fish on a spit: The crow would eat the sacrificial cake and the dog would lick the sacrificial viands, and ownership would not remain with any one, the lower ones would (usurp the place of) the higher ones." [6] Thus "punishment alone governs all created beings, punishment alone protects them, punishment watches over them while they sleep." [7] Indeed, "punishment is . . . the king." [8]

The rulers of ancient Mesopotamia claimed that they received their power from the great Enlil.[9] This terrifying god symbolizes "the power of force, of compulsion. Opposing wills are crushed and beaten into submission." [10] Although he is supposed to use his cruel might judiciously,[11] "man can never be fully at ease with Enlil but feels a lurking fear." [12] This being so, the sovereign's readiness to identify himself with Enlil or with deities descended from him is deeply significant. The Sumerian kings usually identified themselves with Enlil directly.[13] The Babylonians upheld the basic idea, but modified it. Hammurabi pictured himself as having been "called" by Enlil; and he names Enlil's son, Sin, as his divine father.[14] In both cases the Mesopotamian rulers stressed the terroristic quality of their position.

The terror inherent in Pharaonic despotism is symbolized by the poisonous Uraeus snake, which lies coiled on the ruler's forehead and threatens his enemies with destruction.[15] The king's actions are also compared with those of the fear-inspiring lion goddess, Sekhmet.[a]

Chinese statecraft learned to express its need for terrifying punishment in the rational and moral form of Confucianism. But punishment was the primary weapon of the so-called Legalists and of such Legalist-influenced Confucianists as Hsün Tsŭ. And it remained a cornerstone of official policy throughout the imperial period. What we would call the Ministry of Justice was known in traditional China as the Ministry of Punishments.

The Islamic ruler saw to it that he was both respected and feared.[16] The *Arabian Nights,* which depicts Harun al-Rashīd usually accompanied by his executioner, presents in fictional dress a historic truth. The executioner was a standard feature of the Abbassid court.

3. THE MORPHOLOGY OF VIOLENCE

To be sure, all governments deserving the name have ways of imposing their will on their subjects, and the use of violence is always among them. But different societies develop different patterns of integrating (or fragmenting) violence and of controlling (or not controlling) it.

a. Integrated versus Fragmented Patterns of Violence

IN ancient Greece, free men ordinarily wore arms—according to Thucydides, "because their homes were undefended." [17] In other words, the government did not monopolize the use of force. With the growth of public safety the early custom disappeared in most city states; [18] but the citizens, who were potential warriors, were still permitted to keep the tools of violence in their homes. Pictorial evidence portraying the start of a campaign shows "mostly the woman bringing the weapons from the home to the departing man." [19]

In Medieval Europe the semi-independent feudal lords from the beginning represented important secondary centers of military action, and in the course of time many towns developed their own armed forces. These feudal and urban nuclei of political and military life were free to use violence both within their own jurisdictions and against one another. The vassal, who appeared before his sovereign

---

a. See Breasted, 1927, I: 327, and cf. II: 92, and IV: 166; Erman, 1923: 78 ff.; and Wilson, 1950: 11. According to one story, Sekhmet emerged as the suppressor of a conspiracy. When the supreme god Re "perceived the things which were being plotted against him by mankind," he conjured up a force to crush the evil schemers. Then "Sekhmet came into being." She quickly "prevailed over mankind," and desiring to drink human blood—or what she believed to be human blood, "she drank, and it was good in her heart" (Wilson, 1950: 11). Cf. Erman, 1923: 78 ff.

with his sword at his side, expressed strikingly the fragmented and balanced pattern of violence that characterized feudal society.

Concentration of the legitimate uses of force in the hands of the state does not occur under conditions of total power only. Modern constitutional government restricts private violence more and more. But it differs from agrarian and industrial apparatus states in that the size, quality and use of coercion (army and police) are determined by the nongovernmental forces of society. The experiences of classical Greece and the modern West show that a country may rally powerful armies without its citizens losing control over them.

b. Controlled versus Uncontrolled Violence

ARMY discipline requires unquestioning subordination; and the commander in chief of a well-coordinated army—which the feudal hosts were not—rules absolutely within the limits of his jurisdiction. However, in a democratic country he remains responsible to the citizens who control the government. General Eisenhower's comments on the Soviet method of attacking through mine fields indicate the institutional alternatives. In "a matter-of-fact statement" Marshal Zhukov explained to the American general: "When we come to a mine field our infantry attacks exactly as if it were not there. The losses we get from personnel mines we consider only equal to those we would have gotten from machine guns and artillery if the Germans had chosen to defend that particular area with strong bodies of troops instead of with mine fields." Eisenhower adds drily: "I had a vivid picture of what would happen to any American or British commander if he pursued such tactics, and I had an even more vivid picture of what the men in any one of our divisions would have to say about the matter had we attempted to make such a practice a part of our tactical doctrine." [20]

The Soviet way saves materiel and time; and it suits to perfection the rulers' tactical optimum. Obviously this optimum can be realized only when organized violence is wielded by the masters of an unchecked state. The social quality of organized violence, like that of other governmental functions, changes with the over-all setting in which it develops.

C. THE TERROR OF HYDRAULIC DESPOTISM

THE subjects of an agrarian apparatus state have little opportunity to argue the problem of uncontrolled violence. They may be permitted the possession of small and simple weapons, particularly in the villages, which have to ward off bandits. But the organized and military use of coercion is essentially concentrated in the hands of the absolutist rulers, who usually give audience only to unarmed men. In hydraulic society the monster with "a black hue and red eye" is no watch-dog tied up by the people, but a tiger that moves at will.

1. Its Physical Aspect

LIKE the tiger, the engineer of power must have the physical means with which to crush his victims. And the agromanagerial despot does indeed possess such means. He exercises unchecked control over the army, the police, the intelligence service; and he has at his disposal jailers, torturers, executioners, and all the tools that are necessary to catch, incapacitate, and destroy a suspect.

2. Its Psychological Aspect

a. Unpredictability

FURTHERMORE, he can employ these devices with maximum psychological effect. Everywhere persons wielding great governmental or proprietary power like to shroud certain of their acts in secrecy; but the procedures of a despotic government are enigmatic because of the very nature of the regime. Accountable only to themselves, the men of the apparatus tend to handle even insignificant matters with secretiveness; and they raise mystification to an art when they want to intimidate and surprise. Unpredictability is an essential weapon of absolute terror.

b. Lenin: ". . . power not limited by any laws"

LENIN defined the dictatorship of the proletariat—which he held to be the heart of the Soviet regime—as "a power not limited by any laws." [1] Like other utterances of Lenin, this formula combines an impressive half-truth with important fallacies. First, the Soviet dictatorship was never controlled by the Russian workers; and there is ample evidence that Lenin knew this. Second, no regime, however dictatorial, operates without normative regulations or laws of some kind; and this, too, was well known to Lenin. Before he made the just-quoted statement, his dictatorial government had already issued many revolutionary statutes and decrees.[2] The despot's right to interpret, change, and override previously established laws is a fundamental constitutional and legal principle of absolutist rule. Lenin's definition stresses with brutal frankness the dictator's unchecked power to use laws as he wishes. In the sphere of terror he may go so far that it becomes difficult to distinguish between lawless terror and terror by law.

c. Lawless Terror and Terror by Law

A CHIEF or ruler does not necessarily override the laws of his hydraulic community when he himself commits—or gives orders to commit—acts of terrifying brutality.

In smaller hydraulic tribes autocratic cruelty is no issue, because the chief, being close to his fellow tribesmen, is unable to exert power over and above his directing functions. This is the case among the Suk and their hydraulic neighbors and throughout the American Pueblos.

In larger hydraulic tribes the chief may seek to bolster his incipient autocracy by the employment of spectacular terror. A Chagga chief, for instance, may commit all manner of cruelties against his subjects. Ndeserno is said to have torn the hearts from his victims' bodies while they were still alive and to have had them roasted for his children.[3] A chieftain who went to such extremes was contemplated with grave apprehension, but, according to Gutmann, "such cruelties against individuals did not harm his prestige." On the contrary, the fear they inspired cemented the stability of the regime.[4]

The spectacular terror directed by the rulers of ancient Hawaii may well have served the same purpose;[5] and the so-called Cannibal Texts of the Old Kingdom suggest a similar situation in prehistoric Egypt. One of these texts, found in a pyramid, reveals a dead ruler killing, dissecting, and cooking human beings in the nether world for his gustatory pleasure;[6] and another reveals him as taking "the wives from their husbands whenever he wants to and according to his heart's desire."[a]

In more differentiated hydraulic civilizations, there is less need to bulwark the ruler's exalted position by spectacular acts of autocratic ruthlessness. Although such acts do not completely cease, they are now initiated mainly by excessively cruel (and/or insecure) sovereigns and by the heads of dynasties which operate below the rulers' rationality maximum. Gaudefroy-Demombynes describes the irrationally terroristic quality of the Abbassid caliphate as follows: "Improvised executions and the exhibition of heads are part of the regular life of the Abbassid court. Beginning with the reign of El Mançour, when a person is urgently summoned to the palace by the guards of the caliph, he feels that he has a good chance not to

---

a. Sethe, PT, II: 354 ff. The Chagga chiefs seem to have made a like claim on all girls and women of their realm (Widenmann, 1899: 48; cf. Gutmann, 1909: 25).

return alive. He makes his testament, says farewell to his family, and carries his shroud under his arm." [b]

In these and other instances, the ruler's terroristic behavior was above rather than against the law. On the other hand, officials who resorted to extreme brutalities often went beyond even the broadest possible interpretation of the law. At times they might be held accountable. But many "lawless" bureaucratic terrorists were criticized only after they were dead.

The excesses of autocratic and bureaucratic terror are an extreme manifestation of human behavior under total power. Institutionally, however, they are probably less important than the innumerable acts of terror that were perpetrated as a matter of routine and within the flexible frame of despotic law. It was this routine terror in managerial, fiscal, and judicial procedures that caused certain observers to designate the government of hydraulic despotism as "government by flogging."

3. "Government by Flogging"

a. Terror in Managerial Procedures

"The language of the whip" seems to have been employed regularly in the state corvées of ancient Sumer.[7] Under the Pharaohs, every government administrator could resort to corporal punishment.[8] The pictorial records of ancient Egypt show men conducting all manner of public enterprises with sticks in their hands.[9] In the later part of the 19th century, when the British began to abolish "government by flogging," the whip was still standard equipment for insuring the success of the hydraulic corvée.[10] Present-day writers who are greatly impressed by the planned economy of the Incas would do well to remember that the Inca prince, Garcilaso de la Vega, glorying in his forebears' achievements, took it for granted that the one sure way to make people industrious was to threaten them with beating.[11]

b. Terror in Fiscal Procedures

Since the days of the Pharaohs, reluctance in paying taxes was overcome by force. A famous satire of the New Kingdom tells that the Egyptian peasant who failed to deliver his quota of grain was "beaten, tied up, and thrown into the ditch." [12] Irregularities in

b. Gaudefroy-Demombynes, 1931: 384. The friend of an Abbassid caliph, who went to the court every Friday, was "gripped by an intense fear" when he was summoned on a different day. Had he been maligned? Had he been found wanting? His "anguish and fear" increased until he discovered to his immense relief that the sovereign merely wanted him to share an hour of idleness and pleasure (Sauvaget, 1946: 62).

handling state and temple property also called for corporal punishment.[13]

The Sacred Law of Islam prohibited torture; but the tax officials of the caliphs apparently found it impossible to fulfill their task without resorting to violence.[14] Under the Abbassid dynasty, torture was a concomitant of tax gathering until the year 800; and after a short interlude of about twelve years it was invoked again, and as brutally as ever. Government agents "beat the people, imprisoned them, and suspended heavy men by one arm so that they almost died."[15]

The *Arthashāstra* made it mandatory for police and court judges to see that rural taxes were duly paid, and to use force if necessary.[16] The Law Code of imperial China prescribed beating as the standard punishment for persons who failed to fulfill their fiscal obligations.[17]

c. Terror in Judicial Procedures

THE Chinese Code carried the issue of violence beyond the spheres of fiscal action. In case of continued resistance and/or inability to deliver, the defaulter might be taken before a judge; and if necessary, fiscal terror might be replaced by judicial terror. Judicial torture to extort evidence—and frequently also to punish—was employed in virtually all hydraulic civilizations.

In Pharaonic Egypt beating was a regular adjunct of judicial procedures.[18] "He was examined with the rod" was standard phrasing in the New Kingdom.[19]

Indian, Chinese, and Islamic sources describe judicial terror in considerable detail. The *Arthashāstra* states that "Those whose guilt is *believed to be true* shall be subjected to torture."[20] With the exception of the Brahmins,[c] they could be given the "six punishments," the "seven kinds of whipping," the "two kinds of suspension from above," and the "water-tube."[21] Regarding persons "who have committed grave offences," the famous book is still more specific. They could be given the

> nine kinds of blows with a cane: 12 beats on each of the thighs; 28 beats with a stick of the tree (nakta-mala); 32 beats on each palm of the hands and on each sole of the feet; two on the knuckles, the hands being joined so as to appear like a scorpion; two kinds of suspensions, face downwards (ullambane chale); burning one of the joints of a finger after the accused has been

c. They could not be tortured to extort evidence; but if found guilty of a very grave crime, they could be branded (*Arthaśāstra*, 1923: 270).

made to drink rice gruel; heating his body for a day after he has been made to drink oil; causing him to lie on coarse grass for a night in winter. These are the 18 kinds of torture. . . . Each day a fresh kind of the torture may be employed.[22]

In particularly serious cases, such as attempts to seize the king's treasury, the accused could be "subjected once or many times to one or all of the above kinds of torture." [23]

The Chinese Law Code describes a number of instruments used to extract evidence; [24] and the writings of sincere administrators elaborate on proper and improper methods of torture.[25]

Canonic prohibitions notwithstanding, the secular courts of the caliphs extorted evidence by employing "the whip, the end of a rope, the stick, and the strap on the back and belly, on the back of the head, the lower parts of the body, feet, joints, and muscles." [26]

Similar methods seem to have persisted in the Near East until recent days. In 19th-century Egypt, "justice, such as it was, was almost as much a terror to the innocent witness as to the accused person against whom testimony was borne." [27]

d. Western Correspondences Noteworthy for Their Temporary Strength and Their Limitations

MANIFESTLY, judicial torture is widespread in the hydraulic world. But is it specific? After all, torture had a definite place in Roman law. It appears prominently in late feudal and postfeudal Western legal procedures and in the Inquisition. And it survives today in the third degree.

All these phenomena must indeed be recognized for what they are. They remind us grimly that human nature is the same everywhere and that man succumbs to the corrupting influence of power whenever circumstances permit. Fortunately, the shape of Western institutions kept these inclinations from asserting themselves lastingly. But the momentum they gained at certain times and in certain places precludes the complacent assumption that what happened under hydraulic governments—and what is happening today in the totalitarian states—cannot happen here.

The indigenous free men of ancient Greece and republican Rome did not employ managerial or fiscal terror against their fellow citizens—the citizens did not render corvée service nor did they pay substantial taxes—and "as a rule" they were not subjected to judicial torture.[28] Their societal order was too balanced for this; yet it was not sufficiently balanced to prevent the use of managerial and judicial terror against certain alien and unfree elements. In Greece, the position of most slaves was "not much different from that of domestic animals." [29] Their masters were free to punish them physically; [30] and the not too numerous state slaves occupied in public works were directed by foremen, who, frequently slaves themselves, "had a name for being very hard." [31] In Greece both slaves and free aliens were the targets of judicial torture.[32] In republican Rome only slaves were so treated.[33]

The crystallization of absolutist power under the empire deprived the Roman citizens of the protection which their forefathers had enjoyed against judicial and other forms of governmental terror. Roman law in late Roman and Byzantine times extended judicial torture to the bulk of all free persons.[34]

A similar change occurred in the later part of the Middle Ages. Early Frankish (Salic) law permitted only persons of servile status to be tortured.[35] Conflicts between free men were handled by courts composed of peers. Serious legal issues were settled by ordeal or judicial combat; [36] and the burghers in medieval towns, who originally followed these procedures, soon preferred more humane and rational methods of determining guilt or innocence.[37]

The introduction of judicial torture—significantly bulwarked by references to Roman law—coincides with the rise of centralized and despotic power on a territorial and national scale.[38] Most historians point out that the procedures of the absolutist courts superseded the feudal methods of ordeal and combat.[d] Less frequently do they mention the equally important fact that the new judicial torture also replaced the significant beginnings of rational judicial procedure developed in the burgher-controlled towns.[e]

Changes in judicial procedures were certainly intensified by the Inquisition; and anyone who studies this period is struck by the elaborate and cruel tortures employed in questioning heretics. However, three points deserve attention: First, the Church, which based itself on medieval Canonic Law, did not originally recommend the use of extreme measures against heretics.[39] Second, judicial torture was probably initiated by secular agencies.[f] Third, terroristic procedures were equally harsh under those absolutist governments of Europe which, in the course of the Reformation, had dissociated

d. Cf. Petit-Dutaillis, 1949: 309; Lea, 1892: 480, 487 ff., 500 ff., 505. Lea describes in some detail what he calls the "resistance of feudalism" to the development of judicial torture (1892: 494 ff.). See also Williams, 1911: 72.

e. In the 14th century the Italian communities continued to combat the increasing use of torture (Lea, 1892: 506 ff.); and in Lübeck, Germany's foremost city of burgher independence, legal orders discouraging ordeal, judicial duel, and torture yielded but slowly to the new absolutist law (ibid.: 483).

f. Lea, 1908, I: 221; cf. Guiraud, 1929: 86. In the 12th century, long before judicial torture was institutionalized, heretics had been tortured to death (Helbing, 1926: 106 ff.).

themselves from Rome.[40] No doubt the disintegration of medieval society stimulated both heretic tendencies and the fanatic desire to eradicate them; but it was only within the framework of rising absolutist state power that this desire took the form of the Inquisition.

The limitations of Western absolutism also determined the point beyond which the representatives of despotic power could not subdue their own subjects. For a time they were able to employ judicial terror in secular and religious matters, but managerial and fiscal terror were not invoked against the bulk of the population. With the rise of modern industrial society judicial torture was eliminated in the heartlands of European absolutism, and eventually also in the terror-ridden slave economy of our southern states. Presently, public opinion is crusading against such police actions as the third degree. These methods were never legal; their illegal use is receding before the growing vigilance and strength of public-minded citizen organizations.

Pre-Mongol ("Kievan") Russia accepted many elements of Byzantine law, but not the use of corporal punishment. This device, as well as judicial torture, seems to have emerged in Russia only when an Oriental type of despotism arose during and after the Tatar period.[41] Third degree methods continued to be employed until the last decades of the Tsarist regime; [42] but torture as a means of getting evidence was discarded early in the 19th century, when the growth of property-based industrial forms of life promoted the restriction of many absolutist features of Russian law and society.[g] It was left to the masters of the Communist apparatus state to reverse the humanizing trend and to reintroduce the systematic infliction of physical pain for the purpose of extracting "confessions." [h]

4. Varying Configurations of Terror in the Hydraulic World

a. Relatively Lenient Developments

IN different areas and phases of the hydraulic world the methods of terror differed. The indigenous Babylonian government, for in-

g. Lea, 1892: 581; Williams, 1911: 79. For occasional late occurrences see Williams, *loc. cit.*, and Scott, 1943: 264. George Kennan, who at the close of the 19th century, studied the life of political prisoners and exiles in Siberia, draws attention to the arbitrary methods employed by the Tsarist police: unjust arrests and imprisonment, beating and torturing (Kennan, 1891, II: 52 ff.). These methods were certainly brutal, but the growing strength of public opinion restricted them increasingly; and a comparison of the conditions described by Kennan and those to which Soviet prisoners are subjected today reveals an abysmal retrogression in judicial procedure.

h. The Communist methods of judicial terror vary with time, space, circumstance,

stance, proceeded close to the rulers' rationality maximum; and
Babylonian laws known to us mention, as means of establishing guilt
or innocence, the ordeal, the oath, and witnesses, but not torture.[43]
To be sure, judicial torture may well have been employed in cases
involving the security of the regime (the Code does not discuss these
matters); even for minor offenses against the interests of the government punishment was terrifyingly harsh; [i] and there is no reason
to assume that the "language of the whip," which accompanied the
Sumerian corvée, was not used by Babylonian master builders and
master irrigators. But while the Babylonian state, local administrative councils notwithstanding, remained an absolutist regime, it acted
as rationally in judicial and many other matters as could be expected
under the conditions of an agromanagerial system of total power.

b. Average and Excessive Developments

IN most hydraulic civilizations the rulers employed fully all major
forms of terror, the managerial, the fiscal, and the judicial. In doing
so, they established procedural averages, which occasionally were
codified. These averages usually sufficed to satisfy the needs of the
regime; but not infrequently those who applied them resorted to
methods of extreme brutality, which besides producing quicker results, yielded a surplus income for the officials who perpetrated
them.

As shown above, not all officials went to such lengths; and for
various reasons extreme malpractice might be punished. But
"moderate" excesses tended to remain unchallenged. And from

---

and purpose; but despite a certain ingenuity in applying psychological devices, the
main techniques can hardly be claimed as inventions. The "keeping-awake" torture, a
seemingly mild but actually irresistible way of breaking the will of a person under
interrogation, appeared in the Roman arsenal of planned cruelty under the name
tormentum vigiliae (Helbing, 1926: 45). It was re-"invented" in 1532 by Hippolytus de
Marsiliis (Williams, 1911: 77). The starvation torture was known as *tormentum famis*
(Helbing, 1926: 45). Certain Communist methods parallel procedure used by the
Inquisition. Compare the abrupt changes from bad to good treatment and from
good treatment to bad, and the facing of the prisoner with confessions or alleged
confessions of others (Lea, 1908, I: 415 ff.). Cruder methods of torture, beginning with
simple beating—Roman forerunner: the *verbera* (Helbing, 1926: 45)—attain their goal
faster than the more "cultivated" *tormentum vigiliae*. They seem to be extensively
employed particularly in times of crisis, such as the Great Purge, World War II, and
the period of continued stress that followed this war (see Beck and Godin, 1951: 53 ff.;
Weissberg, 1951: 238 ff., 242, 246, 296; SLRUN, 1949: 56, 67, 74 ff.). Of course, many
Soviet modes of torture were foreshadowed by Ivan IV and his successors.

i. Stealing government or temple property was punished with death (Hammurabi,
Secs. 6, 8. See also translator Meek's note 45.

the standpoint of the commoner, the despotic apparatus remained irrationally formidable even when it employed only the standard methods of terror. It became frightening when it exhausted its terroristic potential.

D. TOTAL SUBMISSION

1. MAN'S RESPONSE TO THE THREAT OF TOTAL TERROR

a. The Postulate of Common Sense and the Virtue of Good Citizenship: Obedience

LIVING under the threat of total terror, the members of a hydraulic community must shape their behavior accordingly. If they want to survive, they must not provoke the uncontrollable monster. To the demands of total authority common sense recommends one answer: obedience. And ideology stereotypes what common sense recommends. Under a despotic regime, obedience becomes the basis of good citizenship.

Of course, life in any community requires some degree of coor-dination and subordination; and the need for obedience is never completely lacking. But in the great agrarian societies of the West obedience is far from being a primary virtue.

In the democratic city states of ancient Greece the good citizen was expected to display four major qualities: military courage, religious devotion, civic responsibility, and balanced judgment.[1] Prior to the democratic period, physical strength and courage were particularly valued.[2] But neither the Homeric age nor the classical period considered unquestioning obedience a virtue in a free man, except when he served in the army. Total submission was the duty—and the bitter fate—of the slave. The good citizen acted in accordance with the laws of his community; but no absolute political authority controlled him absolutely.

Nor did the loyalty which the medieval knight owed his overlord result in total submission. The feudal contract bound him to follow his sovereign only in a qualified and limited way. Among the virtues of the good knight, good horsemanship, prowess in arms, and courage ranked high.[3] Unquestioning obedience was conspicuously lacking.

In hydraulic society the relation between the ordinary members of the community and their leaders was regulated very differently. The quest for integrated subordination appears even at the tribal level. In the American Pueblos submissiveness and a yielding dis-position are systematically cultivated.[4] Among the Chagga, "respect for the chief is the first command, which the parents impress upon their children." [5]

In state-centered hydraulic civilizations the supreme holders of power are not as close to the people as they are in Pueblo society, nor are they, as in certain Pueblos and among the Chagga, restrained by clan influence. The masters of an agrarian apparatus state make greater demands than the Pueblo leaders; and their means for enforcing their will far surpass the modest political devices of Chagga chieftainship.

Thorkild Jacobsen, discussing society and religion in ancient Mesopotamia, lists obedience as the prime virtue. Essentially "in Mesopotamia the 'good life' was the 'obedient life.' " [6] Unlike the warriors of Medieval Europe, who often fought in small bands and with little concern for a ranking leader, the Mesopotamians felt that "soldiers without a king are sheep without their shepherd," "peasants without a bailiff are a field without a plowman," and "workmen without a foreman are waters without a canal inspector." [7] Thus the subject was expected to carry out the orders of his foreman, his bailiff, and—of course—his king. "All these can and must claim absolute obedience." [8] Submission which cannot be avoided is conveniently rationalized: "The Mesopotamian feels convinced that authorities are always right." [9]

Similar concepts can be found in Pharaonic Egypt. A ship must have its commander, a gang its leader; [10] and whoever wants to survive—and to succeed—must fit himself into the edifice of superordination and subordination: "Bow thy back to thy superior, thy overseer from the palace [the government]. . . . Opposition to a superior is a painful thing (for) one lives as long as he is mild." [11]

The law of Hindu India prescribes subordination to both secular and priestly authority. Those who oppose the king's commands suffer "various kinds of capital punishment." [12]

The Koran exhorts believers to obey not only Allah and his prophet but also "those in authority amongst you." [13] In the absolutist states established by Mohammed's followers, this passage was invoked to emphasize the basic importance of obedience in maintaining governmental authority. [14]

Confucius envisioned an authority that would realize the ruler's rationality maximum. He therefore insisted that every official should judge the propriety of the ruler's actions; and when conflict became serious, a top-ranking minister might retire. [15] Normally, however, the ideal functionary obeyed his ruler; [16] and reverence toward a superior was a basic duty. [17] The commoner was given no choice whatsoever. Since he could not understand the issues involved, he had to be "made to follow" what superior authority and insight dictated.[18] In Confucius' good society, as in its Indian and Near Eastern variants, the good subject was the obedient subject.

2. PREPARATION FOR TOTAL OBEDIENCE: DISCIPLINARY EDUCATION

THE good subject was also the obedient son. For Confucius an education that demands absolute obedience to parent and teacher forms the ideal foundation on which to build absolute obedience to the masters of society.

No similar correlation can be established for Medieval Europe. The son of a feudal knight was mercilessly disciplined. At an early age he was compelled to ride a high horse, while tied to the saddle; and to toughen him further he was buried in horse manure.[19] Curses and blows were frequent accompaniments to growth. Feature for feature, the early education of the young feudal knight seems to have been as harsh, or harsher, than the education of the young son of an Oriental official. And the apprenticeship of the young European craftsman was no bed of roses either.[20]

But the behavior of the young burghers on festive occasions showed that the educational disciplines to which they had been exposed were not seriously inhibiting,[21] and the behavior of young knights remained equally carefree. Both groups matured under conditions that were built on contractual relations rather than on absolute authority, and they took their early frustrations as the passing experience that it actually was.

Conversely, similar—or even less harsh—disciplines may be eminently effective for assuring total submission. In ancient Mesopotamia, "the individual stood at the center of ever wider circles of authority which delimited his freedom of action. The nearest and smallest of these circles was constituted by authorities in his own family: father and mother, older brother and older sister." [22] And "obedience to the older members of one's family is merely a beginning. Beyond the family lie other circles, other authorities: the state and society." Each and every one of them "can and must claim absolute obedience." [23]

The wisdom of ancient Egypt consciously interlinks obedience at home to obedience to the official. The obedient son "will stand well in the heart of the official, his speech is guided with respect to what has been said to him." [24] In Hindu India the demand for subordination to the secular and priestly authorities is reenforced by the demand for subordination in the personal spheres of life. Obedience is particularly due "the teacher, the father, the mother, and an elder brother." [25]

Confucianism describes filial piety as a unique preparation for civic obedience: "There are few who, while acting properly toward their parents and older brothers, are inclined to oppose their superiors. And there is nobody who, while averse to opposing his superiors, is inclined to making a rebellion." [26]

3. THE GREAT SYMBOL OF TOTAL SUBMISSION: PROSTRATION

EDUCATION teaches man to obey without question, when despotic authority so demands. It also teaches him to perform gestures of reverence when the symbol rather than the submissive action is required. True, all cultures have ways of demonstrating respect; and many gestures indicate subordination.[27] But no symbol has expressed total submission as strikingly, and none has so consistently accompanied the spread of agrarian despotism, as has prostration.

Total submission is ceremonially demonstrated whenever a subject of a hydraulic state approaches his ruler or some other representative of authority. The inferior man, aware that his master's wrath may destroy him, seeks to secure his good will by humbling himself; and the holder of power is more than ready to enforce and standardize the symbols of humiliation.

The inferior person may indicate his submissiveness by placing one hand over the other, as if they were tied together.[28] He may raise his open hands as a gesture of self-disarmament.[a] Or going to extremes, he may fall forward on all fours like an animal, strike his head on the ground, and kiss the dust. Under the shadow of Oriental despotism, prostration is an outstanding form of saluting the sovereign or other persons of recognized authority. The details vary; and occasionally symbols with similar intent are used. Generally speaking, however, prostration is as characteristic for hydraulic society as it is uncharacteristic for the higher agrarian civilizations of classical antiquity and the European Middle Ages.

The absence of prostration in primitive hydraulic societies indicates the limitations of chiefly authority under tribal conditions. The Pueblo Indians hold their *cacique* in the highest esteem; but there are no evidences of the demonstrative submission that found open expression in the higher hydraulic civilizations of Aztec Mexico or Inca Peru. The Chagga tribesmen hail their chieftain;

a. Østrup, 1929: 28 ff. Cf. the modern "hands up."

and they murmur respectfully when he arrives or rises.[29] But this apparently is as far as their display of deference goes.[30]

In state-centered hydraulic civilizations prostration occurred almost everywhere. In ancient Hawaii political power was sufficiently terrifying to make the commoners crawl before their rulers.[b] In Inca Peru, even the highest dignitary approached his sovereign like a bearer of tribute, his back bent under a load.[31] In pre-Conquest Mexico supreme reverence was expressed by prostration. Taught in the "colleges," [32] it was performed before royalty, men of distinction,[33] and persons believed to be divine.[34]

In China prostration was practiced from the early days of the Chou dynasty—that is, during the pre-empire period of the territorial states; [35] and it prevailed throughout all subsequent phases of Chinese history. The experiences of the European envoys, who were asked to kowtow before the Manchu emperor, reveal both the importance of the custom and the embarrassment it caused Western visitors.

In the classical days of Hindu India great respect was shown by embracing a person's feet; and the king seems to have been approached in an attitude of prayer.[36] Prostration was performed before deities and the teacher's young wife.[c] However, in the later part of the Hindu period, the prime gesture of total submission was also performed before the sovereign.[37] Under Muslim rule both the sovereign [38] and venerable Hindus [39] were so honored.

The importance of prostration in the Near East can be amply documented. The records of Pharaonic Egypt describe the whole country as "prone upon the belly" before a representative of the king.[40] Faithful subordinates are shown crawling, and kissing (or sniffing) the monarch's scent.[41] Pictorial evidence suggests that in the New Kingdom high dignitaries employed other gestures of reverence; [42] but contemporary sources do not say that they ceased prostrating altogether. They indicate clearly that lowly persons and subject peoples continued to prostrate.[43]

In ancient Mesopotamia prostration was performed before the gods, the ruler, and other distinguished personalities,[44] and it was performed also in Achaemenian Persia.[45] It persisted in the Hel-

b. Fornander, HAF, VI: 12, 34 (religious prostration), 26 (before the king's idol); prostration before ruler: Kepelino, 1932: 12; Alexander, 1899: 26 ff.; Blackman, 1899: 23.

c. Cf. Manu, 1886: 69. In the second case, prostration obviously was performed in order to prevent bodily contact. For religious prostration, see *Jātakam*, III: 284; IV: 231; V: 274; VI: 302.

lenistic empires of the Seleucids [46] and the Ptolemies,[47] and also in Sassanid Persia.[48] It became the standard gesture of reverence in Eastern Rome on the eve of the Byzantine period.[49] Needless to say, it fitted the social climate of Byzantium to perfection.[50]

The followers of Mohammed originally prostrated only in prayer. Eventually, however, the "Orientalized" Arabs, like the Greeks before them, prostrated also in secular life.[51] In Ottoman Turkey the practice prevailed until close to the end of the Sultanate.[d]

Thus in the hydraulic world prostration was the outstanding expression of submission and reverence. Occasionally, equivalent gestures were used for the same purpose; and in a number of cases prostration spread to countries that were not ruled by Orientally despotic governments. However, the fate of the *proskynesis* in Medieval Europe shows how difficult it was to force this humiliating salutation on a politically balanced society. Some rudiments of the Byzantine ceremony survived in the ceremonial of the Western Church; yet the attempt of certain Carolingian rulers to uphold it as a secular ritual did not succeed. In Sicily under Roger II and Frederick II prostration was practiced temporarily probably under the influence of the Byzantines,[52] or the Arabs, who immediately preceded the Norman rulers.[53]

No doubt usage dulled man's sensitivity to the humiliating intent of prostration, and aesthetic accomplishment sweetened performance. But no matter how much prostration was rationalized, it remained through the ages a symbol of abject submission. Together with managerial, fiscal, and judicial terror, it spectacularly marked the range—and the total power—of agrarian despotism.

E. TOTAL LONELINESS

1. LONELINESS CREATED BY FEAR

DEMONSTRATIVE and total submission is the only prudent response to total power. Manifestly, such behavior does not gain a superior's respect; but other ways of proceeding invite disaster. Where power is polarized, as it is in hydraulic society, human relations are equally polarized. Those who have no control over their government quite reasonably fear that they will be crushed in any conflict with its masters.

And the formidable might of the state apparatus can destroy not merely objectionable nongovernmental forces—with equal thoroughness it may also overwhelm individual members of the ruling

d. Østrup, 1929: 32; Lane, 1898: 211 (kissing the feet as a sign of abject submission).

group, the ruler himself included. Many anxieties darken the path of life; but perhaps none is as devastating as the insecurity created by polarized total power.

a. The Ruler: Trust No One!

THE ruler, being most illustrious, is also most to be envied. Among those near him, there are always some who long to replace him. And since constitutional and peaceful change is out of the question, replacement usually means one thing and one thing only: physical annihilation. The wise ruler therefore trusts no one.

For obvious reasons the innermost thoughts of despots have been little publicized. But observable behavior and utterances confirm our assumption. Egyptian papyri preserve what is said to be a Pharaoh's advice to his son. The message reads: "Hold thyself apart from those subordinate to (thee), lest that should happen to whose terrors no attention has been given. Approach them not in thy loneliness. Fill not thy heart with a brother, nor know a friend. . . . (EVEN) WHEN THOU SLEEPEST, GUARD THY HEART THYSELF, because no man has adherents on the day of distress." [1]

The *Arthashāstra* specifies the dangers which surround the ruler, and it discusses the many means by which they can be averted. His residence must be made safe. Measures must be taken against poisoning.[2] All members of his entourage must be watched and controlled. The king must spy on his prime minister.[3] He must beware of his close friends,[4] of his wives,[5] of his brothers,[6] and most particularly of his heir apparent. According to an authority frequently quoted in the classic of Indian despotism, "Princes, like crabs, have a notorious tendency of eating up their begetter." [7] To prevent this from happening, the manual lists numerous ways by which a ruler can protect himself against his son.[8]

b. The Official: Eternal Suspicion

NOR does the official live securely. "Self-protection shall be the first and constant thought of a wise man; for the life of a man under the service of a king is aptly compared to life in fire; whereas fire burns a part or the whole of the body, if at all, the king has the power either to destroy or to advance the whole family." [9]

A Persian variant stresses particularly the danger that lurks behind seeming bureaucratic safety and success: "Should [the ruler] at any time pretend to you that you are completely secure with him, begin from that moment to feel insecure; if you are being fattened by someone, you may expect very quickly to be slaughtered by him." [10]

And the need for eternal suspicion is by no means confined to those occupying the top of the bureaucratic pyramid. In traditional China, as in other hydraulic civilizations, "high officials cannot but be jealous of those below them, for it is from that quarter that their rivals are to be dreaded. The lower officials, on the other hand, are not less suspicious of those above them, for it is from that quarter that their removal may be at any moment effected." [11]

c. The Commoner: the Fear of Being Trapped by Involvement

THE commoner is confronted with problems of a very different kind. He is not worried by the pitfalls inherent in autocratic or bureaucratic power, but by the threat which this power presents to all subjects. A regime that proceeds unchecked in the fields of taxation, corvée, and jurisprudence is capable of involving the commoners in endless predicaments. And caution teaches them to avoid any unnecessary contacts with their government.

Smith ascribes the mutual distrust that, according to him, prevails in traditional China to the people's fear of getting involved.[12] In the *Arabian Nights*, a corpse is shoved from door to door, because each house owner is convinced that the authorities will hold him responsible for the death of the unknown man. The frequently observed reluctance to help a drowning stranger is caused by similar reasoning: If I fail to rescue the poor devil, how shall I prove to the authorities that I did not plan his submersion?

Those who walk away when they can be of help are neither different from nor worse than other human beings. But their behavior makes it clear that voluntary participation in public matters, which is encouraged in an open society, is extremely risky under conditions of total power. The fear of getting involved with an uncontrollable and unpredictable government confines the prudent subject to the narrow realm of his personal and professional affairs. This fear separates him effectively from other members of the wider community to which he also belongs.

2. THE ALIENATION POTENTIAL OF TOTAL POWER

OF course, separation is not necessarily alienation: an artisan whose forebears left their rural community may consider himself different from the inhabitants of his home village. Or an intellectual may feel himself out of tune with his co-nationals, or in times of crisis he may completely reject a social order that apparently has no use for him. In such situations he may know loneliness. But as long as he can join with others of like mind, his alienation from society will be only partial.

And this partial alienation differs profoundly from total alienation. Only when a person believes he is deserted by all his fellows and when he is unable to see himself as an autonomous and inner-directed entity, only then can he be said to experience total alienation. Under the terror of the semimanagerial agrarian apparatus state he may know total loneliness without total alienation. Under the terror of the modern total managerial apparatus state he may suffer total alienation. Persistent isolation and brainwashing may bring him to the point where he no longer realizes he is being dehumanized.

3. EVERY-DAY ADJUSTMENTS

THERE were many lonely people among the free men of classical Greece; [a] and there are many lonely people in the democratic countries of today. But these free individuals are lonely in the main because they are neglected and not because they are threatened by a power that, whenever it wants to, can reduce human dignity to nothingness. A neglected person can maintain associations of some kind with a few relatives or friends; and he may overcome his passive and partial alienation by widening his associations or by establishing new ways of belonging.

The person who lives under conditions of total power is not so privileged. Unable to counteract these conditions, he can take refuge only in alert resignation. Eager to avoid the worst, he must always be prepared to face it. Resignation has been an attitude of many free individuals at different times and in different segments of open and semi-open societies. But prior to the rise of the industrial apparatus state it was a predominant attitude mainly within the realm of Oriental despotism. Significantly, stoicism arose in antiquity when the balanced society of classical Greece gave way to the Hellenistic system of total power initiated by Alexander.

4. TOTAL LONELINESS IN THE HOUR OF DOOM

THE hour of doom realizes what every-day life foreshadows. The methods of final destruction operate in one way in a democratically balanced world and in another under the rule of total power.

The free citizen of an open society may fear severe punishment

a. The tragic and permanent alienation of the slave is too obvious to need elaboration.

at the hands of a state whose laws he has violated. But after arrest he expects to be visited and aided by his friends and legal counsel. He expects to be tried before a court that is not the tool of government. Moreover, he can insist that he is not guilty as charged; and the court will not prevent him from continuing to do so, even after it has sentenced him to death. Execution will destroy him physically, but the government that has thus shown its authority will not keep his friends from extolling his virtues or reasserting their belief in his innocence.

Socrates' end was unique in several ways, but it was typical for one aspect of enforced death in an open society. Sentenced to die for politically "corrupting" the youth of Athens, he was not made to denounce his acts publicly. Nor was he deprived of the company and admiration of his friends. His ordeal, far from alienating him from his followers—or from his ideas—cemented his union with both.[b]

In an open society governmental disapproval may leave the criti-

b. Plato's description of Socrates' death may have been colored by the affectionate reports of eyewitnesses. Yet it is accepted as substantially true, and it certainly shows that even those who were saddened by the verdict considered it legally proper. The jailer brought the cup of hemlock, and Socrates, after listening to his directions, raised the vessel to his lips and "quite readily and cheerfully . . . drank off the poison." Plato's narrator continues:

> And hitherto most of us had been able to control our sorrow; but now when we saw him drinking, and saw too that he had finished the draught, we could no longer forbear, and in spite of myself my own tears were flowing fast; so that I covered my face and wept over myself, for certainly I was not weeping over him, but at the thought of my own calamity in having lost such a companion. Nor was I the first, for Crito, when he found himself unable to restrain his tears, had got up and moved away, and I followed; and at that moment, Apollodorus, who had been weeping all the time, broke out into a loud cry which made cowards of us all.
>
> Socrates alone retained his calmness: What is this strange outcry? he said. I sent away the women mainly in order that they might not offend in this way, for I have heard that a man should die in peace. Be quiet then, and have patience. When we heard that, we were ashamed, and refrained our tears; and he walked about until, as he said, his legs began to fail, and then he lay on his back, according to the directions, and the man who gave him the poison now and then looked at his feet and legs; and after a while he pressed his foot hard, and asked him if he could feel; and he said, No; and then his leg, and so upwards and upwards, and showed us that he was cold and stiff. And he felt then himself and said: When the poison reaches the heart, that will be the end. He was beginning to grow cold about the groin, when he uncovered his face, for he had covered himself up, and said (they were his last words)—he said: Crito, I owe a cock to Asclepius; will you remember to pay the debt? The debt shall be paid, said Crito; is there anything else? There was no answer to this question; but in a minute or two a movement was heard, and the attendants uncovered him; his eyes were set, and Crito closed his eyes and mouth.
>
> Such was the end, Echecrates, of our friend, whom I may truly call the wisest, and justest, and best of all men whom I have ever known [Plato: 270 ff.].

cized citizen cold; but under conditions of total power, official displeasure may bring disaster. The Chinese official and historian, Ssŭ-ma Ch'ien, was not accused of high treason. He only dared to differ with his emperor's evaluation of a defeated general, and he was only sentenced to be castrated. Living on, he described in an extraordinary letter the abject loneliness he suffered during the time of his ordeal.

According to the law of the then ruling Han dynasty, Ssŭ-ma Ch'ien's punishment could have been remitted by the payment of a sum of money; and this could have been done, for he had wealthy and high-ranking friends. But no one dared to aid him. No one dared to show sympathy for a man who had angered the emperor. Ssŭ-ma Ch'ien writes "My friends did not come to my assistance. Those who were near and intimate with me did not say a single word in my favor." [c] So he was led into the dark room and mutilated as if he had been an animal.

The tragedy of a bureaucratic Timon of Athens has not as yet been written. But Ssŭ-ma's fate shows what can happen to a man who, shunning a basic principle of bureaucratic prudence,[d] contradicts the holder of total power. It shows that what is expected behavior in an open society approaches madness under the shadow of total terror. Ssŭ-ma Ch'ien's environment being what it was, his intervention on a friend's behalf was the glorious exception; his friend's failure to intervene on his the sad norm.

Measured by the standards of an open society, the Chinese historian suffered appallingly. Measured by the standards of his own world, he was not without luck. Although he was emasculated, he remained alive; and being of no political significance, he could continue to work on his history. He even commented critically on the treatment accorded him in a letter, which, however, was cautiously kept out of sight until he was dead.[13]

When persecution is total, the victim of hydraulic terror may be separated not only from his friends but from his good name as well. The great Persian vizier and writer Rashīd ad-Dīn was accused by envious and rival officials of having poisoned the young sultan's father. The crime which Rashīd was said to have committed did not fit his personality, and it was contrary to his most elementary interests. Rashīd ad-Dīn was the outstanding Asiatic historian of his period, "the author of Ghazan's famous code of laws (*kanun*), the greatest vizier of the Ilkhan dynasty, and one of the greatest men the East has produced." [14] The sovereign he was accused of having mur-

---

c. *Han Shu* 62. 18b. Our translation of this passage differs somewhat from that of Chavannes, who has rendered the whole letter (see Chavannes, MH, I: ccxxxii).

d. According to the *Arthaçāstra* (1926: 387) the prudent official avoids "those who have been forced out of position and favor."

dered esteemed him so highly that he is believed to have made him a gift of gold that exceeded the amount Alexander bestowed on Aristotle.[15] Indeed, Rashid ad-Din's talents were said to be "as indispensable to the State as salt was to meat." [16]

It is difficult to see why a man should kill his generous admirer. It beggars comprehension why he should willfully destroy the source of his power, security, and wealth. But no such considerations stayed the hands of Rashīd's enemies. They declared him guilty. They executed his son before his eyes. They cut his own body in two—certainly without permitting him any last comfort from friends or relatives. Thus Rashīd died, a lonely man, deprived of both worldly and spiritual honor. For at the end he was also denounced as a religious imposter.[17]

But no matter how cynically Rashīd's accusers proceeded, they did not force him to confess publicly to crimes he was alleged to have committed. On the contrary, he seems to have maintained his innocence to the end.[18] No such leniency has been shown in the great political trials of the modern total managerial states.

The difference does not arise from any lack of terroristic efficiency on the part of hydraulic despotism. Those who tortured for the hydraulic rulers could have broken anyone, and they certainly could have extorted public confessions if they had wanted to. But the masters of the hydraulic regime saw no reason to publicize their conflicts in the villages or guild quarters where semi-autonomous Beggars' Democracies vegetated in a subpolitical atmosphere. Thus there was no need to promote the spectacular and articulate self-alienation in which the totalitarian "People's" courts now specialize.

The last days of the Soviet Communist Bukharin indicate how, under modern conditions, a victim may be made to cooperate publicly in his own debasement. Lenin, in his "Testament," had written that Bukharin was "the most valuable and biggest theoretician of the party," that he "may legitimately be considered the favorite of the whole party." [19] But the favorite of today is the monster of tomorrow. Framed and sentenced to die during the Great Purge of the 1930's, Bukharin overnight lost his popularity and fame. Vyshinsky, the then State Prosecutor, voiced the opinion of the party leaders when he called Bukharin a "theoretician in quotation marks," [20] a "damnable cross of a fox and a swine," [21] to be listed among the spies and traitors who "must be shot like dirty dogs." [22] And the psychological engineers of the Soviet government handled the defendant so skillfully that he confessed publicly and at length to treasonable acts that he could never have committed.

Manifestly total loneliness, like total terror, also has its varieties.

CHAPTER 6

The core, the margin, and the submargin of hydraulic societies

A. PRELIMINARY STOCK-TAKING IN THE MIDDLE OF THE JOURNEY

1. SOME BASIC RESULTS

OUR inquiry has led to several basic conclusions. First, the institutional order, hydraulic society, cannot be explained by reference to geographical, technological, and economic factors alone. While response to the natural setting is a key feature, it plays a formative hydraulic role only under very specific cultural conditions. And it involves organizational rather than technological changes. Second, some features of hydraulic society appear also in other agrarian orders. But hydraulic society is specific in the quality and weight of two of its features (hydraulic organization and agrohydraulic despotism). And it is their effective combination that brings into being an operational whole, a "going concern" which is able to perpetuate itself over millennia. The historian of human freedom must face this fundamental empirical fact: among the world's higher preindustrial civilizations, hydraulic society, the most despotic of them, has outlasted all others.

2. THREE PROBLEMS DESERVING FURTHER INVESTIGATION

WHY does hydraulic society show such persistence? Is it because of its state-managed system of hydraulic agriculture? An upholder of the economic interpretation of history will believe this; indeed Marx himself argued so.

But it is significant that Marx and Engels viewed the Tsarist government of post-Mongol Russia as Orientally despotic,[1] although both certainly knew that Russian agriculture was not hydraulic. The difficulty from the standpoint of the economic determinist is manifest; and it is increased when we realize that, beside Tsarist Russia, certain other agrodespotic states fulfilled the vital organizational and acquisitive functions of hydraulic society without maintaining a hydraulic economy proper. The capacity of these regimes to perpetuate themselves successfully suggests a decisive developmental role for the organizational and power features of the agromanagerial order.

Obviously the issue is highly important, not only theoretically and for the past, but politically and for the present. It is for this reason that in this chapter we shall examine the peculiarities and the interrelation of the core and the margin of hydraulic society. In the chapters immediately following we shall analyze two other aspects of the matter: the power-determined character of private property and class rule in the hydraulic world.

3. PROBLEMS OF HYDRAULIC DENSITY

How hydraulic was hydraulic society? Obviously there are areas of maximum hydraulic density and others which, although they are hydraulically less dense, may still be considered hydraulic societies proper. What is the institutional pattern of the margin of hydraulic society? And at what point does this margin lose its societal identity? Is there an institutional divide beyond which features of hydraulic society occur only sporadically in a submarginal form?

Assuming that such shades of institutional density exist, are they static and permanent? Or did hydraulic civilizations shift from the margin to the submargin and vice versa? With these questions in mind we shall now discuss the core areas, the margin, and the submarginal zones of the hydraulic world.

B. HYDRAULIC CORE AREAS

THE institutional quality of a hydraulic area varies in accordance with its spatial cohesiveness and the economic and political weight of its hydraulic system. It may be modified further by the relative significance of the second major element of hydraulic operation: flood control.

1. How CONTINUOUS Is THE HYDRAULIC SYSTEM OF A GIVEN HYDRAULIC AREA?

THE spatial (and organizational) cohesiveness of a given hydraulic economy is primarily determined by the continuous or discontinuous form of its water supply. A hydraulic commonwealth is apt to create a single more or less continuous system of irrigation and flood control in a landscape that contains only one major accessible source of humidity. Such a development frequently occurs in oasis-like regions crossed by a river that gathers the bulk of its water in a more humid hilly or mountainous hinterland. The river-valley states of ancient coastal Peru maintained continuous hydraulic systems. In the Old World, Sindh and the Nile Valley civilization of Egypt are classical variants of the same pattern.

If an arid landscape includes several not too widely separated rivers, the canals leading from them may form a relatively continuous hydraulic network. However, few arid regions are so privileged. Lower Mesopotamia is more the exception than the rule.

In most cases the rivers of a potentially hydraulic landscape lie too far apart to permit interlocking through connecting canals. Consequently a hydraulic commonwealth covering a multi-river area generally maintains a discontinuous system of embankments and canals. Individuals depending on a limited and single water supply may reproduce a limited tribal or national culture for a long period of time. This happened in the Rio Grande area and, on a much more impressive scale, in Pharaonic Egypt. But the self-perpetuating hydraulic tribes played an insignificant part on the stage of human history; and even such national complexes as Egypt eventually outgrew their early political isolation. The great majority of all historically conspicuous hydraulic nations and empires include regions which depend on a continuous hydraulic unit; yet, taken as a whole, the hydraulic system of these larger political units have a definitely discontinuous form.

2. How Great Is the Economic and Political Weight of a Given Hydraulic Economy?

SINCE most of the larger hydraulic civilizations maintain discontinuous hydraulic systems, lack of cohesiveness obviously is no reliable index for establishing hydraulic density. The economic and political weights of a discontinuous hydraulic system must be established by other means.

In arid areas a discontinuous hydraulic system occurs occasionally; in semi-arid areas it is virtually the rule, at least for societies that have outgrown their most primitive beginnings. As indicated above, the semi-arid areas which have given rise to hydraulic developments are numerous and large; and within them the relation between hydraulic agriculture and nonhydraulic (small-scale irrigation and rainfall) farming varies enormously.

Three major shades of this relation can be distinguished:

1) The hydraulically cultivated land may comprise more than half of all arable land. Since hydraulic agriculture tends to produce

yields that, by and large, are as high as those produced by small-scale irrigation and definitely higher than the average yields of the rainfall farmers, a hydraulic agriculture which covers more than 50 per cent of all arable land may be said to be in a position of *absolute economic superiority*.

This condition is found most frequently in arid regions; and frequently, although not necessarily, it is found together with a continuous hydraulic system. In most Rio Grande Pueblos the bulk of all land is irrigated; and the bulk of irrigation water is drawn from communally operated irrigation ditches. In Egypt, from the dawn of history, the great majority of all fields was irrigated either by inundation or through canals.[1] In the delta a meager crop can be grown by methods of rainfall farming; [a] and throughout the country, wells can be used to water vegetables, gardens, and orchards.[2] But as in the case of the Rio Grande Pueblos, these supplementary forms of cultivation do not challenge the overwhelming economic superiority of the hydraulic economy.

2) The hydraulically cultivated land, even when it comprises less than half the country's arable acreage, may nevertheless yield more than all other arable land. In this case, hydraulic agriculture may be said to hold a position of *relative economic superiority*. On the eve of China's unification the state of Ch'in enormously strengthened its agrarian heartlands (in present Shensi) by constructing the Chêng Kuo irrigation works; and this action made Ch'in richer and more powerful than any other territorial state. In the subsequent period, the whole area of what had been Ch'in [b] comprised about one-third of the empire's area, but, according to Pan Ku, it accounted for 60 per cent of its wealth.[3] Ssŭ-ma Ch'ien considered the former Ch'in territory "ten times as rich as [the rest of] the empire." [4] Neither of these statements can be verified, and they certainly should not be pressed. Yet they illustrate what we mean by the relative economic superiority of a vigorous hydraulic system of agriculture.

3) The hydraulically cultivated land, even if it is inferior both in acreage and yield to the remaining arable land, may nevertheless be sufficient to stimulate despotic patterns of corvée labor and government. In this case the larger, nonhydraulic area essentially produces food, whereas the smaller, hydraulic area, in addition to producing

a. After mentioning the cultivation of barley in the Nile delta as one of the examples of rainfall agriculture close to the minimum limit, the *Agricultural Yearbook* of 1941 concludes: "Production year after year with these small amounts of moisture is possible only where the distribution of rainfall during the year and other climatic conditions are favorable and where the moisture falling in two or more years is stored for one crop" (CM: 322).

b. In addition to the Chêng Kuo complex, this included among other regions the classical irrigation plain of Szechwan.

food, produces power, and it produces power that is sufficiently strong and sufficiently despotic to control both sectors of the agrarian society.

This evidently happened in numerous semi-arid regions that were suitable—in key areas—for hydraulic operations. During the formative period of many great hydraulic civilizations despotic power probably arose under exactly such conditions; and the pattern has been perpetuated in historic times. Assyria and Mexico applied methods of mass control that were imperative only in relatively small hydraulic regions to large areas of small-scale irrigation and rainfall farming. Under these conditions the hydraulic economy, though predominant neither in acreage nor yield, nevertheless occupied a position of *organizational and political superiority*.

3. How Strong Is the Second Major Element of Hydraulic Operation: Flood Control?

WHERE the hydraulic system prevails economically, the relative strength of protective (as compared with productive) water works is of little concern. An elaborate hydraulic agriculture involves an elaborate bureaucratic development; and the despotic regime is thus conveniently bulwarked.

Things are different when the hydraulic system, although sufficient to establish political supremacy, involves only modest bureaucratic developments. To be sure, the maintenance of large installations for flood control always necessitates comprehensive operations of mobilization and on-the-spot direction; and it also heightens the quasimilitary authority of the managerial government in situations of absolute or relative economic hegemony. But the protective factor becomes particularly important when economic hegemony is lacking. The fight against large and disastrous floods tends to expand government-directed mass mobilization further than would productive hydraulic action alone. And the disciplinary measures involved in protective enterprises do much to cement the power of a government that derives only a limited managerial authority from its agromanagerial achievements. In the lake area of ancient Mexico the struggle against periodic and devastating floods probably re quired much larger corvée teams than did the regional irrigation works. The significance of this fact for the aggrandizement of government power can be easily imagined.

4. Compact and Loose Hydraulic Societies

OUR argument does not exhaust all morphological possibilities. But it establishes one point beyond doubt: The core areas of the hydraulic world manifest at least two major types of hydraulic density. Some are hydraulically compact, whereas others are hydraulically loose.[5] A hydraulic society may be considered "compact" when its hydraulic agriculture occupies a position of absolute or relative economic hegemony. It may be considered "loose" when its hydraulic agriculture, while lacking economic superiority, is sufficient to assure its leaders absolute organizational and political hegemony.

This primary division may be supplemented by some important secondary divisions. A hydraulic society, whose hydraulic agriculture is economically dominant and spatially continuous, is an extreme variant of the compact pattern (C 1). A hydraulic society whose hydraulic agriculture is economically dominant but discontinuous is a less extreme variant of this same pattern (C 2). Distinction between absolute (a) and relative (r) economic hegemony enables us to carry the differentiation still further (Ca 1 and Cr 1, Ca 2 and Cr 2).

A loose hydraulic society may include among its installations large units which are compact within their immediate locale or which go beyond the borders of a single region. The relatively great hydraulic weight of this pattern may be indicated by the symbol "L 1." A loose hydraulic society whose largest hydraulic units fail to achieve economic hegemony even regionally represents the lowest hydraulic density type (L 2). Another differentiating factor, the relatively strong development of *protective* hydraulic works, may be indicated whenever this seems desirable by the formula "+ prot."

A few examples indicate, on a tribal or national scale, the four main categories of hydraulic density:

Compact 1: Most Rio Grande Pueblos, the small city states of ancient coastal Peru, Pharaonic Egypt.

Compact 2: The city states of ancient Lower Mesopotamia, probably the state of Ch'in on the eve of the Chinese empire

Loose 1: The Chagga tribes, ancient Assyria, the old Chinese state of Ch'i (L 1 + prot.), and perhaps Ch'u.

Loose 2: Tribal civilizations: The Suk of East Africa, the Zuni of New Mexico. State centered civilizations: indigenous Hawaii, many territorial states of ancient Mexico (L 2 + prot.).

5. THE GREAT AGROMANAGERIAL EMPIRES—USUALLY LOOSE HYDRAULIC SOCIETIES

DOMINION of one city state over a number of other city states leads to the establishment of rudimentary empires. Conformations of this kind arose in ancient Lower Mesopotamia, on the coast of ancient Peru, in Chou China, and in Buddhist India.

In the first two cases the components were of the compact hydraulic type; and the quasi-imperial units were also hydraulically compact. Usually, however, military and political expansion resulted in the creation of larger and less homogeneous conformations. The great hydraulic empires tended to include territorial and national units of different hydraulic densities. They formed loose hydraulic societies, which frequently included compact hydraulic subareas. The Babylonian and Assyrian empires, China during the periods of unification, the great empires of India, Achaemenian Persia at the height of its expansion, the Arab caliphate, Ottoman Turkey, the Inca empire, and the federation of Aztec Mexico—all were hydraulic societies, and all, perhaps with the exception of Mexico, belonged to the category L 1.

The hydraulic glands of the great agromanagerial empires have been accorded little systematic attention. A morphological study of the hydraulic order of traditional China reveals many density patterns and significant super-regional arrangements.[c] Mez' thoughtful analysis of Abbassid power indicates the number and variety of the great hydraulic areas that for shorter or longer periods lay within the jurisdiction of the Baghdad caliphate: Egypt, South Arabia, Babylonia, Persia (northeast and south Transoxania and Afghanistan).[6] All these areas posed "great irrigation problems,"[7] and the Arab sources note both the technological means and the numerous personnel required to solve them.[8]

6. DEGREES OF HYDRAULIC DENSITY AND DEGREES OF BUREAUCRATIC DENSITY

a. The Principle

THE bureaucratic density of an agromanagerial society varies with its hydraulic density. This correlation is affected by such factors as the institutional weight of large nonhydraulic constructions (the Zuni Pueblos, the territorial states of Chou China, the Roman empire) and the dimensions of communicational and/or military organizations (Assyria, the state of Ch'in, Aztec Mexico). But such factors modify rather than negate the basic hydraulic-bureaucratic relation. Pharaonic Egypt was highly bureaucratized long before it developed a comprehensive military officialdom. And while both the Incas and the Aztecs maintained strong military organizations, there

c. For a discussion of the varying territorial dimensions and character, as well as the interarea relations, in the "loose" hydraulic order of traditional China, see Wittfogel, 1931: 252–72.

can be little doubt that the former had a more comprehensive managerial bureaucracy than the latter.

On the acquisitive level correlations also vary. To be sure, an agrarian despotism, no matter what its hydraulic density pattern, insists upon its right to tax universally. Yet the way in which this right is exercised differs significantly. Although a loose hydraulic society with a strong government may be able to gather in a larger percentage of the estimated revenue than a compact hydraulic society with a weak government, other conditions being equal, the more comprehensive bureaucracy of an intensively managerial state is better equipped over time to handle the business of taxation than is the less comprehensive bureaucracy of a less intensively managerial state.

The collecting of the rural surplus was more centralized in Inca Peru than in Aztec Mexico, where local affairs were handled not by representatives of the government but by heads of the local *calpulli*. In the compact hydraulic societies of the ancient Near East the bulk of the revenue seems to have been gathered by government functionaries, although intermediaries are known to have been used in certain periods in Pharaonic Egypt.[9] Under Greek and Roman influence respectively, tax farming appeared in the Hellenistic and Roman Near East;[10] but the absolutist regimes soon asserted their power, first by modifying the system of tax farming and later by reducing it to insignificance.[11] State-appointed (liturgical) tax collectors, mostly wealthy townsmen, supplemented the fiscal bureaucracy; and big (bureaucratic) landowners fulfilled a similar function with more advantage as well as less danger to themselves.[12] Thus the hydraulically loose Roman empire discarded the independent tax farmers of ancient Greece and republican Rome without reverting to the old Egyptian and Babylonian ways of directly and bureaucratically collecting the revenue.

This step was taken by the Arab masters of the Near East, whose power was rooted in such hydraulic centers as Damascus, Cairo, and Baghdad. Under the Umayyads the bureaucratic fiscal system prevailed; and the tax farmers, whom the Abbassid government began to employ, were still closely integrated in the bureaucratic order. In Mesopotamia they were part of the officialdom.[13] In China some local tax collectors were not members of the regular officialdom;[14] but bureaucratic methods of tax collection seem to have prevailed throughout the ages.

b. Changing Bureaucratic Density of a Hydraulic Territory

THE inclusion of incipiently hydraulic or nonhydraulic territories in a loose hydraulic society is usually followed by the development of a bureaucratic network in these territories. This is what happened when the ancient centers of Chinese culture conquered certain "barbarian" regions in Central and South China.

The inclusion of a compact hydraulic territory in a hydraulically loose empire tends to have the opposite effect. The rulers, who are accustomed to operate with a less compact officialdom, may also reduce the bureaucratic apparatus of the hydraulically compact area. This is what happened when the Nile Valley became part of the Roman empire.

7. HYDRAULICALLY CONCERNED AND HYDRAULICALLY UNCONCERNED MASTERS OF HYDRAULIC SOCIETY

A SECOND FACTOR that may change the bureaucratic density of a hydraulic society is the rulers' concern (or lack of concern) for hydraulic management. As discussed previously, a hydraulic society may sink to a low rationality level if it is ruled by conquerors who take little interest in managerial agriculture or if its indigenous masters slacken their productive efforts. The conquerors' lack of hydraulic concern is usually a consequence of their nonhydraulic background. Internal decay may be due to a reduction in government revenue resulting from the excessive growth of proprietary forces or from the degeneration of a ruling group that reveled in the luxury of total power.

The spatial relation between the main areas of political power and hydraulic economy also plays a part. Rulers may establish their capital close to the major regions of agricultural wealth and surplus; or they may establish it at a considerable distance from these regions. Defense is often given as the reason for the latter decision, and at times it may indeed be the whole reason. Often, however, the rulers—particularly conqueror-rulers—preferred to set up their capitals in a nonhydraulic frontier, because they had a stronger affinity to the periphery than to the core areas of the hydraulic world.

In China the centers of political direction and hydraulic economy coincided more or less until the first millennium A.D., when the growing fertility of the Yangtze area conflicted with the defense needs of the vital northern border zone. From then on, the seat of the central government shifted back and forth; but the northern region never ceased to be hydraulic to some extent, and the northern capitals were ingeniously and hydraulically connected with the main rice areas of Central China through the Grand Canal.

In India the great northern plain, which was the main area of hydraulic agriculture, was also the logical place for the political metropolis; and the Muslim masters of India, like their Hindu predecessors, established their capitals there. But they exhibited less hydraulic concern than had the previous indigenous rulers. Although they were not lacking in managerial interest, and although they created and maintained large irrigation works, they never fully restored the grandiose hydraulic economy that appears to have flourished in the Maurya empire. The role they assigned to local "chiefs" and tax farmers reflects the relatively low bureaucratic density of Muslim India.

The later Roman emperors responded to the lure of the East. Yet they established their new capital, not in one of the great classical areas of hydraulic agriculture (Egypt, Syria, or Mesopotamia) but at the Hellespont, the classical divide between the Orient and the non-hydraulic West. And despite the fact that long acquaintance with managerial despotism stimulated them to plan and build on a large scale, they were content to administer their hydraulic possessions from afar. Immensely bold in the creation of nonhydraulic constructions (highways and frontier walls), they exhibited much less initiative in the agromanagerial sphere. While by no means lacking in hydraulic concern, they aimed at gathering as large a rural revenue as possible with as small a bureaucracy as possible. Rational rulers though they were, they did not realize the rationality maximum of the hydraulic world they controlled.

The Romans, who made Constantinople the capital of their empire, had behind them five hundred years of practical experience with the Hellenistic version of hydraulic statecraft. The Turks, who had conquered Adrianople in 1362, Constantinople in 1452, Egypt in 1517, and Mesopotamia in 1534, were not unacquainted with higher agrarian civilizations of the hydraulic type either; as a matter of fact, they had lived at the edge of the hydraulic world since the dawn of history. But perhaps because of their pastoral background they were less interested in the promotion of agriculture [15] than in military enterprises; and they preferred extending the non-hydraulic margin to intensifying the hydraulic core. True, the great irrigation works of Mesopotamia lay in ruins when the Turks came; but the history of China and India shows that hydraulic effort can restore quickly what antihydraulic action has destroyed. The Turks did not break with agromanagerial tradition in Egypt or Syria; but they furthered no significant reconstruction work in Irak. Speaking generally, they displayed no effective zest for hydraulic development.[16] As Orientally despotic organizers of war, peace, and fiscal exploitation, they were extraordinarily successful; and in some few major administrative centers they employed many officials. Being managerially unconcerned, however, they governed their far-flung empire with a relatively small professional bureaucracy.

8. PERIODS OF AGROMANAGERIAL ADJUSTMENT, DEGENERATION, AND RESTORATION

OF COURSE, the economic ethos (the *Wirtschaftsgesinnung*) of a ruling group is not unchangeable. Great differences in cultural and social assimilation notwithstanding, this is true also for pastoral invaders.

The tribal conquerors of China were usually willing to uphold the indigenous tradition in certain spheres of nonhydraulic construction and management; and many of them became at least superficially aware of the importance of irrigation agriculture. Perhaps none of the northern conquerors equaled the active hydraulic concern of the Manchus, who had practiced irrigation in their homeland prior to their conquest of China.[17] In the Near East the Umayyads, who consolidated a conquest regime established by the first followers of the Prophet, also showed extraordinary hydraulic concern.[18]

Pastoral and semipastoral conquerors who develop an interest in hydraulic matters do so, as a rule, not during the first period of their dominion but later; and often they grow managerially lazy and negligent before their rationality potential has been exhausted. Indigenous rulers, on the other hand, frequently show the greatest hydraulic concern during the earlier periods of their regime, tending to grow managerially less insistent when their power is consolidated. In either case, decay may be retarded by challenging external circumstances; or it may be accelerated by the expansion of large proprietary forces, whose representatives arrogate to themselves an increasing part of the national surplus.[d] When one segment of the despotic elite (primarily the court and clusters of officials close to it) succumbs to the corrupting influence of total power, another segment (other members of the officialdom and their relatives and friends among the bureaucratic "gentry") may seize power. As the result of this process, excessively irrational features may be eliminated in a "cathartic" and "regenerative" revolution.

---

d. For an attempt to explain the great agrarian and political crises in Chinese society by means of this and other social factors see Wittfogel, 1927: 322 ff., 328 ff.; *ibid.*, 1935: 53. Cf. Wittfogel and Fêng, 1949: 377. For an analysis of agrarian crises as a general feature of Oriental society see Wittfogel, 1938: 109 ff.

A development of this type does not change the traditional hydraulic and despotic order; it merely restores its vitality. The first rulers of many Egyptian, Babylonian, Chinese, Indian, Persian, Islamic, and Mexican dynasties have been praised for their vigor and efficiency. Regenerative upsurges may also occur during a later phase of a dynastic reign; and then, as during the formative period, serious attempts may be made at effective hydraulic management and rational fiscal administration. In both cases the more farsighted and less compromised elements within the ruling bureaucracy demonstrate that they can run the country in a more effective way than their self-indulgent and "corrupt" rivals.

9. The Staying Power of Deteriorated Agro-managerial Hydraulic Societies

THE dominant myths of Oriental despotism ascribe regenerative achievements to almost every founder of a new dynasty; but an unbiased evaluation of the evidence leads to less flattering conclusions. Under conditions that permit no independent criticism or political pressure, the immediate benefits of total power have a much greater appeal to the masters of the absolutist apparatus than do the potential fruits of rational—albeit, selfishly rational—managerial effort. Self-indulgence is, therefore, a more typical motive for behavior than the desire to maintain the rulers' rationality optimum.

And this is true not only for most later sovereigns but also for many a dynasty's founding father. Such persons, however vigorous, are often more sensitive to the political weaknesses of the old regime than to the managerial possibilities of the new. Having won over the bulk of the military and civil officials, they readily correct the most glaring abuses in taxation, forced labor, or jurisdiction, and they make the most urgent constructional and agromanagerial improvements; but they have neither the vision nor the personnel to raise the hydraulic government to a conspicuously higher level of hydraulic and fiscal management. In the many dynastic changes that characterize the history of agromanagerial civilizations, thorough regenerative upsurges are probably more the exception than the rule.

Of course, a stoppage of all hydraulic operations would paralyze agricultural life, and this not only in areas of full aridity but in many semi-arid regions as well. Consequently, even a hydraulically unconcerned Oriental government will devote some effort to its managerial duties. It has to carry on somehow, even if it must depend largely and not too rationally on local groups. During the last phase of Byzantine rule over Egypt, influential landlords, most of whom had bureaucratic connections,[19] are said to have maintained the dikes and canals in many localities.[20] To what extent governmental hydraulic action was reduced by this arrangement is hard to decide. Even during this critical period, however, Egypt's irrigation economy was sufficiently continuous and sufficiently effective to feed the people and to furnish a huge revenue. Somehow it succeeded in perpetuating itself. When the Arabs appeared in 639, they found in the Nile Valley a population of about seven millions,[e] that is, about as many persons as had lived there under Ptolemaic rule.

C. THE MARGIN OF THE HYDRAULIC WORLD

IN arid or semi-arid landscapes sedentary agrarian civilizations can persist permanently and prosperously only on the basis of a hydraulic economy. Along the moderately humid periphery of the arid and semi-arid world agrarian life is not so conditioned. Here Oriental despotism may prevail with little or no dependence upon hydraulic activities.

1. VARYING OPERATIONAL AND BUREAUCRATIC DENSITY PATTERNS IN MARGINAL AREAS OF THE HYDRAULIC WORLD

IN the hydraulic core areas degrees of hydraulic density provide a crucial means for distinguishing degrees of institutional density. In the margins, however, this criterion loses its significance. Instead, degrees of bureaucratic density are best determined by an approach that evaluates the relative development of absolutist methods in the spheres of construction (mostly nonhydraulic), organization, and acquisition.

Comparison between the states of Middle Byzantium and post-Mongol Russia reveal significant differences. Byzantium maintained considerable hydraulic installations, in the main for providing drinking water;[a] and these have no parallel in Muscovite Russia. Nor did the Muscovite Russians engage in comprehensive nonhydraulic constructions as did the Byzantines. The founders of Eastern Rome reshaped the earlier network of roads;[1] and their highways were the foundation of the Byzantine system of communications,[2] which in a limited way continued in use even under the Turks.[3]

e. For the beginning of the Arab era see Johnson and West, 1949: 263 (6,000,000, plus children and old people); cf. Munier, 1932: 84. For Ptolemaic Egypt see Diodorus, I, sec. 31 (7,000,000); cf. Josephus, JW 2.16 (7,500,000); Wilcken, 1899, I: 489 ff.

a. Bréhier, 1950: 90 ff. For a description of some of these works see Ritter, 1858: 155, 160, 167, 202, 346, 378, 406, 496, 547. Most of the local and regional hydraulic works that existed under the Turks probably go back to the Byzantines.

The Byzantines also made enormous building efforts for purposes of defense. They protected their borders by a great chain of fortifications; and here, as in the sphere of communications, corvée labor was mobilized for the task.[4] After the victory of the Seljuq Turks at Manzikert (in 1071), the absolutist state still functioned; and the road corvée was still levied in the 12th century;[5] but the vigor of the early days was gone. The great military road, which in the preceding years had had its periods of decay and reconstruction, appears to have been properly maintained only "until the eleventh century."[6]

When the Mongols established their rule over Russia, they did not construct massive roads, nor did they erect frontier walls or chains of border fortresses. They were satisfied to establish organizational and acquisitive methods of total control. It is in these two last fields of action that Byzantium and absolutist Russia, although not identical, were similar.

The Byzantines kept account of their country's wealth in elaborate cadasters.[7] They monopolized quick communication and intelligence by means of the state post.[8] They closely controlled the major sectors of handicraft and commerce, again until the 11th century.[9] And they maintained armies whose orderly integration contrasted strikingly with the amorphous hosts of feudal Europe.[10]

All these features have parallels in Muscovite Russia. The mature Muscovite state registered the mass of its population for fiscal and military purposes;[11] it operated an elaborate "postal" (relay) system;[12] it occupied a key position in the country's trade;[13] and it despotically drafted and directed its fighting men.[b]

During the earlier periods of both absolutist regimes office land was assigned to persons serving the state. In Byzantium this system emerged on the eve of the Arab conquest in a time of turmoil and invasion and as a means of strengthening defense against the Persian attack. Rooted in earlier Roman institutions[14] and set in its classical form by Heraclius I (610–641), it continued patterns that had existed in the ancient Orient from the days of Sumer and Babylon and that prevailed also in contemporary Persia.[15] Under the system of *themes*, each Byzantine soldier received a farm which, like his service, was hereditary and indivisible.[16]

This plebeian version of an absolutist office land system lasted until the 11th century. Then, after the catastrophic defeat at Manzi-

---

b. For the principle see Herberstein, NR, I: 95 ff.; for its full development, Staden, 1930: 58; cf. Kluchevsky, HR, II: 48, 111, 115. As will be shown below, all these institutions existed before Ivan III (1462–1505), during whose reign the Tatar Yoke collapsed.

kert, the state placed at the center of its reorganized military (and office land) system the big landowners, who, with the development of a heavy cavalry, were more useful militarily than the *themes* peasants.[c]

Hand in hand with this transformation went the transformation of the acquisitive order. From the 7th to the 11th century the government collected the bulk of its revenue through its officials. The *themes* soldiers, who lived essentially off their service land, presented no major fiscal problem.[d] The holders of the *pronoia*, the larger land units that constituted the core of the later office land system, provided a certain number of heavily armed soldiers and collected taxes from the peasants of the *pronoia*.[17] Together with the newly established tax farmers,[18] the *pronoetes* formed a group of semi-official tax collectors, who were less directly controlled by the state than were the members of the regular fiscal bureaucracy.

The corresponding Russian development has certain distinct features. The Muscovite holders of office land, the *pomeshchiki*, insofar as they rendered military service, were from the beginning and in the main heavily armed horsemen, and because of the greater burden of their equipment they were usually assigned estates larger than a peasant farmstead. Within their *pomestye* they collected taxes from their peasants. Consequently their government, like the government of later Byzantium, gathered only a part of its revenue through professional fiscal officials.

Both regimes employed despotic methods of government in the organizational and acquisitive fields. In the constructional field such methods were used to a major degree only by Byzantium, and there essentially during the middle period (until the 11th century). The shrinking range of constructional operations in post-Manzikert Byzantium was interestingly paralleled by the shrinking range of its fiscal bureaucracy. In Muscovite Russia constructional activities were irrelevant from the start; and the fiscal system was, also from the start, characterized by a large nonbureaucratic sector.

Thus a positive correlation between operational and bureaucratic density can be formulated for the margin as well as for the core areas of hydraulic society. This correlation may be influenced by other factors, and strongly so. But experience bears out what theoretical considerations suggest: Other conditions being equal, the

c. Cf. Ostrogorsky, 1940: 262. Ostrogorsky describes the military difference between the two groups, which I correlate here with the two types of office land.

d. Ostrogorsky, 1940: 58. According to the *Tactica leonis* 20.71, they seem to have paid some minor imposts (*ibid.*: 48).

density of the despotic bureaucracy tends to increase or decrease with the increase or decrease of its functions.

2. THE GROWTH OF PROPRIETARY FORCES

In Byzantium and post-Mongol Russia the state controlled the bulk of the land either fiscally or administratively, a large part of it being assigned as office land to the soldiers of the *themes,* the *pronoetes,* or to the *pomeshchiki.* Socially and economically, the *pronoia* holders were more powerful than the plebian peasant warriors of the *themes;* but they bore a closer resemblance to the Russian *pomeshchiki* than to the feudal lords of Western Europe. Both the *pronoetes* and *pomeshchiki* delivered part of their rural revenue to the state. Both owed absolute obedience to their respective governments. And both lacked the decisive capacity of feudal and postfeudal landlordism— the capacity to organize independent nationwide political corporations (estates, *stände*).

However, these conditions did not prevail unaltered. They existed in Late Byzantium up to 1204, the year in which the completely defeated empire was replaced by the Latin Empire; and they underwent a great change in the final period of Byzantium, which ended in 1453. In Russia they existed up to 1762, the year in which the former *pomestye* land became the private property of its holders.

In later Byzantium and in post-Muscovite Russia private property and enterprise gained considerable strength. In view of this fact we may ask first, is such a development typical of agrarian despotisms and second, to what degree was the growth of proprietary forces responsible for the societal changes that occurred in Byzantium from 1261 to 1453 and in Russia from 1861 to 1917?

In Byzantium big landownership was an important factor even before 1071; but its significance increased greatly when, at the end of the 11th and at the beginning of the 12th century, the landlord-*pronoetes* were given additional economic and judicial power. After the fall of the Latin Empire, the *pronoetes,* who formerly had held their grants for a limited time only, achieved the "hereditary and unrestricted ownership" of their lands. And they also obtained tax exemptions far greater than anything that had been customary.[19] The corresponding shrinkage in the government revenue was a decisive factor in the weakening of the Byzantine empire, which eventually was unable to resist the Turks.

In Tsarist Russia events took a different course. Here industrialization made substantial advances in the 18th and particularly in the 19th century; and this development was closely related to the growth of private property, first immobile (land) and ultimately also mobile (capital).

3. THE INSTITUTIONAL STAYING POWER OF MARGINAL ORIENTAL DESPOTISM

BUT the growth of proprietary forces did not bring about a transformation in Byzantine society like that achieved in Western Europe. Nor did it, prior to 1917, enable the Russian men of property to prevail over the men of the state apparatus. Why not? Were the beneficiaries of total power fully aware of the issue involved? And did they aim at isolating and crippling the representatives of property?

It is easy to juxtapose neatly separated camps. The real conditions, however, were much more complicated. In Byzantium, in Tsarist Russia, and in most other Orientally despotic countries the men of the apparatus were frequently also men of property. Consequently the conflict between the interests of the absolutist regime and the interests of private property and enterprise appear also—and often primarily—as a conflict between different members of the same ruling class or even as a conflict between different interests of individual members of this class. Why do such persons—as a group and over time—place their bureaucratic above their proprietary interests?

a. Bureaucratic Interests Favoring the Reproduction of the Despotic Order

THE civil or military official of an agrarian despotism is part of a bureaucratic hierarchy, which, taken in its entirety, enjoys more power, revenue, and prestige than any other group in the society. Of course, the post he holds today and the one he hopes to hold tomorrow carry with them the risk of total destruction; and he is therefore never safe. However, under the shadow of total power the man of property is never safe either; and the dangers of his position are not outweighed by satisfactions derived from active participation in the gambles and privileges of total power. Thus, not even the members of the bureaucratic class who hold no office challenge the principles of the absolutist regime, which they may rejoin tomorrow. And the officiating members of this class, confronted with the Big Conflict, aggressively uphold the privileges of bureaucratic power, revenue, and prestige which they are enjoying now.

Narrow and oversimplified interpretation has obscured the issue by formulating it only in terms of the interests of a single person, the autocratic ruler. To be sure, the despot is eager to perpetuate his absolute power, but, lacking an effective governmental apparatus, he cannot achieve this aim. The kings of Medieval Europe found absolutist power as sweet as did their Byzantine confrères. But the latter succeeded where the former failed, because the integrated Byzantine bureaucracy upheld the system of total power that favored both the sovereign and the men of the apparatus, whereas the enfeoffed vassals of the Western kings safeguarded and reproduced their privileges by keeping the king's power fragmented and checked.

To what extent can the prominence of the army in certain agro-managerial countries be taken as a sign of feudal decentralization? Military officials are as much men of the state apparatus as are their civil opposites; and if the first centuries of the Roman empire demonstrate anything, it is exactly this. For it was just when military leadership was prominent that Roman absolutism attained its maturity. The crystallization of despotic power in Muscovite Russia involved considerable bureaucratic activity; but the overwhelming majority of the new serving men wielded the sword and not the pen. The fact that in later Byzantium the heads of the military sector of the state apparatus figured prominently also as political leaders reflects the increasing pressure of foreign aggression. But it does not mean that these individuals served their government in a limited and conditional way as members of a baronial and feudal class.

b. Late Byzantium: Marasmus rather than Creative Transformation

WE must remember all this when we try to evaluate the effect of big property on the society of later Byzantium. Landed property increased during the first centuries of the Middle Empire; yet state protection of peasant holdings and periodic confiscations of large estates [20] notably retarded this development. After 1071, controls grew looser, but the state still had a rein on the country's rural economy. Contrary to corresponding developments in feudal Europe, conversion of the cadaster from a public to a private institution "*never* occurred in the East." [21] And the *pronoetes,* however they may have benefited personally, had to deliver a large part of the taxes they collected to the government.[22]

After the interlude of the Latin Empire, the state of Byzantium never regained its earlier authority. The landowners were now strong enough to withhold a much greater proportion of the national surplus than they had done previously, but they did not consolidate their ranks. Neither the great landowners nor the representatives of mobile urban wealth established nationwide corporations: estates. Private property became big; but it remained politically unorganized. Contrary to corresponding developments in the West, the growth of big private property in Byzantium did not give birth to a new society. It succeeded only in weakening and paralyzing the old one.

c. The Extraordinary Staying Power of Tsarist Bureaucracy

AFTER 1204 the Latin Empire temporarily replaced the traditional despotic regime. Could it be that the quasifeudal institutions of this empire (and of the Western enemies of Constantinople in general) influenced the bureaucratic absolutism of Byzantium so seriously that it was never able to regain its former superiority? In other words, did the rural and urban proprietors succeed in paralyzing the Byzantine government in the last centuries only because external forces broke the backbone of despotic power?

In terms of the fundamental issue the experiences of Tsarist Russia are eminently instructive. Post-Mongol Russia was invaded several times; but prior to the democratic revolution of 1917 the absolutist government was never completely broken. Russia's industrialization was strongly stimulated by Western developments. Foreign money flowed into private (capitalist) enterprises, increasing the weight of the proprietary sector. And Western methods and ideas notably affected Russian thought and performance. But all these external influences did not destroy the absolutist character of the state. The relation of the Tsarist bureaucracy to the forces of property—and eventually also to labor—continued to be determined by conditions that had long been operative in traditional Russian society. And this relation was, and remained, a relation of absolute bureaucratic superiority.

The masters of the despotic state apparatus responded to the changing historical situation with changing attitudes, but until 1917 they did not relinquish their total power. When in the early 18th century it became obvious that industrialization was vital for the country's defense, the Tsarist government was not satisfied with supervising and regulating the new industries, as the absolutist governments of Western Europe were doing. Instead, it directly managed the bulk of the heavy industry and, in addition also, part of the light industry,[e] probably employing for these purposes the

---

e. In 1743 the state had some 63,000 male "souls" ascribed to its (Ural) Mountain Works and 87,000 "souls" to its potash works (Mavor, 1925, I: 441), plus an unknown number of individuals who labored outside of these two main spheres of government production, whereas private workshops and factories occupied some 30,000 (ascribed) male "souls" (ibid.: 493). Under Elizabeth (1741–62) the sector of state-majority of all industrial workers in the form of ascribed labor.[f]

The machine age posed many new problems both in the agrarian and in the industrial spheres of life. The ruling bureaucracy solved them—clumsily, no doubt, but successfully insofar as the preservation of its hegemony was concerned. The Tsarist regime emancipated the serfs, but it maintained a tight control over the villages, which were administered in a quasi-Oriental manner. During the last decades of the 19th century the Russian government, by direct and indirect taxes, seems to have taken from the peasants almost the whole of their agricultural produce proper—almost 50 per cent of the entire peasant income.[23] And the same bureaucracy, which so effectively upheld its acquisitive interests, was perfectly willing to let the landed aristocracy lose a large part of its estates. Between 1861 and 1914 the land owned by this group shrank by over 40 per cent.[24] And Stolypin's reform program of 1908 showed the absolutist officialdom considerably more interested in creating a class of strong peasant owners than in protecting the landed prerogatives of its proprietary wing.

In the nonagrarian sector of economy the adjustments were similarly ingenious. The government encouraged private capitalist enterprise in industry and commerce and—to a lesser extent—also in communications and banking. But at the beginning of the 20th century it managed the bulk of the country's railroads; it maintained fiscal control over the comprehensive "monopoly" industries, and it occupied a key position in foreign investments. By means of state guarantees it influenced something like a third of the nonmonopolized light industry, and in 1914 no less than 90 per cent of the core of heavy industry, mining.[25]

These data indicate the strategic position that the Tsarist regime occupied in the economy of Russia at the beginning of the 20th century. In conformity with the majority of other analysts, the prominent Soviet economist, Lyashchenko, notes that the Russian banking system prior to the revolution "differed materially from the

---

managed industry temporarily shrank (*ibid.:* 440 ff.), but it rose again impressively during the later part of the century. The fourth census reports that for 1781–83 there were about 210,000 "souls" ascribed to the state-owned Mountain Works and 54,000 "souls" to private units (*ibid.:* 441). The somewhat less complete report of the Manufactures Collegium noted for 1780, 51,000 ascribed "souls" for the private Mountain Works and about 24,000 ascribed "souls" outside the key region of Russian industry, the "Mountains" (*ibid.:* 493).

f. Heavy industry formed the core of the state works, and until "the beginning of the nineteenth century, the iron mines and smelting works were manned exclusively by forced labor" (Mavor, 1925, I: 534).

banking system of the Western capitalist countries. . . . The state
bank was the central bank of the entire Russian credit system," and
the director of the credit department of the treasury "controlled the
entire financial apparatus of the country." [26]

There is no need to rest the evaluation of Russia's societal order
on the single criterion of financial control; but it certainly is worth
noting that one bureau of the Tsarist state apparatus did control
the country's entire financial system. Considering the role of the
Tsarist bureaucracy in rural and urban society, it is difficult to
avoid the decision that even at the beginning of the 20th century
the men of the state apparatus were stronger than society.[27]

d. Ottoman Turkey

THE later development of Ottoman Turkey combines features of
the Byzantine and the Russian patterns. The Turkish empire resembled Byzantium, with whose territory it was largely congruent,
in that it also originally controlled classical areas of hydraulic
economy; and it resembled Tsarist Russia in that it was also deeply
influenced by the industrial society of modern Europe. It differed
from Byzantium in that the loss of its hydraulic provinces virtually
coincided with the decline of its political prominence; and it differed
from Russia in that the growing economic and cultural influence of
the industrial West was accompanied, and partly preceded, by a
successful encroachment upon Turkey's sovereignty.

e. Diversified Final Evolutions

IN all three countries outside aggression was a crucial factor in the
weakening of the despotic regime; and this indirectly confirms the
staying power of the Orientally despotic order.

In the case of Byzantium, it is not entirely clear whether the final
marasmus of the despotic regime was caused primarily by external
or internal factors—that is, by the conquest of 1204 or by the excessive growth of landlordism. It is clear, however, that the growing
proprietary forces did not dissociate themselves sharply and creatively
from the decaying state. The impact of the West was sufficiently
strong to paralyze the traditional despotic government, but it was
not strong enough to pave the way for the growth of a new balanced
and property-based (capitalist) society.

In the case of Russia, bureaucratic absolutism suffered a mortal
blow from outside only in 1917. Prior to this date a marginal
Oriental despotism adjusted itself successfully to the conditions of

an advancing industrialization. The Tsarist government made more and more concessions to mobile and immobile property; and during the last period of its existence it even permitted a number of political organizations to operate on a national scale.[28] But these developments notwithstanding, the bureaucratic regime perpetuated itself until the beginning of the year 1917.

In the case of Turkey, foreign powers broke the backbone of Ottoman independence in a series of wars; and although Russia participated in the military defeat of Turkey, Western European influence prevailed in the ensuing transformation. It was under Western European influence that Turkey undertook important constitutional reforms. Due to the lesser significance of independent proprietary developments both in land and capital, the Turkish reforms were at first even more superficial than the reforms accomplished in the Tsarist empire, and this despite the fact that a first parliament was established in Turkey as early as 1876/7. But the weakness of the independent internal forces was to some degree compensated for by the increasing decay of the traditional state apparatus, which finally collapsed after the defeats suffered in the Second Balkan War and in World War I.

4. MARGINAL AGRARIAN DESPOTISMS CONTAINING CONSPICUOUS HYDRAULIC ELEMENTS

AMONG marginal agrarian despotisms Muscovite Russia and Middle Byzantium, which exhibit numerous cultural similarities, share one trait that is particularly relevant to our inquiry: in neither civilization did agrohydraulic operations play a significant role. On the other hand, Liao and Maya society, which culturally had little in common, are alike in that hydraulic features were clearly apparent in both of them.

a. The Liao Empire

THE Liao empire deserves special attention for a number of reasons. It is one of the few Far Eastern societies of conquest in which "barbarian" (pastoral) conquerors—in this case, the Ch'i-tan—ruled over part of China without shifting their political center from their Inner Asiatic grazing grounds to the subdued (North) Chinese territories. Liao is the first of the four great historical Chinese dynasties of conquest, the three others being Chin (ruled by the Jurchen), Yüan (ruled by the Mongols), and Ch'ing (ruled by the Manchus). Liao institutions therefore have significant parallels in the Chin, Yüan, and

Ch'ing dynasties, and it would seem also in other dynasties of conquest and infiltration in China and elsewhere.[g]

During the two hundred years of their rule, the Ch'i-tan acquired no real understanding of the potentialities of hydraulic agriculture. Instead, and not dissimilar to other mounted "barbarians," they eyed with suspicion the irrigated fields which impeded the free sweep of their cavalry.[29] The greater part of their agrarian territories, however, had a long hydraulic tradition. Canals had been dug and rivers diked prior to the establishment of Liao power in North China and Manchuria; [30] and the Ch'i-tan conquerors seem to have been perfectly willing to preserve this hydraulic heritage. When a flood inundated thirty villages in present Hopei, "an imperial decree ordered the old canals dredged"; [31] and when in 1074 excessive rains threatened the population of the Liao River basin, "the northern chancellor [ordered] large-scale mobilization of the able-bodied men along the river in order to complete the river dikes." An experienced official warned that such "large-scale works" would not be advantageous at this moment and he asked that the labor corvée be stopped. "The imperial court approved it and discontinued the work." Subsequent events indicated both the soundness of the official's warning—the river caused no calamity—and the dimension and weight of the hydraulic corvée: "Along the shores of the river for a thousand *li* there was not a person who was not highly pleased." [32]

The Liao government was equally well equipped—and considerably less reluctant—to employ its manpower for nonhydraulic constructions. Highways were maintained and repaired [33]—once with a huge corvée of two hundred thousand men; [34] chains of fortifications were erected along the frontier; [35] and two new capitals and many palaces, temples, and tombs were built north of the old seats of Chinese culture.[36] Literary descriptions and archaeological finds make it clear that the Liao labor service was as effective from the standpoint of the rulers as it was onerous from the standpoint of the people.[37]

Being great builders, the Liao rulers were also great organizers. Their offices registered the population for purposes of taxation, labor service, and military recruitment.[38] Their postal system was both elaborate and fast.[39] And their army was a well-coordinated fighting

---

g. This study was facilitated by the fact that the Chinese subjects of Liao, being trained in historiography, recorded the institutions of Liao society more fully than the scribes of most other conquest societies of Asia that were dominated by pastoral rulers. The reasons for this phenomenon are discussed in Wittfogel, 1949: *passim.*

machine. We have reason to believe that Chingis Khan shaped his own terrifying military organization after the Liao pattern.[40]

These constructional and organizational developments were supplemented by genuinely hydraulic methods of acquisition. True, some "entrusted" territories delivered only their wine tax to the central government; [41] but these regions comprised a mere fraction of the realm; [42] and eventually most of them came under full government control.[43] In the great majority of all administrative subdivisions the state insisted on its subjects paying taxes,[44] just as it insisted on their rendering labor and military services. Powerful families and monasteries sought to have households living on their land struck from the public registers, but evidently the state made no concessions in its claim to tax them.[45]

The final crisis of Liao power has all the earmarks of a dynastic crisis under a typical agrarian despotism. Here, as in similar circumstances, the landowners increased their acquisitive [46] but not their organizational strength. The collapse of the dynasty led to no property-based industrial order. Instead it led to the restoration and rejuvenation of the old agromanagerial society.

b. Maya Society

MAYA civilization presents ecological and cultural features that in several ways are unique. But these "unique" features overlay constructional, organizational, and acquisitive conditions remarkably similar to those of other marginal agromanagerial societies.

The ancient Maya were spread over a wide area, which comprised the greater part of present Guatemala, the western part of the Republic of Honduras, all of British Honduras, and Yucatan. Like most of Central America this area has a sharply divided rain year. From May to October precipitation is heavy, while during the remaining period there is little rain. This dichotomy encouraged elaborate hydraulic developments in territories that border the Lake of Mexico and also in several highland regions further to the south, the Maya-inhabited zones of Guatemala and Honduras among them. However, in large sections of the Maya area geological peculiarities decisively shaped and limited hydraulic enterprise. Almost the entire lowland plain of Yucatan and a great part of the hill zone between this plain and the highlands are composed of an extremely porous mineral: limestone; consequently precipitation quickly sinks below an easily accessible level.

A landscape which precludes the formation of rivers and lakes is of course entirely unsuitable for irrigation agriculture. Worse. The lack of natural storage places for drinking water, other than some well-like waterholes, presents a serious obstacle for any permanent or populous settlements. Persons desirous of establishing such settlements would therefore have to make concerted efforts not for purposes of irrigation but for the gathering and preservation of drinking water. As a result of such efforts we can expect to find hydraulic installations that play only a minor role in other agrarian societies.

When, in 1519, Cortez briefly visited Yucatan, he noted wells (*pozos*) and water reservoirs (*albercas*) in the residential compounds of the "nobles." [47] And in 1566 Landa, in the first systematic description of Maya civilization, stressed both the unique water difficulties of the area and the way in which moisture was provided "in part by industry and in part by nature." [48] It is significant that Landa, like the authors of the *Relaciones de Yucatán*,[h] places the man-made devices for providing water first.

The installations for providing drinking water were (1) artificial wells (*pozos* or *cenotes* in the primary sense of the Maya word),[49] (2) cisterns (*chultuns*), and (3) man-made large reservoirs (*aguadas*). The *Relaciones* report artificial *pozos* everywhere in the lowland; [50] and the early observers fully understood the difficulties of digging and maintaining good wells without the aid of metal tools.[51] Even after the introduction of iron implements, the maintenance and use of the man-made wells often required ingenious communal action.[52] In some cases the methods employed were intricate "past belief," [53] involving the active participation of "the population of a city." [54]

But important as the *cenotes* were, they did not as a rule provide water for large populations. Says Casares, a modern Yucatan engineer: "If we were to depend on the wells only for the supply of water, the greater part of our peninsula could not be inhabited." [55] This being so, the cisterns and *aguadas* of Yucatan become crucially significant.

Bottle-shaped subterranean constructions with circular openings, *chultuns*, have been discovered in several places. At Uxmal, Stephens noticed "so many of them, and in places where they were so little to be expected, that they made rambling out of the cleared paths dangerous, and to the last day of our visit we were constantly finding new ones." [56] These constructions seem to have provided "immense reservoirs for supplying the city with water." [57]

In part. Besides the *cenotes* and the cisterns,[i] the ancient Mayas

h. RY, I: 116, 144, 182, 206, 210, 221, 248, 266. Occasionally major emphasis is placed on the natural *pozos* (*ibid.*: 47, and perhaps 290).

i. Stephens (1848, I: 232) assumes that the *chultuns* of Uxmal had provided water for the people of the ruined city—"in part at least." Casares (1907: 227) also com-

constructed large pools or lakes, *aguadas*. Even in the hilly regions where the terrain provided natural waterholes or cavities, *sartenejos*, Casares considers the *aguadas*, whether natural or artificial, much more important. Those that were man-made differed greatly in shape and quality: "Some have a bottom made out of stones and some have not such stones, and they are of all sizes—true works of art they are—that show the ingenuity and attainments of their builders." [58]

Few students have searched for these *aguadas* as eagerly as did the pioneer explorer, Stephens. At first glance, many of them seemed natural,[59] and Stephens' informants felt sure—and recent research has proven them to be right [60]—that "hundreds are perhaps now buried in the woods, which once furnished this element of life to the teeming population of Yucatan." [61]

From the standpoint of hydraulic organization the importance of this fact can scarcely be overrated. The *cenotes* usually required the cooperative efforts of smaller communities only; and the urban cisterns were probably constructed and maintained by the work teams that "built at their own expense the houses of the lords." [62] But in the case of the *aguadas* large-scale cooperation was imperative. In the midnineteenth century a ranchero, who wanted the *aguada* near his estate cleaned, "secured the co-operation of all the ranchos and haciendas for leagues around, and at length fairly enlisting them all in the task, at one time he had at work fifteen hundred Indians, with eighty superintendents." [63] This much coordinated labor was required when a single *aguada* had to be cleaned with iron tools. Under the stone-age conditions of the ancient Maya, the cleaning, and still more the building, of a chain of *aguadas* certainly involved huge work teams.

Further studies must be made before the institutional weight of the man-made *cenotes*, cisterns, and *aguadas* can be fully determined. But even our present limited knowledge entitles us to state that the constructional operations of the Maya include a not inconsiderable hydraulic sector. *Aguadas* were in use not only in the lowlands but also in the hill zone,[64] where some of the most ancient centers of Maya civilization were located.[65] And irrigation canals, artificial lakes, and other familiar types of hydraulic works have been discovered in the highland sector of the Maya area [j] and, of course, also in the hill zone.[k]

---

ments on the limited capacity of these cisterns to satisfy the water needs of most of the ancient cities.

j. In the old Maya city of Palenque, Stephens discovered the remains of a water channel faced with large stones (Stephens, ITCA, II: 321 and 344). Blom found an elaborate drainage system "in other parts of the ruins" (Blom and La Farge, TT, I:

The nonhydraulic constructions of the ancient Maya have been frequently described. The early Spanish records stress the magnitude of the "houses" and "edifices," which the people built for their secular and priestly masters; [66] and grandiose ruins confirm the early written evidence. Massive stone highways connected a number of cities, and like the pyramids, palaces, and temples they must have required great levies of corvée labor.[67]

No compensation was given for certain types of the construction corvée; [68] and a similar policy may have prevailed also with regard to other corvée services, including agricultural labor for "the lords." [69] But whether the pay arrangements for labor services were uniform or not, there can be little doubt that the commoners worked for their masters in a disciplined manner. Prominent men, obviously officials, "who were very well obeyed," [70] acted on the ruler's behalf. And the power of the sovereign, who controlled either a single city-state or a cluster of such units, can be judged from the fact that local officials received no share of the tax they collected for delivery to the center.[m] The so-called "town councilors," who assisted the highest local official, were "in charge of certain subdivisions of the town, collecting tribute and attending to other municipal affairs." [71] According to a regional description, the officials of the town wards had "to attend to the tribute and services (communal labor?) at the proper time and to assemble the people of their wards for banquets and festivals as well as for war." [72] In addition to a variety of civil officials, who used a hieroglyphic script and who, among other things, kept land records,[73] there were military officials, some holding their posts for life, some being appointed for three-year

189). He also noticed a "fairly elaborate" irrigation system in Amatenango, Chiapas (*ibid.*, II: 396), a region which was formerly part of the Old Maya empire. Further to the east, in Guatemala, Stephens (ITCA, I: 206) encountered "a large artificial lake, made by damming up several streams." A canal in Honduras, probably prehistoric, may have "served to irrigate a large portion of the lower plain" near Lake Yojoa (Strong, Kidder, and Paul, 1938: 101).

k. The hill zone, intermediate between the mountain region and Northern Yucatan, contains troughlike depressions, whose clay bottoms hold "lakes, swampy lowlands, and streams" (Lundell, 1937: 5; Ricketson, 1937: 9; Cooke, 1931: 287), but even here the greater part of the terrain is composed of a limestone so porous that the natural precipitation quickly sinks below a readily accessible level, creating a dangerous deficiency during three or four months of every year (Ricketson, 1937: 10). Bottle-shaped *chultuns*, "excavated in the solid limestone throughout the region," may have been used for storing water, if their walls were "rendered impervious by plaster" (*ibid.:* 9 ff.). An *aguada* near Uaxactun is "doubtless the remains of an ancient reservoir, and excavation in its bottom would probably lay bare the stone flooring with which it originally had been paved" (Morley, 1938: 139).

m. The local officials were supported by the people, who worked their fields, maintained their houses, and served them personally (Tozzer, 1941: 62 ff., n. 292; Roys, 1943: 62).

terms.[74] Picked men, who did most of the fighting and who received a special compensation, seem to have constituted cadre troops, but "other men could also be called out." [75] The rulers determined (and limited) the duration of a campaign in accordance with pragmatic considerations, October to the end of January, the agricultural slack season, being considered the most suitable time for waging war.[76]

In the acquisitive sphere the power of the regime over its subjects was equally unchecked; and there is no reason to doubt that the rulers used their opportunities to the full. It has been said that "tribute" was light; [77] and the amounts requested from individual households may indeed have been modest. But it must be remembered that under Mexican and Inca dominion, subjects who cultivated the fields for the state and the temples paid no taxes. In contrast to this, the Maya commoners who worked the fields of their masters delivered in addition "maize, beans, chile, poultry, honey, cotton cloth, and game." [78] One regional report implies that such tributes were voluntary, but another dealing with the same locality notes that anyone who failed to pay would be sacrificed to the gods.[79]

5. "Loose 2" or "Marginal 1"?

Our survey of Byzantium and Russia and of the Liao empire and Maya civilization leads to several conclusions. The hydraulic density of the four institutional complexes differs greatly: it is very low or zero in the first two cases and relatively high in the last two. As a matter of fact, a reasonable argument can be made for classing Liao and the Maya as borderline cases of loose hydraulic societies— variants of "Loose 2," to use our symbols. For the time being we shall view them conservatively as marginal Oriental societies with substantial hydraulic elements, "Marginal 1" (M 1), as juxtaposed to "Marginal 2" (M 2), that is, Oriental societies with little or no hydraulic substance.

The closeness of M 1 to L 2 and the gap between M 1 and M 2 are as significant as the fact that all variants of the marginal type utilize the organizational and acquisitive methods of despotic state-craft. Thus, however marginal they may be hydraulically, their methods of social control place all of them definitely in the "Oriental" world.

6. Fragmenting Patterns of Inheritance and a Government-Dependent Dominant Religion

Many supplementary data can be adduced to strengthen our basic classification. But here we shall refer only to two particularly significant criteria: the fragmenting system of inheritance and the dependence of religious authority.

The Justinian Code—*Novella* 118—prescribes the equal division of property among the children of a deceased person. This provision, whatever its origin, fits to perfection the needs of agrarian despotism.

In Russia proprietary conditions changed as greatly as the institutional patterns of which they were a part. *Votchina* land, a pre-Mongol form of strong noble property, was not subjected to fragmentation; and this continued to be the custom until long after the noble owners of such land were compelled to serve the state. *Pomestye* land was office land. Originally it passed from father to one son; [80] but since all adult males were obliged to render civil or military service, the *pomestye* estate was finally considered a family possession to be divided among the father's several heirs.[81] When the growing importance of firearms changed the aristocratic cavalry army into a plebeian infantry army, fewer noble serving men were needed, and Peter I, who merged *pomestye* and *votchina* land, made the use of the new type of service (state) land hereditary.[82] The law of 1731 is an important milestone in the process of making *pomestye* land private. From this year on, *pomestye* land was divided among all the children and, according to the Law Book, "equally among all of them." [83]

In Western Europe the nobles emerged from a period of contractual and limited (feudal) state service with their landed property strengthened through primogeniture and entail. Contrary to this, and contrary also to the indigenous *votchina* tradition, the nobles of Tsarist Russia emerged from a period of compulsory and unlimited state service with their landed property weakened through a law of inheritance that prescribed fragmentation.

In Liao society the ruling tribal stratum—except in the matter of imperial succession—seems to have rejected primogeniture,[84] thus maintaining its pastoral *mores,* which permitted all sons to share in the family property. In its Chinese sector the regime was careful to uphold the traditional Chinese laws.[85] Many edicts praised Chinese subjects who conformed to what were considered ideal patterns of Chinese familism.[86] This being so, we have no reason to doubt that the government also upheld the fragmenting Chinese law of inheritance.

A fragmenting pattern of inheritance certainly prevailed among the Maya. Says Landa: "These Indians did not permit their daughters to inherit with their brothers, except it was through kindness or good will; and in this case they gave them some part of the accumulation, and the brothers divided the rest equally, except that to the one who had aided the most notably in increasing the property, they gave the equivalent." [87]

In Byzantium the Church, being nationally organized from the beginning, was well prepared to strive for independence. But the rulers of Eastern Rome and Early Byzantium treated religion as part of the *jus publicum;* and even after the catastrophies of the 7th century, the Byzantine government was able to combat the Church's drive for autonomy. In the 10th century the emperor still played a decisive role in the selection of the Patriarch. And by virtue of his judicial position he could also interfere in church administration.[88]

Significantly, the Church became more independent in the last phase of the Middle Empire; but even then the emperor could still force an obstructing Patriarch to abdicate.[n] It was only after the period of the Latin Empire that a completely shattered autocracy was compelled to tolerate an almost autonomous Church.[89]

In Tsarist Russia the bureaucratic regime expressed its enormous vitality by its victory over the Eastern Church, which after the fall of Byzantium shifted its center to Moscow, the "Third Rome." At the end of the Mongol period the increasingly powerful Russian state exerted an ever-increasing authority over the Church. Ivan III seized half the monasterial land in Novgorod; Ivan IV, the Terrible, required more taxes and services from Church land; [90] and in 1649 a new "department of monasteries" further tightened the state's control over the Church.[91] In 1721, Peter I abolished the Patriarchate and placed the Church under a government body, the Holy Synod.[92] And a few decades later, in 1764, the state seized most of the Church land without compensation, assigning only one-eighth of the revenue from the land to the clergy.[93] In consequence of these combined political, religious, and economic measures, "the church became more and more a part of the administrative machinery of the state." [94]

In Liao society the problem of an independent Church never arose. Government officials, headed by the emperor, shared leadership in religious ceremonies with a variety of shamans, who, like the priests of the Buddhist temples, obviously were not coordinated in any nationwide and independent organization ("church").[95]

The close relation between secular and religious authority among the Maya has already been mentioned. The ruler of a territorial state, the *halach uinic,* is believed to have fulfilled "definite religious functions"; [96] and certain priests might also be war chiefs.[97] But

---

n. A serious conflict was finally decided in favor of the Church, not because the Church was such a strong independent factor but because the high bureaucracy turned against the sovereign (Ostrogorsky, 1940: 239 ff.).

nothing indicates that the priests of the great temples were bound together in any single organization, except insofar as they participated in the work of the government. Says Scholes: "In many cases priestly and political functions had been combined in such a manner that it was difficult, if not impossible, to differentiate them." [98]

7. LOCATION, GENESIS, AND INSTITUTIONAL VULNERABILITY
   OF MARGINAL AGRARIAN DESPOTISMS

MIDDLE and Late Byzantium, the Liao empire, and the Maya point up some of the institutional diversities among marginal agrarian despotisms. Discussion of other pertinent civilizations would differentiate further the picture we have of this significant subtype. The Hopi Indians of Arizona, for instance, engage in extremely modest hydraulic enterprises—mainly communal spring cleaning [99]—but their building activities are impressive.

Tibet was faced with certain irrigation tasks in the river valleys of the high plateau,[100] but the hydraulic weight of these tasks was probably not great. Nevertheless, the "monk officials" [101] did operate a well-functioning labor service [102] and an elaborate and fast postal system also.[103] Holders of land grants served the government unconditionally and as regular officials; [104] and the fiscal apparatus insisted on taxing the bulk of the population.[105]

The kings of ancient Asia Minor and certain territorial rulers in early China were more outstanding as builders and organizers than as hydraulic engineers. But once the common institutional denominator is understood, it is easy to recognize that all these civilizations are variants of the marginal type of hydraulic society.

How did these marginal configurations come into being? And how open were they to change? Before trying to answer these questions, we must consider their relative location—that is, their spacial relation to the major hydraulic areas of the world.

a. Location

TAKING the major hydraulic zones of the Old and the New World as coordinates, we find marginal developments, as for instance the nonhydraulic territorial states of ancient China, interspersed between definitely hydraulic areas. Many other marginal developments (the Hopi Pueblos, the kingdoms of ancient Asia Minor, Middle Byzantium, Tibet, Liao, and the Maya) appear at the geographical periphery of a hydraulic zone.

Russia, however, does not. Russia had no close hydraulic neighbors when, in the 13th century, the Mongols began to introduce

Orientally despotic methods of government. Cases like Russia are more the exception than the rule; but they serve to demonstrate that marginal agrarian despotisms may arise at a great distance from the nearest conspicuous center of hydraulic life.

b. Genesis

THE relative location of most marginal agromanagerial states is highly suggestive of their origins. The bulk of all such regimes obviously came into being not earlier—and often demonstrably later —than the area's oldest hydraulic civilizations. In some cases, such as Byzantium, the marginal territory split off from an older (loose) hydraulic complex. In others, the marginal territory was adjacent to a hydraulic society proper; and while interrelation cannot always be documented, it seems probable that it was the second type which stimulated the first.

The constructional, organizational, and acquisitive patterns of the hydraulic center may have been transferred directly to nonhydraulic regions during periods of temporary control. Or native leaders may have adopted the power techniques of their hydraulic neighbors, which from the standpoint of the ruling group had much to recommend them and which could be easily imposed on a society that lacked strong, well-organized, and independent proprietary, military, and ideological forces. Or experts in managerial and despotic control may have gone from their hydraulic homeland to adjacent nonhydraulic territories either in flight or on invitation to become teachers or co-leaders in their new environment.

On an institutional checkerboard familiarity with the hydraulic techniques of organization and acquisition was probably all that was needed to encourage a changeover from a loosely coordinated nonhydraulic tribe to a nonhydraulic managerial community. Thus it is easy to understand why the Hopi Indians built fortress-like villages similar to those of the more properly hydraulic Pueblos; why, like the inhabitants of other Pueblos, they integrated their work teams under communal leaders; and why they cultivated the fields of their supreme chieftain.

A combination of state-centered hydraulic and marginal agromanagerial societies may emerge from a composite tribal root. In prehistoric and protohistoric China such a development may have been stimulated by varied and prolonged culture contacts: visits, alliances, trade relations, and conquests.

The introduction of marginal agromanagerial institutions by nonagrarian tribal conquerors presents another genetic pattern. In this case, the conquerors employ and transfer organizational and acquisitive methods of hydraulic statecraft, although they themselves do not, to any relevant extent, practice agriculture, not even in its nonhydraulic form. And being nomadic, they may carry these methods far beyond the political and cultural borders of any major hydraulic area. The Mongol conquest of Russia demonstrates both points.[o]

The power of the Ch'i-tan differed from that of the Golden Horde in character as well as in origin. The bulk of the agricultural regions of the Liao empire had previously been part of the old, loosely hydraulic world of China; and the Ch'i-tan masters found it easy to perpetuate the traditionally absolutist administration with the aid of Chinese officials, who were ready to act as junior partners in a somewhat uneasy, but workable, alliance. Like the Mongols of the Golden Horde, the Ch'i-tan tribesmen in their great majority remained pastoralists; but their ruling group integrated itself closely with Orientally despotic officials, who directed huge nonhydraulic constructions and even considerable hydraulic operations.

The marginal agromanagerial societies discussed in our survey came into being in various ways; but they all seem to have derived from compact or loose hydraulic societies. In many instances, such an origin is certain, and in others it is likely. But is it the necessary and only way?

By no means. It is entirely possible that some agrodespotic societies emerged independently. But obviously we can assume such a development only when the despotic order in question fulfills the organizational and acquisitive functions of a hydraulic government and when, for geographical and historical reasons, institutional diffusion can be excluded as altogether unlikely. Having acknowledged the possibility of independent origin, I must add that the cases in which agrodespotic regimes in the terms of our inquiry certainly or probably have a hydraulic ancestry are so numerous that the cases in which independent origins can be established will not substantially change our basic contention. Virtually all historically significant agrodespotisms that

o. The attempt to explain the rise of Muscovite despotism as the consequence of external military pressure usually results in the view that this pressure was exerted in the main by Eastern nomadic aggressors (see Kluchevsky, HR, II: 319 ff.). The imitation of despotic power techniques by a non-"Oriental" government is of course conceivable, particularly if the nongovernmental sector of society lacks "strong, well-organized, and independent proprietary, military, and ideological forces." However, the noble owners of *votchina* land, although not organized in a corporation, were not without strength; and the actual events of the Mongol period show that the Great Princes of Moscow, who set out to subdue them, were for a considerable time directly under Tatar leadership.

fulfill no hydraulic functions seem to have been derived from hydraulic societies.

c. Institutional Vulnerability

DIRECT or indirect connection with an agrohydraulic center seems to have been necessary for the rise of virtually all marginal agrarian despotisms. But a continued connection is not imperative for their perpetuation. Apart from Late Byzantium, which was critically weakened by external forces, marginal Oriental societies have been able to reproduce their patterns of power amazingly well.

Obviously it is enormously difficult to create an effective counterweight to an apparatus government, which has succeeded in repressing, crippling, and fragmenting those proprietary, military, and ideological forces that enabled Medieval (feudal) Europe to evolve into an industrial society. Serious political crises occurred in all hydraulic societies. But the way in which the men of the apparatus overcame them demonstrates the staying power of their methods of organization and exploitation. Purposeful political activists strove to reestablish the only thoroughly tested type of government, which, at the same time, promised them total power and total privilege. And their restorative endeavors were greatly facilitated by the political and organizational ineptitude of their nongovernmental rivals. Among the big landowners, even if they were many, politically ambitious elements were much more eager to seize than to restrict total power. And the representatives of mobile (capitalist) property, even if they were many, were so unaccustomed to think in terms of property-based state power that they were satisfied to get on with their business without making the bid for political leadership that was so characteristic of the differently conditioned bourgeoisie of the West.

In this context, Middle and Late Byzantium and post-Mongol Russia pose crucial questions. Contrary to Maya civilization and the Liao empire—and of course, contrary to all hydraulic societies proper—these two great Eurasian countries fulfilled no relevant agromanagerial functions. And the nonagricultural managerial functions which the Tsarist regime performed did not involve the broad organizational penetration usual even in loosely hydraulic societies.

Did these circumstances reduce the institutional staying power of either marginal Oriental despotism? As stated before, the Byzantine case is not altogether conclusive; but even here it may be asked whether a more intensely managerial regime could have beaten off the external attacks without yielding so much to the proprietary forces within its borders. In Russia the absolutist bureaucracy reproduced itself ingeniously, but it permitted the growth of democratic forces of property and labor that in 1917 temporarily prevailed over the men of the apparatus.

Evidently, marginal agrarian despotisms, like hydraulic societies proper, tend to reproduce their basic power system, and this over a period of time. Like hydraulic societies proper they have a stationary quality. But they seem somewhat more open to structural change, particularly if they entirely lack hydraulic substance.

D. THE SUBMARGINAL ZONE OF
THE HYDRAULIC WORLD

1. THE PHENOMENON

THE effective coordination of absolutist methods of organization and acquisition is the minimum requirement for the maintenance of a genuine agrarian despotism. Outside this margin we find civilizations that, although lacking such a combination, exhibit stray features of hydraulic statecraft. The areas in which such stray features occur in other societal orders constitute the submarginal zone of the hydraulic world.

2. CASES

a. Protohistorical Greece

AN institutional analyst of protohistorical Greece cannot fail to be struck by the hydraulic quality of Minoan Crete. This civilization certainly owed its international prominence to its maritime relations; but while acknowledging this, we must not forget that nearness to the sea alone explains little. The ancient Cretans, like other seafaring peoples, established their thalassocracy on the basis of specific internal conditions.

To what extent Aegean patterns of "fetching water by artificial means" and of using canals and ditches for the purposes of refined agriculture [1] made Minoan society hydraulic is not clear. It is clear, however, that the islanders accomplished miracles regarding matters of drainage and probably also of water supply.[2] We do know that Crete was covered with a network of excellent roads.[3] And we have reason to believe that the supervisor of public works occupied a high position [4] in the country's complex and centralized administration.[5] The Minoan script is still undeciphered, but the government certainly employed it widely for "bureaucratic methods of registration and accounting which were handed down from century to century and were perfected in the process." [6]

These and other facts support the view that "the Minoan civilization was essentially non-European." [7] And although the Minoans had too many cultural peculiarities to be called "part of the East," [8] they were connected through "a few clear and even close bonds with Asia Minor, Syria and Egypt." [9] Ehrenberg concludes that "in particular the sultan-like life of the kings of Cnossus and Phaestus, their courts, their officials, their economy, displayed features which were similar to those of their opposite numbers in the Near East; they were equally unlike anything Western." [10]

The proto-Greek Mycenaean civilization, which rose when Minoan power decayed, accounts for significant quasihydraulic developments in Argolis and Boeotia, and probably also in other parts of eastern Greece. Between the middle and the close of the second millennium B.C. Mycenaean engineers executed great drainage works around the Lake of Copais in Boeotia; and they covered Argolis with an elaborate network of roads. [11] Their rulers lived in huge castle-like edifices, and they erected monumental tombs. [12] Bengtson compares their constructional achievements to "the great creations of the ancient Orient, the pyramids and the *ziqqurats*." [13] True, we hear nothing of a bureaucracy, and the use of the early script seems to have been restricted. [14] But despite such limitations, Bengtson believes that "only a strong central power could plan and execute these works," which, considering their magnitude, in all probability required the services of both native corvée laborers and captured slaves.[a]

Moreover, an Oriental origin has been suggested for the worship of the earth gods and the stars which the historical Greeks inherited from their Mycenaean ancestors, and it was indeed in connection with such religious observances that they practiced prostration. [15] But when the Greeks of the classical period refused to perform before an Oriental despot the act of submission they considered appropriate to the gods, [16] they demonstrated that even if Mycenaean Greece was marginally hydraulic, post-Mycenaean Greece belonged to the submarginal zone of the hydraulic world. In the classical period also the monumental edifices of Argolis [17] had long lost their significance; and the grandiose temple city of Athens, the Acropolis, whose beginnings go back to Mycenaean times, [18] was administered by a government that delegated even the management of its public works to private entrepreneurs. [19]

a. Bengtson, 1950: 41. Bengtson mentions the slaves before he mentions the native corvée laborers, but he calls the latter as numerous as the former.

b. Early Rome

PRIOR to Roman times the Etruscans, who apparently came from the marginal hydraulic zone of Asia Minor,[20] are known to have engaged in stupendous building activities. Their waterworks in the Po Plain are impressive,[21] and others undertaken in Central Italy are equally worthy of attention.[22] While under Etruscan dominion, the Romans learned how to construct "monumental works."[23] Later, but before they established their first colony on Hellenistic ground, they began to build solid overland roads.[24] But although such developments are more characteristic of a hydraulic than a relatively simple rainfall-based agrarian order, Rome at this period manifestly was an aristocratic variant of a multicentered non-Oriental society.

c. Japan

IN ancient Greece and Rome Oriental elements have often been overlooked. In Japan they have frequently been overestimated, and this for a good reason. Japan is part of the Asian continent, and Japanese civilization shares important features with China and India. Furthermore, the Japanese have developed one of the most subtle systems of irrigation farming known to man. Nevertheless, Japanese society never was hydraulic in the terms of our inquiry.

Why did Japan's rice economy not depend on large and government-directed water works? Any competent economic geographer can answer this question. The peculiarities of the country's water supply neither necessitated nor favored substantial government-directed works. Innumerable mountain ranges compartmentalized the great Far Eastern islands; and their broken relief encouraged a fragmented (hydroagricultural) rather than a coordinated (hydraulic) pattern of irrigation farming and flood control. According to the institutional historian, Asakawa, the Japanese landscape permitted "no extensive *Bewässerungskultur* as in Egypt and in parts of western Asia and China."[25] Japan's irrigation agriculture was managed by local rather than by regional or national leaders; and hydraulic trends were conspicuous only on a local scale and during the first phase of the country's documented history.

The rulers of the dominant political center effected a loose political unification at a rather early date, but they were not faced with hydraulic tasks that required the coordinated operation of large corvée teams. Nor were they conquered by the forces of an Orientally despotic state. They therefore failed to establish a comprehensive managerial and acquisitive bureaucracy capable of controlling the nongovernmental forces of society as did the men of the apparatus on the Chinese mainland.

The attempt to establish a centralized and bureaucratic despotism in Japan reached its first spectacular climax in the Taikwa Reform of 646. From the standpoint of our key criteria, its objectives can be listed as follows:

I. Construction
    A. Hydraulic. An edict of 646 demanded uniform procedures relating to dikes and canals.[26]
    B. Nonhydraulic. The basic reform edict ordered the creation of a system of roads for the imperial post.

II. Organization
    A. The population was to be counted periodically and census registers were to be kept.
    B. A government corvée replaced older local (and quasi-feudal) obligations.
    C. A state post was to be operated.

III. Acquisition
    A. The peasants were to be taxed on the basis of the land which the government assigned to them.
    B. Service in the state corvée could be commuted by the payment of a tax.[27]
    C. A number of officials, particularly local and high-ranking dignitaries, were to be supported from land holdings, which had often been previously owned by the new appointees and which were tax exempt.

Compared with the Merovingian and Carolingian attempts at absolute rule, the Japanese program of 646 was much more Oriental. This fact cannot be explained by Japanese contact with T'ang China alone. For centuries the Japanese had practiced irrigation farming [28] and their rulers had engaged in constructing works of a non-hydraulic type. Thus the effort of the masters of the Reform government to do as the Chinese emperors did was rooted in indigenous trends that were definitely, if rudimentarily, hydraulic.

But these quasi-Oriental trends were unable to shape Japanese society. The hydraulic innovations suggested in the Reform lacked the dynamism that characterized similar attempts in early hydraulic societies. The Reform favored the execution of "public works"; but while three of the six T'ang ministries (taxation, war, and justice) were taken over with little modification and two others (administrative personnel and rites) were successfully modified, the sixth (the Board of Public Works) found no counterpart in the new Japanese set-up.[29]

This omission was no accident. A canal that was dug in 656 struck the people as "mad"; and its critics compared it with a useless colossal hill that was built at the same time.[30] Moreover, the decrees that proclaimed a universal state labor service required many less days of corvée work than did T'ang regulations. And the provisions for commuting the corvée by paying a tax showed the Japanese government more interested in revenue than in labor.[31]

The assignment (and/or reassignment) of tax-free land to important officials was perhaps the Reform government's greatest concession to the feudal forces of Japanese society. Behind the new bureaucratic facade a fierce fight was being made to extend and consolidate tax-free land. And so successful were the representatives of the centrifugal forces that the official grantees eventually established themselves as hereditary landowners who, like their European counterparts, introduced a single-heir system of succession.[32]

As the system of tenure changed, universal census taking collapsed; and attempts to reestablish it led nowhere.[33] General taxation met the same fate. Many elements of Chinese culture notwithstanding, the decentralized and property-based society of the Japanese Middle Ages resembled much more closely the feudal order of the remote European world than the hydraulic patterns of nearby China. The poets of feudal Japan, like their confrères in feudal Europe, glorified the heroic deeds of individual warriors or groups of warriors. But the loosely agglomerated armies of Medieval Japan did not stimulate tactical or strategic thinking. The Japanese writers of the period quoted Chinese military authorities, such as Sun Tzŭ; but feudal Japan, like feudal Europe, failed to develop the art of war.[b] Prior to 1543, the Japanese armies "were made up of small, independent bands of soldiers who fought more as individuals than as units of a tactical formation." [c]

---

b. The reader will remember that the term "art of war" connotes the practice and theory of strategy and tactics. A recent survey of ancient and medieval military organization ascribes "the beginnings of an acknowledged art of war" in postfeudal Europe to Maurice of Nassau (Atkinson, 1910: 599), who played a decisive role in the latter part of the Dutch War of Independence.

c. Brown, 1948: 236 ff. A collection of early Japanese texts, Gunsho Ruijū, contains many references to Sun Tzŭ and other military theoreticians of his period. But the Japanese treatment of warfare is "a rather scattered melange quite unlike Sun Tzŭ. . . . The first integrated treatment of the subject comes in a work by Takeda Shingen (1521–1573)" (from a letter of February 16, 1954, from Dr. Marius Jansen, University of Washington, Seattle, who established this point in collaboration with his colleague, Dr. Richard N. McKinnon)

The absolutist concentration of government power, which characterized the Tokugawa period (1603–1867), again resembled more closely Western absolutist developments, both in its economic aspect (the slow rise of property-based commercial and industrial capitalism) and in its political limitations. It was during this period—actually in 1726—that "the first tolerably exact census" was taken.[34] It was then that the road system spread vigorously;[35] and it was then that the government, like certain of the prominent feudal lords, dug a number of locally important canals.[36]

But despite these and other activities—which, except for the irrigation works, find illuminating parallels in absolutist Europe—the absolutist regime of Japan was not strong enough to establish its acquisitive power over the whole empire. Out of a national revenue of twenty-eight or twenty-nine million *koku,* the representatives of supreme power, the Tokugawa shoguns and the court, arrogated to themselves only about eight million *koku,* while by far the larger part of the revenue remained in the hands of great feudal vassals.[37] Japanese absolutism sharply restricted the power of the feudal lords. But until 1867 it was unable to eliminate them.

While stressing the similarities between traditional Japanese society and the feudal and postfeudal West, we must be careful not to oversimplify the picture. The Oriental quality of many Japanese institutions and ideas is beyond doubt. On the lower and local level, Japanese irrigation agriculture required quasihydraulic coordination and subordination; and the feudal lords' insistence upon absolute obedience may, at least in part, reflect such quasihydraulic relations. Rudiments of a postal system seem to have existed prior to the Tokugawa period;[38] and the symbol of total submission, prostration, persisted until modern times.[d] The members of the ruling group, although strongly imbued with a military spirit, continued to think in terms of a somewhat adjusted Confucianism;[39] and although they invented simplified phonetic symbols, they employed with genuine pride the Chinese script, which, like Confucius' conception of the gentleman-bureaucrat, was better suited to a civil and learned officialdom than to a war-minded knighthood.

To sum up: traditional Japan was more than Western feudalism with wet feet. While the Far Eastern island society gave birth to a property-based and genuinely feudal order, its many and cherished elements of Chinese policy and thought show that, in a submarginal way, it was related to the institutional patterns of the hydraulic world.

---

d. During my stay in Japan in 1935 a number of university professors greeted each other in my presence—and prior to an official banquet—by prostration.

d. Pre-Mongol (Kievan) Russia

RUSSIAN society prior to the Mongol conquest (1237–40) presents another and equally illuminating aspect of the hydraulic submargin. In pre-Kievan and Kievan days the subsistence economy of the "Rus" included stock-raising; [e] but its mainstay was agriculture, rainfall agriculture.[40] Under the conditions of a primarily natural economy this agriculture favored the development of a broadly spread landed nobility, which was subordinated to the territorial princes in a loose way.[f] Below this stratum, but above the slave-like *kholopi*,[41] a class of free cultivators moved with comparative ease; [42] and the townspeople were even less restricted. Their "council," the *veche*, could take independent political action not only in the great northern republic of Novgorod [43] but also in such capital cities as Vladimer,[44] and even in Kiev.[45] Prior to the establishment of the Kievan state (*ca.* 880) [g] legal transactions could be consummated, and without interference from any princely authority, by the heads of the rural— and urban—communities, which in the most ancient Russian law code extant are called *mir*.[h] And even in the Kievan era (*ca.* 880–1169), the government, although considerably stronger than previously, was far from being absolutist—indeed as far from such a condition as the government of any feudal state in the contemporary West. Institutionally speaking, Kievan society manifestly belonged to the protofeudal and feudal world of Europe.

It belonged to this world, but in a way that requires special investigation. Like hydraulic society, feudal society, too, has an institutional margin; and Russia's tribal civilization, which arose on the eastern periphery of the feudal world, was for centuries, and particularly after 880,[46] dominated by the Varangians,[47] who were rooted in—and repeatedly supported by—a northern fringe area: Scandinavia. But although Rurik had once received a fief from the Frankish emperor,[48] he did not impose the Western European system of land tenure on the Eastern Slavs. Nor did his successors.

e. The oldest known version of the Russian law, *Russkaya Pravda*, mentions crimes pertaining to oxen, sheep, goats, horses, calves, and lambs (Goetz, RR, I: 15 ff.).

f. This fact has been established through the pioneer investigations of Pavlo-Silvansky. For a survey of his major conclusions see Borosdin, 1908: 577. For an independent study arriving at similar conclusions for the early Russian society see Hötzsch, 1912: 544.

g. Vernadsky (1943: 368) places Oleg's conquest of Kiev "between A.D. 878 and 880 (tentatively, 878)."

h. Russkaya Pravda, I, 17 = Goetz, RR, I: 8, 9. Cf. Vernadsky, 1948: 134. In the third version of the Law, the early term, *mir*, is replaced by *gorod*, city (*Russkaya Pravda*, III: 40 = Goetz, RR, I: 28, 29, cf. 272 ff.).

The native nobles and the members of the princely retinue, the *druzhina,* operated under no feudal contract.[49] Their freedom to "ride away" [50] indicates a type of independence that in Western feudalism was more the exception than the rule.[51] On the other hand, the princely rulers of the various territorial states drew their maintenance not from royal domains, as was usual in most feudal countries, but from a general tax, custom fees, and legal fines.[52]

Thus Kievan society resembled the feudal order of the West in that the rulers shared the power of making political decisions "with the popular assembly (*veche*) and the senate (*boyarskaya duma*)"; [53] and the nobles were able to establish a form of absolute landownership that the lords of Western Europe matched only at the close of the Middle Ages. As in the feudal West, the cities—at least the large ones—and the nobles paid no taxes.[54] But this extremely loose arrangement interlocked with a fiscal system that permitted the sovereign to tax the entire rural population. The principle of levying a tax on each fireplace was employed in Byzantium; [55] and the semi-pastoral Khazars applied it to those Eastern Slavs over whom, prior to the victory of the Varangians, they had control. The Varangians followed the fiscal procedure of the Khazars,[56] and they continued to do so with modifications during the whole Kievan period.[57] They also adopted other "Asiatic" features from the Khazars or related tribes. For a time their rulers referred to themselves as "khagans"; [i] and prior to the introduction of Christianity they apparently kept their numerous concubines in harem-like confinement.[j]

Direct Byzantine influence made itself felt relatively early. In addition to many literary and artistic elements, the Russians adopted Eastern Christianity and Byzantine law, both of which affected the political climate of Kiev. The Byzantine ("Greek") priests, who came to Russia, carried with them significant ideas of theocratic rule and subordination. Accustomed to act as part rather than as rivals of the secular government, they certainly enhanced the power of the prince.[k] The introduction of Byzantine law further strength-

i. Vernadsky (1943: 282) assumes borrowing from the Khazars. The title *khaghan* was borne by "the first Kievan princes." Apart from Vladimir, his son Yaroslav is also known to have been thus addressed by the Metropolitan Hilarion (*ibid.:* 370, and n. 302).

j. Prior to his conversion, Vladimir is said to have had about 800 concubines (Nestor, 1931: 55).

k. This fact has been stressed by a number of historians. Platonov points out that the "Christian and Byzantine conception of the prince as a ruler by divine right . . . was opposed to the pagan view that the prince was a mere leader of a *druzhina,* and could be driven out and killed" (Platonov, 1925: 40). The Soviet academician Grekov quotes fully the pertinent statement in the Nestor Chronicle: "God gives the power to

ened the Kievan sovereigns. In the second Constantinople-influenced version of the Russian law the ruler and his functionaries emerge clearly as the possessors of supreme judicial authority.[58]

But Kievan society did not accept the legal notions of the great Eastern empire *in toto*. The Byzantine code prescribed corporal punishment for horse stealing; but the revised Russian law continued to demand a fine for this act.[59] Despite its great prestige, Byzantine law did not supersede the Kievan view that a free man should not be beaten.

3. COMMENT

EVIDENTLY, the civilizations in the submargin of hydraulic society exhibit a wide institutional range; and their basic structures can be understood only if they are viewed first in their primary institutional context. However, certain secondary qualities, which link them to the hydraulic world, must not be overlooked:

1) A civilization that was once part of this world may, in a later nonhydraulic phase, still preserve certain traces of its previous condition, which, although not necessary to the new configuration, are compatible with it. Post-Mycenaean Greece probably belongs to this category.

2) The voluntary adoption of desirable "Oriental" features accounts for such phenomena as Taikwa Japan and Kievan Russia.

Another point that is valid for marginal hydraulic societies is also valid for the submargin. It would be incorrect to view as submarginally hydraulic an agrarian society which exhibits certain despotic features of organization and acquisition but which has no known link to the hydraulic world. Individual features of hydraulic statecraft, such as the levying of a general tax or the collection of a general tribute, certainly have emerged in civilizations which had little or no contact with this world. In a number of tribal societies this obviously happened; and if we did not know of the Asiatic background of the Khazars, we might also feel tempted to place their system of tribute gathering in this independent and residual category. Comparative analysis must in each instance decide whether we are dealing with submarginally hydraulic or independent trends.

---

whomever he wishes; the Supreme Being appoints whomever he desires as the caesar or prince." Each state should be headed by a caesar or prince, and state power is of divine origin—these are indeed "the familiar features of the Byzantine conception of state power." Grekov underlines the authoritarian spirit of the famous Christian chronicle: "Anyone who attacked the authority—according to the theory—opposed God." And "Yaroslav's merit lies in the restoration of a single authority in the state" (Grekov, 1947: 133 ff.).

E. SOCIETIES WHICH CROSS
THE INSTITUTIONAL DIVIDE

THE submarginal zone of the hydraulic world cannot be explained by a simple formula. Nor is it necessarily self-perpetuating. A number of historically prominent civilizations of the submargin have crossed the institutional divide and become either marginal hydraulic societies or hydraulic societies proper. Others have moved in the opposite direction.

The civilizations discussed so far have been essentially agrarian. The very concept of a hydraulic economy implies agriculture. But the history of the Ch'i-tan, the Mongols, and other tribal conquerors demonstrates that Oriental despotism is not confined to agrarian societies. Nonagricultural peoples, too, may adopt and transmit techniques of despotic government; and they may "Orientalize" nonagricultural as well as agricultural groups. The importance of this fact for the understanding of many despotic conquest societies and of the dynamics of the institutional divide is obvious.

1. NONAGRICULTURAL PEOPLES ADOPTING AND TRANSMITTING POWER DEVICES OF AGRARIAN DESPOTISM

REPRESENTATIVES of many extractive modes of subsistence—gathering, hunting, and fishing—have lived at the fringe of the hydraulic world. In this respect, the margin of Pueblo society [1] and the early phases of Aztec history are instructive. But no primitive nonagricultural group has played as important a role as the pastoralists. The New World lacked animals suitable for drawing carts and carrying men. The Old World had several species that could be so used. Their domestication greatly benefited the plant breeders; but primarily it benefited the pastoralists, who, after the invention of riding, became the military equals, and at times the masters, of large and wealthy agrarian commonwealths.[2]

a. Such Devices Not Necessary for, but Compatible with, Nomadic Pastoralism

PASTORAL nomads frequently supplement their herding economy by farming.[3] Yet the need to move their herds prevents them from giving more than casual attention to whatever crops they plant near their camping grounds. Their migratory way of life, however well regulated, excludes the construction of elaborate and permanent works of water control, which form the foundation of hydraulic agriculture.

But this mode of life does not prevent them from adopting Orientally despotic methods of organization and acquisition. To be sure, such methods do not grow out of the needs of pastoral life. Although some coordination and subordination are imperative for effective camping and trekking, and although disciplined procedure is highly advantageous for hunting and warfare,[4] these practices do not necessarily lead to the establishment of a political apparatus stronger than all nongovernmental forces of society. Technical factors (the ever-recurring need for dispersing herds and men) and social factors (the resistance of the free tribesmen to the demand for total submission) work in the opposite direction. Even subordination under a strong military leader is essentially voluntary. Limited in time and not bulwarked by irreversible organizational arrangements, it rarely, if ever, destroys the loose and fluid character of the tribal society.[5]

The chiefly leader and those close to him are eager to place themselves in a position of permanent and total power; but as a rule they attain this goal only after submission to, or conquest of, a hydraulic country. In the first case the overlords of the agrarian state may apply their own patterns of political control (registration, corvée, taxation) to the submitting herders, whose chieftain usually emerges as the absolute and permanent master of his tribe. In the second case the supreme chieftain (khan, khaghan, etc.) seizes the power devices of the agromanagerial civilizations he has conquered. Bulwarked by indigenous officials who maintain the traditional administration and by a group of tribal followers whose number grows with his successes, he reduces his noble rivals to a shadow of their former importance, if he does not annihilate them altogether.

In both cases the tribesmen may lose their cultural—and eventually also their sociopolitical—identity. This happened to many Arab groups under the Abbassid caliphate. In such a situation the problem itself ceases to exist. However, submitting tribesmen are usually not eager to relinquish their old way of life; nor are tribal conquerors as easily absorbed as legend has it.[6] With proper modifications, the tribal masters of a compound hydraulic empire may maintain their social and cultural identity; and while doing so, they may impose their newly acquired power techniques to outlying nonhydraulic countries. This happened when the Mongols conquered Kievan Russia.

The disintegration of a compound hydraulic empire may again make all or some of its tribal elements autonomous; and it is at this moment that the perpetuation of despotic power, under conditions of tribal pastoralism, is put to the test. At times the despotic regime dissolves as completely as the empire of which it was a part. But historical experience shows that the beneficiaries of absolutist government continued in a privileged position, at least to some extent and for some time. Obviously then, despotic methods of organization and acquisition, although not a necessary adjunct of nomadic pastoralism, are definitely compatible with it.

b. The Brittleness of Orientally Despotic Power at the Pastoral Fringe of the Hydraulic World

RECENT studies have provided a wealth of data concerning all these processes for the Ch'i-tan tribes, who, as Liao rulers, were the temporary masters of the northeastern fringe of China. Many monographs have clarified corresponding aspects of Mongol history; and future investigations of the tribal conquest societies of the Near East, of Persia, India, and pre-Spanish America will certainly bring to light many other varieties of this important institutional conformation.

Already our present knowledge enables us to juxtapose the pastoral and the agrarian forms of a marginal hydraulic society. Without doubt, the staying power of genuine despotism is much greater under agricultural than under tribal, pastoral, or nomadic conditions. The fluidity of a steppe economy encourages diffusion and separation and, as a corollary, the growth of independent centers of animal wealth and military power. Natural calamities or serious military reverses weaken and dissolve a pastoral despotism as quickly as the fortunes of war and conquest bring it into being. The meteoric rise and fall of many steppe empires in Inner and West Asia and in Southeast Europe illuminate the brittleness of pastoral despotism.

The "Black" Ch'i-tan tribes, who grazed their herds in Northern Mongolia a hundred years after Liao fell, revealed few traces of the coordinated political order maintained by their forebears either in the Far East or in Turkestan.[7] After the collapse of the Great Khan's empire, Mongol power shrank to a shadow of its former self, but it did not disappear altogether. In 1640 the Mongol-Oirat were still restrained by laws which, although considerably milder than Chingis Khan's *Yasa*,[8] forced the tribesmen to participate in a relatively heavy transport corvée.[9] Manifestly, postempire Mongol society was not entirely lacking in cohesiveness when attachment to the rising Manchu star gave their secular and religious masters a chance to support, in a privileged if secondary way, another ambitious attempt to establish a despotic regime, first in the margin and later in a great core area of the hydraulic world.

2. Agricultural Civilizations Crossing the Institutional Divide

THE changeover of pastoral societies from a nonhydraulic to a hydraulic order proceeds, as a rule, on a geographical as well as on an institutional level. In contrast to this, changing agrarian societies do not change their locale. They move from one order to another exclusively on the institutional level.

A second difference concerns the potential range of the changeover. Pastoral societies, which preserve their economic identity, may shift from the submarginal to the marginal zone of the hydraulic world and vice versa. Agrarian societies that were originally submarginal may become marginal hydraulic or full-fledged hydraulic societies and vice versa.

Like pastoral societies, agrarian societies change their institutional quality most frequently at the geographical periphery of agromanagerial areas; for it is here that the forces of the hydraulic and the nonhydraulic world have wrestled with each other for millennia. The societal transmutations of Greece, Rome, Spain, and Russia are all part of this gigantic interaction.

a. Greece

FROM a marginal or submarginal hydraulic position, Mycenaean Greece evolved into a civilization whose aristocratic and democratic energies prevented the state from exerting unchecked control over the nongovernmental forces of society. The Greeks of Homer, Hesiod, and Sophocles prostrated before certain of their gods; but they refused to recognize the supreme representative of state power as their master (*despotes*).

For many centuries, and despite their proximity to the hydraulic world, the Greek cities in Western Asia upheld within their limits the principles of a multicentered society. Only in the wake of Alexander's conquests did the old constitutional freedoms begin to shrink. The Hellenistic sovereigns of the Orient reduced the political independence of their own co-nationals in Asia and at home. Together with their Macedonian-Greek aides, they readily donned the robes of Orientally despotic power.

The early Roman empire and Byzantium completed what the Hellenistic dynasties had initiated. The Greeks of the Near East—

and those of the motherland—became part of a hydraulic empire, which included impressive areas of loose (Syria) and compact (Egypt) hydraulic economy. During the 7th century this empire shifted to the margin of the hydraulic world. Later the conquering Turks restored it once more to a loosely hydraulic position.

The Byzantine and Turkish Greeks were no longer the Hellenes of Hesiod, Pericles, and Aristotle. This is probably true ethically, and it is certainly true institutionally. The scions of Mycenae, who during the classical period and for the free members of their community created exemplary models of democratic citizenship, were the ancestors of the Byzantine Greeks, whose elaborate court ceremonial made "Byzantinism" a catchword for man's total, if ritualized, submission to total power.

b. Rome

i. THE RISE OF A HELLENISTIC VERSION OF ORIENTAL DESPOTISM

In Greece the shift to hydraulic forms of state and society was initiated by Alexander's conquest. In Rome the establishment of absolute and monarchic rule by Augustus signals not the beginning but a relatively advanced stage of a process that had been under way for about two hundred years.

In the institutional history of Rome the year 211 B.C. is a fateful date. It was in this year that in the subdued Sicilian kingdom of Syracuse the Romans "encountered for the first time a subtly elaborate legal system of a primary agrarian state patterned after Egyptian and general Hellenistic models." [10] The victorious Italian republic made this system, the so-called Lex Hieronica, "the basis for the organization of its first provincial economy." [11] By so doing, it adopted a basic principle of Hellenistic statecraft, which declared the state the holder of absolute power and the owner of all land. [12]

As the successors of Hieron, the Roman conquerors made their state, the *populus Romanus,* the supreme master of Sicily's agrarian economy. And they acted similarly also in the other territories of their growing empire. In the regions of the Eastern Mediterranean this involved little change. But in the western areas of Roman expansion nonhydraulic conditions prevailed. It is therefore extremely significant that the Italian conquerors, with proper modifications, transferred the Hellenistic system "also to the West." [13]

From the Roman point of view the Hellenistic principle of general taxation was "a complete innovation." And this innovation was a success because it was supplemented by a periodic and comprehensive census. According to Hieron's plan, which the Romans adopted, "it was the duty of the city magistrates every year to take a census of all the farmers of the district . . . recording both the complete acreage . . . and the acreage of each crop actually under cultivation." [14]

These external developments did not automatically create a state stronger than society in the Roman homeland; but the metropolis underwent internal changes which devastatingly weakened the traditional aristocratic republic. On the one hand, the unending wars of conquest enriched the senatorial landlords, who employed an ever-increasing number of slaves; on the other hand, these wars exhausted the peasantry. Together with the land-hungry veterans, the impoverished peasants offered an ideal mass basis for the policies of the *populares* and of the victorious generals, who did not hesitate to confiscate and redistribute the estates of their erstwhile opponents.[15] The civil wars also increased the vulnerability of the wealthy businessmen, the *equites,* some of whom as tax farmers, *publicani,* profited greatly from the growth of the Roman realm. During the advancing crisis the *equites* enjoyed as little personal and proprietary safety as did the members of the senatorial group.

Evidently, the internal changes were so closely tied up with the country's territorial expansion that any attempt to explain the fall of the republic exclusively on the basis of either internal or external factors must prove inadequate. The generals who dominated the political scene, particularly in the 1st century B.C., rose to power because of the size and peculiarity of the territories they occupied. It was in these areas that they secured their material support; and it was in these areas that they tested the effectiveness of Hellenistic methods of government.

How much did any single individual contribute to the changes that occurred in Roman society? For the purpose of our inquiry it is sufficient to note that in Caesar's time the senate had already lost both its social homogeneity and its uncontested political hegemony and that Caesar, who like other great politician-generals of the period gave land to the veterans, challenged the senatorial representatives of large landed property as a "man of the people," a *popularis.* Here, as elsewhere, absolute power was established through the agency of men who used a popular cause to advance their political aims.

At the time of Caesar's assassination the strongest proprietary force in Rome, the senatorial group, had been so shaken that Augustus, who officially controlled a number of "imperial" provinces (among them the old hydraulic areas of Egypt and Syria) was able to control the "senatorial" provinces too.[16] From 29 B.C. on, the senators, who previously had been the decisive force behind the administration, had to get a permit from Augustus before they could leave Italy; and "if the object of their travel was a visit to Egypt, [the request] was refused on principle." [17] During the subsequent period the once dominant aristocratic landowning senators were more and more replaced by persons who became members of the senate because they were in the emperor's service. And the representatives of mobile wealth and capitalist enterprise, who, as *publicani*, had collected taxes and customs fees for the government and, as contractors, had executed certain "public works," were plundered by Pompey, weakened by Caesar, and subordinated by Augustus.[18] Eventually they lost their significance altogether.[19] Thus the Roman metropolis, which temporarily had ruled a huge Hellenistically hydraulic empire without itself being hydraulic,[a] eventually caved in under the hammer blows of forces which drew their ultimate strength from this very empire.

In this gigantic process of transformation Augustus was not only the grave digger of the old social forces, but also the pioneer in administrative and managerial change. Despite great loyalty to the cultural values of Rome, the first emperor (*princeps*) patterned his absolutist state not on early Rome or classical Greece—from which, indeed, he would have gotten little inspiration—but on the Hellenistic Orient.[b] By laying the foundations for a salaried officialdom,[20] he initiated a bureaucratic development that rapidly gained momentum in the 1st century A.D.[21]

Agromanagerial methods of acquisition and organization had already been employed in the provinces under the Republic; now they were elaborated and systematized. Confiscations became a standard feature of the empire's economic and political life. General taxation was bulwarked by the periodic registration of the population, which under Augustus became regular administrative procedure.[22] Initiating the great nonhydraulic constructions that are still associated with the name of Rome, Augustus started to build a truly agromanagerial system of roads. He established the state post, the

---

a. Of course, the Roman metropolis was not hermetically sealed off from its Oriental environment. The growing influence of Hellenistic statecraft was significantly accompanied by the growing influence of Eastern religion, art, technology, and customs. The advance of a Hellenistically Oriental culture and the pathetic attempts to resist it are among the most illuminating developments of the 2d and 1st centuries B.C. (see Voigt, 1893: *passim*).

b. At this time the Roman statesmen began "to look for guidance not to Athens or Sparta but to the Persian Empire and the Hellenistic monarchies which succeeded it" (Stevenson, 1934: 183).

cursus publicus, and very consistently, he combined it with an elaborate intelligence service.[23]

These steps were supplemented by such developments as the employment of former slaves, "freedmen," in the service of the state,[24] the use of eunuchs for political purposes,[25] the worship of the emperor, and the gradual decay of independent commercial and industrial enterprise. Long before the close of the 2d century A.D., when Septimius Severus through wholesale slaughter and confiscation made the despotic center the "owner of most of the good arable land throughout the empire," [26] the old society had lost its identity. It was only logical that the "Semitic emperor," who despised Italy and "spoke Latin with a Punic accent," [27] wanted to be called *dominus,* "master." [c]

Thus when Diocletian established a spectacularly Eastern court, the actual Orientalization of the empire had already been accomplished. A prominent economic historian summarizes the great transformation as follows: "In the second and third centuries . . . not only was the State (or the emperor) the largest landed proprietor, it was also the biggest owner of mines and quarries, and in course of time came to be the greatest industrialist." [28] Furthermore, "trade—wholesale and retail—became increasingly subject to governmental control" [29] and "transport was also largely nationalized." [30] In this single-centered economic setting, "the idea of the omnipotence of the State" evolved readily. It took shape essentially "under the influence of orientalizing-hellenistic and other theories of the State." The wholesale "replacement of one economic system by the other, and the substitution of a new civilization and attitude to life for the old took more than a century and a half. It was completed by the end of the third century." [31]

A comparative analysis of the Orientalization of the Roman Empire leads to certain basic conclusions:

1) The institutional meaning of this process appears clearly only if its study is based on the understanding of hydraulic society and agromanagerial (Oriental) despotism.

2) Hellenization means Orientalization. The Hellenization of Rome started almost two hundred years before the establishment of the principate.

c. "It was as if the spirit of ancient Assyria had taken possession of the palace to make the Empire subject to a bureaucracy which should be the executive of a divine authority transmitted through a dynastic succession. In such a system there would be no place for a Senate or for the principle of delegation by the State, and it was a sign that this notion of government now tended to prevail that the title *dominus* came to be generally applied to the emperor" (Miller, 1939: 35).

3) As a societal type, imperial Rome must be equated not with the proto-industrial absolutisms of the West, but with the great agro-managerial absolutisms of the East.

ii. THE FALL OF AGROMANAGERIAL DESPOTISM IN WESTERN ROME

DIFFERENT from the absolutist rulers of post-Medieval Europe, the Roman administrators of Spain, Gaul, Western Germany, and England were not restricted by nationally organized property-based corporations (estates). And although they preserved as far as possible the indigenous political leadership and culture, they operated the political apparatus in accordance with the great traditions of agro-managerial statecraft. As elsewhere, they created huge nonhydraulic constructions, primarily state roads and frontier walls. By means of their state post they monopolized quick communications. And they counted and taxed the inhabitants of the Western provinces in much the same way as they did in the East.[32]

No innate Iberian, Celtic, or Germanic urge for freedom kept the ancestors of modern Western Europe from accepting—at first under coercion but later as a matter of course—the yoke of a state which gave the nongovernmental forces of society little chance to participate in shaping their political and economic fate. Over several centuries Oriental despotism in its Hellenistic-Roman form spread into the woodlands of Germany, to the Atlantic shores of Spain and Gaul, and to the southern borders of Scotland.

These Eastern institutions did not disappear when, in the 4th century, Western Rome, for all practical purposes, became independent of the hydraulic East. The despotic state, which had tolerated no strong and organized proprietary classes—although it did tolerate large property of all kinds—continued to reproduce itself even after its managerial and bureaucratic apparatus shrank. Indeed, until the end, the government of Western Rome insisted upon its absolutist position. Its last prominent political figure, Heraclius, was a typical representative of hydraulic statecraft, a eunuch.[33]

As in Late Byzantium, the decline of Western Rome was largely due to external factors. The loss of revenue from the wealthy eastern provinces seriously weakened the Italian metropolis, which was also having great difficulty in adjusting itself to the collapse of its slave economy. The East, being agriculturally more intensive, never had relied on slave labor as had the West. And consequently the West suffered severely when the sources of cheap slave labor dried up.

The political impotence of Rome became blatantly apparent at the beginning of the 5th century: Rome lost Gaul in 406, England in 407, Spain in 415, and Africa in 429. Within the truncated metropolis, the forces of big landed property, as represented by a new senatorial group, increased in importance. However, the emerging proprietary leaders lacked the strength to set up a non-Oriental type of government. This objective was achieved only when they joined the Germanic king, Odovacar, who in 476 formally terminated the worn-out absolutism of Western Rome.[34]

c. Europe after 476

i. UNSUCCESSFUL ATTEMPTS TO RULE ABSOLUTELY

CERTAIN symbols of hydraulic statecraft, such as the vassals' obligation to kiss the sovereign's foot, persisted for a considerable time, even outlasting the Merovingian period; [35] but lacking substantial societal foundations, they eventually ceased to be invoked. And the political development, instead of following the Roman model, produced the decentralized protofeudal system of government which characterized the first period of the Middle Ages.[36]

ii. THE "UNPARALLELED" CASE OF THE DOMESDAY BOOK

IN this period, which is assumed to have lasted until the end of the 12th century,[37] there appeared in 1086 the Domesday Book, a register of the lands of England, which was ordered in 1085 by the Norman king, William the Conqueror. European historians have indicated institutional roots of the Domesday both in England [38] and Normandy.[39] But while these roots are entirely authentic, they do not adequately explain the great English-Norman land register. Not only was this type of public cadaster unknown in the area from which William and his men came ("Normandy had no Domesday and no dooms"),[40] but it was also unknown in other parts of non-Oriental Europe. According to Maitland, it represents "an exploit which has no parallel in the history of Europe." [41]

What then inspired this unparalleled achievement? Conquest, which Maitland suggests,[42] provides no plausible explanation, since Medieval Europe saw many conquests but only one Domesday Book. The Normans of Normandy are a case in point. They did not, to our knowledge, institute a Domesday, but they certainly settled in the north of France through conquest. Could it be that by 1085 the Normans had become familiar with administrative methods which were unknown to them in the 10th or even in the earlier part of the 11th century?

When in 1066 the Normans conquered England, some of their countrymen had already set themselves up as the masters of southern Italy, an area which, with interruptions, had been under Byzantine administration until this date; and some of them had established a foothold in Sicily, an area which had been ruled by Byzantium for three hundred years and after that by the Saracens, who combined Arab and Byzantine techniques of absolutist government.

We have no conclusive evidence regarding the effect of this Byzantine-Saracen experience on William and his councilors. But we know that in 1072—that is, thirteen years before William ordered the *descriptio* of England—the Normans had conquered the capital of Sicily, Palermo, and the northern half of the island. And we also know that there were considerable "comings and goings" [43] between the Italian-Sicilian Normans and their cousins in Normandy and England, particularly among the nobility and clergy. The latter happened also to be actively engaged in administrative work.[44] No wonder, then, that on the basis of his knowledge of the period Haskins, the leading English expert on English-Sicilian relations in the Middle Ages, suggests "the possibility of a connexion between Domesday Book and the fiscal registers which the south had inherited from its Byzantine and Saracen rulers." [45]

Haskins' hypothesis explains well why a typically hydraulic device of fiscal administration appeared in feudal Europe. It also explains why for hundreds of years afterward this "magnificent exploit" had no parallel in that area. Evidently, systematic and nationwide registration was as out of place in feudal society as it was customary in the realm of Oriental despotism.

d. Spain

i. ORIENTAL CONQUEST

BUT neither the failure of the Frankish attempts nor the singularity of the English Domesday implies that after 476 the institutional divide between the hydraulic and nonhydraulic parts of Europe remained fixed. The history of southern Italy and Sicily prior to the Normans reveals two major forces of Eastern expansion: the Byzantines, who tried to uphold their way of government in certain former provinces of the Roman empire, and, far more significantly, the Arabs, who, inspired by a dynamic new creed and equipped with new methods of warfare,[46] extended their power from the Near Eastern centers of hydraulic society throughout Northwest Africa, Spain, and —temporarily—Sicily.

This colossal eruption resembled the westward growth of the Roman empire in that it, too, spread Orientally despotic patterns of government. But for a variety of reasons the institutional effects of the Islamic conquest were much more far-reaching. Under Roman influence Western Europe became part of a loosely hydraulic Oriental society without, however, adopting hydraulic agriculture; and eventually it returned to a submarginally hydraulic or altogether non-hydraulic position. Under the influence of the Arabs, the swing was considerably greater. Prior to the Islamic invasion, the Iberian peninsula was the home of a protofeudal civilization, which had small-scale irrigation agriculture but probably few hydraulic enterprises.[d] In sharp contrast to the Romans, who seized Western Europe, the Arab conquerors of Spain were entirely familiar with hydraulic agriculture, and in their new habitat they eagerly employed devices that had been extremely profitable in the countries of their origin. Under Muslim rule "artificial irrigation . . . was improved and extended . . . on Oriental models," and this included government management: "its superintendence was the business of the state." [47]

Thus Moorish Spain became more than marginally Oriental. It became a genuine hydraulic society, ruled despotically by appointed officials [48] and taxed by agromanagerial methods of acquisition. The Moorish army, which soon changed from a tribal to a "mercenary" body,[49] was as definitely the tool of the state as were its counterparts in the Umayyad and Abbassid caliphates. A protoscientific system of irrigation and gardening [50] was supplemented by an extraordinary advance in the typically hydraulic sciences of astronomy and mathematics.[51] Contemporary feudal Europe could boast of no comparable development. Reconstructing the impressions of the great Arab geographer, Ibn Hauqal, who visited Spain in the 10th century, Dozy comments on the organizational power of the Muslim state, whose police, like its hydraulic agriculture, penetrated the most remote parts of the country: "The foreigner noticed with admiration the universally well cultivated fields and a hydraulic system, which was coordinated in such a profoundly scientific manner that it created fertility in the seemingly least rewarding soils. He marvelled at the perfect order that, thanks to the vigilant police, reigned even in the least accessible districts." [52]

d. Hirth, 1928: 57 ff.; Hall, 1886: 363, 365; Lévi-Provençal, 1932: 166; Laborde, 1808: 29, 107. Laborde's memoir claims complete lack of agricultural interest for the Gothic conquerors of Spain (Laborde, 1808: 107).

In the second half of the 14th century the leading town of the Hanseatic League, Lübeck, numbered 22,000 inhabitants,[53] and London about 35,000.[54] At the height of the Western caliphate the Moorish capital, Cordoba, may have harbored a million persons,[55] and Seville in 1248 more than 300,000.[56] At the close of the Muslim period Granada was probably at least as populous. The *Encyclopedia of Islam* estimates the dwellers of this beautiful last Islamic capital in Spain at "half a million." [57]

No wonder then that the absolutist state, at the peak of its prosperity, collected a stupendous revenue.[58] And no wonder either that this state, which like other hydraulic regimes freely used eunuchs,[59] was ruthless in purging dignitaries who fell from favor. When these unfortunates were liquidated, the state was quick to confiscate whatever property they possessed.[60]

ii. THE RECONQUISTA

THE *reconquista,* which in the 13th century reestablished Christian control over the greater part of Spain, transformed a great hydraulic civilization into a late feudal society. Students of Russia, who see the rise of an Orientally despotic state in Muscovy as the consequence of an armed struggle against powerful Eastern enemies, will do well to compare the Russian story with what happened in Spain—and for that matter, in Austria.

To begin with the latter country. For several centuries, Austria was threatened by one of the greatest Oriental empires known to history: Ottoman Turkey; and extended parts of Hungary were occupied by the Turks for more than one hundred and fifty years. But the main political and military base of the counterattack, Austria, remained free; and the protracted struggle against the mighty Eastern foe did not convert the Austrian state into an Oriental despotism. Like other countries of Europe, Austria advanced toward a definitely Western type of absolutism: until the middle of the 18th century the Austrian diets (*Landtage*) had a decisive voice concerning taxation and the drafting of soldiers,[61] and even after 1740 the estates played an essential role in the fiscal administration.[62] Hungary stubbornly maintained a semi-autonomous government, whose *Landtag,* consisting of an upper house (clerical and secular magnates) and a lower house (lower nobles and urban deputies), "exerted a great influence on the country's administration." [63]

In Spain, too, the base of the Reconquest was never Orientalized. The rulers of the small northern states that had withstood the Arab onslaught depended for their military strength on the support of the nobles, the clergy, and the towns; [64] and at the end of the main phase of the Reconquest these groups, far from being politically pulverized, were able, because of their privileges, to maintain a semi-autonomous existence.[65] Similar to the development in late feudal and postfeudal France, England, Germany, Italy, and Scandinavia, Spain also developed an absolutist government.[66] This government was strong enough to prevail over the nobles, the Church, and the towns; [67] but it was unable to wipe out the entailed aristocratic landholdings [68] and the semi-autonomy of the Church; and it was unable to break the pride and dignity of the Spanish people. The estates of Aragon that had declared the recognition of their privileges to be the condition of their homage to the king (*"si no, no."*) repeated this daring formula again in 1462,[69] that is, more than a hundred years after the greater part of the Peninsula had been reconquered. And although the assemblies (*cortes*), which in Castille essentially represented the free municipalities, had ceased to exist in 1665, the absolutist regime failed to instill in its subjects the submissive attitude habitual under hydraulic regimes.

To state this is not to deny the extraordinary strength of Spanish absolutism. This phenomenon may at least in part be explained by the exigencies of the Reconquest "frontier," which enhanced the growth of royal authority in Catalonia, Navarre, and Aragon.[70] However, the *Wirtschaftsgesinnung* of the Christian kings may have been even more decisive. The northern base of the Reconquest greatly favored pastoralism; and the European demand for wool—which increased with the advance of the Reconquest [71]—led the Spanish kings one-sidedly to promote sheep breeding also in the liberated areas of central Spain, and even in parts of southern Spain.[72] While the kings gave all manner of privileges to the towns and nobles, they established a tight fiscal and jurisdictional control over the sheep breeders, who, from the 13th century on, were combined in a special organization, the Mesta.[73]

In Spain, as in England, the sheep "ate" the people. But Spain differed from England in that, almost from the beginning, the princes profited enormously from the rapidly expanding pastoral economy. State revenues from this source were large.[74] Eventually the monarchs considered "the exploitation and conservation of the pastoral industry . . . the principal sustenance of these kingdoms." [75]

The huge revenues which the Crown received from its colonial empire have frequently been held responsible for the decline of the Spanish population in the 16th century.[e] However, the depopulation

e. Seville, which in 1247 had over 300,000 inhabitants, numbered in the 16th century 200,000. Cordoba, which under the caliphs may have harbored a million people, now

of the villages, which certainly was a major cause for the depopulation of the cities, cannot be satisfactorily explained thus, since the influx of gold and silver would have enabled the enriched townspeople to buy more rather than fewer rural products.

In all probability the downward trend was caused primarily by the replacement of labor-intensive irrigation farming by labor-extensive cattle breeding. This development, stimulated by the soaring export of wool,[f] led to the promulgation of the *Leyes de Toro*, which completed the "subjection of agriculture to large scale pasturage" [76] fourteen years before Cortez took Mexico and twenty-eight years before Pizarro took Cuzco. And it also accounts for the great reduction in the Indian farming population in post-Conquest Mexico, Yucatan, and Peru.[g]

In the Spanish countryside, herds and herders now made their

---

numbered 60,000 (Laborde, 1808: 9). The population of Granada decreased from perhaps 500,000 to 80,000 (see above, and Laborde, 1808: 9). These decreases resulted in part from military destruction; but in part they express the transformation of the rural order. Some sections of the countryside never recovered from the pestilence and the Reconquest (Klein, 1920: 337). Others were allowed to lie fallow during the 16th and 17th centuries (*ibid.*: 320, 342 ff.), until the formerly flourishing fields were "smitten with the curse of barrenness" (Prescott, 1838, III: 461, n. 85), because sheep breeding had been allowed "to run riot throughout the land and to annihilate almost the last vestiges of agriculture that still remained" (Klein, 1920: 343).

The known ruins of former settlements in Catalonia, Aragon, Leon, Valencia, Mancha, Castille, etc. numbered more than 1141. The region of the Guadalquivir had boasted 1200 villages under the Caliph of Cordoba. In 1800 only 200 survived. Of the fifty villages of Malaga, only sixteen were left. One section of the diocese of Salamanca had only 333 villages out of its former 748, while of 127 villages which existed near *des partidos de Banos peña del rey* only thirteen remained (Laborde, 1808: 8). The area of the kingdom of Granada that prior to 1492 had supported three million people numbered only 661,000 by 1800 (*ibid.*: 9).

f. The rise continued until the latter part of the 16th century (Klein, 1920: 37–46).

g. Ships were small and freight expensive; and nothing much was to be gained by exporting grain to Europe. Silver was the most highly prized export article; but handsome profits could also be made in sugar and cacao, dyewoods, dyestuffs, and hides (Humboldt, 1811, IV: 368 ff.). Within a few decades "oxen, horses, sheep, and pigs multiplied to a surprising degree in all parts of New Spain" (*ibid.*, III: 224). By 1570, when Acosta arrived in America, some individuals owned as many as 70,000 and even 100,000 sheep (Acosta, 1894, I: 418; Obregon, 1928: 151). Wherever the increase of cattle was not checked, the herds grew rapidly, not only in Central America but also in the Southwest of North America (Obregon, 1928: 151), in Peru (cf. Markham, 1892: 163; see also Juan and Ulloa, 1806, I: 300, 318, and *passim*), and in Yucatan (Shattuck, Redfield, and MacKay, 1933: 15). When Cortez set up a princely estate in Oaxaca, he at once "imported large numbers of merino sheep and other cattle, which found abundant pastures in the country around Tehuantepec" (Prescott, 1936: 671). Consistently, it was Cortez who in the New World organized a Mesta patterned after the Mesta of Castille (Mendoza, 1854: 225).

lonely way over vast grasslands. It was in this landscape that Don
Quixote urged on his stumbling nag. And in the cities no spectacle
was so popular as the bullfight. In Valladolid, in 1527, Charles V
celebrated the birth of his son, Philip II, by himself entering the
ring to challenge the bull.

e. The Introduction of Oriental Despotism into Russia

"THE TATARS had nothing in common with the Moors. When they
conquered Russia, they gave her neither algebra nor Aristotle."
Pushkin was doubtless correct in lamenting the negative cultural
consequence of the Tatar [h] conquest. He might have gone even
further and noted the devastating political consequences of their
fabulous military success. The Tatars, who by 1240 had crushingly
defeated the Eastern Slavs, controlled their new subjects so effectively
that no independent Russian power undertook to liberate them.

Nor did any internal Russian force engage in a systematic and
open struggle against the Horde. The isolated military victory at
the Don River, which the Grand Duke of Moscow, Dmitry, won
over a Tatar army in 1380, backfired sadly: the subsequent reprisals
discouraged armed resistance for another hundred years.[i] Even when,
in 1480, Ivan III refused allegiance to the enfeebled Tatars, he
avoided battling against them. The Tatars, while still able to lead
an army against the Muscovite host, were equally reluctant. Inde-
cision on both sides resulted in "an unbelievable spectacle: two
armies fleeing from each other without being pursued by anyone."
To quote Karamsin further: "So ended this last invasion of the
Tatars." [j]

h. The name "Tatar" originally referred to peoples living in the eastern part of
Inner Asia (see Wittfogel and Fêng, 1949: 101 ff.). After the great expansion of Mongol
power during the 13th century, the name began, in Eastern Europe, to denote those
Mongols and Turks who together formed the core of the Golden Horde. Merging
with older Turkish and Finnish groups, these "Tatars" spoke Turkish, a language
which by then had become the most important ethnic and cultural trait of the
westernmost sector of the Mongol world (Spuler, 1943: 11 n.). In the present discussion
the terms "Tatar" and "Mongol" are used interchangeably to designate the people
of the Golden Horde.

i. After 1380 the leading principality, Muscovy, "for the time being did not think
of fighting the Tatars" (Kliuchevskii, *Kurs,* II: 20).

j. Karamsin, HER, VI: 195–6. Karamsin considers this the most plausible version
of "the course of the great event." When the Khan, irritated by the Grand Duke's
disobedience and the smallness of his presents, advanced toward the Don River, Ivan
mobilized his troops and, after some weeks, moved them close to the Khan. But he
remembered the aftermath of the victory which Dmitry Donsky had won at the same
river a hundred years before. "Dmitry had triumphed over Mamai to see afterwards

So indeed ended Tatar rule over Russia. It had lasted for almost two hundred and fifty years; and the Grand Duchy of Muscovy, which rose to prominence during this period, did so not as an independent force but as the instrument of the Khan.

This fact is not disputed. Nor is it seriously denied that 16th-century Muscovy cannot be equated with Western absolutism. However, opinions differ fundamentally concerning the origin of Muscovy's despotism. Was Ivan's autocratic control over land and people due to external conditions, namely to a continually fought-over frontier? Or was it due primarily to internal and direct Oriental influence, above all to Tatar rule?

Historians who uphold the "external" interpretation lean heavily on the authority of the foremost modern Russian historian, Kliuchevsky. I fully share the esteem in which Kliuchevsky is held by scholars of the most diverse opinion; but I find his views on the emergence of Muscovite despotism less one-sided than is generally assumed.

True, Kliuchevsky has paid little attention to the Tatar Yoke,[k] and his understanding of Oriental despotism is limited.[m] But he

Moscow covered with smoking ashes and to pay a shameful tribute." The memory made him proceed with "prudent circumspection." He left his troops and returned to Moscow, where some of his followers accused him of having first infuriated the Khan and of now refusing to defend his country. "Finally the Grand Duke yielded to the general desire and promised to oppose the Khan." He returned to the front, and after some minor combats sent an envoy to negotiate with the Tatars. But no understanding was reached. After fifteen days Ivan ordered his army to withdraw to what he believed to be a more suitable place for combat. His soldiers, however, thought his command was inspired by fright. They lost their nerve and "fled in the greatest disorder." At this point, Karamsin's source notes, a miracle occurred: the Khan suspected the Russians of planning to ambush him; and "gripped by a panic of fear, he hastened to take his departure" (*ibid.*: 176–95).

k. Florinsky criticizes him for suggesting that when studying the political organization of northeastern Russia, one "should forget for a time . . . that Russia was conquered by the Tartars" (Florinsky, 1953, I: 78); and Vernadsky (1953: 333 ff.) notes that except for "a few general remarks on the importance of the khans' policies for the unification of Russia . . . [Kliuchevsky] paid little attention to the Mongols."

m. Kliuchevsky was not too familiar with the institutions of Oriental society and with such of its variants as traditional China. Otherwise he would not have contrasted the service-based class system of Muscovite Russia and the conditions of Oriental despotism (Kluchevsky, HR, III: 52). In another context, however, he notes the similarities in the Muscovite methods of liquidating potentially dangerous relatives and methods of Oriental despotism in like situations (*ibid.*, II: 88). And his description of state service and land tenure in post-Mongol Russia clearly indicates institutional affinities to Ottoman Turkey and Muslim India. His discussion of Peter's efforts to develop industry is a major contribution to our understanding of the Russian version of an agrobureaucratic despotism. The omnipotent state, based on enforced service and claiming ultimate control over all land, has also been viewed as a key element of

was too great a student to overlook the crucial institutional changes which, under Tatar rule and because of it, occurred in Russia's state and society. According to his own account, these changes definitely preceded the rise of the "frontier," with whose formative role he is so impressed.

Indeed, Kliuchevsky, in his "frontier" thesis, deals essentially with the post-Tatar period. He describes the changes involved in the recruiting of "a numerous military-official class" as being closely connected with "the territorial expansion of the empire," whose new frontiers had "placed the state in direct contact with such external and alien foes of Russia as the Swedes, the Lithuanians, the Poles, and Tatars. This direct contact had put the state in such a position that it had come to resemble an armed camp surrounded on three sides by enemies." [77] Manifestly, the Tatars of whom Kliuchevsky is speaking are those that confronted 16th-century Muscovy, and the frontier of which they form a part is the 16th-century frontier. Kliuchevsky says so expressly,[78] and several times he refers specifically to the years from 1492 to 1595.[79]

In view of these facts we cannot help feeling that Kliuchevsky's "frontier" thesis raises more questions than it answers. Why should a non-Oriental Russia evolve into an enforced-service despotism, because Russia was fighting such Western countries as Sweden, Lithuania, and Poland? Many European governments dealt with comparable enemies without establishing Orientally despotic patterns of control over land and people. Or why should a non-Oriental Russia become Orientally despotic when the Oriental forces she was combating were, relatively speaking, no stronger than the Turks, with whom the Austrians and Hungarians fought, or the Moors, with whom the Spanish reconquerors were engaged in a life and death struggle? Neither Hungary and Austria nor Spain became Orientally despotic because of their Oriental "frontier." We may therefore well ask: Could the Muscovite development of the 16th century have occurred because Russia, prior to this period and as the result of her long subjection to Oriental domination, had already taken decisive organizational and acquisitive steps in the direction of a despotic "service" state?

Kliuchevsky's frame of reference prevents him from giving a consistent answer to these questions. But it is amazing how far his account

---

Tsarist society by Sumner, who considers Tsarism to be rooted in the "ideas and ritual" of Byzantium and "the fact and practice of the Tatar khans." Elaborating this point, Sumner observes that it was under the influence of the Golden Horde rather than "far-away Byzantine administration" that the Muscovite government and military system originated (Sumner, 1949: 82 f.).

of 13th-, 14th-, and 15th-century Russia goes in affirming the socio-historical significance of the Tatar period.

According to Kliuchevsky, it was during this period that the towns, which had played a prominent role in Kievan Russia,[80] lost, with a few exceptions (Novgorod, Pskov), their political importance; [81] and it was in this period that the territorial princes and independent boyars, after a temporary improvement in their conditions, were sharply curbed by the grand dukes of Muscovy. Many princes became the serving men of Muscovy, whose new prince-officials by 1500 "overlaid, if they did not crush, the older stratum of Muscovite non-titled boyars." [82]

Why did this happen? In the matter of the political emasculation of the towns, Kliuchevsky shuts his eyes to the effects of Tatar rule,[n] which were pointed out earlier by Karamsin.[o] In the matter of the fate of the boyars and territorial princes, he recognizes that Tatar power enabled Muscovy to subdue them.

Kliuchevsky is aware that for more than two generations the Tatars operated the fiscal organization that they had erected in Russia: "After their conquest of Rus, the Tartars themselves first collected the tribute they imposed on Rus." [83] He is also aware that political and jurisdictional power accrued to Moscow when, in 1328, the Khan transferred this function to his Muscovite deputy: "The simple trustee-agent in charge of collecting and delivering the tribute of the Khan, the Prince of Moscow, was then made plenipotentiary leader and judge of the Russian princes." Subsequently the Khan's commission became "a powerful instrument for the political unification of the territorial states of Rus." [84]

In all these instances, Tatar influence is clear. It becomes still more impressive when we recognize the bureaucratic innovations that accompanied the political change. Kliuchevsky knows that the methods of registering land and tax payers which were used throughout

n. Kliuchevsky views this development as the result of the colonization of northern Russia (Kluchevsky, HR, I: 269). "Rus" did indeed expand northward, but this is only half the story. In Western Europe many towns, which were founded by princes or feudal lords, emancipated themselves. Why was it that in 13th- and 14th-century Russia princely authority grew at the expense of the towns? And why did the *veche* cease to function, even where it had previously prevailed?

o. Karamsin (HER, V: 451) ascribes the change to the increased authority with which the princes were endowed by the Tatars. Recently Vernadsky noted that "the destruction of most of the major cities of East Russia during the Mongol invasion" was followed by an equally devastating, and even more successful, political campaign against the towns and that in this campaign the Russian princes and boyars supported their Mongol masters. In the middle 14th century, the *veche* "had ceased to function normally in most East Russian cities and could be discounted as an element of government" (Vernadsky, 1953: 345).

the 16th and 17th centuries [85] had existed at the close of the 15th century and long before.[p] He knows that after the conquest of Russia the Tatars "during the first thirty-five years of the Yoke three times took a census, *chislo*, of the entire Russia people, with the exception of the clergy, by means of *chislenniki* [census takers] sent from the Horde." [86] Subsequent studies have thrown additional light on the original Tatar organization,[87] which may have served military as well as fiscal purposes.[88] Vernadsky plausibly suggests that *"it was on the basis of the Mongol patterns that the grand ducal system of taxation and army organization was developed in the late 14th to 16th centuries."* [89] His conclusion elaborates what Kliuchevsky had intimated fifty years before.

When describing the state post of 16th-century Moscow,[90] Kliuchevsky does not expressly connect it with earlier developments. But his remark, "the *Jamskoi prikaz*, the Department of Posts, which was known from the beginning of the 16th century," [91] in all likelihood points to Ivan III,[92] that is, to the close of the Tatar period. Other scholars have connected the postal system, *yam*, which the Tatars maintained in Russia,[93] with the Muscovite institution of the same name.[q]

The rise of Muscovite despotism coincides with the rise of the new type of civil and military serving men, who, as temporary holders of state land (*pomestye*), were unconditionally and unlimitedly at the disposal of their supreme lord. From the later part of the 14th century on, the grand dukes of Muscovy began to reduce the territorial princes to the position of serving men; [94] and in the 15th century they assigned office land—which was previously given only to unfree retainers [95]—to free serving men as well, mainly to warriors but also to civil ("court") officials.[96] Kliuchevsky is fully cognizant that this type of compulsory service differs from the conditions of Western Europe; [97] and it is therefore not surprising that in his discussion of the legal principles involved in the institution of the *pomestye*

p. Kluchevsky, HR, III: 228. The Tatar origin of the Muscovite system of census taking has been stressed among others by Miljukov (1898: 128) and Kulischer (1925: 404), the latter of whom, not without reason, assumes ultimate Chinese influence.

q. Brückner, 1896: 521 ff.; Milukow, 1898: 81; Kulischer, 1925: 405; Grekov, 1939: 216 ff. The Altaic term *yam*, "post," and *jamči*, "postmaster" (Spuler, 1943: 412) appeared in Russian as *jam* and *jamshchik* (Brückner, 1896: 503, 522). During the Mongol period, "the yam was a special tax for the upkeep of post-horse stations" (Vernadsky, 1953: 221). When in the early part of the 16th century Herberstein used the Muscovite state post, he had relay horses assigned to him "by the post-master, who in their language is called 'jamschnik' [sic!]." The relay stations were called *"jama"* (Herberstein, NR, I: 108). In the 16th century the Postal Chancellery was first called *jamskaja izba*, then *jamskoj prikaz* (Staden, 1930: 13, n. 4; cf. 15, 59).

he considers only two roots, both Oriental: Byzantium and the Tatar Horde. Rejecting the former, he is left with the Tatar alternative, suggested by Gradovski. According to this view, "the idea of the prince as the supreme landowner originated only during the Mongol period. As representatives of the authority of the Khan, the Russian princes enjoyed, in their territories, the same rights as the Khan himself enjoyed in all the territory under his rule. Later the Russian princes inherited these state rights from the Khan completely; and this shattered the incipient private ownership of land." [98]

It is characteristic for Kliuchevsky's ambivalence toward the Tatar issue that he fails to verbalize what, from the standpoint of his own premises, is the only logical conclusion. But he does not hesitate to stress the rapid growth of the *pomestye* institution at the close of the Tatar period. Evidently, "traces of an intensive and systematic distribution of public land in *pomestye* tenure can already be found during the second half of the 15th century." [99] The Muscovite princes established *pomestye* lands on a large scale first in newly conquered territories such as Novgorod; but in the early 16th century "a great development of *pomestye* tenure" also took place in the vicinity of Moscow.[100]

The comparative economic historian, Kovalevsky, expressly claimed a Tatar origin for the fateful institution: "It is a fact that prior to the 15th century we never hear of Russian princes paying for services except by the distribution of money and objects taken as war loot, whereas the assignment of military tenures under the name of *iktaa* was known in the entire Mohammedan world and especially among the Tatars for centuries prior to the appearance of this practice in Muscovy. These considerations led the author to state that this kind of practice was introduced to Muscovy and the other Russian principalities through the imitation of the Tatar khanates." [101] Vernadsky does not claim a direct link; but he too calls the Mongol age the "incubation period" of the *pomestye* system.[102]

In view of these facts it is hard to reject Vernadsky's conclusion that in the days of the Tatars the old free society of Kievan Russia was "persistently chipped away without at first affecting the facade," and that when Ivan III broke with the Horde, "the framework of the new structure was all but ready and the new order, that of a service-bound society, became clearly noticeable." [103]

It became clearly noticeable indeed. And a few decades after Ivan's death, the forces of despotism had gained sufficient strength to destroy ruthlessly the obsolete facade. The time lag between incubation and maturation reflects the contradictory interests of the Tatars, who wanted their Muscovite agency to be sufficiently strong to carry

out the will of the Khan but not strong enough to override it. Without foreseeing the ultimate consequences of their action, they built
an institutional time bomb,[r] which remained under control during
their rule but which started to explode when the "Yoke" collapsed.

Byzantium's influence on Kievan Russia was great, but it was
primarily cultural. Like China's influence on Japan, it did not seriously alter the conditions of power, class, and property. Ottoman
Turkey's influence on 16th-century Russia stimulated a regime that
was already Orientally despotic,[104] but it did not bring it into being.
Tatar rule alone among the three major Oriental influences affecting
Russia was decisive both in destroying the non-Oriental Kievan
society and in laying the foundations for the despotic state of Muscovite and post-Muscovite Russia.

F. STRUCTURE AND CHANGE IN THE DENSITY PATTERNS OF THE ORIENTAL WORLD

THUS Greece, Rome, Spain, and Russia all crossed the institutional
divide. In Greece, Rome, and Spain the pendulum swung back and
forth. In Tsarist Russia the reverse movement (away from a despotic
state) came close to bringing the country back into the Western orbit.
The changes that occurred in each of these cases were enormous;
but their character cannot be clearly understood unless the affected
institutional structures are clearly defined. Our analysis has tried
to do this. Approaching both structure and change from the standpoint of varying hydraulic and bureaucratic density, we can draw
the following major conclusions.

1. STRUCTURE

a. Density Subtypes of Hydraulic Society

THERE are two subtypes of hydraulically compact areas: one with
economically predominant and continuous hydraulic systems (Compact 1), the other with economically predominant but discontinuous
hydraulic systems (Compact 2). There are two subtypes of hydraulically loose areas: one with an organizationally predominant hydraulic system, which comprises major and regionally compact
hydraulic units (Loose 1), the other without major compact units
(Loose 2). And there are two subtypes of the margin of hydraulic
society: one containing conspicuous hydraulic elements (Margin 1),
the other lacking such elements (Margin 2). A seventh subtype, the
submargin, belongs to the fringe of the hydraulic world, because its

r. Vernadsky (1953: 335) appropriately speaks of "influence through delayed action."

representatives employ conspicuous elements of Orientally despotic statecraft. But since its dominant institutions are of a definitely non-hydraulic character, it must be placed on the outer fringe of this world.

b. Differing Frequencies of Occurrence

THE hydraulically densest subtypes of hydraulic society, Compact 1 and 2, are not the most frequent ones. Nor can the other subtypes be called less "advanced," if this term is meant to imply that eventually and necessarily they will become compact. Among the historically prominent hydraulic societies, and particularly among their larger representatives, the compact patterns are more the exception than the rule.

c. Decreasing Importance of Hydraulic Economy Proper

THE decreasing importance of hydraulic economy proper becomes clearly apparent when the agromanagerial world is viewed in its spatial and temporal entirety. There is little doubt that representatives of this world had a greater hydraulic density during their formative and primary phase than during their later and secondary developments.

In the formative phase, relatively small hydraulic commonwealths arose in semi-arid and arid settings. And if our genetic hypothesis is correct, we are safe in assuming that while, during this phase, a number of marginal hydraulic societies originated through diffusion, few such societies originated through the disintegration of larger, loosely hydraulic units, which were then practically nonexistent. The greatest number of marginal hydraulic societies—both absolutely and in proportion to the number of hydraulic societies proper—appeared therefore not during the formative phase, but after it.

This developmental peculiarity is accompanied by another which, although independent of it, aggravates its effects. For reasons which in the Old World are closely connected with the spread of nomadic conquest and globally with the lessening of hydraulic concern, hydraulic societies proper tend to reduce rather than increase their hydraulic intensity.

The specific density patterns of industrial and hydraulic society develop in different ways. The representatives of industrial society tend to become more industrial without of necessity becoming industrially compact. Conversely, the representatives of agromanagerial society seem to reach their highest hydraulic density coefficient during a relatively early phase of their growth. Afterward they hold their own or recede. Taken in its entirety, agromanagerial society apparently "advances" not to higher but to lower levels of hydraulic density.

2. CAPACITY FOR SOCIETAL CHANGE

OUR density analysis clarifies both structure and change. And it clarifies change—or lack of change—not only within the same societal type, but also from one societal type to another.

1) The formation of hydraulic society apparently depends on the presence of a hydraulic economy proper as an essential condition.

2) The perpetuation of hydraulic society is assured by a plurality of factors, among which hydraulic enterprise may play a minor part, and marginally no part at all.

3) The history of hydraulic society records innumerable rebellions and palace revolutions. But nowhere, to our knowledge, did internal forces succeed in transforming any single-centered agromanagerial society into a multicentered society of the Western type.

4) More specifically: neither in the Old nor in the New World did any great hydraulic civilization proper spontaneously evolve into an industrial society, as did, under nonhydraulic conditions, the countries of the post-Medieval West. In the marginal hydraulic civilization of Late Byzantium the rise of big private property led only to societal paralysis. In Russia, after severe attacks *from the outside,* the forces of private property (and their concomitant, free labor) prevailed in 1917 for a number of months over the system of despotic state power.

CHAPTER 7

ℐatterns of proprietary complexity in hydraulic society

NOT all hydraulic societies comprise independent proprietary forces of consequence. When such forces are present, they seem to be more of a threat to the margin than to the hydraulic heartlands, although even in these latter, strong proprietary developments intensify social differentiations and periodic political crises.

Hence, an institutional analysis of hydraulic society should deal not only with the density of its agromanagerial apparatus but also with the complexity of its proprietary development. Having explored the major patterns of hydraulic and bureaucratic density, we shall now examine the major complexity patterns of private property and enterprise which emerge under the shadow of agromanagerial despotism.

A. THE HUMAN RELATION CALLED "PROPERTY"

PROPERTY is the individual's recognized right to dispose over a particular object. Like other rights, the right called property involves more than a relation between a person and a thing. It involves a relation between the proprietor and other individuals who, through the former's prerogative, are excluded from disposing over the object in question.

The relation also involves the representatives of government, who, on the one hand, share the restrictions placed on the private non-proprietors and, on the other, are concerned with maintaining the existing property regulations. Thus in addition to being a legal and social institution, property is a political phenomenon. And property rights in different societies, even when they are similar in form, need not be similar in substance.

Strong property develops in a societal order which is so balanced that the holders of property can dispose over "their" objects with a maximum of freedom. Weak property develops in a societal order that is not so balanced.

The preceding chapters have described those peculiarities of hydraulic society which, by making the state inordinately strong, tend to make private property inordinately weak. Of course, weakness is not nonexistence. Hydraulic society has given rise to many forms of private property that, as far as external appearance goes, have their parallels in other societies. Some of these forms show a different degree of development in different hydraulic civilizations, and these distinctions are so regular—and so manifest—that we can establish several subtypes of proprietary (and societal) complexity.

B. OBJECTS OF PROPERTY RIGHTS

THE concepts of mobile and immobile property present obvious difficulties, but they have great advantages for our inquiry. Immobile property (essentially land) is the basis of private enterprise in the main branch of hydraulic economy: agriculture; and mobile property (tools, raw materials, merchandise, money) is the basis of its two most important secondary branches: industry (handicraft) and commerce. Persons, too, may become the object of a proprietary relation. Like many other institutional conformations, hydraulic society also knows slavery. But unlike mobile and immobile property, slavery under agromanagerial despotism does not establish specific patterns of independent enterprise and social position. We shall therefore discuss the peculiarities of this type of slavery in the next chapter, which deals with classes.

C. THE POTENTIAL SCOPE OF PROPRIETARY RIGHTS

A HOLDER of strong property may dispose over his property in a variety of ways.

He may put his property to whatever use he wants, as long as he does not interfere with the rights of other members of the commonwealth. He may employ it actively, either in the economic sphere (for purposes of subsistence and material gain) or in the sphere of physical coercion (for purposes of promoting his and his group's material or political interest); or he may employ it passively, consuming it for purposes of maintenance and pleasure.[a] Occasionally he may decide not to use it at all. He may make a piece of wood into a bow to serve him in a hunt or raid, or into a digging implement for farming. He may employ a piece of land for raising what crops he wishes, or for grazing or hunting, or he may let it lie fallow.

The holder of strong property whose active property produces gains

---

a. The distinction between productive and nonproductive property is a narrow, if important, economic variant of the wider dichotomy.

because he, either alone or with, or through, others, employs it effectively, is free to enjoy these gains fully. He owns the calf as well as the cow. He is free to alienate his property at will. And he is free to determine who shall inherit it when he dies.

D. THREE MAJOR COMPLEXITY PATTERNS IN HYDRAULIC CIVILIZATIONS

1. SIMPLE, SEMICOMPLEX, AND COMPLEX PATTERNS OF PROPERTY

THE holder of weak property may enjoy only a shadow of these prerogatives, but this does not destroy his desire to act as freely as he can. He exercises his modest rights with respect to both mobile and immobile, passive and active property. In the sphere of mobile and active property they become institutionally important when the holders of such property employ it professionally and independently in industry and commerce. Those who engage in handicraft or trade take a decisive step forward when they begin to devote themselves to these pursuits professionally, that is, full time. However, such an advance effects no major societal change, as long as the professional craftsmen and traders constitute only a new subsection within the class of government functionaries. It is only when they use their property to operate professionally *and* independently that they appear as a new class. The difference is not one of the "mode of production"—which may not change at all—but of the producers' and traders' political (and politically conditioned societal) position.

Land is tilled professionally (that is, by peasants who spend most of their time farming) as soon as agriculture becomes an essential basis of subsistence. And elements of private (independent) land-ownership emerge relatively early. But the landowners, who often do not till their soil themselves, are in many Oriental societies prevented from expanding the sphere of private agrarian property, since most of the land is, in one way or another, regulated by the government. It is only when free (nonregulated) land becomes the dominant form of land tenure that private landownership becomes a societal phenomenon comparable to the predominance of independent professional handicraft and trade.

Independent active property advances unevenly in its mobile and immobile sectors. These developmental differences are sufficiently clear and regular to permit distinction between at least three major patterns of proprietary complexity in hydraulic society:

1) When independent active property plays a subordinate role in both its mobile and immobile forms, we are faced with a relatively

simple pattern of property. We shall call this conformation a simple hydraulic society.

2) When independent active property develops strongly in industry and commerce but not in agriculture, we are faced with a semicomplex pattern of property. We shall call this conformation a semicomplex hydraulic society.

3) When independent active property develops strongly in industry and commerce and also in agriculture, we are faced with the most complex pattern of property to be observed in hydraulic society. We shall call this conformation a complex hydraulic society.

2. SUPPLEMENTARY REMARKS

a. "Simple I" and "Simple II"

How far can private and independent property advance in industry and commerce? And when does private ownership in land prevail over all other forms of land tenure? We shall attempt to answer both questions when we discuss the peculiarities of semicomplex and complex configurations of Oriental property.

Another question, however, must be settled first. Are there, within hydraulic society, conditions under which professional representatives of industry and commerce are altogether absent or, for all practical purposes, as good as absent? Such conditions do exist indeed. They occur essentially in hydraulic tribes, which for this and other reasons represent the most rudimentary variant of a simple Oriental society. We distinguish the tribal type of simple hydraulic society, "Simple I," from the state-centered type of simple hydraulic society, "Simple II."

TABLE 4. *Patterns of Proprietary Complexity in Hydraulic Society (Schematized)*

PATTERNS OF PROPERTY	SPHERES OF PROPRIETARY DEVELOPMENT			
	Agriculture Pursued:		*Industry and Commerce Pursued:*	
	Professionally	*Predominantly with Privately Owned Land*	*In the Main [1] Professionally*	*On Basis of Private Property and in the Main [1] Independently*
Simple				
I	⊕[2]	—	—	+[3]
II	+	—	⊕	—
Semicomplex	+	—	+	⊕
Complex	+	⊕	+	+

Key	
+ Feature conspicuous	1. The meaning of the qualification is explained in the text, p. 233.
— Feature inconspicuous or absent	2. The circle ⊕ indicates a developmentally new feature.
	3. Farmer-craftsmen and producer-traders.

b. Proprietary Complexity and Hydraulic Density

CORRELATIONS between the patterns of proprietary complexity, on the one hand, and patterns of hydraulic density, on the other, are less easily established. The rise of property-based enterprise and social classes is due to several factors, among which hydraulic density is only one, and one that in a given area tends to change its quality very slowly and usually only because of changing relations with other areas.

This, however, does not imply the absence of significant correlations between hydraulic density and proprietary complexity. Of the two major evolutionary steps that hydraulic property may take, at least the first—the transition from a simple to a semicomplex pattern —may be greatly retarded, if not altogether blocked, when the underlying agrarian order is hydraulically compact. Like the correlation between the rise of a state-centered simple hydraulic society and the advance of professional industry and commerce, this correlation will be clarified when we systematically discuss the characteristics of simple, semicomplex, and complex patterns of Oriental property.

E. NONSPECIFIC AND SPECIFIC ASPECTS IN THE PROPRIETARY CONDITIONS OF TRIBAL HYDRAULIC SOCIETIES

1. NONSPECIFIC ASPECTS

AGRICULTURAL tribes handle their property in many different ways; and this is as true for hydraulic as for nonhydraulic communities.[1] In the simpler farming communities of Melanesia, South America, and Africa "movables are privately owned, but not land."[2] Similar trends exist also among important groups of the American Northwest;[a] but in Melanesia and West Africa a more differentiated pattern has made its appearance. "As a rule, land was common property of the village, but in regard to cultivated land we find the beginnings of sib, family, or individual ownership."[3]

Up to a point conditions of land tenure are similar in hydraulic tribes. Among the smaller irrigation tribes of equatorial Africa land can be bought and sold. This is the case among the Suk[4] and the Endo.[5] Among the En-Jemusi it was originally "marked out by the chief," but now, when division after the father's death excessively reduces an allotment, an owner can augment his holdings by pur-

a. The Iroquois have a saying: "Land cannot be bought and sold, any more than water and fire can" (Lips, 1938: 516).

chase, as do the Suk; or following the earlier pattern, he may be given additional fields by his chief.[6] In the American Pueblos communal patterns of land tenure prevailed until modern times. In the Rio Grande area "unused agricultural land reverts to the town, to be reallotted by Town chief [*cacique*] or Governor." [7] Among the hydraulically marginal Hopi a "clan system of land tenure was universally in vogue"; [8] and the village chief, who was "the theoretical owner of all the village lands," [9] asserted his authority "most frequently . . . in the settlement of land disputes." [10]

Thus in both nonhydraulic and hydraulic small farming communities the forms of land tenure vary; and the tendency toward communal control is strong but not universal. Corresponding resemblances can be discovered also with respect to mobile property. Weapons as well as tools that are used in hunting and gathering are usually owned individually by hydraulic tribesmen; but the objects thus obtained are so perishable that their passing possession does not favor the development of class distinctions, whatever the methods of distribution.

Nor, under such conditions, do industry and trade lead to significant social differentiations. This is eminently clear with regard to trade. The exchange of privately owned goods is undertaken privately; but this does not require special training or full-time handling. As in the small nonhydraulic farming communities, there is trade in hydraulic tribes, but there are no professional traders.[b]

2. Specific Aspects

IN industry conditions are not so simple. Property-based crafts are practiced primarily to satisfy the farmers' personal needs; and those who, because they command particular skills or have access to particular materials, produce goods for exchange usually do so on a part-time basis, their major efforts still being devoted to agriculture. This is the prevailing pattern in both nonhydraulic and hydraulic tribes, and it is a pattern that is not fundamentally altered by the presence of a few professional craftsmen, such as smiths.[c]

b. Among the Pueblo Indians exchange between the various villages or with non-Pueblo peoples is maintained by individuals (Parsons, 1939, I: 35; Beaglehole, 1937: 81) or by trading parties (Parsons, 1939, I: 34 ff.). Market-like gatherings are organized, usually by women (Beaglehole, 1937: 82 ff.; Parsons, 1939, I: 36 ff.) and, it seems, spontaneously (Beaglehole, 1937: 81 ff.). For earlier conditions see Espejo, 1916: 183; Bandelier, FR, I: 101, 163; Parsons, 1939, I: 33 ff.; Hackett, 1923, II: 234, 236, 240, 242 ff.; for recent developments, see Parsons, 1939, I: 34 ff. For the Chagga see Widenmann, 1899: 69; Gutmann, 1926: 425, 431.

c. Beech, 1911: 18. The potters mentioned by Beech (p. 17) obviously give only part of their time to their craft.

Large-scale constructions are a different matter. Small farming communities of the nonhydraulic type usually lack the organizational integration for the execution of such enterprises; and some hydraulic tribes, such as the Suk and the Endo, have not applied the organizational methods they employ in hydraulic work to nonhydraulic objectives, as the American Pueblo Indians have done with amazing success. To be sure, the tools of the Pueblo builders were privately owned; but their building materials were secured under communal leadership, and the work was done by communal labor. Such arrangements do not promote a property-based private industry nor the growth of a group that derives its strength from private industrial property and enterprise. On the contrary. They clear the way for patterns of operation that retard the rise of nongovernmental proprietary forces in industry as well as in other sectors of society.

In the sphere of hydraulic works these antiproprietary forces appear regularly. A primitive peasant, using his own tools, cultivates land that may or may not be communally regulated, and the seeds for his crops may belong to him personally or to his kin group. Under nonhydraulic conditions this is the whole story. In a hydraulic setting cultivation proper follows a similar pattern; but the "preparatory" operations do not. The tools are privately owned, but the raw materials for making the hydraulic installations (earth, stone, and perhaps timber) either are communal property—that is, owned by nobody or everybody—or, if they are to be found on land held by a particular individual, family, or clan, are taken over by the community. And the end products of the community's coordinated effort, the ditches or canals, do not become the property of the individual farmers or farming families that participate in the work, but, like the water which they carry to the individual fields, they are controlled ("owned") by the community's governing agency.[d] This proprietary peculiarity can be discerned in the incipient hydraulic communities of the Hill Suk, whose "irrigation ditches are the property of the tribe, not of the individual." [11] In the irrigation villages of the En-Jemusi the irrigation ditches are also the property of the tribe; [12] and this is equally the case with the larger, communally built, irrigation installations of the Pueblo Indians.

To evaluate these facts properly we must remember that the communities discussed so far are small farming societies—that is, communities in which the basic unit of tribal activity is almost always the village. In a nonhydraulic setting the headmen of the small units do not, as a rule, have authority over any substantial communally

d. Small ditches that require the labor of only a few individuals or a kin group are the property of those who make them.

owned and communally managed property. Such property, however, characterizes the hydraulic village; and in most cases it is administered by ceremonial and/or operational leaders.[e]

This proprietary development has another aspect, which has already been noted but which in the present context assumes a new significance. In small nonhydraulic farming societies a headman, who exerts little functional leadership, does not have his fields tilled for him by the community. Among small hydraulic tribes the headman, even when his leadership is overtly recognized, is not always so privileged either.[f] However, among the Pueblo Indians, who in most cases combined a compact hydraulic agriculture with large nonhydraulic constructions, the chief's fields were cultivated for him, even in villages that numbered only a few hundred inhabitants.

Among larger hydraulic tribes, such as the Chagga, the existence of the chief's fields cannot be considered specific, since such land arrangements occur in large nonhydraulic communities. But in large hydraulic tribes the chief's fields tend to be extensive; and work on them (and on the chief's houses) is done not by a limited number of retainers but by all able-bodied tribesmen.[g] Another proprietary peculiarity is entirely specific: the chief's privileged claim on the tribe's irrigation water.[13]

The extraordinary concentration of land, water, agricultural and

e. For the Pueblos the directing authority of the *cacique* and the war chief is well established. The situation among the Hill Suk is less clear. Beech (1911: 15) recognized that communal discipline was invoked in hydraulic work, but he was unable to discover any directing secular leader, or for that matter any religious leaders: "medicine men" (*ibid.:* xiv, n. 1). However, an "Elder" plays a prominent role in two crucial agricultural ceremonies, one pertaining to the clearing of the land, the other to the opening of the irrigation ditches (*ibid.:* 15 ff.). Sir Charles Eliot doubts the validity of Beech's anarchistic picture (*ibid.:* xiv, n. 1); and he does so by citing military requirements. No doubt the need for military leadership exists in almost all independent communities, but Eliot's military argument would be equally valid for the small nonhydraulic farming communities, whose chiefs rarely have more than a "purely representative position" (Lips, 1938: 515). In the Pueblos tribal leadership is definitely linked to leadership in communal activities, and among them hydraulic work ranks first. Expanding Eliot's reservations, we suggest that the germs of an operational authority were present among the Hill Suk, particularly in the matter of the tribe's most important property, its hydraulic installations.

f. The chief occupies a conspicuously strong position among the En-Jemusi (Beech, 1911: 37), but there is no evidence of any public fields being tilled for him.

g. The Chagga chieftain demands corvée labor from the tribe's adult males, from the women, and from the adolescent boys. These three groups work for the chief, in agriculture: cutting the bush (men), burning (men), hoeing (women), watering the seeds (men), raking and weeding (women), irrigating (men), and harvesting (women) (Gutmann, 1926: 376); in construction work: cutting and transporting timber (men), building proper (men), carrying of heavy loads of straw for the roofs (women), bringing up material for fences, etc. (the "boys") (*ibid.:* 376, 368).

industrial labor in the hands of the chiefs does not enhance personal, family, or clan ownership.[h] It does not benefit the social position of private craftsmen, who in the larger hydraulic tribes become somewhat more numerous.[i] Nor does it favor private professional merchants.[j] Specifically, it hampers the expansion of private property in what is frequently an important secondary branch of the subsistence economy: herding.

The tribal history of many European civilizations shows how, in an agrarian economy, growing cattle wealth is a factor in establishing societal leadership. In East Africa animal wealth is similarly esteemed; and in a predominantly pastoral community, such as the Masai, this wealth, which is eagerly displayed,[14] is an essential means of determining the owners' social position.[k] Not so among the Chagga. Cattle, which under the peculiar conditions of the Chagga area were largely stall-fed,[15] increased substantially; and some tribesmen owned as many as eighty head.[16] But in Chagga society the owners of large herds did not necessarily enjoy a higher social status, although they certainly enjoyed added material advantages. The Chagga chieftain, thanks to his quasidespotic powers, easily found a pretext for ac-

h. Until recent colonial times the bulk of all Chagga land was controlled, first by the clans and subsequently, and increasingly, by the chieftain. The clans yielded to the chief some of their authority over the banana lands, which were probably the first to be cultivated and required some irrigation (Gutmann, 1926: 303; Dundas, 1924: 300 ff.). The fields of eleusine millet, which had always required intensive irrigation "are marked out and allotted by the Chief himself. So are the maize fields in the plains, and this allotment is one of the important duties of the Chief" (ibid.: 301). For recent colonial developments in the chieftain-controlled maize sector see Gutmann, 1926: 307.

i. Among the Chagga, even more exclusively than in the Pueblos, trade is in the hands of women (Widenmann, 1899: 69; Gutmann, 1926: 425).

j. Among the Chagga the only professional craftsmen are the smith and perhaps the tanner (Widenmann, 1899: 84; Gutmann, 1909: 119; Dundas, 1924: 270 ff.). The smiths live in special localities and they may only marry women from families of smiths (Widenmann, 1899: 84; Gutmann, 1909: 119; Dundas, 1924: 271).

k. Merker, 1904: 28. Among the Pastoral Suk, who "rather look down upon them [the Agricultural (Hill) Suk] on account of their poverty" (Beech, 1911: 15), cattle wealth seems to be decisive for the establishment of communal prominence. A certain Karôle, who had the reputation of being the "richest" of the Suk (ibid.: 7, n. 1), rose as high politically as the undifferentiated conditions of his tribe permitted; he became his group's "most important advisor" (ibid.). But the overt authority of the "advisors" was extremely slight; and it is doubtful whether, among the Pastoral Suk, any of them exerted more power covertly, since no communal enterprise known to us provided an opportunity for invoking generally accepted disciplinary methods. It is probably no accident that the poorer but incipiently hydraulic Hill Suk prosecuted persons who violated the tribal laws more severely than did the wealthier plainsmen: "The punishments for crime in the hills are far stricter than in the plains" (ibid.: 27, n. 1).

cusing conspicuous cattle owners of some malfeasance or other and for confiscating some or all of their animals.[17] And the Chagga herders, instead of boasting of their growing cattle wealth, became increasingly secretive and fearful. An earlier practice of farming out cattle to poorer tribesmen for foddering [18] became a convenient device for hiding their valuable but insecure property. The animals were now handed over to their temporary keepers furtively and by night; [19] and the owners' sons, who originally had played an important role in the transfer,[20] were at times not even informed as to where the cattle were placed. Says Dundas: "So secret does he keep the whereabouts of his stock, that he will not even tell his sons where it is." [21] This trend gained strength with the growth of chiefly power, which occurred prior to the establishment of colonial rule. It was further aggravated when, under this rule, the chief started to raise a general cattle tax.[22]

In this setting private wealth does not necessarily, or even primarily, establish public prominence.[m] Among the qualities that in the earlier time favored chieftainship, wealth probably was a desirable but not a necessary factor; and the chief's property certainly grew not in proportion to what wealth he or his forefathers may have had originally but in proportion to his growing agromanagerial and military power. For his aides the ruler chose men who were prominent in their locality [23] or—and increasingly—men whose personal qualifications fitted them for the job.[24] In both cases selection involved a conspicuous improvement in the material conditions of the chosen, for the chief provided his serving men with cattle and women.[25] In fact, Merker found that only persons in government positions were rich.[26]

3. SIMPLE I . . .

MANIFESTLY, hydraulic tribes like nonhydraulic agrarian tribes develop private property. Both conformations present undifferentiated forms of property (as in handicraft and trade) and a trend to-

---

m. Gutmann (1909: 7) says that rich tribesmen may withhold irrigation water from the poor, but in a later and more detailed study he describes the equalitarian way in which all members of a given hydraulic unit are provided with water (1926: 418).

He also refers to certain "nobles" who obviously owned cattle and who helped a chieftain obtain office (*ibid.:* 462). But no details are given regarding this incident, which occurred at the beginning of the 19th century (*ibid.:* 461), that is, before the chief's leadership in communal affairs had been fully established. And the clan leaders did not owe their rank to wealth, though, once chosen, some of them probably had opportunities for improving their economic condition (*ibid.:* 15). A clansman became ceremonial leader because he was the oldest male in the group (*ibid.:* 13), and the political leader, the "speaker," achieved his position on the basis "not of his age, nor of his wealth, but of his political shrewdness" (*ibid.:* 14).

ward regulated forms (as in farming with respect to land). At the same time, however, significant differences may be observed. Under hydraulic circumstances, political property already emerges in small hydraulically compact communities (the chief's land in the Pueblo villages). In larger tribes political property expands one-sidedly, and it retards and cripples private property in important spheres of activity (such as herding).

The difference between this one-sided accumulation of property in the hands of the governing authorities and the pluralistic patterns of proprietary growth in nonhydraulic agrarian tribes reflects perfectly the differences in the character and weight of political authority.[n] In the German tribes observed by Caesar and Tacitus the chieftain, although recognized as the top-ranking political leader and expected to devote much of his time to his governmental duties, was unable to restrict or tax the wealth of his nobles. Nor did he demand corvée labor or taxes from his tribesmen, who would have considered such a request an insult and who, like the nobles, participated in the public discussions of the tribe's affairs.[27]

Thus in tribal hydraulic societies property is simple, but it is simple with a specific tendency toward the predominance of political, power-based, property. This tendency increases with the size of the community. It becomes decisive in simple hydraulic commonwealths that are no longer directed by a primitive (tribal) government, but by a state.

F. PATTERNS OF PROPERTY IN STATE-CENTERED SIMPLE HYDRAULIC SOCIETIES

1. STATEHOOD VERSUS PRIMITIVE GOVERNMENT

CONTROL over a distinct territory has been considered a basic aspect of statehood. This aspect is indeed essential; but it has little value in the present context, since it is not specific. (As a rule, primitive governments also claim control over their territory.) Nor does the criterion of sovereignty help much. (Primitive governments also strive to establish sovereignty; and like states, they are not always able to.)

The differences between a primitive government and a state seem inconsequential so long as we confine comparison to external relations. They become significant when we compare internal conditions.

---

n. As elaborated above, in most nonhydraulic communities tribal coordination is required mainly for military and ceremonial purposes, whereas the heads of hydraulic tribes, in addition to exerting military and/or religious leadership, fulfill specific, vital agromanagerial functions.

Primitive governments are operated in the main by nonprofessionals —that is, by functionaries who devote the bulk of their time not to the civil, military, or religious affairs of the community but to their own hunting, fishing, farming, or raiding. States are operated in the main by professionals—that is, by functionaries who devote the bulk of their time to "public" affairs. From the standpoint of human relations a state means government by professionals.

Certain communal functions, such as the maintenance of internal order and the organization of defense, are vital for the perpetuation of all types of society. Consequently, man's political activities are as essential as those involved in the securing of food and shelter; and the professionalizing of government is as important an aspect of social differentiation as is the professionalizing of those economic or intellectual pursuits that under more primitive conditions are handled only by persons who are primarily engaged otherwise.

It goes without saying that a statelike government with its full-time civil and military officials, its soldiery and police can invest much more time and energy in administrative and coercive activities than a primitive government. It is this power potential of the state that makes its control by responsible and effective nongovernmental forces the only guarantee against the rise of a totally powerful (and totally corrupt) apparatus state.

Many Marxists, following Marx' and Engels' interpretation of the Western state and disregarding their stress on the peculiarity of Oriental despotism, have described "the state" as an institution that *always* serves the special interests of a property-based ruling class. This interpretation, which today, in its Soviet version, is part of an extremely widespread—and extremely potent—political myth, is not true even for modern parliamentary governments, whose plutocratic potential it generalizes and whose capacity for growth and democratization it denies. Nor does it fit the states of Western absolutism and feudalism, nor indeed the democratic states of ancient Greece. And it is completely absurd when it is applied to the agrarian and industrial apparatus states that are characterized not by the strong influence of nongovernmental proprietary forces on the state, but by the abysmal lack of any such influence.

2. Steps in the Professionalizing of Government

a. Chagga Chieftainship and the State of Ancient Hawaii

THE difference between primitive government and statehood becomes unmistakably clear when we juxtapose the single full-time and

community-supported leader of a Pueblo village and the large staffs
of government functionaries in Pharaonic Egypt, imperial China, or
Ottoman Turkey. The almost complete predominance of nonprofessionals in the first case is as manifest as the almost complete predominance of professional apparatus men in the second. The
difference is less obvious, but perhaps even more informative, when
we compare the regimes of large hydraulic tribes, such as the Chagga,
with the state of a relatively crude neolithic hydraulic civilization,
such as ancient Hawaii.

The absolutist acts of a Chagga chief are impressive: he kills, [a]
spies, seizes his subjects' cattle,[b] and keeps as many girls as he wishes
in his palace.[c] In addition and more importantly, he is the commander in chief of the tribe's laboring and fighting force.[d] Nevertheless, his ability to rule the lives of his subjects is limited by the small
number of his full-time functionaries. Highest among them is "a
person who may best be described as his prime minister, and on
whom much of the executive work devolves."[1] Below this tribal
version of a vizier are certain helpers and advisors, *akida,*[2] who "receive the chief's orders, convey them to the people, using for this
purpose special helpers, and supervise and organize their execution.
Such orders pertain, for instance, to the making and repairing of
canals, work for the chieftain . . . payment of taxes and religious
affairs."[3] The *akida,* who are expected to spend a considerable part
of their time at the chief's palace,[4] apparently have one assistant each;[5]
but the professional officialdom ends here. Clan heads may advise
the chief,[6] staying at his palace for this very purpose, and most of
the on-the-spot directing remains in the hands of the clans. The
hornblower, the actual leader of the corvée, is selected by members of
his clan and only confirmed by the chieftain.[7] Obviously, he is
not a full-time salaried functionary.[8]

a. To demonstrate his loyalty a Chagga dignitary was ready to burn his sister to
death when ordered to do so by his chieftain (Gutmann, 1914: 219).

b. As punishment for an alleged crime, Chieftain Mapfuluke is said to have seized
the cattle of one of his fathers-in-law. Later, and quite unexpectedly, he returned some
part of them (Gutmann, 1914: 231).

c. Gutmann (1926: 388 ff.) estimates that, in one instance, the chieftain assembled
from among rank-and-file families more than 5 per cent of all girls. These young
females were then assigned to his wives; but the chieftain maintained his sexual rights
over all of them: "None of the girls entered marriage untouched, the chieftain used
them as he pleased."

d. The Chagga chieftain makes the supreme decisions concerning the hydraulic
corvée and other large-scale secular enterprises. He commands his tribesmen in war;
he assigns residences to all; and he fixes the dates for sowing and harvesting (Gutmann,
1909: 25).

Nor does the chieftain have at his disposal professional guards or policemen. The warriors who protect his person—and this is particularly demanded at night—are ordinary members of the tribe who return home after their shifts are done.[9]

The supreme head of the Chagga government is occasionally referred to as a "monarch" or "king." [e] However, the majority of all observers designate him as "chieftain." [10] Conversely, the ancient Hawaiian rulers are sometimes called "chiefs," but in more scholarly treatises they are designated as "kings." The preferred titles reflect the general conviction that the Chagga ruler presides over a more primitive type of government than does his Hawaiian counterpart. This conviction seems well founded. In the first case we are faced with a primitive government that has elements of incipient statehood, in the second with a crude but genuine state.

The Hawaiian kings disposed over a much more differentiated staff of top-ranking aides than did the Chagga chieftains. In addition to a chief councilor, the Hawaiian ruler had a chief war leader, a chief steward, a treasurer, and "land experts." [11] There is no evidence that clan heads acted as his advisors or that his guards served part time. Besides a "body guard," the king had at his beck and call a detachment of armed men headed by an executioner—official terrorizers who were always ready in the king's name to accuse, arrest, and kill.[12]

In the Hawaiian government the professionals were not confined to the top echelon. Below the leading officials there were primarily and most importantly the *konohiki*. In contrast to the Chagga *akida,* who spent much of their time near their chieftain, the *konohiki* seem to have resided and officiated for the most part in the regions of their jurisdiction, directing the regime's constructional, organizational, and acquisitive operations. They kept count of the population; [13] they mobilized the corvée; [14] they directed the hydraulic enterprises; [15] they supervised agriculture; [16] they gathered the tax,[17] retaining some of it for their own use and for the use of their underlings, but passing on most of it to the higher authorities, and eventually to the king.[18]

Manifestly, the *konohiki* and their aides were government-supported full-time functionaries. The organizational and acquisitive network that they spread over the countryside probably contributed more than any other political institution to making the government of ancient Hawaii a crude, agrobureaucratic hydraulic despotism.

e. Gutmann, 1909: 10 ff. Lowie (1938: 302) calls him the head of a "monarchical system."

b. Proprietary Consequences

CONTROLLING a much more fertile territory and a much larger population—the largest Hawaiian kingdom had five times the population of the largest Chagga tribe *f*—the Hawaiian rulers were in a better position to establish and maintain a permanent officialdom. And this larger officialdom in turn enabled them to control their subjects' property more completely. In Hawaii the government's jurisdiction over the land was not restricted by any clan rights, as was the case among the Chagga.[19] Nor did a clan head stand between tax-collecting officials and individual taxpayers, as in Chaggaland.[20] Indeed the Hawaiian regime functioned so well that the masters of the apparatus state were able to syphon off over half of the entire rural produce. According to one estimate, "the common laborers did not receive on an average more than one third of the avails of their industry." *g*

On a smaller scale the difference between the two types of government appear also in the sphere of circulation. The Chagga markets were policed by the chief's wives and regional officials;[21] but a market tax on agricultural products and salt was collected by a member of one particular clan.*h* In Hawaii we find no trace of such divided authority. The functionaries who sanctioned the transactions and taxed the goods were toll collectors—that is, government officials.[22]

Thus the kings of Hawaii exerted a much more formidable power

f. In the 18th century some 300,000 Hawaiians were organized in a few sovereignties, the largest of which, Hawaii proper, numbered more than 85,000 people (Lind, 1938: 60). Lind's figure harmonizes well with an estimate made by Ellis in 1826 (Ellis, 1826: 8). Ellis considered the total of 400,000 inhabitants suggested by the earliest observers "somewhat above the actual population of that time, though traces of deserted villages, and numerous enclosures formerly cultivated, but now lying waste, are everywhere to be met with." In 1826 there were between 130,000 to 150,000 people on the archipelago (Ellis, 1826: 8). Fornander, although suggesting smaller figures than Cook and King, sees "no valid reasons for assuming a greater or more rapid depopulation between 1778 and 1832, when the first regular census taken gave an approximately correct enumeration of 130,000 than between the latter year and 1878, when the census gave only 44,088, exclusive of foreigners" (Fornander, PR, II: 165). At the beginning of the 19th century Bali had a population of about 760,000 persons, with some of the island's major kingdoms accounting for more than 100,000 persons each (Lauts, 1848: 104–5). The largest Chagga tribes numbered less than 20,000, 10,000, or 5,000 persons respectively (Gutmann, 1926: 1).

g. Alexander, 1899: 28 n. Blackman (1899: 26) presents this estimate as "the opinion of careful observers."

h. Gutmann, 1926: 426 ff. The clan functionary grasps a handful of taxable goods. The trading women have the right to kick him once; but they cannot prevent him from seizing the fee, which "at a well attended market amounts to fairly sizable loads" (*ibid.*: 427).

over their subjects' life and property than did the Chagga chieftains. Difference in the form of reverence strikingly expresses the difference in autocratic power. As already mentioned, the Chagga tribesmen hold their ruler in great esteem, but unlike the Hawaiians they do not perform before him the classical gesture of total submission: prostration.

3. Simple Patterns of Property in Land, Industry, and Commerce

In the early phases of state-centered hydraulic societies, private property in land is not necessarily lacking; its origins go back much further than was assumed by the pioneer institutionalists of the 19th century. But the greater part of all cultivable land is regulated, and thus kept from being privately owned, even after private and independent property emerged notably in industry and commerce. For this reason, we shall discuss the problems of hydraulic land tenure later. With respect to the simple patterns of hydraulic property we need only state here that, within the framework of these patterns, the forms of land tenure are many but that regulated land always prevails (and generally by a substantial margin) over privately owned ("free") land.

Property-based and independent handicraft and commerce, however, must be examined immediately, for their occurrence makes, as we see it, a change in the patterns of property and society. This development is not uniform.

It advances unevenly in the spheres of

A. Industry, in
1. The extractive industries (mining, quarrying, certain forms of salt production)
2. The processing industries
   a. Constructions
   b. Others

and also in

B. Commerce, in
1. Foreign trade
2. Domestic trade, dealing with
   a. Easily supervised goods (such as salt, iron, tea, wine, oil, etc.)
   b. Others.

In all hydraulic societies proper and in most marginal hydraulic societies, the government engaged in comprehensive constructions. Employing a large labor force, the agrarian apparatus state enjoys what amounts to a monopoly of all large-scale construction work.

Often it also manages those extractive operations which provide the bulk of all raw materials for the large government constructions. Other extractive industries, such as mining and certain forms of salt production, may either be directly managed by the government or, and particularly under the conditions of a money economy, they may be controlled through monopolistic licensing.

Thus property-based and independent action cannot hope to prevail in the most important sector of hydraulic industry: large-scale constructions. Nor can it hope to operate freely in the large extractive enterprises. Only in the nonconstructional sector of the processing industries is there a chance for property-based free handicraft to become significant. Indeed, apart from the making of coins, only a few manufacturing pursuits, such as the production of weapons and certain luxury goods, may be directly managed by the government, while most other crafts are handled entirely by private and independent entrepreneurs.

Free private enterprise, however, does not necessarily mean large enterprise. Large-scale industries are extremely vulnerable on the fiscal level, and except for government-protected units do not prosper under the shadow of total power. The many private and independent crafts which have emerged in certain hydraulic societies are essentially confined to small shops and small-scale operations.

The development of independent private trade may be retarded under conditions of great hydraulic and bureaucratic density (compactness), but it is not blocked by the state's managerial predominance, which, with regard to the construction industries, appears in all hydraulic societies proper and also in many marginal hydraulic societies. Above the level of the producer-trader, commercial business is transacted over significant distances, either overland or oversea. This favors large-scale action, particularly since the merchandise so handled is less conspicuous and therefore less vulnerable fiscally than a fixed and conspicuous industrial plant.

When the law of diminishing administrative returns induces a state to limit its own commercial operations, independent merchants tend to appear both in foreign and domestic trade; and governmental attempts to maintain direct and indirect controls in both sectors at a particular level or to restore them to an earlier level are based for the most part on short-range considerations.[i]

---

i. This is why government policy in this regard in China, India, and the Near East oscillated so considerably. The student of Chinese history will recall the discussions which Han administrators conducted concerning the way in which the sale of salt and iron should be handled. The problem arose in pre-Han days, and different solutions were found at different times. The administrative history of India is not

Hydraulic society outgrows the simple patterns of property, when private and independent handicraft becomes prominent in the processing industries (excluding, of course, large-scale construction) and when big and independent merchants handle as much or more business than all government-managed and government-controlled commerce taken together.

The almost complete absence of pertinent statistical data compels us to formulate our criteria broadly. In some branches the relative proportions are evident. In others we can at least establish prevailing trends.

4. VARIANTS OF SIMPLE PATTERNS OF HYDRAULIC PROPERTY AND SOCIETY

a. Hawaii

THE Hawaiian archipelago is so distant from the more southerly regions of the Polynesian world that after an early period of daring expeditions, "all intercourse with the southern groups seems to have ceased, for there is no further evidence of it in any of the ancient legends, songs, or genealogies for five hundred years." [23]

Nor were the relations between the various Hawaiian kingdoms sufficient to stimulate the development of commerce above the producer-trader level.[24] Internal circulation consisted in the main in the transfer of rural surpluses from the peasant and fishermen producers to the local and central representatives of the government. Exchange between individuals occurred either in the form of "gifts" [25] or barter; [26] and in both instances without the aid of professional middlemen. Markets and fairs provided ample opportunity for such activity. Ellis' descriptions of what was then considered the most famous fair makes no reference at all to any professional merchants. The only professional person noted by the observer was the government official who supervised and taxed the transactions between the barterers.[27] When, in the early 19th century, contact with the outside world opened up a new outlet for sandalwood, it was the king and his lieutenants and not independent private

---

so well documented as that of China, but what we know about Indian fiscal policy suggests similar oscillations.

The history of state and private commerce in the great hydraulic countries of the Near East is still in its infancy; and attempts, such as that made recently by Leemans, reveal the institutional importance of this phenomenon as well as the difficulties of investigating it. The Near Eastern data show again that in contrast to the great hydraulic works and the big nonhydraulic constructions, large-scale commerce can readily be handled by private and independent merchants.

Hawaiian merchants who handled the resulting international trade.[28]

The undeveloped conditions of circulation reflect the undeveloped industrial conditions, and these in turn are closely connected with the paucity of suitable raw materials. The volcanic islands of Hawaii lack metals; and this deficiency kept the islanders, as long as they were separated from technically more advanced civilizations, at a relatively crude level of neolithic life. The archipelago had useful plants (such as taro and the coconut tree) but none of the world's major cereals; and there were no animals that could be used to ease man's labors. Lava was the only important workable stone.

The technical skill which the Hawaiians developed in this natural and cultural setting was admirable.[29] However, even maximum ingenuity produced only a modest differentiation in the crafts. Specialists built canoes [30] and houses,[31] made nets, fish lines, tapa cloth,[32] and many other articles,[33] yet the economic and political position of these artisans is none too clear. A number of them may well have worked for their own account.[j] But neither Hawaiian tradition nor early non-Hawaiian observers suggest that these private artisans could compare in importance with the craftsmen who served the king and his functionaries. The government, which controlled an enormous percentage of the country's surplus, was able to support many artisans, *poe lawelawe*. The supreme *poe lawelawe* was a member of the central government.[34] He seems to have directed the industrial activities undertaken for the benefit of the government and obviously through the use of corvée labor. In addition, he was in charge of the numerous artisans who were permanently attached to the court. Says Kepelino: "At the chief's [king's] place there were many workers or *Poe-lawelawe* of every description." [35]

Thus in ancient Hawaii professional artisans appeared most significantly as persons who, supported by the government, worked under government functionaries for the ruler and his serving men. This constellation, together with the complete absence of independent professional merchants, created in ancient Hawaii a very rudimentary variant of simple patterns of hydraulic property and society.

b. Inca Peru

THE masters of the Inca empire drew upon natural resources that were richer than those of Hawaii but poorer than those of Egypt, Mesopotamia, China, or India. The agriculturists of the Andean area entered the metal age at a relatively late date; and even then they did not process iron. Nor did they domesticate animals for use in farming. To be sure, in hydraulic civilizations the absence of labor

j. Several trades had special patron gods (Alexander, 1899: 37, 62 ff.; Blackman, 1899: 32).

animals is of less importance to crop-raising [k] than to transportation, which is basic to the spread of military and political control, to the collection of taxes, and to the growth of trade. However, compared with the donkey, the mule, the ox, the horse, and the camel—the chief labor animals of the Old World—the llama, although useful for its wool, was a poor instrument of locomotion. The absence of navigable rivers, in addition to a rugged coastline, discouraged experiments in shipping, except on primitive rafts; and a scarcity of culturally advanced neighbors discouraged international trade much more decisively than was the case in Pharaonic Egypt.

TABLE 5. *Factors Stimulating Commerce and Regional Division of Labor in Industry*

HYDRAULIC CIVILIZATIONS	LABOR ANIMALS	NAVIGABLE RIVERS AND BOATS	CULTURALLY ADVANCED NEIGHBORS INVITING INTERNATIONAL TRADE
Inca Peru	(—)	—	—
Pharaonic Egypt (particularly the Old and Middle Kingdoms)	+	+	(—)
The various states of ancient China	(+) [1]	+	+
Sumer	+	+	+

Key
+   Present
—   Absent
( ) Development limited

1. The ox was used for plowing only at the close of the Chou period.

Our analysis has revealed a number of factors that stimulate commerce and regional division of labor in industry. We indicate in Table 5 the uneven development of these factors for a number of major simple hydraulic civilizations. Although by no means the only formative features, they aid us in recognizing the uneven development of trade and industry in these civilizations.

In the Andean area transportation was further discouraged by the desert-like conditions in large segments of the coast and by the high and steep elevations in the strategically located mountain regions. For all these reasons, effective and long-distance communication proceeded essentially on land and not on water; and it depended

k. An approach which recognizes the crucial role of hydraulic operations in the development of agriculture cannot be content with Lowie's otherwise suggestive typology of subsistence economies: "hunting, farming with hoe or dibble, farming with plow and livestock, and stockbreeding without farming (pastoral nomadism)" (Lowie, 1938: 283). The Near East, India, and China shared the plow and labor animals with Europe and Japan; and the reason for the differences between the stationary hydraulic civilizations and other agrarian civilizations that were not stationary must therefore be looked for elsewhere, and most decisively, it would seem, in the presence or absence of hydraulic agriculture.

to an extraordinary degree on roads that were built and controlled by the omnipotent hydraulic state. There were a few foreign-merchants; [36] and some of the trade in salt and fish reported for the northern border zone [37] may have been handled by professionals. But such developments were so peripheral and of so little importance that serious scholars, such as Means, have completely overlooked their occurrence. Within the empire government officials directed the transfer of enormous quantities of goods—corn, beans, cotton, timber, metal, textiles, etc.—along the coast, on the *altiplano,* and from one zone to the other; and small producer-traders exchanged products by barter at the many fairs that were held regularly throughout the country.[38] But there is no evidence that any private agency competed with the government in long-distance transportation and distribution of goods. Trade there was, and on a local level obviously plenty of it. But there were almost no independent professional traders.

The industrial sphere of Inca life was much more differentiated, but the private artisans remained inconspicuous in comparison with government-employed craftsmen. The mines were managed either by the local heads of formerly independent territories or by nonlocal members of the imperial officialdom.[m] In both cases they were controlled by professional officeholders who, in one way or another, were part of the over-all agromanagerial apparatus.

More precise information exists concerning certain aspects of the processing industries. The large construction teams were directed by prominent Inca functionaries; and the work patterns of Hawaii, Pharaonic Egypt, and early China suggest that here, too, special officials may have been in charge of the permanent government workers and those craftsmen who, for two months or "at most" three months,[n] rendered industrial labor service in the state workshops. Among the permanent craftsmen that the government occupied there were apparently many silversmiths [39] and also not a few carpenters.[40] Weavers, shoemakers, lumbermen, and makers of copper tools are mentioned as working at home after having fulfilled their corvée obligations.[41] Garcilaso's description does not make it clear whether all, or most, of these last worked exclusively at their specialities or whether some—or even most of them—were farmer-artisans. If we assume that most of them were professional craftsmen, it is even more noteworthy that the early accounts of rural and urban

m. Local mining of gold in accordance with directions from Cuzco is indicated by Polo de Ondegardo (1872: 70 ff.). Cf. Cieza, 1945: 269; Sarmiento, 1906: 100; Rowe, 1946: 246; Garcilaso, 1945, I: 253; Sancho de la Hos, 1938: 181.

n. Notable overtime was deducted from the following year's corvée labor (Garcilaso, 1945, I: 255).

life do not mention them. It was only as permanent workers for the state or as members of the industrial corvée that the artisans became a conspicuous feature of Inca society.

The "virgins," who were selected by officials from among the young and attractive females of the empire, provided the regime with a unique, but eminently useful, labor force. The "Selected Ones" were kept under strict supervision in special houses, where they spent the greater part of their time weaving, spinning,[42] and preparing beverages.[o] The sovereign included some of them in his harem; and he assigned others to prominent dignitaries. But there were always large numbers of them confined to the "houses." Apparently there were many such establishments in the Inca empire: some had two hundred inmates,[43] the one in Caxa had five hundred,[44] the one on Lake Titicaca one thousand,[45] and the one in Cuzco usually more than fifteen hundred.[46] Economically, the Inca "houses" constitute an interesting parallel to the textile shops of 17th- and 18th-century Europe. Few of these latter employed more persons, and those employed were in the main women, who often worked only part of the year.[47]

Despite a not inconsiderable technical development, Inca society developed no conspicuous, independent, private-property-based classes. The sinecure land, which the Incas assigned to certain members of the ruling group, created no full-fledged landownership; [48] and professional private enterprises were virtually absent in the spheres of transport and trade, which in other civilizations favored the rise of independent rich merchants. Professional private artisans, who certainly existed, remained an insignificant force even in the processing industries, when compared with the numerous craftsmen who permanently or temporarily practiced their skills in the government workshops and "houses." An interesting if feeble trend toward private handicraft notwithstanding, the Inca empire represents a simple pattern of hydraulic property and society.

o. CPLNC: 309. The two Spaniards who gave Sancho de la Hos (1938: 181) a first-hand report on the Lake Titicaca temple mentioned only the preparation of sacred wine by the women, if the chronicler recorded their story correctly. But whatever the accuracy of the initial report, it seems most unlikely that the thousand "selected" women of the Lake Temple made nothing but *chicha* the year round, and this in the classical region of llama-breeding and wool production. Our doubts are strengthened by *The Anonimo's* comment on the dual activities of the women at Caxa (CPLNC: 309) and by Garcilaso's description of the institution in the Inca capital. Obviously the virgins also had to prepare *chicha* and certain ceremonial foodstuffs, but their main operation (*il principal exercicio*) was spinning and weaving (Garcilaso, 1945, I: 188 ff.). There were many other houses of the same kind throughout the country. Their inmates engaged in the same economic activities. They "spun and wove and made an enormous amount of cloth for the Inca" (*ibid.*: 189).

c. Pharaonic Egypt

A UNIQUELY serviceable river provided the masters of Pharaonic
Egypt with excellent facilities for internal communication; shipping
was therefore well advanced at the dawn of written history. But
scarcity of raw materials did not necessitate a regular foreign trade;
nor was such trade stimulated by culturally advanced neighbors. The
Egyptian ships and beasts of burden permitted the establishment of
some external contacts, but these contacts remained intermittent—
and essentially government managed—until the close of the Middle
Kingdom.

During the New Kingdom, and particularly in the days of the
empire, private merchants emerged. But often they were attached
to the temples [49] and apparently they were no match for the state.
According to Kees, during a great part of the New Kingdom the
Pharaoh remained "the only big merchant." [50]

To be sure, foreign merchants did business in Egypt, but native
middlemen were given even less opportunity in domestic than in
foreign trade.[51] In the local markets producer-traders exchanged their
goods directly, and in the main by barter.[52] A market official of the
New Kingdom significantly bore the title "Scribe of Barter." [53]

Handicraft offered more room for the development of private
enterprise. No matter to what extent the census data of the Old
Kingdom imply the presence of independent trades during that
period,[p] the cases of Hawaii and Inca Peru show that professional
artisans operated in state-centered hydraulic societies that were technically less advanced than the Old Kingdom. And a number of
records from the Middle and the New Kingdom definitely speak of
private artisans.[54]

These Egyptian private artisans were more conspicuous than their
colleagues in the Inca empire; but, like them, they probably catered
essentially to the every-day needs of small consumers.[55] Did they, at
least numerically, equal the many craftsmen who in the processing
industries were permanently or temporarily employed by the government and the temples? Even this is not certain. But there can be
little doubt that economically they were less significant.

The government engaged particularly in three kinds of industrial
work: (1) extractive and preparatory operations requiring much
labor, some of it skilled, but most of it unskilled; (2) big construction
enterprises, requiring a combination of skilled and unskilled labor;
and (3) processing industries, carried out in the main by skilled

---

[p]. Kees (1933: 164 ff.) hesitates to accept E. Meyer's interpretation of these data
as proving the existence of free artisans and merchants.

craftsmen who were gathered together in larger or smaller workshops.

In all three sectors the skilled craftsmen, who included artists of great ability,[56] seem to have been largely government employees. The "chiefs of work" [57] probably had supreme jurisdiction over them. In the branch industries they operated under specially designated foremen.[58]

On the basis of carefully weighed evidence Kees concludes that "the economic life of [Pharaonic] Egypt constituted a not very appropriate soil for an estate of *independent* free artisans." [59] He finds the concept of free handicraft, except for lowly producers who satisfied lowly needs, "poorly suited for the economic picture of the Old Kingdom." [60] After the interlude of the Middle Kingdom, during which territorial courts became outstanding centers of the arts and crafts,[61] the New Kingdom increasingly forced the artisans into state-regulated workshops and subjected them to the rigid control of the state storehouses that allocated the raw materials.[62]

Documents from the New Kingdom show the state artisans eager for promotion to higher posts. Their foremen considered themselves fairly distinguished members of the bureaucratic hierarchy.[63]

To summarize: the power of the Pharaohs was so all embracing that private and independent handicraft made little headway, and independent professional commerce during the greater part of the period even less. The prevalence of state trade and the weight of government-managed industry, together with the dominance of state-regulated landed property created—and maintained—in Pharaonic Egypt a historically and institutionally significant variant of the simple pattern of hydraulic property and society.

d. Ancient China

THE most archaic Chinese inscriptions, the divination texts of the Shang dynasty, mention sets of shells, which in all probability were used as means of exchange. But they do not clearly refer to professional merchants. Neither do merchants play a conspicuous role in the inscriptions and literary texts of the Chou dynasty. Although in early China there certainly was trade, there seem to have been few, if any, professional traders.

Big merchants, who traveled overland, are reported for the first part of the later Chou period, the time of the "Spring and Autumn Annals" (721–481 B.C.). But those on whom the data are fullest cooperated so closely with their rulers that they can probably be considered to have been government attached.[64]

During the last phase of the Chou dynasty, the time of the Warring

States, independent merchants increased in importance—so much so, in fact, that in the 4th century B.C. the state of Ch'in took measures to restrict them.[65] By the time Ch'in had welded "all-under-heaven" into an empire, the great Unifier, Ch'in Shih Huang-ti, decimated the ranks of the merchants by sentencing them to guard the frontier, at first the merchants themselves and then their sons and grandsons.[66] This policy demonstrates both the economic importance and the political weakness of nongovernmental professional traders at the end of the Chou period.

The early Chinese records that have so little to say about professional traders are more articulate about craftsmen. The beautiful bronze artifacts of Shang and early Chou reveal extraordinary industrial refinement. However, and different from conditions in feudal Europe, the Chinese crafts developed not on many and separated manorial estates or in guild-controlled burgher towns but rather in big administrative centers controlled by the Son of Heaven, the territorial rulers, or their high ranking officials. Artisan-officials, the "hundred artisans," are mentioned in the oldest literary texts as well as in the early bronze inscriptions.[67] Apparently government artisans employed their skills under the supreme direction of the Minister of Works, the *ssŭ-kung*,[68] and alongside the "people," who as part of their corvée duty constituted the unskilled labor force of the government's large constructional enterprises.

Government-attached artisans may have prevailed until the time of the "Spring and Autumn Annals";[69] and perhaps it was only during the subsequent period of the Warring States that private artisans became increasingly important.

We have no conclusive evidence that, under the Chou dynasty and under the first imperial dynasties, private merchants or artisans organized independent professional corporations (guilds).[q] The retarded development in this regard is surprising when we remember that private handicraft and particularly private trade flourished at the close of and after the Chou period. Whatever the reasons for this unevenness, we are probably safe in suggesting that a simple Oriental society prevailed in ancient China until the end of Early Chou (722 B.C.) and probably also in the first centuries of Later Chou.

q. Shops dealing with the same goods were apparently assembled in the same locality from the close of the Chou period on or from Early Han days (Kato, 1936: 79), and probably also prior to this time. But it "was not until after the Sui period that the expression 'hang', used in the sense of a street of shops of the same trade, came into general use"; and it was only "at the close of the T'ang period, or even later, that they [the Chinese merchants] came to organise a real merchants' association" (*ibid.*: 83).

e. Sumer

THE agricultural civilizations of Lower Mesopotamia originated in a setting that was as lacking in certain industrial materials as it was encouraging to interarea exchange. The alluvial landscape, which because of its well-watered rivers offered ideal opportunities for hydraulic development, lacked stone, timber, and metals. However, these materials, which were essential to technical, military, and political growth, were available in adjacent lands, and from the standpoint of wealth, security, and power the incentives to obtain them were enormous.

The ancient Hawaiians did not get from abroad the raw materials that they lacked at home; and the Andean Indians and early Egyptians created urban civilizations mainly on the basis of their own resources. The Sumerians developed a flourishing urban life, because they succeeded in establishing and maintaining an elaborate system of international relations and exchange.

Needed raw materials can be obtained by organized force: war. But this is not always appropriate, and particularly not when the sources of supply are remote and those in control strong. In many cases the sought-for goods had to be acquired by peaceful means—that is, primarily by trade.

Long distance trade requires the services of specialists in transportation and exchange. In Lower Mesopotamia merchants appeared early. While traders played an insignificant role in almost all other simple Oriental civilizations, they were conspicuously mentioned in the Sumerian protohistorical inscriptions of Fara; [70] and in later and more detailed inscriptions they were depicted as important professionals.

The development of urban centers of administration and religion also involved a fairly advanced division of industrial labor; and the Sumerian inscriptions contain many references to artisans, who practiced their skills professionally. How developed were private property and private enterprise in early Lower Mesopotamia?

Deimel's elaborate investigations suggest that from the dawn of history on,[r] the Sumerian temple cities probably offered less opportunity for independent craftsmen than did ancient Hawaii, Peru, and Pharaonic Egypt. Like the other members of the temple com-

---

r. According to Deimel, the ancient Sumerians apparently depended as much on the temples, when the Fara texts were written, as they did three or four hundred years later, when Urukagina ruled Lagash. "The population then too served the temple and lived on it" (Deimel, 1924a: 42).

munity, the artisans received land,[71] and like them also, they rendered corvée service,[72] which, according to Schneider's tentative estimate, may have lasted some four months a year.[73] A number of craftsmen were employed permanently in temple workshops,[74] as were certain slaves (in the main female).[75] The majority of all artisans, however, seems to have worked for the temples through the operation of a putting-out system: temple storehouses provided them with raw materials, which they processed at home and for a wage.[76] The position of these artisans was not unlike that of many European craftsmen who during the first centuries of industrial capitalism worked in a similarly decentralized way for their commercial or industrial employers.

Were all domestic artisans of early Mesopotamia so engaged? And did any of them engage at least in some independent business? The second question is more easily answered than the first. The fact that all (or some?) of the workmen offered the temples certain tax-like "gifts" [77] is best explained by the assumption that they were able to produce something for their own account.[s]

The private activities of the Sumerian merchants were apparently much more extensive. No doubt these merchants were not independent of the city or temples either. They, too, were assigned land, but much more than the artisans—in fact, as much as a middle official or officer.[t] They could have their fields cultivated for them by tenants, wage laborers, or slaves; and their landed possessions, instead of handicapping them in their commercial activities, probably provided them with additional means for their business enterprises. As merchants, they were attached either to the supreme authority of the city state,[78] or to a temple, the second most important unit of power.[79] And obviously and in the main, they traded for the "palace" or the temples.[80]

In their transactions the great merchants, *gal damkar,* and the ordinary merchants, *damkar,* enjoyed considerable freedom; [81] and

---

s. A. Schneider assumes that the artisans who worked at home for the temples "apart from this, and perhaps already against a remuneration, also executed orders from other members of the temple community" (1920: 85).

t. According to inscriptions collected by Hussey, a *damkar* of the Bau Temple received 19 *gan* of land (Schneider, 1920: 66). One *gan* could support more than one person and two *gan* a small family (*ibid.*: 35 ff.). A top-ranking temple executive, mentioned in Hussey's material, received 43 *gan* (*ibid.*: 35). Another text gives much higher totals for the land assigned to high officials: 90 *gan* and even 138¾ *gan* (*ibid.*). Heads of military detachments or other prominent warriors received 23, 24, 26, and 18 *gan,* and a temple official *engar* 17¾ *gan* (*ibid.*: 110 ff.). Among the artisans, a carpenter was given 1 *gan,* a chariot maker 1 to 2 *gan,* a tanner 3 *gan,* and cooks and bakers from 2¼ to 6 *gan* (*ibid.*).

in addition they were permitted to trade for their own account. They might have business dealings with the ruler,[82] with the queen,[83] with members of the ruling family,[u] and with less highly situated persons.[84] Manifestly the opportunities for amassing wealth were vast.[85]

Thus in contrast to ancient Hawaii, China, and Pharaonic Egypt, Sumer saw a very early development of private enterprise in trade. And whereas the country's artisans, even when they were engaged in domestic industry, were closely tied to the temple economy, the merchants, who were neither trading officials nor governmental commercial agents but something in between, were much less so. Few simple hydraulic societies moved as conspicuously toward a property-based and independent commerce as did ancient Sumer.

5. ORIGINS OF BUREAUCRATIC CAPITALISM

THE great merchants of Sumer, who had funds of their own and who traded directly with their sovereign, occupied a position very different from that of the commercial specialists of the Pharaohs. The representatives of the Pharaohs, who traded with Punt,[86] Phoenicia,[87] Mesopotamia,[88] and Cyprus,[89] handled government property for the advantage of the government. They accomplished an exchange of goods often under the guise of diplomatic "presents," but they had a keen eye for the values involved. They asked for specific items,[90] they carefully examined the objects offered them,[91] they criticized inadequate gifts,[92] and they stressed the need for reciprocity.[93] Whatever presents were given them during, or át the end of, their expeditions were given them as servants of the king and not as independent businessmen. In short, they were governmental trading officials not too different in their position from the members of a Soviet Trade Mission.

In contrast to such trading officials, the government-attached merchants used their own capital largely, or exclusively, in the service of their rulers, who—while providing them with excellent opportunities for doing business—might also set the conditions (prices, profits) under which these opportunities could be utilized. To invoke a designation that originally pleased the Chinese Communists but that now embarrasses them, these merchants were "bureaucratic capitalists." [94]

In a wider sense, the designation "bureaucratic capitalists" is applicable to several groups: (1) tax collectors, who act as fiscal agents

u. Scholtz, 1934: 59. Princes or princesses occupied a number of artisans, servants, and slaves (Deimel, 1929: 126, 128; *ibid.*, 1931: 110).

for a ruling bureaucracy; (2) officiating or nonofficiating members of such a bureaucracy, who on the strength of their political position engage in private enterprises, such as trading, money lending, and tax farming; (3) private businessmen, who as commercial agents or contractors do business for the ruling bureaucracy; and (4) private businessmen, who attach themselves to individual members of the bureaucracy to assure the success of their transactions. Bureaucratic capitalists, then, are owners of capital who act as commercial or fiscal agents for an apparatus state, no matter whether they are members of the officialdom or functionaries of the dominant religion, or persons of wealth who are neither.

The records of ancient China are not clear on the subject of trading officials, although it seems likely that in the Shang and Early Chou periods certain functionaries of the early territorial states fulfilled commercial tasks. They are more articulate on the presence of government-attached commercial agents. Indeed such persons are sufficiently conspicuous to justify our tentatively classing Chou China, up to the period of the "Spring and Autumn Annals," as a simple Oriental society.

For Inca Peru the very problem does not arise seriously. Officials of the frontier districts may have traded government-owned goods against goods produced abroad; and some transactions may well have been concluded privately. But Inca society seems to have had little need for trading officials and still less for government-attached commercial agents.

The Sumerian inscriptions contain many references to foreign trade (internal exchange was mainly confined to barter).[95] Unfortunately, however, the texts leave many questions unanswered. What kinds of commercial transactions were involved in the many government expeditions that were undertaken to acquire stone,[96] wood,[97] metal,[98] bitumen,[99] and other items? Were the majority of all merchants primarily trading officials or governmental commercial agents? No matter what the answer to these questions may be, the character of ancient Sumerian society provides scant justification for interpreting the "merchants" of the oldest inscriptions thus far deciphered as independent entrepreneurs.

6. THE HYDRAULIC SPONGE

MOST of the hydraulic civilizations that achieved considerable proprietary differentiation seem to have maintained simple patterns of property at an earlier time. In some cases, such as India, simple conditions of property and society gave way relatively quickly to semicomplex configurations. In other cases, such as Egypt and Lower Mesopotamia, they prevailed for millennia. In the Andean area they were (still or again?) dominant when the conquistadores arrived.

The variations in the persistence of simple patterns of property assume a new meaning as soon as they are correlated with variations in hydraulic density. The hydraulic centers of Peru, Egypt, and Lower Mesopotamia all gave birth to compact systems of hydraulic agriculture, whereas many of the territorial states of India and China and, for that matter, of Mexico relied on loose or marginal types of Oriental agriculture. We do not, in this context, cite Hawaii, because in that archipelago the perpetuation of extremely simple patterns of Oriental property was obviously due to an extraordinary combination of internal and external circumstances. However, in the first instances the contrast in hydraulic density patterns is too striking to be dismissed as irrelevant. In all probability the early independent hydraulic communities of the Andean zone traded beyond their borders, and this early trade may well have been handled not only by commercial officials but also by government-attached private merchants, who may to some extent have acted for their own account. But Sumerian history demonstrates that strong hydraulic regimes can keep the bulk of all traders attached to the government even in separated city states. Thus it is not impossible that in the Andean area (as in Sumer and Pharaonic Egypt, but perhaps with more marked oscillations) there prevailed, even prior to the Incas, simple conditions of power, property, and class.

In Peru these conditions may have endured as long as state-centered and hydraulic civilizations were present in the area. In Egypt they outlasted the relative isolation of the hydraulically complex Nile Valley. And in Lower Mesopotamia they persisted even after the compact hydraulic heartland had been incorporated into larger and looser hydraulic conformations. Leemans assumes a high development of private property and trade [100] when the second Sumerian empire under Ur III for a brief period reached to the Mediterranean Sea, Assyria, and Persia. However, according to the same authority, state trade prevailed again under the last Larsa ruler, Rim-Sin,[101] under the Babylonian king, Hammurabi,[102] who defeated him, and for over four centuries under the Kassites.[103]

In these compact hydraulic societies the "dense" bureaucratic apparatus obviously acted like a powerful hydraulic sponge, whose capacity to absorb vital functions of industry and trade was superior, other conditions being equal, to that of less compact hydraulic communities.

G. SEMICOMPLEX PATTERNS OF HYDRAULIC PROPERTY AND SOCIETY

BUT such compact and self-perpetuating simple hydraulic societies are not too numerous. In many hydraulic civilizations the agromanagerial apparatus state, while keeping the bulk of the cultivable land from becoming private property, did not so seriously restrict the growth of nongovernmental, property-based, and professional handicraft and commerce.

1. OCCURRENCES

a. Pre-Conquest Meso-America

THE rise of independent professional artisans and merchants in Aztec Mexico contrasts illuminatingly with conditions in Inca Peru. A complete lack of transport animals handicapped the inhabitants of Meso-America; but this deficiency was largely compensated for by a number of other ecological advantages. The terrain was far more suitable for interterritorial communication; navigable lakes, rivers, and an extended and approachable coast stimulated the circulation of goods by boat. The Sumerians enjoyed similar advantages; and we should not be surprised to learn that like them the Aztecs and their predecessors, the Toltecs, had private professional merchants and carried on an extensive international commerce.[1] These conditions also promoted a technical and regional division of industrial labor. But neither the city states nor the larger territorial units of pre-Conquest Mexico were as hydraulically compact as were their Sumerian counterparts. Thus the professional artisans and merchants of Mexico were not equally dependent upon the hydraulic state. Their plots of land were allotted by the *calpulli,* local and stratified units that possessed a limited autonomy; [2] and apparently neither group rendered extended labor services. Except for references to houses in which females were assembled,[a] we have little evidence for government workshops.[b] According to Zurita and other early sources, the artisans rendered no corvée labor but paid over part of their produce

---

a. According to Torquemada, houses with females, "nuns," were "widespread" (Torquemada, 1943, II: 189, 191). Diaz, who observed traditional Aztec society before it disintegrated, asserts that there were "nunneries" in a number of Central American countries. In Mexico proper he knew of only one, in the capital (Díaz, 1944, I: 349 ff.).

b. Díaz (1944, I: 346) mentions government-managed bakeries. Sahagun (1938, III: 75) speaks of persons who made shoes for the lords. Was the work in the government shops performed by serving men, who, while hereditary members of the *calpulli,* worked exclusively for the sovereign? (Monzon, 1949: 41.) Is this what Torquemada (1943, II: 488) had in mind when he said that certain work was done by artisans as tax.[3] Except for the time they spent in tilling their fields, the many Mexican craftsmen [4] seem to have deployed their special skills for their own account, preparing articles to be sold at the markets that were held in the large communities.[5]

The small traders were probably as independent as they were insignificant.[c] But the big interterritorial merchants, the *pochteca*, were close to the governmental apparatus. Permitted to rent out their plots of land [6] and to render tax instead of labor service,[7] the *pochteca* could engage in full-time commerce. They served the government as diplomats [8] and spies.[9] Occasionally they conducted military campaigns on behalf of their sovereign.[10] Tezozomoc says that the king's own brothers and uncles were *pochteca*.[11]

Manifestly, these big merchants were part of the ruling class.[12] But they were not commercial officials. Being rich, they operated with their own funds, and essentially, it would seem, for their own account. They might also collect taxes for the government,[13] and at such times, they were bureaucratic capitalists in the narrow sense of the term. However, this was no universal practice, for we know that as a rule the taxes were levied by full-time officials.

And there is still less evidence that the Mexican *pochteca* and/or their aides traded largely on order of the ruler and the temples, as did the Sumerian *damkar*. Thus, however close the *pochteca*'s associations with the "lords" may have been socially and politically, professionally they do not seem to have been part of the state apparatus. It is for this reason and because of the independence of the artisans that we view Aztec Mexico as a semicomplex hydraulic society.

The exact position of the Maya artisans is not easily determined. Clearly they were given fields, *milpa*,[14] and contrary to practice in Aztec Mexico they seem to have received allotments, not from semiautonomous heads of the *calpulli* but from regional representatives of the central government.[15] The Maya commoners who built "houses" for the "lords" may well have included artisans; but the records are not articulate on this point. They are even less articulate on government-managed workshops, which as in Mexico were probably not absent altogether. But as in Mexico, the Maya craftsmen probably produced and traded mainly for their own account.[16]

Lacking a comprehensive agromanagerial officialdom, the Maya rulers did not maintain an elaborate state trade. Some "rich" men were members of the governing class,[17] but it is doubtful whether the

---

"for the lords"? Or are we faced with residual forms of an industrial corvée, which, although still invoked, had ceased to be institutionally relevant?

c. Apparently they dealt in foods, cloth, and cacao on a modest scale and for a lowly clientele (Sahagun, 1938, III: 40, 53, 77).

big Maya merchants in their entirety were as close socially to the secular and priestly leaders as were the *pochteca*. According to Landa, men of wealth lived near the "lords" and priests, but not in the same quarter.[18] Could it be that the crystallization of a property-based and nongovernmental group of professional merchants had advanced further in the hydraulically marginal lowlands of Yucatan than in the hydraulic core of Mexico?

b. India, China, the Near East

IN India semicomplex patterns of hydraulic property and society prevailed throughout the greater part of its recorded history. In China and the Near East simple patterns of property yielded to more complex configurations and with differing results. China operated on a semicomplex level at least twice, once during the last centuries of the Chou period and again from the later part of the 5th century to the 8th century A.D. In the Near East complex patterns of property possibly prevailed only during a certain phase of Roman rule, whereas semicomplex configurations were prominent both before and after that time.

Thus varying forms of semicomplex hydraulic property and society prevailed in India almost from the dawn of written history to the 19th century, in China altogether for some five hundred years, and in the Near East for two long periods covering two thousand years or more.

c. Byzantium and Russia

IN Byzantine society there was no lack of private craftsmen and merchants. As a matter of fact, Byzantine trade was both comprehensive and flourishing during the middle and later part of the first millennium.[19] But the Byzantine artisans and merchants no longer had the freedom of action that their predecessors had enjoyed in the Greek cities of Western Asia or in Rome prior to the victory of bureaucratic absolutism. Administrative and fiscal restrictions burdened the craftsmen and traders of Byzantium until the 11th century,[20] pressing them into a peculiarly crippled variant of a semicomplex pattern of hydraulic property.

In post-Mongol Russia private property in land evolved unevenly and as far as the peasants were concerned, very late. Professional and free handicraft recovered slowly from the setbacks instituted under the Mongol yoke. Commerce offered much greater opportunities to those who controlled it, and the masters of the Muscovite apparatus state were eager to manipulate it either directly, through trading officials, or indirectly, through commercial agents. In the sphere of domestic trade government functionaries first purchased wax, honey, and other items, "taking them at smal prices what themselves list, and selling them againe at an excessive rate to their own marchants, and to marchants strangers. If they refuse to buy them, then to force them unto it." [21] The government also sold goods that it received as taxes or tributes and obviously with a similar disregard for the buyer, for such goods were "forced upon the marchants to be bought by them at the emperours price, whether they will nor no." [d]

Foreign merchants too had to submit to government regulations. Once inside the Russian realm they had to display all their commodities before the officials, who "put a value on them"; [22] and they could not trade with private individuals before the Tsar was given an opportunity to buy what he wanted. [23]

But the Muscovite state was unable to manage the bulk of all large-scale circulation as did the regimes of Pharaonic Egypt or Inca Peru. The Tsar comprehensively employed the services of a number of rich merchants, particularly the *gosti*. These bureaucratic capitalists, who collected taxes and custom fees for the government, [24] usually acted as the Tsar's commercial councilors and agents. [25]

Outside the government trade proper, commerce was carried on, among others, by the *pomeshchiki*. These holders of office land sold the surplus grain and other surplus products of their estates for their own account, [26] thus constituting a group of bureaucratic capitalists *sui generis*. The monasteries, which were linked and subordinated to the state, also engaged in commercial transactions, not infrequently on a large scale. [27]

All this did not leave much room for the operations of professional and independent trade. The *gosti* and a small number of other privileged merchants controlled a large segment of the market, [28] seeing to it that "nowhere free commerce be permitted." [29] Such at least was the opinion of the ordinary merchants, who played a decidedly inferior role and hated the *gosti* bitterly. [30]

Privileged merchants of the Muscovite period could amass great wealth, but neither this wealth nor their semi-official position protected them against the confiscatory actions of their despotic masters. Fletcher reports a case in which three brothers of unusual energy and daring built up a thriving trade that yielded them "300,000 rubbels in money, besides landes, cattels, and other commodities." Fletcher ascribes this initial success partly to the fact that the brothers lived more than a thousand miles from Moscow. For a while they

d. The government profited particularly from the quasimonopolistic sale of furs, grain, and wood (Fletcher, 1856: 57 ff.).

stood well with the authorities, who charged them with the administration of certain customs along the Siberian border. The Tsar was
"content to use their purse, till such time as they got ground in
Siberia." Finally, however, the government took away their fortune
"by pieces, sometimes 20,000 rubbels at a time, sometime more; till
in the end their sonnes that now are, are well eased of their stocke,
and have but small parte of their fathers substance: the rest being
drawen all into the emperours treasurie." [31]

Private property and property-based enterprise suffered immensely
from this ruthless policy. "The great oppression over the poore
commons," so Fletcher,

> maketh them to have no courage in following their trades: for
> that the more they have the more daunger they are in, not onely
> of their goods but of their lives also. And if they have any
> thing, they conceale it all they can, sometimes conveying it
> into monasteries, sometimes hiding it under the ground and
> in woods, as men are woont to doo where they are in feare of
> forreine invasion. . . . I have seene them sometimes when they
> have layed open their commodities for a liking . . . to look
> still behind them and towards every doore: as men in some
> feare, that looked to be set upon and surprised by some enimie.[32]

Under such conditions most of the commoners preferred immediate
satisfaction to long-range planning: "This maketh the people (though
otherwise hardened to beare any toile) to give themselves much to
idlenes and drinking: as passing for no more then from hand to
mouth." [33] It is difficult to find a more colorful and more depressing
picture of private mobile property under the conditions of a crippled
semicomplex hydraulic society.

2. How Powerful Could the Representatives of Private Mobile and Active Property Become in Semicomplex Hydraulic Societies?

How much power may the potentially wealthiest representatives of
mobile property, the big merchants, wield in semicomplex hydraulic
societies? Can they ever dominate, or run, an absolutist government?
Wealthy merchants certainly may control absolutist governments;
and this may be the case even in commonwealths that contain elements of hydraulic statecraft. Elements. As long as such governments
fail to keep private property legally and economically weak, so long
will the patterns of property and power remain hydraulically submarginal. This is always so when the interests of private property
dominate the society; and it is so even when large hydraulic enter-

prises and/or quasi-Oriental devices of political control are present. The city state of Venice built enormous protective waterworks, but Venice remained a nonhydraulic aristocratic republic, in which big commercial property gained a maximum of strength and security.

Carthaginian society in the 4th and 3d centuries B.C. included a number of Oriental institutions. The Carthaginians certainly knew irrigation agriculture.[34] Their government was strong enough to tax the Lybian peasants of their agrarian hinterland.[e] To the disgust of their Roman enemies, they invoked the symbol of total submission, prostration, not only before their gods "as is the custom with other men," but also before their fellow men.[35] But as we have seen in Japan, irrigation techniques and prostration may occur also at the submarginal fringe of the hydraulic world; and in Carthage commercial interests were manifestly paramount[f] and private property was the key means for attaining high political office.[g] On the basis of our present knowledge we may therefore say that at least at the time of Aristotle the rich merchants probably dominated Carthaginian society and that similar submarginal configurations in all likelihood emerged in a number of other places, particularly—although not necessarily—at the geographical fringe of the hydraulic world.

In independent commonwealths based on commerce, rich merchants—who may also be big landowners—can certainly achieve social and political prominence. But while recognizing this possibility, we must ask: how much power can the representatives of independent commercial property wield in semicomplex Oriental societies?

a. Miscellaneous Developments

UNDER semicomplex conditions of property, the bulk of cultivable land is not owned privately; the big merchants must therefore derive their societal strength primarily from their mobile wealth. In a number of cases their combined wealth was enormous; but even under rational despots, such as the kings of Babylonia, commercial property generally remained subject to fragmenting laws of inheritance, to comprehensive taxation, and, insofar as transportation was concerned, not infrequently also to government regulation of oxen, carts, and

---

e. Gsell assumes that normally the government claimed 25 per cent of the crops as tax. Polybius (1.72.2) shows that in emergencies as much as 50 per cent might be collected (Gsell, HA, II: 303).

f. Meyer (GA, III: 644) calls the Carthaginian government a "commercial autocracy."

g. Aristotle, *Politics* 2.11.1273a. Aristotle, who noted that in Carthage the greatest offices, such as those of kings and generals, were bought, considered this "a bad thing." "The law which allows this abuse makes wealth of more account than virtue." For an elaboration of these points see Gsell, HA, II: 235 ff.

hired men.[36] It has been said before, and because of the importance of the issue it must be said again: the holders of active mobile property might organize in guilds, and often the state compelled them to do so; but neither the merchants nor the craft guilds were integrated in independent political machines on a local or national basis.

The gentlemen traders of Aztec Mexico seem to have been content to act as a commercial appendage to the secular and religious rulers; and nothing is known regarding any attempts on their part to dominate Mexican society. The "rich" Maya, whose quarters were close to, but not identical with, those of the masters of the state, operated at the outer edge of the power system. Commoners, "apparently men of wealth or influence," sometimes "insinuated themselves into political positions considered to be above their station," but "the official hierarchy was purged from time to time of the pretenders and upstarts, who were not versed in the occult knowledge of the upper class." [37]

In the Old World, the marginal hydraulic societies of Byzantium and Russia differed greatly from Maya society, but their private traders also failed to become politically dominant. In Byzantium the merchants, however wealthy they were individually, remained politically and socially restricted until the 11th century. During the final phases of Byzantine history, the men of property who succeeded in paralyzing the absolutist apparatus were not merchants or artisans, but landlords.

In Muscovite Russia the merchants were little more than economically useful domestic animals; nor did the big merchants in China rise to political prominence when semicomplex patterns of property prevailed at the end of the Chou period and during the middle part of the first millennium A.D.

b. Hindu India

THE corresponding developments in early India are particularly instructive because the Aryan conquest was accomplished by a group that, although aware of the importance of irrigation canals,[38] emphasized cattle wealth, trade, and traders. The Vedas speak respectfully of merchants.[h] In a hymn in the *Atharva-Veda-Samhita* merchants pray to the god Indra as "the merchant par excellence." [39] The great epics that were composed very much later [40] confirm the relatively high and influential position of the Vedic merchant in what Hopkins calls "the Aryan state." [41] However, they leave no doubt that

h. Grassmann, RV, I: 197; II: 113; cf. Banerjee, 1925: 155. Less esteemed, although equally prosperous, was the *pani,* a businessman who sought gain "either through trade or through usury" (Banerjee, 1925: 156).

"in distinction from noble and priests," the merchants, together with the Aryan peasants, belonged to "the people." [42] Thus whatever the status of the Aryan commoners, the Vaisyas, may have been in prehistoric times, in the Vedic era they were "oppressed by the princes." It was in this era—or even later in the subsequent Buddhist period [43] —that professional associations of merchants began to appear.[44]

Of course, the rise of such bodies proves nothing about their political independence. In simple Oriental societies—and often also under more complex conditions—the professional corporations are useful tools of government. The epics voice the king's concern with the merchants, particularly in times of war and crisis; but the merchants' chief political importance may well have been derived from their possible conspiratorial value to enemy countries.[45]

There can be no doubt regarding the prospering of trade and traders during the Buddhist period; and there can be no doubt either regarding the social prominence of the government-attached chief merchants, the *setthi*. However, this does not justify the claim that the merchants, as a group, were able in the major centers of what was then Hindu India to normally and conspicuously influence —or control—the political decisions of their respective governments.

These governments were not necessarily monarchies. In the homeland of Buddhism, northeast India, there were several republics, in which the ruler discussed public affairs in full and frequent assemblies.[46] But the merchants were not included in these bodies. The meager information we have on eight of the ten republics listed by T. W. Rhys-Davids [47] shows all of them to have been dominated by members of the warrior caste, Kshatriyas.[48] Buddha considered their assemblies an ancient institution; [49] and it may well be that the patterns of Aryan society [i] persisted somewhat longer in the northeastern area, in which hydraulic action, although highly advantageous, was not so crucial as in the more arid western parts of the north Indian plains.[j] However, irrigation agriculture and hydraulic enterprises were by no means absent in the northeast; [50] and the aristocratic republics clearly moved toward a monarchical form of power [51] which was already widespread in the days of Buddha [k] and which, after a transitional period of turmoil and conquest, came to prevail throughout the heartlands of Aryan culture.[52]

i. For the original role of an aristocracy of warriors see Hopkins, 1888: 73; Keith, 1922: 98.

j. Cf. Stamp, 1938: 299 ff. Oldenburg (1915: 284) regrets that the studies of Vedic and Buddhist India have neglected the solidly Brahmin development in the west and the great susceptibility of the east to the anti-Brahmin movement of Buddhism.

k. For the despotic character of these Indian monarchies see Law, 1941: 169 ff. Cf. Fick, 1920: 105 ff.

In the restless and changing Indian society of this important period many governments availed themselves of the services of a *setthi*. Apparently a man of means,[53] the *setthi* often advised and aided the ruler in economic matters.[54] His position, though not that of an official,[55] was distinguished and hereditary,[56] vacancies being filled by the king.[57]

The term *setthi* means "best, chief." [58] Manifestly he was a "representative of the commercial community," [59] but it is most important to note that he did not operate as the constitutionally established spokesman of organized merchant power. Nor does he seem to have been regularly—or primarily—concerned with guild affairs. His title "may possibly imply headship over some class of industry or trading"; [60] and a famous *setthi* mentioned in the *Jataka* tales apparently "had some authority over his fellow-traders." [61] But this authority, even if real, was rooted in a body whose organizational effectiveness has not yet been clearly established. In Buddhist and post-Buddhist India there certainly were merchant corporations, but C. A. F. Rhys-Davids warns against over-estimating the degree to which the traders were syndicalized.[62] To repeat her conclusion: "There is . . . no instance as yet produced from early Buddhist documents pointing to any corporate organisation of the nature of a gild or Hansa league." [63]

All this does not preclude the political prominence of merchants in some Orientally submarginal cities or city states of classical India; but it stresses the need for a most careful examination of the sources adduced to prove such prominence.

Hopkins, the well-known Sanscritist, cites a Nepalese legend of the 3d or 4th century A.D. as offering particularly valuable data on the political power of a merchant guild.*[m]* In his opinion this legend "records that Thana was ruled by a strong merchant guild." [64] Turning to the *Bombay Gazetteer* which Hopkins consulted,[65] we find that it makes a significantly more limited claim: "A strong merchant guild ruled *the trade of the city*." [66] The city in question is Sopara, one of several settlements located on the coast of Thana,[67] south of modern Bombay. Turning to the legend itself, we find that the merchants in question, far from controlling the government of the city, did not even control its trade. A single powerful outsider prevailed over the "500" merchants who were trying to corner the market, and he did so after both parties were summoned to appear before the king, who manifestly was the undisputed ruler of the city and the merchants.[68]

The Indian development is instructive in several respects. The

---

m. "Later literature down to our own time contains frequent reference to such bodies, but no thorough treatment of them is to be found" (Hopkins, 1902: 175).

Kshatriya republics show that hydraulic regimes need not be monarchic; but their final phases also underline the tendency toward a concentration of power that inheres in such regimes. The fate of the merchants is equally worth noting. During the formative days of the Aryan conquest society, traders enjoyed considerable social prestige. But subsequently their position deteriorated, and this happened despite the fact that they were tightly organized.

c. Ancient Mesopotamia

WERE the merchants more successful in the great Western Asiatic cradle of Oriental trade, ancient Lower Mesopotamia? Sumerian legends speak of elders and assembly-like gatherings, which the legendary king, Gilgamesh, consulted before making decisions.[69] What do these tales mean? Boas has convincingly argued that myths contain fictitious as well as realistic features and that realistic elements may be exaggerated or transformed into their opposites.[70] There may very well have been proto-Sumerian assemblies similar to the warrior assemblies of the Aryan conquest republics in northeast India. Kramer assumes the existence of a military aristocracy during the formative period of prehistoric Sumer.[71] But whatever the institutional quality of these legendary assemblies may have been, no such gatherings dominated the Sumerian city states when they emerged in the light of recorded history. To quote Jacobsen: "The political development in early historical times seems to lie under the spell of one controlling idea: concentration of political power in as few hands as possible." [72] In each of the early Mesopotamian city states "one individual, the ruler, united in his hands the chief political powers: legislative, judiciary, and executive." [73] In each of them the king handled the despotic state apparatus through the agency of an effective secular and priestly bureaucracy, "the court and temple administrators and intellectuals," as Kramer calls the new core of the "ruling caste." [74]

Significantly there are few, if any, traces of assemblies in the simple hydraulic society of historical Sumer. With regard to Babylonia the situation is otherwise. Babylonian inscriptions refer to assemblies, to elders, and—in the same context—to merchants. Could it be that the growth of Babylonian trade also increased the power of its representatives, the big merchants?

The possible extent, and the limitations, of merchant power are indicated by the Assyrian merchant colonies, which flourished in Cappadocia during the earlier part of the second millennium B.C. These Assyrian settlements were established in an area which, al though lacking political unity,[75] comprised a number of territorial governments.

The Assyrian traders who settled far to the north of their homelands did not dwell inside the Cappadocian towns. The walled sections were reserved for the native population and for the palaces of the ruler.[76] Moreover, the local authorities [77] inspected the trader's commodities in the palace and also, it seems, had a first claim on any goods they wanted to sell.[78] The presence of such local authorities did not mean that the colonies were independent of the Assyrian metropolis. In the end it was Assur that decided legal cases and that had the power to impose taxes: [79] "The authorities of Assur and ultimately the king were therefore the superiors of the Assyrian authorities in the commercial centers." [80]

Within this over-all frame the colonies dealt with their judicial matters in "a general assembly of all colonists," [81] the *karum;* and this body also settled other communal problems.[82] Evidently the members of these Assyrian trade colonies enjoyed a greater autonomy than did the merchants of Assyria or Sumer, or—after the close of the Sumerian period—Babylonia; but they did not dominate the Cappadocian towns, nor were they politically independent in their own quarters.

Babylonian absolutism, like that of Sumer, was rooted in a compact agromanagerial economy; and private property probably played a secondary role in agriculture as well as in commerce.[n] In any case, no serious institutional analyst claims that the assemblies, and through them the merchants, controlled the Babylonian government. The king and his men dominated the administration, the army, and the fiscal system. The king was also the lawgiver. Furthermore, he and his functionaries were strategically situated in the judiciary. At the king's service "judges of the king" ruled according to the "legal practice of the king." [83] But the royal judges, who frequently combined administrative, military, and legal activities,[84] re-

n. Probably. The reasons for the second part of our assumption have been given above; the reasons for the first will be given below when we discuss the extent of private landownership. Dr. Isaac Mendelsohn, in a personal communication and on the basis of an independent examination of the inscriptions, believes that in both spheres of Babylonian economy private property was more extended than the combined property of the state and the temples. No doubt the facts of the matter have to be decided by the period specialists; and our tentative classification of Babylonian society is therefore open to whatever adjustments future research may postulate. But assuming for the sake of the argument that the private property sector exceeded the public sector, there is still no need to change our evaluation of the subordinate political position of the Babylonian merchants. In the same personal communication, Dr. Mendelsohn rejects an interpretation of Babylonian society as democratic.

lied for the settlement of local issues heavily on local assemblies. These bodies dealt primarily with legal matters.[85] Operating under the king's control, they constituted "a kind of civil jury." [o]

The members of these assemblies were "elders," "notables," "merchants" (under a head merchant), and "men of the gate." [86] According to Cuq, these designations refer to separate groups that acted either alone or in combination.[87] Whether Cuq's interpretation is correct or not and whatever the terms "elders," "notables," or "men of the gate" may mean, for our present purpose it is sufficient to know that the assemblies were essentially judicial bodies and that among their members there were merchants headed by an *akil tamgari*.

In early Babylonia the *akil tamgari* seems to have been the director of the Department of Commerce or the Department of Finance, and as such the chief of the fiscal bureaucracy.[88] He headed the ordinary merchants, who undertook commercial expeditions, "at times exclusively in the interest of the crown." [p] He thus was a prominent official through whom the absolutist regime exerted control over the country's traders.

Occasionally an assembly dealt with issues that concerned a whole town; and its merchant members would therefore be participating in matters of considerable local importance. However, since the assembly was presided over by a royal governor or town prefect and since it acted essentially as a civil jury, it certainly did not control the town government; and the merchants, who were under the authority of the *akil tamgari*, were not free to control even their own professional spheres, the country's trade.

d. Conclusions

THE lessons of all this are obvious. Powerful groups of rich merchants may control the government of their commonwealth; and this may happen even in communities that fulfill substantial hydraulic functions. But as far as we know, such developments did not result in anything that can be called the rule of hydraulic merchants. The great merchants of Venice operated in a societal setting in which hy-

---

o. Cuq, 1929: 361. Occasionally they also handled political crimes, but the case cited by Jacobsen involves no deeds, but words only: "seditious utterances" (Jacobsen, 1943: 164).

p. Krückmann, 1932: 446. Was the head merchant of the king, *rab tamgar sa šarri,* who is mentioned in the Neo-Babylonian inscriptions, the successor of the *akil tamgari?* His activities were obscure. Ebeling (1932: 454) places him among the "high officials," adding that he "probably conducted commercial and monetary transactions for the king."

draulic institutions were submarginal. And Carthage, although certainly more hydraulic than Venice, may well have belonged, either from the start or eventually, to the submarginal zone of the hydraulic world.

Carthage-like or Venice-like commercial commonwealths flourished in considerable numbers at the geographical fringe of hydraulic society; and there is no reason why such commonwealths should not have constituted independent heterogeneous enclaves also within certain zones of the hydraulic world. We therefore do not reject Max Weber's assumption that independent commercial communities may have flourished in Buddhist India.[89] But the evidence adduced is not conclusive; and in a number of cases reexamination reveals that the position of the merchants is far from being politically dominant.

Further inquiries into the political role of merchants in institutionally peripheral regions will certainly deepen our insight into the diversities that exist within the margin and the submargin of the hydraulic world. They may also shed more light on the limitations of mobile private property even in those hydraulic societies in which private-property-based commerce became more important than government-managed and government-attached trade.

H. COMPLEX PATTERNS OF PROPERTY IN HYDRAULIC SOCIETY

1. HYDRAULIC LANDLORDISM, PAST AND PRESENT

THE limitations of immobile property in hydraulic society are equally significant—and equally misunderstood. The institutional pioneers who viewed the despotic state as the only major landowner tended to neglect the problem of private landownership altogether. Modern observers, who have noted the paralyzing influence of absentee landlordism in the Orient, are inclined to treat as a basic feature of hydraulic society what in many cases is only a feature of hydraulic society in transition. And they are quick to interpret in terms of past (feudal) or present (capitalist) Western institutions what is actually a specific Oriental development.[a]

a. To mention just one key issue: the establishment of private peasant land by means of a thoroughgoing land reform has one meaning when it is undertaken by the separate forces of a relatively decentralized postfeudal or industrial society and quite another when it is undertaken by the government-controlled forces of a disintegrating hydraulic order or, for that matter, by a totalitarian state of the Soviet type. Major changes in the system of land tenure that occurred in modern Japan, in Russia under the Tsars or under the Bolsheviks, in Nehru's India, or in Communist

More will be said on this subject in our concluding chapter. In the present context we are concerned essentially with the roots of the modern development: the extent and peculiarities of private landownership prior to the dissolution of hydraulic society.

2. GOVERNMENT-CONTROLLED AND PRIVATE LAND IN HYDRAULIC SOCIETY

THE extent and the peculiarities of private land in hydraulic society can be properly viewed only when we remember the extent and the peculiarities of hydraulic state power. In the majority of all hydraulic societies the despotic regime kept private land in a quantitatively subordinate position. In all hydraulic societies the despotic regime limited the freedom of the private land it permitted to exist.

a. Types of Government-controlled Land

IN order to establish the extent of private land we have to clarify the extent of government-controlled land. This last comprises three main types: (1) government-managed land, (2) government-regulated land, and (3) government-assigned land.

All land that is kept by government measures from being alienated either to or by private landowners is regulated land in the broad sense of the term, and in this sense all government land is regulated land. In a narrow sense, the term "regulated land" will be applied essentially to that part of government-controlled land that is managed not by the government but by possessors, who work for, or pay tax or rent to, the government. The term "government-managed land" will be applied to land that is farmed under the direction of government functionaries and for the immediate and exclusive benefit of the government. The term "assigned land" will be applied to land that is temporarily, or indefinitely, assigned to officials (office land), to representatives of the dominant religion (sacred or temple land), or to some distinguished persons who do not, in return, fulfill any special secular or religious functions (sinecure land).

i. GOVERNMENT-MANAGED LAND

GOVERNMENT-MANAGED "public" land was never more than a minor part of all regulated land, since the peasants who cultivated the "public" fields also needed land for their own support. Above a certain agronomical level and except in some strategically important

---

China are frequently treated as if they were more or less identical, though in their societal substance and effect they are entirely different phenomena.

regions, the hydraulic state preferred the payment of a land tax from the individually cultivated fields to products from public fields.

Imperial China, although favoring private ownership of land, maintained farm colonies for the support of the army, primarily in border areas, but at times also in critical inland areas: at places that were being "pacified" and along vital lines of communication. The tilling in these colonies was done either by soldiers (in which case they were generally called "garrison fields," *t'un-t'ien*) or by civilians (in which case they were frequently called "camp fields," *yin-t'ien*). The two types of fields together occasionally comprised as much as one-tenth of all cultivable land, but in most dynasties the fraction was much smaller.

Apart from military colonies, there were government domains for the growing of special crops, and parks and gardens for the rulers' pleasure. These secluded retreats were often built with corvée labor, but usually they were cared for by professional cultivators, palace laborers, and slaves *b*—that is, they were government-managed. But while remarkable in this respect, they were spatially insignificant. They were tiny islands in a sea of peasant farms, whose occupiers or owners supported the government not by their labor or public fields but by their tax payments.

ii. GOVERNMENT-REGULATED LAND

THE most important type of all government-controlled land is perhaps the least clearly defined: peasant land which is neither managed by government officials nor assigned to groups of grantees, nor owned by the cultivators. This type of land cannot be simply equated with the land of village communities, since not all peasants who possess regulated land live in integrated village communities—that is, in communities that distribute and redistribute the land. Nor are all village communities under the control of the government.

Regulated peasant land, in terms of the present inquiry, is land that a holder cannot alienate freely. Often, and particularly when the land is periodically redistributed, a holder may be allowed to lease it to other villagers,*c* but he cannot sell it.*d* In other cases he

b. Royal or imperial gardens and parks have been described by many authors. For the Mexican lake area see Ixtlilxochitl, OH, II: 209 ff.; for Pharaonic Egypt, Erman and Ranke, 1923: 206 ff.; for ancient Mesopotamia, Meissner, BA, I: 201, 292; Contenau, 1950: 53 ff.; for the Islamic Near East, Mez, 1922: 362 ff.; for Muslim Spain, Lévi-Provençal, 1932: 223; for India, *Jātakam: passim* and Smith, 1926: 402 ff.; for Chou China, Legge, CC, II: 127 ff.

c. This was customary among the *calpulli* members of Aztec Mexico. See Zurita, 1941: 88; Monzon, 1949: 39.

d. For an elaborate description of the regulated village community in Tsarist Russia, the *obshchina* or *mir*, see Haxthausen, SR, I: 129 and *passim*.

may sell it but only to other villagers—that is, to fellow peasants. In Byzantium earlier directives were restored and reenforced in 922 by a law which permitted the peasants to sell land to the following groups and in this order: (1) co-possessing relatives, (2) other co-possessors, (3) persons whose land was adjacent to the land to be sold, (4) neighbors who shared the seller's fiscal responsibility, and (5) other neighbors.[1] These regulations made it impossible for a landlord to purchase peasant land except in villages where he was already an owner.[2] As long as they worked, they protected the bulk of the peasant land from falling prey to the expanding forces of land-lordism.

Similar principles were employed in Hindu [e] and Muslim India. Bulwarked by the law-enforcing powers of the state, the Indian village community "protected small farming against the invasion of capitalistic interests," and it did so "by maintaining [for the villagers] the rights of entail, pre-emption, and pre-occupation." [3]

The cases of Byzantium and India, which could be supplemented by data from other civilizations, demonstrate the negative effects of regulated land on the growth of private landownership. Wherever the Orientally despotic state insisted on keeping the bulk of all land regulated, private ownership of land was kept in a secondary and not infrequently in an irrelevant position.

iii. GOVERNMENT-ASSIGNED LAND

THE despotic regime that is able to regulate all or a large part of the land is also able to assign portions of it to any individual or group of individuals. Such land assignments may differ in purpose and duration, but usually the two aspects interlock. Persons who serve the government may hold their office land for life or even hereditarily. Others may hold their offices only for a short term; in such cases tenure over their office land is equally brief. Serving men who fulfill military functions are particularly apt both to obtain and to lose their office land suddenly.

Land grants made to those who serve the gods are more stable. Enduring religious organizations, such as temples and mosques, are almost always permitted to retain their grants indefinitely.

Sinecure land is given for a variety of reasons to a variety of persons. The grantees may be so distinguished because of their meritori-

---

e. See Appadorai, 1936, I: 133 ff. The alienability of land has been seen as a sign of ownership, whereas it may merely be indicative of a flexible form of possession. Jolly's (1896: 94) interpretation makes allowance both for the (externally) regulated and the (internally) fluid conditions of village land. He assumes "that generally the villages were shut off from the outer world, but that within the individual villages there existed private property of land."

ous acts or merely because they are the ruler's relatives, friends, or favorites.[f] In all instances the land is assigned unconditionally. The grantees do not render service for the revenues which the sinecure land yields. This is also true for the holders of pension land. But whoever the beneficiary may be, the government remains the master of the assigned land.

Sacred (temple) land is usually supervised and/or managed by secular government officials. This has been established for Pharaonic Egypt,[4] for Ptolemaic Egypt,[5] for Babylonia,[6] and of course, for pre-Conquest Peru and Mexico. In the Islamic world, direct or indirect state control over the various types of religious property persisted, with many modifications in detail, until recent times.[7]

Control over office land is guaranteed by the government's operational control over the landholders. A normally functioning despotic regime determines the fate of its serving men and the lands allotted to them. When, at the close of the Chou period, the chancellor of the state of Ch'in made merit rather than inheritance the essential basis for office,[g] he met with no conspicuous resistance; and throughout late Chou China the decrease of areas administered by holders of office land [8] were accepted with equal meekness. No organized group of "barons" rose against the imperial unifier of China when he finally and decisively discarded the office land system in its entirety. Nor did Akbar's decision to substitute in large part salaries for office land [9] meet with any greater challenge. Akbar went far, but not so far as the Turkish Sultan Suleiman, who spectacularly demonstrated that a well-functioning despotism could abolish office land as easily as it could create it.[10]

Sinecure land might be given without any limitation as to time. In this case possession might come to an end when the ruling dynasty fell. In Pharaonic Egypt this seems to have been the rule; [11] and it is not unlikely that the land grants in ancient Peru would have suffered the same fate if the Inca regime had been replaced by other native rulers. Often sinecure land was intended to support the recipient as long as he lived, but the grantor's death might terminate the assignment earlier. The land grants of ancient Hawaii were apparently so conditioned.[12]

---

f. Cf. *Jātakam*, I: 56 (grant given to the king's barber); II: 193 (to a Brahmin), 270 (to a princess), 457 ff. (to a princess); IV: 116 (to a Brahmin), 309 (reward for finding a precious antelope), 415 (to a princess), 480 (reward for singing a special verse); V: 21 (reward for useful advice), 35 (to ascetics), 45 (to a hunter), 374 (to a hunter); VI: 135 (to a barber), 355 (to the king's brother or son), 422 (to a *setthi*), 438 (to good advisors), 447 (to an advisor). Cf. *ibid.*, I: 362 ff., 424, 462.

g. *Shih Chi* 68.4a; Duyvendak, 1928: 15, 61. The "nobles" whom he restricted more

b. Private Land

i. DEFINITIONS

LAND that is government-managed, government-regulated, or government-assigned is obviously not the property of private landowners; and it cannot be so viewed, even when possession is prolonged. Permanency of possession is not enough (hereditary tenants also enjoy this privilege); nor is the right to alienate enough (holders of regulated land are sometimes permitted to alienate it within their social group). Only when the proprietor has the right both to hold his land indefinitely and to alienate it to persons outside his social group do we encounter what, in conformance with established usage, can be called full private landownership.

ii. ORIGINS

THE commoners and nobles of early Greece, Germany, Gaul, and England owned their land not because of the decision of an autocratic ruler but because of differentiations within a tribal society, which produced multiple patterns of private property and political leadership. In hydraulic society it was essentially the ruler and his functionaries who established private landholding by transferring to individual owners what was previously government-controlled land.

Individuals usually became landowners through gifts or sale. Entire groups were made landowners by government decree. After a piece of land had been recognized as private property, it could, within government-set social limits, be transferred from one private owner to another. Large-scale conversions of regulated land into private land are relatively rare in the history of Oriental society. They seem to have occurred only where private-property-based handicraft and trade were well developed.

c. Types of Landownership

i. PEASANT LANDOWNERSHIP

WHO then are the potential owners of land in hydraulic society? In Oriental as in other agrarian societies the key figure in the basic subsistence economy is the peasant. We can therefore expect him to play an important role in the expanding sector of private landownership; and indeed in China the establishment of free private land involved the emergence of a large class of peasant owners.

---

and more (*ibid.*: 27; *Shih Chi* 68.8b) are said to have hated him (Duyvendak, 1928: 23; *Shih Chi* 68.6b), but his measures led to no organized "baronial" rebellion.

ii. BUREAUCRATIC LANDLORDISM

BUT the Chinese development is the exception rather than the rule. In the majority of all cases it is not the peasant owner but the nonpeasant owner who first and prominently appears in the private land sector. Evidently the more complex a hydraulic society becomes, the greater the number of social groups that seek to be landed proprietors. But one group among them is outstanding: the civil and military functionaries of the government and their relatives, the bureaucratic gentry.

Under simple conditions of property few others are rich enough to buy land. And even where there are wealthy merchants or traders, the bulk of the surplus, and consequently the bulk of the purchasing power, remains in the hands of the governing class. Furthermore, it is to members of the governing class that the ruler is most likely to make gifts of land.

Bureaucratic landlordism therefore tends to appear in all types of hydraulic society, whatever their complexity. It prevails completely in those simple hydraulic societies in which private land is at all relevant. It is a significant feature in many semicomplex hydraulic societies. And it is crucial in complex hydraulic societies where privately owned land outweighs state-controlled land.

Data on landed property in Pharaonic Egypt are vague even for the New Kingdom.[13] A few statements that are specific speak essentially of princes, viziers, and other members of the governing class as owners of private land.[14]

In Aztec Mexico private lands were held by the rulers, their officials, and some merchants.[15] In Hindu India the Brahmins did not, as was the case with priesthoods in many other hydraulic societies, live on large and permanently granted temple lands. Consequently, in Hindu India land grants to individual Brahmins fulfilled a special function, and it is not surprising to find that they were numerous. Many of them carried only the right of possession, but a number of Brahmins seem to have owned land at least in the last phase of Hindu rule.[16] In Byzantine Egypt the "powerful ones" who had large estates were most frequently officials;[17] and this pattern is repeated in Islamic times. Among the persons who, during the Mamluk period, acquired private land, actual or former holders of office land were prominent.[18] In Ottoman Turkey some office lands became the private property of former holders.[19]

In Middle Byzantium functionaries were for a time forbidden without special imperial permission to purchase land while they held office. The restriction retarded the growth of bureaucratic landownership but did not prevent it.[20] In Tsarist Russia the edict of 1762 converted the *pomeshchiki*, who had been possessors of office land, into landowners. In later imperial China government functionaries were forbidden to purchase land in the district in which they officiated.[21] Nothing was said regarding the purchase of land outside this area; and the evidence at hand suggests that among the owners of land officiating and nonofficiating members of the government class were outstanding.

iii. OTHER SOCIAL GROUPS

To be sure, members of other social groups also owned land, if they had the necessary means and if they were permitted to. In semicomplex and complex hydraulic societies rich merchants particularly were likely to acquire land; and information on Aztec Mexico,[22] India,[23] and China shows clearly that they did so. Moreover, the measures invoked by the Han dynasty reveal both how well entrenched this type of landlordism might become and how ruthlessly a ruling bureaucracy might combat it.[24] Of course, even persons of modest wealth might buy land. In traditional China persons from all walks of life owned small pieces of land.[25]

iv. ABSENTEE LANDLORDISM (THE GENERAL TREND)

OCCASIONALLY a nonpeasant owner of land, who for some reason or other was deprived of his occupation, might assure his support by personally turning to farming.[h] Generally, however, nonpeasant landowners left the tasks of cultivation to tenants. In many cases they were absentee landlords.

In Medieval and post-Medieval Europe tenancy and absentee landlordism were also widespread. However, many landlords personally managed their large estates (*Güter*) or employed stewards for this purpose.

The small incidence of large-scale farming in hydraulic society is due primarily to the high crop yield obtained by labor-intensive methods, which are in part required and in part stimulated by irrigation agriculture.[26] These methods provide extraordinary advantages for small-scale peasant farming on a family basis. The advantages are so striking that the dominant hydraulic "economic ethos" (*Wirtschaftsgesinnung*) discouraged large-scale and "manorial" methods, even when they might have been profitably applied.

The significance of this attitude for hydraulic society in transition

---

h. For Brahmins who tilled their land either with or without the aid of farmhands, see *Jātakam*, II: 191 ff.; III: 179, 316; IV: 195, 334 ff.; V: 70.

is obvious. The consolidation of landlordism in postfeudal Europe encouraged many owners of large farms to cultivate their land scientifically. The recent growth of landlordism in many hydraulic countries intensified the acquisitive zeal of the absentee landlords without increasing the rationality of tenant farming.

V. ABSENTEE LANDLORDISM (TRADITIONAL RUSSIA)

AN interesting variant of absentee landlordism appeared in Tsarist Russia. The *pomeshchiki* of Muscovite and post-Muscovite Russia were kept so busy rendering military or civil services that they could not pay much attention to farming, as did the landed nobles of England or Germany. In consequence, large-scale and scientific farming was extremely limited among landholding aristocrats in Russia prior to 1762, and despite some expansion it remained the exception long after this date.

Baron Haxthausen, who made his famous study of rural Russia in the 1840's, was struck by the difference between landlords in Russia and in the rest of Europe. Although unaware of the peculiarities of Oriental despotism, he clearly recognized that Russia's landowning aristocracy lacked a feudal tradition:

> The Russian, the Great-Russian nobility, is not a landed nobility [*Landadel*] now, nor in all probability was it ever one; it had no castles, it did not pass through a period of knighthood and [private] feuding. It always was a serving nobility, it always lived at the Courts of the Great Princes and the smaller princes and in the cities, rendering military, Court, or civil services. Those among them, who lived in the countryside, peacefully pursued agriculture; but in actuality they were either insignificant or unfit. Even today the majority of the Great-Russian nobles have no rural residences, no [manorial] economies as we see them in the rest of Europe. All the land that belongs to the noble—cultivated land, meadows, forests—are left to the peasant village community that works it and pays the lord for it. Even if the lord owns, and lives in, a country house, he still does not have a [manorial] economy, but rather lives like a *rentier*. Most nobles have country houses, but they live in town and visit the country house only for weeks or months. This is the old Russian way of life of the aristocracy! [27]

The Russian nobles' peculiar detachment from the land they owned—together with the fragmenting law of inheritance—kept them from becoming "a real landed aristocracy," as Haxthausen knew it in Central and Western Europe. "I do not think that there is, in any major country in Europe, less stability of their land than in Great Russia." [28]

It is against this background that we must view the two great agrarian changes accomplished by the Tsarist bureaucracy in the second half of the 19th and the beginning of the 20th century: the emancipation of the serfs from their former landlords (in 1861) and Stolypin's reform (in 1908). In both cases resistance was great; but in both cases the new measures were introduced by members of the same governing class that comprised the bulk of all landlords.

vi. BORDERLINE CASES OF REGULATED AND PRIVATE LAND TENURE

ABSENTEE landlordism is quickly apparent, more quickly than the exact proprietary quality of a particular piece of land. How many of the land "grants" of Pharaonic Egypt or Buddhist India were given with the intention of establishing possession? How many with the intention of establishing ownership? The records often fail to provide definite information on these points. And even when they suggest the right of ownership—how secure was this right? Segrè, in comparing the proprietary developments under Oriental absolutism and in classical Greece, concludes that "private property in a sense approaching to classical ownership could not exist as long as the king could exercise the power of withdrawing rights either to land or to liberties or change these terms at will." [29]

Brahmin property was believed to be safe from confiscation. But this did not prevent Hindu rulers from seizing Brahmin land for "treason," which the king's judiciary had no difficulty in establishing when it suited his purposes.[30] In Pharaonic Egypt private landownership, although perhaps more extensive than in Hindu India, was equally insecure. Indeed it was "basically nothing but an exceptional transfer of royal prerogatives, a transfer which as a matter of principle could be reversed at any time and which was often reversed when a new dynasty came into being." [31] In such cases it is manifestly hard to draw a sharp line between possession and ownership.

Another difficulty arises from the fact that in certain hydraulic societies the right to alienate private property in land is spread unevenly. Nonpeasant landlords may be free to buy land from other landlords, whereas the peasants who live in a regulated rural order enjoy no corresponding right of alienation. In hydraulic society such mixed patterns create a major classificatory problem only when, as in Late Byzantium and in Russia after 1762, the land held by landlords comprises a large part (perhaps more than one-half) of all cultivated land. When this is the case, we can speak of an incipient pattern of complex hydraulic property and society.

d. The Extent of Private Landownership in Various Subtypes of Hydraulic Society

THE categories of government and private land developed so far enable us to advance beyond our initial tentative position and to correlate with greater precision and fuller evidence the advance of mobile and immobile private property in various hydraulic civilizations. Germs of private landownership were present even in hydraulic societies in which private-property-based industry and commerce were of little consequence, but they did not assume major dimensions. This confirms the validity of our concept of "simple" patterns of hydraulic property and society. In hydraulic civilizations with a substantial sector of mobile property and enterprise, private landownership frequently remained a secondary feature, and occasionally an insignificant one. This confirms the validity of our concept of semicomplex patterns of hydraulic property and society. Furthermore it confirms our contention concerning the relative scarcity of the complex configuration—a configuration in which immobile private property is as prominent in agriculture as, in its peculiar way and with its peculiar limitations, mobile property is prominent in industry and trade.

On the basis of these results, we shall contemplate briefly the extent of private landownership in some of the major hydraulic civilizations. In this survey certain crucial data that were adduced in the discussion of our key criteria have to be mentioned again. But they now appear in a new context and, in a number of cases, they are supplemented by important additional information. In accordance with our previously established concepts we shall advance from simple to semicomplex and eventually to complex conditions of property and society.

i. SIMPLE HYDRAULIC SOCIETIES

Hawaii: Ancient Hawaii certainly knew private possession of land. But it is doubtful whether there existed full landownership, since the "estates" even of the most powerful territorial "chiefs," the governors, "reverted to the king" after the holder's death and since "at the accession of a new king . . . all the lands of an island" were reassigned.[32]

Inca Peru: As stated above, sinecure lands were held privately and indefinitely, but the holders of such lands lacked the right to alienate them. Thus they were not owners but permanent occupiers.

Sumer: At the close of the Sumerian period, genuine private land-ownership emerged.[33] However, the governments of the earlier temple cities seem to have exercised a strict control over the cultivable land. The records so far deciphered fail to reveal the existence even of such private landed possessions as have been documented for Inca society.

Pharaonic Egypt: In addition to government land proper and to government-assigned land (temple land and office land), there was private land which could be alienated,[34] but the king could cancel a holding at any time. Generally speaking, private landownership was more the exception than the rule.[35]

ii. SEMICOMPLEX HYDRAULIC SOCIETIES

India: Numerous inscriptions document for the last southern phase of Hindu India what was already certain for the Buddhist and post-Buddhist periods,[36] namely that "most villages" were occupied by *ryotwāri* [37]—that is, by peasants who were under the direct control of the state. This implies that private landownership can have existed only in a (not very large) minority of all villages.

Mesopotamia: At the end of the Sumerian period and in Babylonian society private landownership is clearly apparent. Did it become the dominant form of land tenure? Evidence to this effect would lead us to class this period not as semicomplex but as complex. However, available data seem at best to indicate semicomplex patterns of property. At best. If state trade equaled or exceeded private trade during a large part of the Babylonian period, we would be faced with an advanced simple or an incipient semicomplex situation.

For Late Sumer—the Third dynasty of Ur—the texts frequently mention private property in fields a well as in houses and gardens.[38] But although the temples were no longer alone in leasing land, they are still most frequently mentioned in this respect.[i] For Babylonia, Meissner finds that the best and largest tracts of lands were in the hands of the government and the temples. "What still remained of the land was private property." [39] Schawe's analysis of the tenancy conditions of the period seem to confirm Meissner's view: in Babylonia land was rented out "primarily by the state and temple domains and then also by private individuals." [40]

i. Schneider, 1920: 58. Hackman's (1937: 21 ff.) numerous references to fields unfortunately are often vague concerning their property position.

Cuq stresses the specific position of land that was made private through royal gift.[41] At the same time he mentions among the features that led to differentiations in land tenure the emergence (or reemergence?) under the Kassites of communities which he characterizes as tribal and kinship-based,[42] but which he also compares with the Russian *mir* [43]—that is, with a purely administrative type of village community. The details of the Kassite rural units are still obscure,[44] but we know that they were interlinked with the governmental apparatus through certain of their leaders and that they regulated the landed possessions of their members in ways not too different from those of the Mexican *calpulli* and the Inca *ayllus*.

During the last phase of Babylonian history the two types of government-controlled land still prevailed—if what the Persians found in Mesopotamia is indicative of the Neo-Babylonian conditions. In Persian Mesopotamia there were (1) state lands that in large part were assigned to individuals, (2) "large tracts of land" held by the temples, and (3) lands "held in fee simple by the individuals." The first two categories were obviously very extensive: "With much of the land held by the state and the temples, the number of land transactions is not so large as that of other sales." [45] Again we lack statistical data, but the above statement suggests that the process of "privatization" had gone further in mobile than in landed property.

Persia: The Persians used the government-controlled land (and outside the Greek cities this was the bulk of all cultivated land) very much as had the Babylonians and Sumerians before them. They assigned it to members of the royal house and to friends of the king (obviously as sinecure land), to officials, resettled soldiers, and persons obligated to provide contingents for the army (obviously as office land).[46] Knowing the conditions under which office land was held in other Oriental despotisms, we have no reason to doubt that this land, like the regulated peasant land, was what Rostovtzeff takes it to be: state land.

The Persian office land was not a feudal institution, nor did it inspire a feudal order among the Parthians. The big Parthian landholders were no semi-autonomous fief-holders who spent most of their time attending to their personal affairs. Instead, and very much like their Persian predecessors, they were government officials.[j]

j. Christensen, 1933: 307. According to Christensen, the Parthian government was "despotic" in form, at least as long as the Parthian monarchy was united (*ibid.*). Did the political order change when the monarchy disintegrated into several territorial kingdoms? This is, of course, possible but it is by no means certain. On the basis of comparable cases, it seems more likely that the smaller and later Parthian kingdoms

Hellenistic Monarchies of the Near East: Private landownership was confined essentially to the Greek cities,[47] which were few in Egypt but numerous in Western Asia. Outside these Greek enclaves, the land was controlled by the government and by government-attached temples.

The Seleucid rulers established considerable private land through grant or sale [48] "on condition that the grantee joined his land to some city and made of it city-land"; [49] and, of course, they assigned office land to soldiers and probably also to civil functionaries.[50]

The kings of Pergamum do not seem to have reduced the royal land at all. "Like the Ptolemies, they must have gifted the (revocable) user of estates on King's land to officials." [51]

In Ptolemaic Egypt "private land originally meant house, gardens, and vineyard; even the house and garden of a Royal peasant were 'private.' Greeks sometimes called it property, but it was, like every other Ptolemaic form, not property but user; apart from the Greek cities, the property or legal estate in any land in Egypt never left the king." [52]

It is in the light of this statement that we have to view the existence of certain "private" grain land. Rostovtzeff suggests that this type of land had existed in Pharaonic Egypt; [53] and what we know of the earlier period confirms his assumption. However, we must remember first the instability that in Pharaonic times characterized landed property generally, and second the loose way in which the Ptolemaic (Greek) masters of Egypt employed the term "private."

The "private" land, whose spread the Ptolemies encouraged, was "regulated emphyteutic" tenure [54]—that is, a lease of "deserted land" "for a long period (hundred years) or in perpetuity." The rights over this kind of property were "transferable by alienation or succession and enjoyed in a certain measure the same protection as ownership." [55] By developing emphyteutic tenure, the Ptolemies strengthened the trend toward landownership. But until the Roman era, this trend does not seem to have gone beyond a relatively strong form of "landed possession." [56]

The Roman Interlude: Under the Romans private property emerged on a large scale.[57] The reasons for this extraordinary development—and for its limited success—are treated below in connection with the discussion of complex patterns of property.

The Islamic Near East (the first centuries): The Arab conquerors

---

were smaller Oriental despotisms, with certain leading families hereditarily holding the top-ranking positions in government and occupying very substantial tracts of office land.

of Egypt and Syria perpetuated most of the Byzantine institutions,[58] including patterns of land tenure. For obvious reasons many former holders of estates fled,[59] and those who stayed [60] lost the right to collect the taxes for the government.[61] Alongside them, prominent Arab landholders established themselves on deserted estates and the old state domain.[62] These new holders bought and sold land, and they held their property, *qati'a*,[63] hereditarily.[64] But the *qati'a* represented an emphyteutic form of possession; [65] and it is doubtful whether holders could enlarge them by freely buying peasant land. Their Byzantine predecessors had been forbidden by law to do so; [66] and the new Arab state was certainly as eager as the officials of Eastern Rome—and probably better able—to protect the regulated villages. Apparently, the *qati'a* possessions increased in extent,[67] but they remained in the hands of a limited group of leaders. The mass of the Arab tribesmen lived in military camps; [68] and it was only after several generations that the *qati'a* were spread into the villages.[69]

We need not follow here the step-by-step rise of a new system of landed property, whose beneficiaries were both tax collectors and holders of office land.[70] This system appears clearly and consistently in Mamluk society.

Mamluk Society: At the beginning of Mamluk power virtually all the cultivable land of Egypt was divided into twenty-four units, which were either controlled directly by the sultan or assigned as office land.[71] Private land, *mulk,* was "almost absent." [k] Its later growth was accomplished "mostly" by an intricate process which required a holder of office land to surrender part of it to the treasury before he purchased it from the government, either directly or through a middleman.[72]

But while *mulk* continued to increase until the end of the period, it remained only one of a number of types of land that an official (and usually a military official) might control. In addition to his office land (*iqtā'*) and to his *mulk,* he might possess pension land,[73] and he might also be the manager of a *waqf* which he had founded [74] and which in all likelihood would yield him and his family a steady income.

Ottoman Turkey: The Turkish sultans demonstratively established the hegemony of state land by officially abolishing the bulk of privately owned land.[m] Some "landowners proper" seem to have

k. Poliak, 1939: 36. Poliak assumes that private lands were, at the beginning of the Mamluk period, "numerous" in Syria.

m. Gibb and Bowen, 1950: 236, 258, n. 4; cf. Poliak, 1939: 46. This refers essentially to cultivable land and pastures. The farmhouses and the land around it were always *mulk;* and vineyard and orchards were usually so considered (Gibb and Bowen, 1950: 236).

existed from the start; [75] and local "notables" (a'yāns) acquired mulk, perhaps through conversion of office and other land.[76] But until the recent period of transition, most of the land was controlled by the government, which assigned part of it as office land or waqf and taxed the remainder through the agency of its tax farmers.[n]

The tax farmers had many prerogatives. In the non-Arab provinces they might transfer a vacant peasant farm [o] to a resident of another village, but "only after offering it to the peasants of the village to which the land in question was attached." [77] In the Arab provinces their position, by the 18th century, approached that of holders of military office land. In Egypt they were given one-tenth of all village land under the name of waṣîya. They could sell this waṣîya land, but only to another tax farmer and only when they, at the same time, transferred to the buyer a corresponding amount of their jurisdictional domain.[78] In the Arab provinces the fellahs could alienate their land "to other fellâhs." [79] Regarding the Arab territories, Gibb and Bowen expressly state that the person responsible for collecting the taxes "might not deprive a fellâh of his land, except for non-payment of taxation." [80] Thus in both the non-Arab and Arab provinces the majority of all peasants were hereditary occupiers of assigned or regulated state land.[81]

The prerogatives of tax farmers and of holders of assigned lands present important problems; but all of them arise within the context of government-controlled land. Since land of this type comprised the bulk of all cultivated acreage, we feel justified in saying that the Islamic Near East, up to the 19th century, was characterized by a semicomplex pattern of Oriental property and society.

Maya Society: The Maya system of land tenure is not clear.[82] There probably was some individual landownership,[83] but most of the cultivable land seems to have been "common" (regulated) land.[84]

Pre-Conquest Mexico: Early sources agree that the bulk of all land in this area, as in Yucatan and Peru, was government controlled. The great majority of all peasants (and townspeople) lived in regulated communities (calpulli).[85] But there were also certain private lands, *tierras proprias patrimoniales*,[86] which were tilled by *mayeques*,[87] peasants attached to the soil.

According to Zurita, private land had long been in existence.[88] Did it originate through grant or sale? And how freely could those who held it dispose of it? Local officials were permitted to sell

n. Gibb and Bowen, 1950: 237. The authors cite a statement according to which the "Sipāhīs" used to convert the state land they held into private property "in later times" (*ibid.*: 188, n. 6). Unfortunately the reference specifies neither the approximate date nor the extent of the development.

o. A farm whose deceased owner was without heirs (Gibb and Bowen, 1950: 239).

calpulli lands, if they were not burdened with obligations; and as
stated above, the buyers of these tracts—which were then alienable—
were either members of the ruling families or "some officials or
merchants." [89] However, most of the *calpulli* land was burdened
with serious and lasting obligations in that its yield was destined
to support either the members of the *calpulli* themselves or officials
of the local or central government, garrisons, or temples.[90] In consequence, the amount of land available for sale was probably small.[91]

It is not clear to what extent the *tierras proprias patrimoniales*
originated from the sale of *calpulli* land. Some, or perhaps even
many, of these private holdings may well have been grants made by
the rulers to distinguished individuals. In contrast to the allodial
estates of feudal Europe, the *tierras proprias patrimoniales* remained
under the jurisdiction of the government; [92] and in contrast to the
serfs of allodial or feudal estates the Mexican *mayeques* served the
government "in time of war or need." [93] This formula is comprehensive. In Aztec Mexico, as in other hydraulic societies, the government determined one-sidedly what kind of services it needed.

Not being office lands, the private holdings were not kept intact
by the will of the government. And not being allodial or feudal
estates, they were not entailed by the will of the owner: *"no son de
mayorazgo."* [94] In fact, the private lands of ancient Mexico were as
similar to the sinecure lands of other Oriental societies as they
were dissimilar to the strong landed property of feudal and postfeudal Europe. In all probability they represented a smaller percentage of all cultivated land than did private lands in Babylonia
or in early Islamic society. According to one estimate, the private
holdings in ancient Mexico amounted to little.[95] According to another, they may have comprised somewhat more than 10 per cent of
the total cultivated area.[p]

iii. COMPLEX PATTERNS OF HYDRAULIC
PROPERTY AND SOCIETY

ORIENTAL societies in which there was less private land than
government-controlled land are many. Private land was insignificant
in the higher civilizations of South and Meso-America when they
were overrun by the Spaniards. It remained a secondary feature in
India, Sumer, Babylonia, Persia, the Hellenistic monarchies of the
Near East, and Islamic society. In the early phases of state-centered
Chinese society it appears to have been as unimportant as it was in

p. This figure was suggested in a memorandum on land tenure in pre-Conquest
Mexico prepared for the present inquiry by Dr. Paul Kirchhoff.

pre-Conquest America; and when China, under the impact of Inner Asian forces, temporarily discarded the free forms of landed property that had prevailed at the end of the Chou period and throughout the imperial dynasties of Ch'in and Han, regulated patterns of land tenure prevailed again.

Thus, our survey confirms what we tentatively suggested at the start of our discussion of hydraulic land tenure. Prior to the recent period of institutional disintegration and transition, private land may have prevailed in the Near East under Roman rule; it certainly prevailed in China from the later part of the first pre-Christian millennium to the 5th century A.D. and, after an interlude of almost three centuries, again and until our time.

The Roman Near East: Did such classically hydraulic countries as Egypt, under Roman rule, actually develop complex patterns of property? The conquerors did indeed establish private landed property within the terms of Roman provincial law; [96] and in Byzantine Egypt prior to the Arab conquest large estates were certainly held by the "powerful ones," the *dynatoi.* But how widespread was land-ownership at the beginning of the Roman empire? And to what extent did it prevail during the 5th and 6th centuries?

Under Roman influence private land was created through grants,[97] through transfer of cleruchic land (military office land),[98] and through the sale and grant of other government land.[99] This was a far cry from Hellenistic conditions; but even scholars who emphasize the qualitative differences [100] are usually careful also to indicate the quantitative limitations. The greater part of the former cleruchic land was taken back by the government immediately after the conquest; [101] and out of the private estates that temporarily came into being as the result of grants or sales "the majority" soon again became imperial property.[102] Thus "the best land continued for the most part to form the royal domain and to bear the name royal land." [q] And since, in the main, it was the larger estates that were confiscated, private land seems essentially to have been held by small owners. This is particularly true for Egypt and Asia Minor. A greater incidence of large estates is suggested for Syria and Palestine.[103]

The existence of private landownership is said to have reached a

---

q. Bell, 1948: 73. On the basis of several decades of additional research Bell confirms what Mommsen had cautiously noted in 1885, namely that the imperial domain constituted "a considerable part of the entire area in Roman as in earlier times" (Mommsen, 1921: 573). Johnson and West (1949: 22) refer to "the retention of the great bulk of arable land as the property of the [Roman] crown"; and Johnson (1951: 92) calls "the amount of privately owned land in Roman times . . . slight."

second peak on the eve of the Arab conquest, especially in Byzantine
Egypt. What actually were the conditions of land tenure in Egypt
during this period? The peasants, who because of extreme fiscal
pressure had become increasingly reluctant to farm—not a few ran
away from their villages—became the targets of elaborate "reform"
measures. Government control in the form of compulsory permanent
tenancy (epibolē) became more and more strict.[104] Increasingly the
peasants were permanent holders of land which they were forbidden
to leave. As coloni, they were attached to the land which, from
then on and within the confines of a rigidly regulated village community, became their "private" possession.[105] The continuing fiscal
burdens caused many villages to look to "powerful" protectors,
primarily members of the governing class, and to the church.[106]
These individuals, who were designated patroni until 415,[107] did not
exert authority everywhere—many villages remained directly subordinated to the fiscus and the imperial administration.[108] Nor did
they integrate "their" peasants into a typical and large-scale manorial
economy,[109] although for lack of a better term their holdings are
usually referred to as "estates."

The edict of 415, which acknowledged the position of the estate
holders, also reaffirmed the government's claim on the fiscal and corvée
services that the landholding coloni had previously fulfilled.[110] The
holders of the new estates were delegated to collect taxes for the
government from their coloni. But although this function endowed
the new landlords with great power,[111] the state upheld its fiscal
rights without compromise: "the rate of taxation was the same for
all." [112] Thus with regard to the most crucial fiscal aspect the estate
holders were not privileged: "that their tax rate was less than others,
there is no evidence whatsoever." [r]

Under Justinian (to be precise: in 538) the Byzantine government

r. Johnson and West, 1949: 240. In the 2d and 3d centuries the tax collectors seem
to have been in the main municipal groups or individual businessmen who had their
fiscal duties imposed upon them as a "liturgy." The government used these liturgical
obligations to destroy the economic strength of propery-based groups (Wallace, 1938:
347 ff.); and it transferred the fiscal tasks to the bureaucratic landlords, who, being
politically better connected, succeeded where the private entrepreneurs had failed. But
these estate-holders were in no sense feudal lords, who could appropriate the bulk of
the peasant surplus they collected. From the 4th to the 6th century the Byzantine
collectors were generally allowed commissions of some 2 per cent on the collection
of wheat, 2½ per cent on barley, and 5 per cent on wine and pork (Johnson and
West, 1949: 328, cf. 290). Whether these rates were valid for Egypt we do not know
(ibid.); but we do know that the Egyptian tax collector was entitled to a fee of one-
eighth to one-twelfth of the money tax he raised (ibid.: 268, 284), that is, to a commission of 8 to 15 per cent. By manipulation he could raise his share to from 10 to
20 per cent of the money tax (ibid.: 268, 284 ff.).

expected a tax revenue from Egypt that was larger than that mentioned for the time of Augustus.[113] This fact involves a number of
questions which have not as yet been solved.[114] For our purpose,
however, it is enough to know that the Byzantine government was
able to tax the Egyptian peasants as comprehensively and successfully as did the Romans under their powerful first emperor.

To be sure, there were in Egypt at the close of the Byzantine
period large units of private landed property: estates. These estates
arose under a bureaucratic government; they were held mainly by
bureaucratic landlords; and they were organized in a conspicuously
bureaucratic way.[s]

All this we know. We do not know, however, "whether these estates
of Egypt were privately owned or were leaseholds from imperial and
ecclesiastical properties, or even from small farmers." [115] We do not
know either whether these estates, prior to the Arab conquest, comprised more than one-half of the cultivable land. The law forbade
the estate holders to purchase peasant land at will, and according to
Johnson,[116] "there is no evidence" that this legislation "was ever
a dead letter." The landlord's proprietary position, even if it had
the character of ownership, was legally limited. The freedom of the
villagers, it need scarcely be repeated, was even more severely restricted.

The historical data known today suggest that in such Near
Eastern countries as Egypt private landownership did not prevail
at the beginning of the Roman period and they give little reason to
assume that this type of ownership spread later in such a way as to
even temporarily establish complex patterns of property and society.

China: Authentic historical records state that in the 4th century
B.C. in the state of Ch'in the traditional regulated field system was
abolished and that from then on, land could be bought and sold
freely.[117] The records dealing with the imperial dynasties of Ch'in
and Han imply that after the unification of China private landownership prevailed generally.[118] When, in the first century B.C.,

---

s. Bell finds that in contrast to feudal lordship in the West, which "was a replica
in little of the kingdom to which it belonged," the estate of Byzantine Egypt "reproduced in little the bureaucratic empire of which it formed a part; its organization and
its hierarchy of officials were modelled on the Imperial bureaucracy. Indeed it is
sometimes impossible, in dealing with a papyrus document of this period, to be
certain whether the persons whose titles are mentioned in it were Imperial officials
or the servants of some great family" (Bell, 1948: 123 ff.). This overlapping of titles,
far from being accidental, reflects an overlapping in positions. The proprietors of
these estates were for the most part, if not exclusively, officiating or nonofficiating
members of the governing class, who even in their capacity as landlords functioned
as semi-officials: tax collectors and leaders of the hydraulic and nonhydraulic corvées.

merchants accumulated substantial mobile and immobile property, the government took strong fiscal measures to reduce their wealth, and an edict in 119 B.C. forbade them to own land; [119] but this edict did not interfere with land transfers between other classes, and even in the case of the merchants it seems to have been maintained only temporarily.

Unfortunately the historical sources leave important aspects of the agrarian development unexplained; and this is true both for the first period of complex property relations and for the subsequent regulated agrarian order that was instituted in the 5th century A.D. and endured until the middle of the 8th century. However, the information at hand is sufficient to illuminate at least the main trends in these periods.[120] During the last millennium, dynasties of conquest reserved lands for their tribal supporters and for some Chinese who had joined their conquering armies; but for the bulk of their Chinese subjects they upheld private landownership. It has been estimated that during the last phase of the Ch'ing (Manchu) dynasty the combined bannerland of the Manchu, Mongol, and Chinese bannermen amounted to some 4 per cent and privately owned land to almost 93 per cent.[t]

Although prior to this phase nongovernment land may at times have amounted to no more than one-half of all land,[121] and although a variety of legal clauses gave the right of preemption (primarily) to relatives,[122] it seems evident that China went further than any other major Oriental civilization in maintaining private ownership in land.

The reasons for this extraordinary development are by no means clear. But certain facts are suggestive. In China the critical changes occurred after the middle of the first millennium B.C., when several important culture elements appeared simultaneously: plowing with oxen, the use of iron, and the art of horseback riding. We hesitate to dismiss this coincidence as inconsequential. None of these elements emerged in the hydraulic areas of pre-Conquest America; and in the Near East and India they emerged separately in the course of a drawn-out development. In both areas plowing with labor animals was known from the dawn of written history, whereas the use of iron spread later, and the art of horseback riding later still. Could

---

t. Buck, 1937: 193. The estimate used by Dr. Buck puts privately owned land at 92.7 per cent, land assigned to Manchu nobles together with some "crown land" at 3.2 per cent, "state land" (land set aside for the maintenance of schools, religious purposes [state cult]) at 4.1 per cent. These data are approximate. They do not make allowance for private ancestral and temple land, which, according to the same source, amounted to less than .05 per cent.

it be that the simultaneous rise of new techniques of agricultural production and of military coercion and fast communication (and the assurance the two last gave to the maintenance of government control) encouraged the masters of Chinese society to experiment confidently with extremely free forms of landed property? Whatever the reason for the fateful step may have been, once taken it was found to be politically workable and agronomically and fiscally rewarding.

The Chinese development—which requires further investigation —is remarkable not only for its success but also for its geographical limitations. It seems to have affected certain southwestern neighbors, especially Siam. But many cultural contacts with more remote Asian countries notwithstanding, the Chinese system of private landowner- ship remained essentially confined to the area of its origin.

3. How Free Is Private Landed Property in Hydraulic Society?

THUS private landownership was present in many hydraulic civiliza- tions; but except for a brief and recent period of transition, the combined private lands were less extensive than the combined public lands. More. Even where private landownership did prevail, it in- variably was prevented from achieving the kind of freedom which is possible in a multicentered nonhydraulic society.

a. Despotically Imposed versus Democratically Established Restrictions of Private Property

To be sure, in no society does an owner absolutely dispose over his property. Even under conditions of strong property the owner of bricks, who may sell or store them or use them in building his house, may not throw them at his neighbor. The early Roman emphasis on the proprietor's sovereign position, although meaningful fiscally, is not valid societally.

Even fiscally the holder of strong property is not necessarily without burdens. In most free commonwealths some public func- tionaries have to be supported, and when this is the case, the citizens may have to draw upon their property to satisfy this need. Contribu- tions from private property for the maintenance of the government will be used only for proven essentials when the property-based forces of society can keep government in a serving position. Such contributions will increase, and be spent more freely, when an im- perfectly controlled government partially determines its own budget. They will be determined one-sidedly and with primary concern for the interests of those in power when a state stronger than society prevents the representatives of property from protecting their interests. It is under conditions of the first type that we find strong, though never absolute, property. And it is under conditions of the third type that property is weak. In hydraulic society immobile property, like mobile property, remains weak even where private landownership quantitatively outweighs public land tenure.

b. Restrictions Imposed upon the Freedom to Enjoy, to Use, to Transfer, and to Organize

ORIENTAL despotism one-sidedly restricts the landowner's freedom to enjoy the fruits of his property, to decide on its use, to will it freely (through testament), and to protect it by means of political organization.

The agrodespotic government demands payments from all landholders, either for its own use or for the use of especially privileged persons or institutions (temples, mosques, churches); and it determines the land tax one-sidedly, according to its own (the rulers') rationality standard. Tenancy may stratify the proprietary sector; and the changing strength of local and central authorities may alter the distribution of state revenues within the bureaucratic order. But neither condition affects the fundamental arrangement that compels owners and/or possessors of land generally to surrender a substantial part of their revenue to the representatives of the state.

Directly, this arrangement aims at the fruits of operational landed property. Indirectly, it also influences (and limits) the use to which a given piece of land may be put. The government bases its fiscal demands on the expectation that the peasant occupiers (or owners) will grow a crop capable of yielding a certain return. This demand forces the cultivator to grow the standard crop or an acceptable substitute. Occasionally, and particularly in regulated agrarian orders, the government may expressly prescribe that certain plants or trees (rice, corn, olives, hemp, cotton, or mulberry trees) be cultivated; and in these cases the proprietor's freedom to determine how his land should be used is nil. Frequently, however, the government is content to prescribe how much should be paid over to it. In both cases the result is a crude type of planned economy, which substantially limits the cultivator's freedom of choice and action.

Restrictions on the freedom to will property and to organize for its protection have been discussed in an earlier chapter. Hydraulic laws of inheritance fragment privately owned land. The landowner's inability to strengthen his proprietary position through independent national and politically effective organizations is as apparent in complex as in semicomplex or simple hydraulic societies.

This does not mean to say that the predominance of private land-ownership and the spread of landlordism in such civilizations as traditional China were societally irrelevant. They were not. But the spread of landlordism, which significantly modified the relations between the officiating and nonofficiating (gentry) segments of the ruling class, did not result in the consolidation of landed property or in independent organizations of landed proprietors. From the fiscal, legal, and political points of view private landownership was as weak at the final collapse of traditional Chinese society as it had been at its birth.

I. THE EFFECT OF PRIVATE PROPERTY ON HYDRAULIC SOCIETY

1. The Perpetuation of Hydraulic Society Depends on the Government's Maintenance of its Property Relations

On the basis of these facts certain general conclusions seem justified. First of all, hydraulic society, like other institutional conformations, knows private property. Human existence over any considerable period of time is impossible without the public recognition and standardization of relations between persons and things or services. Even the convict possesses his clothes while he wears them; and many slaves possess not only their clothes but certain other articles as well. A serf possesses a great variety of things in addition to his land.

In most cases possession—and, of course, ownership—are recognized by custom. Where written laws exist, important forms of property may be recognized and regulated by special statutes.

This is true for all societies, including those ruled by despotic regimes. The most elementary considerations of rationality require that even those who make—and change—laws one-sidedly and despotically should emphasize their validity by not abrogating them unnecessarily. A ruler's rationality coefficient is the higher, the more strictly he himself observes the regulations which he has imposed upon his subjects. This also includes regulations concerned with private property.

The Oriental despot may buy and sell land.[1] He may have private artisans producing goods for him and at times he may pay them generously. And he may also buy directly from merchants. In all these cases he may—though he need not—set a low price. In Muscovite Russia this seems to have been the rule,[2] and in classical Hindu

India merchants had to accept whatever figure the king's appraiser deemed appropriate.[3] But the fact that the ruler and his officials paid for certain goods and services does not negate the despotic character of the regime. It only shows that by and large the despotic regime proceeds on the basis of the legal and proprietary regulations it has established.

What is true for Oriental despotism is no less true for the modern industrial apparatus state. Superficial observation may be satisfied with the presence of laws that deal with property. But no realistic analyst will call the Hitler government democratic because it dealt with Jewish property in accordance with the Nüremberg laws. Nor will he deny the absolutist character of the early Soviet state because it bought grain at a government-fixed price from individually producing peasants.

2. THE GROWING COMPLEXITY OF PROPERTY AND THE GROWING COMPLEXITY OF SOCIETY

IN addition to being an essential feature of hydraulic society, hydraulic property is also characterized by a variety of forms. Considerable private property and enterprise may appear in industry and commerce; and private ownership may spread, and even prevail, in agriculture. The representatives of semicomplex and complex patterns of property maintain relations to one another and with the state that differ substantially from those maintained by representatives of simple patterns of property. This fact enables us to distinguish, on the basis of different patterns of property, different subtypes of the over-all societal order.

3. SMALL PROPERTY OFFERS A CONSIDERABLE ECONOMIC INCENTIVE, BUT NO POLITICAL POWER

a. Incentives Inherent in Private Possession and Ownership

THE technical advantages accruing from devices that can be employed only by large teams may equal or outweigh what is achieved by individual effort or by the labor of a few kinsmen working together. But when the technical advantages are insignificant or lacking, the incentives for individual action tend to become more effective.

Individual action need not be based on ownership. The occupier of a piece of land may only be its possessor, but in premachine days and under comparable technical conditions he is likely to outproduce a member of a team who is working for hire. Throughout the hydraulic world we therefore find the peasants tilling their land individually rather than collectively; and where labor animals increased the advantages of individual cultivation, small-scale peasant work also replaced the only relevant system of collective agriculture, the public field system. In handicraft and commerce private enterprise is generally based on private ownership. In agriculture private possession is usually sufficient to make the peasant proceed with great care. Tenancy, like peasant ownership, has created a horticulture-like intensity of farming.

To be sure, the tenant's desire to own his land is enormously strong. Even under the most frustrating fiscal conditions most peasant owners cling to their fields in the hope that the irrational tax pressure will be lightened before they are forced to abandon their property.

Property-based private handicraft created many of the beautiful objects (textiles, wood-, leather-, and metal-work) that delight the student of hydraulic civilization; and the hydraulic peasants who individually tilled their fields surpassed in skill and productivity the serfs of Medieval Europe. This was so even when these peasants were only the hereditary occupiers of regulated land; and it was even more so when they were tenants or private landowners. Indeed it is not at all unlikely that the exceptional intensity of agriculture in traditional China derived from the fact that private peasant land-ownership was more widespread there than in any other major hydraulic civilization.[a]

b. The Beggars' Property

SMALL private property, both possessed and owned, was conspicuous in hydraulic societies of the semicomplex type. It became much more so, and particularly in the agrarian sphere, in complex Oriental societies. Did it in either case become an important political force?

From the standpoint of a multicentered property-based society, the question is entirely reasonable. Small proprietors (artisans and peasants) played an ever increasing political role in classical Greece.

a. The feudal landholders of Japan did not engage in large-scale manorial farming as did their European peers; and the Japanese peasants cultivated their land individually and under conditions which resembled tenancy rather than serfdom. On the basis of a highly refined irrigation economy, they too engaged in a semihorticultural type of farming. This cannot be explained entirely by geographical proximity. The Japanese did not adopt the semimanagerial bureaucratic absolutism of China; nor did they adopt their system of private landownership from their continental neighbors. But within a feudal framework of power and social relations, the Japanese nobles gave their peasants as great a proprietary incentive as the over-all pattern of their society permitted.

Independent artisans were prominent in many guild cities of Medieval Europe; and, together with the peasants, they constituted a significant element in the democratic governments of Switzerland. In a number of the predominantly agrarian states of the United States which are not given over to giant farms and large-scale production the farmers' vote is a decisive factor. Although today the farmers account for no more than one-fifth of America's manpower, they are better organized than ever, and they continue to be a substantial political force, both regionally and nationally.

There is no need here to stress the potential political importance of labor—a group whose essential economic asset is the capacity to work. Free labor became a political force during the final democratic phase of ancient Greece, and under new conditions it emerged again in the property-based industrial society of our time. Organized both professionally and politically, the representatives of this form of individual property have in some industrial countries, such as Australia, Sweden, and England, assumed political as well as economic leadership; and in many others, including the United States, their political position has improved rapidly.

Small property and labor played no comparable role in the hydraulic world. With regard to labor the issue is simple. Personally free, hired laborers have existed in many hydraulic civilizations.[4] Unskilled workers were for the most part unorganized. Skilled workers were frequently organized in local and separate professional units. But even when they were not under strict government supervision, they constituted only a politically irrelevant form of self-government, a Beggars' Democracy.

And the peasant proprietors? Whether they possessed or owned their land, they remained the representatives of a fragmented type of property and enterprise. At best they were permitted to handle their essentially local affairs within the rural version of a Beggars' Democracy, the village community.

From the standpoint of the absolutist bureaucracy, the property of both artisans and peasants was Beggars' Property, property that was economically fragmented and politically impotent.[b]

b. Did the peasants constitute an economic and political threat during the first period of the Soviet regime? Long before 1917 Lenin stressed the danger of any private property (peasant land included) for a socialist regime (cf. Lenin, S, IX: 66–7, 213–14, and passim); and he did not change his opinion after his party established its dictatorial power with the support of the peasants who had been "given" land (ibid., XXVII: 303 ff.; XXXI: 483 ff.). He insisted that property transforms men into "wild beasts" (ibid., XXX: 418); and he called the petty bourgeois and small peasants potential breeders of capitalism and thus an inherent danger to the Soviet state (ibid., XXVII: 303 ff.; XXXI: 483). In 1918, and again in 1921, Lenin viewed these petty

4. PRIVATE COMMERCIAL PROPERTY POLITICALLY INCONSEQUENTIAL EVEN WHEN PERMITTED TO BECOME LARGE

UNDER certain conditions, the representatives of Oriental despotism found it economically advisable to have the bulk of all trade handled by private businessmen. When this was the case, some merchants grew fabulously rich, and a few enjoyed distinguished social positions.

We do not exclude the possibility that big merchants as a group could have participated in the running of despotic governments; but the evidence at hand fails to document this development as a significant feature in any of the major representatives of semicomplex or complex hydraulic societies. In Babylonia, in Buddhist India, in pre-Conquest Meso-America, in the Islamic Near East, and in imperial China big merchant property, even when involved in large-scale operations, remained politically inconsequential.

5. PROBLEMS OF WEALTH WITHIN THE GOVERNING CLASS

PROPERTY problems of a very different kind arise within the governing class. In simple hydraulic societies almost the entire national surplus is appropriated by the ruler and his serving men. And even when intermediary groups, such as the merchants, are permitted to derive considerable profit from their transactions, the governing class continues to monopolize the greater part of the country's wealth. The members of the court and the officials may receive their share of this wealth either as revenue from assigned (office or sinecure) lands or as salary (in kind or cash). In both cases the income is based on the government's power to control land and to tax people. And in both cases it becomes private (bureaucratic) property. Its recipients may use all of it for consumption; or they may set some part of it aside as savings or for investments. Both types of use involve the problem of bureaucratic hedonism; the second raises in addition the problem of bureaucratic landlordism and capitalism.

---

bourgeois forces as his regime's "principal enemy" (*ibid.*, XXXII: 339). On the eve of the First Five-Year Plan, Stalin repeated Lenin's formula that the small producers are "the last capitalist class" (*ibid.*, XXXII: 460). He insisted that this class "will breed capitalists in its ranks, and cannot help breeding them, constantly and continuously" (Stalin, 1942: 102). There is no evidence that either Lenin or Stalin based his views on a serious study of the political position of small peasant landholders under absolutist state power. Stalin's pseudoscientific accusations of 1928 only served to prepare the Soviet bureaucracy and the Soviet people for the total liquidation of private peasant property.

a. Bureaucratic Hedonism

BUREAUCRATIC hedonism can be defined as the enjoyment of wealth without provoking the envy of high officials or the crushing wrath of the despot.[5] Such hedonism may be complicated by opportunities for saving and investing. While the members of the governing class are generally eager to enjoy their property as long as the enjoying is good, they express this desire differently under different circumstances. But the wish to consume pleasantly and to live well prevails everywhere, even in those complex hydraulic societies in which the possibility of owning land encourages economy and thrift.[c] Often and particularly in the case of very highly placed and continually endangered officials, such as viziers, chancellors, or "prime ministers," the bureaucratic *joie de vivre* is spectacularly manifested.[6]

b. Bureaucratic Landlordism and Capitalism

EVEN the most luxury-loving functionary usually tries to save part of his income. After all, he may not be in office forever; his family will always have to eat; and his children will have to be trained for the most desirable of all goals: a government career. Thus the thoughtful official buries precious metals and jewels in the ground. Or better still he converts some of his passive private property into active property. He buys land for rental and/or he uses his funds profitably as a government contractor (especially as a tax collector), or as a money lender, or as a partner in private commercial enterprise. On the basis of his bureaucratic property he becomes a bureaucratic landlord and/or a bureaucratic capitalist.

Of course, there are others who are landlords also. Wherever land can be freely alienated, small proprietors are eager to purchase it.[7] And there may also be nonbureaucratic capitalists. But since the uniquely powerful state apparatus surpasses all other forces of hydraulic society in acquiring agricultural and nonagricultural revenue, officials figure prominently as tax farmers and, wherever land can be bought, as landowners.

In imperial China predominance of private landownership enabled the officials to invest a considerable part of their income in land. A recent analysis of officialdom and bureaucratic gentry in 19th-century China suggests that at the close of the Ch'ing dynasty present and former officials, holders of official titles, and holders of high examination degrees together may have received land rents

---

c. The pleasures of bureaucratic consumption in late imperial China were depicted in great detail in such novels as the *Dream of the Red Chamber*.

amounting to 165 million taels annually and about 81.5 million taels from entrepreneurial activities. At the same time all lower degree-holders together received about 55 millions from the first source and 40 millions from the second.[d] These figures indicate that by far the greater part of the rent income of the official-literati went to the upper echelon of this group, which was predominantly bureaucratic (present and former officials and quasi-officials outweighed the holders of high degrees by three to one).[e] The members of this echelon received an average of 1100 taels in rent annually. The lower degree holders received from this source only about 44 taels; and this despite the fact that over a third of all members of this group were wealthy enough to purchase their degree.[f]

The civil and military officials may have derived an annual income of 91 million taels from their government positions. This suggests for the ranking official an average bureaucratic income of about 1700 taels [g]—that is, 65 per cent more than the average income from rent.

Under Oriental as well as under Occidental despotism, landlord-ism and officialdom overlap. But the seemingly similar configurations differ profoundly in their institutional substance. The bureaucratic landlords of Oriental society derived their political power essentially from the absolutist government, of which they themselves

d. These and many other illuminating data have been taken from a comprehensive study of the Chinese "gentry" in the 19th century by Dr. Chang Chung-li, University of Washington, Seattle, who has generously permitted their inclusion in the present study. The officials and degree-holders are classed together, because during the later part of imperial China they constituted a status group, *shên-shih* (see below, Chap. 8). Their entrepreneurial income stemmed mainly from investments in native banks, pawnshops, and the salt trade (Chang, GI, Pt. II). Dr. Chang's study shows that the *shên-shih*—"a privileged group with managerial abilities and functions"—received "from 'government services,' 'professional services' and 'gentry services' together" an income larger than that from rent or mercantile activities (letter from Dr. Chang, March 20, 1954).

e. Prior to the Taiping Rebellion, the "officials, officers and holders of official titles" together constituted 67 per cent of the upper group; after the Taiping period, the figure rose to 75 per cent (Chang, CG, Pt. II).

f. A lower degree attained through examination opened the door to regular advancement on the ladder of higher examination degrees and government office. The purchased degree carried with it no such advantages.

g. It is assumed that out of a total of 50,000 incumbent and former civil officials (Chang, CG) about 40,000 held office (see below, Chap. 8, sec. C, n. 3); and that among the 17,000 military officers (*ibid.*) a similar proportion prevailed. According to Dr. Chang, the figure of 40,000 civil officials, suggested by Mrs. Lienche Tu Fang, probably includes "expectant officials who gathered around the governors and governor-generals" and who "were often given temporary assignments." Although not listed in the registers of the central government, they were responsible to, and paid by, the provincial authority (letter from Dr. Chang, March 1, 1954).

or their officiating relatives formed an active part. It was only as officials that the members of the agrobureaucratic gentry were politically organized. The noble landlords of postfeudal Europe or Japan did not necessarily hold government office. And they did not need government salaries to periodically restore their landed property, since their estates were kept intact by primogeniture and entail.

The land of the bureaucratic (Oriental) gentry might facilitate a government career for certain of its members and thus give renewed access to power; but essentially this land was revenue property. Conversely, the land of the feudal (Occidental) gentry involved the perpetuation of organized political power, independent of, and at times openly conflicting with, state power. In a way unparalleled by hydraulic property (bureaucratic and other) and in addition to being revenue land, feudal property was conspicuously and significantly power property.

6. CONCLUSIONS LEADING TO NEW QUESTIONS

a. Hydraulic Property: Revenue Property versus Power Property

WHETHER hydraulic property is large or small or whether or not it belongs to a member of the governing class, it provides material advantages. But it does not enable its holders to control state power through property-based organization and action. In all cases, it is not power property but revenue property.

b. The Importance—and Limitation—of Private Property in Determining Class Differentiations within Hydraulic Society

THIS does not mean to deny the importance of property in establishing social (class) differentiations. The emergence of property-based handicraft and commerce and the spread of private landownership involve the emergence of new social elements, groups, and classes. Thus it is not only legitimate but necessary to show in which ways patterns of social differentiation correlate with patterns of private property.

However, it is quickly apparent that in hydraulic society the problem of social differentiation involves more than the question of the presence or extent of private property. Once established, bureaucratic wealth is private property, but it is rooted in, and derives from, government property, and its intrabureaucratic distribution is based on political conditions that cannot be explained in terms of private property.

CHAPTER 8

Classes in hydraulic society

A. THE NEED FOR A NEW SOCIOLOGY OF CLASS

MODERN institutional analysis emerged in a society that was decisively shaped by conditions of property. Consequently, the pioneers in the modern sociology of class saw the major segments ("orders") [1] of society as determined essentially by major types of private property and by corresponding types of revenue. According to Adam Smith, "the whole annual produce of the land and labour of every country . . . naturally divides itself . . . into three parts; the rent of land, the wages of labour, and the profits of stock; and constitutes a revenue to three different orders of people; to those who live by rent, to those who live by wages, and to those who live by profit. These are the three great, original and constituent orders of every civilized society, from whose revenue that of every other order is ultimately derived." [2] The representatives of government are supported to an extent from "public stock and public lands"; but the greater part of their expenses is met by the three major orders which render some of their revenue to the state in the form of taxes. [3]

According to this view, the representatives of government constitute not a major order of society but a secondary and derivative one. And whenever conflicts concerning property arise, civil government becomes a weapon of the propertied classes against the economically under-privileged groups. To quote Smith again: "Civil government, so far as it is instituted for the security of property, is in reality instituted for the defence of the rich against the poor, or of those who have some property against those who have none at all." [a]

This statement, which was written in a period of unbridled

---

a. Smith, 1937: 674. Smith supplements this statement by a citation from his "Lectures": "Till there be property there can be no government, the very end of which is to secure wealth and to defend the rich from the poor." He adds a reference to Locke, *Civil Government*, sec. 94: "Government has no other end but the preservation of property."

proprietary privilege, presents a crude economic interpretation of the state. It makes no allowance for power as an independent determinant of class or for the socio-economic prominence of the state in the hydraulic civilizations with which Smith was familiar.[b] Smith's successors defined the peculiarity of Asiatic society more clearly; but they, too, treated "Asia" as a residual category in a socio-economic system which considered private property and the revenue derived from it the decisive factors in the formation of class.

Despite its obvious deficiencies, the proprietary concept of class greatly stimulated the social sciences up to the beginning of the 20th century. Without doubt, this concept is essential for the understanding of societies in which strong independent private property prevails; and it remains important also for the understanding of certain secondary aspects of power-based societies. But it is insufficient when it is unqualifiedly applied to formations of the first type. And it is altogether inadequate when it is used as the essential means for explaining formations of the second type.

The growth of big government in many modern industrial countries and the rise of totalitarian states in the USSR and Germany enable us to recognize state power as a prominent determinant of class structure, both in our time and in the past. They also enable us to recognize more clearly than before the importance of power in the establishment of the ruling class in hydraulic society.

B. CLASS STRUCTURE IN HYDRAULIC SOCIETY

1. THE KEY CRITERION: RELATION TO THE STATE APPARATUS

THE pioneers of a property-based sociology of class viewed the Asiatic state as a gigantic landowner. In most hydraulic societies the bulk of all cultivated land is indeed regulated; and although the state's proprietary right over the regulated fields is hidden behind the façade of a seemingly self-governing village community, it operates negatively when the government prevents outsiders from purchasing these fields, and positively when the government assigns or sells land (or villages) at will. However, the classical formula is definitely unsatisfactory in at least one respect: It overlooks irrigation water, which in hydraulic societies is a major agent of production.

b. Smith, 1937: 789 ff. On a number of occasions Smith tries to remove the inconsistency by limiting his scheme to "civilized" societies. But he makes no effort to establish a concept of class that adequately mirrors the specific position of the state and its representatives in either the Eastern or the Western world.

Does the despotic state "own" the great accumulations of water? This has been claimed in many but not all hydraulic civilizations. I prefer to view the state as controlling rather than owning the country's "big" water.

The same approach may also be taken with regard to land. Some hydraulic states, such as imperial China, tolerated the predominance of privately owned land over a long period of time, and in this case the state restricted the owner's proprietary position by means of heavy taxation, directives as to what crops should be grown, and a fragmenting law of inheritance. Thus the hydraulic state, which frequently owned the bulk of all cultivable land, generally kept landed property weak. Its position is again best viewed as one of control.

In hydraulic society the first major division into an order of superior and privileged persons and an order of inferior and under-privileged persons occurs simultaneously with the rise of an in-ordinately strong state apparatus. The masters and beneficiaries of this state, the rulers, constitute a class different from, and superior to, the mass of the commoners—those who, although personally free, do not share the privileges of power. The men of the apparatus state are a ruling class in the most unequivocal sense of the term; and the rest of the population constitutes the second major class, the ruled.[a]

Within the ruling class different individuals and groups differ greatly in their ability to make decisions and handle personnel. In the civil administration, as in the army, major directives originate at the top level. But, again, as in the army, minor decisions are made by men in the middle brackets. And decisions concerned with the final execution of orders and regulations are made by the noncoms and the buck privates of the power hierarchy. Such decisions may be insignificant from the standpoint of a superior, but they are often vitally important for the commoners whose fate they affect.

The parallel between the lower strata of the apparatus hierarchy and the small businessmen of a capitalistic society is obvious. A small capitalist has little influence on the conditions of supply, marketing, or finance, except when he combines with others of his kind; but whether he does so or not, he can usually decide where and what he wants to buy and/or produce. In fact, he makes many small decisions

a. Max Weber drew attention to the fact that under the conditions of supreme bu-reaucratic power the mass of the population are all reduced to the level of "the ruled,' who see themselves confronted by "a bureaucratically stratified ruling group" that actually, and even formally, may occupy "an altogether autocratic position" (Weber, WG: 667; cf. 669, 671).

respecting the small affairs that are his world. Similarly, middle and even lower functionaries in hydraulic society are, like the top-ranking leadership, part of the power apparatus; and with proper grading they, too, enjoy advantages that accrue essentially from the unrestricted authority of the regime.

In terms of income, lower members of the apparatus hierarchy may be compared to the employees of a capitalistic enterprise who do not share in the surplus they help to realize. A property-based sociology of class would therefore consider them commoners rather than members of the upper class. Such an approach, however, over-looks the human relations that usually and specifically characterize the operations of a bureaucratic order. These operations make the lowest representatives of the apparatus state participants in the exercise of total power. In contrast to the employees of a commercial or industrial enterprise who proceed under the give-and-take con-ditions of the market and thus in a formally equal way, even the most lowly men of the apparatus proceed on the basis of coercion, that is, in a formally unequal way. Their position in the power hierarchy provides some of the lowest functionaries with particular opportunities for personal enrichment; and it provides all of them with a specific sociopolitical status. As representatives of the despotic state, even the lowest functionaries arouse in the commoners a mixture of suspicion and fear. They therefore occupy a social posi-tion which places them, in terms of power, prestige, and sometimes also of revenue, outside of, and ambivalently above, the mass of the ruled.

The natives of a conquered country consider the occupying army a unit; and they do so knowing full well that the power of the rank-and-file soldier is extremely restricted. Similarly, the subjects of a hydraulic despotism view the men of the apparatus as a unit, even when it is clear that individual members vary immensely in power, wealth, and social status.

2. THE MULTIPLE CONDITIONING OF SOCIAL SUBSECTIONS

THE ruling class is differentiated from the earliest beginnings of hydraulic civilizations. The ruled class is usually undifferentiated in simple hydraulic societies. It is always differentiated in semicomplex and complex hydraulic societies.

The subsections of the two classes are differently conditioned. Within the ruling class position in the power hierarchy is the primary determinant, and wealth, although at times significant, remains secondary. Within the ruled class types and dimensions of active property are the primary determinants of social status, whereas differences in relation to the government tend, in this apolitical world, to play a minor role or no role at all.

C. THE RULERS

1. THE MEN OF THE APPARATUS

a. *The Basic Vertical Structure*

THE ruling class of hydraulic society is represented first by its active core, the men of the apparatus. In virtually all hydraulic countries these men are headed by a ruler, who has a personal entourage (his court) and who controls and directs his numerous civil and military underlings through a corps of ranking officials. This hierarchy, which includes the sovereign, the ranking officials, and the underlings, is basic to all Orientally despotic regimes. Horizontal developments, which occur under certain conditions, complicate the basic vertical structure.

i. THE RULER AND THE COURT

THE despot's arbitrary cruelties and his equally arbitrary generosities form the themes of many records. His arbitrary cruelties indicate that subject to obvious physical and cultural limitations he can make or break anyone if he wants to. His arbitrary generosities indicate that, subject to obvious economic limitations, he can spend wastefully and without being restricted by any constitutional agency. The proverbial glamour of Oriental courts is merely an economic expression of the ruler's despotic control over his subjects.

In his person the ruler combines supreme operational authority and the many magic and mythical symbols that express the terrifying (and allegedly beneficial) qualities of the power apparatus he heads. Because of immaturity, weakness, or incompetence, he may share his operational supremacy with an aide: a regent, vizier, chancellor, or "prime minister." But the exalted power of these men does not usually last long. It rarely affects the symbols of supreme authority. And it vanishes as soon as the ruler is strong enough to realize the autocratic potential inherent in his position.

The unique importance of the ruler's whims and actions give unique importance to individuals who may influence him. In addition to the vizier—and sometimes more consequential than he— the best situated to do so are the members of the ruler's personal entourage: his wives and concubines, his blood relatives and affinals, his courtiers, servants, and favorites. Under the conditions of despotic autocracy, any one of them may temporarily and irrationally wield excessive power.

ii. THE RANKING OFFICIALS

IN speaking of officials, we refer to persons who are assigned a particular type of government task. Among sedentary peoples the regular duties involved in such a task tend to be permanently and physically located in an "office" or "bureau." And usually the holder of such an office keeps a record of his dealings.

Linguistically, the word "bureaucracy" is a monstrosity.[1] But the importance of some of its connotations has made it popular, despite the disapproval of the purists. Semantically, a bureaucrat is a person who "rules through bureaus." In a wider sense, the term is also applied to any official who uses secretarial devices ("red tape") to delay action, to make himself important, or to idle on the job. When Stalin criticized "bureaucracy," he particularly stressed "bureaucracy and red tape," officials who indulge in "idle chatter about 'leadership in general,'" "incorrigible bureaucrats and chairwarmers."[2]

Certainly bureaucratic chair-warmers can be annoying and harmful; and even serving and controlled governments are plagued by them. But a bureaucracy becomes truly formidable only when its offices are the organizational centers of ruthless and total power. For this reason Stalin's effort to hide the bureaucratic Frankenstein of the Soviet regime behind the semihumorous facade of inefficient "chair-warmers" is nothing more than a clumsy attempt at totalitarian myth making.

The ranking officials include civil and military functionaries of recognized status. They do not include the bureaucratic underlings. The civil officials resemble their military colleagues in that both are in positions of command and able to make limited and intermediate decisions, that both are parts of centrally directed bodies, that both unconditionally (and usually full time) serve their ruler, and that both are government-supported either by salary or by revenue derived from state-assigned office lands.

An army is essentially an instrument of coercion, and as such not necessarily a bureaucratic institution. But the management of centrally directed armies of the Oriental type involves considerable organizational planning, which in literate civilizations is usually carried out through bureaus. Many officers are both fighters and administrators; but often the fighting officials are functionally separated from the bureaucratic officials (*Militärbeamte*). In any case officers are not feudal knights but government functionaries, and as such part of the ranking officialdom.

iii. THE UNDERLINGS

THE underlings of the bureaucratic hierarchy are either scribes or menial aides. The scribes account for the bulk of all the secretarial work done at the court, in the central government, and in the provincial and local offices. The menial aides act as gate keepers, runners, servants, jailers, and, in a semimilitary capacity, as policemen.

In all sizable agrobureaucratic despotisms the underlings are numerous. During the last period of imperial China about 40,000 ranking (civil) officials had at their disposal over 1,200,000 clerks and over 500,000 runners—that is, a total of more than 1,700,000 underlings, or something more than forty underlings to one ranking official.[3]

b. Horizontal Developments

THE bureaucratic network may spread over a large territory. But as long as the central government appoints the bulk of the ranking officials and directs the provincial bureaus, no special problems of horizontal authority arise, even when the regional functionaries, for reasons of distance or political expediency, are given a relatively free hand in the conduct of their business.

Max Weber was struck by the relatively loose way in which the central government of imperial China controlled the provincial bureaucracy;[4] and indeed, in accordance with the law of diminishing administrative returns, regional and local officials were given considerable freedom of decision in matters of detail. But as Weber himself recognized, the central government appointed and transferred these officials at will; and it determined the major lines of their action.[5]

Of course, from time to time dynastic authority declined; and when the inner crisis was serious, the high territorial officials became temporarily the semi-autonomous, or even the autonomous, masters of the areas they administered. But except for periods of disruption, the most distinguished provincial dignitaries were merely prominent members of the centrally established and centrally manipulated ranking bureaucracy.

i. SATRAPS

THE Persian empire of the Achaemenids differed from the Chinese empire both in origin and structure. The unification of China was prepared for by centuries of institutional growth; and the core areas of Chinese culture were sufficiently populous and strong to make their domination over the outlying and colonized regions relatively easy. Conversely, the Persians in a single generation extended their rule beyond the confines of their homeland to four sizable countries, each of which had a well-defined culture: Media (549), Lydia (546), Babylonia (538), and Egypt (525). They abolished the ruling houses in all four of these regions and in addition changed the political map by carving them up into a number of provinces, each governed by a satrap.[6]

The heterogeneity and size of their new acquisitions compelled the Persian conquerors to give their satraps unusual freedom in the handling of political affairs. A satrap might retain his position for a long period; and at times he might be succeeded by his son.[7] Moreover, he appointed the subsatraps [8] and probably also the local officials, who were usually natives.[9] He hired mercenary troops and his bodyguard. He commanded militia-like levies raised in his territory.[10] He administered the taxes of his province.[11] He maintained diplomatic relations with neighboring states.[12] And he might organize a military expedition against a neighbor country—usually, however, with the permission of the Great King.[13] Surrounded by his court, he ruled with kinglike splendor.[14] This quasiroyal status of the satrap was actively encouraged by the Persian sovereign,[15] who apparently considered this as good a way as any to maintain his prestige in distant regions.

Nevertheless, in several crucial respects, the Great King exerted strict control over his satraps. Definitely and conspicuously, he was the master, the satrap the serving man who owed him absolute obedience. A central system of communication and intelligence,[16] inspection by metropolitan officials,[17] and the maintenance of Persian garrisons at strategic points [18] prevented the satrap from attaining military or fiscal independence. The satrapies were taxed according to centrally devised principles and with definite obligations toward the capital. "The proceeds of this taxation were forwarded annually by the satraps to Susa, where the surplus that remained, after defraying the annual outgoings, accumulated in the king's treasury as a reserve fund." [19]

The Great King considered his satrap not a feudal vassal but a top-ranking territorial agent. "The king is the master over all his

subjects and the satrap his representative; they can arbitrarily interfere everywhere, not only where this is required by the realm's
interest, but wherever they want." [20]

Thus the Persian empire was "a bureaucratic state" (*ein Beamten-*
staat); [21] and the satrap's administrative and military freedom of
action did not destroy the basic structure of the bureaucratic hierarchy of which the satrap was a part.

ii. SUBORDINATE PRINCES, CURACAS, RĀJAS

A SATRAP might be a native of the region over which he had jurisdiction. But this was not typical. Only in Cilicia did the Great King
permit a member of the former ruling house to become the governor
of a newly established province.[22] Princes who voluntarily accepted
Persian sovereignty were generally permitted to continue ruling as
vassals. Like the satraps and subsatraps, they owed the Great King
military services and tribute; [23] but they seem to have enjoyed more
political and cultural freedom than did many other native rulers who
fell under the sway of powerful hydraulic empires.

The builders of the Inca empire permitted rulers who had surrendered voluntarily to hold official position; but these *curacas*
were subordinated to Inca governors.[a] Moreover, the shrines of the
region's highest deities were transferred to Cuzco; and the main
features of Inca religion were imposed upon the new subjects.[24]
While in some ways perpetuating the appearance of native rule, the
curacas were, for all practical purposes, integral parts of the imperial
officialdom.[b]

In Muslim India a number of native "chiefs" or rulers (*rāīs, rājas*)
were also, if somewhat differently, included in the ruling order. A
rāja was permitted to preserve many secondary features of his
previous power, if he vowed unconditional political (and fiscal)
submission to his new overlord. Says Moreland: "His [the chief's]
tenure depended on his loyalty, which meant primarily the punctual
payment of tribute." [25] The *rājas* were more or less free to determine
how, in their regions, the tribute should be raised.[26] In Akbar's
time the six older provinces, which constituted the core of the empire, were almost completely administered by the central govern-

a. Usually their sons were taken as hostages to Cuzco, where they were taught the
Inca way of life (Rowe, 1946: 272).

b. They were chiefs of 10,000, 5,000, 1,000, or 500 corviable men. See Rowe, 1946:
263. The chiefs of 100 were apparently the lowest ranking officials. Like the higher
functionaries, they might ceremonially participate in communal agriculture; but essentially they supervised and directed the chiefs of ten, who as foremen worked with
the peasants (Rowe, 1946: 263, 265).

ment, whereas the outlying provinces presented a mixed picture, some being headed by centrally appointed officials, some by *rājas*.[27]

The Persian satraps, the Inca *curacas,* and the *rājas* of Muslim India constitute a series of variants on the scale of political subordination. The relations between a satrap or *curaca* and their sovereign were definitely noncontractual; in substance, as well as in form, the ruler demanded total submission. The position of certain *rājas* included elements of a contractual arrangement; but these were expressed factually more than formally. Only with regard to the most loosely attached dependencies did a despotic overlord accept, under the cloak of an alliance, a quasicontractual relationship.

The contrast to feudal patterns of subordination is manifest. Under a feudal regime the contractual relationship is essential; and it characterizes the core of the feudal order. Under a hydraulic despotism relations of total submission characterize the core of the bureaucratic system and they also prevail in its horizontal extensions. Only in the loosely dependent periphery do quasicontractual (quasifeudal) features make their appearance.

The sociology of hydraulic despotism recognizes relevant differences between an ordinary member of the centrally directed bureaucracy and a satrap (or *curaca*), and between such dignitaries and a *rāja* or a loosely dependent ally. In all cases the determining force is the agrarian apparatus state; but the degree of operational dependency creates significant subdivisions in the edifice of despotic power.

iii. GRADATIONS OF POWER IN
MODERN TOTALITARIAN STATES

ANALYSTS of modern industrial apparatus states are equally concerned with differences between the officials of the totalitarian heartland and the heads of the satellite countries. In these cases too it is essential to recognize both the supreme role of the metropolis and the structural differentiations that characterize its horizontal extensions.[c] It is also essential to recognize the tendency toward

c. In 1921 Stalin characterized the horizontal gradations in the newly established USSR as follows: "The Russian experiment in applying various forms of federation, in passing from federation based on Soviet autonomy (the Kirghiz Republic, the Bashkir Republic, the Tatar Republic, the Gortsi, Daghestan) to federation based on treaty relations with independent Soviet republics (the Ukraine, Azerbaidjan), and in allowing intermediate phases (Turkestan, White Russia), has fully proved the significance and flexibility of federation as a general form of state government for the Soviet republics" (Stalin, S, V: 22). Stalin considered this allegedly voluntary association a transitional step to a future and "supreme" unity; and indeed as far as the then

intensified subjugation in periods of imperialistic growth and co-ordination. The quasi-independent ally of yesterday may be the dependent ally of today and the satellite, satrap, or run-of-the-mill official of tomorrow.

In hydraulic society this trend has its counterpart in retrogressive developments that may ultimately replace one unified despotic regime by several such systems. Pharaonic Egypt fell temporarily into a number of quasi-independent territories; and post-T'ang China was even more seriously dismembered. But in both cases the new political units perpetuated despotic methods of statecraft, and the term "feudal," which may with a certain poetic licence be applied to the relation between the weakened center and its larger sub-units, is completely inappropriate when used to designate sub-units which are actually nothing but detached and smaller replicas of the larger despotic model.

The control mechanism of the modern apparatus states makes separation extremely difficult as long as the despotic metropolis itself persists. The defection of Tito's Yugoslavia was made possible by exceptional geomilitary circumstances.[28] Manifestly, the horizontal extensions of the modern apparatus state are not identical with—although they offer instructive parallels to—the territories of satraps, *rājas,* or dependent allies in hydraulic society.

2. SUBCLASSES ATTACHED TO THE MEN OF THE APPARATUS

THE manipulators of the despotic state apparatus are the core, but not the whole of the ruling class. A biosocial supplement—blood relations and affinals—must be included, and frequently also an operational supplement—persons who enjoy a semi-, quasi-, or pre-official status.

a. Attachment Based on Kinship

i. THE RULING HOUSE

POLYGAMY was a recognized institution in the great majority of all hydraulic societies;[d] and for obvious reasons the sovereign had

---

"autonomous" and "independent" republics were concerned, he and his comrades worked successfully to bring this about: "This voluntary character of the federation must absolutely be preserved in the future, for only such a federation can become a transitional form to that supreme unity of the workers of all countries in a single universal economic system, the necessity for which is becoming ever more perceptible" (*ibid.:* 23).

d. Interesting exceptions: Christian Byzantium and Russia. The prevalence of

unique opportunities to utilize it. His many relatives (by blood or marriage) usually enjoyed a distinguished social status, and usually they also enjoyed considerable material advantage. If and to what extent the despot employed them in the government depended on a number of circumstances. But when employed, they had an excellent chance to rise to positions of prominence and power.

In the Inca empire the male descendants of the sovereigns were organized in *ayllus,* whose number increased with the advance of the dynasty. The members of these *ayllus* "formed a useful court circle of educated men trained in the imperial ideology, and interested in its perpetuation. The emperors chose their top administrators from this group when possible." [29]

In certain Chinese dynasties, such as Han, the consort family played an enormous political role; and in the conquest dynasty of Liao the members of the consort clan, Hsiao, were apparently more trusted than those of the imperial Yeh-lü clan.[30] But whether the sovereign's blood relatives or his affinals were numerous or not in the bureaucratic hierarchy, the members of these two groups were generally a distinguished component of the ruling class.

ii. THE BUREAUCRATIC GENTRY

ON a less exalted level, the families of the ranking officials are equally significant. Like the relatives of the sovereign, although not entirely for the same reasons, the members of what may be called the bureaucratic gentry did not necessarily hold office. Some were too young, some too old, some inept, some women; and some who had the qualifications could not find a government post, first, because there were usually more candidates than vacancies and second, because some of the vacancies might be filled by outsiders rather than by sons of officials.

The amount and form of family possessions are important differentiating factors. Mobile passive wealth (gold, jewels, etc.) shrinks more quickly than landed property, which, although it is fragmented through equal division among the heirs, may during the owner's lifetime remain undiminished, if the rents are large enough to support him and his family. Thus hydraulic societies with highly developed private landownership provide the bureaucratic gentry with optimal, if gradually diminishing, opportunities for living on

---

monogamy in Byzantium and Russia shows that this form of marriage, despite the restrictions it imposed on the rulers, was nevertheless compatible with the main political, economic, and social trends of Oriental despotism.

the amassed family wealth. The Chinese saying that a family may rise from rags to riches in three generations and go back to rags in the next three well describes the trend toward declining wealth that in contrast to the feudal gentry characterizes the bureaucratic gentry of hydraulic society. Equally important is the speed with which a return to government service can reestablish (or increase) family wealth. No doubt, if members of an impoverished gentry family held office for three generations, the family fortune (and landholdings) at the end of that time would certainly be large. But often one family member who served the government even for a limited time was able to restore his family's property. In a Chinese case with which I am personally familiar a three-year stint in a county magistracy did the trick.

The political significance of the bureaucratic gentry is indicated by the fact that members of this group are frequently invited to fulfill auxiliary administrative, judicial, or priestly functions. In Pharaonic Egypt remunerative positions in the temple service were often given to children of notables.[31] In the judicial assemblies of Babylonia some "notables" were officeholders, others had a gentry-like status.[32]

For Buddhist India Fick assumes the existence of a "gentry of the land" that formed a part of the *gahapatis,* the "householders." [33] In his opinion these householders were neither warriors, Kshatriyas, nor Brahmins; [34] rather they were identical with, or overlapped, a "lower-land-owning nobility." [35] Fick's interpretation of the householders is open to doubt. Dutoit considers them members of the third order, the Vaisya.[e] The texts which Fick has translated show clearly that Brahmins could be householders; [36] and this indeed was

e. *Jātakam,* II: 143, n. 1; cf. IV: 541, n. 1. At this period, castes, *jati,* already existed. But the *jati,* which later increased to several thousand, are not identical with the four major *varṇa,* the Kshatriyas, Brahmins, Vaisyas, and Sūdras. The use of the word *varṇa* ("color") as a designation for these great divisions, goes back to the period covered by the Rigveda—that is, to the days when the Aryans, the persons of "the light color," subdued the indigenous Dasyus, the persons of "the dark color" (Rapson, 1922: 54; see also Renou, 1950: 63). After this period the term *varṇa* "denotes 'a social order' independently of any actual distinction of colour" (Rapson, 1922: 54) or a "class" or "order." Smith (1928: 36), following Shama Sastri, suggests these or "some equivalent term." Cf. also Rhys-Davids, 1950: 46. The rules of castes, *jati,* which most prominently regulate diet and marriage, shaped with increasing rigidity the four orders, among which, however, only the Brahmins persisted throughout India and until modern times: "No four original castes ever existed at any time or place, and at the present moment the terms Kshatriya, Vaisya, and Sūdra have no exact meaning as a classification of existing castes. In northern India the names Vaisya and Sūdra are not used except in books of disputes about questions of caste precedence. In the south all Hindus who are not Brahmans fall under the denomination of Sūdra, while

their regular condition when, after having completed their education, they married and founded a family.[37]

Fick's classification seems valid to this extent: a householder enjoyed no "special privileges," [38] and when he lived essentially off his lands he generally belonged to the lower nobility—that is, to a segment of the ruling class that was less distinguished than the officeholding Kshatriyas, Brahmins, or Vaisyas. But land grants were made primarily to secular serving men and to Brahmins; [39] and the nonofficiating members of these groups certainly constituted a bureaucratic or priestly gentry. This was the case whether they held land grants hereditarily or for life, or not at all.[40]

In Byzantine Egypt the relatives of prominent functionaries seem to have been eager to assume office when opportunity offered. While living on their estates, they fulfilled a variety of semi-official functions in their locality.[41]

The Inca state took elaborate measures to support meritorious dignitaries and other persons of distinction. The lands assigned to them were also intended to benefit their descendants.[42] This suggests that, as in other hydraulic civilizations, a sizable bureaucratic gentry flourished in Inca society. In pre-Conquest Mexico, too, sinecure lands were held for long periods of time, not only by relatives of the ruling house but also by the families of ranking officials.[43]

In China individuals who achieved social distinction because of their bureaucratic family background can be documented as early as the Chou period; and at least since T'ang times and with due consideration for the degree of relationship, the kinsmen of ranking officials enjoyed legally established advantages.[44] Thus they constituted a bureaucratic gentry within the terms of our definition.

In a somewhat different way, Western writers have applied the term "gentry" to the shên-shih, the sash bearers, a group that overlaps but is not identical with the bureaucratic gentry of the present inquiry. As far as we know, the designation shên-shih is found only in official documents of the last dynasties. The lists of shên-shih included natives of a particular region who were or had been officials, and in addition persons who had attained a degree either, and in the main, through examination or through purchase, but who, as yet, had not held office.

The examination system appears relatively late in Chinese history; and the classing of holders of examination degrees as a social group

---

the designations Kshatriya and Vaisya are practically unknown" (Smith, 1928: 35). The consolidation, social rise, and persistence of the Brahmins in Hindu and Muslim India is a crucial aspect of the long and complicated history of Indian society.

appears even later. But whatever the initial date, the bureaucratic orientation of the *shên-shih* is clear. As noted above, *shên-shih* status was determined not by relations to land but to government office.[f] The top echelons of the *shên-shih* hierarchy were composed of present or former officials and holders of high degrees who expected to be in office soon. Much larger was the number of lower *shên-shih*, who, holding lower degrees, would have a long wait. However, like the high-degree holders, who had not as yet entered government service, the members of the lower *shên-shih* engaged in all kinds of semi-official activities, such as the promotion of local public works, local defense and security measures, management of relief and welfare enterprises, and the collection of contributions and fees for the government.[g] And they were, of course, always ready to accept a government position, which, in addition to opening the way to greater political and social influence, was incomparably more rewarding materially.

f. In an analysis of the Chinese gentry published in 1946, H. T. Fei emphasized both its proprietary and bureaucratic aspects; but his formulation of the second point remains somewhat vague: "Not until one of the family members [of a landlord] enters the *scholar group and into officialdom* is their position in the gentry consolidated" (Fei, 1946: 11; italics mine). In 1948 in a book which he wrote prior to joining the Communist camp, Fei, defining the gentry, mentions their connections to government office *before* landownership: "The gentry may be returned officials or the relatives of officials or simply educated landowners" (Fei, 1953: 32). To fully appreciate Fei's statement it should be remembered that he sharply rejected any idea of a self-perpetuating landlordism in China. The law of inheritance dissolved even large holdings; and traditionally the major road to acquiring land was through government office (see Fei and Chang, 1945: 302). This implies that the bulk of China's landowners, and particularly the large and educated landowners, were bureaucratic landlords—that is, typical members of a bureaucratic gentry.

Eberhard in a recent definition of the Chinese gentry mentions their "landed property" first; he refers to the proprietary aspect again, and prominently, when he describes "the gentry class" as comprising "landowners, scholars and politicians *in one and the same class*," normally with "representatives of all three occupations *in one family*" (Eberhard, 1952: 16; cf. 14. italics in original.). Eberhard "feels not qualified to write about Egypt, Mesopotamia and India" (*ibid.:* 35, n. 2); and he does not consider Rüstow's concepts of the "Hellenistic-Oriental sultanate" and of the bureaucratic state slavery of the later Roman empire (Rüstow, OG, II: 169, 187). Lacking crucial tools for a comparative study of Oriental government and property, he remains unaware of the peculiar character (and strength) of the former and of the peculiar character (and weaknesses) of the latter.

g. Chang (GI, Pt. II). A number of these tasks, such as construction and repair of local roads, irrigation canals, and river dikes and the collection of contributions and fees for the government, belong to the intermediate type of enterprises, which in hydraulic society are sometimes handled by the bureaucracy, sometimes by private persons (cf. Wittfogel, 1931: 413 ff., 445 ff.). These private persons are mostly members of the bureaucratic ruling class, and their work assumes a semi-official character when it is backed by government authority for the collection of funds and for the mobilization of people.

The average ranking civil official may have derived about 1700 taels from his office.[h] The average member of the lower *shên-shih* probably had an annual income in the neighborhood of 200 taels from "gentry services."

For some hydraulic societies our evidence on the existence of a bureaucratic gentry is merely suggestive; for others it is conclusive. But even where documentation is scanty, the presence of privileged members of the ruling house and of a similarly, if less conspicuously, privileged bureaucratic gentry seems indicated. The ranking officials were eager to share the advantages of their positions with their relatives. And within the range of their power they certainly did so.

iii. THE RELATIVES OF CIVIL UNDERLINGS AND RANK-AND-FILE SOLDIERS

AND then there are the relatives of the civil underlings and rank-and-file soldiers. About the day-to-day life of this numerous group we know little. In the 17th century in China a bureaucratic racketeer, Li San, lived splendidly because he was able to cash in on his own and his father's and grandfather's experience as government clerks.[45] His success, although short-lived and exceptional, underlines the benefits that intelligent and ambitious relatives of civil underlings could derive from their position.

The families of professional soldiers constituted a more or less analogous group. Some of their problems are indicated in Hammurabi's Code,[46] and a comparative study of the Ptolemaic cleruchs and the peasant soldiers of the Byzantine *themes* would probably reveal similar conditions.

For the most part, the relatives of these civil and military underlings were as modestly situated economically as the bulk of the artisans and peasants. But politically and socially they shared the ambivalent prestige of their serving family members. The social position, which the father, wife, or son of a policeman enjoys in a police

h. According to Dr. Chang, at the close of the 19th century the "lower" *shên-shih* group numbered about 1,250,000 persons; and it derived about 94 million taels annually from "gentry services" (see Chang, GI, Pt. II). Dr. Chang estimates the total annual income of the lower *shên-shih* as 239 million taels (55 million from rent, 40 million from various private enterprises, 50 million from professional services—mainly teaching—and 94 million from "gentry services") and that of the upper *shên-shih* as 365.5 million taels (165 million from rent, 81 million from private enterprises, 91 million from office, 5 million from professional services, and 21 million from "gentry services") (Chang, GI, Pt. II). This suggests an income of 192 taels for the average member of the lower *shên-shih* as against an income of over 1800 taels for an average member of the upper *shên-shih*.

state, gives some indication of the place occupied by the relatives of underlings in an Orientally despotic state.

b. Attachment Based on Semi-, Quasi-, or Pre-official Status

NOT all relatives of the men of the apparatus share to the same degree the social privileges of their officiating kinsmen. Relative closeness to the bureaucratic activists and the peculiarities of the prevailing kinship system define the beneficiaries' specific position within the ruling class. But whatever the variations, this position, other conditions being equal, derives from the prominence that the apparatus state gives its functionaries.

In a different way this is true also for groups that have a semi-, quasi-, or pre-official status. Although they are not properly officials, members of such groups work for the government as economic agents or they are granted official or quasi-official status because as functionaries of the dominant religion they magically bolster the security of the regime.

i. SECULAR SEMI-OFFICIALS (COMMERCIAL AND FISCAL AGENTS)

PERSONS who spend all or most of their time serving the government as economic agents (*damkar, setthi*) are sometimes included among the officials. In this case their status need not be argued. Often, however, commercial agents are not so listed; and fiscal agents (tax farmers) are rarely if ever considered part of the bureaucratic hierarchy. But although these men are denied official rank, they are recognized as servants of the government. In this capacity they are supported and given authority, sometimes even coercive authority, and to compensate them for their services they are granted a fee or commission. In Ptolemaic Egypt tax farmers were granted a fee of 5 per cent, and later 10 per cent; [47] in Byzantium of one per cent, 2.5 per cent, or 5 per cent; [48] in Muslim India up to 10 per cent.[49] In Ottoman Egypt they had assigned to them, in addition to cash income, about 10 per cent of all cultivable village land, the so-called *waṣîya*.[50]

To be sure, commercial agents and tax farmers might succeed in gathering and keeping more than the prescribed quota. But this tendency, which was vigorously combated by strong rulers, does not distinguish the economic agents from the commercial or fiscal officials, who were equally eager to gather and keep more than they should.

The commercial and fiscal agents were private entrepreneurs in

that both used private means and, in some part, privately hired employees. But in acting for the government they enjoyed the advantages of government authority, and when necessary they could mobilize government personnel to impose their will. The population
respected and feared them, not as private individuals but as extensions of government power.

If these persons were officials or members of the bureaucratic gentry, who sought to increase their wealth through semi-official operations, their bureaucratic position was established *a priori*. In any
event, the government-based character of their functions made them
semi-officials and placed them in, although often at the periphery of,
the ruling class.

ii. RELIGIOUS QUASI-OFFICIALS (FUNCTIONARIES OF THE DOMINANT RELIGION)

IN a previous chapter we examined the methods by which the agrodespotic state closely attached to itself the dominant religion and its
functionaries. In China and in the earlier period of Pharaonic Egypt
government officials performed many of the major tasks of the dominant cult. In other Oriental civilizations the government appointed
the priests of the dominant religion and from the standpoint of administration treated them like secular officials (*Staatsbeamte*).[51]

The religious functionaries of Islam lived for the most part on
endowments (*waqfs*) that were controlled directly or indirectly by
the government.[52] In this respect they were more closely attached to
the state than were the Brahmins of Hindu India, who only on occasion received land grants. In both cases, however, the state enforced
the sacred law of the dominant religion, which bestowed a quasi-
official position of authority on the religious functionary.

To be sure, any religious functionary enjoys a special kind of awe
among the believers; but his prestige may be weakened or enhanced
by the over-all setting in which he operates. The priest of a secondary
and underprivileged creed may have difficulty in asserting his authority even among his own followers, who are constantly exposed to
the disparaging value judgments of an unfriendly environment. The
priest of a dominant creed is not faced with such difficulties. On the
contrary. The respect of the rulers enhances his prestige; and the
more so, the stronger the government happens to be. Under hydraulic
despotism the functionaries of the dominant religion, even where
they are not appointed officials, enjoy on the social level a quasi-
official status.

iii. PERSONS OCCUPYING A PRE-OFFICIAL STATUS (TRAINEES AND DEGREE-HOLDING CANDIDATES FOR OFFICE)

THE intricacies of ideology and script, and most hydraulic civilizations above the tribal level had a script, tended to make the training for office a drawn-out affair, and those who participated in it often constituted a special group. If they were accepted in official "colleges" or "universities," they were carefully selected and restricted in number. This was the situation in Aztec Mexico and Byzantium, under the Mamluks in Ottoman Turkey and during certain periods of Chinese history such as Han.

Where the students were educated in temples and/or by priests, their training was not specifically bureaucratic but their number was similarly restricted. Where competitive examinations were open to the public generally, as was the case under the later Chinese dynasties, the students were numerous, and the lower degree-holders many. Exposed to a long and intensive process of indoctrination, the students may well have been even more sensitive to the benefits and eminence of the bureaucratic life than the office-holders. Bureaucratic class consciousness could be further consolidated if degree-holders were permitted to carry out certain semi-official functions. The members of the Chinese *shên-shih,* who held examination degrees but had not yet attained office, are a classical example of a pre-bureaucratic group.

iv. A COMPARATIVE NOTE (PROFESSIONAL IDEOLOGISTS IN THE USSR)

IN hydraulic society the rulers rarely manipulated the sacred doctrine, even if they were its high priests. In the Soviet Union the Orthodox Church, although still tolerated, is no longer a dominant creed; and when the openly expressed Soviet designs materialize, the Church will be replaced altogether by the secular state doctrine. The standard bearers of this doctrine are the masters of the apparatus state; they—and they alone—interpret and change it. The country's top-ranking ideologists are the top-ranking members of the ruling bureaucracy; and the great bulk of all professional intellectuals are, like them, government officials.

A few outstanding artists and writers may produce their works without holding office. But they follow state directives, they execute state orders, they are paid as are high officials; and since they serve

the state well and without reservation, they enjoy similar prerogatives. For all practical purposes, they have a quasi-official status.

Thus, while in hydraulic society the quasi-official ideological
(religious) functionaries are many and relatively free insofar as
doctrine is concerned, in the USSR the quasi-official intellectuals are
few and their freedom in matters of doctrine is nil. The rulers of
the total managerial state have nationalized the ideology as well as
the ideologists.

c. Subdivided, but Still an Entity

OUR survey reveals that even under the simplest conditions the
ruling class in hydraulic society is divided into several subsections.
Under more differentiated conditions it tends to be a fairly complex
entity. How conscious of the peculiarity and superiority of their class
position are the members of the various subsections?

Class consciousness is probably a less general—and certainly a less
dynamic—factor than Marxism would have us believe. But there
can be little doubt that the masters of hydraulic society, who enjoyed extraordinary privileges of power, revenue, and status, formed
one of the most class-conscious groups in the history of mankind.

To be sure, their class-consciousness did not always express itself
in images which underlined their greatness as ranking officials. The
serving men of Ottoman Turkey were proud to be the "slaves" of
their sultan. The glory of the ruling class, as they saw it, rested upon
its autocratic ruler. The political ideologists of Hindu India stressed
the prominence of the king as the supreme protector of the dominant
religion. The glory of the ruling class, as they saw it, rested upon its
priestly advisors. The Confucian philosophers paid homage to their
absolute sovereign; but they extolled the gentleman-scholar, who,
because of his training, was likely to become a gentleman-bureaucrat.
The glory of the ruling class, as they saw it, rested upon its properly
educated officials.

Confucianism presents the sociopolitical aspect of the matter with
unusual clarity. By designating the gentleman-scholar as *chün-tzŭ*,
Confucius emphasized the political quality of his ideal man. The
chün-tzŭ was thoroughly versed in the cultural tradition of the
hereditary ("noble") officialdom, but his qualifications had an
essentially political intent. The word *chün-tzŭ* originally connoted
"a ruler," "a man engaged in the business of ruling." After being
properly trained, the *chün-tzŭ* was ready to be "used" as a government official.[53] He was ready to rule the "little men," the mass of the
population.

The dichotomy between the two groups finds expression in the Chinese terms *shih* and *min*. The *shih* are those individuals who, by their training in ethical, military, and ceremonial matters, are qualified to serve their ruler and who do so when this is possible. The *min* are "the people," who are ruled by the sovereign and the officiating members of the *shih*.[i] The values placed on civil and military qualifications have varied over time.[j] But the glorification of the *shih* endured until the end of the imperial era.

Whatever the nomenclature, the *shih-min* distinction operates in all hydraulic societies. In all of them the potential and the actual rulers are deeply aware of their superiority to, and difference from, the mass of the ruled—the commoners, the "people."

D. THE RULED

1. PROPERTY-BASED SUBSECTIONS OF COMMONERS

BELOW the rulers spreads the vast world of the commoners. Its members share a negative quality: none participates in the affairs of the state apparatus. They also share a positive quality: none are slaves.

Chinese tradition distinguishes three main groups of commoners: peasants, artisans, and merchants. The sequence reflects the order of their appearance on the historical scene; but it is doubtful whether this was in the minds of those who listed them so. More likely they were concerned with relative economic importance, agriculture being the root (*pên*) and handicraft and commerce the branches (*mo*) of their agrarian civilization.[a]

i. The *Classic of History* frequently refers to the officials as *shih* (Legge, CC, III: 275, 367, 369, 626), as also do the Odes (*ibid.*, IV: 360, 409, 429 ff., 569). More narrowly the term *shih* connotes lower ranking officials (cf. *ibid.*, I: 401). As persons of proper training, the *shih* are frequently mentioned, particularly in the Confucian writings (cf. *ibid.*, I: 168, 274, 276). The ultimate test of their education is revealed in government service (*ibid.*, I: 271 ff., 339). To be sure, the friendship of a *shih* should be sought even when he is not in office (*ibid.*, I: 297).

Frequently the *shih* are juxtaposed to the *min*. The former serve elegantly at the royal ancestral temple (*ibid.*, IV: 569) or the court, while the latter look on and admire them (*ibid.*, IV: 409 ff.). Taken together, the *shih* and the *min* constitute the whole population. In periods of unrest both groups suffer (*ibid.*, IV: 560).

j. Confucius was primarily interested in the civil qualifications of the *shih;* and this obviously modified an earlier tradition (see Legge, CC, I: *passim;* cf. Wittfogel, 1935: 49, n. 3).

a. The Chinese classification which places the *shih* before the peasants, artisans, and merchants does not recognize a class of persons whose position rests essentially on landownership.

The root and the branches correspond to two basic forms of property: immobile and mobile. In our survey of the complexity patterns of property we discussed the rise, development, and social position of the three just-mentioned groups in considerable detail; [1] and there is no need to recapitulate our conclusions here. However, to round out the inquiry, we shall at this point examine the position of the most lowly social group: the slaves. Slaves played only a very limited role in hydraulic society. Why?

2. SLAVES

SOIL, water, and plants are manipulated with great care by persons who profit personally from their labors: peasant members of village communities, owner-cultivators, and tenant farmers. But no such care can be expected from full slaves—that is, from persons, who, in addition to being personally unfree, possess neither family nor property. This is true for agrarian conditions generally, and it is especially true for areas where the agronomy is largely determined by irrigation farming.

In irrigation-based hydraulic agriculture slave labor was little employed. Occasionally when easy access to slave labor suggested its use in farming (or in handicraft), such labor remained an auxiliary force. To assure the necessary care the slaves were usually given a share in what they produced, and at times they could marry.

The costs of supervision inhibited the use of great numbers of slaves in the most typical of all public works in hydraulic society: the construction and maintenance of canals, embankments, roads, and walls. It was only in spatially restricted enterprises, such as mines and quarries, the building of palaces and temples, and the transport of bulky objects that slave labor could be easily supervised and therefore advantageously employed. [2]

This explains why state slaves are found primarily at the court, in government offices, workshops, and mines, and in special types of building activities. It explains why privately owned slaves were essentially employed domestically and by wealthy persons, who could afford the luxury of lavish consumption. [3] It explains why occasional attempts to use slaves in subtler tasks compelled their public and private masters to provide conspicuous incentives and to replace full slavery by semislavery.

A victorious war might, of course, produce a sizable slave reservoir. And while the conquerors of agricultural regions usually hastened to assign the bulk of their peasant captives to farming, the occupation in which they would best profit their new masters, some might be kept as government slaves or sold to private persons.

The Aztecs, who frequently fought their neighbors, had little use for slave labor in their communally organized *calpulli* villages. But as sacrifices at the great state ceremonials many captives served the purposes of spectacular terror, a major device for keeping the crudely coordinated Mexican empire united.

In ancient Mesopotamia warfare between the independent states was also an important source of slaves; and in Babylonia slaves were used to some extent in agriculture and handicrafts. But here, too, slave labor remained a secondary feature; and usually it was employed under conditions of semislavery: the slaves could acquire property and marry.[4] In Pharaonic Egypt slavery seems to have assumed some importance only in the New Kingdom, when major wars and conquest flooded the country with unfree foreign labor.[5]

After examining the history of ancient Mesopotamia and Egypt in their entirety, Westermann finds that in these civilizations slave labor was predominantly domestic;[6] and Meyer, in his evaluation of Near Eastern slavery, asserts that "scarcely anywhere in the Orient did slavery play a major economic role."[7] Mendelsohn's recent study on slavery in the ancient Orient confirms the earlier findings. Whatever slave labor was used in agriculture "was of no great weight. On the whole, slaves were used primarily in domestic service."[8]

Studies of other Oriental countries reach the same conclusions. There were many slaves in India, China, and the Islamic world, but in none of these large civilizations did slave labor dominate agriculture or handicraft.[b]

Some slaves and freedmen were raised to positions of prominence by Oriental despots, and others were given important supervisory tasks by private slave owners. But their careers were not representative of the conditions of their group. While the domestic slaves of hydraulic society in their majority were not chattel slaves,[9] they were personally unfree and they remained at the mercy of their masters. In the case of the female slaves it was usually taken for granted that their masters had access to them.

b. For India, see C. A. F. Rhys-Davids, 1922: 205; Fick, 1920: 306 ff. Appadorai (1936, I: 317 ff.) does not correlate his findings on the use of slaves in late Hindu South India with his analysis of agriculture and industry. But his description of these two branches of economy imply what Dr. Rhys-Davids has explicitly noted for Buddhist India. In both fields slave labor was insignificant (C. A. F. Rhys-Davids, 1922: 205). For Chinese society in general, see Wittfogel, 1931: 393 ff.; for the Han period, see Wilbur, 1943: 174 ff., 195 ff. For Abbassid society, see Mez, 1922: 152 ff.; for pre-Mongol Persia, see Spuler, 1952: 439 ff.

In a society that polarized total authority and total submission individuals who lacked every personal freedom were not to be envied. Their position was little improved by the fact that in certain hydraulic civilizations and in wealthy families they were, at times, numerous.

E. MODIFICATIONS OF CLASS STRUCTURE THAT OCCUR IN CONQUEST SOCIETIES

SLAVERY affects the bottom rung of Oriental society, conquest the top. Indeed, conquest may change the traditional structure of a conquered area so greatly that we are justified in designating the institutional result as a conquest society.[1] The sociology of conquest has essentially stressed the relation of conquest to the beginnings of stratified societies (primary conquest in our terms); and this process, although not too fully recorded, certainly deserves attention. But conquest may further differentiate already stratified societies (secondary conquest in our terms); and this process, which is more fully recorded and which generally involves more recent developments, deserves particular attention.

1. CONQUEST INVOLVING THE FORMATION OF STRATIFIED SOCIETIES (PRIMARY CONQUEST)

WAR between independent political commonwealths is as old as human life. But devices for keeping a given population permanently subdued developed only when permanent subjection was both rewarding and feasible. Was this possibility exploited first and in all cases by conquerors? Or did the increasing facilities of production first lead to the emergence of a native upper group, a tribal nobility or a professional officialdom?

Lowie, who considers "internal conditions" sufficient "to create hereditary or approximately hereditary classes," [2] cautiously evaluates the possible range of internal differentiation and conquest by stating that the two factors "need not be mutually exclusive." [3]

An essentially endogenous development has been documented in a number of cases,[4] but there seems to be no question that in other cases conquest created a conspicuous social stratification and very often intensified and advanced incipient endogenous differentiation. Conquest of this kind—primary conquest—apparently occurred throughout the hydraulic world, in ancient Greece and Rome, in Japan, and in Medieval Europe. It is a general and not a specific factor, and therefore it cannot be held responsible for the diverse patterns of power, property, and class, which characterized these civilizations.[a]

2. Conquest Involving the Further Differentiation of Stratified Societies (Secondary Conquest)

SECONDARY conquest does not always lead to the establishment of a conquest society. The bulk of all members of the conquering group may remain in their homeland; and their leaders may be satisfied to exercise remote control either by placing their own nationals directly over those they have subjugated, or by utilizing native collaborators, or by establishing strategically placed garrisons. Rule by satraps, *curacas*, or *rājas* is usually an end product of military conquest; and it involves significant horizontal gradations of power. But the resulting institutional order is not a conquest society in the sense of the present inquiry.

I speak of a conquest society only when the conquerors take up residence in the lands they have seized, when they neither liquidate nor expel the native population, and when they are sufficiently numerous to establish a cohesive and distinct alien ruling body apart from, and above, their new subjects.

a. For the history of the relation of conquest to the origin of class structure, see Rüstow, OG, I: 84 ff. The phenomenon has been systematically discussed from a sociological standpoint by Gumplowicz (1905: 190 ff., 195 ff.) and Oppenheimer (1919: 32 ff.), both of whom promoted the thesis that class differentiation is generally initiated by conquest. This thesis has been convincingly challenged by the anthropologists MacLeod (1924: *passim*) and Lowie (1927: 33 ff.). Without consideration for their arguments, Rüstow (OG, I: 66 ff., 74 ff., 95 ff.) accepts in the main the earlier conquest thesis; but he admits the possibility of social differentiations resulting from internal and peaceful development (OG, I: 88 ff., 90 ff.), and he recognizes that the conquest-created societies are diversely structured. Although he suggests that these societies be called " 'medieval' or 'feudal' in the widest sense" (OG, I: 79), he notes that the term "feudal" in its "political and narrower meaning" fits essentially Medieval Europe (OG, I: 312), that in ancient Rome a big-peasant aristocracy formed the dominant class (OG, II: 166), and that in Egypt from the dawn of history a planned economy doomed the mass of the population to "state slavery" (OG, II: 187).

In view of this, it is unfortunate that Eberhard, who "accepts the theory of A. Rüstow of the power factor, which creates feudal societies by superstratification" (Eberhard, 1952: 3) and who considers Rüstow's ideas "the so far most complete theory on the origin of feudalism" (*ibid.*) fails to familiarize his readers with the structural diversity of Rüstow's feudal societies. Eberhard sees "no principal difference between Oriental and Western feudalism" (*ibid.*: 2). But we have only to confront Eberhard's feudal system "based essentially on land which the vassal held as a fief" (*ibid.*: 1) with the Oriental reality and Rüstow's concept of Egypt's "spiritual feudalism" with its ruling priesthood and planned state slavery (OG, II: 17, 31, 187) to realize the inadequacy of Eberhard's view both from the standpoint of institutional facts and from that of his alleged authority, Dr. Rüstow.

Incipient conquest societies have emerged as the result of primary conquests. Full-fledged conquest societies appeared in many parts of the world and under a variety of circumstances. Their rise was inevitably stimulated by the attractiveness of the target country and by the military strength and mobility of the conquerors. Agricultural civilizations (and particularly "wealthy" hydraulic economies) were highly desirable objectives; and until modern times powerful nomadic tribes (especially pastoralists who could ride and use the saddle and stirrup) have been optimally successful in seizing them.[5]

3. CLASS MODIFICATIONS IN HYDRAULIC CONQUEST DYNASTIES

a. The Chinese Did Not Always Absorb Their Conquerors

GREAT and culturally persistent peoples, such as the Chinese, have pointed to the speed with which their "barbarian" conquerors adopted many features of their way of life. Easy-going generalizations from this cultural fact originated the widespread legend that the Chinese "always" absorbed their conquerors. However, reality contradicts this legend. Instead of relinquishing their privileges of power, prestige, and revenue the conquerors invariably sought to maintain them by all manner of political, military, and legal devices. And where they found it desirable to do so they also preserved particular features of their own cultural tradition.

Comparative analysis shows that none of the four major conquest dynasties of China confirms the myth of absorption, not even the last. The Manchus had already adopted many Chinese customs prior to the conquest;[6] but in their case, as in the others, basic differences in political and social status were maintained to the end.[b]

b. Devices for Preserving the Conquerors' Hegemony

THE reasons for this are easily understood. The "barbarian" conquerors depended for many details of civil administration on native experts and bureaucrats. But they protected their political, social, and economic hegemony by placing their own nationals above the indigenous officialdom, by concentrating their tribal soldiers in special cadres, camps, *ordus* (hordes), or banners, by making intermarriage with the subdued population difficult or impossible, and

b. Under conditions of conquest, cultural change is closely interlinked with political change. Our Chinese findings are therefore suggestive for conquest societies in general: "full cultural amalgamation obviously occurred only when the disappearance of the social divide permitted the cultural divide to disappear also—that is, after the period of conquest had come to an end" (Wittfogel, 1949: 15).

by preserving their tribal religion even when, for purposes of prestige, the ruler and his lieutenants performed the great indigenous ceremonies.[c]

The Arab warriors, who were the military mainstay of the Umayyad dynasty, lost their social prominence when that dynasty collapsed,[d] just as in China the Ch'i-tan, Jurchen, Mongols, and Manchus lost their privileged position when their respective conquest dynasties (Liao, Chin, Yüan, and Ch'ing) came to an end.

c. Duplications of Class

THUS conquest societies tend to involve a curious duplication of social strata. As a rule, an exogenous upper class (nobility) is superimposed upon a native bureaucracy; and tribal warriors become a distinguished stratum of plebeian underlings in the political hierarchy. The newly organized banners, camps, or *ordus* replace the former cadre troops, and definitely outrank the native troops which the regime may decide to maintain.

F. MANY SOCIAL ANTAGONISMS BUT LITTLE CLASS STRUGGLE

FOR obvious reasons the representatives of the despotic state are significant in any study of class structure; and this not because the men of the apparatus form the bulk of the population—which they certainly do not—but because state power, more than any other factor, shapes the fate of both the members of the ruling class and the commoners. This becomes crystal clear when we consider the three major types of social antagonisms that arise in hydraulic society: antagonisms between the members of different subsections of commoners, antagonisms between the commoners and the state, and antagonisms between the members of the various subsections of the ruling complex.

1. SOCIAL ANTAGONISM AND CLASS STRUGGLE

SOCIAL antagonism is not identical with class struggle. A conflict may be considered social when it involves members of different social groups and when it arises essentially out of the social position of those concerned. But a social conflict which is limited to a few

---

c. This, for instance, happened in the case of the Manchus, whose emperors performed the traditional Chinese sacrifices, while within the privacy of the palace they continued to worship their tribal gods (Wittfogel, 1949: 14).

d. Wellhausen, 1927: 557. The Umayyads did not conquer the Near East, but they consolidated the conquests accomplished under the first caliphs.

persons cannot reasonably be called a class struggle. The term "class" connotes a group—and usually a relatively large group—of socially homogeneous individuals; and a social conflict assumes the character of a class conflict only when those who participate in it represent a recognizable and representative fraction of such a group.

Class struggle involves mass action. Such a struggle may reach a point where it challenges existing social and political conditions. Marx, who perhaps more than any other social scientist of the 19th century studied classes, stressed this aspect of the matter by saying that "every class struggle is a political struggle." [1]

2. PARALYSIS OF CLASS STRUGGLE BY TOTAL POWER

THE meaning of all this for an understanding of hydraulic society is far-reaching. An agrarian despotism which is strong enough to prevent independent political organization does not need to tolerate mass action as a means of settling social conflicts. The men of the apparatus easily control the secular and religious variants of the Beggars' Democracy. They are suspicious of all rallies of socially dissatisfied persons. And usually they hasten to break up incipient mass movements.

During the middle period of the Ch'ing dynasty, in 1746, some Fukienese tenants joined together in requesting an adjustment of their rents. Apparently this was nothing but an argument between two groups of private persons, yet the local officials quickly intervened, arrested, and punished the leaders. [2] A subsequent edict blamed the provincial officials for the fact that "stupid people assemble and violate the law." [3]

A Han discussion of state and private enterprise in the manufacture of salt and iron objected to private businesses that employed more than a thousand workers, since such an accumulation of manpower might provide opportunities for treacherous action. [4] At the close of the imperial period an edict noted emphatically that there had "always been a law of this dynasty forbidding the establishment of societies and associations of any sort whatsoever." [5] The statement is significant both for its hostility to popular associations and for its lack of concern for the existing craft and trade guilds. Obviously the government did not count these organizations among the politically relevant societies and associations.

Such attitudes precluded political mass action (class struggle) as a legitimate form of social protest. And they did so even in the ruling class. Conflicts between members of different subsections of this class were often politically colored in that they involved antagonistic claims to power-based privileges; but they rarely led to open and political mass action. The history of hydraulic society suggests that class struggle, far from being a chronic disease of all mankind, is the luxury of multicentered and open societies.

G. ANTAGONISM BETWEEN MEMBERS OF DIFFERENT SUBSECTIONS OF COMMONERS

IN simple hydraulic societies peasants constitute almost the whole of the "ruled," and they continue to be the most numerous sub-section of commoners in semicomplex and complex hydraulic societies. How much opportunity is there for social antagonism between them and other commoners?

Poor (and tenant) farmers may clash with rich (landowning and well-to-do) farmers, with traders, or with money lenders. However, the possibility of such frictions is minimal in the regulated village communities that prevail in the majority of all hydraulic societies. For in these communities tenancy is either a nonexistent or a marginal issue; and the economic differences between the similarly situated peasant households are slight. Moreover, the limited economic flexibility of the average community member restricts the extent to which he may deal—and clash—with nonpeasant commoners: artisans, traders, and/or money lenders.[a]

a. W. C. Smith in his article "Lower-class Uprisings in the Mughal Empire" says nothing about social conflicts of this inter-commoner type. Several times he mentions "landlords" as involved in class struggles with peasants. But in one instance he only surmises the existence of such persons (1946: 28); in others he uses the word "land-lords" as an equivalent for zamīndārs (ibid.: 27, 30). Until the 18th century the zamīndārs were essentially tributary rājas (Moreland, 1929: 279); and the "nobility" which, according to Smith, seized "approximately one-third of the country's agricultural produce" did so "in the form of what is called 'taxes' or 'revenue'" (1946: 23). That is, these "nobles" were actually government functionaries who lived on government revenue. This pattern is altogether different from the system of land tenure of feudal Europe; and it is regrettable that Smith, who was aware of this (1946a: 308), nevertheless designated the Indian conditions as "feudalism" (ibid.).

Peasants apparently participated in rebellions of various kinds, but those that can be clearly recognized as involving secular issues seem mostly to have arisen from fiscal conflicts. As may be expected in a country dominated by rulers of an alien creed, religious conflicts frequently merged with secular ones; and in many cases the former probably gave voice or increased intensity to the latter (see Smith, 1946: 27 ff.). But we have no reason to doubt that certain conflicts were genuinely—or primarily—religious. In 1672 members of a small sect clashed with the authorities, defeated the local police and several contingents of regular troops, and temporarily controlled the city of Narnâwl. Smith, who views this event as a "desperate class struggle" (ibid.: 29), fails to mention any secular issue which would justify such a classification.

And then there were struggles that essentially concerned national or territorial issues. The Pathan rebellion, which Smith designates as "perhaps the most formidable

Rural conflicts increased as private landownership increased. In Tsarist Russia large peasant uprisings flared up in the 18th century when the *pomeshchiki* became the owners of their former service land and when the peasants, encouraged by rumors of all kinds, hoped also to become the owners of the land they were tilling.[1] The reform of the *pomeshchik* land in 1762 was followed by serious peasant disturbances,[2] which reached their climax in the great rebellion led by Pugachev (1772–75).[3]

Conflicts arising out of the usurious lending of grain or money and out of oppressive tenancy are well documented for Ptolemaic and Roman Egypt, for traditional China, and, of course, for many hydraulic societies in transition.

Recent studies have often concentrated on these property-based conflicts and as a consequence have paid little attention to the extraordinary forces of bureaucratic power and property that underlie and complicate the tensions between various groups of wealthy and poor commoners. But however much such studies have misunderstood the character of hydraulic society, they provide us with valuable data on conflicts arising from property; and they relieve us of the need to repeat here what their authors have industriously, if one-sidedly, said on this subject.

The rise of private property and enterprise in handicraft and commerce created conditions that resulted in social conflicts of many kinds among urban commoners. In Medieval Europe such conflicts were fought out with great vigor. Not infrequently the social movements assumed the proportions of a mass (and class) struggle, which in some towns compelled the merchants to share political leadership with the artisans and which in others assured the hegemony of the craft guilds.[4]

The contrast with the hydraulic world is striking. Although the guilds of hydraulic society have a much longer history than their Western counterparts, they rarely, if ever, engaged in militant and political activities of comparable scope.[b]

---

people's movement" of the Mogul period was the prolonged and pathetic endeavor of proud border tribesmen to resist "the attempt to impose . . . [on them] the rule of the Mughal State" (*ibid.*: 33, 34). And in the district of Kishtwar it was obviously a semi-independent group of local rulers that combated the Moguls' infringement upon them. The protagonists of the Kishtwar rebellion, local *zamīndārs*, defended the cause of their prince, who eventually was reinstated. The fact that the "lower classes" also "fought and suffered" and that the *ryots* and inhabitants of nearby Kashmir "complained" about the harshness of the Mogul commander (*ibid.*: 27) is scarcely a reason for including this affair among the "lower-class uprisings" of the period.

b. Cf. above, Chap. 4. The Kārimī merchants of Mamluk Egypt accumulated great fortunes in the international spice trade and as bankers; and their commerce with

H. THE "PEOPLE" VERSUS THE
MEN OF THE APPARATUS

THE disproportion between the intensity of social antagonism and the frequency of class struggle becomes particularly striking when we view the relations between the two main classes of hydraulic society: the "people" and the men of the apparatus. In the normal course of events the commoners suffer periodically from the demands made on them by representatives of the despotic state. Generally those who are oppressed or exploited do not dare to resist openly; and frequently they do not even dare to resist covertly. The Oriental subject's proverbial eagerness to avoid any contact at all with the feared organs of government underlines his acceptance of defeat in a contest that he never dares to enter.

Avoidance, however, is not always possible. The commoner may not lay his complaints before a judge or magistrate; but often he must render services and usually he must pay a tax. He may bitterly resent both demands, and being unable to protect himself by constitutional means, he may feign compliance. But behind this facade he will combat the men of the apparatus with all the weapons of indirect and passive resistance at his command.

When he performs his corvée labor, he will work as slowly as the overseer's control (or the stick or whip) permits.[1] When he renders his tax, he will seek to conceal certain of his assets. And not infrequently he will hand over his quota only after being severely beaten. Writers in Pharaonic Egypt have satirized this aspect of the battle of the land tax;[2] and a 19th-century account shows the Egyptian peasant's attitude in these matters to be unchanged: "All the felláheen are proud of the stripes they receive for withholding their contributions, and are often heard to boast of the number of blows which were inflicted upon them before they would give up their money." [a]

When taxation becomes unusually burdensome, the peasant may reduce his cultivated acreage,[3] and when the heavy demands continue, he may become a fiscal fugitive,[b] abandoning his fields alto-

---

such countries as Yemen may occasionally have influenced the foreign policy of the Mamluk government, which derived great revenues from it. But their economic importance notwithstanding, the Kārimī merchants failed to attain an independent political position comparable to that of the guild merchants of feudal Europe. See Fischel, 1937: 72 ff., 76 ff., 80 ff.; cf. Becker, IS, I: 186, 214.

a. Lane, 1898: 143 ff. Lane adds: "Ammianus Marcellinus gives precisely the same character to the Egyptians of his time." Ammianus lived in the 4th century A.D.

b. The founder of the Mogul Dynasty, Bābur, was infuriated by the Indian peasants,

gether. He may wander in despair, look for work elsewhere, or turn bandit or rebel.[c]

As stated above, open conflicts between peasants and government were rare where land tenure was regulated; and even in imperial China they assumed major proportions mainly during periods of disintegration which initiated the collapse of a dynasty.

Conflicts between urban commoners (or groups of commoners) and the government occurred in a different context. They frequently centered around tax issues; but the administrative (and garrison) character of most hydraulic towns generally prevented the discontented townspeople from resorting to armed rebellion. The individual merchants or artisans defended themselves as well as they could against restrictive regulations and fiscal exploitation; and the guilds of craftsmen and traders, headed by government-appointed or government-supervised functionaries, not infrequently appealed to the authorities for the adjustment of excessive demands At times artisans ceased to work and merchants closed their shops; [4] and occasionally a crowd might start a riot.[d] Government officials who

---

who, typical fiscal refugees, hid in the woods and "trusting to their inaccessible situation, often continue in a state of revolt, refusing to pay their taxes" (see Bābur, 1921: 208).

c. Chinese historiography relates many such cases (cf. Wittfogel and Fêng, 1949: 420). An incident that occurred in the Ming dynasty is illuminating in several respects. Between 1436 and 1448 a tenant, Têng Mao-ch'i, became a person of influence among his fellow villagers, whom he is said to have gotten to "work for him." His prestige was greatly enhanced through his leadership in a movement that urged the tenants not to make the customary gift to their landlords when they paid their rent. The landlords approached the local magistrate, and it may well be that some of them were members of the court or the officialdom, since in Ming days these groups were extremely successful in appropriating peasant land. In any case, the magistrate dispatched armed forces; but Têng defeated them with a rebel army, which eventually numbered several tens of thousands. Soon his power spread over twenty counties, and he received further assistance from people who escaped from the "unbearable" oppression of a "greedy and cruel" official. Subsequent developments revealed excessive corvée labor as a major reason for their discontent. After several military successes the rebels were defeated; and Têng, together with some of his followers, was beheaded (Ming Shih 165.5a–b). An episode in the middle of the fight characterizes both the strength of the government and the limited objectives of the revolt. Negotiating with a courageous official, the rebels are reported to have asked only that their lives be spared and that they be exempted from labor service "for three years." If these conditions were granted, they would lay down their arms and again be "good people" (Ming Shih 165.5b). At the close of the dynasty the government would probably have been more ready to compromise and the rebels less eager to submit. During the last phase of the Ming period rebels appeared everywhere; and the many local conflicts were merged in the final battle for the overthrow of the dynasty.

d. For Mamluk Egypt cf. Poliak, 1934: 267 ff. The members of the Indian sect who, in 1672, started an uprising are said to have been "goldsmiths, carpenters, sweepers, tanners, and other ignoble beings" (commoners?). Some apparently engaged in agri-

were charged with maintaining the rulers' rationality minimum, were expected to heed such warnings. And indeed they often did. But they were most ready to do so where private, and not state, business was involved,[5] and any sporadic moderation on their part did not keep them from exerting their authority fully and coercively in matters of consequence—for instance, over artisans and laborers who rendered corvée labor [6] or over particular persons whose wealth they wished to syphon off.

In the great majority of all cases the artisan or merchant who aroused the greed of a ranking official or underling maneuvered prudently. Whenever he could he paid his way out of his impasse. Obviously, an accommodating lie or a well-placed bribe are not exactly weapons in a war of liberation. And the unending small conflicts between the bureaucratic hunter and his petty-bourgeois or capitalist game made it unmistakably clear that in this chase the urban commoners might survive, but they could not win.

Traditional Chinese statecraft gave more leeway to private property than did the absolutist regimes of most other hydraulic civilizations; but under its shadow capitalist enterprise was as cagey as elsewhere. An edict of the short-lived reform government of 1898 puts the blame for this fact on the officials, particularly—and somewhat hypocritically—on the underlings. When a firm is in diffi-

---

culture (Elliot and Dowson, 1877: 185, 294). Smith (1946: 29) suggests that the urban sectarians were workers or poor traders: "petty traders and workers, either propertyless proletariat or men with a very small professional 'property.'" His second source speaks of trade "on a small scale" or, according to another translation, "their trade is on a small capital" (ibid.: 29 ff.). In Muslim India, as elsewhere, propertyless persons certainly participated in urban riots; but in this case the cited data point to artisans who owned their means of production rather than to proletarian elements.

Another insurrection of the period is even farther removed from being proletarian. According to Smith (ibid.: 25 ff.), the town of Patna was seized in 1610 "by a proletarian mob" whose leader impersonated "the popular hero Khusraw." After the success of this coup "numbers of the lower-class aligned themselves with him. These proletarians even organized a minor army from amongst themselves, which they were foolish enough to send out against the upper-class army advancing under the irate governor." This account is greatly at variance with the facts as given in Smith's own sources. The popular hero Khusraw was the emperor's oldest son, who was kept prisoner after he had made an armed attempt to seize the throne (Jahāngīr, 1909: 56–68). Khusraw had based his rebellion primarily on the support of members of the imperial army (ibid.: 52, 55, 58); and temporarily his chances of success had been considerable (ibid.: 58). It is therefore not surprising that the impostor found adherents among "a number of foot- and horsemen." These soldiers—and no "proletarian mob"— seized Patna and its fort (ibid.: 174); and there is no specific evidence that the "wretched creatures," who later joined the rebellion (ibid.: 174), were "proletarians" either. Jahāngīr applies the term "wretch" indiscriminately to rebels, including persons of the highest political and social status (ibid.: 55, 65, 123).

culties, "the demands and extortions of the yamen underlings are invariably so great and exorbitant that merchants become discouraged and dare not venture further afield into trade enterprise, thereby causing trade to stand immovable." [7]

The covert conflicts between state slaves and their bureaucratic masters were numerous and, generally speaking, unnoticed. Like the domestic slaves of private owners, the unfortunate bondsmen of the government tried to ease their fate by cunning and well-camouflaged devices; and like them also they were employed essentially as single individuals or in small groups and with little opportunity to revolt *en masse*.

The slave war that started in southern Mesopotamia in 869 drew its initial strength from the unusually large number of slaves employed by unusually large private enterprises [8] in the production of salt, east of Basra. The magnitude of these enterprises made them an ideal breeding ground for mass action. The revolt, which lasted some fourteen years, owed much of its temporary success to the fact that during these years the Abbassid state was shaken by civil wars between certain generals and high territorial officials and between both and the caliphate.[9]

I. SOCIAL CONFLICTS WITHIN THE RULING CLASS

EXCEPT for the peasant uprisings that occasionally, and particularly in hydraulic societies with strongly developed private landownership, challenged the authority of the officialdom, only the social conflicts within the ruling class had a definitely political quality. The military rebellions of dissenting members of the ruling family or of ambitious generals or governors against a weak monarch usually involved conflicts between persons of different grades and positions within the power hierarchy. But they occurred only sporadically and at long intervals; and when they did, they tended to evolve quickly into military tests of strength between two or more independent territories or regions.

Much more frequent, and much more difficult to discern, are the undercover conflicts that arose between ranking officials and bureaucratic underlings, between various groups of ranking officials, between officials and the bureaucratic gentry, and between ranking officials and the despot and his personal entourage, the court. These conflicts were usually concerned with political power or influence, and while most of them affected only a few individuals, some of them involved the privileges of larger groups, subsections or strata within the bureaucratic order. But although such conflicts might touch the interests of a considerable number of persons, they lacked the organized cohesiveness which characterized the great social movements of the ancient, medieval, and modern West.

1. RANKING OFFICIALS VERSUS UNDERLINGS

BROADLY speaking, the ranking officials determine the operations of their secretarial and menial underlings. But often an administrative (or fiscal or police) problem can be solved to the advantage of either the ranking officials or their underlings. Ambivalent situations of this kind are inherent in all organizations whose functions are vertically divided. But in the hydraulic setting these situations were particularly consequential because the actions of the *apparatchiki* were not checked by effective outside forces and because those involved in the conflicts disposed over the resources of a uniquely powerful state apparatus.

The ranking officials, as well as the underlings, aimed at a maximum of control over details of procedure and personnel, partly for the sake of power and partly for the sake of increasing their share of the government revenue. Status was no major issue, although the underlings, by increasing their power, also increased their social prestige. A critical examination of the Chinese government under the Manchus suggests that the underlings for some time arrogated to themselves something like 30 per cent of the government revenue.[1] Since this estimate was made by a member of the ranking officialdom,[2] it may be too high, but it indicates the dimension of the economic problem involved in the day-to-day struggle between the gentlemen-functionaries and their plebeian aides.

In this struggle the underlings could and did draw advantage from their intimate knowledge of local affairs, their familiarity with the know-how of the office, and their physical control over the ultimate execution of all administrative work. The officials could and did draw advantage from the various methods of supervision, from control over the hiring and firing of the staff personnel, and in serious cases from the power to invoke all manner of punishment.

An official Chinese statement of 1899 reveals how in the tug-of-war between the ranking officials and the underlings certain functionaries might become dependent on strategically placed scribes: "In all matters of promotion, transfer, appointment, merit or demerit, or of taxes and legal decisions, provincial officials sought to gain favors by bribing clerks in the various Boards. And officials who were charged with the delivery of revenue, or copper, or dye materials to the central government were especially harried by their demands.

From the day they reported deliveries to the time they were given the receipts the clerks found many reasons for making extortions. The sums asked reached hundreds and thousands of taels. This was known as the 'Board of Expenses' and was collected with little effort at concealment." [3]

The runners exerted their power on a different plane and, of course, with different methods. They controlled access to government buildings; they arrested people and guarded the jails. Thus they could alleviate a prisoner's lot or make it more miserable; they could regulate the force of a flogging; they could claim resistance to arrest.[4] The power and possible material benefits inherent in these situations are manifest.

The ranking officials, who wished to maintain their control over the numerous and well-entrenched host of underlings, brought into play all the administrative and disciplinary means with which they were invested. The functionaries of Ch'ing China attempted to limit the duration of the underlings' employment. But while such control strengthened the hold of the ranking officials over the lower functionaries, the costs in skill and experience could be considerable.

Underlings who abused their power to the manifest detriment of the government were to be severely punished. This aspect of the matter has been clearly defined in the *Arthashāstra,* in the dynastic regulations of China, and in other manuals of agrodespotic statecraft. For scribes and runners who were dishonest or resorted to extortion the last Code of imperial China established penalties ranging from fines to permanent exile and execution by strangulation. The attached cases show that the higher officials did not hesitate to strike when they saw fit.[5]

In the struggle between the officials and the underlings the latter could never be completely subdued. But neither could they upset the structure of the bureaucratic apparatus, which enabled the ranking officials to emerge over time, not as total victors but as the holders of superior legal, administrative, and economic authority.

2. BUREAUCRATIC COMPETITION

a. Patterns of Competition Different in Different Societies

COMPETITION in the market is only one of many forms of competition. And hydraulic and feudal society differ from capitalism not because in them competition is absent, but because it is differently shaped.

In the medieval world of the West serfdom reduced competition in most villages to insignificance, whereas the feudal knights openly and violently competed with their fellows for land and glory. The guilds severely restricted competition in the crafts but not in large-scale and international trade.[6]

The regulated villages of Oriental society had little opportunity for economic rivalries. In traditional China the advance of private peasant landownership encouraged competition in economic affairs, without, to be sure, making Chinese agriculture capitalist. In all types of hydraulic society the members of the ruling class competed for power, prestige, and income; and this is true not only for the ranking officials but also, and with proper modifications, for the bureaucratic underlings.

Within the capitalist system we find competition on both the employer and employee levels. But while the expansion of this system increases the quality of goods and the number of persons involved, it reduces the number of competing and bargaining elements through the rise of corporations and labor unions. In addition, legal controls tend to restrict the methods of the competitive struggle, which generally is more violent in the early than in the later phases of capitalist economy.

The difference between the three types of competition appears also as a difference in their results. The medieval knight who makes a crucial mistake while competing with his fellows (on the battle field) may forfeit his life, but his property and honor usually remain untouched. The modern businessman who makes a crucial mistake while competing with his fellows (on the market), may lose his property, but his honor is rarely besmirched, and he certainly will not forfeit his life. The official of an agrarian despotism who makes a crucial mistake while competing with his fellows (in a bureaucratic or court intrigue) is likely to lose his honor, his property, and his life. Where power is fragmented and balanced, punishment for a crucial mistake is limited. Under conditions of total power, it is total.

b. Bureaucratic Competition in Hydraulic Society

ALL bureaucratic organizations have certain technical features in common; and some methods of intrabureaucratic competition appear universally in serving, controlled, and ruling bureaucracies. However, this makes it all the more imperative to recognize, behind the familiar trees, the peculiarity of the woods of which they form a part.[a]

a. Universals of warfare appear in the military enterprises of feudal Europe as well as in the hydraulic and modern industrial societies. But no one concerned with institutional specification will, for this reason, deny the peculiarities of organization and procedure that distinguish the three patterns.

The functionaries of Occidental absolutism are closest to those of Oriental absolutism insofar as the chance for a meteoric rise or fall is concerned; but under Western absolutism there are non-bureaucratic roads to social prominence. And the government officials of an open modern society have legally established rights which guarantee that the loser in an intrabureaucratic fight need suffer nothing more than the frustration of not being promoted.

Under the conditions of total power bureaucratic life is as competitive as it is dangerous. A statistical study of the officials of the first long-lasting dynasty of imperial China, Han, shows that among those whose careers can be traced in some detail [7] about 21 per cent at one time or another were imprisoned for derelictions during their official career, and about 35 per cent died a violent death outside the battlefield. More than 12 per cent were murdered or died after torture in prison, 14 per cent were executed, and 9 per cent committed suicide.[b]

3. CIVIL VERSUS MILITARY OFFICIALS

BUREAUCRATIC competition occurs not only between members of the same office or administrative unit but also between members of different branches of the state apparatus. Among these branches, the army, for obvious reasons, poses special problems.

a. The Autocrat and the Army

THE army, as the compact machine of institutionalized coercion, plays a different role in different phases of hydraulic society. During the formative period the supreme military leader is also apt to control the new political economy, since his organizational and disciplinary position prepares him uniquely to head the emerging agromanagerial apparatus. Once established, the over-all political apparatus tends to prevail over the various branches, because the heads of the former through their control over personnel and com-

---

b. A study of 19th-century China suggests that at the close of the imperial period the career of an official was still beset with many dangers, although the character of these dangers had changed in several respects. On the basis of the *Tung-hua-lu,* Dr. Hellmut Wilhelm assumes that between 1821 and 1895 "almost every high official was punished at least once during his career." Extremely severe punishments (execution, banishment, enslavement, corporal punishment, or imprisonment) were imposed in about 22 per cent of all cases brought to the emperor's attention, dismissal in 42 per cent, and lighter punishments (reprimands, fines, and/or demotion) in the remaining cases. The survey, which considers both Manchu and Chinese officials, was made under Dr. Wilhelm's direction, at the University of Washington, Seattle, by Cecil Cody, Robert Crawford, Chen-i Wang, and Lincoln Wong.

munication penetrate all segments, which, no matter what their economic weight or coercive potential may be, remain compartmentalized and thus strategically inferior to the coordinating center. To elaborate upon our previously established thesis we may say: it is not the technical specialist or the hydraulic manager or the head of the police, or the commander of the army, but the master of the all-pervasive political apparatus who maintains supreme power over the compartmentalized technicians, managers, police chiefs, and generals. Only during periods of political disintegration and civil war will a vigorous general seize control of the entire country or a number of generals simultaneously in separated territories become military and political leaders: bureaucratic warlords.

The agromanagerial despot is usually very much aware of the power potential inhering in the armed forces; and he therefore takes every precaution to keep them subdued. He is the supreme master of the military, first because he makes the crucial decisions concerning its organization, its personnel, and (often also) its supply, and second because he heads the centralized apparatus of communications and intelligence.

Similar sociostrategic advantages favor the political masters of modern industrial apparatus states. They largely explain why, in the 1930's Stalin was able to liquidate the discontented heads of the Soviet army and two subsequent chiefs of the GPU, and why, in 1944, the National Socialist center prevailed over the generals who sought to overthrow Hitler.

b. Civil versus Military Officials

THE military functionaries, like their civil colleagues, are part of the over-all officialdom, and not infrequently the duties of the two groups overlap. When essential civil and military tasks are concurrently executed by the same higher officials (a governor, a satrap, etc.), conflicts between military and civil functionaries occur only on lower levels of authority. Often, however, the two spheres of action are represented by two distinct groups; and then such conflicts appear in the top echelons of the hierarchy.

Outside of periods of formation, decay, and crisis, military leaders in the hydraulic world have a chance to establish positions of prominence under several conditions: (1) in all areas—core and margin—which, being situated between strong neighbors, for international reasons require strong protection; (2) in marginal areas, because the lesser importance of the managerial bureaucracy increases the weight of the army; and (3) in conquest societies, in which the army is an essential factor not only for the establishment of the regime but for its perpetuation.

A number of the states of Buddhist India fall into the first category, Middle and Late Byzantium and post-Mongol Russia in the second, and many conquest societies of the Old and the New World in the third.

The struggle between the civil and military officialdom can be clearly observed in several hydraulic civilizations. In Pharaonic Egypt functionaries who specialized in the military arts proper ("front" officers) were during prolonged periods subordinated to military administrators—that is, to officials who kept the military records and who organized supply and equipment.[8] But in another context the front officers might successfully counterbalance members of the civil administration. The king placed some of them in important government positions, where, as socially inferior homines novi, they could be relied upon to uphold his interests against the ambitions of the ranking civil officials.[9]

Under the Mamluks the military officers, who were exclusively Mamluks, remained apart from, and above, the native bureaucracy. They could—and did—expropriate, imprison, and execute civil officials when they felt the latter were overstepping their authority.[10]

During the last period of the Roman republic successful generals rose to the top of the political hierarchy; and under the empire the army played a dominant, although varying, role for centuries.[11]

Ostrogorsky considers "the struggle between the competing forces of the metropolitan civil aristocracy and the provincial military aristocracy" the basic trend of Byzantine society.[12] The meaning of this statement becomes clear when we remember that the Byzantine civil aristocracy was a Beamtenadel, an aristocracy of officials,[13] and that both groups competed within the framework of a Beamtenstaat, a bureaucratic state, which was "constantly swelling and which, as the ruling stratum, made ever-greater demands."[14]

The intragovernmental struggles in T'ang China and in comparable periods in the history of other hydraulic civilizations were largely struggles between the civil and military branches of the ranking officialdom.

4. THE BUREAUCRATIC ACTIVISTS VERSUS THE BUREAUCRATIC GENTRY

CONFLICTS between the officiating functionaries and members of the bureaucratic gentry resemble the intrabureaucratic struggles in that they, too, are frequently linked with the intrigues and machinations of competing court cliques. However, they have important peculiarities of their own. The active bureaucrats wield power; the members of the bureaucratic gentry exert influence. The officiating executives have excellent opportunities to accumulate wealth; the bureaucratic rentiers have fair opportunities to preserve, at least during their lifetime, what wealth they have. These differences in position go far to explain the conflicts that occur between members of the two groups.

If the individuals concerned are of the same rank, then, other things being equal, power will prevail over influence and the executive over the rentier. Not infrequently, however, a local official of minor rank may find himself in opposition to members of the gentry, who are able to prevail because they belong to a bureaucratically powerful family. The study of powerful families in hydraulic society [15] reveals the decisive role that power plays in this society in determining status, influence, and revenue.

A gentry-bureaucracy conflict may involve only a single member of the gentry, a person, let us say, who seeks through influence to decrease his fiscal obligations or increase his landholding. Occasionally it may involve all the members of a local gentry who are seeking to shape local politics according to their interests. Members of the gentry may stress (and actually represent) the ruler's rationality maximum; and they may dramatize their intentions by getting commoners to demonstrate against the local officials. To support their interests at the local level they may even appeal to top-ranking members of the hierarchy.

In the province of Anhui, after the T'ai-p'ing Rebellion, members of the gentry, together with other landowners, were temporarily able "to cheat the government yearly of a large proportion of income from land revenue." The local officials accepted this condition for a time because they feared that an insistence on full tax payments would cause the people, "incited by the landed gentry," to rebel against the newly arrived magistrate. Eventually, however, some undaunted members of the bureaucracy suggested the restoration of the destroyed cadaster in order to reestablish government control over the revenue. [16]

Conversely, several members of the gentry of a certain region in the province of Chekiang were dissatisfied with the district magistrate because of his "extortions." They complained to his superiors, requesting his demotion. [17]

An imperial decree of April 14, 1890, deplored "the common practice among the provincial gentry and literati of mixing themselves up in matters of public business, and sometimes even bringing pressure to bear on the authorities." The former justified their actions by stating that they promoted the public good. However, according to the official view these actions were "in reality designed for selfish purposes." [18] The publication of the edict shows that the local officials, who were temporarily at a disadvantage, eventually and through the support of the central government, prevailed over the gentry.

In periods of political decay the gentry asserts itself in various ways, but officials of a strong regime usually insist that it meet their demands. This last was the case in Early and Middle Byzantium and in 19th-century Russia, where the negotiations concerning the emancipation of the serfs revealed the relative strength of the bureaucratic and the proprietary (gentry) wings of the ruling nobility. Theoretically speaking, the (bureaucratic) landowners, or the absolutist state and its functionaries, or the peasants might have become the chief beneficiaries of the Emancipation of 1861. Actually, the government one-sidedly determined that the "Editing Commission" was to be "composed of officers of the various departments which had to do with peasant affairs, together with a number of experienced landowners." [19] Thus the terms of the Emancipation were "settled by discussion in the bureaucratic field"; [20] and both the bureaucratic landowners and the officials presented their respective arguments, which were based "not upon any ideal, but upon the recognition of the needs of the landowners or of the State." [21] The bureaucratic quality of the nobles' landed interests was expressed in the person of the man who finally headed the Commission, Count Panin. Panin owned enormous estates and twenty-one thousand serfs, but he also had a prominent role in the juridical affairs of the government. Pressured by the Tsar and his aides, Panin readily subordinated the proprietary aspirations of the nobility to its bureaucratic interests. [22]

The relations between the bureaucratic activists and the rentier-like bureaucratic gentry recall patterns of conflict occurring in the big corporations of modern industrial society. Shareholders of a company, who are not among its officers, have the right at the annual meeting to comment on, or question, company policy. But such casual and optative participation is far from effective control. Satisfied with their dividends, the majority of the shareholders are willing to leave the actual management to the executive officers. These functionaries exert supreme power over decision making and personnel; and even if originally they possessed little stock, they have incomparably greater opportunities for improving their material position than do the shareholders. [23]

In contrast to the corporation shareholders, who have the right to assemble, to rally public opinion, and to resort to legal action, the members of the hydraulic gentry, even when they owned considerable amounts of land, could not organize or gather freely. These privileges were restricted to the men in office, who, controlling the bulk of the country's surplus and monopolizing coercive power, had no difficulty in stressing the bureaucratic against the proprietary interests of the ruling class. And they did so, even when, as in the case of Count Panin, they were both officials and big landowners.

Thus the conflicts between the bureaucratic gentry and the ranking officials once more thrust into sharp relief the unique power position enjoyed in hydraulic society by the men of the state apparatus.

5. Conflicts between the Autocrat and Other Members of the Ruling Class

THE autocrat has been likened to the life-giving sun, to fierce animals, and to the merciless forces of lightning, storm, and flood. To his subjects he is indeed all these, and those among them who act in his name are eager both to execute his will and to influence it.

But the master of a tool is also its servant. The autocrat depends operationally upon the persons who implement his orders. The history of Oriental courts records endless attempts to influence the autocrat and equally endless attempts by the ruler to prevail over all personal and impersonal (bureaucratic) forces. The resulting conflicts are many. Contemplating the autocrat's antagonistic relations with his relatives on the one hand and with his ranking officials on the other, we can distinguish several types of conflict and also several major devices that the antagonists employ to further their respective aims.

a. The Autocrat versus His Relatives

i. BLOOD RELATIVES

THE ruler's relatives (who they are depends upon the prevailing patterns of kinship) are ever-ready to use their socially privileged position for political purposes. To name a successor outside the established tradition or to replace a ruler in his lifetime is a risky venture; but attempts to do so have frequently been made and not always without success.

Serious problems may arise even when the established tradition is upheld. How does an autocrat control his crown prince? How does he control his kinsmen? The Han emperors granted them much property but little power. Such a policy cannot eliminate all conflicts, but it will restrict them greatly, and to the decided advantage of the autocrat.

ii. AFFINALS

THE ruler's affinals are an equally ambivalent asset. They attain political prominence because one of their female members is his wife. They thus have a vested interest in the person of the ruler, who on his part may trust them more than his blood relatives. The Han rulers almost invariably kept their blood relatives out of office, but many members of the empress' family were given high positions in the bureaucracy. The Liao emperors were less discriminatory, but they, too, often turned to their in-laws when key political positions were to be filled.[24] Of course, such a policy has its dangers. Affinals who wield great power may reduce the ruler to a figurehead during his lifetime. Or after his death they may install a child as his successor and then reign in his stead. During a great part of the Liao dynasty the empire was ruled by empress dowagers.[25]

How does an autocrat control his affinals? The limiting of political eunuchism tends to decrease the influence of the ruler's wives, and measures designed to protect the heir apparent also have obvious advantages. The Toba ruler went to extremes: He killed his wife after she bore him an heir.[26] But such radical means were rarely invoked. More often, instead of killing the mother of his son (or sons), the ruler filled his harem with slave girls. Their relatives were usually persons of lowly status, and although some among them might rise to high station, they were much less of a threat, as a group, than noble and well-established consort families. Several Chinese emperors were the sons of former "singing girls," [27] and the majority of all caliphs [e] and Turkish sultans had former slave girls as mothers.[28]

The problems raised by the blood relatives contrast sharply with those raised by the affinals. With regard to the former the ruler could narrow the basis of hostility; with reward to the latter he could, under optimal circumstances, remove it altogether.

c. All Abbassid caliphs except three had slave mothers (Goldziher, 1889: 124; cf. Mez, 1922: 140, and Kremer, CGO, I: 393).

b. The Autocrat versus the Ranking Officials

i. ONCE MORE THE PROBLEM OF AUTOCRACY

THE despot's effort to control his relatives is only a particular expression of his over-all effort to control his serving men. Neither indicates the absence of autocratic authority. As developed above, a ruler who in his person concentrates "all the power over major decisions" [29] is by no means above and beyond the influence of those who serve him. And since the interests of the officialdom frequently suggest one decision and the ruler's interests another, there is considerable room for conflict. Needless to say, the sovereign will prevail the more completely, the more he determines the choice of his civil and military functionaries, and the more he controls their executive procedures.

The fact that the ruler in peace or war may insist on an irrational policy, even when it endangers the very existence of the state, underlines the extent to which power is concentrated in his person. The fact that his minor decisions may profoundly affect the prestige, income, and security of his officials underlines the unique political sensitiveness of the ruling class under the conditions of total power.

ii. HUMAN (SOCIAL) RELATIONS EXPRESSED THROUGH INSTITUTIONAL ARRANGEMENTS

THE despot establishes horizontal checks by giving equal authority to two or more officials. He maintains vertical checks by a multiple system of reporting and supervising. And he demonstrates his supreme power by ruthless methods of discipline and punishment. Thus he is able to counter the strivings of his ranking officials for more influence (as advisors and memorialists), for more freedom (as executives and judges), for more wealth (as manipulators of the government revenue), and for more group advantage (as the beneficiaries of hereditary privileges).

The resulting institutional arrangements are not merely organizational and technical, as some observers believe. Rather they express human (social) relations between two crucial and antagonistic subsections of the ruling class. These relations are always slanted in favor of the despot, and this is so even where the officials enjoy hereditary privileges. It is particularly so where the ruler appoints his officials without the need to consider a self-perpetuating (noble) bureaucracy.

6. Autocratic Methods of Controlling the Bureaucratic Personnel

a. The Ruler's Control over a Hereditary Officialdom (a Bureaucratic Nobility)

MEMBERS of hereditary (noble) official families usually have a hereditary claim on an office, but not necessarily a claim on a special office or one of equal rank. If a hereditary serving man blunders seriously or is disloyal, the ruler can cancel the family privilege altogether and enslave or exterminate the culprit.[30] The ruler, who is limited with respect to the group from which he chooses his officials, nevertheless asserts his power by promoting or demoting its members at will.

b. Autocratic Means of Weakening or Destroying the Self-perpetuating Quality of the Ranking Officials

BUT "despotism itself has its varieties." [31] The despot may reduce the social homogeneity of the ranking officials by the appointment of outsiders; he may place men of lowly origin above officials of upper-class background; he may give precedence to priests, "barbarian" nobles, eunuchs, or slave officials. In the sovereign's hand such devices become the weapons for asserting his autocratic power against the will, and the unending political intrigues, of the ranking officialdom.

i. PRIESTS

THE inclusion of professional religious functionaries in the government was an important means of preventing a homogeneous officialdom. Under the Mayas, priests seem to have been regularly employed as officials.[32] In India the leading position of the "warrior-rulers," the Kshatriyas, was weakened by the appointment of Brahmins to government offices [33] and by the institution of the *purohita*. The royal house-priest, who was his sovereign's main advisor, could be expected to promote the selection of priests as officials whenever circumstances permitted. Even the Muslim rulers of India used to "make a Brahmin their secretary of state." [34] The prominence of priests among the king's councilors probably goes far in explaining why both in Hindu and Muslim India eunuchs had little opportunity to advance to the top-ranking advisory positions which they attained in other Oriental civilizations.

ii. COMMONERS (GENERAL OBSERVATIONS)

THE professional functionaries of the dominant religion were members of the ruling class; and the ruler who employed them—or for that matter his relatives by blood or marriage—counterbalanced the trend toward a self-perpetuating bureaucracy without drawing upon "the people."

In the wider sense "the people" included commoners and slaves. But it is characteristic of the peculiarities of social mobility under agromanagerial despotism that in this type of regime slaves (and eunuchs) were more systematically appointed to key political positions than were commoners.

The hereditary officials and the priests in government posts laid great stress on the educational qualifications required for the execution of their bureaucratic tasks; and their overlord had little reason to discard prerequisites which, from the standpoint of effectiveness and prestige, seemed eminently desirable. These prerequisites provided serious arguments against the indiscriminate placing of commoners into government positions.

In India the Sūdras, as a group, were not permitted to study the sacred books; [35] the Vaisyas were not so restricted.[36] But how many of them actually attained as thorough an education as a Brahmin or Kshatriya? Among the Maya, wealthy commoners were employed in government positions, but, as noted above, from time to time the official hierarchy was purged of those who were "not versed in the occult knowledge of the upper class." [37] Confucius accepted commoners as disciples,[d] but like their noble colleagues, these commoners had to be thoroughly familiar with the classics and the secular and religious ceremonial before they could be "used" in office.

iii. COMMONERS: SOCIAL EFFECTS AND LIMITATIONS OF THE CHINESE EXAMINATION SYSTEM

THE Chinese examination system has frequently been viewed as an institution which, throughout the period of imperial rule, gave the commoners access to office. Since participation in the examinations was based not on invitation from above but on the would-be candidate's spontaneous application, the Chinese bureaucracy may well seem, during this period, to have been recruited in large part from "the people."

d. One, Tzŭ-kung, is known to have been a businessman (*Shih Chi* 129.5a; cf. Legge, CC, I: 144, 242). For Tzŭ-kung's prominent position among Confucius' followers see Creel, 1949: 66 ff.

The Chinese examination system did in fact make it possible for a number of qualified commoners to enter the bureaucracy; but its social effects were much more modest than popular legend would have us believe. What actually did happen? The question is sufficiently important for an understanding of mobility in hydraulic society to justify a brief statement of the function—and the limitation—of the Chinese examination system.

First of all, the Chinese examination system provided the absolutist governments of China with candidates for office only during a limited and relatively late period. In Chou times and probably also under the Shang dynasty the bulk of all officials held positions because their forefathers had done so. During the Han dynasty (206 B.C.–A.D. 220) entry upon a government career depended essentially on appointment by the emperor or by a special official; in addition, office-holding fathers might recommend their own sons. The method of "recommending sons" (jên tzŭ) [38] favored the self-perpetuation of particular families in the bureaucracy, while appointment favored the self-perpetuation of the ranking officialdom generally. An examination of the biographical data included in the dynastic histories of the Han period gives considerable insight into the effects of these procedures, which are in fact a bureaucratic variant of the aristocratic principle of cooptation. [39] Basing ourselves on this source, we find that no more than 8 per cent of all officials of known social background were commoners, the remainder being relatives of the emperor (in the main, affinals), members of other noble families, or—and in their great majority—the relatives of officials. [40]

The period of disruption which ended in A.D. 589 modified earlier patterns of government. Although wars and conquest provided opportunities for the rise of social outsiders, a limited number of families were able to perpetuate their hold on the state apparatus. Under the infiltration and conquest dynasties [41] of North China, nobles of Inner Asian origin prevailed; and in the South indigenous "hereditary families" (shih chia) were similarly prominent. The biographies of the Southern Chin dynasty (216–419) indicate that about 9.5 per cent of all officials with known background may have been commoners.[e]

---

e. In 1935–36, in Peiping, I organized a study of the social background of the officials listed in the biographical sections of the official histories of several imperial dynasties. In 1938 I summarized the results of a preliminary analysis of our findings as follows: "Some 'fresh blood' may have been absorbed from the lower strata of society by means of the examination system; but on the whole the ruling officialdom reproduced itself socially more or less from its own ranks. The Chinese system of examinations had a very definite function; but, as in the case of the family, this

The much-discussed examination system was established only in the time of the re-unified empire by the short-lived Sui dynasty (581–618). It was fully developed by the subsequent T'ang dynasty—that is, it came into being something like seventeen hundred years after the beginning of the Chou dynasty and eight hundred years after the beginning of the imperial era. And even during the first half of the thirteen hundred years of its existence its influence on the social composition of the imperial bureaucracy was seriously restricted by institutionalized social discrimination, by hereditary claims to office (the *yin* privilege), and, under the conquest dynasties, by the politically prominent nobles of the "barbarian" master nationality.

The Chinese examination system was established not by democratic forces but one-sidedly by a despotic ruler. The ranking officials certainly influenced the original plan; and they implemented it, once it was established. Anyone who was eligible to participate in the examinations could take the initiative in applying; and this is a significant deviation from the earlier appointment system. However, even under the examination system the emperor and his officials ultimately decided whom they would employ, and how they would employ them. The government determined in advance how many degrees would be conferred; and even the holders of the most important degree, the *chin-shih*, originally were admitted to office only after they had also passed a sort of civil service test.[42]

The insistence upon a thorough classical education gave the members of official families—and, of course, also the relatives of the ruling house—an enormous cultural and social advantage. This advantage was enhanced by measures that, on the one hand, restricted the commoners' access to office and, on the other, provided the relatives of higher and middle officials with institutionalized claims to office.

The Sui statutes that initiated the examination system expressly excluded "artisans and merchants" from holding office. A similar policy of discrimination prevailed under the T'ang, and, with certain modifications, also under the Sung dynasty.[43] Since commerce, more than any other occupation, provided commoners with opportunities

---

function is by no means, what popular legend has thus far made us believe it was" (Wittfogel, 1938a: 11 ff.).

From 1939 on, the Chinese History Project, New York, has investigated several aspects of Chinese officialdom, including the *yin* system. It has examined in detail the selection of officials in the Liao dynasty (Wittfogel and Fêng, 1949: 450 ff.); and it greatly refined an earlier statistical analysis of the biographies of the Han dynasty. For several reasons it has not yet been possible to process the biographies of the other major dynasties as fully; but since the problem of mobility is a very important one, I have felt justified in presenting above some of the results of my original pilot inquiry together with some of our more recent findings.

for acquiring wealth and education, discrimination against merchants excluded from government exactly those commoners who were materially best equipped to prepare for the examinations.*

Moreover, the statutes that restricted the artisans and merchants gave added advantages to the bureaucracy. On the basis of their governmental position, higher and middle officials were granted the "protective" (yin) privilege of having one or several of their sons *g* enter the civil service without having to pass an examination.[44] This privilege, which in a new guise reestablished time-honored prerogatives, emerged in the Sui and T'ang dynasties—that is, as soon as the examinations were instituted. The yin system underwent considerable change during the Sung period, but it continued to play a significant role at this time [45] and also under the two first of the four great dynasties of conquest, Liao and Chin.[46]

The Mongols were deeply suspicious of their Chinese subjects. They therefore preferred appointment for their Chinese officials to any other method of selection. During the great part of their rule the Mongols held no examinations; and when eventually the examinations were re-instituted, the number of chin-shih degrees remained grotesquely low: "averages totaled not more than seventy (including a number of 'barbarians')." [47] They also restricted the number of yin sons and grandsons to one, as compared with ten and twenty beneficiaries under Sung rule and six under Chin rule. But they favored those who held the yin privilege by permitting them to enter the bureaucratic hierarchy in the fifth rank, a higher level than that granted in T'ang days.[h] The Ming and Ch'ing emperors reduced the yin prerogative to a shadow of its former self. They granted it only to the descendants of higher officials; and its beneficiaries could attain high positions only if they had passed the examinations.[48]

f. Under the Sung dynasty, government positions might be granted to persons who contributed grain for famine relief. This policy, which amounted to an indirect sale of office, gave some merchants a chance to enter the state service. But "it seems to have been practiced only in connection with a specific emergency" (Kracke, 1953: 76).

g. The number varied from period to period.

h. Wittfogel and Fêng, 1949: 459, 463. At the same time, "the Mongols raised the level of entry into the official hierarchy for yin claimants from the seventh to the fifth rank." Originally the yin son of a father who occupied one of the three highest ranks could begin his career in the seventh rank, and yin sons of fathers who occupied posts in the fourth or fifth rank could enter in the eighth rank, whereas the holders of the distinguished chin-shih degree might apply for positions only in the lowest or ninth rank. Yin officials might rise to the highest positions, including those of prime minister; and while in T'ang times this supreme post was, in most cases, held by men with a chin-shih degree, many yin sons seem to have attained posts in the middle or upper middle brackets (ibid.: 458).

The role of the holders of the *chin-shih* degree indicates one crucial function of the examination system. The intensive knowledge of the Chinese classics required for the examinations saturated the students both with the social philosophy of the ruling bureaucracy and with the great traditions of its semimanagerial and absolutist statecraft. Thus the competitive examination system was an excellent means for thoroughly indoctrinating ambitious commoners and for compelling the talented sons of officials and bureaucratic gentry families to submit to a most·comprehensive professional ideological training.

The examinations were open to commoners during the first six hundred years with serious restrictions, and during the last six hundred years without such hindrances. But how many commoners did actually rise to official position in the government of imperial China through this method? Again the biographies, included in each of the official dynastic histories, provide us with invaluable, if selective, information. The biographies are numerous, more numerous in fact than any other collection of corresponding data in any other agrarian civilization, and they deal essentially with high and middle officials, who are listed not because of their rank, but because of their achievements.

Our preliminary effort to determine the social background of the official biographies in some of the more important imperial dynasties indicates that during the T'ang period (618–907) some 83 per cent of all socially definable officials had an upper-class background: about 70 per cent were from the families of officials and 13 per cent from the ruling house or other noble families. Almost 7 per cent were "barbarians" (the T'ang ruling house was, at least in part, of Turkish origin). And less than 10 per cent were commoners.

The corresponding figures for the Sung dynasty (960–1279) suggest a minimum figure of some 85 per cent of officials with an upper-class background: 72 per cent descended from the families of officials and 13 per cent from the ruling house. About 15 per cent were commoners.

Our survey of the biographies of the Mongol dynasty (1234–1368) suggests that about 85 per cent of all socially definable officials had an upper-class background: 74 per cent were descended from the families of officials and 11 per cent from the ruling house. About 15 per cent were descended from commoners.

The indigenous rulers of the Ming dynasty were not at all eager to restore the pre-Mongol privileges of the bureaucracy. They controlled the officials from above through political eunuchism. And they made it easier for commoners to enter the state service by crippling the *yin* privilege and by not discriminating against artisans and merchants, as the Sui, T'ang, and Sung governments had done. Under the Ming dynasty 77 per cent of all socially definable officials had an upper-class background: 63 per cent were descended from the families of officials, 14 per cent from the ruling house. And about 23 per cent were descended from commoners.

The Manchu rulers were no more inclined than their Ming predecessors to favor the bureaucracy's tendency toward self-perpetuation. They controlled their Chinese officials from above through tribal nobles, whose political position was bulwarked by the preservation of their hereditary prerogatives. And they facilitated the access of commoners to examinations and office, as the Ming rulers had done, through curtailing the *yin* privilege and through not discriminating against artisans and merchants. They particularly stressed purchase of degrees as a means of preventing the *shên-shih* (the officials and degree-holders) from becoming a socially homogeneous body.

An imperial edict of 1727 expressed sharp criticism of many persons who attained office through examinations. "If the official career should be left completely to those who rise through examinations, they would just firmly join together and work for their private interest against the public interest. This is of great harm to the public welfare and to the livelihood of the people. The purchase system should be appropriately expanded." [49]

According to a recent analysis of the social background of *chin-shih* candidates, the percentage of candidates whose forebears were neither officials nor degree-holders increased greatly during the 19th century.[i] And a study of the 19th-century *shên-shih* reveals that persons who joined this group not through examination but through purchase of a degree constituted about 32 per cent of the "lower gentry" during the first half of the century and about 36 per cent after 1854.[j]

The results of our analysis are confirmed for the Sung period by two lists of *chin-shih* graduates for 1148 and 1256 respectively, which, although incomplete as to social background data,[k] throw additional

i. See the unpublished study of the Ch'ing officialdom undertaken by Dr. C. K. Yang for the Modern Chinese History Project, Far Eastern and Russian Institute of the University of Washington, Seattle.

j. Chang, CG. For further data on the position of the *shên-shih* at the close of the Ch'ing dynasty see below, and Chap. 7 above.

k. For details concerning the two lists see Kracke, 1947: 107 ff. The second list has conspicuous gaps (*ibid.*: 113), and both, like the dynastic biographies, provide only selected data concerning the protagonists' official background. In his thoughtful study of this background, Kracke considered only relatives in the direct line up to, and including, the great-grandfathers (*ibid.*: 115). However, besides such individuals the list of 1256 mentions regularly the brothers of "graduates" who held degrees or offices.

light upon our problem. Assuming that during the thirty-year period from 1142 to 1171 almost forty-five hundred persons [m] passed the examinations, that all these persons and an equal number who "presumably entered the service by other methods" [50] achieved government positions, that at least one-half of all *chin-shih* graduates, as relatives of the emperor, acting officials, or members of the bureaucratic gentry, belonged to the ruling class,[n] and that the average length of office tenure was something like twenty years,[o] we find among the

In two cases, in which no direct forebears had held public office, five (69a) and seven (66a) brothers respectively did so. And both lists note brothers, uncles, granduncles, and great-great-grandfathers whenever they are family heads. Differing from Kracke, we view graduates with such relatives as having an official background; and in consequence we add sixteen more cases for 1148 and twenty more for 1256 to his graduates with official background. This raises the percentages of graduates with known official background from 42.1 to 45.6 per cent in the first case and from 43.7 to 49.5 per cent in the second.

m. The exact figure, according to Kracke (1947: 120), is 4428.

n. In his 1947 study, Dr. Kracke distinguishes essentially between graduates with and without an official background. Our figures, therefore, can be expected to be somewhat larger than his. All graduates of 1148 who are members of the imperial family, Chao, are listed in the Sung account as having relatives who held official position; and they are therefore included by Dr. Kracke. However, in the 1256 record only the names of the Chao graduates, who numbered twenty-seven, are listed. Dr. Kracke is consistent in not including them; but we are equally consistent in doing so. We thus find that 50.3 per cent of all graduates of 1256 belonged to the ruling class. In view of the limited character of the background data contained in both lists, our above estimate that "at least one half of all *chin-shih* graduates . . . belonged to the ruling class" is probably a conservative one. I should like to take this opportunity to thank Mr. Fang Chao-ying for calling my attention to the imperial relatives mentioned in the lists and Professor Tung-tsu Chu for his careful reexamination of the social data contained in the two Sung lists.

o. Dr. Kracke assumes that the (civil) officials "served an average of some thirty years each (the examinations were passed by men commonly ranging in age from the twenties to the fifties)" (Kracke, 1947: 120). The last mentioned fact indicates that part of the candidates were physically and mentally vigorous until their fifties; but it tells us nothing about the political conditions that determine and shorten an official career under Oriental despotism. Lacking pertinent Sung statistics, I revert to the biographical data of the Han period, which has been analyzed in detail by the Chinese History Project. Among the Han officials for whom such information is given, about 45 per cent were in office for less than ten years, and more than 18 per cent from ten to nineteen years. This suggests an average office tenure of not more than ten years. At the end of Northern Sung, in 1119, the *yin* privilege was sharply, if temporarily, reduced by granting it only to civil and military functionaries, who had held office for more than fourteen and nineteen years respectively (*Wên-hsien T'ung-k'ao* 34: 325). Obviously, these terms of tenure were not considered excessively short (or the measure would have had little restrictive value) or excessively long (or it would have been forbidding). Assuming that the average office tenure in Sung time was definitely higher than during the Han dynasty and somewhat higher than the figures mentioned for 1119, an average of twenty years seems a reasonable estimate.

thirty-three thousand civil and military officials [p] a total of 9 per cent who may have come from the rank of commoners. These figures are well below the 15 per cent suggested by our earlier analysis. To adjust them, we would have to assume that the Sung emperor appointed more than the above-suggested number of commoners without benefit of a degree.

Many details of the Chinese examination system still need clarification, but this much seems certain: if the Sui and T'ang emperors established the examination system, in part at least, in order to alter the social composition of the ranking officialdom, then it must be said that the system failed to achieve this purpose. The examinations provided the ambitious core of the ruling class with a most intensive intellectual and doctrinal training; and they added a varying amount of "fresh blood" to the ranking officialdom. But they did not destroy the trend toward sociopolitical self-perpetuation which dominated the thoughts and actions of this group.

iv. EUNUCHS: THE PRINCIPLE

A VERY different method of strengthening the ruler's autocratic grip on his officials was provided by the employment of castrated persons —political eunuchs.

Castration was probably first used on large domesticated animals. In ancient America, which knew no such animals, there is no evidence of eunuchism. In the Near East, however, references to castrated animals appear in the middle of the 2d millennium B.C., and perhaps before that time.[q] Castration of human beings as a form of punish-

---

p. Chinese tradition views both civil and military functionaries as government officials (po kuan); and throughout the imperial period civil officials were time and again given military posts and military officials civil posts. (For Sung see Kracke, 1953: 56). Accepting for the sake of the argument an average office tenure of thirty years (an improbably high estimate on the basis of our data) and considering only civil officials (according to Kracke some 11,000 persons), we find that as graduates of the examinations, commoners might constitute 20.4 per cent of the civil officialdom. An average office tenure of twenty years would reduce the figure to 13.6 per cent. Our calculation is based on Chin Yü-fu's "combined numbers of civil and military [Sung] officials" given by Kracke in the next to last note of his study (Kracke, 1947: 122, n. 31).

q. A few passages in the Pyramid Texts have been considered as possibly referring to castration; but the Berlin Dictionary and such outstanding Egyptologists as Sethe indicate the problematic character of such an interpretation (Sethe, PT, III: 213, 215, 216; Wb, IV: 43, 264; V: 410). The caution exercised by these authorities should pertain also to passage 1462c (see Mereer, 1952, II: 323; III: 712 ff.). The inscriptions that refer to tribute bullocks from Syria (Breasted, 1927, II: 191, 199, 203) originated under Pharaoh Thutmose III (15th century). Thus in the middle of the second millennium B.C. castration of animals was known in Egypt and obviously also in Western Asia, but we have no equally reliable evidence for the castration of humans.

ment was used in Assyria in the second half of the 2d millennium. But political eunuchism is clearly evidenced in the Near East and China only from the first millennium B.C. on.[r]

In all likelihood eunuchs were used as harem guards before they became political functionaries. It is not difficult to see how a ruler who as a boy had known eunuchs as his mother's personal servants would be inclined to rely on such trusted attendants when he came to power and was faced with an elaborate and alien bureaucracy. Having been castrated as adults (and then usually for a crime) or as children (and then usually after being sold off by poor parents), eunuchs, unlike the regular officials, did not come from prominent families. Socially rootless, they owed everything they had and everything they were to their ruler; and their doglike devotion to him therefore resulted as consistently from their position as did their detachment from, or their open hostility to, the regular members of the officialdom. The Achaemenian Persians, who employed political eunuchs exclusively,[51] told Greek visitors that such persons were the most reliable tools a ruler could have.[52]

Oriental despots were pleased to use eunuchs in many semipersonal and semipolitical spheres of court life and in government proper. Often the eunuchs were entrusted with confidential tasks of intelligence. Not infrequently they were responsible for their sovereign's personal safety (as heads of his bodyguard); and at times they were placed in command of important armies or navies, or in charge of the royal treasury.

Such arrangements proved highly satisfactory since, although mutilated in body and spirit,[53] a eunuch retained his intellectual powers and his ability to act. One of their number, Ts'ai Lun, is credited with having invented paper;[54] and the most eminent Chinese historian, Ssŭ-ma Ch'ien, completed his great historical work after he had been castrated. Eunuch generals and admirals seem to have been no less ingenious and daring than those who had not been emasculated. In the political arena eunuch cunning at times astounded veterans of Oriental court intrigue. It was here that they were most

---

r. Meissner (BA, I: 120) is not sure whether the *girsequm* of Hammurabi's Code (secs. 187, 192, 193) were eunuchs. The Code punishes adultery with death (Hammurabi, secs. 129, 130), whereas the Middle Assyrian Laws order castration for this and other sex crimes (Meek, 1950: 181). The tables on which these laws are recorded originated in the 12th century B.C., but the laws themselves "may go back to the 15th century" (*ibid.*: 180). Assyrian references to what seem to be political eunuchs are contained in inscriptions made under Adad-Nirari II (911–891 B.C.) and Sargon (724–705 B.C.) (Luckenbill, AR, I: 116); but as far as pictorial representations of beardless men are concerned, Meissner (BA, I: 411) warns that these need not always indicate eunuchs.

feared, because it was here that they came closest to the nerve centers of despotic power.

V. EUNUCHS: A FEW HISTORICAL FACTS

THUS institutionalized eunuchism seems to have been altogether absent in ancient America. Domestic eunuchism was known in many major areas of Old World Oriental society. Political eunuchism was weakly developed in Hindu India, where an enormously influential priesthood provided the most important group of non-Kshatriya candidates for government office. In China and the Near East it temporarily became a formidable weapon of autocracy for supervising and controlling the ranking officialdom.

In China eunuchs emerged as political advisors and heads of armies during the second half of the Chou period—that is, at a time when the ranking officials still constituted a hereditary (noble) bureaucracy.[55] The founder of the empire, Ch'in Shih Huang-ti, had at the close of his life as his most intimate companion the eunuch, Chao Kao. After the emperor's death, Chao Kao succeeded in destroying the great chancellor, Li Ssŭ, and many other prominent functionaries. And so powerful was this eunuch that after having brought about the suicide of the second emperor he, and not a high-ranking official, chose the new emperor.[56]

The first sovereigns of the long-lasting imperial dynasty, Han, soon began to use eunuchs to maintain their autocratic rule. Under Empress Dowager Lü (188–180 B.C.) the eunuch Chang Shih-ch'ing handled the edicts and commands.[57] Under Emperor Wên (180–157) two eunuchs enjoyed considerable favor.[58] Emperor Wu (141–87) left political matters to his trusted eunuchs when he withdrew to his harem,[59] and two eunuchs, Hung Kung and Shih Hsien, played a prominent role in the government of Emperor Yüan (48–33 B.C.).[60]

Under these rulers of Early Han individual eunuchs were prominent. During the Later Han period (A.D. 25–220) eunuchs were merged in a powerful group. Their influence increased notably in the second half of the first century A.D. and, in the second century they held in their hands "kingdoms and noble ranks and they had in their mouths the decrees of Heaven." [61] As tools of the emperor or of his wives or in-laws, they temporarily exerted an almost unlimited control over the bureaucracy.[62]

Similar developments also characterized the "typically" Chinese [63] dynasties, T'ang and Ming. The prominence of political eunuchs in T'ang times coincided significantly with the establishment of the examination system, and in Ming times with the restrictions of the *yin* prerogative. Under the Ming emperors [s] eunuchs were in charge of special agencies for supervising the metropolitan officials and commoners. The eunuch Liu Chin, the most famous of the "Eight [eunuch] Tigers," systematically persecuted his bureaucratic opponents, and he was equally merciless in his dealings with members of the bureaucratic gentry.[64] Although Liu was eventually executed, eunuchs remained powerful until the dynasty fell under the combined onslaught of Chinese rebels and Manchu invaders.

The Sung emperors relied less on political eunuchism than did the Han, T'ang, and Ming rulers; but at the beginning of the 12th century the eunuch T'ung Kuan was raised to the highest military rank and set over the empire's supreme defense council.

In Western Asia eunuchism flourished under the Achaemenids. It receded under the Hellenistic monarchs, but it acquired great strength as the Roman empire became increasingly Orientalized.

In strong contrast to earlier custom the emperors Claudius, Nero, Vitellius, and Titus included eunuchs in their entourage. Claudius was influenced by two, Posides and Halotus; and Nero, who "married" the eunuch Spores, placed the eunuch Pelago in charge of a terror squad.[65] Under Elagabalus and Gordian eunuchs became a permanent feature of the administration.[66] Diocletian gave them a prominent place in his new court hierarchy.[67]

Of the eighteen ranks of Byzantine officialdom eunuchs could hold eight, among them the distinguished Patrikios; and eunuch patricians were rated above ordinary patricians.[68]

Runciman calls the employment of eunuchs "Byzantium's great weapon against the feudal tendency for power to be concentrated in the hands of a hereditary nobility, which provided so much trouble for the West." [69] Since eunuchism was already fully institutionalized in Byzantium in the 4th century, it cannot have been instituted as a weapon to combat a feudal tendency, which was certainly no issue in the bureaucratic regime of Eastern Rome and which, even in the West, only became an issue several centuries later. The suggestion that the eunuchs "gave the Emperor a governing class he could trust" [70] comes closer to the heart of the matter. As elsewhere the political eunuchs of Byzantium constituted an entirely trustworthy control group within the absolutist bureaucracy. And they functioned so well that Byzantium became a "eunuch's paradise." [71] Among the eunuch generals, Narses, Solomon,[72] and Nicephorus Uranus [73] were

---

s. The rise of the eunuchs in Ming times began soon after the founding of the dynasty (1368). Eunuchs were entrusted with the defense of the northern border in 1403, and in 1406 the eunuch Chêng Ho commanded the large imperial fleet that visited India, Arabia, and East Africa.

outstanding, among the eunuch admirals Eustathius Cymineanus [74] and Nicetas, who commanded the Byzantine fleet in the battle for Sicily in 963.[75] After the military and political catastrophe of Manzikert, a eunuch, Nicephorus the Logothete, "managed to reform the army." [76] "No religious or secular office, however high—with the imperial dignity as the only exception—was closed to them as a matter of principle." [77] "A large proportion of the Patriarchs of Constantinople were eunuchs." [78] At times eunuchs exerted unlimited power over the sovereign. Constantius II (d. A.D. 361) was so completely dominated by the eunuch Eusebius that the historian Ammianus quipped: "To speak truly, Constantius had much influence with him." [t]

Political eunuchism flourished during and after the Abbassid caliphate in the centers of Muslim power. From the 9th century on, the caliphs placed eunuchs in important positions at the court and in the army and navy. The Abbassid general Munis, the Samanid general Fa'ig, and the Muslim admiral Thamil were eunuchs. How high, at this time, eunuchs might rise in the military hierarchy is illustrated by the fact that when the naval forces of Baghdad and Fatimid Egypt fought each other in 919, both fleets were commanded by eunuch admirals.[79]

vi. THE DESPOT'S PERSONAL AGENCY NO INCIPIENT PARTY

UNDER the conditions of advancing industrialization and intensive communications between the various segments of society and the ruling center, an all-pervasive superorganization, such as the Communist or Fascist state party,[80] provides unique means for maintaining total autocratic power.

Oriental despotism needed no such superorganization. The compartmentalized peasant or urban communities, and also the individual officials who lacked modern facilities for communication and potential conspiracy, could be satisfactorily controlled by the postal and intelligence service, by the ruler's "men," and by special segments of his officialdom, such as the eunuchs. The intelligence service took care of the country's vital administrative and military centers, the eunuchs in the main of the court and, often also, of the capital. It is interesting to note that the eunuchs never formed a very large group. In many hydraulic societies a limited number of personal agents sufficed to assure the ruler's autocratic position.

t. Ammianus Marcellinus 18.4.3: "Eusebi . . . apud quem - - si vere dici debeat— multa Constantius potuit."

vii. THE TRIBAL NOBLES OF CONQUEST DYNASTIES

IN many Oriental societies, but not in all. To mention only one exception: even in the hydraulic societies of the Old World that knew institutionalized eunuchism, political eunuchs were of no great importance in conquest societies.

We have already commented on the peculiar role played in Oriental conquest societies by the nobles and commoners of the conquering nationality. Alien commoners were ideal instruments of coercion, and alien nobles, ranking above the native bureaucracy, formed a social elite whose prominence and security depended on their loyalty to the ruler and their ability to control the native officials. Alien nobles regularly commanded the cadre armies and usually headed strategic civil offices. They were political agents who, as faithfully as any eunuch, upheld the interests of the conquering dynasty—which indeed was substantially identical with their own.

Why did the Umayyad caliphs have little use for political eunuchs? Religion has been invoked to explain this interesting phenomenon.[81] But the Abbassid development shows that theological difficulties could be easily overcome, if the ruler wanted it so. More probably, the Umayyads, as a conquest dynasty, found it quite satisfactory to base their autocratic power essentially on their Arab nationals, nobles and commoners.

The Ch'i-tan masters of the Liao empire established their domination over northeastern China without engendering an excessive antagonism between pastoral victors and sedentary subjects. Nevertheless, they prudently reserved for themselves the key positions of power, and the emperor personally handled both strategic communications and the supreme command.[82] The only high-ranking Chinese who was thoroughly trusted (because of his great achievements in the war against the Sung empire) did not shift the center of authority to the Chinese sector of the government. Instead, he was given a Ch'i-tan clan name, a symbol of his inclusion in the "barbarian" nobility of the conquerors. When the last Liao emperor, in desperation and already deprived of a great part of his realm, offered the command of the remnants of his eastern forces to a Chinese, the man of his choice declined, noting bitterly and correctly that "under the old system Chinese did not participate in the important military and state policies . . ."[83] Indeed under the old system the major military and civil decisions were made by the alien ruler and his "barbarian" nobles. No wonder then that "eunuchs . . . were marginal men in Liao society. . . . no real political influence was ever concentrated in the hands of any Liao eunuch mentioned in the historical records." [84]

In the Manchu dynasty, too, the Manchu nobles made eunuchs superfluous. The T'ai-p'ing Rebellion (1850–1863) weakened, but did not destroy, the hegemony of the tribal aristocrats, and the short-lived attempt of 1898 to modernize the government, which under a heretic Manchu emperor was undertaken by Chinese reformers, was crushed by the Empress Dowager. In her first restoration edicts she significantly appointed a number of Manchus to positions of power.[85] Thus even the Manchus who had accepted more of Chinese culture than any of the three preceding conquest dynasties relied not so much on eunuchs as on "barbarian" nobles. These nobles came as close to constituting a totalitarian "quasiparty" as any dominant segment in the ruling class of hydraulic society anywhere.[u]

viii. SLAVES

IN nonconquest societies eunuchs are a formidable weapon of autocratic policy. However, slaves (and ex-slaves) may serve similarly, since they too are socially rootless. And they may fulfill their purpose even more effectively, since their more normal physique makes them seem more suitable to represent the despot's authority everywhere.

Some early Roman emperors employed freed slaves (*libertini*) in important political positions; [86] but later emperors preferred eunuchs, who, unlike the slaves, were traditionally associated with the power of Oriental despotism.

The use of slaves as the ruler's serving men was more frequent in the Islamic Near East, where quickly changing conditions of war and political alignments strongly encouraged experiments with hired soldiers. In contrast to the Umayyads, who maintained their conquest regime essentially by means of tribal supporters, the Abbassids relied increasingly on mercenaries. Eventually, and particularly for the caliph's bodyguard, they bought Turkish slaves. The Samanid and Seljuk rulers of Persia followed the Abbassid example.[87] In the Mamluk empire an alien elite of ex-slave warriors perpetuated itself by systematically filling vacancies with slaves purchased abroad. When entering upon their official careers, these slaves were solemnly enfranchised; but they remained a socially self-contained stratum.[88] In

---

u. Political eunuchs emerged temporarily under Emperor Shih-tsu (d. 1661) (Hummel, ECCP, I: 256 ff.). But the trend was stopped abruptly and never showed strength again except under the last Empress Dowager (cf. Hummel, ECCP, I: 296; II: 724; cf. also I: 298). Even this extraordinary woman despot, however, sought to enhance her power not by intensifying eunuchism, but by restoring Manchu control over the Chinese officialdom.

Ottoman Turkey tribute boys and persons of slave or slavelike origin were trained to be cadre warriors and top-ranking administrators.

These Turkish "slave" functionaries were offered many incentives: substantial earnings, honors, opportunities for advancement, and, at times, also a chance to marry. They were no chattel slaves but highly privileged half-slaves, if they were not completely enfranchised. But even as ex-slaves, they remained closely attached to the ruler.[v] More favorably situated in many ways than the great majority of the free population, they considered it an honor to be his personal property.

But the distinctions they enjoyed did not remove the basic deficiency of their position—their essential rootlessness. True, they might at the height of their career invite certain of their relatives to share their glory and wealth, but this was more the exception than the rule. In any case—and this was to the benefit of the ruler—the fortunate relatives were almost always persons of humble status; and thus they formed no link to an ambitious and self-perpetuating (noble) bureaucratic gentry.

Their rootlessness was further aggravated when the ruler selected his slave functionaries from among the children of nonbelievers, particularly from among the children of Christians. Of course, they were given a thorough Muslim education, but their special training widened the gap between them and the upper-class believers, from whom they were already separated by accidents of origin.

The social effects of the system of slave officials appeared with classical clarity in Turkey. During the heyday of Ottoman power the administrative and military functionaries did not establish a hereditary officialdom,[89] and they prevented the hereditary leaders of the militia cavalry, who were supported by office land (*khasses, ziamets,* and *timars*),[90] from attaining more than secondary and subordinate positions of power.

In this set-up political eunuchs were not altogether absent,[w] but they only bulwarked an autocratic edifice that was essentially a "government by a slave class." [91] The functionaries of this government were so thoroughly disciplined and, even in the civilian sphere, so well integrated that Machiavelli saw no chance of upsetting the Turk-

v. The Turkish word *"kul"* like the Arab word *"mamluk"* means "slave."

w. In the Mamluk empire eunuchs were in charge of the training of the Mamluks (Ayalon, 1951: 14 ff.). The Turkish sultans made the chief White Eunuch the head of the Palace School, where the military and administrative leaders of the state were educated (Miller, 1941: 64, 88). Another high-ranking White Eunuch guarded the treasures in the sultan's private treasury (Miller, 1941: 38). The chief White Eunuch, in addition to being in charge of the Palace School and Harem and acting as the grand master of ceremonies, was also the sultan's confidential agent (Miller, 1941: 88).

ish regime through cooperation with dissenters (today we would say a fifth column) as could be done in feudal France. For "in kingdoms governed like that of France . . . it is easy to enter them by winning over some baron of the kingdom, there being always malcontents, and those desiring innovations. These can, for the reasons stated, open the way to you and facilitate victory." [92] Not so with the Turks. "Because, being all slaves and dependent, it will be more difficult to corrupt them, and even if they were corrupted, little effect could be hoped for, as they would not be able to carry the people with them for the reasons mentioned. Therefore, whoever assaults the Turk must be prepared to meet his united forces, and must rely more on his own strength than on the disorders of others." [93]

Contemplating the struggle between the supreme ruler and his serving men, we are not so much surprised that the Turkish office holders advanced eventually to hereditary or semihereditary tenure,[94] but that, over a considerable period, the sultan was able to successfully block these trends by maintaining a socially rootless class of "slave-officials." [z]

7. "Regular" Officials, Control Groups, and the People

SLAVE officials were among the most effective tools that the ruler of a hydraulic state could muster. Political eunuchs or a nobility of tribal conquerors might supervise, weaken, and restrict the "regular" officialdom, but slave officials could replace it. Despite obvious differences, the three groups resembled each other in one significant way. Each of them constituted a control group, which from the autocrat's standpoint was manifestly more effective than the commoners who might be included in the ranks of the officialdom. The priests, who in ancient America, India, and elsewhere were placed in important government positions, most probably fulfilled a similar function.

z. The autocratic master of the new class society in the USSR exerts supreme control over the ranking *apparatchiki* by a variety of methods, among them the periodic purging of established groups of functionaries (the "old guard," the "old cadres") and the introduction of technically and politically suitable commoners. From the standpoint of the supreme autocrat, the functionaries' reliability may be expected to be greater, the less they are rooted in any prestige group that preserves elements of social cohesion. The Great Purge of the thirties liquidated the bulk of the Old Bolsheviks, and subsequent purges many other persons of prominence in the party, government, and army. Vyshinsky, who was a Menshevik until the early days of the regime, was ideally fitted to prosecute the Old Bolsheviks. No bonds of comradeship tempered his assault; and his heterodox past made him particularly vulnerable—and particularly ready to please the supreme Party leadership.

The regular officials were remote from, and above, the people. But the members of the control groups, who were particularly close to the despot, were also particularly removed from the people. A well-intentioned regular official or a member of the bureaucratic gentry might develop quasipatriarchal relations to the local population. This was much less likely to be the case with priest officials, slave officials, alien nobles, or eunuchs.

J. SOCIAL PROMOTION

THE political careers of eunuchs, slaves, ex-slaves, and commoners in hydraulic society have a further significance. They demonstrate that social (vertical) mobility means one thing in open and balanced societies, and another in societies which exist under the shadow of total power. Obviously there is more than a single pattern of social mobility. And any discussion of the phenomenon will be satisfactory only to the degree that the facts are placed in their specific institutional setting.

1. RESERVOIRS AND MAINSPRINGS OF SOCIAL PROMOTION

IN open and property-based societies a commoner may rise above his original station, either through political or economic achievement. Members of the upper class may try to prevent his ascent, but they cannot forbid it. They may discriminate against the power *parvenu* or the *nouveau riche* personally, but usually the newcomer's children or grandchildren achieve social acceptance. This was the general pattern in the democratic city states of ancient Greece. And it is increasingly typical for such modern industrial countries as England, Scandinavia, Australia, and the United States.

This pattern of democratic and spontaneous social mobility differs fundamentally from the patterns of social mobility that characterize hydraulic society. In hydraulic society the lowly ones who entered the ruling class rarely came from the ranks of free and prominent commoners. In China the number of persons who could obtain a higher examination degree was carefully restricted; and even this Chinese pattern was by no means typical for the majority of all Oriental civilizations. In general, a vigorous commoner was not likely to become a member of the ruling class. The eunuchs, freedmen, and slaves who rose to political prominence originally ranked below the free commoners. And this was true also for the slave girls, who in the ruler's harem could become the mothers of future rulers.

Members of these groups rose to positions of distinction, not because they overcame barriers of established wealth and power through their own efforts, but because their ruler was sufficiently strong to select whom he pleased and to place the person of his choice where he pleased. What vertical mobility there was in hydraulic society resulted from manipulation from above.

To be sure, there are active elements in passive behavior, just as there are passive elements in active behavior.[a] But this does not negate the validity of the conclusion that under Oriental despotism social mobility was essentially a passive process.

It may be said, of course, that in certain complex and semicomplex Oriental societies some commoners have risen from poor and humble origins to wealth and distinction within their class, improving their status in a way that is typical for property-based open societies. True enough. However, in many hydraulic societies such patterns are almost entirely lacking, and where they do occur they do not involve ascent into the ruling class.

2. CRITERIA FOR SOCIAL PROMOTION (APTITUDES "PLUS" . . .)

TOTAL power promotes prudently and discriminatingly. And it promotes those who may be expected to satisfy the needs of the apparatus state. In such a process the candidate must possess aptitudes "plus." . . . What is this "plus"?

Some who are selected for promotion may be unusually talented; and this certainly is desirable. But all must excel in the key virtue of totalitarianism: total and ingenious servility. This qualification may be expressed in either an ideologically or a ceremonially subtle way (as was the case in Confucian China and Hindu India) or pragmatically and directly (as was the case in many other hydraulic civilizations). But the substance was everywhere the same; and the supreme manipulators of total power would have considered themselves fools if they had not insisted on a qualification that, from their standpoint, was vital.

3. SOCIAL PROMOTION ON A SLAVE PLANTATION

SOCIAL mobility in hydraulic society is not identical with social mobility on a slave-operated plantation. Nevertheless, some features of the latter are not without interest for the former. A plantation owner may raise the most lowly slaves to be his foremen or personal servants,

a. Cf. Wittfogel, 1932: 474 ff. This study has tried to define the potential influence of an object upon the operations to which it is exposed.

but an awareness of this possibility does not favor an independent spirit among their fellows. On the contrary. The fact that promotion is offered essentially to those who are unquestionably submissive tends to stimulate among the opportunistic majority of all slaves attitudes of spectacular servility.

K. THE TOTAL RULING CLASS—A MONOPOLY BUREAUCRACY

1. The Ruling Class of Hydraulic Society and the Upper Classes in Other Stratified Societies

FROM still another angle, the peculiarity of social mobility in hydraulic society indicates the peculiarity of its ruling class. For all practical purposes this ruling class is a closed class. Only by the will of its recognized representatives can members of lower classes be incorporated into it. In this respect it is like the feudal nobility and unlike the upper classes of a modern property-based industrial society.

The peculiarity of the hydraulic variant of a closed ruling class derives mainly from the manner in which it is organized. The active core of the ruling class of hydraulic society is a rigidly cohesive body; in this respect it differs not only from the modern bourgeoisie but also from the feudal nobility. Even where entrepreneurial monopolies coordinate prominent elements of the *haute bourgeoisie,* we do not find the business class as a whole hierarchically and formally organized, as were the vassals of feudal countries. The organizational unity of the feudal lords reached its peak in their combined (national) military actions; but both the scope of these actions and the disciplinary controls exercised by the supreme leader were very restricted. For the most part the lords were independently concerned with their own military, economic, and social affairs.

The serving men of hydraulic despotism were organized as a per manently operating and highly centralized "apparatus." In contrast to the bourgeois upper class, which has no recognized head, and in contrast also to the feudal lords, whose recognized head was the first among equals in a conspicuously decentralized order, the men of the hydraulic apparatus state held their ruler to be the supreme leader, who always and unconditionally determined their position and tasks.

Prior to the rise of the modern industrial apparatus state, the men of a hydraulic government were the only major example of a ruling class, whose operational core permanently functioned as an organized, centralized, and semimilitary entity.

2. AUTHORITARIAN BODIES DO NOT NECESSARILY EXERT TOTALITARIAN POWER

EVEN a formidable authoritarian body cannot prevail totally as long as significant countervailing forces exert a restraining or controlling influence on it. Both in Periclean Athens and in a modern industrial democracy the army is an authoritarian organization; its commanders expect, and have the means to enforce, unquestioning obedience. But in each case it is subordinated to the decisions of an over-all and democratically established political body.

Manifestly no society is without its authoritarian segments, but in a democratic society such segments can be supervised and controlled. Awareness of this fact is essential for a proper evaluation of the effects (and the limitations) of authoritarian patterns in Big Business, Big Labor, and Big Government that appear in modern property-based civilizations.

The absolutist governments of late and postfeudal Europe had to cope with such forces as an organized nobility, the Church, the guilds, and the rising capitalist middle classes. These governments were authoritarian enough, and they strove hard to exert exclusive ("totalitarian") power. But on the whole they were unable to do so, because they were unable to attain a monopoly of societal leadership.

3. MONOPOLY VERSUS COMPETITION IN SOCIETAL LEADERSHIP

SOCIETAL leadership may be exerted by several groups or classes that in various ways offset one another. Or it may be exerted monopolistically by a single group or class. Manifestly, a group that exerts monopolistic leadership behaves differently from a group that, despite its superior strength, is unable to crush its rivals.

In postfeudal Europe and Japan state power and active (entrepreneurial) property gave rise to several upper classes; and no class succeeded in establishing exclusive (total) prominence. More recently the owners of land and capital are being confronted with a new type of rival: the owners of a special kind of property, labor. Today labor openly contests the political and social leadership of the old upper classes.

In hydraulic society development took a different course. There the rise of propertied classes—artisans, merchants, and landowners—did not involve the rise of competing upper classes. In semicomplex and complex hydraulic societies the ranking officials accepted as inevitable, and in some measure as desirable, the presence of men of wealth who were detached from government. But even when these men were numerous enough to constitute a class, they did not compete with the bureaucratic upper class for social and political leadership. They did not compete because they had no opportunity to engage in a substantial political struggle. Neither at the start nor later did these holders of independent small or large property succeed in coordinating their forces into a national and politically effective rival organization.

In all probability the men of the apparatus were not clearly aware of the threat that a rival organization might pose. Most hydraulic societies originated prior to, and far away from, the balanced agrarian societies that crystallized in ancient Greece and Rome and in Medieval Europe and Japan. And in most simple hydraulic societies the independent propertied groups were too feeble to make their political will felt either in general political assemblies or in estate-like corporations. Democratic tribal traditions—where they existed —were apparently abandoned either when, or before, they became a serious threat to the masters of the agromanagerial regime. This may have happened in proto-Sumerian society, but even in this case the evidence is weak. As a rule the representatives of the young despotic states seem to have kept the owners of private mobile or immobile property politically atomized, sometimes by resorting to violence, but more often without exerting any untoward physical or political effort.

In late medieval and postmedieval times the Orientally despotic states of the Near East and Russia co-existed with European states that were characterized by multiple political organizations. But except for post-Muscovite Russia and 19th-century Turkey, there is little to show that the Western pattern was consciously imitated in these nearby Eastern lands. The Christian crusaders weakened the absolutist power of Late Byzantium, but its men of property were unable to create independent and effective feudal or burgher corporations. In Turkey and Russia multiple political organizations appeared only when the industrial revolution and the impact of Western power created an altogether new national and international situation.

4. Monopoly of Societal Leadership Appears in Oriental Despotism as Monopoly of Bureaucratic Organization ("Monopoly Bureaucracy")

THE freedom to compete involves the freedom to organize; and it involves the freedom, when conditions permit, to use bureaucratic devices for developing and perpetuating organizational bonds. The corporate barons and burghers of the feudal world utilized bureaucratic means only to a modest degree. But the history of the medieval Church shows that during that era a powerful nongovernmental body could erect, if it wanted to, impressive bureaucratic structures.

In the modern countries of central and western Europe, in America, Australia and Japan, many smaller and larger bureaucracies exist outside and independent of government. Aristocratic landlords, where they still survive, may employ bureaucratic devices to protect their interests. Merchants, industrialists, and bankers run large enterprises with bureaucratically organized staffs; and when they combine to achieve comprehensive political goals, they create or support bureaucratically organized lobbies or parties. Farmers, too, are resorting more and more to bureaucratically coordinated action. And trade unions and labor parties are gaining economic and political prominence, because they effectively use bureaucratic methods to realize the organizational potential inherent in the concentration of workers in large plants.

Of all these developments, the expansion of large business enterprises into monopolistic giants has been particularly commented upon by certain analysts, who viewed it as so outstanding a feature of our time that they decided to speak of an entire period of "monopoly capitalism."

The concept "monopoly capitalism" is as provocative as it is misleading, but its very deficiencies aid us in putting into proper relief the peculiarities of the Oriental monopoly bureaucracy. The modern giant enterprises are indeed formidable, both in dimension and influence; and they certainly have crushed or absorbed many medium-sized and small rivals. But only rarely have they been able to prevent the operations of other giants in different branches of economy. And never have they been able to prevent the rise of big societal rivals, such as Big Government and Big Labor. "Monopoly capitalism" is therefore a misnomer for an institutional conformation in which multiple societal forces, however monopolistically inclined, counterbalance each other so as to preclude the exclusive leadership of any one of them.

No such checks weaken the monopolistic claims of a total apparatus state. The masters of hydraulic society permit no conspicuous and bureaucratically organized rivals. They exert exclusive leadership by ruthlessly and continually operating as a genuine monopoly bureaucracy.

CHAPTER 9

The rise and fall of the theory of the Asiatic mode of production

SUCH is hydraulic society, as it emerges from our inquiry. This society persisted over millennia—indeed until it suffered the impact of the rising industrial and commercial West. Then chain reactions were set in motion that gave the old order a new shape and a new direction. Does our analysis of traditional hydraulic society enable us to understand these recent developments?

At this point the reader who has followed us so far may want to ask some questions. The concept of hydraulic society, he may say, seems to have been eminently productive for the study of the past. But is it also useful for evaluating the present and the future? Isn't the "feudal" interpretation of Oriental conditions equally appropriate? Certainly it indicates the vigorous condemnation of an evil heritage—and already it is widely employed in the East and in the West.

This may well be so. However, in our context vigor and currency can scarcely be decisive criteria. The history of social and racial demagoguery shows that false slogans pervert man's thoughts and deeds—the more disastrously, the more often and the more insistently they are uttered. By equating the Orient and feudal Europe, we lose sight of basic differences. And by ignoring the existence of major non-Western societies, we run the danger of abandoning the freedom of historical choice, because we are paralyzed by the fiction of a unilinear and irresistible development.

No such danger resulted from the efforts of the 19th-century unilinealists whose errors are easily recognized. Essentially it is a product of contemporary Marxism-Leninism, which combines ideological and political means to liquidate both the theory of Oriental society and the concept of a multilinear development.

Unidentified, this Marxist-Leninist force may block the analysis of hydraulic society in transition—not by open argument, but by creating an enervating atmosphere of ambivalence and distrust. Prop-

erly identified, it will give a new impetus to the study of the facts—
and the potentialities—of a multiform and changing world.

A. OLD AND NEW CONSTRUCTS OF A UNILINEAR DEVELOPMENT DISREGARD HYDRAULIC SOCIETY

1. 19TH-CENTURY UNILINEALISTS

THE unilinealists of the 19th century disregarded hydraulic society,
not because they shunned the reality of bureaucratic despotism but
because they were inspired by the stupendous consequences of the
industrial revolution. Overgeneralizing the experience of a rapidly
changing Western world, they naively postulated a simple, unilinear,
and progressive course of societal growth.

Man seemed to move irresistibly toward freedom (Hegel), toward
universal harmony (Fourier), toward a just and rational society
(Comte), toward general happiness (Spencer). Archaeologists began
to distinguish a scale of "ages" based on the use of stone, bronze, and
iron; and ethnologists arranged selected features of primitive life in
consecutive "stages." By defining the "Paleolithic" and "Neolithic"
as forerunners of the "Metal Age," Lubbock completed in 1865 what
Thomson had initiated in 1836. And in 1877 Morgan formulated his
much cited typological sequence: Old Stone Age (savagery), New
Stone Age (barbarism), and Iron Age (civilization).

2. NEGATIVE CRITICISMS

THE 19th-century evolutionists should certainly be praised for their
efforts to find structure and orderly change in the turbulent currents
of history. But their performance can hardly be deemed satisfactory,
for they were able to depict the higher civilizations as progressing
unilineally only by disregarding the fate of over one-half of the people of the globe. Nor did the criticism that was subsequently leveled
against them close the gap, for it, too, failed to take into account the
stagnation of the hydraulic world.

A wealth of new anthropological and archaeological data enabled
scholars such as Boas to demonstrate that the 19th-century theoreticians "erred in assuming a single unilinear evolution." [1] But the new
insights were accompanied by a stubborn reluctance to draw upon the
facts of Western and Oriental institutional history for a new multilinear pattern of development. Said Boas: "Laws of development,
except in most generalized form, cannot be established and a detailed
course of growth cannot be predicted. All we can do is to watch and
judge day by day what we are doing by what we have learned and

to shape our steps accordingly." [2] True, even this cautious statement suggests a "course of growth" of some kind. But instead of trying to determine its character, Boas contented himself with an impressionistic "day by day" evaluation of man's experience.

3. A THEORETICAL VACUUM

BOAS' arguments carried great weight both inside and outside his discipline. And his adevelopmental attitude gained wide support among social scientists generally during the first decades of the 20th century. A sociologist of knowledge, observing this agnosticism, could have quickly discerned the resulting theoretical vacuum. And he could have predicted that major conflicts and crises would inspire new questions and, ultimately, new answers.

Spengler's concept of compartmentalized civilizations that grow and decay like living organisms was so obviously based on biological rather than historical premises that it failed to satisfy the social scientists. For a different reason Toynbee's attempt failed also. Being a historian by profession, Toynbee approached the fate of mankind historically. But a lack of incisive major concepts handicapped his analysis. Overemphasis on details prevented him from recognizing major patterns of societal change. Overemphasis on the peculiarities of individual "societies" prevented him from recognizing the common institutional denominators that compel their classification in larger units. In the realm of taxonomy the "splitter" is as likely to err as is the lumper.[3] The intriguing trees that dot Toynbee's landscape [a] do not reveal the character of the woods of which they form a part.

4. THE SPREAD OF A "MARXIST-LENINIST" NEO-UNILINEALISM

BUT the demand for new historical vistas arose even before the appearance of Toynbee's *Study of History*. Economic and political earthquakes, starting with the Depression, had made Spengler's romantic speculations appear as unrealistic as the findings of an overmethodologized, overcompartmentalized and overquantified sociology.

Impressed by the brutal directness with which Marxism-Leninism discussed the burning conflicts of the day, numerous writers accepted

---

a. A landscape, let it be added, that was rich and suggestive in many ways. Toynbee's attempt to see structure and process in the life of "societies" will be acknowledged also by those who find the major conclusions of his sociohistorical studies intellectually problematic or morally paralyzing.

significant elements of the Soviet scheme of societal development together with the Marxist-Leninist explanation of capitalism and imperialism. They did not hesitate to call the traditional institutions of China, India and the Near East "feudal." They equated post-Mongol Russia and Western feudalism. And they were convinced that Communist Russia—and recently also mainland China—had attained a higher socialist or protosocialist level of development, because they had prevailed over both "feudalism" and capitalism.

5. THE NEED FOR A REEXAMINATION OF MARX', ENGELS', AND LENIN'S VIEWS ON THE "ASIATIC SYSTEM" AND ORIENTAL DESPOTISM

THIS being so, no responsible student of hydraulic society will deny the importance of reviewing the ideas of Marx, Engels, and Lenin about the "Asiatic system," Oriental despotism, and societal development. Manifestly such an examination is necessary from the standpoint of our subject matter. And it is highly dramatic, because Marx and Engels, and even the pre-October Lenin, accepted the very Asiatic concept that the high priests of Marxist-Leninist ideology are rejecting today.

B. MARX, ENGELS, AND LENIN ACCEPT THE ASIATIC CONCEPT

1. MARX FOLLOWS HIS CLASSICAL PREDECESSORS WITH REGARD TO THE INSTITUTIONAL STRUCTURE AND THE DEVELOPMENTAL POSITION OF THE ORIENT[a]

MARX' concept of Asiatic society was built largely on the views of such classical economists as Richard Jones and John Stuart Mill, who in their turn had developed generalized ideas held by Adam Smith and James Mill. Adam Smith noted similarities of hydraulic enterprise in China and "several other governments of Asia"; and he commented particularly on the acquisitive power of the rulers in China, ancient Egypt, and India.[1] James Mill considered the "Asiatic model of government" a general institutional type;[2] and he rejected forced analogies to European feudalism.[3] Richard Jones outlined

---

a. Marxist writers have seldom troubled to trace the sources of Marx' Asiatic concept (see Kautsky's note to Plechanoff, 1891: 447; Kautsky, 1929, II: 209 ff.; and Plekhanov, FPM: 40, 50). In my earlier writings I pointed to the geographer Ritter and to Hegel as possibly having influenced Marx (Wittfogel, 1929: 492–496; ibid., 1931a: 354); but I did not then realize the fundamental dependence of Marx on the classical economists.

an over-all picture of Asiatic society in 1831,[4] when Marx was thirteen years old. And John Stuart Mill placed this society in a comparative frame in 1848,[5] when the authors of the *Communist Manifesto,* despite an occasional reference to the "East," [6] betrayed no awareness of a specific Asiatic society. It was only after Marx resumed his study of the classical economists in London [b] that he emerged as a vigorous adherent of the "Asiatic" concept.

From 1853 until his death Marx upheld the Asiatic concept together with the Asiatic nomenclature of the earlier economists. In addition to the formula "Oriental despotism," he employed for the whole institutional order the designation "Oriental society," used by John Stuart Mill,[7] and also (and with apparent preference) the designation "Asiatic society," used by Richard Jones.[8] He expressed his specific concern for the economic aspect of Asiatic society by speaking of an "Asiatic system" of landownership,[9] a specific "Asiatic mode of production," [10] and, more concisely, "Asiatic production." [11]

In the 1850's the notion of a specific Asiatic society struck Marx with the force of a discovery. Temporarily abandoning party politics, he applied himself intensely to the study of industrial capitalism as a distinct socio-economic and historical phenomenon. His writings during this period—among others, the first draft of *Das Kapital* which he set down in 1857–58 [c]—show him greatly stimulated by the Asiatic concept. In this first draft as well as in the final version of his *magnum opus,* he systematically compared certain institutional features in the three major types of agrarian society ("Asia," classical antiquity, feudalism) and in modern industrial society.[12]

b. In London, Marx resumed his economic and sociohistorical studies by reading Mill's *Principles of Political Economy* (from September 1850 on), Smith's *Wealth of Nations* (March 1851), Jones' *Introductory Lecture* [on Political Economy] (June 1851), Prescott's *Conquest of Mexico* and *Conquest of Peru* (August 1851), Bernier's *Voyages* (May–June 1853), James Mill's *History of British India* (probably—mentioned on July 7, 1853) (KMCL: 96, 103, 107, 110, 139; cf. also MEGA, III, Pt. 1: 133; Marx, NYDT, July 7, 1853).

c. In its original form this draft appeared in print for the first time in two volumes in 1939 and 1941 respectively. Marx rewrote and published part of it in 1859 under the title, *Zur Kritik der Politischen Ökonomie.* In the preface to this book he made his most systematic statement on social structure and change, a statement which ended with the enumeration of four major socio-economic orders, the Asiatic, the ancient, the feudal, and the capitalist modes of production. From the summer of 1863 on, Marx reorganized and reworked his earlier draft into what he now called *Das Kapital* (see Grossmann, 1929: 310 ff.). The history of pertinent theories, which Marx planned to publish as the fourth volume of *Das Kapital* (ibid.: 311), was eventually published as a separate work under the title *Theorien über der Mehrwert* (*Theories on Surplus Value*).

2. MARX' ASIATIC INTERPRETATION OF INDIA, CHINA, AND POST-MONGOL RUSSIA

WE need not in the present context examine every aspect of Marx' views on Asiatic society. For our purposes it is enough to underline his Asiatic interpretation of three countries that today are again prominent on the global political scene: India, China, and Russia.

a. India ("Asiatic Society" . . .)

IN two articles published in the *New York Daily Tribune* in 1853 [d] Marx discussed the character of Asiatic society and the possibilities of its progressive dissolution. In these articles he cited India as a representative of "old Asiatic society" and the Hindus as having certain crucial institutions in common with "all Oriental people." He argued that "climate and territorial conditions" made "artificial irrigation by canals and waterworks the basis of Oriental agriculture." And he observed that water control "necessitated in the Orient, where civilization was too low and the territorial extent too vast to call into life voluntary association, the interference of the centralizing power of the government."

Thus it was the need for government-directed water works that according to Marx gave birth to the Asiatic state. And it was the "dispersed" condition of the "Oriental people" and their agglomeration in "self-supporting" villages (combining small agriculture and domestic handicraft) that permitted its age-long perpetuation.[13]

Factually, the second statement requires qualification. Ideologically, it is most consequential. Only when we keep Marx' notion of the role of the "dispersed" Oriental villages in mind can we fully understand Marx' own, as well as Engels' and Lenin's, characterization of Oriental despotism.

b. China (". . . Asiatic Production" and Private Peasant Landholding)

LIVING in England, as he did for the greater part of his adult life, Marx was more alert to conditions in India than in China. But from the 1850's on he viewed China, like India, as characterized by "Asiatic" institutions,[14] and he found "the economic structure of Chinese society depending upon a combination of small agriculture and domestic industry (1859).[15] In Volume 3 of *Das Kapital*, while dis-

---

d. Marx, NYDT, June 25 and August 8, 1853. In his correspondence with Engels, Marx had gone far in clarifying his concept of an "Asiatic" or "Oriental" society (see MEGA, III, Pt. 1: 445 ff., 470 ff., and especially 475 ff., 480 ff., and 486 ff.).

cussing the impact of English trade on India and China, he made this point again. But here he also commented on the absence of a communal system of land tenure in contemporary China. In India and China "the broad foundation of the mode of production is shaped by the unity of small agriculture and domestic industry, to which, in India, is added the pattern of *the village community based on communal property, which, by the way, was also the original form in China.*" And remarking on the slow dissolution of the self-sufficient rural economy in contemporary India (where Britain intervened directly) and the slower dissolution of this economy in China ("where no direct political power aids it"), he concluded that "different from English trade, the Russian trade leaves the economic foundations of *Asiatic production* untouched." [16]

As early as the 1850's Marx was aware of the fact that the Chinese "Crown" permitted most of the peasants to "hold their lands, which are of a very limited extent, in full property." [17] And the just cited passage from *Das Kapital* shows clearly that in his opinion the disappearance of "communal landownership" in China had not, in any significant way, undermined "the economic foundations of Asiatic production."

c. Russia ("Oriental Despotism" . . . Perpetuated)

To the best of my knowledge, Russia was first called a "semi-Asiatic" country in an article signed by Marx, but written by Engels, which appeared in the *New York Daily Tribune* on April 18, 1853.[18] On August 5, 1853, and this time in an article that was genuinely his, Marx contrasted certain "semi-Eastern" developments involving Tsarist Russia with "completely Eastern" events in China. From the start the term "semi-Asiatic," as applied by Marx and Engels to Russia, referred not to that country's geographic location but to its "traditions and institutions, character and conditions." [19]

The articles of 1853 did not discuss Russia's institutional peculiarity in detail. However, in 1881 Marx spoke of Russia's isolated villages and the strongly centralized form of despotism that had arisen everywhere on this foundation.[20] Shortly before, Engels had emphasized this point. Indeed the Marxian interpretation of Russia received its greatest currency through two statements made by Engels in the 1870's. The first, written in 1875, reads as follows: "Such a complete isolation of the individual [village] communities from each other, which in the whole country creates identical, but the exact opposite of common, interests, is the natural foundation of Oriental despotism, and from India to Russia this societal form, wherever it prevailed, has always produced despotism and has always found therein its supplement. Not only the Russian state in general, but even its specific form, the despotism of the Tsar, far from being suspended in mid-air, is the necessary and logical product of the Russian social conditions." [21] The second, contained in his critique of Dühring, expresses the same idea more briefly: "The ancient communes, where they continued to exist, have for thousands of years formed the basis of the most barbarous form of state, Oriental despotism, from India to Russia." [22]

How long did Russian Oriental despotism endure? Marx insisted that Peter the Great, far from eliminating it, "generalized" it. [23] And he expected the emancipation of the serfs to strengthen the absolutist regime, because it would destroy both the power of the nobles over the serfs and the self-government of the rural communities. [24]

Marx did not explain how in Russia modern capitalism could develop under Oriental rule. His failure to do so is one of the most serious deficiencies in his treatment of marginal and transitional patterns of hydraulic society. But in terms of his views on the position of capitalism in the Orient, [25] he was consistent when, in 1881, he considered Russia's modern quasi-Western capitalism a predatory, middleman-like force. [26]

3. MARX WARNS AGAINST CONFUSING THE STATE-CONTROLLED AGRARIAN ORDER OF ASIA WITH SLAVERY OR SERFDOM

RETURNING to the over-all problems of the Asiatic mode of production, we may say: no matter what Marx thought about the exact nature of landownership in the Orient, he felt certain it was not feudal. In 1853, when Engels noted "that the Orientals did not advance toward landownership,[e] not even to a feudal one," Marx warned against a too sweeping assumption of the absence of Oriental landownership. [27] But while he then saw some evidence of private landholding in India, [28] and later also in China, he did not call their systems of land tenure "feudal."

Oversimplifying a complicated pattern of proprietary relations, Marx, nevertheless, recognized a basic trend when he noted that under the "Asiatic system" the state was "the real landlord." [29] Later he refined this early notion. In Das Kapital, Volume 3, he explained that under the Asiatic system there existed "no private landowner-

---

e. Engels means private landownership, as can be seen from Marx' preceding letter, which, taking up Bernier's view, expressly speaks of Privatgrundeigentum (MEGA, III, Pt. 1: 477).

ship, but both private and communal possession and usage of the soil." [30]

This position led Marx to brand the confusion of Asiatic-Egyptian land tenure with systems based on slavery and serfdom as the worst mistake that can be made in the analysis of ground rent.[31] And it immunized him against viewing the Indian *zamindars* as a variant of European feudal landlords. He classified the traditional *zamindars* as "native tax-gatherers." And he ridiculed the attempt to equate the British-made *zamindar*-landlords with England's landed gentry: "A curious sort of English landlord was the zemindar, receiving only one-tenth of the rent, while he had to make over ninetenths of it to the Government." [f]

4. "General Slavery"

Thus in the "Orient" the state ruled supreme over both the labor and property of its subjects. Marx commented on the despot's position as the actual and apparent coordinator of the population's labor for hydraulic and other communal works; [32] and he considered the individual land-possessing peasant *"au fond* the property, the slave" of the head of the Oriental community.[33] Consistently he spoke of the "general slavery of the Orient." [34] In contrast to the private slavery of classical antiquity, a type whose insignificance in the Orient he understood,[35] and in contrast to the decentralized patterns of feudal control, which he also understood,[36] Marx viewed the relation between Oriental despotism and the most important group in the population as one of *general* (state) slavery.[g]

5. For Many Years Lenin Also Upheld the Asiatic Concept

It is difficult to harmonize these statements with the "feudal" interpretation of the Orient offered today by persons calling themselves

---

f. Marx, NYDT, August 5, 1853. For reasons that will be discussed below, the Indian Communist edition of *Karl Marx: Articles on India* (cited as Marx, 1951) which attached "feudal" comments to Marx' Asiatic views contains neither this piece nor the one published on June 7, 1858, also dealing with the Indian land system.

g. In an elliptic remark made in 1887, Engels said that "class oppression" in both Asiatic and classical antiquity had the form of "slavery." Since Engels, like Marx, recognized the irrelevance in the Orient of private slavery (see below), he was obviously referring to the "general slavery" of Oriental despotism. His claim that in both cases slavery involved "not so much the expropriation of the masses from the land as the appropriation of their persons" (Engels, 1887: iii) fits the Orient, but not classical antiquity.

"Marxists." It is even difficult to present such an interpretation in the name of Leninism. Starting as an orthodox Marxist, Lenin upheld the idea of a special "Asiatic system" for the better part of three decades, speaking precisely, from 1894 to 1914.

a. "Asiatic Despotism," a Totality of Traits "with Special Economic, Political, and Sociological Characteristics"

THE young Lenin joined the Social Democratic movement in 1893. After a zealous study of Marx' and Engels' writings, he accepted, in 1894, the "Asiatic mode of production" as one of the four major economic configurations of society.[37] In his first important book, *The Development of Capitalism in Russia,* published in 1899, he began to designate his country's Asiatic conditions as the *Aziatchina,*[38] the "Asiatic system." And he termed Tsarist control over land and peasants a "fiscal land ownership." [39]

In 1900 he referred to the government of traditional China as "Asiatic"; [40] and he rejected as "pharisaic" the equation of European and Asiatic institutions.[41] In 1902 he noted the crushing character of Asiatic oppression.[42] In 1905 he denounced "the cursed heritage of bondage of the *Aziatchina* and the shameful treatment of man," [43] and he contrasted the retarded development of "Asiatic capitalism" and the comprehensive and fast development of European capitalism.[44] In 1906 and 1907 he engaged in a passionate debate with Plekhanov which underlined his awareness of the Asiatic system and its implications for a "semi-Asiatic" Russia.[45] In 1911 he reemphasized the peculiarity of "the Oriental system," the "Asiatic system," and the stagnation of the Orient.[46]

In 1912, on the occasion of the Chinese revolution, he recognized the "Asiatic" quality of traditional China by speaking of "Asiatic China" [47] and of the "Asiatic" president of China.[48] In 1914 in a discussion with Rosa Luxemburg, he defined "Asiatic despotism" as a "totality of traits" with special "economic, political, and sociological characteristics," and he ascribed its great stability to "utterly patriarchal pre-capitalist traits and an insignificant development of commodity production and class differentiation." [49] In the fall of that year he wrote an article on Marx for the *Encyclopaedia Granat,* in which once more he listed Marx' four major socio-economic configurations, "the Asiatic, the ancient, the feudal, and the modern bourgeois modes of production." [50]

Thus from 1894 to 1914 Lenin upheld basic features of Marx' concept of Asiatic society, the Asiatic mode of production, and Oriental despotism.

b. Lenin Elaborates Marx' Semi-Asiatic Interpretation of Tsarist Russia

LENIN, however, approached the Asiatic problem more narrowly and more broadly than Marx. Marx defined the peculiarities of pre-capitalist societies in order to deepen his understanding of capitalist society; and his comments on the Asiatic mode of production primarily served this end. But he did not employ the Asiatic concept either to analyze or to influence his sociopolitical environment.

Lenin was much less interested in macrohistorical comparisons. Living in a society which Marx had characterized as semi-Asiatic, and fighting a state which Marx had characterized as Orientally despotic, Lenin was vitally interested in applying the Asiatic concept to his immediate environment. Most of his references to "Asiatic" conditions pertain to Russia.

Following Marx and Engels, Lenin called Russian society "semi-Asiatic," [51] and the Tsarist regime "Oriental despotism." Western socialists loathed Bismarck because of his antisocialist measures; and some Russian socialists, such as Ryazanov, equated Russian and Prussian absolutism.[h] But Lenin considered Bismarck's repressive state a "pygmy" compared to Russian absolutism, which, probably remembering Marx' characterization of Tatar despotism,[52] he called a "monster." [53]

c. Lenin Holds the Term "Feudal" Unsuited to Traditional Russia

LENIN expressed his acceptance of the Asiatic concept positively by using such terms as *Aziatchina* and "Asiatic" and negatively by his reluctance to apply the term "feudal" to traditional Russia. The Russian peasants lived under conditions of *krepostnichestvo*, literally "attachment"; [i] and Lenin thus designated the Russian system of land tenure. We translate it "bondage."

Lenin made his position clear in 1902, when he criticized the first

h. A Western interpretation of historical Russia was suggested by the scholarly Ryazanov, who perhaps more than any other Russian socialist familiarized Western Marxists with Marx' Asiatic views on Russia. Ryazanov explained the rise of Muscovite autocracy as a spontaneous response to "the Tatar danger," comparable to Austria's response to "the Turkish danger." The analogy is manifestly faulty, since the Austrians never lived under a Turkish "yoke." But Ryazanov made it the starting point for his equation of Russian and Austrian absolutism, and he bracketed Prussian absolution and Tsarist Russia (Rjasanoff, 1909: 28).

i. Readers unfamiliar with the Russian language are warned against relying on the official Communist translations of Lenin's and Stalin's works. These translations almost always render *krepostnichestvo* as "feudal." Disregarding a distinction that

draft of the program of the Russian Social-Democratic party for having "almost intentionally" confused the issue by ascribing a "feudal-craft period" to Medieval Russia. Noting that the appropriateness of the term "feudalism" to the Russian Middle Ages was being questioned, he found it "least applicable to Russia." [54] In 1905 he again, with reference to Russia, insisted that the word *krepostnichestvo* be employed instead of *feodalisma*.[55] In 1911 he apologized for using the term "feudal" in the Russian context, since this was "a not quite exact general *European* expression." [56]

C. RETREAT FROM TRUTH

DOES all this mean that Marx, Engels, and Lenin upheld the classical concept of Asiatic society fully and without oscillation? It does not. Several times Lenin came close to withdrawing from his original Asiatic position before abandoning it altogether in 1916. But the retrogressive trend began prior to Lenin. Significantly, the first Marxist to accept the concept of an Asiatic society was the first to cripple it: Marx himself. Significantly also, he crippled it by dropping the idea of a bureaucratic ruling class.

1. MARX

a. Marx "Mystifies" the Character of the Ruling Class

IN his effort to determine class rule Marx, like Adam Smith and his successors, asked: Who controls the decisive means of production and the "surplus" created by them? And he found that these advantages were enjoyed in antiquity by the "slaveholders," in feudal society by the "feudal landlords," in modern industrial society by "the capitalists," and in Asiatic society by "the sovereign" or "the state." [1] Thus in the three types of private-property-based society of his schema, Marx established a ruling class as the main beneficiaries of economic privilege, whereas with regard to government-dominated Oriental society he was satisfied to mention a single person, the ruler, or an institutional abstraction, "the state."

This was a strange formulation for a man who ordinarily was eager to define social classes and who denounced as a mystifying "reification" the use of such notions as "commodity" and "the state," when the underlying human (class) relations were left unexplained.[a]

---

for many years Lenin deemed essential, they misrepresent his view of Russian society during these years.

a. When Marx discussed the "fetishistic" character of commodities, he stereotyped ideas already formulated by his classical predecessors. He admitted this none too

But it may be said, perhaps Marx did not know of any persons who, in Asiatic society, shared the surplus with the sovereign? No such plea can be made. Marx had thoroughly studied John Stuart Mill's *Principles*,[2] which, in addition to the ruler's household and favorites, listed as the beneficiaries of the Asiatic state revenue "the various functionaries of the government." [3] And in his historical survey of the theories of surplus value, he had inserted *verbatim* Jones' statement that "The surplus revenue from the soil, the only revenues except those of the peasants of any considerable amount, were (in Asia, and more especially in India) distributed by the state and its officers," [4] as well as Bernier's comment that in India the state revenues supported large numbers of serving men.[5]

Marx' interest in the class issue, the data at his disposal, and his objection to the mystification of social relations point to one conclusion, and one conclusion only. They all suggest that from his own standpoint Marx should have designated the functional bureaucracy as the ruling class of Oriental despotism. But Marx did nothing of the kind. Instead of clarifying the character of the Oriental ruling class he obscured it. Measured by the insights reached by Bernier, Jones, and Mill, Marx' mystification (reification) of the character of the ruling class in Oriental society was a step backward.

b. Further Retrogressions

MARX took this step backward in the 1850's, at the very time he was accepting the classical concept of Asiatic society. In the '60's and '70's he regressed further. A comparison of the first volume of *Das Kapital* and his writings of 1853 and 1857–58 shows him in the early years more precise on the hydraulic aspect of Oriental despotism. The many passages in *Das Kapital* and the *Theorien über der Mehrwert* that contrast Oriental and ancient, feudal, and/or capitalist conditions reveal both the later Marx' determination to view Asiatic society as a specific institutional conformation and his reluctance to discuss the managerial aspect of Oriental despotism.[6]

In the writings of the later period he emphasized the technical side of large-scale water works,[7] where previously he had emphasized their political setting. He now lumped together control of water "in Egypt, Lombardy, Holland, etc.," [8] where previously he had distinguished the centralized and despotic governments of the Orient from the

gracefully in Volume I of *Das Kapital* (I: 47 n.). But he was more generous in Volume III, where he commented that the exposure of the false "personification of things and the reification of production relations" was "the greatest merit of classical economy" (Marx, DK, III, Pt. 2: 366).

private-enterprise-based "voluntary associations" of Flanders and Italy.[9] He now mentioned the agrohydraulic function of a single state, India,[10] where previously he had spoken of this "economic function" as devolving upon "all Asiatic governments." [11]

A frequently cited passage in *Das Kapital*, Volume 1, appears to face the problem of the ruling class in Oriental society. Actually, however, it blurs the issue by introducing what, from the Marxian point of view, is a most peculiar determinant of economic dominance. Attached to the phrase "The regulation of water in Egypt" is the following note: "The necessity to calculate the periodic movements of the Nile created Egyptian astronomy and with it the rule of the priest caste as leader of agriculture." By making astronomy the basis for economic leadership, Marx dropped his standard criterion: control over the means of production. And by stressing the hereditary ("caste") status of the "leaders" rather than their class, he further confused the matter.[b]

Moreover, in Volume 3 of *Das Kapital* he asserted that "in despotic states, the labor of supreme supervision and the ubiquitous interference of the government" is demanded in "the execution of the common tasks evolving from the nature of *all* [sic!] commonwealths as well as the specific functions that stem from the antagonisms between the government and the mass of the people." [12]

In writing thus, Marx obscured the specific managerial functions of the despotic state of the Orient, which in the '50's had intrigued him so greatly.

2. ENGELS

a. Asiatic Society—Yes! (Engels' Basic Attitude)

MARX' retrogressions in the treatment of Asiatic society are little known. Those of Engels have been widely publicized. Indeed the frequent references to certain passages in his book, *The Origin of the Family, Private Property, and the State,* have beclouded the fact that from 1853 until his death in 1895 Engels upheld, in largest part, the theory of Oriental society.

Engels' early role in clarifying Marx' understanding of the hydraulic aspect of the Orient and the validity of an "Asiatic" interpretation of India and Russia [c] has already been noted. In his critique of Eugen

b. Marx, DK, I: 478, n. 5. The sentence is followed by a quotation from Cuvier's *Discours sur les revolutions du globe,* which relates the need for astronomy to the annual rise of the Nile and the [seasonal] agricultural activities of the Egyptians.

c. See above. Since neither Marx nor Engels had explained how, under the influence of foreign capitalism, an Orientally despotic government could encourage modern

Dühring (the *Anti-Dühring*) he went further than Marx by suggesting that the execution of important "socio-administrative functions" [13] might lead to the formation of a "ruling class." And he underscored this point by noting that each of the many "despotic governments which rose and fell in India and Persia . . . knew full well that it was first of all the total entrepreneur [*Gesamtunternehmerin*] of irrigation in the river valleys, without which no agriculture is possible there." [14] In his critique of Dühring as well as in his book on the family Engels contrasted the "domestic slavery" of the Orient and the "work slavery" of antiquity.[15] And in a passage inserted in *Das Kapital,* Volume 3, published in 1894, eleven years after Marx' death, he described the peasants of both India and Russia as being exploited by the mercilessly grinding "tax-screw of their despotic governments." [16]

b. Asiatic Society—Yes and No! (The Anti-Dühring)

THIS long-range trend was interrupted by two major lapses—one manifested in the *Anti-Dühring,* the other in *The Origin of the Family, Private Property, and the State.*

In the *Anti-Dühring* Engels suggested a dual origin for the state and for its ruling class. In the first case, these two forces came into being because of excessive political power, in the second because of the growth of private property and private-property-based production. The first development involved the rise of important socio-administrative functions and the ability of the governing persons to defy control to the extent that the original "servant" of society became its "master." [17]

In this context Engels mentioned "an Oriental despot or satrap, the Greek tribal prince, the chieftain of a Celtic clan and so on." His two Western examples bring to mind Marx' ideas on societal dominance based on political-military function.[18] According to Marx, this

---

capitalist forms of private enterprise, Engels was introducing a new concept when in 1894 he called Russia's new bourgeoisie a dominant force (Marx and Engels, 1952: 240). He did not elaborate this point, nor did he reconcile it with a statement made four years earlier on the incompatibility of Oriental despotism and capitalism: "Turkish, like any other oriental domination, is incompatible with a capitalistic economy; the surplus value extorted is not safe from the hands of greedy satraps and pashas. The first basic condition of bourgeois acquisition is lacking: the security of the person and the property of the trader" (Marx and Engels, 1952: 40). Engels' statement of 1894 also contradicts the insertion in *Das Kapital,* III, in which he described Russia's despotic government as the great exploiter of the peasantry (Marx, DK, III, Pt. 2: 259 ff.). But however different their emphasis, Engels' various utterances on post-Emancipation Russia had one thing in common: they all implied that Tsarist despotism was still a going concern.

type of dominance soon yielded to dominance based on private property and private-property-rooted labor (slave labor and serf labor).[19] Only in the form of Oriental despotism did societal dominance based on public function spread far and last long.

Although Engels, in the *Anti-Dühring*, twice noted the enormous staying power of Oriental despotism ("thousands of years"),[20] in neither instance did he elaborate this point. But he did list the Oriental despot first; and later in speaking of the despotic regimes of Persia and India he did specify their "socio-administrative" function: their "first duty was the general maintenance of irrigation throughout the valleys."[21] Engels even noted that dominance based on socio-administrative function united the "individual ruling persons into a ruling class."[22]

Thus far Engels' presentation, despite its lack of subtlety, was scientifically legitimate and in agreement with Marx' version of the classical concept of Oriental society. Equally legitimate, and again in agreement with relevant ideas of Smith, Mill, and Marx, was his statement on the second origin of classes and the state:[23] the rise of slave-based production and of private property in slaves involved the rise of a private-property-based ruling class; and this development paved the way for an evolution that led via classical Greece and the Roman Empire to "modern Europe."[24] And it also involved the rise of a type of state which, because of irreconcilable contradictions in the new private-property-based economy, was used by the propertied classes to protect their privileged position.[25]

We need not criticize here the primitive ideas on the relation of wealth and government that Marx shared with John Locke, Adam Smith, and others.[26] In the present context we are interested only in the fact that Engels, in the earlier part of the *Anti-Dühring*, indicated two different patterns of societal development ("Side by side with this [the socio-administrative] origin of class there occurred still another")[27] and that in the last part of this same book, he abruptly abandoned this notion of a multilinear development. There he spoke of state and class rule as if they had resulted exclusively from antagonisms based on conditions of private property. And he climaxed his slanted presentation by listing only three class societies based respectively on slavery, serfdom, and wage labor.[28]

c. Asiatic Society—No! (The Origin of the Family, Private Property, and the State)

IN Engels' much quoted book on the family, which links the basic ideas of Morgan's *Ancient Society* and certain Marxian views, Asiatic society as a major societal order has altogether disappeared. Here Engels discusses the origin of the state as if he had never heard of the "socio-administrative" state in general and of Oriental despotism in particular.

This omission cannot be ascribed to any lack of interest in societies of the "barbarian" type, for Engels elaborated on the conditions of "barbarism" [d] in ancient Greece, Rome, and the Celtic and Germanic Middle Ages.[29] Nor can it be ascribed to the general exclusion of matters pertaining to the Orient. Although more remiss in this respect than Morgan [30] (Engels refrained for reasons of "space" from dealing with the pertinent history of "Asiatic" peoples),[31] he did speak of Asia, the Asiatics, and Oriental institutions; [32] and as already related, he contrasted the "domestic slavery" of the Orient with the "work slavery" of antiquity.[33] But unconcerned with what he had formerly designated as the "new division of labor"—a division which, subsequent to the natural division of labor within a community,[e] caused the rise of "functional" governments and power-based ruling classes —and also unconcerned with what both he and Marx had written regarding the exploitative quality of Oriental despotism, Engels now asserted categorically that *"the first great social division of labor initiated the first great division of society into two classes: masters and slaves, exploiters and exploited."* [34]

The slavery-based society was governed by a state of slave owners, just as the feudal and capitalist types of society were governed respectively by a state of feudal nobles and a state of capitalists.[35] In all these societies economic dominance led to political dominance.[36] And eco-

d. Marx and Engels adopted the terms "barbarism" and "civilization" not from Adam Smith (see Smith, 1937: 666, 669, esp. 735), but from Fourier, whose typology of development Engels praised in the forties [MEGA, I, Pt. 4: 413 (1846); I, Pt. 6: 398 ff. (1848)], and again with undiminished enthusiasm in the seventies (Engels, 1935: 269). Even in 1884, when he adopted Morgan's schema, Engels still referred to Fourier's "brilliant critique of civilization," and he commented on the fact that Fourier, like Morgan, viewed private landownership as a key feature of this phase (Engels, 1921: 187 n.).

Under the influence of Morgan, Marx and Engels modified these categories. But they did not discard them. It was with these categories in mind that Engels, in 1848, spoke of "semi-barbarous" countries, such as India and China (MEGA, I, Pt. 6: 506), that Marx, in the fifties, spoke of the "barbarism" of China and the "semi-barbarian" emperor of China (Marx, 1951a: 48, 50, 55) and its "patriarchal constitution" (*ibid.*: 56), of "barbaric" Turkey and Persia (*ibid.*: 47), of the "semi-barbarian, semi-civilized communities" of India (Marx, NYDT, June 25, 1853), of Eastern "barbarism" (*ibid.*, April 12, 1853), and "the barbarian" sovereign of Russia (Marx and Engels, 1920, I: 251).

e. Engels, 1935: 165. In the same work Engels referred to the "primeval division of labor in the agricultural family" (*ibid.*: 183). Marx (DK, I: 44 and 316) considered the division of labor according to sex and age its primeval form.

nomic dominance, as Engels stressed, involved *private ownership of the decisive means of production.*[37]

Thus societal leadership and exploitation were essentially rooted in private property. The despotic masters of the functional state, whose ruthless methods of exploitation Engels had once so eloquently described, remained unnoted. "With *slavery,* which in civilization developed most fully, there occurred *the first great split of society into an exploiting and an exploited class.* This cleavage lasted throughout the whole period of civilization. *Slavery is the first form of exploitation,* which is specific for the ancient world; it was succeeded by serfdom in the Middle Ages and wage labor in more recent times. These are the three great forms of servitude, characteristic of the three great epochs of civilization." [38]

The references to "civilization" do not correct the notion of a unilinear pattern of development created by these sentences. But they show Engels aware of what he was doing—or better: of what he was hiding. In Engels' terminology, "civilization" was identical with the predominance of private property. Through his qualifying clause, he backhandedly admitted that his statement did not include the "barbarian" world of Oriental despotism.

d. Retrogressive Trends in a Supposedly Progressive Position

i. MARX DEFENDS SCIENTIFIC OBJECTIVITY AGAINST ALL EXTRANEOUS CONSIDERATIONS

THIS is not a pretty picture. The founding fathers of scientific socialism, who claimed to be basing their political practice on the most advanced theory of societal development, harmed rather than helped the cause of truth when they were confronted with the most important historical manifestation of total power. Why? Did Marx have so little regard for scientific truth that he bent it easily? This certainly was not the case. The care with which he documented his own economic views and the elaborate way in which he presented opposing views demonstrate that he fully recognized the demands of scholarship.

And Marx himself was explicit on this point. Commenting on the scientific behavior of Malthus and Ricardo, he condemned all who abandoned scientific truth and the interest of mankind in general for special interests of any kind. A scholar, he held, should seek the truth in accordance with the immanent needs of science, no matter how this affected the fate of any social class: capitalists, landowners, and workers. Marx praised Ricardo for taking this attitude,[39] which he called

"not only scientifically honest, but also scientifically required." [40]
For the same reasons, he condemned as "mean" anyone who subordinated scientific objectivity to extraneous purposes: "a man who
tries to accommodate science to a standpoint which is not derived
from its own interest, however erroneous, but from outside, alien,
and extraneous interests, [such a man] I call 'mean' (gemein)." [f]

Marx was entirely consistent when he held the refusal to accommodate science to the interests of any class to be "stoic, objective, scientific." [41] He was entirely consistent also, when he concluded on a note
which from the standpoint of Leninist-Stalinist partisanship sounds
heretically humanitarian: "As far as this can be done without sin
against his science, Ricardo is always a philanthropist, as he indeed
was in practice." [42] And he was equally consistent when he branded
the reverse behavior a "sin against science." [43]

ii. MARX' AND ENGELS' "SIN AGAINST SCIENCE"

IN view of these strongly worded principles, Marx' retrogressions in
analyzing Asiatic society assume special significance. Obviously the
concept of Oriental despotism contained elements that paralyzed his
search for truth. As a member of a group that intended to establish
a total managerial and dictatorial state and was ready to use "despotic
measures" [44] to achieve its socialist ends, Marx could scarcely help
recognizing some disturbing similarities between Oriental despotism
and the state of his program.

The classical economist John Stuart Mill, who, in his Principles,
wrote about the Oriental state, warned in the same book against an
all-interfering state, against the dangers of an intellectually elitist despotism ("the government of sheep by their shepherd, without anything like so strong an interest as the shepherd has in the thriving of
his flock"), against "political slavery," [45] and a "dominant bureaucracy." [46] Did these and other academic exhortations induce Marx in
the '50's to hide the bureaucratic aspect of Oriental despotism? This
we do not know. But we do know that in the '60's and '70's anarchist
writers leveled much less academic criticisms at the Marxian principles of state socialism.

When Marx was writing the final version of Das Kapital, Volume
1, he was in open conflict with the Proudonists.[47] And from the late
'60's on, both he and Engels were manifestly disturbed by the claim
of the Bakunists that state socialism would inevitably involve the despotic rule of a privileged minority over the rest of the population, the

f. Marx, TMW, II, Pt. 1: 312 ff. In this context the German word gemein, like
the related English "mean," has the connotations "vicious," "shabby."

workers included.[48] In 1873 Bakunin continued the attack in his book *Statism and Anarchism,* which insisted that the Marx-envisaged socialist state "begets despotism on the one hand and slavery on the other." [49] The Marxist theory "is a falsehood, behind which lurks the despotism of a governing minority, a falsehood which is all the more dangerous in that it appears as the ostensible expression of the people's will." [50]

The political solutions offered by the anarchists were without doubt Utopian. But their criticism cut deep, as can be inferred from Marx' interpretation of the Paris Commune (which the Anarchists held to be a clownish reversal of his earlier position),[51] and from the secrecy with which, in 1875, Marx and Engels shrouded their ideas on state socialism and the dictatorship of the proletariat.[52] In his personal copy of *Statism and Anarchism* Marx made extensive notes, but he never answered Bakunin's acid arguments in public.

Engels confused the issue of Oriental despotism most seriously in the years following the appearance of Bakunin's book. His insertion in *Das Kapital,* Volume 3, dealing with the exploitative despotic regimes of Russia and India was made in the '90's [53]—when, according to Engels' own statement, he was no longer bothered by the anarchists.[g]

iii. FROM PROGRESSIVE TO REACTIONARY UTOPIANISM

THE authors of the *Communist Manifesto* accused the "Utopian" socialists of giving a "fantastic description of the society of the future." [54] But Marx and Engels did exactly this when they pictured their socialist state. The fathers of "scientific socialism," who realistically, if imperfectly, analyzed the problems of capitalist economy, failed to make any comparable effort to analyze the problems of the dictatorial and functional state, a socialist variant of which they were seeking to establish. Substituting "fanatical superstitions" [55] for scientific inquiry, they made the very mistake for which they had so harshly criticized the early Utopians.

And they suffered the same fate. The Utopian views, which in Marx' and Engels' opinion originally had a progressive ("revolutionary") quality, lost "all practical value and all theoretical justification," when new progressive societal forces emerged. Their significance bore "an inverse relation to historical development." Eventually they became outright "reactionary." [56]

g. For the later Engels' evaluation of the anarchist criticism as a past issue, see his foreword to *The Critique of the Gotha Programme,* published in 1891: "These considerations do not now exist" (Marx, 1935: 41).

Under different circumstances and in a much more devastating way, the Utopian state socialists also closed the circle. Their economic and functional approach to history stimulated the social sciences of the 19th and early 20th centuries. And their social criticism stimulated the struggle against the monstrous conditions that characterized the earlier phases of the modern industrial system.[57] But the original vision lost its progressive quality as realization neared. On the theoretical plane its reactionary potential was manifested early in Marx' and Engels' retrogressive attitude toward the Asiatic variant of managerial and bureaucratic despotism. On the practical plane this reactionary potential was manifested on a colossal scale when, nine months after the fall of the semimanagerial apparatus state of Tsarism, the Bolshevik revolution paved the way for the rise of the total managerial apparatus state of the USSR.

3. LENIN

a. Lenin Further Cripples Marx' Crippled Version of the Asiatic Concept

i. CONSISTENT DISREGARD OF THE MANAGERIAL ASPECT OF ORIENTAL DESPOTISM

THE factors which increasingly distorted Marx' and Engels' views of Oriental despotism increasingly produced retrogressive results in the case of Lenin.

During the first twenty years of his political career Lenin had generally accepted Marx' version of the classical concept of Asiatic society, but from the start his attitude was peculiarly selective. He never mentioned the managerial functions of Oriental despotism, although he certainly knew Engels' pertinent statements in the *Anti-Dühring* (from which he frequently quoted) and although these functions were emphasized in the correspondence between Marx and Engels (with which he was familiar). Nor was his disinclination to explore the functional aspect of Asiatic despotism weakened by the knowledge that this aspect was stressed by Kautsky, whose "orthodox" Marxism he admired, and by Plekhanov, whom he considered the leading authority on Marxist philosophy even after they broke politically.

Lenin thus closed his eyes not only to crucial realities in traditional Asia but also to essential features of the Tsarist regime, whose managerial activities he could observe at close range. In his *Development of Capitalism in Russia* (1899), he accomplished the extraordinary feat of describing the rise of a private-property-based industry in his native land without indicating the dimension of the state-managed enterprises which for almost two hundred years had dominated Russia's large-scale industry and which, with significant modifications, were still extremely important.

By neglecting the managerial role of Tsarist despotism, Lenin seriously falsified the picture of Russia's economic order. By underplaying its exploitative role, he falsified it still more. In 1894 Engels noted the crushing effect of taxation on the Russian peasants. And a few years later, Nicolai-on and Milyukov showed that the government, through direct—and indirect—taxes, was depriving the Russian peasants of about 50 per cent of their income.[58] Although he dealt with Nicolai-on's work at length, Lenin said nothing about the indirect taxes, which were numerous and heavy, and this procedure led him to the problematic conclusion that among the peasant group on which he had detailed data the taxes absorbed only about 15 per cent or "one seventh of the gross expenditure." [59]

ii. A CONFUSED PRESENTATION OF RUSSIA'S RULING CLASS

LENIN'S treatment of the ruling class under Oriental despotism was equally unsatisfactory. Marx' retrogressions in this respect, although enormously important for the interpretation of managerial despotism in general, did not seriously affect his analysis of modern Western society, which after all was his major concern. On the other hand, Lenin's discussion of the ruling class of Oriental despotism was anything but academic. It pertained to the very society which he was endeavoring to revolutionize.

If, as Lenin assumed, Tsarism was a variant of Oriental despotism, and if under Oriental despotism landlordism originated from a non-feudal form of state dependency, then he could be expected to hold that Tsarist society was controlled not by feudal or postfeudal landowners but by bureaucrats; and if this was his opinion, he could be expected to say so. If it was not, he could be expected to give substantial reasons for rejecting this view.

Actually he did neither. Instead he described Russia's ruling class now in one way, now in another. At times he spoke of a "dictatorship of the bureaucracy," [60] and he saw its officials towering "over the voiceless people like a dark forest." [61] At times he spoke of the Tsarist government as having "bourgeois" tendencies [62] and being subservient to the "big capitalists and nobles." [63] Most frequently he described it as being dominated by noble landowners.[64]

b. A Power-Strategist's Treatment of Truth

OBSERVING these inconsistencies, we may well wonder how a revolutionary leader whose ideas on the ruling class were so blurred could seize power. But we have only to recall Hitler's perverted interpretation of German conditions and his smashing victories over his internal enemies to realize that enormous political successes can be won on the basis of ideas that are at best semirational.

Lenin's stress on objective and absolute truth [65] did not prevent him from demanding that socialist writers and artists follow the principle of partisanship, *partinost*.[66] Throughout his career he himself did so even when it meant the abrogation of the most elementary rules of scientific propriety.[67]

Certainly Lenin's inconsistency in defining Russia's ruling class had no scientific justification. And his tricky verbal acrobatics in and after the Stockholm debate on Russia's Asiatic Restoration foreshadow his later readiness to blackout the truth completely.[h]

c. The Threat of the Asiatic Restoration (1906–07)

PREPARING for the Stockholm Congress of the Russian Social Democratic party in 1906, Plekhanov, speaking for the Mensheviks, challenged Lenin's plan for the nationalization of the land. Both the debate at the Congress itself and Lenin's subsequent utterances show him seriously upset by Plekhanov's argument, which, recalling Russia's Asiatic heritage, warned of the possibility of an Asiatic restoration.

The reason for Plekhanov's apprehensions can be quickly told. Encouraged by the experiences of 1905, Lenin believed that the Social Democratic party would be able to seize power if it could rally behind it Russia's small working class and the numerically strong peasantry. To win the support of the latter, he suggested that the nationalization of the land be made part of the revolutionary program. Plekhanov branded the idea of a socialist seizure of power as premature and the plan to nationalize the land as potentially reactionary. Such a policy, instead of discontinuing the attachment of the land and its tillers to the state, would leave "untouched this survival of an old semi-Asiatic order" and thus facilitate its restoration.[68]

This was the dreaded historical perspective that Lenin alternately designated as "the restoration of the Asiatic mode of production," [69] "the restoration of our old 'semi-Asiatic' order," [70] the restoration of

h. Plekhanov in 1906 compared Lenin to a brilliant lawyer who, in order to bulwark a problematic case, defies logic (*Protokoly*, 115).

Russia's "semi-Asiatic nationalization," [71] "the restoration of the semi-Asiatic order," [72] "the return to the *Aziatchina*," [73] and Russia's " 'Asiatic' restoration." [74]

Plekhanov, in developing his theme, adhered to Marx' and Engels' idea that under Mongol rule Russia became semi-Asiatic and that despite important modifications it remained so even after the Emancipation.[75] He noted that eventually [in 1762] the *pomeshchiki* were made the owners of their former service land without any further obligation to serve the government, while the peasants were still allotted their land [by the state and the *pomeshchiki*]. Resenting the striking injustice of the situation, the peasants wanted the old system of state control over the land restored.

Plekhanov, who recognized the revolutionary aspect of this position, at the same time dreaded what he considered its reactionary implications. Through a restoration of Russia's old economic and governmental order "the wheel of Russian history would be powerfully, very powerfully reversed." [76] Invoking the example of the Chinese statesman Wang An-shih, who allegedly sought to make the state the owner of all land and the state officials the managers of all production,[i] Plekhanov exclaimed: "We expect nothing but damage from the projects of Russian Wang An-shihs, and we bend all our efforts to make such projects economically and politically impossible." [77] "We want no *kitaishchina*"—no Chinese system.[78]

With these experiences in mind, Plekhanov fought Lenin's program to establish a dictatorial government based on a small proletarian minority that could do little to prevent a restoration. Instead he advocated the municipalization of the land, a measure that would place "organs of public self-government . . . in possession of the land" and thus "erect a bulwark against reaction." [79]

Would the "bulwark" of municipalization have been strong enough to counter the infinitely greater power of the new state that Lenin intended to create? It hardly seems so. Would it have been strong enough to hold in bounds a variant of the old-fashioned despotic bureaucracy that Plekhanov apparently saw as the beneficiaries of a possible future restoration? This is not quite as unlikely as Lenin made it appear.

But whatever the effect of municipalization might have been, Plekhanov certainly was on firm ground when he pointed to Russia's Asiatic heritage and when he stressed "the necessity to eliminate that economic foundation through which our people have approached

i. Plekhanov took up the argument as it was presented by Reclus (1882: 577 ff.). For a historically more correct evaluation of Wang An-shih's aims, see Williamson, WAS, II: 163 ff.

more and more closely the Asiatic people." [80] This formulation implies what Plekhanov in the same debate and in conformity with Marx' and Engels' views said explicitly—that in Russia, Oriental despotism, although very much weakened, still persisted after the Emancipation. And he was only drawing the logical conclusion from this premise when he warned that the decay of the hoped-for revolution would lead to an Asiatic restoration.

The significance of Plekhanov's arguments explains why Lenin kept reverting to them at the Stockholm Congress, in a subsequent *Letter to the Petersburg Workers,* in a lengthy pamphlet on the Party's agrarian program, published in 1907, and in a digest of this pamphlet for a Polish Socialist paper. Manifestly, his revolutionary perspective was being challenged by the very Asiatic interpretation of Russian society that until then had been for him a Marxist axiom.

But although Lenin was greatly disturbed by this fact, he could not, in the then climate of Russian Marxism, abandon the Asiatic concept. Despite his aggressive rejection of Plekhanov's arguments, he admitted the reality of Russia's Asiatic heritage when he demanded that "the restoration of our old semi-Asiatic order must be distinguished from the restoration that took place in France, on the basis of capitalism." [81] He admitted it when he noted that the "shell" of the old order was "still strong in the Peasant Reform," and that, even after the '80's the bourgeois development of rural Russia advanced "very slowly." [82] And he admitted it when he asserted that land nationalization would "far more radically eliminate the economic foundations of the Aziatchina" than municipalization.[83]

These are important affirmations. And they become even more important when we recall Lenin's conviction that because of Russia's backwardness a protosocialist revolution there was bound to fail if it was not supported by a socialist revolution in one or more of the industrially advanced countries of the West. "The only guarantee against restoration is the socialist revolution in the West." [84] In view of the just-cited statements, the dreaded Russian restoration could only be an Asiatic restoration.

Plekhanov, in harmony with socialist teachings which Lenin also accepted, condemned Lenin's plan to seize power as "Utopian," and he referred to Napoleon's remark that a general who counts on the simultaneous occurrence of all favorable conditions is a bad general.[85] But Lenin was determined to take the Great Gamble. And it was for this reason that during and immediately after the Stockholm Congress, he minimized and obscured Russia's Asiatic heritage.

In his concluding speech at Stockholm and in his digest of the subsequent pamphlet in the Polish paper he discussed the problem of the restoration without mentioning the possibility of an Asiatic restoration. In his *Letter to the Petersburg Workers* he mentioned the issue, but he belittled its significance by describing the Asiatic mode of production in Russia as a phenomenon of the past. If the dreaded restoration should occur, it would not be a restoration of the Asiatic mode of production or even a restoration of the 19th-century type. For "in Russia from the second half of the 19th century on, the capitalist mode of production became stronger, and in the 20th century, it became absolutely predominant." [86]

Recalling Lenin's remark in 1905—that so far Russia had developed only a restricted "Asiatic" capitalism—this statement seems fantastic, and in his 1907 pamphlet, he did not repeat it. Indeed, as noted above, he admitted here that Russian agriculture developed along the bourgeois path "very slowly." And his assertion that the "medieval system of landownership" presented obstacles to the growth of bourgeois farming in Russia explains what he meant when he said that the foundations of the *Aziatchina* still needed eliminating.

A leader who in one year deals with the facts of a crucial problem in four different ways (by omission, ambiguity, denial of their importance, and recognition of their importance) is not too sure of his course. From Stockholm on, Lenin increasingly avoided the "Asiatic" nomenclature, and this even when he was dealing with Asiatic institutions.[87] He increasingly called the "Asiatic" heritage "medieval," "patriarchal," or "precapitalist." And although he still spoke of Russian "bondage" (*krepostnichestvo*), he increasingly spoke of Russian "feudalism." [j]

d. Further Oscillations (1907–14)

DESPITE these oscillations, Lenin stuck by a concept for which apparently he knew no substitute. In the fall of 1910 he again drew closer to Plekhanov,[88] and in January 1911 he demonstrated his continued adherence to the Asiatic views by characterizing the Russia of Tolstoy's writings as a land in which "the Oriental system, the Asiatic system" prevailed until 1905, this year being "the be-

---

j. Lenin employed the term "state feudalism" for the Asiatic land system in his 1907 pamphlet, naming Plekhanov and "subsequently also" Martynov as persons who had used this formula (Lenin, S, XIII: 301). Martynov did indeed say at Stockholm "our feudalism is a state feudalism" (*Protokoly*, 90), but I have not found any similar phrase in Plekhanov's speeches. However, even if Plekhanov had occasionally used this formula, throughout the year 1906 he kept insisting that Russia's institutional heritage was not feudal but semi-Asiatic (see esp. *Protokoly*, 116).

ginning of the end of 'Oriental' stagnation." [k] In 1912 he discussed traditional China in "Asiatic" terms; [89] and in 1914, he spoke of the Asiatic despotism of Russia as a living reality.[90]

e. Full Retreat (1916–19)

i. LENIN'S IMPERIALISM (1916)

WORLD WAR I abruptly terminated Lenin's adherence to the Asiatic concept. In October 1914 he expressed the hope that the war would permit the radical socialists to initiate a comprehensive political and social revolution.[91] And in 1915 he was convinced that a gigantic cataclysm was in the making.[92] To prepare his followers for their daring revolutionary role, he wrote two small books that evidence a crucial turn in his sociohistorical views: *Imperialism: the Highest Stage of Capitalism* in 1916 and *State and Revolution* in 1917.

In *Imperialism* Lenin depicted capitalism as a "monopolistic" and imperialistic system which, as its sterile and stationary condition revealed, had reached the end of its historical road. And following Hilferding, he viewed "finance capital" as the master of a modern country's credit system and, on this account, also the master of its economy. The next logical step, or so it seems, would have been the demonstration that these ideas had validity not only for Western Europe and America but also for Russia, the chief target of his theoretical and political concern. In the case of Russia such a demonstration would have been both simple and instructive, for it was generally known that the Tsarist government had supreme control of the Russian credit system. The "Asiatic" interpretation of Russian society suggested that this circumstance gave the Tsarist bureaucracy supreme control over the country's economy.

Lenin recognized the premise, but he dodged the conclusion. He mentioned the financial key position of the Tsarist government; [93] but he did so without emphasis and without explaining its implications for the economy, as he had done for the private-property dominated West. Having failed to stress the managerial functions of the Russian state for the past, he also failed to stress them for the

k. Lenin, S, XVII: 31. This periodization appeared again in an article in 1916 by Zinoviev, then a close collaborator of Lenin, who wrote that the analysis made by Engels in 1890 met with the general approval of the Russian socialists (Zinowjew, 1919: 46). The Revolution of 1905, he added, initiated a new situation. Then, the rise of a politically conscious proletariat and the pro-Tsarist turn of the bourgeoisie (*ibid.:* 46 ff., 49, 60, 70 ff.) "changed the entire social structure of Russia, the relative strength of the various classes" (*ibid.:* 69). Tsarist autocracy now faced a new enemy; but Zinoviev did not deny that in 1916 it had still existed.

present. He thus hid an essential institutional feature that might link the country's "semi-Asiatic" past either with a state-Socialist or with an "Asiatic" future.

ii. STATE AND REVOLUTION (1917)

STATE AND REVOLUTION carried the deception still further. In this treatise Lenin explained the need for replacing the existing state, which was dominated by the ruling class, by a new type of a state which, like the Paris Commune, would be controlled from below. He based this significant decision not on an examination of the facts of history but on Marx' relevant comments.

To make good his claim to restore Marxist orthodoxy, Lenin promised to present "the totality" of Marx' and Engels' views on the state. For this purpose, "all, or at least all the most decisive, passages in the works of Marx and Engels on the subject of the state must necessarily be given as fully as possible." [94]

A reader interested in certain ideas of a certain author will want to be introduced first to that author's major work, if these ideas are discussed there, and then to his other pertinent writings. How did Lenin proceed in State and Revolution? As shown by his remark in 1907, the coming Russian revolution still had to eliminate the economic foundations of Oriental despotism. As shown by his remark in 1912, the year 1905 was only "the beginning of the end" of Russia's stationary "Oriental" conditions. And as shown by his remark in 1914, he still considered the contemporary "state system of Russia" as characterized by a "totality of traits which as a whole produces the concept 'Asiatic despotism.'" Thus in 1916–17, when Lenin promised to give all of Marx' and Engels' important observations on the state, we could expect him to give, along with Marx' ideas on the proprietary foundations of the state, his ideas on its functional foundations and on the related Russian state system. We could expect him to cite from Das Kapital, Marx' major work, which contains many significant references to the Asiatic state, as well as from those among his other writings which deal with this topic. And of course we could expect him to cite from Engels' writings also, giving special attention to his statement in 1875 on Russia's Oriental despotism.

But Lenin did nothing of the kind. In the book in which he allegedly was going to present all of Marx' decisive comments on the state, Das Kapital is not even mentioned. And all other comments of Marx and Engels on the functional state in general and on Russia's Oriental despotism in particular are equally shunned. In fact, Marx' and Engels' idea of a functional despotic state disappeared.

The only kind of state to which Lenin referred was Marx' and Engels' private-property-based variant: the non-Oriental state.

Consistent in his selectivity, Lenin cited only three statements which were concerned with the three private-property-based societal orders of the Marxist schema: antiquity, feudalism, and capitalism. And these statements he found most readily at hand not in Marx but in the later sections of Engels' *Anti-Dühring* and in the weakest link of Engels' sociohistorical writings: *The Origin of the Family, Private Property, and the State.*[95]

iii. LENIN'S LECTURE ON THE STATE (1919)

IN 1916, when Lenin was organizing his notes for *State and Revolution,* Russian absolutism, however weakened, still persisted. In the summer of 1917, when the book was completed, the Tsar had fallen; the Bolsheviks were trying to carry out Lenin's program of 1905–06, including the nationalization of the land which, according to Plekhanov, would greatly increase the chance of an Asiatic restoration.

Thus Lenin misled his readers on the key issues of the revolution he was promoting. And he continued to do so immediately after the October revolution and later when the Bolsheviks were consolidating their monopolistic managerial power. The climax of his ideological turnabout came in a lecture, "On the State," delivered on July 11, 1919.

In *State and Revolution* Lenin had failed to cite *Das Kapital;* but he had at least quoted some of Marx' secondary writings. In his lecture "On the State" he mentioned neither Marx' name nor the word "Marxism." Instead he gave Engels as his only authority in the matter of "contemporary Socialism." And he recommended Engels not for his many insights on the Asiatic state and Russia's Oriental despotism, or even for his *Anti-Dühring,* but only for his 1884 popularization of Morgan. Said Lenin: "I trust that concerning the question of the state you will familarize yourselves with Engels' work, *The Origin of the Family, Private Property, and the State.* This is one of the basic works of contemporary [m] Socialism, every phrase of which can be accepted with confidence."[96]

But even though Lenin recommended every phrase of this book as authoritative, he distorted some of its key ideas. Two instances are of particular interest to our inquiry, both involving the significance of slavery and both tending to strengthen the belief that societal development was a unilinear process.

m. Note that Lenin did not use the formula "scientific" socialism, usually associated with Marxist socialism.

As stated above, Engels indicated in his book on the family that slavery was not an essential element of production either in the "Orient" or in the European Middle Ages (the Orient knew only "domestic slavery"; and the Celtic and Germanic tribes, avoiding the "morass" of slavery, moved directly from a primitive "gens" society to feudal serfdom). Lenin, however, brushed aside these important distinctions and defined the "slave-owning society" as a virtually universal phase of development. "Through this [phase] passed *all* of contemporary civilized Europe—slavery ruled supreme two thousand years ago. Through this passed the great majority of the peoples in other parts of the world." [97] And one allegedly general type of private-property-based order necessarily led to the next: slave-owning society to serf-owning society; serf-owning society to capitalism; and capitalism to socialism.[98]

This unilinear scheme of development left no room for an Asiatic society and an Asiatic restoration. Rather it demonstrated "scientifically" that the Bolshevik revolution, by crushing the evil forces of private property, initiated the inescapable next stage of human progress: socialism.

f. Lenin's Last Period: the Specter of the Aziatchina Reemerges

IF Lenin had discarded his earlier convictions entirely, our account of the Big Myth could stop here. But Lenin was a "subjective socialist." And although the regime he headed from its inception bore little resemblance to the protosocialist government envisaged by Marx or by himself before the October revolution, he continued to reassert his earlier convictions. Thus while for the sake of power he betrayed his socialist principles, there is no doubt that he did so with a bad conscience. And there is no doubt either that he was uneasy when he obscured the Asiatic issue.

In *State and Revolution* Lenin indirectly recognized the existence of Oriental despotism, the decisive "barbarian" system of oppression and exploitation, by attaching the qualifying phrase "in the period of civilization" [99] to his remarks on the private-property-based state. This gesture did little to counteract the misleading effect of his main thesis, but it did show him aware of his "sin against science."

In his lecture "On the State" Lenin used the term "bondage" (*krepostnichestvo*) where Engels had used "feudalism." And he concluded his discussion of the bondage state by saying: "This was the bondage state, which in Russia, for instance, or in completely (*sovershenno*) [n] backward Asiatic countries, where bondage prevails until today—it differed in form—was either republican or monarchical." [100] Obviously, Lenin still knew that "Asiatic countries" had a special form of bondage. And he still distinguished between "completely" backward Asiatic countries and other (semibackward, semi-Asiatic?) countries, among which he included Russia. Again he made significant admissions, but again he hid his admissions so carefully that they were barely recognizable. And this also continued to be his method after the October revolution.

From the standpoint of Lenin's premises, the Bolshevik seizure of power in the fall of 1917 had little chance to initiate a protosocialist and socialist development. For in his own opinion the internal "relative" guarantees provided by a state of the Commune type (no bureaucracy, no police, no standing army) could only prevent the dreaded restoration, if the new regime had the support of a revolution in some industrially advanced Western countries. Hence Lenin was overjoyed when a revolution broke out in Germany in November 1918.

But the assassination of the two German Communist leaders, Karl Liebknecht and Rosa Luxemburg, on January 15, 1919, grimly demonstrated the weakness of the revolutionary forces in the West whose aid he craved. Lenin was profoundly shaken. Five days later, in a strange speech before the Second All-Russian Trade Union Congress, he assessed the achievements of the Bolshevik revolution. The French revolution in its pure form, he noted, had only lasted a year—but it accomplished great things. The Bolshevik revolution in the same time did much more.[101] His rambling sentences, however, scarcely veiled his fear that the Bolshevik revolution, like the French revolution before it, was headed for a restoration.

We do not know exactly what kind of a restoration Lenin was envisaging then, but in a speech on April 20, 1921—immediately after the Kronstadt uprising—he drew attention to the antisocialist and antiproletarian dangers inherent in the new Soviet bureaucracy. This bureaucracy was no bourgeois force but something worse. His comparative scale of societal orders suggests what he had in mind: "Socialism is better than capitalism, but capitalism is better than medievalism, *small production, and a bureaucracy connected with the dispersed character of the small producers.*" [102]

Lenin's statement may puzzle those who are unfamiliar with the

n. Lenin's formula recalls the distinction Marx had made between the "completely" Eastern troubles in the China of the fifties and the "semi-Eastern" troubles caused by Tsarist Russia (Marx, NYDT, August 5, 1853).

Marxist definition of Oriental despotism. But the initiated will recall Marx' and Engels' view that self-sufficient, dispersed, and isolated rural communities form the solid and natural foundation of Oriental despotism.[103] And they will recall Lenin's statement in 1914 that the "insignificant development of commodity production" was the economic cause of the great stability of Asiatic despotism.[104]

A few paragraphs later, and as if to dispel all doubt as to what he was driving at, Lenin went still further in characterizing the new Soviet bureaucracy. To his own question, "What are the economic roots of bureaucracy?" he answered, "There are two main roots: on the one hand, the developed bourgeoisie needs a bureaucratic apparatus, primarily a military apparatus, and then a judicial apparatus. . . . This we have not got. Our bureaucracy has a different economic root: *it is the fragmented and dispersed character of the small producer, his poverty, the lack of culture, the absence of roads, illiteracy, the absence of exchange between agriculture and industry, the absence of connection and interaction between them.*" [105]

True, Lenin did not put a label on the phenomenon he was describing. But the details he cited all elaborated the dispersion and isolation of the villages over which the new regime ruled. In Aesopian language [o] he was obviously expressing his fear that an Asiatic restoration was taking place and that a new type of Oriental despotism was in the making.

No wonder then that at the end of his political career Lenin several times called Russia's institutional heritage "bureaucratic" and "Asiatic." He noted that Russian society had "not yet emerged" from its "semi-Asiatic" lack of culture.[106] He juxtaposed the "Asiatic" way in which the Russian peasant traded to the "European" way.[107] And he criticized the Soviet regime for being unable to "go along without the particularly crude types of pre-bourgeois culture, i.e. bureaucratic or bondage culture." [108] Bondage culture—not feudal culture. And shortly before he suffered the stroke that altogether removed him from the political arena, he went so far as to call the Soviet state apparatus "to a large extent the survival of the old one. . . . It is only slightly repainted on the surface." [p]

---

o. Originally Lenin used an "Aesopian" (slave) language to speak to those oppressed by the government in such a way that the rulers would not realize what he was saying (cf. Lenin, S, XXII: 175). Now, as the head of the new ruling stratum, he used the same device to hide his meaning from those who were being ruled.

p. Lenin, S, XXXIII: 440; cf. Lenin, SW, IX: 382. See also Lenin, S, XXXIII: 404 ("We still have the old apparatus") and 434 ("Our apparatus . . . which we took over in its entirety from the preceding epoch").

4. STALIN

LIKE the first Roman emperor, Augustus, the founding father of the Soviet Union, Lenin, upheld in words what he destroyed by deeds. But words, too, have their history, and under a regime that fits its ideas into a rigid frame, words of the official doctrine makers are not easily cast out. It is no accident that in the USSR arguments defending the concept of an Asiatic society continued to be made openly as long as "subjective socialists" (members of the "Old Guard") openly fought the rise of the new totalitarian bureaucracy. And it is no accident that Stalin, who inherited and developed Lenin's incipient apparatus state, also inherited and developed Lenin's readiness to destroy inconvenient truths, even when these truths were uttered by Marx and Engels—or by Lenin himself.

a. The Old Guard Objects

IN 1925 Ryazanov, who was then director of the Marx-Engels Institute, published an article, "Marx on India and China," which brought together Marx' ideas on Asiatic society and the Asiatic mode of production.[109] In the same year the top economist, Varga, declared that government-controlled productive and protective water works were the basis of Chinese society and that the scholarly administrators, the *literati,* and not the representatives of private property, such as the landowners, constituted China's ruling class.[110] In 1928 the *Program of the Communist International,* which was drafted under Bukharin's guidance, found in the economy of colonial and semi-colonial countries "feudal medieval relationships, or 'Asiatic mode of production' relationships prevailing"; and Varga, in an article in *Bolshevik,* the theoretical organ of the Communist Party of the USSR, again defined traditional China as an Asiatic society and pointed out that in this society the peasants, both owners and tenants, occupied a very different position from that of the serfs in feudal society.[111] In 1930 he publicly criticized the Comintern official Yolk and those editors of the *Problemy Kitaia* who sided with him for calling the Asiatic mode of production an Asiatic variant of the feudal mode of production: If Marx had been of this opinion, "he would have said so." [112] The change suggested by Yolk involved no less than a "revision of Marxism." Varga therefore demanded that the underlying problem be made the topic of an organized discussion.

Such a discussion was indeed held in Leningrad in February 1931 —that is, shortly after the enforced collectivization which enormously strengthened the new Stalin-led *apparatchiki* but before the Purges, which ruthlessly decimated the Old Guard. The date explains why Ryazanov, Varga, Bukharin, and Madyar (the leading younger proponent of the Asiatic concept) were not invited to participate. And it also explains why those who called the great Asian civilizations "feudal" proceeded with a certain restraint when they attacked the defenders of "the theory of the Asiatic mode of production."

b. A Half-hearted Criticism of the Theory of Oriental Society

i. THE LENINGRAD DISCUSSION (1931)

POLITICALLY speaking, the advocates of the "feudal" interpretation of Oriental society were in a strong position, for since 1926 Stalin had repeatedly designated China's agrarian order as "feudal." [113] But Stalin had been more apodictic than convincing when he spoke of China's feudal conditions. He had not driven home his ideas by reference to the known facts of Chinese economy and society. Nor had he shown how to deal with Marx', Engels', and Lenin's utterances concerning the Asiatic system and the Asiatic mode of production.

This lack of direction is reflected in the Comintern statements on China, India, and other Asiatic countries. And it accounts for the caution with which those who stressed Stalin's "feudal" view proceeded during the Leningrad discussion. It was no easy matter to uphold a party line that was fraught with serious doctrinal difficulties.

However, in the course of the Leningrad conference, a few points did emerge clearly.

1) The critics of the Asiatic concept rejected as un-Marxist the idea that a functional bureaucracy could be the ruling class. [114]

2) They rejected the Asiatic-bureaucratic interpretation of the Chinese "gentry." [q]

3) They claimed that the theory of the Asiatic mode of production imperiled the work of the Communist International in the colonial and semicolonial countries of Asia. [r]

q. DASP: 68, cf. 181. It was in this respect that I was singled out for criticism as having stressed the "Asiatic" quality of the Chinese gentry. This indeed I did when I described the group in question as the nonofficiating wing of the bureaucratic ruling class (Wittfogel, 1931: 730). For the elaboration of my earlier view see above, pp. 312 ff.

r. Godes charged that the idea of the "exceptionality" (the non-Western character) of the Orient implied in the theory of Asiatic society tended to encourage some Asian nationalists to reject the doctrinal authority of the Communists and that the idea of a stationary Asia conceded to European capitalism the possibility of a "Messianic" role (DASP: 34). Such a "Messianic" argument was suggested by Marx' evaluation of British

The spokesmen for the feudal interpretation of the Orient bolstered their position by invoking those utterances of Engels and Lenin that ignored Asiatic society. The defenders of the theory of the Asiatic mode of production, on their part, cited supporting statements from Marx, Engels, and Lenin. But they did not mention Marx' or Engels' Oriental interpretation of Russia; and they shied away from Lenin's concept of the *Aziatchina* and his comments on the possibility of an Asiatic restoration.

In this battle of quotations the defenders of the "Asiatic" theory did not fare too badly. The party-line spokesmen, who before the conference had surely consulted with the Politburo, were obviously not instructed on how to deal with Marx' concept of an Asiatic mode of production, as presented in his *Preface* to the *Critique of Political Economy*. Thus Godes and Yolk, who dared to dissociate themselves from the "Asiatic" clause in the Comintern program,[115] still faithfully quoted Marx' famous pronunciamento.[s]

Their doctrinal insecurity found expression also in their political behavior. At the outset Yolk had asserted: "I want to warn against this theory. What is really important is to unmask it politically, and not to establish the 'pure truth' as to whether the 'Asiatic mode of production' existed or not." But his contempt for even the appearance of scientific objectivity was as premature as it was imprudent. Godes tactfully rephrased Yolk's comment,[116] and the printed minutes give only an emasculated version of the original statement.[t] Moreover, while both Godes and Yolk reprimanded some members of the "antifeudal" camp for "Trotskyite" leanings,[117] Godes warned against labeling all members of the group as Trotskyites.[118]

This restraint was certainly not due to the fact that Trotsky had never invoked the Asiatic concept in his fight against Stalin.[u] No

rule in India. Marx' attitude greatly embarrassed the Comintern, as may be seen from the heated debate on the problems of "industrialization" and "decolonization" in colonial and semi-colonial countries (see *Inprecor*, 1928: 1225 ff., 1247 ff., 1276, 1312, 1320 ff., 1350, 1352 ff., 1365, 1395 ff., 1402, 1405 ff., 1409 ff., 1412 ff., 1421 ff., 1424, 1425, 1471 ff.).

s. Yolk minimized its importance (DASP: 71), but Godes criticized him for doing so (*ibid*.: 164 ff.).

t. DASP: 59. In the printed report of the Leningrad conference Yolk stresses only the political importance of the Asiatic theory. Happily, however, the editors slipped up on their job. They reproduced not only Godes' rephrasing of Yolk's statement, which showed that Yolk had raised the issue of truth, but also, in the speech of another conferee, a citation of Yolk's exact words (*ibid*.: 89).

u. In the introductory chapters of his books on the Russian revolutions of 1905 and 1917, Trotsky succinctly explained the managerial and exploitative quality of the Tsarist regime which, in his opinion, approached "Asiatic despotism" (Trotsky, 1923:

such contingency would have stopped a Bolshevik propagandist. But if the "feudalists" had denounced the whole "Asiatic" camp as Trotskyite, they would have given the discussion a finality which, at that time, the ideological master strategists apparently did not want. Even the rude Yolk found it necessary to say that the defenders of the Asiatic concept were not repeating bourgeois theories. He merely found that, objectively, "their erroneous positions reflect alien influences." [119]

Thus the political propriety of the upholders of the theory of the Asiatic mode of production was not questioned. Their heresy was a minor one, and it did not deprive them of their good Communist standing.

ii. THE SIGNIFICANCE OF THE 1931 DISCUSSION

FROM the standpoint of immediate results, the Leningrad conference was inconclusive. From the standpoint of the student of the sociology of knowledge, it was highly rewarding. For this conference was the only one in which, to my knowledge, Soviet ideologists discussed the political implications of the theory of Asiatic society with any degree of frankness. Its singularity is underlined by two facts: unlike the other discussions of controversial matters—economic, literary, or biological—the Leningrad conference was not publicized in the international Communist press, nor were the issues involved comprehensively debated in Communist parties outside the USSR.

To summarize these issues briefly: The theory of Asiatic society endangered Communist leadership in Asia in that it depicted the "capitalist" West as capable not only of oppressive, but also of constructive, action. It endangered Communist leadership in that it enabled the nationalist leaders of Asia to reject Moscow-rooted doctrine as their guide. And it endangered the Communist attempt to one-sidedly stress secondary, if serious, problems of property and thus to hide the primary problem of bureaucratic class rule and general state slavery.

The delicate nature of these issues necessitated cautious procedures. But the top leadership of World Communism knew that whatever

---

18 ff.; *ibid.*, 1931: 18 ff.). But in the twenties and thirties he did not discuss Chinese society in "Asiatic" terms, nor did he use the criteria of Oriental despotism when he criticized Stalin's bureaucratic despotism. In 1938 Trotsky wrote a survey of what he held to be Marx' ideas. In his discussion of the types of social relations he mentioned only three—slavery, feudalism, and capitalism (Trotsky, 1939: 8)—just as Stalin did in the same year and Lenin had done in 1919.

the delays, the concept of a managerial-bureaucratic "Asiatic" state ultimately had to wither away.

c. Ideological Twilight

THE ideological erosion of the theory of the Asiatic mode of production advanced unevenly. The Chinese Communists rejected the concept of an Asiatic mode of production for traditional China before the Leningrad conference. They took this step in 1928 at their Sixth National Congress (held in Moscow) in a resolution on Agrarian Relations and the Struggle for Land in China, whose wording showed them more eager to embrace Stalin's "feudal" views than to do justice to Marx' "Asiatic" comments on China.[v] True, the first draft of this resolution had employed the concept of an Asiatic mode of production.[120] But this pathetic effort—which was probably spearheaded by Ch'ü Ch'iu-pai [121] and which led to nothing—only underlined the lack of a serious Marxist tradition in the Chinese Communist movement.

In other parts of the Marxist-Leninist world the idea of an Asiatic society survived in an ideological twilight that endured until the appearance of Stalin's *Dialectical and Historical Materialism* in 1939 and in some Anglo-Saxon countries even after.

It would be interesting to show how, during the 1930's, Soviet writers tried to find a "feudal" explanation for phenomena which they knew Marx considered expressions of an Asiatic mode of production. Note the efforts of Prigozhin (1934),[w] Grinevitch (1936),[x] and Struve (1938).[y] It would be interesting to show how, even within

v. In his study on Mao Tse-tung, B. Schwartz mentioned two theoretical decisions of the Sixth Congress of the CCP, one rejecting the Trotskyite stress on capitalist relations in the Chinese villages, the other rejecting the interpretation of Chinese society as an Asiatic society (Schwartz, 1951: 122 ff.). It is regrettable that *A Documentary History of Chinese Communism* (1952), which Schwartz edited together with John K. Fairbank and C. Brandt, failed to inform its readers on the latter point. According to the *History*, "the only innovation in the 'theoretical' sphere" was "the new estimate of the revolutionary situation" (Brandt, Schwartz, and Fairbank, 1952: 125). The omission is all the more regrettable since only a few years previously Dr. Fairbank in his book, *The United States and China*, had devoted a whole chapter to the discussion of "China as an Oriental Society" (Fairbank, 1948: 53–8).

w. Prigozhin explained the Asiatic mode of production as a special type of feudalism and he spoke of "the so-called Asiatic mode of production" (Prigozhin, 1934: 80, 86).

x. See the *Great Soviet Encyclopaedia*, 1936, XXXII: "China" (esp. pp. 538, 530), where Grinevitch speaks of the "bureaucratic feudalism" and the "bureaucratic despotism" of imperial China.

y. See Struve's ten points on the Asiatic mode of production in Struve, 1940 (1st ed. 1938): 22.

the Comintern itself, the Asiatic concept could still be employed. Note the article "The Flood Disasters in China," by Madyar in the Comintern organ, *International Press Correspondence,* published on September 3, 1931,[z] and Fox' 1935 praise of Marx' "brilliant grasp on the Indian . . . problem" in the same journal.[a] It would be interesting to show how English Marxism, as set forth in Burns' *A Handbook of Marxism,* spread the hydraulic interpretation of the Orient. Note the stress on the managerial and despotic peculiarities of "Oriental societies" in Gordon Childe's *Man Makes Himself.*[b] And it would be interesting to show how in the United States certain writers who based their thinking on Marx' Asiatic-hydraulic concept influenced non-Marxist students of the Orient. Note the impression made by Chi Ch'ao-ting's *Key Economic Areas in Chinese History, as Revealed in the Development of Public Works for Water-Control,* and by myself on Owen Lattimore.[c]

But a detailed review of this many-sided development is outside the scope of the present book. For our purpose it is sufficient to state that during the 1930's and especially in the Anglo-Saxon world Marxism in its most actively proselytizing form reproduced and spread an Asiatic-hydraulic interpretation of Oriental civilizations.

z. Protected by a thin veil of "feudal" verbiage (China's "feudal dismemberment"), Madyar stressed the "tremendous importance" of hydraulic works and the organizing function that, because of them, devolved upon "the Oriental despotism of the Chinese ruling class" (*Inprecor,* 1931: 865).

a. *Inprecor,* 1935: 1336. Fox, who in 1930 had published a comprehensive collection of Marx' statements on the Asiatic mode of production (*Letopis Marksizma,* 1930, XIII: 3–29), drew attention to Marx' ideas on India in a review of *A Handbook of Marxism.* It is a curious accident—if it is an accident—that this *Handbook,* which brought together fifty-two writings by Marx, Engels, and Stalin and which was distributed in the U.S.A. as well as in Great Britain, reproduced Marx' two main articles on India but not Lenin's lecture "On the State."

b. Childe acknowledged the significance of Marx' "realistic concept of history" in this book. And although his notion of the "urban revolution" is a deterioration of Marx' and Engels' (originally: Adam Smith's) ideas on the separation of town and village, and although his notion of the "arrested growth" of Oriental societies (Childe, 1952: 181, 186) lacks the incisiveness of Jones', Mill's, and Marx' statements on this phenomenon, his emphasis on the crucial significance of hydraulic operations for the rise of Oriental societies in Egypt, Mesopotamia, and early India definitely follows the classical Asiatic concept.

c. In his *Inner Asian Frontiers of China* (completed in 1939), Lattimore related that Chi's book first impressed on him "the importance of irrigation and canal transport in Chinese history" (Lattimore, 1940: xxi). In the same book he stated that over two millennia ago China's early feudalism had been superseded by "a bureaucratically administered empire" (*ibid.:* 369 ff., 375 ff.; cf. 368 ff., 373); and he added that "the prime factors" of this transformation had been "authoritatively classified by Wittfogel" (*ibid.:* 370).

d. Stalin "Edits" Marx

HOWEVER, while this development stimulated a number of social historians, from the standpoint of Russia's new totalitarian bureaucracy it was dynamite. Stalin had probably already sensed the danger in the late 1920's, but he probably also sensed the difficulty of abandoning a key idea of Marx that was still being upheld by respected Old Bolsheviks. Significantly, it was only after the Great Purges (1935–38), which liquidated the bulk of these traditionalists, that Stalin dared to lay hands on Marx' decisive statement on the Asiatic mode of production.

But wasn't Stalin himself an Old Bolshevik? Stalin had indeed been schooled in orthodox Marxism. In 1913 he described the Russia of the 1830's as dominated by "a gross Asiatic social and political regime," and he spoke of contemporary Russia as a "semi-Asiatic country." [122] But Stalin wrote these lines under Lenin's influence.[123] And while, on occasion, he employed the term "Asiatic" to characterize particularly oppressive features in his homeland, Georgia,[124] it is doubtful whether he was ever greatly concerned with Marx' theory of Asiatic society. During the Stockholm Party Congress of 1906 Stalin outdid Lenin in pleading for the "black" transfer of the landowners' land to the peasants; [125] but the possibility of an Asiatic restoration, which so deeply stirred Lenin and Plekhanov, evoked no comment from him. In his first popular presentation of Marxism in 1906–07 he listed among the types of society above the level of primitive communism, matriarchy, and patriarchy—slavery, "bondage," and capitalism.[126]

After the middle 1920's Stalin began to emphasize the "feudal" character of China's agrarian order. In 1926 he spoke of China's "medieval feudal survivals," [127] and in 1927, he elaborated the standard formula "feudal survivals" [128] by referring to China's "medieval-feudal forms of exploitation and oppression" [129] and "feudal-bureaucratic apparatus." [130]

There is little reason to believe that an early and complete acceptance would have kept Stalin from discarding the Asiatic concept. Lenin abandoned cherished ideas when strategy demanded it. But his lack of strong "Asiatic" convictions certainly made it easier for Stalin to promote the "feudal" view, just as his lack of subtlety in general made it easier for him to achieve his ends without any concern for consistency.

As discussed above, Engels had not, in his most problematic non-Asiatic statements, denied the socio-evolutionary importance of the ecological factor which he and Marx had emphasized in their earlier comments on Asiatic society. And neither Engels nor Lenin had tampered with Marx' programmatic statement on the four antagonistic modes of production as set forth in his famous *Preface*.

Stalin did both. He rejected the "geographical environment" as a *"determining* cause of social development, for that which remains almost unchanged in the course of tens of thousands of years cannot be the chief cause of development." [d] And instead of by-passing Marx' programmatic declaration as others had done, he brazenly invoked—and mutilated—it. Having pontifically presented his unilinear scheme of development, which included only three types of class societies (slave-holding, feudal, and capitalist), he fulsomely praised the "brilliant formulation of the essence of historical materialism given by Marx in 1859 in his historic *Preface* to his famous book, *Critique of Political Economy*." And he quoted the "historic" passage word for word—until just before the sentence which contains Marx' reference to the Asiatic mode of production.[131] Stalin thus demonstrated for all concerned that Marx, too, could be "edited," when necessary, *modo Tatarico*—with a meat cleaver.

e. Delayed Reaction in the Anglo-Saxon World

THE supreme judge of Marxist-Leninist doctrine had spoken—the Asiatic concept need no longer embarrass the faithful. However, the *Short Course* appeared in book form and in many foreign languages in the spring of 1939 [e]—at a time when the world was tense with the fear of an approaching catastrophe. From September 1939 on, the spreading war prevented the political strategists of the Soviet Union from pressing doctrinal issues. In fact, during these years they made substantial ideological concessions to the peoples of the USSR as well as to the Western democracies.

These circumstances go far to explain why, in 1940, the leading

---

d. Stalin, 1939: 118 ff. In rejecting environment and population growth as major determinant factors, Stalin was closely following the argument of Bukharin (Bukharin, 1934: 121, 124), who, shortly before his execution in 1938, had been publicly ridiculed by Vyshinsky as a "theoretician in quotation marks" (see above, p. 160). In Chap. 1 of the present inquiry I noted that the Marxian view of the relation between man and nature underrated the cultural factor, but this limitation notwithstanding, Marx' concept of the historically changing character of nature is far removed from the static view promoted by Bukharin, and following him, Stalin. Obviously, both Lenin and Plekhanov were closer to Marx' than to Bukharin's position (see Wittfogel, 1929: 504–21 and 698–724).

e. In the USSR the work began to appear in installments in the fall of 1938 (see *Inprecor*, 1938: 1067, 1108, 1132, 1157, 1197).

British Marxist-Leninist theoretician, R. P. Dutt, in a book *India To-day*, and in an Introduction to *Karl Marx, Articles on India*, enthusiastically reproduced Marx' ideas on Asiatic society in general and Indian society in particular.*f* They also go far to explain why, in 1942, Childe in another general sociohistorical study, *What Happened in History*, carried his discussion of the peculiarities of "Oriental societies" still further than he had in 1936.[132] In his second study he noted that the Bronze and Iron ages gave birth to four distinct institutional orders: irrigation-based agrarian societies, whose surplus "was concentrated in the hands of a relatively narrow circle of *priests and officials*"; classical Graeco-Roman civilizations, in which the primary producers and artisans were ultimately impoverished or enslaved; European feudalism; and the modern "bourgeois capitalist" world.[133] Semantically these four orders are identical with Marx' four major antagonistic societal conformations.

f. The Rout of the Notorious Theory of the Asiatic Mode of Production

WHEN the war ended, the ideological twilight ended also. Dutt, who a few years previously had vigorously recommended the application of the theory of the Asiatic mode of production to the scientific analysis of India and China, no longer discussed this theory, which he had once found singularly rewarding.*g*

f. Dutt presented Marx' pertinent articles of 1853 as "among the most fertile of his writings, and the starting-point of modern thought on the questions covered" (Dutt, 1940: 93). Marx' ideas on Asia that for half a century were almost unknown now begin "increasingly to influence current thought on Indian questions. To-day modern historical research is increasingly confirming the main outlines of their approach" [*ibid.*: 92. Cf. Dutt, 1951 (written 1940): *passim*]. An approving digest of *India To-day*, including Marx' "Asiatic" argument, by T. A. Bisson, was published in *Amerasia*, IV, No. 9, 1940.

g. In 1942 Dutt still upheld his earlier position, if in a diluted way [Dutt, 1943 (Engl. ed. 1942): 38 ff., 43, 71, 73 ff., 76 ff., 87]. He stopped doing so after the end of the War. While he still on occasion pointed to Marx' writings on India (*Labour Monthly*, XXXII, 1950: 43; XXXV, 1953: 105), the reader can draw no "Asiatic" conclusion from his vaguely phrased remarks. Viewed isolatedly, Dutt's scattered comments on "feudal" conditions in India (*ibid.*, XXVIII, 1946: 321; XXIX, 1947: 211) may not have created a new, non-"Asiatic" image. However, Dutt glorified Stalin, the great Marxist theoretician and author of the *Short Course* (*ibid.*, XXXI, 1949: 357); he dutifully praised S. A. Dange's crudely unilinear historical sketch, *India, from Primitive Communism to Slavery* (*ibid.*, XXXII, 1950: 41 ff.); and he reproduced in his magazine, and at length, the 1952 Soviet discussion on the Eastern countries, which was very specific in its emphasis on the "feudal survivals" and the "feudal" or "semi-feudal" character of rural India (*ibid.*, XXXV, 1953: 40, 41, 44, 84, 86). All this, taken together, definitely encouraged the feudal interpretation of traditional India.

Chi Ch'ao-ting, too, lost interest in the hydraulic-bureaucratic thesis that underlay his study of China's *Key Economic Areas*. Neither as an employee of the Chinese Nationalist government nor as a high-ranking official of the Chinese Communist regime did he elaborate his earlier "Asiatic" arguments.

And Lattimore, who in the 1930's was so impressed by Chi's and my own hydraulic-bureaucratic views and who still in 1944 considered the loosely used terms "semi-feudal" and "feudal survivals" scientifically obscuring, in the later '40's characterized the traditional societies of Asia as "feudal." [h]

The case of Childe is different. Childe, who since the '30's identified himself with Marx' interpretation of history, who in the '40's began to invoke Stalin's sociological authority,[134] and who in 1951 hailed Stalin as "the leading exponent of Marxism today," [135] established a frame of reference that makes his recent changes ideologically quite understandable. Having previously spoken of four major types of class societies, Childe in 1951 mentioned only three: classical, medieval, and modern.[i] And having previously stated that *"priests*

h. In 1936, Lattimore, as the then editor of *Pacific Affairs*, published a bibliography of the Chinese Soviet Movement, prepared by the staff of the American Council of the Institute of Pacific Relations. The authors of the bibliography described the position that "characterizes Chinese economy as 'semi-feudal'" as "the viewpoint adopted by official documents of the Communist International and the Communist Party of China"; but they also indicated that Madyar, who upheld the idea of an "Asiatic Mode of Production," although officially criticized for doing so, nevertheless, had exerted in the USSR "considerable influence . . . in the field" (*Pacific Affairs*, IX, 1936: 421 ff.).

As noted above, Lattimore, in his *Inner Asian Frontiers of China* (1940), upheld the "bureaucratic" against the feudal interpretation of imperial Chinese society. And in March 1944 he still classed Stalin's concept of "feudal survivals" among the "paramount Communist theses" that "a Communist writer has . . . to maintain" when he discusses Chinese society (Lattimore, 1944: 83). Commenting on a number of recent Soviet studies on China, he objected to the "emphasis on 'feudal' thought later than the Christian era" (*ibid.:* 87) for China, and he held that "the social data are somewhat obscured by loosely used terms like 'semi-feudal' and 'feudal survivals'" (*ibid.:* 85, 87). In 1948 members of a research group directed by Lattimore published a survey of Sinkiang which applied to the typically hydraulic conditions of that area a variety of "feudal" terms: "semi-feudal agrarian relations," "the purely feudal system of the past," "the survival of feudal land" (*Far Eastern Survey*, March 10, 1948: 62 ff.). And in 1949 Lattimore himself spoke of Asia's "feudal land tenure" (Lattimore, 1949: 67). Of course, Lattimore is free to hold whatever sociohistorical ideas he wants and to change them in whatever way he deems fit. But in view of his previous statements concerning the politically motivated and scientifically harmful character of the feudal interpretation of China, he may legitimately be asked to explain his recent position in the light of his earlier appraisal.

i. In his 1951 study Childe claimed that Marx had developed his sociohistorical concepts "from historical data furnished by civilized societies—classical, medieval, and

and officials" were the controllers of the surplus in the Orient, Childe in 1953 ascribed this prerogative—the prerogative of the ruling class —to "the divine king and *a very small class of noble landowners."* [136] In the new formulation, the emphasis on private property replaced the emphasis on bureaucratic functions that Childe had clearly recognized in the past

Behind the Iron Curtain the enforced withdrawal from the theory of Asiatic society was part of an intellectual tragedy whose scope and intensity are difficult for the outsider to comprehend. A complaint made in 1942 that "for a long time" the young Soviet Orientalists had been excessively interested in the problem of the socioeconomic character of the Orient—which included the problem of "the so-called Asiatic mode of production [137]—is indicative of a trend that obviously persisted after that year. In 1950 an official report on recent Soviet Oriental studies listed as the outstanding achievement in the field "the rout of the notorious theory of the 'Asiatic mode of production.' " [138]

D. THREE FORMS OF THE BLACKOUT OF THE THEORY OF THE ASIATIC MODE OF PRODUCTION

THE fall of the theory of the Asiatic mode of production was as extraordinary as its rise. In 1748 Montesquieu opened up an area of inquiry that included Oriental despotism as an important issue. In 1848 John Stuart Mill, drawing upon the earlier classical economists, hammered out a new concept of Oriental society. And in the 1850's, Marx, who sought to predict the future of societal development by determining its past, added the idea of a specific Asiatic mode of production.

However, the managerial-bureaucratic implications of the Asiatic concept soon embarrassed its new adherent, Marx. They also increasingly disturbed his friend Engels. And they caused a complete ideological retreat in the movement which, under the banner of Marxism-Leninism, engaged in establishing a totalitarian "socialist" state. What one hundred years previously had seemed a highly illuminating idea and what, for a time, had been an accepted Marxist concept, became the "so-called" and eventually the "notorious" theory of the Asiatic mode of production.

The resulting ideological blackout has three major forms. It is

---

modern" (Childe, 1951: 10). Invoking the term "civilized," as Engels and Lenin had done under similar circumstances, Childe by-passed "barbarian" Oriental society, which certainly influenced Marx' sociohistorical thinking—and which happened also to be a major concern of Childe's own studies.

overt and official in the Communist third of the world. It is covert and limited in most private-property-based industrial societies. And it is thinly camouflaged and disturbingly successful in many non-Communist countries of the Orient.

The third condition will occupy our attention when we discuss the institutional and ideological aspects of hydraulic society in transition. The first condition is largely beyond the reach of our influence. It is part of the general intellectual blackout that results from total managerial power; and it is not substantially relieved by modifications in detail. Sundry attempts may be made to improve on the Engels of 1884, the Lenin of 1919, and the Stalin of 1939. Of course they, too, will bulwark the total managerial regime that initiates them, and they, too, will remain inconsistent. However, even a torn rag can smother a helpless victim. For all practical purposes the official blackout is sufficient to keep the people behind the Iron Curtain ideologically paralyzed.

The second condition is our most immediate concern. In the property-based industrial societies some elements of the Soviet scheme of development have been widely circulated, but the scheme in its entirety is so contrived that recognition usually leads to rejection. This being the case, critical explanation serves a vital purpose. In the rational treatment of big ideas, as in the control of big water, protective and productive action go hand in hand.

CHAPTER 10

Oriental society in transition

RECOGNITION of the peculiarity of hydraulic society is the decisive stumbling block for any unilinear scheme of development. It is crucial in the formulation of a multilinear pattern of societal evolution. And it is the starting point for any institutional analysis of the recent changes in the East.

The many students who, examining Oriental civilizations, found them to be substantially different from feudal societies often did not draw the developmental consequences suggested by their research. Others, using the comparative method, perceived hydraulic society as part of a multilinear pattern of development. John Stuart Mill was one of the first to do this conspicuously.[1] Max Weber's relevant observations, although never integrated, were global in scope and trail blazing in detail. Childe's use of Marx' ideas confused rather than refined the underlying concepts. But even in Childe's version, these concepts proved extremely productive. And the friendly reception they received indicates the need to deepen our understanding of societal structure and function ("type") and change ("development").

This state of affairs gives particular importance to the recent search for developmental regularities undertaken by archaeologists such as J. O. Brew [2] and G. R. Willey [3] and to the recent efforts to establish the principles of a multilinear development undertaken by science-philosophers such as J. S. Huxley [4] and ethnologists such as J. H. Steward.[a]

Having employed, and elaborated, the concept of multilinear development in the course of the present inquiry, I will now briefly emphasize some key aspects which may help in clarifying the position and perspective of hydraulic society in transition.

---

a. Steward, 1949: 2 ff.; *ibid.*, 1953: 318 ff.; *ibid.*, 1955: 1 ff. Willey (1953: 378) mentions as students of "developmental parallelism" on an area level: W. C. Bennet, R. Larco Hoyle, W. D. Strong, J. Bird, P. Armillas, and himself (we might add D. Collier, R. Adams, and A. Palerm). And he singles out Steward for having made "world-wide comparative evaluations."

413

A. BASIC CONCEPTS OF SOCIETAL TYPE AND DEVELOPMENT

1. SOCIETAL TYPES

a. Essential, Specific, and Nonspecific Elements of Society

SOCIETY changes in an orderly and recognizable way. This thesis implies the existence of social entities whose structure and transformation can be discerned. The present inquiry is based on this thesis. It accepts in substance John Stuart Mill's principle of the "Uniformity of Co-existence," [5] which postulates a definable relation between the major aspects of society. But it rejects the assumption concerning the necessity for coexistence.

Among the ideological, technical, organizational, and social features that appear in any given society, some are essential for the society's proper functioning, some are not. Among the essential features some are specific, some are not. A third group is neither essential nor specific.

Agromanagerial despotism is essential to hydraulic society, and as far as we know it is specific to it. The feudal system of limited and conditional service (not unconditional subservience), vassalage (not bureaucracy), and fief (not office land) is essential to the medieval societies of Europe and Japan. It occurs so rarely elsewhere that it may be considered specific to these societies.

Corvée labor is an essential element of hydraulic and feudal societies, and serfdom (the attachment of the peasant to his land or village) is essential to the helotage-based [6] societies of ancient Greece, to feudal society, and to most simple and semicomplex Oriental societies. That is, both institutions are essential to more than one type of society and specific to none.

Large government-managed works of irrigation and flood control are probably essential to all primary hydraulic societies, and they remain essential to the core areas of secondary hydraulic societies. But they are not specific to either. Hydraulic installations were built in ancient Greece and Rome, and hydraulic enterprises of various kinds appear also in postfeudal Western societies. Slavery may have been essential to the agriculture of late republican and early imperial Rome. It was compatible with, but not essential to, many other societies.

Innumerable elements of technology, custom, art, and belief occur widely and without being either essential or specific to the conditions of power, status, and property—that is, to the crucial relations within any society. These elements may fulfill an essential cultural function, human life being organized not only in societal but also in cultural "going concerns"; [7] and their interrelations within a specific societal order may color their appearance. But being compatible with several types of societies, they are more or less free floating. The ease with which certain elements of Chinese culture—such as the script, Confucianism, and architecture—flowed to Japan, and the persistence with which China's bureaucratic patterns of power, property, and class were kept out of Japanese society illustrate this point. A similar flow of societally irrelevant elements characterized the relations between classical Greece and Western Asia, between Kievan Russia and Byzantium, between Christian and Muslim Spain, and between nonhydraulic Egypt and the hydraulic areas in general. A comparison of the German part of Switzerland and Hitler Germany demonstrates strikingly that civilizations may share many technological, artistic, literary, and religious features and yet, from the standpoint of societal structure, be worlds apart. Recognition of these facts should go far in correcting the idea of a "necessary relation between *all* possible aspects of the same social organism." [b]

Evidently, then, the discrete cultural traits of a given civilization do not always clearly and surely reveal its specific societal structure. Nor is this structure necessarily clarified by the recognition of unique and specific essential institutional features. Specific occurrence is more the exception than the rule. Usually an essential element becomes specific through its dimension and/or through the type of configuration in which it occurs. The corvée is not confined to hydraulic societies; forced labor of nonslaves appears also in other societal types. It is specific in that in agrohydraulic civilizations, different from feudalism, corvée labor is imposed on the mass of the population by the state.

But specific or not, essential features are usually not numerous. Nor do they occur in many combinations. It is a basic fact of history that the key institutions of power, property, and social relations have constituted only a limited number of effective going concerns— societies.

Hydraulic society is such a going concern. Its dimension and staying power have made it prominent in the history of man. Yet it is only one among several types of stratified societies that emerged prior to the rise of the modern industrial world. A brief glance at these other types will aid us in defining more clearly the peculiarity of hydraulic society.

b. Comte, approvingly quoted by Mill, 1947: 599, cf. 600 (italics mine). For a one-sidedly economic version of the same thesis see Marx, 1939: 27.

b. Pre-industrial Stratified Societies

i. PASTORAL SOCIETY

STATE-CENTERED hydraulic societies may have preceded all other stratified civilizations; but in all probability the early hydraulic societies were soon confronted by groups which combined nonhydraulic farming with extensive stock raising and which were dominated by tribal aristocracies. The Aryan conquerors of India apparently were semipastoralists of this kind.[8]

However, it was only after the first great cavalry revolution, when man learned to ride the horse and the camel, that he gained easy access to the steppe and established powerful societies based essentially on herding. Interacting with hydraulic and nonhydraulic sedentary neighbors, stratified pastoralists [c] affected the course of history greatly, persisting mainly in Inner Asia and the Near East until modern times.[d]

ii. SEVERAL TYPES OF ANCIENT SOCIETIES

THE higher agrarian civilizations of Greece and Rome, which existed side by side with the self-perpetuating East for almost a millennium,

c. We cannot discuss here the possible subtypes of stratified pastoral societies. Max Weber's stress upon the social peculiarities of "small cattle pastoralism" as practiced by the early Jews (Weber, RS, III: 44 ff.) indicates the possibility of at least one subdivision.

d. Why did Marx omit Mill's stratified pastoral societies from his list of "progressive epochs in the economic system of society"? (see Marx, 1921: lvi). As explained in Chap. 9, above, Marx did not, in this context, view "progress" in terms of an actual historical development; and Plekhanov's efforts to correct Marx on this point therefore sought to remove an obstacle that was not there (Plekhanov, FPM: 50). Reminiscent in a way of Hegel's "worlds," which differed from each other in the degree of freedom they enjoyed and which did not constitute a developmental sequence, Marx set up a series of "antagonistic" societies, which, although different with respect to the increase and importance of private property, also did not constitute a developmental sequence. The despotic states of Asiatic society controlled the villages, and they did not break up their communal landed property (Marx, 1939: 376 ff., 380, 383). The societies of Greece and Rome made the first major attempts to establish private property, but they also preserved a part of the communally held landed property as *ager publicus* (ibid.: 378 f., 380, 382). Medieval ("feudal") society went further in reducing communal property (ibid.: 380 ff., 399 ff.). And in modern "bourgeois" society private ownership of the means of production prevails completely (ibid.: 375, 402 ff.).

Marx' famous scheme did not take into account the fact, of which he later became aware (cf. Marx, DK, III, Pt. 1: 318), that certain Asiatic societies, such as China, abolished the communal system of land tenure. Moreover, it is contrived with regard to "ancient" and feudal land tenure. The inclusion of another stratified and property-based conformation, pastoral society, would have made his typology even more artificial.

were neither hydraulic nor feudal. Nor can they be subsumed under a single major societal type, which was penetrated and, finally, ruined by slave labor.

A well-integrated upper stratum maintained its hegemony in Crete, Sparta, Thessaly, and also, under different conditions, in Rome, while in the Greek city states of the Athenian type loosely associated aristocracies eventually lost their political dominance. In Sparta native serfs tilled the fields for their alien masters, and the free peasants of Rome were ultimately, and largely, replaced by slaves. Conversely, in the city states of the Athenian type, farming remained predominantly in the hands of free peasants, and the increase of slave labor primarily affected urban industry.[9]

Without trying to disentangle all the threads of this institutional tissue, we are probably safe in saying that prior to the spread of Hellenism, the civilizations of Greece and Rome—and for that matter Spain and France—embraced more than a single societal type. Among them the helotage-based Spartan type is noteworthy for both the stability of its over-all pattern and the insignificance of slave labor.[10]

iii. FEUDAL SOCIETY

THE ancient societies of Greece and Rome, whatever their original form, were eventually Orientalized. The agrarian societies of Europe and Japan were not. In fact, these latter developed specific feudal relations which, on the agrarian level, are unmatched both in their multicenteredness and in their capacity for growth. It was this feudal order that led to a limping and multicentered type of absolutism and, eventually, to multicentered and private-property-based industrial society.

The similarities between the feudal civilizations of Europe and Japan are evident. In both cases there existed, alongside and below the sovereign, numerous lords (vassals) who rendered only limited and conditional services and who were not members of a bureaucratic state apparatus. But the two institutional configurations were not identical. Along the western flank of the Eurasian continent agriculture, being based on rainfall, was extensive, and it was conducive to a manorial economy that gave rise to centers of large-scale farming. Along the eastern flank farming, being based on irrigation, was intensive and definitely favored small-scale production. Furthermore, the independent Church and the guild cities of Europe had no parallel in Japan.

Thus we find in Japan and in the early phase of Medieval Europe a simpler form of feudal society in which the ruler shared societal leadership exclusively with his vassals. In Europe this simpler form gave birth to a more complex form in which the ruler had to reckon with a powerful corporated clergy and a variety of burgher associations.

These two variants do not exhaust the subtypes of feudal society. In Medieval Sweden and Kievan Russia the decisive social relations, as expressed in feudal investiture and enfeoffment, never seem to have matured. We may therefore view them as belonging to a third subtype: "marginal" feudal society.

iv. UNWIELDY HYDRAULIC SOCIETY

HYDRAULIC society surpasses all other stratified pre-industrial societies in duration, extent, and the number of persons dominated. This may largely explain why it comprises so many subtypes. Taxonomically speaking, hydraulic society is an unwieldy giant. Should we not then treat certain of its major subtypes as discrete major societal conformations?

Such a decision would be justified if we were faced with basic structural differences in social relations and societal leadership. However, no such differences can be demonstrated, since agromanagerial despotism and a monopoly bureaucracy prevail in all known subtypes of the hydraulic world. In consequence, arbitrary "splitting" would obscure the crucial sociohistorical fact that hydraulic society dwarfed all other agrarian societies in dimension and institutional diversity.

Biological taxonomists, faced with similar problems, have refused "to split up big genera simply because they contain a larger number of species than some other genera and may look 'unbalanced' " or "unwieldy." Knowing that the biological world is characterized by inequality, they feel that scientific "classification should reflect this inequality faithfully." [11]

v. RESIDUAL STRATIFIED PRE-INDUSTRIAL SOCIETIES

THE problem of taxonomical residues, another concern of biotaxonomy, is also suggestive for our inquiry. "It is estimated that less than 2 per cent of the total number of species of birds of the entire world remain still unknown." [12] This optimum is reached only by "a few genera of mammals, butterflies, beetles, mollusks and so forth." [13] Most biologists consider their investigations well advanced when they can establish, in the field of their researches, the major outlines of structure (system) and change (evolution).

Taking the stratified pre-industrial civilizations in their entirety how many specific societies can be discerned? Assuming that Greek and Roman antiquity embraced at least two types, we arrive at a minimum of five such conformations. And there is good reason to believe that there are others. The nonhydraulic parts of the "classical" and preclassical Mediterranean could well be further scrutinized. So could certain neglected areas of Asia, Africa, the Pacific Islands, and America.

But while making full allowance for possible new disclosures, we must warn against overrating their historical significance. The records of the past and present-day observations indicate that above the level of primitive tribal life and below the level of modern industrial society, the great majority of all human beings lived in already identified institutional settings—in stratified pastoral societies, in hydraulic societies, in helotage-, free peasant-, or slavery-based nonfeudal societies, or in feudal societies.

2. SOCIETAL CHANGES

a. Forms

THE fate of these different types of societies is instructive in several ways. As stated above, the stratified pastoral societies underwent a variety of experiences. Some raised crops; some became predominantly agricultural. This may well have been the origin of the early Greek tribal aristocracies, and it manifestly was the background of Germanic tribal society. Other herding groups were in contact with hydraulic civilizations. Some merged with them completely, some, after a period of conquest or subjugation, withdrew to the steppe. Some, without an "Oriental" interlude, persisted in their semi-arid grasslands, remaining in a state of developmental stagnation, until under the influence of modern neighbor societies they began to lose their institutional identity.

The higher agrarian societies of ancient Greece and Rome attacked the Oriental world. But while their conquests brought material advantages to many of their citizens and a great increase in power to a few, the price paid was the general Orientalization of their society. This transformation offers a striking example of "diversive" (*externally* conditioned) as juxtaposed to "developmental" (*internally* conditioned) [14] change.

Feudal society was sufficiently strong to hold its own against hydraulic society. It was sufficiently open to initiate a commercial and manufacturing way of life. Among higher civilizations it is the outstanding case of societal development.

Hydraulic society is the outstanding case of societal stagnation. Probably originating in several ways [15] and under favorable circumstances developing semicomplex and complex patterns of property and social stratification, hydraulic society did not abandon its basic structures except under the impact of *external* forces.

b. Values

THESE facts show that the morphology of societal change is far from simple. They also show that behind the problems of form lie crucial problems of value which a naive, or politically motivated, developmental optimism is unable or unwilling to see.

Societal change is not identical with development. Development, the transformation effected essentially by internal forces, is only one form of societal change. Equally important is diversive change, the transformation effected essentially by external forces.

Moreover, neither developmental nor diversive change is necessarily progressive: neither necessarily improves the condition of man. Man's control over nature is an enormously significant factor in civilization; but as a criterion of progress it must be examined together with man's relation to his fellow men and to his own convictions (secular and religious). The three relations interlock, and any two are as likely to clash as to harmonize.

The wishful thinker may be frightened by such conflicts. The realist, who accepts tragedy as an inevitable element of life, will accept the possibility of diverse value developments in diverse historical circumstances. He will understand that simultaneous progress in all three relations is less frequent than legend has it and that from the standpoint of human values development may be progressive, ambivalent, or outright retrogressive. To the technologist the emergence of Western absolutism and early industrialism will appear spectacularly progressive. In our opinion this development probably destroyed as many values as it created. To the apologist of Soviet rule the diversive change that laid the groundwork for Muscovite despotism will appear as predominantly progressive.[16] In terms of human values it was definitely retrogressive.

Processes that transform a given society into a society of a different type can be considered *primary* societal changes. For obvious reasons their number is limited. *Secondary* societal changes may produce a new subtype of the same over-all conformation; or they may be circular, leading eventually to the restoration of the original order or suborder. They may—but they need not—be cathartic (regenerative). Certain dynastic changes and many institutional reforms have been of this kind.

Restorative developments occur in all institutional conformations. They are particularly frequent in societies that perpetuate themselves over long periods of time. Above the level of primitive civilizations, hydraulic society therefore offers the richest opportunities for studying societal stagnation and circular change.

B. HYDRAULIC SOCIETY IN TRANSITION

1. Four Aspects of the Self-perpetuation of Hydraulic Society

a. The Potential for Institutional and Cultural Growth

THE power nuclei of hydraulic society surpassed all other agrarian commonwealths in their capacity for subduing and controlling outlying areas. After a local "formative" period and where opportunity permitted, these nuclei assumed territorial or national dimensions. Under particularly favorable conditions, territorial "florescence" was followed by "imperial" expansion and "fusion." [a] Hydraulic society enduring over millennia had unique opportunities to exhaust the creative potential of each of these situations. The culture history of hydraulic civilization shows how thoroughly these opportunities were realized.

The growth in the magnitude of a sociocultural unit, however, does not necessarily involve a corresponding institutional and cultural growth. Loose interaction between numerous independent units proves more stimulating than island- or oasis-like isolation. It also proves more stimulating than imperial fusion, which tends to give the initiative for experiment and change to a single center. This probably accounts for the fact that the foremost representatives of hydraulic civilization generally achieved the peak of their creativeness when they were part of a cluster of loosely related territorial states.

Virtually all great Chinese ideas on the "Way" (tao), on society, government, human relations, warfare, and historiography, crystallized during the classical period of the territorial states and at the beginning of the imperial period. The establishment of the examination system and the psychologically slanted reformulation of Con-

---

a. See Wittfogel, 1955: 47 ff. The terms "formative," "florescence," and "empire" have recently been used to distinguish "periods" in the development of societies ("culture types"). A "formative" period on a local scale may be followed by a "florescent" or "classical" period (growth and maturation on a regional or territorial scale), and this eventually by a period of interarea expansion: "Empire" or "Fusion" (see Steward, 1949: 7 ff.; *ibid.*, 1953: 323).

fucianism followed the reunification of the empire, the transfer
of the economic center to the Yangtze Valley, and the building of an
artificial Nile, the Grand Canal.[1] Other significant changes occurred
during later periods of imperial China in the field of the drama and
the popular novel; but they were partly due to a new influence, the
complete subjugation of China by two "barbarian" conquest dynasties. And none of them shook the Confucian foundation of Chinese
thought.

The climax of creative expression in India is similarly located.
Religion, statecraft, law, and family patterns originated and reached
their "classical" maturity either when India was a network of independent states or during the early phase of imperial unification.

The Arab-dominated conquest societies of the Near East began
on an empire-like level. In this case most of the great ideas concerned with law, statecraft, and man's fate were formulated during
the first and early middle periods of Islamic society.

b. Stagnation, Epigonism, and Retrogression

WITHIN a given framework, creative change does not continue indefinitely. The growth potential of a society varies with its natural
and cultural setting, but when the possibilities for development
and differentiation have in great part been realized, the creative
process tends to slow down. Maturation becomes stagnation. And
given time, stagnation results in stereotyped repetition (epigonism)
or outright retrogression. New conquests and territorial expansions
favor acculturation. But the ensuing changes do not necessarily alter
the existing pattern of society and culture. Eventually they also will
yield to stagnation, epigonism, and retrogression.

The trend toward epigonism and retrogression may merge—and
in the Oriental conquest societies of the Old World it did merge
—with a trend toward reduced hydraulic intensity and increased
personal restriction. In terms of managerial action, personal freedom,
and cultural creativeness, most hydraulic societies of the late "Empire" period probably operated on a level lower than that reached
during the days of regional and early "Empire" florescence.

c. The Staying-Power of Hydraulic Society

BUT whether the institutional and cultural level was lowered or
whether periodically regenerative changes restored earlier "classical"
conditions, hydraulic society, as an institutional configuration, persisted. Dominated by its monopoly bureaucracy, it continued to
muster the technical and intellectual skills necessary to its perpetua-

tion. Its officials frequently possessed learning and subtlety. Its peasants grew their crops with more care than did the serfs of Europe,[b]
and its artisans handled the materials of their crafts with the greatest
refinement. These groups responded to a variety of incentives, but
they did not demand political independence or a popular form of
government.

Nor did the irrational features of hydraulic despotism prevent the
monopoly bureaucracy from perpetuating itself. Measured by the
people's rationality standard, an apparatus state may be overorganized
economically. It may be overdefended militarily. And its masters
may be overprotected police-wise. But as long as the regime maintains
the masters' rationality minimum, it will continue as a going concern. And it will hold its own against open societies with a much
higher rationality coefficient as long as its armed forces are a match
for theirs.

d. Societal Change Dependent on External Influence

ONE important developmental consequence of this fact has already
been discussed. Since the agrarian monopoly bureaucracy prevented
hydraulic society of and by itself from developing a multicentered
type of society, it is clear that when such a transformation occurred,
it occurred only through the direct or indirect influence of external
forces.

Western Rome was crushed by tribal invaders from the north, and
Moorish Spain fell to the feudal warriors of the Iberian Peninsula.
In both cases, internal crisis facilitated the institutional victory of
the aggressors. In Byzantium the European attackers, who were strong
enough to overthrow the decaying absolutist regime, were too weak
to initiate a multicentered order with corporated barons, powerful
guild cities, and an independent Church, such as existed at that time
in their feudal homelands. The external nonhydraulic forces had to
penetrate hydraulic society thoroughly in order to accomplish a full
diverse transformation.

2. RECENT PATTERNS OF EXTERNAL INFLUENCE

DID the impact of the commercial and industrial West produce such
a transformation? John Stuart Mill was convinced that this would be
the case. The "civilized [industrial] nations" [2] would make "all other
countries" follow the course they had taken [3] in technology and
material prosperity, personal security, and voluntary cooperation.[4]

b. Japanese farming, based on small-scale irrigation and stimulated by the Chinese
example, was, during the feudal period, as intensive as Chinese farming.

Marx also was convinced that in such colonial countries as India,
"England has to fulfill a double mission . . . one destructive, the
other regenerating—the annihilation of old Asiatic society and the
laying the material foundations of Western society in Asia." [5] And
even if he expected the Indians to reap "the fruits of the new elements
of society" only after they had attained freedom through labor rule
in Great Britain or through their own efforts,[6] he spoke enthusiastically of the newly introduced Western features, mentioning especially political unity, modern communications (telegraph, railways,
steamships), a Western-trained army, a free press, private landownership,[c] and a class of modern civil servants.[7]

With regard to Tsarist Russia he was still more optimistic. Although well aware of Russia's Oriental heritage, he nevertheless
believed it possible that Russia might cross "the threshold of the
capitalist system" and then "submit to the implacable laws of such
a system, like the other Western nations." [8]

Mill and Marx were expressing opinions that many of their contemporaries shared. But manifestly they did not know how their
predictions would be fulfilled. To the best of my knowledge, Mill
did not elaborate on his statement of 1848; and Marx, who in the
50's presented the British-promoted dissolution of India's old rural
order as a *fait accompli* and "the only social revolution ever heard
of in Asia," [9] noted in Volume 3 of *Das Kapital* that this dissolution
was proceeding "only very slowly (*nur sehr allmählich*)." [10] To be
sure, in the meantime much has happened in the West as well as in
the East, and much has been said about the "changing" (and the
"unchanging") Orient. The contrived interpretations of events given
by the Communist International do not mean that a truly scientific
analysis is not needed. Such an analysis is very much needed, since
the issues involved are both complex and momentous.

a. Patterns of Interrelation

To begin with, present-day developments in the hydraulic world
follow no single pattern. Different types of interrelation with the
West and different conditions within both the influencing and the
influenced side inevitably affect the result. Thus on the basis of different intensities of cultural contact and different degrees of military
aggression and political control we may distinguish at least four pat-

---

c. Marx called the *zamindar* and *riotwar* forms of land tenure, which the British
had created, "abominable"; but he still welcomed them as "two distinct forms of private property in land—the great desideratum of Asiatic society" (Marx, NYDT, August
8, 1853).

terns of interrelations between the commercial and industrial West and various countries of the Oriental world.

Type I: Aloof independence (representative: Thailand).[d] Thailand suffered only minor military defeats at the hands of the West; and there was no direct, and little indirect, Western interference in the country's internal affairs. Nor was there, until recently, much Western contact of any kind. In consequence, Thailand remained an independent and more or less aloof hydraulic society, which was free to adopt or disregard Western institutions and culture.

Type II: Proximity and independence (foremost representative: Russia). Russia was geographically and culturally close to Western Europe. But in contrast to Ottoman Turkey, its policy was not decisively influenced by foreign "councils"; and in contrast to China, its major cities were not compelled to tolerate foreign settlements. Three disastrous military events—the Crimean War, the war against Japan, and World War I—shook Russia deeply, but they did not force it into a colonial or "semi-colonial" position. A minimum of direct foreign interference was combined with a maximum of peaceful interaction.

Type III: Complete and simple dependency (outstanding representatives: Mexico, Peru, Indonesia, and India). All these countries suffered complete military defeat at the hands of the West, which led to their outright political subjugation (colonization).

Type IV: Limited and multiple dependency (major representatives: Ottoman Turkey and China). Both countries suffered severe military defeats at the hands of the West, and both were subjected to substantial political and economic interference from several foreign powers. But the Turkish and Chinese governments preserved their armies, and although under great pressure from the outside, they still made policy decisions.

b. The Influencing Side

On the cultural level, diffusion was by no means a one-way process. In the 19th and early 20th centuries Russian literature had a great fascination for the Western world. And long before Turgeniev, Dostoievsky, and Tolstoy, Islamic architecture and poetry and Indian and Chinese philosophy were admired and studied in far-away Western lands. However, in the spheres of technology, government, property, and class, influences moved essentially in one direction, and hydraulic society was definitely on the receiving end.

But these influences were neither identical nor static. In the 16th

d. Prior to 1939 called "Siam."

century, when the Spaniards seized "the Americas," Europe had just outgrown the feudal way of life, and absolutist governments were consolidating themselves throughout the continent. In the 17th century, when the Dutch and English were spreading their domination in South Asia, capitalist elites became socially significant in a few economically advanced countries. But it was only during the 18th and 19th centuries that the new bourgeois middle class in its entirety achieved sociopolitical prominence and that representative government came to prevail in the Western world.

This timetable, which by necessity is simplified, throws light on the colonial history of three major areas of hydraulic society. The conquest of the Americas was organized, not by private merchant adventurers, but by an absolutist government, which was enormously strengthened by its war against the Moors and by its fiscal control of the Spanish sheep-herding economy. The colonization of Indonesia and India was accomplished by small groups of privileged businessmen, whose government-supported and quasigovernmental East India companies came closer to representing a genuine monopoly capitalism than certain recent formations that have been thus designated.

The Dutch East India Company was dissolved in 1798; and Dutch colonial policy was liberalized after the revolutions of 1848, which to some extent shifted the center of gravity also in Dutch society.[11] The British East India Company lost its monopoly in India in 1813 (after the Napoleonic Wars) and its monopoly of the China trade in 1833 (after the passing of the Reform Bill). Spain's American empire came to an end before the constitutional development of the 19th century made itself felt in the Iberian Peninsula. Yet it is worth noting that the later phase of Spanish absolutism, especially the reign of Charles III (1749–88), saw an encouragement of private enterprise in the form of companies, which until then had played no role in Spain.[12]

In all these instances Western impact upon a traditionally hydraulic civilization involved direct colonial domination. In others, several commercial and manufacturing powers competed for the control of an economically attractive Oriental territory. Under such circumstances, the relation between the changing conditions in the industrial camp and the form and intensity of the interference are complex. Nevertheless, certain causal relations can be established. It was only after the Industrial Revolution that the West was able to force an open-door policy upon the remote Chinese empire; and it was only from the second half of the 19th century on, that Western advisors seriously suggested constitutional and representative governments in Turkey and China.

c. Institutional Differences in the Target Societies

As demonstrated throughout our inquiry, conditions also varied greatly in the hydraulic countries.

In Mexico hydraulic enterprises were of the "Loose 2" type.[13] In Turkey the metropolis gradually lost control over its hydraulic provinces. Kievan Russia had no agrohydraulic enterprises; and the Tatar Yoke produced no change in this respect. In pre-Spanish Peru and in Siam large-scale private native trade played no role; in Indonesia and Ottoman Turkey it was extremely limited. In Muscovite Russia businessmen other than bureaucratic capitalists were greatly restricted. In Aztec Mexico independent commerce flourished, and in China it assumed large proportions.

In some of these countries there were substantial groups which, given a chance, could have been expected to evolve into a modern middle class. And in some there existed forms of private landownership which, under the impact of private-property-based industrial society, could also have been expected to further the growth of a modern multicentered society. In what manner and to what extent were these possibilities realized?

3. SOCIETAL RESULTS

TRACING the results of the recent Western impact, we need not deal here at length with Thailand.[e] Suffice it to say that despite a number of technical and political innovations, an independent and aloof Thailand has thus far developed neither an indigenous middle class [f] nor a genuinely representative system of government.

a. Russia

LIKE Thailand, Russia remained politically free, but it suffered much more seriously from military attacks. Like the Chinese mandarins, the masters of Russian society were greatly disturbed by the defeats of their armies, but being closer to the West, they were quicker to comprehend the institutional and cultural basis of its military and technical strength. They, therefore, promoted Western forms of strong property, private enterprise, public discussion, and

e. For obvious reasons, we must in the present context refrain altogether from discussing the development of Japan. Never having been hydraulic, Japan speedily evolved from a "simple" feudal order into a modern multicentered industrial society.

f. The Chinese business community, which has many features of an incipient middle class, is increasingly excluded from Thailand's economic life. Unless the present trend is reversed, this group will be prevented from playing the developmental role for which it is otherwise well prepared.

local self-government. They introduced these institutions grudgingly —not because they wanted them to prevail but because they deemed them necessary and susceptible to continued control.

The deficiences of the emancipation of the serfs have already been discussed.[14] The *zemstvos*, elected bodies of local self-government, were, after a brief bloom (1864–66), severely restricted.[15] But even in their crippled form they wielded much more power than the Beggars' Democracies of hydraulic despotism. Count Witte was entirely justified in asserting that autocracy and the *zemstvos* could not coexist for any considerable length of time.[g]

To be sure, the absolutist bureaucracy remained supreme. But its prestige was weakened by the Turkish war of 1877–78,[16] and it was deeply shaken by the disasters of the Russo-Japanese War of 1904–05.

State control and oppressive taxation severely handicapped the growth of a modern economy.[17] But private property now became secure, and private enterprise, which prior to the middle of the 19th century was already significant in certain light industries,[18] now advanced vigorously on many fronts.

Between 1893 and 1908, 2,965 million rubles of Russian capital were invested in industry as compared to 874 million rubles of foreign capital.[19] By 1916–17 government-directed foreign capital prevailed almost completely in mining; but Russian capital was equally strong, or prevailed, in most other branches of industry. In the chemical industry it constituted 50 per cent of all capital, in metal smelting and processing 58 per cent, in wood processing 63 per cent, and in textiles 72 per cent.[20] The State Bank remained the supreme master of the credit system; but many private banks came into existence. Private banks increased their own capital plus deposits from 1,289 million rubles in 1909 to 3,375 million rubles in 1913.[21]

This expansion of Russia's modern economy was accomplished not with forced labor and spectacular police terror but with an increasingly free working class and in an atmosphere of receding despotism. Take the country's heavy industry: during the two decades before World War I "the output of coal in the Russian Empire increased fourfold, and if we exclude Poland, sixfold."[22] From 1893 to 1913 the output of copper "multiplied nearly nine times."[23] Between 1890 and 1913 the output of iron within the empire increased six times; in the crucial industrial centers of South Russia it increased "twentyfold."[24] Or take light industry: in 1913 the spindles in the cotton industry "were two and a half times as numerous, the amount

g. Florinsky, 1953, II: 900; cf. Mavor, 1928: 30. Tsar Nicolas II was therefore right when he harshly rebuked the representatives of the *zemstvos* for fostering "*senseless dreams* of . . . sharing in the conduct of internal affairs" (see Birkett, 1918: 488 ff.).

of raw cotton employed three times as great, and the amount of cotton yarn produced two and a half times as great as in 1890." [25]

Russia's first revolution brought about important changes in the political sphere. The Tsar's manifesto of October 1905, although upholding the principle of absolutist power, granted significant constitutional checks and balances. Max Weber, who was deeply aware of the lack of decisive Western phases of development in Russia [26] and who stressed the "Asiatic" or "Mongol" spirit of the Tsarist regime,[h] recognized clearly the enormous advance made by the introduction of even a limited constitution.[i] And indeed, a parliament that could influence the budget and openly criticize the government, political parties that could appeal to the population, a press that enjoyed almost complete freedom of speech,[27] an educational system that was rapidly expanding,[j] commoners who could organize over ten million persons in cooperatives,[28] and workers and other employees who, while prevented from maintaining free trade unions, could share in the administration of health insurance funds [29]—these developments taken together presented a serious challenge to the old single-centered society.

After 1905 Russia's anti-absolutist forces were still not strong enough to establish an open, multicentered society by their own efforts. But when World War I paralyzed the Tsarist army, these forces were sufficiently strong to establish in the spring of 1917 a short-lived but genuinely anti-absolutist and democratic government.

h. Weber spoke of the "cunning Mongol deceit" of the Tsarist bureaucracy (Weber, 1906: 249) and of the regime's "veritable Mongol deceit" (*ibid.:* 394). He criticized the Tsarist police for employing "the most tricky means of the most cunning Asiatic deceit" (*ibid.:* 396).

i. Weber used the not altogether appropriate designation, "pseudoconstitution" (Weber, 1906: 249).

j. Like other countries that had entered the Industrial Age, Russia energetically fostered general education. In 1874, out of one hundred army recruits 21.4 per cent are said to have been literate, in 1894 37.8 per cent, in 1904 55.5 per cent, and in 1914 67.8 per cent. In 1918 among industrial workers aged twenty or below, 77.1 per cent were listed as literate; among those between thirty and thirty-five, 64.8 per cent; and among those over fifty 43.4 per cent (Timasheff, 1946: 35). The high literacy rate of the youngest workers reflects the inauguration by law in 1908 of general secondary education. On the basis of this law almost all children should have been attending school by 1922 (Florinsky, 1953, II: 1237). Florinsky states that progress was slower than anticipated; but he too considers "the modernization and expansion of the school system" impressive (*ibid.:* 1237, 1232). According to the last prerevolutionary estimate, 78 per cent of all Russians were expected to be literate by the late 1930's (Timasheff, 1946: 34, 313). War and revolution retarded performance, but subsequent policy speeded things to some degree. The Soviet census of 1939 asserts that literacy at this time had reached 81.1 per cent (*ibid.:* 314).

b. Colonized Hydraulic Countries

THE Russian experience shows that even in an independent country ruled by a despotic bureaucracy, under favorable international conditions, the germs of a multicentered society may grow fast. This was not the case in the hydraulic areas that, as colonies, fell completely under the sway of Western powers. The Spanish, Dutch, and English colonizers, and also the Portuguese and French, whose ventures we shall not pursue, attempted no thorough modernization of their Oriental possessions. Congruent with their special interests, they introduced Western institutions in a selective and limited way.

The reasons for this are not hard to find. The major areas in hydraulic civilization, being densely populated and for the most part located in tropical and subtropical regions, offered little opportunity for a mass immigration of Europeans. Consequently the conquerors were usually content to establish in their hydraulic colonies a strong administrative apparatus, plus whatever public or private arrangements seemed expedient for economic exploitation.

The Spaniards took this course in the agromanagerial areas of America.[k] The Dutch in Indonesia and the British in India acted similarly. The result was a system of human relations which, despite its differences from traditional hydraulic society, was far from being a replica of Spain, Holland, or England.

Whether the colonizers perpetuated the traditional rural order in a crippled form, as did the Spaniards in Peru and Mexico, whether they left it practically intact, as did the Dutch in Indonesia, or whether they converted communal landholdings into private property, as did the British in India, the administrative masters kept the villages politically impotent. And whether they discarded the native merchants (Mexico and Java), whether they prevented their rise (Peru), or whether they tolerated them (India), the new overlords did little to alter the single-centered society which they had inherited.

Linked to nonhydraulic absolutist or aristocratic regimes, the colonial governments were a curious mixture of Oriental and Occidental absolutism. They were this, despite—or perhaps, to some extent, because of—their continued use of native dignitaries (princes, *caciques, curacas*), who with certain modifications perpetuated long-established agromanagerial patterns of political, social, and religious control.

k. And also in the nonhydraulic regions. The determination of policy at the center and the excessive strength of the state in the colonial societies in these regions is largely responsible for the continued prominence of the government bureaucracy and for the extraordinary power of its coercive branch, the army.

This roughly was the state of affairs up to the Industrial Revolution, which, in Europe, stimulated the spread of representative governments and which also affected the colonial regimes—where such regimes persisted. The qualification is significant, for India remained a colony until 1949, whereas Spain's American possessions gained their independence shortly after the Napoleonic era.

In postcolonial Mexico and Peru, parliamentary republics were speedily set up. But the innovations benefited primarily the bureaucracy, and still more the army, which in these countries, as in other former Spanish colonies, exerted extraordinary political and economic power.

In Indonesia and India administration was in the hands of a civil service that reflected changing social and political conditions in Holland and England. In both countries popular control over the government increased, and the peculiarities of colonial rule notwithstanding, this fact also influenced the attitudes of the colonial officials toward the native populations. True, the Dutch admitted Indonesians to the regular civil service only in the 20th century,[30] and even then they were reluctant to put them in places of authority. Nevertheless, on the eve of World War II, Indonesians occupied 60.6 per cent of all lower-middle, 38 per cent of all middle, and 6.4 per cent of all higher government positions.[31]

In India a like trend began much earlier and went considerably further. A year after the passage of the Reform Bill, which did so much to strengthen the English middle class, offices in the Indian civil service were opened to all Indians, "irrespective of caste, creed, or race." [32] The Act of 1833 was not much more than a declaration of principle, but subsequent events lent it substance. The British maintained their control over the central government,[33] but they increased Indian authority over the local and provincial administrations until, in 1935, the provinces were given complete self-government.[34]

An ever-larger number of Indians and Indonesians went to Europe to study. Democratic procedures were therefore well known in India and Indonesia before the two countries gained their independence. Indeed the first acts of the new governments showed them eager to promote a parliamentary government, political parties, and free associations of workers, businessmen, peasants, and intellectuals.

What is the developmental meaning of all this? To what extent do the imperfect democracies of Mexico and Peru and the technically advanced democracies of India and Indonesia reveal the rise of new forces that aim at replacing their old single-centered societies with a genuinely multicentered system of human relations?

In Mexico and Peru, Spanish colonial rule did not—except during a short interlude—encourage the growth of private enterprise or the rise of a modern middle class. The independent republics remained governmentally top-heavy. In Mexico the potentials of power and wealth inherent in a bureaucratic or military career further retarded, although they did not block, the spread of independent private enterprise. In Peru the Indians had much less opportunity to engage in middle-class activities than in Mexico. Yet the country's hydraulic and managerial past did not prevent the emergence of large private enterprises in agriculture and industry. Peru's entrepreneurial upper class was (and is) strongly interlinked with foreign capital. And while some of its members profit from close attachment to the government, the group as a whole cannot be viewed as an Andean variant of bureaucratic capitalism.[m]

The Inca empire had no merchant class when the Spaniards came. In Mexico the Spaniards seem to have wiped out the prominent *pochteca* merchants. The Portuguese and their successors, the Dutch, "suppressed Javanese commerce"; and native "merchants and ship-builders lost their occupation." [35] Thereafter, the Dutch controlled the bulk of big enterprise in Indonesia; and they permitted a group of "Oriental foreigners," the Chinese, to operate on an intermediate level as traders and money lenders. When Indonesia became free, the Dutch were eliminated as administrators and in large part also as businessmen. The Chinese remained distrusted outsiders.[n] And in their own ranks the Indonesians never evolved a sizable industrial, commercial, or banking middle class that could close the gap between the large peasant population and the educated, and mainly bureaucratic, elite.[36] Thus in Indonesia a democratic shell covers a societal structure that is much closer to the single-centered hydraulic patterns of the past than to a modern multicentered industrial society.

The Indian development differs from the Indonesian development in several significant respects. Prior to the arrival of the British, some capitalist enterprise existed in India—probably not so much as is suggested by recent legend [37] but not so little as is claimed by Bernier, who measured Mogul India by Occidental standards. While the British crippled indigenous business activities, they did not forbid them. During the colonial period Indian businessmen organized a number

m. For a comprehensive study of the uneven growth of a modern middle class in the various parts of modern Latin America, see Crevenna, *MECM: passim*.

n. In Indonesia, as in Thailand and other countries of Southeast Asia, there is a substantial Chinese business community. But as in Thailand, the Chinese capitalists of Indonesia are considered aliens; and for this reason they have been unable to fulfill the political functions of a recognized indigenous middle class (see Furnivall, 1944: 414; Kahin, 1952: 28, 475).

of finishing industries, especially cotton, and certain heavy industries, especially steel,[38] and by the time India gained its independence the private sector had increased considerably. However, according to all estimates, this sector—and the modern middle class which reflects its growth—is still small.

Of course, the British also introduced private ownership of land. But contrary to Marx' expectation, this reform did little to aid the growth of Western society in India. Private landownership prevailed in a few hydraulic societies, and was present in lesser degree in many It tended to lead to bureaucratic and absentee landlordism.[39] In general the British recognized the erstwhile holders of office land, the *jagidars,* as landowners. In certain regions they made the previous tax collectors, the *zamindars,* the owners of the lands over which they had exercised fiscal jurisdiction, and in many others they converted the peasant occupiers, the *ryotwari,* into full owners of the land they cultivated. But a land reform that does not protect the peasant owners by appropriate educational, political, and economic measures, especially in the sphere of credit, tends to benefit them only temporarily. The new Indian peasant owners soon fell prey to the money lender. And eventually many were forced to sell their land to an official, *zamindar,* or other person of wealth, who, as an absentee landlord, took half, or more than half, of the crop as rent. In 1950 "about 80 per cent of the land [was] in the hands of absentee landlords, or in other words four-fifths of the land [was] cultivated by people who do not own it." [40] Instead of Westernizing the Indian villages, the British imposed on them one of the worst features of Oriental land tenure: bureaucratic and absentee landlordism.

c. Semidependent ("Semicolonial") Countries

THE recent history of the Near East (roughly the orbit of the former Turkish empire) and of the continental Far East (China) reveals the development of hydraulic countries which, although not colonized, were conspicuously under pressure from the industrial West. In both cases several great powers struggled for control, but none was sufficiently strong to establish its hegemony. In both cases the negative effects of Western interference, which were grave, were to some extent mitigated by the fact that the target areas remained independent and that their governments played an active role in modernizing their countries.

In the Near East a series of military defeats weakened the authority of Constantinople over the Turkish provinces where local masters were seeking to buttress their position, first by abolishing the privileges of such government-attached functionaries as tax collectors and holders of office land, and second by assigning the bulk of the land to those who were tilling it. As in India, many poorly equipped, poorly educated, and poorly organized peasants were soon compelled to sell their newly acquired property to persons of wealth: former tax collectors, civil and military serving men, village sheiks,[41] and rich townsmen with loose or no government ties.

As a result of this process, bureaucratic and absentee landlordism has prevailed until today in Egypt, Syria, Iraq, Lebanon, and other parts of the Near East.[o] And the introduction of certain technical innovations went hand in hand with the perpetuation of quasihydraulic patterns of society that did little to encourage the growth of a modern middle or laboring class or a literate and politically organized peasantry.

The core area of Ottoman power, Anatolia, had a different history. More than the outlying provinces, which gradually broke away, the region was subjected to serious and direct interference from the Great Powers. The Capitulations, which gave privileged foreigners judicial and economic extraterritoriality, were particularly apparent in Constantinople, where most of the beneficiaries lived. Together with the foreign administration of Turkey's debts and the International Council, they did much to lower the country's economy and international prestige.[42]

But the scene of Turkey's greatest humiliation also became the scene of its strongest political and intellectual resurgence. In 1876 a parliamentary constitution was temporarily adopted in Constantinople. Later, the Young Turks began their reform movement in the old metropolitan area. And it was also in this area that Kemal Ataturk and his followers laid the foundations for the new Turkish national state.

Present-day Turkey has almost no middle class in the modern sense.[43] But on the political level a multiparty system has been established, and on the socio-economic level private property and enterprise have been encouraged. An experienced observer, who in 1952 still saw the old vicious circle of bureaucratic power, exploitation, and privilege prevailing in most parts of the former Ottoman empire, found "strong evidence that this circle has at last been broken in one Middle [Near] Eastern country," Turkey.[44]

Has the circle really been broken? Only time will tell. But this

---

o. See Cooke, 1952: 40. Cooke does not interpret the relation between bureaucratic position and landlordism in these countries as a consequence of traditional bureaucratic rule. But he too recognizes that in the Ottoman empire civil and military office, religious leadership, and landownership overlapped (*ibid.:* 281).

much can be said. The development of modern Turkey, which is both free and closely interlinked with the West, shows significant similarities to later 19th- and early 20th-century Russia, and significant dissimilarities to pre-Communist China.

If the presence of large segments of private property and enterprise were decisive for transforming hydraulic society into a multi-centered Western society, then no country could have been better prepared than China to take this road. In China private property in land was incomparably older than in Turkey or Tsarist Russia, and the tradition of private handicraft and commerce, including big commerce, was equally ancient. But the case of China demonstrates beyond doubt that the emergence of a modern middle class of the Western type depends on more than big private property and enterprise.

From 1840 on, China suffered from outside pressures. Unequal treaties, international concessions, extraterritoriality, and foreign control over the maritime customs weakened the absolutist government to the point where internal enemies were able to overthrow it and set up a republic. But the events which followed the revolution of 1911 revealed both the country's political cohesiveness and its societal inertia. Although temporarily broken up into a number of territorial regimes headed by bureaucratic warlords, China did not evolve a strong modern middle class, and this despite the fact that not a few native business communities in the concessions and abroad supported Dr. Sun Yat-sen's efforts at modernization.

This situation did not change fundamentally when, in 1927–28, the Kuomintang under Chiang Kai-shek accomplished a loose reunification of China proper. Continued foreign interference, aggravated by Soviet-directed Communist operations, prevented the Nationalist government from gaining full control of the country. And while modern bourgeois forces temporarily exerted some influence over the central government, they remained weak in the provincial administrations, which continued to be largely dominated by a traditional agromanagerial bureaucracy.[45]

But all these obstacles notwithstanding, China did not stand still. Western technology was increasingly welcomed; and Western ideas found expression in education, in the rising position of women, and in a relatively free press. Quit of foreign fetters, the country might have greatly accelerated its cultural and societal transformation.

World War II put an end to the many Western privileges that had crippled China. But relief came too late. It came during a war in which the Japanese, by occupying the treaty ports and the industrial cities, were able to weaken China's modern middle class.[46]

It came during a war in which the Communists were able to thoroughly penetrate the loosely integrated and sorely burdened Chinese society.

In Turkey, when semidependency ended, the road to a modern non-Communist society was clear and open. In China, when this period ended, the opportunities for diversive change, while broadened by the Western powers, were blocked by the Communists.

d. A New Developmental Force Arises: Soviet Communism

IN the 1920's the Soviet Union was too weak to affect decisively even such countries as Turkey, to whom it gave considerable economic aid. In the '30's it began to play a major role in international diplomacy. And after World War II it openly competed with the West for world leadership.

Thus the rise of the USSR presents the heirs of hydraulic society with a new alternative. Where formerly those who strove for institutional change saw only one goal, they now see two, and this because of the Bolshevik revolution. What is the developmental meaning of this revolution?

4. HYDRAULIC SOCIETY AT THE CROSSROADS

a. The Developmental Issue Underlying the Bolshevik Revolution

AMONG the major countries of the Oriental world that were breaking away from their agrodespotic past, the first to turn its back on Western society was Russia. This is of crucial importance because, prior to 1917, Russia had gone far in its Westernization and because, after 1917, it became the most influential source of anti-Western action in Asia and elsewhere.

The extent of Russia's Westernization in the spring of 1917 is indicated by the political prominence of the middle-class party of the "Cadets," the peasant party of the Socialist Revolutionaries, and the Mensheviks, all of whom wanted a parliamentary and democratic government. It was these groups, and not the Bolsheviks, who after the February revolution were supported by the majority of the peasants, workers, and soldiers. The bulk of the peasants followed the Socialist Revolutionaries; [47] the bulk of the workers followed either the Socialist-Revolutionaries or the Mensheviks. (In April 1917 Lenin admitted that "in most of the Soviets of Workers' Deputies" the Bolsheviks constituted "a small minority.") [48] And among the soldiers, who in the main came from the peasantry, the situation was similar.

Even in the elections to the Constitutional Assembly, which were held in the fall of 1917, more soldiers voted for the Socialist Revolutionaries than for the Bolsheviks.[49] In fact, on that occasion the former received 58 per cent of the total vote.[50]

The intelligentsia were even less inclined to follow the Bolsheviks. The pro-Tsarists among them were politically discredited; and the liberals and socialists were "equally alien to Tsarism and to Bolshevism."[51] No wonder then that after the February revolution the democratic parties prevailed not only in the civilian government and army[52] but also in the first soviets,[53] in the new peasant organizations,[54] and in the trade unions.[p]

In their agrarian program the Socialist Revolutionaries had requested the distribution of all "alienated" land to the rural toilers.[55] This was infinitely more attractive to the peasants than Lenin's demand that after the "nationalization of all land" the large estates should be operated as "model farms . . . under the control of the Agricultural Workers' Deputies and for the public account."[q]

As for the war, all the democratic groups, with different arguments, rejected a separate peace with Germany. And while the Bolsheviks introduced a sharp anticapitalist note into the debate, they, too, originally made no such recommendation. In his April Theses Lenin outlined the conditions for a "revolutionary war." While strongly objecting to the prevailing policy of a "revolutionary defence," he urged the utmost patience with the masses who were honestly accepting the war "as a necessity and not as a means of conquest."[56] And as late as June he refused a separate peace, which he held would mean "an agreement with the German robbers, who are plundering just as much as the others."[57]

Lenin's formula of the workers' control over industrial production[58] became increasingly popular in the factory committees.[59] But it did not, prior to the October revolution, make the Bolsheviks the masters of the trade unions.

Manifestly then, there existed in Russia in 1917 a genuinely open historical situation. Had the new leadership defended and developed the new freedoms in a truly revolutionary way, they would have had more than a sporting chance of completing Russia's transformation into a multicentered democratic society. But they lacked both

p. It was the Mensheviks, not the Bolsheviks, who at first controlled the quickly growing labor unions (Florinsky, 1953, II: 1421).

q. Lenin, S, XXIV: 5. In making this demand in his April theses, Lenin repeated a principle of Marxism that had been particularly elaborated by the leading orthodox Marxist, Kautsky. By implication, this policy withholds the land of the large estates from the peasants.

experience and resolve. Afraid of alienating their Western allies, they continued a war they had no strength to fight. And afraid of violating the rules of orderly legal procedure, they postponed the much needed land reform until after the opening of their Constituent Assembly, which was never able to function.

Thus the Bolsheviks got their big chance largely through default. After the July insurrection Lenin, revising his previous position, decided that in the war against the Germans an *"immediate and unequivocal peace must be proposed."* [60] And he soon made an equally daring *volte face* on the internal front. Discarding his orthodox plan to convert the big landed estates into model farms, he took over *in toto* (his opponents said "stole") the Socialist Revolutionary program for distributing land to the peasants, a program which he had recently rejected and which, he openly intimated, he still did not approve of.[61] In addition, he dropped the principle of majority support, which until this time he had considered a basic prerequisite for the seizure of power. Seeing the majority of the population discouraged and confused by the policies of the Provisional Government, which still had their votes, Lenin rallied to his side a minority of urban and rural activists who proved strong enough to place him and his party at the helm of a Soviet dictatorship.

More favorable international conditions—and more understanding and helpful democratic allies—might have tipped the scales in the opposite direction. But the situation being what it was, the political weakness of Russia's Western-oriented forces paralyzed the country's diversive revolution and opened the way for an entirely different type of development.

b. The USSR—Russia's Asiatic Restoration?

WHERE did this lead? Surely not to a socialist order in the sense of Marx and the pre-October Lenin. As shown in Chapter 9, Lenin himself at the close of his life believed that Russia was well on the way to an Asiatic restoration. Lenin's pessimism followed logically from his earlier views and later experiences. It followed from his knowledge of Marx' insistence on primitive democratic control over the protosocialist state, as exemplified in the Paris Commune. It followed from his acceptance of Marx' and Engels' notion that the dispersed rural communities constituted the economic foundation of Oriental despotism generally, and of its Tsarist version particularly.[62] It followed from his own notion that there was only one "absolute" guarantee that would prevent the hoped-for Russian revolution from turning into an Asiatic restoration: the victory of socialism in the highly industrialized West, and only one "relative" guarantee: the strict maintenance of democratic control over the new revolutionary government (no bureaucracy, no army, no police). And it followed from the developments after the October revolution: no socialist revolution occurred in the great industrial countries of the West, and the Soviet regime rapidly set up a new bureaucracy, standing army, and police.

Bukharin, then a top-ranking Bolshevik, had cried out against the new "bureaucratic centralization" and the threatening "enslavement of the working class" as early as the spring of 1918.[63] The Communist party had attacked "the partial revival of the bureaucracy" in its program of 1919. And in 1921 Lenin had depicted the new Soviet bureaucracy in a way that had one meaning and one meaning only: the new bureaucracy was the monster force that was driving Russia toward an Asiatic restoration. In 1922 the "nonproletarian" and "alien" representatives of the new "bureaucratic machine" were so strong that Lenin was no longer certain whether they or the small "Old Guard of the Party" were in the saddle. "Who controls whom?"[64] Only the "undivided prestige" of the Old Guard had so far prevented the complete victory of the new "alien" social forces. And this prestige could be destroyed by "a very slight internal struggle within this structure."[65] It was destroyed shortly after Lenin's death.

This, of course, does not mean that Soviet society originally had a protosocialist quality that was lost by 1922 or shortly thereafter. Lenin's belated warnings indicate the problem, but they show him unwilling to face the reality fully. According to Marx and the pre-October Lenin, socialism is economic planning plus effective popular control over the planners. The Bolsheviks permitted no such control when, after their revolutionary seizure of power, they engaged in economic planning on an ever-growing scale. Measured by Marxist-Leninist standards, there were subjective socialists in Soviet Russia, but there was never socialism.

Nor was there an Asiatic restoration. It is understandable why, in 1921, Lenin had viewed the new Soviet bureaucracy as ruling over fragmented and dispersed small producers. At the end of the civil war, in 1920, large-scale industry was producing not much more than 10 per cent of its prewar output,[66] and most of the industrial workers had returned to their villages. The country relied mainly on a fragmented peasant economy and whatever small-scale industry [r] survived in the villages and shrunken towns.[s] Lenin went so far as to say in 1921, "The proletariat has vanished." [67]

These conditions explain why, between 1921 and 1923, Lenin interpreted the new bureaucracy in terms that Marxists used to designate Oriental despotism. They explain why he spoke of the country's "semi-Asiatic" lack of culture and of the "Asiatic way" in which the peasants traded.[68] Nevertheless, his belief that the men of the new state apparatus were establishing a new version of Russia's old Asiatic system was profoundly wrong.

It was wrong because it underrated the economic mentality of the men of the new apparatus. These men were not satisfied with ruling over a world of peasants and craftsmen. They knew the potential of modern industry. Possessed by a quasireligious socialist vision,[t] they strove to realize it, first within the frame of Russia's previous production maximum and, from the First Five Year Plan on, far beyond it.

Thus while the masters of Soviet Russia perpetuated a key feature of an agrodespotic society, the monopolistic position of its ruling bureaucracy, they did much more than perpetuate that society. Even prior to the collectivization of agriculture, the Soviet *apparatchiki* disposed over a mechanized system of communication and industry that made their semimanagerial position different from and potentially superior to the semimanagerial position of an agro-hydraulic bureaucracy. The nationalized industrial apparatus of the new semimanagerial order provided them with new weapons of organization, propaganda, and coercion, which enabled them to liquidate the small peasant producers as an economic category. The completed collectivization transformed the peasants into agricultural workers who toil for a single master: the new apparatus state.[u]

The agrarian despotism of the old society, which, at most, was semimanagerial, combines total political power with limited social and intellectual control. The industrial despotism of the fully developed and totally managerial apparatus society combines total political power with total social and intellectual control.

Remembering Lenin's emphasis on the significance of the "apparatus" as a means for seizing and defending total power, I have

r. In 1920 Russia's small-scale industry still produced around 44 per cent of the output of 1913 (Baykov, 1947: 41).

s. The towns lost from one-third to over one-half of their populations (Baykov, 1947: 41).

t. For the discussion of Marxism-Leninism as a secular religion see Gurian, 1931: 192 ff.

u. For a pioneering analysis of the Soviet Union as a new class society, see Meyer, 1950: *passim*.

designated the genuinely despotic state an "apparatus state." This term covers both the agrarian and industrial forms of total statism. Is there any Marxist label that may be applied specifically to the new industrial apparatus society?

This new apparatus society has been called "neofeudalism" and "state capitalism." Neither formula is appropriate. "Feudalism" certainly does not fit the most highly centralized political order so far known, and "state capitalism" does not fit a conformation that precludes private means of production and an open market for goods and labor.

Marx clearly overrated the oppressiveness of Oriental society, which he held to be a system of "general slavery." [69] Ironically, but suitably, this designation can, however, be used for the new industrial apparatus society. We can truly say that the October revolution, whatever its expressed aims, gave birth to an industry-based system of general (state) slavery.

c. Communist China—the Product of a Genuine "Asiatic Restoration"?

BUT what about Communist China? In contrast to Russia, which in the 20th century made great strides toward industrialization, China was still a predominantly agricultural country when the Communists entered the arena some time after World War I. And there was not much of a modern Chinese middle class when the Communists made their final bid for power after World War II. Is it therefore not a fact that Mao Tse-tung and his followers established an agrarian despotism which, despite superficial modifications, bore a close resemblance to the great despotic regimes of China's past?

Indeed not a few observers have taken Mao's temporary retreat into the countryside as an agrarian deviation from an industry-oriented Marxism-Leninism. But such an interpretation disregards both the strategic aims of the Communist International and the reasons that made the Chinese Communists cling to them during the agrarian phase of their operations.[70]

Man is an ideological animal; he acts in accordance with his innermost conviction; and this is true whether religious or secular issues are at stake. A comprehensive philosophical and political creed, such as Communism, provides its adherents with a map of the world, an arsenal of operational directives (a "guide to action"), a flag, and a powerful political myth. It inspires those who hold it with supreme confidence and paralyzes those among their enemies who are impressed by it.[71]

From the standpoint of the Chinese Communists, the Soviet ideology has proved eminently effective. True, certain features of the developmental scheme have been adjusted; and the new proto-"socialist" or "socialist" order does not fit the Marxian concept of socialism. But these changes involve aspects of the Communist doctrine that probably never were real to the Chinese Communists—or, for that matter, to Communists in "backward" countries generally. We can find tragedy in the career of a Lenin, whose Aesopian warnings against the neo-"Asiatic" trends in Soviet society reveal a pained awareness of having betrayed the principles of his socialist creed. But there is no similar tragedy in a Mao's career, because there is no similar awareness. Mao did not betray the principles of socialism, to which he adhered officially, for the simple reason that for him these principles never had any meaning.

While Lenin's doubts did not bother the Chinese Communists, Moscow's power strategy attracted them immensely. Here was a revolutionary system with popular appeal which, accompanied by proper organization and action, could result in conclusive victory. It had done so in Russia. And properly adapted—the Comintern analysis of global conditions is very detailed—it might prove equally successful in other countries. This system required industrialization in all Communist-dominated areas, not for academic reasons but because ultimately Communist success in the sociopolitical sphere depended directly on Communist success in the industrial sphere.

The relation of these ideas to the long-range perspective of the Chinese Communists is evident. A Mao Tse-tung who viewed entrenchment in the countryside as a permanent principle and not as a temporary strategic device would be no deviant Communist, but merely a fool. He would be like the man who always prefers a stick to a gun, because once in the woods he had only a stick to fight with.

But Mao is no fool. He and his followers never considered themselves leaders of a peasant party,[v] whose actions were motivated, and limited, by the interests of the villages. When the conditions of the civil war forced the Chinese Communists to operate in the countryside, they always expected to return to the cities. And when they seized the cities, they did exactly what the Bolsheviks had done after the October revolution. They restored, consolidated, and developed whatever industries there were; and they were noticeably eager to

v. Lattimore claimed that during the ten years preceding the Sino-Japanese War the Chinese Communists, "cut off from cities and urban workers, had become a peasant party" [Lattimore, 1947 (1st ed. 1945): 108].

control modern industry [w] and mechanized communication. Thus they were as little interested in an Asiatic restoration as were the bureaucratic masters of the Soviet apparatus.

With due consideration for the peculiarities of their country's "backward" and "semicolonial" situation, the Chinese Communists moved quickly to establish a new semimanagerial order, which differs both in structure and developmental intent from the semimanagerial order of agrarian despotism. The rapid integration of the Chinese peasants into primitive collectives, called Producers' Cooperatives, indicates that Communist China is moving quickly from a semi-managerial to a total managerial order. According to an account given by Mao on December 27, 1955, the mass of all Chinese peasants may be members of semisocialist cooperatives (which still recognize a certain tie between the land and the farmer-peasant owner) by the end of 1956; and by 1959 they may be organized in a "completely" socialist way.[x]

C. WHITHER ASIA?

FOR obvious reasons the rise of a Communist regime in China affected the colonial and ex-colonial countries of the Orient much more directly than did the rise of the USSR. The Russia in which Lenin seized power appeared to the Eastern observers as a European country—and one that until recently had exercised imperialist control over vast expanses of Asia. The China in which Mao's party seized power was still an Oriental country and one that had suffered seriously from Western and Japanese imperialism.

Of course, Communist anti-imperialism appealed to the national revolutionists of Asia before the Chinese Communists took over the mainland. The Soviet Union established friendly relations with Ataturk's Turkey as early as 1920 and with Sun Yat-sen and his Canton government in 1923. And Nehru was conspicuous in the Communist-organized First Congress of the League against Imperialism at Brussels in 1927.[1]

But while, in the 1920's, the Asian national revolutionists were

w. Five years after the establishment of the Chinese People's Republic, 71 per cent of the output of all industrial enterprises, in terms of value, came from state-owned "joint state-private" and cooperative enterprises, the first complex supplying 59 per cent of the total, the second 12 per cent, and the third 4 per cent. At that time the value of the output of private industry had shrunk to 25 per cent of the total (*Jen-min Jih-pao*, September 23, 1955, Peking).

x. For Mao's above cited statement see *Izvestia*, January 13, 1956. Cf. Wittfogel, 1955a: Walker, 1955: 149 ff.; Tang (MS).

able to disregard the Soviet conquest of Georgia and Turkestan, they could not remain blind to Moscow's expansion in Eastern Europe after World War II and to Peiping's occupation of Tibet, a large Inner Asian country, whose right to be free Mao Tse-tung had publicly recognized in the 1930's.[2] They responded to these developments by resorting to a semi-anti-imperialism [a] which is as quick to attack the insecure forces of an old and shrinking capitalist imperialism as it is reluctant to criticize the brazen operations of the young and growing Communist imperialism.

Such behavior makes it clear that hostility to Western imperialism is only one reason for the popularity of the Communist regimes in non-Communist Asia. Another enormously compelling reason is the affinity to, and admiration of, the Communist system of managerial statism.

The political scientist who considers only the form of government may argue that today almost all non-Communist countries of the Orient have parliamentary governments and that in several countries, such as India, the leading policy makers take their democratic creed very seriously. Quite so. But the political scientist, who examines the phenomenon of government in depth, knows that in different institutional contexts the same form may have entirely different meanings. The Roman senate in the heyday of the republic had little in common with the body which, under the same name, operated in the empire; and Augustus' sentimental concern for Rome's glorious traditions did not restore the republic, for Augustus was careful to keep the supreme center of power outside and above all effective control.

Whither Asia? When answering this question, we must remember that capitalist colonization during the three hundred years of its dominance failed in the Orient to develop multicentered societies based on a strong middle class, organized labor, and an independent peasantry. We must remember that most constitutions of the new sovereign Asian nations, directly or indirectly, proclaim statism as a basic feature of their government.[b] We must remember that in many cases—we exclude Ataturk [3]—the will to statism was bulwarked

---

a. An excellent example of this semi-anti-imperialist attitude is Panikkar's *Asia and Western Dominance*. The Indian author is very outspoken in his criticism of Western imperialism in Asia and very gentle with Communist imperialism. Citing Lattimore, Panikkar finds kind words also for Tsarist imperialism, which he obviously considers the forerunner of modern Soviet imperialism (Panikkar, AWD: 249 ff.).

b. The principle of statism is solemnly proclaimed in Article 2 of the Turkish Constitution. Semantically, this principle is also invoked in the constitutions of Nationalist China, India, Burma, and Indonesia.

by democratic-socialist principles and that, in most of these cases —we exclude Sun Yat-sen—the professed democratic socialists were also professed admirers of Marx.

The student of Asia naturally wants to know how seriously the Asian socialists take Marx' Asiatic ideas: his theory of the Asiatic mode of production, which stresses private property as a key necessity for overcoming state-heavy Asiatic society; his multilinear concept of development, which warns against any simple scheme of unilinear development; his definition of socialism, which includes popular control as an essential element and which makes it impossible to call Communist Russia and Communist China socialist or proto-socialist; and his "Oriental" interpretation of Tsarist Russia, which made Plekhanov and Lenin consider the dangers of an Asiatic restoration.

Strange as it may seem, the Asian socialists are as indifferent to these ideas as are the Asian Communists. And this is true for the spokesmen of socialist parties as well as for socialists like Nehru who do not belong to any such organizations. Nehru, who found "Marx's general analysis of social development . . . remarkably correct," [4] apparently was unimpressed by Marx' analysis of the social development of India, which he can hardly have missed seeing, since Marx' writings on this subject circulated in India in several editions.

To be sure, the official representatives of the various Asian socialist parties sharply attack Russian and Chinese Communism for their totalitarianism. But disregarding Marx' views on Asiatic society and socialism, they disregard what, from the standpoint of "scientific socialism," would be the decisive critical test. And they hide the grave implications of their own societal past by calling this past "feudal" and by placing it into a crude scheme of unilinear development.[5]

Such procedures cannot be excused by asserting that the democratic Marxists of Europe also neglected Marx' Asiatic views. For while the European socialists did not draw the political conclusions Plekhanov drew, they certainly recognized Marx' concept of the Asiatic mode of production. In fact, Rosa Luxemburg, who is highly esteemed by the leading Indian Socialist Mehta,[6] expressly discussed the hydraulic and stationary character of Oriental societies.[7]

But even if the European socialists had neglected these societies, which to them constituted a remote issue, this would not excuse the Asian socialists. Being concerned primarily with Asia, they should have paid particular attention to what Marx had to say on this subject. However, instead of doing this, they remain stubbornly aloof from Marx' and Engels' theory of Asiatic society.

This omission does not keep the Asian socialists from opposing the "excessive growth of bureaucracy" in their own part of the world [8] and from rejecting the Russian and Chinese Communist regimes.[9] However, it gives tacit support to a policy which endeavors to abandon as soon as possible what Marx called "the greatest desideratum of Asian society"—private property in land.[10]

And far from precluding, it indirectly encourages a sympathetic appraisal of the managerial statism of the USSR and Communist China. In the 1930's Nehru viewed the Soviet Union as "run by representatives of the workers and peasants" and as being "in some ways . . . the most advanced country in the world." [11] In the 1940's he approvingly cited Tagore's opinion that the USSR "is free from all invidious distinction between one class and another," its regime being based not on exploitation but on cooperation.[12] And in the 1950's he equated the despotic masters of Communist Russia and China and their peoples; and he depicted Mao and his lieutenants as advancing the freedom of those they rule.[13]

Like his Indian counterpart, the prime minister of Burma, U Nu, is not unaware of the dangers of Communist expansion. But in 1954 he noted with pride the internal and external strength of Mao's regime. And he lauded the Chinese Communists for having abolished corruption and for improving the condition of the "downtrodden teeming millions." [14] He said this about a regime which openly and repeatedly had admitted being plagued by corruption. And he said it at a time when Mao's policy of enforced "cooperativization" was breaking the backbone of the Chinese peasantry.[15]

Excepting Japan—which never was a hydraulic civilization—and making full allowance for regional differences, we find most non-Communist nations of the Orient institutionally ambivalent and influenced by a semi- or crypto-Communist ideology which, by enhancing the authority of Marxism-Leninism, as the Leningrad discussion of 1931 explained, tends to weaken their political independence.

Does this mean that one after the other the ideologically penetrated countries will cease resisting the political erosion to which Communist strategy is exposing them? Such a turn is entirely possible. And although its consequences would entail far more than an "Asiatic restoration," in one respect it deserves this title: it would be a spectacular manifestation of a retrogressive societal development.

D. WHITHER WESTERN SOCIETY—WHITHER MANKIND?

CAN the West prevent this development, which would extend the system of bureaucratic state slavery to two-thirds of mankind? The history of pre-Bolshevik Russia shows that countries of the Oriental type which are independent and in close contact with the West may vigorously move toward a multicentered and democratic society. As described above, a diversive transformation of this kind has begun in many non-Communist countries of the Orient; and given time and opportunity, it may assume momentous dimensions. But will there be time? Will there be opportunity?

Time is already running out. And opportunity, if it is to be seized with any chance of success, presupposes a West whose attitude toward bureaucratic totalitarianism is both informed and bold. Today, the attitude of the West is neither.

Public opinion in the leading Western countries is ambivalent about the form and function of managerial bureaucracy; and it is ambivalent also about the form and function of private property and enterprise. The Second Industrial Revolution, which we are now experiencing, is perpetuating the principle of a multicentered society through large bureaucratized complexes that mutually— and laterally [a]—check each other: most importantly, Big Government, Big Business, Big Agriculture, and Big Labor. But the destruction of one major nongovernmental complex may bring about the downfall of others. Under Fascism and National Socialism, the liquidation of Big Labor so strengthened Big Government that eventually Big Business and Big Agriculture were also threatened.[b] And in Soviet Russia the liquidation of Big Business and Big Agriculture quickly enabled Big Government to subdue labor.

These experiences should alert us to the dangers inherent in unchecked bureaucratic dominance. To what extent can we trust the members of any "Big" group to use supreme and total power, once

a. The decrease of vertical controls from below (by voters, shareholders, and rank-and-file trade union members) goes hand in hand with the increase of lateral controls. These last are not new (cf. the history of factory legislation in England). But while their significance has grown, the recent Communist and Fascist revolutions show that their capacity to prevent a totalitarian accumulation of power is limited.

b. Before the end of World War II some attempts were made to analyze the institutional trends in Italian and German Fascism; but comparison with Communist totalitarianism was superficial or avoided altogether. In recent years there has been little interest in comparative studies of modern totalitarianism that include Fascism. Moscow's role in Hitler's rise to power is a similarly neglected issue.

they gain it, to serve the people's interest and not their own? To what extent can we trust the judgment of officiating or nonofficiating members of our segmented bureaucracies who view the Communist monopoly bureaucracy as a progressive form of totalitarianism? [c]

Western writers, teachers, and practicing politicians who do not understand the meaning of their institutional and cultural heritage are poorly equipped to unleash its creative potential. And they are also poorly equipped to combat Communist totalitarianism. For however necessary military preparedness and a courageous economic policy may be, they are only two among several essentials. Equally important is the judicious implementation of institutional change. And most important, because most fundamental, is a thorough grasp of the multiform course of history and of the opportunities and responsibilities it imposes on free man.

No doubt we are in the midst of an open historical situation, and no doubt there is freedom of effective choice. But our past blunders and present deliberations show that so far we have not used our opportunities competently. We did not give full scope to the antitotalitarian forces in the Western world. And failing to do this, we did little to strengthen the antitotalitarian forces in the hydraulic societies in transition.

But while the realm of freedom is rapidly shrinking, the desire to defend and expand it is growing. Shocked into a vigorous reappraisal of our position, we may still learn how to wrest victory from defeat. A new insight that is fully perceived, convincingly communicated, and daringly applied may change the face of a military and ideopolitical campaign. It may change the face of a historical crisis. Ultimately, the readiness to sacrifice and the willingness to take the calculated risk of alliance against the total enemy depend on the proper evaluation of two simple issues: slavery and freedom.

The good citizens of classical Greece drew strength from the determination of two of their countrymen, Sperthias and Bulis, to resist the lure of total power. On their way to Suza, the Spartan envoys were met by Hydarnes, a high Persian official, who offered to make them mighty in their homeland, if only they would attach themselves to the Great King, his despotic master. To the benefit of Greece—and to the benefit of all free men—Herodotus has preserved their answer. "Hydarnes," they said, "thou art a one-sided counselor. Thou hast experience of half the matter; but the other

---

c. When John K. Fairbank stressed "the distinction between fascist-conservative and *communist-progressive forms of totalitarianism*" (Fairbank, 1947: 149; italics mine), he expressed in print, and very succinctly, an opinion shared today by many intellectuals and officials.

half is beyond thy knowledge. A slave's life thou understandest; but, never having tasted liberty, thou canst not tell whether it be sweet or no. Ah! hadst thou known what freedom is, thou wouldst have bidden us fight for it, not with the spear only, but with the battle-axe."

NOTES

Intro.

1. For documentation concerning these statements, see below, Chap. 7, notes to first part.
2. Mill, 1909: 210.
3. *Ibid.:* 211.
4. Bury, 1910: 1.
5. See below, Chaps. 4 and 8.
6. See below, Chap. 4.
7. DASP, 1931: 89.
8. Tolstov, 1950: 3.
9. Marx, TMW, II, Pt. 1: 310 ff.
10. For documentary evidence for the above statements see Chap. 9, *passim.*
11. Wittfogel, 1924: 122, cf. 49.
12. *Ibid.:* 117.
13. *Ibid.,* 1926: 25.
14. *Ibid.:* 16.
15. *Ibid.:* 20–7.
16. *Ibid.,* 1927: 314, 315 ff., 320 ff., 324 ff.
17. *Ibid.,* 1929: 606.
18. *Ibid.,* 1931: *passim.*
19. *Inostrannaya Kniga* (Moscow), No. 1, 1931: 20.
20. Marx, NYDT, June 22, 1853.

1, C

1. Widtsoe, 1926: 64.

1, D

1. Nelson, 1938: 8.
2. Widtsoe, 1926: 5.

2, A

1. Wittfogel, 1956: 157.
2. Wittfogel, 1931: 312, 424, 337–44. *Ibid.,* 1956: 158.
3. Buck, 1937: 61.
4. See Wittfogel, 1931: 253 ff., 261 ff., 267 ff.
5. Buckley, 1893: 10. Cf. Marshall, 1931, I: 6.
6. RRCAI: 359. Cf. Saha, 1930: 12.
7. See Strabo 16.1.10.
8. Wittfogel and Fêng, 1949: 661, n. 52.
9. Willcocks, 1904: 70.
10. See Humboldt, 1811, II: 193 ff.
11. Beech, 1911: 15.
12. Parsons, 1939, I: 111.
13. Gutmann, 1909: 20.
14. Eck and Liefrinck, 1876: 228 ff.
15. Deimel, 1928: 34. *Ibid.,* 1931: 83.
16. Sethe, 1912: 710 ff.
17. *Arthaçāstra,* 1926: 60. *Arthaśāstra,* 1923: 51 ff.

18. Blas Valeras = Garcilaso, 1945, I: 245.
19. Sahagun, 1938, I: 292, 296.
20. Ramirez, 1944: 52, 75. Tezozomoc, 1944: 381, 385.
21. Willcocks, 1889: 274.
22. *Ibid.:* 279.
23. *Ibid.*
24. Gutmann, 1926: 369, 374.
25. Parsons, 1939, I: 124–6. Wittfogel and Goldfrank, 1943: 29.

2, C

1. Cf. Wittfogel, 1931: 456 ff., 680 ff. *Ibid.*, 1938: 98 ff. Wittfogel and Fêng, 1949: 123, 467.
2. Herodotus 2.109.

2, D

1. Reed, 1937: 373. Robins, 1946: 91 ff., 129 ff.
2. For Palenque see Stephens, ITCA, II: 321, 344. For Aztec Mexico see Tezozomoc, 1944: 23, 379 ff.; Chimalpahin Quauhtlehuanitzin: 117, 128.
3. Cf. Pietschmann, 1889: 70.
4. Cf. Cahen, 1940: 132.
5. Jacobsen and Lloyd, 1935: 31. Luckenbill, AR, II: 150. Cf. Olmstead, 1923: 332; Thompson and Hutchinson, 1929: 129 ff.
6. See below, Chap. 6.
7. Heichelheim, 1938: 728. See also below, Chap. 7.
8. Williams, 1910: 168. Cf. Sombart, 1919, I: 396; II: 252.
9. Kulischer, AW, II: 381 ff.
10. Williams, 1910: 168.
11. Sombart, 1919, II: 251.
12. Williams, 1910: 168.
13. Kees, 1933: 129, cf. 109. Breasted, 1927: 147 and *passim*.
14. Thompson, 1941: 515.
15. See *Shih Chi*, 29.3a–b, 4b–5a, 5b–6a, 7b–8a, 126.15b. *Han Shu*, 29.2b–3a, 4a–b, 5a–b, 7a–8a, 89.14b–15a. For translation and comment see MS HCS, Ch'in-Han, II (3) (4) (36) (43) (54) (55) (56) (72).
16. See *Shih Chi*, 29.2a–b, 4a–b. *Han Shu*, 29.1b–2a, 3b–4a, 64A.6b. *Hou Han Shu*, 35.3b. For translation and comment see MS HCS, Ch'in-Han, IV (1) (6) (32) (66).
17. *Sui Shu*, 3.11a, cf. 5a.
18. Kulischer, AW, II: 6.
19. King, 1927: 97 ff.
20. Dundas, 1924: 73; cf. Widenmann, 1899: 63 ff.
21. Dundas, 1924: 73.
22. *Ibid.:* 95 ff.
23. *Ibid.* Cf. Widenmann, 1899: 63 ff.
24. Cortes, 1866: *passim*. Díaz, 1944: *passim*. Cf. Vaillant, 1941: 135.
25. Armillas, 1944: *passim*. Vaillant, 1941: 219.
26. Jerez, 1938: 38. Sancho de la Hos, 1938: 177 ff. Cieza, 1945: 206 ff., 245. Ondegardo, 1872: 75 ff. Garcilaso, 1945, II: 31, 146 ff. Espinosa, 1942: 565 ff. Cobo, HNM, IV: 65 ff., 207 ff. Cf. Rowe, 1946: 224 ff.
27. Cobo, HNM, III: 272. Garcilaso, 1945, II: 147.
28. *Arthaśāstra*, 1923: 54 ff.
29. *Shih Chi*, 88.1b.
30. Meissner, BA, I: 340.

31. *Ibid.:* 340 ff. Olmstead, 1923: 334.
32. Herodotus 5.52 f.; 8.98. Cf. Xenophon 8.6.17.
33. Rostovtzeff, 1941, I: 133, 135, 173 ff., 484, 517.
34. For Diocletian's achievements in this sphere see Bury, 1931, I: 95 ff.; and Ensslin, 1939: 397.
35. Mez, 1922: 461.
36. For the Mamluks see Sauvaget, 1941: 35. For the Ottoman Turks see Taeschner, 1926: 203 ff.
37. *Arthaçāstra*, 1926: 60, and esp. 74. Strabo 15.1.50.
38. Cf. Smith, 1914: 135.
39. Appadorai, 1936, I: 424 ff.
40. Sabahuddin, 1944: 272 ff.
41. Haig, 1937: 57.
42. Smith, 1926: 413 ff.
43. *Kuo Yü*, 2.22 ff.
44. *Han Shu*, 51.2a. For translation and comment see MS HCS, Ch'in-Han, IV (4).
45. Jerez, 1938: 55. Estete, 1938: 83 ff., 97 ff., 244 ff. Sancho de la Hos, 1938: 175. Pizarro, 1938: 259. CPLNC: 310. Cieza, 1945: *passim*. Sarmiento, 1906: 88. Ondegardo, 1872: 12. Cf. Garcilaso, 1945, II: 242 and *passim;* Cobo, HNM, III: 260 ff.
46. Pizarro, 1938: 259.
47. *Chin Shih Ts'ui Pien*, 5.13a–b. For translation see MS HCS, Ch'in-Han, IV (75), n. 305.
48. Widenmann, 1899: 70.
49. Ixtlilxochitl, OH, II: 174.
50. I Kings 5: 14. For ancient Mesopotamia see Schneider, 1920: 92; Mendelsohn, 1949.
51. Marshall, 1928: 587 ff.
52. *Shih Chi*, 6.31a–b. For translation and comment see MS HCS, Ch'in-Han, III (12).
53. *Shih Chi*, 6.13b–14a, 24a–25a. For translation and comment see MS HCS, Ch'in Han, III (10) (11).
54. See above.
55. *Sui Shu*, 3.9b.
56. *Sui Shu*, 24.16a.
57. Barton, 1929: 3 ff. Thureau-Dangin, 1907: 3 and *passim*. For epigraphic references to the temples of Babylonia and Assyria see Meissner, BA, I: 303 ff.; and Luckenbill, AR: *passim*.
58. Breasted, 1927, I: 186, 244, 336; II: 64, 72, 245, 311, 318; III: 96 ff.; IV: 116 ff., 179 ff., and *passim*.
59. Ramirez, 1944: 39.
60. Ixtlilxochitl, OH, II: 184.
61. Chimalpópoca, 1945: 49.
62. *Ibid.:* 52.
63. Cieza, 1943: 150 ff.
64. *Ibid.:* 241. Cf. Garcilaso, 1945, I: 245, 257 ff.

2, E

1. Cf. Bengtson, 1950: 38.

2, F

1. Glotz, 1926: 152, cf. 267.
2. Kulischer, AW, I: 224.
3. Sombart, 1919, II: 792. Cf. Cole, 1939, II: 458 ff.
4. Cf., for Ottoman Turkey, Anhegger, 1943: 5, 8 ff., 22 ff., 123 ff., 126 ff.

5. Boulais, 1924: 728.
6. Pant, 1930: 70.

2, G

1. See below, Chap. 6.

3, A

1. Milukow, 1898: 111.

3, B

1. Garcilaso, 1945, II: 23 ff., 25 ff. Cobo, HNM, III: 295 ff. Rowe, 1946: 264.
2. Torquemada, 1943, II: 546 ff.
3. *Kuo Yü*, 1.8 ff.
4. *Shih Chi*, 6.50a. See MS HCS, Ch'in-Han, I, 3, n. 17.
5. *Kuan Tzŭ*, 3.17–18.
6. *Hou Han Shu*, 10A.4a. For translation and comment see MS HCS, Ch'in-Han, I, 3 (8).
7. *Kuan T'ang Chi Lin*, 11.5b–6a. See MS HCS, Ch'in-Han, I, 3, n. 21.
8. *Han Shu*, 28A, 28B. *Hsü Han Chih*, 19–23. See MS HCS, Ch'in-Han, I, 1, Tables.
9. *Arthaçāstra*, 1926: 86 ff.
10. Smith, 1926: 376.
11. Strabo 15.50 f.
12. Appadorai, 1936, II: 683 ff.
13. Deimel, 1924: *passim. Ibid.*, 1927, 1928.
14. Breasted, 1927, I: 54, 59, and *passim.* Cf. Meyer, GA, I, Pt. 2: 159 ff.
15. Wilcken, 1912: 173 and n. 3.
16. *Ibid.:* 173.
17. *Ibid.:* 178 ff., 206.
18. *Ibid.:* 192 ff.
19. *Ibid.:* 237 ff. For further data on the cadasters under Arab rule see de Sacy, 1923, II: 220 ff.
20. Gaudefroy-Demombynes, 1923: xli. Wiet, 1937: 482. *Ibid.*, 1932: 257. Cf. Björkman, 1928: *passim.*
21. Wright, 1935: 119. Cf. Lybyer, 1913: 167 ff.; and Gibb and Bowen, 1950: 167 ff.
22. *Chou Li*, 16.5a. cf. Biot, 1851, I: 367.
23. Herodotus 3.117.
24. Eck and Liefrinck, 1876: 231.
25. Wirz, 1929: 13.
26. *Ibid.*
27. *Ibid.:* 14.
28. *Ibid.*
29. Eck and Liefrinck, 1876: 230.
30. Wittfogel, 1931: 263.
31. Willcocks, 1889: 339.
32. Sombart, 1919, II: 373 ff.
33. Cf. Grant, 1937: 241.
34. Prescott, 1936: 29.
35. Torquemada, 1943, II: 536.
36. Cieza, 1943: 125. Rowe, 1946: 231.
37. Cieza, 1943: 126.
38. Herodotus 5.52 f.; 7.239; 8.98. Cf. Christensen, 1933: 283 ff.; Olmstead, 1948: 299.
39. Herodotus 7.239.
40. Xenophon 8.6.17.

41. Cf. Seeck, 1901: 1847 ff.
42. Suetonius Augustus, 1886: 61.
43. Riepl, 1913: 459. Hudemann, 1878: 81 ff.
44. Bréhier, 1949: 324.
45. Procopius, *Anecdota* 3.1.30 = Bréhier, 1949: 326.
46. Christensen, 1944: 129.
47. Gaudefroy-Demombynes, 1923: 239, n. 1. Björkman, 1928: 40.
48. Mez, 1922: 461.
49. Ibn Khordādhbeh, 1889: 114.
50. Mez, 1922: 70.
51. *Ibid.:* 71.
52. Björkman, 1928: 41.
53. Sauvaget, 1941: *passim.* Gaudefroy-Demombynes, 1923: 239 ff. Grant, 1937: 239.
54. Björkman, 1928: 43. See also Sauvaget, 1941: 44 ff.
55. Grant, 1937: 243.
56. Strabo 15.1.48.
57. *Arthaśāstra*, 1923: 256 ff., and *passim;* Manu, 1886: 387 ff. Cf. Vishnu, 1900: 17.
58. Saletore, 1943: 256 ff.
59. Cf. Sabahuddin's instructive account of the postal system in Muslim India (Sabahuddin, 1944: 273 ff., 281). Cf. also Ibn Batoutah, 1914: 95; Bābur, 1921: 357.
60. Smith, 1926: 382.
61. *Ibid.:* 414.
62. See *Kuo Yü*, 2.22 ff.
63. *Hou Han Shu*, 86.5a, 89.22b, 87.22b–23a. For translation and comment see MS HCS, Ch'in-Han IV (73).
64. *Han Shu*, 63.11a. For translation and comment see MS HCS, Ch'in-Han IV (43).
65. *Hou Han Shu*, 16.34b–35a. For translation and comment see MS HCS, Ch'in-Han IV (77).
66. Wittfogel and Fêng, 1949: 161 ff.
67. *Ibid.:* 162.
68. Marco Polo, 1929, I: 434 ff.
69. *Ibid.:* 435.
70. MS HCS, Ch'ing IV.
71. Delbrück, GK, III: 102 ff., 172. Lot, 1946, I: 303, 305. Stubbs, CHE, I: 432; II: 277. Vinogradoff, 1908: 61 and nn. 2, 3.
72. Lot, 1946, I: 303 ff.
73. Delbrück, GK, III: 103, 172.
74. Tout, 1937: 140 ff.
75. Full list in Lot, 1946, II: 212.
76. Delbrück, GK, III: 260 ff., 263 ff., 304 ff.
77. Herodotus 9. 62.
78. Herodotus 7. 104. Cf. Delbrück, GK, I: 38 ff.
79. Oman, 1924, I: 204.
80. *Ibid.:* 204–5.
81. *Ibid.:* 205.
82. *Ibid.:* 251.
83. *Ibid.:* 252. Cf. Delbrück, GK, III: 305, 307, 333, 338 ff.
84. Atiya, 1934: 71.
85. Rowe, 1946: 274.
86. Herodotus 7. 25.
87. Oman, 1924, I: 190 f.
88. Cf. Fries, 1921: 12 ff.; Horn, 1894: 57 ff.; Løkkegaard, 1950: 99; and Gibb, 1932: 39.

89. See Wittfogel and Fêng, 1949: 523 ff., 526 ff. Cf. MS HCS, Ch'in-Han and Ch'ing, sec. XV.

90. Delbrück, GK, III: 303, 333 ff.

91. *Arthaçāstra*, 1926: 64 ff., 399 ff., 406 ff., 522, 526 ff.

92. Delbrück, GK, III: 207–9. Wittfogel and Fêng, 1949: 536. Huuri, 1941: 71 ff.

93. Koran, 61. 4. For discipline in Muhammad's army see Buhl, 1930: 242, n. 97.

94. Wüstenfeld, 1880: *passim*. Ritter, 1929: 116, 144 ff. Huuri, 1941: 94 ff.

95. *Ca.* 500 B.C. See Wittfogel and Fêng, 1949: 534, n. 438.

96. *Han Shu*, 30. 25b ff.

97. Sun Tzŭ, 1941: 39.

98. *Han Shu*, 30. 25b–28a.

99. Bandelier, 1877: 131, 133 ff.

100. Cobo, HNM, III: 270; Rowe, 1946: 278.

101. Wittfogel and Fêng, 1949: 519.

102. *Ibid.*: 532 ff.

103. Lot, 1946, I: 98, 122 ff.

104. Kremer, CGO, I: 223 ff. Lot, 1946, I: 59 ff.

105. See Kremer, CGO, I: 213, 216, n. 4.

106. *Ibid.*: 244.

107. Lot, 1946, II: 257, n. 1.

108. *Ibid.*: 257.

109. *Ibid.*, I: 56.

110. Herodotus 7. 184.

111. *Ibid.* 7. 83.

112. Delbrück, GK, I: 41.

113. Smith, 1914: 125.

114. *Ibid.*

115. *Ibid.* Cf. Strabo 15. 1. 52.

116. Smith, 1914: 126 and n. 2.

117. Horn, 1894: 40 ff.

118. *Chan-kuo Ts'ê*, 8. 76, 14. 20, 19. 56, 22. 94, 26. 30, 29. 55.

119. Wittfogel and Fêng, 1949: 516, 519.

120. Williamson, WAS, I: 185.

121. *Ch'ing Shih Kao*, 137. 13b, 13b–19a, 19a–20b.

122. *Han Shu*, 24A.11a. Cf. MS HCS, Ch'in-Han, II (18).

123. For this figure see Kahrstedt, 1924: 660.

124. For the data on which these percentages are based see *ibid.*: 660 ff.

125. For the basic data see Inama-Sternegg and Häpke, 1924: 672, 680.

3, C

1. Parsons, 1939, I: 157–8, 495, 534; II: 790, 893, 901, 904, 909, 1131.

2. Gutmann, 1909: 111.

3. Deimel, 1922: 20, 22. Cf. *ibid.*, 1931: 83.

4. Poma, 1936: 1050.

5. Legge, CC, IV: 600 ff.

6. Breasted, 1927, IV: 194, cf. 157, 178, 185. Cf. also Kees, 1933: 45 ff.

7. Wan, KT, 1933: 38. Ma, SF, 1935: 218–19.

8. Glotz, 1926: 154.

9. *Ibid.*: 153 ff.

10. Stubbs, CHE, I: 583. See below, Chap. 6.

11. Meissner, BA, I: 125.

12. Genesis 47:24. Cf. Kees, 1933: 46.

13. *Arthaçāstra,* 1926: 372.

14. Meissner, BA, I: 125.

15. *Arthaśāstra,* 1923: 72 ff.

16. *Ibid.*: 77.

17. See Kees, 1933: 42, 47, 223 ff., 226. For the system of land tenure during this period see below, Chap. 7.

18. Kees, 1933: 42, 226.

19. Wilson, 1950: 212. Cf. Kees, 1933: 47, n. 7, 224.

20. Hummel, ECCP, I: 289.

21. *Arthaśāstra,* 1923: 75 ff.

22. *Ibid.*: 74.

23. *Ibid.*: 75.

24. *Ibid.*: 72.

25. *Ibid.*: 76. *Arthaçāstra,* 1926: 100.

26. *Arthaçāstra,* 1926: 100. *Arthaśāstra,* 1923: 77.

27. *Arthaśāstra,* 1923: 70.

28. *Ibid.*: 76 and n.

29. *Mez,* 1922: 109.

30. *Ibid.*: 110.

31. *Ibid.*

32. *Ibid.*: 127 ff.

33. *Arthaçāstra,* 1926: 373.

34. *Ibid.*: 374.

35. *Ibid.*: 378.

36. *Ibid.*: 380.

37. *Arthaśāstra,* 1923: 296.

38. *Ibid.*

39. *Mez,* 1922: 107.

40. *Ibid.*: 110 ff.

    3, D

1. Mitteis, 1912: 231. Kreller, 1919: 182. Taubenschlag, 1944: 158. Kees, 1933: 83.

2. Hammurabi, sec. 165. Cf. Meissner, BA, I: 159.

3. Meek, 1950: 185, 188. Meissner, BA, I: 178.

4. *Arthaçāstra,* 1926: 255 ff., 456 f. Keith, 1914, I: 232, 191. Cf. Hopkins, 1922: 244; Āpastamba, 1898: 134 ff.; Gautama, 1898: 303 ff.; Vasishṭha, 1898: 88 ff.; Manu, 1886: 348 and n. 117; Rangaswami, 1935: 30 ff.; Baudhāyana, 1898: 224 ff.; Vishnu, 1900: 40; Nārada, 1889: 201; and Yājnavalkya, 53 ff., 68 ff.

5. Cf. Juynboll, 1925: 253 ff.; Kremer, CGO, I: 527 ff.; and Schacht, 1941: 513 ff.

6. Boulais, 1924: 199.

7. Ondegardo, 1872: 37 ff.

8. Zurita, 1941: 144.

9. Fei and Chang, 1945: 302.

10. Schacht, 1941: 516.

11. Ondegardo, 1872: 38.

12. Glotz, 1926: 247.

13. *Ibid.*: 248.

14. Myers, 1939: 20.

15. Morris, 1937: 554 ff.

16. *Ibid.*

17. Aristotle, *Politics* 2.7.

18. Pöhlmann, 1912, I: 206 ff.

19. Jefferson, 1944: 440.
20. Beard, 1941: 149.
21. Beard, 1927, I: 292.
22. *Ibid.:* 413.
23. Bloch, 1949, II: 244.
24. Tout, 1937: *passim.*
25. McIlwain, 1932: 673.
26. *Ibid.*
27. *Ibid.*
28. Morris, 1937: 554.
29. *Ibid.:* 553 ff.
30. Murdock, 1949: 37 ff.
31. *Shih Chi* 53.4b–5b. For translation and comment see MS HCS, Ch'in-Han, II (14).

3, E

1. Weber, WG: 241 ff.
2. Deimel, 1920: 21.
3. *Ibid.:* 31.
4. *Ibid.:* 21. Cf. Meissner, BA, II: 53.
5. Deimel, 1920: 31.
6. *Ibid.*
7. Glotz, 1929: 39.
8. Bury, 1937: 46. Cf. Stengel, 1920: 33 ff.; and Bengtson, 1950: 97.
9. Bengtson, 1950: 62.
10. Busolt, GS, I: 515.
11. *Ibid.:* 498.
12. Lamprecht, DG: 17 ff., 34. Petit-Dutaillis, 1949: 23.
13. Petit-Dutaillis, 1949: 92.
14. *Ibid.:* 333.
15. Cf. Ranke, 1924, I: 32.
16. Garcilaso, 1945, I: 58 ff. Cobo, HNM, III: 122 ff. Means, 1931: 370. Rowe, 1946: 257.
17. Garcilaso, 1945, I: 61. Means, 1931: 370.
18. Means, 1931: 370, 374. Rowe, 1946: 265. Cf. Garcilaso, 1945, I: 84.
19. Garcilaso, 1945, I: 84, 175 ff. Means, 1931: 407, 370. Rowe, 1946: 299.
20. Ondegardo, 1872: 18 ff. Cobo, HNM, III: 246 ff. Rowe, 1946: 265 ff.
21. Cobo, HNM, III: 254 ff. Rowe, 1946: 266 ff.
22. Sethe, PT, II: 139. Breasted, 1927, I: 108, 114, 242, 327; II: 11, 25, and *passim;* III: 17 and *passim;* IV: 15, 27 and *passim.*
23. Breasted, 1927, II: 12 and *passim;* III: 17 and *passim;* IV: 28 and *passim.*
24. Breasted, 1927, I: 70, 114, and *passim.*
25. *Ibid., passim.*
26. *Ibid.,* II: 80 and *passim;* III: 56 and *passim.*
27. Erman and Ranke, 1923: 73.
28. Engnell, 1943: 5 ff.
29. Erman and Ranke, 1923: 73.
30. Breasted, 1927, I: 100 and *passim.* Kees, 1933: 242 ff.
31. Cf. Breasted, 1927, I: 103.
32. Kees 1933: 252.
33. See above, p. 89.
34. Breasted, 1927, IV: 346 and *passim,* 419, 452, 482.
35. Engnell, 1943: 4.
36. *Ibid.:* 16.

37. Barton, 1929: 31 ff., 37, 43, 99. Labat, 1939: 53 ff. Engnell, 1943: 16 and nn.
38. Labat, 1939: 63.
39. Cf. Labat, 1939: *passim;* Engnell, 1943: 16 ff., 33; McEwan, 1934: 7 ff.; and Nilsson, 1950: 129 and n. 2.
40. Barton, 1929: 31, 35, 97, 137 ff., 325.
41. Labat, 1939: 131.
42. Engnell, 1943: 31. Cf. Labat, 1939: 202 ff.
43. Cf. Deimel, 1920: 21 ff.
44. Meissner, BA, I: 68. Labat, 1939: 135.
45. Labat, 1939: 202.
46. *Ibid.:* 168.
47. *Ibid.:* 234.
48. Meissner, BA, II: 59 ff.
49. *Ibid.:* 60.
50. *Ibid.*
51. Cf. Christensen, 1944: 229; and McEwan, 1934: 18 and n. 116.
52. McEwan, 1934: 17.
53. *Ibid.:* 19.
54. Nilsson, 1950: 145 ff., 149 ff., 156 ff.
55. *Ibid.:* 161 ff.
56. Taylor, 1931: 58 ff.
57. *Ibid.:* 185 ff.
58. Bury, 1931, II: 360.
59. Bréhier, 1949: 61 ff.
60. See below, p. 97.
61. De Groot, 1918: 141 ff.
62. *Ibid.:* 180 ff. Cf. Wittfogel, 1940: 123 ff.
63. De Groot, 1918: 182 ff.
64. *Ibid.:* 219 ff.
65. *Ibid.:* 226 ff.
66. *Ibid.:* 247 ff.
67. *Ibid.:* 270 ff.
68. *Ibid.:* 276 ff.
69. Seler, GA, III: 332 ff.
70. *Ibid.:* 107 ff.
71. Seler, 1927: 238, 171. Cf. Sahagun, 1938, I: 211.
72. Seler, 1927: 104. Cf. Sahagun, 1938, I: 139.
73. Seler, 1927: 354.
74. Paul Kirchhoff, personal communication.
75. Priests as warriors: Seler, 1927: 115. *Ibid.,* GA, II: 606, 616. For priests as judges see *ibid.,* GA, III: 109.
76. Christensen, 1933: 257, 291.
77. *Ibid.:* 289.
78. Bréhier, 1949: 61.
79. Ostrogorsky, 1940: 18.
80. Cf. Arnold, 1941: 291 ff.
81. *Ibid.:* 295.
82. Pedersen, 1941: 445.
83. Fick, 1920: 98 ff.
84. Manu, 1886: 14.
85. *Ibid.:* 216 f.
86. Keith, 1922: 127 ff. Cf. *ibid.,* 1914, I: 109, 279; II: 599 ff.

87. Fick, 1920: 166 ff.
88. Manu, 1886: 228.
89. Baudhāyana, 1898: 200.
90. Manu, 1886: 26.
91. *Ibid.*: 509.
92. *Ibid.*: 253 f. Gautama, 1898: 237 ff.
93. Fick, 1920: 174.
94. *Ibid.*: 173 ff.
95. Dubois, 1943: 290.
96. *Ibid.*
97. Fick, 1920: 79 ff.

4, A
1. Cf. Têng and Biggerstaff, 1936: 139 ff.
2. Cf. Hopkins, 1922: 277 ff.
3. Hsieh, 1925: 34.
4. Rangaswami, 1935: 103 ff.
5. Bury, 1910: 26.
6. Arnold, 1924: 53.
7. Schacht, 1941: 676 f. Cf. Laoust, 1939: 54; Horster, 1935: 5 ff.; and Gaudefroy-
    Demombynes, 1950: 154.
8. Arnold, 1924: 47. Cf. Gaudefroy-Demombynes, 1950: 110.
9. Rangaswami, 1935: 69.
10. Wittfogel and Goldfrank, 1943: 30 and n. 139.
11. Krause and With, 1922: 26 ff.
12. For Hindu India see Manu, 1886: 397 ff.; Fick, 1920: 103; and *Arthaçāstra*, 1926:
    lxiii ff., 822. For Muslim thoughts see al-Fakhrî, 1910: 56. Cf. Hasan Khan,
    1944: 36 ff.
13. For the contrary view see Hsieh, 1925: 11.
14. Wittfogel and Fêng, 1949: 398 ff.
15. Reid, 1936: 25.
16. Mommsen, 1875: 1034.
17. Bury, 1910: 9.
18. Diehl, 1936: 729.
19. Bury, 1910: 8.
20. *Ibid.*: 8 ff.
21. Kornemann, 1933: 143.
22. Boulais, 1924: 464.
23. For Egypt see Kees, 1933: 184. For India see *Arthaśāstra*, 1923: 28 ff.; and Manu,
    1886: 224 ff. For China see Hsieh, 1925: 83.
24. For China see Ch'ü, TT, 1947: 206–8.

4, B
1. Cf. Clark, 1937: 145 ff.
2. Garcilaso, 1945, I: 246.
3. De Groot, 1940: *passim.*
4. For intermediate constellations see below, Chap. 7.
5. Marx, 1939: 371, 375, 386, 429.
6. Manu, 1886: 24.
7. Legge, CC, I: *passim.*
8. For Chagga see Gutmann, 1909: 167; and Dundas, 1924: 158 ff. For Hawaii see
    Alexander, 1899: 66 ff., 72 ff.

9. Ch'ü, TT, 1947: 7 ff.
10. *Ibid.:* 20.
11. Hammurabi, sec. 117.
12. Koran, 17.24 ff. Cf. Daghestani, FM: 134.
13. Daghestani, FM: 136. Cf. Gaudefroy-Demombynes, 1950: 128.
14. Jolly, 1896: 78.
15. Vāsishṭha, 1898: 75.
16. Rowe, 1946: 263 ff. Cobo, HNM, III: 232 ff.
17. Zurita, 1941: 90.
18. Breasted, 1927, II: 278 ff. Kees, 1933: 36 ff.
19. Cf. Wiedemann, 1920: 68.
20. Jouguet, 1911: 59 ff., 62. Wilcken, 1912: 275. San Nicolo, PR, I: 162 ff. Johnson and
    West, 1949: 98. Tomsin, 1952: 117 ff.
21. Jouguet, 1911: 59.
22. San Nicolo, PR, I: 171.
23. Jouguet, 1911: 213.
24. Harper, 1928: 142 ff.
25. Cf., for the end of the "ancient" period, Rostovtzeff, 1910: 259; and San Nicolo,
    PR, I: 160, n. 1. Cf. also below, Chap. 7.
26. Rostovtzeff, 1910: 259.
27. *Ibid.:* 258. Broughton, 1938: 629.
28. Johnson, 1951: 133.
29. Steinwenter, 1920: 52 ff.
30. *Ibid.:* 49 ff.
31. *Ibid.:* 54.
32. Gibb and Bowen, 1950: 262.
33. *Ibid.:* 263. Cf. Kremer, 1863, I: 255.
34. Kremer, 1863, I: 255.
35. Fick, 1920: 160 ff. Rhys-Davids, 1950: 35.
36. Rhys-Davids, 1950: 35. Jolly, 1896: 93. Cf. Matthai, 1915: 10.
37. Fick, 1920: 114, n. 1.
38. Jolly, 1896: 93. Fick, 1920: 161.
39. Matthai, 1915: 15.
40. Smith, 1899: 227 ff. Yang, 1945: 173.
41. Smith, 1899: 228.
42. Williams, 1848: 384 ff.
43. Smith, 1899: 233 ff.
44. Smith, 1897: 230.
45. Rostovtzeff, 1941, II: 1062 f. (italics mine).
46. Stöckle, 1911: 82.
47. For the market inspector see Ibn al-Ukhuwwa, 1938: 5. Cf. Gaudefroy-Demom-
    bynes, 1938: 450 ff.; and Lévi-Provençal, 1947: 42 ff.
48. Maurer, GSD, III: 30 ff. Inama-Sternegg, 1901: 353–4.
49. Gibb and Bowen, 1950: 278.
50. *Jātakam, passim.* Fick, 1920: 257 ff.
51. Fick, 1920: 285. Cf. Hopkins, 1902: 172.
52. Hopkins, 1902: 171.
53. Fick, 1920: 285.
54. C. A. F. Rhys-Davids, 1922: 210 ff.
55. *Chiu T'ang Shu,* 48.11b.
56. Kato, 1936: 62.

57. *Ibid.*
58. Grunebaum, 1946: 179.
59. *Ibid.:* 185.
60. Scheel, 1943: 8, 16.
61. Grunebaum, 1946: 185.
62. Wittfogel and Fêng, 1949: 292 and n. 19.
63. De Groot, 1940, I: 102 ff.
64. *Ibid.:* 107.
65. *Ibid.:* 109 ff.
66. *Ibid.:* 113.
67. *Ibid.:* 116.
68. For China see Ch'ü, TT, 1947: 18–19. For India see Manu, 1886: 260.
69. Harper, 1928: *passim.*
70. Johnson, 1951: 133.
71. Gibb and Bowen, 1950: 263.
72. Dubois, 1943: 88 ff.
73. *Ibid.:* 89.
74. See Appadorai, 1936, I: 152.
75. *Ibid.*
76. Fick, 1920: 120. Baden-Powell, 1896: 441 ff.
77. Letter of January 15, 1954, of Dr. K. C. Hsiao.
78. Smith, 1899: 229.
79. *Ibid.:* 228.
80. Manu, 1886: 260 and n. 41.
81. For Ottoman Turkey see Gibb and Bowen, 1950: 227. For Byzantium see Stöckle, 1911: *passim.* For China see Ch'üan, HS, 1934: *passim.*
82. Gibb and Bowen, 1950: 277.
83. *Ibid.:* 278.
84. *Ibid.:* 277 (italics mine).
85. De Groot, 1940, I: 116.
86. Macdonald, 1941: 96.
87. Smith, 1899: 229.
88. De Groot, 1940: *passim.*
89. Grunebaum, 1946: 184.
90. Stöckle, 1911: 138.
91. Massignon, 1937: 216.
92. Gibb and Bowen, 1950: 281, n. 5.
93. C. A. F. Rhys-Davids, 1922: 210 ff.
94. Wittfogel, 1931: 572 ff. Cf. Hintze, 1941: 152 ff.
95. Wittfogel, 1931: 580 ff.

4, c

1. *Yüan Shih,* 146.4a. Cf. Wittfogel, 1949: 10.
2. Koran, 2.266 (267). For irrigation in ancient Arabia see Grohmann, 1933: 19 ff. For irrigation near Mecca see Lammens, 1922: 141 ff.
3. Wittfogel, 1949: 10.
4. Garcilaso, 1945, I: 43.
5. Legge, CC, I: 215.
6. *Ibid.,* II: 128 ff.
7. Garcilaso, 1945, II: 21.
8. *Ibid.:* 9.
9. Garcilaso, 1945, II: 81.

10. For Ch'ing see *Ta Ch'ing Lü Li*, 17.26a ff.; Boulais, 1924: 389 ff. Cf. Ch'ü, TT, 1947: Chap. 3.

11. Manu, 1886: 37 ff. Āpastamba, 1898: 9 ff. Gautama, 1898: 176 ff. Baudhāyana, 1898: 150. Vāsishṭha, 1898: 56 ff. Vishnu, 1900: 114 ff.

12. Erman and Ranke, 1923: 238 ff.

13. Meissner, BA, I: 130 ff.

14. Porphyrogénète, 1939: 34 ff. Cf. Stein, 1949: 844; Lopez, 1945: 2.

15. Kremer, CGO, II: 218 ff.; Mez, 1922: 217.

16. Makrizi, 1845: 72.

17. Björkman, 1941: 756.

18. *Han Shu*, 24A.11b–12a. For translation and comment see MS HCS, Ch'in-Han VII, 1 (18).

19. Bernier, 1891: 225.

20. *Ibid.*: 226.

21. Cf. Meissner, BA, I: 147 ff.

22. Locke, 1924: 162–3.

23. *Ibid.*: 162.

24. Acton, 1948: 364.

25. *Arthaśāstra*, 1923: 296.

26. Stalin, S, XII: 368.

5, A

1. Fromm, 1941: *passim.*

5, B

1. Manu, 1886: 219.

2. Legge, CC, I: 267.

3. Manu, 1886: 218.

4. *Ibid.*: 220.

5. *Ibid.*: 219 (italics mine).

6. *Ibid.*

7. *Ibid.*

8. *Ibid.* (italics mine).

9. Barton, 1929: 31 and *passim.*

10. Jacobsen, 1946: 143.

11. *Ibid.*: 144.

12. *Ibid.*

13. Barton, 1929: 31 and *passim.*

14. Hammurabi: Prologue.

15. Erman and Ranke, 1923: 64, 460.

16. al-Fakhrî, 1910: 36.

17. Thucydides 1.6.

18. *Ibid.*

19. Bauer, 1893: 350.

20. Eisenhower, 1948: 467 ff.

5, C

1. Lenin, S, XXVIII: 216.

2. Vyshinsky, 1948: 92 ff.

3. Gutmann, 1909: 26.

4. *Ibid.*

5. Alexander, 1899: 26 ff. Blackman, 1899: 22 ff.

6. Sethe, PT, II: 137 ff., 156 ff.

7. Price, 1927: 17, 60.

8. Kees, 1933: 224.

9. Mallon, 1921: 137 ff.

10. Cromer, 1908, II: 402.

11. Garcilaso, 1945, I: 246.

12. Erman, 1923: 247.

13. Kees, 1933: 23, 220, cf. 224.

14. Mez, 1922: 126 ff. Cf. Goldziher, 1905: 108; Juynboll, 1925: 317, n. 1; Schacht, 1935: 117; Santillana, 1938: 48.

15. Mez, 1922: 126.

16. *Arthaçāstra*, 1926: 228.

17. Boulais, 1924: 215 ff.

18. Kees, 1933: 224.

19. Breasted, 1927, IV: 270. Cf. Spiegelberg, 1892: 85.

20. *Arthaśāstra*, 1923: 269 (italics mine). Cf. *Arthaçāstra*, 1926: 343.

21. *Arthaśāstra*, 1923: 269. Cf. *Arthaçāstra*, 1926: 344.

22. *Arthaśāstra*, 1923: 269.

23. *Ibid.*: 270.

24. *Ta Ch'ing Lü Li* 2.34b. Boulais, 1924: 5 ff.

25. Cf. Doolittle, 1876, I: 335–46.

26. Mez, 1922: 349. The quotation is taken from Masçudi, VIII: 154.

27. Cromer, 1908, II: 403.

28. Busolt, GS, I: 555 ff.

29. *Ibid.*: 280.

30. Glotz, 1926: 281.

31. *Ibid.*

32. Busolt, GS, I: 555 ff.; II: 1180. Cf. Aristotle, *Rhetoric* 1.15; Freudenthal, 1905: 14.

33. Schiller, 1893: 223. Mommsen, 1905: 5. Hitzig, 1905: 43.

34. Hitzig, 1905: 43 ff. Williams, 1911: 73 ff.

35. Helbing, 1926: 46 ff.

36. Brunner, 1905: 58. Cf. Lea, 1892: 275 ff., 117 ff.

37. Lea, 1892: 200 ff., 483.

38. Helbing, 1926: 101 ff.

39. Lea, 1908, I: 217 ff. Helbing, 1926: 112. Williams, 1911: 74.

40. Williams, 1911: 75 ff. Lea, 1892: 483, 527 (Protestant Germany), 566 ff. (Protestant England without formal integration in the law), 572 ff. (Scotland).

41. See below, Chap. 6.

42. Cf. Kennan, 1891, II: 52.

43. Hammurabi: *passim*.

5, D

1. Jaeger, 1939: 104.

2. *Ibid.*: 88 ff.

3. Díaz, 1949: 91 ff.

4. Parsons, 1939, I: 53, 108. Goldfrank, 1945: 527 ff. Wittfogel and Goldfrank, 1943: 30.

5. Gutmann, 1909: 21.

6. Jacobsen, 1946: 202.

7. *Ibid.*: 202 ff.

8. *Ibid.*: 202.

9. *Ibid.*: 203.

10. Grapow, 1924: 150, 153.

11. Wilson, 1950: 414.

12. Manu, 1886: 391.
13. Koran, 4.62.
14. al-Fakhrî, 1910: 44.
15. **Legge, CC, I: 245.**
16. *Ibid.:* 246.
17. *Ibid.:* 178.
18. *Ibid.:* 211.
19. Bühler, 1948: 175 ff.
20. *Ibid.:* 296 ff.
21. *Ibid.:* 298.
22. Jacobsen, 1946: 202.
23. *Ibid.*
24. Wilson, 1950: 414.
25. Manu, 1886: 71.
26. *Lun Yü,* 1.1b.
27. Østrup, 1929: 27 ff.
28. *Ibid.:* 27.
29. Dundas, 1924: 282.
30. Cf. Gutmann, 1926: 531.
31. Cobo, HNM, III: 279–80. Rowe, 1946: 259.
32. Seler, 1927: 328.
33. *Ibid.*
34. Sahagun, 1938, IV: 51. Seler, 1927: 483.
35. Kuo, MJ, 1935: 20b, 30b, 39a, 46a, 55a–b, 57a, 60b, 61a–b, 62b, 65b, 68a ff. Legge, CC, III: 424, 432, 437 f., 446, 449, 508, 511.
36. Strabo 15.1.67. Manu, 1886: 43, 54.
37. Saletore, 1943: 179 ff. Beal, *Si-yu-ki,* I: 85. *Ta T'ang Hsi-yü Chi,* Chap. 1.
38. Jahāngīr, 1909: 203.
39. Dubois, 1943: 132.
40. Breasted, 1927, I: 214.
41. Grapow, 1924: 121 ff. Cf. Erman and Ranke, 1923: 82; Kees, 1933: 183; and Østrup, 1929: 31.
42. Erman and Ranke, 1923: 82.
43. *Ibid.* Breasted, 1927, IV: 204, 422, 427 f., 430, 437 ff.
44. Barton, 1929: 27. Meissner, BA, I: 70. Østrup, 1929: 32. Cf. Horst, 1932: 55.
45. Herodotus 1.134.
46. Horst, 1932: 103 ff.
47. *Ibid.:* 27, 103.
48. Ṭabarī, 1879: 93, 367.
49. Kornemann, 1933: 142.
50. Bréhier, 1949: 70.
51. Mez, 1922: 135 ff. Sauvaget, 1946: 62. Gaudefroy-Demombynes, 1950: 110. Kremer, CGO, II: 247.
52. Schramm, 1924: 220.
53. Kantorowicz, 1931: 76, 91.

    5, E
1. Wilson, 1950: 418.
2. *Arthaśāstra,* 1923: 42, 45.
3. *Ibid.:* 24.
4. *Ibid.:* 42.
5. *Ibid.:* 43.

6. *Ibid.*

7. *Ibid.:* 34.

8. *Ibid.:* 34 ff.

9. *Ibid.:* 302.

10. Kai Kā'ūs ibn Iskandar, 1951: 191.

11. Smith, 1897: 257.

12. *Ibid.:* 242. Cf. Doolittle, 1876, I: 346.

13. *Han Shu,* 62.14a–22a.

14. Howorth, HM, III: 588 ff.

15. *Ibid.:* 561.

16. *Ibid.:* 588.

17. *Ibid.:* 588 ff.

18. *Ibid.*

19. Trotsky, 1928: 322.

20. ASBRT: 627.

21. *Ibid.:* 644.

22. *Ibid.:* 697.

6, A

1. For Marx' and Engels' ideas concerning the Asiatic issue see below, Chap. 9, *passim.*

6, B

1. Westermann, 1921: 169 ff. *Ibid.,* 1922: 22 ff. Schnebel, 1925: 8 ff.

2. Westermann, 1922: 27. Erman and Ranke, 1923: 203 ff. Schnebel, 1925: 11, 274. Kees, 1933: 32, 40, 49.

3. *Han Shu,* 28B.20b. MS HCS, Ch'in-Han, I, 2 (3).

4. *Shih Chi,* 8.16b. Cf. MS HCS, Ch'in-Han, I, 2 (4).

5. See Wittfogel, 1931: 454; *ibid.,* 1938: 110.

6. Mez, 1922: 423–8.

7. *Ibid.:* 423.

8. *Ibid.:* 423–8.

9. Gardiner, 1948, II: 9, 69, 88, 163.

10. Wilcken, 1912: 182 ff., 212 ff.

11. *Ibid.:* 183 ff., 212 ff., 230. Wallace, 1938: 286 ff. Johnson and West, 1949: 299, 321 ff.

12. Wilcken, 1912: 230–1.

13. Mez, 1922: 125. Cf. Becker, IS, I: 237, 239, and *passim.*

14. See above, Chap. 4.

15. Cf. Lybyer, 1913: 147.

16. For occasional and exceptional efforts see Longrigg, 1925: 127.

17. Wittfogel, 1949: 10.

18. Lammens, 1907: 131 ff., 140. *Ibid.,* 1914: 179 ff. Miles, 1948: 236 ff. Wellhausen, 1927: 252 and n. 1, 331 ff. Gabrieli, 1935: 12 ff., 22, 128 ff.

19. See below, pp. 276 and 288.

20. Hardy, 1931: 59 ff., 113. Johnson and West, 1949: 11.

6, C

1. Ramsay, 1890: 74 ff.

2. *Ibid.* Cf. Bréhier, 1949: 328 ff.

3. Cf. Ramsay, 1890: 74. Taeschner, 1926: 202 ff.

4. Ostrogorsky, 1940: 261. Honigmann, 1935: 44 and *passim.* For the character and purpose of these fortifications see Ramsay, 1890: 200.

5. Ostrogorsky, 1940: 261.

6. Ramsay, 1890: 199.

7. Bréhier, 1949: 262.

8. *Ibid.*: 328 ff. Cf. the description of the Byzantine post at the close of the 9th century given by Hārūn b. Yaḥyā (Marquart, 1903: 207 ff.).

9. Bréhier, 1950: 220 ff.

10. See above, Chap. 3.

11. See Karamsin, HER, VI: 439 (Ivan III); Herberstein, NR, I: 95 (Vasili III); and Staden, 1930: 57 (Ivan IV). Cf. Kluchevsky, HR, II: 126 ff., 138; III: 235 ff.; and Milukow, 1898: 129 ff.

12. Karamsin, HER, VI: 448 (Ivan III). Herberstein, NR, I: 108 (Vasili III).

13. Herberstein, NR, I: 111. Staden, 1930: 52 ff. Fletcher, 1856: 57 ff. Cf. Kulisher, 1925: 345 ff.; and Lyashchenko, 1949: 224 ff.

14. Ostrogorsky, 1940: 57, n. 4.

15. Stein, 1920: 50 ff. Cf. Ostrogorsky, 1940: 57, n. 4.

16. Ostrogorsky, 1940: 57 ff., 87.

17. *Ibid.*: 262.

18. *Ibid.*: 232.

19. *Ibid.*: 344.

20. *Ibid.*: 216. *Ibid.*, 1942: 209.

21. Dölger, 1927: 94 n.

22. Ostrogorsky, 1940: 262 ff.

23. See Stepniak, 1888: 155 ff.; and Nicolai-on, 1899: 171. Cf. Milukow, 1898: 142 ff.

24. See Robinson, 1949: 129 ff., 268, 270.

25. Wittfogel, 1950: 452. Cf. Prokopowitsch, 1913: 17 ff., 31, 39 ff.; and Lyashchenko, 1949: 534 ff., 716.

26. Lyashchenko, 1949: 701, 706.

27. Cf. Wittfogel, 1950: 453.

28. See below, Chap. 10.

29. Wittfogel and Fêng, 1949: 123 ff., 136.

30. *Ibid.*: 365, 371, 373 f.

31. *Ibid.*: 371.

32. *Ibid.*: 373.

33. *Ibid.*: 160, 165.

34. *Ibid.*: 370.

35. *Ibid.*: 365, 373, 522.

36. *Ibid.*: 367 ff.

37. *Ibid.*: 366.

38. *Ibid.*: 112 ff., 370 ff., 520, 559.

39. *Ibid.*: 162.

40. *Ibid.*: 533.

41. *Ibid.*: 65 ff.

42. *Ibid.*: 66 ff.

43. *Ibid.*: 45, 65, n. 29.

44. *Ibid.*: 310 ff.

45. *Chin Shih*, 96.4b. Cf. Wittfogel and Fêng, 1949: 296.

46. Wittfogel and Fêng, 1949: 124, 296, 572.

47. Cortes, 1866: 24.

48. Landa, 1938: 225. Cf. Tozzer, 1941: 187 and n. 975.

49. Roys, 1933: 75, 175.

50. RY, I: 116 and *passim*.

51. Landa, 1938: 226.

52. Stephens, 1848, I: 335; II: 144 and *passim*.

53. *Ibid.*, I: 357.

54. *Ibid.* Casares (1907: 221) agrees with this conjecture.
55. Casares, 1907: 217.
56. Stephens, 1848, I: 231.
57. *Ibid.,* ITCA, II: 429.
58. Casares, 1907: 218.
59. Stephens, 1848, I: 250.
60. See Ruppert and Denison, 1943: 3 and *passim.*
61. Stephens, 1848, II: 213.
62. Tozzer, 1941: 86 = Landa, 1938: 104.
63. Stephens, 1848, II: 211 ff.
64. Ruppert and Denison, 1943: *passim.*
65. *Ibid.* Cf. Morley, 1947: 43.
66. Landa, 1938: 104, 209. Tozzer, 1941: 85 ff., 170 ff. Cf. Morley, 1947: 174.
67. Tozzer, 1941: 174, n. 908. Landa, 1938: 212. Morley, 1947: 339 ff. and plate 55. Roys, 1943: 51.
68. Landa, 1938: 104.
69. *Ibid.*
70. Tozzer, 1941: 87 = Landa, 1938: 105.
71. Roys, 1943: 63.
72. *Ibid.*
73. Tozzer, 1941: 28 and n. 154; 64, n. 292.
74. Roys, 1943: 66.
75. *Ibid.:* 67.
76. *Ibid.*
77. *Ibid.:* 61.
78. *Ibid.*
79. *Ibid.*
80. Kljutschewskij, 1945, I: 162.
81. *Ibid.:* 163.
82. *Ibid.:* 164 ff.
83. *Ibid.,* II: 91.
84. Wittfogel and Fêng, 1949: 398 ff.
85. *Ibid.:* 466 ff., 502.
86. *Ibid.:* 213, 259, and *passim.*
87. Tozzer, 1941: 99 = Landa, 1938: 114.
88. Ostrogorsky, 1940: 173.
89. *Ibid.:* 348.
90. Sumner, 1949: 177.
91. *Ibid.:* 178.
92. *Ibid.:* 184.
93. *Ibid.:* 178.
94. *Ibid.:* 184.
95. Wittfogel and Fêng, 1949: 217 ff.
96. Roys, 1943: 60.
97. *Ibid.:* 79.
98. Tozzer, 1941: 27, n. 149.
99. Beaglehole, 1937: 30. Wittfogel and Goldfrank, 1943: 25. Titiev, 1944: 186. Parsons, 1939, I: 111.
100. Das, 1904: 52, 98, 102. Cf. Hedin, 1917: 280, 295, 299, 320.
101. For this term see Das, 1904: 233.
102. *Ibid.:* 234, 244 ff.
103. *Ibid.:* 245 ff.

104. *Ibid.*: 231. Bell, 1927: 158.
105. See Rockhill, 1891: 292 ff. Das, 1904: 241 ff.

6, D

1. Glotz, 1925: 10.
2. *Ibid.*: 115–17.
3. *Ibid.*: 117, 186 ff., 402.
4. *Ibid.*: 151.
5. *Ibid.*: 119, 150 ff.
6. *Ibid.*: 150.
7. Ehrenberg, 1946: 8.
8. *Ibid.*
9. *Ibid.* Cf. Meyer, GA, I, Pt. 2: 776, 779. Glotz, 1925: 202 ff.
10. Ehrenberg, 1946: 8.
11. Bengtson, 1950: 41. Meyer, GA, II, Pt. 1: 244 ff.
12. Bengtson, 1950: 41.
13. *Ibid.*
14. *Ibid.*: 42.
15. Horst, 1932: 23.
16. Herodotus 7.136. Arrian 4.10 ff.
17. Bengtson, 1950: 38.
18. *Ibid.*
19. Cf. Glotz, 1926: 268, 271.
20. Ehrenberg, 1946: 22.
21. Homo, 1927: 110.
22. Voigt, 1893: 274, 358.
23. Homo, 1927: 120.
24. *Ibid.*: 217, 243.
25. Asakawa, 1929: 71.
26. Nihongi, 1896, II: 225 ff.
27. See Sansom, 1938: 93 ff.; and Reischauer, 1937, I: 146 ff.
28. Nihongi, 1896, I: 164, 183, 283. Asakawa, 1929a: 193 and n. 6.
29. Asakawa, 1903: 270. See also Sansom, 1938: 101, contradicting his statement on p. 159.
30. Nihongi, 1896, II: 250 ff., 255. Cf. Florenz, 1903: 163.
31. Nihongi, 1896, II: 208, 241.
32. Asakawa, 1911: 178 ff. Cf. Rathgen, 1891: 142.
33. Takekoshi, 1930, I: 161.
34. Sansom, 1938: 457.
35. Takekoshi, 1930, III: 394, 412.
36. *Ibid.*
37. Sansom, 1938: 455 ff. Takekoshi, 1930, I: 253.
38. Honjo, 1935: 241.
39. Sansom, 1938: 470.
40. Vernadsky, 1943: 327.
41. Struve, 1942: 421.
42. *Ibid.*
43. Nestor, 1931: 101.
44. *Ibid.*: 180.
45. *Ibid.*: 122, 124.
46. Hötzsch, 1912: 545.
47. Nestor, 1931: 11, 16. Cf. Vernadsky, 1943: 276 ff. For a recent Soviet presentation cf. Grekov, 1947: 130.

48. Vernadsky, 1943: 338.
49. *Ibid.:* 168 ff.
50. Borosdin, 1908 (presenting the finds of Pavlov-Silvansky): 577. Hötzsch, 1912: 546. Struve, 1942: 427.
51. Mitteis, 1933: 87 ff., 528.
52. Vernadsky, 1948: 190.
53. Struve, 1942: 422.
54. Vernadsky, 1948: 191.
55. Ostrogorsky, 1940: 130.
56. Nestor, 1931: 11, 56, cf. 43; cf. also 14.
57. *Ibid.:* 43; Miakotine, 1932: 101.
58. Goetz, RR, II: 228.
59. *Ibid.,* I: 247 ff.; IV: 144.

6, E

1. Goldfrank, 1945a: *passim.*
2. Wittfogel and Fêng, 1949: 505 ff.
3. *Ibid.:* 120 ff.
4. Vladimirtsov, 1948: 102.
5. *Ibid.:* 101 ff.
6. Wittfogel, 1949: 5 ff.
7. Wittfogel and Fêng, 1949: 664.
8. Riasanovsky, 1937: 102.
9. *Ibid.:* 95.
10. Rostovtzeff, 1910: 230 ff.
11. *Ibid.:* 230.
12. *Ibid.:* 237.
13. *Ibid.:* 237 and n.
14. Frank, 1928: 795.
15. Gelzer, 1943, II: 49 ff.
16. Stevenson, 1934: 211 ff.
17. Jones, 1934: 180.
18. Stevenson, 1934: 191 ff.
19. *Ibid.:* 216. Cf. Last, 1936: 428 ff.
20. Stevenson, 1934: 185 ff.
21. Charlesworth, 1934: 686 ff.
22. *Ibid.:* 123. Stevenson, 1934: 192 ff.
23. Riepl, 1913: 435 ff., 459.
24. Stevenson, 1934: 189. Charlesworth, 1934: 686 ff.
25. See below, Chap. 8.
26. Frank, 1940: 300.
27. Miller, 1939: 24.
28. Oertel, 1939: 272.
29. *Ibid.*
30. *Ibid.:* 273.
31. *Ibid.:* 256.
32. Cf. (for Spain) Van Nostrand, 1937: 127 ff.; (for Gaul) Grenier, 1937: 493 ff.; (for England) Collingwood, 1937: 14 ff.
33. Stein, 1928: 515–17.
34. *Ibid.:* 343.
35. Reiske, 1830: 271.
36. See Lot, 1951: 405 ff.

37. Bloch, 1937: 209.
38. Maitland, 1921: 1 ff.
39. Haskins, 1918: 5 ff.
40. *Ibid.*: 4.
41. Maitland, 1948: 9.
42. *Ibid.*
43. Haskins, 1911: 435.
44. *Ibid.*: 436.
45. *Ibid.*: 664 ff.
46. Wittfogel and Fêng, 1949: 507 ff.
47. Koebner, 1942: 52.
48. Sánchez-Albornoz, EM, I: 281. Cf. Lévi-Provençal, 1932: 99 ff.
49. Sánchez-Albornoz, EM, I: 213 ff.
50. Cf. Mieli, 1938: 205 ff. *Ibid.*, 1946: 165 ff. Lévi-Provençal, 1932: 173 ff.
51. Mieli, 1938: 184 ff., 197 ff. *Ibid.*, 1946: 132, 141 ff.
52. Dozy, 1932, II: 173.
53. Bücher, 1922, I: 382.
54. Rogers, 1884: 117.
55. al-Makkari, 1840, I: 215, cf. 214.
56. *Primera Crónica General:* 767 (chap. 1124). Cf. Laborde, 1808: 9; and Schirrmacher 1881: 410.
57. Seybald, 1927: 176. Cf. Lafuente Alcantara, 1845: 136.
58. Dozy, 1932, II: 173.
59. *Ibid.*: 200, 222. Sanchez-Albornoz, EM, I: 344.
60. See Sanchez-Albornoz, EM, I: 349, 351.
61. Hintze, 1901: 406.
62. *Ibid.*: 413.
63. *Ibid.*: 411.
64. Altamira, 1930: 61.
65. *Ibid.*: 104 ff.
66. See *ibid.*: 62 ff.
67. *Ibid.*: 160.
68. *Ibid.*: 138.
69. Hintze, 1930: 241.
70. Altamira, 1930: 63.
71. See Klein, 1920: 34 ff.
72. *Ibid.*: 17 ff., see esp. the map following p. 18.
73. *Ibid.*: 75, 77 ff., 157 ff., 170, 173, 175 ff.
74. *Ibid.*: 279.
75. Quoted by *ibid.*: 317.
76. *Ibid.*: 325.
77. Kliuchevskii, *Kurs,* II: 260.
78. Kluchevsky, HR, II: 112.
79. *Ibid.*, II: 112 ff.
80. *Ibid.*, I: 117.
81. *Ibid.*, I: 269.
82. Kliuchevskii, *Kurs,* II: 174.
83. *Ibid.*, II: 22–3.
84. *Ibid.*, II: 23.
85. Kluchevsky, HR, II: 126 ff., 138; III: 235 f., 237 ff., 241.
86. Kliuchevskii, *Kurs,* II: 23.
87. Spuler, 1943: 333, 338. Vernadsky, 1953: 219 ff.

88. Vernadsky, 1953: 357 ff.
89. *Ibid.*: 358 (italics mine).
90. Kluchevsky, HR, III: 227.
91. Kliuchevskii, *Kurs,* II: 436.
92. See Karamsin, HER, VI: 448.
93. Spuler, 1943: 409 ff. Karamsin, HER, IV: 393 ff. Vernadsky, 1953: 221, 357.
94. Kluchevsky, HR, I: 304 ff.
95. *Ibid.,* II: 123.
96. *Ibid.*: 124 ff.
97. *Ibid.,* III: 52.
98. Kliuchevskii, *Kurs,* II: 272–3.
99. *Ibid.*: 277.
100. *Ibid.*: 278.
101. Kovalewsky, 1903: 43.
102. Vernadsky, 1953: 372.
103. *Ibid.*: 367.
104. See Wipper, 1947: 15, 30, 37, 42 ff.

7, E

1. See Murdock, 1949: 38 ff.
2. Lips, 1938: 516.
3. *Ibid.*
4. Beech, 1911: 16.
5. *Ibid.*: 34.
6. *Ibid.*
7. Parsons, 1939, I: 20.
8. Titiev, 1944: 184. Cf. Beaglehole, 1937: 15.
9. Titiev, 1944: 61.
10. *Ibid.*: 64.
11. Beech, 1911: 15.
12. *Ibid.*: 34.
13. Dundas, 1924: 302.
14. Merker, 1904: 217.
15. Widenmann, 1899: 68. Dundas, 1924: 266. Gutmann, 1926: 440 ff
16. Gutmann, 1926: 455.
17. *Ibid.*: 442.
18. *Ibid.*
19. *Ibid.*: 442, 448.
20. *Ibid.*: 446 ff.
21. Dundas, 1924: 298.
22. Gutmann, 1926: 382 ff.
23. Gutmann, 1909: 12.
24. Dundas, 1924: 286.
25. Widenmann, 1899: 87.
26. Merker, 1903: 34.
27. Waitz, 1880, I: 338 ff.

7, F

1. Dundas, 1924: 287.
2. Widenmann, 1899: 87.
3. Gutmann, 1909: 12. Cf. Widenmann, 1899: 87.
4. Widenmann, 1899: 87.

5. Gutmann, 1926: 368.
6. Dundas, 1924: 287.
7. Gutmann, 1926: 370.
8. See *ibid.*: 369 ff.
9. *Ibid.*: 497 ff.
10. So also, with a few exceptions, Gutmann, 1909: 9 and *passim; ibid.*, 1914: *passim;* and *ibid.*, 1926: *passim.*
11. Kepelino, 1932: 122, 124, 134. Cf. Fornander, HAF, V: 72, 478.
12. Kepelino, 1932: 122, 126, 146.
13. Lydgate, 1913: 125.
14. Alexander, 1899: 28. Cf. Fornander, HAF, V: 208 ff., 262; and Perry, 1913: 93 ff.
15. Perry, 1913: 92, 95. Handy, 1940: 36.
16. Malo, 1903: 84. Cf. Fornander, HAF, IV: 356; Kepelino, 1932: 146; and Handy, 1933: 34.
17. Ellis, 1826: 395. Alexander, 1899: 28, 59 ff. Kepelino, 1932: 148, 150. Handy, 1933: 34.
18. Kepelino, 1932: 150.
19. Gutmann, 1926: 302 ff.
20. *Ibid.*: 16.
21. *Ibid.*: 428.
22. Ellis, 1826: 296 ff.
23. Alexander, 1899: 24.
24. *Ibid.*: 88. Blackman, 1899: 55.
25. Lind, 1938: 140.
26. Ellis, 1826: 401. Alexander, 1899: 88.
27. Ellis, 1826: 296 ff.
28. Cf. Alexander, 1899: 156; and Blackman, 1899: 188.
29. Cook, 1944: 337.
30. Fornander, HAF, V: 478, 610 ff., 630. Vancouver, 1798, II: 116. Ellis, 1826: 89.
31. Alexander, 1899: 82.
32. Malo, 1903: 105; Cook, 1944: 436.
33. For lists of such objects see Blackman, 1899: 54 ff.; Alexander, 1899: 80 ff.; and Cook, 1944: 337 ff.
34. Kepelino, 1932: 124.
35. *Ibid.*: 134.
36. Sarmiento, 1906: 90.
37. Cieza, 1945: 180, 116 ff.
38. *Ibid.*: 272. Garcilaso, 1945, II: 82. Cf. Cobo, HNM, III: 43 ff.; and Means, 1931: 314 ff.
39. Cieza, 1945: 243, 278 ff. Cf. Garcilaso, 1945, I: 237, 180.
40. Estete, 1938: 94.
41. Garcilaso, 1945, I: 251.
42. CPLNC: 309. Jerez, 1938: 38. Garcilaso, 1945, I: 187, 189 ff.
43. Cieza, 1945: 144, 165.
44. CPLNC: 309. Cf. Jerez, 1938: 38.
45. Sancho de la Hos, 1938: 181.
46. Garcilaso, 1945, I: 185.
47. Sombart, 1919, II: 769 ff., 837. Kulischer, AW, II: 156 ff.
48. See above, pp. 79 f.
49. Breasted, 1927, IV: 164. Spiegelberg, 1896: 21, 25.
50. Kees, 1933: 103.
51. *Ibid.*: 103–4.
52. *Ibid.*: 104.
53. Newberry, BH, I: 46.

54. Erman and Ranke, 1923: 112. Kees, 1933: 164. Cf. Klebs, 1915: 116; and Erman, 1923: 102 ff.
55. See Kees, 1933: 165.
56. *Ibid.*
57. Breasted, 1927, II: 401 and *passim*.
58. *Ibid.: passim.* Kees, 1933: 166 ff.
59. Kees, 1933: 103.
60. *Ibid.:* 165.
61. *Ibid.:* 164.
62. *Ibid.:* 167.
63. *Ibid.*
64. Ch'ü, TT, 1937: 200–1.
65. Duyvendak, 1928: 49, 177, 179, 183.
66. *Shih Chi,* 6.21b. For translation and commentary see MS HCS, Ch'in-Han, VII, 1 (7).
67. See Legge, CC, III: 381, 439; and Kuo, MJ, 1935: 102b, 114a, 125b.
68. Legge, CC, III: 414, 516; IV: 439, cf. 582. Kuo, MJ, 1935: 118a.
69. Ch'ü, TT, 1947: 200.
70. Falkenstein, 1936: 58 ff.
71. Schneider, 1920: 21, 23.
72. Deimel, 1924b: 25. Schneider, 1920: 108 ff.
73. Schneider, 1920: 92.
74. Deimel, 1927: 58 ff., 61. *Ibid.,* 1928: 116 ff. *Ibid.,* 1929: 82, 85 f. Cf. Schneider, 1920: 80, 85.
75. Deimel, 1927: 60 ff. *Ibid.,* 1931: 108 f., 112.
76. Schneider, 1920: 83.
77. *Ibid.:* 32.
78. Scholtz, 1934: 36, 137.
79. Deimel, 1931: 39. Schneider, 1920: 66 ff. Cf. Scholtz, 1934: 79, 92.
80. Schneider, 1920: 67 ff. Scholtz, 1934: 115. Leemans, 1950: 45 ff.
81. Schneider, 1920: 68.
82. Scholtz, 1934: 171.
83. *Ibid.:* 115.
84. Schneider, 1920: 68.
85. Leemans, 1950: 46.
86. Sethe, 1908: 8. Breasted, 1927, I: 209; II: 208 ff.; III: 20 ff.
87. Sethe, 1908: 8 ff.; Breasted, 1927, IV: 284.
88. TEA, I: 83 ff.
89. *Ibid.:* 279 ff.
90. *Ibid.:* 75, 89, 97, 281, 287, 291.
91. *Ibid.:* 93. Breasted, 1927, II: 114.
92. TEA, I: 93.
93. *Ibid.:* 93, 99, 281, 283, 297. Breasted, 1927, IV: 282 ff.
94. Cf. Wittfogel, 1951: 34.
95. Schneider, 1920: 66 ff.
96. Thureau-Dangin, 1907: 67 ff., 77, 103 ff. Barton, 1929: 181 ff., 217 ff., 143. Price, 1927: 58 ff., 16.
97. Thureau-Dangin, 1907: 31, 103, 105–7. Barton, 1929: 47, 131, 145. Price, 1927: 63, 71 19 ff.
98. Thureau-Dangin, 1907: 71, 107. Barton, 1929: 185, 221. Price, 1927: 63, 20–1.
99. Price, 1927: 20.
100. Leemans, 1950: 113.

101. *Ibid.:* 118.
102. *Ibid.:* 120 ff.
103. *Ibid.:* 122.

7, G

1. Acosta, 1945: 39 ff.
2. Bandelier, 1878: 426 and n. 98. *Ibid.,* 1880: 600. Monzon, 1949: *passim*
3. Zurita, 1941: 146. Oviedo, HGNI, II, Pt. 2: 535 ff. Cf. Bandelier, 1880: 602 and n. 73.
4. For various categories of Aztec craftsmen see Sahagun, 1938, III: 28 ff.; II: 385, 394; Díaz, 1944, I: 349; Torquemada, 1943, II: 486; and Motolinia, 1941: 243.
5. Motolinia, 1941: 206. Oviedo, HGNI, II, Pt. 2: 536. Tezozomoc, 1944: 105. Torquemada, 1943, II: 555, 559. Cf. Cortes, 1866: 103.
6. Monzon, 1949: 44. Bandelier, 1878: 426, n. 98.
7. Zurita, 1941: 146 ff. Monzon, 1949: 26.
8. Tezozomoc, 1944: 100, 105, 123, 148.
9. Sahagun, 1938, II: 356 ff. Tezozomoc, 1944: 143, 156.
10. Sahagun, 1938, II: 341, 344 ff., 354 ff., 359.
11. Tezozomoc, 1944: 125.
12. Cf. Sahagun, 1938, II: 102, 196.
13. Ramirez, 1944: 86. Tezozomoc, 1944: 148.
14. Roys, 1943: 46.
15. See above, Chap. 6.
16. See Roys, 1943: 46.
17. *Ibid.:* 51.
18. Landa, 1938: 94 ff.
19. Bréhier, 1950: 183 ff., 201 ff.
20. Stöckle, 1911: 11, 16, and *passim.* Bréhier, 1950: 182 ff., 221.
21. Fletcher, 1856: 57.
22. Herberstein, NR, I: 111. Cf. Staden, 1930: 11 ff.
23. Herberstein, NR, I: 111.
24. Kulischer, 1925: 349 ff.
25. Kilburger, quoted by Kulischer, 1925: 350. Lyashchenko, 1949: 224 ff.
26. Kulischer, 1925: 343 ff. Mavor, 1925, I: 118 ff.
27. Kulischer, 1925: 344 ff.
28. *Ibid.:* 349 ff. Lyashchenko, 1949: 224 ff.
29. Kilburger, quoted by Kulischer, 1925: 350.
30. *Ibid.*
31. Fletcher, 1856: 62 ff.
32. *Ibid.:* 61.
33. *Ibid.:* 62.
34. Gsell, HA, I: 98.
35. Polybius 15. 1. 6 f.
36. Hammurabi, sec. 271. Cf. Meissner, BA, I: 153, 361, 163, 230 ff.
37. Roys, 1943: 34.
38. Grassman, RV, I: 341. Whitney, 1905: 899. Cf. Keith, 1922: 100; and Banerjee, 1925: 115.
39. Banerjee, 1925: 155. Cf. Whitney, 1905: 111.
40. Hopkins, 1922: 258 ff.
41. *Ibid.:* 267.
42. *Ibid.*
43. Fick, 1920: 277.
44. Banerjee, 1925: 192.

45. Hopkins, 1902: 173.
46. Buddhist Suttas: 3.
47. Rhys-Davids, 1922: 175.
48. *Ibid.*: 178. Law, 1923: *passim.* Ibid., 1941: 163 ff. Buddhist Suttas: 131.
49. Buddhist Suttas: 3.
50. *Jātakam*, I: 155; III: 317; IV: 195; V: 35 and esp. 441 ff.
51. Fick, 1920: 137 ff. Rhys-Davids, 1950: 13, 16. Law, 1923: 116, 138 ff., 172 ff., 180, 196, 202.
52. Rhys-Davids, 1950: 1. *Ibid.*, 1922: 190 ff. Law, 1941: 119–38.
53. See *Jātakam*, I: 65, 79; II: 378 ff.; III: 66, 144, 321 ff.; IV: 1; V: 185, 210, and *passim.* Cf. C. A. F. Rhys-Davids, 1922: 207.
54. Fick, 1920: 258 ff. Cf. *Jātakam*, I: 336, 342 ff.; II: 59, 74; III: 134, 322; IV: 74; V: 414 and *passim.*
55. Fick, 1920: 257 ff.
56. See *Jātakam*, I: 178, 203; II: 268, 491; III: 523 ff.; IV: 80 and *passim.*
57. See *Jātakam*, I: 436, 438.
58. C. A. F. Rhys-Davids, 1922: 207.
59. Fick, 1920: 260. Cf. *Jātakam*, V: 412 ff.; VI: 391 ff.; VII: 224.
60. C. A. F. Rhys-Davids, 1922: 207.
61. *Ibid.*
62. *Ibid.*: 211.
63. *Ibid.*: 210 ff.
64. Hopkins, 1902: 175.
65. *Ibid.*: 175, n. 2.
66. GBP, 1882: 406 (italics mine).
67. *Ibid.*: 405.
68. See Burnouf, 1876: 220.
69. Speiser, 1942: 60. Jacobsen, 1943: 165 ff. Kramer, 1950: 45 ff.
70. Boas, 1938: 610. Wittfogel and Goldfrank, 1943: 17.
71. Kramer, 1948: 156 ff.
72. Jacobsen, 1943: 159 ff.
73. *Ibid.*: 160.
74. Kramer, 1948: 162.
75. Götze, 1933: 67.
76. *Ibid.*: 67, 71.
77. Landsberger, 1925: 10, 23.
78. Götze, 1933: 71 and nn. 18–20.
79. Landsberger, 1925: 9.
80. Götze, 1933: 70 and nn. 22–25.
81. Jacobsen, 1943: 161. Cf. Götze, 1933: 70.
82. Landsberger, 1925: 9.
83. Jacobsen, 1943: 162. Cf. Walther, 1917: 12 ff.; and Cuq, 1929: 354 ff.
84. Cf. esp. Walther, 1917: 22 ff.
85. Jacobsen, 1943: 164 ff.
86. Cuq, 1929: 358.
87. *Ibid.*
88. Cf. Krückmann, 1932: 446; and Walther, 1917: 74, 75 ff.
89. Weber, RS, II: 88 ff.

7, H
1. Ostrogorsky, 1940: 192.
2. *Ibid.*

3. Mukerjee, 1939: 219.
4. Edgerton, 1947: 156. Kees, 1933: 45.
5. Wilcken, 1912: 278 ff.
6. Cuq, 1929: 363.
7. See above, Chap. 4.
8. For the main date see Bodde, 1938: 238 ff. For a fuller treatment of the matter see MS HCS, Ch'in-Han, I, 1.
9. Smith, 1926: 365.
10. Gibb and Bowen, 1950: 254 ff.
11. See Kees, 1933: 42.
12. Alexander, 1899: 29.
13. Edgerton, 1947: 159 ff.
14. See Kees, 1933: 23, 42, 44; and Breasted, 1927, I: 76 ff., 93, 166 ff.; II: 6, 9; IV: 405.
15. Zurita, 1941: 148 ff. Oviedo, HGNI, II, Pt. 2: 535. Monzon, 1949: 44.
16. Appadorai, 1936, I: 135 ff.
17. Hardy, 1931: 22, 25. Johnson and West, 1949: 22 ff., 65.
18. Poliak, 1939: 36, 39.
19. Gibb and Bowen, 1950: 253.
20. Ostrogorsky, 1940: 179, 194.
21. Boulais, 1924: 244.
22. Oviedo, HGNI, II, Pt. 2: 535.
23. *Jātakam*, II: 427; VI: 98.
24. *Shih-chi*, 30.11a. For translation and comment see MS HCS, Ch'in-Han II (45)
25. Lang, 1946: 87, 94.
26. See Wittfogel, 1956: 157 ff.
27. Haxthausen, SR, III: 46 ff.
28. *Ibid.*: 47.
29. Segrè, 1943: 107.
30. Appadorai, 1936, I: 115.
31. Kees, 1933: 42.
32. Alexander, 1899: 29.
33. Leemans, 1950: 53.
34. Seidl, 1951: 46.
35. Kees, 1933: 42.
36. Jolly, 1896: 94.
37. Appadorai, 1936, I: 152.
38. Leemans, 1950: 53.
39. Meissner, BA, I: 188.
40. Schawe, 1932: 434.
41. Cuq, 1929: 105.
42. *Ibid.*: 92 ff.
43. *Ibid.*: 103.
44. *Ibid.*: 100.
45. Dubberstein, 1939: 36.
46. Rostovtzeff, 1941, I: 465. Christensen, 1933: 271.
47. Rostovtzeff, 1910: 246 ff.
48. Segrè, 1943: 88, 133.
49. Tarn, 1927: 113 ff. Cf. Bikerman, 1938: 183 ff.; and Rostovtzeff, 1910: 249 ff.
50. Tarn, 1927: 123, 150 ff.
51. *Ibid.*: 131.
52. *Ibid.*: 150. Cf. Bell, 1948: 46; Schubart, 1922: 229 ff.; and Johnson, 1951: 67 ff.
53. Rostovtzeff, 1941, I: 289.

54. *Ibid.:* 290.
55. Berger, 1950: 314.
56. Wilcken, 1912: 285 ff. Cf. Tarn, 1927: 150.
57. Wilcken, 1912: 307. Cf. Bell, 1948: 74.
58. Wellhausen, 1927: 32.
59. Becker, IS, I: 237.
60. Cf. Tritton, 1930: 146 ff.
61. Steinwenter, 1920: 51.
62. Becker, IS, I: 237. Cf. *ibid.,* 1903: 94.
63. Cf. Wellhausen, 1927: 275.
64. Becker, 1903: 94.
65. Becker, IS, I: 238.
66. Johnson, 1951: 86.
67. Becker, IS, I: 237.
68. Becker, 1903: 121 ff. Wellhausen, 1927: 31 ff.
69. Becker, 1903: 121 ff.
70. *Ibid.:* IS, I: 239 ff.
71. Poliak, 1939: 24.
72. *Ibid.:* 36 ff.
73. *Ibid.:* 32 ff.
74. *Ibid.:* 39.
75. Gibb and Bowen, 1950: 238.
76. *Ibid.:* 256.
77. *Ibid.:* 239.
78. *Ibid.:* 261.
79. *Ibid.:* 258.
80. *Ibid.*
81. *Ibid.*
82. Roys, 1943: 36.
83. *Ibid.:* 37.
84. Landa, 1938: 111. Tozzer, 1941: 96 and n. 429. Roys, 1943: 37.
85. Monzon, 1949: 45 ff.
86. Zurita, 1941: 148.
87. *Ibid.:* 143 ff., 148 ff., 152 ff.
88. *Ibid.:* 144.
89. Oviedo, HGNI, II, Pt. 2: 535.
90. Monzon, 1949: 41 ff. Cf. Oviedo, HGNI, II, Pt. 2: 535 ff.
91. Monzon, 1949: 45.
92. Zurita, 1941: 153, cf. 144.
93. *Ibid.:* 153.
94. *Ibid.:* 144.
95. Monzon, 1949: 45.
96. Mommsen, 1921: 573, n. 1. Wilcken, 1912: 287. Bell, 1948: 74.
97. Johnson and West, 1949: 18, 39.
98. Wilcken, 1912: 298, 303.
99. *Ibid.:* 298, 307 ff. Bell, 1948: 74.
100. Wilcken, 1912: 287, 302, 307.
101. *Ibid.:* 303.
102. *Ibid.:* 298, 302. Johnson and West, 1949: 18.
103. Cf. Johnson, 1951: 72 ff.
104. Wilcken, 1912: 312, 319 ff., 322.

105. See *ibid.:* 322.
106. *Ibid.:* 322 ff. Hardy, 1931: 22, 25, 136, 138. Johnson and West, 1949: 22 ff., 65. Johnson, 1951: 97. Cf. Bell, 1948: 122 ff.
107. Cf. Wilcken, 1912: 323; Johnson and West, 1949: 46; and Hardy, 1931: 230.
108. Hardy, 1931: 54 ff. Bell, 1948: 124. Johnson, 1951: 86, 97.
109. Hardy, 1931: 82 ff. Johnson, 1951: 83 ff.
110. Cf. Hardy, 1931: 23; and Johnson and West, 1949: 46.
111. See Hardy, 1931: 59 ff.; Bell, 1948: 124 ff.; and Johnson and West, 1949: 30.
112. Johnson and West, 1949: 240.
113. *Ibid.*
114. Cf. *ibid.;* and Johnson, 1951: 123.
115. Johnson, 1951: 86.
116. *Ibid.*
117. *Han Shu,* 24A.14b.
118. *Ibid.:* 11a–b, 14b–15a.
119. *Shih Chi,* 30.11a, 15a ff. *Han Shu,* 24B.12a, 14a ff. MS HCS, Ch'in-Han, II (45) (50).
120. Wan, KT, 1933: 163 ff. Cf. Balázs, BWT, I: 43 ff.
121. *Agrarian China:* 2.
122. *Ibid.:* 23 ff.

7, I

1. Scheil, 1900: 86, 99. Meissner, BA, I: 367. Cuq, 1929: 130. Cf. Speiser, 1942: 59.
2. See above, Chap. 6.
3. *Jātakam,* II: 37 ff. For the function of the appraiser see also IV: 160 ff.
4. See Kees, 1933: 48; Hammurabi, secs. 273 ff.; Meissner, BA, I: 163, 231; and *Jātakam* III: 316, 443, 488, 490.
5. Cf. *Arthaśāstra,* 1923: 76.
6. Cf. *Jātakam, passim;* and *Arabian Nights: passim.*
7. For China see Lang, 1946: 94.

8, A

1. Smith, 1937: 248.
2. *Ibid.*
3. *Ibid.:* 776.

8, C

1. For the history of the term see Emge, 1950: 1205 ff.
2. Stalin, 1942: 352 ff.
3. These facts have been established by Lienche Tu Fang through an analysis of bureaucratic underlings in the Ch'ing dynasty as part of the Ch'ing work of the Chinese History Project (MS).
4. Weber, RS, I: 331 ff.
5. *Ibid.:* 332.
6. Cf. Meyer, GA, IV, Pt. 1: 45 ff. and n.; and Christensen, 1944: 137, n. 1.
7. Cf. Gray and Cary, 1939: 196; and Meyer, GA, IV, Pt. 1: 49.
8. Meyer, GA, IV, Pt. 1: 48.
9. *Ibid.:* 50.
10. *Ibid.:* 49, 67 ff. Gray and Cary, 1939: 198.
11. Gray and Cary, 1939: 198.
12. Cf. Herodotus 5.96; Gray and Cary, 1939: 197; and Meyer, GA, IV, Pt. 1: 49.
13. Herodotus 5.32, Meyer, GA, IV, Pt. 1: 49.
14. Xenophon 8.6.10. Gray and Cary, 1939: 196. Meyer, GA, IV, Pt. 1: 49.

15. Xenophon 8.6.10 ff.
16. Gray and Cary, 1939: 197.
17. *Ibid.*
18. *Ibid.:* 198.
19. *Ibid.:* 199.
20. Meyer, GA, IV, Pt. 1: 50, cf. 53.
21. *Ibid.:* 59 and n. 1.
22. Gray and Cary, 1939: 196.
23. Meyer, GA, IV, Pt. 1: 51.
24. Rowe, 1946: 273.
25. Moreland, 1929: 9.
26. *Ibid.:* 8.
27. *Ibid.:* 119 ff.
28. Wittfogel, in *Commentary*, October 1950: 337.
29. Rowe, 1946: 267.
30. Wittfogel and Fêng, 1949: 441.
31. Kees, 1953: 4.
32. See above, Chap. 8.
33. Fick, 1920: 253.
34. *Ibid.*
35. *Ibid.*
36. *Jātakam*, IV: 541 ff.; VI: 317.
37. Jolly, 1896: 148 ff. Cf. Vishnu, 1900: 190 ff.
38. See C. A. F. Rhys-Davids, 1922: 205.
39. See above, Chap. 7.
40. For the social position of landholders see *Jātakam*, I: 130, 167, 185, 232 ff., 376; II: 73, 98, 234 ff., 300, 384, 388, 425; III: 59, 105, 171, 222 ff., 224, 554; IV: 449; V: 168, 475, 506 ff.; VI: 317.
41. See Stein, 1951: 131. Cf. Hardy, 1931: 25 ff.
42. Ondegardo, 1872: 37 ff.
43. See above, Chap. 7.
44. Ch'ü, TT, 1937: 172.
45. See above, sec. C, n. 3.
46. See esp. Hammurabi, secs. 28 ff.
47. Wilcken, 1912: 184.
48. Johnson and West, 1949: 290.
49. Cf. Poliak, 1939: 49.
50. Gibb and Bowen, 1950: 261.
51. Cf. Otto, PT, II: 243 ff.
52. See above, Chap. 4.
53. Legge, CC, I: *passim.*

8, D

1. See above, Chap. 7.
2. Cf. above, Chap. 2.
3. Wittfogel, 1931: 393 ff. *Ibid.*, 1938: 96 ff.
4. Meissner, BA, I: 180, 377. Mendelsohn, 1949: 66 ff.
5. Kees, 1933: 48, 130. Cf. Erman and Ranke, 1923: 144.
6. Westermann, 1937: 75.
7. Meyer, 1924, I: 190.
8. Mendelsohn, 1949: 121.
9. Wittfogel, 1931: 408 ff.

8, E

1. For this term see Wittfogel, 1949: 15.
2. Lowie, 1927: 42. Cf. MacLeod, 1924: 12, 39.
3. Lowie, 1927: 38.
4. See MacLeod, 1924: *passim*. Cf. Lowie, 1927: 33 ff.
5. Wittfogel and Fêng, 1949: 505 ff.
6. Wittfogel, 1949: 10 ff.

8, F

1. MEGA, I, Pt. 6: 534.
2. *Ch'ing Shih Kao*, 11.2a.
3. *Ibid.*, 11.4b.
4. *Yen T'ieh Lun*, I: 14a. Cf. Gale, 1931: 35.
5. *Peking Gazette*, 1898: 92.

8, G

1. Mavor, 1925, I: 306 ff.
2. Lyashchenko, 1949: 279.
3. *Ibid.*: 280. Cf. Mavor, 1925, I: 306, 310.
4. Wittfogel, 1924: 93. Cf. Lamprecht, DG, IV: 200 ff.

8, H

1. See above, Chap. 5. Cf. Gutmann, 1909: 111.
2. Cf. Erman and Ranke, 1923: 138; and Erman, 1923: 247.
3. Kees, 1933: 46.
4. For China see Wittfogel, 1931: 578 ff. For Mamluk Egypt see Poliak, 1934: 268.
5. For China see Wittfogel, 1931: 579, nn. 355 f.
6. Boulais, 1924: 184.
7. *Peking Gazette*, 1898: 43.
8. Nöldeke, 1892: 158, 162.
9. *Ibid.*: 155, 158.

8, I

1. See above, sec. C, n. 3.
2. *Huang-ch'ao Ching-shih Wên Hsü-p'ien.*
3. See above, sec. C, n. 3. Reference to *Ch'ing Shih Lu* (Chia-ch'ing), 55.18a–19a.
4. *Ibid.*
5. Boulais, 1924: 654 ff.
6. See Kulischer, AW, I: 280 ff.
7. "The Han Officials, a Statistical Study," MS prepared by the Chinese History Project. The basic data were collected by Mrs. Ch'ü Tseng-ch'iu and analyzed by Esther S. Goldfrank.
8. Helck, 1939: 14 ff.
9. *Ibid.*: 71 ff.
10. Wiet, 1937: 399.
11. See Kornemann, 1949: 257 ff.
12. Ostrogorsky, 1940: 225.
13. *Ibid.* Cf. Stein, 1951: 129.
14. Ostrogorsky, 1940: 241 (italics mine).
15. For the concept of powerful families see Wittfogel and Fêng, 1949: 285.
16. *Peking Gazette*, 1896: 60.
17. *Ibid.*, 1872: 4.
18. *Ibid.*, 1890: 55.

19. Mavor, 1925, I: 398.
20. *Ibid.:* 415.
21. *Ibid.*
22. *Ibid.:* 410 ff.
23. See Berle and Means, 1944: 94, 117, 121; and Gordon, 1945: 28, 49, 52, 108 ff.,
    272 ff., 301 ff.
24. Wittfogel and Fêng, 1949: 441.
25. *Ibid.:* 199 ff.
26. *Ibid.:* 416, n. 51.
27. *Han Shu,* 97A.21b–23a. *San Kuo Chih, Wei* 5.1a.
28. Lybyer, 1913: 58 and n. 2.
29. See above, Chap. 4.
30. *Tso Chuan Chu Shu,* 42.6a–b. *Shih Chi,* 68.9b.
31. Jones, 1831: 113.
32. See above, Chap. 3.
33. Cf. *Jātakam,* III: 369; and Fick, 1920: 173.
34. Dubois, 1943: 290. See above, Chap. 3.
35. Manu, 1886: 141.
36. *Ibid.:* 24.
37. Roys, 1943: 34.
38. Wittfogel, 1947: 24.
39. See Aristotle, *Politics* 4.15.1300b.
40. See MS "The Han Officials."
41. For this phrase see Wittfogel, 1949: 15 ff.
42. Wittfogel and Fêng, 1949: 454.
43. Wittfogel, 1947: 25 and nn. 57–61. Cf. Kracke, 1953: 70 and n. 61.
44. Wittfogel, 1947: 26.
45. *Ibid.:* 30 ff.
46. *Ibid.:* 32–8.
47. Wittfogel and Fêng, 1949: 463.
48. *Ibid.*
49. For a discussion of this edict see MS Chang, CG.
50. Kracke, 1947: 120.
51. See Olmstead, 1948: 90, 227, 267, 312, 314, and *passim.*
52. Herodotus 8.105. Xenophon 7.5.64.
53. Cf. Mez, 1922: 336.
54. *Hou Han Shu,* 78.6b–7a. For translation and comment see MS HCS, Ch'in-Han
    III (76).
55. See Wittfogel, 1935: 55, n. 2.
56. *Shih Chi,* 87.22b ff. Cf. Bodde, 1938: 52 ff.
57. *Hou Han Shu,* 78.2b.
58. *Han Shu,* 93.1a.
59. *Hou Han Shu,* 78.2b.
60. *Han Shu,* 93.4b.
61. *Hou Han Shu,* 78.3b.
62. *Ibid.,* 68.4a ff.
63. For this term see Wittfogel, 1949: 24.
64. *Ming Shih,* 304.21b–28a.
65. Hug, 1918: 451 f.
66. *Ibid.:* 452.
67. *Ibid.*
68. Ostrogorsky, 1940: 175.

69. Runciman, 1933: 204.
70. *Ibid.*
71. *Ibid.:* 203. Schubart, 1943: 27, 220.
72. Schubart, 1943: 206, 102. Mez, 1922: 335.
73. Runciman, 1933: 203 ff.
74. *Ibid.*
75. Amari, 1935: 301, 312. Mez, 1922: 335.
76. Runciman, 1933: 203.
77. Ostrogorsky, 1940: 175.
78. Runciman, 1933: 203.
79. Mez, 1922: 335.
80. For this term see Fischer, 1948: 634.
81. Mez, 1922: 332.
82. Wittfogel and Fêng, 1949: 529, 560 ff.
83. *Ibid.:* 569.
84. *Ibid.:* 464.
85. *Peking Gazette*, 1899: 82, 84 ff., 86, 87 f.
86. Stevenson, 1934: 188 ff. Charlesworth, 1934: 686. Momigliano, 1934: 727. Last, 1936: 426 ff., 432. Duff, 1936: 757 ff.
87. Miller, 1941: 14.
88. Ayalon, 1951: 16 ff., 27 ff., 29 ff., 31 ff., 34 ff.
89. Lybyer, 1913: 39, 117 ff. Miller, 1941: 70, 73.
90. Lybyer, 1913: 100 ff.
91. Miller, 1941: 71.
92. Machiavelli, 1940: 16 ff.
93. *Ibid.:* 16.
94. Lybyer, 1913: 69, 92, cf. 49.

9, A

1. Boas, 1937: 102.
2. *Ibid.*, 1928: 236.
3. See Arkell and Moy-Thomas, 1941: 397, 408. Mayr, 1942: 280 ff., 286, 289.

9, B

1. Smith, 1937: 645 ff., 687 ff., 789.
2. See Mill, 1820, I: 175 ff.
3. *Ibid.*, II: 175 ff.; cf. I: 182 ff., and II: 186. For other references to the nonfeudal conditions of India see II: 25 ff., 166 ff., 176, 189 ff., 202.
4. Jones, 1831: 7 ff., 109 ff.
5. Mill, 1909: 12 ff.
6. MEGA, I, Pt. 6: 630.
7. Mill, 1909: 20.
8. Jones, 1859: 447. Cf. *ibid.*, 1831: 111 ff.
9. Marx, NYDT, August 5, 1853.
10. Marx, 1921: lvi. *Ibid.*, DK, I: 45; III, Pt. 1: 318.
11. Marx, DK, III, Pt. 1: 318.
12. See Marx, DK, I: 42 ff.; III, Pt. 1: 310, 315, 317, n. 50; III, Pt. 2: 136, 174, 324. *Ibid.*, 1921, II: 482 ff.
13. For the above cited passages see Marx, NYDT, June 25, 1853.
14. Marx and Engels, 1920, I: 197.
15. Marx, NYDT, December 3, 1859.
16. Marx, DK, III, Pt. 1: 318 (italics mine).
17. Marx, NYDT, December 3, 1859.

18. MEGA, III, Pt. 1: 455, 459. See Marx and Engels, 1920, I: 475.
19. Marx and Engels, 1920, I: 160.
20. Marx, 1927: 333.
21. Engels, 1894: 56.
22. Engels, 1935: 165.
23. Marx, 1857: 227.
24. Marx, 1927: 144.
25. Marx, DK, III, Pt. 1: 315; III, Pt. 2: 136.
26. Marx and Engels, 1952: 225.
27. MEGA, III, Pt. 2: 487.
28. *Ibid.*
29. Marx, NYDT, August 5, 1853.
30. Marx, DK, III, Pt. 2: 324.
31. *Ibid.*: 174.
32. Marx, 1939: 376 ff.
33. *Ibid.*: 393.
34. *Ibid.*: 395.
35. *Ibid.*: 392 ff.
36. *Ibid.*, DK, I: 683 ff.
37. Lenin, S, I: 121.
38. *Ibid.*, III: 56.
39. *Ibid.*: 58.
40. *Ibid.*, IV: 351.
41. *Ibid.*: 390.
42. *Ibid.*, VI: 13.
43. *Ibid.*, IX: 43.
44. *Ibid.*: 33, 32.
45. *Ibid.*, XIII: 300 ff.
46. *Ibid.*, XVII: 31.
47. *Ibid.*, XVIII: 144.
48. *Ibid.*: 145.
49. *Ibid.*, XX: 375.
50. *Ibid.*, XXI: 40.
51. *Ibid.*, II: 312; XIII: 300 ff.
52. Marx, 1857: 218.
53. Lenin, S, V: 345.
54. *Ibid.*, VI: 28.
55. *Ibid.*, IX: 114.
56. *Ibid.*, XVII: 118 (italics mine).

9, c

1. Marx, DK, I: 104; III, Pt. 1: 316; III, Pt. 2: 237. *Ibid.*, TMW, I: 371; III: 452 ff., 479 ff.
2. MEGA, III, Pt. 1: 133.
3. Mill, 1909: 12 ff.
4. Marx, TMW, III: 501. For the original version see Jones, 1859: 448 ff.
5. MEGA, I: 476 ff. See Bernier, 1891: 220, 381, cf. 204 ff., 205 ff., 213 ff.
6. See Marx, DK, I: 45 ff.; III, Pt. 1: 316 f.; III, Pt. 2: 136, 157, 174, 323 ff., 337, 367. *Ibid.*, TMW, I: 397; II, Pt. 1: 205; III: 451, 452 ff., 473 ff., 479 ff., 482 ff., 495 ff., 497, 498 ff.
7. Marx, DK, I: 478.
8. *Ibid.*

9. Marx, NYDT, June 25, 1853.
10. *Ibid.*
11. *Ibid.* Cf. Marx, 1939: 337.
12. Marx, DK, III, Pt. 1: 370 (italics mine).
13. Engels, 1935: 183.
14. *Ibid.*
15. Engels, 1935: 183. *Ibid.*, 1921: 185.
16. Marx, DK, III, Pt. 2: 259 ff.
17. Engels, 1935: 183.
18. Marx, 1939: 378.
19. *Ibid.:* 391.
20. Engels, 1935: 164, 185.
21. *Ibid.:* 183.
22. *Ibid.*
23. *Ibid.*
24. *Ibid.:* 184.
25. *Ibid.:* 291.
26. See above, Chap. 8, sec. A, n. *a.*
27. Engels, 1935: 183.
28. *Ibid.:* 291.
29. Engels, 1921: *passim.*
30. Morgan, 1877: 372 ff.
31. Engels, 1921: 132.
32. *Ibid.:* 165 f., 44 ff.
33. *Ibid.:* 185. Cf. Engels, 1935: 184 ff., 395.
34. Engels, 1921: 167 (italics mine).
35. *Ibid.:* 180.
36. *Ibid.*
37. *Ibid.:* 181.
38. *Ibid.:* 331 (italics mine).
39. Marx, TMW, II, Pt. 1: 310.
40. *Ibid.*
41. *Ibid.*, II, Pt. 1: 313.
42. *Ibid.*
43. *Ibid.*
44. MEGA, I, Pt. 6: 545.
45. Mill, 1909: 949.
46. *Ibid.:* 961.
47. MEGA, III, Pt. 3: 217, 224, 302, 341.
48. Guillaume, IDS, I: 78 ff. Bakunin, 1953: *passim.*
49. Bakunin, 1953: 288.
50. *Ibid.:* 287.
51. Guillaume, IDS, II: 192.
52. Cf. Wittfogel, 1953: 358, n. 34.
53. See Engels and Kautsky, 1935: 306, 310, 313 ff.
54. MEGA, I, Pt. 6: 554.
55. *Ibid.*
56. *Ibid.:* 555.
57. Cf. Mill, 1909: 208.
58. See above, p. 180.
59. Lenin, S, III: 126.
60. *Ibid.*, V: 271, 275 f.

61. *Ibid.*, VI: 334.
62. *Ibid.*, I: 272, n. 2.
63. *Ibid.*, IV: 350.
64. *Ibid.*, II: 103–4; VI: 333, 343.
65. *Ibid.*, XIV: *passim.*
66. *Ibid.*, X: 27 ff.
67. See below, p. 396.
68. *Protokoly:* 116.
69. Lenin, S, X: 303.
70. *Ibid.*, XIII: 300.
71. *Ibid.*
72. *Ibid.*, XIII: 301.
73. *Ibid.:* 302.
74. *Ibid.:* 303.
75. Plekhanov, 1906: 12 ff. *Protokoly:* 44.
76. Plekhanov, 1906: 16.
77. *Ibid.:* 14.
78. *Ibid.:* 17 (italics mine).
79. *Protokoly:* 45.
80. *Ibid.:* 116.
81. Lenin, S, XIII: 300.
82. *Ibid.*, XIII: 302.
83. *Ibid.:* 301.
84. *Protokoly:* 103 ff. See also Lenin, S, XIII: 299.
85. *Protokoly:* 45.
86. Lenin, S, X: 303.
87. *Ibid.*, XIII: 301, 387.
88. Lenin, 1937: 288.
89. See above, sec. B, nn. 47, 48.
90. See above, sec. B, n. 49.
91. Lenin, S, XXI: 17.
92. *Ibid.:* 17 ff., 78 ff., 257, 336.
93. *Ibid.*, XXII: 226.
94. *Ibid.*, XXV: 357 ff.
95. *Ibid.:* 358 ff.
96. *Ibid.*, XXIX: 436. Cf. *ibid.*, SW, XI: 642.
97. Lenin, S, XXIX: 438 (italics mine).
98. *Ibid.:* 438 ff.
99. *Ibid.*, XXV: 362.
100. *Ibid.*, XXIX: 445.
101. *Ibid.*, XXVIII: 401.
102. *Ibid.*, XXXII: 329 (italics mine).
103. See MEGA, III, Pt. 1: 487; Marx, DK, I: 323; and Marx and Engels, 1952: 211 ff.
104. See above, sec. B, n. 49.
105. Lenin, S, XXXII: 330 (italics mine).
106. *Ibid.*, XXXIII: 423.
107. *Ibid.:* 430.
108. *Ibid.:* 445.
109. Rjasanoff, 1925: 374 ff.
110. *Inprecor,* 1925: 1280 ff.
111. Varga, 1928: 19 ff.
112. *Problemy Kitaia* (Moscow), Nos. 4–5, 1930: 223.

113. See below, p. 407.
114. DASP: 2 ff., 14 ff., 66 ff.
115. *Ibid.:* 72, 181.
116. *Ibid.:* 182.
117. *Ibid.:* 5, 62.
118. *Ibid.:* 20, 24.
119. *Ibid.:* 74.
120. *Ibid.:* 3.
121. See *Inprecor,* 1928: 1249, 1254.
122. Stalin, S, II: 337 f.
123. See Wolfe, 1948: 582 ff.
124. Stalin, S, II: 118, 124 f., 128.
125. *Ibid.,* I: 237 ff.
126. *Ibid.:* 311.
127. *Ibid.,* VIII: 359.
128. *Ibid.,* IX: 240 ff., 285 ff., 290, 336 ff.
129. *Ibid.:* 240.
130. *Ibid.:* 241.
131. Stalin, 1939: 131.
132. Childe, 1946 [originally 1942]: 76, 161, 203, 223, 272, and *passim.*
133. *Ibid.:* 18 ff. (italics mine).
134. Childe, 1944: 23.
135. Childe, 1951: 35.
136. Childe, 1953: 72 (italics mine).
137. Guber, 1942: 275, 279.
138. Tolstov, 1950: 3.

      10, A
1. Mill, 1909: 10–20.
2. Brew, 1946: 44 ff.
3. Willey, 1953a: 378 ff.
4. Huxley, 1955: 9 ff., 15, 21.
5. Mill, 1947: 959.
6. For this term see Westermann, 1937: 76, 13.
7. For this term see Veblen, 1947: 133.
8. Piggott, 1950: 263 ff.
9. Westermann, 1937: 75 ff.
10. *Ibid.:* 76.
11. Arkell and Moy-Thomas, 1941: 408.
12. Mayr, 1942: 5.
13. *Ibid.*
14. See Kroeber, 1948: 261.
15. See above, Chap. 1.
16. See Wipper, 1947: 39, 81.

      10, B
1. See Wittfogel, 1935: 52.
2. Mill, 1909: 696 ff., 701. Cf. Smith, 1937: 736.
3. Mill, 1909: 697, 701.
4. *Ibid.:* xlvii, 699–701.
5. Marx, NYDT, August 8, 1853.
6. *Ibid.*
7. *Ibid.*

8. Marx and Engels, 1952: 217.
9. Marx, NYDT, June 25, 1853.
10. *Ibid.*, DK, III, Pt. 1: 318.
11. Furnivall, 1944: 148. Vandenbosch, 1949: 81.
12. Altamira, 1930: 168 ff.
13. See above, p. 166.
14. See above, Chap. 6.
15. Florinsky, 1953, II: 900.
16. *Ibid.:* 1067, 1081 ff.
17. Prokopowitsch, 1913: 52 ff.
18. Tugan-Baranowsky, 1900: 70 ff., 76 ff., 85 ff.
19. Prokopowitsch, 1913: 58. Cf. Lyashchenko, 1949: 716.
20. *Ibid.*
21. *Ibid.:* 703.
22. Zagorsky, 1928: 7.
23. *Ibid.:* 8.
24. *Ibid.*
25. *Ibid.:* 6.
26. Weber, 1906: 324, cf. 398.
27. Florinsky, 1953, II: 1238. Wolfe, 1948: 564.
28. Kayden, 1929: 14.
29. Florinsky, 1953, II: 1228.
30. Furnivall, 1944: 252.
31. Kahin, 1952: 35.
32. *Imperial Gazetteer of India,* II: 514.
33. Appleby, 1953: 51.
34. Schuster and Wint, 1941: 72.
35. Furnivall, 1944: 43.
36. Kahin, 1952: 471, cf. 29 ff.
37. Nehru, 1946: 283 ff.
38. *Ibid.:* 332 ff., 415 ff., cf. 420 ff.
39. See above, Chap. 7.
40. *Agriculture in India:* 35.
41. Warriner, 1948: 15, 85 ff. Bonné, 1948: 188.
42. Jäckh, 1944: 78 ff.
43. See *ibid.:* 187, 191; Thornburg, Spry, and Soule, 1949: 180, 199: and Bismarck-
    Osten, 1951: 9.
44. Cooke, 1952: 283.
45. See Taylor, 1936: 13.
46. *Ibid.,* 1942: 132.
47. Chamberlin, 1935, I: 248 ff.
48. Lenin, S, XXIV: 4.
49. *Ibid.,* XXX: 237.
50. *Ibid.:* 230 ff.
51. Chamberlin, 1935, I: 281.
52. See *ibid.:* 229.
53. *Ibid.:* 159.
54. *Ibid.:* 249 ff.
55. See Lenin, S, XXVI: 227 ff.
56. *Ibid.,* XXIV: 4.
57. *Ibid.,* XXV: 20.
58. *Ibid.,* XXIV: 5.

59. Chamberlin, 1935, I: 266 ff.
60. Lenin, S, XXV: 267.
61. *Ibid.*, XXVI: 228.
62. See *ibid.*, XX: 375. For Marx' and Engels' basic statements see above; Chap. 9, see B, nn. 20 ff.
63. Lenin, SWG, XXII: 646 ff.
64. *Ibid.*, S, XXXIII: 258.
65. *Ibid.*, XXIII: 229.
66. Baykov, 1947: 8.
67. Lenin, S, XXXIII: 43.
68. *Ibid.*: 423, 430.
69. Marx, 1939: 395.
70. See Mao, 1954: 64, 122, 172, 188, 267, 269–71, 278, cf. 105 ff., 189, 196. *Ibid.*, 1945: 35. *Ibid.*, 1945a: 58.
71. See Wittfogel, 1950: 335.

10, C

1. See *Inprecor*, 1927: 292, 328, 330 ff.; 1942: 123 ff. Cf. Nehru, 1942a: 123 ff.
2. See Wittfogel, 1951: 33.
3. See Jäckh, 1944: 191.
4. Nehru, 1946: 19.
5. See *Socialist Asia*, II, No. 10: 2; III, No. 2: 10; III, No. 3: 5; III, No. 8: 17; Rangoon Tracts, I: 5, 7 ff., 11, 13, 16, 20 ff. See also Mehta, 1954: 40, 59, 149, 152 ff., 165. For statements made by Nehru about India's "feudal" heritage see Nehru, 1946: 284, 307, 319, 320 ff., 324 ff., 334, 352 ff.
6. See Mehta, 1954: 43 ff.
7. Luxemburg, 1951: 604 ff.
8. Rangoon Tracts, I: 5.
9. *Ibid.*, I: 4.
10. See *ibid.*, I: 8, 9.
11. Nehru, 1942: 597.
12. *Ibid.*, 1946: 376.
13. *Hindu Weekly Review* (Madras), November 1, 1954.
14. *Socialist Asia*, III, No. 4: 3, 4.
15. See Wittfogel, 1955a: *passim.*

BIBLIOGRAPHY

THE TITLES LISTED BELOW refer to books and articles cited in this study. In our notes these works are cited by the author's name and date of publication. However, those of more than one volume whose publication was spread over several years (e.g. Meissner, BA) and articles published serially over several years (e.g. Bandelier, DH) are designated by author and title initials. Abbreviations appearing in the notes without an author's name (e.g. RDS) should be found in proper alphabetical position in the list. Titles of collections or periodicals which appear more than twice in the list are cited by the following symbols:

AA	*American Anthropologist.*
ANET	*Ancient Near Eastern Texts, Relating to the Old Testament,* ed. James B. Pritchard. Princeton, 1950.
ASS	*Archiv für Sozialwissenschaft und Sozialpolitik.*
BCPP	*Biblioteca de Cultura Peruana-Premera,* Ser. 2, *Los Cronistas de la Conquista,* ed. Horacio H. Urtega. Paris, 1938.
CAH	*The Cambridge Ancient History,* ed. S. A. Cook, F. E. Adcock, and M. P. Charlesworth. 12 vols. Cambridge, 1923-39.
CEHE	*The Cambridge Economic History of Europe from the Decline of the Roman Empire,* ed. J. H. Clapham and Eileen Power. 2 vols. Cambridge, 1942-52.
CHI	*The Cambridge History of India,* ed. E. J. Rapson. Vols. 1, 3, 4. New York and Cambridge, 1922-37.
CIW	Carnegie Institution of Washington Publications.
CMH	*The Cambridge Medieval History,* planned by J. B. Bury, ed. by H. M. Gwatkin and J. P. Whitney. 8 vols. Cambridge, 1913-36.
ESAR	*An Economic Survey of Ancient Rome,* ed. Tenney Frank in collaboration with T. R. S. Broughton, R. G. Collingwood, A. Grenier, and others. 5 vols. Baltimore, 1933-40.
ESS	*Encyclopaedia of the Social Sciences,* ed. Edwin R. A. Seligman and Alvin Johnson. 15 vols. New York, 1937.
HWI	*Handwörterbuch des Islam,* ed. A. J. Wensinck and J. H. Kramers. Leiden, 1941.
HZ	*Historische Zeitschrift.*
IC	*Islamic Culture.*
JNES	*Journal of Near Eastern Studies.*
NZ	*Die Neue Zeit.*
OCRAA	*Orientalia commentarii de rebus Assyro-Babylonicis, Arabicis, Aegyptiacis,* etc.

PMAAE   Peabody Museum of American Archaeology and Ethnology, Harvard University.

PM   *Dr. A. Petermanns Mitteilungen aus Justus Perthes Geographischer Anstalt.*

RA   *Reallexikon der Assyriologie,* ed. Erich Ebeling and Bruno Meissner. 2 vols. Berlin and Leipzig, 1932–38.

SBE   Sacred Books of the East, ed. F. Max Müller. 50 vols. Oxford and New York, 1879–1910.

SIBAE   Smithsonian Institution, Bureau of American Ethnology Publications.

UBM   *Unter dem Banner des Marxismus.*

Acosta, Fray Joseph de. 1894. *Historia natural y moral de las Indias,* published in Seville, 1590. 2 vols. Madrid.

Acosta Saignes, Miguel. 1945. *Los Pochteca.* Acta Anthropologica, I, No. 1. Mexico City.

Acton, John Emerich Edward Dalberg-. 1948. *Essays on Freedom and Power.* Boston.

Agrarian China. Selected Source Materials from Chinese Authors, comp. and trans. by the Institute of Pacific Relations, with an introduction by R. H. Tawney. Chicago (preface dated 1938).

Agriculture in India. The Publications Division, Ministry of Information and Broadcasting, Government of India, Delhi. April 1950.

Aitken, Barbara. 1930. "Temperament in Native American Religions," *Journal of the Royal Anthropological Institute of Great Britain and Ireland,* LX: 363–400.

Alexander, W. D. 1899. *Brief History of the Hawaiian People.* New York, Cincinnati, and Chicago.

Altamira, Rafael. 1930. *A History of Spanish Civilization,* trans. P. Volkov. London.

Amari, Michele. 1935. *Storia dei Musulmani di Sicilia,* II. 2nd ed. Catania.

Amerasia. A review of America and Asia. 1938–47.

Ammianus Marcellinus. *Ammiani Marcellini rerum gestarum libri qui supersunt,* ed. V. Gardthausen. 2 vols. Leipzig, 1874–75.

Anhegger, Robert. 1943. *Beitraege zur Geschichte des Bergbaus im osmanischen Reich,* I. Istanbul.

Âpastamba. 1898. In *Sacred Laws of the Âryas,* trans. Georg Bühler. SBE, II. New York.

Appadorai, A. 1936. *Economic Conditions in Southern India (1000–1500 A.D.).* 2 vols. Madras University Historical Series, 12 and 12-bis. Madras.

Appleby, Paul H. 1953. "Report of a Survey," *Public Administration in India.* Cabinet Secretariat. New Delhi.

Aristotle. "Politics," in *Basic Works of Aristotle,* ed. Richard McKeon: 1114–1316. New York, 1941.

───── "Rhetoric," in *Basic Works of Aristotle:* 1317–1451.

Arkell, W. J. and Moy-Thomas, J. A. 1941. "Palaeontology and the Taxonomic Problem," in *The New Systematics,* ed. Julian Huxley: 395–410. London.

Armillas, Pedro. 1944. "Revista Mexicana de estudios anthropologicos," in *Sociedad Mexicana de Anthropologia,* VI, No. 3, September 1942– December 1944. Mexico City.

───── 1948. "A Sequence of Cultural Development in Meso-America," in *A Reappraisal of Peruvian Archaeology,* assembled by Wendell C. Bennett. Society of American Archaeology, *Memoirs,* IV: 105–11. April 1948.

───── 1951. "Tecnología, formaciones socio-económicas y religión en Mesoamérica," *Selected Papers of the XXIXth International Congress of Americanists:* 19–30. Chicago.

Arnold, Thomas W. 1924. *The Caliphate.* Oxford.

───── 1941. "*Khalīfa,*" HWI: 291–296. Leiden.

Arrian. *The Anabasis of Alexander* in *The Greek Historians,* trans. Edward J. Chinnock, II: 402–620. New York, 1942.

Árthaçāstra. 1926. *Das altindische Buch vom Welt- und Staatsleben des Arthaçāstra des Kauṭilya,* trans. Johann Jakob Meyer. Leipzig.

Arthaśāstra. 1923. *Kauṭilya's Arthaśāstra,* trans. R. Shamasastry. 2d ed. Mysore.

Asakawa, Kanichi. 1903. *The Early Institutional Life of Japan. A Study in the Reform of 645 A.D.* Tokyo.

───── 1911. "Notes on Village Government in Japan after 1600, II," *Journal of the American Oriental Society,* XXI: 151–216.

───── 1929. *The Documents of Iriki,* Yale Historical Publications, X. New Haven.

───── 1929a. "The Early *Sho* and the Early Manor: a Comparative Study," *Journal of Economic Business History,* I, No. 2: 177–207.

ASBRT. Report of Court Proceedings in the Case of the Anti-Soviet "Bloc of Rights and Trotskyites," heard before the Military Collegium of the Supreme Court of the USSR, Moscow, March 2–13, 1938, *in re* N. I. Bukharin etc. Moscow, 1938.

Atiya, Aziz Suryal. 1934. *The Crusade of Nicopolis.* London.

Atkinson, Charles Francis. 1910. "Army," *Encyclopaedia Britannica,* II: 592–625. 11th ed. New York.

Ayalon, David. 1951. *L'Esclavage du Mamelouk.* Israel Oriental Society Publications, No. 1. Jerusalem.

Bābur. 1921. *Memoirs of Zehīr-ed-Dīn Muhammed Bābur,* II, trans. John Leyden and William Erskine, annotated and revised by Sir Lucas King. London, etc.

Baden-Powell, B. H. 1892. *The Land-Systems of British India*. 3 vols. London and New York.

―――― 1896. *The Indian Village Community*. London, New York, and Bombay.

Bakunin. 1953. *The Political Philosophy of Bakunin: Scientific Anarchism,* comp. and ed. G. P. Maximoff. Glencoe, Ill.

Balázs, Stefan. BWT. "Beiträge zur Wirtschaftsgeschichte der T'ang-Zeit (618–906)," *Mitteilungen des Seminars für orientalische Sprachen,* XXXIV: 1–92; XXXV: 1–73; XXXVI: 1–62. 1931–33.

Bandelier, Adolph E. DH. "Documentary History of the Rio Grande Pueblos, New Mexico," *New Mexico Historical Review,* IV: 303–34; V: 38–66, 154–85. 1929, 1930.

―――― FR. *Final Report of Investigations among the Indians of the Southwestern United States, Carried on Mainly in the Years from 1880 to 1885,* Archaeological Institute of America, American Series, *Papers,* III, 1890; IV, 1892. Cambridge, Mass.

―――― 1877. "On the Art of War and Mode of Warfare of the Ancient Mexicans," PMAAE, *Reports,* II: 95–161. Cambridge, Mass.

―――― 1878. "On the Distribution and Tenure of Lands, and the Customs with Respect to Inheritance, among the Ancient Mexicans," PMAAE, *Reports,* II, No. 2: 385–448. Cambridge, Mass.

―――― 1880. "On the Social Organization and Mode of Government of the Ancient Mexicans," PMAAE, *Reports,* II: 557–699. Cambridge, Mass.

Banerjee (Narayan Chandra Bandyopadhyaya). 1925. *Hindu Period*. Vol. I of *Economic Life and Progress in Ancient India*. Calcutta.

Barton, George A. 1929. *The Royal Inscriptions of Sumer and Akkad.* New Haven and London.

Baudhāyana. 1898. In *Sacred Laws of the Âryas,* trans. Georg Bühler. SBE, II: 143–336. New York.

Bauer, Adolf. 1893. "Die griechischen Kriegsaltertümer," in *Die griechischen Privat- und Kriegsaltertümer* by Iwan von Müller and Adolf Bauer: 270–469. Munich.

Baykov, Alexander. 1947. *The Development of the Soviet Economic System.* Cambridge and New York.

Beaglehole, Ernest. 1937. *Notes on Hopi Economic Life.* Yale University Publications in Anthropology, XV.

Beal, Samuel. *Si-yu-ki. Buddhist Records of the Western World.* 2 vols. in one, London, no date.

Beard, Charles A. 1941. *An Economic Interpretation of the Constitution of the United States.* New York.

Beard, Charles A. and Mary R. 1927. *The Rise of American Civilization.* 2 vols. New York.

Beck, F. and Godin, W. 1951. *Russian Purge and the Extraction of Confession*. New York.

Becker, Carl H. IS. *Islamstudien*. 2 vols. Leipzig, 1924–32.

—— 1903. *Beiträge zur Geschichte Ägyptens unter dem Islam*, II. Strassburg.

Beech, Merwyn W. H. 1911. *The Suk, Their Language and Folklore*. Oxford.

Bell, Sir Charles. 1927. *Tibet Past and Present*. London.

Bell, H. Idris. 1948. *Egypt from Alexander the Great to the Arab Conquest*. Oxford.

Bengtson, Hermann. 1950. *Griechische Geschichte*. Munich.

Berger, Adolph. 1950. "Emphyteusis," *Oxford Classical Dictionary*: 314. Oxford.

Berle, Adolf A., Jr., and Means, Gardiner C. 1944. *The Modern Corporation and Private Property*. New York.

Bernier, François. 1891. *Travels in the Mogul Empire* A.D. *1656–1668*. Rev. ed. based upon Irving Brock's trans., by Archibald Constable: *Constable's Oriental Miscellany, I: Bernier's Travels*. Westminster.

Bhagavadgītā. 1900. Trans. Kāshināth Trimbak Telang. SBE, VIII. New York.

Bikerman, E. 1938. *Institutions des Seleucides*. Paris.

Biot, Edouard. 1851. *Le Tcheou-Li ou Rites des Tcheou*. 2 vols. Paris.

Birkett, G. A. 1918. "From 1801 to 1917," in *Russia from the Varangians to the Bolsheviks*, by Raymond Beazley, Nevill Forbes, and (introduction by) Ernest Barker: 347–557. Oxford.

Bismarck-Osten, Ferdinand von. 1951. *Strukturwandlungen und Nachkriegsprobleme der türkischen Volkswirtschaft*. Kieler Studien, XVI. Kiel.

Björkman, Walther. 1928. *Beiträge zur Geschichte der Staatskanzlei im islamischen Ägypten*. Abhandlungen aus dem Gebiet der Auslandskunde, 28. Hamburg University.

—— 1941. "Turban," *HWI*: 754–8. Leiden.

Blackman, William Fremont. 1899. *The Making of Hawaii*. New York and London.

Bloch, Marc. 1937. "Feudalism: European," *ESS*, V: 203–10. New York.

—— 1949. *La Société féodale*. Paris.

Blom, F. and LaFarge, O. TT. *Tribes and Temples*. 2 vols. New Orleans, 1926–27.

Boas, Franz. 1928. *Anthropology and Modern Life*. New York.

—— 1937. "Anthropology," *ESS*, II: 73–110. New York.

—— 1938. "Mythology and Folklore," in *General Anthropology*, ed. Boas: 609–26. Boston and New York.

Bodde, Derk. 1938. *China's First Unifier*. Leiden.

Bonné, Alfred. 1948. *State and Economics in the Middle East*. London.

Borosdin, J. 1908. "Eine neue Arbeit über den Feudalismus in Russland," review of N. Pawlow-Silwansky, *Der Feudalismus im alten Russland*, in *Vierteljahrschrift für Social- und Wirtschaftsgeschichte*, VI: 572–8.

Boulais, Guy. 1924. *Manuel du Code Chinois*. Shanghai.

Brandt (Conrad), Schwartz (Benjamin), and Fairbank (John K.). 1952. *A Documentary History of Chinese Communism*. Cambridge, Mass.

Breasted, James Henry. 1927. *Ancient Records of Egypt*. 5 vols. Chicago.

Bréhier, Louis. 1949. *Les Institutions de l'Empire Byzantin. L'Evolution de l'humanité*. Paris.

—— 1950. *La Civilisation Byzantine. L'Evolution de l'humanité*. Paris.

Brew, John Otis. 1946. *Archaeology of Alkali Ridge, Southeastern Utah*. PMAAE, *Reports*, XXI. Cambridge, Mass.

Broughton, T. R. S. 1938. "Roman Asia," in *ESAR*, IV: 499–916. Baltimore.

Brown, Delmer M. 1948. "The Impact of Firearms on Japanese Warfare, 1543–98," *Far Eastern Quarterly*, VII, No. 3: 236–53.

Brückner, A. 1896. *Geschichte Russlands bis zum Ende des 18. Jahrhunderts*. Gotha.

Brunner, H. 1905. "Antworten: Germanisch," in Mommsen, 1905: 53–62. Leipzig.

Bücher, Karl. 1922. *Die Entstehung der Volkswirtschaft*. 2 vols. Tübingen.

Büchner, V. F. 1941. "*Madjūs*," *HWI*: 378–82. Leiden.

Buck, John Lossing. 1937. *Land Utilization in China*. Chicago.

Buckley, Robert Burton. 1893. *Irrigation Works in India and Egypt*. London and New York.

Buddhist Suttas. Trans. T. W. Rhys-Davids, SBE, VII, Pt. 2. New York, 1900.

Buhl, Frants. 1930. *Das Leben Muhammeds*, trans. Hans Heinrich Schaeder. Leipzig.

Bühler, Johannes. 1948. *Die Kultur des Mittelalters*. Stuttgart.

Bukharin, Nikolai. 1934. *Historical Materialism*. New York.

Burnouf, E. 1876. *Introduction à l'histoire du Buddhisme Indien*. 2d ed. Paris.

Bury, J. B. 1910. *The Constitution of the Later Roman Empire*. Cambridge.

—— 1931. *History of the Later Roman Empire*. 2 vols. London.

—— 1937. *A History of Greece to the Death of Alexander the Great*. Modern Library. New York.

Busolt, George. GS. *Griechische Staatskunde: Handbuch der klassischen Altertums-Wissenschaft*, ed. Iwan von Müller (Vol. I) and Walter Müller (Vol. II). Munich, 1920, 1926.

Cahen, Claude. 1940. *La Syrie du Nord à l'époque des croisades,* Institut Français de Damas Bibliothèque Orientale, I. Paris.

Casares, David. 1907. "A Notice of Yucatan with some Remarks on its Water Supply," *Proceedings of the American Antiquarian Society,* new ser., XVII: 207–30.

Castañeda. 1896. "Translation of Narrative of Castañeda" in George Parker Winship, "Coronado Expedition 1540–1542," SIBAE, *Fourteenth Annual Report,* Pt. 1: 470–546. Washington.

Chamberlin, William Henry. 1935. *The Russian Revolution 1917–1921.* 2 vols. New York.

Chan-kuo Ts'ê. Commercial Press, Shanghai, 1934.

Chang Chung-li. GI. "Gentry Income." MS.

——— CG. *The Chinese Gentry. Studies on Their Role in Nineteenth-Century Chinese Society.* Introduction by Franz Michael. University of Washington Press, Seattle. 1955. (This book was cited from the manuscript.)

Charlesworth, M. P. 1934. "The Triumph of Octavian, Parts II and III" and "Gaius and Claudius," CAH, X: 116–26 and 653–701. Cambridge.

Chavannes, Edouard. MH. *Les Mémoires historiques de Se-ma Ts'ien.* 5 vols. Paris, 1895–1905.

Chi Ch'ao-ting. 1936. *Key Economic Areas in Chinese History.* London.

Childe, V. Gordon. 1944. "Archaeological Ages as Technological Stages," *Journal of the Royal Anthropological Institute of Great Britain and Ireland,* LXXIV: 7–24.

——— 1946. *What Happened in History.* Penguin Books, New York (Published originally in 1942).

——— 1951. *Social Evolution.* London.

——— 1952. *Man Makes Himself.* Mentor Book, New York (published originally in 1936).

——— 1953. *What Is History?* Schuman's College Paperbacks, New York.

Chimalpahin Quauhtlehuanitzin. *Annales de Domingo Francisco de San Anton Muñon Chimalpahin Quauhtlehuanitzin,* trans. Remi Simeon, Bibliothèque Linguistique Américaine, XII. Paris, 1889.

Chimalpópoca, Códice. Anales de Cuauhtitlan y leyenda de los soles, trans. Primo Feliciano Velazquez. Publicaciones del Instituto de Historia, Ser. 1, No. 1. Mexico, 1945.

Chin Shih. Po-na ed. Commercial Press.

Chin Shih Ts'ui Pien, by Wang Ch'ang. *Ching-hsün t'ang* edition, 1805.

Ch'ing Shih Kao. Published by Ch'ing Shih Kuan.

Chiu T'ang Shu. Po-na ed. Commercial Press.

Chou Li Chu Shu. Ssǔ-pu Pei-yao. Shanghai, 1936.

Christensen, Arthur. 1933. "Die Iranier," in *Kulturgeschichte des alten Orients,* by A. Alt, A. Christensen, A. Götze, A. Grohmann, H. Kees, and B. Landsberger. Vol. III, Pt. 1: 203–310. Munich.

——— 1944. *L'Iran sous les Sassanides.* 2d ed. Copenhagen.

Ch'ü T'ung-tsu. 1937. *Chung-kuo Fêng-chien Shih-hui.* Commercial Press, Shanghai.

——— 1947. *Chung-kuo Fa-lü Yü Chung-kuo Shih-hui.* Commercial Press, Shanghai.

Ch'üan Han-shêng. 1934. *Chung-kuo Hang-hui Chih-tu Shih.* Hsin-shêng-ming, Shanghai.

Cieza de León, Pedro. 1943. *Del Señorío de los Incas,* prologue and notes by Alberto Mario Salas. Buenos Aires.

——— 1945. *La Crónica del Perú.* Buenos Aires and Mexico.

Clark, John Maurice. 1937. "Diminishing Returns," *ESS,* V: 144–6. New York.

CM. *Climate and Man.* Yearbook of Agriculture, Washington, D.C. 1941.

Cobo, Bernabé. *HNM. Historia del Nuevo Mundo . . .* ed. Marcos Jiménez de la Espada. Sociedad de Bibliófilos Andaluces. 4 vols. Seville, 1890–95.

Cole, Charles Woolsey. 1939. *Colbert and a Century of French Mercantilism.* 2 vols. New York.

Collingwood, R. G. 1937. "Roman Britain," in *ESAR,* III: 1–118. Baltimore.

Contenau, Georges. 1950. *La Vie quotidienne à Babylone et en Assyrie.* Paris.

Cook, James. 1944. *Captain Cook's Voyages of Discovery,* ed. John Barrow. Everyman's Library, London and New York.

Cooke, C. Wythe. 1931. "Why the Mayan Cities of the Péten district, Guatemala, Were Abandoned," *Journal of Washington Academy of Science,* XXI: 283–7.

Cooke, Hedley V. 1952. *Challenge and Response in the Middle East.* New York.

Cortes, Don Pascual de Gayangos. 1866. *Cartas y relaciónes de Hernán Cortés al Emperador Carlos V.* Paris.

CPLNC. "La Conquista del Perú llanda la nueva Castilla," in *BCPP:* 307–28. Paris, 1938.

Creel, H. G. 1949. *Confucius, the Man and the Myth.* New York.

Crevenna, Theodore T. *MECM. Materiales para el estudio de la clase media en la America Latina.* 6 vols. Washington, D.C., 1950–51.

Cromer, Earl of. 1908. *Modern Egypt.* 2 vols. London.

Crum, W. E. 1925. "Koptische Zünfte und das Pfeffermonopol," *Zeit-*

schrift für ägyptische Sprache und Altertumskunde, LXX: 103–11.

Cuq, Edouard. 1929. *Etudes sur le droit Babylonien. Les Lois Assyriennes et les lois Hittites.* Paris.

Daghestani, Kazem. FM. *La Famille Musulmane contemporaine en Syrie.* Paris, no date.

Das, Sarat Chandra. 1904. *Journey to Lhasa and Central Tibet.* New York.

DASP. 1931. *Diskussia ob Aziatskom Sposobe Proizvodstva* (Discussion of the Asiatic Mode of Production). Moscow and Leningrad.

DCF. *Die chinesische Frage. Auf dem 8. Plenum der Exekutive der Kommunistischen Internationale Mai 1927.* Hamburg and Berlin, 1928.

De Groot, J. J. M. 1918. *Universimus.* Berlin.

———— 1940. *Sectarianism and Religious Persecution in China.* 2 vols. Reprint.

Deimel, Anton. 1920. "Die Reformtexte Urukaginas," *OCRAA,* No. 2: 3–31.

———— 1922. "Die Bewirtschaftung des Tempellandes zur Zeit Urukaginas," *OCRAA,* No. 5: 1–25.

———— 1924. *Wirtschaftstexte aus Fara.* Leipzig.

———— 1924a. "Die Vermessung der Felder bei den Šumerern um 3000 v. Chr . . . " *OCRAA,* No. 4:1–55.

———— 1924b. "Die Verarbeitung des Getreides," *OCRAA,* No. 14: 1–26.

———— 1927. "Listen über das Betriebspersonal des $é^d$ Ba-ú (Konscriptionslisten)," *OCRAA,* No. 26: 29–62.

———— 1928. "Die Lohnlisten aus der Zeit Urukaginas und seines Vorgängers: I sě-ba-Texte d. h. Gerste-Lohn-Listen . . ." *OCRAA,* No. 5, 34–35: 1–129.

———— 1929. "Die Lohnlisten aus der Zeit Urukaginas und seines Vorgängers (Fortsetzung)," *OCRAA,* Nos. 43–44.

———— 1931. "Šumerische Tempelwirtschaft zur Zeit Urukaginas und seiner Vorgänger," Analecta Orientalia, No. 2.

———— 1932. "Beamter," *RA,* I: 441–4. Berlin and Leipzig.

Delbrück, Hans. GK. *Geschichte der Kriegskunst im Rahmen der politischen Geschichte.* 5 vols. Berlin, 1900–27.

Díaz del Castillo, Bernal. 1944. *Historia verdadera de la conquista de la Nueva España,* with introduction and notes by Joaquin Ramirez Cahanas. 3 vols. Mexico.

Díaz de Gámez. 1949. "The Chivalric Ideal," in *The Portable Medieval Reader,* ed. James Bruce Ross and Mary Martin McLaughlin. New York.

Diehl, Charles. 1936. "The Government and Administration of the Byzantine Empire," *CMH,* IV: 726–44. Cambridge.

Diodorus. *Diodorus of Sicily,* with an English trans. by C. H. Oldfather. 10 vols. London and New York, 1933.

Dölger, Franz. 1927. "Beiträge zur Geschichte der byzantinischen Finanzverwaltung besonders des 10. und 11. Jahrhunderts," *Byzantinisches Archiv,* IX.

Doolittle, Justus. 1876. *Social Life of the Chinese.* 2 vols. New York.

Dozy, R. 1932. *Histoire des Musulmans d'Espagne,* new ed. revised by E. Lévi-Provençal. 3 vols. Leiden.

Dubberstein, Waldo H. 1939. "Comparative Prices in Later Babylonia," *American Journal of Semitic Languages and Literature,* LVI: 20–43.

Dubois, J. A. 1943. *Hindu Manners, Customs and Ceremonies,* trans. Henry K. Beauchamp. Oxford.

Duff, J. Wight. 1936. "Social Life in Rome and Italy," *CAH,* XI: 743–74. Cambridge.

Dundas, Charles. 1924. *Kilimanjaro and Its People.* London.

Dutt, R. Palme. 1940. *India To-day.* London.

—— 1943. *The Problem of India.* New York.

—— 1951. Introduction to *Karl Marx: Articles on India.* Bombay. See also below, *Labour Monthly.*

Duyvendak, J. J. L. 1928. *The Book of Lord Shang.* London.

Ebeling, E. 1932. "Beamte der neubabylonischen Zeit," *RA,* I: 451–7. Berlin and Leipzig.

Eberhard, Wolfram. 1952. *Conquerors and Rulers. Social Forces in Medieval China.* Leiden.

Eck, R. van, and Liefrinck, F. A. 1876. "Kertâ-Simâ op Gemeente- en Waterschaps-Wetten op Bali," *Tijdschrift voor Indische Taal-, Land- en Volkenkunde,* XXIII: 161–215.

Edgerton, William F. 1947. "The Government and the Governed in the Egyptian Empire," *JNES,* VI: 152–60.

Ehrenberg, Victor. 1946. *Aspects of the Ancient World.* New York.

Eisenhower, Dwight D. 1948. *Crusade in Europe.* Garden City.

Elliot, Sir H. M. and Dowson, John. 1877. *The History of India,* VII. London.

Ellis, William. 1826. *Narrative of a Tour through Hawaii, or Owhyee.* London.

Emge, Carl August. 1950. "Bürokratisierung unter philosophischer und soziologischer Sicht," *Akademie der Wissenschaften und der Literatur. Abhandlungen der Geistes- und Sozialwissenschaftlichen Klasse,* XVIII: 1205–23. Mainz.

Engels, Friedrich. 1887. *The Condition of the Working Class in England in 1844,* Appendix written in 1886, preface in 1887, trans. Florence Kelley Wischnewetzky. New York.

Engels, Friedrich. 1894. "Soziales aus Russland (Volksstaat, 1875)" in *Internationales aus dem Volksstaat (1871–75)*: 47–60. Berlin.

—— 1921. *Der Ursprung der Familie, des Privateigenthums, und des Staats.* 20th ed. Stuttgart.

—— 1935. *Herrn Eugen Dührings Umwälzung der Wissenschaft. Dialektik der Natur. 1873–1882.* Moscow.

Engels, Friedrich and Kautsky, Karl. 1935. *Aus der Frühzeit des Marxismus. Engels Briefwechsel mit Kautsky.* Prague.

Engnell, Ivan. 1943. *Studies in Divine Kingship in the Ancient Near East.* Uppsala.

Ensslin, W. 1939. "The Senate and the Army," *CAH*, XII: 57–95. Cambridge.

Erman, Adolf. 1923. *Die Literatur der Aegypter.* Leipzig.

Erman, Adolf, and Ranke, Hermann. 1923. *Aegypten und aegyptisches Leben im Altertum,* revised by Ranke. Tübingen.

Espejo, Antonio. 1916. "Account of the Journey to the Provinces and Settlements of New Mexico. 1583," in *Spanish Explorations in the Southwest 1542–1706,* ed. Herbert Eugene Bolton: 163–92. New York.

Espinosa, Antonio Vázquez de. 1942. *Compendium and Description of the West Indies,* trans. Charles Upson Clark. The Smithsonian Institution, Washington, D.C., Miscellaneous Collections, CII.

Estete, Miguel de. 1938. "La Relación del viaje que hizo el Señor Capitán Hernando Pizarro por mandado del Señor Gobernador, su hermano, desde el Pueblo de Caxamalca a Pachacama y de allí a Jauja" and "Noticia del Perú," in *BCPP:* 77–98, 195–251. Paris.

Fairbank, John King. 1947. "China's Prospects and U. S. Policy," *Far Eastern Survey,* XVI, No. 13: 145–9.

—— 1948. *The United States and China.* Cambridge, Mass.

al-Fakhrî. 1910. Ibn aṭ-Tiqṭaqâ. al-Fakhrî. *Histoires des dynasties musulmanes,* trans. Emile Amar. Archives Marocaines, XVI. Paris.

Falkenstein, Adam. 1936. *Archaische Texte aus Uruk bearbeitet und herausgegeben von . . . Ausgrabungen der deutschen Forschungsgemeinschaft in Uruk-Warka,* II. Berlin.

Fei Hsiao-tung. 1946. "Peasantry and Gentry: an Interpretation of Chinese Social Structure and its Changes," *American Journal of Sociology,* LII: 1–17.

—— 1953. *China's Gentry.* Essays in Rural-Urban Relations, revised and ed. Margaret Park Redfield, with an introduction by Robert Redfield. Chicago.

Fei Hsiao-tung and Chang Chih-i. 1945. *Earthbound China.* Revised Engl. ed. prepared in collaboration with Paul Cooper and Margaret Park Redfield. Chicago.

Fick, Richard. 1920. *The Social Organisation in North-East India in*

Buddha's Time, trans. Shishirkumar Maitra. University of Calcutta.

Fischel, Walter J. 1937. *Jews in the Economic and Political Life of Mediaeval Islam.* London.

Fischer, Ruth. 1948. *Stalin and German Communism.* Cambridge.

Fletcher, Giles. 1856. "Of the Russe Common Wealth: or Maner of Government by the Russe Emperour etc.," in *Russia at the Close of the Sixteenth Century,* Hakluyt Society, XX. London.

Florenz, Karl. 1903. *Japanische Annalen,* A.D. *592–697 Nihongi,* supplement of *Mitteilungen der deutschen Gesellschaft für Natur- und Völkerkunde Ostasiens.* Tokyo.

Florinsky, Michael T. 1953. *Russia. A History and an Interpretation.* 2 vols. New York.

Fornander, Abraham. HAF. *Fornander Collection of Hawaiian Antiquities and Folk-lore,* Memoirs of Bernice P. Bishop Museum, IV–VI. Honolulu, 1916–20.

—— PR. *An Account of the Polynesian Race, Its Origin and Migrations and the Ancient History of the Hawaiian People to the times of Kamehameha I.* 3 vols. London, 1878–85.

Frank, Tenney. 1928. "Rome after the Conquest of Sicily," *CAH,* VII: 793–821. Cambridge.

—— 1940. *Rome and Italy of the Empire. ESAR,* V. Baltimore.

Freudenthal, Berthold. 1905. "Antworten, Griechisch," in Mommsen, 1905: 9–19. Leipzig.

Fries, Nicolaus. 1921. *Das Heereswesen der Araber zur Zeit der Omaijaden nach Ṭabarî.* Tübingen.

Fromm, Erich. 1941. *Escape from Freedom.* New York.

Furnivall, J. S. 1944. *Netherlands India,* intro. by A. C. D. De Graeff. Cambridge and New York.

Gabrieli, Francesco. 1935. *Il Califfato di Hishâm.* Memoires de Société Royale d'Archéologie d'Alexandrie, VII, No. 2. Alexandria.

Gale, Esson M. 1931. *Discourses on Salt and Iron.* Leiden.

Gallegos. 1927. "The Gallegos Relation of the *Rodriguez Expedition to New Mexico,*" trans. George P. Hammond and Agapito Rey, Historical Society of New Mexico, Publications in History, II: 239–68, 334–62.

Garcilaso de la Vega, Inca. 1945. *Commentarios Reales de los Incas,* ed. Ángel Rosenblat. 2d ed. 2 vols. Buenos Aires.

Gardiner, Alan H. 1948. *The Wilbour Papyrus.* 3 vols. Published for the Brooklyn Museum at the Oxford University Press.

Gaudefroy-Demombynes, Maurice. 1923. *La Syrie à l'époque des Mamelouks d'après les auteurs Arabes.* Paris.

—— 1931. "Le Monde Musulman," in *Le Monde Musulman et Byzantin jusqu'aux Croisades,* by Gaudefroy-Demombynes and Platonov: 29–451. Paris.

Gaudefroy-Demombynes, Maurice. 1938. "Sur quelques ouvrages de *ḥisba*," *Journal Asiatique*, CCXXX: 449–57.

——— 1950. *Muslim Institutions*, trans. John P. MacGregor. London.

Gautama. 1898. In *Sacred Laws of the Āryas*, trans. Georg Bühler. SBE, II. New York.

GBP. 1882. *Gazetteer of the Bombay Presidency*, XIII, Pt 2: "Thána." Bombay.

Gelzer, Matthias. 1943. *Vom roemischen Staat.* 2 vols. Leipzig.

Gibb, H. A. R. 1932. *The Damascus Chronicle of the Crusades.* London.

Gibb, H. A. R. and Bowen, Harold. 1950. *Islamic Society and the West.* Vol. I: *Islamic Society in the Eighteenth Century.* London, New York, and Toronto.

Glotz, Gustave. 1925. *The Aegean Civilization.* London and New York.

——— 1926. *Ancient Greece at Work.* New York.

——— 1929. *The Greek City and Its Institutions.* London and New York.

Goetz, Leopold Karl. RR. *Das russische Recht.* 4 vols. Stuttgart, 1910–13.

Goldfrank, Esther S. 1945. "Socialization, Personality, and the Structure of Pueblo Society," *AA*, XLVII, No. 4: 516–39.

——— 1945a. "Irrigation Agriculture and Navaho Community Leadership: Case Material on Environment and Culture," *AA*, XLVII, No. 2: 262–77.

Goldziher, Ignaz. 1889. *Muhammedanische Studien*, I. Halle.

——— 1905. "Antworten: Islam," in Mommsen, 1905: 101–12. Leipzig.

Gordon, Robert Aaron. 1945. *Business Leadership in the Large Corporation.* Washington, D.C.

Götze, Albrecht. 1933. "Kleinasien," in *Kulturgeschichte des alten Orients*, by A. Alt, A. Christensen, A. Götze, A. Grohmann, H. Kees, and B. Landsberger. III, Pt. 1: 3–199. Munich.

Grant, Christina Phelps. 1937. *The Syrian Desert.* London.

Grapow, Hermann. 1924. *Die bildlichen Ausdrücke des Aegyptischen; vom Denken und Dichten einer altorientalischen Sprache.* Leipzig.

Grassman, Hermann. RV. *Rig-Veda.* 2 vols. Leipzig, 1876–77.

Gray, G. B. and Cary, M. 1939. "The Reign of Darius," *CAH*, IV: 173–228. Cambridge.

Grekov, B. D. 1939. "La Horde d'Or et la Russie," Pt. 2 of B. Grekov and A. Iakoubovski: *La Horde d'Or*, trans. François Thuret: 163–251. Paris.

——— 1947. *The Culture of Kiev Rūs*, trans. Pauline Rose. Moscow.

Grenier, Albert. 1937. "La Gaule Romaine," *ESAR*, III: 379–644. Baltimore.

Grohmann, Adolf. PAP. "Probleme der arabischen Papyrusforschung, II," *Archiv Orientální*, V: 273–83; VI: 377–98. Prague, 1933–34.

——— 1933. *Südarabien als Wirtschaftsgebiet*, Pt. 2. Schriften der Philosophischen Fakultät der Deutschen Universitat in Prag, XIII. Brünn, Prague, Leipzig, and Vienna.

Grossmann, Henry. 1929. "Die Änderung des ursprünglichen Aufbauplans des Marxschen 'Kapital' und ihre Ursachen," *Archiv für die Geschichte des Sozialismus und der Arbeiterbewegung*, XIV: 305–38.

Grunebaum, Gustave E. von. 1946. *Medieval Islam*. Chicago.

Gsell, Stephane. HA. *Histoire ancienne de l'Afrique du Nord*. 8 vols. Paris, 1914–28.

Guber, A. A. 1942. "Izuchenie Istorii Stran Vostoka v SSSR za 25 let," in *Dvadtsat pyat let istoricheskoi nauki v SSSR:* 272–84. Academy of Sciences of the USSR. Moscow and Leningrad.

Guillaume, James. IDS. *L'Internationale. Documents et souvenirs (1864–1878)*, I and II. Paris, 1905–07.

Guiraud, Jean. 1929. *The Mediaeval Inquisition*, trans. E. C. Messenger. London.

Gumplowicz, Ludwig. 1905. *Grundriss der Soziologie*. Vienna.

Gurian, Waldemar. 1931. *Der Bolschewismus*. Freiburg im Breisgau.

Gutmann, Bruno. 1909. *Dichten und Denker der Dschagganeger*. Leipzig.

——— 1914. *Volksbuch der Wadschagga*. Leipzig.

——— 1926. *Das Recht der Dschagga*. Munich.

Hackett, Charles Wilson. 1923. *Historical Documents Relating to New Mexico, Nueva Vizcaya, and Approaches Thereto, to 1773*, collected by A. F. A. and F. R. Bandelier. 2 vols. CIW, CCCXXX. Washington, D.C.

Hackman, George Gottlob. 1937. *Temple Documents of the Third Dynasty of Ur from Umna. Babylonian Inscriptions in the Collection of James B. Nies, Yale University*, V. New Haven and London.

Haig, Wolseley. 1937. "Sher Shāh and the Sūr Dynasty. The Return of Humāyūn," *CHI*, IV: 45–69. Cambridge.

Hall, W. H. 1886. *Irrigation Development Report*, Pt. 1. Sacramento.

Hammurabi. "Collections of Laws from Mesopotamia and Asia Minor," trans. Theophile J. Meek, *ANET:* 163–80. Princeton, 1950.

"The Han Officials." A statistical study prepared by the Chinese History Project (MS).

Han Shu. Po-na ed. Commercial Press.

Handbook of Marxism. 1935, ed. Emile Burns. New York.

Handy, E. S. Craighill. 1933. "Government and Society," in *Ancient Hawaiian Civilizations:* 31–42. Honolulu.

——— 1940. *The Hawaiian Planter, I: His Plants, Methods and Areas of Cultivation*. Bernice P. Bishop Museum Bulletin, CLXI.

Hardy, Edward Rochie. 1931. *The Large Estates of Byzantine Egypt*. New York.

Harper, George McLean, Jr. 1928. "Village Administration in the Roman Provinces of Syria," *Yale Classical Studies*, I: 105–68. New Haven and London.

Hasan Khan, M. 1944. "Medieval Muslim Political Theories of Rebellion against the State," *IC*, 18: 36–44.

Haskins, Charles Homer. 1911. "England and Sicily in the Twelfth Century," *English Historical Review*, XXVI: 433, 447, 641–65.

—— 1918. *Norman Institutions*. Harvard Historical Studies, XXIV. Cambridge, Mass.

Haxthausen, August Freiherr von. SR. *Studien über die innern Zustände, das Volksleben und insbesondere die ländlichen Einrichtungen Russlands*. 3 vols. Hanover and Berlin, 1847–52.

HCS, Ch'in-Han. "History of Chinese Society, Ch'in-Han" (in preparation by the Chinese History Project).

HCS, Ch'ing. "History of Chinese Society, Ch'ing" (in preparation by the Chinese History Project).

Hedin, Sven. 1917. *Southern Tibet, II: Lake Manasarovar and the Sources of the Great Indian Rivers*. Stockholm.

Heichelheim, Fritz M. 1938. *Wirtschaftsgeschichte des Altertums*. 2 vols. Leiden.

Helbing, Franz. 1926. *Die Tortur*, revised by Max Bauer, with postface by Max Alsberg. 2 parts. Berlin.

Helck, Hans-Wolfgang. 1939. *Der Einfluss der Militärführer in der 18. Ägyptischen Dynastie*, Untersuchungen zur Geschichte und Altertumskunde Aegyptens, XIV. Leipzig.

Herberstein, Sigismund von. NR. *Notes upon Russia; Being a Translation of the Earliest Account of That Country Entitled Rerum Moscoviticarum Commentarii*, trans. and ed. R. H. Major. 2 vols. Hakluyt Society, X, XII. London, 1851–52.

Herodotus. 1942. "The Persian Wars," trans. George Rawlinson in *The Greek Historians*, I: 1–563. New York.

Hewitt, James Francis. 1887. "Village Communities in India, Especially Those in the Bengal Presidency, the Central Provinces, and Bombay," *Journal of the Society of Arts*, XXXV: 613–25.

Hintze, Otto. 1901. "Der österreichische und der preussische Beamtenstaat im 17. und 18. Jahrhundert," *HZ*, LXXXVI, new ser., L: 401–44.

—— 1930. "Typologie der ständischen Verfassungen des Abendlandes," *HZ*, CXLI: 229–48.

—— 1941. *Staat und Verfassung*. Leipzig.

Hirth, Paul. 1928. *Die künstliche Bewässerung*. Kolonial-Wirtschaftliches Komitee, XXI, No. 3. Berlin.

Hitzig, H. F. 1905. "Antworten: Römisch," in Mommsen, 1905: 31–51. Leipzig.

Homo, Léon. 1927. *Primitive Italy and the Beginnings of Roman Imperialism.* New York.

Honigmann, Ernst. 1935. *Die Ostgrenze des byzantinischen Reiches von 363 bis 1071.* . . . Brussels.

Honjo, Eijiro. 1935. *The Social and Economic History of Japan.* Kyoto.

Hopkins, Edward Washburn. 1888. *The Social and Military Position of the Ruling Caste in Ancient India as Represented by the Sanskrit Epic,* reprinted from the *Journal of American Oriental Society,* XIII.

———— 1902. *India Old and New.* New York and London.

———— 1922. "Family Life and Social Customs as They Appear in the Sūtras," "The Princes and Peoples of the Epic Poems," and "The Growth of Law and Legal Institutions," *CHI,* I: 227–95. New York.

Horn, Paul. 1894. *Das Heer- und Kriegswesen der Grossmoghuls.* Leiden.

Horst, D. Johannes. 1932. *Proskynein.* Gütersloh.

Horster, Paul. 1935. *Zur Anwendung des islamischen Rechts im 16. Jahrhundert.* Stuttgart.

Hötzsch, Otto. 1912. "Adel und Lehnswesen in Russland und Polen und ihr Verhältnis zur deutschen Entwicklung," *HZ,* CVIII: 541–92.

Hou Han Shu. Po-na ed. Commercial Press.

Howorth, H. H. HM. *History of the Mongols.* 4 vols. London, 1876–1927.

Hsiao, K. C. "Rural China, Imperial Control in the Nineteenth Century" (MS).

Hsieh, Pao Chao. 1925. *The Government of China (1644–1911).* Baltimore.

Hsü Han Chih. Po-na ed. Commercial Press.

Huang-ch'ao Ching-shih Wên Hsü-p'ien. Edition of 1888.

Hudemann, E. E. 1878. *Geschichte des römischen Postwesens während der Kaiserzeit.* Berlin.

Hug. 1918. "Eunuchen," *Pauly-Wissowa-Kroll,* Suppl. 3: 450–5. Stuttgart.

Humboldt, Al. de. 1811. *Essai politique sur le royaume de la Nouvelle-Espagne.* 5 vols. Paris.

Hummel, Arthur W. ECCP. *Eminent Chinese of the Ch'ing Period.* 2 vols. Washington, D.C., 1943–44.

Huuri, Kalervo. 1941. *Zur Geschichte des mittelalterlichen Geschützwesens aus orientalischen Quellen.* Helsinki.

Huxley, Julian S. 1955. "Evolution, Cultural and Biological," in the *Yearbook of Anthropology,* Wenner-Gren Foundation for Anthropological Research: 3–25. New York.

Ibn Batoutah. 1914. *Voyages d'Ibn Batoutah,* III, trans. C. Defrémery and B. R. Sanguinetti. Paris.

Ibn Khordādhbeh. 1889. *Kitāb a-Masālik wa'l-Mamālik (Liber viarum et regnorum)* by Ibn Khordādhbeh (Arabic and French translation), ed.

and trans. M. J. de Goeje in *Bibliotheca geographorum arabicorum,*
VI: vii–xxiii and 1–144, Arabic text 1–183. Leiden and Batavia.

Ibn al-Ukhuwwa. 1938. *The Ma'ālim al-Qurba,* trans. and ed. Reuben
Levy. E. J. W. Gibb Memorial New Series, XII. London.

Imperial Gazetteer of India. The Indian Empire. new ed. 4 vols. Oxford,
1907–09.

Inama-Sternegg, Karl Theodor von. 1901. *Deutsche Wirtschaftsgeschichte,*
III. 2. Leipzig.

Inama-Sternegg and Häpke. 1924. "Die Bevölkerung des Mittelalters und
der neueren Zeit bis Ende des 18. Jahrhunderts in Europa," *Handwörterbuch der Staatswissenschaften,* II: 670–87. 4th ed. Jena.

Inostrannaya Kniga, No. 1, 1931. Moscow.

Inprecor. International Press Correspondence. English ed. Vienna and
London, 1921–38.

Ixtlilxochitl, Don Fernando de Alba. OH. *Obras Historicas,* ed. Alfredo
Chavero. 2 vols. Mexico, 1891–92.

Jäckh, Ernest. 1944. *The Rising Crescent, Turkey Yesterday, Today, and
Tomorrow.* New York and Toronto.

Jacobsen, Thorkild. 1943. "Primitive Democracy in Ancient Mesopotamia," *JNES,* II, No. 3: 159–72.

—— 1946. "Mesopotamia: the Cosmos as a State" in *The Intellectual
Adventure of Ancient Man* by Frankfort, Wilson, Jacobsen, and Irwin:
125–219. Chicago.

Jacobsen, Thorkild, and Lloyd, Seton. 1935. *Sennacherib's Aqueduct at
Jerwan.* Chicago.

Jaeger, Werner. 1939. *Paideia: the Ideals of Greek Culture,* trans. Gilbert
Highet. New York.

Jahāngīr. 1909. *The Tūzuk-i-Jahāngīrī,* or *Memoirs of Jahāngīr,* trans.
Alexander Rogers and ed. Henry Beveridge. Oriental Translation
Fund, new ser. XIX. London.

Jātakam. Trans. from the Pali by Julius Dutoit. 7 vols. Leipzig and
Munich, 1908–21.

Jefferson, Thomas. 1944. *Basic Writings of Thomas Jefferson,* ed. Philip S.
Foner. New York.

Jen-min Jih-pao. Peking.

Jerez, Francisco de. 1938. ". . . la Conquista del Perú . . . " in *BCCP:*
15–115. Paris.

Johnson, Allan Chester. 1951. *Egypt and the Roman Empire.* Ann
Arbor.

Johnson, Allan Chester, and West, Louis C. 1949. *Byzantine Egypt: Economic Studies.* Princeton.

Jolly, Julius. 1896. "Recht und Sitte" in *Grundriss der Indo-Arischen*

Philologie und Altertumskunde, II, Fasc. 8, ed. G. Bühler. Strassburg.

Jones, Sir Henry Stuart. 1934. "Senatus Populusque Romanus," *CAH,* X: 159–81. Cambridge.

Jones, Richard. 1831. *An Essay on the Distribution of Wealth, and on the Sources of Taxation.* London.

―――― 1859. *Literary Remains, Consisting of Lectures and Tracts on Political Economy,* with a prefatory notice by William Whewell. London.

Josephus, Flavius. JW. *The Works of Flavius Josephus, Containing Twenty Books of the Jewish Antiquities, Seven Books of the Jewish War,* I, trans. William Whiston, revised by Samuel Burder. New York, no date.

Jouguet, Pierre. 1911. *La Vie municipale dans l'Egypte Romaine.* Bibliothèque des Ecoles Française et de Rome, Fasc. 104. Paris.

Juan, George, and Ulloa, Antonio de. 1806. *A Voyage to South America,* trans. John Adams. 2 vols. London.

Juynboll, Th. W. 1925. *Handleiding tot de Kennis van De Mohammedaansche Wet volgens de Leer der Sjāfi'itische School.* 3d ed. Leiden.

Kahin, George McTurnan. 1952. *Nationalism and Revolution in Indonesia.* Ithaca, New York.

Kahrstedt, Ulrich. 1924. "Die Bevölkerung des Altertums," *Handwörterbuch der Staatswissenschaften,* II: 655–70. 4th ed. Jena.

Kai Kā'ūs ibn Iskandar. 1951. *A Mirror for Princes. The Qābus Nāma by Kai Kā'ūs Ibn Iskandar,* trans. Reuben Levy. New York.

Kantorowicz, Ernst. 1931. *Kaiser Friedrich der Zweite.* Berlin.

Karamsin, M. HER. *Histoire de l'empire de Russie,* trans. St.-Thomas and Jauffret. 11 vols. Paris, 1819–26.

Kato, Shigeshi. 1936. "On the Hang or the Associations of Merchants in China," *Memoirs of the Research Department of the Toyo Bunko,* VIII: 45–83.

Kautsky, Karl. 1929. *Die Materialistische Geschichtsauffassung.* 2 vols. Berlin.

Kayden, Eugene M. 1929. "Consumers' Cooperation," in *The Cooperative Movement in Russia during the War,* Vol. VI of *Economic and Social History of the World War,* Russian Series: 3–231. New Haven.

Kees, Herman. 1933. *Ägypten.* Munich.

―――― 1938. "Herihor und die Aufrichtung des thebanischen Gottesstaates," *Nachrichten von der Gesellschaft der Wissenschaften in Göttingen,* Philologisch-Historische Klasse, new ser., Section I: *Nachrichten aus der Altertumswissenschaft,* II: 1–20.

―――― 1953. *Das Priestertum im ägyptischen Staat.* Vol. I of *Probleme der Ägyptologie.* Leiden and Cologne.

Keith, Arthur Berriedale. 1914. *The Veda of the Black Yajus School En-*

titled Taittiriya Sanhita. Harvard Oriental Series, XVIII, XIX. 2 vols. Cambridge.

―――― 1922. "The Age of the Rigveda," *CHI*, I: 77–113. New York.

Kennan, George. 1891. *Siberia and the Exile System.* 2 vols. New York.

Kepelino. 1932. *Kepelino's Traditions of Hawaii,* ed. Martha Warren Beckwith. Bernice P. Bishop Museum Bulletin, XCV. Honolulu.

King, F. H. 1927. *Farmers of Forty Centuries.* London.

Klebs, Luise. 1915. *Die Reliefs des alten Reiches (2980–2475 v. Chr.), Material zur ägyptischen Kulturgeschichte,* Abhandlungen der Heidelberger Akademie der Wissenschaften, Philologisch-Historische Klasse, III.

Klein, Julius. 1920. *The Mesta. A Study in Spanish Economic History 1273–1836.* Cambridge.

Kliuchevskii, V. O. *Kurs russkoi istorii.* 5 vols. Moscow, 1908–37.

Kljutschewskij, W. O. 1945. *Russische Geschichte von Peter dem Grossen bis Nikolaus I,* trans. Waldemar Jollos. 2 vols. Zurich.

Kluchevsky, V. O. HR. *A History of Russia,* trans. C. J. Hogarth. 5 vols. London, 1911–31.

KMCL. *Karl Marx Chronik Seines Lebens in Einzeldaten.* Moscow, 1934.

Koebner, Richard. 1942. "The Settlement and Colonisation of Europe," *CEH,* I: 1–88. Cambridge.

Koran, the (Qur'an), trans. E. H. Palmer. London, New York, and Toronto, 1942.

Kornemann, Ernest. 1933. "Die Römische Kaiserzeit," in *Römische Geschichte* by J. Vogt and E. Kornemann: 57–186. Leipzig and Berlin.

―――― 1949. *Von Augustus bis zum Sieg der Araber.* Vol. II of *Weltgeschichte des Mittelmeer-Raumes.* Munich.

Kovalewsky, Maxime. 1903. *Institutions politiques de la Russie,* trans. from the English by Mme. Derocquigny. Paris.

Kracke, E. A., Jr. 1947. "Family vs. Merit in Chinese Civil Service Examinations under the Empire," *Harvard Journal of Asiatic Studies,* X: 103–23.

―――― 1953. *Civil Service in Early Sung China, 960–1067.* Cambridge.

Kramer, Samuel Noah. 1948. "New Light on the Early History of the Ancient Near East," *American Journal of Archaeology,* LII, No. 1: 156–64.

―――― 1950. "Sumerian Myths and Epic Tales," in *ANET:* 37–59. Princeton.

Krause, Gregor, and With, Karl. 1922. *Bali.* Hagen i. W.

Kreller, Hans. 1919. *Erbrechtliche Untersuchungen Aufgrund der graeco-aegyptischen Papyrusurkunden.* Leipzig and Berlin.

Kremer, Alfred von. CGO. *Culturgeschichte des Orients unter den Chalifen.* 2 vols. Vienna, 1875–77.

―――― 1863. *Aegypten.* 2 parts, Leipzig.

Kroeber, A. L. 1948. *Anthropology*. Rev. ed. New York.

Krückmann, O. 1932. "Die Beamten zur Zeit der ersten Dynastie von Babylon," *RA*, I: 444–51. Berlin and Leipzig.

Kuan T'ang Chi Lin by Wang Kuo-wei. 1927. In *Wang Chung Ch'üeh Kung I Shu, Ch'u-chi*.

Kuan Tzŭ. Commercial Press, Shanghai, 1934.

Kulischer, Josef. AW. *Allgemeine Wirtschaftsgeschichte des Mittelalters und der Neuzeit*. 2 vols. Munich and Berlin, 1928–29.

——— 1925. *Russische Wirtschaftsgeschichte*, I. Jena.

Kuo Mo-jo. 1935. *Liang Chou Chin Wên Tz'ŭ Ta Hsi K'ao Shih*. Tokyo.

Kuo Yü. Commercial Press, Shanghai, 1935.

Labat, René, 1939. *Le Caractère religieux de la royauté Assyro-Babylonienne*. Paris.

Laborde, Alexandre de. 1808. *Itinéraire descriptif de l'Espagne* etc., IV. Paris.

Labour Monthly. Ed. R. Palme Dutt. London.

Lafuente Alcantara, D. Miguel. 1845. *Historia de Granada* etc., III. Granada.

Lambton, Ann K. S. 1938. "The Regulation of the Waters of the Zāyande Rūd," *Bulletin of the School of Oriental Studies* (University of London), IX: 663–73.

——— 1948. "An Account of the Tārīkhi Qumm," *Bulletin of the School of Oriental Studies*, XII: 586–96.

Lammens, Henri. 1907. "Etudes sur le règne du calife Omaiyade Mo'awia Ier," *Mélanges de la Faculté Orientale* (Université Saint-Joseph, Beyrouth), II: 1–172.

——— 1914. *Le Climat—les Bédouins*. Vol. I of *Le Berceau de l'Islam*. Rome.

——— 1922. "La Cité Arabe de Ṭāif a la veille de l'Hégire," *Mélanges de l'Université Saint-Joseph Beyrouth (Syrie)*, VIII: 115–327.

Lamprecht, Karl. DG. *Deutsche Geschichte*. Vol. II, 1909; Vol. IV, 1911. Berlin.

Landa, Diego de. 1938. *Relación de las cosas de Yucatan*, with introduction and notes by Hector Perez Martinez. 7th ed. Mexico.

Landsberger, Benno. 1925. "Assyrische Handelskolonien in Kleinasien aus dem dritten Jahrtausend," *Der Alte Orient*, XXIV, Fasc. 4.

Lane, Edward William. 1898. *An Account of the Manners and Customs of the Modern Egyptians*. London.

Lang, Olga. 1946. *Chinese Family and Society*. New Haven.

Laoust, Henri. 1939. *Essai sur les doctrines sociales et politiques de Taḳi-d-Dīn Aḥmad b. Taimīya*. Recherches d'Archéologie, de Philologie et d'Histoire, X. Cairo.

Last, Hugh. 1936. "The Principate and the Administration," *CAH*, XI: 393–434. Cambridge.

Lattimore, Owen. 1940. *Inner Asian Frontiers of China*. New York.

—— 1944. "A Soviet Analysis of Chinese Civilization," *Pacific Affairs*, XVII: 81–9.

—— 1947. *Solution in Asia*. Boston (first published February 1945).

—— 1949. *The Situation in Asia*. Boston.

Lauts. 1848. *Het eiland Balie en de Balienezen*. Amsterdam.

Law, Bimala Charan. 1923. *Some Kṣatriya Tribes of Ancient India*, with a foreword by A. Berriedale Keith. Calcutta and Simla.

—— 1941. *India as Described in Early Texts of Buddhism and Jainism*. London.

Lea, Henry Charles. 1892. *Superstition and Force*. Philadelphia.

—— 1908. *A History of the Inquisition of the Middle Ages*, I. New York and London.

Leemans, W. F. 1950. *The Old-Babylonian Merchant, His Business and His Social Position*. Leiden.

Legge, James. CC. *The Chinese Classics*. 7 vols. Oxford 1893–95.

Lenin, Vladimir Ilych. S. *Sochinenia*, 4th ed. 35 vols. Moscow, 1941–50.

—— SW. *Selected Works*. 12 vols. New York, 1943.

—— SWG. *Sämtliche Werke*. Vienna and Berlin, later Moscow and Leningrad.

—— 1937. *The Letters of Lenin*, trans. Elizabeth Hill and Doris Mudie. New York.

Letopis Marksizma. Moscow.

Lévi-Provençal, E. 1932. *L'Espagne Musulmane au Xème siècle*. Paris.

—— 1947. *Séville Musulmane au debut du XIIe siècle. Le Traite d'ibn 'Abdun sur la vie urbaine et les corps de métiers*. Paris.

Lind, Andrew W. 1938. *An Island Community. Ecological Succession in Hawaii*. Chicago.

Lips, Julius E. 1938. "Government," in *General Anthropology*, ed. F. Boas: 487–534.

Locke, John. 1924. *Of Civil Government*. Everyman's Library. London and New York.

Løkkegaard, Frede. 1950. *Islamic Taxation in the Classic Period*. Copenhagen.

Longrigg, Stephen Hemsley. 1925. *Four Centuries of Modern Iraq*. Oxford.

Lopez, R. S. 1945. "Silk Industry in the Byzantine Empire," *Speculum*, XX, No. 1: 1–42.

Lot, Ferdinand. 1946. *L'Art militaire et les armées au moyen âge en Europe et dans le Proche Orient*. 2 vols. Paris.

Lot, Ferdinand. 1951. *La Fin du monde antique et le debut du moyen âge.* L'Evolution de l'humanité, XXXI. Paris.

Lowie, Robert H. 1927. *The Origin of the State.* New York.

—— 1938. "Subsistence," in *General Anthropology,* ed. F. Boas: 282–326.

Luckenbill, Daniel David. AR. *Ancient Records of Assyria and Babylonia.* 2 vols. Chicago, 1926–27.

Lun Yü Chu Shu in *Ssŭ Pu Pei Yao.* Shanghai, 1936.

Lundell, C. L. 1937. *The Vegetation of Petén.* CIW, 478. Washington, D.C.

Luxemburg, Rosa. 1951. *Ausgewählte Reden und Schriften,* with a foreword by Wilhelm Pieck. 2 vols. Berlin.

Lyashchenko, Peter I. 1949. *History of the National Economy of Russia,* trans. L. M. Herman. New York.

Lybyer, Albert Howe. 1913. *The Government of the Ottoman Empire in the Time of Suleiman the Magnificent.* Cambridge and London.

Lydgate, John M. 1913. "The Affairs of the Wainiha Hui," *Hawaiian Almanac and Annual for 1913:* 125–37.

Ma Shêng-fêng. 1935. *Chung-kuo Ching-chi Shih* I. Nanking.

Macdonald, D. B. 1941. "*Dhimma,*" HWI: 96. Leiden.

Machiavelli, Niccolò. 1940. *The Prince and the Discourses.* Modern Library. New York.

MacLeod, William Christie. 1924. *The Origin of the State Reconsidered in the Light of the Data of Aboriginal North America.* Philadelphia.

Maitland, Frederic William. 1921. *Domesday Book and Beyond.* Cambridge.

—— 1948. *The Constitutional History of England.* Cambridge.

al-Makkarí, Ahmed Ibn Mohammed. 1840. *The History of the Mohammedan Dynasties in Spain,* extracted from the *Nafhu-t-tíb min Ghosni-l-Andalusi-r-rattíb wa Tárikh Lisánu-d-din Ibni-l-khattíb,* trans. Pascual de Gayanges y Arce, I. Oriental Translation Fund. London.

Makrizi, Taki-eddin-Ahmed- . 1845. *Histoire des sultans Mamlouks, de l'Egypte,* II, Pt. 4, trans. M. Quatremere. Oriental Translation Fund. Paris.

Mallon, Alexis. 1921. "Les Hebreux en Egypte," *OCRAA,* No. 3.

Malo, David. 1903. *Hawaiian Antiquities.* Honolulu.

Manu. 1886. *The Laws of Manu,* trans., with extracts from seven commentaries, by G. Bühler. SBE, XXV. Oxford.

Mao Tse-tung. 1945. *China's New Democracy.* New York.

—— 1945a. *The Fight for a New China.* New York.

—— 1954. *Selected Works of Mao Tse-tung,* I. London.

Marco Polo. 1929. *The Book of Ser Marco Polo,* trans. Colonel Sir Henry Yule, 3d ed. Revised by Henri Cordier. 2 vols. New York.

Markham, Clements R. 1892. *A History of Peru.* Chicago.

Marquart, J. 1903. *Osteuropäische und ostasiastische Streifzüge.* Leipzig.

Marshall, Alfred. 1946. *Principles of Economics.* London.

Marshall, John. 1928. "The Monuments of Muslim India," *CHI,* III: 568–640. New York and Cambridge.

—— 1931. *Mohenjo-daro and the Indus Civilization.* 3 vols. London.

Marx, Karl. DK. *Das Kapital.* 4th, 2d, and 1st ed. 3 vols. Hamburg, 1890–94.

—— NYDT. Articles in the *New York Daily Tribune.*

—— TMW. *Theorien über den Mehrwert.* From the posthumous manuscript "Zur Kritik der politischen Ökonomie," published by Kaul Kautsky. 3 vols. Stuttgart, 1921.

—— 1857. "Revelations of the Diplomatic History of the Eighteenth Century," *The Free Press,* IV: 203–4, 218, 226–8, 265–7. Feb. 4, 18, 25; April 1.

—— 1921. *Zur Kritik der Politischen Ökonomie.* 8th ed. Stuttgart.

—— 1927. *Herr Vogt,* trans. J. Molitor. 3 vols. Paris.

—— 1935. *Critique of the Gotha Programme.* New York.

—— 1939. *Grundrisse der Kritik der Politischen Oekonomie* (Rohentwurf), 1857–58. Moscow.

—— 1951. *Articles on India,* with an introduction by R. P. Dutt. Bombay.

—— 1951a. *Marx on China 1853–1860.* Articles from the *New York Daily Tribune,* with an introduction and notes by Dona Torr. London. See also KMCL.

Marx, Karl, and Engels, Friedrich. 1920. *Gesammelte Schriften 1852 bis 1862,* ed. N. Rjasanoff. 2 vols. Stuttgart.

—— 1952. *The Russian Menace to Europe,* a collection of articles ed. Paul W. Blackstock and Bert F. Hoselitz. Glencoe, Ill. See also below, *MEGA.*

Massignon, Louis. 1937. "Guilds," *ESS,* VII: 214–16. New York.

Matthai, John. 1915. *Village Government in British India.* London.

Maurer, Georg Ludwig von. GSD. *Geschichte der Städteverfassung in Deutschland.* 4 vols. Erlangen, 1869–71.

Mavor, James. 1925. *An Economic History of Russia.* 2d ed. 2 vols. London, Toronto, and New York.

—— 1928. *The Russian Revolution.* London.

Mayr, Ernst. 1942. *Systematics and the Origin of Species.* New York.

McEwan, Calvin W. 1934. *The Oriental Origin of Hellenistic Kingship,* The Oriental Institute of the University of Chicago, Studies in Ancient Oriental Civilization, XIII. Chicago.

McIlwain, C. H. 1932. "Medieval Estates," *CMH,* VII: 665–715. New York and Cambridge.

Means, Philip Ainsworth. 1931. *Ancient Civilizations of the Andes*. New York and London.

Meek, Theophile J. 1950. "The Middle Assyrian Laws," in *ANET*: 180–8. Princeton.

MEGA. Karl Marx and Friedrich Engels. *Historisch-kritische Gesamtausgabe*. Marx-Engels Institute, Moscow, 1927–

Mehta, Asoka. 1954. *Democratic Socialism*. 2d ed. Hyderabad.

Meissner, Bruno. BA. *Babylonien und Assyrien*. 2 vols. Heidelberg, 1920–25.

Mendelsohn, Isaac. 1949. *Slavery in the Ancient Near East*. New York.

Mendoza, Juan González de. 1854. *The History of the Great and Mighty Kingdom of China*, II. Hakluyt Society, XV. London.

Mercer, Samuel A. B. 1952. *The Pyramid Texts*. 4 vols. New York, London, and Toronto.

Merker, M. 1903. "Rechtsverhältnisse und Sitten der Wadschagga," *PM*, XXX, No. 138.

———— 1904. *Die Masai*. Berlin.

Meyer, Eduard. GA. *Geschichte des Altertums*. 4 vols. Stuttgart and Berlin, 1926–39.

———— 1924. *Kleine Schriften*. 2d ed. 2 vols. Halle.

Meyer, Peter. 1950. "The Soviet Union: a New Class Society" in *Verdict of Three Decades*, ed. Julien Steinberg: 475–509. New York.

Mez, Adam. 1922. *Die Renaissance des Islams*. Heidelberg.

Miakotine, V. 1932. "Les Pays russes, des origines à la fin des invasions tatares," *Histoire de Russie*, by Paul Milioukov, Ch. Signobos, and L. Eisenmann, I: 81–124. Paris.

Mieli, Aldo. 1938. *La Science Arabe et son role dans l'évolution scientifique mondiale*. Leiden.

———— 1946. *Panorama general de historia de la ciencia*. Madrid.

Miles, George C. 1948. "Early Islamic Inscriptions Near Ṭa'if in the Hijāz," *JNES*, VII: 236–42.

Mill, James. 1820. *The History of British India*. 2d ed. 12 vols. London.

Mill, John Stuart. 1909. *Principles of Political Economy*. London, New York, Bombay, and Calcutta.

———— 1947. *A System of Logic Ratiocinative and Inductive*. London, etc.

Miller, Barnette. 1941. *The Palace School of Muhammad the Conqueror*. Cambridge.

Miller, S. N. 1939. "The Army and the Imperial House," *CAH*, XII: 1–56. Cambridge.

Milukow, Paul. 1898. *Skizzen Russischer Kulturgeschichte*, I. Leipzig.

Ming Shih. Po-na ed. Commercial Press.

Minorsky, V. 1943. *Tadhkirat al-Mulūk.* E. J. W. Gibb Memorial Series, new ser., XVI. London.

Mitteis, Heinrich. 1933. *Lehnsrecht und Staatsgewalt. Untersuchungen zur mittelalterlichen Verfassungsgeschichte.* Weimar.

Mitteis, L. 1912. *Juristischer Teil, erste Hälfte: Grundzüge.* Vol. II of *Grundzüge und Chrestomathie der Papyruskunde,* by L. Mitteis and U. Wilcken. Leipzig and Berlin.

Momigliano, A. 1934. "Nero," *CAH,* X: 702–42. Cambridge.

Mommsen, Theodor. 1875. *Römisches Staatsrecht,* II, Pt. 2. Leipzig.

―――― 1905. *Zum ältesten Strafrecht der Kulturvölker. Fragen zur Rechts-vergleichung gestellt von . . .* Leipzig.

―――― 1921. *Römische Geschichte,* V. 9th ed. Berlin.

Monzon, Arturo. 1949. *El Calpulli en la organización social de los Tenochca.* Mexico City.

Moreland, W. H. 1929. *The Agrarian System of Moslem India.* Cambridge.

Morgan, Lewis H. 1877. *Ancient Society or Researches . . . through Barbarism to Civilization.* Chicago.

Morley, S. C. 1938. *The Inscriptions of Petén,* CIW, 437. Washington, D.C.

―――― 1947. *The Ancient Maya.* 2d ed. Stanford University.

Morris, Richard B. 1937. "Entail," *ESS,* V: 553–6. New York.

Motolinia, Fr. Toribio de Benavente o. 1941. *Historia de los Indios de la Nueva España* (1541). Mexico City.

Mukerjee, Radhakamal. 1939. "Land Tenures and Legislation," in *Economic Problems of Modern India,* I: 218–45. London.

Munier, Henri. 1932. "L'Egypt Byzantine de Dioclétien à la conquête Arabe," *Précis de l'Histoire d'Egypte,* II: 3–106. Cairo.

Munro, J. A. R. 1939. "Xerxes' Invasion of Greece," *CAH,* IV: 268–316. Cambridge.

Murdock, George Peter. 1949. *Social Structure.* New York.

Myers, Gustavus. 1939. *The Ending of Hereditary American Fortunes.* New York.

Nârada. 1889. In the *Minor Law-Books,* trans. Julius Jolly, Pt. 1: 1–267. SBE, XXXIII. Oxford.

Nehru, Jawaharlal. 1942. *Glimpses of World History.* New York.

―――― 1942a. *Toward Freedom.* New York.

―――― 1946. *The Discovery of India.* New York.

Nelson, N. C. 1938. "Geological Premises" and "Prehistoric Archaeology," in *General Anthropology,* ed. F. Boas: 7–16, 146–237.

Nestor. 1931. *Die Altrussische Nestorchronik Povest' Vremennych Let,* trans. Reinhold Trautmann, Slavisch-Baltische Quellen und Forschungen, VI. Leipzig.

Newberry, Percy Edward. BH. *Beni Hasan. Archaeological Survey of Egypt,* Pts. 1–4. London, 1893–94.

Nicolai-on. 1899. *Die Volkswirtschaft in Russland,* trans. Georg Polonsky. Munich.

Nihongi. 1896. *Nihongi, Chronicles of Japan from the Earliest Times to* A.D. *697.* Transactions and Proceedings of the Japan Society, London, Suppl. 1. 2 vols. London.

Nilsson, Martin P. 1950. *Geschichte der Griechischen Religion.* Vol. II of *Die Hellenistische und Römische Zeit.* Munich.

Nöldeke, Theodor. 1892. *Orientalische Skizzen.* Berlin.

Obregon. 1928. *Obregon's History of the 16th Century Explorations in Western America,* trans. G. P. Hammond and A. Rey. Los Angeles.

Oertel, F. 1939. "The Economic Life of the Empire," *CAH,* XII: 232–81. Cambridge.

Oldenberg, Hermann. 1915. *Die Lehre der Upanishaden und die Anfänge des Buddhismus.* Göttingen.

Olmstead, A. T. 1923. *History of Assyria.* New York and London.

——— 1948. *History of the Persian Empire.* Chicago.

Oman, Charles. 1924. *A History of the Art of War in the Middle Ages.* 2d ed. 2 vols. London.

Ondegardo, Polo de. 1872. "Relación de los fundamentos acerca del notable Daño que resulta de no guardar á los Indios sus fueros," in *Coleccion de Documentos Inéditos . . . de América y Oceania,* XVII: 5–177. Madrid.

Oppenheimer, Franz. 1919. *Der Staat.* Frankfurt am Main.

Ostrogorsky, Georg. 1940. *Geschichte des byzantinischen Staates.* Munich.

——— 1942. "Agrarian Conditions in the Byzantine Empire in the Middle Ages," *CEHE,* I: 194–223. Cambridge.

Østrup, J. 1929. *Orientalische Höflichkeit,* trans. K. Wulff. Leipzig.

Otto, Walter. PT. *Priester und Tempel im hellenistischen Ägypten.* 2 vols. Leipzig and Berlin, 1905–08.

Oviedo y Valdes, Gonzalo Fernandes de. HGNI. *Historia general y natural de las Indias,* ed. Jose Amador de los Rios. 3 pts. in 4 vols. Madrid, 1851–55.

Pacific Affairs. Published by the Institute of Pacific Relations.

Palerm, Ángel. 1952. "La Civilización urbana," *Historia Mexicana,* II: 184–209.

——— 1954. "La Distribución del regadío en el área central de Mesoamérica," *Ciencias Sociales,* V: 2–15, 64–74.

——— 1955. "La Base agricola de la civilización urbana en Mesoamérica," in *Las Civilizaciónes antiguas del Viejo Mundo y de América.* Estudios Monograficos, 1. Union Panamericana, Washington, D.C.

Panikkar, K. M. AWD. *Asia and Western Dominance.* A survey of the Vasco Da Gama epoch of Asian history 1498–1945. New York, no date.

Pant, D. 1930. *The Commercial Policy of the Moguls.* Bombay.

Parsons, Elsie Clew. 1932. "Isleta, New Mexico," SIBAE, *Forty-seventh Annual Report:* 201–1087.

—— 1939. *Pueblo Indian Religion.* 2 vols. Chicago.

Pedersen, J. 1941. "*Masdjid,*" *HWI:* 423–48. Leiden.

Peking Gazette. English translation. Shanghai, 1872–99.

Perry, Antonio. 1913. "Hawaiian Water Rights," *The Hawaiian Almanac and Annual for 1913:* 90–9. Honolulu.

Petit-Dutaillis, Ch. 1949. *The Feudal Monarchy in France and England,* trans. E. D. Hunt.

Pietschmann, Richard. 1889. *Geschichte der Phönizier.* Berlin.

Piggott, Stuart. 1950. *Prehistoric India.* Pelican Books. Harmondsworth.

Pizarro, Hernando. 1938. "A Los Magnificos señores, los señores oidores de la audiencia real de Su Majestad, que residen en la cuidad de Santo Domingo," *BCPP:* 253–64. Paris.

Plato. *The Trial and Death of Socrates.* Vol. III of *The Dialogues of Plato,* trans. J. Jowett. New York, no date.

Platonov, S. F. 1925. *History of Russia,* trans. E. Aronsberg. New York.

Plekhanov, G. V. FPM. *Fundamental Problems of Marxism.* Marxist Library, I. ed. D. Riazanov. New York, no date.

—— 1891. (Plechanoff). "Die Zivilisation und die grossen historischen Fluesse," *NZ,* IX, No. 1: 437–48.

—— 1906. "On the Agrarian Question in Russia," *Dnevnik Sotsial-Demokrata,* No. 5, March.

Pod Znamenem marxizma. Nos. 2–3, 6, 7–8, 1929.

Pöhlmann, Robert von. 1912. *Geschichte der sozialen Frage und des Sozialismus in der antiken Welt.* 2 vols. Munich.

Poliak, A. N. 1934. "Les Révoltes populaires en Egypte à l'époque des Mamelouks et leurs causes économiques," *Revue des Etudes Islamiques,* VIII: 251–73.

—— 1939. *Feudalism in Egypt, Syria, Palestine, and the Lebanon, 1250–1900.* London.

Polybius. *The Histories,* with an English trans. by W. R. Paton. 6 vols. New York, 1925.

Poma de Ayala, Felipe Guaman. 1936. *Nueva corónica y buen gobierno.* Travaux et mémoires de l'Institut d'Ethnologie, XXIII. Paris.

Porphyrogénète, Constantin VII. 1939. *Le Livre des cérémonies,* II, Bk. 1, chaps. 47–92, trans. Albert Vogt. Paris.

Prescott, William H. 1838. *History of the Reign of Ferdinand and Isabella, the Catholic.* 3 vols. Boston.

—— 1936. *History of the Conquest of Mexico and History of the Conquest of Peru.* Modern Library. New York.

Price, Ira Maurice. 1927. *The Great Cylinder Inscriptions A and B of Gudea*, Pt. 2. Leipzig and New Haven.

Prigozhin, A. G. 1934. "Karl Marks i problemy istorii Dokapitalisticheshikh formatsiy," in *Sbornik k pyatidesyatiletiyu so dnya smerti Karla Marxa*, ed. N. Ya Marr. Moscow and Leningrad.

Primera crónica general ó sea estoria de España que mandó componer Alfonso el Sabio y se continuaba bajo Sancho IV en 1289, I, ed. Ramón Menéndez Pidal. Madrid, 1906.

Problemy Kitaia, Nos. 4, 5, 1930. Moscow.

Prokopowitsch, Sergej. 1913. "Uber die Bedingungen der industriellen Entwicklung Russlands," *ASS*, Suppl. X.

Protokoly Obyedinitelnovo Syezda Rossyskoi Sotsialdemokraticheskoi Rabochei Partii (Protocols of the Unification Congress of the RSDRP), held in Stockholm, 1906. Moscow, 1907.

Ramirez, Codice. 1944. *Codice Ramirez. Manuscrito del Siglo XVI intitulado: Relación del origen de los Indios que habitan esta Nueva España, segun sus historias*, ed. Manuel Orozco y Berra. Mexico City.

Ramsay, W. M. 1890. *The Historical Geography of Asia Minor.* Supplementary Papers of the Royal Geographical Society, IV. London.

Rangaswami Aiyangar, K. V. 1935. *Considerations on Some Aspects of Ancient Indian Polity.* 2d ed. University of Madras.

Rangoon Tracts, 1. *Resolutions of the First Asian Socialist Conference, Rangoon, 1953.* Asian Socialist Conference, Rangoon.

Ranke, Leopold. 1924. *Deutsche Geschichte im Zeitalter der Reformation.* 3 vols. Munich and Leipzig.

Rapson, E. J. 1922. "Peoples and Languages and Sources of History," *CHI*, I: 37–64. New York and Cambridge.

Rathgen, Karl. 1891. "Japan's Volkswirtschaft und Staatshaushalt," *Staats- und socialwissenschaftliche Forschungen*, ed. Gustav Schmoller, X, No. 4. Leipzig.

RDS. 1896. "Translation of the *Relacion del Suceso*, account of what happened on the journey which Francisco Vazquez made to discover Cibola," in George Parker Winship, "Coronada Expedition 1540–1542," *SIBAE, Fourteenth Annual Report*, 1892–93, Pt. 1: 572–9.

Reclus, Elisée. 1882. *L'Asie Orientale.* Vol. VII of *Nouvelle geographie universelle.* Paris.

Reed, Thomas H. 1937. "Water Supply," *ESS*, XV: 372–7. New York.

Reid, J. S. 1936. "The Reorganisation of the Empire," *CMH*, I: 24–54. Cambridge.

Reischauer, Robert Karl. 1937. *Early Japanese History*. 2 vols. Princeton.

Reiske, J. J. 1830. *Constantinus Porphyrogenitus. Constantini Porphyrogeniti Imperatoris de Cerimoniis Aulae Byzantinae*, II. Bonn.

Renou, Louis. 1950. *La Civilisation de l'Inde ancienne*. Paris.

C. A. F. Rhys-Davids (Mrs.). 1922. "Economic Conditions according to Early Buddhist Literature," *CHI*, I: 198–219. New York.

Rhys-Davids, T. W. 1922. "The Early History of the Buddhists," *CHI*, I: 171–97. New York.

—— 1950. *Buddhist India*. 1st Indian ed. Susil Gupta.

Riasanovsky, V. A. 1937. *Fundamental Principles of Mongol Law*. Tientsin.

Ricketson, Oliver G. 1937. "The Excavations," Pt. 1 of *Uaxactun, Guatemala Group E, 1926–31*, CIW, 477: 1–175.

Riepl, Wolfgang. 1913. *Das Nachrichtenwesen des Altertums mit besonderer Rücksicht auf die Römer*. Leipzig and Berlin.

Ritter, Carl. 1858. *Klein-Asien*. Vol. IX, Pt. 1, of *Die Erdkunde von Asien*, Berlin.

Ritter, H. 1929. "La Parure des Cavaliers und die Literatur über die ritterlichen Künste," *Der Islam*, XVIII: 116–54.

Rjasanoff, N. (Ryazanov). 1909. "Karl Marx über den Ursprung der Vorherrschaft Russlands in Europa," Suppl. to *NZ*, XXVII, Pt. 1, No. 5.

—— 1925. "Introduction to *Marx über China und Indien*," *UBM*, I, No. 2: 370–8.

Robins, F. W. 1946. *The Story of Water Supply*. London, New York, and Toronto.

Robinson, Geroid Tanguary. 1949. *Rural Russia under the Old Régime*. New York.

Rockhill, William Woodville. 1891. *The Land of the Lamas*. New York.

Rogers, James E. Thorold. 1884. *Six Centuries of Work and Wages*. New York.

Rostovtzeff, M. (Rostowzew). 1910. *Studien zur Geschichte des Römischen Kolonates*. Leipzig and Berlin.

—— 1941. *The Social and Economic History of the Hellenistic World*. 3 vols. Oxford.

Rowe, John Howland. 1946. "Inca Culture at the time of the Spanish Conquest," *Handbook of South American Indians*, II: 183–330. SIBAE, CXLIII.

Roys, Ralph L. 1933. *The Book of Chilam Balam of Chumayel*. CIW, 438.

—— 1943. *The Indian Background of Colonial Yucatan*. CIW, 548.

RRCAI. *Report of the Royal Commission on Agriculture in India, Presented to Parliament by Command of His Majesty*, June 1928. Abridged.

Runciman, Steven. 1933. *Byzantine Civilisation*. New York and London.

Ruppert, Karl and Denison, John H., Jr. 1943. *Archaeological Reconnaissance in Campeche, Quitana Roo, and Peten*. CIW, 543.

Rüstow, Alexander. OG. *Ortsbestimmung der Gegenwart*. 2 vols. Erlenbach-Zurich, 1950–52.

RY. "Relaciones de Yucatán," in *Colección de documentos inéditos relativos al descubrimiento conquista y organización de las antiguas posesiones Españolas de Ultramar*, ser. 2, Vols. XI, XIII. Madrid, 1898 and 1900.

Sabahuddin, S. 1944. "The Postal System during the Muslim Rule in India," *IC*, XVIII, No. 3: 269–82.

Sacy, Silvestre de. 1923. *Bibliothèque des Arabisants Français contenant les mémoires des Orientalistes Français relatifs aux études Arabes*, published under the direction of George Foucart, Ser. 1, Vol. II. Cairo.

Saha, K. B. 1930. *Economics of Rural Bengal*, with a foreword by Sir Jehangir Coyajee. Calcutta.

Sahagun, Bernardino de. 1938. *Historia general de las cosas de Nueva España*. 5 vols. Mexico City.

Saletore, Rajaram Narayan. 1943. *Life in the Gupta Age*. Bombay.

San Kuo Chih, Wei. Po-na ed. Commercial Press.

Sánchez-Albornoz, Claudio. EM. *La España Musulmana*, I. Buenos Aires, no date.

Sancho de la Hos, Pedro. 1938. "Relación para S. M. de lo Sucedido en la conquista y pacificación de estas provincias de la Nueva Castille y de la Calidad de la Tierra," *BCPP*: 117–93. Paris.

San Nicolò, Mariano. PR. *Ägyptisches Vereinswesen zur Zeit der Ptolemäer und Römer*. 2 vols. Munich, 1913–15.

Sansom, George B. 1938. *Japan, a Short Cultural History*. New York and London.

Santillana, David. 1938. *Teoria Generale delle obbligazione*. Vol. II of *Istituzioni di diritto Musulmano Malichita*. Rome.

Sarmiento de Gamboa, Pedro. 1906. "Geschichte des Inkareiches," ed. Richard Pietschmann, in *Abhandlungen der Königlichen Gesellschaft der Wissenschaften zu Göttingen, Philologisch-Historische Klasse*, VI, Fasc. 4.

Sauvaget, J. 1941. *La Poste aux chevaux dans l'empire des Mamelouks*. Paris.

———— 1946. *Historiens Arabes*. Paris.

Schacht, Joseph. 1935. *G. Bergsträsser's Grundzüge des islamischen Rechts*. Berlin and Leipzig.

———— 1941. "*Mīrāth*" and "*Sharī'a*," *HWI*: 511–17, 673–8. Leiden.

Schawe, J. 1932. "*Bauer*," *RA*, I: 434. Berlin and Leipzig.

Scheel, Helmuth. 1943. "Die staatsrechtliche Stellung der ökumenischen Kirchenfürsten in der alten Türkei," *Abhandlungen der Preussischen Akademie der Wissenschaften, Philologisch-Historische Klasse*, Fasc. 9.

Scheil, V. 1900. *Textes Elamites-Sémitiques*, Ser. 1. Delegation en Perse, *Mémoires*, II. Paris.

Schiller, Herman. 1893. "Staats- und Rechtsaltertümer," *Die römischen Staats-, Kriegs- und Privataltertümer*, by Schiller and Moritz Voigt: 1–268. Munich.

Schirrmacher, Friedrich Wilhelm. 1881. *Geschichte von Spanien*, Vol. IV of *Geschichte der europäischen Staaten*, ed. A. H. L. Heeren, F. A. Ufert, and W. von Giesebrecht. Gotha.

Schnebel, Michael. 1925. *Der Betrieb der Landwirtschaft*, Vol. I of *Die Landwirtschaft im hellenistischen Ägypten*. Munich.

Schneider, Anna. 1920. *Die Anfänge der Kulturwirtschaft: die sumerische Tempelstadt*. Essen.

Scholtz, Rudolf. 1934. *Die Struktur der sumerischen Engeren Verbalpräfixe (Konjugationspräfixe). Speziell dargelegt an der I. and II. Form (E- und Mu-Konjugation)*. Mitteilungen der Vorderasiatisch-Aegyptischen Gesellschaft, XXXIX, No. 2. Leipzig.

Schramm, Percy Ernst. 1924. "Das Herrscherbild in der Kunst des Frühen Mittelalters," *Bibliothek Warburg, Vorträge 1922–23*, I: 145–224. Leipzig.

Schubart, Wilhelm. 1922. *Ägypten von Alexander dem Grossen bis auf Mohammed*. Berlin.

——— 1943. *Justinian und Theodora*. Munich.

Schuster, Sir George, and Wint, Guy. 1941. *India & Democracy*. London.

Schwartz, Benjamin I. 1951. *Chinese Communism and the Rise of Mao*. Cambridge, Mass.

Scott, George Ryley. 1943. *The History of Torture throughout the Ages*. London.

Sears, Paul B. 1951. "Pollen Profiles and Culture Horizons in the Basin of Mexico," *Selected Papers of the XXIXth International Congress of Americanists*: 57–61. Chicago.

Seeck, Otto. 1901. "Cursus Publicus," *Pauly-Wissowa*, IV: 1846–63. Stuttgart.

Segrè, Angelo. 1943. *An Essay on the Nature of Real Property in the Classical World*. New York.

Seidl, Erwin. 1951. *Einführung in die ägyptische Rechtsgeschichte bis zum Ende des neuen Reiches*. Glückstadt, Hamburg and New York.

Seler, Eduard. GA. *Gesammelte Abhandlungen zur Amerikanischen Sprach- und Alterthumskunde*. 5 vols. Berlin, 1902–23.

Seler, Eduard. 1927. *Fray Bernardino de Sahagun*. Stuttgart.

Seligman, Edwin R. A. 1914. *Principles of Economics*. New York and London.

Sethe, Kurt. PT. *Übersetzung und Kommentar zu den altägyptischen Pyramidentexten*. 4 vols. Glückstadt, Hamburg and New York, 1935–39.

—— 1908. "Zur ältesten Geschichte des ägyptischen Seeverkehrs mit Byblos und dem Libanongebiet," *Zeitschrift für ägyptische Sprache und Altertumskunde*, XLV: 7–14.

—— 1912. "R. Weill, Les Décrets royaux de l'ancien empire égyptien," *Göttingische gelehrte Anzeigen*, CLXXIV: 705–26.

Seybald, C. F. 1927. "Granada," *Encyclopaedia of Islam*, II: 175–7. Leiden and London.

Shattuck (George Cheever), Redfield (Robert), and MacKay (Katheryn). 1933. "Part I: General and Miscellaneous Information about Yucatan," chaps. 1–5 of *The Peninsula of Yucatan*, CIW, 431.

Shih Chi. Po-na ed. Commercial Press.

SLRUN. *Slave Labor in Russia. The Case Presented by the American Federation of Labor to the United Nations*. A. F. of L., 1949.

SM. *Soils and Men. Yearbook of Agriculture, 1938*. Washington, D.C.

Smith, Adam. 1937. *An Inquiry into the Nature and Causes of The Wealth of Nations*. Modern Library, New York.

Smith, Arthur H. 1897. *Chinese Characteristics*. Edinburgh and London.

—— 1899. *Village Life in China*. New York.

Smith, Vincent A. 1914. *The Early History of India*. 3d ed. Oxford.

—— 1926. *Akbar, the Great Mogul, 1542–1605*. 2d ed. Oxford.

—— 1928. *The Oxford History of India*. 2d ed. Oxford.

Smith, Wilfred Cantwell. 1946. "Lower-class Uprisings in the Mughal Empire," *IC*, XX, No. 1: 21–40.

—— 1946a. *Modern Islam in India*. London.

Socialist Asia. Published monthly by the Asian Socialist Conference, Rangoon.

Sombart, Werner. 1919. *Der moderne Kapitalismus*. 2 vols. Munich and Leipzig.

Speiser, E. A. 1942. "Some Sources of Intellectual and Social Progress in the Ancient Near East," in *Studies in the History of Science*: 51–62. Philadelphia, 1941. Revised reprint.

Spiegelberg, Wilhelm. 1892. *Studien und Materialen zum Rechtswesen des Pharaonenreiches*. Hanover.

—— 1896. *Rechnungen aus der Zeit Setis, I*. Text. Strassburg.

Spuler, Bertold. 1943. *Die Goldene Horde. Die Mongolen in Russland 1223–1502*. Leipzig.

—— 1952. *Iran in Früh-Islamischer Zeit*. Wiesbaden.

Staden, Heinrich von. 1930. *Aufzeichungen über den Moskauer Staat,* ed. Fritz Epstein. Hamburg University, Abhandlungen aus dem Gebiet der Auslandskunde, XXXIV. Hamburg.

Stalin, Joseph. S. *Sochinenia.* 13 vols. Moscow, 1946–51.

—— 1939. "Dialectical and Historical Materialism," in *History of the Communist Party of the Soviet Union* (Bolsheviks), *Short Course,* ed. by a Commission of the Central Committee of the CPSU (B.), and authorized by the Central Committee of the CPSU (B.). New York.

—— 1942. *Selected Writings.* New York.

Stamp, L. Dudley. 1938. *Asia, a Regional and Economic Geography.* 4th ed. New York.

Stein, Ernst. 1920. "Ein Kapitel vom persischen und vom byzantinischen Staate," *Byzantinisch-Neugriechische Jahrbücher,* I: 50–89.

—— 1928. *Vom römischen zum byzantinischen Staate. Geschichte des spätrömischen Reiches,* I. Vienna.

—— 1949. *De la Disparition de l'empire d'Occident à la mort de Justinien* (476–565). Vol. II of *Histoire du Bas-Empire.* Paris, Brussels and Amsterdam.

—— 1951. "Introduction à l'histoire et aux institutions byzantines," *Traditio,* VII: 95–168.

Steinwenter, Artur. 1920. *Studien zu den koptischen Rechtsurkunden aus Oberägypten.* Leipzig.

Stengel, Paul. 1920. *Die griechischen Kultusaltertümer.* Munich.

Stephens, John L. ITCA. *Incidents of Travel in Central America, Chiapas, and Yucatan.* 12th ed. 2 vols. New York, 1863–77.

—— 1848. *Incidents of Travel in Yucatan.* 2 vols. New York.

Stepniak. 1888. *The Russian Peasantry.* New York.

Stevenson, G. H. 1934. "The Imperial Administration," *CAH,* X: 182–217. Cambridge.

Steward, Julian H. 1949. "Cultural Causality and Law: a Trial Formulation of the Development of Early Civilizations," *AA,* LI: 1–27.

—— 1953. "Evolution and Process," in *Anthropology Today,* ed. Kroeber: 313–26. Chicago.

—— 1955. "Introduction: the Irrigation Civilizations, a Symposium on Method and Result in Cross-Cultural Regularities," in *Irrigation Civilizations: a Comparative Study:* 1–5. Social Science Monographs, 1. Pan-American Union, Washington, D.C.

Stöckle, Albert. 1911. *Spätrömische und byzantinische Zünfte. Klio. Beiträge zur alten Geschichte.* Leipzig.

Strabo. *The Geography of Strabo,* with an English trans. by Horace Leonard Jones. 8 vols. New York, 1917–32.

Strong (William Duncan), Kidder (A.), and Paul (A. J. D., Jr.). 1938. *Harvard University Archaeological Expedition to Northwestern Honduras,*

1936. Smithsonian Miscellaneous Collections, XCVII, No. 1. Washington, D.C.

Struve, Peter. 1942. "Russia," in *CEHE,* I: 418–37. Cambridge.

Struve, V. V. 1940. "Marksovo opredelenie ranneklassovogo obshchestva," *Sovetskaya Etnografia, Sbornik Statei,* Fasc. 3: 1–22.

Stubbs, William. CHE. *The Constitutional History of England.* 2 vols. Oxford, 1875–78.

Suetonius Augustus. *C. Suetoni Tranquilli quae supersunt omnia,* ed. Karl Ludwig Roth. Leipzig, 1886.

Sui Shu. Po-na ed. Commercial Press.

Sumner, B. H. 1949. *A Short History of Russia.* Revised ed. New York.

Sun Tzu. 1941. "On the Art of War," in *Roots of Strategy,* ed. Thomas R. Phillips: 21–63, trans. Lionel Giles. Harrisburg, Pa.

Ta Ch'ing lü-li hui chi pien lan. Hupeh, 1872.

Ta T'ang Hsi-yü Chi in *Ssŭ-pu Ts'ung K'an.*

Tabari. 1879. *Geschichte der Perser und Araber zur Zeit der Sasaniden aus der arabischen Chronik des Tabari,* trans. T. Nöldeke. Leiden.

Taeschner, Franz. 1926. "Die Verkehrslage und das Wegenetz Anatoliens im Wandel der Zeiten," *PM,* LXXII: 202–6.

Takekoshi, Yosoburo. 1930. *The Economic Aspects of the History of the Civilization of Japan.* 3 vols. London.

Tang, Peter. MS. "Communist China Today: Domestic and Foreign Policy." In press.

Tarn, W. W. 1927. *Hellenistic Civilisation.* London.

Taubenschlag, Raphael. 1944. *The Law of Greco-Roman Egypt in the Light of the Papyri.* New York.

Taylor, George E. 1936. *The Reconstruction Movement in China.* Royal Institute of International Affairs, London.

———— 1942. *America in the New Pacific.* New York.

Taylor, Lily Ross. 1931. *The Divinity of the Roman Emperor.* Middletown, Conn.

TEA. 1915. *Tell-el-Amarna Tablets. Die El-Amarna-tafeln . . .* ed. J. A. Knudtzon, revised by Otto Weber and Erich Ebeling. 2 vols. Leipzig.

Têng Ssŭ-yü and Biggerstaff, Knight. 1936. *An Annotated Bibliography of Selected Chinese Reference Works.* Harvard-Yenching Institute, Peiping.

Tezozomoc, Hernando Alvarado. 1944. *Crónica Mexicana escrita hacia el ano de 1598,* notes by Manuel Orozco y Berra. Mexico City.

Thompson, R. Campbell, and Hutchinson, R. W. 1929. *A Century of Exploration at Nineveh.* London.

Thompson, Virginia. 1941. *Thailand: the New Siam.* New York.

Thornburg (Max Weston), Spry (Graham), and Soule (George). 1949. *Turkey: an Economic Appraisal.* New York.

Thucydides. 1942. "The Peloponnesian War," *The Greek Historians,* trans. Benjamin Jowett, ed. Francis R. B. Godolphin: 567–1001. New York.

Thureau-Dangin, F. 1907. *Die sumerischen und akkadischen Königsinschriften,* Vorderasiatische Bibliothek, I, Pt. 1. Leipzig.

Timasheff, Nicholas S. 1946. *The Great Retreat. The Growth and Decline of Communism in Russia.* New York.

Titiev, Mischa. 1944. *Old Oraibi—a Study of the Hopi Indians of the Third Mesa.* PMAAE, *Reports,* XXII, No. 1. Cambridge, Mass.

Tolstov, S. 1950. "For Advanced Soviet Oriental Studies," *Kultura i zhizn,* Aug. 11, trans. in *Current Digest of the Soviet Press,* XI, No. 33: 3–4.

Tomsin, A. 1952. "Etude sur les πρεσβύτεροι des villages de la χώρα égyptienne," *Bulletin de la Classe des Lettres et des Sciences Morales et Politiques, Académie Royale de Belgique,* Ser. 5, XXXVIII: 95–130.

Torquemada, Fray Juan de. 1943. *Monarquia Indiana.* 3d ed. 3 vols. Mexico City.

Tout, T. F. 1937. *Chapters in the Administrative History of Mediaeval England,* II. Manchester University Press.

Tozzer, Alfred M. 1941. *Landa's relación de las cosas de Yucatan,* trans. with notes, PMAAE, *Reports,* XVIII, Cambridge, Mass.

Tritton, A. S. 1930. *The Caliphs and Their Non-Muslim Subjects.* London and Madras.

Trotsky, Leon. (Trotzki). 1923. *Die russische Revolution 1905.* Berlin.

—— 1928. *The Real Situation in Russia,* trans. Max Eastman. New York.

—— (Trotzki). 1931. *Geschichte der russischen Revolution. Februarrevolution.* Berlin.

—— 1939. *The Living Thoughts of Karl Marx Based on Capital: a Critique of Political Economy.* Philadelphia.

Tso Chuan Chu Shu. Ssŭ-pu Pei-yao.

Tugan-Baranowsky, M. 1900. *Geschichte der russischen Fabrik,* ed. B. Minzes. Suppl. to *Zeitschrift für Sozial- und Wirtschaftsgeschichte,* V–VI.

Vaillant, George C. 1941. *Aztecs of Mexico.* Garden City, New York.

Vancouver, Captain George. 1798. *A Voyage of Discovery to the North Pacific Ocean and Round the World.* 3 vols. London.

Vandenbosch, Amry. 1949. "Indonesia," in Mills and Associates, *The New World of Southeast Asia:* 79–125. New York.

Van Nostrand, J. J. 1937. "Roman Spain," in *ESAR,* III: 119–224. Baltimore.

Varga, E. 1928. "Osnovniye problemy kitaiskoi revolyutsii" (Fundamental Problems of the Chinese Revolution), *Bolshevik*, VIII: 17–40. Moscow.

Vâsishtha. 1898. In *Sacred Laws of the Âryas*, trans. Georg Bühler, SBE, II: 1–140. New York.

Veblen, Thorstein. 1945. *What Veblen Taught*, selected writings, ed. Wesley C. Mitchell. New York.

———— 1947. *The Engineers and the Price System*. New York.

Vernadsky, George. 1943: *Ancient Russia*. 1948: *Kievan Russia*. 1953: *The Mongols and Russia*. Vols. I–III of *History of Russia*, by G. Vernadsky and M. Karpovich. New Haven.

Vinogradoff, Paul. 1908. *English Society in the Eleventh Century*. Oxford.

Vishnu. 1900. "The Institutes of Vishnu," trans. Julius Jolly, SBE, VIII. New York.

Vladimirtsov, B. 1948. *Le Régime social des Mongols. Le Féodalisme nomade*, trans. Michel Carsow. Paris.

Voigt, Moritz. 1893. "Privataltertümer und Kulturgeschichte," *Die römischen Staats-, Kriegs- und Privataltertümer*, by Herman Schiller and Voigt: 271–465. Munich.

Vyshinsky, Andrei Y. 1948. *The Laws of the Soviet State*, trans. Hugh W. Babb, with an intro. by John N. Hazard. New York.

Waitz, Georg. 1880. *Deutsche Verfassungsgeschichte*, I. 3d ed. Berlin.

Walker, Richard L. 1955. *China under Communism. The First Five Years*. New Haven.

Wallace, Sherman Le Roy. 1938. *Taxation in Egypt*. Princeton.

Walther, Arnold. 1917. "Das altbabylonische Gerichtswesen," *Leipziger Semitistische Studien*, VI: Fasc. 4–6.

Wan Kuo-ting. 1933. *Chung-kuo T'ien Chih Shih*. Nanking.

Warriner, Doreen. 1948. *Land and Poverty in the Middle East*. Royal Institute of International Affairs. London and New York.

Wb. *Wörterbuch der ägyptischen Sprache*, IV–VI, ed. Adolf Erman and Hermann Grapow. Berlin and Leipzig, 1930–31, 1950.

Weber, Max. RS. *Gesammelte Aufsätze zur Religionssoziologie*. 3 vols. Tübingen, 1922–23.

———— WG. *Wirtschaft und Gesellschaft. Grundriss der Sozialökonomik*, Pt. 3. Tübingen, 1921–23.

———— 1906. "Russlands Übergang zum Scheinkonstitutionalismus," *ASS*, V: 165–401.

Weissberg, Alexander. 1951. *The Accused*. New York.

Wellhausen, J. 1927. *The Arab Kingdom and its Fall*, trans. Margaret Graham Weir. University of Calcutta.

Wên-hsien T'ung-k'ao. Commercial Press, Shanghai.

Werner, E. T. C. 1910. *Descriptive Sociology: or, Groups of Sociological*

Facts, Classified and Arranged by Herbert Spencer. Chinese. Compiled by E. T. C. Werner, ed. Henry R. Tedder. London.

Westermann, William Linn. 1921. "The 'Uninundated Lands' in Ptolemaic and Roman Egypt," Pt. 2, *Classical Philology,* XVI: 169–88.

———— 1922. "The 'Dry Land' in Ptolemaic and Roman Egypt," *Classical Philology,* XVII: 21–36.

———— 1937. "Greek Culture and Thought," and "Slavery, Ancient," *ESS,* I: 8–41; XIV: 74–7.

White, Leslie A. 1932. "The Acoma Indians," SIBAE, *Forty-seventh Annual Report:* 17–192.

———— 1942. *The Pueblo of Santa Ana, New Mexico.* Memoir Series, American Anthropological Association, LX.

Whitney, William Dwight. 1905. *Artharva-Veda Saṁhitā,* revised by Charles Rockwell Lanman. Harvard Oriental Series, VII. Cambridge.

Widenmann, A. 1899. "Die Kilimandscharo-Bevölkerung Anthropologisches und Ethnographisches aus dem Dschaggalande," *PM,* Suppl. XXVII, No. 129.

Widtsoe, John A. 1926. *The Principles of Irrigation Practice.* New York and London.

———— 1928. *Success on Irrigation Projects.* New York and London.

Wiedemann, A. 1920. *Das alte Ägypten.* Heidelberg.

Wiet, Gaston. 1932. "L'Egypte Musulmane de la conquête Arabe à la conquête Ottomane," *Précis de l'Histoire d'Égypte,* II: 107–294.

———— 1937. *L'Egypte Arabe de la conquête Arabe à la conquête Ottomane,* Vol. IV of *Histoire de la Nation Egyptienne.* Paris.

Wilbur, C. Martin. 1943. *Slavery in China during the Former Han Dynasty.* Chicago.

Wilcken, Ulrich. 1899. *Griechische Ostraka aus Aegypten und Nubien.* 2 vols. Leipzig and Berlin.

———— 1912. *Historischer Teil: Grundzüge,* Vol. I, Pt. 1, of *Grundzüge und Chrestomathie der Papyruskunde,* by L. Mitteis and U. Wilcken. Leipzig and Berlin.

Willcocks, W. 1889. *Egyptian Irrigation.* London and New York.

———— 1904. *The Nile in 1904.* London and New York.

Willey, Gordon E. 1953. *Prehistoric Settlement Patterns in the Virú Valley, Perú.* SIBAE, CLV.

———— 1953a. "Archeological Theories and Interpretation: New World," *Anthropology Today,* ed. A. L. Kroeber: 361–85. Chicago.

Williams, Sir Edward Leader. 1910. "Canal," *Encyclopaedia Britannica,* V: 168–71. 11th ed.

Williams, James. 1911. "Torture," *Encyclopaedia Britannica,* XXVII: 72–9. 11th ed.

Williams, S. Wells. 1848. *The Middle Kingdom*. 2 vols. New York and London.

Williamson, H. B. WAS. *Wang-An-Shih, a Chinese Statesman and Educationalist of the Sung Dynasty*. 2 vols. London, 1935–37.

Wilson, John A. 1950. "Egyptian Myths, Tales, and Mortuary Texts," "Documents from the Practice of Law: Egyptian Documents," and "Proverbs and Precepts: Egyptian Instructions," in *ANET*: 3–36, 212–17, 412–25. Princeton.

—— 1951. *The Burden of Egypt*. Chicago.

Wipper, R. 1947. *Ivan Grozny*, trans. J. Fineberg. Moscow.

Wirz, Paul. 1929. *Der Reisbau und die Reisbaukulte auf Bali und Lombok*. Leiden.

Wittfogel, Karl August. 1924. *Geschichte der bürgerlichen Gesellschaft*. Vienna.

—— 1926. *Das erwachende China*. Vienna.

—— 1927. "Probleme der chinesischen Wirtschaftsgeschichte," *ASS*, LVIII, No. 2: 289–335.

—— 1929. "Geopolitik, geographischer Materialismus und Marxismus," *UBM*, III: 17–51, 485–522, 698–735.

—— 1929a. "Voraussetzungen und Grundelemente der chinesischen Landwirtschaft," *ASS*, LXI: 566–607.

—— 1931. *Wirtschaft und Gesellschaft Chinas, Erster Teil, Produktivkräfte, Produktions- und Zirkulationsprozess*. Leipzig.

—— 1931a. "Hegel über China," *UBM*, V: 346–62.

—— 1932. "Die natürlichen Ursachen der Wirtschaftsgeschichte," *ASS*, LXVII: 466–92, 579–609, 711–31.

—— 1935. "The Foundations and Stages of Chinese Economic History," *Zeitschrift für Sozialforschung*, IV: 26–60.

—— 1936. "Wirtschaftsgeschichtliche Grundlagen der Entwicklung der Familienautorität," *Studien über Autorität und Familie, Schriften des Instituts für Sozialforschung*, V. Paris.

—— 1938. "Die Theorie der orientalischen Gesellschaft," *Zeitschrift für Sozialforschung*, VII: 90–122.

—— 1938a. *New Light on Chinese Society*. International Secretariat, Institute of Pacific Relations.

—— 1940. "Meteorological Records from the Divination Inscriptions of Shang," *Geographical Review*, XXX: 110–33.

—— 1947. "Public Office in the Liao Dynasty and the Chinese Examination System," *Harvard Journal of Asiatic Studies*, X: 13–40.

—— 1949. "General Introduction," *History of Chinese Society, Liao*: 1–35. Philadelphia.

—— 1950. "Russia and Asia," *World Politics*, II, No. 4: 445–62.

—— 1951. "The Influence of Leninism-Stalinism on China," *Annals of* the *American Academy of Political Science*, CCLXXVII: 22–34.

—— 1953. "The Ruling Bureaucracy of Oriental Despotism: a Phenomenon That Paralyzed Marx," *Review of Politics*, XV, No. 3: 350–9.

—— 1955. "Developmental Aspects of Hydraulic Societies," in *Irrigation Civilizations: a Comparative Study*: 43–52. Social Science Monographs, 1. Pan-American Union, Washington, D.C.

—— 1955a. *Mao Tse-tung. Liberator or Destroyer of the Chinese Peasants?* Published by the Free Trade Union Committee, A. F. of L., New York.

—— 1956. "Hydraulic Civilizations," *Man's Role in Changing the Face of the Earth*," ed. William L. Thomas, Jr., Wenner-Gren Foundation. Chicago.

Wittfogel, Karl A., and Fêng Chia-shêng. 1949. *History of Chinese Society, Liao*, American Philosophical Society, *Transactions*, XXXVI. Philadelphia.

Wittfogel, Karl A., and Goldfrank, Esther S. 1943. "Some Aspects of Pueblo Mythology and Society," *Journal of American Folklore*, January–March 1943: 17–30.

Wolfe, Bertram D. 1948. *Three Who Made a Revolution*. New York.

Wright, Walter Livingston, Jr. 1935. *Ottoman Statecraft*. Princeton.

Wüstenfeld, F. 1880. "Das Heerwesen der Muhammedaner nach dem Arabischen," *Abhandlungen der Historisch-Philologischen Classe der Königlichen Gesellschaft der Wissenschaften zu Göttingen*, XXIV, No. 1.

Xenophon. 1914. *The Education of Cyrus*. Everymans Library. London and New York.

Yājnavalkya Smṛiti. With Mitâkṣarâ. *The Law of Inheritance*, trans. Pandit Mohan Lal, in Sacred Books of the Hindus, II, No. 2. Allahabad City, no date.

Yang, Martin C. 1945. *A Chinese Village*. New York.

Yen T'ieh Lun by Huan K'uan. Shanghai, 1934.

Yüan Shih. Po-na ed. Commercial Press.

Yüeh Hai Kuan Chih. Tao-Kuang edition.

Zagorsky, S. O. 1928. *State Control of Industry in Russia during the War*, Vol. II of *Economic and Social History of the World War*, Russian Series. New Haven.

Zinowjew, G. 1919. "Der russische Sozialismus und Liberalismus über auswärtige Politik der Zarismus," *Archiv für die Geschichte des Sozialismus und der Arbeiterbewegung*, VIII: 40–75.

Zurita. 1941. "Breve relación de los señores de la Nueva España," *Nueva colección de documentos para la historia de Mexico*, XVI: 65–205.

GENERAL INDEX

Abbreviations: HS—hydraulic society; OD—Oriental despotism; OS—Oriental society

Absolutism
  insufficiently studied, 2
  genuine in OD, 103
  limited Western, 45 ff., 78
    multicentered society, 45 and *passim*;
    strong property, 82 ff., 189, 300, 360
  limited Japanese, 200, 366
  and autocracy, 106
  See also Autocracy, Europe, Japan, Mercantilism, OD, Total power
Absorption of conquerors, legend and
  reality, 326. *See also* Conquest societies
Acton, Lord, 133
Administrative returns
  law of changing, 109 ff.
    in hydraulic economy, 109 ff.; in
    sphere of social control, 111 ff.
  law of diminishing, 109 f., 113
Aesopian language
  originally used by slaves, 400
  used by masters of USSR, 400, 442
Agriculture
  essential natural conditions for, 13 ff.
  rainfall, 18 ff.
  hydroagriculture, 3, 18
    primary and secondary origin, 17
  hydraulic, 3
    origins, 18 ff.; multiple, 19 ff.; intensive, 23, 322
  See also Division of labor, Hydraulic
  economy
Agrobureaucratic regime, synonymous
  with OD, 3, 8, and *passim*
Agrodespotic regime. *See* Oriental despotism
Agromanagerial society, synonymous with
  HS, 3, 8
Akbar, 48, 274, 309
Alexander the Great, 44, 157, 160, 207 f.
Akida (Chagga official), 240 f.
Alienation
  patterns of, 156 ff.
  partial, 157
  total, 157, 160
  See also Loneliness
Altiplano. See Andean zone, Inca society
America, ancient (pre-Conquest)
  hydraulic civilizations, 3
  masters of, great builders, 42 f.
  priests, 362

no evidence of eunuchism, 354 f.
institutional effect on Latin America,
  8, 430
See also Andean zone, Inca society,
  Maya society, Mexico, Pueblo Indians
Anarchists, criticize Marxist state socialism
  for involving despotism and slavery,
  388
Andean zone
  hydraulic landscape, 19, 24, 247
  hypothetical origin of HS, 19
  coastal area, 163, 166
  aqueducts, 31
  trade, 257
  pre-Inca conditions, surmised, 163, 257
  See also Inca society
Apparatus state
  term, 440 f.
  ruling class a monopoly bureaucracy,
  368
Apparatchiki, 335 and *passim*
Arab civilizations
  origins, 127, 154, 359
  Umayyad Caliphate
    a conquest dynasty, 359; upheld by
    tribal supporters, 359 f.; eunuchs insignificant, 359; army, 64, 215, 327; hydraulic concern of, 127, 171; taxation,
    168; prostration, 154; collapse, 205,
    327
  Abbassid Caliphate
    hydraulic core areas, 167; hydraulic
    management, 53; tribal support discarded, 205; army, 215; bureaucratic
    density, 167; eunuchs, 358; terror, 139,
    142 ff., 156; taxation, 168; confiscation,
    76 f;. slaves as bodyguards, 360; slave
    girls, mothers of caliphs, 344
  See also Islamic civilizations, Near East
Architecture, hydraulic
  monumental pubiic structures, 43 ff.
  introvert private edifices, 86
  compared with that of Medieval Europe,
  44 ff.
Aristotle, 160, 208, 219, 263
Army. *See* Military organization
Artisans
  part time, 233
  professional, 246
  government-attached, 246, 248 ff., 250

Rome (*continued*)

post, 56, 210 f.; intelligence service, 211; judicial torture, 146; the autocratic and divine ruler, 101 f., 211; power of freedmen and eunuchs, 211 f., 357, 360; the state the biggest landowner and entrepreneur, 211; prominence of military leaders, 178; from capitalist to bureaucratic tax farmers, 168

Western

absolutism, 212; eunuchism, 211, 357, 360; decline, 212 f.; role of external impact, 423

Eastern

the shift to the East, 211; emperor "*dominus*," 211; roads, 170, 173; big walls, 170; office land, 174; eunuchs, 357

See also Byzantium, Diocletian

Russia

Kievan

rainfall agriculture, 201; marginal feudal society, 201, 418; retainers could "ride away," 202; power of towns, 222; free men not to be beaten, 147, 203; influence of Byzantine culture, 202, 225, 415; Khazar influence, 202; on submarginal zone of HS, 202 ff.

Mongol

introduction of organizational and acquisitive methods of OD, 174, 191, 193, 205; census, 223; state post, 223; office land (*pomestye*), 223 f.; judicial torture, 147; Muscovy, the Khan's agency, rises to prominence, 224; towns lose their power, 222; independent boyars weakened, 222; crucial role of Mongols in this transformation, 222 ff.

Tsarist, Muscovite

pattern of OD, 174 f.; government control of trade, 260 f.; bureaucratic capitalists, 261; weak private property, 262

Tsarist: Peter I and after

state-directed industrialization, 179; forced labor prevailing in heavy industry until 19th century, 180; military pattern changed, 174 f.; landlordism established, 176; a serving rather than a landed nobility, 278; fragmenting pattern of inheritance, 189, 278 f.; no corporations ("estates"), 176; regulated villages, 272 f.; bureaucratically

directed emancipation of serfs, 180, 342

See also Church

Tsarist, Modern

state control over economy perpetuated, 180; acquisitive power of government perpetuated, 180; bureaucratic credit control, 181, 395; external impact, 425, 428; development of private property and enterprise, 428; rise of bourgeoisie and labor, 429, 436; increasing political freedom, 429; growth of anti-absolutistic forces, 429, 436 f.; the *zemstvos*, 428; political parties, 428, 436

democratic revolution

breakthrough to multicentered society, 429, 437; an open historical situation, 437 ff.; Bolshevik power strategy, 437; Communist victory by default, 438

See also Asiatic restoration, Engels, Lenin, Marx, Plekhanov, USSR

Ryazanov, 379, 401 f.

Ryotowari, 281, 433

Satraps, 308 f., 325

Self-government in HS

limited but extant in groups of secondary importance

family, 116 ff., 122 ff.; guilds, 120, 124; secondary religions, 121-2, 124; village communities, 117 ff., 123 ff.

Beggars' Democracy, 125 ff.

See also Guilds

Seleucids

landownership, 283

religious and secular authority combined, 94

prostration, 154

Semi-Asiatic order

conceptualized by Marx and Engels, 5

in Tsarist Russia, 5, 375, 391 ff., 399

inherited by Soviet Union (Lenin), 400

Semi-officials, 289, 315

Septimius Severus, 211

Serfdom, compatible with several types of societies, 414

Setthi, 120, 265 f., 317

Sher Shāh, 37

Shih, 320 f.

Sicily

Syracuse under Hieron, Hellenistic regime, 208

seized by Rome, 208

INDEX OF AUTHORS AND WORKS

For full reference to each see the Bibliography

Three views of a new town: Tai Po in 1952

Tai Po growing in 1972

Tai Po today

HONG KONG *1993*

A REVIEW OF 1992

HONG KONG 1993

Editor:	Hugh Witt, Government Information Services
Creative Director:	Allan Cheung, Government Information Services
Artist:	Liu Chiu-tsan, Government Information Services
Photography:	Stone Chiang, Augustine Chu, Daniel Wong, David Ho and other staff photographers Other photographs by arrangement with International (Elite) Divers Training Centre, World Wide Fund for Nature (Hong Kong) and Reuter.
Special Contributor:	Burton Levin (Chapter 1)
Statistical Sources:	Census and Statistics Department

The editor acknowledges all contributors and sources

Code No.: F30019300E0 (ISBN 962-02-0125-6)

Price: HK$52.00   US$17.00   UK £16.00

Cover: *Hong Kong Ballet Group in rehearsal for a 'Celebration Gala' at Queen Elizabeth Stadium, Wan Chai.*

Frontispiece: *Three views of the development of Tai Po New Town in the New Territories.*

CONTENTS

ILLUSTRATIONS

END-PAPER MAPS

Front:

The Territory of Hong Kong

Back:

The Interdependence of Hong Kong and China

APPENDICES

When dollars are quoted in this report, they are, unless otherwise stated, Hong Kong dollars. Since October 17, 1983, the Hong Kong dollar has been linked to the US dollar, through an arrangement in the note-issue mechanism, at a fixed rate of HK$7.80 = US$1.

*   *   *

Some figures in the text are estimated; actual figures appear in the appendices.

CALENDAR OF EVENTS IN 1992

5.1	Director of the Hong Kong and Macau Affairs Office of China's State Council Lu Ping visits Hong Kong.
9.1	Governor of Macau General Rocha Vieira visits Hong Kong at the invitation of Governor Sir David Wilson.
24.1	A two-day promotion of Hong Kong in London is concluded with the performance of 'Hong Kong Heartbeat' at the Barbican Centre, attended by the Princess of Wales.
30.1	First meeting of the Economic Advisory Committee which is set up to advise the Financial Secretary on strategic issues concerning the economy.
31.1	The Government announces the construction of Container Terminal No. 9 on Tsing Yi with work to start in 1993.
14.2	The Governor adopts his new title as Baron Wilson of Tillyorn of Finzean in the District of Kincardine in Deeside, Scotland, and of Fanling in Hong Kong.
18.2	The Government issues a public consultation paper on a bank deposit protection scheme.
20.2	A delegation from the Guangdong Provincial Bureau of Water Conservancy and Hydro-Power arrives for the third annual business meeting on water supply to Hong Kong.
24.2	The Government publishes the 1992–3 Draft Expenditure Proposals of over $121 billion.
26.2	The Governor visits Guangdong for two days to view economic development in the province.
4.3	Financial Secretary Hamish MacLeod presents the 1992–3 Budget in the Legislative Council (LegCo).
17.3	The Financial Secretary confirms a plan by the Hongkong and Shanghai Banking Corporation Holdings to merge with the United Kingdom's Midland Bank.

1

18.3	The Industry and Technology Development Council holds its first meeting and discusses a $200 million scheme for applied research and development.
20.3	The Health and Medical Development Advisory Committee is formed to replace the Medical Development Advisory Committee to reflect increased emphasis on primary health care.
3.4	Treasury Secretary Yeung Kai-yin leads a delegation to China at the invitation of the Chinese State Council's Hong Kong and Macau Affairs Office.
	The Governor-in-Council authorises the reclamation of land at the Central waterfront to accommodate the Hong Kong terminus of the Airport Railway.
15.4	Secretary for Security Alistair Asprey announces the disbandment of the 1 000-strong Royal Hong Kong Regiment (The Volunteers) by September 1995.
23.4	Departure of the 100th flight organised by the United Nations High Commissioner for Refugees (UNHCR) under its voluntary repatriation programme for Vietnamese migrants.
24.4	Sham Shui Po District Board by-election held in the Pak Tin constituency.
26.4	The Governor visits the UK to brief British Government Officials and his successor, Mr Christopher Patten.
	Director of the Chinese Foreign Ministry's Hong Kong and Macau Affairs Office Zhao Jihua begins a seven-day visit to Hong Kong.
29.4	The Government announces the granting of the Colvin House site for use as the British Consulate after 1997.
8.5	An intense rainstorm brought a deluge of 109.9 millimetres of rain in one hour, the highest ever recorded, and caused flooding and mudslips.
12.5	The British, Hong Kong and Vietnamese Governments sign an agreement on the repatriation of Vietnamese migrants who arrived in Hong Kong before October 29, 1991.
15.5	Provincial Governor of Guangdong Zhu Senlin arrives for a five-day visit.
18.5	Secretary for Home Affairs Michael Suen leads a delegation to China for five days at the invitation of the Hong Kong and Macau Affairs Office of the State Council.
24.5	New Foreign and Commonwealth Office Minister with Special Responsibility for Hong Kong Alastair Goodlad visits Hong Kong.
2.6	The Government awards a $3.5 billion contract for the construction of the Tai Ho Section of the North Lantau Expressway, which will link up the new airport and the urban areas.

7.6	The Governor visits China to bid farewell to Chinese officials.
23.6	The Education Commission Report No. 5 is released and makes recommendations on the status, training and workloads of teachers.
24.6	Political Adviser William Erhman and Shenzhen officials meet to review progress of an agreement to open up Shenzhen–Hong Kong links.
26.6	The Governor makes a farewell visit to Macau.
1.7	Clearance of residents of the Kowloon Walled City is completed.
3.7	Governor Lord Wilson retires and leaves Hong Kong for the UK with his family.
9.7	The Rt Hon Christopher Patten arrives and is sworn in as the 28th Governor of Hong Kong.
10.7	The Governor visits Mongkok, Sha Tin and Wong Tai Sin.
21.7	The 20 000th Vietnamese illegal immigrant returns home under the UNHCR voluntary repatriation programme.
26.7	Secretary of State for Foreign and Commonwealth Affairs Douglas Hurd arrives in Hong Kong for a three-day visit.
29.7	The Government announces its decision to introduce licences for the operation of local fixed communication networks to compete with the Hong Kong Telecommunication Company.
20.8	First meeting between the Governor and the Director of the New China News Agency (Hong Kong Branch) Zhou Nan.
30.8	The New Territories West Legislative Council by-election is held in Tuen Mun and Yuen Long.
8.9	Hong Kong and Canada sign a Memorandum of Understanding on Environmental Collaboration, under which the two signatories agree to exchange information on environmental issues.
14.9	The Governor visits London to met with the Prime Minister and the Foreign and Commonwealth Secretary.
26.9	A five-city Festival Hong Kong '92 is launched in Canada.
5.10	A Regional Council by-election is held in Tuen Mun.
7.10	The Governor delivers his first policy address in LegCo and announces plans for constitutional development in the territory.
8.10	The Governor participates in a radio phone-in programme on RTHK, holds his first question time in LegCo and meets members of the public at the City Hall to answer questions on the policy address.

9.10	The Governor meets members of the public at Sha Tin Town Hall to answer questions on the policy address.
11.10	A Tuen Mun District Board by-election is held.
13.10	The Governor meets members of the public at Tsuen Wan Town Hall to answer questions on the policy address.
16.10	The Governor meets members of the public at the Cultural Centre to answer questions on the policy address.
20.10	The Governor leaves for a four-day visit to Beijing.
28.10	Inaugural meeting of the Governor's Business Council.
29.10	The Governor pays his first official visit to Macau.
3.11	An agreement is initialled for an extension of the Hong Kong/European Community Textiles Agreement for one year until December 31, 1995.
5.11	The Prince of Wales arrives in Hong Kong for a four-day visit.
10.11	The Government announces the granting of development rights for Container Terminal No. 9 to three companies by private treaty.
	Joseph Yam is appointed the first Chief Executive of the Hong Kong Monetary Authority.
11.11	The Governor leaves for Canada to attend the Festival Hong Kong '92 closing ceremony.
16.11	The Governor starts a five-day visit to London.
	The Government awards a $1.64 billion contract for the design and construction of the Kap Shui Mun Bridge and Ma Wan Viaduct on the Lantau Fixed Crossing, linking the new airport with the urban areas.
18.11	Eight Chinese officials, led by Deputy Director of the Chinese Foreign Ministry's Hong Kong and Macau Office Wang Guisheng, start a three-day visit to Hong Kong.
19.11	An agreement on the encouragement and protection of investments is signed between Hong Kong and the Netherlands.
23.11	The Governor leaves for a four-day visit to Japan.
24.11	The Government announces that coins and bank notes of a new design will be issued from 1993.
27.11	The Finance Committee of LegCo approves $6.699 billion for site preparation for the new airport at Chek Lap Kok.
14.12	The third meeting of the Hong Kong–Guangdong Environmental Protection Liaison Group is held in Hong Kong from December 14 to 15.

Above: *Hong Kong's new Governor, the Right Honourable Christopher Patten, accompanied by his wife Lavender and daughters Laura (left) and Alice, arrived at Hong Kong International Airport on July 9.*

Right: *The Governor was greeted by well-wishers at Queen's Pier.*

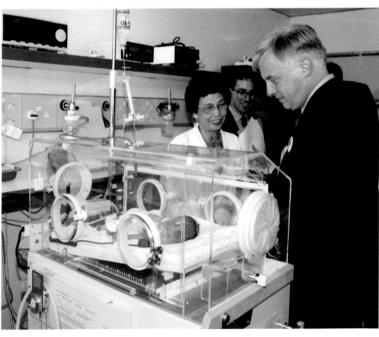

Preceding Pages: *Mr Patten plunged into a hectic round of "getting to know you" visits, including* **(top row, left to right)** *Mong Kok District in Kowloon, the David Trench Home for the Elderly and an estate flat in Upper Wong Tai Sin;* **(bottom row left to right)** *the control tower at Hong Kong International Airport, the cargo terminal at the airport and Tai Kok Tsui.*

Top row, left to right: *Mr Patten at Tseung Kwan O, at Tsuen Wan New Town and visiting the Kowloon-Canton Railway rolling stock maintenance centre.*

Bottom row, left to right: *The Governor at the maternity ward of Queen Elizabeth Hospital and on a visit to an Industrial Estate at Tai Po.*

Above: *Mr Patten in London with British Prime Minister Mr John Major.*

Right (top): *Mr Patten met Canadian Prime Minister Mr Brian Mulroney in Ottawa during Festival Hong Kong 92.* **(Bottom):** *Mr Patten called on Mr. Kiichi Miyazawa, Prime Minister of Japan, during a visit to Tokyo.*

Following page: *Mr Patten held four public meetings to explain his policies to the community. During them he invited questions from his audiences.*

1
THE HONG KONG–CHINA PHENOMENON

WHEN asked to reflect upon the relationship between Hong Kong and southern China in 1993, my thoughts turn to a phenomenon unimaginable to the young of Hong Kong today. Well into the 1970s, one of the highlights of a tourist stay in Hong Kong was a visit to Man Kam To, then a sparsely populated outpost not far from Lo Wu. From a vantage point there, the visitor thrilled at the opportunity to peer into inscrutable, unreachable 'Red China'. What mysteries lay beyond that barbed wire fence? Few could imagine, and fewer had ventured beyond the border. To the visitor, the rare glimpse of a peasant or even a water buffalo or bird (crossing the fence at will) provided the basis for many a tale told to friends and family at home.

For nearly three decades, the curious had no choice but to settle for the vicarious thrill of such a fleeting look across the border. A relatively small number of people did have contact – like the amahs and construction workers who would return for Spring Festival, Ching Ming or Chung Yeung heavily laden with packages for family and friends. Private residents crossing the border did not number more than a few hundred thousand per year. For those who made the trip, the crossing of a few short kilometres was not a simple affair. It was not until 1979 that a nonstop train service between Hong Kong and Guangzhou was introduced, cutting what was previously an all-day ordeal (including an obligatory stop at Lo Wu and a walk over the railway bridge to the Chinese side), to under three hours. In 1978 1.3 million Hong Kong residents entered China while there were 24 800 visitor arrivals from the PRC to Hong Kong, including PRC nationals residing in the PRC and overseas. In 1990, by contrast, Hong Kong residents made over 16 million trips to China, while more than 370 000 People's Republic of China residents visited the territory.

Official contact was limited to the customs officials checking shipments of choy sum, pigs, or chickens as they crossed the border, or those responsible for ensuring the flow of water to Hong Kong, so vital to a still rapidly growing population. From time to time, an accident at sea or (more frequently) illicit border crossings would bring the need for contact and co-operation among security officials, which promptly ended at the conclusion of the incident in question. A combination of China's self-imposed isolation and outside suspicion of the regime assured an absence of contact between higher-ranking Hong Kong officials and their counterparts to the north.

In Guangdong, attempts were made to limit awareness of what lay across the banks of the Shenzhen River in Hong Kong. Official propaganda portrayed life in Hong Kong as a sad affair, with the common man oppressed by colonialist masters and capitalist exploiters.

Despite this, word of the impressive economic gains that were transforming Hong Kong society and lifestyles spread steadily.

Trade was also a victim of this mutual hostility and suspicion. The imposition of a United Nations trade embargo following China's entry into the Korean war struck a serious blow to Hong Kong's traditional entrepôt role. The meagre level of trade that continued in those years was attributable to Hong Kong's need for food imports. With little arable land or natural resources, Hong Kong has long relied on the relative abundance in China.

Despite the decades of estrangement and a heavily guarded border, there was still a sizeable influx from China to Hong Kong throughout the period. Fleeing the chaos of the Cultural Revolution and attracted by economic opportunity in Hong Kong, illegal immigration into the territory continued well into the 1980s. This influx provided a valuable source of labour for an expanding Hong Kong industry. There are many who believe that the refugee mentality so common to Hong Kong has been a substantial contributor to the territory's economic dynamism over the years. Though accurate figures on immigration from Guangdong are hard to come by, best estimates are that the '60s and '70s saw tens of thousands arriving every year. By mutual agreement, this flow was cut off almost entirely following 1978, though the legal daily limit of 75 is no doubt far from the true number, with many continuing to cross into Hong Kong illegally in search of economic gains.

Increased contact for ordinary Guangdong citizens with their Hong Kong relatives and compatriots began to grow in the mid to late seventies. Nearly all of the province has links to Hong Kong, and increased travel to the homeland brought closer personal ties and awareness of the outside world along with gifts of money, television sets, and other electronics.

With the death of Mao Zedong and the overthrow of the Gang of Four, Chinese leaders took stock of the destruction and widespread poverty that were the result of years of ideological excess. Realising the extent of China's backwardness and need for change, Deng Xiao Ping boldly proclaimed new policies designed to speed economic development and the country's re-entry into the world economy. The economic reforms and the opening of China's door to the outside world, embodied in the Third Plenum of the Eleventh Central Committee of the Chinese Communist Party in December 1978, provided the framework for forward-looking policies which would uplift the Chinese people, forever change the country's pattern of isolation, and bring Hong Kong and China ever closer to each other. Over the past 14 years, what was once an impermeable barrier has become a two-way flow of people, capital, ideas, and indeed, increasing goodwill.

An end to collectivised agriculture, the encouragement of small-scale private enterprise, and the unleashing of entrepreneurial abilities brought a rapid improvement in living standards to the Chinese countryside. Greater economic incentives and a reduction in the bureaucratic and ideological obstacles in the way of economic development engendered a new spirit and hope that would transform Chinese society. Along with greater opportunities for Chinese citizens, new policies also included the encouragement of foreign investment, which would serve to accelerate the development process through the introduction of capital, new technologies and modern management techniques.

In the ensuing years, as it became clear that China's new policies toward foreign investment were here to stay, Hong Kong's own economy was also expanding, and its manufacturers felt the pressures of rising land and labour costs affecting their competitiveness. The migration of the territory's manufacturing base across the border proceeded apace. Today, with some four-fifths of local manufacturers having transferred production to the mainland, Hong Kong is said to be responsible for more than 80 per cent of the foreign investment in Guangdong province. Some 60 000 Hong Kong people, now managing factories and other investments in southern China, are responsible for much of the cross-border traffic increase, while between three and four million workers in southern China are directly or indirectly employed by Hong Kong firms.

With well earned pride, Hong Kong can share the credit for transforming what was a relationship of suspicion and ignorance on either side of the border to what is now emerging as perhaps the single greatest economic takeoff in world history. Hong Kong manufacturers have benefited enormously from the proximity of Guangdong. The cultural and linguistic similarities they share with China have enabled them to take full advantage of what can seem a somewhat daunting environment for other foreign investors. In initial forays into the Chinese market many foreigners have lacked the patience required to forge the relationships and trust considered so important by their Chinese joint venture partners or other counterparts. Sharing a cultural heritage and language despite their differences, Hong Kong investors have an understanding of how their mainland partners think, as well as what their counterparts might appreciate from them to make ventures successful. Modern technology, new manufacturing techniques, and different financial and managerial skills have added to the speed with which landscape and attitudes alike are changing.

This successful pattern is perhaps best illustrated by a concrete example.

A prominent businessman of my acquaintance, managing director of a major toy manufacturing company, has long considered himself fortunate to call Hong Kong home, having come from China with his parents in 1950. Just two years old then, he grew up in Hong Kong feeling little personal identification with his native land. In 1976, he and a friend joined forces to go into business on their own. With the company's growth and rising production costs, a move into China clearly emerged as the only viable alternative for the firm to remain competitive. Ironically, having been born in China and raised in Hong Kong, his first return visit to China was not until his initial trip in search of industrial space and a new factory in 1984.

With some 300 000 square feet of factory space and operations in eight Guangdong locations today, the company's success is clearly evident. Early negotiations over where and how to set up the first operation, however, were a test of patience and persistent negotiating skills, as the government offices, departments and officials with the authority to offer attractive investment terms had to be identified.

In retrospect, the negotiating process for this first factory may have been faster had my friend opted to set up in Shenzhen or one of the other Special Economic Zones (SEZs) in Guangdong. With toy manufacturing a highly seasonal business, however, the more restrictive environment and higher costs of the SEZs were inappropriate to the company's needs. During the peak June–September buying period, it employs some 2 500 workers in its manufacturing and assembly operations. In Dongguan, the ability to negotiate directly with the local *danwei* (work unit) enables the firm to reduce or expand the labour force with relative ease. An agreement with the *danwei* also allows for payment of overtime directly to workers, an arrangement that provides important incentives to the work force. With the direct payment system the firm employs, practiced by some 70 per cent of Hong

7

Kong companies in Guangdong today, motivation comes through direct incentive and recognition for work done.

With few if any comparable toy firms remaining in Hong Kong, the savings to a firm like I have described from having its operation across the border are difficult to quantify. Between 70 and 80 per cent of the toy industry worldwide, and some 95 per cent of all plastic toys produced, are manufactured in China today. Alternative production sites cannot rival China when it comes to competitiveness in the toy industry.

As China's economic reforms have taken hold and outside investment has increased, better living standards and higher expectations are evident among officials and ordinary citizens alike. Small village officials are negotiating fewer outward processing plants and more joint ventures, which can give the Chinese side a greater economic stake in inward investment. People in the countryside, once looked down upon by their urban neighbours, are earning small fortunes through land leases and often substantial side businesses. People in the Special Economic Zones, often unwilling to take menial clerical jobs, opt instead for the more glamorous positions in hospitality and other boom industries. More and more, manufacturing workers in Guangdong factories are being hired from less prosperous inland provinces. The same trend is taking place in more technically-orientated positions. Many of the small, family-owned firms operating in Guangdong have had difficulty expanding in the past, since competing with larger firms for key management positions is difficult. With the lure of south China, however, an increasing number of firms are getting around the problem by hiring highly-qualified northern Chinese managers eager to hone their skills and gain experience in international business.

Modernisation of cross-border transportation and communications facilities have helped to make this partnership possible. In contrast to the tortuous travel difficulties of the past, transport options to and from south China have now been expanded to include several non-stop trains each day to Guangzhou, ferry services to various points in the Pearl River Delta, hoverferries, and several daily flights to Bai Yun airport from Kai Tak. Today, Taiwanese businessmen crowd the flights to Xiamen, where special zones have been established to accommodate their investment projects. Travel and business within the region will receive a further boost in the near future with the inauguration of the superhighway linking Hong Kong to Guangzhou, expected to cut the time between the two cities to little more than one hour. Even with the existing road network, 20 153 freight trucks cross the border each day compared with 17 000 in January 1992 and there is great demand for expansion of opening hours at the various border checkpoints to accommodate the huge volume of goods moving in both directions. The three land border control points at Man Kam To, Sha Tau Kok and Lok Ma Chau are now open for a total of 41 hours daily, five and a half hours longer than in January 1992.

Added to the flow of foodstuffs crossing the border today is an enormous volume of textiles and light industrial items, raw materials, machinery, spare parts, and high-technology goods. Any recent traveller between Hong Kong and Shenzhen can attest to the changes that have come to the once sleepy border. By 1990, Hong Kong/China trade had exceeded HK$400 billion – a fifty-fold increase in just over a dozen years. Hong Kong's domestic exports to China amounted to just two-tenths of one per cent of the territory's total exports in 1978. The percentage as of 1991 was some 24 per cent and in 1992 was 26 per cent. The volume of goods being transported today boggles the mind, and more often than not the traveller between Hong Kong and Guangzhou finds colossal traffic jams where a few years ago the water buffalo enjoyed virtual unimpeded access to the road.

The 'open door policy', the introduction of Special Economic Zones, and the easing of foreign travel for ordinary Chinese, have meant changes not just in how the country will do business, but in the way people view their role in the world as well. Mainland citizens now visit Hong Kong in large numbers, not only on official business, but in holiday tour groups – unthinkable just a few years ago. For officials and private visitors alike, Hong Kong serves as a model in its internationalism, modernity, and as the paradigm of a highly successful Chinese society.

The growth of mainland investment in Hong Kong has come about for several reasons. While Chinese investment in a variety of goods and services in Hong Kong have been undertaken for sound business reasons, highly visible mainland involvement in the territory's economy also conveys to the world China's commitment to Hong Kong's future and to its role in the global economy. Several PRC companies, established in Hong Kong well before the signing of the Sino-British agreement, have long been household names. Expertise gained by employment in the early Hong Kong-based firms has been an important contributor to the modernisation process on the mainland. China Merchants' Steam Navigation, begun as a shipping firm and agent, later expanded into activities as diverse as trading, construction, tourism and hospitality. China Resources, registered as a Hong Kong company in 1983, was originally established in 1948 as the Ministry of Foreign Economic Relations and Trade's Hong Kong trading arm. China Travel Service, established in 1928, now handles most of China's tourist trade from Taiwan, as well that of visitors from around the world. CITIC, established in 1979, stood out among the early PRC firms for its vision and professionalism. It is now a major shareholder in flagship Hong Kong firms such as Cathay Pacific and Hong Kong Telecom. The Bank of China group, building on success in retail banking, expanded quickly into merchant banking, foreign exchange, bullion trading and loan syndication. The sleek and modern Bank of China Tower is a distinctive addition to Hong Kong's famous skyline.

These large and prominent PRC firms are no longer alone as a myriad of mainland interests have joined them in Hong Kong since the late 1970s. All of China's 21 provinces and many municipalities now operate companies in Hong Kong, handling foreign trade, attracting inward investment, and seeking investment opportunities both in Hong Kong and abroad. Many mainland-invested firms have even taken advantage of the Open Door to re-invest in China, enjoying all the preferential terms granted foreign investors. With the wide variation of activities in which mainland firms are engaged, the value of their Hong Kong investments is not easy to quantify. An oft-quoted figure today is of US$10–15 billion, though many analysts believe China's investment in the territory may already well outpace that of Japan and the United States. Mainland property investments have received the most attention of late, with prime Central buildings going to PRC consortia.

Looking beyond the economic sphere, the mainland presence in Hong Kong today is also clearly evident in the arts. The greater number and variety of musical performances, dance, drama, and exhibitions of painting and calligraphy now available to the public are a welcome reminder of Hong Kong's Chinese heritage in an otherwise business-minded and fast-paced society. An increase in the number of tea houses and other shops provide locals and tourists a welcome respite in a traditional Chinese atmosphere. One even hears more Mandarin on the street, as greater mobility allows mainlanders to visit Hong Kong in

9

greater numbers and more Hong Kong people make an effort to learn Putonghua, in recognition of China's growing importance to the territory's future.

While influences from the north are growing, the converse is also true. The ties are clearly multiplying, with changes in the very social fabric on both sides of the border taking place as a result. Shanghai, as China's manufacturing, financial, and commercial centre, was long considered China's most cosmopolitan city, and the symbol of modernity and chic. While Shanghai is again on the rise, Hong Kong has taken its place as a model, particularly among youth on the mainland. The appeal of Hong Kong's food, music, fashion, and even dialect is influencing trends across China today. I have even been told the Cantonese accent, once considered vulgar and the object of derision, has grown in popularity in parts of the north.

Thus, after decades of separation, isolation, and distrust, the common culture shared by Hong Kong and China, with its history of 3 000 years, is again evolving in tandem on both sides of an increasingly symbolic border, despite still sizeable disparities in income. Television and other media, broadcast both locally and from Hong Kong, has brought a profusion of new ideas and material incentives to the counties of Guangdong and beyond. Mass media is greatly accelerating a process that is blurring the social and cultural differences separating Hong Kong from China.

These growing contacts have also encouraged a breakdown of the social and psychological barriers separating people. Materialism aside, these closer ties and a recognition of shared values and heritage are helping to alleviate Hong Kong's concerns about the future on a very human level. While governments talk, people are getting on with things in true Hong Kong (and increasingly mainland) fashion. Hong Kong's relationship with China, which has often been a cause of great concern, is increasingly seen as the territory's greatest advantage. A better understanding of this relationship and its inherent opportunities is having a lubricating effect on the transition, despite the inevitable bumps in the road. At the same time, the overseas Chinese communities in countries elsewhere in the region keep a watchful eye, with Hong Kong such an indispensable link in their economic activity throughout Asia.

Greater access and exposure to new ideas means subtle changes in thinking, in what may be seen by some as not just a period of transition, but of some confusion as well. New lifestyle patterns are emerging, as people move into cities and large portions of society become less agrarian in nature. Most clearly in the south, but further north to a growing degree, as people are acquiring more materialistic tastes, Chinese have increasingly come to resemble their counterparts in the industrialised world. Hong Kong has provided (and continues to provide) a neutral meeting point for China and the world in business, the arts, and in a broad sense, education. It is a place for cultural exchanges of many kinds, and for a sharing of views on limitless subjects. A contrast and a model for China's planners, it endures with a unique combination of East and West, modern and traditional. Offering China the best in technology, expertise and world markets, it does so with the familiarity and shared ancestry no other country or territory can match. While still playing its traditional role, that of China's window on the world, Hong Kong has helped its mother country find its own windows to the world.

Burton Levin

2
CONSTITUTION AND ADMINISTRATION

HONG KONG is administered by the Hong Kong Government, which is headed by the Governor. He is the representative of the Queen in Hong Kong. Under the terms of the Joint Declaration of the British and Chinese Governments on the Question of Hong Kong which entered into force on May 27, 1985, Hong Kong will become, with effect from July 1, 1997, a Special Administrative Region of the People's Republic of China.

Hong Kong operates a three-tier system of representative government. At the central level is the Legislative Council. There are two municipal councils: the Urban Council and the Regional Council, at the regional level. In addition, there are 19 District Boards at the district level which cover the whole territory.

There are direct elections on the basis of universal franchise at all the three tiers of representative government: two-thirds of District Board members, 38 per cent of Urban Council members, 33 per cent of Regional Council members, and 30 per cent of Legislative Council members, are returned through direct elections.

Constitution

The Letters Patent establish the basic framework of the administration of Hong Kong and, together with the Royal Instructions passed under the Royal Sign Manual and Signet which lay down procedures that must be followed, form the written constitution of Hong Kong.

The Letters Patent create the office of Governor and Commander-in-Chief of Hong Kong and require him to observe laws and the instructions given to him by the Queen or the Secretary of State. They also deal with the constitution of the Executive and Legislative Councils, the Governor's powers in respect of legislation, disposal of land, the appointment of judges and public officers, pardons, and the tenure of office of Supreme Court and District Court judges.

The Royal Instructions deal with the appointment of members of the Executive and Legislative Councils, the nature of proceedings in the Executive Council, the Governor's responsibility to consult the Executive Council on important policy matters, and his right to act against its advice (a right only exercised once in 1946). They also deal with the membership of, and election to, the Legislative Council, the nature of proceedings there, and the nature of legislation which may not be passed.

There are various well-established practices which determine the way in which these constitutional arrangements are applied. Hong Kong is governed by consent and through

11

consultation with the community. For instance, although from the constitutional instruments described above Her Majesty's Government would appear to have substantial control over the way in which Hong Kong is run, in practice the territory largely controls its own affairs and determines its own policies. Similarly, the Governor, by convention, rarely exercises the full extent of his powers.

Role of the Governor
The Governor is appointed by the Queen and derives his authority from the Letters Patent. He has ultimate direction of the administration of Hong Kong and is also the titular Commander-in-Chief of the British Forces stationed in Hong Kong. He makes policy decisions on the advice of the Executive Council, and makes laws by and with the consent of the Legislative Council. As head of the government he presides at meetings of the Executive Council. The present Governor, the Rt Hon Christopher Patten, assumed office on July 9, 1992, and is the 28th incumbent.

Central Government
Executive Council
The Executive Council comprises four *ex-officio* members – the Chief Secretary, the Commander British Forces, the Financial Secretary and the Attorney General – together with 12 other members including three members who are officials and appointed by the Governor with the approval of the Secretary of State. The council normally meets once a week, and its proceedings are confidential although many of its decisions are made public. (With effect from February 19, 1993 the Commander British Forces ceased to be an *ex-officio* member of the Executive Council).

The Governor is required by the Royal Instructions to consult the council on all important matters of policy. The Governor in Council – the Governor acting after consulting the Executive Council – is Hong Kong's central and highest executive authority on policy matters. In practice, decisions are arrived at by consensus rather than by division. Members tender their advice on individual capacity, and the council is collectively responsible for the decisions made by the Governor in Council. Individual non-official members do not hold personal responsibility for given subjects or portfolios. This is a matter for the government.

In addition to policy matters, the Governor in Council determines appeals, petitions and objections under those ordinances which confer a statutory right of appeal. The council also considers all principal legislation before it is introduced into the Legislative Council, and is responsible for making subsidiary legislation under numerous ordinances. The council's advice on matters of policy involving the expenditure of public funds is subject to the approval of the necessary funds by the Finance Committee of the Legislative Council.

Legislative Council
Starting from the session of the Legislative Council which began on October 9, 1991, the council has an elected majority. It consists of 60 members – three *ex-officio* members, namely the Chief Secretary, the Financial Secretary and the Attorney General; 18 appointed members, (including one appointed as the Deputy President of the council;) and 39 elected members. The appointed members are appointed by the Governor with the

approval of the Secretary of State. Among the elected members, 21 are elected by functional constituencies, each representing an economic or social sector, and 18 elected by direct elections in geographical constituencies which cover the whole territory. The Governor is the President of the Legislative Council. During his policy address to the Legislative Council in October 1992, the Governor announced that, as a move to enable the Legislative Council to manage its own affairs, he had decided to hand over as soon as practicable the Presidency to a member elected by all Legislative Councillors themselves.

The chief functions of the Legislative Council are to enact laws, control public expenditure and put questions to the government on matters of public interest. The government is responsible for initiating legislative and public funding proposals to the Legislative Council for consideration.

Legislation is enacted in the form of bills. Most business, including bills, is transacted by way of motions, which are decided by the majority of votes. Private bills, not representing government measures and intended to benefit particular persons, associations or corporate bodies, are introduced from time to time and enacted in the same way. A bill passed by the Legislative Council does not become law until the Governor gives his assent to it. After the Governor's assent a bill becomes an ordinance without being subject to external approval, although the Queen has reserve powers to disallow an ordinance. The power of disallowance has not been used for many years.

Apart from the enactment of legislation, the business of the council includes two major debates in each legislative session: a wide-ranging debate on government policies which follows the Governor's Address at the opening of the new session of the council in October each year, and the budget debate on financial and economic affairs concerning the annual Appropriation Bill which takes place in April.

Members of the council may also question the government on policy issues for which the government is responsible, either seeking information on such issues or asking for official action on them. Members may request either oral or written answers to the questions asked, and supplementary questions for the purpose of elucidating an answer already given may also be asked.

The council normally meets in public once a week. There is a House Committee which consists of all non-official members (excluding the Deputy President), which meets regularly in public, to discuss the council proceedings and make preparatory work for meetings of the full council.

Finance Committee
The Finance Committee of the Legislative Council consists of the Chief Secretary (Chairman), the Financial Secretary and all members other than the other *ex-officio* members. It scrutinises public expenditure, both at special meetings held in March at which members examine the draft Estimates of Expenditure, and at regular meetings held throughout the year to consider requests which entail changes to the provisions agreed by the Legislative Council in the estimates each year, or to note financial implications of new policies. Both the special and regular meetings are held in public. The Finance Committee has two sub-committees: the Establishment Sub-Committee and the Public Works Sub-Committee, whose meetings are also held in public.

The Establishment Sub-Committee consists of 28 members of the Legislative Council, one of whom is the chairman. Representatives of the Secretary for the Civil Service and the Secretary for the Treasury are in attendance. It examines mainly the creation, redeployment and deletion of permanent and supernumerary posts remunerated from the directorate pay scales and changes to the structure of Civil Service ranks and grades (including pay scales, new grades and new ranks), and makes recommendations on them to the Finance Committee. It also reports to the Finance Committee on changes in departmental establishments and on the size and cost of the Civil Service.

The Public Works Sub-Committee consists of 32 members of the Legislative Council and the Financial Secretary (Chairman). The Secretary for Planning, Environment and Lands, the Secretary for Works, the heads of all works departments and the Environmental Protection Department and two representatives from the Finance Branch are in attendance at all meetings to provide technical advice. The sub-committee reviews the progress of capital works projects in the Public Works Programme, and makes recommendations to the Finance Committee in the upgrading of projects to Category A of the programme which indicates their readiness for commencement, and on changes to the scope and approved estimates of projects already in that category.

Public Accounts Committee

The Public Accounts Committee, established by resolution of the Legislative Council in 1978, is a standing committee consisting of a chairman and six members, none of whom is an *ex-officio* member of the council. Their main function is to examine and report on the findings of the Director of Audit's Reports on the audit of the government's annual statements of account prepared by the Director of Accounting Services, on any matters relating to the performance of the Director of Audit's duties and the exercise of his powers under the Audit Ordinance, and on any matters relating to value-for-money audits carried out by the Director of Audit. Value-for-money audits are carried out under a set of guidelines tabled in the Legislative Council by the chairman of the Public Accounts Committee in November 1986. These guidelines were agreed between the committee and the Director of Audit and have been accepted by the government.

The committee's prime concern is to see that public expenditure has not been incurred for purposes other than those for which the funds were granted, that full value has been obtained for the sums expended, and that the government has not been faulty or negligent in its conduct of financial affairs.

The Director of Audit submits two reports to the Governor as President of the Legislative Council during the course of the year. The first, tabled in April, relates to value-for-money audits; the second, tabled in November, relates to the audit of the government's annual statements of account and also value-for-money audits. Following the tabling of the report, the committee holds public hearings and controlling officers for different heads of public expenditure give evidence. The committee's report based on these hearings is laid on the table of the Legislative Council within three months of the laying of the Director of Audit's report to which it relates. The government's response to the committee's reports is contained in the government minute, which describes the measures taken to give effect to the committee's recommendations or reasons why these recommendations cannot be accepted. The government minute is also laid on the table of the Legislative Council within three months of the laying of the Public Accounts Committee's report.

Committee on Members' Interests
The Committee on Members' Interests, established by resolution of the Legislative Council in 1991, is a Standing Committee consisting of a chairman and six members. It examines the arrangements for the compilation, maintenance and accessibility of the Register of Members' Interests, considers matters pertaining to the declaration of interests by members and matters of ethics in relation to the conduct of members in their capacity as such, and it makes recommendations on matters relating to members' interests. Sittings of the committee are held in public unless the chairman otherwise orders in accordance with any decision of the committee.

Select Committees
The Legislative Council may appoint select committees to consider matters or bills in depth. The purpose is to enable small groups of members to examine complex problems and to report their findings and recommendations to the council. A Select Committee on Legislative Council Elections was appointed in January 1992 to review the arrangements for the 1991 Legislative Council elections and to report its recommendations on the arrangements for future Legislative Council elections. The Select Committee tabled its Report in the Legislative Council on July 8, 1992 and was subsequently dissolved.

OMELCO
OMELCO stands for Office of the (non-government) Members of the Executive and Legislative Councils. Until October 1992, there was cross membership on the two Councils and hence the need for a link between them. This link was provided by OMELCO.

Members of OMELCO play a significant role in the administration of Hong Kong. They advise on formulation of and change to government policy, consider complaints from members of the public, and monitor the effectiveness of public administration. Members of the Legislative Council also scrutinise, process and enact legislation, as well as approve public expenditure.

Through their work, members are involved in the consideration of major public issues. They study and comment on bills and major policy initiatives proposed by the government, taking into account the views of the public through members' contacts with various constituencies and district boards, as well as representations received from members of the community. Important issues which require the attention and endorsement of all members are discussed at fortnightly in-house meetings. There are 16 standing panels formed by members, which regularly monitor the policy and progress of work in different areas of activity. These include: community and New Territories affairs, constitutional development, recreation and culture, economic services and public utilities, education, environmental affairs, finance, taxation and monetary affairs, health services, housing, lands and works, manpower, public service, security, trade and industry, transport, and welfare services. Besides meeting among themselves, panel members hold sessions with senior government officials and interest groups to hear their views.

Non-government Members of the Legislative Council formed a number of *ad hoc* groups and working groups to study bills introduced into the Legislative Council and issues which concern the community at large, including the arrangements for the 1995 elections, financial arrangements for the new airport and related projects, occupational retirement schemes and protection of women and juveniles.

15

In September 1992, non-government members of the Legislative Council adopted a new committee structure for the Legislative Council. Under the new structure, the in-house meetings were replaced by the House Committee which comprises all members of the Legislative Council other than the President, the Deputy President and the *ex-officio* members. Bills Committees were formed to replace *ad hoc* groups. Bills are allocated to these committees for scrutiny by the House Committee. The House Committee and the Bills Committees normally hold their meetings in public and may call any person to appear before them and to give evidence or information.

Until October 1992, non-government members of the two councils were serviced by the OMELCO Secretariat which is independent of the Administration. Following the withdrawal of members of the Executive Council from OMELCO in October 1992, the OMELCO Secretariat continues to provide supporting services to members of the Legislative Council, pending review of the future status and functions of OMELCO Secretariat by Members.

With effect from October 1992, the House Committee of the Legislative Council decided that the OMELCO standing panels would become panels of the Legislative Council and the OMELCO Complaints Division would become the Complaints Division of Members of the Legislative Council. A working group comprising 10 members was formed to discuss changes necessitated by the winding up of OMELCO, including the development of an appropriate supporting organisation which would give members financial and managerial autonomy in handling their affairs, the future of the OMELCO London Office, the future of the OMELCO redress system, and further development of the Legislative Council's committee system.

Urban Council

The Urban Council is a statutory council with responsibilities for the provision of municipal services to almost 3.28 million people in the urban areas. These services include street cleansing, refuse collection, control of environmental hygiene, and ensuring the hygienic handling and preparation of food in restaurants, shops, abattoirs and other places.

The Urban Council is also the authority for the control of hawkers and street traders, although some of this devolves on the police as the council does not have the manpower or finance to shoulder the whole burden.

Within the urban area, the council provides and manages all public recreation and sporting facilities such as swimming pools, parks, playgrounds, indoor and outdoor stadia, tennis courts, football grounds, squash courts and basketball courts, and promotes a large number of sports at district level.

The Hong Kong Stadium is undergoing redevelopment funded by the Royal Hong Kong Jockey Club. When completed, its seating capacity will increase to 40 000 for major sporting, entertainment and cultural events.

The council manages museums, public libraries and several major cultural venues and multi-purpose facilities, including the City Hall, the Queen Elizabeth Stadium and the Hong Kong Coliseum, the Science Museum and the Museum of Art. The Hong Kong Cultural Centre, opened in November 1989, contains a 2 100-seat concert hall, a theatre seating 1 700 and a studio theatre accommodating about 500 persons. Despite the new facilities, the City Hall Concert Hall and Theatre continue to be heavily booked. The council promotes cultural performances and runs a comprehensive programme of public entertainment throughout the urban area.

The council consists of 40 members, 15 elected from district constituencies, 15 appointed by the Governor and 10 representative members from the urban district boards. It meets in public once a month when it passes by-laws and deals with finances, formal motions and questions on its activities. The routine business of the Urban Council is conducted by the Standing Committee of the whole council, supported by 12 select committees and 23 working groups or sub-committees.

As from November 1, 1991, all the council's select committees as well as the Keep Hong Kong Clean Committee have opened their meetings to the public.

The council's chief executive is the Director of Urban Services, who controls the operations of the Urban Services Department with a staff of 16 300. The director is charged with carrying out the council's policies and implementing its decisions.

The council is financially autonomous and during 1991–2 spent about $3,888 million on council-controlled activities and projects. It is financed by a share of the rates which forms the main part of its income, with the balance coming from various licence fees and other charges.

The council has ward offices spread throughout the urban area where councillors deal with and answer complaints from the public on a wide variety of matters. Since December 1991, members of the public may also make their complaints and views known to the council through the 'Members Duty Roster System'. Under this system, members of the council are placed on a duty roster to meet the public, by appointment, twice a week.

Regional Council

The Regional Council is the statutory municipal authority for the New Territories where some 2.5 million people live. It is responsible for all matters concerning environmental hygiene, public health, sanitation, liquor licensing and the provision of recreation, sports and cultural facilities and services within its jurisdiction.

The Regional Council consists of 36 members. Twelve are elected directly, nine are elected as representatives of the nine district boards within the Regional Council area and 12 are appointed by the Governor. The remaining three are *ex-officio* members, being the chairman and two vice-chairmen of the Heung Yee Kuk. The chairman and vice-chairman of the council are elected by members among themselves.

The council's policies are implemented by its executive arm, the Regional Services Department, which is headed by the Director of Regional Services and has a staff of about 10 000.

The council is financially autonomous. Its main source of revenue comes from rates collected in the council area which in 1991–2 provided about 80 per cent of total revenue, with the remainder being fees and charges, investment income (mostly interest from bank deposits). In 1991–2, total revenue amounted to $1,991 million while total expenditure amounted to $2,237 million.

The council meets monthly to deal with policy issues, formal motions and members' questions on its activities. It has set up four functional select committees, nine geographically-based district committees and a Liquor Licensing Board. The four select committees deal with finance and administration, capital works, environmental hygiene, and recreation and culture, while the district committees deal with and monitor the provision

17

of services and advise on the management of council facilities in individual districts. The select committees meet monthly, the district committees meet bi-monthly and the Liquor Licensing Board meets quarterly. All meetings of the council, its select committees, district committees, as well as the Liquor Licensing Board, are open to the public.

The Regional Council maintains close liaison with the district boards in the New Territories and the Heung Yee Kuk to ensure that local aspirations and views are taken into account in its deliberations. Four members from district boards as well as other personalities are co-opted to each of the district committees of the council, thus providing an opportunity for the views of district representatives to be taken into account in the planning and provision of services and facilities.

The council is represented on a number of organisations whose work is closely related to that of the council. These organisations include the Council for the Performing Arts, the Sports Development Board, the Hong Kong Arts Centre, the Chung Ying Theatre, the Antiquities Advisory Board, the Hong Kong Ballet and the Hygiene Services Advisory Committee.

District Administration

District Boards are statutory bodies established in 1982 to provide an effective forum for public consultation and participation in the administration of the districts.

There are 19 district boards throughout the territory. Each board consists of appointed non-government members, elected members from the respective constituencies and, in the case of the New Territories, rural committee chairmen. The elected members are in the majority. For the present term of the district boards (1991–4), there are altogether 274 elected and 140 appointed members.

The last district board general election was held on March 3, 1991. A by-election was held in Tuen Mun on October 11, 1992 to fill a seat vacated by a member who had passed away. Three candidates were nominated for the seat. Of the 12 036 registered voters in the constituency where the seat was contested 29.58 per cent turned out to vote.

The functions of the district boards are basically to advise the government on a wide range of matters affecting the well-being of the people living and working in the districts. Through their advice, they make important contributions to the management of district affairs. They also help monitor the work of government departments at district level. In addition, they are often invited to give views on important territory-wide issues, such as the broadcasting policy review, deposit protection scheme and review of the housing subsidy policy.

Where funds are available, they undertake minor environmental improvement projects and help organise and sponsor activities to promote community involvement in the districts. In 1992–3, $66.8 million was provided, partly with the assistance of the two Municipal Councils, for these purposes.

Each district board operates a 'meet-the-public' scheme under which residents may, by appointment, meet the board members face-to-face to express their views on any district problems and suggest ways for improvement. The scheme has been well received by the general public and proved effective in providing a direct channel for collecting public views on local issues and reflecting them to the government.

The 20 Public Enquiry Service Centres throughout the territory provide a wide range of free services to members of the public, including answering general enquiries on government services, distributing government forms and information materials, administering oaths and declarations for private use, and referring cases under the Meet-the-Public Scheme, Free Legal Advice Scheme and Rent Officer Scheme. During the year, a total of 9 498 480 cases were handled. To strengthen the public enquiry service and enable members of the public to make enquiries without having to travel to a public enquiry centre, a Central Telephone Enquiry Centre is also provided by the City and New Territories Administration.

In each district there is a district management committee, chaired by the district officer, comprising representatives of departments providing essential services in the district. It serves as a forum for inter-departmental consultation on district matters and co-ordinates the provision of public services and facilities to ensure that district needs are met promptly. The committee works closely with the district board and, as far as possible, follows the advice given by the board.

Area Committees and Mutual Aid Committees have become an important component of the district administration scheme. They were set up in the early 1970s throughout the territory in support of the Keep Hong Kong Clean Campaign and Fight Violent Crime Campaign. Each area committee serves a population of about 40 000 to 50 000, and members are appointed from a wide spectrum of the community. Mutual aid committees are building-based resident organisations established to improve the security, cleanliness and general management of multi-storey buildings. At present, there are over 120 area committees and 4 100 mutual aid committees. They provide an extensive and effective network of communication between the government and the people at the local grass-root level.

During the year, the administration conducted a review of the district administration scheme. Improvement measures are implemented to enhance its effectiveness.

Links Between the Representative Institutions
The Urban Council and the Regional Council are closely linked to the district boards. Each district board in the urban area has a representative member on the Urban Council. In addition to a similar arrangement between the Regional Council and the district boards in the New Territories, members of the latter are also included in the district committees under the Regional Council. Through these channels, the district boards are consulted on a wide range of council matters affecting their areas.

New Territories district boards maintain a close relationship with the Heung Yee Kuk (a statutory advisory body which represents the indigenous population of the New Territories). Seats are reserved on the district boards for rural committee chairmen who are also *ex-officio* members of the Heung Yee Kuk's executive committee.

The Regional Council also has a formal link with the Heung Yee Kuk, through the *ex-officio* membership of the Kuk's chairman and the two vice-chairmen on the council.

The Urban Council and the Regional Council, which cover much the same fields in their respective areas, have, during the year, held liaison meetings and have also instituted joint ventures such as the Keep Hong Kong Clean Campaign. The annual Flower Show is also a responsibility of both councils and is held in each council's area in alternate years.

Starting from the 1991–2 Legislative Council session, the two municipal councils as well as the Heung Yee Kuk became functional constituencies, each returning one member to the Legislative Council.

Electoral System for the Urban Council, Regional Council and District Boards

Elections to the Urban Council, Regional Council and District Boards are on a geographical constituency basis and through a broad franchise. Practically everyone who is 21 years of age or over and who is a Hong Kong permanent resident, or has been resident in Hong Kong for the preceding seven years, is eligible to apply for registration as an elector in the constituency in which he lives. An applicant should be ordinarily resident in Hong Kong at the time of application. Registration is conducted between April and June while applications for registration can be made at any time of the year. The 1992 electoral roll carried 1 933 821 names, representing 52.5 per cent of an estimated potential electorate of 3.68 million.

There are 210 constituencies, each having one or two seats for District Board elections, returning 274 District Board members. In constituencies where there are two seats (64), each elector can cast two votes. For elections to the Urban Council and Regional Council, there are 15 and 12 single-seat constituencies respectively. Election is by simple majority.

An elector must be registered under the Electoral Provisions Ordinance before he can exercise his right to vote. He may vote only in the constituency in which he has been registered. He may, however, stand for election to the Urban Council, the Regional Council or a District Board in any constituency, provided he has been resident in Hong Kong for the preceding 10 or more years and his nomination is supported by 10 electors in that constituency.

Electoral System for the Legislative Council

The electoral system for the Legislative Council comprises both geographical and functional constituencies. There are nine double-seat geographical constituencies returning a total of 18 members. These constituencies follow closely the boundaries of District Boards and are: Hong Kong Island East, Hong Kong Island West, Kowloon East, Kowloon Central, Kowloon West, New Territories North, New Territories South, New Territories East and New Territories West.

There are 15 functional constituencies consisting of 20 electoral divisions, which cover the commercial, industrial, finance, financial services, labour, tourism, real estate and construction, social services, medical and health care, teaching, accountancy, legal, engineering, architectural and associated professions, the municipal councils and rural sectors. They return a total of 21 members (the Labour Functional Constituency returning two members).

The franchise for Legislative Council geographical constituency elections is the same as for the direct elections to the District Boards and the municipal councils. They use the same electoral roll. For functional constituency elections, an elector can be either a corporate or an individual. An individual elector is also required to be registered as an elector for the geographical constituency elections. A corporate elector must appoint an authorised representative to vote on its behalf. The authorised representative is not allowed to represent more than one elector in the same constituency. No individual elector or authorised representative may be registered in more than one functional constituency. However, if eligible, an individual may be registered as an elector in one functional constituency and serve as an authorised representative for a corporate elector in another functional constituency. For 1992, the electoral roll for functional constituencies carried 69 976 entries, compared to the registered electorate of 69 825 in 1991.

The qualifications for candidature in geographical constituency elections are the same as in the District Board and municipal council elections. In functional constituency elections, a candidate must have in addition a substantial connection with the relevant functional constituency. Each nomination requires 10 subscribers, except for the municipal council functional constituencies which require only five subscribers due to the small electorate size of the constituencies. Except for one electoral division (Labour) which has two seats, all electoral divisions are single-seat.

Election is by simple majority for geographical constituencies; and by a preferential elimination voting system for all functional constituencies. In constituencies where there are two seats, each elector can cast two votes.

Advisory Committees

The network of government boards and committees is a distinctive feature of the system of government which seeks to obtain, through consultation with interested groups in the community, the best possible advice on which to base decisions. Thus advisory bodies of one kind or another are found in nearly all government departments and quasi-government bodies. In general, advisory bodies may be divided into five categories: statutory bodies which give advice to a head of department (such as the Endangered Species Advisory Board); statutory bodies which give advice to the government (such as the Board of Education); non-statutory bodies which give advice to a head of department (such as the Labour Advisory Board), non-statutory bodies which give advice to the government (such as the Transport Advisory Committee), and committees which are executive in nature (such as the Hong Kong Examinations Authority).

Government officials and members of the public are represented on these committees. About 5 750 members of the public are appointed to serve on a total of 469 boards and committees, and some serve on more than one of these advisory bodies. These members are appointed in view of their specialist knowledge or expertise, or their record or interest in contributing to community service. Increasing importance has been attached to the contribution they make to the formulation and execution of government policies and, in order to utilise their potential to the full, the composition and effectiveness of these bodies are regularly monitored. Where appropriate, the government broadens the cross-section of representation and encourages an inflow of new ideas through a reasonable turnover of membership.

The Administration

Role of the Chief Secretary

The Chief Secretary is principally responsible to the Governor for the formulation of government policies and their implementation. He is the head of the Public Service. The Chief Secretary, together with the Financial Secretary and the Attorney General, are the Governor's principal advisers.

The Chief Secretary exercises direction primarily as head of the Government Secretariat, the central organisation comprising the secretaries of the policy branches and resource branches and their staff. He deputises for the Governor during his absence and is the Senior Official Member of the Executive and Legislative Councils and Chairman of the Finance Committee.

21

Role of Financial Secretary

The Financial Secretary, who reports directly to the Governor, is responsible for the fiscal and economic policies of the Hong Kong Government. He is an *ex-officio* member of both the Executive and Legislative Councils. He is, in addition, a member of the Finance Committee of the Legislative Council and chairman of the Public Works Sub-Committee of the Finance Committee. As the government official with primary responsibility for Hong Kong's fiscal and economic policies, the Financial Secretary oversees the operations of the Finance, Monetary Affairs, Trade and Industry, Economic Services and Works Branches of the Government Secretariat and the new Hong Kong Monetary Authority.

The Financial Secretary is responsible under the Public Finance Ordinance for laying before the legislature each year the government's Estimates of Revenue and Expenditure. In his capacity as an *ex-officio* member of the Legislative Council, he delivers a major speech each year, outlining the government's budgetary proposals and moving the adoption of the Appropriation Bill, which gives legal effect to the annual expenditure proposals contained in the Budget. He is also responsible under a number of ordinances for carrying out executive duties, such as setting levels of certain charges and remunerations, and overseeing the accounts of certain trust funds and statutory bodies.

Role of the Central Policy Unit

Although the CPU forms part of the Government Secretariat, it is not a policy branch and does not have responsibility for a defined programme area of its own. Its role is to undertake in-depth examinations of complex policy issues, to analyse options, and to recommend solutions. These issues are assigned to it by the Governor, Chief Secretary and Financial Secretary and are specified on a case-by-case basis. They are mostly issues of a long-term, strategic nature, or issues which cut across, or fall between, the boundaries of several policy branches or government departments.

Role of the Efficiency Unit

The Efficiency Unit (EU) was established in May 1992. The unit takes direction from the Public Sector Reform Policy Group and is a part of the Government Secretariat. Its role is to secure improvements in the formulation of policy objectives and priorities, management and motivation of staff; control over the use of resources; and the delivery of services to customers. The key principles on which these improvements are to be brought about are openness, responsibility and accountability. In other words the role of the unit is to put into practice the Public Sector Reform philosophy.

The Structure of the Administration

The Administration of the Hong Kong Government is organised into branches and departments. The branches, each headed by a secretary, collectively form the Government Secretariat. There are currently 12 policy branches, and two resource branches concerned with finance and the Public Service.

The policy branches whose secretaries report directly to the Chief Secretary are: City and New Territories Administration (headed by the Secretary for Home Affairs); Constitutional Affairs; Education and Manpower; Health and Welfare; Planning, Environment and Lands; Recreation and Culture; Security; and Transport. The Civil Service Branch, a resource branch, also comes under the aegis of the Chief Secretary. The policy branches whose secretaries report directly to the Financial Secretary are: Economic Services, Monetary Affairs, Trade and Industry, and Works. The Finance Branch, a resource branch, is also responsible to the Financial Secretary.

With certain exceptions, the heads of government departments are responsible to the branch secretaries for the direction of their departments and the efficient implementation of approved government policy. The exceptions are the Audit Department and the Independent Commission Against Corruption, whose independence is safeguarded by their heads reporting directly to the Governor, the Judiciary, which is the responsibility of the Chief Justice, and the Legal Department, which is the responsibility of the Attorney General. There are currently 68 departments and agencies in this structure.

To assist in the co-ordination of government policy, there are, under the umbrella of the Chief Secretary's Committee, seven policy groups which bring together branch secretaries in related programme areas. The six, which are chaired by the Chief Secretary, are: Community Affairs; Constitutional Affairs; Lands, Works, Transport, Housing and Environmental Protection; Public Service; Social Services; Legal and Security. The Legal Affairs Policy group is chaired by the Attorney General.

Office of the Commissioner for Administrative Complaints

The Commissioner for Administrative Complaints (COMAC) is an independent authority established in 1989 under the Commissioner for Administrative Complaints Ordinance to provide for citizens some means whereby an independent person outside the public service can investigate and report on grievances arising from administrative decisions, acts, recommendations or omissions. COMAC has jurisdiction over all government departments and the Hospital Authority, except the Royal Hong Kong Police and the Independent Commission Against Corruption for which there are separate systems to deal with complaints from the public. A complaint lodged with the Commissioner has to be referred to him by a member of the Legislative Council other than an official member and with the complainant's agreement to such a referral.

Between January 1 and December 31, 1992, a total of 143 complaints were received by the office. Together with 54 cases carried over from the previous year, there were in all 197 cases for investigation. During the year, 154 cases were completed. Of these, 113 were investigated, and nine (8.0 per cent) were found to be substantiated in whole and 32 (28.3 per cent) in part. In 72 cases (63.7 per cent), the complaints were found to be unsubstantiated.

In the cases received during the year, the areas which attracted substantial numbers of complaints related to error or wrong decision, followed by lack of response to complaint, negligence or omission, rudeness, delay and faulty procedures. In terms of complaints by department, the Building and Lands Department, the Housing Department and the Inland Revenue Department received most complaints, followed by the Urban Services Department, the Correctional Services Department, the City and New Territories Administration, the Government Secretariat, the Fire Services Department and the Hospital Authority. These departments have much contact with members of the public and are more vulnerable to complaints than the others.

In mid-1992, the government undertook a review of the COMAC redress system to identify areas where improvements might be made to strengthen its role as a safeguard against government maladministration. After a three-month public consultation exercise, the government proposed to make a number of major changes to the system. They include replacing the existing referral system to enable the public to take their complaints directly to the Commissioner, extending the Commissioner's jurisdiction to major statutory bodies, and allowing the Commissioner to publicise investigation reports of public interest subject to the names of the individuals involved in the complaint being anonymised. Legislative proposals are being introduced to put these recommendations into effect.

Office of the Director of Audit
The necessity for an audit presence was recognised in the very early days of Hong Kong and the Audit Department is in fact one of the oldest departments, an Auditor-General having been first appointed in 1844, only three years after cession of the territory.

The audit of the accounts of the Hong Kong Government is carried out under the terms of the Audit Ordinance enacted in 1971, which provides for the appointment, security of tenure, duties and powers of the Director of Audit, for the submission of annual statements by the Director of Accounting Services, for the examination and audit of those statements by the Director of Audit, and for the submission of the latter's report thereon to the Governor as President of the Legislative Council. Certain specific duties relating to the examination, audit, reporting and certification of the government's accounts, are pre-scribed in the ordinance and wide powers are given to the director regarding his access to books, documents and records, and the explanations which he may require. Moreover, as in the performance of his duties and the exercise of his powers the director is not subject to the direction or control of any other person or authority, considerable discretion is given to him in the conduct of his inquiries and he is free to report publicly as he sees fit. Therefore, the director functions independently of the Administration.

The audit of all the government's accounts is carried out by the Director of Audit and his staff. He also audits the accounts of the Urban Council, the Regional Council, the Vocational Training Council, the Housing Authority, the ex-Government hospitals of the Hospital Authority and more than 50 statutory and non-statutory funds and other public bodies, as well as reviewing the financial aspect of the operations of the multifarious government-subvented organisations in Hong Kong.

Government auditing practised in Hong Kong falls into two main categories, respectively termed 'regularity' audit and 'value-for-money' audit. The regularity audit, which is intended to provide an overall assurance of the general accuracy and propriety of the government's financial and accounting transactions, is carried out by means of selective test checks and reviews designed to indicate possible areas of weakness. The audit is designed to ensure as far as reasonably possible that the accounts are accurate and correct, although, with the considerable volume and variety of government revenue and expenditure, it cannot hope to disclose every accounting error or financial irregularity. Value-for-money audit is carried out according to guidelines tabled in the Legislative Council by the chairman of the Public Accounts Committee on November 19, 1986. The audit is intended to provide independent information, advice and assurance about the economy, efficiency and effectiveness with which any branch, department, agency, other public body, public office, or audited organisation has discharged its functions. This involves going beyond the normal accounting records. In line with contemporary developments in both government and commercial auditing elsewhere, it is also becoming increasingly relevant to ascertain whether efficient and economical practices are being followed in pursuing prescribed goals and whether these goals are being achieved.

The Director of Audit's report, after it has been submitted to the Governor as President of Legislative Council and laid before the council, is considered by the Public Accounts Committee. In 1992, the Director submitted two reports. The first report was tabled on April 29, covering the results of value-for-money audits completed, and the second report on November 18, covering the audit certification of the government's accounts for the preceding financial year as well as the results of value-for-money audits completed.

The director's reports on the accounts of other public bodies are submitted to the relevant authority in accordance with the legislation governing the operation of these bodies.

Foreign Relations
The Role of the British Government
Because of Hong Kong's status as a dependent territory, the Secretary of State for Foreign and Commonwealth Affairs is constitutionally responsible to the British Parliament for the actions of the Hong Kong Government and he has authority to give directions to the Governor of Hong Kong. In practice, however, such formal directions have not been issued in living memory, and Hong Kong conducts its affairs with a high degree of autonomy in all domestic matters.

The relationship between London and Hong Kong is also essentially one of co-operation. For example, one important task regularly undertaken by the Foreign and Commonwealth Office is to ensure that Hong Kong's interests and views (which are not always identical with those of the United Kingdom) are properly considered within the British Government machinery, particularly when new policies are being formulated by other Whitehall departments.

Hong Kong's foreign relations are constitutionally the direct responsibility of the British Government. Thus the British Government is internationally responsible for ensuring that the Hong Kong Government fulfils its obligations under the many international conventions and agreements which extend to Hong Kong as well as to the United Kingdom. But, in the day-to-day conduct of external affairs, Hong Kong in practice enjoys a considerable degree of autonomy, and full autonomy regarding trade matters. It is a contracting party to the General Agreement on Tariffs and Trade in its own right.

The Role of Political Adviser
The Political Adviser is a senior member of the British Diplomatic Service, seconded to the Hong Kong Government principally to advise the Governor and the Chief Secretary on matters concerning Hong Kong's relations with China. His office is part of the Hong Kong Government. Following extensive involvement in the Sino-British negotiations which culminated in the Joint Declaration, the Political Adviser's office, in conjunction with the Constitutional Affairs Branch, is closely involved in the work of implementing the Joint Declaration. In addition, the Political Adviser's office continues to offer advice, and, in some cases, to co-ordinate action on many other matters, notably in promoting the wide range of contacts between Hong Kong Government departments and their counterparts in Guangdong Province, particularly in the Shenzhen Special Economic Zone.

Close and effective cross-border co-operation has developed in such diverse areas as immigration, crime, smuggling, transport, environment, customs, postal services and telecommunications. The Political Adviser's office is also one of the channels of communication between the Hong Kong Government and foreign and Commonwealth missions in Hong Kong. These missions do, however, deal directly with the relevant departments of the Hong Kong Government over most day-to-day matters.

Public Service

The Public Service provides staff for all government departments and other units of the administration. With Hong Kong's centralised form of government, the Public Service operates a wide range of services which in many countries would be administered by other public authorities. These include public works and utilities, public health, education, fire services and the police force. The departments in charge of these areas, namely, the Lands and Works group of departments (24 509 posts), the Municipal Services group of departments (26 618), the Education Department (6 976), Fire Services Department (7 954), and the Royal Hong Kong Police (32 811) account for 52 per cent of the establishment of the whole Public Service. As at October 1, 1992, the total strength of the service was 183 374 or about 6.6 per cent of Hong Kong's work force. Over 98 per cent are local officers. The service is structured into some 420 grades or job categories in the administrative, professional, technical and manual fields, with about 1 210 ranks or job levels.

Overall responsibility for the management of the Public Service lies with the Civil Service Branch of the Government Secretariat. The branch deals with such matters as appointments, pay and conditions of service, staff management, manpower planning, training and discipline. It is also the focal point for consultation with the principal staff associations. There are five departmental divisions each responsible for the full range of personnel management matters of a group of departments; and three functional divisions dealing with service-wide issues such as training, staff relations and pensions.

Recruitment and promotion to the middle and senior ranks of the Public Service are subject to the advice of the Public Service Commission which is independent of the government. The commission has a full time chairman and prominent citizens serving as members.

The government is advised on matters relating to pay and conditions of service by four independent bodies. The Standing Committee on Directorate Salaries and Conditions of Service advises on matters affecting directorate officers (the 1 000 or so most senior public servants). The Standing Committee on Judicial Salaries and Conditions of Service advises on matters affecting judicial officers. The Standing Committee on Disciplined Services Salaries and Conditions of Service advises on the salaries and conditions of service of the disciplined services. The Standing Commission on Civil Service Salaries and Conditions of Service advises on matters affecting all other civil servants.

A civil service housing package, which comprises a Home Financing Scheme, an Accommodation Allowance Scheme and an improved Home Purchase Scheme, was introduced in October 1990. The objective of the housing package is to make more effective use of the resources provided for civil service housing benefits and to encourage home ownership among public servants. Over 17 000 officers are currently receiving benefits under the schemes.

The government fully recognises the value of regular communication with staff. There are four central consultative councils, namely, the Senior Civil Service Council, the Model Scale 1 Staff Consultative Council, the Police Force Council and the Disciplined Services Consultative Council. Departmental consultative committees, established in most government departments, constitute an important part of the consultative machinery. In addition, individual members of the public service or staff associations have ready access to the departmental or grade management, as well as to the Civil Service Branch. Staff are also encouraged to make suggestions to improve the efficiency of the service under the Staff Suggestion Scheme.

In recognition of staff commitment and contributions, long serving civil servants are granted awards under the Long Service Travel Award Scheme and the Long and Meritorious Service Certificate Scheme. Those with 30 years of meritorious service are also presented with a gold pin. A retirement souvenir was also introduced recently for civil servants who have had 20 or more years of service on retirement.

Continued efforts were made in 1992 to improve productivity and the quality of management. Further value-for-money studies and work improvement studies were carried out in various departments. At the same time, departments were given greater control in more aspects of financial and personnel management. They now have greater authority in matters such as non-directorate appointments and promotions, leave and passage, and professional training. Possibilities of further devolution are being examined on a continuing basis. Reforms in the way public services are delivered continued under the Public Sector Reform initiatives. Public Sector Reform aims to bring about long-term productivity improvements in the public service and better services to the community. The application of modern information technology and office automation were also effective means of achieving high efficiency and productivity. These efforts brought about not only improvements in the quality of service but also significant savings in resources.

The quality of service is maintained by way of a disciplinary code which applies to all public servants. It provides sanctions against misconduct and sub-standard performance where other staff management measures fail, while safeguarding the interests and rights of individual public servants. A major initiative was launched by the Governor in his Policy Address to improve the quality of service further by engendering a culture of public service which treats clients as customers.

The government is developing its use of manpower planning techniques and practices in order to ensure that the public service possesses the right mix of officers in terms of numbers, experience, qualifications and skills to achieve its objectives and goals. Particular care and attention are paid to the selection and grooming of senior government officials.

Civil Service Training
The government attaches great importance to the training of public servants in order to increase efficiency and effectiveness and to help them meet new challenges. Induction and refresher training is provided by many departments to equip staff with the skills to carry out their duties effectively. Where the need arises, staff are also sponsored on overseas training courses or attachments so that they can keep abreast of the latest developments in their specialised fields. To meet common departmental needs, the Civil Service Training Centre conducts a wide range of management, language and computer courses, and co-ordinates the management training undertaken by public servants at local and overseas institutes. As the central training agency, it also provides advice and assistance to departments.

The government has introduced a China Studies Programme which aims to provide officers with a better understanding of various aspects of life and government in China. It includes seminars and talks for officers at various levels. Familiarisation visits to China are

27

also arranged to give officers first-hand experience of China. The existing management development programmes have also been expanded to include a China dimension.

An important component of the training and development offered to senior public servants is the three-month programme run by the Senior Staff Course Centre. The centre emphasises 'learning from doing'. Each year participants examine about 100 problems, some with significant policy implications. Study tours to other countries in the region help to broaden perspectives and foster much goodwill with host governments.

Government Records Service

The Government Records Service is responsible for the broad management of government records.

It undertakes two different but related programmes: the Records Management Office for a record management programme to handle records at their current and non-current stages and the Public Records Office for an archives administration programme to look after the preservation and use of permanent records.

A record is the basic unit of administration and its appropriate management will have a significant impact on the efficiency of government business. It is the responsibility of the Records Management Office to oversee and develop a comprehensive system concerned with everything that happens to records from their productive 'life' as a means of accomplishing the government agency's functions to their 'death' or destruction as non-current records when all useful purposes have been served. The aim is to have fewer records to store, better records to use and more economical record management costs to finance.

The Public Records Office is one of the largest local sources of information for historical and other studies relating to Hong Kong.

Language

The official languages of Hong Kong are English and Chinese. The Official Languages Ordinance enacted in 1974 provides that both languages possess equal status and enjoy equality of use for the purposes of communication between the government or any public officer and members of the public. Correspondence in Chinese from the public is replied to by government departments either in Chinese or in English accompanied by a Chinese version. Major reports and publications of public interest issued by the government are available in both languages. Simultaneous interpretation is provided at meetings of the Legislative Council, Urban Council, Regional Council other government boards and committees where English and Chinese are used. A Bilingual Laws Advisory Committee was set up in October 1988 to advise the Governor in Council, among other things, on the authentication of Chinese texts of existing laws which are being translated. With the declaration of the Chinese version of Chapter 1 of the Law of Hong Kong, the Interpretation and General Clauses Ordinance, made authentic in July 1992, the Chinese version of other existing laws are being processed sequentially for authentication. Since April 1989, all new principal legislation has been enacted in both English and Chinese. Cantonese (the Guangzhou dialect) is the most commonly-spoken dialect among the local Chinese community while Putonghua (Mandarin) has gained popularity as closer ties with China are being developed. English continues to be used not only by the expatriate community but also by a wide cross-section of the local community in commercial, financial and professional circles.

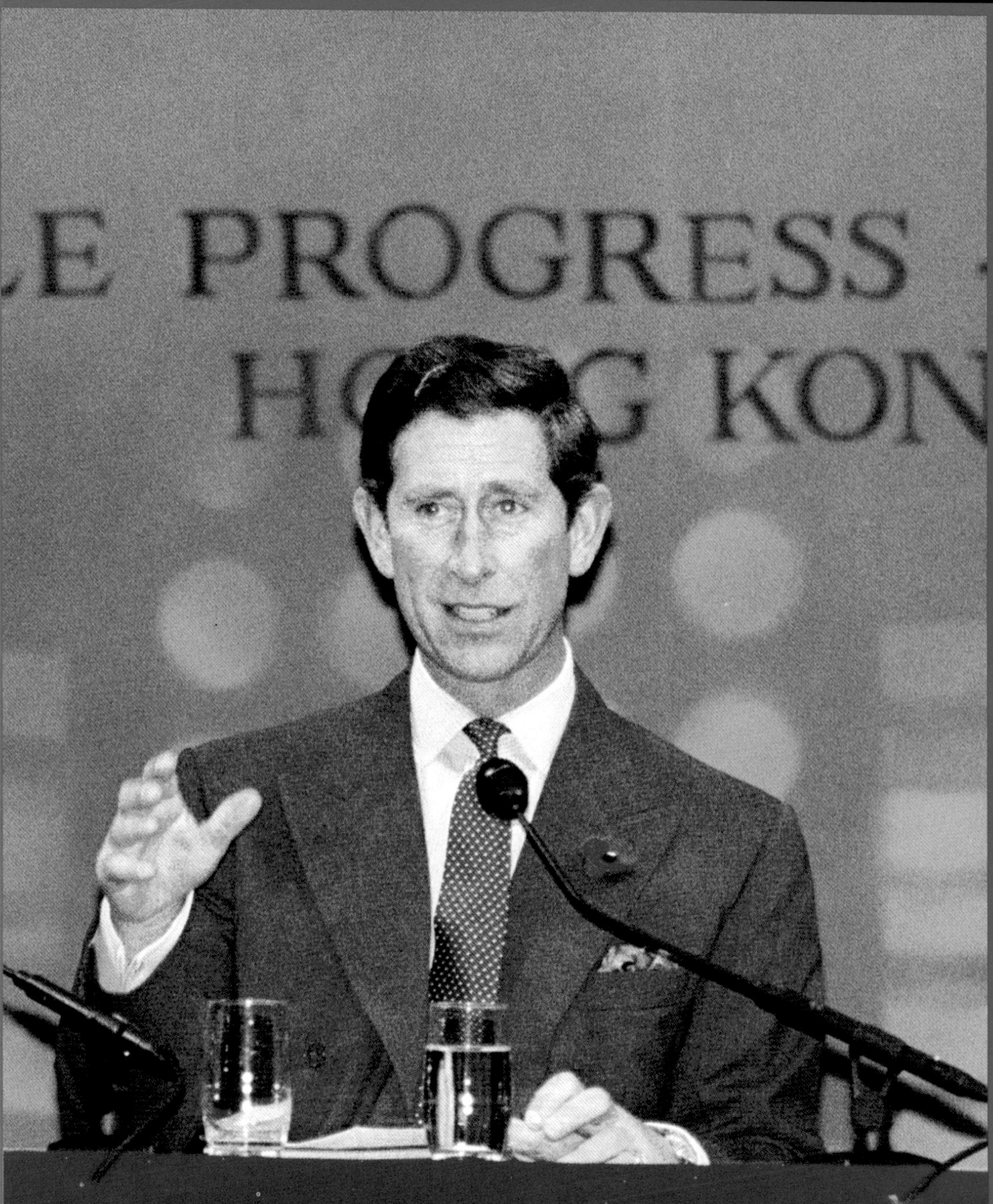
LE PROGRESS
HO G KON

Preceding page: *During a visit to Hong Kong His Royal Highness the Prince of Wales addressed the plenary session of the Business Leaders' Forum.*

Above: *Her Royal Highness the Princess of Wales met Hong Kong entertainers at a reception in London during the 'Hong Kong Heartbeat' trade seminar.*

Left: *Mr Victor Fong, Chairman of Hong Kong Trade Development Council, addressed the business conference 'Hong Kong -- Britain's Bridge to Asia'.*

Right: *Lions Club International held its 75th International Convention in Hong Kong.*

WELCOME TO HONG KONG
75TH LIONS CLUBS
INTERNATIONAL CONVENTION
----
00 00 00

LONGINES

Left: *The Asian Development Bank held its 25th meeting in Hong Kong, during which delegates inspected a model and illustrations of the new international airport at Chek Lap Kok,* **(below)**.

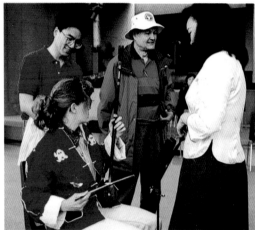

Extreme left: *A spectacular parade marked the opening ceremony of Festival Hong Kong 92 in Toronto. The festival, with its theme 'Bridge Across the Pacific' was also held in Vancouver, Ottawa, Montreal and Calgary.*

Left and above: *Scenes of celebration and ceremony in Hong Kong and Canada before and during 'Festival Hong Kong 92'.*

Following page: *The 'Regco 92' festival staged in the New Territories by the Regional Council opened with a colourful float procession.*

3
THE LEGAL SYSTEM

THE law of Hong Kong generally follows that of England. The Application of English Law Ordinance declares the extent to which English law is in force in the territory. The ordinance provides that the common law of England and the rules of equity shall be in force in Hong Kong so far as they are applicable to the circumstances of Hong Kong or its inhabitants, subject to such modifications as such circumstances may require. The ordinance applies some English Acts, such as the Justices of the Peace Act of 1361, to Hong Kong.

United Kingdom legislation may be applied to Hong Kong either directly or by order of Her Majesty in Council under the legislation. In addition, the power of Her Majesty to make all such laws as may appear necessary for the peace, order and good government of the territory is expressly reserved by Article IX of the Letters Patent. In practice, the exercise of these powers is largely confined to matters which have a bearing on Hong Kong's international position. For example, the Multilateral Investment Guarantee Agency (Overseas Territory) Order 1988 is an Order in Council implementing in Hong Kong a treaty to which the United Kingdom is a party.

In order to ensure that by 1997 Hong Kong will possess a comprehensive body of law which owes its authority to the Legislature of Hong Kong, it is necessary to replace such United Kingdom legislation which applies to Hong Kong by local legislation on the same topics. The Hong Kong legislature has been empowered under the Hong Kong Act 1985 to repeal or amend any enactment so far as it is part of the law of Hong Kong and to make laws having extra-territorial operation, if the enactment relates to civil aviation, merchant shipping, or admiralty jurisdiction or is required in order to give effect to an international agreement which applies to Hong Kong. Legislation has already been enacted to localise laws in the fields of admiralty jurisdiction, marine pollution and merchant shipping, and work in other areas is in progress.

A Localisation and Adaptation of Laws Unit has been established in the Attorney General's Chambers. This unit's role is to co-ordinate and speed up work in the localisation of United Kingdom legislation which now applies to Hong Kong. It also advises on the adaptation of the Laws of Hong Kong to ensure compatibility with the Basic Law of the Hong Kong Special Administration Region which was promulgated in April 1990. A review by policy branches of all ordinances within their spheres of responsibilities is being undertaken and, where appropriate, drafting instructions will be prepared with a view to appropriate amendments being enacted before July 1, 1997.

The Governor, acting with the advice and consent of the Legislative Council, has plenary powers to enact laws for the peace, order and good government of Hong Kong. Most of the legislation applicable in Hong Kong is, and has been since its earliest days, enacted in the form of ordinances or as subsidiary legislation made under an ordinance.

Until 1989, the laws of Hong Kong were published in a 32-volume compilation known as the Laws of Hong Kong. This was updated annually. A new loose-leaf edition of the Laws of Hong Kong is in the course of preparation and about one-third of the volumes have been issued. The new edition will be based upon the 1989 revised edition as amended by laws taking effect since and will be updated continuously. In addition, all new laws are published in the Hong Kong Government Gazette.

The Attorney General's Chambers are responsible for drafting new legislation in both Chinese and English, and translating existing legislation into Chinese. Both the Chinese and English texts are authentic versions of the laws. The first bilingual ordinance was enacted on April 13, 1989. Since then, all new principal legislation has been enacted bilingually. In October 1988 the government set up the Bilingual Laws Advisory Committee to advise on the publication of Chinese texts of existing ordinances. The committee examines Chinese texts prepared by the Law Drafting Division of the Attorney General's Chambers. If it approves them, it recommends the Governor in Council to declare those texts an authentic version of the laws. The first Chinese text of existing legislation was declared authentic in July 1992. Some 520 ordinances remain to be translated or authenticated.

Bill of Rights
Since 1976, the International Covenant on Civil and Political Rights (ICCPR) and the International Covenant on Economic, Social and Cultural Rights (ICESCR) have been extended to Hong Kong. The Joint Declaration guarantees that the provisions of the two covenants as applied to Hong Kong shall remain in force after 1997.

Until recently, the provisions of the ICCPR, like those of the ICESCR, were implemented in Hong Kong through a combination of common law, legislation and administrative measures. In view of the strong support in the community for the embodiment of basic civil and political rights in a justiciable Bill of Rights, the Hong Kong Bill of Rights Ordinance was enacted in June 1991. This ordinance gives effect in local law to the provisions of the ICCPR as applied to Hong Kong.

To complement the protection afforded by the Bill of Rights, the Letters Patent for Hong Kong have been amended so as to ensure that no law can be made in Hong Kong that restricts the rights and freedoms enjoyed in Hong Kong in a manner which is inconsistent with the ICCPR as applied to Hong Kong. The amendment came into operation at the same time as the Bill of Rights Ordinance.

Judiciary
The Chief Justice of Hong Kong is head of the Judiciary. He is assisted in his administrative duties by the Registrar, seven Deputy Registrars and one Assistant Registrar of the Supreme Court. The Assistant Registrar is designated Chief Magistrate.

The Judiciary operates on the principle, fundamental to the common law system, of complete independence from the executive and legislative branches of government. This applies equally whether a dispute is between the government and an individual, or whether it involves only private citizens or corporate bodies.

The most senior court in Hong Kong is the Supreme Court, comprising the Court of Appeal and the High Court. Sitting in the Supreme Court in addition to the Chief Justice are nine Justices of Appeal and 22 High Court Judges. The Registrar and Deputy Registrars also have jurisdiction as Masters of the Supreme Court in civil trials in the High Court. The jurisdiction of the High Court is unlimited in both civil and criminal matters, and the Court of Appeal is the highest court in Hong Kong. The Court of Appeal hears both civil and criminal appeals from the High Court and from the District Court. Further appeal lies to the Judicial Committee of the Privy Council in London; however this is infrequent as leave to appeal is granted only on stringent conditions.

High Court Judges usually sit alone when trying civil matters, although there is a rarely-used provision for jury trials in certain cases including defamation. For criminal trials they sit with a jury of seven, or nine on special direction of the judge. The issue of guilt is determined by the jury, which must have a majority of at least five to two, except with charges attracting a death sentence when unanimity is required.

The District Court has both civil and criminal jurisdiction. Its civil jurisdiction is limited to disputes of a value up to $120,000, and its criminal jurisdiction up to seven years' imprisonment. Its judges sit without a jury and may try the more serious cases, save principally for murder, manslaughter and rape, which are reserved to the High Court. There are 29 judges of the District Court.

The Magistrates' Courts try annually some 90 per cent of all the cases heard in the territory. There are 60 professional magistrates sitting in 10 magistracies, two of which are on Hong Kong Island, four in Kowloon and four in the New Territories.

Magistrates have a purely criminal jurisdiction covering a wide range of offences. Professional magistrates are generally restricted in sentence to two years' imprisonment and $10,000 fines, however a number of statutes allow increased sentences. Professional magistrates also try cases in the Juvenile Court, which has jurisdiction in charges against children and young persons up to 16 years, except in cases involving homicide.

In addition to the professional magistrates, there are 11 Special Magistrates who are not legally qualified. They handle routine cases, such as littering and minor traffic offences, and their powers of sentence are limited to fining up to $20,000. They are all Cantonese speaking and usually conduct their cases in that language.

In addition to the principal courts of civil and criminal jurisdiction, there are five specialised tribunals. The Coroner's Court handles enquiries into unusual circumstances causing death; the Small Claims Tribunal hears civil claims up to a limit of $15,000; the Labour Tribunal hears individual civil claims arising from contracts of employment, and the Lands Tribunal has jurisdiction in matters of rating and valuation and in assessing compensation when land is resumed by government or reduced in value by development. Finally, the Obscene Articles Tribunal has jurisdiction to determine whether or not an article is obscene and to classify it into statutory categories of acceptability or otherwise.

The Small Claims and Labour Tribunals provide the public with inexpensive recourse to litigation, as their proceedings are informally conducted and professional representation is not permitted.

The official language of the court is English in the Court of Appeal, the High Court and the District Court; in the other courts and tribunals the court may use Chinese. Whichever language is used, a party or witness in any court in Hong Kong may use Chinese or English or any other language permitted by the court.

Arbitration and Alternative Dispute Resolution

Arbitration has been a popular method of dispute resolution in Hong Kong for some time. Arbitration is governed by the Arbitration Ordinance which has two distinct regimes, a domestic regime based on English Law and an international regime which includes the UNCITRAL Model Law, the model law adopted by the United Nations Commission on International Trade Law. Arbitral awards made in Hong Kong can be enforced in more than 80 other jurisdictions which are signatories to the New York Convention on the Recognition and Enforcement of Foreign Arbitral Awards.

The Hong Kong International Arbitration Centre (HKIAC) was established in 1985 to act as an independent and impartial focus for the development of all forms of dispute resolution in Hong Kong and South-East Asia. The HKIAC provides information on dispute resolution and arbitrations both in Hong Kong and overseas. It operates panels of international and local arbitrators and maintains lists of mediators. The HKIAC premises, situated at 1 Arbuthnot Road, have purpose-built hearing rooms and have full support facilities. The number of cases involving the HKIAC has tripled in the last two years and it is anticipated, given the increasing popularity of arbitration and mediation as a means of dispute resolution, that there will be an increase in such cases in the future.

Attorney General

The Attorney General is the Governor's legal adviser. The Royal Instructions provide for him to be an *ex-officio* member of both the Executive Council and the Legislative Council. He is chairman of the Law Reform Commission of Hong Kong and a member of both the Judicial Services Commission and Operations Review and Complaints Committees of the Independent Commission Against Corruption.

All government departments requiring legal advice receive it from the Attorney General. He is the representative of the Crown in all actions brought by or against the Crown. He is also responsible for the drafting of all legislation.

The Attorney General is responsible for all prosecutions in Hong Kong. It is his responsibility to decide whether or not a prosecution should be instituted in any particular case, and if so to institute and conduct the prosecution.

The Attorney General is chairman of the Legal Affairs Policy Group, one of several policy bodies established under the umbrella of the Chief Secretary's Committee to bring together branch secretaries in related programme areas. The group plays an important co-ordinating role in legal policy matters, decision-making and allocation of responsibility for legislative initiatives which have a substantial legal policy content. Often, the group will call upon the Attorney General to take responsibility as sponsor and spokesman for legislative proposals to be submitted to the Executive and Legislative Councils.

The Attorney General's Chambers have six divisions, five of which are headed by a Law Officer to whom the Attorney General delegates certain of his powers and responsibilities. The remaining division deals with administrative matters concerning chambers.

The Civil Division, headed by the Crown Solicitor, provides legal advice to government on civil law and conducts civil litigation, arbitration, and mediation, on behalf of government.

The International Law Division, headed by the Law Officer (International Law), deals with all external legal matters arising out of the Sino-British Joint Declaration and other international agreements, and advises upon questions of international law.

The Law Drafting Division, headed by the Law Draftsman, is responsible for drafting all legislation (including subsidiary legislation) in Chinese and English, and assists in steering legislation through the Executive and Legislative Councils.

The Solicitor General heads the Legal Policy Division which includes the Law Reform Commission Secretariat. The division services the professional needs of the Attorney General, and provides legal input on a wide variety of topics being considered by the government.

The Prosecutions Division is headed by the Crown Prosecutor who is commonly known as the Director of Public Prosecutions. Counsel from this division conduct the prosecution in the majority of High Court and District Court trials and often appear before magistrates when an important point of law is involved. This division also provides legal advice to police and other government departments responsible for prosecuting offences.

Law Reform Commission

The Law Reform Commission was appointed by the Governor in Council to consider and report on such topics as may be referred to it by the Attorney General or Chief Justice. Its membership includes Legislative Councillors, academic and practising lawyers, and prominent members of the community.

Since its establishment in 1980, the commission has published 22 reports covering subjects as diverse as Commercial Arbitration, Homosexuality, Bail, Sale of Goods and Supply of Services, and Illegitimacy. The recommendations in 10 of those reports have been implemented either in whole or in part and others are still under consideration.

The commission is currently considering references on Evidence in Civil Actions, Copyright, Fraud, Privacy, Codification of the Criminal Law, Guardianship and Custody, Insolvency, Description of Flats on Sale, and Interpretation of Statutes.

Registrar General

The Registrar General, a statutory office established by the Registrar General (Establishment) Ordinance, combines the statutory offices of Land Officer and Registrar of Companies. Previously, the Registrar General also combined the statutory office of Official Receiver but on June 1, 1992, a new department entitled the Official Receiver's Office was established by the enactment of the Official Receiver's Ordinance 1992 (No. 39 of 1992). In addition, the Registrar General, in his capacity as Land Officer, was previously responsible for the operation of the Legal Advisory and Conveyancing Section of the Land Division of the Registrar General's Department. However, on December 1, 1992, responsibility for that section was transferred to the Legal Advisory and Conveyancing Office of the Buildings and Lands Department under the Director of Buildings and Lands.

The Registrar General's Department is therefore now divided into two main divisions. The Land Division operates a land registration service under the provisions of the Land Registration Ordinance (the Land Registry) and also a registry of owners corporations under the Multi-Storey Buildings (Owners Incorporation) Ordinance. The Companies Division comprises the Companies Registry and the Money Lenders Registry. The

Companies Registry administers the provisions of the Companies Ordinance, while the Money Lenders Registry regulates money lenders under the Money Lenders Ordinance.

The Registrar General is also an *ex-officio* member of the Standing Committee on Company Law Reform, and represents the Financial Secretary as an *ex-officio* member of the Council of the Hong Kong Society of Accountants.

Director of Intellectual Property

The Director of Intellectual Property was established on July 2, 1990, as a statutory office by the Director of Intellectual Property (Establishment) Ordinance, to take over from the Registrar General the statutory offices of Registrar of Trade Marks and Registrar of Patents. The Intellectual Property Department includes the Trade Marks and Patents Registries which provide and administer a system of trade mark and patents registration and protection under the provisions of the Trade Marks Ordinance and Registration of Patents Ordinance. In addition, the department is responsible for other forms of intellectual property protection and will serve as a focal point for further development of Hong Kong's intellectual property regime.

The Legal Profession

The Law Society is the governing body for solicitors. It has wide responsibilities for maintaining professional and ethical standards and for considering complaints against solicitors. There are around 2 400 solicitors and 400 local law firms in Hong Kong. In addition there are around 30 foreign law firms in Hong Kong which advise on foreign law.

The Bar Committee is the governing body for barristers. The conduct and etiquette of the Bar are governed by the Code of Conduct for the Bar of Hong Kong. There are around 460 barristers in Hong Kong.

Legal Aid

Hong Kong has developed over the years a very comprehensive system of legal aid, advice and assistance funded by the government through two organisations: the Legal Aid Department and Legal Advice and Duty Lawyer Scheme administered by the Law Society and the Bar Association. The Legal Aid Department administers highly sophisticated and extensive schemes for legal representation in both civil and criminal cases heard in the District Court, the High Court, the Court of Appeal and the Judicial Committee of the Privy Council in London. Legal aid is available to eligible persons in Hong Kong, resident or non-resident, either free of charge or upon payment of a graduated contribution if they satisfy the Director of Legal Aid on financial eligibility and justification for legal action.

Applications for legal aid are subject to means testing. With effect from July 1, 1992, a person whose disposable financial resources, including both income and capital, do not exceed $120,000 is financially eligible. In calculating an applicant's disposable financial resources, the value of his owner-occupied home, tax payments and contributions to retirement schemes, apart from various allowances to cater for the support of himself and his dependants, are deducted. Also since July 1, 1992, the Director of Legal Aid has the discretion to grant legal aid in criminal cases in the interests of justice to an applicant who fails the means test.

If a person is granted legal aid, the Director of Legal Aid will assign his case either to a private lawyer, or to one of the department's own lawyers in its litigation division.

The Official Solicitor

Following the entry into force of the Official Solicitor Ordinance on August 1, 1991, the Director of Legal Aid was appointed the first Official Solicitor and a separate office with a senior lawyer and support staff was established to represent persons under legal disability in court proceedings in Hong Kong. Since inauguration and up to July 1992, the Official Solicitor received a total of 76 such requests in receivership, unclaimed estates, adoption, guardianship, and other issues. The Official Solicitor assigned less than 10 per cent of the cases to private legal practitioners for litigation and litigated the balance himself.

Civil Legal Aid

In civil cases, apart from financial eligibility an applicant must satisfy the Director of Legal Aid that he has reasonable grounds for taking or defending an action. Legal aid is available for a wide range of civil proceedings, such as traffic and industrial accident claims, employees' compensation, immigration matters, professional negligence, family law, and Admiralty proceedings for seamen's wages. An applicant who is refused legal aid may appeal to the Registrar of the Supreme Court or in Privy Council cases to a committee of review. The total estimated expenditure for 1992 was $86 million in civil cases. During the year, 5 378 applications out of 17 294 applications were granted legal aid and $254 million was recovered for the aided persons.

An independent counselling agency, the Hong Kong Catholic Marriage Advisory Council, funded by the Royal Hong Kong Jockey Club, provides counselling service to legal aid applicants in matrimonial cases in the department's Kowloon Branch Office.

Since October 1984, the Director of Legal Aid has operated a Supplementary Legal Aid Scheme for people whose resources exceed the financial limits under the ordinary legal aid scheme but are not sufficient to meet the high costs of conducting litigation on a private basis. It is available for claims in the High Court and certain claims in the District Court for damages for death, personal injuries and employees' compensations. Since July 1, 1992, an applicant with financial resources exceeding $120,000 but not exceeding $280,000 is eligible to apply. A successful litigant under the supplementary scheme pays back 10 per cent to 12.5 per cent of the damages he recovers to the scheme to assist other litigants in future litigation. The total estimated expenditure of the scheme in 1992 was $5 million. During the year, 71 applications out of 86 applications were granted legal aid.

Legal Aid in Criminal Cases

In criminal cases, legal aid is available for representation in proceedings in the Supreme and District Courts, and in the Magistrates' Court where the prosecution is seeking committal of a defendant to the High Court for trial. The department also provides assistance in preparing petitions for clemency to the Governor in Council and in conducting pleas in mitigation of sentence.

For appeals against conviction for murder, the grant of legal aid is mandatory to ensure that all relevant matters are placed before the court by the appellant's legal representative. For all other criminal appeals, legal aid will be given subject to financial eligibility if the Director of Legal Aid is satisfied that there are arguable grounds of appeals.

The total estimated expenditure for 1992 was $72 million in criminal cases. During the year, 2 708 applications were granted legal aid out of 4 225 applications received.

Legal Advice and Duty Lawyer Schemes

The Legal Advice and Duty Lawyer Schemes comprise three programmes to provide free legal representation, legal advice and legal information. The government funds the entire operation of the schemes and the subvention in 1992–3 was about $57 million.

Until June 1991, the Duty Lawyer Scheme provided free legal representation to defendants charged with one of nine 'specified' offences in the Magistrates' Courts. Upon the enactment of the Bill of Rights Ordinance in June 1991, the scheme was expanded to offer free legal representation to virtually all defendants in the Magistrates' Courts who meet certain criteria (such as those in jeopardy of losing their liberty or where a substantial question of law is involved) and subject to a simple means test. The Administrator of the Duty Lawyer Scheme has a discretion to grant legal representation to defendants whose gross annual incomes exceed the specified financial limit (of gross annual income of $90,000). There are approximately 600 remunerated barristers and solicitors on the Duty Lawyer roster. In 1992, 32 632 defendants facing charges received advice and representation at trial.

The Legal Advice Scheme provides free advice without means testing at five advice centres located in District Offices. Members of the public can make appointments to see the volunteer lawyers through one of the 120 referral agencies which include all District Offices, Caritas Services Centres and many others. There are approximately 408 lawyers in the scheme. Some 2 800 people are advised each year.

The Tel-Law Scheme was introduced in March 1984. It provides taped legal information by telephone. Each taped message is available in both English and Chinese. The main purpose of the service is to provide basic information on the legal aspects of everyday problems, and to encourage people who have such problems to use the Legal Advice Scheme. The tapes cover aspects of matrimonial, landlord and tenant, criminal, financial, employment, environmental and administrative law. Tapes are added when a new subject is identified as being of interest to the public. During the year, Tel-Law handled over 53 184 calls.

4
IMPLEMENTATION OF THE SINO-BRITISH JOINT DECLARATION

DISCUSSIONS on the implementation of the Sino-British Joint Declaration on the Question of Hong Kong continued. Progress has been made in the work of both the Sino-British Joint Liaison Group (JLG) and the Sino-British Land Commission.

The Sino-British Joint Liaison Group
The Joint Liaison Group was established in accordance with the provisions of Annex II to the Joint Declaration. Its functions are to conduct consultations on the implementation of the Joint Declaration, to discuss matters relating to the smooth transfer of government in 1997, and to exchange information and conduct consultations on such subjects as may be agreed by the two sides. The JLG is an organ for liaison and not an organ of power. It plays no part in the administration of Hong Kong.

The JLG comprises a senior representative and four other members on each side. Supporting staff and experts also attend meetings as appropriate. In accordance with the provisions in Annex II to the Joint Declaration, the JLG has taken Hong Kong as its principal base since July 1, 1988. Both sides have established offices here and their respective senior representatives are resident in Hong Kong. This has helped closer liaison and further progress on many issues. The JLG continues, nevertheless, to hold plenary sessions at least once every year in Beijing, London and Hong Kong.

During the year, four plenary sessions were held. Expert talks on a number of items also took place. Progress was made in several important areas.

Defence and Public Order
Both in the JLG itself and in talks at expert level, discussions on the implementation of the Joint Declaration in respect of defence and the maintenance of public order were held. Information and views on a wide range of practical matters relating to this issue were exchanged. Such exchanges are necessary for developing understanding between the two sides to allow for a smooth transfer of defence responsibilities from Britain to China in 1997.

Court of Final Appeal
The Joint Declaration provides for the establishment of a Court of Final Appeal in the Hong Kong Special Administrative Region. At the 20th meeting of the JLG (September 1991), the two sides reached agreement in principle on the establishment of the Court of

Final Appeal. Draft legislation and a package of arrangements for establishing the court are being considered.

Localisation of Laws

As explained in Chapter 3, a large number of United Kingdom laws currently apply to Hong Kong. These laws will cease to have effect in Hong Kong after June 30, 1997. It will be necessary therefore to 'localise' them, that is, replace them by legislation enacted in Hong Kong which will survive that date. At the eighth meeting of the JLG (November 1987), the two sides agreed on the general principles for consultation on the localisation of United Kingdom legislation. Since then good progress has been made. As at December 31, 1992, five localising ordinances have been enacted and 31 sets of localising regulations have been made.

Air Service Agreements

In order to maintain Hong Kong's status as an international civil aviation centre after 1997, there is an on-going Air Service Agreement (ASA) separation programme, whereby provisions involving Hong Kong in United Kingdom ASAs are separated into discrete Hong Kong ASAs. So far Hong Kong has concluded eight ASAs, with the Netherlands, Switzerland, Canada, Brunei, France, New Zealand, Malaysia and Brazil. Negotiations with a number of other aviation partners are at an advanced stage. New ASAs will be signed when the need arises.

Sub-Group on International Rights and Obligations

The Sub-Group on International Rights and Obligations, set up by the Joint Liaison Group, was formally established in July 1986 to examine and discuss matters relating to the continued application after 1997 of international rights and obligations affecting Hong Kong and to report its conclusions to the JLG. The sub-group, which is based in Hong Kong, consists of three experts on each side, supplemented as necessary by other experts and supporting staff.

There is a considerable number of treaties and international obligations applying to Hong Kong. The sub-group has to examine each individually. The consequence is that the work of the sub-group will take a number of years to complete. So far the two sides have reached agreement in the JLG on Hong Kong's continued participation in 29 international organisations (including the General Agreement on Tariffs and Trade). The sub-group has also been discussing the continued application after 1997 of multilateral treaties currently applying to Hong Kong and has so far reached agreement on a number of treaties on customs, conservation, health, trade, postal services, marine pollution, transport, drugs, private international law, science and technology and international crime.

Land Commission

The Sino-British Land Commission was established in 1985 in accordance with Annex III to the Joint Declaration. Its function is to conduct consultations on the implementation of the provisions of Annex III on land leases and other related matters. The commission is composed of three officials on each side. The meetings are held in Hong Kong.

During 1992, the Land Commission held two formal meetings. The two sides agreed to make available, during the 1992–3 financial year, a total of about 164.3 hectares of land. This includes 60 hectares for the development of Container Terminal No. 9.

Under the terms of paragraph 6 of Annex III to the Joint Declaration, premium income obtained by the Hong Kong Government from land transactions is, after the deduction of the cost of land production, to be shared equally between the Hong Kong Government and the future Hong Kong Special Administrative Region Government. The average cost of land production is adjusted by the commission annually, and for the 1992–3 financial year the agreed figure was $3,950 per square metre. The Hong Kong Government's share of premium income is put into the Capital Works Reserve Fund for financing public works and land development. The future SAR Government's share is held in a trust fund, called the Hong Kong Special Administrative Region Government Land Fund, established by the Chinese side of the Land Commission. The fund is managed under the direction and advice of an investment committee, which includes prominent bankers in Hong Kong, as well as a monetary expert from the Hong Kong Government. Over $34,223 million, representing the future SAR Government's share of premium income for the period May 27, 1985 to September 30, 1992, has been transferred to the fund.

The Basic Law
The Joint Declaration provides that the basic policies of the People's Republic of China regarding Hong Kong will be stipulated in a Basic Law of the Hong Kong Special Administrative Region (HKSAR) by the National People's Congress (NPC) of the People's Republic of China. After deliberation and consultation extending over five years, the Basic Law was promulgated in April 1990 by the NPC, together with the designs for the flag and emblem of the HKSAR. The Basic Law will come into effect on July 1, 1997. It prescribes the systems to be practised in the HKSAR, and provides that the HKSAR will enjoy a high degree of autonomy.

Adaptation of Laws
Article 8 of the Basic Law, which reflects paragraph 7 of Annex I to the Joint Declaration, provides that after the establishment of the HKSAR, the laws previously in force in Hong Kong shall be maintained, except for any that contravene the Basic Law, and subject to any amendment by the legislature of the HKSAR. The laws of Hong Kong therefore need to be reviewed and if necessary amended to ensure their compatibility with the Basic Law, so that they can continue to be in force in the HKSAR from July 1, 1997. Agreement on principles for consultation relating to the adaptation of laws was reached at the 17th meeting of the JLG (December 1990) and work on the review is now in progress.

5
THE ECONOMY

THE growth momentum of the Hong Kong economy was strengthened further in 1992. While the marked increase in re-exports continued to provide the main impetus to growth, domestic exports remained virtually static. Domestic demand was robust throughout the year. The renewal of China's Most Favoured Nation status in the United States for another year and the satisfactory resolution of the market access negotiations between China and the United States under Section 301 of the US Trade Act boosted business confidence. However, the protracted negotiations with China on the financing arrangements for the new airport and related projects gave rise to some uncertainty. Political differences over the proposals on constitutional development also aroused concern in the business community.

In the external sector, domestic exports, after showing virtually no change in the first quarter, picked up slightly during the second and third quarters. However, the performance slackened again in the fourth quarter. Re-exports continued to show a strong increase. Many of these re-exports were products of outward processing arrangements made between Hong Kong companies and manufacturing entities in China. In the domestic sector, both consumption and investment expenditures were buoyant. Reflecting these developments, the gross domestic product (GDP) grew by 5.0 per cent in 1992, with increases of 4.9 per cent in the first half and 5.1 per cent in the second half. The corresponding growth rate in 1991 was 4.2 per cent.

After a temporary easing in the early part of the year, the labour market tightened up again in the subsequent months as economic activity continued to grow steadily. The seasonally adjusted unemployment rate was 2.4 per cent in the first half of 1992, while in the second half it was 2.0 per cent. Labour resources continued to shift from manufacturing to services, reflecting the on-going structural transformation of Hong Kong into a more service-orientated economy. Average earnings in all major sectors showed significant increases in money terms in 1992, with appreciable gains after discounting inflation.

Consumer price inflation was generally on a moderating trend in 1992. The inflationary pressures remained mainly generated domestically rather than imported. The rate of increase in the Consumer Price Index (A) for the year as a whole was 9.4 per cent, comprising 9.6 per cent in the first half and 9.2 per cent in the second half. The corresponding increase in 1991 was 12 per cent.

Statistical data are given at Appendices 7–11.

Structure and Development of the Economy

Because of limited natural resources, Hong Kong has to depend on imports for virtually all its needs, including food and other consumer goods, raw materials, capital goods, fuel and even water. It must therefore export on a sufficient scale to generate foreign exchange earnings to pay for these imports, and the volume of exports must continue to grow if the population is to enjoy a rising standard of living.

The externally-orientated nature of the economy can be seen from the fact that in 1992 the total value of visible trade (comprising domestic exports, re-exports and imports) amounted to 254 per cent of the GDP. If the value of imports and exports of services is also included, this ratio becomes 288 per cent. Between 1982 and 1992, Hong Kong's total exports grew at an average annual rate of 17 per cent in real terms, which was roughly twice the growth rate of world trade. The corresponding average annual increase was 16 per cent for imports. With a gross value of $1,880 billion in overall visible trade in 1992, Hong Kong ranks high among the world's trading economies.

Contributions of the Various Economic Sectors

The relative importance of the various economic sectors can be assessed in terms of their contributions to the GDP and to total employment.

Primary production (comprising agriculture and fishery, mining and quarrying) is small in terms of its contributions to both the GDP and employment.

Within secondary production (comprising manufacturing; the supply of electricity, gas and water; and construction), manufacturing still accounts for the largest share in terms of both the GDP and employment. The contribution of the manufacturing sector to the GDP declined steadily from 31 per cent in 1970 to 21 per cent in 1982. It then increased to 23 per cent in 1983 and to 24 per cent in 1984, before stabilising at around 22 per cent during the period 1985 to 1987. It fell again thereafter to about 16 per cent in 1991, reflecting partly the slow-down in domestic exports and partly the continued expansion of the service sectors. The share of the construction sector in the GDP increased from four per cent in 1970 to eight per cent in 1981. It then declined to seven per cent in 1982 and six per cent in 1983, before settling at about five per cent during the period 1984 to 1991.

The contribution of the tertiary service sectors as a whole (comprising the wholesale, retail and import/export trades; restaurants and hotels; transport, storage and communications; finance, insurance, real estate and business services; and community, social and personal services) to the GDP increased from 60 per cent in 1970 to 65 per cent in 1982. It fell to around 62 to 64 per cent during the period 1983 to 1986, before rising steadily to 73 per cent in 1991.

With regard to employment, the most notable change since the early 1970s was the continuous decline in the share of the manufacturing sector in total employment, from 47 per cent in 1971 to 41 per cent in 1981, and further to 24 per cent in 1992. On the other hand, the share of the tertiary service sectors as a whole in total employment increased from 41 per cent in 1971 to 47 per cent in 1981, and further to 66 per cent in 1992.

The Manufacturing Sector

Although Hong Kong's domestic exports are still concentrated in a number of major product groups, there has been continuous upgrading of quality and diversification of items within these groups. The pressure of protectionism and growing competition from

41

other economies have resulted in local manufacturers intensifying their efforts to diversify, in respect of not only products but also markets. A major proportion of Hong Kong's manufacturing output is eventually exported.

Manufacturing firms in Hong Kong must be flexible and adaptable in order to cope with the frequent changes in demand patterns and to maintain their external competitiveness. The existence of a large number of small establishments providing an extensive local sub-contracting system has greatly facilitated the necessary changes in production and has helped to increase the flexibility of the manufacturing sector. Moreover, increasing use has been made of the outward processing facilities in China for handling the relatively labour-intensive production processes. Because of the land and space constraint, Hong Kong's manufacturing industries are mostly those which can operate successfully in multi-storey factory buildings. This, in practice, implies concentration in the production of light manufactures.

Over the past 30 years, many industries have emerged and grown, the most notable ones being plastics and electronics. The textiles and clothing industries remain prominent despite their continuous decline in relative importance. Other industries of importance include fabricated metal products, electrical appliances, watches and clocks, toys, jewellery, and printing and publishing.

Of particular note is the significant upgrading in labour productivity within the manufacturing sector over the years. During the period 1973 to 1990, the value of net output by the manufacturing sector grew at an average annual rate of 15 per cent, while manufacturing employment grew at an average annual rate of less than one per cent. Even after taking into account the effect of price increases on the output value, a significant secular improvement in labour productivity was evident.

Within the manufacturing sector, the most significant change occurred in the textiles industry. The share of this industry in the net output of manufacturing declined from 27 per cent in 1973 to 15 per cent in 1990, while its share in manufacturing employment fell from 21 per cent to 15 per cent. Against this decline was the expansion of the electrical appliances and electronics, and watches and clocks industries. Between 1973 and 1990, their shares in the net output of manufacturing increased from nine per cent to 12 per cent, and from one per cent to three per cent respectively. In terms of employment, the share of the former, however, decreased slightly from 11 per cent in 1973 to 10 per cent in 1990, while that of the latter increased from one per cent to two per cent.

Domestic exports in 1992 consisted principally of wearing apparel and clothing accessories (33 per cent of the total value), electronics (26 per cent), textiles (seven per cent), watches and clocks (seven per cent), plastic products (three per cent), metal products (three per cent), and electrical household appliances (one per cent). In terms of the share in the total value of domestic exports, the most significant change over the past decade was the decline in the relative importance of clothing, from 35 per cent in 1982 to 33 per cent in 1992. On the other hand, increases were recorded in the relative importance of such commodities as telecommunications and sound recording and reproducing equipment, electrical machinery and appliances, and office machines and data processing equipment. The combined share of these three commodity groups in the total value of domestic exports rose from 17 per cent in 1982 to 23 per cent in 1992.

Market diversification over the years has been the combined result of initiatives taken by local manufacturers and exporters, and promotion efforts supported by the government.

Over the past five years, the share of the United States in Hong Kong's total domestic exports has been declining, although it still remains as the largest market. On the other hand, the shares of domestic exports going to China, Germany, Japan, Canada and Australia, and to the South East Asian economies have increased. Moreover, Hong Kong has also diversified into other new markets, including countries in the Middle East, Eastern Europe, Latin America and Africa.

The Service Sectors
Over the past decades, the rapid growth in external trade has not only enabled Hong Kong to build up a strong manufacturing base, it has also provided the underlying conditions for the service sectors to flourish and diversify. Of particular note was the rapid growth and development in finance and business services, including banking, insurance, real estate, and a wide range of other professional services.

The significance of entrepôt trade re-emerged in the late 1970s as China embarked on its open door policies to facilitate its modernisation programmes. Rapid economic growth in the Asia-Pacific region over the past decade provided an added stimulus. Hong Kong, with its strategic location and well-established transport and communications network, was in a favourable position to take advantage of these opportunities. Trading and other economic links between Hong Kong and the region generally, and China in particular, increased rapidly.

Over the years, Hong Kong has developed an efficient wholesale and retail network to cater for the growing consumption needs of a more affluent population. Supermarkets, large department stores, convenience stores and modern shopping centres have become increasingly popular. This development was reinforced by the rapid growth in tourism. Restaurants and hotels have also experienced a substantial increase in business. Furthermore, with higher household incomes, there has been a growing demand for services of a better quality to meet the rising standard of living. Thus, services in the community, social and recreational fields have also grown substantially.

Analysed by sectors, the contribution of the wholesale, retail and import/export trades, restaurants and hotels to the GDP varied between 19 and 21 per cent in 1970 to 1983, before rising to 25 per cent in 1991. The contribution of transport, storage and communications to the GDP was stable at around seven to eight per cent until 1986, before rising to 10 per cent in 1991. The contribution of finance, insurance, real estate and business services to the GDP experienced considerable fluctuations. It rose from 15 per cent in 1970 to 24 per cent in 1981, but fell back to 16 per cent in 1984, mainly reflecting the slump in the property market. Thereafter it rose steadily, to 23 per cent in 1991.

Within the service sectors, the most notable increase in employment was in the wholesale, retail and import/export trades, restaurants and hotels sector, with its share in the total employed workforce rising from 16 per cent in 1971 to 19 per cent in 1981 and further to 27 per cent in 1992. This was followed by finance, insurance, real estate and business services, with its employment share rising from three per cent in 1971 to five per cent in 1981 and further to 20 per cent in 1992.

Between 1982 and 1992, exports of services rose at an average annual rate of nine per cent in real terms, while imports of services were higher by 11 per cent per annum. The major components of Hong Kong's trade in services are shipping, civil aviation, tourism and various financial services. The shares of transportation services in total exports and

43

total imports of services were 48 per cent and 32 per cent respectively in 1991. Travel services accounted for 33 per cent of the total value of exports of services and 48 per cent of the total value of imports of services. The corresponding shares for financial and banking services were six per cent and three per cent respectively.

Increasing Economic Links between Hong Kong and China
Since the adoption of open door policies by China in late 1978, Hong Kong's economic relations with China have undergone rapid growth and development.

Hong Kong and China are now each other's largest trading partner. In 1992, the total value of visible trade between Hong Kong and China amounted to $628 billion, representing an increase of 25 per cent over 1991. This rapid growth reflected partly the buoyant economic conditions in China and partly the sustained growth in outward processing trade.

In 1992, China was the second largest market for Hong Kong's domestic exports, accounting for 26 per cent of the total. China was also the largest market for, as well as the largest supplier of, Hong Kong's re-exports. About 86 per cent of the goods re-exported through Hong Kong were either destined for, or originated from, China.

In addition to trade in goods, Hong Kong also serves as an important service centre for China generally and South China in particular. This includes the provision of infrastructural facilities such as the port and airport, as well as institutional supports such as financial and related business services. This is evidenced, among other things, by the increasing importance of Hong Kong as a centre for entrepôt, transhipment and other supporting activities involving China.

Hong Kong has always been a convenient gateway to China for business and tourism. In 1992, 21 million trips to China were made by Hong Kong residents, and another 1.7 million trips to China were made by foreign visitors through Hong Kong. These represented increases of 13 per cent and 28 per cent respectively over 1991.

Besides visible and invisible trade, Hong Kong is also the most important source of external investment in China, accounting for about two-thirds of the total. While Hong Kong's direct investment in China has been concentrated in light manufacturing industries, investment in hotels and tourist-related facilities, property and infrastructure has also been increasing. As can be expected, Guangdong occupies a highly important position in this respect. It has been estimated that, in Guangdong Province, around three million people are working for Hong Kong companies either through joint ventures or in tasks commissioned by Hong Kong companies in the form of outward processing arrangements and compensation trade. This, in effect, provides Hong Kong with a substantial production base.

Concurrently, China has also been investing heavily in Hong Kong. Its investment ranges from traditional activities like banking, import/export, wholesale/retail, and transportation and warehousing, to newer areas like property development, financial services, manufacturing and infrastructural projects.

Increasing financial links between Hong Kong and China are reflected by the rapid growth in financial transactions with China in recent years. While the Bank of China Group is the second largest banking group in Hong Kong, after the Hongkong Bank Group, the latter group is the best represented foreign bank in China, followed by the Standard Chartered Bank.

Hong Kong is a major funding centre for China. Most of China's fund-raising activities in Hong Kong have taken the form of syndicated loans. Although in some cases Hong Kong is not the direct source of funds, it serves as a window through which China can have access to external borrowing. These loans are mostly for financing China's own economic development, but some of them are used by China-interest companies in Hong Kong to finance their investment activities in Hong Kong or abroad. In addition to syndicated loans, China-interest banks and other enterprises have been making greater use of negotiable certificates of deposit, bonds, commercial paper, and share issuance to raise funds.

The prospects for further development of economic links between Hong Kong and China continue to be good, given the firm foundation that has been established over the years as well as the broadened open door policies, accelerated economic reforms and rapid economic growth in China.

The Economy in 1992

The economy continued to grow steadily in 1992. Re-exports surged further, while domestic exports recorded virtually no growth. Locally, both consumption and investment expenditures remained robust throughout the year.

Consumer price inflation was generally on a moderating trend in 1992. For 1992 as a whole, the rate of increase in the Consumer Price Index (A) averaged 9.4 per cent, appreciably lower than the 12 per cent recorded in 1991. The GDP deflator, as a broad measure of overall inflation in the economy, rose slightly faster than the consumer price indices, by 10.3 per cent in 1992. This faster increase was, however, largely due to an improvement in the terms of trade, with the prices of imports rising more slowly than those of exports.

According to the preliminary estimate, the growth rate in real terms of the GDP was 5.0 per cent in 1992, with increases of 4.9 per cent in the first half and 5.1 per cent in the second half. In 1990 and 1991, the GDP grew by 3.2 per cent and 4.2 per cent respectively in real terms.

External Trade

In 1992, re-exports grew markedly, by 29 per cent in value terms over a year earlier. After discounting for an estimated one per cent increase in prices, there was a 28 per cent increase in real terms. The corresponding growth rates in 1991 were 29 per cent and 26 per cent respectively. The robust performance of re-exports was in line with the on-going structural shift of domestic exports to re-exports.

China remained the largest source of, as well as the largest market for, Hong Kong's re-exports. Supported by the expansion of outward processing activities across the border and by the increase in China's external trade, re-exports involving China in both directions continued to rise rapidly in 1992. Meanwhile, re-exports not related to China showed a more moderate increase. The other major re-export markets were the United States, Japan, Germany, Taiwan and the United Kingdom. The major suppliers of Hong Kong's re-exports, apart from China, were Japan, Taiwan, the United States and the Republic of Korea.

Analysed by end-use categories, Hong Kong's re-exports comprised mostly consumer goods, and raw materials and semi-manufactures, which represented 55 per cent and 27 per cent respectively of the total value of re-exports in 1992. Analysed the major commodity

45

items, re-exports of footwear, electrical machinery and appliances, telecommunications and sound recording and reproducing equipment, clothing, and textile fabrics, showed faster increases than other commodity items.

The value of domestic exports was one per cent higher in 1992 than in 1991. After discounting for an estimated one per cent increase in prices, there was virtually zero growth in real terms. This compared with an increase of two per cent in value terms or virtually no growth in real terms in 1991. On a year-on-year comparison, domestic exports grew by one per cent in real terms in the first half of 1992, but fell by one per cent in the second half.

Domestic exports to the various major markets showed a mixed performance in 1992. Compared with 1991, domestic exports to China surged further, by 13 per cent in real terms. A large proportion of these domestic exports were related to outward processing arrangements commissioned by Hong Kong companies. Domestic exports to the United States eased back in the second half of 1992, after a pick-up in the first half. For the year as a whole, there was no growth in real terms. On the other hand, domestic exports to Germany and the United Kingdom showed marked declines amid a slack demand, but the rates of decline had moderated somewhat in the latter part of the year. For 1992 as a whole, domestic exports to these two markets declined by 20 per cent and eight per cent respectively in real terms. For domestic exports to Japan, a moderate decrease of five per cent in real terms was recorded in 1992.

Analysed by major product categories, domestic exports of textiles fell by three per cent in real terms in 1992, while those of clothing fell by two per cent. Their shares in the total value of domestic exports in 1992 were seven per cent and 33 per cent respectively. In 1992, domestic exports of electronic components recorded a sharp growth of 31 per cent in real terms. On the other hand, domestic exports of watches and clocks, and electrical appliances fell, by nine per cent, and 38 per cent respectively in real terms. Domestic exports of metal manufactures recorded virtually no growth.

Imports grew rapidly, by 23 per cent in value terms or by about 22 per cent in real terms in 1992. This compared with an increase of 21 per cent in value terms or 19 per cent in real terms in 1991. The major sources of Hong Kong's imports were China, Japan, Taiwan, the United States, the Republic of Korea and Singapore. Most of the growth in imports was attributable to the continued surge in re-export trade. To a lesser extent, it was also supported by imports retained in Hong Kong for local use.

Retained imports increased by 14 per cent in value terms in 1992. The increase in real terms was also 14 per cent. Among the various end-use categories, retained imports of consumer goods recorded the fastest growth, by about 23 per cent in real terms. Retained imports of capital goods also grew sharply, by 19 per cent in real terms. Within this category, retained imports of industrial machinery for manufacturing use registered an increase of about 11 per cent in real terms. Retained imports of food, fuels and raw materials and semi-manufactures increased by about nine per cent, 18 per cent, and seven per cent respectively in real terms.

As the value of total exports (domestic exports plus re-exports) was smaller than that of imports, a visible trade deficit of $30,342 million, equivalent to 3.2 per cent of the total value of imports, was recorded in 1992. This compared with a deficit of $13,096 million, equivalent to 1.7 per cent of the total value of imports, recorded in 1991. As the prices of total exports increased at a faster rate than those of imports in 1992, the terms of trade showed a small improvement.

Domestic Demand

Indicative of a generally buoyant economy, domestic demand rose by 10 per cent in real terms in 1992, following a nine per cent growth in 1991. Private consumption expenditure grew by nine per cent in real terms in 1992, and government consumption expenditure by eight per cent in real terms. Their corresponding growth rates in 1991 were eight per cent and seven per cent. Investment demand, measured in terms of gross domestic fixed capital formation, grew by 11 per cent in real terms in 1992, having increased by 10 per cent in 1991. Among its major components, expenditure on plant and machinery was higher by 23 per cent in real terms, while expenditure on building and construction showed a marginal increase of one per cent in real terms.

The Labour Market

The labour market, after showing some easing in the early part of 1992, tightened up again in the latter part of the year. The seasonally adjusted unemployment rate rose to around 2.4 per cent in the first half of 1992, before falling to about 2.0 per cent in the second half. The underemployment rate exhibited a broadly similar trend. It rose to 2.2 per cent in the first half of the year, and then fell to 2.0 per cent in the second half.

Between September 1991 and September 1992, employment in the manufacturing sector decreased by 13 per cent to 571 200, while employment in the service sectors as a whole increased by four per cent to 1 621 800. Labour resources thus continued to shift from manufacturing to services. Among the various service sectors, employment in water transport, air transport and services allied to transport increased by eight per cent; that in finance, insurance, real estate and business services by six per cent; that in restaurants and hotels by four per cent; and that in the wholesale, retail and import/export trades by three per cent. On building and construction sites, employment decreased by one per cent. However, for the building and construction industry as a whole, employment of site workers and non-site workers taken together still showed an increase of two per cent. As the employment situation in the manufacturing sector remained slack, vacancies in this sector declined markedly, by 18 per cent over a year earlier to 19 100 in September 1992. Nevertheless, vacancies in the service sectors as a whole rose by 10 per cent to 54 100.

Local manufacturing output, as measured by the index of industrial production, increased by two per cent in the first three quarters of 1992 over the same period in 1991. This compared with an increase of one per cent in 1991 over 1990. The attainment of this level of performance, notwithstanding a significant reduction in manufacturing employment, showed that labour productivity in the manufacturing sector had risen significantly. This was attributable partly to the marked increase in investment in machinery and equipment, and partly to the relocation of the more labour-intensive production processes to China.

The generally tight labour market conditions boosted labour incomes. Average earnings in all major sectors recorded further significant increases in money terms during the twelve months ending September 1992. When expressed in real terms, earnings in all major sectors except restaurants and hotels increased.

Between September 1991 and September 1992, average earnings of manufacturing workers increased by 15 per cent in money terms. After adjusting for inflation, this amounted to an increase of four per cent in real terms. Average earnings for the service

47

sectors as a whole rose by 14 per cent in money terms, or by four per cent in real terms over the same period. Of the various service sectors, earnings in the wholesale, retail and import/export trades; finance, insurance, real estate and business services; and transport, storage and communication all rose by about 12 per cent in money terms. After adjusting for inflation, the increase in real earnings in these three sectors were two per cent, two per cent and one per cent respectively. Earnings in restaurants and hotels rose by only nine per cent in money terms, which was equivalent to a decrease of one per cent in real terms.

The Property Market
The residential property market underwent some consolidation in 1992. The anti-speculation measures introduced by the government in late 1991 and the tight mortgage lending policy pursued by the banks continued to have their restraining effect. Transactions were considerably less in 1992 than in 1991. The prices of residential flats, after showing a further increase during the first half of the year eased somewhat during the second half, amid more sluggish trading. But the rentals on new lettings of residential flats remained stable, with some increases recorded in more favoured areas. In the market for shopping space, demand was supported by the pick-up in consumer spending and the growth in tourism. Prices and rentals rose further. The demand for office space revived along with a modest gain in rentals in most districts, while supply remained abundant. The sales market for office strata was active as buyers' interest continued to shift from residential flats to office premises. The market for older conventional factory space remained sluggish. However, well-located modern industrial buildings designed also for ancillary office uses were more favoured. As to land sales, response to the auctions of residential sites during 1992 remained generally favourable. However developers were cautious about acquiring industrial sites.

Inflation
The rate of inflation at the consumer level, as measured by the Consumer Price Index (A), rose by an average of 9.4 per cent in 1992. This compared with the corresponding increase of 12 per cent in 1991. Continuing the moderating trend since April 1991, the rate of inflation eased further in the first eight months of 1992, to 8.3 per cent in August. It rebounded to 9.9 per cent in September, partly due to the volatile movements in the prices of certain essential foodstuffs. In December, the rate of inflation stood at 9.4 per cent.

Among the various components of the CPI(A), the cost of housing recorded the fastest increase, by an average of 13 per cent in 1992 over 1991. This was followed by charges for services (12 per cent), alcoholic drinks and tobacco (10 per cent), food (nine per cent) and clothing and footwear (eight per cent). Taken together, these five components accounted for 87 per cent of the overall increase in the CPI(A). On the other hand, relatively more moderate increases were recorded in the prices of transport, miscellaneous goods, fuel and light and durable goods by an average of seven per cent, seven per cent, five per cent and two per cent respectively in 1992 over 1991. As faster price increases were generally recorded for items with a larger local input content, which was to be expected when the local resource situation was tight, it showed that inflation in 1992 was mostly generated domestically rather than imported.

Economic Policy and Public Finances
Economic Policy
Economic policy in Hong Kong is to a large extent dictated, and constrained, by the special circumstances of the economy. Owing to its small size and open nature, the economy is vulnerable to external factors, and government actions designed to offset unfavourable external influences are of limited effectiveness. Moreover, the government considers that, except where social considerations are over-riding, the allocation of resources in the economy is best left to market forces with minimal government intervention in the private sector.

This basically free-enterprise, market-disciplined system has continued to contribute to Hong Kong's economic success. A relatively simple tax structure with low tax rates provides good incentive for workers to work and for entrepreneurs to invest. Both workers and entrepreneurs are highly motivated. The primary role of the government is to provide the necessary infrastructure and a sound legal and administrative framework conducive to economic growth and prosperity.

Structure of Government Accounts
In accounting terms, the public sector is taken to include the Hong Kong Government itself, the Housing Authority and Urban and Regional Councils. Government grants and subventions to institutions in the private or quasi-private sectors are included but expenditure by organisations in which the government has only equity, such as the Mass Transit Railway and Kowloon-Canton Railway Corporations, is not included.

The government controls its finances through a series of fund accounts. The General Revenue Account is the main account for day-to-day departmental expenditure and revenue collection. Four other funds exist mainly to finance capital investment and expenditure and to make loans. They are the Capital Works Reserve Fund, Capital Investment Fund, Loan Fund and Lotteries Fund.

The Capital Works Reserve Fund finances the Public Works Programme, land acquisitions, capital subventions, and major systems and equipment items and computerisation. On May 27, 1985, when the Sino-British Joint Declaration came into effect, the fund was restructured to enable the premium income obtained from land transactions to be accounted for in accordance with the arrangements in Annex III to the Joint Declaration. The income of the fund is derived mainly from land premia and appropriations from the General Revenue Account.

The Capital Investment Fund is used to finance the government's capital investments in public bodies, such as equity injection in the Mass Transit Railway Corporation, capital investment in the Hong Kong Housing Authority and advances to the Provisional Airport Authority. Its income is derived mainly from interest and dividends on investments, disposal of investments, repayments of loans, and appropriations from the General Revenue Account.

The Loan Fund is used to finance schemes of government loans such as student loans and housing loans. Transfers are made from the General Revenue Account to enable the fund to meet its commitments. The other main sources of income are interest and dividends on loans and investments and loan repayments.

The Lotteries Fund is used to finance development of social welfare services through loans and grants. Its regular source of income is derived mainly from the sharing of the proceeds of Mark Six lotteries.

Management of the Budget

The government manages its finances against the background of a rolling five-year Medium Range Forecast of expenditure and revenue. This models the consolidated financial position of the General Revenue Account and of all the funds except the Lotteries Fund.

The most important principle underlying the government's management of public expenditure is that the growth rate of public expenditure should over a period be close to that of gross domestic product.

The Budget presented by the Financial Secretary to the Legislative Council each year is developed against the background of the Medium Range Forecast to ensure that full regard is given to these principles and to longer-term trends in the economy.

Public Expenditure

Public expenditure in 1991–2 was $108.0 billion. The government itself accounted for $90.0 billion excluding equity injections in the Mass Transit Railway Corporation, the Housing Authority, the Provisional Airport Authority and other bodies. The growth rate over the preceding year was 13.5 per cent in nominal terms or 2.9 per cent in real terms. Some $27.5 billion or 25.5 per cent of the public expenditure in 1991–2 was of a capital nature. An analysis of expenditure by function is at Appendix 8.

The growth rate of public expenditure is compared with the rate of economic growth at Appendix 9. Public expenditure has been around 15 to 17 per cent of the gross domestic product since 1987–8. It is estimated that this will rise to about 19 per cent in 1992–3.

Total government revenue in 1991–2 was $113.6 billion and the consolidated cash surplus was $22.5 billion including net borrowing of $1.1 billion. Details of revenue by source and of expenditure by component for 1991–2 and 1992–3 (estimate) are at Appendix 10.

The draft Estimates of Expenditure on the General Revenue Account are presented by the Financial Secretary to the Legislative Council when he delivers his annual Budget Speech. In the Appropriation Bill introduced into the Legislative Council at the same time, the administration seeks appropriation of the total estimated expenditure on the General Revenue Account.

The Estimates of Expenditure contain details of the estimated recurrent and capital expenditures of all government departments, including estimates of payments to be made to subvented organisations and estimates of transfers to be made to the statutory funds. They also provide for the repayment of public debt.

With the exception of only five years (1974–5, 1982–3, 1983–4, 1984–5 and 1990–91) in the past 20 years, the General Revenue Account has shown a surplus of income over expenditure at the end of each year. The accumulated net surpluses on the General Revenue Account and on the Funds together form the government's fiscal reserves. These secure the government's contingent liabilities and ensure that it is able to cope with any short-term fluctuations in expenditure relative to revenue.

The Urban Council and Regional Council, which operate through the Urban Services Department and Regional Services Department respectively, are financially autonomous. They draw up their own budgets and expenditure priorities. The expenditures of the two councils are financed mainly from a fixed percentage of the rates from property in the Urban Council area (Hong Kong, Kowloon and New Kowloon) and in the Regional Council area (New Territories). Additonal income derives from fees and charges for the services the councils provide.

The Housing Authority, operating through the Housing Department, is also financially autonomous. Its income is derived mainly from rents. If the Authority's cash flow is inadequate to meet the construction costs of new estates, it may request an injection of capital by the government. The authority is provided with land on concessionary terms for the construction of public rental housing. Part of the authority's recurrent expenditure, for such activities as clearances and squatter control, is financed from the General Revenue Account. The authority is also responsible for carrying out a programme of squatter area improvements which are funded from the Capital Works Reserve Fund.

Revenue Sources
Hong Kong's tax system is simple and relatively inexpensive to administer. Tax rates are low, but the government accords a high priority to curbing tax avoidance and evasion. The principal direct taxes are salaries tax and profits tax. Important indirect taxes include rates on property, stamp duty on property and stock market transactions, betting duty and duties on certain specified commodities (see Appendix 11).

The Inland Revenue Department is responsible for the collection of over 60 per cent of general revenue including earnings and profits tax, stamp duty, betting duty, estate duty, hotel accommodation tax, and entertainments tax. Revenue from these sources are collectively described as 'internal revenue'.

Earnings and profits tax, which alone accounted for about 44 per cent of general revenue in 1991–2, is levied under the Inland Revenue Ordinance. Persons liable to this tax may be assessed on three separate and distinct sources of income, namely business profits, salaries and income from property.

Profits tax is charged only on net profits arising in Hong Kong, or derived from a trade, profession or business carried on in Hong Kong. Profits of unincorporated business are currently taxed at 15 per cent and profits of corporations are taxed at 17.5 per cent. Tax is payable on the actual profits for the year of assessment.

Tax is paid initially on the basis of profits made in the year preceding the year of assessment and is subsequently adjusted according to profits actually made in the assessment year. Generally, all expenses incurred in the production of assessable profits are deductible. There is no withholding tax on dividends paid by corporations and dividends received from corporations are exempt from profits tax. In 1991–2, the government received some $25 billion in profits tax, amounting to about 25 per cent of the general revenue.

Salaries tax is charged on emoluments arising in or derived from Hong Kong. The basis of assessment and method of payment are similar to the system for profits tax. Tax payable is calculated on a sliding scale which progresses from two per cent to 17 per cent on the first three segments of net income (that is, income after deduction of allowances) of $20,000 each and then to 25 per cent on remaining net income. No one, however, pays more than 15 per cent of their total income. The earnings of husbands and wives are reported and assessed separately. However, where either spouse has allowances that exceed his or her income, or when separate assessments would result in an increase in salaries tax payable by the couple, they may elect to be assessed jointly. Salaries tax contributed some $17 billion, or 17 per cent of total general revenue, in 1991–2.

Owners of land or buildings in Hong Kong are charged property tax at the standard rate of 15 per cent on the actual rent received, less an allowance of 20 per cent for repairs and maintenance. There is a system of provisional payment of tax similar to that for profits tax and salaries tax. Property owned by a corporation carrying on a business in Hong Kong is exempt from property tax (but profits derived from ownership are chargeable to profits tax). Receipts from property tax totalled $1.2 billion in 1991–2.

The Stamp Duty Ordinance imposes fixed and *ad valorem* duties on different classes of documents relating to assignments of immovable property, leases and share transfers. The revenue from stamp duties accounted for about nine per cent of general revenue, or $9.6 billion, in 1991–2.

Betting duty is imposed on bets at the Royal Hong Kong Jockey Club and on the proceeds of Mark Six lotteries – the only legal forms of betting in Hong Kong. The duty now accounts for about seven per cent of general revenue. The rate of duty is 11.5 per cent or 17.5 per cent of the amount of the bet, depending on the type of bet placed, and 30 per cent on the proceeds of lotteries. Yield in 1991–2 totalled some $7 billion.

Other taxes collected by the Inland Revenue Department include estate duty, imposed on estates valued at over $4 million at levels ranging from six per cent to a maximum of 18 per cent; hotel accommodation tax of five per cent, imposed on expenditure on accommodation by guests in hotels and guest-houses; and entertainments tax, imposed on the cost of admission to race meetings at an average rate of about 28 per cent.

The Customs and Excise Department is responsible for collecting and protecting duty revenue. The Dutiable Commodities Ordinance imposes controls on the import, export, manufacture, sale and storage of dutiable items. In 1991–2, $6.8 billion was collected in duties, accounting for about seven per cent of general revenue. Duties are levied on five groups of commodities – hydrocarbon oils, alcoholic liquor, methyl alcohol, tobacco and cosmetics.

Duties are imposed irrespective of whether the product concerned is locally manufactured or imported. There is no discrimination on the grounds of geographical origin. The levels of duties take into account consumers' ability to pay: champagne is taxed more heavily than beer.

The Rating and Valuation Department is responsible for assessing and collecting rates which are levied on landed property at a fixed percentage of its rateable value. The revenue raised helps finance the various public services provided by the Urban Council and Regional Council, as well as providing a stable and reliable revenue stream to the Government.

Rateable value is an estimate of the annual rent at which a property might be expected to let as at a designated date, and general revaluations are conducted at intervals to keep rateable values up to date. The current lists of rateable values came into force on April 1, 1991 and reflect rental values at July 1, 1990.

The percentage charge is fixed annually by the Legislative Council in accordance with the financial requirements of the Government, the Urban Council and Regional Council. The percentage charge is now fixed at 5.5 per cent. Of this amount, three per cent of the revenue collected from Hong Kong Island and Kowloon is credited to the Urban Council and 3.75 per cent of that collected from the New Territories goes to the Regional Council. The remainder, amounting to $3.5 billion in 1991–2, is credited to general revenue.

Exemptions are few although the government generally provides financial assistance towards payment of rates to non-profit making educational, charitable and welfare organisations, if their premises are being run in accordance with approved guidelines. No refunds of rates are allowed for vacant domestic properties, but half the rates paid may be refunded in the case of unoccupied non-domestic premises.

The government derives significant amounts of revenue from a number of other sources. Fees and charges for services provided by government departments generated a total of about $7.2 billion in 1991–2. The government's general policy is that the cost of the service provided should be fully covered by the level of relevant fees or charge. Certain essential services are, however, subsidised by the government or provided free.

A further $6.7 billion was generated by government-operated public utilities. The most important of these, in revenue terms, are water supplies, postal services and Kai Tak Airport. Significant sums also accrued to general revenue from the tax imposed for the registration of motor vehicles under the Motor Vehicles (First Registration Tax) Ordinance. This revenue, amounting to approximately $3.4 billion in 1991–2, is collected by the Commissioner for Transport.

Finally, about $0.9 billion was received in the same year by way of royalties and concessions. These are paid by certain major companies holding franchises, such as the Cross Harbour Tunnel Company and television broadcasters, as well as holders of concessions to operate taxis and petrol stations.

The cumulative effect of all these (as well as a number of minor) revenue sources is to provide the government with a stable and fairly broad-based tax system, which is able to ensure that adequate funds are available for the implementation of its medium-term expenditure programmes, as well as the maintenance of adequate fiscal reserves.

6

FINANCIAL AND MONETARY AFFAIRS

HONG KONG'S financial sector comprises an integrated network of institutions and markets which, under various forms of regulation, provide a wide range of products and services to local and international customers and investors.

Financial Institutions

Hong Kong maintains a three-tier system of deposit-taking institutions: licensed banks, restricted licence banks and deposit-taking companies.

Banking licences are granted at the discretion of the Governor in Council, in accordance with the provisions of the Banking Ordinance. In September 1992, the Governor in Council made a number of changes to the criteria for bank licence applications as part of the regular review of such criteria. In the case of a local applicant incorporated in Hong Kong, the criterion that it should be predominantly beneficially owned by Hong Kong interests has been broadened to enable close association and identification with the territory to be taken into consideration. Apart from the requirements of a paid-up capital of at least $150 million and a minimum of 10 years in the business of taking deposits from and granting credit to the public, which have remained unchanged, an applicant has also to satisfy minimum requirements on assets (net of contra items) and public deposits. The latter two requirements were increased to $4,000 million and $3,000 million respectively. In the case of a bank incorporated outside Hong Kong applying to establish a branch in the territory, the asset size requirement (net of contra items) was increased to US$16,000 million. A licence may still be granted in exceptional circumstances, however, if the bank is of exceptionally high standing or if banks from its country of incorporation are under-represented in Hong Kong. The criterion dealing with home country supervision has also been changed to the effect that the home supervisor must demonstrate the necessary capabilities for meeting the minimum standards for supervision of international banks published by the Basle Committee of Supervisors in June. In general, there should be some acceptable form of reciprocity in an overseas applicant's home country to banks from Hong Kong.

At the end of 1992, there were 164 licensed banks in Hong Kong, 30 of which were locally incorporated. They maintained a total of 1 409 offices in Hong Kong. In addition, there were 148 representative offices of foreign banks. The total deposit liabilities of all the licensed banks to customers at the end of the year was $1,449 billion.

Only licensed banks may operate current or savings accounts. They may also accept deposits of any size and any maturity from the public. The interest rate rules of the Hong Kong Association of Banks (of which all licensed banks are required, under their licensing conditions, to be members) result in the setting of maximum rates payable on bank deposits of original maturities up to 15 months less a day, with the exception of deposits of $500,000 or above with a term to maturity of less than three months, for which banks may compete freely.

Restricted banking licences are granted at the discretion of the Financial Secretary. Companies are required to have a minimum issued and paid-up capital of $100 million, and to meet certain criteria regarding ownership, general standing, and quality of management. If incorporated overseas, the applicants must also be subject to adequate home supervision. Restricted licence banks may take deposits of any maturity from the public, but in amounts of not less than $500,000. There are no restrictions on the interest rates they may offer. At the end of 1992, there were 56 restricted licence banks and their total deposit liabilities to customers was $35 billion.

Restricted licence banks are able to use the word 'bank' in describing their business in promotional literature and advertisements but this must be qualified by adjectives such as 'restricted licence', 'merchant', or 'investment'. To avoid confusion with licensed banks, descriptions such as 'retail' or 'commercial' are not allowed. Overseas banks seeking authorisation as restricted licence banks may operate in branch or subsidiary form. If in branch form, they may use their registered name even if it includes the word 'bank' or a derivative, but in this case it must be qualified prominently by the words 'restricted licence bank' in immediate conjunction.

The authority to register deposit-taking companies rests with the Commissioner of Banking. Since April 1981, the Commissioner has, at the direction of the Governor, restricted new registrations to companies which, as well as meeting certain basic criteria, are more than 50 per cent owned by banks in Hong Kong or elsewhere. Deposit-taking companies are required to have a minimum paid-up capital of $25 million. They are restricted to taking deposits of not less than $100,000 with a term to maturity of at least three months. At the end of 1992, there were 147 deposit-taking companies, and their total deposit liability to customers was $19 billion.

Apart from deposit-taking, conventional lending and foreign exchange dealing, banks and deposit-taking companies in Hong Kong are increasingly diversifying into other financial services, including securities business, fund management and the provision of investment advice.

Dealers in securities, investment advisers, commodity dealers and commodity-trading advisers and their representatives are required to be registered with the Securities and Futures Commission. To obtain registration, they must comply with the requirements (including the 'fit and proper' test) stipulated in the Securities Ordinance, the Commodities Trading Ordinance and the Securities and Futures Commission Ordinance. At the end of 1992, there were 9 242 registered persons. Of the 311 registered corporate securities dealers, 150 were from overseas. Of the 105 commodities dealers, 41 were from overseas.

Only members of the Stock Exchange of Hong Kong Limited are permitted to trade on the Stock Exchange. At the end of 1992, the Stock Exchange had 620 corporate and individual members. Only shareholders who have applied for and been granted membership of the Hong Kong Futures Exchange Limited can trade on the Futures Exchange. At the end of 1992, the Futures Exchange had 90 members.

Under the Insurance Companies Ordinance, insurance companies are authorised by the Insurance Authority to transact business in Hong Kong. At the end of 1992, there were 233 authorised companies. Of these, 127 were overseas companies from 29 countries.

Financial Markets

Hong Kong has a mature and active foreign exchange market, which forms an integral part of the corresponding global market. The link with other major overseas centres enables foreign exchange dealing to continue 24 hours a day round the world. With an average daily turnover of around US$61 billion in April 1992, Hong Kong is among the largest markets in Asia, along with Tokyo and Singapore. Besides the Hong Kong dollar, most major currencies are actively traded in Hong Kong, including the US dollar, Deutschemark, Yen, Sterling, Swiss franc, Australian dollar and Canadian dollar. As a market in foreign exchange, Hong Kong is favoured by a host of factors such as a favourable time zone location, a large volume of trade and other external transactions, the presence of a large number of international banks with experience in foreign exchange transactions, the absence of exchange controls, and a highly advanced telecommunications system.

Equally well established and active is the interbank money market which had an average daily turnover of HK$38 billion in November 1991. Wholesale Hong Kong dollar deposits and foreign currency deposits (mainly in US dollars) are traded both among authorised institutions in Hong Kong, and between local and overseas institutions. The interbank money market is mainly for short-term money, with maturities ranging from overnight to 12 months for both Hong Kong dollars and US dollars. The traditional lenders of Hong Kong dollars in the market tend to be the locally-incorporated banks, while the major borrowers are those foreign banks without a strong Hong Kong dollar deposit base. As an indication of the size of the market, at the end of 1992, Hong Kong dollar interbank liabilities accounted for 33 per cent of the total Hong Kong dollar liabilities of the banking sector and foreign currency interbank liabilities accounted for 77 per cent of total foreign currency liabilities of the banking sector.

The launch of the Exchange Fund Bills programme in March 1990 has invigorated the local capital markets. Commencing with the weekly issue of 91-day bills, the programme was expanded to include fortnightly issues of 182-day bills in October 1990 and issues of 364-day bills every four weeks in February 1991. The bills are issued in paperless form for the account of the Exchange Fund and are used as a monetary market instrument. They are available in minimum denominations of HK$500,000 and are issued on a discount basis by tenders which are open to recognised dealers selected from institutions authorised under the Banking Ordinance. To promote secondary market activity, 22 recognised dealers have additionally been appointed as market makers. One of their obligations is to quote two-way yields for the bills during normal money market trading hours. At the end of 1992, outstanding issues of 91-day, 182-day and 364-day bills amounted to $12.5 billion, $4.5 billion and $3.4 billion respectively.

The Government Bond Programme launched in mid-November 1991 marked another significant development in the local capital markets. As with the Exchange Fund Bills Programme, both recognised dealers and market makers have been appointed under the bond programme. The bonds are available in minimum denominations of HK$50,000. They are issued in paperless form through tenders which are open to recognised dealers and market makers. Initially, two-year bonds have been introduced to provide continuity in the maturity spectrum of the government debt market. Longer-term bonds may be issued later, having regard to the government's requirements and the development of the bond programme. At the end of 1992, outstanding value of the bonds stood at $3.0 billion. Unlike the Exchange Fund Bills which are issued for the purposes of creating an additional money market instrument to assist in maintaining exchange rates stability, the bonds are issued for the purposes of financing capital expenditure incurred by the government. The bond proceeds therefore are credited to the Capital Investment Fund and Capital Works Reserve Fund.

The local capital markets are also an important source of finance for corporate borrowers. The two main types of negotiable debt instruments traded in the market are certificates of deposit issued by authorised institutions and commercial paper issued by other organisations and companies. Although the majority of issuers are locally-based institutions, a number of non-resident institutions have also come to tap the local capital markets. Some examples were the four issues of Hong Kong dollar bonds issued by the World Bank during 1989 to 1991; the Hong Kong dollar and US dollar bonds issued by the Asian Development Bank in November 1991, May 1992 and October 1992, as well as the Hong Kong dollar bonds issued by the International Finance Corporation in August 1992. All these issues have been well received by the market.

The stock market provides another important source of capital for local enterprises. It attracts both local and overseas investors. At the end of 1992, 413 public companies, with a total market capitalisation of $1,332 billion, were listed on the Stock Exchange of Hong Kong Limited. This has made Hong Kong the second largest stock market in Asia after Japan.

The Hong Kong Futures Exchange has offered futures contracts in sugar, soya beans, gold, Hang Seng Index and Sub-Indices and interbank interest rate. Trading in each of the Hang Seng Sub-Indices, – Commerce and Industry, Properties, Finance and Utilities – commenced in the second half of 1991. Helped by the active local stock market, trading in Hang Seng Index futures increased markedly during the year. Trading in soya beans futures and sugar futures ceased on March 1, and October 1, 1992 respectively. The Hong Kong Futures Exchange introduced trading in stock index options on March 5, 1993.

The Chinese Gold and Silver Exchange Society operates one of the largest gold bullion markets in the world. Gold traded through the society is of 99 per cent fineness, weighed in taels (one tael equals approximately 1.2 troy ounces) and quoted in Hong Kong dollars. Prices follow closely those in the other major gold markets in London, Zurich and New York.

There is another active gold market in Hong Kong, in which the main participants are banks, major international bullion houses and gold trading companies. It is commonly known as the Loco-London gold market, with prices quoted in US dollars per troy ounce of gold of 99.95 per cent fineness and with delivery in London. Trading in this market has expanded in recent years.

Regulation of the Financial Sector

The government has consistently worked towards providing a favourable environment in the financial sector, with sufficient regulation to ensure as far as possible sound business standards and confidence in the institutional framework, but without unnecessary impediments of a bureaucratic or fiscal nature.

The authority for the prudential supervision of banks, restricted licence banks and deposit-taking companies, collectively called authorised institutions, is vested in the Commissioner of Banking. His authority is derived from the Banking Ordinance which replaced earlier banking and deposit-taking companies ordinances in 1986. The provisions of the ordinance relate to the regulation of banking business, particularly the business of taking deposits, and the supervision of authorised institutions, so as to provide a measure of protection to depositors and to promote the general stability and effective operation of the banking system.

The Commissioner's Office has broadened its approach to supervision which has hitherto been reliant on on-site examinations. Examinations are still an integral part of the supervisory process, but are supplemented by off-site reviews and prudential meetings with authorised institutions. Off-site reviews involve the analysis of the regular statistical returns, and accounting and other management information supplied by institutions with a view to assessing their performance and compliance with the Banking Ordinance. Such reviews are followed by prudential interviews with institutions' senior management, at which the business, prospects and potential areas of concern of institutions are discussed. This broader approach to supervision is enhancing the office's ability to identify potential areas of concern which can be followed up by on-site examinations. The principles of the revised concordant issued by the Committee on Banking Regulations and Supervisory Practices, which meets regularly at Basle in Switzerland, and the principles of worldwide supervision of banking groups based in Hong Kong, are accepted and practised.

Following a review of the arrangements for the co-ordination of banking supervisors in the supervision of international banking groups, the Basle Committee issued in June 1992 a set of minimum standards that the G-10 countries have agreed to apply in the supervision of international banking groups and their cross-border establishments. These standards are designed to provide greater assurance that no international bank can operate in future without being subject to effective consolidated supervision. Hong Kong's authorisation and supervisory regime are already largely in conformity with these standards. To ensure full compliance with the new standards, changes were introduced in September to the criteria dealing with home supervision for bank licence applications from overseas incorporated banks. The home supervisor of a foreign applicant must have established, or be working to establish, the necessary capabilities to meet the minimum standards.

The Securities and Futures Commission, which was established in May 1989 in response to the weakness in Hong Kong's financial markets at the time of the October 1987 world stock market crash, exercises prudential supervision of the securities, financial investment and commodities futures industry in Hong Kong. It administers the Securities and Futures Commission Ordinance, the Securities Ordinance, the Protection of Investors Ordinance, the Commodities Trading Ordinance, the Stock Exchanges Unification Ordinance, the Securities (Disclosure of Interests) Ordinance and the Securities (Insider Dealing) Ordinance.

The Securities Ordinance and the Stock Exchanges Unification Ordinance, together with the Securities and Futures Commission Ordinance, provide a framework within which dealings in securities are conducted and the Stock Exchange operates, enabling trading in securities to be regulated. They require the registration of dealers, dealing partnerships, investment advisers and other intermediaries and provide for the investigation of suspected malpractice in securities transactions and the maintenance of a compensation fund to compensate clients of defaulting brokers.

The Protection of Investors Ordinance prohibits the use of fraudulent or reckless means to induce investors to buy or sell securities, or to induce them to take part in any investment arrangement in respect of property other than securities (the latter being controlled by the Securities Ordinance). It regulates the issue of publications related to such investments by prohibiting any advertisement inviting investors to invest without the advertisement first being submitted to the commission for authorisation.

The Commodities Trading Ordinance, together with the Securities and Futures Commission Ordinance, provides a regulatory framework within which the Futures Exchange operates and dealers, commodity trading advisers and representatives conduct their business. It includes provisions for the registration of dealers and their representatives and the maintenance of a compensation fund to compensate clients of defaulting commodity dealers.

Two important components of the regulatory framework in Hong Kong are the Securities (Insider Dealing) Ordinance and the Securities (Disclosure of Interests) Ordinance, which were brought into operation in September 1991. The Securities (Insider Dealing) Ordinance provides much stricter penalties for insider dealing than those previously applicable. The Securities (Disclosure of Interests) Ordinance requires that company shareholders with 10 per cent or more of the voting shares of a listed company disclose their interests and dealing publicly and that directors and executives disclose certain dealings.

The Office of the Commissioner of Insurance exercises prudential supervision of the insurance industry in Hong Kong. It administers the Insurance Companies Ordinance which brings all classes of insurance business under a comprehensive system of regulation and control by the Commissioner of Insurance (Insurance Authority). Conducting insurance business in or from Hong Kong is restricted to authorised companies, to Lloyd's and to certain underwriters approved by the Governor in Council. All new applications for authorisation are subject to careful scrutiny by the Insurance Authority to ensure that only insurers of good repute who meet all the criteria of the ordinance are admitted. The ordinance stipulates minimum share capital and solvency requirements for all authorised insurers and requires them to submit financial statements and other relevant information to the authority annually. It provides that any person who is not considered by the authority to be a fit and proper person to be associated with an authorised insurance company cannot acquire a position of influence in relation to such company. It also empowers the authority to intervene in the conduct of the business of insurance companies in certain circumstances. Where the authority has cause for concern, it may take remedial or precautionary measures to safeguard the interests of policy holders and claimants, including the limitation of premium income, the restriction of new business, the placing of assets in custody and petitioning for winding-up the company involved.

The Office of the Commissioner of Insurance will assume responsibility for the regulation of private sector retirement schemes when the Occupational Retirement Schemes Ordinance is brought into operation in mid 1993. The object of the ordinance is to provide greater certainty that retirement benefits promised to employees will be paid when they fall due. The regulatory framework is based on the four guiding principles of separation of assets, sufficient funding, independent audit and disclosure of information. It is estimated that over 20 000 schemes will be registered within the prescribed two-year transitional period on commencement of the ordinance.

Self-regulatory measures to strengthen discipline in the insurance market have been formulated by the insurance industry after consultation with the government. The measures comprise the adoption by the insurance industry in 1989 of two Statements of Insurance Practice governing the writing of insurance contracts for long term and general insurance business, and the establishment in February 1990 of an Insurance Claims Complaints Bureau which provides an independent avenue for resolving claims disputes arising from personal insurance policies. The government is also in dialogue with the industry over the proposals for the self-regulation of insurance intermediaries (i.e. agents and brokers). The self-regulatory system will benefit Hong Kong as a developing international insurance centre.

The Securities and Futures Commission
The Securities and Futures Commission (SFC) was established on May 1, 1989, following enactment of the Securities and Futures Commission Ordinance. The enactment of the ordinance represented a first important phase in the overhaul of securities legislation in Hong Kong and the implementation of some of the major recommendations made by the Securities Review Committee in May 1988.

The ordinance transfers the functions of the former Securities Commission, the Commodities Trading Commission and the Office of the Commissioner for Securities and Commodities Trading to the SFC. It provides a general regulatory framework for the securities and futures industries, leaving certain elements to be provided by regulations, administrative procedures and guidelines developed by the commission.

The SFC was established as an autonomous statutory body outside the civil service. It has 10 directors, half executive and half non-executive. The Governor appoints the directors and may give policy directions to the commission. Each year the commission must present the Financial Secretary with a report and an audited statement of its accounts, which are laid before the Legislative Council.

The SFC seeks advice on policy matters from its Advisory Committee, whose 12 independent members are appointed by the Governor and are broadly representative of market participants and relevant professions. Decisions of the SFC relating to matters concerning the registration of persons and intervention in their business are subject to appeal to the Securities and Futures Appeals Panel.

The SFC is funded largely by the market and partly by the government. Market contribution is in the form of fees and charges for specific services and functions performed (on a cost recovery basis), plus a statutory levy on transactions recorded on the Stock and Futures Exchanges. The annual budget is estimated at about $180 million. As of December 31, 1992, the SFC had a total establishment of 225.

In its first three years of operation, the SFC has taken steps to develop a detailed framework of securities regulation that brings Hong Kong in line with inter-nationally-accepted standards of market regulation and practice. As part of this exercise, it has issued revised versions of the Code on Unit Trusts and Mutual Funds and the Code on Takeovers and Mergers. The revised versions bring the codes in line with the increasingly sophisticated investment environment and incorporate a number of features designed to deal with situations which are unique to Hong Kong. Two new Codes, a Code on Investment-Linked Assurance and Pooled Retirement Funds and a Code on Immigration-Linked Investment Schemes, have also been issued, enhancing the level of

Preceding page: *American singer Diana Ross appeared in concert at Hong Kong Coliseum.*

Left and right: *Illusionist David Copperfield amazes his Hong Kong audiences.*

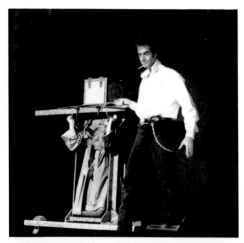

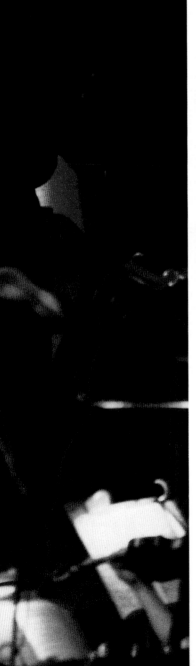

Left: *French pianist Richard Clayderman is accompanied by his own orchestra.*

Below: *'Spanish Passion' is the apt title of the entertainment presented by guitarist Paco Peña and his Flamenco Dance Company.*

The world famous Vienna Boys' Choir.

protection for investors of these funds within the framework of the Protection of Investors Ordinance.

The SFC has been encouraging the development of more efficient equity trading systems and a greater variety of securities and futures products. It has been working closely with the Hong Kong Securities Clearing Company in order to implement the proposed new automated book-entry central clearing and settlement system, which began clearing stock market transactions on a continuous net settlement basis in October 1992. The new clearing and settlement system is a major achievement for the Hong Kong market, allowing the development of an automated transaction and execution system (which is well underway), while at the same time improving settlement efficiency, enhancing risk management capability, and increasing trading capacity. In the first six months of 1992, capacity problems caused by the sharp increases in transaction volume on the Stock Exchange of Hong Kong highlighted the absolute necessity of a more modern system for clearing and settling trades, as well as the necessity for an automated trading system.

The SFC and the Stock Exchange have taken steps to develop the necessary systems for introducing short-selling and stock borrowing and lending, and are working towards the development of new financial products such as traded options. The Stock Exchange is also examining the viability of listing PRC-based companies in Hong Kong, while maintaining adequate standards of investor protection. The SFC is also working on a rationalisation and updating of Hong Kong's legislative framework for securities and futures regulations into a coherent, well-organised and user-friendly body of securities law.

Hong Kong as an International Financial Centre

The favourable geographical position of Hong Kong, which provides a bridge in the time gap between North America and Europe, together with strong links with China and other economies in the South-East Asian region as well as excellent communications with the rest of the world, have helped Hong Kong to develop into an important international financial centre. The absence of any restrictions on capital flows in and out the territory has also contributed to this.

Foreign banks in Hong Kong tend to be the premier banks in their countries of incorporation and this is illustrated by the fact that 79 of the top 100 banks in the world in 1992 have operations in the territory. In addition, many merchant banks or investment banks of world standing operate in Hong Kong. A substantial proportion of the transactions in the banking sector are international in nature: more than 60 per cent of the sector's aggregate assets and liabilities are external, spreading over more than 100 countries. The financial markets, particularly in foreign exchange and gold, form an integral part of the corresponding global markets. Moreover, Hong Kong serves as an important centre for the intermediation of international flows of savings and investment, particularly through the syndication of loans and international fund management. International investors play a significant and increasing role in Hong Kong, and Hong Kong investment overseas is also believed to be considerable.

The Financial Scene

A mutual agreement was announced on February 19, 1992 by the Provisional Liquidator of the Bank of Credit and Commerce Hong Kong Ltd. (BCCHK) and the Hong Kong

Chinese Bank to terminate negotiations on the Provisional Agreement for the transfer of the assets and recorded liabilities of BCCHK which had come into effect on November 22, 1991. The termination of the agreement was necessitated by the emergence of large claims from the liquidators of the various BCCI group operations in other parts of the world which could not be researched or evaluated within a time-frame consistent with the take-over of the business, and in the absence of a sufficient guarantee against unrecorded liabilities. It was deemed necessary by the Provisional Liquidator in the interests of preserving assets of the bank to seek an order for the liquidation of the bank as an early solution to the problem appeared unlikely. Subsequently, the High Court ordered the formal liquidation of the bank on March 2, 1992.

In July 1992, the Liquidator announced a Scheme of Arrangement which would enable any unsecured creditor whose claim was HK$100,000 or less to receive the full amount in priority, or to continue to rank for dividend *pari passu* if his claim was greater than HK$100,000 unless he elected to accept HK$100,000 in full satisfaction of his claim. A simple majority in number and 75 per cent in value of creditors who would be receiving less than full payment (i.e. those with deposits in excess of HK$100,000) voting in favour of the scheme was required by law.

The scheme was approved at a meeting of scheme creditors on September 1 and was formally approved by the Court on September 14 with no opposition lodged. Payment under the scheme to the 30 000 creditors owed $100,000 or less began on September 21, 1992, while the other large creditors owed more than $100,000 are being paid a first dividend of 41 per cent from the same date as their claims are adjudicated and admitted, and further payments will be made to them in the course of the liquidation when further assets are recovered. This represented an unprecedented bank liquidation in that 85 per cent of creditors by number received payment in full only six months after the winding-up order was made. This was made possible by the relatively high liquidity and asset quality of BCCHK which had been ringfenced from the rest of the BCCI Group by effective supervisory measures.

Following the closure of BCCHK in July 1992, there was renewed pressure for the introduction of a deposit protection scheme (DPS) in Hong Kong, principally for the protection of the interests of small depositors in the event of bank failures.

To assess public opinion on the matter, a consultation paper was published in February 1992 inviting submissions by end of May. About 50 submissions from various organisations and individuals were received, and the views expressed were divergent. At the same time, other alternatives were also considered, including a proposal to afford priority claim to small depositors in the event of a bank liquidation. The Standing Committee on Company Law Reform was consulted at the end of October on the proposal. The Standing Committee gave its support to the concept. A decision was taken in January 1993 that a DPS should not be pursued, but instead legislative amendments should be sought to give effect to the proposal.

In 1992, the local financial scene was characterised by the following features. Firstly, the exchange rate of the Hong Kong dollar against the US dollar remained stable under the linked exchange rate system throughout the year. Secondly, local interest rates remained low and moved downward in line with the interest rates in the US. Thirdly, the growth rate of Hong Kong dollar domestic loans and advances slowed down during the year, while the growth in Hong Kong dollar deposits picked up strongly since the second quarter.

During 1992, the market exchange rate of the Hong Kong dollar against the US dollar moved within a narrow range of HK$7.72 and HK$7.78 to US$1. During the second quarter, the exchange rate of the Hong Kong dollar strengthened to around HK$7.73 in April from 7.78 at end-91. Such a move could have been triggered by the enthusiasm of foreign investors in the Hong Kong stock market. The exchange rate then moved around the range between HK$7.73 to 7.76 during May to August 1992. At the end of the year, it closed at HK$7.74.

Under the linked exchange rate system, the overall exchange value of the Hong Kong dollar, as measured by the effective exchange rate index, is influenced predominantly by the movements of the US dollar against other major currencies. Reversing the trend in the latter part of 1991, the US dollar rebounded strongly during the first quarter of 1992. The effective exchange rate index of the Hong Kong dollar rose from 109.2 at the end of 1991 to 113.2 on April 21. However, in the face of a slow recovery pace of the US economy and the substantial interest rate differential in favour of the European currencies, the US dollar weakened against other major currencies during the second quarter and the first part of the third quarter. In mid-September, the US dollar rebounded briefly amid the chaos in the foreign exchange market in Europe. Reflecting the movement of the US dollar, the effective exchange rate index fell from a high of 113.2 to 108.3 in early September before picking up to close the year at 114.2.

During the first four months of 1992, the three-month Hong Kong Interbank Offered Rate (HIBOR) generally stayed above the corresponding Euro-Dollar deposit rate. The HIBOR eased markedly in late April subsequent to two liquidity injections by the Exchange Fund on April 28 and 29. Overnight HIBOR dropped from 5.750 per cent on April 28 to 4.125 per cent on April 29 and the three-month HIBOR dropped from 4.625 per cent to 4.250 per cent. The interest rate gap between the three-month HIBOR and the corresponding Euro-Dollar was completely closed in mid-May. Since then, the former has fallen below the latter. In August, influenced by several large share flotation exercises, the three-month HIBOR firmed up and rose above the Euro-Dollar rate. But it fell below the Euro-Dollar rate again following a liquidity injection of HK$512 million into the system by the Exchange Fund on August 6. Since mid-September, the three-month HIBOR moved closely with the corresponding Euro-Dollar rates. Their average differential for 1992 was 0.13 of a percentage point, compared with the corresponding 0.29 percentage point recorded in 1991.

During the year, in line with the movements in local money market interest rates, deposit rates administered by the Hong Kong Association of Banks were adjusted downward across-the-board on three occasions, by half of a percentage point on May 4, by one percentage point on May 25 and by another half of a percentage point on July 6.

Hong Kong dollar deposits grew by 13.2 per cent during 1992, lower than the growth rate of 16.2 per cent in 1991 but was still broadly consistent with the growth in gross domestic product in money terms. On the other hand, the annual increase of foreign currency deposits slowed down to 6.3 per cent in 1992 from 8.3 per cent in 1991. The growth of offshore deposits booked in Hong Kong probably slackened during the year, largely reflecting the sharp deceleration in monetary expansion in the USA and Japan as a result of their slowing economies. Taken together, total customer deposits (in all currencies) increased by 9.3 per cent in 1992, compared with 11.6 per cent in 1991. The relative share of Hong Kong dollar deposits to total deposits rose to 45.5 per cent at end-1992, from 44.0 per cent at end-1991.

Hong Kong dollar M1, M2 and M3 rose by 24.8 per cent, 14.3 per cent and 13.7 per cent respectively in 1992. The corresponding increases for total M1, M2 and M3 were 21.1 per cent, 10.8 per cent and 9.5 per cent.

Hong Kong dollar loans recorded a growth of 12.2 per cent in 1992 while foreign currency loans increased by 9.0 per cent. Analysed by major categories, loans for use in Hong Kong (including those for trade financing) increased by 10.9 per cent. Reflecting measures announced by the government in November 1991 to cool down the overheated property market, growth in residential mortgage loans slowed down from 35.4 per cent in 1991 to 13.6 per cent in 1992. Moreover, banks generally maintained a tight credit policy on mortgage loans. In particular, the maximum loan-to-valuation ratio was kept at 70 per cent. The quarterly growth rate of these mortgage loans slowed down from 8.8 per cent in the second quarter in 1991 to an average of 4.0 per cent in the first two quarters of 1992. Loans for trade financing recorded a moderate decrease of 4.0 per cent during 1992. Loans to other major sectors, including wholesale and retail trades, building, construction, property development and investment, transport, manufacturing and financial concerns, all recorded some increases during the year.

Turning to the financial markets, the expansion in the government borrowing programme facilitated the further development of the local capital markets. The Exchange Fund Bills market was expanded in February 1991 to include 364-day bills and the government bonds programme was first launched in November 1991. Both the bills and the government bonds were well received by the market with tenders invariably several times oversubscribed. The yields for the bills were around 20 to 60 basis points below the corresponding Hong Kong interbank offered rate at end 1992, depending on the maturity of the bills while the yields for the bonds were around 90 basis points above the corresponding US Treasury bonds. Daily turnover of the bills and bonds, taken together, in the secondary market averaged $8.2 billion, or 35 per cent of the total amount of bills and bonds outstanding, at $23.3 billion at end-1992.

New issue activity in respect of other debt instruments in 1992 remained relatively moderate as funds can be raised through the buoyant stock market. A total of 99 new issues of negotiable certificates of deposit were launched during 1992, of which 87 were denominated in Hong Kong dollars. Of these 87 issues, 66 were arranged on fixed-rate terms and the remaining 21 on floating-rate terms. At the end of 1992, the outstanding value of Hong Kong dollar-denominated negotiable certificates of deposit amounted to $26.9 billion, compared with $23.2 billion at end-1991; 52.3 per cent of them were held outside the local banking sector.

Of the six new issues of commercial paper and other debt instruments reported to the Securities and Futures Commission during 1992, five were denominated in Hong Kong dollars. Following a successful issue of US dollar bonds last year, the Asian Development Bank launched in May 1992 its first issue of Hong Kong dollar bonds, amounting to HK$500 million, which will mature in 1999. The Asian Development Bank launched another five-year Dragon bond issue in Hong Kong in October 1992 to raise US$300 million. These bonds are listed on the stock exchanges of Hong Kong, Singapore and Taipei. In August, the International Finance Corporation, a World Bank affiliate, also launched a maiden issue of five-year Hong Kong dollar bonds involving an issue size of HK$500 million.

In the local stock market, the shares prices gathered strong upward momentum since early 1992. Supported by favourable corporate results, the Hang Seng Index rose and rallied further in the second quarter. Continuing the upward trend established during the first two quarters and partly stimulated by the release of the impressive Exchange Fund size on July 15, local stock market prices rallied to 6 163 points on July 16. However since then the market underwent a period of consolidation. It then rebounded in early September and rose to a record high of 6 447 on November 12 before closing the year at 5 512, 28.3 per cent higher than the level at the end of 1991. The gain in the Hang Seng Index during the year of 28 per cent has outperformed those in many overseas stock markets. Average daily turnover in the local stock market increased notably to $2.8 billion in 1992, compared with $1.3 billion in 1991.

The number of newly listed companies increased markedly to 64 in 1992, raising a total of $12 billion. The more optimistic market sentiment as well as the reduction in the minimum requirements regarding issue capital and the length of track record by the Stock Exchange contributed to this increase. In addition to new share issues, funds were tapped through rights issues and open offers ($11.2 billion) and private placements ($26 billion).

The Hong Kong Futures Exchange launched futures contracts based on the four Hang Seng sub-indices (Commerce and Industry, Finance, Properties and Utilities) in the second half of 1991. Turnover in these contracts was moderate. Trading in the Hang Seng Index futures was more active. Daily turnover averaged 4 470 contracts in 1992, compared with 2 295 contracts in the preceding year.

Trading in commodity futures and interest rate futures remained modest. For the year as a whole, total turnover in gold futures amounted to 1 000 lots (100 troy ounces each), while turnover in interest rate futures was 205 contracts. Due to decreasing turnover, the Hong Kong Futures Exchange decided to terminate the trading of soya bean contracts in April and sugar contracts in October 1992. Turnover in soya bean futures amounted to 4 688 lots (30 000 kg each) from January to March, while turnover in sugar futures amounted to 8 598 lots (112 000 lb each) from January to September.

The price of Loco-London gold moved within a narrow range between US$360 to US$331 in 1992. Partly affected by the chaotic situation in the European forex markets around mid-September, the price of Loco-London gold rose, from US$336 at mid-August to US$352 per troy ounce at mid-September and closed the year at US$333. The price of gold at the Chinese Gold and Silver Exchange Society showed similar movements. At the end of 1992, it was HK$3,078 per tael. Turnover on the exchange totalled 24 million taels in 1992, similar to the level in 1991.

The number of unit trusts and mutual funds picked up to 900 at end-1992 from 854 at end-1991. Of the 112 newly authorised funds approved by the Securities and Futures Commission during the year, nine were China funds. Among the different types of funds, Hong Kong equity funds recorded the best performance in terms of investment return in the past year.

Following the conclusion of the Gulf war and in line with moves by the international community, Hong Kong lifted on March 15 the freeze on certain assets of Kuwait, introduced on August 6, 1990. The restrictions on certain Iraqi assets are still in place in accordance with the Hong Kong (Control of Gold, Securities, Payments and Credits; Kuwait and Republic of Iraq) Order 1990. In line with the resolution adopted by the United Nations Security Council on May 30, 1992, the Serbia and Montenegro (United

Nations Sanctions) (Dependent Territories) Order 1992 came into force on June 5, 1992 imposing restrictions on a number of transactions with Serbia and Montenegro and persons connected with Serbia and Montenegro. Guidelines on the operation of the Order were also published on July 18, 1992.

Monetary Policy

A linked exchange-rate system was introduced on October 17, 1983 after a period of much instability in the exchange rate of the Hong Kong dollar. Under the system, certificates of indebtedness (CIs) issued by the Exchange Fund which the two note-issuing banks are required to hold as cover for the issue of Hong Kong dollar notes are issued and redeemed against payments in US dollars at a fixed exchange rate of HK$7.80 to US$1. In practice therefore any increase in note circulation is matched by a US dollar payment to the Exchange Fund, and any decrease in note circulation is matched by a US dollar payment from the Exchange Fund. The two note-issuing banks in turn extend this fixed exchange rate to their note transactions with all other banks in Hong Kong. In the foreign exchange market, the exchange rate of the Hong Kong dollar continues to be determined by forces of supply and demand. However, the interplay of arbitrage and competition between banks ensures that the market exchange rate stays close to the rate of HK$7.80 to US$1 fixed for the CIs.

With the adoption of the linked rate system, the exchange rate is no longer a variable in the economy's adjustment process. Interest rates, the money supply and the level of economic activity over time adjust automatically to balance of payments pressures. If there is an outflow of money, caused for example by a tendency for the balance of payments to be in deficit, there will be a contraction in the money supply and higher interest rates. These will, on the one hand, induce an inflow of funds to offset the original outflow arising from the balance of payments deficit and, on the other hand, reduce domestic demand, restrain imports and enhance export competitiveness and thereby also contribute to restoring the external balance. Alternatively, if there is an inflow of money, caused for example by a tendency for the balance of payments to be in surplus, there will be an expansion in the money supply and lower interest rates. These will, on the one hand, induce outflow of funds and, on the other hand, increase domestic demand and imports and erode export competitiveness, again restoring the external imbalance.

When there is a tendency for the Hong Kong dollar to weaken relative to the US dollar, Hong Kong dollar interest rates will rise relative to US dollar interest rates. They may rise to a level where the interest rate gap between the Hong Kong dollar and the US dollar is large enough to stem or reverse the outflow from the Hong Kong dollar. Similarly, when there is a tendency for the Hong Kong dollar to strengthen relative to the US dollar, Hong Kong dollar interest rates will fall relative to US dollar interest rates. They may fall to a level where the interest rate gap between the Hong Kong dollar and the US dollar is large enough to stem or reverse the inflow into the Hong Kong dollar. From the monetary policy point of view, it is sometimes desirable to expedite this adjustment process in order that the economy is not unduly disrupted by speculative flows of funds aimed at manipulating the value of the Hong Kong dollar. So that the interest rate gap could be large enough to produce the corrective inflows or outflows, there therefore should ideally be no limit on how low or high interest rates can move.

The lower limit for interest rates was eliminated when the Hong Kong Association of Banks, after consultation with the Financial Secretary, introduced in January 1988 revised interest rate rules whereby banks may impose deposit charges ('negative interest rates') on large Hong Kong dollar credit balances maintained by their customers, if the need arises. The purpose of the revised rules was to deter persistent speculation on a revaluation of the Hong Kong dollar which emerged in late 1987 and continued in early 1988. In practice however there has been no need to impose the deposit charges, as the mere threat of their imposition has been effective in deterring speculation.

The upper limit for interest rates was removed in July 1988 when the Money Lenders Ordinance was amended to exempt all authorised institutions under the Banking Ordinance from the restriction on lending money at an effective interest rate exceeding 60 per cent per annum.

To enable the government, through the use of the Exchange Fund, to exercise more effective influence over liquidity and interest rates in the interbank market and thus to assist it in maintaining exchange rate stability within the framework of the linked exchange rate system, the Accounting Arrangements were entered into in mid-July 1988 between the Exchange Fund and the Hongkong and Shanghai Banking Corporation Limited (HSBC) as the Management Bank of the Clearing House of the Hong Kong Association of Banks. Under these arrangements, HSBC maintains a Hong Kong dollar account with the Exchange Fund. The government uses the account at its discretion to effect settlement of its Hong Kong dollar transactions with HSBC or with other banks. HSBC is required to ensure that the net clearing balance (NCB) of the rest of the banking system does not exceed its balance in the account and that the NCB is not in debit. Otherwise it will have to pay interest to the Exchange Fund.

Consequently, the Exchange Fund effectively became the ultimate provider of liquidity in the interbank market, a role which was previously performed by HSBC. Through its borrowing Hong Kong dollars in the interbank market, or selling foreign currencies for Hong Kong dollars in the foreign exchange market, the fund is able to reduce the supply of Hong Kong dollars and hence raise interest rates in the interbank market, thereby offsetting a weakening of the exchange rate of the Hong Kong dollar against the US dollar. Similarly, it may increase interbank liquidity and lower interest rates by taking action in the opposite direction, thereby offsetting a strengthening of the exchange rate.

Under these accounting arrangements, the government can also influence monetary conditions in the interbank market through its buying or selling of Hong Kong dollar financial assets of acceptable quality. For this purpose, the government has developed a programme for the issue of short-term paper for the account of the Exchange Fund (the so-called Exchange Fund bills). The bills are designed to complement the Accounting Arrangements by providing the Exchange Fund with an additional instrument for conducting money market operations.

In June 1992, the Liquidity Adjustment Facility was introduced to assist banks in making late adjustments to their liquidity positions. Bid rate (for taking overnight deposits from banks) and offer rate (for lending overnight money to banks) are set, having regard to the level of interest rate appropriate for maintaining exchange rate stability. These rates provide an additional tool for the government to influence the movements of the interbank interest rates.

The Exchange Fund

The Hong Kong Government's Exchange Fund was established by the Currency Ordinance of 1935 (later renamed the Exchange Fund Ordinance). Since its inception, the fund has held the backing to the note issue. In 1976, its role was expanded, with the assets of the Coinage Security Fund (which held the backing for coins issued by the government) as well as the bulk of foreign currency assets held in the government's General Revenue Account, being transferred to the fund. On December 31, 1978, the Coinage Security Fund was merged with the Exchange Fund.

In 1976, the government began to transfer the fiscal reserves of its General Revenue Account (apart from the working balances) to the fund. This arrangement was introduced for the safety, economy and advantage of these monies so as to avoid fiscal reserves having to bear the exchange risk arising from investments in foreign currency assets and to centralise the management of the government's financial assets. The fiscal reserves are not permanently appropriated for the use of the Exchange Fund. They are repaid to the General Revenue Account when they are required to meet the obligations of the general revenue.

Thus, the bulk of the government's financial assets are now with the fund, which holds its assets mainly in the form of bank deposits in certain foreign currencies and in Hong Kong dollars, and of marketable interest-bearing instruments in foreign currencies. The principal activity of the fund on a day-to-day basis is management of these assets. Its statutory role as defined in the Exchange Fund Ordinance is to influence the exchange value of the Hong Kong dollar and it intervenes when necessary in the local money market or foreign currency markets to maintain stability. The functions of the fund were extended on the enactment of the Exchange Fund (Amendment) Ordinance 1992 by introducing a secondary and subsidiary role of maintaining the stability and integrity of the monetary and financial systems.

Another function related to the Exchange Fund is the supply of notes and coins to the banking system. Apart from a very small fiduciary issue, which is backed by gilt-edged securities, currency notes in everyday circulation (currently of $10, $20, $50, $100, $500 and $1,000 denominations) may only be issued by the Hongkong and Shanghai Banking Corporation Limited and Standard Chartered Bank, against holdings of certificates of indebtedness issued by the fund.

These non-interest-bearing liabilities of the fund are issued or redeemed as the amount of notes in circulation rises or falls. The fund bears the costs of maintaining the note issue (apart from the proportion of the costs relating to the fiduciary issue), and the net profits of the note issue accrue to the fund. Coins of $5, $2, $1, 50 cents, 20 cents and 10 cents denominations, and currency notes of one-cent denomination, are issued by the government. The total currency in circulation at the end of 1992, with details of its composition, is shown at Appendix 13.

As at December 31, 1991 total assets of the fund stood at $236 billion, of which foreign currency assets amounted to US$29 billion. Accumulated earnings of the fund amounted to $99 billion. The financial position of the fund for the five years 1987–91 is shown at Appendix 13.

Establishment of the Hong Kong Monetary Authority

In order to maintain the continuity and professionalism in Hong Kong's monetary and reserves management and banking supervision, in a way which will command the confidence of the people of Hong Kong and the international financial community, the government announced its decision in October 1992 to seek to establish a Hong Kong Monetary Authority (HKMA). It is planned that the HKMA will be formed by merging the Office of the Exchange Fund with the Office of the Commissioner of Banking and headed by a Chief Executive. The use and management of the Exchange Fund would remain the statutory responsibility of the Financial Secretary although he would delegate his authority to the senior staff of the HKMA as appropriate.

The HKMA would be an integral part of the government and it would initially be staffed mainly by civil servants. The HKMA would, though, be able to employ staff on terms different from those of the civil service in order to attract personnel of the right calibre, experience and expertise. The staff and operating costs of the HKMA would be charged directly to the Exchange Fund instead of to the general revenue, thus taking the HKMA outside the resource allocation constraints of other government departments.

The HKMA would be responsible for the development and execution of monetary policy; overseeing operation of both the money and foreign exchange markets and carrying out money market operations, whenever there is a need to do so, to maintain stability in the market; managing the assets of the Exchange Fund; developing the financial markets in Hong Kong; running the market for government debt; and supervising authorised institutions under the Banking Ordinance. The establishment of the HKMA would not entail the assumption of further central banking functions by the government. There is neither the need nor intention for the two residual central banking roles (i.e. bank notes issue and cheque clearing) to be assumed by the new body.

The HKMA would be accountable to the Financial Secretary, who would continue to be advised by the Exchange Fund Advisory Committee on matters relating to the control of the Exchange Fund. But reinforcing a trend over recent years, the involvement of the committee in monetary and investment matters would become much closer and the committee would function very much like a management board, including advising the Financial Secretary on the annual budget of the HKMA. To reflect the wider ambit of the fund and the increased responsibility of the committee, the membership of the committee would be suitably expanded to include additional distinguished members of the financial and related sectors.

The Exchange Fund (Amendment) Ordinance 1992 providing for the establishment of the Monetary Authority was enacted on December 10, 1992. The ordinance also gave statutory recognition to the monetary policy objectives of Hong Kong. Apart from the primary use of the Exchange Fund to affect the Hong Kong dollar exchange rate, the ordinance made clear that the Financial Secretary could use the Exchange Fund to maintain the stability and the integrity of the monetary and financial systems of Hong Kong, with a view to maintaining Hong Kong as an international financial centre. This secondary purpose would be subordinate to the primary purpose of affecting the exchange value of the Hong Kong dollar. Should there be any conflict, the primary purpose would prevail.

7
INDUSTRY AND TRADE

HONG KONG's trade policy seeks to promote a free, open and stable multilateral trading system; to safeguard Hong Kong's rights and fulfil its obligations as a contracting party to the General Agreement on Tariffs and Trade (GATT) and a party to the Multi-Fibre Arrangement (MFA); within the context of the GATT, to secure, maintain and improve access for Hong Kong's exports and to ensure and maintain the integrity of all measures adopted by Hong Kong to meet its obligations under multilateral and bilateral trade or trade-related agreements.

The role of the government is to facilitate industrial and trade activities within the framework of a free market. It neither protects nor subsidises manufacturers. It nevertheless recognises a responsibility to provide an acceptable industrial infrastructure, particularly in terms of industrial land and manpower for industry, and to make available services which enable industry to become more competitive through productivity growth, quality improvement and product innovation. It also encourages technology transfer through an inward investment promotion programme.

Industrial policies are kept under review by the Trade and Industry Branch of the Government Secretariat, which acts on the advice of the Industry and Technology Development Council (ITDC). Members of the council include prominent industrialists and businessmen, academics, representatives of major industry and trade organisations, and government officers. The ITDC advises the government on the overall development of industry and technology in Hong Kong. To this end, it is assisted by the Technology Review Board and the Technology Committee. The role of the former is to review broad strategic directions in technology development having regard to global technology trends and the local circumstances, while that of the latter is to identify key enabling technologies deemed crucial to sustaining a competitive and healthy economy in Hong Kong. Industry specific committees have also been set up under the council. In addition, the council helps the government to administer the Applied Research and Development (R&D) Scheme which provides funding support to worthwhile applied R&D projects undertaken by private companies. Productivity, product innovation and quality improvement services are mainly provided by the Hong Kong Productivity Council and the Industry Department. The Industry Department also promotes inward investment in Hong Kong's manufacturing industries. Responsibility for providing an efficient infrastructure within which industry can operate successfully rests with a number of government departments and other organisations, but the responsibility for monitoring the adequacy of provision rests with the Industry Department.

On the external relations front, Hong Kong joined the Asia Pacific Economic Co-operation (APEC) forum in November 1991. APEC is an inter-governmental economic forum inaugurated in 1989. The main objectives are to strengthen the multilateral trading system, to assess prospects for and obstacles to increased trade and investment flows within the Asia Pacific region and to identify a range of practical common economic interests. Apart from Hong Kong, current members include the United States, Canada, Australia, New Zealand, Japan, South Korea, China, Chinese Taipei and the six countries of the Association of South-East Asian Nations (ASEAN). Hong Kong became a full member of the Pacific Economic Co-operation Conference (PECC) in May 1991. PECC is a non-governmental organisation comprising tripartite membership drawn from academia and private and public sectors, seeking to develop closer cooperation on trade and economic policy issues within the Asia Pacific region.

In the industrial field, although total employment in manufacturing fell by 13 per cent in 1992 from the previous year's figure, the total value of Hong Kong's manufactured exports rose by one per cent, compared with an increase of two per cent in 1991. Besides confirming its worldwide reputation as a manufacturer and exporter of manufactured consumer goods, Hong Kong also reinforced its growing role as a major service and sourcing centre for the Asian region. The value of the territory's re-exports grew by an impressive 29 per cent in 1992.

Hong Kong's continuing success as a leading manufacturing and commercial centre is due to a simple tax structure and low tax rate, a versatile and industrious workforce, an aggressive and innovative managerial class, efficient transport facilities, a fine harbour, excellent international communications, and the government's firm commitment to free trade and free enterprise. These factors remained as important as ever during the year.

Faced with increasing competition from low-cost economies in the region, rising labour costs at home, and demand in its major export markets for ever-higher standards of quality, Hong Kong's manufacturers can no longer compete in the territory's major export markets on price and speed of response alone. Manufacturers are moving decisively away from labour-intensive production into the manufacture of high-value-added products which can compete on quality. In this respect, the Hong Kong Productivity Council continued to feature in the past year as the government's principal agent in helping the manufacturing sector improve its productivity and move up the value-added ladder. With its expertise in different disciplines, the council offers diversified services including management consultancies, training programmes and technological support services.

At the same time, this restructuring is supported by the government, which is implementing a comprehensive quality improvement programme to develop the territory's existing quality infrastructure and to encourage the greater use of quality assurance in manufacturing through a Quality Awareness Campaign. In addition, the Hong Kong Quality Assurance Agency (HKQAA) has been established to provide third party assessment of companies' quality management systems according to the ISO 9000 standards and to award ISO 9000 certification to companies that meet the necessary standards. These quality improvement activities have helped to enhance the quality of Hong Kong's products and services.

Science and Technology

Science and technology are transforming the way that business is conducted in all areas of economic activity. Constant advancement in science and technology is essential to Hong Kong's continued prosperity. To ensure that Hong Kong can respond to the rapidly changing technological environment and to underline the vital connection between industry and technology, the Government established in early 1992 an Industry and Technology Development Council (ITDC), which replaced the Industry Development Board and the Committee on Science and Technology. With its expanded terms of reference and a more focussed and co-ordinated approach, this new council is better placed to advise the Government on the overall development of industry and technology in Hong Kong.

Hong Kong has a skilled workforce, ready access to information and technology from overseas, and a sound infrastructure to take advantage of opportunities in technology-based industries. The government is investing substantially in infrastructure to support the use and development of technology in Hong Kong. The key elements of this infrastructure include the provision of education and training in science and technology; the provision of land at development cost to high technology industries; the provision of services and facilities to help manufacturers acquire new technologies; the provision of funding support to applied research and development in industry; and the promotion of technology transfer through inward investment.

In June 1992, in recognition of the need for Hong Kong to improve its technological infrastructure, the Industry Department commissioned a study to examine the case for establishing a science park in Hong Kong. The study was completed in November 1992.

The government has also released a $250 million grant and committed another $188 million as an interest bearing loan to meet the initial costs of developing a technology centre in Hong Kong to encourage the growth of technology-based firms. The centre, to be called the Hong Kong Industrial Technology Centre, will be established as a statutory corporation, and will provide accommodation and services for established and fledgling technology-based companies. During the year the Provisional Hong Kong Industrial Technology Centre Company Limited, an interim body pending the establishment of a statutory corporation, began work on planning and developing the technology centre, which is intended to become fully operational in mid-1994.

Electronic Data Interchange

Electronic data interchange, the computer to computer exchange of business information in a standard format, is one of the techniques being implemented worldwide in an attempt to curb the amount of paperwork involved in business and to improve efficiency.

Hong Kong's use of electronic data interchange has expanded considerably during the last few years. The government is keen to encourage this trend as electronic data interchange is seen as an important means of maintaining Hong Kong's competitiveness in international markets.

A particularly important area is the processing of statutory trade documents, such as the lodgement of trade declarations and applications for import and export licences. Following a joint study with Tradelink Electronic Document Services Limited, a group of 11 leading trade-related organisations in Hong Kong, the government agreed to take a substantial shareholding in the company. Tradelink, with government as one of its shareholders, will fund and manage a Community Electronic Trading Service. The service will act as the electronic gateway between the trading community and the relevant government departments, checking and validating electronic submissions before passing them through for approval.

Tradelink will also establish a way for non-computer users to access the service. In this way, both government and the wider trading community can enjoy the full benefits of electronic data interchange as rapidly as possible. An initial service is expected to commence in mid-1994. The service will bring about a significant increase in the number of companies using electronic data interchange and will help generate more demand for other electronic trading services.

In the interest of compatibility, the government agreed that the United Nations Electronic Data Interchange for Administration, Commerce and Transport, a standard language developed by the United Nations for electronic trading, will be adopted for government transactions wherever applicable.

The Industrial Scene

Hong Kong enjoys a worldwide reputation as a producer and exporter of manufactured consumer goods. Although the territory has a thriving construction industry and, as a major trading economy, has developed shipbuilding, ship repair and aircraft engineering industries, light manufacturing industries predominate. About 8.0 per cent of Hong Kong's manufactured products are exported, and clothing, electronic products, watches and clocks, textiles, and plastic products (particularly toys) have for many years accounted for the bulk of this output. The total value of Hong Kong's manufactured exports in 1992 was $234,123 million, and its major export markets were the United States (27.6 per cent), China (26.5 per cent), Germany (6.8 per cent), and the United Kingdom (5.4 per cent). In 1991, the territory was the world's largest exporter (including domestic exports and re-exports) by value of clothing and toys and games, and the second largest exporter of watches.

Manufacturing developed on a large scale in Hong Kong in the 1950s. The territory's small size limited the amount of land which could be made available for industry and precluded the development of heavy or land-intensive industries; its manufacturing industries were therefore characterised by small-scale firms, mostly operating from premises in multi-storey buildings, and manufacturing light consumer goods for export.

For many years, manufacturing was both the territory's largest employer and its most important economic sector, but lost this dominating position in the 1980s. Manufacturing employment fell from 904 709 in 1984 (41.7 per cent of total employment) to 571 181 (23.3 per cent) in 1992, and its contribution to the Gross Domestic Product (GDP) fell from 24.1 per cent in 1984 to 15.5 per cent in 1991. During these years manufacturers took advantage of China's open door policy to shift labour-intensive jobs into China to reap the benefits of the lower land and labour costs there. Manufacturing is now the territory's second largest employer, and makes the third largest contribution to GDP after financial and business services.

There were 41 937 manufacturing establishments in Hong Kong in 1992, of which 36 381 employed fewer than 20 persons, and 39 882 fewer than 50 persons. The remaining 2 055 establishments accounted for more than half Hong Kong's total manufacturing employment. Many smaller establishments are linked with larger factories through an efficient and flexible subcontracting network, which has enabled Hong Kong's manufacturing sector to respond swiftly to changes in external demand.

Clothing

The clothing industry is the largest employer and export-earner. In 1992, it employed 186 743 workers (33 per cent of total manufacturing employment) and earned $77,156 million in exports (33 per cent of Hong Kong's total domestic exports). Hong Kong is one of the world's leading suppliers of clothing, and produces a wide variety of products, from simple accessories to expensive and high-quality fashion wear.

Electronics

The electronics industry (including the manufacture of electronic watches and clocks, and electronic toys) is the second largest employer and export-earner. In 1992, it employed 60 653 workers (11 per cent of total manufacturing employment), and earned $60,291 million in exports (25.8 per cent of total domestic exports). The industry produces a wide range of sophisticated finished products and components, including radio and television sets, calculators, wired and cordless telephones, modems, photocopying equipment, micro-computers, computer memory systems, dot matrix printers, talk-back toys, switching power supplies, multi-layer printed circuit boards, electronic modules, liquid crystal displays, quartz crystals and semiconductor devices, and surface-mounted devices.

Textiles

The textiles industry is the third largest export-earner. It comprises four main sectors: spinning, weaving, knitted fabrics manufacturing and finishing. In 1992, it employed 53 204 workers (nine per cent of total manufacturing employment), and earned $17,226 million in exports (7.4 per cent of total domestic exports). On top of its role as an exporter, the textiles industry is a major supplier of yarns and fabrics of various fibres and blends (mostly cotton) to the local clothing manufacturers who are actually the textiles sector's largest customer.

Watches and Clocks

In 1992, the watches and clocks industry employed 18 995 workers (three per cent of total manufacturing employment) and earned $15,476 million in exports. Besides complete electrical and mechanical watches and clocks, the industry also produces high quality components and accessories. The world's first water watch was manufactured in Hong Kong in 1987.

Plastics

In 1992, the plastic products industry employed 35 347 workers (six per cent of total manu-facturing employment), and earned $7,508 million in exports (3.2 per cent of total domestic exports). Plastic household articles and plastic toys together accounted for 40 per cent of domestic exports of plastic products. Other major export items included travel goods, handbags, footwear, and plastic flowers.

Toys

Hong Kong's toy industry has an international reputation, but its various segments are classified under the plastics, electronics, metal products and other industries in official publications. Considered as a separate industry, the toys industry employed 15 617 persons in 1992, and earned $3,723 million in exports. The manufacture of plastic toys accounted for 77 per cent of employment in the toy industry and 70 per cent of its exports.

Other Industries
Other important light manufacturing industries include metal products, printing, food and beverages, jewellery, industrial machinery, household electrical appliances, and photographic and optical goods. The development of the metal products and industrial machinery industries has enabled Hong Kong to produce sophisticated parts and components and other semi-manufactures of high quality. This has benefited the manufacturing sector in general, as the quality of finished products depends heavily on the capability of the linkage industries which service them.

Hong Kong's shipyards provide a competitive repair service and build a variety of vessels. Several large shipbuilding and repair yards on Tsing Yi Island provide services to the shipping industry and construct and service oil rigs. Hong Kong's aircraft engineering industry has a high international reputation and provides extensive maintenance and repair services. Facilities are available for the complete overhaul of airframes and engines for many types of aircraft.

Overseas Investment in Manufacturing
As at end-1991, there were 536 manufacturing companies in Hong Kong with overseas investment. The total value of direct overseas investment was $34,399 million, and the 536 companies concerned employed 80 736 workers (12.8 per cent of total manufacturing employment) and accounted for 25 per cent of Hong Kong's total domestic exports. The main sources of investment were Japan (32 per cent), the United States (28 per cent), China (11 per cent), and Australia (six per cent). More than three-fifths of this investment was concentrated in five industries: electronics (32 per cent), electrical products (13 per cent), textile and clothing (nine per cent), tobacco (five per cent) and chemical products (five per cent).

Industry Department
One of the main tasks of the Industry Department is to carry out regular studies of Hong Kong's main manufacturing industries, to enable the government to identify constraints on their efficiency and assess where support is needed. In 1992, studies were conducted on the metals and light engineering industries, textiles and clothing industries and on the pace of industrial automation in Hong Kong. The department also conducts annual surveys to estimate the value of overseas investment in Hong Kong's manufacturing industries, and to assess the investment climate in the manufacturing sector.

The department provides information on available industrial support services to manufacturers through its Industrial Extension Service (IES), and encourages them to upgrade their operations by making use of these services. In 1991 a total of 293 visits were made by engineers of the IES, and 67 referrals were made to organisations which could help to solve the problems encountered by the companies concerned. In a number of other cases IES engineers dealt with the problems themselves.

Another major responsibility of the Industry Department is to monitor the availability of land and trained manpower for industry. Industrial land is normally sold by public auction or tender. Land can be sold on special terms where industries are land and capital intensive, or use advanced technology, and where their presence is considered to be economically desirable.

Two industrial estates in Tai Po and Yuen Long have been developed and managed by the Hong Kong Industrial Estates Corporation to accommodate manufacturing processes which employ advanced technology and which cannot be carried out efficiently in ordinary multi-storey buildings. Construction of a third industrial estate at Tseung Kwan O began in August 1991. The first phase with 18 hectares of serviced sites will be available by early 1994. A total of 68 hectares of industrial land will be provided upon completion of site formation work over the rest of the area in early 1995.

Additional land and accommodation were also made available for industry during the year. The government put up for sale by auction or tender 11 pieces of industrial land with a total area of 46 942 square metres, and about 545 000 square metres of flatted factory space were completed by private developers.

Regarding manpower training for industry, technical education and industrial training is available in eight technical institutes and three industrial training centre complexes run by the Vocational Training Council. In addition, the Clothing Industry Training Authority also runs two training centres. To further strengthen manpower training, the Vocational Training Council has decided to convert the Chai Wan Technical Institute into a Technical College and build a new Technical College at Tsing Yi. Both of these are scheduled to commence operation in 1993–4. Technological training at higher levels is provided in Hong Kong's two polytechnics and three universities.

In June 1992 the New Technology Training Scheme was launched. This is providing financial assistance to employers to train, either locally or overseas, their technologists and managers in new technologies strategically important for industrial and economic development. The scheme is administered by the Vocational Training Council and assistance is provided by the Industry Department and the Hong Kong Productivity Council.

During the year the Industry Department played an active role in assisting local manufacturers to comply with environmental measures. In March 1992, the department commissioned a consultancy study on support to industry on environmental matters. The objective of the study is to assess the effects of current and planned environmental legislation on manufacturing in Hong Kong, to identify any weaknesses in the prevailing support mechanisms and to recommend a coherent support strategy. The study is scheduled to be completed by March 1993. The Department also published in March 1992 a booklet entitled 'A Guide to Pollution Control Legislation Affecting Manufacturing Industries 1992'. This will assist manufacturers by providing them with basic information on environmental legislation and where technical advice can be obtained. This booklet will be published annually.

The department was also actively involved in a number of environmental measures outlined in the 1989 White Paper on Pollution in Hong Kong. The department's role is to liaise closely with the concerned industrial organisations to ensure that they are fully aware of the government's proposals on environmental issues and to take their views into account when commenting on the implications of the proposals for Hong Kong's manufacturing industry. Issues covered during the year included the proposed controls on the handling and disposal of chemical waste under the Waste Disposal Ordinance; the proposals for the Chemical Waste Treatment Centre; the extension of MARPOL Annex III (an international convention for the prevention of pollution of marine water by ships) to Hong Kong; and Air Pollution Control (Amendment) Bill.

Promoting inward investment in Hong Kong's manufacturing industries is another important area of the Industry Department's work. The department provides information and assistance to potential overseas investors in Hong Kong and through overseas Industrial Promotion Units based in Tokyo, San Francisco, New York, Brussels and London.

Much of the recent manufacturing investment has been from multinationals at the forefront of technological development, and this has helped to raise technology and skill levels in the local manufacturing sector. Two projects in particular, involving the manufacture of polystyrene and compact discs respectively, were good examples of the introduction of state-of-the-art technology into Hong Kong.

In recent years an increasingly important part of the Industry Department's work has been to promote wider application of quality assurance in the manufacturing sector. The department has therefore developed a range of services to assist manufacturers to improve the quality of their products. The Hong Kong Government Standards and Calibration Laboratory holds Hong Kong's official standards of measurement, and provides a calibration service to manufacturers to enable them to meet measurement standards required for their products. The laboratory has measurement capabilities for a wide range of electrical, temperature, mechanical, pressure, volume and humidity measurements. A new laboratory is being built to provide a force calibration service for the construction industry.

The department's Product Standards Information Bureau provides advice and information to manufacturers on both national and international standards affecting their products. The bureau also maintains a reference library of the national standards issued by Hong Kong's trading partners and the international standards published by the International Organisation for Standardisation (ISO) and the International Electro-technical Commission (IEC). To improve the storage and retrieval of product standards information, a direct computer link with the databases of overseas standards institutions and a computerised information retrieval system have been established.

The Industry Department also operates the Hong Kong Laboratory Accreditation Scheme (HOKLAS), designed to improve the standard of testing and management in Hong Kong's laboratories and provide official recognition for those assessed as competent. HOKLAS has so far accredited 43 laboratories for testing such items as toys, textiles, electrical and electronic goods, food and construction materials. Several laboratories were accredited in 1992 in the important field of environmental testing. A number of important mutual recognition agreements have been concluded with overseas laboratory accreditation schemes, including the National Measurement Accreditation Service of the United Kingdom, the National Association of Testing Authorities of Australia, the American Association for Laboratory Accreditation and the Testing Laboratory Registration Council of New Zealand. Under such agreements, Hong Kong products may not be required to undergo further testing in these countries if they have already been tested and issued with a HOKLAS endorsed test report in Hong Kong.

Since March 1990 the department has been running a Quality Awareness Campaign, whose basic message, disseminated through quality management seminars and workshops, and through a range of promotional literature, is that investment in quality is profitable.

Since Hong Kong's economy is heavily dependent on exports, higher quality in production will increase its competitiveness in the market place. The campaign is part of a wider quality improvement programme aimed at encouraging more manufacturers to adopt quality assurance in their companies. The other components of the programme include strengthening the department's existing range of quality services and developing a quality management certification scheme.

Under the certification scheme, government recognition is conferred on companies which adopt quality management systems conforming to the international standard ISO 9000. An independent subvented organisation, the Hong Kong Quality Assurance Agency, was established in 1990 to audit factories for the award of certificates. Response to the scheme has been very enthusiastic, involving both manufacturing and service sector companies.

The Governor's Award for Industry, established in 1989, rewards and recognises outstanding achievements in industrial competitiveness. In 1992, the number of award categories was increased from four to six. Different organisations are responsible for arranging annual competitions in each of these categories. The Federation of Hong Kong Industries is responsible for the consumer product design category; the Chinese Manufacturers' Association of Hong Kong for machinery and equipment design; the Hong Kong Productivity Council for productivity; the Industry Department for quality; the Private Sector Committee on the Environment for environmental performance; and the Hong Kong Trade Development Council for export marketing.

Hong Kong Productivity Council
The Hong Kong Productivity Council (HKPC) was established by statute in 1967 to promote increased productivity of industry in Hong Kong. It is financed by an annual government subvention and by fees earned from its services. The council consists of a chairman and 21 members appointed by the Governor. Its membership is drawn from the management, labour, academic and professional fields and from appropriate government branches and departments.

The HKPC has about 500 staff members with expertise in a wide range of disciplines. It provides a variety of training programmes, industrial and management consultancies and technical support services, using resources available in its 16 operational divisions: Computer Services, Electronics Services, Engineering Services, Systems and Organisation, Computer-Aided Design Services, Chemical and Metallurgy, Manufacturing Engineering, Textiles and Apparel, Industrial Consultancy, Training, Environmental Management, Information Services, Development and Administration, Public Relations, Marketing and Accounting.

The HKPC moved to its new building in Kowloon Tong in February 1991. The new HKPC building places all the council's operations under a single roof and contains a display area, an auditorium, a technical reference library, electronics data processing facilities, a computer-aided design service centre, a surface mount technology laboratory, a radio frequency and digital communication laboratory, photo-chemical machining, metal finishing and industrial chemistry laboratories, an environmental management laboratory, sheet metal processing, precision machining and die casting laboratories.

There was a growing demand during the year for HKPC's consultancy and technical support services. The council undertook 1 120 consultancy projects, including feasibility studies, production management, new plant projects, environmental management, quality management, product design and development, and industrial automation services. It completed 2 100 laboratory-based assignments.

To facilitate the transition to high value-added products, HKPC invited local companies to join consortia to share the design and development costs of new products, namely a notebook computer, a 900-megahertz indoor cordless telephone and a palmtop computer. Thirty companies took part in these projects.

The HKPC organised 622 training courses for 11 900 participants, covering management and supervisory techniques, advanced programming and electronic data processing, and a range of technology programmes for various industries. In-plant courses continued to be popular and 114 programmes were organised during the year to meet the specific training needs of individual companies.

Eight overseas study missions were organised during the year for local industrialists to gain first-hand information on the latest technology in various areas, including precision machining, textile machining and clothing manufacturing technology, quality control circles, total quality control and just-in-time systems, die casting technology, wastewater treatment technology and environmental and pollution control technology.

HKPC is the government's agent for all matters concerning the Asian Productivity Organisation (APO). During the year, under the sponsorship of the APO, HKPC held three regional seminars on managerial productivity, industrial pollution control and strategic information technology management. In addition, HKPC hosted the 32nd Workshop meeting of Heads of National Productivity Organisations in February 1992.

Hong Kong Industrial Estates Corporation

Hong Kong Industrial Estates Corporation is responsible for developing and managing industrial estates in Hong Kong. It offers developed land in its industrial estates at cost to companies with new or improved processes and products which cannot operate in multi-storey factory buildings. The corporation now has two industrial estates in the New Territories, at Tai Po and Yuen Long. A third is under construction at Tseung Kwan O. The industrial estates are fully serviced with roads, drains, sewers, electricity and water. Companies on the estates design and construct their own factory premises to meet their specific requirements. They are required to adopt appropriate environmental protection measures to meet current standards.

Currently, 108 factories are operating in the Tai Po and Yuen Long Estates while more are being built. On the Tai Po Estate, which has 73 hectares of industrial land, only one site of about 1.6 hectares is vacant. The Yuen Long Estate has 67 hectares of land in total, of which 22 hectares are still available for leasing. The land premia are $1,650 and $1,500 per square metre for Tai Po and Yuen Long respectively.

Construction of a third industrial estate at Tseung Kwan O began in August 1991. The first phase will be completed by early 1994, making available 18 hectares of serviced sites. A total of 68 hectares of industrial land will be provided in early 1995. This new industrial estate is only three kilometres from the centre of the Tseung Kwan O New Town. Water-front sites and berthing facilities will be available for ocean-going ships. Applications for sites on this new estate are now being invited and the initial land premium has been fixed at $1,700 per square metre.

The corporation's estates are held under leases from the Hong Kong Government. In accordance with the Sino-British Joint Declaration, such leases have been extended from

1997 to 2047. The corporation in turn grants sites also up to 2047 to enable investors to plan with certainty.

External Trade

Hong Kong is among the top 10 traders in the world. Overall, its trade is normally in balance and in 1992 it showed a deficit. Its largest trading partner is China, followed by the United States and Japan. Its external trade was generally buoyant in 1992. Total merchandise trade amounted to $1,880,248 million, an increase of 22 per cent over 1991. Imports rose by 23 per cent to $955,295 million. Domestic exports and gross total value of re-exports increased by one and 29 per cent to $234,123 and $690,829 million respectively; together they represented an increase of 21 per cent.

Appendices 15 and 16 provide summary statistics of external trade.

Imports

Hong Kong is almost entirely dependent on imported resources to meet the needs of its population of 5.9 million and its diverse industries. In 1992, imports of consumer goods, valued at $394,543 million, constituted 41 per cent of total imports. The major consumer goods imported were: clothing, ($80,078 million); radios, television receivers, gramophones, records, amplifiers and tape recorders, ($47,662 million); footwear, ($31,689 million); baby carriages, toys, games and sporting goods, ($31,145 million); and travel goods, handbags and similar containers, ($18,883 million).

Imports of raw materials and semi-manufactured goods totalled $329,950 million, representing 35 per cent of total imports. The principal items imported were transistors, diodes, semi-conductors and integrated circuits, ($43,602 million); woven fabrics of man-made fibres, ($30,609 million); plastic materials, ($29,262 million); iron and steel, ($15,523 million) woven cotton fabrics, ($15,131 million); and watch and clock movements, cases and parts, ($14,418 million).

Imports of capital goods amounted to $167,798 million, or 18 per cent of total imports. Imported capital goods consisted mainly of electrical machinery, ($21,928 million); transport equipment, ($17,514 million); office machines, ($16,612 million); scientific, medical, optical, measuring and controlling instruments and apparatus, ($6,709 million); and textile machinery, ($6,279 million).

Imports of foodstuffs were valued at $45,351 million, representing five per cent of total imports. The principal imported food items were fish and fish preparations, ($10,728 million), fruit, ($6,604 million); meat and meat preparations, ($5,398 million); and vegetables, ($4,485 million).

Mineral fuels, lubricants and related materials, worth some $17,653 million were imported in 1992, representing two per cent of total imports.

China and Japan were principal suppliers of imports, providing 37 per cent and 17 per cent respectively of the total. China alone supplied 32 per cent of Hong Kong's imported foodstuffs. Taiwan ranked third, providing nine per cent, followed by the United States, the Republic of Korea, Singapore, Germany and the United Kingdom.

Exports

Clothing remained the largest component of domestic exports, valued at $77,156 million or 33 per cent of the total. Exports of miscellaneous manufactured articles consisting mainly of jewellery, goldsmiths' and silversmiths' wares, plastic toys and dolls, and plastic articles were valued at $22,152 million, representing nine per cent of domestic exports. Exports of office machines and automatic data-processing equipment valued at $20,530 million, contributed another nine per cent to the total. Electrical machinery, apparatus and appliances mainly of household-type appliances, transistors and diodes amounted to $20,138 million or nine per cent of the total. Photographic apparatus, equipment, supplies and optical goods, watches and clocks were valued at $18,879 million (eight per cent of the total). Other important exports included textiles (seven per cent) as well as telecommunications and sound recording and reproducing apparatus and equipment (six per cent).

The direction and level of Hong Kong's export trade is much influenced by economic conditions and commercial policies in major overseas markets. In 1992, 46 per cent of all domestic exports went to the United States and the European Community. The largest market was the United States, ($64,600 million or 28 per cent of the total); China, ($61,959 million or 26 per cent); Germany, ($15,956 million or seven per cent); and the United Kingdom, ($12,541 million or five per cent). Domestic exports to Japan and Singapore increased to $10,997 million and $10,360 million respectively. Other important markets were Taiwan, Canada, the Netherlands and France.

Re-Exports
Re-exports showed a very significant increase in 1992. Their gross total value accounted for 75 per cent of the combined total of domestic exports and re-exports. Principal commodities re-exported were miscellaneous manufactured articles, ($97,316 million); clothing, ($78,095 million); textiles, ($67,744 million); telecommunications and sound recording and reproducing apparatus and equipment, ($55,763 million); electrical machinery, apparatus and appliances, ($53,746 million); as well as footwear ($35,327 million). The main origins of these re-exports were China, Japan, Taiwan, the United States and the Republic of Korea. Largest re-export markets were China, the United States, Japan, Germany and Taiwan.

External Commercial Relations
Hong Kong possesses full autonomy in the conduct of its external commercial relations. The Governor has been formally entrusted with executive authority to conduct external relations on behalf of Hong Kong, namely to conclude and implement trade agreements, whether bilateral or multilateral, with states, regions and international organisations and to conduct all other aspects of external commercial relations.

Hong Kong is a contracting party to the General Agreement on Tariffs and Trade (GATT), the basic aim of which is to liberalise world trade and ensure the conduct of trade in a non-discriminatory and stable manner. The Hong Kong Government, which pursues a free trade policy, is one of the best examples of GATT principles in action. The success of the policy is evidenced by the steady rise in the value and sophistication of Hong Kong's exports in recent years. Within the context of this free trade policy, Hong Kong's commercial relations are designed to ensure that Hong Kong's trading rights in overseas markets are protected and its international obligations are fulfilled.

GATT is the cornerstone of Hong Kong's external trade relations, while the Multi-Fibre Arrangement (MFA), which aims at the orderly development and expansion of 81 international trade in textiles, provides the framework within which Hong Kong negotiates bilateral restraint agreements with textile importing countries.

GATT

Hong Kong is the world's 10th largest trading entity in terms of the value of its merchandise trade. Given the externally-orientated and open nature of its economy, Hong Kong contributes to, and relies on, the healthy functioning of the multilateral trading system. Hong Kong has, therefore, always been a staunch supporter of the GATT and the free trade principles it espouses. Hong Kong participated in the activities of the GATT for many years as a British dependent territory before becoming a separate contracting party to the GATT in 1986. This status, which underlines Hong Kong's autonomy in the conduct of its external commercial relations, will extend beyond 1997.

During the year, Hong Kong continued to participate actively and constructively in the extended GATT Uruguay Round of multilateral trade negotiations. The draft final package of agreement reached in late 1991 was used as a basis for further negotiation and progress was made in various negotiating areas although some major problems remain unsolved.

Hong Kong has continued to work closely with other exporters of textiles and clothing in the International Textiles and Clothing Bureau to press for the phasing out of MFA restrictions and the integration of the textiles sector into the GATT disciplines. Hong Kong has played a pivotal role in forging consensus on the extension of the MFA, aimed to bridge the gap between the expiry of the MFA and the implementation of a Uruguay Round agreement.

Textiles

Bilateral agreements negotiated under the MFA govern Hong Kong's textile exports to Austria, Canada, the European Community (EC), Finland, Norway and the United States.

In September 1991, the United States Government published new classification guidelines for knitted tights for women. The Hong Kong Government considered that the guidelines amounted to a reclassification of the products concerned as trousers. Consultations were held between the two governments from November 1991 to July 1992. A settlement was subsequently reached in July 1992 with quota adjustments for women's and girls' cotton and man-made fibre trousers.

Pursuant to the Canadian proposal to introduce a new textile categorisation system based on the Harmonised Commodity Description and Coding System, three rounds of consultations were held between Hong Kong and Canada. Agreement was reached in October 1992 and the new Canadian categorisation system was implemented on January 1, 1993.

The bilateral textiles agreement with Norway expired in June 1992. Consultations in March 1992 resulted in a new 18-month Hong Kong/Norway Textiles Agreement from July 1, 1992 to December 31, 1993 with reduction in restraint and respectable improvements in growth. The number of categories under restraint was cut from five to three. In December 1992, Hong Kong also reached agreement with Austria on an eleven months' extension of the current Hong Kong/Austria textiles agreement which expired in January 1993. The new agreement, which represents meaningful improvements in market access over the current agreement, will be automatically extended to end-1994 if the Uruguay Round Agreement is not in force by January 1, 1994.

The bilateral textiles agreement with the EC expired at the end of 1992. Consultations in early November 1992 resulted in the extension of the agreement for two years up to December 31, 1994 extendable until end-1995. The new agreement will automatically terminate upon the entry into force the Uruguay Round Agreement. The terms of the new agreement are basically the same as those of the previous one but with regional restrictions removed.

Non-Textiles Issues

In September 1992 the EC initiated new anti-dumping proceedings against Hong Kong companies in respect of 3.5″ magnetic floppy discs. The case is under investigation by the EC Commission.

The relatively uncertain developments in trade relations between the United States and China have cast a shadow over Hong Kong's economic well being. The areas of concerns include, *inter alia*, the uncertainty of renewal of China's most-favoured-nation (MFN) trading status and the US market access 301 action against China. The failure of the Senate to override the Presidential veto of the MFN conditionality bill as well as the successful conclusion of the market access negotiations between the United States and China are welcome news to Hong Kong. Nevertheless, the United States has to renew MFN trading status for China annually under the present United States laws. The Hong Kong Government and the private sector will continue to emphasise to the United States Administration and Members of Congress as well as the Chinese authorities the adverse effects on Hong Kong's economy that withdrawing or conditioning of China's MFN status will bring about.

In December 1991, Turkey completed its anti-dumping investigation in respect of woven cotton fabrics originating from Hong Kong and decided that no anti-dumping duty should be levied.

In 1992, the Mexican authorities initiated anti-dumping proceedings against Hong Kong companies in respect of woven cotton fabrics, excluding denim, and candles originating from China and re-exported from Hong Kong. The investigation against woven cotton fabrics, excluding denim, was subsequently terminated in December 1992 because the Mexican authorities found that there was insufficient evidence to establish the existence of dumping. The case for candles is still under investigation by the Mexican authorities.

The Mexican authorities have completed investigation initiated in 1991 against Hong Kong in respect of tableware and kitchenware of ceramic, porcelain or china originating from China and re-exported from Hong Kong. Final compensatory rates of 26 per cent of the declared import price for porcelain or china and 23 per cent for ceramic on tableware/kitchenware originating from China, regardless of the country of re-export, were imposed.

In November 1992, the Mexican authorities initiated a review on the final resolution made in September 1991 to impose anti-dumping duties on imports from Hong Kong of denim of 85 per cent cotton or more. The review is in progress.

In March 1992, the New Zealand authorities initiated an anti-dumping investigation against Hong Kong companies in respect of certain men's footwear. No evidence of material injury caused by the importation of the goods from Hong Kong could be established and the proceedings were terminated.

In April 1992, the New Zealand authorities initiated another anti-dumping investigation against Hong Kong companies in respect of certain non-leather women's footwear originating from China and re-exported from Hong Kong. Final duties equal to the amount by which the normal value exceeded the value for duty of the footwear when entering for home consumption in New Zealand were imposed in September 1992.

In August 1992, the South Korean authorities initiated anti-dumping investigation against Hong Kong companies in respect of phosphoric acid originating from China and re-exported from Hong Kong. Provisional duties were imposed in October 1992.

In September 1992, the Australian authorities initiated anti-dumping proceedings against Hong Kong companies in respect of plastic cutlery. The case is under investigation by the Australian authorities.

In all these cases the Hong Kong Government worked closely with the industries alleged to have dumped to ensure that each was given a fair chance to present its case fully and accurately to the investigating authorities, and to see that the principles and provisions of the GATT Anti-Dumping Code were adhered to.

Trade Department

The Trade Department is responsible for Hong Kong's commercial relations with foreign governments. It implements trade policy and agreements and procedures for import and export licensing and origin certification. On matters of policy affecting trade, the Director-General of Trade takes advice from the Trade Advisory Board and the Textiles Advisory Board, both of which are appointed by the Governor and chaired by the Secretary for Trade and Industry.

The department consists of five divisions, three of which deal with bilateral commercial relations with Hong Kong's trading partners of different geographical areas. Their work includes the conduct of trade negotiations and the implementation of textiles agreements, as well as collection and dissemination of information on developments which may affect Hong Kong's external trade, especially those relating to trade policies and measures adopted in its major markets. One of these divisions has, in addition, responsibility for economic co-operation with the Asia-Pacific region and also the computerisation of the department's licensing systems and the introduction of electronic data interchange. The fourth division deals with the multilateral aspects of Hong Kong's external commercial relations, such as its participation in the GATT and in the negotiation of the Multi-Fibre Arrangement. The fifth division is responsible for the textiles export control system, common services, origin certification, the import and export licensing of commodities other than textiles, and a rice control scheme.

The department's work is assisted by eight overseas Hong Kong Government Offices administered by the Trade and Industry Branch of the Government Secretariat.

Hong Kong Representation Overseas

The Trade and Industry Branch oversees offices in Geneva, Brussels, London, Washington, New York, San Francisco, Toronto and Tokyo, mainly to safeguard and advance Hong Kong's economic and commercial interests overseas. (Address details are at Appendix 6.) They work closely, on a day-to-day basis, with departments and organisations concerned to represent Hong Kong's economic and commercial interests overseas and to promote goodwill for Hong Kong. The offices also monitor and collect information on international developments which may affect Hong Kong and provide information on Hong Kong affairs and developments to its trading partners and the overseas communities.

The Geneva Office represents Hong Kong as a contracting party to the GATT. The office participates in the regular activities of the GATT as well as in the ongoing multilateral trade negotiations (generally known as the Uruguay Round) which were launched in September 1986. The Brussels Office represents and promotes Hong Kong's economic, commercial and public relations interests to the European Commission and the member states of the European Community (other than the United Kingdom) and to Switzerland. Hong Kong's commercial relations with the United Kingdom, Austria and the Nordic countries (Finland, Sweden and Norway) are handled through the London Office. The London Office is also responsible for monitoring the economic and political developments in the United Kingdom that are of interest to Hong Kong, for promoting Hong Kong's interests, enhancing understanding of Hong Kong affairs and advancing Hong Kong's image in the United Kingdom. In this connection, the office maintains close liaison with the business and commercial sectors, politicians and the media in the United Kingdom. The Washington, New York and San Francisco offices closely monitor economic and trade developments, proposed legislation and other matters in the United States of America that might affect Hong Kong's economic and trading interests in general. The Toronto Office does something similar in respect of Canada. The Tokyo Office conducts similar activities in Japan, looking after Hong Kong's commercial, economic and public relations interests there.

With the exception of Geneva, all offices act as a point of direct contact between Hong Kong and the host country, and the local media and organisations with an interest in Hong Kong. They monitor commercial, economic and industrial developments and official thinking on international trade policies and advise the Hong Kong Government on the likely repercussions of such developments. (See also the section on Hong Kong's Image Overseas in Chapter 21.)

The Brussels, London, New York, San Francisco and Tokyo offices also contain Industrial Promotion Units which promote direct investment in manufacturing. The Washington, New York and San Francisco offices also assist in the recruitment of administrative officers from the United States and Canada. The London and Toronto Offices act as a point of contact for Hong Kong Chinese communities (including Hong Kong students) in the United Kingdom and Canada respectively and provide advisory services and assistance to them as appropriate. The London Office also undertakes recruitment in the United Kingdom of civil servants for the Hong Kong Government. The Marine Adviser based in London is Hong Kong's permanent representative to the International Maritime Organisation. He acts as a focus in London for all technical, legal and general maritime matters pertaining to Hong Kong, particularly the autonomous Hong Kong Shipping Register.

Hong Kong Trade Development Council
The Hong Kong Trade Development Council (TDC) is the territory's statutory body responsible for promoting and developing Hong Kong's trade. As the marketing arm for local manufacturers, exporters and importers, it plays a vanguard role in opening new or difficult markets for Hong Kong companies and in helping them to increase market share. It also publicises business opportunities in Hong Kong.

The council's chairman is appointed by the Governor. The other 18 members include representatives of major trade associations, leading businessmen and industrialists, as well as two senior government officials. Seven specialised Industry Advisory Groups, with a

85

membership of more than 200, provide a direct link between TDC and the business community it serves.

Established in 1966, the council is headquartered in the Hong Kong Convention and Exhibition Centre and has 33 branch offices in 24 countries. For the convenience of local users, it also operates TDC Datashops in Tsuen Wan, Kwun Tong, Mong Kok and Central. Another datashop will be opened in Tsim Sha Tsui.

All TDC offices locally and overseas handle trade enquiries, provide up-to-date trade and economic information, and market intelligence. Through a computerised Trade Enquiry Service, which is on-line to its global network of offices, the TDC 'matchmakes' buyers with sellers. There are 48 000 Hong Kong manufacturers and exporters registered in the TDC database, along with 215 000 overseas buyers and importers. The Trade Enquiry Service handled more than 300 000 overseas and local trade enquiries in 1992. The council also operates Hong Kong's largest electronic information network, TDC-Link. Its 2 000 subscribers are able to access the TDC's business information databank from their office or home computer.

More than 240 major international trade promotion projects were organised by the TDC in 1992. Among them were the European Watch, Clock and Jewellery Fair in Basel, the Berlin International Audio and Visual Fair, the International Toy Fair in Nuremburg, the Tokyo Toy Show and the Japan Electronics Show. The TDC also participated in many important fairs in the United States, including the Summer Consumer Electronics Show in Chicago, the Winter Consumer Electronics Show in Las Vegas, and the American International Toy Fair in New York.

To strengthen Hong Kong's position as a regional business hub, the TDC is developing Hong Kong as Asia's convention and trade fair capital. In 1992 it staged 16 trade fairs and consumer expos at the Hong Kong Convention and Exhibition Centre. These included Hong Kong Fashion Week, the Hong Kong Toys and Games Fair, the Hong Kong International Jewellery Show, the Hong Kong Book Fair, Food Expo and Hong Kong Showcase. The TDC's Exhibition Services Centre in Yuen Long continued to design and construct exhibition stands for the council's local trade fairs, and provide special designs and contracting services for other fairs.

As a matter of priority, the TDC is helping Hong Kong manufacturers upgrade their products and encouraging them to market their brand names locally. In 1992 the council expanded its popular TDC Design Gallery, a retail outlet which is located in the Hong Kong Convention and Exhibition Centre. It increased the range of products for sale and intensified the promotion of Hong Kong brand labels. Design Gallery outlets were also opened in four Wing On department stores, in Sheung Wan, Central, Tsim Sha Tsui and Mong Kok.

The TDC's Research Department published more than 70 special market surveys and detailed product reports in 1992, identifying specific opportunities for Hong Kong products in overseas markets. TDC's research unit also organised export management and practical training courses for local executives, as part of an ongoing programme.

The TDC publishes a total of 10 product magazines. In 1992 the TDC reaffirmed its position as one of Hong Kong's biggest trade publishers by setting new world records. The 1 356-page January 1992 issue of *Hong Kong Toys* was accepted in June by the London-based Guinness Book of Records as the 'Largest Periodical' title in the 1993 edition. This was subsequently eclipsed by the TDC's flagship product publication, *Hong Kong Enterprise*, whose October issue had 1 374 pages. Besides, the council produces *Hong*

Kong Apparel, Hong Kong Garments and Assessories, Hong Kong Jewellery Biannual, Hong Kong Watches and Clocks, Hong Kong Household, and *Hong Kong Gifts and Premiums* biannually, the quarterly *Hong Kong Electronics* and the annual *Hong Kong Optical.* Together, these product magazines reach an audience of two million buyers, importers and business decision-makers in more than 100 overseas markets. The TDC's monthly newspaper *Hong Kong Trader* is circulated by airmail to target readers around the world, as well as the business class travellers on selected airlines. The TDC also distributes *Hong Kong For the Business Visitor,* which it publishes in eight languages.

The TDC's international network of contacts includes 19 Hong Kong Business Associations whose 7 000 members are business leaders in their own communities. They provide strong endorsement of the advantages of Hong Kong as a business partner. The TDC's Overseas Associations Section also administers the Hong Kong/United States Economic Co-operation Committee and the Hong Kong–Japan Business Co-operation Committee. They are high-level committees of business and government leaders.

To further develop Hong Kong's external trade relations, the TDC organises visits to overseas markets by Hong Kong economic missions and business groups. These missions and groups visit both established and emerging markets and their activities range from calls on government leaders, press interviews and speeches at business seminars, to the staging of product exhibitions. The TDC also organises and receives inward business missions from overseas markets. These numbered more than 440 in 1992.

Hong Kong Export Credit Insurance Corporation
The year 1991 marked the 25th anniversary of the Hong Kong Export Credit Insurance Corporation (ECIC), which is a statutory corporation established in 1966 to provide insurance protection to exporters and manufacturing exporters against the risk of monetary loss arising from non-payment by their overseas buyers for goods exported and services rendered on credit which are not normally covered by commercial insurers. The maximum percentage of indemnity against country and buyers risks is 90 per cent.

The ECIC's paid-up capital of $20 million was provided by the government which also guarantees the payment of all moneys due by the corporation. The maximum contingent liability arising from its insurance and guarantees operations which may be assumed by the corporation is $7,500 million. Within the limits of the Hong Kong Export Credit Insurance Corporation Ordinance, Chapter 1115, the corporation is autonomous in its day-to-day operations and is run on a commercial basis. It is assisted by a 12-member Advisory Board comprising prominent members from the business sector and representatives from the government.

In 1991, the corporation continued to work hard to improve its services to exporters and manufacturers under the leadership of a new Commissioner. Following a series of meetings with bankers, policyholders, trade associations and staff of all levels, guidelines and manuals on operations and management have been revised and updated to improve the efficiency and productivity of the ECIC. Studies have been undertaken with a view to widening the scope of insurance cover, introducing new facilities, reducing premiums and giving premium rebates.

During 1991–2, the ECIC underwrote $15,291 million and received premiums amounting to $90 million, both being increases of 11 per cent over 1990–91. It paid out $39 million as gross claims. The excess of income over expenditure was $28 million in the year 1991–2.

Being a member of the International Union of Credit and Investment Insurers (Berne Union), ECIC has regular access to confidential and updated economic and market information on all major trading countries. The corporation stays close to exporters and manufacturers in order to understand their needs. It holds seminars for banks, trade associations and individual exporters.

The ECIC's activities fall into three main categories. The first category is the protection provided by the corporation to indemnify policyholders up to 90 per cent of their losses. Besides domestic exports and re-exports, shipments from third countries direct to overseas buyers are also covered. Protection is provided to exporters against non-payment due to buyers' insolvency and default, war or civil disturbance and transfer delays. Cover can also be extended to outward processing operations against confiscation and non-repatriation of raw materials, work-in-progress and finished products. For export of capital goods and services sold on medium or long-term credits, the ECIC can provide tailor-made insurance policies.

The second category of ECIC's activities is the provision of credit advisory services to its policyholders. On request by a policyholder, the corporation will investigate the prospective buyer's creditworthiness, having regard to the market trading environment and the terms of payment of the proposed transaction, and advise the policyholder on the amount of credit that can be prudently extended to the overseas buyer.

Finally, the ECIC provides a risk management service when a policyholder experiences payment problems. A policyholder is advised on possible courses of action either to prevent or minimise any loss.

Other Trade and Industrial Organisations
A number of associations have been established in Hong Kong to represent the interests of industry and commerce. Among the larger, older, and more influential associations are the Federation of Hong Kong Industries, the Chinese Manufacturers' Association, the Hong Kong General Chamber of Commerce and the Chinese General Chamber of Commerce. Other important organisations include the Hong Kong Management Association, the Hong Kong Exporters' Association, the American Chamber of Commerce, the Indian Chamber of Commerce, and the Hong Kong Japanese Chamber of Commerce and Industry.

The Federation of Hong Kong Industries is a statutory body, established by the government in 1960 to promote and protect the interests of Hong Kong's manufacturing industry. It offers a wide range of services, covering certificates of origin, the Hong Kong Quality Mark Scheme, a custom-built multi-risks insurance policy, consultancy work on quality assurance, trade enquiries and economic research.

With a membership spanning all industrial sectors, the federation services the Hong Kong Toys Council, Chemical and Pharmaceutical Industries Council, Transport Services Council, Hong Kong Watch and Clock Council, Hong Kong Electronics Industry Council, Hong Kong Plastics Industry Council and the Hong Kong Mould and Die Council. It also runs an annual Young Industrialist Award of Hong Kong and is responsible for organising the consumer product design award category of the Governor's Award for Industry.

The Chinese Manufacturers' Association of Hong Kong (CMA), established in 1934, is a non-profit-making chamber of commerce and industry. It is also a member of the

International Chamber of Commerce. With a membership of over 3 600 industrial and trade establishments, the CMA is authorised by the government to issue certificates of origin. It also provides trade information, handles trade enquiries, organises missions, fairs and exhibitions, and is active in encouraging product development and quality improvement. The CMA Testing and Certification Laboratories provide technical back-up services, including materials and product testing, pre-shipment inspection and technical consultancy services. The CMA also organises various seminars and training courses and operates two pre-vocational schools to provide technical education and training for more than 2 200 students. The CMA provides scholarships annually to outstanding students of technical colleges and post-secondary institutions. Since 1989, the CMA has been appointed by the government to organise the machinery and equipment design award category of the Governor's Award for Industry.

The Hong Kong General Chamber of Commerce is the oldest internationally-recognised trade association in Hong Kong and one of the 10 largest chambers in the world. Founded in 1861, its membership of over 3 100 member companies is representative of every sector of commerce and industry. The chamber organises trade and goodwill missions overseas and receives inbound delegations. It handles trade enquiries and extends assistance to individual visiting business people. It is authorised by the government to issue certificates of origin and is the sole local issuing authority for international Association Temporarie Admission (ATA) Carnets, through its seven local certification offices.

Although an independent, autonomous organisation receiving no subvention, the chamber is represented on a wide range of official advisory committees and bodies. The chamber founded and formed the Hong Kong Article Numbering Association, the Hong Kong Coalition of Service Industries, the Hong Kong Franchise Association and sponsors the Hong Kong Committee of the Pacific Basin Economic Council.

Established in 1900, the Chinese General Chamber of Commerce is an association of local Chinese firms, businessmen and professionals. It has a membership of over 6 000, representing a wide spectrum of trade as well as industry. It provides a variety of services including certification of origin, organisation of seminars, exhibitions, trade missions and other trade promotional activities. It maintains close links with trade organisations both in Hong Kong and China. Since 1957, it has been authorised by the Chinese Export Commodities Fair authorities to issue invitations on their behalf to local Chinese firms. It has been operating courses for senior government officials of China since 1982. These courses are designed to enable participants to better understand the various aspects of Hong Kong's economy.

The Hong Kong Management Association is a professional management organisation incorporated in 1960 for the purpose of improving the efficiency and effectiveness of management in Hong Kong. It organises over 1 500 training programmes and provides various management services such as translation, recruitment and exhibition.

The Hong Kong Exporters' Association was formed in 1955. It has a membership of 300 export and manufacturing companies. Its members together account for about one third of Hong Kong's total domestic exports. Its objectives are to protect and promote the interests of its members, to disseminate trade information, and to act as a representative body to voice members' concerns and to assist in solving any trade problems which they may encounter.

Documentation of Imports and Exports

As a free port, Hong Kong keeps its import and export licensing requirements to a minimum. Products over a wide range do not need licences to enter or leave Hong Kong. Where licences are required, they are intended to achieve two main objectives. First, they help Hong Kong to fulfil its international obligations to restrain exports of textiles products, and to monitor the flow of these products into Hong Kong. Secondly, they help Hong Kong to control, on health, safety or security grounds, exports and imports of a few non-textiles products such as strategic commodities, reserved commodities, pharmaceuticals, agricultural pesticides and ozone-depleting substances.

As a measure to curb smuggling, the government amended the Import and Export (General) Regulations in May. With the amendments, the import and export of left-hand-drive vehicles and outboard engines exceeding 111.9 kilowatts are subject to licensing control. Separately, import and export licensing control was introduced in May for biological warfare agents and any article or equipment which is used for the design, development or deployment of mass destruction weapons.

Hong Kong maintains a certification of origin system which enables the origin of goods which Hong Kong exports to be established, in order to meet the requirements of importing authorities. The Trade Department administers this system and issues certificates of origin where required. Other certificate-issuing organisations which have government approval are the Hong Kong General Chamber of Commerce, the Indian Chamber of Commerce, the Federation of Hong Kong Industries, the Chinese Manufacturers' Association of Hong Kong and the Chinese General Chamber of Commerce.

Participation in International Organisations

Being an integral part of the Asian-Pacific economy and an important regional services centre, Hong Kong has a role to play and a contribution to make in regional economic co-operation. Hong Kong's economic linkages with the region have been expanding. In 1992, some 78 per cent of Hong Kong's total external trade was accounted for by the other 14 APEC member economies.

During the year, Hong Kong participated actively in the work of Asia-Pacific Economic Co-operation culminating in the 4th APEC Ministerial Meeting held on September 10–11, 1992 in Bangkok. As to PECC, the Hong Kong Committee, set up in March 1990 with the objective of advising on Hong Kong's participation in and co-ordinating the territory's input to the PECC process, continued to participate actively in the various task forces. The highlight of the year was the PECC 9th General Meeting held on September 23–25 in San Francisco.

Hong Kong continued to play an active part in the informal dialogue initiated by the Organisation for Economic Cooperation and Development (OECD) with the dynamic Asian economies (Hong Kong, Singapore, South Korea, Taiwan, Thailand and Malaysia). Hong Kong participated in all six workshops held between March and November in Paris, Bangkok, Seoul and Sydney, with topics covering foreign direct investment, economic integration, short term economic prospects, bond market, taxation and investment.

Customs and Excise Department

The Trade Controls Branch of the Customs and Excise Department is responsible for trade-related enforcement activities. It enforces legislation concerning certification of origin, textile import and export controls, import and export licensing controls of strategic and reserved commodities, weights and measures and other consumer protection programmes. It also verifies and assesses import and export declarations.

Consistent with its obligations under international conventions and trade agreements, Hong Kong enforces an effective origin certification and licensing control system on import and export of textiles and clothing products and strategic commodities. The branch works closely with the Trade Department to ensure the integrity of the system.

To tackle the growing incidence of country of origin fraud and illegal transhipments in textile trade, the branch has established a special task force to conduct more physical checks on textile imports and exports and keep vigil over suspected consignments and traders and cargo forwarders involved in illegal transhipment.

The branch has continued to play an active role in enforcing weights and measures legislation. In addition to investigating complaints of short weights and measures, it has initiated spot checks with a view to deterring the fraudulent use of inaccurate weighing and measuring equipment as well as the sale of prepackaged foodstuffs with incorrect weights or quantities. The branch will also be responsible for the enforcement of the Toys and Children's Products Safety Bill when enacted.

Trade in Endangered Species
In Hong Kong, the importation, exportation and possession of endangered species of animals and plants, including parts and derivatives, are strictly regulated by the Animals and Plants (Protection of Endangered Species) Ordinance which gives effect to the Convention on International Trade in Endangered Species of Wild Fauna and Flora (CITES). The licensing policy follows closely the principles of the convention. Commercial trade in highly-endangered species is prohibited and trade in less endangered species is subject to strict licensing requirements.

The ordinance is administered by the Agriculture and Fisheries Department and enforced by officers of the department and the Customs and Excise Department through checking at entry points, markets, shops and restaurants, as well as inspection of endangered species shipments. All suspected offences are thoroughly investigated and prosecutions follow if there is evidence of a breach of the ordinance. During 1992, there were 297 seizures and 153 prosecutions under the ordinance.

Government Supplies Department
The Government Supplies Department is the Government's central organisation for procurement and supply of stores and equipment required by government departments and certain subvented agencies.

Since 1979 the department has represented the Hong Kong Government as an entity in the Agreement on Government Procurement of the General Agreement on Tariffs and Trade. Under the agreement, except for special requirements, all purchases exceeding Special Drawing Rights 130 000 (HK$1,370,000 in 1992) are widely advertised and open to competitive bidding internationally. All purchases, ranging from simple office sundries to complex computer systems, are made entirely on the basis of 'best value for money', regardless of the source of supply. Due to its open procurement policy, goods and services are purchased from over 40 countries and some 4 000 registered local and overseas suppliers.

To ensure continuity of supply, the department maintains goods which are generally required by other departments in its main stores in Hong Kong and Kowloon and four sub-stores specially established to serve the engineering workshops. It also seconds supplies staff to other departments to ensure a professional approach to acquisition and maintenance of stores and equipment.

In 1991–2, the department placed orders to a total value of HK$3,207 million. The top major sources of supply were the United States, United Kingdom, China, Japan and Hong Kong. Major items of purchase included computer systems, rations and pharmaceuticals.

Trade Marks and Patents

The Intellectual Property Department provides a focal point for the development of Hong Kong's intellectual property regime and includes the Trade Marks and Patents Registries.

The Trade Marks Registry is a registry of original registration. Trade Marks are registered under the Trade Marks Ordinance, the provisions of which are similar to trade marks legislation in the United Kingdom. Since March 2, 1992, it has been possible to register trade marks for services as well as goods. The procedure in applying for registration is laid down in the Trade Marks Rules, and the prescribed forms may be obtained free from the Trade Marks Registry, Intellectual Property Department. Every mark, even if already registered in the United Kingdom or any other country, must satisfy the requirements of the Trade Marks Ordinance before it may be accepted for registration. During 1992, 16 456 applications were received, 10 586 of which were in respect of goods and 5 870 in respect of services. Applications totalling 5 859, including many made in previous years, were accepted and allowed to be advertised. A total of 5 500 marks were registered in 1992, compared with 4 340 in 1991. The principal places of applicants' origin were:

United States	1 355	United Kingdom	290
Hong Kong	973	Germany	287
Japan	759	Switzerland	237
France	362	Taiwan	141
Italy	317	Singapore	83

The total number of marks on the register at December 31, 1992 was 62 866.

Unlike the Trade Marks Registry, the Patents Registry, which also forms part of the Intellectual Property Department, is not a registry of original registration. It registers patents that have been granted in the United Kingdom and European Patents (UK). The Registration of Patents Ordinance provides that any grantee of a United Kingdom Patent or European Patent (UK) may, within five years from the date of its grant, apply to have the patent registered in Hong Kong.

A total of 1 069 patents were registered in Hong Kong during the year, compared with 1 079 in 1991. Registration of a United Kingdom Patent or European Patent (UK) in Hong Kong confers on the grantee the same privileges and rights as if the patent had been granted in the United Kingdom with an extension to Hong Kong. The privileges and rights run from the commencement of the term of the patent in the United Kingdom, and continue for as long as the patent remains in force there.

Preceding page: *Two hundred artists exhibited works of wide-ranging skills at the Contemporary Hong Kong Art Biennial Exhibition.*

Left: *Among imaginative exhibits by students at the Joint School Science Exhibition was a project exploring the possibility of human migration to the bottom of the sea.*

Below: *Young members of a school environmental awards scheme explained their ideas to His Royal Highness the Prince of Wales at Government House.*

Bottom: *After studying chemical engineering in the United States, Katia Tam returned to Hong Kong as operations engineer of an oil company.*

Right: *Shirley Loong was prima ballerina in 'Swan Lake', one of the ballets presented by Hong Kong Ballet Group as part of the 30th anniversary of Hong Kong City Hall.*

Below: *Other scenes from the anniversary celebration.*

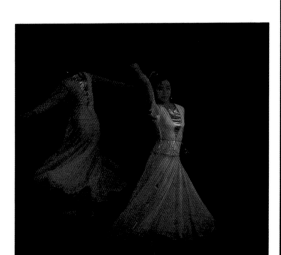

Left: *Hong Kong Fashion Week 92 showcased the talents of young local designers.*

Below: *One of the eye-catching costumes on show.*

Bottom: *Fashion design award winner Carol Lee.*

Following page: *Lee Lai-shan was lady champion and overall first runner-up in the Mobil Hong Kong Circuit Stanley Windsurfing Championships.*

Companies Registry

The Companies Registry of the Registrar General's Department keeps records of all companies incorporated in Hong Kong and of all overseas companies that have established a place of business in Hong Kong.

Local companies are incorporated under the Companies Ordinance, which is similar to, but in some aspects quite different from, the United Kingdom Companies Acts. The ordinance is subject to continual revision and improvement on the advice of the Standing Committee on Company Law Reform which was set up in 1984. The primary task of the committee is to ensure that Hong Kong's company law meets the up-to-date needs of government and business.

A recent amendment to the ordinance is the Companies (Amendment) Ordinance which was enacted in December 1992 and will come into operation on a day to be appointed by the Governor. It will transfer the responsibility for the vetting of prospectuses from the Companies Registry to the Securities and Futures Commission and the Stock Exchange of Hong Kong.

During 1992 a new and more powerful computer system with twice the capacity of the previous system was installed in the Companies Registry. It commenced its live run on June 1, 1992. As a result of this enhanced system, the Companies Registry is considering the implementation over the next few years of a series of new computerised programmes beginning with the computerisation of the Document Index and the Control Book of incoming documents. During the year, other improvements achieved in the Registry's operational efficiency included the availability for search of an index of charges pending registration in the form of a computer print out, the printing of some certificates of registered charges by personal computer, the printing of certificates of incorporation of companies by computer, and further improvements in office accommodation and layout. Officers from the Finance Branch of the Government Secretariat and consultants from Coopers and Lybrand were invited to study the procedures undertaken in the Registry's Charges and Public Search Sections. As a result of implementing their recommendations, there have been significant improvements in the productivity and service levels of these sections.

On incorporation, a company pays a registration fee of $1,000 plus $6 for every $1,000 of nominal capital. In 1992, 58 110 new companies were incorporated, 14 135 more than in 1991. The nominal capital of new companies registered totalled $5,208 million. Of the new companies, 235 had a nominal share capital of $5 million or more. During the year, 11 657 companies increased their nominal capital by amounts totalling $45,574 million on which fees were paid at the same rate of $6 per $1,000. At the end of 1992, there were 358 129 local companies on the register, compared with 304 538 in 1991.

Companies incorporated overseas are required to register certain documents with the registry within one month of establishing a place of business in Hong Kong.

A registration fee of $500 and some incidental filing fees are payable in such cases. During the year, 550 of these companies were registered and 185 ceased to operate. At the end of the year 3 193 companies were registered from 72 countries, including 656 from the United States, 365 from the United Kingdom and 299 from Japan.

The registry also deals with the incorporation of trustees under the Registered Trustees Incorporation Ordinance, and with the registration of limited partnerships.

93

Plans are under way to give the independent Companies Registry trading fund status which would give it a considerable degree of financial and managerial autonomy in carrying out its functions.

Money Lenders

Under the Money Lenders Ordinance, which came into force in December 1980 and was amended in July 1988, anyone wishing to carry on business as a money lender must apply to a Licensing Court for a licence. The ordinance does not affect bankers and deposit-taking companies authorised under the Banking Ordinance.

Any application for a licence is, in the first instance, submitted to the Registrar General as Registrar of Money Lenders and a copy is sent to the Commissioner of Police, who may object to the application. The application is advertised, and any member of the public who has an interest in the matter also has the right to object. During the year, 560 applications were received and 504 licences were granted. At the end of 1992, there were 537 licensed money lenders.

The ordinance provides severe penalties for a number of statutory offences, such as carrying on an unlicensed money-lending business. It also provides that any loan made by an unlicensed money lender shall not be recoverable by court action. With certain exceptions (primarily authorised institutions under the Banking Ordinance), any person, whether a licensed money lender or not, who lends or offers to lend money at an interest rate exceeding 60 per cent per annum commits an offence. Agreement for the repayment of any such loan or any security given in respect of such loan shall be unenforceable.

Bankruptcies and Compulsory Winding-up

The Official Receiver's Office administers estates of personal bankrupts and companies ordered to be compulsorily wound up by the court.

Once a Receiving Order is made against the property of a personal bankrupt, or a Winding-Up Order by the court is made against a company, the Official Receiver becomes the receiver or provisional liquidator respectively.

In estates where the assets realised are less than $200,000, the Official Receiver applies to the court for a summary procedure order and is appointed as trustee or liquidator. In other cases a meeting of creditors in bankruptcy, or of creditors and contributories in compulsory liquidations, is held to decide whether the Official Receiver or another person from the private sector should be appointed as trustee or liquidator. If a debtor makes a proposal for a composition in satisfaction of his debts or a proposal for a scheme of arrangement of his affairs, he will not be adjudged bankrupt if the proposal is accepted by his creditors and the court. As in past years, the Official Receiver was appointed trustee or liquidator in most cases.

During the year the court made 295 Receiving Orders and 342 Winding-up Orders, which is an increase of 1.43 per cent over the previous year. The assets realised by the Official Receiver during 1992 amounted to $131.4 million, and $221.3 million in dividends were paid to creditors in 205 insolvency cases.

Hitherto part of the Registrar General's Department, the Official Receiver's Office was established as a separate legal entity starting from June 1, 1992. At the same time a new grade of Insolvency Officer was introduced and the work of the office was reorganised from a function-orientated to an overall case management approach in order to streamline procedures and improve efficiency.

Consumer Council

Established in 1974, the Consumer Council is the statutory body charged with protecting and promoting the interests of consumers of goods and services. The council comprises a chairman, vice-chairman and 20 members appointed by the Governor from a wide cross section of the community. It has an office, headed by a Chief Executive, with a staff establishment of 107. It is a council member of the International Organisation of Consumer Unions.

The council provides a comprehensive consumer protection service embracing consumer representation and legislation, advice and complaints, research and testing, and information and publications. It maintains close liaison with the government through the Trade and Industry Branch and is consulted on major policies affecting the interests of the consumer public. It is represented on many committees dealing with specific consumer issues and concerns. Its head office was relocated to new premises which it bought this year.

To cope with an increasing demand for its service and a changing environment, the council has to focus its resources on the areas of work that will best benefit the consumer in the years ahead. Four broad areas were identified for special attention. They include monitoring monopolistic tendencies in the marketplace and their impact on the livelihood of the ordinary consumers, and trade practices which leave consumers in a weak bargaining position. The council remains an active ally of environmental protection and green consumerism, and the international consumer movement.

The Consumer Council continued its efforts to safeguard the interests of property buyers. For example, the council investigated consumer grievances relating to the practices of estate agents and studied whether and how to regulate estate agent practices. For the first time, it named specific developers and sales agents for the significant difference between the gross and saleable floor areas of the properties sold by them. In addition, it is devising ways and means to hold developers liable to purchasers for the rectification of defects in new buildings and to extend such defect liability period from the existing six months to a more reasonable length of time following occupation.

The Council's efforts in the field of consumer product safety are beginning to bear fruit. In June 1992, the legislation requiring registration of electrical contractors and workers in order to enhance the safety of fixed electrical installations was implemented. Legislation governing the safety of toys and children's products is now being processed in the Legislative Council. In addition, the council is helping to examine legislating controls on consumer products safety.

The council's call to improve consumer representation and consultation in the provision of public utility and public transport services was well-received and a number of these companies have set up consumer consultative groups or the likes. To counter the excessive speculation in the public tender for taxi licences and to encourage ownership by *bona fide* taxi drivers, the council proposed a relaxation of restriction on the number of licences issued and a tightening of the free transfer of licences. In addition, the council recommended changes to the motor insurance industry, including the scrapping of the basic tariff rate set by the Accident Insurance Association and a review of the basic commission structure for agents and brokers. The council will continue to periodically review the situation to safeguard the interests of motorists.

The council also participated in a review of the regulatory system of the outbound travel industry which has led to important changes to the existing self-regulatory structure and an increase in the level of *ex-gratia* compensation payments to consumers in the event of default by travel agents. The council remains firmly committed to its support for the introduction of a Deposit Protection Scheme as it not only will offer protection to smaller depositors in the event of bank failure, but will facilitate financial and social stability and enhance competition in the banking sector. The council is also strongly behind a campaign to assert patients' rights and to demand that medical practitioners disclose their schedule of charges and inform patients about the medicines they have prescribed.

During the year, 9 282 complaints and 249 097 enquiries for advice and information were received at the 16 Consumer Advice Centres throughout the territory. The diversity of topics of consumer interest, published in the council's monthly magazine *CHOICE*, reflected both the quality and quantity of other ongoing activities in research, survey and product testing. Numerous consumer education activities involving the community at large were organised throughout the year in a constant effort to raise consumer awareness.

Metrication

The government's metrication policy is to promote and facilitate the progressive adoption of the International System of Units (SI) in Hong Kong. The Metrication Ordinance, enacted in 1976, provides for the eventual replacement of non-metric units by SI units in all legislation in Hong Kong. Government departments are now using metric units exclusively.

A Metrication Committee, consisting of representatives of industry, commerce, management and consumer affairs, and government officials, is the focal point of liaison for all matters concerning metrication. It advises and encourages the commercial and industrial sectors in the development and implementation of their metrication programmes.

During the year, the committee continued to direct its efforts towards the retail trade. A publicity campaign was launched to encourage the use of metric units in public markets. Concurrent with the campaign, weighing scales with triple calibrations (metric, imperial and Chinese units) were provided for use by members of the public to familiarise them with metric units. Publicity materials and metric conversion tables were distributed to members of the public. A poster and slogan design competition for primary and secondary school students was organised to stimulate new ideas from the younger generation on the promotion of metrication. In arranging these promotional activities, the committee invited members from the Junior Police Call organisation to assist in the promotion of metrication and appointed them as 'Metrication Ambassadors' in recognition of their voluntary efforts.

8
EMPLOYMENT

COMPENSATING for the lack of natural resources, Hong Kong's best asset is its people. A stable and motivated workforce is essential to Hong Kong's economic growth. As of the third quarter of 1992, Hong Kong had a workforce of 2.8 million, of whom 64 per cent were male and 36 per cent female. Of this workforce, 27.9 per cent were engaged in wholesale and retail trades, restaurants and hotels; 10.8 per cent in transport, storage and communications; 8.6 per cent in construction; 8.6 per cent in financing, insurance, real estate and business services; and 23.5 per cent in manufacturing. According to the survey of employment, vacancies and payroll in the manufacturing sector conducted in September, 571 181 people were engaged in 41 937 establishments, including some 239 947 people in the textile and wearing apparel sectors, which are the largest employers in the manufacturing industry, with the electronics and fabricated metal products industries being the next two largest employers.

Details of the distribution of manufacturing establishments and of the number of people engaged in them are at Appendices 17 and 18.

Unemployment for the third quarter of 1992 was 1.9 per cent, and underemployment 1.9 per cent. Compared with 1991, the unemployment rate decreased slightly. This showed that Hong Kong's labour market remained tight during the year as a result of economic activities continuing at a relatively high level albeit with signs of easing off at times.

New approaches were being adopted by employers to tackle the problem of staff recruitment and retention. Higher wages were offered while a limited number of foreign workers were allowed to be brought in. The new airport project is likely to further tighten the labour supply in the construction industry and a small number of foreign workers have already been recruited.

Wages

Wage rates are calculated on a time basis, either daily or monthly, or on an incentive basis depending on the volume of work performed. These rates continued to increase in money terms during the year. The average wage rate for all employees, including wage earners and salaried employees up to the supervisory level, increased by 10.2 per cent in money terms, or by 0.3 per cent in real terms between September 1991 and September 1992.

The average wage rate in the manufacturing sector rose by 10.3 per cent in money terms between September 1991 and September 1992. After allowing for rises in consumer prices, the wage rate increased in real terms by 0.4 per cent during the same period.

In September, 75 per cent of manual workers in the manufacturing sector received a daily wage, including fringe benefits, of $174 or more, and 25 per cent received $261 or more. The overall average daily wage was $224.

Employee Benefits

The Employment Ordinance provides for benefits including statutory holidays, annual leave, rest days, maternity leave, sickness allowance, severance payment, long service payment and other entitlements for employees. In addition, some employers provide employees with various types of fringe benefits such as subsidised meals or food allowances, good attendance bonuses, free medical or subsidised treatment and free or subsidised transport. Many employees also enjoy a year-end bonus of one month's pay or more under their employment contracts, usually paid just before the lunar new year.

While there is no central provident fund in Hong Kong, the government has encouraged employers to establish their own provident fund schemes and in recent years, an increasing number of employers have done so to provide improved long-term security for their employees. Up to the end of 1992, a total of 13 008 private retirement schemes had been approved by the Inland Revenue Department.

In November 1991, an inter-departmental working group on retirement protection was set up under the chairmanship of the Secretary for Education and Manpower to review the options, other than a central provident fund, which would enable workers to secure better retirement protection. In October 23, 1992, a consultation paper on *A Community-Wide Retirement Protection System* was issued to the general public and their views on it were invited.

Under the long service payment scheme, employees who have completed five years' service or more are entitled to long service payment upon dismissal other than by way of summary dismissal or redundancy, or upon retirement on grounds of ill-health. The payment is payable also to the families of eligible employees who die in service. Retirement at the age of 65 or above with at least 10 years' service will also attract long service payment. The amount of long service payment is calculated at the rate of two-thirds of a month's wages for each year of service. The amount receivable is reduced at a rate which takes into account the factors of age and years of service.

The Employment Ordinance was amended in July 1992 to better protect an employee who is dismissed due to removal of the workplace. Before the amendment, an employee who was dismissed in such circumstances was entitled to severance payment if the workplace were moved across Victoria Harbour. The ordinance amendment enables a dismissed employee to claim severance payment if the removal causes him undue hardship, even though the removal is not across the harbour.

To discourage exploitation of workers, the maximum penalty for late or non-payment of wages by unscrupulous employers was increased tenfold in May 1992. An imprisonment term of one year for the offence was also introduced.

Labour Conditions

Children below the age of 15 are prohibited from working in any industrial undertaking. Children aged 13 and 14 may be employed in non-industrial establishments subject to their having completed nine years' education and other conditions which aim to protect their safety, health and welfare. However the vast majority of children in this age group are still in the formal education sector.

Working hours, night work, rest periods, overtime work for young persons aged below 18 and women in industrial establishments and work in dangerous trades are strictly regulated by law.

The Labour Inspectorate of the Labour Department is responsible for monitoring employers' compliance with labour standards and statutory benefits in respect of employment of women and young persons, payment of wages, leave, sickness allowance and maternity protection as stipulated in the Employment Ordinance which applies to both local and foreign workers.

In addition to regular inspections of workplaces six special teams are deployed to enforce the provisions of the Employment Ordinance for both local and foreign workers.

Special campaigns are organised each year to tackle particular subjects. In 1992, nine campaigns involving 26 100 establishments were conducted to deter the employment of children and illegal immigrants.

Labour Legislation

The Commissioner for Labour is the principal adviser to the government on labour affairs and is responsible for initiating proposals for new labour legislation and amendments to existing legislation. In respect of labour matters, the government's policy is to achieve a level of safety, health and welfare for employees in Hong Kong broadly equivalent to those provided in neighbouring countries at a similar stage of economic development. This objective has been achieved through legislative enactments totalling 125 in the past decade. During 1992, 17 pieces of labour legislation were enacted.

Labour Advisory Board

The Labour Advisory Board, a non-statutory advisory body on labour matters, plays an active role in the formulation of labour policies and legislation. Established in 1927, the board has six members representing employers and another six representing employees, with the Commissioner for Labour or her deputy as the *ex-officio* chairman. Of the employer representatives, five are nominated by five major employer associations and one appointed *ad personam*. Five of the employee representatives are elected by registered employee trade unions and one appointed *ad personam*. All 12 members are appointed by the Governor.

To cope with the increasing range and complexity of work and to encourage greater participation by employers and employees, committees have been set up under the Labour Advisory Board on special subject areas such as employment services, industrial safety and health, labour relations, employees' compensation and the implementation of international labour standards. A number of employers and employees are co-opted to serve on these committees. The process of consultation through the Labour Advisory Board ensures that the views of the employers and employees can be sufficiently canvassed in the formulation of labour policies to provide a progressive yet balanced programme of labour legislation for the benefit of all concerned.

International Labour Conventions

The International Labour Organisation adopts international labour conventions which set out the standards on matters relating to basic human rights, employment, social policy, labour administration, labour relations, conditions of work and social security. As a dependent territory of the United Kingdom, Hong Kong's declarations on the application of the conventions are made by the United Kingdom Government after consultation with the Hong Kong Government. The Commissioner for Labour ensures that Hong Kong's obligations under International Labour Conventions are observed.

International Labour Conventions have significant influence on the formulation of labour legislation in the territory. Hong Kong now has a comprehensive body of labour law governing the conditions of employment, safety and health and employees' compensation. As at December, Hong Kong applied 48 conventions, 29 in full and 19 with modification, and compared favourably with most members of the International Labour Organisation in the region.

Trade Unions

In Hong Kong, trade unions must be registered under the Trade Unions Ordinance, which is administered by the Registrar of Trade Unions. Once registered, a trade union becomes a corporate body and enjoys immunity from certain civil suits.

During the year, 17 new unions were registered. At the end of the year, there were 522 unions, comprising 481 employees' unions, 27 employers' associations and 14 mixed organisations of employees and employers, and their total memberships were about 488 000, 2 900 and 15 400 respectively.

The majority of employees' unions are affiliated to one of the six local societies registered under the Societies Ordinance – Hong Kong Federation of Trade Unions (87 affiliated unions with about 181 900 members); Hong Kong and Kowloon Trade Unions Council (69 affiliated unions with about 30 600 members); Hong Kong Confederation of Trade Unions (27 affiliated unions with about 71 100 members); the Joint Organisation of Unions, Hong Kong (18 affiliated unions with about 9 900 members); Hong Kong Trade Union Education Centre (13 affiliated unions with about 65 000 members); and the Federation of Hong Kong and Kowloon Labour Unions (18 affiliated unions with about 23 800 members). The remaining 249 employees' unions have a total membership of about 105 700.

Labour Administration and Services

Headed by the Commissioner for Labour, the Labour Department is responsible for formulating proposals on labour legislation, promoting good labour relations, protecting the safety and health of workers, providing assistance to job seekers and to employees injured at work and persons suffering from occupational diseases in obtaining compensation, and enforcement of legislation regulating employment conditions. During 1992, there were 6 799 prosecutions for breaches of ordinances and regulations administered by the Labour Department. Fines totalling $19,420,700 were imposed.

Labour Relations

In 1992, the Labour Relations Division of the Labour Department conciliated in 137 trade disputes (each involving 21 or more workers) which involved 11 work stoppages, with a loss of 3 296 working days. The service also dealt with 17 130 claims for wages and other employment-related payments.

The Labour Relations Ordinance provides the machinery for special conciliation, voluntary arbitration and boards of enquiry to settle trade disputes which cannot be resolved through ordinary conciliation.

The Labour Relations Division endeavours to promote harmonious labour-management relations in the private sector through a variety of activities such as promotional visits to individual establishments, employers' associations and employees' trade unions; organising training courses, seminars and exhibitions; and publishing newsletters, information leaflets and pamphlets on a wide range of labour matters. Four territory-wide seminars on case studies of the Employment Ordinance and two seminars on the community-wide retirement protection system were organised in 1992. These seminars attracted 1 000 participants.

Two industry-wide committees comprising representatives from employers' associations, trade unions and government have been set up in the catering and construction industries to provide meeting points for relevant parties to discuss labour relations matters of mutual concern.

The Labour Tribunal

The Labour Tribunal, which is part of the judiciary, is intended to provide a quick, inexpensive and informal method of adjudicating certain types of disputes between employees and employers.

In 1992, the tribunal heard 3 949 cases involving employees as claimants, and a further 426 cases initiated by employers. More than $42 million was awarded by the presiding officers. Of these cases, 87 per cent were referred by the Labour Relations Service after unsuccessful conciliation attempts.

Protection of Wages on Insolvency Fund

The Protection of Wages on Insolvency Fund is financed by an annual levy of $250 on each business registration certificate. Employees who are owed wages and other termination benefits by their insolvent employers may apply to the fund for *ex-gratia* payment. It covers wages not exceeding $8,000 for services rendered during a period of four months preceding the date of application. It also covers seven days' wages in lieu of notice, up to $2,000. In respect of severance payment, it covers an applicant's entitlement in full up to $8,000 (which is the priority claim limit in a winding-up or bankruptcy) plus 50 per cent of his entitlement in excess of $8,000.

Finding Employment

The Employment Services Division of the Labour Department provides free placement services to help employers recruit staff and job-seekers to find suitable employment. Its Local Employment Service operates from 10 offices which are linked by a facsimile system for the rapid exchange of vacancy information. Starting from 1992, employers wishing to employ foreign workers under the importation of labour scheme are required to notify the service of vacancies. This requirement ensures that local job-seekers have priority to fill those vacancies.

As a result of economic restructuring in recent years, there is a growing need for local workers to be retrained so that they can obtain employment in another trade or a higher level job in the same trade. During the year, the government established an Employees Retraining Scheme which was financed by a levy imposed on employers of imported workers. Under this scheme, a local employee undergoing retraining is paid a retraining allowance. The Employees Retraining Board comprising representatives of employers, employees, training authorities and government was established to manage the funds and advise on the planning and implementation of the scheme. The Local Employment Service is responsible for processing applications under the scheme and assisting the retrainees in finding employment.

The Selective Placement Division helps disabled persons integrate into the community by providing a free employment counselling and placement service for hearing impaired, sight impaired, physically disabled, mentally retarded and ex-mentally ill persons seeking open employment.

The division launched various activities to promote its work and the employability of the disabled. These included district-based exhibitions, presentation of awards to employers and disabled employees, and quarterly newsletters for distribution to employers of various trades and industries. Pamphlets concerning employment of people with various disability types were also issued to members of the public. Promotional visits were made regularly in order to widen the employment opportunities of disabled job-seekers.

Careers Guidance

The Careers Advisory Service of the Labour Department is responsible for promoting careers education in Hong Kong.

The service operates careers information centres, each equipped with a reference library, an audio-visual unit with sound-on-slides, cassette tapes and videos, and an enquiry service on employment and training opportunities. It also produces written and audio-visual resource materials including careers pamphlets, job sheets, slide presentations and films. These materials are made available to the public free of charge.

The service organises a wide range of careers activities for young people including careers seminars, quizzes, exhibitions and visits to commercial and industrial establishments. In February, it joined hands with the Hong Kong Trade Development Council for the first time in staging the *Education and Careers Expo '92* which attracted more than 160 000 visitors.

The service also helps in the training of careers teachers. Every year it organises a seminar on careers education in conjunction with the Education Department and Hong Kong Association of Careers Masters and Guidance Masters, and runs a certificate course for careers teachers jointly with the Education Department and the University of Hong Kong.

Foreign Workers

The Immigration Department is responsible for controlling the entry of foreign workers. Generally speaking, a foreigner may be permitted to work or invest in Hong Kong if he possesses a special skill, knowledge or experience of value to and not readily available in Hong Kong, or if he is in a position to contribute to the economy. To maintain Hong Kong's economic competitiveness, the Immigration Department always ensures that the policy is well understood by employers and is flexibly applied. Genuine businessmen and entrepreneurs are welcome to establish a presence in Hong Kong, bringing with them the needed capital and expertise. Qualified professionals, technical staff, administrators and managerial personnel are also admitted with minimum formalities.

During the year, 13 859 professionals and persons with technical, administrative or managerial skills from more than 50 countries were admitted for employment.

To remove manpower shortage in certain bottleneck areas, a separate scheme for the importation of skilled workers at the supervisory, technician, craftsman and operative level was introduced in 1989 and repeated in 1990. After a review, it was decided in January 1992 that the scheme should be expanded in such a way that the total number of such workers in Hong Kong did not exceed 25 000 at any one time. Discounting those 13 000 workers who came under the previous schemes and whose contracts were still valid, employers were allowed to import 12 000 workers in 1992. This scheme received overwhelming response from employers. Despite the quota of 12 000 workers, the Immigration Department received some 8 350 applications from employers, involving a total of 92 600 workers.

In addition, to facilitate the construction of the new airport and related projects, a scheme to import initially 2 000 construction workers was introduced in May 1990. A quota of 1 247 has so far been allocated.

Foreign Domestic Helpers

The entry of foreign domestic helpers is subject to the condition that they have experience in that field of work, that their employers are *bona fide* Hong Kong residents who are prepared to offer reasonable terms of employment including wages and accommodation, and that the employers are willing to provide for the helpers' maintenance in Hong Kong as well as the costs for repatriation to their country of origin. Because of the affluence of Hong Kong, the demand for foreign domestic helpers has increased steadily. In 1992, there were 101 182 such helpers in Hong Kong, representing an increase of 19.6 per cent when compared with 84 619 in 1991. About 88.1 per cent of these domestic helpers were citizens of the Philippines.

Attestation of Employment Contracts for Foreign Domestic Helpers

For the purpose of controlling and protecting the employment conditions of foreign domestic helpers in Hong Kong, the Foreign Domestic Helpers Service of the Labour Department attested 80 823 employment contracts in 1992.

The service is frequently consulted by the public on application procedures for the employment of foreign domestic helpers and interpretation of the terms of employment contracts. It also provides a conciliation service in wage claims arising out of such contracts.

Employment Agencies

The Employment Agencies Administration of the Labour Department is responsible for administering Part 12 of the Employment Ordinance and the Employment Agency Regulations, which were amended in May 1992 to facilitate more effective control on the licensing and operation of employment agencies in Hong Kong. The service issued 1 000 licences in 1992.

Employment Outside Hong Kong

The External Employment Service is responsible for enforcing the Contracts for Employment Outside Hong Kong Ordinance, which was amended in May 1992 to extend the requirement for such contracts to be attested by the Commissioner for Labour from manual workers to include non-manual workers with monthly wages not exceeding $20,000. The service attested 85 new contracts in 1992.

Industrial Safety

The Factory Inspectorate of the Labour Department is responsible for enforcing the Factories and Industrial Undertakings Ordinance and its subsidiary regulations. These regulations provide for the safety and health of workers in factories, restaurants, catering establishments, building and engineering construction sites and other industrial undertakings. Advice and assistance are given to managements on various safety and health aspects, including the adoption of safe working practices and factory layouts to achieve a better working environment. The inspectorate also investigates industrial accidents and dangerous occurrences.

The Factories and Industrial Undertakings (Cargo Handling) (Amendment) Regulations and the Factories and Industrial Undertakings (Noise at Work) Regulations were enacted in July 1992. The former extends the requirements on safe handling and storage of containers from container ports to all container yards, and the latter provides better protection for employees engaged in noisy work processes.

To promote self-regulation, the Safety Programme Promotion Unit helped industry develop in-plant safety committees. The unit assisted management and workers in identifying and assessing hazards at work and in devising and improving their safety and health programmes. The unit also assisted in organising seminars, safety training courses and other promotional activities. A two-day symposium on safety and health management with training workshops for trainers was organised jointly with the Regional Office for Asia and the Pacific of the International Labour Organisation in May.

The Factory Inspectorate placed much emphasis on the regulatory activities in high-risk areas of factories and construction sites. Special enforcement campaigns were launched in the year to promote machinery safety, fire prevention and construction safety. During these campaigns 23 568 factories, 669 restaurants and catering establishments and 1 246 construction sites were inspected and 1 536 summonses were taken out.

Throughout the year, the Industrial Safety Training Centre conducted courses for workers, supervisors and managers from various industries. Talks on safety at work were organised for teachers and students of technical institutes and special talks were arranged with the Education Department as part of the Summer Job Safety promotional activities. The centre also gave talks on safety management to medical and engineering students of the University of Hong Kong and business students in post-secondary institutions. In collaboration with Hong Kong Polytechnic, the centre continued to organise evening courses leading to the award of a post-experience certificate in industrial safety. It also assisted the Construction Industry Training Authority in running certificate courses for construction safety officers.

The inspectorate, in conjunction with the Information Services Department, continued its publicity programme for the promotion of industrial safety and health. It also assisted the new airport projects co-ordination office in publishing the airport core programme site safety manual for promoting the safety of the new airport projects. Four large-scale symposia and conferences on safety and health management, construction safety, printing safety and safety auditing were held.

A construction site safety award scheme was organised later in the year jointly by the Factory Inspectorate, Housing Department, Hong Kong Construction Association Ltd and Hong Kong Construction Industry Employees General Union.

The Pressure Equipment Division of the Labour Department administers the Boilers and Pressure Vessels Ordinance and the Gasholders Examination Ordinance to ensure the safe use and operation of all equipment covered by the two ordinances.

The Boilers and Pressure Vessels Ordinance stipulates that boilers, including thermal oil heaters, steam receivers, steam containers, air receivers and pressurised cement tanks mounted on trucks or trailers must be approved and registered with the division and must be examined periodically by qualified engineers who are on the approved list as boiler inspectors/air receiver inspectors. The division also investigates accidents involving pressure equipment.

The Pressure Equipment Advisory Committee advises the Boilers and Pressure Vessels Authority, presently the Commissioner for Labour, on the effective control of pressure equipment. The authority accords recognition to local inspection bodies, who meet the criteria, for issue of certificates of inspection during construction of the equipment under the ordinance. The authority also issues advice in the form of code of practice and guides on the operation and maintenance of different types of pressure equipment.

Under the Gasholders Examination Ordinance, the division approves the design of gasholders and carries out inspection during fabrication and repairs, and subsequently conducts annual inspections.

The division provides technical advice to the Director of Fire Services on approval of pressurised containers and storage installations for compressed gases within the provisions of the Dangerous Goods Ordinance. The expertise in the field of pressure equipment is available, free of charge, to any organisation in private or public sectors.

Occupational Health and Hygiene

The Occupational Health Division of the Labour Department protects workers against health hazards arising from employment. It provides an advisory service to government and the public on matters concerning the health of workers and the hygiene of the work-place, and complements the Factory Inspectorate Division in supervising health standards and practices in industry.

During the year, the division took part in a number of seminars to promote occupational health. With sponsorship from the Occupational Safety and Health Council, it also organised a week-long exhibition on *Occupational Health Perspective – Industrial Chemicals and You* which attracted some 30 000 visitors. It continued to publish a series of booklets and codes of practice on occupational health and the prevention of occupational diseases. Occupational health promotion and education activities were carried out by nursing officers.

A major responsibility of the division is to investigate notified occupational diseases and potential health hazards reported by the Factory Inspectorate and to determine preventive action. Surveys were conducted in various industries and a number of epidemiological studies on health and hygiene conditions were completed. Programmes to monitor various chemicals, dusts and other occupational health hazards were also carried out.

The division carries out medical examinations on personnel exposed to ionising radiation, users of compressed-air breathing apparatus, and government employees working in compressed air or engaged in diving or pest control. It also deals with cases of silicosis under the Pneumoconiosis (Compensation) Ordinance. The registered nurses of the division handle medical clearance for employees' compensation cases and its occupational health officers are appointed as members of special assessment boards and prostheses and surgical appliance boards under the Employees' Compensation Ordinance.

The laboratory of the division, which is a member of the Hong Kong Laboratory Accreditation Scheme, continued to carry out analytical tests on biological samples collected from workers and on other environmental samples taken during site visits.

Occupational Safety and Health Council

The Occupational Safety and Health Council aims to promote a safer and healthier working environment through education and training, promotion of the use of modern technology, dissemination of technical knowledge, provision of consultancy services, and encouragement of co-operation and communication among government and non-government bodies having such common goals.

The council comprises 20 members appointed by the Governor and drawn from employers and employees, academic and professional fields, and the government. It is financed by a levy on the premium of all employees' compensation insurance policies.

To assist the council in routine operation, five functional committees have been formed to deal with publicity, staffing, finance, education and research, and general affairs. There are also nine industry-based committees covering the catering, construction, electronics, metalware, ship building and ship repairing, plastics, printing, transport and physical distribution industries. One additional advisory committee specialising in chemicals was established in the year.

The year under review ended with a significant expansion in the training activities of the council in that agreement was reached to transfer general safety and health training courses by stages from the Labour Department to the council. Other training courses for safety and health supervisors; health and safety management for civil engineers; competence programmes on ionising, radiation protection and safe handling of asbestos; management of dangerous substances; laser safety; and noise assessment were also conducted with gratifying feedback from the public. A total of 3 858 employees or professionals were trained through the courses.

Throughout the year, the council organised 13 seminars which focused on selected technical topics for professionals and interested members of the public. Research projects were also undertaken by the council to improve occupational safety and health in Hong Kong. Consultancy services of the council, which are provided on a cost recovery basis, also experienced increased demand.

The council also produced safety and health literature, codes of practice and guidebooks, Green Cross (a bi-monthly magazine), safety advice pamphlets, bulletins for individual industries and posters. A comprehensive library housing a wide collection of safety and health journals, technical reference books and an advance data base on occupational safety and health is open for public use.

In addition, the council launched campaigns to arouse public interest in occupational safety and health. A major campaign was the *Occupational Safety and Health Week* staged from November 9 to 15.

The council's occupational safety and health employees' participation scheme continued to offer financial assistance to employees' organisations running safety and health activities. During the year, 21 employees' organisations received financial subsidy under the scheme.

Employees' Compensation
The Labour Department administers the Employees' Compensation Ordinance and the Pneumoconiosis (Compensation) Ordinance. The department ensures that injured employees and dependants of deceased employees covered by the Employees' Compensation Ordinance obtain compensation from their employers in respect of injuries or deaths caused by accidents arising out of and in the course of employment, or by occupational diseases. It also ensures that persons covered by the Pneumoconiosis (Compensation) Ordinance obtain compensation as soon as possible from the Pneumoconiosis Compensation Fund which is financed by a levy imposed on the construction and quarry industries.

The Employees' Compensation Assistance Ordinance establishes the Employees' Compensation Assistance Fund to make payments of statutory compensation and damages at common law due to an injured employee or dependants of a deceased employee when an employer defaults or an insurer becomes insolvent. It also covers claims from employers failing to obtain indemnity from their insolvent insurers. The fund, financed by a levy on all employees' compensation insurance premiums, is administered by the Employees' Compensation Assistance Fund Board.

Under the two-tier Employees' Compensation Assessment Board system, employees with work-related injuries which are likely to result in permanent incapacity are assessed by the boards at 10 major hospitals in Hong Kong. In 1992, ordinary assessment boards convened 534 sessions and completed assessment of 16 200 cases referred to them by the Commissioner for Labour and 1 221 review cases. Special assessment boards convened six sessions and completed assessment of six cases referred to them by the ordinary assessment boards.

In 1992, 189 pneumoconiosis cases were awarded compensation amounting to $28,646,875. The Pneumoconiosis Compensation Fund Board also financed research, educational and publicity programmes to enhance awareness of pneumoconiosis and to promote prevention of the disease.

The Employees' Compensation Ordinance was amended in July 1992 to provide for a simplified procedure for the settlement of minor injury cases which only incapacitate the injured employees for seven days or less. Under this new procedure, an employer may agree with his employee on the amount of compensation to be paid without recourse to the Labour Department or the Court.

The coverage of the ordinance has been expanded to include part-time domestic helpers. The definition of 'dependants' has also been extended to include children of an employee born after his death and parents and grandparents who will retire within two years and will then be likely to be dependent on the earnings of the deceased for a living.

Telephone Enquiry Service
In 1992, the staff of the General Enquiry Telephone Service was enhanced to handle 172 486 public enquiries on the Employment Ordinance and its subsidiary regulations, the Protection of Wages on Insolvency Ordinance, the Employees' Compensation Ordinance, and matters relating to the employment of foreign domestic helpers. Where appropriate, pre-recorded tapes in both English and Chinese were used to supplement the information given.

9
PRIMARY PRODUCTION

EVERY day in Hong Kong, people consume about 920 tonnes of rice, 1 020 tonnes of vegetables, 8 060 pigs, 410 head of cattle, 280 tonnes of poultry, 550 tonnes of fish and 1 460 tonnes of fruit. Based on these figures, Hong Kong people, according to the United Nations Food and Agriculture Organisation, are among the world's highest consumers of protein.

Most of Hong Kong's food supplies are imported and China alone supplies about 49 per cent of Hong Kong's total requirements. Local production enables Hong Kong to maintain some degree of self-sufficiency and helps to stabilise the price and supply of fresh produce. In terms of quantity, local farmers and fishermen produce about 26 per cent of fresh vegetables, 27 per cent of live poultry, six per cent of live pigs, 12 per cent of freshwater fish and 63 per cent of all live and fresh marine fish consumed. Local produce is highly regarded in the marketplace for its freshness and quality and so tends to fetch higher prices.

While local agricultural and fisheries production plays an important role in supplying Hong Kong with fresh food, the government, as with other sectors of the economy, does not give direct subsidies to the primary industries or seek to protect them from the free operation of market forces. It does, however, provide infrastructural and technical support services to facilitate their development.

The Agriculture and Fisheries Department is the co-ordinator and main provider of these services, the purpose of which is to help the primary industries to increase their productivity and efficiency and take advantage of new market opportunities. The department studies the business efficiency of different sectors of the industries to establish and update productivity standards and identify areas for improvement.

Local production statistics are given at Appendix 22.

Agricultural Industry
In Hong Kong, only about eight per cent of the total land area is suitable for farming, so local agriculture is directed towards the production of high quality fresh foodstuffs through intensive land use.

The most common crops are vegetables and flowers although a small quantity of fruit and other high-yield field crops is also grown. The area of land under vegetable and flower cultivation was about 1 810 hectares in 1992. The value of crop production was about $442 million.

Main vegetable crops are white cabbage, flowering cabbage and lettuce. They are grown throughout the year, with peak production in the cooler months. Some exotic temperate vegetables including tomatoes, sweet corn and celery are also grown. Straw mushrooms are produced using industrial cotton waste as the growing medium.

Common types of flowers such as gladioli, chrysanthemums and ginger lilies are grown throughout the year. A wide range of ornamental plants is produced in the various commercial nurseries. Peach blossom and ornamental citrus are grown specially for the lunar new year.

Because there is insufficient land for extensive grazing, pigs and poultry are the principal animals reared for food. Pigs in Hong Kong are mostly crosses of imported breeds. The value of locally-produced pigs in 1992 amounted to $155 million and that of poultry, including chickens, ducks, pigeons and quails, amounted to $525 million. Local production of pigs and poultry is declining as the industry adjusts to the progressive implementation of environmental pollution controls under the livestock waste control scheme.

Agricultural Development

The Agriculture and Fisheries Department conducts investigations and applied research into modern methods of crop and livestock production and the control and prevention of plant and animal diseases. One of the more important fields of study is pest management without the use of toxic pesticides. New farming techniques, particularly those requiring less labour, are evaluated and promoted if found suitable for development under local conditions. Experiments are conducted with a view to improving quality and yield. Good quality seeds and breeding stocks of pigs and poultry are produced and made available for commercial propagation.

To help farmers comply with the livestock waste control scheme, the department has introduced the rearing of pigs on sawdust litter, an innovative non-polluting and cost-effective pig husbandry technique. The simple technique involves using a special bedding material comprising sawdust and bacterial products in the pig shed to decompose the pig manure *in situ*. Studies have also been conducted on the recycling of spent sawdust litter for horticultural and landscaping use.

Local vegetable growers are encouraged to cultivate premium vegetables including traditional Chinese types, exotic varieties and vegetables produced through organic farming and hydroponics. Technical advice and marketing services are provided to help interested farmers.

Agricultural extension officers are posted by the department throughout the New Territories to deal with farming problems and to liaise with co-operative societies and rural associations. Vocational training and seminars on special topics of interest and importance are conducted.

Technical assistance is made available to farmers, who are also frequently advised about the proper handling and safe use of pesticides. Visits are arranged for farmers to see government experimental farms and farming projects.

Low interest loans administered by the department are available to the agricultural industry from the Kadoorie Agricultural Aid Loan Fund, the J.E. Joseph Trust Fund and the Vegetable Marketing Organisation Loan Fund. By December 31, 1992, loans issued since the inception of these three funds had reached $292 million, with $287 million having been repaid.

There are 65 co-operative societies and two federations among the farming community with a total membership of some 11 548 farmers. These societies help to promote agriculture and the Director of Agriculture and Fisheries acts as their registrar. His powers and duties relate to such matters as the registration of co-operative societies and their by-laws, the auditing of accounts, inspection and enquiry, and general supervision of operations.

An agricultural land rehabilitation scheme aimed at bringing fallow arable land back to efficient cultivation is being implemented by the department. Infrastructural improvements in irrigation, drainage and farm road access are being effected and a package of assistance including advance payment of rent, soil improvement and marketing facilities offered. The results of a pilot scheme at Cheung Po in Yuen Long and another at Hok Tau in Fanling have been satisfactory. Plans are in hand to extend this scheme to other suitable areas.

Fishing Industry

Marine fish constitute one of Hong Kong's most important primary products. In 1992, total production from marine capture and culture fisheries was estimated at about 223 400 tonnes with a wholesale value of $2,510 million. This represented a decrease of three per cent in weight and a decrease of one per cent in value compared with 1991. In weight terms, marine capture contributed 98 per cent towards total production while the remainder came from culture operations.

The Hong Kong fishing fleet, manned by 21 000 fishermen, comprises some 4 500 vessels of which 4 200 are mechanised. It plays a vital role in primary production, catching over 150 species of commercially important food fish and supplying over 55 per cent of all marine produce consumed locally. Golden thread, bigeyes, lizard-fishes, squid, melon seed, conger pike eels, croakers, hairtail, scads and yellow belly are the most important species landed.

Major fishing methods include trawling, lining, gill-netting and purse-seining. About 60 per cent of the vessels are between 10 and 34 metres in length comprising mainly trawlers, liners and gill-netters that operate on the continental shelf of the South China Sea between the Gulf of Tonkin and the East China Sea. The remaining 40 per cent of the vessels are less than 10 metres long, consisting primarily of gill-netters, hand-liners, and purse-seiners which operate in shallow coastal waters.

Trawling accounted for 73 per cent or 160 000 tonnes of marine fish landed in 1992. The total landed catch of live and fresh marine fish available for local consumption amounted to 96 000 tonnes with an estimated wholesale value of $1,050 million.

Marine fish culture is practised within 26 designated fish culture zones, most of which are to be found around the coast of the eastern New Territories. Fish culture licences are issued by the Agriculture and Fisheries Department. At the year-end, there were 1 651 licensed mariculturists. Young fish are reared in cages suspended from buoyed rafts. Grouper, seabream and snapper are the most common culture species. In 1992, this sector supplied 3 400 tonnes of live marine fish valued at $210 million.

Freshwater fish are also cultured. Fish ponds covering 1 350 hectares are located in the New Territories, mostly around Yuen Long. Several different species of carp are cultured in the same pond, each with a different food requirement to maximise utilisation of the nutrients introduced. The land area devoted to fish ponds has gradually declined because of increasing urbanisation of the New Territories. During the year, pond culture yielded 5 400 tonnes, or 13 per cent of the local consumption of freshwater fish.

Fisheries Development

The Agriculture and Fisheries Department conducts a wide spectrum of studies on marine resources, aquaculture and the environmental impact of development activities on fisheries to assist the development of the local fishery industry.

Marine resource studies emphasise optimising production from currently exploited fisheries resources and exploring the potential of under-developed resources. Efforts to develop a deep sea prawn resource located in the South China Sea at depths between 500 to 1 000 metres continued. In addition, pair trawl fishermen were directed towards a deep sea prawn species occurring at 200 metres depth. This was pursued by interested fishermen with onboard freezing equipment provided by the Fish Marketing Organisation.

Large scale development projects involving construction works affecting the foreshore and seabed exert adverse impact on the marine environment and marine resources. To offset such impact and to enhance recovery, the department is actively investigating the feasibility of deploying artificial reefs.

Aquaculture studies are directed towards the development of more efficient culture systems and improved husbandry techniques to increase productivity and minimise impact on the environment. The feasibility of open sea cage culture is being explored with a view to introducing marine fish culture to more exposed coastal waters. Marine environment studies are conducted to assess the impact of pollution and red tides on fisheries, particularly mariculture operations, to help the industry minimise production loss.

Fisheries development work includes modernising fishing craft and introducing more efficient fishing gear and navigational aids. A free advisory service on fishing vessel hull design, fishing methods and fishing equipment is available to fishermen while studies are conducted to assess the suitability of new fishing gear and methods for local application. Training classes in navigation, engineering, radiotelephony, use of ancillary equipment such as radar and weather facsimile, and seminars on safety on board fishing vessels at sea are organised regularly at major fishing ports.

The department also advises local fishermen interested in building steel-hulled fishing vessels and organises sea-fishing endorsement courses to train and qualify them to operate these vessels.

The department administers four loan funds servicing the fishing fleet. The Fisheries Development Loan Fund with a capital of $7 million provides long-term capital for the development of improved vessels, gear and equipment. The World Refugee Year Loan Fund, the Fish Marketing Organisation Loan Fund and the Co-operative for American Relief Everywhere Loan Fund with total capital of $26.52 million at the end of 1992, are revolving funds which provide shorter-term financing mainly for recurrent purposes. By December 31, loans issued since the inception of the four funds totalled $237 million, with $220 million having been repaid.

At the end of the year, 2 067 fishermen were members of co-operative societies and there were 64 societies and four federations supported by fisherfolk.

Close contact with the fishing community is maintained by liaison with producer associations and fishermen's co-operative societies through eight Fish Marketing Organisation liaison offices at the major fishing ports.

Marketing

Much of the wholesale marketing of primary products – particularly fresh foods – is the responsibility of the Agriculture and Fisheries Department and the Vegetable and Fish Marketing Organisations. This year, 47 per cent of the total quantity of locally-produced vegetables, and 68 per cent of the total landings of marine fish were sold through the organisations.

The Vegetable Marketing Organisation operates under the Agricultural Products (Marketing) Ordinance, which also provides for the establishment of a Marketing Advisory Board to advise the Director of Marketing (the Director of Agriculture and Fisheries). It seeks to maximise returns to farmers by minimising marketing costs. The organisation is responsible for transporting locally-produced vegetables from the New Territories to the wholesale market in Kowloon, providing marketing facilities, and supervising sales and financial transactions in the market. Revenue is obtained from a 10 per cent commission on sales. The organisation is non-profit-making. Surpluses are ploughed back in the development of marketing services and the farming industries. It provides ancillary services such as the acquisition and sale of agricultural supplies to farmers and the awarding of secondary and tertiary education scholarships to their children. It also monitors and checks pesticide residue levels in both the imported and locally produced vegetables handled by the organisation, to safeguard public health. During the year, 44 400 tonnes of local vegetables valued at $122 million were sold through the organisation.

The Fish Marketing Organisation operates under the Marine Fish (Marketing) Ordinance, which also provides for the establishment of a Fish Marketing Advisory Board. The ordinance provides for the control of the landing, transport, wholesale marketing, and import and export of marine fish. The organisation operates seven wholesale fish markets. Revenue comes from a commission on the proceeds of sales. Surplus earnings are channelled back into the industry in the form of services such as low-interest loans to fishermen, improvements to the markets, financial support for schools for fishermen's children, and scholarships for secondary and tertiary education.

In 1992, the wholesale fish markets handled 68 000 tonnes of marine fish, crustacea and molluscs which were sold for $590 million. This included 3 300 tonnes of imported marine fish sold through these markets.

The wholesale marketing of imported vegetables, fruit, poultry, eggs, freshwater fish and crustacea takes place at various Agriculture and Fisheries Department wholesale markets located in different parts of Hong Kong Island, Kowloon and the New Territories.

Facilities provided in some of these markets have already become dilapidated, congested and unable to cope with the increasing throughput. Marketing activities have spilled onto adjacent areas, causing obstruction, traffic congestion and environmental problems. To improve the situation, a long-term programme has been devised to replace the outdated markets by establishing large modern wholesale market complexes on Hong Kong Island and in Kowloon to centralise the wholesale marketing of fresh foodstuffs. In the first of these, phase one of the wholesale market complex on Hong Kong Island has been completed and the fruit, freshwater fish and egg markets subsequently relocated to the complex which became fully operational by the end of 1991. Construction work for phase two which includes poultry and vegetable markets is progressing satisfactorily and is expected to be completed by early 1994. Steady progress has also been made in the planning of the Kowloon complex which is to be built on the new West Kowloon reclamation. The complex is to be constructed in two phases and works for phase one started during the year are expected to be completed in late 1993. Pending the eventual completion of the complexes, the department continues to operate a number of temporary wholesale markets – at Western District on Hong Kong Island for poultry, at North District in the New Territories for agricultural products and at Cheung Sha Wan in Kowloon for imported vegetables, freshwater fish and poultry.

Mining and Quarrying

The Mines and Quarries Division of the geotechnical engineering office of the Civil Engineering Department enforces legislation relating to mining, quarrying and explosives. It processes mining and prospecting applications and inspects mining and prospecting areas, stone quarries, blasting sites and explosives stores.

There was no mining activity in 1992, but there was an application for a prospecting licence. During this year, Hong Kong's total consumption of sand, aggregates and other rock products amounted to 19 million tonnes. Around one half of the territory's demand for aggregates and sand is met locally, the balance is imported from China. The local quarries and stone processing sites are supervised by the division.

The Mines and Quarries Division controls the possession, conveyance, storage, manufacture and use of explosives in Hong Kong, and issues shotfirers' blasting certificates. In addition, it manages two government explosives depots, which provide bulk storage facilities for imported as well as locally-manufactured explosives, and undertakes the delivery of explosives from government depots to blasting sites.

Quarrying and site formation works were the largest users of explosives in 1992. Sewerage tunnel construction and seismic surveys also used explosives, albeit in smaller quantities. Overall consumption of explosives in the territory was 4 000 tonnes.

Storage space was provided for imported fireworks for the lunar new year fireworks display in February. The division continued to provide transit storage facilities for explosives and temporary storage for confiscated fireworks awaiting destruction.

10
EDUCATION

A STRONG foundation to develop Hong Kong's human resources for the next century is being laid by a series of reforms to school education and by increasing opportunities at the tertiary level. To maintain Hong Kong's position as one of the economic powerhouses of Asia, education continues to be given high priority in the government budget, where it receives a larger share of resources than any other programme.

With targets of provision almost fully achieved at the school level, and with the tertiary expansion programme well on course, attention during the year was focussed on measures to ensure that schools can deliver the quality of education needed to sustain continued social and economic progress. New policies were implemented in several areas relating to the school curriculum, school management and learning assessments. Major proposals for improving the professional development, status and working environment of teachers were unveiled in the Education Commission's fifth report (ECR5), published in June.

The Structure of the Education System

Formal educational opportunity encompasses kindergartens, primary schools, secondary schools (including technical and prevocational schools), technical institutes, and tertiary level institutions. The great majority of places from primary school upwards are provided either free or at highly-subsidised rates in the public sector. All kindergarten provision is in the private sector, and other areas with strong private support include international schools and schools providing language, computer, and business courses.

All children are required by law to be in full-time education between the ages of six and 15. The core of the education system is thus formed by the primary and secondary schools. However, there is a large demand for formal education both before and after universal education.

Pre-school education begins for most children in a kindergarten, at the age of three. Primary school begins at the age of six, and lasts for six years. At about 12, children progress to a three-year course of junior secondary education in a grammar, prevocational or technical school. After Secondary 3, most stay on for a two-year senior secondary course leading to the first public examination, the Hong Kong Certificate of Education Examination (HKCEE). Others join a full-time craft course of vocational training; while a small number choose to leave formal education at this point.

Following the HKCEE, opportunities for progression include a two-year sixth form course leading to the Hong Kong Advanced Level Examination (HKALE); two or three-year vocational courses leading to a certificate or diploma; and a three-year course of teacher training. After the HKALE, students may gain a place on a degree or diploma course, or on a course of teacher training normally lasting two years. Those leaving full-time education at the end of the senior secondary or sixth form course have opportunities for part-time study or vocational training all the way up to degree level.

Although most educational provision is in the public sector, the government directly manages only a small proportion of primary and secondary schools. Most are operated by non-profit-making voluntary organisations receiving public funds under a code of aid. Tertiary institutions (except for the self-funding Open Learning Institute) are autonomous statutory bodies receiving public funds through the University and Polytechnic Grants Committee (UPGC). A comprehensive system of technical education and vocational training is provided, with public funds, by the statutory Vocational Training Council (VTC).

The Legislative Framework

Any institution offering education to 20 or more pupils in a day must operate in accordance with statutory requirements. The operation of schools (including kindergartens, primary and secondary schools, and commercial colleges) is governed by the Education Ordinance, which provides for the registration of schools, teachers and managers, and for attendance by children between the ages of six and 15. The subsidiary Education Regulations cover a wide range of matters including health and safety provisions, fees and charges, and the qualifications of teachers.

The Post-Secondary Colleges Ordinance covers institutions offering post-secondary courses but outside the tertiary sector. The VTC Ordinance covers technical colleges, technical institutes, industrial training centres, and skills centres for the disabled. Two bodies with an important quality control role, the Hong Kong Examinations Authority (HKEA) and the Hong Kong Council for Academic Accreditation (HKCAA), have been established under their own ordinances. The Education Scholarships Fund Ordinance provides for the administration of the large number of scholarships donated by generous members of the public.

The Director of Education is responsible for supervising education at kindergarten, primary and secondary level. He also supervises institutions registered under the Post-Secondary Colleges Ordinance. He directly controls all government schools, the four colleges of education, the Institute of Language in Education (ILE) and the Curriculum Development Institute.

The main responsibilities of the Education Department relate to the planning and provision of public sector school places; the allocation of pupils to these places; support for curriculum development; professional training for non-graduate teachers; language education for teachers; the setting of academic targets and related assessments; the monitoring of teaching standards; and the administration of funding to public sector schools and some private institutions. The department also plays an important role in policy development and review.

The following figures give some idea of the size and importance of the education system. About 1.2 million students, or 21 per cent of the total population, were in full-time education during the year. They attended 1 900 institutions, and were taught by 54 000 teachers supported by a large number of support staff. There were some 297 000 candidates for local public examinations, with a further 219 000 candidate entries for 18 overseas

115

examinations. The total public budget for education in 1992–3 was $22,860 million. An unknown but certainly very large additional amount was spent privately on education.

Community Participation

Members of the community play an important part in the planning, development and management of the education system at all levels, sitting on advisory bodies such as the Education Commission, Board of Education, Curriculum Development Council, UPGC, and Research Grants Council; on executive bodies like the VTC, HKEA and HKCAA; on management committees of schools; and on the governing bodies of tertiary institutions.

The Education Commission

The Education Commission, the highest advisory body on education, advises the government on the development of the education system in the light of community needs. Its terms of reference are to define overall objectives; to formulate policies, and recommend priorities for implementation having regard to the resources available; to co-ordinate and monitor the development of education at all levels; and to initiate educational research.

The commission has 13 members, of whom 11, including the chairman, are appointed from outside the government to bring a wide range of personal and professional experience to bear on the issues under review. They include the chairmen of the Board of Education, UPGC and VTC. The two government members are the Secretary for Education and Manpower, who is the vice-chairman, and the Director of Education.

In June the commission published its fifth report, containing extensive recommendations for improving the professional development, status and working environment of teachers. Among the major proposals were the upgrading of the colleges of education and Institute of Language in Education into an autonomous Institute of Education; the creation of a new in-service qualification, the Advanced Teacher's Certificate; measures to upgrade 35 per cent of primary teacher posts to graduate status within 15 years; and improvements in teacher/pupil ratios. The report also proposed the creation of three new advisory bodies: an advisory committee on teacher education and qualifications; a committee on home-school co-operation; and a council on professional conduct in education. Following widespread public support during the consultation period, the government made plans to begin implementing the recommendations during 1993.

In October the commission published a draft statement of aims for school education in Hong Kong. This too was well received by the public, and preparations were made to issue a revised version as an official statement of government policy.

The Board of Education

The board is a statutory body appointed to advise the government, through the Director of Education, on educational matters at school level. Its focus is on the implementation of approved policies, and the need for new or modified policies relating to school education. Its members include the chairmen of advisory and executive bodies concerned with the school system: the Curriculum Development Council (CDC); the HKEA; the Private Schools Review Committee, and advisory committees on school guidance and support services, school administration and finance, and school allocation systems. Other members have experience in kindergartens, special schools, school administration, vocational training, tertiary education, business and the professions. Two government officials sit on he board: the Director of Education as vice-chairman, and the Deputy Secretary for Education and Manpower.

The Curriculum Development Council

The CDC was reconstituted in January 1992, along lines recommended in the Education Commission's fourth report (ECR4). It became a free-standing committee appointed by the Governor to advise the government through the Director of Education on curriculum matters. Its members include not only educators, but also employers and parents.

The CDC continued many of the curriculum development activities undertaken by the former Curriculum Development Committee, and examined new curriculum needs. During the year it continued to consolidate syllabus development, conduct research on curriculum issues, and develop school-based curricula. The development of teaching targets and target-related assessments in the three core subjects progressed well, as did the preparation of new subjects: general studies for primary students; and travel and tourism and science for non-science students at the secondary level. Curriculum guides, which help in developing subject syllabuses in compatible directions, were produced for each educational level and issued to schools. Guidelines on environmental education in schools were also issued.

Curriculum Development Institute

The Curriculum Development Institute (CDI) was set up in April 1992 as a new division within the Education Department. It is responsible for developing curricula, and for helping schools to implement curriculum policies and innovations. It provides a secretariat for the CDC; conducts research, experimentation and evaluation in curriculum planning; issues updated curriculum guides and subject syllabuses; develops resource materials, manages resource centres and provides resource library services; liaises with the HKEA, the Advisory Inspectorate of the Education Department and teacher training institutions on the development and evaluation of the curriculum; and reviews school textbooks.

The CDI is staffed by both civil servants and experts from outside the civil service. This arrangement ensures a regular infusion of new ideas to sustain the creative and innovative approach needed for good curriculum development; and also enables the CDI to draw on the practical experience of its civil service members, including their close links with schools. During the year, over a hundred officers were redeployed from the Inspectorate Division to the CDI, and the first non-civil servant experts were recruited.

The University and Polytechnic Grants Committee

The UPGC, appointed by the Governor, advises on the development and funding of higher education, and administers public grants to the tertiary institutions. Its members, all prominent in their field, include 10 academics from overseas, three local academics and five local professional and business people. No government officer sits on the committee, but its secretariat is staffed by civil servants.

Since 1965, when the then University Grants Committee was created, student numbers have increased more than tenfold, from about 4 000 full-time equivalent in two universities to about 48 000 in seven institutions. These, in order of age as a tertiary institution, are the University of Hong Kong, the Chinese University of Hong Kong, Hong Kong Polytechnic, Hong Kong Baptist College, City Polytechnic of Hong Kong, Hong Kong University of Science and Technology, and Lingnan College.

117

In 1992, in the light of the latest population forecast and estimates of the supply of matriculants over the next few years, the government took the view that planned provision of first-year first degree places for 1994–5 could be revised from 15 000 to 14 500, without affecting the target of places for 18 per cent of the mean of the 17–20 year old population. The UPGC, in consultation with the institutions, then formulated a revised expansion scenario in which growth in first-year places during the 1992–5 triennium would be 12 per cent each year, rather than the previously planned 14.5 per cent. As a result, the UPGC was able to return to the government $509 million from the $18,200 million of approved recurrent funding for the triennium.

Recruiting and retaining academic staff of the right calibre is crucial to the tertiary expansion programme. To help train local students for future careers in Hong Kong's institutions, the UPGC strategy includes a substantial increase in research student places, from about 1 300 in 1991–2, to almost 2 800 in 1994–5.

During the year the UPGC continued to monitor progress towards a revised structure of tertiary education, with a unified admission point following Secondary 7. A simplified procedure for the joint university and polytechnic admissions system was designed, applicable to those entering the sixth form in 1992 and aiming for a tertiary place in 1994, when the revised structure will be fully in place.

The UPGC also started a major review of the development of tertiary education, to take stock of progress achieved and formulate advice to the government on further development after 1994–5.

The Research Grants Council
The RGC, established in 1991, advises the government through the UPGC on the needs of institutions for academic research and the funding required, and monitors the use of public research funds. It comprises six locally-based academics, five overseas academics, and three local professionals and industrialists. Three specialist panels comprising mostly local academics consider grant applications in the areas of physical science and engineering, biology and medicine, and humanities and social science. An independent network of academic referees gives impartial advice on research proposals. In 1992 the RGC disbursed $122 million in earmarked grants, and received government approval to increase funding to $144 million in 1993. The RGC and the British Council also jointly sponsored the United Kingdom/Hong Kong Joint Research Scheme, aimed at strengthening links between tertiary institutions in the UK and Hong Kong.

The Vocational Training Council
Established under the Vocational Training Council Ordinance and funded by a subvention from the government, the VTC advises the Governor on measures to ensure a comprehensive system of technical education and industrial training suited to the developing needs of Hong Kong, and administers technical colleges, technical institutes, industrial training centres and skills centres for the disabled. (Two industry sectors, construction and clothing, operate training centres funded by levies under separate statutory authorities). The VTC also administers the statutory apprenticeship scheme. The 23 members of the council include prominent industrialists and academics and four government officers: Secretary for Economic Services, Director of Education, Commissioner for Labour and Director-General of Industry.

To ensure that the VTC's advice and operations meet the needs of industry and the service sector, the government has appointed, on the VTC's advice, 20 training boards and seven general committees with members representing those who use the graduates of VTC training courses. Each training board is responsible for training in one sector of the economy, such as electronics, textiles or insurance; while general committees are concerned with training relevant to several sectors, such as precision tooling, translation and the training of technologists.

During the year, the VTC continued preparations for taking over 6 670 sub-degree places from the polytechnics in September 1993, as part of the government's plans for tertiary expansion. Construction work started on a new technical college on Tsing Yi Island and on the conversion of the technical institute at Chai Wan to another technical college. A new industrial training complex at Pok Fu Lam became operational, and the modification and upgrading of existing technical institutes was completed in late 1992.

Hong Kong Examinations Authority

The HKEA is an independent statutory body, with membership drawn from the teaching profession, tertiary institutions and members of the business community. It is self-funding and non-profit-making. The authority's main role is to operate local public examinations: the HKCEE; the HKALE; and the Hong Kong Higher Level examination.

The HKEA also offers proficiency tests, aimed at adults, in Putonghua and in English language speaking skills, and basic proficiency tests for school-leavers in English language, Chinese language and mathematics. On behalf of overseas examining bodies it conducts a large number of examinations leading to academic, professional or practical qualifications.

In 1992, a total of 128 457 candidates entered for the HKCEE, 2 165 for the higher level examination, and 16 879 for the HKALE. The basic proficiency tests attracted 1 996 candidates. A total of 219 000 candidates sat for overseas examinations: 65 900 for the London Chamber of Commerce and Industry, 45 100 for the Associated Board of the Royal Schools of Music, and 27 000 for the Test of English as a Foreign Language (TOEFL).

With the phasing out of the Higher Level examination, held for the last time in 1992, from September 1992 all sixth form courses will be for two years, and will lead to the HKALE, the entry route to all tertiary institutions other than the Open Learning Institute. In 1992, for the first time, most HKALE subjects were offered in both Chinese and English. Previously they were offered in English only. Preparations continued for offering advanced supplementary subjects in the 1994 HKALE.

Hong Kong Council for Academic Accreditation

The HKCAA was established by ordinance in June 1990 to undertake academic accreditation activities for non-university degree awarding institutions, to ensure that the degrees they award meet internationally recognised standards. The council has 22 members including experts in accreditation, local and overseas academics, and local industrialists and business people. Its activities are administered by a small secretariat.

During the first two years of operation, the HKCAA has reviewed the standards of four institutions, scrutinised 73 degree programmes and monitored a number of other programmes. It has stimulated the creation of an international network of similar agencies, for which it provides administrative support. Other activities include seminars and

119

professional development workshops on quality assurance in higher education; and advice and assistance in response to relevant requests from the tertiary sector, government, and individuals. This includes advising on overseas institutions advertising or operating in Hong Kong, and on the development of teacher education.

The HKCAA maintains a register of subject specialists, which now includes nearly a thousand names of local and overseas academics and experts. Members of institutional review and validation teams are drawn from this register.

School Management Committees

Under the Education Ordinance, each school is managed by its own management committee, which employs the staff and is responsible for the proper education of the pupils and the operation of the school. One of the managers must be registered as the supervisor, whose main role is to be the point of contact between the management committee and the Education Department.

Each aided primary or secondary school is operated, under a letter of agreement, by its sponsoring body, which contributes the full cost of furnishing and equipping the premises, and nominates the first supervisor of the school. In September 1992, a total of 856 schools were in the care of 254 sponsoring bodies, with between one and 72 schools operated by any one body.

The School Management Initiative (SMI) was introduced in 1991 to give school managements in the public sector more decision-making power in return for more formal procedures for planning, implementing and evaluating their activities. The 21 aided secondary schools which joined the scheme in September 1991 made good progress in developing a new school management framework, and came under more flexible funding arrangements in September 1992. A further 13 secondary schools (10 government and three aided schools) joined the SMI in September 1992. An advisory committee, whose members provide a wide range of education and management expertise, offered advice and support to schools taking part in the SMI. During the year the committee produced reference materials on the school plan, school profile, staff appraisal, school policies and procedures and financial management. A newsletter, the *SMI Quarterly*, publicised the scheme and provided a forum for sharing experiences in school management reform.

Governing Bodies of Tertiary Institutions

Each tertiary institution has its own structure of governance, set out in its ordinance. In all cases the structure includes a governing body (called the Court, the Council, or the Board of Governors) and a body to regulate academic affairs (called the Senate or the Academic Board). Some institutions operate under three bodies: a governing body, an executive body, and a body dealing with academic affairs.

In addition to representatives of the institution's staff, a majority of members of the governing bodies are drawn from the community. Some institutions are required by their ordinance to include experienced businessmen or industrialists on the governing body. This helps to ensure that the institution's services are relevant to Hong Kong's needs.

Funding of Education

Approved public spending on education in the 1992–3 financial year, at HK$22,860 million, represented 23 per cent of the government's total recurrent expenditure and 7 per cent of capital expenditure. Public funds cover about 90 per cent of the capital cost of an aided primary or secondary school and virtually the full cost of tertiary institution campuses; the entire recurrent cost of providing tuition from Primary 1 to Secondary 3; and about 85 per cent of the recurrent cost from Secondary 4 up to degree level.

Non-profit-making kindergartens are eligible for rent and rates rebates, and parents of kindergarten pupils may apply for assistance towards fees. Private primary schools and pupils receive no public funding, on the grounds that there are sufficient places in the public sector; but some private secondary schools receive public funds under two schemes. Under the Direct Subsidy Scheme (DSS), any private secondary school meeting a specified standard may receive a recurrent subsidy, related to the cost of an aided school place and the fee charged by the school; while secondary schools in the Bought Place Scheme (BPS), from which the government buys places to make up shortfalls in government and aided school places, are given financial assistance to raise their standards.

The site for an aided school is granted to the sponsor by private treaty at a nominal premium, except where it lies within a Housing Authority estate, in which case the school operates under a tenancy agreement between the sponsor and the authority. International schools meeting specified criteria may also be granted land at a nominal premium.

During the year, the government continued to develop a linked series of computer models for the financing of education. These will help planners to evaluate the resource implications of different policy scenarios, as an aid to policy formulation.

Student Finance

The Student Financial Assistance Agency administers various financial assistance schemes and scholarships, described below. The aim of financial assistance is to ensure as far as possible that students are not denied access to education because of lack of means. Scholarships are awarded on the basis of academic merit.

Student Travel Subsidy

Students aged between 12 and 25 in full time study up to first degree level are eligible for a subsidy to cover part of their study-related travelling expenses. During the year, 172 735 students received assistance totalling $131 million.

Textbook Assistance

Primary or junior secondary students who need help to meet the cost of textbooks and stationery may apply for a grant. During the year 102 440 students received a total of $29.6 million.

Fee Remission

The policy on fees for public-sector places beyond Secondary 3 is to balance the benefit to the community and to the individual of the higher level of education. The Fee Remission Scheme, by relieving students of half or all the standard school fee, helps to ensure that those in need can continue their education without undue financial strain on their families. During the year 49 585 students benefited under the scheme.

A kindergarten fee remission scheme was introduced in August 1990. Assistance available ranges from 25 to 100 per cent of the weighted average of fees charged by non-profit-making kindergartens. During the year, a total of $24.74 million was granted to 10 988 kindergarten pupils.

Local Student Finance Scheme
Full-time students in local tertiary institutions funded by the UPGC may apply for means-tested assistance under the Local Student Finance Scheme. This provides for loans to meet living expenses, and for grants to cover tuition fees, faculty expenses and student union dues. During the year, 11 865 students received loans totalling $128.7 million. Of these, 8 976 also received grants totalling $68.2 million.

United Kingdom-Hong Kong Joint Funding Scheme
A joint funding arrangement between the governments of the United Kingdom and Hong Kong provides grants on a means-tested basis to full-time students attending first degree or higher national diploma courses in the United Kingdom. The grant meets the difference between fees for home students and fees for overseas students. During the year grants of £4.4 million and loans of $29 million were made to 1 797 students.

United Kingdom-Hong Kong Scholarships
These scholarships aim to provide educational opportunities at tertiary level in the United Kingdom for outstanding students from Hong Kong. The scholarship fund is contributed equally by the United Kingdom Government and the Royal Hong Kong Jockey Club on behalf of the Hong Kong Government. Nine scholarships were awarded in the 1991–2 academic year.

Sir Edward Youde Memorial Fund
The fund was established in April 1987 to manage public donations made in memory of the late Governor, Sir Edward Youde, who passed away in service in December 1986. The fund promotes education and learning among Hong Kong people, and encourages research. In the 1991–2 academic year $6 million was disbursed. Thirteen students were awarded fellowships or scholarships for postgraduate or undergraduate study overseas. Locally, 43 postgraduate research students were awarded fellowships, and 82 under-graduate, diploma and certificate students received scholarships. Awards from the fund were also made to five students excelling in public examinations, nine disabled students at tertiary, secondary and post-secondary level, and 597 outstanding senior secondary students nominated by school heads.

Education Scholarships Fund
In addition to the above schemes, a large number of scholarships for school students have been endowed by private benefactors. These are administered by the department under the Education Scholarships Fund Ordinance. Certain other charitable trust funds also provide scholarships.

Schools and Kindergartens
Kindergartens
In September 1992, 189 730 children aged three to five were enrolled in 743 kindergartens. All kindergartens are privately operated. An increasing number are run on a non-profit-making basis which renders them eligible for rent and rates rebates. They may also

be allocated premises in public housing estates. Most kindergartens operate two half-day sessions, but the number of whole-day places is increasing.

A fee remission scheme is available to needy parents with children in kindergartens. Assistance ranges from 25 to 100 per cent of the weighted average of fees charged by non-profit-making kindergartens. In 1992, 10 988 children benefited from the scheme.

The department gives professional advice to kindergarten managers, teachers, parents and the public. It produces curriculum development materials and runs basic training courses, seminars, workshops and exhibitions to help heads and teachers develop their professional skills. The department also publishes guidelines to help teachers organise the curriculum and learning activities.

Primary Schools
Primary schooling, beginning at the age of six and lasting six years, has been provided free of tuition fees in all government schools and in nearly all aided schools since 1971. Although enough places are available in the public sector, about 10 per cent of parents prefer to send their children to private primary schools. Admission to Primary 1 in the public sector is processed through a central allocation system, administered by the department. This has helped to eliminate pressure on children caused by intense competition for entry to popular schools.

In September 1992, 501 625 children were enrolled in 652 primary schools. Four new school buildings were completed during the year to provide for the growing population in the new towns.

A standard primary school consists of 24 classrooms and two special rooms. A new design was introduced in 1990 to provide more accommodation needed as a result of various changes in education policy. This provides 30 classrooms, four special rooms and three remedial teaching rooms, accommodating 60 classes in two half-day sessions. It can be converted into a secondary school, if necessary, by adding a special room block. The standard class size is 40 pupils where conventional teaching methods are used, and 35 for 'activity approach' classes, which offer a more child-centred teaching method.

Most primary school buildings accommodate two half-day sessions, a system adopted since the 1950s to meet demand from an increasing school population in a situation of severe space constraints. The Education Commission's Report No. 4 recommended a programme for phasing in whole day operation for all Primary 5 and 6 classes over a number of years. But this was not fully supported by the public. During the year, the government accepted the Education Commission's revised recommendation that whole-day schooling should remain a long term goal. In the meantime, any primary school wishing to convert to whole-day operation will be allowed to do so, wherever this will not adversely affect the supply of places in the district concerned.

The primary curriculum aims to provide a broad, balanced and general education appropriate to the age group and the local environment. While the core curriculum (Chinese, English, mathematics, social studies, science, health education, music, physical education, and art and craft) is followed by all primary schools, other learning programmes may be offered on a cross-curricular basis or as separate optional subjects. A syllabus for each core subject is prepared by the CDC, and is regularly revised and updated to meet changing educational and community needs. Awareness of the benefits of the 'activity approach' method is growing and it is now used in 262 schools.

123

All teaching posts in primary schools are in non-graduate ranks. The primary pupil: teacher ratio is about 27:1, and the staffing ratio is 1.2 teachers per class. This allows for remedial teaching to help slow-learning pupils. Additional teachers may be provided so the school can operate revised resource classes for pupils in need of special educational help.

Chinese is the language of instruction in most primary schools, with English taught as a second language. In many schools Putonghua is taught as either a timetabled subject or an after-school activity. A few schools use English as the language of instruction.

As recommended in the Education Commission's Report No. 4, a framework of teaching targets and target-related assessments (TTRA) has been developed to set a clearer direction for teaching, learning and assessment. The TTRA initiative will be introduced first to primary schools in the three basic subjects of Chinese, English and mathematics. Seminars were held for all primary school heads, and teachers taking classes at Primary 4 to Primary 6, to prepare them for implementing TTRA at Primary 4 level in 1993.

The class library scheme provides supplementary reading materials for pupils to support classroom learning, promote a more exploratory approach to learning, develop the habit of leisure reading, and pave the way for effective use of the library in secondary schools. A reading award scheme is organised annually for Primary 5 and 6 students, and a booklet containing the winning book reports is issued to all schools. In 1992, 44 000 students from 227 primary schools took part in the scheme.

At the end of the primary course, pupils are allocated to government or aided secondary schools, or to private schools with bought places. The Secondary School Places Allocation System is based on internal school assessments, scaled by a centrally administered academic aptitude test, and on parental choice. For allocation purposes the territory is divided into 19 school nets. A total of 84 696 primary pupils took part in the 1992 allocation, of whom 74 549 (88.02 per cent) found places in government and aided grammar schools, 4 886 (5.77 per cent) in prevocational schools, and 5 261 (6.21 per cent) in private schools in the Bought Place Scheme (BPS).

Secondary Schools

In 1978 universal free education was extended to junior secondary classes. The policy for public sector provision after Secondary 3 is broadly to meet the demand for places on a senior secondary or vocational course. In 1992 the number of subsidised Secondary 4 places was equivalent to 82 per cent of the 15-year-old population, with places for a further eight per cent on full-time craft courses of vocational training. The target for sixth form education is to provide one public sector Secondary 6 place for every three public sector Secondary 4 places two years earlier.

Secondary 3 leavers are selected for subsidised places in Secondary 4 or on a vocational course according to internal school assessments and parental preference. One objective of the selection process is to enable as many students as possible to progress to Secondary 4 within the same school. In 1992, 74 748 students took part in the process, of whom 63 253 secured a Secondary 4 place and 3 999 were admitted to craft courses.

The Secondary 6 admission procedure introduced in 1991 was expanded to include sixth form places in prevocational and BPS schools. Over 99.5 per cent of the 21 993 places available were filled.

To meet provision targets new secondary schools are built and places are bought from private schools. During the year, seven new secondary schools were completed, providing

8 120 places. Another 19 schools will be completed between 1993 and 1995 to meet increasing demand and to reprovision schools from areas of surplus to areas of shortfall. The majority of these schools will be built to a new standard design introduced in 1990, which provides additional teaching spaces and better facilities.

There are three main types of secondary school in Hong Kong: grammar, technical and prevocational. In 1992, the 410 grammar schools had a total enrolment of 403 619. They offer a five-year secondary course in a broad range of academic, cultural and practical subjects leading to the HKCEE. Most offer in addition a two-year sixth form course leading to the HKALE. The 22 technical schools, which prepare students for the HKCEE with an emphasis on technical and commercial subjects, had an enrolment of 21 967. Qualified candidates can continue their studies in the sixth form or in technical institutes.

The 23 prevocational schools had an enrolment of 20 199. These offer an alternative form of secondary education suited to students with an aptitude for practical and technical subjects. They provide a solid foundation of general knowledge and a broad introduction to technical and practical education upon which future vocational training may be based. The curriculum in Secondary 1 to 3 is made up of about 40 per cent technical and practical subjects and 60 per cent general subjects. The technical and practical content is reduced to about 30 per cent in Secondary 4 and 5. Students completing Secondary 3 in a prevocational school may enter approved apprenticeship schemes or continue their studies to Secondary 5 and take the HKCEE. Qualified candidates can continue their studies in polytechnics or technical institutes. In September some prevocational schools started to provide sixth form classes, to prepare students for technical or other studies in the polytechnics, universities or other tertiary institutions.

The Direct Subsidy Scheme (DSS) was introduced in 1991 to strengthen the private secondary school sector, as a means to improve the quality and diversity of education. Under the scheme private secondary schools meeting specified standards can receive a public subsidy for each eligible student. They are free to decide their own curriculum and to set entrance requirements and fee levels. Nine schools were admitted to the DSS during the 1991–2 school year, and a sixth form college was admitted in September 1992.

As part of the same policy package, the BPS will end in the year 2000. Schools in the scheme will be helped before then to raise their standards so that they may if they wish apply to join the DSS. Twenty private schools were operating under contracts with the government which specify improvements in such areas as whole day operation, the class structure, teacher qualifications and school facilities. The contracts will expire in August 2001, unless terminated earlier by either party.

The curriculum for secondary education is divided into two levels: junior and senior. The junior secondary curriculum aims to provide a well-balanced and basic education suitable for all students in Secondary 1 to 3, whether or not they continue formal education beyond Secondary 3. It is designed to follow on from the primary curriculum, to form an integral learning framework for the nine years of free and universal education.

The senior secondary curriculum aims to prepare students for education beyond Secondary 5 as well as the world of work, and offers a diverse range of subjects from which schools and students select according to individual needs and interests, school traditions and the facilities available.

The new sixth form curriculum introduced in schools in September 1992 aims to provide a more broadly-based and balanced programme of study for students intending to proceed to tertiary education or join the workforce after Secondary 7. The range of choices in the HKALE was enlarged by new practical and technical subjects at A-Level, and by 17 new Advanced Supplementary (AS) subjects. To help teachers prepare for the new AS-level subjects, short courses, seminars and workshops were organised and run by the Advisory Inspectorate, and by tertiary institutions with financial help from the department.

The CDC prepares, and keeps under review, teaching syllabuses for all subjects offered at the secondary level. During the year, the syllabuses for computer studies, mathematics, and home economics were revised.

Teaching guidelines and supporting materials are provided to schools for cross-curricular studies such as civic education, moral education, sex education and environmental education. Civic and moral education are promoted by making use of learning opportunities across the curriculum and in the extra-curricular life of the school. Sex and AIDS education is integrated into various subjects in primary and secondary schools. The aim is to enable pupils to understand sex as part of overall personal and social well-being, and not as something isolated from other aspects of behaviour. Resources for sex and AIDS education were developed and issued to schools. A newsletter, *Sex Education News*, was published regularly to inform teachers about sex education resources and activities. A learning pack on AIDS was issued to secondary schools in July to help teachers discuss with their pupils moral and social issues related to AIDS. A calendar card design competition was organised in December in support of the World AIDS Day.

Environmental education is promoted through relevant topics and themes in subjects such as social studies and science in primary schools; and social studies, integrated science, economics and public affairs, geography, biology, physics and chemistry in secondary schools. It is supplemented by extra-curricular activities. Guidelines on environmental education in schools were issued in July, and various activities to promote environmental education were organised by the department, some in conjunction with other government departments or voluntary agencies.

In September, two new computer subjects for the sixth form, computer studies at A-level and computer applications at AS-level, were introduced to 21 public sector schools. Senior secondary students in 370 schools took the HKCEE computer studies course, while computer literacy for Secondary 1–3 was taught in 189 schools. Students in over 75 per cent of special schools were also given the chance to learn through computers and to employ the new technology in communication and rehabilitation.

The school-based Curriculum Project Scheme, introduced in 1988, encourages practising educators to develop projects which adapt the centrally designed curriculum to meet the varied abilities and needs of pupils. Apart from producing useful curriculum materials, the scheme helps to develop curriculum development and planning skills among teachers. The scheme provides production expenses, and an award on satisfactory completion of a project. In the 1991–2 school year, 47 schools were involved and 54 projects were completed.

The school library service promotes good reading habits, cultivates the ability to study independently, and supports teaching and learning in schools. All public sector secondary schools may appoint a teacher-librarian. The annual Reading Award Scheme for secondary students attracted 33 000 participants from 212 schools. A booklet containing the winning book reports was sent to all schools for students' reference. An inter-school project competition was organised to encourage among pupils a positive attitude towards ife, and an exhibition of the winning projects was held in November 1992. A newsletter for school libraries is published half-yearly.

Chinese and English are both used as mediums of instruction in secondary schools. Some schools use Chinese, some use English, while others use both languages. The government accepted recommendations in the Education Commission's Report No. 4 to establish a framework for grouping secondary students according to their ability in the two languages. Objective target-related assessments in the two languages were being developed, to help schools and parents decide on the most appropriate medium of instruction for each student. To enable school authorities to prepare for a clear policy on their medium of instruction before the new assessments are available, they were given information from existing assessment instruments on the language abilities of past intake cohorts.

Target-related assessments were also being developed for mathematics. The assessments in English, Chinese and mathematics will eventually supersede the standardised Hong Kong attainment tests, which now help schools to assess the achievement of students at each year level from Primary 1 to Secondary 3.

In government and aided secondary schools, the staffing ratio is 1.3 teachers per class in Secondary 1 to 5 and two teachers per class in the sixth form, with additional teachers to help schools strengthen language teaching; provide remedial teaching, careers guidance, counselling, extra-curricular activities and library services; and offer split class teaching of such subjects as second language, domestic science, woodwork, metalwork, computer studies, art and design and music. The ratio of graduates to non-graduate teachers is about 7:3. The pupil to teacher ratio is about 20:1. The class structure of a standard government or aided secondary school is six classes each in Secondary 1–3, four classes each in Secondary 4–5 and two classes in each sixth form year.

Extra-Curricular Activities

Extra-curricular activities are an integral part of school education. They usually take place outside school hours, in the school premises or elsewhere, under teacher supervision. The department provides professional guidance and advice to teachers through in-service training programmes and school inspections, and also subsidises certain activities. Inter-school programmes and activities organised or co-ordinated by the department include the Community Youth Club, the Duke of Edinburgh's Award Scheme, the Sister Schools Scheme, the Lions Clubs International Hong Kong Secondary Schools Adoption Scheme, and the Schools Drama Festival.

The Community Youth Club, established in 1977 to help build a strong community spirit among students through organised activities, had a membership of about 120 000 students from 1 064 primary and secondary schools. Up to June 1992, 46 293 members had gained awards under the CYC Merit Award Scheme. In recognition of their outstanding service, 19 primary school members were taken on a tour to Singapore during the summer holiday, and 24 secondary school members visited England.

The department is the largest of the 20 operating authorities of the Duke of Edinburgh's Award Scheme in Hong Kong, with 20 370 members from 181 schools. Over 130 training courses and functions at bronze, silver and gold levels were organised during the year.

The Sister Schools Scheme which started in 1981 under the auspices of Lions Club International District 303, matches ordinary and special schools to promote social inter-action and friendship among students. In 1992, 43 special schools and 45 ordinary schools were made sister schools, and about 20 000 pupils took part in activities sponsored by the scheme.

The Hong Kong Secondary Schools Adoption Scheme was devised jointly by the department and Lions Club International District 303, to encourage links between Hong Kong schools and Lions Club districts around the world. It was launched at the International Lions Club Convention held in Hong Kong in June. The aim is to promote mutual understanding, co-operation, assistance and cultural exchange.

The department also supports inter-school activities in music, speech, drama and sports. In the 1991–2 academic year the music festival organised by the Hong Kong Schools Music and Speech Association attracted 63 900 students from 923 schools, while 52 800 took part in the speech festival. The Schools Drama Festival, organised under the guidance of the School Drama Council, encouraged drama productions involving about 3 200 students from 109 schools. Sporting activities organised by the Hong Kong School Sports Association and the New Territories School Sports Association attracted over 111 200 participants from more than 1 200 schools.

Special Education

The main policy objective of special education is to integrate the disabled into the community through the co-ordinated efforts of the government and voluntary agencies.

Early identification is an important preventive measure. Screening and assessment services identify special educational needs among school age children so that appropriate follow-up and remedial treatment can be given before problems develop into educational handicaps. Under the combined screening programme, all Primary 1 pupils are given hearing and eyesight tests. Teachers are provided with checklists and guides to help them detect children with speech problems and learning difficulties. Children requiring further assessments are given audiological, speech, psychological or educational assessments at special education services centres, or are referred for ophthalmic advice.

Children identified as having special educational needs are as far as possible integrated into ordinary schools. They are placed in special schools only when their handicaps are such that they cannot benefit from the ordinary school programme. There are altogether 62 special schools (including a hospital school) for the blind, deaf, physically handicapped, mentally handicapped, maladjusted, socially deprived and children with learning difficulties. Sixteen schools provide residential places. Apart from teachers, special schools are staffed by specialists such as educational psychologists, therapists and social workers.

Special education classes in ordinary schools cater for partially-sighted or partially-hearing children, or children with learning difficulties. Remedial services for children integrated into ordinary classes include centre-based remedial support outside school hours, a peripatetic teaching service, as well as advice for ordinary teachers on how to cope with handicapped students.

In general, special schools and classes follow the ordinary school curriculum, with adaptations or special syllabuses where appropriate to cater for the varied learning needs of the children. Special attention is given to daily living skills. The CDC's Special Education Co-ordinating Committee, with members from government departments and schools, advises on special educational needs. Special schools also offer extra-curricular activities to enrich the practical life experiences of day and residential pupils.

In response to recommendations in the Education Commission's Report No. 4, a research project was commissioned on education for the gifted, and improvements began to be implemented in services for less able pupils.

International Schools

In keeping with Hong Kong's international character, a number of schools offer curricula designed for the needs of a particular cultural, racial or linguistic group.

The English Schools Foundation (ESF) was established by ordinance in 1967. It operates nine primary schools (known as junior schools), five secondary schools for children whose first language is English, and a special education centre for English-speaking pupils with moderate to severe learning difficulties. The education provided is similar in content and method to that available in Britain, and is aimed at British public examinations. To meet the heavy demand for places on Hong Kong Island, one of the secondary schools operated during the year in temporary premises pending completion of a new building. The ESF receives public grants based on grants paid to local aided schools, and charges fees to meet additional staffing and administrative costs.

Other international schools provide education on the American, Canadian, French, Japanese, German, Swiss and Singaporean patterns. In the school year 1992–3, there were 12 schools operating up to secondary level, 13 at primary level and 16 kindergartens. Some of these schools have received help from the Hong Kong Government in the form of favourable land grants and reimbursement of rates. Some are sponsored by their own governments or communities while some have received assistance from both sources. Four international secondary schools have joined the DSS.

Teacher Education

Four colleges of education offer pre-service professional training for non-graduate teachers in primary and secondary schools, as well as in-service initial training for primary, secondary and kindergarten teachers. To acquaint serving teachers with modern teaching methods and approaches, the colleges offer refresher courses in primary and secondary teaching, and advanced courses of teacher education for non-graduate teachers of cultural, practical and technical subjects in secondary schools. Full time pre-service courses last three years for those with HKCEE qualifications, and two years for those with two A-levels. In October 2 144 trainees were on full time courses and 2 356 were on part time or short courses.

The University of Hong Kong and the Chinese University of Hong Kong offer post-graduate certificate of education courses for graduates who are, or who wish to become, teachers. They also offer short courses for teachers covering areas like curriculum innovation, resource development, educational psychology, student guidance and counselling, professional development of teachers, and educational administration.

The Institute of Language in Education (ILE) offers full time and part time language-related courses and seminars for serving teachers of Chinese (including Putonghua) and English; conducts policy-focused research and development; provides a resource centre for language teachers; publishes a professional journal, books and newsletters; offers consultancy services on languages in education; and organises an annual international conference. During the year 671 teachers attended full time courses, and 859 attended part time courses. Of these, 118 attended a summer immersion programme in the United Kingdom. The ILE international conference in December, on the theme of language and content, attracted over 300 local and overseas scholars, and over 100 papers were delivered.

The four colleges and the ILE are run directly by the Education Department. By the year's end, preparations were in hand to implement the recommendation, in Education Commission Report No. 5, that the colleges and ILE should be upgraded into an autonomous Institute of Education.

Support Services
Teaching and learning in schools is backed up by a wide range of services, mostly provided or supported by the department.

The Advisory Inspectorate advises schools on curriculum, teaching methods and educational resources, and offers short courses, seminars and workshops for teachers. Its teaching and resource centres offer resources and advice to kindergarten, primary and secondary teachers in the areas of language, mathematics, science, social and cultural subjects, computer education, technical subjects, civic education, religious, ethical and moral education, sex education, and kindergarten teaching.

Changes to the student guidance service, to implement the 'whole school approach' recommended in Education Commission Report No. 4, began in September 1992, when the first batch of aided primary schools were provided with their own student guidance teachers. The department's student guidance section provides training in student guidance at primary level, enforces compulsory education, and ensures an adequate provision of study room facilities.

Educational television programmes, produced jointly by the department and Radio Television Hong Kong, are transmitted to schools by the two local commercial television stations. Syllabus-based programmes for students in Secondary 1 to 3 cover Chinese language, English language, mathematics, social studies and science while those for pupils in Primary 3 to 6 cover the same five subjects plus health education. A new series of programmes, called *Value of Life*, was produced in response to the increased number of student suicides during the 1991–2 school year.

Starting in July, microcomputers began to be installed in government and aided schools to help in their administration work. By the year's end, computers were installed in 350 schools, and their staff trained to use the standard software including Chinese and English word processing, spreadsheet, and database packages. The project is expected to be completed by the end of 1993. In December, consultants delivered a plan for an information systems strategy, aimed at making better use of information technology to support the school education service.

The Hong Kong Teachers' Centre, established in 1989, promotes professionalism and a sense of unity among teachers. It is supervised by an advisory management committee with wide representation from schools, teacher organisations and educational bodies, and is staffed by the department. During the year, the centre organised or was associated with over 600 activities with 50 000 participants. The centre maintains a professional library and publishes news bulletins.

The department's Educational Research Establishment (ERE) conducts research, develops tests and monitors educational standards. During the year, the ERE completed development of Series 4 of the standardised Hong Kong Attainment Tests for Primary 4 to Primary 6 in the three core subjects of Chinese, English and mathematics. Such tests are administered each year by primary and secondary schools. The results enable schools to diagnose areas of strength and weakness in these subjects, so that appropriate guidance, counselling and remedial teaching can be provided. Test results also help the department to monitor standards across years and levels. Research projects conducted by ERE in 1992 included studies into the continuity of curriculum and teaching practices between the various levels of education; the effects of the change of medium of instruction at junior secondary level; and the efficacy of different curriculum approaches. The ERE also participated in the international reading literacy study project of the International Association for the Evaluation of Educational Achievement.

The department's 19 district education offices, each headed by a senior education officer, provide advice and assistance to schools, teachers, parents and students, and act as channels of communication between them and the department. District education officers attend district board meetings to assist in discussions on educational matters.

The department's Careers and Guidance Services Section gives advice and information on educational establishments overseas. During the year, 4 408 students went to study in Britain, 3 583 to Canada, 5 410 to the United States, and 2 866 to Australia. Exhibitions promoting overseas education were staged by American, Australian, British and Canadian organisations.

The Students Division of the Hong Kong Government Office in London promotes the interests of Hong Kong students in the United Kingdom. It maintains close liaison with universities, polytechnics and colleges, and also with official and unofficial bodies including government departments concerned with the welfare of overseas students. The division monitors developments in education in the UK. It works closely with the department to help students wishing to further their studies in the UK, and with the Student Financial Assistance Agency to administer the UK-HK Joint Funding Scheme. It also maintains close contact with the Hong Kong student community through college-based student societies.

Technical Education and Industrial Training

A comprehensive system of technical education and industrial training offers school leavers an alternative to further academic study, and helps to prepare them for specific careers. Publicly funded technical education is provided through the VTC, which operates seven technical institutes and provides industrial training for the major industrial and service sectors. Two other training authorities operate levy-funded training schemes for the clothing and construction industries.

The manpower needs of each economic sector are assessed by regular manpower surveys, conducted by the VTC training boards and general committees. During the year 14 sectors were surveyed. Based on survey findings, proposals are formulated for new or modified training courses. Other measures adopted by the VTC and its boards and committees to help employers meet their needs include assistance with in-house staff training schemes, organisation of out-centre training courses, training seminars and trade tests, and the preparation of job specifications, trade test guidelines, training curricula, and glossaries of common technical terms.

Technical Education

Technical education at technician and craft level is provided by the VTC's seven technical institutes. Disciplines cover environmental studies, chemical technology, clothing technology, commercial studies, accountancy, computing studies, construction, design, electrical engineering, electronic engineering, child care, hairdressing, hotel-keeping and tourism studies, marine engineering and fabrication, manufacturing engineering, mechanical engineering, motor vehicle engineering and printing and textiles.

Courses leading to a recognised qualification are offered with several modes of attendance. Courses for craft apprentices, usually Secondary 3 leavers, are offered on a part time day release or block release basis. At technician level, full time, part time day and part time evening courses are offered, mostly for Secondary 5 leavers. Most technician courses are validated by the UK Business and Technology Education Council. Students completing them may register for BTEC awards.

In September 1992, the institutes offered 321 courses taught by 792 full-time teaching staff and about 730 supporting staff. Evening courses were delivered by 1 930 part time lecturers. Enrolment in the 1992–3 academic year totalled 9 400 full time, 15 800 part time day and 25 600 part time evening students. In addition, about 9 000 serving employees attended 198 short courses to upgrade their knowledge and skills.

In July, 6 000 full time, 5 300 part time day and 9 800 evening students graduated from the institutes. The employment of graduates from full time courses was surveyed during the year. Findings again showed that graduates had little difficulty in finding jobs, and that most found work relevant to the training they had received.

Industrial Training

The VTC's 19 industrial training centres provide basic training or skills upgrading for industrial craftsmen and technicians, and for clerical and supervisory personnel in the service sector. In 1992, over 30 000 trainees attended full time or part time courses. Trade tests for serving employees were offered in six industries, including automobile, building and civil engineering, electrical, machine shop and metal working, plastics and printing. Training boards in conjunction with educational and training institutions organised out-centre training courses to upgrade or update serving employees.

The Engineering Graduate Training Scheme, administered by the VTC, helps engineering students and graduates complete the professional training which will gain them recognition by the Hong Kong Institution of Engineers or other professional bodies. In 1992, 85 engineering firms took part in the scheme, which provided 280 training places.

The VTC's Management Development Centre conducts research and development projects, and promotes management training. The centre's projects include work with owner-managers and various entrepreneurial firms, development of learning materials, and activities with management trainers and business executives.

Two statutory authorities operate industrial training schemes in two important sectors. The Clothing Industry Training Authority operates two training centres funded by a levy on the export value of clothing and footwear. In 1992, 7 700 trainees attended courses. The three training centres of the Construction Industry Training Authority, funded by a levy on the value of construction works exceeding $1 million, provided courses for 4 000 trainees.

Training in New Technology

The Precision Tooling Training Centre houses a precision sheet metal processing unit, set up in 1990 with financial and expert technical help from the Japan International Co-operation Agency under an agreement between the governments of Hong Kong and Japan. The unit plays an important part in the transfer of precision sheet metal technology to local industries.

A new Technology Training Scheme was launched during the year. The scheme will provide matching grants from a special fund to help industrial employees acquire skills in new technologies of benefit to Hong Kong industry.

Retraining for Local Workers

At the request of the government and as part of the employees retraining scheme, the VTC organised specially designed retraining programmes for local workers displaced as a result of economic re-structuring to provide them with opportunities for acquiring new or upgraded skills they need to obtain employment.

Apprenticeship Schemes

The Apprenticeship Ordinance governs the training of craftsmen and technicians in 42 designated trades. Anyone aged between 14 and 18 who is employed in such a trade and has not completed an apprenticeship must enter into a contract with the employer. This must be registered with the Director of Apprenticeship, who is the executive director of the VTC. Contracts in respect of other trades, or for apprentices aged over 18, may be registered voluntarily. An apprenticeship normally lasts three to four years, but qualifications earned before the apprenticeship starts, such as completion of a craft foundation course in a technical institute, may lead to exemption from the first year of the apprenticeship.

The Office of the Director of Apprenticeship advises and helps the employers of apprentices. Inspectors visit workplaces where apprentices are employed to ensure that training schemes are properly implemented, help to resolve disputes arising from registered contracts, and ensure that apprentices receive the required technical education on courses at the polytechnics or technical institutes. The office also provides a free apprentice placement service to job-seekers who are interested in apprentice training. In 1992, 4 300 contracts were registered. Of these, 850 were in non-designated trades. The contracts covered 3 650 craft apprentices, and 650 technician apprentices. By the year's end 9 000 apprentices were being trained.

Vocational Training for the Disabled

Six skills centres, three run by the VTC and three by voluntary agencies, prepare disabled people for open employment or mainstream technical education and industrial training. The centres provide 840 places, of which 358 are residential.

The VTC also provides support services. The vocational assessment service assesses individual potential and helps those assessed to select a suitable vocational training programme. Internationally recognised test batteries, as well as work samples designed to match local industrial skills profiles, are used. All mildly mentally disabled school leavers attend a one-week vocational assessment programme. An eight-week vocational assessment programme is also operated to provide an in-depth assessment for more complex cases.

The Technical Aids and Resource Centre designs and makes technical aids for disabled trainees, students and workers, to enhance their training, employment prospects and productivity. Information and resource materials on vocational rehabilitation are produced and made available to disabled persons and professionals in this field.

The inspectorate unit advises skills centres on administration, curriculum, training methods and standards. It also provides guidance and counselling to disabled students in technical institutes and industrial training centres. The unit works closely with the Labour Department's selective placement service to ensure that training matches the demand for skills in the local employment market. The annual employment survey of disabled students and trainees completing full-time courses in technical institutes and skills centres showed that about 90 per cent either found open employment or were enrolled in mainstream technical education courses.

Tertiary Education

Ten years ago less than five per cent of the 17–20 age group could receive tertiary education locally. By 1992 this figure had increased to 20 per cent, and expansion plans announced by the government in 1989 will take it to 25 per cent by 1994–5. A first year first degree place will be available for about five out of every six matriculants, helping to supply the graduates needed to sustain Hong Kong's economic growth.

Degrees up to PhD level awarded by local institutions are widely recognised around the world. Academic standards are assured by appointing external examiners from prominent overseas institutions. Degrees awarded by non-university institutions are also validated by the HKCAA on behalf of the UPGC.

The Tertiary Institutions

The oldest tertiary institution is the University of Hong Kong, founded in 1911. Its 9 162 full time and 2 254 part time students are enrolled in nine faculties: arts, architecture, dentistry, education, engineering, law, medicine, science and social sciences.

The Chinese University of Hong Kong was established in 1963 by bringing together three colleges: New Asia College, founded in 1949; Chung Chi College (1951) and United College (1956). A fourth college, Shaw College, was founded in 1986. There are 8 363 full time and 2 524 part time students in seven faculties: arts, business administration, education, engineering, medicine, science and social science.

The Hong Kong Polytechnic, founded in 1972, offers postgraduate, first degree and sub-degree courses in six faculties: applied science and textiles; business and information systems; communication; construction and land use; engineering; and health and social studies. The polytechnic's part time and sandwich courses encourage concurrent work and study, and close links are maintained with industry, commerce and the community. Enrolment in October was 10 209 on full time and sandwich courses and 14 989 on part time courses.

The Hong Kong Baptist College was founded in 1956 by the Baptist Convention of Hong Kong. Since 1983 it has been incorporated under its own ordinance and fully funded by the government. In 1986 it became a degree-granting institution. It has 3 634 full time and 64 part time students in five faculties and schools: arts, business, communication, science and social sciences.

The City Polytechnic of Hong Kong, founded in 1984, has 7 729 full time, 5 734 part time and 379 sandwich course students. The four faculties of business, humanities and social sciences, law, and science and technology offer first degree courses, postgraduate diplomas and master's degree courses, as well as MPhil and PhD programmes by research. Diploma and higher diploma courses in commerce, humanities and social sciences, and technology are offered by the College of Higher Vocational Studies.

The Hong Kong University of Science and Technology was incorporated in 1988 and admitted its first class in October 1991. Three schools – science, engineering, and business and management – offer first and advanced degrees. The fourth school, humanities and social science, offers advanced degrees and provides general education to all under-graduates. In October the university had 1 749 full time undergraduate students and 246 full time and 258 part time postgraduate students.

Lingnan College was founded in 1967 to continue the tradition of Lingnan University. The college was upgraded to tertiary status under the aegis of the UPGC in July 1991 and subsequently incorporated under its own ordinance in 1992. It has three faculties – arts, business, and social sciences – and a general education division. In October, enrolment was 1 495 full time students, of whom 371 were pursuing honours degree studies and 1 124 honours diploma studies. Enrolment is planned to increase to 1 800 by 1994, when the college is expected to be relocated to a new campus in Tuen Mun.

The Open Learning Institute of Hong Kong (OLI), established in 1989 as the seventh degree-granting institution, is funded initially by a government subvention, but aims to become self-financing by 1993–4. It provides distance learning courses, under an open-access policy, for adults who want to study for personal development or obtain a further qualification. In April about 15 500 students were actively pursuing studies. Degree programmes are offered in three schools: science and technology, business and administration, and arts and social sciences. In June the OLI established a School of Education to offer degree programmes and professional training courses for serving teachers. A Centre for Continuing and Community Education was also launched, to offer sub-degree and postgraduate studies and short training courses for adults.

Each institution publishes detailed information about admission criteria, courses, staff and other matters in its annual report, calendar and prospectus. Appendix 24 gives additional data about the institutions.

Post-Secondary Colleges
Shue Yan College, registered in 1976 under the Post Secondary Colleges Ordinance, operates a four-year diploma programme. Its faculties of arts, social science and commerce include 13 departments, which offered day and evening courses to 3 070 students in October 1992. The college receives no public funding, but its students may apply for government grants and loans.

Adult Education
Many formal and informal opportunities are available for adults to study in their spare time, either for personal development or to update knowledge and skills relevant to their work. There are numerous private schools offering language, business and computer courses. The British Council, Alliance Francaise, Goethe Institute and Japanese Consulate all offer language courses.

All tertiary institutions except the Hong Kong University of Science and Technology and Lingnan College operate extra-mural departments or divisions of continuing education. These offer an enormous variety of courses, some at degree level, in such areas as languages, translation, business management and professional development for teachers, social workers and others.

The Education Department provides formal courses of remedial and second chance education for adults at primary and secondary level, and courses of personal development at post-secondary level. Less formal activities including hobby and fitness classes are provided in adult education and recreation centres run by the department. During the year government subventions supported 363 adult education projects organised by 67 voluntary agencies.

The British Council

The aim of the British Council in Hong Kong is to offer British skills and expertise in the key areas of science and technology, the arts and English language teaching and learning, to meet the challenge of Hong Kong's changing needs into the next century.

English language teaching is one of the council's major programmes in Hong Kong. Through its general and business English course, distance learning language programmes with Radio Television Hong Kong, summer schools and teacher training courses, the English Language Centre provided English language learning opportunities for over 42 000 Hong Kong residents in 1992. In addition, the council arranged for 100 teacher trainees from the colleges of education to visit the United Kingdom for total immersion courses jointly funded by the Education and Manpower Branch.

The council provides access to British expertise in helping to develop Hong Kong's industry through promoting technology transfer, including working closely with Industry Department and Hong Kong Polytechnic on post-experience training, and a feasibility study on a Science Park for Hong Kong. The council is also working in close collaboration with the government, higher education and other organisations in areas such as the environment, law, planning and accountancy, in some cases through schemes linking Hong Kong and Britain with China. The annual Science Lecture Series for Young People took place at the Science Museum on the theme of the environment and an annual scholarship in environmental science was awarded, co-funded with the Swire Educational Trust and the Aberdeen University Hong Kong Association.

The council's library and information services are open to all Hong Kong residents and cover all aspects of British life and culture, with an emphasis on English literature and English language teaching. The collections include books, magazines, newspapers, videos, CD-ROM, music on CD and audio tapes. The library facilities are computerised and free to students of the council's English Language Centre. Others are charged a nominal annual subscription.

The Educational Counselling Service provides free and impartial advice to students on educational opportunities available in Britain. In 1992, 28 000 students used the service for information on studying in British universities and colleges.

11
HEALTH

THE Department of Health is the health authority and adviser to Government on all matters related to health. It operates a wide range of services to promote health and prevent diseases. These include personal health services such as out-patient clinics, family health and family planning, health education and community health, territory-wide health services for tuberculosis and chest health, social hygiene, child assessment, dental health, occupational health, disease surveillance, public health and special preventive programmes, environmental health, port health, radiation health, drug addiction treatment, pharmaceutical services and hygiene services. Through collaboration with the private sector and teaching institutions, the Department strives to provide a comprehensive range of primary health care services to the community.

The Hospital Authority is an independent statutory body responsible for the management and control of all public hospitals in Hong Kong. The Authority was established in December 1990 to integrate government and government-assisted hospitals with a view to optimising the use of resources, facilitating hospital management reforms and enhancing community participation. A comprehensive range of medical treatment and rehabilitation services is provided to patients through hospitals and specialist clinics operated by the Authority. Starting in 1992, management reforms have been introduced in eight public hospitals with emphasis on defining clear lines of accountability as well as greater devolution of responsibilities.

The Department of Health and the Hospital Authority continued to make progress on an extensive development programme which included the planning of additional public hospitals as well as additional general out-patient clinics and specialist out-patient services. Tuen Mun Hospital opened in 1990 and is now operating with 952 beds to serve the population in New Territories West and will provide a total of 1 607 beds upon full operation. Physical construction of the 1 620-bed Pamela Youde Hospital in Chai Wan is scheduled for completion in late 1992.

For the 1992–3 financial year, the allocation of funds to medical and health services to the public sector amounted to $11,303 million including $10,035 million for the Hospital Authority. In addition, subventions totalling $169 million were provided for other medical institutions and organisations. Capital expenditure on new hospitals and other buildings, including equipment and furniture, was about $935 million.

Health of the Community

The community's good general level of health is attributable to the comprehensive range of preventive, promotive and personal health services, and a comparatively high standard of living. This is reflected by health indices which compare favourably with those of industrialised nations. Infant mortality remained below seven per 1 000 live births and the average life expectancy at birth has increased to 81 for females and 75 for males.

Cancers, heart diseases and cerebrovascular diseases (strokes) continue to be the leading causes of death, accounting for 58 per cent of the mortalities in the territory. These diseases generally affect older people. Given the continual ageing of the population, it is anticipated that these diseases will remain prominent in the near future.

There were three cases of cholera at the end of 1992. One was a local sporadic case while two were imported cases with a history of travel abroad. Prompt control was instituted and no secondary spread was found.

Although communicable diseases are largely under control, they still pose a threat. Viral hepatitis and tuberculosis have re-emerged, both locally and overseas.

In 1992, Hong Kong experienced its biggest hepatitis A epidemic to date. This commenced in December 1991 and continued until July 1992. A total of 3 496 cases were reported, of which 281 cases occurred among Vietnamese migrants. To control the situation, health education and publicity measures were increased and control of food premises (including raiding and prosecution of illegal food hawkers) were stepped up.

There were 6 534 tuberculosis notifications during the year, representing a notification rate of 112 per 100 000 population. A total of 410 deaths were reported.

To protect the population from infectious diseases, children in Hong Kong are immunised against nine important infectious diseases from an early age. These include tuberculosis, diphtheria, pertussis, poliomyelitis, tetanus, hepatitis B, measles, mumps and rubella. As a result of the high coverage of immunisation, diphtheria and poliomyelitis have been virtually eradicated from the territory and the incidence of other diseases among children are kept at low levels.

The immunisation programmes are carried out at maternal and child health centres for children under six, and at primary schools. BCG, polio type 1 vaccine and the first dose of hepatitis B are given to newborn babies in hospitals and maternity homes. The coverage rates are over 97 per cent.

Immunisation for all infants against hepatitis B was first introduced in November 1988. Hepatitis B vaccination was also offered to children born between 1986 and 1988 on a one-off basis in 1992. A total of 141 338 vaccinations were given between July and November 1992.

All new born babies are covered in the Combined Neonatal Screening Programme for congenital hypothyroidism and glucose-6-phosphate-dehydrogenase deficiency. This facilitates early diagnosis and treatment of these conditions which may lead to disability. Parents of children identified through the screening programme are advised on the treatment and management needs of their children.

HIV Infection and AIDS

The influence exerted by HIV (Human Immunodeficiency Virus) and AIDS (Acquired Immunodeficiency Syndrome) virus infection is increasing world-wide. As there is yet no cure for AIDS and no effective vaccine against HIV infection, HIV continues to pose a serious threat. In 1992, 73 cases of HIV infection were reported. This brings the total number of cases reported since the beginning of the surveillance programme in April 1985 to 339. Fourteen new cases of AIDS were reported in 1992, giving a cumulative total of 73 cases, of which 48 have died.

The fight against HIV/AIDS continues with the Advisory Council on AIDS of the Department of Health taking the lead. Under the Council, the Committee on Education and Publicity on AIDS (CEPAIDS) continues to work towards promoting greater community involvement in AIDS education, sustaining awareness of the disease among members of the public, co-ordinating the training of intermediaries to provide education and counselling, promoting respect for the confidentiality of and preventing discrimination against HIV-infected individuals, evaluating the effectiveness of the programmes and co-ordinating activities for special target groups such as students, youth workers, drug abusers and sexually-active persons. To achieve these objectives, seven working groups were formed under CEPAIDS, each responsible for a specific area of the work.

The Scientific Working Group, also under the council, is concerned with the technical aspects of the preventive programmes. The working group concentrates on the production of comprehensive guidelines for the prevention of transmission of HIV in health care settings, oversees HIV surveillance programmes, undertakes quality assurance programmes on HIV antibody testing and carries out studies and scientific research projects.

To foster collaboration with the community, the Hong Kong AIDS Foundation was incorporated in May 1991 as a non-governmental organisation to supplement and complement government's efforts. The Foundation's activities include research, health promotion and education, publicity and counselling services. In particular, it mobilises public support and opens up avenues for community participation.

The AIDS Counselling and Health Education Service continues to provide counselling and medical consultation for persons who are at risk of contracting AIDS. Health talks are arranged for various groups such as students, prison inmates and intravenous drug abusers. Members of the public can use a special telephone hotline to obtain advice in confidence. Blood tests may be arranged under conditions of complete anonymity.

Mass screening of all donated blood for antibodies to AIDS virus has been carried out since 1985 by the Hong Kong Red Cross Blood Transfusion Service. This ensures the safety of blood used in transfusion and transmission of HIV through this route has become unlikely.

Review of Primary Health Care
Primary health care, which emphasises promotion of general health and prevention of disease, is recognised world-wide as the most cost-effective means to provide health care services.

The Working Party on Primary Health Care, whose report was endorsed by the Government in 1991, made 102 recommendations to improve Hong Kong's primary health care service. The key recommendations are being implemented in phases. These include improvements to over 50 general out-patient clinics, the establishment of a well woman clinic, preventive health programmes for the elderly and a clinical information system. A review on occupational health has also been conducted.

Training in family medicine is a priority area for improvement. Several training programmes have been devised. A training and education centre in family medicine was opened in Ngau Tau Kok Jockey Club Clinic.

District Health System
The District Health System is a new organisational framework for the delivery of primary health care services. It attaches importance to the need for efficient co-ordination among various providers of medical and health services and community participation. One of its main features is the decentralisation of health services from the regional to the district level and public involvement in service planning and health promotion.

A pilot District Health System programme was initiated in 1992 in Kwun Tong. To facilitate co-ordination with hospitals and other community service providers and the community, a District Health Committee was set up. Its functions include liaison between different services, provision of a forum for information exchange and enhancing the role of the community in the identification of health needs.

Hospitals and Development Programmes
Hospitals in Hong Kong provide a total of 26 412 beds, representing 4.6 beds per thousand population. Public hospitals provide low-charge services which are easily accessible to the people of Hong Kong. In 1992, 693 200 patients were treated in public hospitals, while 4 251 360 attendances were made at specialist clinics.

Cases of acute illness and accident casualties are handled by the accident and emergency departments of major public hospitals free of charge. In 1992, 1 286 500 attendances were made – an average of 3 515 per day.

During the year, demand for hospital services remained high, as reflected by the consistently large number of attendances at out-patient and specialist clinics, accident and emergency departments, and the number of hospital admissions. In addition, both the Department of Health and the Hospital Authority continue to provide medical care to Vietnamese migrants. In 1992, they accounted for 13 010 attendances at accident and emergency departments and 11 350 hospital admissions, with a total of 69 130 bed days occupied.

Projects in the hospital development programme have progressed satisfactorily with the opening of the Argyle Street Ophthalmic Centre and the Tung Wah Eastern Hospital Paramedical Block. Construction work on the 1 620-bed Pamela Youde Hospital in Chai Wan is scheduled for completion in late 1992.

New or additional services are being progressively introduced in Tuen Mun Hospital, Queen Mary Hospital Extension, Ruttonjee Hospital, Shatin Cheshire Home and Shatin Infirmary and Convalescent Hospital. The accident and emergency service provided by Tuen Mun Hospital has been extended to 24 hours per day since early 1992.

Major projects under construction include extension to the United Christian Hospital, refurbishment and air-conditioning of Queen Elizabeth Hospital, and expansion of the delivery suite and specialist clinic at Prince of Wales Hospital. Future projects include redevelopment of Haven of Hope Hospital, redevelopment of Castle Peak Hospital, relocation of Nethersole Hospital to Tai Po, extension of Kwong Wah Hospital, establishment of a Geriatric Day Hospital at Wong Tai Sin Infirmary and construction of Tai Po Infirmary and Convalescent Hospital.

Clinics
General out-patient services form a vital part of the health care system. Government now operates 63 general out-patient clinics. In the more densely-populated areas with higher

Preceding page: *The abundance of marine life at Pak Sha O attracts many amateur divers.*

Left: *Divers prepare to visit the beautiful flora and fauna of the underwater world.*

Below: *Pak Sha O waters provide a home for Gorgunian Soft Coral* **(top)** *and Castle-like Brain Coral.*

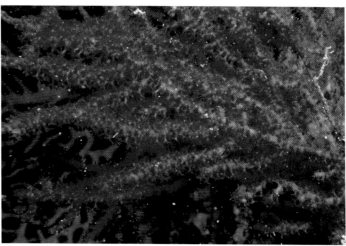

Top to bottom: *the Parasitic Cowry Snail with soft coral; tentacles of anemone; the 'eye' of the long spined sea urchin.*

Right: *A diver encounters a shoal of small fish.*

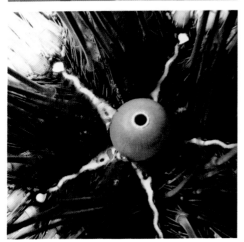

Top row (left to right): *'Peacock' worm; Zoanthid soft coral; Colourful Nudibranch;*
bottom row (left to right): *a Clownfish with its anemone host; a file shell on stony coral; anemone shrimp.*

Above: *The feather star.*
Right: *Pearly soldier fish.*

demand, evening, Sunday and public holiday sessions are also provided. Total attendance was 10.7 million in 1992. To cater for increasing demand, 13 additional clinic projects have been included in the medical development programme in the next decade. Mobile dispensaries and floating clinics provide the necessary medical services to remote areas of the New Territories and outlying islands. Other inaccessible areas are visited regularly by the 'flying doctor' service, with the assistance of the Royal Hong Kong Auxiliary Air Force.

The Department of Health also operates child assessment, tuberculosis and chest, leprosy, social hygiene, dermatology and clinical genetics services, providing both preventive and curative services for different patient groups.

At the end of the year, there were a total of 89 clinics operated by various charity organisations registered under the Medical Clinics Ordinance and 139 registered as exempted clinics. Registered medical practitioners belonging to the Estate Doctors' Association run clinics in housing estates to provide a low-cost service for residents. Private medical practitioners continue to attend to the majority of out-patients.

Family Health
The Family Health Services of the Department of Health operate 46 maternal and child health centres, providing a comprehensive health programme for women of child-bearing age and children below six years. Ante-natal and post-natal medical consultation, as well as family planning services, are offered to women. Immunisation, child health advice and physical examinations are provided for children. During the year, about 90 per cent of newborn babies attended maternal and child health centres.

Under the Comprehensive Observation Scheme, children are assessed at different ages for early detection of developmental abnormalities. They are referred to specialist clinics or child assessment centres for further examination as necessary.

At present, there are four government and one government-assisted assessment centres. These provide comprehensive physical, psychological and social assessment as well as treatment, parental counselling and referral for appropriate placement of children in the various institutions and centres run by the government and voluntary agencies. Three more centres have been included in the Department of Health's medical development programme.

Health education is an essential component of the Family Health Services. In addition to health talks and counselling on child care at centres, health education for expectant mothers is extended to public hospitals, with emphasis on the promotion of breast-feeding. A telephone service is available to answer public enquiries.

The government-subvented Family Planning Association of Hong Kong runs 22 birth control clinics, providing services such as pre-marital counselling, contraception, sterilisation, vasectomy and advice on sub-fertility. There is also emphasis on health education and publicity on family planning and sex education.

School Health
The School Medical Service Scheme is operated by an independent School Medical Service Board. Participation is voluntary and all children from Primary 1 to Form 3 of the participating schools can join the scheme by paying a token fee of $20 a year. As at

December 31, 1992, more than 339 200 children from 1 112 schools have participated – representing about 46 per cent of the eligible school population – and about 490 general medical practitioners have enlisted. Starting from November 1, 1992, each child has to pay $16 for each consultation made at the chosen medical practitioner's office. The government contributes $136 a year for each pupil enrolled and also bears the administrative cost.

School health service deals with the environmental health and sanitation of school premises and the control of communicable diseases. School health officers, health nurses and health inspectors make regular inspections of schools to advise on matters concerning the health of children and organise health education activities and immunisation campaigns.

Port Health
The Port Health Service is the control authority to prevent the entry of quarantinable diseases into Hong Kong via air, land, rail or sea and to enforce the measures stipulated under the Quarantine and Prevention of Disease Ordinance and the International Health Regulations.

A 24-hour health clearance service is provided for all incoming vessels, including those ferrying refugees, and radio pratiques are granted to ships. The service provides vaccination facilities and issues international vaccination certificates. It also inspects and supervises the eradication of rats from ships on international voyages and ensures adequate standards of hygiene and sanitation on board vessels or aircraft. It provides medical assistance to ships and planes within the territory and gives medical advice to vessels at sea.

The food catering service for international airlines is kept under close surveillance by health staff to ensure that food and water supplied to flight kitchens is clean and safe. The hygiene and sanitation of the airport is also under the strict scrutiny of health staff.

The service regularly exchanges epidemiological information with the World Health Organisation in Geneva and its Western Pacific Regional Office in Manila, as well as with neighbouring countries.

Occupational Health
The Occupational Health Division of the Department of Health provides an advisory service to Government and the public on matters concerning the health of workers and the hygiene of workplaces. It also supervises the observance of occupational health standards and practices in the work place. The objectives of the division are to maintain and improve the physical and mental well-being of workers, to protect them against any health hazard arising from employment and to help them adjust to their jobs. The emphasis is on occupational disease prevention and health promotion. In 1992, the division continued to participate in occupational health activities organised to promote public awareness of the importance of health at work. The division itself also organised a large-scale exhibition on *Occupational Health Perspective – Industrial Chemicals and You* in early 1992.

Dental Services
The School Dental Service aims to promote dental health among primary school children. Services include regular dental examination, treatment and oral health education. Participation is voluntary at an annual fee of $10 per child. In the 1992–3 school year,

398 759 children from 991 schools participated, representing 78 per cent of the primary school population.

The Oral Health Education Unit of the Department of Health organises oral health education activities for the community. In 1992, an exhibition on *Healthy Teeth, Happy Life* was organised. The unit has also planned a three-year oral health education programme for pre-school children. This will be launched in February 1993.

The Government Dental Service provides emergency treatment for the public at a number of district dental clinics. Dental treatment is also provided for inmates of correctional institutions and patients in public hospitals.

Services for the Mentally Ill and Mentally Handicapped

Medical services for mentally ill persons include treatment in hospitals, out-patient clinics and day hospitals and out-reaching services. The Mental Health Service, in conjunction with local academic and non-governmental organisations, provides a comprehensive psychiatric service for the territory. Emphasis is placed on continuity of care and integrating rehabilitation with medical treatment.

At the end of 1992, 3 514 beds were provided in psychiatric hospitals, and 879 beds in public psychiatric units of general hospitals, with 871 additional beds being planned for mentally ill persons in various public hospitals. Psychiatric patients are treated, as far as possible, in the community. The community work and aftercare units of the psychiatric hospitals provide multi-disciplinary assistance to patients discharged from these hospitals. Community psychiatric nursing service and domiciliary occupational therapy service in particular aim to provide continual care and treatment programmes for discharged mental patients in their home setting, thereby assisting them in social readjustment and educating patients as well as their families in mental health. There are now nine Community Psychiatric Nursing Service centres and two more are being planned. The various other complementary rehabilitative services include day centres, half-way houses, longstay care homes, vocational training, selective placement and social clubs offered by various government departments and non-government organisations.

Severely mentally handicapped persons requiring intensive nursing care and rehabilitation services are cared for in Tuen Mun Hospital with 200 beds, Caritas Medical Centre with 300 beds and Duchess of Kent Children's Hospital with 10 beds. In order to meet the great demand in this area, a further 676 beds have been planned.

Support Services

The Pathology Service of the Department of Health provides both clinical and public health laboratory services for government clinics and some public hospitals.

The Forensic Pathology Service with its fully-established forensic laboratory works closely with the Royal Hong Kong Police on the medical aspects of criminology and other medico-legal work. It also performs investigations in all homicides and coroners' cases.

The Virus Unit is the central laboratory for the diagnosis and surveillance of viral infections including HIV infections. It provides laboratory support for the screening, assessment and guidance of vaccination programmes against viral diseases. Moreover, the Institute of Immunology undertakes the monitoring and quality control of biological products, including vaccines for use in local health services.

The Central Neonatal Screening Laboratory co-ordinates the laboratory activities of the territory-wide neonatal screening programme on congenital hypothyroidism and glucose-6-phosphate-dehydrogenase deficiency.

The Pharmaceutical Service of the Department of Health is made up of two divisions. The first division provides pharmaceutical service to all government clinics. The second deals with the inspection and licensing of pharmaceutical manufacturers and dealers and the registration and import-export control of pharmaceutical products and medicines. Action is taken against the illegal sale and distribution of pharmaceutical products and medicines. In 1992, there were 65 prosecutions.

Radiation Health

Regular visits are made by the staff of the Radiation Health Unit of the Department of Health to medical, commercial and industrial premises to inspect the working conditions of radiation workers. The unit also issues radiation licences to proprietors in accordance with the Radiation Ordinance and Regulations. It assists in the Background Radiation Monitoring Programme organised by the Royal Observatory to establish an accurate baseline of background radiation levels in Hong Kong.

Community Nursing Service

The Community Nursing Service of the Hospital Authority provides domiciliary and rehabilitation nursing care and treatment to the sick, the elderly infirm and the disabled in their own homes. The service is provided through a network of eight hospital stations and 42 satellite centres. During the year, 20 100 patients were served and 270 200 home visits were made.

Health Education

The Central Health Education Unit of the Department of Health is responsible for the planning, organisation, co-ordination and promotion of health education activities. In 1992, the unit was actively involved in a number of campaigns including those on prevention of communicable diseases such as viral hepatitis and malaria; organ donation; diabetes; self-care; and AIDS.

The theme of the major health education campaign for 1992 was *Healthy Members, Happy Family*. A series of programmes including a 24-hour pre-recorded telephone information service, cartoon wording competition, photo competition and health news were arranged. An exhibition was held in the Science Museum in September.

Special training courses were arranged for students and teachers, notably the 13th Young Health Leaders' Training Course, which was held in July. Health talks and presentations were delivered to schools, voluntary agencies, private companies and government departments. Health education materials like pamphlets, cassettes, slides, videos and exhibits were produced for distribution or loan.

Close liaison is maintained with both government and non-government organisations in promoting health educational activities.

Smoking and Health

The Smoking (Public Health) (Amendment) Ordinance 1992 was passed by the Legislative Council on January 29, 1992. As an important step in the government's on-going antismoking policy, the new law further prohibits smoking in public places and public transport, limits tobacco advertising, restricts the tar content in cigarettes and conveys stronger health warnings to the public. Following this, the government launched a consultation exercise from August to October to solicit views on proposals furthering restrictions on the use, sale and promotion of tobacco products.

The Hong Kong Council on Smoking and Health is an independent statutory body established in 1987 to acquire and disseminate information on the health hazards of using tobacco products and to advise government on matters related to tobacco and health. During the year, the Council conducted publicity campaigns with particular emphasis on discouraging young people from smoking. With a $2 million grant from the Royal Hong Kong Jockey Club, it completed a year-long youth project in collaboration with the Community Youth Club of the Education Department with the aim of promoting a happy and healthy lifestyle among young people without addiction to smoking. More than 500 schools have taken part in various activities, involving hundreds of thousands of students.

Medical Charges

The government is committed to the policy that no one is denied adequate medical treatment through lack of means. Medical charges remain low, reflecting a substantial subsidy from public funds. Patients in general wards of public hospitals are charged $43 a day and the fee covers everything from meals, medicine and investigation tests, to surgery or any other treatment required. The charge may be reduced or waived in cases of hardship certified by a medical social worker. A limited number of private beds are provided at major public hospitals with higher maintenance and treatment charges.

The charge for consultation at general out-patient clinics is $21, while that for specialist clinics is $33. Charges for physiotherapy, occupational therapy and child assessment services are $33. Attendance at geriatric or psychiatric day centres and home visits by community nurses cost $34. These fees may also be waived if warranted.

The charge for injections and dressings in general out-patient clinics is $9, while charges for visits to family planning clinics and methadone clinics remain at $1. These levels of charges reflect substantial subsidies from public funds.

Free medical services continued to be offered at maternal and child health centres, tuberculosis and chest clinics, social hygiene clinics, and accident and emergency departments.

Training of Medical and Health Personnel

The basic training of doctors is provided by the University of Hong Kong and The Chinese University of Hong Kong. Graduates of the two medical schools are conferred degrees which are recognised by the General Medical Council of Great Britain. The medical student intake at the University of Hong Kong was 163 in 1992 and 155 in the Chinese University of Hong Kong.

Under the Licentiate Scheme of the Hong Kong Medical Council, 35 externally-trained doctors passed the local licentiate examination in 1992. After satisfactory completion of an externship programme in public hospitals, they will become registered medical practitioners.

Training in dentistry is available at the University of Hong Kong which produced the eighth batch of 38 graduates in January 1992. The training of dental therapists is provided at the Tang Shiu Kin Dental Therapists Training School.

Three-year basic nursing training is offered by schools of nursing of the Hospital Authority (HA) and one private hospital. The Hong Kong Polytechnic and the Chinese University of Hong Kong also conduct undergraduate degree nursing courses. On completion of either programmes and having registered with the Nursing Board of Hong Kong, graduates are licensed to practise as registered nurses. The three-year training capacity for student nurses in the HA general nursing schools is 3 417 while that of the psychiatric nursing schools is 520. Two-year programmes are also organised to train pupil nurses to become enrolled nurses. The two-year training capacity for HA schools is 991 in the general stream and 160 for the psychiatric. Opportunities for further training in specialised fields are available both locally and overseas.

The departments of Diagnostic Sciences, Rehabilitation Sciences and Health Sciences of the Hong Kong Polytechnic provide training for para-medical and para-dental staff, including radiographers, optometrists, physiotherapists, occupational therapists, medical laboratory technicians and dental technicians. Training for speech therapists is provided by the University of Hong Kong. The Chai Wan Technical Institute of the Technical Education and Industrial Training Department provides training for dispensers which is complemented by in-service training. There is also in-service training for prosthetists, mould laboratory technicians and therapeutic radiographers in the respective units of public institutions. Where local training is not yet available, government training scholarship programmes are offered for supply of audiologists, audiological technicians, orthoptists and chiropodists. There are opportunities for overseas training in specialised areas for medical, nursing, para-medical and para-dental staff.

Government Laboratory

The Government Laboratory provides a wide range of primarily chemical testing services to government departments and other institutions. Much of the work is related to the protection of public health and the environment. The laboratory has statutory responsibilities for testing under a number of ordinances and regulations.

Food and food products are regularly tested over the year for composition, additives, toxic residues and contaminants. Several outbreaks of food poisoning arising from consumption of vegetables contaminated with toxic pesticide residues, have led the laboratory again to be heavily involved in the checking of vegetable samples. Results of analysis are made available within a few hours of sample receipt to enable client departments to take appropriate follow-up action in good time.

Pharmaceutical products for use in public hospitals and clinics are tested for compliance with pharmacopoeia or other specifications. Those intended for use and sale locally are examined for compliance with registration and labelling requirements. Herbal medicines are checked for the presence of synthetic drugs and toxic metals.

In other areas of public health, projects have been conducted with the Consumer Council to test for toxic and carcinogenic substances in several types of consumer products, and a unit was set up to undertake comprehensive testing of toys and products for children for compliance with safety requirements.

A wide range of commodities continued to be examined on behalf of the Customs and Excise Department. These included dutiable commodities tested for duty assessment purposes, weighing equipment for compliance with the weights and measures ordinance, suspected forged commodities for identification, and gold and platinum articles for fineness determination. Research is now underway to study the quality of precious stones.

In the realm of environmental protection more litigation-related samples were examined on top of the bulk of samples analysed on behalf of the Environmental Protection Department for the monitoring of air, river and marine waters and sediments for a variety of pollution level indicators. These samples included industrial fuels for sulphur determination, illegal sewage discharges for microbiological tests, and industrial effluents for the determination of toxic and environmentally harmful substances.

Analytical and advisory services in relation to storage, carriage and classification of dangerous goods continued to be provided to the Fire Services Department. Immediate testing of medical gases was carried out to support their safe use in hospitals. In addition, a 24-hour service was provided to render assistance to fire service personnel at scenes of emergency involving hazardous chemicals.

Drug Abuse and Trafficking

The government's policy is to stop the illicit trafficking of drugs into and through Hong Kong, to develop a comprehensive treatment and rehabilitation programme for drug abusers and to dissuade people, particularly young people, from experimenting with drugs, so as to eradicate drug abuse from the community.

The exact number of drug abusers is not known. However, the government's computerised Central Registry of Drug Abuse and other linked indicators suggest that at the end of 1992 there were about 38 000 'active' drug abusers, which was 0.8 per cent of the population aged 11 and above.

Data collected by the registry, based on 498 000 reports on 70 000 persons, indicate that 90 per cent of drug abusers are male and 10 per cent female. Sixty seven per cent of the 'active' abusers were over 30-years-old at the end of 1992, 25 per cent were in the 21 to 30 bracket and 8 per cent were aged under 21. The most common drug of abuse is heroin, which was used by 93 per cent of the persons reported to the registry in 1992. In the case of young persons below the age of 21, the common drugs of abuse included heroin, cough medicines and cannabis.

A total of 2 500 drug abusers came to the notice of the registry for the first time in 1992. Of the new cases, 85 per cent were male and 15 per cent were female. Most of them, or 70 per cent, were within the age bracket of 16 to 30. The drugs reported to be commonly abused by these new cases were again heroin, cough medicines and cannabis.

Overall Strategy and Co-ordination

The government has a comprehensive anti-drug programme which has achieved considerable success. The programme adopts a four-pronged approach, namely law enforcement, treatment and rehabilitation, preventive education and publicity and international co-operation. Effective law enforcement induces abusers to seek treatment voluntarily as a result of short supply of drugs. Treatment and rehabilitation are undertaken by government and a number of voluntary agencies which offer a wide range of facilities to meet the different needs of drug abusers from varying backgrounds. The

147

effectiveness of these treatment programmes reduces the demand for illicit drugs. At the same time, the government places great emphasis on preventive education and publicity to heighten public awareness of the drug problem and to promote the advantages of a drug-free lifestyle. Co-operation at the international level, through exchange of information and experience and joint action against illicit trafficking, enhances the effectiveness of efforts in these three areas.

These efforts are co-ordinated by the Action Committee Against Narcotics (ACAN), a non-statutory body which includes both non-official and government members. The committee is the government's advisory body on all anti-drug policies and actions undertaken by government and non-government agencies. It is serviced by the Narcotics Division, which is headed by the Commissioner for Narcotics.

Legislation and Law Enforcement
The Dangerous Drugs Ordinance is the main piece of legislation dealing with drug offences. In June, amendments to the ordinance were passed which modified and repealed presumptions which were incompatible with the Bill of Rights, raised the maximum fines for the offences of possession of dangerous drugs and revised the definition of drug trafficking to include the offence of possession of dangerous drugs for the purpose of unlawful trafficking. As a further deterrent to the abuse of psychotropic substances by youngsters, all benzodiazepines liable to abuse were included in the first schedule to the Dangerous Drugs Ordinance in October 1991. The full sanctions and controls provided under the ordinance have been applied, with effect from January 1992, with regard to the possession, import, export, supply and otherwise dealing with benzodiazepines.

The Royal Hong Kong Police and the Customs and Excise Department seized some 580 kilograms of No. 4 heroin, 3 000 kilograms of cannabis and 17 kilograms of methylamphetamine (or 'ice') during the year. These included the seizure of 396 kilograms of No. 4 heroin in June, 1 555 kilograms of cannabis in May and 15 kilograms of methyl-amphetamine in May. Following joint operations with overseas law enforcement agencies, a number of international drug trafficking syndicates were neutralised with substantial quantities of dangerous drugs seized and ringleaders arrested locally and abroad. In 1992, police and customs action resulted in the arrest of 8 900 persons for drug offences.

Treatment and Rehabilitation
The voluntary Methadone Treatment Programme operated by the Department of Health provides both maintenance and detoxification for out-patients. Methadone maintenance is designed to reduce or eliminate an abuser's reliance on heroin or other opiate drugs, while the detoxification programme aims to eliminate dependence on any drug. The programme has proved to be very effective in serving both drug abusers and the community. There are 24 methadone clinics.

The largest voluntary in-patient treatment programme is run by the Society for the Aid and Rehabilitation of Drug Abusers (SARDA) which operates an in-patient treatment centre for up to 380 men on the island of Shek Kwu Chau, and one for up to 40 women at Sha Tin. Linked to these centres are four regional social service centres, five halfway houses, a job skill training laboratory and a clinic which provides pre-admission medical examination, counselling and detoxification services, urine analysis and post-discharge medical care.

A compulsory in-patient treatment programme is operated by the Correctional Services Department under the Drug Addiction Treatment Centres Ordinance. The department runs two addiction treatment centres, one for up to 704 males on the island of Hei Ling Chau and the other for 100 females at Tai Lam Chung. These treatment programmes range from two to 12 months, the actual period being determined by the inmate's progress and the likelihood of continued abstinence from drugs following release. All persons discharged are given one year of statutory after-care.

In 1992, the two voluntary treatment programmes and the Correctional Services Department's compulsory treatment programme admitted 12 200 abusers. On average, 12 800 drug abusers and ex-drug abusers were receiving some form of treatment, rehabilitation or after-care every day.

The counselling centre, PS33, set up in Tsim Sha Tsui in April 1988 to provide counselling and telephone advice for psychotropic substance abusers, handled 113 cases and 1 176 telephone and drop-in enquiries during the year. PS33 is operated by the Hong Kong Christian Service with financial support from the Royal Hong Kong Jockey Club.

Preventive Education and Publicity
The government and the community continued their efforts in promoting anti-drug preventive education and publicity. The main themes of the publicity campaign in 1992 were similar to those for 1991, with more emphasis being placed on alerting youngsters to the harmful effects of abusing drugs and other substances. The publicity message for the year was *Substance abuse can ruin your life, Say NO to drugs.*

Six district campaigns were held involving the community through carnivals, variety shows, competitions and exhibitions.

The Narcotics Division's school talks team gave 295 drug education talks to 100 917 students in 165 secondary schools and technical institutes throughout the territory. Starting from September, drug education talks using different approaches were extended to Primary 6 students and to the four colleges of education. Apart from school students, talks were also organised for members of youth organisations, parents, juvenile offenders at the boys' and girls' homes operated by the Social Welfare Department and Vietnamese illegal immigrants.

To support the annual International Day Against Drug Abuse and Illicit Trafficking, a bus parade was organised and a large-scale exhibition was held in Kwai Fong Metroplaza in June. A simple anti-drug message, *Say NO to Drugs*, was also applied as a post mark on all mail in June.

In 1992, a Community Against Drugs Scheme was established to replace the former Youth Against Drugs Scheme with a view to encouraging more interested groups to plan and implement their own anti-drug education and publicity projects. Under the scheme, financial support up to $5,000 per project will be granted. The 55-member ACAN Youth Volunteer Group took part in district campaigns and organised a number of community involvement projects. The ACAN Youth Advisory Group, comprising a cross-section of young people, continued to give advice on educational and publicity materials and activities.

The ACAN Drug Abuse Telephone Enquiry Service received 2 731 enquiries, the majority seeking information on treatment facilities.

International Action

Hong Kong continued to play an active international role, maintaining close links with the United Nations, inter-governmental agencies such as Interpol and the Customs Co-operation Council, as well as with individual governments. Hong Kong took part in 36 regional and international meetings and seminars concerned with anti-drug policies, law enforcement, treatment and rehabilitation, and preventive education.

The techniques and methods employed in Hong Kong have made it an important venue for training anti-drug personnel from overseas. During the year, 303 people from 25 countries and international bodies came to Hong Kong on study visits and training courses.

As at the end of the year, bilateral agreements had been concluded with 11 foreign jurisdictions with a view to enhancing international co-operation, particularly as regards the tracing and confiscation of the proceeds of drug trafficking.

Environmental Hygiene

The Urban Services Department and the Regional Services Department, working under the Urban Council and the Regional Council, are responsible for street cleaning, collection and removal of refuse and nightsoil, cleansing of gullies, management of public toilets and bathhouses, pest control and services for the dead.

A regular workforce of about 8 500 is employed in cleansing duties, employing a fleet of 550 specialised vehicles which include refuse collection vehicles, street washers, mechanical sweepers, nightsoil collectors and gully emptiers.

Streets are swept, either manually or mechanically, up to six times a day for busy thoroughfares to once every second day for village lanes. Streets and lanes are also hosed down where local conditions warrant. Hawker areas and refuse collection points are washed regularly.

About 4 760 tonnes of refuse and junk are collected daily, including 114 tonnes removed by a contractual barging service from outlying islands for disposal on the mainland. A free nightsoil collection service is also provided every day in those areas without a water-borne sewage and disposal system. These services are provided free.

There are 1 109 refuse collection points and 1 584 bin sites in the territory.

The two departments continued to contract out some of their cleansing services to private contractors to reduce the direct involvement of departmental labour and enhance cost-effectiveness. In the urban areas, the contracts covered 307 public toilets and bathhouses, manual street sweeping of Tai Kok Tsui, part of Wan Chai and two squatter villages. In the New Territories, the contracting-out of street cleansing services was extended to cover selected areas in Tuen Mun, Sha Tin and Sai Kung districts from April 1992. The provision of desludging services for Vietnamese migrant centres was also assigned to a private contractor. As the performance of the private contractors has been found to be satisfactory, contracting out will be extended to other suitable localities. Under active planning are the contracting-out of waste collection in Tai Po township and cleansing for remote areas in Sai Kung.

During the year, the Keep Hong Kong Clean Campaign celebrated its 20th anniversary. To mark the special year, the Joint Urban Council/Regional Council Steering Committee stepped up its efforts to spread the keep clean message by launching a seven-phase clean-up programme, covering the environment, water, roads, schools, homes, squatter areas and illages, as well as the countryside and country parks. The campaign focused on ommunity involvement, education and publicity through all media of communication.

The 20th anniversary celebrations included mass participation events, a parade carnival nd the Keep Hong Kong Clean 20th Anniversary Rally, at the launching and conclusion f the campaign year, involving the active participation of the District Boards.

To encourage greater public participation and achieve wider media publicity, the two nunicipal councils engaged an advertising agency. Along with the 20th anniversary theme, new slogan, *Thanks for Keeping Hong Kong Clean*, was adopted. Television Broadcasts imited was engaged to build up publicity for the campaign through nominating a 'Star of Cleanliness' each month and a grand finale TV spectacular in November.

The Dragon of Cleanliness, the mascot for the campaign, continued to participate ctively in various campaign activities to put across the keep clean message.

Law enforcement remained a major weapon against litter offenders, and special efforts vere made by enforcement officers to deter littering. During the year, 37 000 litterbugs were ined a total of $10.5 million.

Controls

Both municipal councils are the authorities responsible for environmental hygiene and staff f the two municipal services departments enforce the Public Health and Municipal Services Ordinance and its subsidiary legislation to ensure that standards of hygiene in the erritory are well maintained. The staff regularly inspect licensed and permitted premises, common parts of buildings, squatter areas, construction sites and undeveloped land. They espond to complaints about sanitary nuisances, vermin infestation and substandard oods. They also work closely with the Department of Health in the investigation and control of food-poisoning outbreaks and infectious diseases.

To better utilise manpower and resources, the Urban Services Department continued with the Selective Inspection System for the inspection of licensed food premises. Under his system, food business establishments are graded according to their past performance. The frequency of inspection for each establishment is then determined in accordance with ts grading.

In order to maintain standards on food premises and to deter offences against licensing nd hygiene regulations, a Demerit Points System is used under which the accumulation of 15 points for convictions within 12 months forms the basis for suspension or cancellation f a food business licence or permit.

The Regional Services Department continued to exercise strict control over food premises which failed to apply for a licence or which had not complied with the specified equirements. Since 1987, the prosecution of offenders had increased in frequency from nonthly to weekly. This had had the effect of dramatically reducing the number of unlicensed food businesses to 75 in December 1992.

For the prevention of vector-borne diseases, pest control staff of the two departments carried out integrated programmes to control rodents, mosquitoes, flies and other public health pests. Measures taken included environmental improvement, eradication of breeding places, health education and law enforcement. Special surveillance was maintained to prevent outbreaks of malaria in Vietnamese migrant centres. Technical support is provided by the Pest Control Advisory Section of the Department of Health.

Environmental Health Education

An important role of the Health Education Unit of the Hygiene Division of the Department of Health is to promote environmental health and food hygiene through education on a territory-wide basis. Under the auspices of the two Municipal Councils, the unit launched a number of educational campaigns in 1992. Of these campaigns, the most notable were the Environmental and Health Drive held early in the year and the 1992 Food Hygiene Campaign with the theme *Food Safety Is Our Talking Point* organised during the hot summer months for members of the food trade and school teachers. The former aimed at arousing public attention to the importance of keeping a clean home environment while the latter promoted the adoption of good hygiene practices during food preparation in order to prevent food-borne diseases.

In addition, publicity campaigns directed at the prevention of rodent infestation and nuisances caused by mosquitoes and dripping air-conditioners were staged during the year. Apart from talks, broadcasting and hotline services provided by the unit, health messages were disseminated through the mass media. Public health materials including posters and leaflets were also distributed to the general public at the unit's resource centre.

Food Hygiene

The Hygiene Division of the Department of Health consists of three sections, the Food section, Pest Control Advisory Section and Health Education Unit.

The health inspectorate, backed by a hygiene consultant, controls food for sale, both imported and locally produced. Supported by laboratory resources and assisted by a scientific advisory arm, the inspectorate ensures that consumers are able to buy good wholesome food, unadulterated, uncontaminated, properly described and of nutritious quality.

Food samples are taken regularly for chemical analyses, bacteriological examinations and toxicity tests to ascertain their fitness for human consumption. For the purpose of sampling for laboratory testing, food items are prioritised according to the nature of the food and the risks that they may pose to consumers. Complementary to regular laboratory analyses, field tests for pesticide residues are performed on imported vegetables at the points of entry into Hong Kong including Lo Wu, Man Kam To and the airport. Owing to the fast development of transportation across the border, another border checkpoint at Lok Ma Chau was built and became operative in 1992.

The growing number of food establishments and the quantities and variety of food items available on the local market have increased the importance of law enforcement. Parallel to this is the increasing demand for services for health certification of foods for export and re-export.

The review of food legislation has been an on-going exercise with a view to ensuring that laws made are consistent with international standards, guidelines and recommendations based on scientific evidence. This is important in order to provide a high standard of public health protection and at the same time to facilitate international trade in foods.

On the international scene, Hong Kong maintains close ties with the World Health Organisation and the Food and Agriculture Organisation of the United Nations and other international authoritative bodies on foods. As the bulk of local food supply comes from China, Hong Kong has been working closely with Chinese authorities towards promoting food safety and better food hygiene. Regular meetings are held with officials from Guangdong and Shenzhen Commodities Inspection Bureaux.

Market

The Urban Council operated 62 retail markets in the urban areas in 1992. In these markets, 10 035 stalls offered commodities ranging from fresh food to household items.

Old and outdated markets have been replaced gradually by multi-purpose complexes managed by the Urban Council with new markets and cooked food centres on the lower floors. On the upper floors of the 14 existing complexes, a variety of facilities are provided for indoor sports activities, cultural and recreational pursuits.

New markets with food centres are built not only to meet hawker resiting commitments which was the case in the past, but also to meet consumer demand. This approach, together with improvements in design, has been adopted in planning and building more pleasant and viable markets.

The pilot scheme of contracting out cleansing has been implemented in 14 markets – eight on Hong Kong Island and six in Kowloon. The scheme will be extended to more markets.

The Regional Council is responsible for the management of public markets in the New Territories. In 1992, a new market with 35 stalls was completed at Mui Wo and provided space for resiting all the licensed hawkers and eligible unlicensed hawkers trading in the vicinity. The council now manages 46 markets providing 5 222 goods stalls and 378 cooked food stalls.

During the year, the council continued to improve its existing markets. Apart from better ventilation already provided, installation of an additional escalator has been planned for Tung Yick Market in Yuen Long to improve its accessibility. At the Yeung Uk Road Market in Tsuen Wan, a water scrubber system and a jet cleaner were installed at the poultry scalding room and refuse collection chamber to improve their sanitation. Recommendations of the council's working group on market design were adopted for the proposed Shek Wu Hui Market under planning for completion in 1994–5. Another working group formed by the council is currently reviewing market policy and related management matters.

Hawkers

The Urban Council is responsible for the licensing of street hawkers in the urban areas and the Regional Council is responsible for their management in public places in the New Territories. In 1992, there were 14 400 licensed hawkers in the territory, a decline of 1 200 compared with 1991. This was attributable to the policy of not renewing or allowing succession of itinerant hawker licenses and resiting on-street hawkers into new markets. The completion in 1992 of the Nam Cheong Street Temporary Market, the Tung Chau Street Temporary Market and the Java Road Cooked Food Centre made it possible to resite 381 on-street licensed hawkers formerly trading in the vicinity. Moreover, steady progress continued in a scheme introduced in 1990 for itinerant hawkers to voluntarily surrender their licences in exchange for *ex-gratia* payment, a fixed-pitch hawker licence or a mini-stall tenancy. By the end of 1992, 1 550 licences were returned under this scheme.

Following the recommendations of the Urban Council's working party on hawker and related policies, efforts have been made to relax the issue of hawker licences to a limited extent. About 227 fixed-pitch newspaper hawker licences have been issued. The issue of other classes of licences will depend on the availability of suitable sites identified to be viable and acceptable. Both municipal councils have a firm policy of not issuing any new

153

hawker licences to itinerant hawkers, whose trading activities cause serious obstruction to pedestrians and vehicular traffic in highly built-up urban areas.

Control over hawking is maintained by the two municipal services departments through the deployment of general duties teams. These are civilian staff trained in law enforcement duties and number 2 700. During the year, they secured 117 000 court convictions for hawking offences.

Restructuring of the general duties teams in the New Territories was completed during the year. Besides strengthening their capability to make arrests, all squads were equipped with radio transceivers and an additional vehicle to enhance their efficiency. Furthermore, eight special squads were set up under two sub-regional commands to reinforce district-based operations. The Regional Council also formed a working group to examine hawker policies and control strategies against illegal hawking and illegal shop extensions. A computerised hawker offence record system was implemented in April 1992 with which previous conviction records of offenders were computerised and presented to the court for reference and consideration of heavier penalties on recidivists.

Abattoirs
There are two abattoirs in the urban areas and three slaughterhouses in the New Territories, including a new one on Cheung Chau which also serves the nearby islands. With the exception of the Cheung Sha Wan Abattoir which is run by the Urban Council, all the others are managed by licensed private operators. To meet long-term demand, a site has been reserved for a new slaughterhouse in Sheung Shui.

During the year, 2 930 000 pigs, 150 000 head of cattle and 15 000 goats were slaughtered, which accounted for about 100 per cent of the local fresh meat supply. To ensure the wholesomeness of their meat, all slaughtered animals were inspected by qualified health inspectors of the two municipal services departments.

The Regional Services Department also kept vigilance against illegal slaughtering to ensure that only wholesome meat is supplied to the market. In the past year, health inspectors carried out 49 raids on suspected illegal slaughterhouses and nine offenders were successfully prosecuted. Staff also carried out spot checks on meat stalls and 10 persons were prosecuted in 1992 for possession of unstamped carcasses for sale.

Cemeteries and Crematoria
It is government policy to encourage cremation rather than burial for the disposal of the dead. During the year, over 73 per cent of the dead were cremated in the territory. Human remains buried in public cemeteries are subject to exhumation after six years when the exhumed remains are either cremated or re-interred in urn cemeteries.

The Urban Council operates one public funeral parlour in Kowloon which provides free funeral services for the needy. Two service halls at the parlour are also opened for public use free of charge.

In the urban area, the Urban Council manages five public cemeteries and two public crematoria, and monitors 18 private cemeteries. There are also two war cemeteries under the management of the Commonwealth War Graves Commission.

The Regional Council manages six public cemeteries and four public crematoria in the New Territories. It also oversees the operation of nine private cemeteries and six private crematoria, and provides six columbaria for the deposit of cremated ashes. As at December 1992, these columbaria contained 35 000 niches.

Auxiliary Medical Services

The Auxiliary Medical Services (AMS) is a disciplined medical civil defence corps with the primary mission of augmenting the regular medical and health services in times of natural disasters and emergencies, such as typhoons, rainstorms or landslides, aircraft crashes, large-scale fires, major epidemics, civil disturbance and influx of illegal immigrants.

Since its formation in 1950, the AMS has grown from a membership of 2 000 to over 5 800 in 1992. They come from all walks of life, comprising physicians, nurses, pharmacists, dispensers, radiographers, paramedical personnel, civil servants and laymen in the private sector.

By statutory requirement, the Director of Health is the Commissioner of the AMS who is responsible to the Governor for the efficient operation of the corps. Assisting him is a number of deputy and assistant commissioners appointed on a voluntary basis.

With the exception of medical and nursing professionals, volunteer members all receive comprehensive training in the areas covering first-aid, squad drill, basic ambulance aid and practical ambulance manning, casualty evacuation, home nursing, clinical and hospital ward attachment, life saving, leadership and management development.

Under emergency situations, volunteer members would be mobilised and equipped with the necessary medical resources to provide immediate first-aid treatment for the injured at a disaster scene, to convey casualties to hospitals, to render nursing care to patients at both acute and convalescent hospitals and to work in collaboration with other rescue forces.

If paramedical assistance at a scene is required, the AMS Emergency Response Task Force (ERTF/AMS) would be available at short notice. Medical officers, nurses and trained members of the ERTF/AMS are equipped to undertake nursing aid and minor surgery at the spot.

Apart from being in full readiness to perform emergency roles and functions, AMS is committed to provide supplementary medical services to government departments and outside agencies for ambulance manning, life-guard duties, clinical services in methadone clinics and refugee camps, and first-aid coverage at country parks, cycling tracks, school activities and major public functions such as fireworks displays, Community Chest walks, charity shows, local festivals and sports meetings.

During the year, AMS continued to assist in the daily manning of 25 methadone clinics and provide round-the-clock clinical manning at 10 sick bays in seven Vietnamese boat people centres. More than 684 636 man-hours were committed to operational tasks in the year.

The AMS also carries the responsibility of providing first-aid training to civil servants. A total of 2 752 government servants completed the basic first-aid certificate course and qualified as first-aiders in 1992.

The Mui Wo Sub-unit Headquarters and the New Territories Regional Headquarters were set up in April and November respectively to enhance operational efficiency and to provide local training facilities.

12
SOCIAL WELFARE

THE Director of Social Welfare is responsible for carrying out government policies on social security and social welfare, based on the objectives set out in three White Papers – Integrating the Disabled into the Community: A United Effort (1977); Primary Education and Pre-primary Services (1981); and Social Welfare into the 1990s and Beyond (1991).

The government is advised on social welfare policy by two committees – the Social Welfare Advisory Committee, covering the whole area of social welfare, and the Rehabilitation Development Co-ordinating Committee, on matters of rehabilitation. Members of these committees are appointed by the Governor, with non-officials as chairmen.

In the provision of welfare services, the Social Welfare Department maintains a close working partnership with non-governmental organisations, most of which are affiliated to the Hong Kong Council of Social Service. More details about the Hong Kong Council of Social Service are in Appendix 32A.

Continuing its drive to provide more and better welfare services to meet the changing needs of the community, the government increased spending on social welfare in 1992–3 by 11 per cent to $6,384 million.

The Protection of Women and Juveniles (Amendment) Bill 1992 was published in the Hong Kong Government Gazette in March 1992. Among other things, it aims at widening the circumstances in which a child may be considered to be in need of care or protection and providing the Director of Social Welfare with more flexible powers of intervention and investigation.

Arising from widespread public concern over tragedies involving young children left unattended at home, the three-month public consultation exercise on measures to prevent children from being left unattended at home was concluded in January 1992. The majority was of the view that legislation to prohibit parents from leaving children unattended at home should not be introduced but recommended an increase of child care facilities and support services, the promotion of mutual help groups and the enhancement of public education. These recommendations were considered and endorsed by the Social Welfare Advisory Committee. Follow-up actions are carried out by the department.

During the year, seven new day nurseries, two homes-cum-care-and-attention units, six social centres for the elderly, and nine children and youth centres were established.

With improved housing, financial assistance and community support services, the need for self-care hostels for the elderly is now less obvious. To meet the changing trend, some of the self-care/meal places in hostels for the elderly are being converted into meal/care-

and-attention places. This approach is particularly valuable not only in expanding the number of care-and-attention places but also useful in minimising the transfer of elderly residents to a completely new environment when their health deteriorates.

Community Chest
The Community Chest, which organises and co-ordinates fund-raising activities for its member agencies, raised $132 million in 1991–2, compared with $113 million in 1990–91. More details about the Community Chest are in Appendix 32B.

Social Security
Social security is a major social welfare programme aimed at meeting the needs of vulnerable groups in the community requiring financial or material assistance. The Public Assistance Scheme and the Special Needs Allowance Scheme are the key elements in the non-contributory social security system. They are supplemented by three other schemes: Criminal and Law Enforcement Injuries Compensation Scheme, Traffic Accident Victims Assistance Scheme and Emergency Relief.

The Public Assistance Scheme, which is means-tested, provides cash assistance to those in need. It is designed to raise the income of needy individuals and families to a level where essential requirements are met. Persons who have resided in Hong Kong for not less than one year may be eligible if their income and other resources are below the prescribed levels. An able-bodied unemployed person aged 15 to 59 who is available for work is in addition required to register with the Labour Department for job placement in order to qualify for assistance.

Public assistance payments comprise four components: basic allowance, rent allowance, supplements and special grants. Essential needs such as food, clothing, fuel and light, are met by the basic allowance. Rates of the basic allowance were increased across the board by 10.74 per cent in April 1992 to keep pace with inflation. Current rates of the monthly basic allowance are $825 for a single person; $620 for each of the first two eligible members of family; $610 for each of the next two eligible members; and $600 for each additional eligible member. To cover the cost of accommodation, a separate allowance is paid. For personal needs arising from the recipients' particular circumstances, additional supplements are provided. A monthly old-age supplement of $413 is given to those aged 60 to 69, and $470 to those aged 70 and over, who are not receiving a disability supplement or a special needs allowance under a separate scheme. A disability supplement of $413 per month is payable to those who are certified to be partially disabled with at least 50 per cent loss of earning capacity and who are not in receipt of an old-age supplement or a special needs allowance. A child supplement of $205 per month is given to children of public assistance recipients aged below 15 and to those aged 15 to 18 in full-time education and not receiving educational grants. Those who have received public assistance continuously for 12 months are given an annual long-term supplement to enable them to meet the cost of replacing household wares and durable goods: $1,050 for a single person; $2,100 for a family with two to four members; and $3,150 for a family with five or more members. In addition, special grants are given where necessary to meet other needs such as school fees, travelling or special diets. To encourage self-help, an individual's monthly earnings of up to $620 may be disregarded in the calculation of assistance payable.

At the end of 1992, the number of public assistance cases was 79 700, compared with 71 294 in 1991. The majority of recipients were the elderly, the disabled and single parent families. Expenditure on public assistance during the year amounted to $1,339.0 million, representing an increase of 24.0 per cent over the previous year.

The Special Needs Allowance Scheme provides flat-rate allowances for the severely disabled and the elderly. Any person who is certified to be severely disabled and who has resided continuously in Hong Kong for at least one year immediately before application, is eligible for a disability allowance. To be eligible for an old age allowance, a person must have resided continuously in Hong Kong for at least five years prior to attaining the qualifying age.

The rates of allowances were revised upwards by 10.74 per cent in April 1992 to reflect the rise in the cost of living.

A higher disability allowance, which is twice the normal rate, is payable to those severely disabled persons who require constant attendance from others in their daily life but are not receiving such care in a government or subvented institution or a medical institution under the Hospital Authority. The current monthly rate for disability allowance is $825 and, for higher disability allowance, $1,650.

Old age allowance is non-means-tested for those aged 70 and above, and they are entitled to a current rate of $470 per month. For those aged 65 to 69, the monthly allowance is set at a lower rate of $413, subject to a declaration that income and assets do not exceed prescribed levels.

The number of people receiving disability and old age allowances at the end of the year was 501 200, compared with 471 803 at the end of 1991. Expenditure on special needs allowances during the year was $2,860.1 million, representing an increase of 16.7 per cent over the previous year.

The Criminal and Law Enforcement Injuries Compensation Scheme provides cash assistance to people who are injured in crimes of violence or in helping to prevent crime in Hong Kong. It also extends compensation to those injured by law enforcement officers using weapons in the execution of their duties. Payments are made to their surviving dependent family members in the case of persons killed in any one of these circumstances.

This scheme, which is non-means-tested, is administered by the Criminal Injuries Compensation Board and the Law Enforcement Injuries Compensation Board. Both boards consist of the same chairman and members, who are appointed by the Governor, from outside the civil service.

During the year, total payments amounted to $9.0 million, compared with $7.6 million in the preceding year.

The Traffic Accident Victims Assistance Scheme is a no fault and non-means-tested scheme. It provides cash payments to victims of traffic accidents or their dependents. It is administered by the Director of Social Welfare in consultation with an advisory committee.

For a person to be eligible, the traffic accident must be one as defined under the Traffic Accident Victims (Assistance Fund) Ordinance (Cap. 229) and must have been reported to the police. The application must be lodged within six months of the date of the accident. For an injury case, the victim must be medically certified to require at least three days sick leave. Payments cover personal injury and death but not damage to property.

Under the scheme, an applicant retains the right to claim legal damages or compensation from other sources for the same accident. In case of a successful claim, the applicant is required to refund either the payment received from the scheme or the amount of damages or compensation, whichever is the less.

During the year, 5 460 applications were received and 4 970 were approved for assistance, with payments of $69.0 million compared with $55.5 million in 1991.

Emergency relief is provided to victims of natural or other disasters in the form of material aid, such as hot meals, eating utensils and other essential articles. Grants from the Emergency Relief Fund are also paid to disaster victims or their dependents to relieve hardship arising from personal injury or death.

With the exception of burial grant, the rates of grants payable under the Criminal Injuries Compensation Scheme, the Traffic Accident Victims Assistance Scheme and the Emergency Relief Fund were increased in March and September 1992 to cover the rise in living cost and in the average manufacturing workers' wages.

During the year, emergency relief was given to 4 042 registered victims on 98 occasions. The Social Welfare Department also assisted in providing hot meals to refugees and boat people from Vietnam.

To prevent abuse of the various schemes, a special team investigates cases of suspected fraud or difficulties encountered in recovery of overpayment. During the year, the team completed investigations into 19 cases.

Social Security Appeal Board
The Social Security Appeal Board is an independent body comprising non-official members appointed by the Governor. It considers appeals from individuals against decisions by the Social Welfare Department concerning public assistance, special needs allowance and traffic accident victims assistance payments. During the year, 138 appeals were heard by the board. Of these, six were related to public assistance, 130 to special needs allowance and two to traffic accident victims assistance.

Services for Offenders
The Social Welfare Department has several statutory duties in the field of services for offenders. These duties are to put into effect the directions of the courts on the treatment of offenders through social work methods. The overall aim is to rehabilitate offenders through probation supervision, the Community Service Orders Scheme, residential training for young offenders and after-care services.

Probation service is provided in 11 probation offices which serve 10 magistracies, the District and Supreme Courts. Probation officers make inquiries into the background and home surroundings of offenders as the court may direct and of prisoners for consideration of reducing sentences. They also supervise offenders in complying with the requirements of probation orders. Probation applies to offenders of all age groups from seven years onwards. It allows offenders to remain in the community under supervision and subject to prescribed rules set by the courts. The probation officers work closely with the probationers' families with a family-orientated approach. To promote community involvement in the rehabilitation of offenders, volunteers are recruited to befriend probationers and residents of institutions and assist them in activities that do not require professional skills and knowledge.

The Community Service Orders Scheme is a community-based treatment with punitive and rehabilitative aims. It requires an offender over the age of 14 and convicted of an

159

offence punishable by imprisonment, to perform unpaid work of benefit to the community and to receive counselling and guidance from a probation officer. The scheme has been extended to serve all magistrates in the year.

The Young Offender Assessment Panel, run jointly by the Social Welfare Department and the Correctional Services Department, provides magistrates with a co-ordinated view on the most appropriate programme of rehabilitation for convicted young offenders aged between 14 and 25.

The Social Welfare Department operates seven residential institutions with a total capacity of 636 places, each with a slightly different training programme to cater for the needs of the residents. Educational, pre-vocational and character training are provided to assist juvenile offenders to return to the community as law-abiding citizens. The Begonia Road Boys' Home and Ma Tau Wei Girls' Home consist each of a remand home and a probation institution for juvenile offenders and girls in need of statutory care and protection. The Pui Yin Juvenile Home is a remand home for boys. The Pui Chi Boys' Home provides residential training for juvenile probationers. The O Pui Shan Boys' Home and Castle Peak Boys' Home are reformatory schools for boys aged under 16 on admission. The Kwun Tong Hostel is a probation hostel for young men aged between 16 and 21.

Plans are in hand to improve residential and training facilities, including the conversion of a youth centre and hostel into a probation home for girls, building a new workshop block at O Pui Shan Boys' Home and the relocation of the Castle Peak Boys' Home and Begonia Road Boys' Home to Sha Tin and Ngau Chi Wan respectively.

In addition to the work carried out by the Social Welfare Department, several subvented non-governmental organisations also provide hostel, employment, casework and volunteer services to help ex-offenders and young people with behavioural problems to reintegrate into the community.

Family Welfare

The Social Welfare Department and a number of non-governmental welfare organisations provide a variety of family and child care services with the overall objective of preserving and strengthening the family as a unit through helping individuals and families to solve their problems or to avoid them altogether.

The department operates a network of 30 family services centres while the subvented welfare sector operates 23 such centres. The major services provided in family services centres include: family casework and counselling; care and protection of children and young persons aged under 21; and referrals for schooling, housing, employment and financial assistance.

Wai On Home, run by the Social Welfare Department and Harmony House, run by a non-governmental organisation, together provide short-term accommodation with 80 places for women and children who may be victims of domestic violence, and for young girls at risk.

The department continues its efforts to tackle the problem of street sleeping. It has set up outreaching teams dedicated to helping street sleepers. It also assists non-governmental welfare organisations to run temporary shelters, urban hostels and day relief service for street sleepers. The department is identifying suitable premises to set up more hostels for the homeless in the urban area.

A wide range of child welfare services is provided. The Child Protective Services Unit caters for abused children. The Adoption Units are responsible for local and overseas adoption of orphans, abandoned babies and children freed for adoption. The Central Foster Care Unit promotes foster care services in Hong Kong. Furthermore, the Child Custody Services Unit carries out statutory duties in respect of supervision or care arising from custody and guardianship matters handled in Family Courts or the High Court. Chuk Yuen Children's Reception Centre and Sha Kok Children's Home provide for the temporary care of children aged up to eight. The first hostel for girls run by the department, Wai Yee Hostel, started its operation in November 1991. The hostel, located in Tuen Mun, has facilities for 100 girls aged between seven and 18 who are in need of care and protection.

In addition to the work carried out by the Social Welfare Department, subvented welfare organisations also provide residential child care services in children's homes, homes and hostels for boys and girls, foster homes and small group homes.

Child care centres are available for children under the age of six. Such centres must comply with standards laid down in the Child Care Centres Ordinance and Regulations. They are subject to registration and inspection. At the end of the year, there were 34 807 places in day child care centres and 591 places in residential child care centres. New modes of child care services were being tried out as experimental projects to meet the changing needs of families. A flexible and temporary form of child care service on half day or full day basis when carers stay away from home for short periods of time was introduced in March 1992. Families with low incomes and social needs for children to attend a child care centre may make use of the Fee Assistance Scheme in meeting nursery fees. A total of 7 710 children were receiving fee assistance at the end of the year.

Home help service, subvented by the government and operated by non-governmental organisations, provides meal services, personal care and household work service to those who need it. At the end of the year, there were 64 home help teams.

Family aide service, as a complement to casework service, is provided by four family services centres of the Social Welfare Department and non-governmental organisations to develop clients' home management skills and child care techniques and to help families attain self-reliance.

The Department operates a telephone hotline service, answering enquiries and providing professional advice to the public on social welfare matters.

Family life education aims to improve the quality of family life through the promotion of interpersonal relationships and social consciousness which may help to prevent family breakdowns and social problems. There are 59 family life education workers providing a wide range of family education programmes in the territory. The 1991–2 family life education publicity campaign adopted the main theme of *Happy Marriage and Responsible Parenthood*. The campaign aimed at arousing public awareness of the importance of harmonious marital relationships and effective parenting. A wide variety of publicity media, including television, posters, booklets on effective parenting, bus advertisements, a slogan competition, an exhibition and an opening event were organised. In support of the centralised publicity campaign, promotional and educational activities were organised by social workers at the district level. The Family Life Education Resource Centre plays a significant role in supporting social workers in promotional and educational work by providing resource materials and audio-visual equipment on loan.

Medical Social Service

The Social Welfare Department continues to provide medical social service in public hospitals and clinics to help patients and their families deal with the many personal and family problems arising from illness and disability.

Care of the Elderly

The White Paper 'Social Welfare into the 1990s and Beyond' laid down care in the community and by the community as the guiding principle for the planning and development of services for the elderly. A wide range of community support services is provided to help families look after their elderly members and to enable old people to live with dignity in the community for as long as possible. Such community services include home help, day care, social and recreational facilities, canteen services, community education, as well as respite care. At the end of 1992 there were 64 home help teams, 129 social centres, 17 multi-service centres, 10 day care centres and 13 respite care places. Financial assistance, which includes public assistance and special needs allowance and housing assistance comprising compassionate rehousing and priority allocation of public housing, continues to be available for those eligible. To provide timely services to the elderly at risk, two outreaching pilot teams, which started in April 1991, continue to operate.

Residential facilities are provided for those who for health or other reasons are unable to look after themselves and who have no relatives or friends to assist them. At the end of 1992, there were 1 727 hostel places, 5 886 home places and 3 406 care-and-attention places.

In addition sheltered housing is provided in private housing flats as well as in public housing estates for 1 822 elderly people who are capable of living independently.

The Registration Office of Private Homes for the Elderly provides advice and assistance to private homes for the elderly to reach an acceptable service standard. Higher service standards are encouraged through the Voluntary Registration Scheme and through an offer to buy places from registered homes under the Bought Place Scheme.

To provide a regulatory framework and a set of uniform standards for all homes for old people, legislation on residential care homes is in the final stage of drafting.

Services for Young People

Helping young people to become mature and responsible members of society is the main objective of this programme. A wide range of services is designed for young people aged from six to 24 to foster the development of their personality, character, social aptitude, sense of civic responsibility, ability to use their leisure time constructively and to enable those with adjustment problems to direct their energies towards positive goals in society.

At district level, apart from providing group work activities in community centres, the department promotes and co-ordinates youth programmes and encourages the establishment of self-programming and volunteer groups through its youth offices. Since 1974 the department has been running the Opportunity for Youth Scheme. Every year young people are helped with funds to implement a variety of community service projects to meet specific social needs. Awards are given for outstanding projects to recognise the contributions of participants.

Children and youth centres, operated mainly by subvented non-governmental organisations, serve as focal points for a variety of programmes and activities for the personal growth and social development of young people. In 1992 nine combined children and youth centres were opened, making a total of 214 children centres and 215 youth centres.

Outreaching social work attempts to cater to groups of young people at risk who do not normally participate in organised youth activities. In 1992, there were totally 24 outreaching social work teams serving in priority areas with large youth populations, high population density and high juvenile crime rates.

School social work service, provided by social workers in secondary schools, helps students with personal behavioural or family-related problems in adjusting to school life. In 1992, there were totally 150 School Social Work Units covering all secondary schools in the territory.

Uniformed organisations offer young people opportunities to join organised activities with progressive training programmes to help them develop character and leadership so that they can eventually become responsible, self-reliant and caring members of the community. There are eight subvented welfare organisations, with over 85 000 members operating a wide range of activities with different emphasis for different target groups of young people. The Duke of Edinburgh's Award Scheme offers a comprehensive programme focusing on development of the potential of young people, attracting a membership of 36 711 through its 20 operating authorities.

Rehabilitation of Disabled Persons

The objective of Hong Kong's rehabilitation services is to integrate disabled persons into the community. Services provided by government departments and non-governmental organisations aim to enable disabled people to fully develop their physical, mental and social capabilities. These services are co-ordinated by the Commissioner for Rehabilitation, who also conducts regular reviews of the Rehabilitation Programme Plan which projects the requirement for and identifies the shortfall in rehabilitation services for the following 10 years. A Green Paper on Rehabilitation entitled 'Equal Opportunities and Full Participation: A Better Tomorrow for All' was published in March 1992 to consult the public on the way forward for future development of rehabilitation services in Hong Kong. Public comments received are being examined carefully and a White Paper on Rehabilitation will be produced in 1993.

The Department of Health is responsible for providing immunisation programmes against various communicable diseases and promoting health education to prevent disabilities. It also provides screening services for early detection and identification of disabilities. The Hospital Authority is responsible for providing medical rehabilitation services. The Social Welfare Department is responsible for the planning and development of a wide range of social rehabilitation services, either through direct service provision or subvention to non-governmental organisations. The Education Department is responsible for the planning and development of education and related supportive services for disabled children of school age. The Labour Department is responsible for job placements for the hearing and visually impaired, the physically handicapped, the mentally handicapped and ex-mentally ill persons. The Transport Department subvents a 'Rehabus' Service for disabled persons who have difficulties in using public transport. The Vocational Training Council is responsible for providing and co-ordinating vocational training for disabled persons.

By the end of the year, the Social Welfare Department and non-governmental organisations provided a total of 718 integrated programme places, 987 special child care centre places (including 54 residential places) and 905 early education and training centre places for pre-school disabled children. In addition, the service of a clinical psychologist was provided for autistic children in special child care centres as a special provision. For disabled adults, there were 2 033 day activity centre places which provided day care, daily living skills and work training for the mentally handicapped; 4 155 sheltered workshop places to provide employment for disabled persons who were unable to compete in the open job market; and 2 061 hostel places for those disabled persons who could neither live independently nor be adequately cared for by their families, or who lived in areas too remote from their places of training or employment. For aged blind persons unable to look after themselves adequately or in need of care and attention, 339 places in homes and care and attention homes for the aged blind were provided. In addition, 200 long stay care home places, 809 halfway house places and 110 day activity centre places were provided for discharged mental patients and 21 social and recreational centres were provided for all categories of disabled persons.

The supported employment scheme introduced by the Social Welfare Department will continue to provide employment opportunities for disabled persons. Various supported employment service models are being developed.

To improve service quality, professional back-up from clinical psychologists, occupational therapists and physiotherapists is provided to all rehabilitation day centres and hostels. Other support services include respite service which provides short-term relief to families with mentally handicapped persons, and five home-based training teams which help train mentally handicapped persons as an interim measure while they await placement.

The Queen Elizabeth Foundation for the Mentally Handicapped was set up in August 1988. Its purpose is to further the welfare, education and training of mentally handicapped persons and to promote their employment prospects. The management and use of the foundation's funds are determined by a council consisting of prominent members of the community appointed by the Governor. During the year, the foundation allocated $6.7 million in the form of grants or sponsorships to 21 non-governmental organisations and one government department, enabling them to undertake projects for the benefit of mentally handicapped persons. The fund stood at $108 million on March 31, 1992.

Staff Development and Training
Training of professional social workers is provided by the universities, polytechnics and post-secondary colleges. The Social Welfare Department and non-governmental organisations assist in arranging practical work placements for social work students from these institutions. The department, through its Lady Trench Training Centre, conducts various types of in-service training programmes such as orientation courses for newly-recruited staff, basic social work training for non-professional grade staff, induction training for staff transferred to a new service area and staff development programmes to provide knowledge and skills in helping staff handle increasingly complicated social problems.

During the year, the training centre organised 264 programmes, seminars and workshops for 8 281 participants, compared with 184 programmes in 1991. It also operates a child care centre for 113 children aged between two and six years which serves as a training ground for child care centre workers.

To equip staff with updated and specialised skills in the various fields of professional practice, the department sponsors experienced staff to attend advanced local and overseas training courses and international conferences. During the year, 80 staff attended 35 such courses and conferences.

The Social Work Training Fund continues to provide financial assistance for individuals to pursue social work training in Hong Kong or overseas. In 1992, a total of 116 applicants were awarded either full or partial grants. It also provides funding support for other purposes, such as financing overseas experts to provide training and consultation, and the printing of resource training materials for social workers in Hong Kong.

The department is also involved in the work of the Advisory Committee on Social Work Training and Manpower Planning. The committee advises the government, through the Social Welfare Advisory Committee, on all matters relating to the education and training of social workers, including the planning of manpower to meet welfare service needs.

Research and Statistics

The department conducts surveys and maintains data systems for the monitoring and development of social welfare services. Seven surveys were carried out during the year. In conjunction with the Hong Kong Council of Social Service, the department runs the Social Welfare Manpower Planning System which collates information on individual social work personnel and on the demand for and supply of trained social workers for facilitating overall manpower planning in the welfare sector. The department also maintains nine other data systems, these being the Integrated Law and Order Statistical System on offenders under the charge of the department, the Child Protection Registry, the Street Sleepers Registry, the Planned Welfare Projects Registry, and five central referral systems for co-ordinating the referral of clients to various welfare institutions.

Subvention and Evaluation

Financial assistance is given to 159 non-governmental organisations for the provision of social welfare services in accordance with government policies. Financial assistance for capital and special expenditure is also provided through the Lotteries Fund.

The Evaluation Unit of the department is responsible for monitoring and assessing services provided by subvented non-governmental organisations. For this purpose, departmental staff make regular visits to the agencies which are in turn required to submit service statistics at specified intervals. Where appropriate, findings are submitted to the Subventions and Lotteries Fund Advisory Committee which advises on the allocation of subventions and lotteries grants to agencies providing social welfare and rehabilitation services. During the year, the department conducted seven in-depth evaluations of experimental projects and services operated by non-governmental organisations.

Community Building

A number of government departments and voluntary organisations contribute towards the community building programme.

This programme, co-ordinated by the Community Building Policy Committee, serves to foster among the people of Hong Kong a sense of belonging, mutual care and civic responsibility as society undergoes rapid socio-economic changes.

Community building efforts involve the provision of purpose-built facilities for group and community activities, the formation of citizens' organisations and the encouragement of community participation in the administration of public affairs, solving community problems, promoting social stability and improving the quality of life in general.

The City and New Territories Administration and the Social Welfare Department are the two departments principally responsible for implementing this programme. The City and New Territories Administration, through its network of district offices, is primarily concerned with promoting mutual care and community spirit through local organisations, such as area committees, mutual aid committees, rural committees, kaifong welfare associations, women's organisations, and local arts and sports associations.

The Social Welfare Department is responsible for various aspects of group and community work aimed at promoting the development of individuals and groups and at fostering a sense of community responsibility.

Community centres run by the City and New Territories Administration are provided throughout the territory to serve as a base for community building work.

Commission on Youth
The Commission on Youth was established in February 1990 with members appointed by the Governor. The main objectives were to advise the Governor on matters pertaining to youth, to initiate research, to promote co-operation and co-ordination in the provision of youth services and to serve as a focal liaison point with other international youth organisations for exchange programmes.

The commission is developing a Charter for Youth containing important principles and ideals covering the protection, nurture and promotion of young people's interests and stating the roles of all concerned in promoting youth affairs. A consultative document on the draft Charter for Youth was published in February 1992 to seek the views of the public.

The commission also completed two studies in 1992. These are a study on the attitudes and expectations of youth towards their future; and on the influence of the mass media on youth. The commission's recommendations on these two subjects were presented to the relevant government departments. Working groups have also been set up to examine youth participation in community activities as well as their education and career plans. These studies will identify necessary measures to build Hong Kong's youth for the future.

The commission has also started to build up a liaison network with youth and youth-related organisations to facilitate its work and to promote better co-ordination in furthering the well-being of youth.

Committee on the Promotion of Civic Education
In May 1986, the government set up the Committee on the Promotion of Civic Education to encourage all sectors of the community to promote civic awareness and responsibility. Made up largely of non-government members, the committee advises the government and community organisations on the objectives and scope of civic education. It encourages, through sponsorship, community efforts in organising civic education activities among different age groups.

The committee sponsored 29 projects in 1992 with an allocation of over one million dollars. As the committee has chosen 'the rule of law' as one of its major work emphases or 1992–4, an exhibition entitled *Equality Under the Rule of Law* was held to encourage reater understanding of the key concepts of the rule of law among the public.

At the request of the government, the committee has also taken up the responsibility o promote human rights education. Series of human rights-related civic education rogrammes, including seminars and production of teaching kits will be organised in 992–3.

In 1991–2 other promotional activities launched by the committee included seminars, a urvey on voting behaviour and a number of projects to encourage people's participation in olitical and community affairs. The work of the committee has received strong support rom district organisations and voluntary agencies.

13
HOUSING

MORE public sector flats are being built for ownership to meet a growing demand for them reflecting a trend in Hong Kong's economic development.

In helping to meet Hong Kong's public housing demands as projected by the Long Term Housing Strategy, the Housing Authority will be building some 177 000 rental flats and 214 400 flats for sale between now and the year 2001.

Meanwhile, it continues to build at a rate of around 40 000 units a year, producing 27 855 flats – 15 557 for rent and 12 298 for sale – in addition to a wide variety of commercial, community and educational premises and supporting infrastructure.

In all, some 3 000 000 people live in Hong Kong's 146 public sector estates, including nearly 500 000 who live in 110 ownership courts.

Further progress
Progress in housing development during the year included the completion of a redevelopment programme which has provided homes for over 500 000 people.

Some other achievements of direct benefit to the people were: a greater opportunity for home ownership through a higher income limit, temporary rent relief for domestic tenants facing financial hardship, a chance to rent flats with a larger living space per person, an increase in the waiting list income limits, an increase in the production of one-person units, and a higher standard of refurbishment of vacant flats.

Housing Authority
The Housing Authority, which evolved from a number of bodies, was established on April 1, 1973 under the Housing Ordinance.

It was reorganised on April 1, 1988 and given a separate financial identity and autonomy, together with sufficient flexibility to deal with the priorities under the government's Long Term Housing Strategy.

It advises the Governor on all housing policy matters and through its executive arm, the Housing Department, plans and builds public housing estates for rent or ownership, and temporary housing areas.

The authority also manages public housing estates, ownership courts, temporary housing areas, transit centres, flatted factories and ancillary commercial facilities throughout the territory, and administers the Private Sector Participation Scheme and the Home Purchase

Loan Scheme. It acts as the government's agent to clear land, prevent and control squatting and maintain improvements to squatter areas.

It is made up of members appointed by the Governor for a two-year term.

It is chaired by a non-official and supported by 20 other non-official members and four official members whose responsibilities have a bearing on housing matters. There are also 33 non-official committee members who sit on one or more of the various committees which deal with particular housing issues. Many members of the authority and of the committees also serve the Hong Kong community as executive, legislative, urban or regional councillors, or as members of the New Territories Heung Yee Kuk, district boards, area committees and mutual aid committees and other government boards and committees.

Together they have a broad range of experience and representation in community service and professional knowledge in certain areas of activity, and are able to apply a broad and critical perspective in determining public housing policies.

In April 1991, the authority held its first annual open meeting to provide an opportunity for the public and the news media to see the full Housing Authority at work. From September, all regular full meetings were open to them.

Apart from the eight standing committees, the special committee on the clearance of Kowloon Walled City, established in January 1987, is expected to complete its work soon.

Other *ad hoc* committees have completed or are about to complete their tasks of examining the housing needs of the 'sandwich class'; reviewing domestic rent policy and allocation standards; reviewing the policy on housing subsidy; setting out a programme of work on the allocation and standards of vacant flats and reviewing schemes to promote home ownership.

The authority is responsible for its own finance and management and will continue to provide homes at affordable rents and prices to the people. Under an arrangement which came into effect in April 1988, the government continues to ensure the availability of funds required for the housing programmes as set out in the Long Term Housing Strategy.

On March 31, 1992 the government's capital investment and contribution to housing stood at about $110.3 billion, which comprised permanent capital of $25.1 billion, contribution to domestic housing of $75.8 billion and non-domestic equity of $9.4 billion.

In the 1991–2 financial year, recurrent expenditure on the authority's domestic rental properties, covering mostly management and maintenance costs, totalled $5,649.2 million, while income from domestic rents was $4,905.4 million, resulting in a deficit of $743.8 million. This deficit was mainly because the low rents in old estates were insufficient to cover management expenses and the high cost of maintenance and improvements.

The authority was able to offset this deficit partly from income derived from its non-domestic properties which, over the same period, generated a surplus of $478.9 million after charging amortisation and paying interest on permanent government capital and 50 per cent dividends to government.

The authority spent $7,411.5 million on its capital programmes, of which $6,661.5 million (89.9 per cent) was financed by the authority, while the balance of $750.0 million (10.1 per cent) came from the government through supplementary injection of capital.

Construction
With the continued lower levels of private sector workload and an improvement in the labour shortage situation of previous years, tender prices remained very competitive throughout the year.

A total of 198 housing blocks containing 102 540 flats were being built during the year.

The waiting list for public rental housing is being steadily reduced, and, in order to meet increasing public demand, construction work in the coming years will be geared to producing a greater proportion of flats for sale under the Home Ownership Schemes and more fully self-contained flats for smaller or one person households.

The first of the new Harmony range blocks was completed during the year, and 14 more will be completed in 1993.

Quality assurance

The emphasis being placed on quality assurance has received the support of the construction industry, and it is expected that by early 1993 about half of the major companies employed by the authority will be certified as firms capable of complying with the international quality standard ISO: 9000.

Meanwhile, the Housing Authority's Construction Branch is establishing its own quality management system and expects to achieve certification to ISO:9001 in 1993. Other quality measures include the selection of contractors to tender for new works building contracts based on their performance on existing contracts as measured by the performance assessment scoring system, and the further development of a similar system for use in relation to maintenance building contracts.

Quality assured components are now extensively used on the authority's construction projects and these include kitchen and bathroom doorsets, domestic cooking bench sink units and steel collapsible security gates. Staircase balustrades and balcony grilles will be added in 1993 and steps have been taken to increase the use of precast facades on standard domestic blocks.

In addition to this, precast staircases and aluminium windows are now specified in all of the rental blocks.

Site safety

A very successful site safety campaign was carried out during the year to ensure that the work sites and nearby areas were safer places for workers and members of the public.

Research and development are being carried out on a number of projects to ensure that public housing continues to satisfy the needs of Hong Kong in the years ahead. These include measures to meet the increasing demand for small household accommodation by adding special annex wings to existing Harmony blocks, constant upgrading and improvement of design standards, studies on Harmony block thermal and energy performance and individual colour studies for rural and outlying island sites.

Maintenance

Spending on maintenance and improvement works for the year amounted to $1.4 billion.

A notable feature of the year's maintenance works was the emphasis placed on repairs to the newer housing stock, following completion of the structural repair operations which were carried out on older buildings over a five-year period at a total cost of $1.6 billion.

More time was also spent on leaking shower trays, water seepage problems in bathrooms and external mosaic tile finishes.

In the continuing management of materials containing asbestos, abatement works were carried out in 90 blocks at a cost of $40 million, and asbestos cement roofing sheets were removed during demolition of 72 older temporary housing areas as part of the phasing out of this particular form of housing.

Other maintenance activities included completion of the programme for reinforcement of electrical supplies to prevent summer overloading in 122 blocks in 37 estates at a cost of $46 million.

There was also significant improvement in the breakdown rate for lift installations, which was halved from one breakdown per lift each month.

Under the modernisation programme, 52 new lifts were installed and design and contract specifications were drawn up for 55 more.

A major five-year programme was started to upgrade 40 commercial centres with new facilities and finishes in order to meet residents' needs and attract customers. It will cost $300 million.

During the year, liaison with tenants was strengthened, and a new and improved maintenance system referred to as CARE – for Condition, Appraisal, Repair and Examination – was introduced.

In the next five years, the authority will spend $2.7 billion in its commitment to provide a reliable and efficient maintenance service.

Building Works

Meanwhile, building works continue on a large number of estates and commercial premises, in various locations in the urban areas and in the new towns.

In the urban areas, work is being carried out mainly in the eastern and southern parts of Hong Kong Island, and in Central and East Kowloon.

In the new towns, much work is being carried out in Tin Shui Wai, Ma On Shan, Tai Po, Fanling and Tseung Kwan O.

In Tin Shui Wai, one of the newest new towns, intake of tenants began in April for 4 022 rental flats in Phase 1 of Tin Yiu Estate, and, later in the year, 1 824 ownership flats were made available to the public.

Plans for the development of Tiu Keng Leng, as part of Tseung Kwan O New Town, are well underway. Six phases of public housing works will be completed there between 1999 and 2000, providing a total of 12 100 flats for 40 600 people.

And, as part of the North Lantau New Town Development Phase 1 at Chek Lap Kok, 1 710 rental flats and 2 640 ownership flats will be available by mid-1997, together with ancillary facilities. Site formation work on this public housing project started in April, and piling and building works will follow. The design concept places strong emphasis on the visual and physical connections between the public housing development and the adjacent Town Centre as well as segregation of pedestrian and vehicle movements.

Residential buildings will be set back and orientated in such a way as to minimise noise nuisance created by major roads.

Redevelopment

Redevelopment of the older estates to bring them up to current standards is an integral part of public housing development.

During the year, 63 Mark III to VI and former Government Low Cost Housing blocks were redeveloped thereby improving the living conditions of 15 900 families. Under this massive redevelopment programme, which is a continuation of the Mark I/II blocks

171

redevelopment programme completed in 1991, a total of over 500 blocks involving some 720 000 families will be cleared by 2001.

Rent Policy

Despite increasing operating and maintenance costs, rents for domestic premises in public housing estates have been maintained at low levels. This has been possible as a result of government subsidies in the form of free land and average low interest rates.

To meet the demand for more spacious allocation, the *Ad Hoc* Committee to Review Domestic Rent Policy and Allocation Standards recommended in 1991 that in future, upon their moving into public housing, tenants could choose to live at the minimum internal floor area allocation standard of seven square metres per person with the median rent-income ratio not exceeding 18.5 per cent, or at the current minimum standard of 5.5 square metres per person with the income ratio not exceeding 15 per cent. Present rents are $41.8 per square metre for the newest urban estates and $23.1 for the newest New Territories estates.

On average, public housing tenants pay about seven per cent of their income on rent.

Rents are reviewed every two years and adjusted to take account of rate increases, maintenance and other costs, estate values in terms of location, facilities and services provided, and also the tenants' ability to pay.

Owing to the very low rents in old estates where maintenance and improvement costs are high, there is an overall deficit in the Housing Authority's estate working account for domestic properties.

Home Ownership Scheme

More flexible purchase arrangements were introduced for the Home Ownership Scheme (HOS) during the year, allowing buyers to start paying their mortgages before occupation of their flats in return for a discount in the price and about 29 per cent of purchasers chose these immediate mortgage terms. The Home Ownership Scheme was established in the 1970s to provide flats for sale at prices below market value to lower middle income families and housing tenants.

Private sector applicants for these flats may not own domestic property and are subject to a household income limit of $18,000 per month. These restrictions, however, do not apply to public housing tenants, residents of temporary housing areas and cottage areas managed by the authority, households displaced by clearance of squatter areas for development, natural disaster victims and junior civil servants.

Since the scheme started in 1978, a total of 172 944 flats, including 55 984 produced under the complementary Private Sector Participation Scheme (PSPS) have been sold to eligible families. About 55 per cent of these families were public housing tenants who were required to surrender their rental flats to the authority on obtaining HOS flats.

As an encouragement, public housing tenants are accorded higher priority than private sector applicants in selecting HOS flats. This incentive is also extended to prospective tenants, so that more rental flats will be available for applicants in greater need.

In return for the authority's indemnity against loss in case of default, favourable mortgage terms are provided by 50 financial institutions for the purchase of HOS and PSPS flats. The guarantee enables purchasers to borrow between 90 and 95 per cent of the flat price, with repayment periods of up to 20 years.

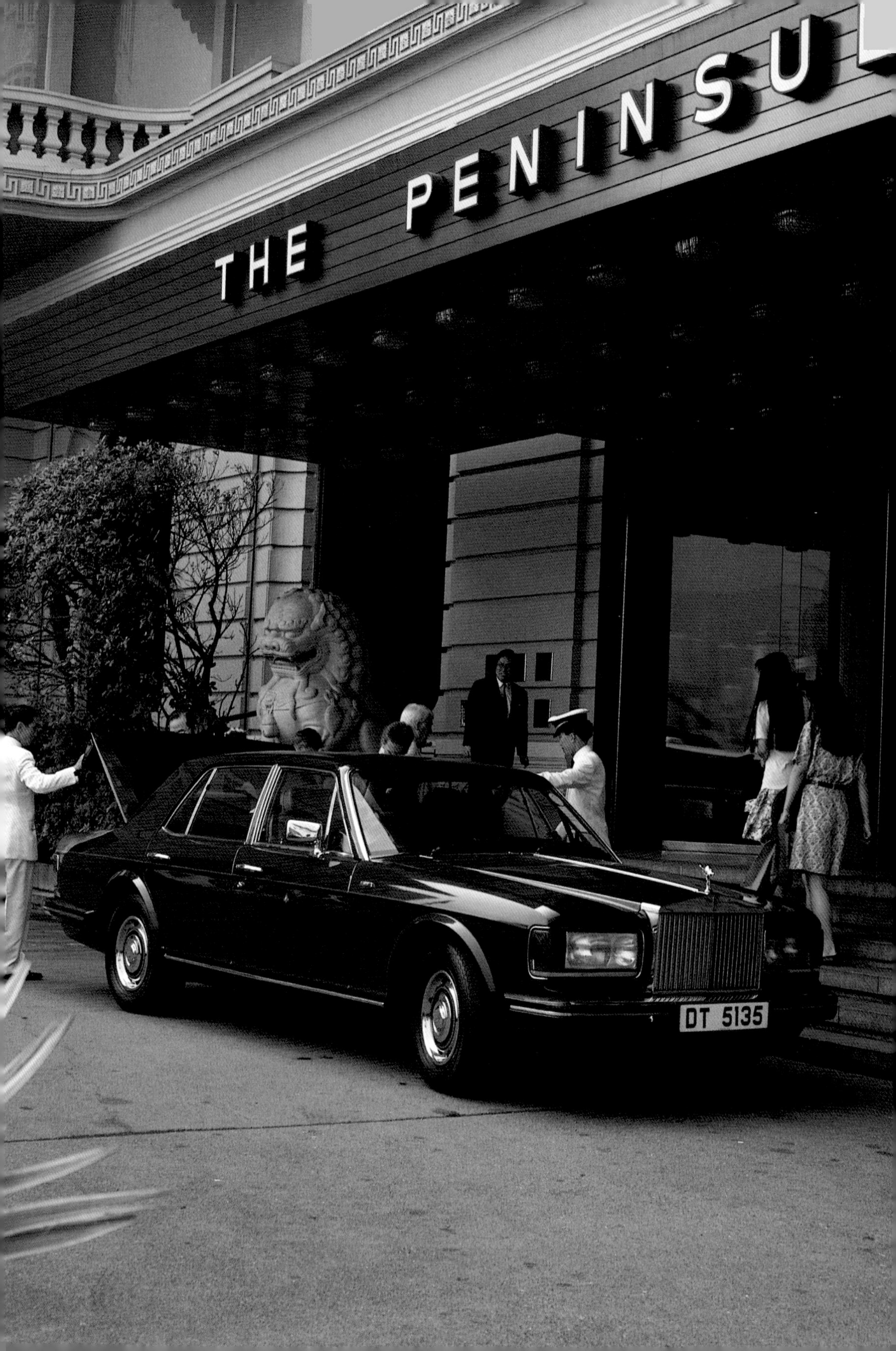
THE PENINSUL
DT 5135

Preceding page: *Luxury cars are a common sight in affluent Hong Kong, although many motorists choose more humble or historical models, shown on this and following pages.*

Above: *A classic car show attracts enthusiasts to Chater Road, in Central, Hong Kong Island.*

Opposite page: *One specialist motoring club is devoted entirely to Volkswagen 'Beetle' owners and another* **(right top)** *to Ferarri owners.* **(Below)** *the 'Auto Show 92' at Hong Kong Covention and Exhibition Centre.*

Above: *An Opel car show at Pacific Place and* **(following page)** *motorists prepare at Shatin Race Course for the start of a classic car drive to China.*

As part of the continuing implementation of the Long Term Housing Strategy, the production of ownership flats will increase from 14 000 flats a year to around 17 000 flats a year from 1991 to 1996. Of these, about 33 per cent of annual production will be upgraded flats in blocks originally intended for rental housing estates, thus providing a wider choice of flat sizes, standards, locations and prices.

During 1992, a total of 19 782 flats were sold, starting in January with 6 452 flats in Phase 13C. Applications were invited for a further 6 474 flats in Phase 14A in April, and nearly 60 000 applications were received.

In August another 6 856 flats were put up for sale, and in December 7 469 more flats were offered.

The prices of flats sold ranged from $294,200 for a flat of 40.9 square metres (saleable floor area) at Tin Yau Court, Tin Shui Wai, to $1,333,700 for a large flat of 58.1 square metres at Po Hei Court, Sham Shui Po.

Home Purchase Loans

Under the Home Purchase Loan Scheme, which is an integral part of the housing programme, lower-middle-income families are given assistance in buying flats of their own in the private sector.

Eligible applicants are offered an interest-free loan of $150,000, repayable in 20 years to help towards the purchase at downpayment or completion stage.

The authority has introduced a new option whereby eligible applicants can opt for a monthly mortgage contribution of $2,000 for 36 months, which is not repayable.

Since the implementation of the loan scheme in 1988, 7 645 loans and 122 subsidies have been granted. As a result, 4 352 public housing units have been recovered for allocation to other families.

Allocation

During the year, 23 000 new flats and 14 000 vacated flats were let to the various categories of eligible applicants. The biggest share went to waiting list applicants (38 per cent), followed by tenants affected by the redevelopment of the older blocks and in the comprehensive redevelopment programme (28 per cent), and families affected by development clearance (11 per cent).

The remainder of the flats went to junior civil servants, victims of fires and natural disasters, occupants of huts and other structures in dangerous locations, compassionate cases recommended by the Social Welfare Department, families affected by the Kowloon Walled City clearance and applicants from temporary housing areas.

In all, the Housing Authority owns and manages some 645 000 rental flats of different sizes, amenities and rent levels in 146 estates.

The public housing waiting list and allocation of rental flats have been computerised, and information on nearly three million applicants and tenants has been stored. This enables housing allocation and duplication checks to be carried out effectively and also produces useful statistical information.

Some 8 000 flats, mainly in Tin Shui Wai and Tuen Mun, were allocated to successful waiting list applicants. The waiting time for these districts is the shortest and has been reduced to about one year.

Applicants for public rental housing through the waiting list are considered in the order of registration and in accordance with the choice of districts indicated by applicants. Accommodation is offered to those who, on investigation, are found eligible in respect of their family income and residence in Hong Kong. The income limits range from $6,700 for a family of two to $18,000 for a family of 10 or more. The number of applications at the end of the year stood at 153 000. In addition, there were 27 000 applications on the Single Persons Waiting List established in January 1985. The income limit for single persons is $3,800.

A priority scheme is provided under which elderly couples or single elderly persons applying in groups of two or more will be allocated public housing within two years. So far, 9 500 flats have been allocated to this category.

There is also an incentive scheme by which families with elderly persons are allocated housing two years ahead of their normal waiting time. So far, 6 400 families have benefited from this scheme.

In 1986, the authority introduced a sheltered housing scheme with a warden service for able-bodied elderly persons.

In 1992, new sheltered housing projects were opened at Tak Tin Estate in East Kowloon, Fung Tak Estate in Central Kowloon and Wan Tau Tong Estate in Tai Po for applicants attaining 60 years of age who were eligible under the compulsory rehousing categories, and to qualified elderly applicants from the Single Persons Waiting List and the Elderly Persons Priority Scheme.

Housing for Elderly

Since 1987, housing units have been provided as a supplementary housing resource for able-bodied elderly persons who are self-reliant and independent. A warden service to deal with emergency situations is also provided.

Cases in which a higher level of health care is required are referred to the Social Welfare Department for transfer to more suitable housing.

Sitting Tenants

An earlier scheme introduced in 1991 having failed to meet with sufficient response, plans are underway to present a revised scheme for the sale of flats to sitting tenants, probably in 1993.

Under the original scheme, tenants in a number of selected rental blocks were offered the chance to buy the flats they occupied, provided that 50 per cent of tenants in each block opted to do so.

It is likely that the relaunch of the scheme will have modifications to ensure its success.

Housing Subsidy Policy

The Housing Subsidy Policy, in effect since 1987, has been generally supported by the public. Criticisms by some groups were reviewed by an *ad hoc* committee whose recommendations were released for public consultation in September. A final report will be prepared for decision by the Housing Authority early next year.

Under this policy, tenants who have lived in public housing for 10 or more years and whose incomes exceed the Subsidy Income Limit (twice the Waiting List Income Limit) are required to pay double net rent plus rates.

There are some 284 000 households with 10 years' residence in public housing, and around 24 per cent of these will be required to pay double rent.

Rent Assistance

A new Rent Assistance Scheme was started in September 1992, to grant temporary rent relief to domestic tenants in public housing estates facing financial hardship.

A public housing domestic tenant whose rent-to-income ratio exceeds 25 per cent as a result of an increase in rent or a reduction in household income after moving in may apply for rent assistance. This will take the form of a rent reduction for a period of six months and be renewable for a further six months if the rent-to-income ratio still exceeds 25 per cent.

The amount of reduction will be 25 per cent for tenants whose ratio exceeds 25 per cent, or 50 per cent for those whose ratio exceeds 33 per cent.

Tenants who still have financial difficulty after 12 months may arrange to transfer to cheaper housing in the same district. They will be entitled to a domestic removal allowance and a rent-free period of one month on transfer.

A family which has already moved to cheaper housing because of hardship but whose ratio still exceeds 25 per cent will be entitled to further rent assistance, subject to review at six-month intervals.

So far, 195 families have benefited from the scheme.

Agency Management Scheme

Under an agency management scheme, 33 Home Ownership Estates are managed by private property management agents appointed and supervised by the authority.

The scheme aims to provide more flexibility and to encourage greater participation by owners in the day-to-day management of their own properties, with the authority remaining ultimately responsible for management standards and policy.

Housing Information Centres

For the benefit of residents of private buildings affected by redevelopment, the authority established two Housing Information Centres in conjunction with the City and New Territories Administration. With the support of the Social Welfare Department, Labour Department, Education Department and Rating and Valuation Department, these centres provide enquiry and advisory services to the residents on matters relating to public housing, education, employment, social welfare, and their rights under existing tenancies.

One centre is located at Mong Kok District Office; the other is at Wan Chai District Office.

Management

Visits are regularly made by the chairman and members of the authority to the estates to meet community representatives and for informal exchanges of views.

Illegal Parking and Hawking

Much attention is given to the problem of illegal parking on the roads in the 138 rental estates, nine factory estates, 44 home ownership courts and 24 temporary housing areas under the control of the authority.

Under the by-laws, the authority is empowered to impose charges for impounding and removing illegally-parked vehicles from housing estates. Meanwhile, steps are being taken to enable fixed penalty tickets to be issued to traffic offenders.

On the other hand, with the proven success of the plan to privatise the authority's car parks in 28 estates, five management contracts have been signed with three private companies to place 27 more estates under the scheme for a period of three years.

Hawking is another perennial problem, and, to keep these activities within estates under control, staff are required to work irregular hours. During the year, there were 12 550 arrests and seizures and 750 prosecutions for hawking activities.

Welfare Services

By the end of the year, 888 welfare premises in Housing Authority estates and courts were let for welfare and community services at a concessionary rent of $25 per square metre per month. Non-domestic premises at less popular locations were also let at a fair market rate to community organisations.

Under another programme, the authority undertakes fitting-out works on some welfare projects in various estates. Since 1984, 120 welfare projects have been fitted out.

In view of the successful experimental project in providing out-reaching services to elderly people in Choi Hung and So Uk Estates, the Estate Liaison Officer Scheme has been extended to Tung Tau and Pak Tin Estates. Housing management staff visit the elderly persons to help them take part in various activities and to render assistance.

Commercial Properties

The Housing Authority manages 1.27 million square metres of commercial space for shops, market stalls, banks, restaurants and flatted factory units, of which 20 000 square metres was completed in 1992.

This commercial space is let under some 30 800 separate tenancies which generated a rental income of $2,460 million during the year, representing one-third of the total rental income of the authority.

The stock includes 17 660 flatted factory units in 17 flatted factories and 4 260 graded shops in the former resettlement estates. These shops were initially let at very low rents which, despite moderate biennial increases since 1976, remain at less than half market levels.

In line with the policy not to subsidise commercial tenants, rents for other commercial premises are fixed at market levels. During the year, 820 commercial premises were let by rental tendering while another 115 premises with a total floor area of 19 000 square metres were let on negotiated terms. Negotiation provides a more flexible approach and assists in attracting anchor tenants, especially those who take large spaces for the operation of superstores, single-operator markets and food courts.

The completion of Tin Yiu and Tin Shui shopping centres in Tin Shui Wai provided a wide variety of retail outlets catering for the daily necessities of the new town residents. Other shopping centres opened during the year include Kwong Tin, Siu Lun Court and Shek Lei where marketing efforts secured satisfactory occupancy.

Improvements were made to 10 existing shopping centres to modernise facilities and provide better services to the estate residents as well as shoppers. In particular, major upgrading schemes were being undertaken at the two large district shopping centres of Lok Fu and Wong Tai Sin. A co-ordinated strategy for improvement of older shopping centres was formulated and a five-year improvement programme was drawn up for the upgrading of some 30 selected centres.

Clearance

During the year, 213 hectares of land were cleared for development. Around 11 330 people affected were given permanent rehousing and 3 690 given temporary rehousing. Some 520 industrial, commercial and agricultural undertakings affected by clearances were awarded *ex-gratia* allowances.

The year also marked the completion of the clearance programme for all the potentially hazardous slopes in the urban areas which began six years ago. About 58 000 squatters were cleared under this programme.

A total of 2 860 people who became homeless as a result of fires and landslips were provided with either permanent or temporary accommodation.

Temporary Housing

Temporary Housing Areas (THAs) are provided for people made homeless by squatter clearances, fire and other natural disasters, but who are not immediately eligible for permanent public housing.

The one-storey or two-storey houses are built of wooden materials, and are partitioned into different sizes to suit requirements. Each unit is provided with electricity and metered water supply and a kitchen and shower area.

During the year, 9 200 persons were given temporary housing. At the same time 10 800 people moved from THAs to permanent public housing through the waiting list, trawling and clearance, or to their own homes purchased under the Home Ownership Scheme or the Home Purchase Loan Scheme in which they had priority.

At the end of the year, there were 55 THAs in the territory housing 65 000 people. Due to reduced demand, construction of new houses has been discontinued.

Transit Centres

There are eight transit centres in the territory with a capacity for 1 300 persons. They provide immediate shelter for persons made homeless by fires or natural disasters.

Cottage Areas

There are six cottage areas, accommodating 9 900 people. The largest, Tiu Keng Leng Cottage Area at Tseung Kwan O, housing some 5 600 people, will soon be cleared.

Squatter Control

The 1982 squatter structure survey provides a baseline for control of new squatting on government land and private agricultural land. Squatter control is carried out by daily patrols and regular hut-to-hut checks, and good control has been maintained.

The squatter population has been reduced to 45 851 in the urban area and 227 978 in the New Territories, as a result of rehousing through clearance and the Waiting List.

Squatter Area Improvements

The Housing Authority continues to undertake repairs and maintenance of services and facilities provided under the squatter area improvement programme. It is also responsible for settling electricity charges for public lights in squatter areas installed under this programme.

Kowloon Walled City

The Kowloon Walled City clearance was completed in July 1992. Some 28 000 residents and 900 commercial undertakings had moved out of the Walled City. About $3 billion cash compensation had been paid out.

The demolition contract, costing about $42 million, was awarded in November 1992. The structures on the 2.7 hectare site are being demolished by conventional methods. Demolition work is due for completion in March 1994. Special measures have been taken to protect the Yamen Building and other antiquity items, namely two Chinese cannons, granite lintel and the couplet of the Longjin Free School, two stone tablets of the Tin Hau Temple and three old wells. They will be preserved and incorporated in a public park with community facilities.

Park development works will commence in April 1994 and be carried out in two phases. The entire development is expected to be completed in the latter half of 1995.

Rent Control in the Private Sector

Statutory controls on rents and security of tenure date back to 1921 in Hong Kong. The legislation governing these matters is the Landlord and Tenant (Consolidation) Ordinance. Parts I and II of this ordinance apply controls over the rent levels and give security of tenure in respect of certain domestic tenancies. For nearly all other domestic tenancies Part IV of the ordinance gives security of tenure but the tenant must pay the prevailing market rent.

Under the ordinance, unless a tenant voluntarily vacates the premises, a landlord must apply on certain specified grounds and obtain an order from the Lands Tribunal before he can recover possession. Heavy penalties are prescribed for harassment of a protected tenant with intent to induce him to leave. However, provisions exist to facilitate an agreed surrender by the tenant of his protected tenancy in exchange for a consideration.

The Rating and Valuation Department publishes explanatory pamphlets to help people understand their position in relation to the legislation. It provides an advisory and mediatory service to deal with the many practical problems arising from rent controls and also operates a scheme under which rent officers attend District Offices on designated days each week to deal with referred cases and answer enquiries on landlord and tenant matters.

The legislation is under constant review to improve its workings and to achieve the objective, recommended in 1981 by a Committee of Review and endorsed by the government, that as soon as circumstances permit, rent controls should be phased out. To this end a bill has been introduced to the Legislative Council to allow controlled rents under Parts I and II to increase progressively up to market levels. However, security of tenure will still be preserved.

Pre-War Premises

Legislation controlling rents and providing security of tenure for pre-war premises was instituted by proclamation immediately after World War Two. In 1947 it was embodied in the Landlord and Tenant Ordinance, since re-enacted as Part I of the Landlord and Tenant (Consolidation) Ordinance.

Part I previously applied to both domestic and business premises, but as from July 1, 1984 it has applied only to domestic premises. Substantially reconstructed buildings are however excluded from Part I controls.

Rent increases under Part I are controlled by reference to the standard rent of the premises (the rent payable in respect of the unfurnished premises on or most recently before December 25, 1941). The rent chargeable under the ordinance is the permitted rent which in 1992, is 48 times the standard rent. However in no case is the permitted rent to exceed the prevailing market rent. The Commissioner of Rating and Valuation is empowered to certify the standard rent and the prevailing market rent.

The legislation provides for the exclusion from control of premises for the purpose of redevelopment, and generally possession is subject to the payment of compensation to the protected tenants. Jurisdiction under Part I is exercised by the Lands Tribunal, while technical functions are performed by the Commissioner of Rating and Valuation.

Post-War Premises

Comprehensive legislation to control rent increases in post-war domestic premises has been in force in one form or another since 1963 – apart from the period between 1966 and 1970 – and this is now contained in Part II of the Landlord and Tenant (Consolidation) Ordinance.

Part II controls rent increases and provides security of tenure to tenancies and sub-tenancies in post-war domestic premises completed or substantially rebuilt after August 16, 1945 and before June 19, 1981. It does not however apply to new lettings created on or after June 10, 1983, nor to tenancies of premises having a rateable value of or above $30,000 as at June 10, 1983.

Under Part II, landlords and tenants are free to agree on an increase in rent, but such agreements must be endorsed by the Commissioner of Rating and Valuation. Increases, except by agreement, are permitted only once every two years. Where an increase is not agreed, the landlord may apply to the commissioner to certify the increase which may be made to the current rent. The permitted increase is arrived at by taking the lesser of (i) the difference between the prevailing market rent and the current rent, or (ii) 30 per cent of the current rent. However, if the increase so determined, when added to the current rent, results in a rent of less than 70 per cent of the prevailing market rent, the permitted increase will be the amount necessary to bring the current rent up to that percentage of the prevailing market rent. Both the landlord and tenant may apply to the commissioner for a review of his certificate and further to appeal to the Lands Tribunal against the commissioner's review.

For nearly all domestic tenancies not subject to Part I or II controls, Part IV of the ordinance provides security of tenure for a sitting tenant who is prepared to pay the prevailing market rent on renewal of his tenancy. However, Part IV does not impose control on rents. Under these provisions, a further tenancy must be granted to the existing tenant unless the landlord can satisfy the Lands Tribunal that he requires the premises for his own occupation, or that he intends to rebuild the premises, or on one of the other grounds specified in the legislation. The parties are free to agree on the rent and terms for the new tenancy but, failing agreement, they can apply to the Lands Tribunal for a determination. Provisions also exist enabling tenancies to be transferred, under certain statutory conditions, from the ambit of Part II to Part IV.

14
LAND, PUBLIC WORKS AND UTILITIES

THE primary objectives of the government's lands and works policies are to ensure an adequate supply of land to meet the short-term and long-term needs of the public and private sectors, to optimise the use of land within the framework of land use zoning and development strategies, and to ensure co-ordinated development in infrastructure and buildings.

Policy responsibility for land, public works and private development rests with two separate policy branches – the Planning, Environment and Lands Branch and the Works Branch, each headed by a secretary. Both secretaries are members of the Land Development Policy Committee, which is chaired by the Chief Secretary, and is responsible for overseeing all aspects of the physical development of the territory and for giving broad approval to all major proposals affecting the development or planned use of land.

The Secretary for Planning, Environment and Lands (SPEL) is Chairman of the Development Progress Committee and the Port Progress Committee. These two committees are responsible for monitoring the general progress of the physical development of the territory as well as considering and approving detailed planning briefs, layouts and development plans. He is also Chairman of the Town Planning Board. In addition, policy responsibility for conservation rests with SPEL.

In addition to his policy functions, the Secretary for Planning, Environment and Lands oversees the operation of the Buildings and Lands Department, Environmental Protection Department, Planning Department and Drainage Services Department, as well as the Land Office of the Registrar General's Department and part of the work of the Territory Development Department, Civil Engineering Department, and Agriculture and Fisheries Department.

The Secretary for Works oversees and has policy responsibility for the operation and works agency activities of the Architectural Services Department, Civil Engineering Department, Drainage Services Department, Electrical and Mechanical Services Department, Highways Department, Territory Development Department and Water Supplies Department. The New Airport Projects Co-ordination Office (NAPCO) was also set up in February 1991 under the Secretary for Works and it co-ordinates the implementation of the massive projects of the Airport Core Programme (ACP).

Planning
Town planning seeks to bring about a good living and working environment for the present and future population of Hong Kong. Given limited land resources relative to

requirements, it is a great challenge to plan for the competing demands from housing, commerce, industry, transportation, utilities, as well as recreational, educational, medical and health, and other community facilities.

The work of town planning is carried out by the Planning Department under policy directives from the Planning, Environment and Lands Branch of the Government Secretariat. The department comprises three functional units: the Territorial and Sub-Regional Planning Branch, the District Planning Branch, the Ordinance Review and Technical Administration Division. Work undertaken by the three units is diverse, complex and interrelated. Major planning tasks undertaken by the department in 1992 include:
- formulation of proposals for the new Planning Ordinance;
- updating and reviewing the Territorial Development Strategy, the North West and South West New Territories Sub-Regional Development Strategies and the Hong Kong Planning Standards and Guidelines;
- follow-up work on the Rural Planning and Improvement Strategy, the Port and Airport Development Strategy and the Metroplan Selected Strategy;
- forward planning and development control for the districts, including co-ordination of various urban renewal efforts; and
- undertaking enforcement actions against unauthorised developments in designated rural areas.

Review of Town Planning Ordinance
The Town Planning Ordinance for Hong Kong was first enacted in 1939. In September 1987, the Executive Council ordered that an overall review of the ordinance should be undertaken with a view to introducing new legislation to replace the existing one, to provide the necessary degree of guidance and control for planning and development in Hong Kong to meet changing circumstances.

Public consultation on the comprehensive review of the Town Planning Ordinance, which commenced in July 1991, concluded in January 1992. A total of 75 written submissions were received from various public bodies, professional and academic institutions, community groups, individuals and academics overseas. The Legislative Council also held a motion debate on the subject on January 15, 1992.

As part of the comprehensive review, the Special Committee which was set up in July 1991 to consider specifically the complex and contentious issue of compensation and betterment arising from planning actions has received 63 submissions. After careful consideration of the submissions and views from various sectors, the Special Committee submitted a report to the Governor in March 1992. The report was published in April 1992.

The Administration has finalised proposals for the new Planning Ordinance in the light of the public comments received.

Hong Kong Planning Standards and Guidelines
The Hong Kong Planning Standards and Guidelines (HKPSG) is a manual for government town planners for determining the quantity, scale, location and site requirements of various land uses and facilities. This manual is applied to planning studies, preparation or revision of town plans and development control. The document is constantly under review to take account of changes in government policies and demographic characteristics as well as

social and economic trends. Major revisions during the year included road standards and internal transport (including parking) facilities, new standard design school buildings, standards and guidelines for industrial development, open space and recreation facilities, and planning guidelines for conservation of natural landscape.

A summary of the standards and guidelines has long been made available to the public. Since 1990, the distribution of the HKPSG has been extended to the libraries of tertiary educational institutions, public libraries and other institutions. To further promote public awareness of planning and to facilitate the use of these guidelines by non-government bodies in their own work, the government decided to publish the document chapter by chapter for public reference. At the end of 1992, nine chapters of the document were available for sale at the Government Publications Sales Centre.

Territorial Development Strategy
The Territorial Development Strategy (TDS) provides a broad long-term land use-transport-environmental framework for the planning and development of the territory. It aims to facilitate the continued growth of the territory as a regional centre and international city. A comprehensive review of the strategy was commenced in 1990 to assess the implications of the proposed port and airport developments and the current policies on environment and transport, taking into account the changing role of the territory in the context of recent economic and infrastructural developments in the Pearl River Delta region and the deeper hinterland of China.

The TDS Review consists of three main streams of work. The first stream, which has been completed, comprises appraisal and review studies, including identification and assessment of goals and objectives, key issues, development constraints and opportunities, evaluation criteria, and sectorial land use studies on industry, housing, office and business park, recreation, rural land, landscape/conservation and environment. The second stream, which is now in progress, comprises formulation and evaluation of TDS development options on the basis of the results of the first stream. The third stream consists of production of a recommended development strategy and a medium term implementation plan. The current review of the TDS is expected to be completed in 1993.

Sub-Regional Development Strategies
The Sub-Regional Development Strategies serve as a bridge between the TDS and district plans. They are prepared to translate the long-term broad-brush territorial goals into district planning objectives for the five sub-regions of Hong Kong, namely Metro area, North East New Territories (NENT), South East New Territories (SENT), North West New Territories (NWNT) and South West New Territories (SWNT). Following the government's decision in October 1989 on the replacement airport at Chek Lap Kok and on port expansion, work on the review for the NWNT and SWNT sub-regions commenced in early 1990. Each of these reviews aims at producing for the sub-region an appropriate land use-transport-environment strategic development framework for the target year 2011.

The review of the NWNT Development Strategy has examined key issues in the NWNT including the protection of Deep Bay and the Mai Po marshes, problems of open storage, flooding and deteriorated agricultural land. Given a long-term land use budget and inputs from other relevant studies such as the Port and Airport Development Strategy (PADS) and the Rural Planning and Improvement Strategy (RPIS), three development scenarios with a range of development patterns were postulated. Under these scenarios, a number of initial and hybrid development options were generated and evaluated in terms of environment, land valuation, engineering costs and transport aspects. A final recommended strategy will be formulated by the end of 1993 pending the results from the TDS. Development statements for individual districts are being produced based on the goals and concepts of the Development Strategy to serve as a basis for district planning, development programming activities and statutory planning control within the NWNT.

In view of development pressures arising from the replacement airport and the port facilities in North East Lantau, the review of the SWNT Development Strategy attempted to reach a balance between future urbanised development and conservation in the SWNT. Three development scenarios with a range of development patterns were postulated. Under these scenarios, a number of initial and hybrid options were generated, evaluated and tested before the formulation of a recommended strategy for SWNT by the end of 1992. Development statements for individual districts would then be produced based on the goals and concepts of the Development Strategy to serve as a basis for district planning, development programming activities and statutory planning control within the sub-region.

Metroplan

The Metroplan Selected Strategy was approved by the Governor in Council in September 1991 to provide a planning framework for public and private sector development with the aim of making Hong Kong city a better place in which to live and work. Rather than a programme by itself, it is a conceptual strategy for developing and upgrading the Metro sub-region including Hong Kong Island, Kowloon and New Kowloon, Tsuen Wan and Kwai Tsing. To further publicise the principal components of the strategy, a mobile exhibition was mounted in four different locations in early 1992.

To achieve the Metroplan objectives, with the help of consultants work started on a series of development statements to provide a planning brief for each district with priorities being given to West Kowloon, South-East Kowloon (including the Kai Tak Airport site), Tsuen Wan–Kwai Tsing and Central–Western. Also as a follow-up to Metroplan, a consultancy study is underway to establish the appropriate institutional framework and map out a coherent strategy to restructure and upgrade the obsolete industrial areas in the Metro sub-region. The results of all these studies will be available in 1993.

District Planning

Most development projects are implemented in accordance with statutory or departmental town plans prepared at the district level. The purposes of these plans are to regulate and provide guidance to development in terms of types of land use, building density and development characteristics of individual sites to ensure developments are compatible with the surrounding environment, to ensure adequate provision of community facilities and public utility services, and to meet the long-term planning objectives of the territory.

Statutory Outline Zoning Plans (OZP) for various districts of the main urban areas and new towns and Development Permission Area (DPA) plans for many parts of the rural areas in the New Territories are prepared by the Town Planning Board (TPB) under the provisions of the Town Planning Ordinance. Planning Department is the executive arm of the TPB. Once exhibited for public inspection under the ordinance, both the OZP and

DPA plans acquire statutory effect. The Building Authority is empowered to disapprove plans of new building works submitted under the Buildings Ordinance if the building proposals contravene the zoning or the development restrictions on the statutory OZP or DPA plans.

At the end of 1992, there were a total of 50 OZPs, covering the main urban areas and new towns. These plans indicate the proposed broad land use patterns, major road systems of individual districts, and specific development restrictions within individual zones, and serve as development guides to public and private investment. In 1992, two new OZPs were published and 12 existing plans were amended by the TPB.

In response to the increasing number of unregulated and haphazard developments in the New Territories, such as open storage and container yards, which have led to the general degradation of the rural environment, DPA plans have been prepared by the TPB since the enactment of the Town Planning (Amendment) Ordinance 1991 which extended the statutory planning jurisdiction to the non-urban areas. DPA plans are transitional plans prepared for areas which require immediate planning control but where time does not allow the preparation of OZPs. Unlike OZPs, zonings on DPA plans are not comprehensive and there are many 'unspecified' areas on these plans where planning permission is required for all types of development other than those listed as always permitted. It is intended that all DPA plans will be replaced by OZPs within three years after publication. At the end of 1992, there were a total of 31 DPA plans exhibited by the TPB.

Attached to and forming part of the OZPs and DPA plans are notes setting out the types of land use which are always permitted as of right under a particular zoning or which may be permitted with or without conditions on application to the TPB. This permission system allows for greater flexibility in land use planning to meet changing community needs and market demand. The ordinance allows an unsuccessful applicant the right to request the TPB to review its decision. During the year, the board considered 608 applications for planning permission and 96 applications for review as compared with 396 and 47 respectively in 1991.

An independent Town Planning Appeal Board was set up in November 1991 under the ordinance to deal with appeals lodged by applicants who felt aggrieved by the decisions of the TPB upon review of their planning applications. Since its establishment, the Appeal Board has received 19 appeal cases and has heard seven cases.

To assist the board in assessing planning applications and to guide applicants in their submission of planning applications, the TPB regularly promulgates guidelines for applications for various types of development. During the year, new guidelines for applications for factory/workshop/warehouse use within the 'unspecified use' area on DPA plans and revised guidelines for composite 'industrial-office' buildings in the industrial zone were released adding to the nine other sets of guidelines for other types of development issued in previous years.

During the year, a survey on the characteristics of offices, showrooms and research and development facilities currently established within existing industrial buildings and a study on underground development of commercial facilities extending beyond private land were completed to provide inputs to the revision of existing TPB guidelines for processing related planning applications. Another consultancy study on the operational characteristics of wholesale activities was also commissioned to provide a basis for formulating new planning guidelines and updating the notes to statutory plans.

Apart from statutory OZPs and DPA plans, the Planning Department prepares outline development plans and layout plans for individual districts to show the planned land use patterns, development restrictions and road network in greater detail. These are non-statutory departmental plans to serve as a guide for land formation, implementation of public work projects as well as subsequent land sales and allocations. At the end of 1992, there were a total of 30 outline development plans and 234 layout plans.

During the year, the Planning Department provided planning inputs to a number of major reclamation and development projects, notably the Central and Wan Chai and the West Kowloon Reclamations. The plan for Hung Hom Bay Reclamation was also reviewed. Various planning studies were in progress, including those for the West Kowloon Development Statement and Tsuen Wan and Kwai Tsing Development Statement, and those on restructuring obsolete industrial areas, future development in Stanley, planning for vehicle repair workshops and density guidelines for private residential areas. The two major district planning consultancy studies commissioned in 1991 on the Comprehensive Review of Special Control Areas and the Review of Building Density and Height Restrictions in Kowloon and New Kowloon were near completion. The recommendations of these studies would be submitted to the TPB for consideration prior to incorporation into the relevant OZPs. Another study was commissioned in late 1992 to examine and assess the redevelopment potential of a number of under-developed government sites. In the New Territories, major forward planning studies covered North Lantau and the Lantau Port Peninsula. Studies were also being undertaken to identify suitable back-up sites to meet the increasing demand for container and open storage sites due to the rapid growth of the cross-border trade and the associated transport and storage activities.

Enforcement

One of the amendments introduced under the Town Planning (Amendment) Ordinance 1991 is the provision of enforcement powers in areas covered by DPA plans. Under the ordinance, no person should undertake or continue development in a DPA unless the development is an existing use, is permitted under the DPA plan or planning permission to do so has been granted. Any development which does not satisfy any of these criteria is an unauthorised development and may be subject to enforcement proceedings by the Director of Planning.

Since July 1991, patrol teams have been established in the Planning Department to carry out regular patrol within the DPAs to identify suspected unauthorised developments. On receipt of public complaints and referrals from other departments, the teams also carried out individual site inspections to ascertain the nature of the suspected unauthorised developments and make recommendations on appropriate enforcement action. After detailed investigation, 476 warning letters were issued in respect of 62 such cases, 47 enforcement notices for 17 cases and three stop notices for three cases were served in 1992.

Rural Planning and Improvement Strategy

The Rural Planning and Improvement Strategy (RPIS) was endorsed by the Executive Council in March 1989. Its main objective is to improve the quality of life in the rural areas of the New Territories. RPIS is being implemented at both strategic and district levels. At the strategic level, land use policies are continuously reviewed to control incompatible developments and provide a more sustainable and cost-effective basis for public and private investments. In this regard, a number of reviews and studies have been or are being undertaken. They included a study on better utilisation of agricultural land and review of the rural upgrading concept.

At the district level, rural improvement projects are undertaken under the Rural Development Programmes to address rural needs. These improvement projects include village improvement and expansion works; provision of sewers and sewage treatment plants; improvement, reconstruction and expansion of village access roads; provision of local recreational facilities in village areas; works related to land drainage, river training and flood prevention schemes; and the provision and improvement of communal irrigation, field drainage and farm access in selected agricultural areas. These rural improvement projects are initiated, implemented and monitored by the various District Rural Development Working Groups, with a budget totalling about $4 billion over a span of 10 years.

The implementation and progress of the rural development programme is overseen and monitored by the Rural Development Steering Committees while the overall policy and development management aspects of the RPIS are monitored by the RPIS Monitoring Group.

Port Development
The Port and Airport Development Strategy (PADS) provided a development strategy for the integrated phased provision of new port facilities along with related infrastructure. The main features of the port development element of PADS include container terminals at Stonecutters Island and South East Tsing Yi, port facilities at the proposed Lantau Port Peninsula, a River Trade Terminal (RTT) at Tuen Mun and provision for industry at Tuen Mun and Tseung Kwan O.

In March 1991 Container Terminal 8 was let by private treaty grant with estimated completion dates between September 1993 and March 1995 for its four berths. During 1992 tenders were invited for the construction of Container Terminal 9 at South East Tsing Yi. Expressions of interest were also sought for the development of the proposed RTT at Tuen Mun Area 38.

The first review of the Port Development Strategy was completed, resulting in the production of an updated Port Development Plan and Programme in June 1992. The Study of Port-related Industrial and Commercial Enterprises (SPICE), which was carried out by the Planning Department with the assistance of the Census and Statistics Department and specialist consultants, was completed in May 1992. It provides a strategic forecast of land required to accommodate a range of industrial and commercial enterprises that are important to the successful operation of the port.

After the production of a series of development statements which set out the development objectives and priorities of each component of PADS, a number of port development studies were initiated. The Lantau Port Peninsula Development Study and the Western Harbour Development Study commenced in August and September 1991 respectively. The main objective of these studies was to plan for a port peninsula at north-east Lantau Island to accommodate container terminals, river trade terminals, cargo handling areas and other waterfront facilities and to provide for additional sheltered waters in the Western Harbour. Also in August 1991, the Tuen Mun Port Development Study commenced. This study was aimed at investigating the feasibility of accommodating deep waterfront industries and cargo working area within the study area. To enable detailed planning and design to proceed for port facilities with deep waterfront industries, including potentially hazardous installations, on the eastern side of Tseung Kwan O, the Engineering Feasibility Study of the Development of Tseung Kwan O Area 137 began in February 1992 with the objective of producing an outline engineering design for the area.

Airport-Related Development

To facilitate the operation of the new airport at Chek Lap Kok, an airport support community was proposed in the PADS to be developed in Tung Chung and Tai Ho areas in the northern part of Lantau Island. In July 1990, consultants were appointed by the government to carry out the planning of this community. It was recommended that a new town should be developed which would incorporate residential, industrial and commercial activities and all the necessary backup infrastructure requirements both for the new town itself and to serve, where practicable, the new airport. The proposed new town would involve about 760 hectares of land with a designed population capacity of 200 000 persons up to 2011.

This new town is likely to be the latest generation of new towns in Hong Kong. It provides a unique opportunity to create a well planned, high amenity living environment which will serve as an important 'gateway' for air travellers to and from Hong Kong. Indeed, in designing the town centre special attention was given to establishing the image of the town.

The new town comprises two discrete urban development areas at Tung Chung and Tai Ho with proposed populations of 150 000 and 50 000 respectively by 2011. Residential and commercial developments are concentrated in the town centre and two district centres in Tung Chung and Tai Ho, each incorporating a Lantau Line railway station and public transport terminus. The town centre provides the retail, commercial and cultural core of the new town. The necessary retail and commercial uses will be distributed in a hierarchy of centres comprising the town centre, district centres serving Tung Chung and Tai Ho, and local centres within housing areas. Land will be reserved at Siu Ho Wan for airport related industrial uses. A number of major utilities including a water treatment works, a sewage treatment works, a railway depot and a refuse transfer station will also be located at Siu Ho Wan.

There will be four phases of development for the new town between now and 2011. The first phase of the development, which is earmarked as one of the Airport Core Programme projects, will be completed by 1997 to coincide with the opening of the new airport and will accommodate about 20 000 residents at Tung Chung. Site formation works, involving substantial reclamation, are in progress.

Two independent authorities have been set up to administer the new airport and the sea port developments. The Provisional Airport Authority is concerned with the Chek Lap Kok airport development, while the Port Development Board deals with sea port plans. See chapters 16 and 17 for details of the airport and sea port respectively.

New Towns and Rural Townships

The programme for Hong Kong's new towns is an expansion of the initial 10-year housing programme aimed at providing proper living conditions for 1.8 million people. Starting from new town development programmes back in 1973 to co-ordinate planning and construction activities for the provision of land, infrastructure and a full range of social, educational and recreational facilities in the New Territories, it has outgrown the public housing-led concept and become more concerned with the 'quality of life' of the populace living in the new towns.

At the end of 1992, about 2.5 million people were housed in the new towns. The present design population capacity of the eight new towns at Sha Tin, Tai Po, Fanling/Sheung Shui, Yuen Long, Tin Shui Wai, Tuen Mun, Tsuen Wan, Tseung Kwan O and rural townships is 3.5 million. The population build up is embodied in programmes extending to the 2000s.

The year 1993 marks the twentieth anniversary of the Territory Development Department, which was created in 1973 (under the name of New Territories Development Department), to plan and implement the new town development programmes. In 1986 the department extended its role to cover works co-ordination and further development in the urban areas. Hence its present title and its readiness for the added emphasis on the urban extension areas.

The department is constituted on a multi-disciplinary basis and includes professional officers with expertise in civil engineering, architecture, landscaping and planning. They work closely with the Housing Department, Planning Department, City and New Territories Administration, Architectural Services Department, Regional Services Department and other government departments to ensure that development objectives are met economically, efficiently and in accordance with the development programmes.

In addition to participation by other works departments and consultants, the private sector has been actively taking part in the development of comprehensive housing schemes within the new towns and rural townships.

Tsuen Wan
Tsuen Wan New Town extends over the areas of Tsuen Wan, Kwai Chung and Tsing Yi Island. Its population is currently estimated to stabilise over the next 10 years at around 710 000. While new development and redevelopment will take place, the gradual reduction in family size and increased provision of larger flats will result in a decrease in population in some areas resulting in no overall increase.

Container Terminal No. 8 (CT8) at Stonecutters Island is already under construction. The first berth is anticipated to be commissioned in September 1993 and the remaining three berths at six-month intervals thereafter. Completion is expected by April 1995. Container Terminal No. 9 (CT9) will be sited at south-east Tsing Yi. Construction work is expected to commence in early 1993. Upon completion of CT9 development in early 1997, Hong Kong's container handling capacity will be increased by about 64 per cent. Detailed design for the duplicate Tsing Yi South Bridge has been completed and the construction work will commence together with the CT9 development. Its timely completion is essential to tie in with the opening of the first berth of CT9 scheduled for mid-1995.

Major highway projects will further extend and improve the principal road network. In Tsuen Wan, with the completion and opening of the flyover for the improvement of Texaco Road (Phase I) at the end of 1991, traffic conditions at the junctions of Texaco Road/Yeung Uk Road and Texaco Road/Sha Tsui Road were greatly improved. Footbridge systems at the junctions of Kwan Mun Hau Street/Castle Peak Road and Yeung Uk Road/Ma Tau Pa Road were also completed and opened to pedestrians in late

1991, resulting in a significant increase in the capacity of the road junctions. In Kwai Chung, with the completion of the contract works for improvements to Kwai Chung Road South and Container Port Road by the end of 1992, the comprehensive scheme for improvements to the Kwai Chung Road Corridor between Castle Peak Road and Mei Foo Bridge has been fully implemented. This has resulted in a significant improvement to the traffic conditions along this main route and in the container port area. Major road improvement works to Hing Fong Road and Texaco Road (Phase II) were progressing satisfactorily.

Community facilities completed in 1991 included Tsuen Wan District Police Head-quarters, two community halls and an urban clinic in Tsing Yi, one special school for the physically handicapped in Kwai Chung, a local open space in Shek Yam and two sitting out areas in Tsuen Wan Sam Tung Uk resite village. The opening of Tso Kung Tam outdoor recreation centre in October 1991 provided dormitories for overnight campers and recreational facilities.

Sha Tin

The development of Sha Tin is virtually complete with much of the remaining works concentrated in Ma On Shan. Works carried out during 1992 aimed at complementing and enhancing the infrastructure and providing community facilities to cater for a population which will increase from the present 550 000 to around 620 000 by the end of the 1990s with 66 per cent of the population living in public housing.

Major road-links with urban Kowloon and the north-eastern New Territories have been completed including the Tate's Cairn Tunnel and the Sha Tin Approaches.

In Ma On Shan, the final reclamation contract to provide 23 hectares of land progressed satisfactorily.

On the pollution-control scene, the water quality of Shing Mun River and Tolo Harbour has improved significantly since the commissioning of facilities for the marine disposal of sludge and modification of the sewage treatment works. A further improvement scheme by exporting the effluent to Kai Tak Nullah is being constructed for commissioning in mid-1993.

Community projects completed in 1992 included a neighbourhood community centre, a sub-divisional fire station, ambulance depot and ambulance training school and a public leisure pool and a district open space. Construction of another primary school, a special school for moderately mentally handicapped children, a district open space and the expansion and reprovisioning of facilities for the Prince of Wales Hospital progressed satisfactorily.

Tai Po

Tai Po New Town is about 20 kilometres north of Kowloon, situated at the head of Tolo Harbour. The harbour and the surrounding hills at Pat Sin Leng and Tai Mo Shan provide Tai Po with an attractive scenic setting. It is well served by the electrified Kowloon-Canton Railway with two railway stations, and the Tolo Highway.

The population of Tai Po is about 244 000 at present and the projected population by the end of the 1990s is around 280 000. Seventy per cent of the population are now accommodated in public housing developments comprising six public rental estates, six home ownership schemes and three private sector participation schemes.

A total of 11 hectares of land was formed and serviced for various uses in 1992. One of the sites was designated for the Nethersole Hospital, which is to be relocated from the urban area in Hong Kong to serve as a general hospital in Tai Po. Construction of the new hospital commenced in 1992 and is scheduled for completion in 1996.

Tai Po Sewage Treatment Works caters for effluent from residential developments in Tai Po as well as from an industrial estate. Since the commissioning of the first stage in 1979, the works have been expanded over the years to cope with the developing new town. The latest expansion was under design for commissioning in 1995.

To serve the growing population, community facilities completed in 1992 included two primary schools, one secondary school, a district open space and a neighbourhood community centre. Construction of another secondary school and a park along the seafront progressed satisfactorily.

Fanling/Sheung Shui

Although Fanling/Sheung Shui is only about four kilometres from China, it is well linked to the urban areas and other parts of the Territory by the electrified Kowloon-Canton Railway and the New Territories Circular Road.

The population of Fanling/Sheung Shui in 1992 was about 153 000 and is expected to reach 220 000 by the end of the 1990s. Formation and servicing works in several areas progressed satisfactorily and 35 hectares of land were produced for various uses in 1992. Another internal transport facility comprising a terminal for buses, mini-buses and taxis was provided at Luen Wo Hui.

To improve flood-control, the training of River Indus Minor and rehabilitation of the moat at Sheung Shui Tsuen progressed to near completion.

Community facilities completed in 1992 include a secondary school while two secondary schools, a rural centre at Ta Kwu Ling, an open space, expansion and improvement to Fanling Hospital Phase I and a market complex were under construction. A district hospital with 720 beds was also being planned.

At Sha Tau Kok, a small township with a population of 4 500 on the border with China, formation and servicing of a security buffer zone near Chung Ying Street to guard against illegal immigrants were progressing.

Tuen Mun

Tuen Mun, in the West New Territories, is developed mainly on land reclaimed from Castle Peak Bay and on platforms formed in the valley between Castle Peak and the Tai Lam Hills. In 1992, about five hectares of additional land were reclaimed for industrial development and district open space.

The present population is about 430 000 of which about 70 per cent live in public housing developments which include 11 public rental estates and 13 home ownership and private sector participation schemes. One more home ownership scheme was completed in late 1992. Within the next five years, three more home ownership and private sector participation schemes will be developed to accommodate a further 23 000 people. Together with some high-density private housing development along the south-eastern coast, the new town will provide homes for about 480 000 people by the mid-1990s.

In the provision of educational facilities, one prevocational school was completed by the end of 1991 and two additional secondary schools were completed in mid-1992. To meet the demand for medical services, the regional hospital providing 1 606 beds with staff quarters and the fifth nurses training school were completed. The first stage of the hospital was put into operation in early 1990 and the last stage in early 1992. One urban clinic is under construction and works will be completed in mid-1993.

A marina along the south-east coast of the town was programmed for completion in mid-1993. This private development consists of residential buildings, hotels, shops and recreational facilities, including berths for 300 boats. Eleven out of 19 residential blocks were completed and occupied.

Main industries in Tuen Mun are light manufacturing such as plastics, garments, metal, electronics and textiles. The existing industrial areas provide floor space for about 2 200 companies and jobs for about 40 000 people. Over 80 per cent of the workers employed in the factories live in the Tuen Mun and Yuen Long areas.

The backbone of the transport service, serving the town and linking it with Yuen Long, is the Light Rail Transit system. Three additional links – Pier Head to Yau Oi, Yau Oi to Sam Shing, and Town Centre to North East Tuen Mun – have been completed and in operation since February 1992.

A feasibility study for the development of a 125-hectare site in the western part of Tuen Mun for the establishment of special industries and a terminal for river trade with China was completed in late 1991. The actual reclamation work for the special industry area was scheduled to commence in 1994 and the river trade terminal was planned to be developed by the private sector. The planning and engineering feasibility study of reclaiming an even larger area to the north of Tap Shek Kok in Tuen Mun West for both deep waterfront industries and cargo working terminal development was scheduled for completion by early 1993.

Yuen Long, Tin Shui Wai and the North-Western New Territories

Development of Yuen Long from its former market town status into a thriving new town community began early in the 1970s. In 1992, the population of the town stood at 130 000 and is expected to grow to 140 000 by the end of the 1990s.

Environmental improvement work for the Yuen Long nullahs was completed in late 1992. Improvements to the water quality in the upper nullahs were quite noticeable and the offensive smell experienced in the past abated.

Three major infrastructure contracts in Tin Shui Wai have been completed, while another three major contracts are in progress. These contracts are to be completed in phases to provide access and services to private and public housing developments. The formation of the first stage of the Light Rail Transit link into Tin Shui Wai was completed in late 1992 and service is due to commence in early 1993. The two public housing estates, Tin Yiu Estate and Tin Shui Estate, were being completed in phases. The first residents started moving into their new flats in April 1992. They were followed shortly afterwards by the residents of the private development, Kingswood Villa. A third public housing development is planned to commence in 1993. After its completion in 1997 the new town population is expected to reach 140 000. The provision of community facilities in Tin Shui Wai has been programmed to coincide with population intake.

Long Tin Road and Long Ping Road, which connect the south east of Tin Shui Wai to Yuen Long were completed in early 1992. The construction of the Tuen Mun–Yuen Long Eastern Corridor was in progress for completion in 1993. Construction of the Yuen Long

191

Southern By-Pass and the Tin Shui Wai West Access commenced in 1992. As these major roads are being completed, the traffic around this area will be progressively improved.

To cope with developments in Yuen Long, Tin Shui Wai and the Tuen Mun–Yuen Long corridor construction of the North West New Territories Sewerage Scheme began in 1989. The main components of the scheme, including a sewage treatment plant at San Wai, a nine-kilometre sewer tunnel underneath Castle Peak and a 3.1-kilometre submarine outfall at Urmston Road, were under construction, to be completed in February 1993.

In the Tuen Mun–Yuen Long Corridor, construction of the infrastructure for a commercial/residential development at Hung Shui Kiu was completed. A contract for developing a village area in Ping Shan, the first pilot scheme for village expansion areas in the Yuen Long district, commenced in early 1992 for completion in late 1993.

Tseung Kwan O and Sai Kung

The development Tseung Kwan O New Town began in 1983. Development of the new town is divided into three phases. The major part of the new development areas is formed by reclaiming Tseung Kwan O Bay. A total of about 66 million cubic metres of earth will be required to complete the land formation of all three phases of the new town development. A major part of Phase I area has been completed. Reclamation for the Phase II development commenced in 1990 for completion in 1997. Reclamation of Phase III started in 1991 and will extend beyond 2000. Population intake into the new town stood at 109 500 towards the end of 1992. The population capacity upon full development will be about 445 000.

About 390 hectares of land have been formed so far together with main drainage and the supporting engineering infrastructure. A large proportion of the formed land has been used for public housing and government facilities. Three public rental estates, four home ownership schemes and three private sector participation schemes have been occupied. Another public rental estate together with the associated urban infrastructures was under construction. Roads and main drainage works in Hang Hau were substantially complete, while the reclamation at the north of the future town centre was in progress.

Works for the provision of land and services for the Tseung Kwan O Industrial Estate started in August 1991. Upon completion in early 1996, 71 hectares of land will be available for industrial use. Reclamation of the southern part of Siu Chik Sha also commenced in December 1991. A study was started to examine the feasibility of developing a site of 120 hectares for deep waterfront industry and storage.

Work commenced on the construction of the first district open space in Tseung Kwan O. Located near the Po Lam housing estate, the project will provide extensive active recreational facilities upon completion in early 1994.

At Sai Kung, the construction of a seawall extension was completed in February 1992. Reclamation of Sai Kung Creek was in progress to provide land upon its completion in late 1993 for a rural public housing estate site.

Islands District

Improvement work on the living environment and facilities for residents and visitors to the Islands district continued during 1992.

Site formation for the first rural public housing estate on Peng Chau was completed and foundation and building works were commenced in late 1992. In Cheung Chau, a loading/unloading area was completed and opened for public use and more open space were formed. Construction of a fire boat berthing point at Mui Wo and upgrading of roads and sewerage at Rural Committee Road and Chung Hau Street commenced in August 1992, for completion within two years.

During the year, community facilities completed were an indoor recreation centre in Cheung Chau and a beach building in Ma Wan.

Urban Development Areas

Six development areas at Aldrich Bay, Siu Sai Wan, Hung Hom Bay, West Kowloon, Central/Wan Chai and Belcher Bay, all involving reclamations in Victoria Harbour, are under planning or construction to meet forecast development needs in the 1990s and beyond.

The Aldrich Bay Reclamation will produce about 18 hectares of land for residential, public housing and open space uses. The newly completed typhoon shelter has already been put into use while reclamation of the old typhoon shelter started in August 1992 for completion in August 1997.

The Siu Sai Wan development includes the formation of about 56 hectares of land for industrial, residential, government/institution/community and other uses. Land formation was complete and developments have already taken place.

Twenty hectares of land have so far been formed at Hung Hom Bay out of a total of 36 hectares, with the remaining area due for completion in 1994. Future uses for this reclamation will include residential, commercial, community facilities, open space, transport interchange facilities and expansion of the existing Kowloon-Canton Railway freight yard. Two new ferry piers and a bus concourse have been constructed near Whampoa Garden and were opened in March 1991.

Steady progress was maintained in the West Kowloon Reclamation scheduled for substantial completion by the end of 1994. In accordance with Metroplan the reclaimed area of some 330 hectares will provide opportunities for thinning-out existing high density development in the West Kowloon hinterland as well as accommodating strategic transport links to serve the new airport at Chek Lap Kok, namely the Airport Railway, the West Kowloon Expressway and Route 3.

Tenders for 20 hectares of reclamation in Central Hong Kong Island between Blake Pier and Rumsey Street multi-story carpark were invited in June 19, 1992. This reclamation will provide land for the Central terminal of the Airport Railway and also provide opportunities for the development of commercial and open space uses.

Belcher Bay reclamation will create about 10 hectares of land mainly for the construction of a dual carriageway connecting the existing upgraded Connaught Road West with Smithfield in Kennedy Town. Both the reclamation and the link were scheduled to commence in January 1993 for completion by 1996 to tie in with the opening of the Western Harbour Crossing.

Urban Renewal

Over the years, government and private developers have been involved in the redevelopment of the older urban districts where buildings are old and in dilapidated condition and where the provision of various community and infrastructural facilities is inadequate. In the course of preparing the Metroplan, the older urban districts are seen as offering redevelopment opportunities for comprehensive urban renewal in order to create a better urban environment.

The Land Development Corporation (LDC) was established in January 1988 to encourage and speed up urban renewal. A section was set up in the Planning Department to serve as the main contact point between the LDC and the government. This section is responsible for processing LDC redevelopment proposals, making planning assessments and preparing planning briefs for various urban renewal schemes, and identifying suitable areas for urban renewal.

Since the inception of the LDC, about 20 projects have been initiated within the designated old urban districts. Up to the end of 1992, there were five comprehensive redevelopment scheme plans drawn up and gazetted under the Town Planning Ordinance.

Of the five redevelopment schemes, the Jubilee Street and Wing Lok Street Schemes were approved by the Executive Council in 1991 and the Queen Street Scheme was approved in September 1992. Resumption of private land and properties in the first two schemes was largely completed and construction works would soon be commenced. On completion, they will provide high quality office/commercial buildings and much needed open space and community facilities for the district. The Queen Street Scheme is to provide residential and commercial/office use, together with a multi-purpose social welfare complex, ample provision of public open space, a cooked food centre and a day nursery. Site assembly work is in progress.

The other two redevelopment schemes were still being processed by the TPB in accordance with provisions of the Town Planning Ordinance. Objections against the Argyle Street/Shanghai Street Scheme were heard by the TPB and the scheme is to be submitted to the Executive Council for approval in early 1993. On the other hand, preliminary consideration of the objections raised against the Sham Chun Street Scheme was held and the TPB decided to uphold the objections.

Apart from the comprehensive redevelopment schemes, a number of smaller commercial and residential redevelopment proposals were also being undertaken by the LDC. On Hong Kong Island, the commercial/office development in Queen's Road Central was completed, and the residential projects at Third Street and Li Chit Street were under construction. In Kowloon, there were two residential projects, one located at Yim Po Fong Street and one at Soy Street, and two commercial projects, one at Dundas Street and the other at Sai Yeung Choi Street South. Land grants for these projects were either completed or being processed.

Another notable LDC scheme was the renovation of the Western Market building at Sheung Wan. The scheme was planned to bring viable uses into a historic building by converting it into a London Covent Garden type of bazaar. The renovated market, opened in late 1991, has brought new life with traditional Chinese trades and crafts which are the prime characteristics of the Sheung Wan district.

To formulate area-specific renewal strategies and identify urban redevelopment opportunities, consultancy studies have been commissioned by the LDC. In 1992, two studies of redevelopment opportunities in Tsuen Wan Town Centre and Hung Hom were completed. The Planning Department also commissioned a survey on social attitudes towards urban renewal in mid-1992. The survey is expected to be completed by the end of the year. The findings will be used by the government as a reference in the formulation of future urban renewal approaches and the implementation of the Metroplan.

The Hong Kong Housing Society has also contributed to the urban renewal process by undertaking a number of urban improvement schemes in the old urban areas. There were three such projects in progress, one in Yau Ma Tei, one in Sheung Wan (both scheduled for completion in 1995) and one in Sham Shui Po (to be completed in 1993).

Building Development – Private Sector

As the property market continued to boom, the number of occupation permits issued for completed buildings was 443, compared with 440 in 1991. The amount of usable floor area provided was 3.1 million square metres and the total costs of new building works were $23,518 million.

The skyline of Hong Kong changed following the completion of a 78-storey office building, the Central Plaza. With a height of 374.30 metres, it is the tallest concrete-framed building in the world, the tallest building in Asia, and the fourth tallest building in the world. Phase I of the Hong Kong University of Science and Technology was completed and Phase II was at an advanced stage of completion. A major residential development was well underway at Ap Lei Chau comprising 38 tower blocks of flats for more than 50 000 people.

As new buildings in Hong Kong become more sophisticated, it is imperative to maintain a high standard of building safety. New Building (Planning) Regulations were introduced in 1992 requiring the provision of easy means of access within new buildings for fire fighting and rescue purposes.

The Buildings Ordinance Office also continued to place great emphasis on building safety in existing buildings. More staff were employed to deal with the problem of potential dangers arising from older buildings. Efforts in publicity and civic education were maintained to promote public awareness of the need for efficient maintenance and repair of buildings. In the on-going enhanced planned survey exercise, 8 624 buildings in suspect condition were inspected resulting in the issue of 910 orders requiring repair or demolition of buildings.

On the morning of May 8, 1992, Hong Kong experienced a severe rainstorm. This event, one of the worst on record, meant that the Buildings Ordinance Office had to attend to a total of 85 emergency cases, resulting in the immediate closure of one building on a permanent basis, and 20 buildings temporarily.

The problem of unauthorised building works remained a problem for the Buildings Ordinance Office. Operations were launched to clear external appendages which threatened the safety of public thoroughfares. Fifty two buildings were targeted for clearance during the year. Of the 11 160 appendages removed, 6 140 were removed voluntarily by the building owners themselves, attesting not only to the success of the operations but also to the willingness of the public to co-operate.

The office played an active role in promoting energy conservation by co-ordinating a study on the use of overall thermal transfer values in air-conditioned buildings as a means to achieve energy efficiency. A draft handbook was prepared and commended to the building industry for use on a trial basis.

The office was also alert to the wasteful use of tropical hardwood in the building industry, to the detriment of the environment. Practice notes were issued to authorised persons, registered structural engineers and registered contractors aiming at encouraging the use of alternatives to timber for construction purposes. An exercise was initiated to examine existing building regulations to further the cause.

195

Building Development – Public Sector

The Architectural Services Department is a multi-disciplinary organisation having responsibility for providing technical advice on building related matters to government departments; financial and project management of public building developments under the Public Works Programme and for monitoring public expenditure on subvented building projects financed by Government. The department provides professional design services for Government, Urban and Regional Council buildings; and maintenance management services for buildings owned or occupied by Government, Urban and Regional Councils, subvented schools and the British Forces in Hong Kong.

During 1991–2, the department had under study, design and construction over 700 projects valued at $39 billion. In addition, the value of subvented projects monitored by the department amounted to $11 billion. Work valued at $5.8 billion was carried out on building projects undertaken or monitored by the department. Expenditure on maintenance and minor alteration works to Government, Urban Council, Regional Council, Hospital Authority, Subvented Schools and British Forces properties amounted to $0.8 billion.

In the 12 month period to March 1992 tender prices dropped by about 15 per cent primarily due to market forces. On the other hand, over the same period, labour and basic material costs rose by 10 per cent and three per cent respectively.

The department is in the preliminary stages of the design of government facilities for the new airport at Chek Lap Kok. At the Kai Tak Airport passenger terminal the refurbishment programme and the transport terminus improvements were completed in August and September 1992 respectively. Part of the south apron development project of the Royal Hong Kong Auxiliary Air Force Headquarters was completed in August 1992.

Under the Airport Core Projects programme, Phase I of the Cheung Sha Wan Wholesale Market commenced in April 1992 and will be completed in September 1993. In conjunction with the second phase it will provide Kowloon and the New Territories with an integrated wholesale market facility.

The Western Wholesale Market, Phase II, at Kennedy Town is also currently under construction and will be completed by April 1994.

Various other market complexes and sports and recreational facilities were completed during the year for the Urban Council including Chai Wan Park and Electric Road Market Complex. Construction started in 1992 included the largest indoor games hall to be built in Hong Kong (on the Western Reclamation) as well as various other facilities.

The Regional Council increased its provision of public facilities with the completion of the Shatin Leisure Pool Complex, the Tai Po Sports Ground and indoor recreation centres at Fanling and Cheung Chau. Construction commenced on an air-conditioned market complex in Shek Wu Hui and two air-conditioned indoor recreation centres in Kwai Chung and Tsuen Wan.

Medical and health projects completed during the year included the Pamela Youde Hospital at Chai Wan, the Block B extension to Queen Elizabeth Hospital, improvement works to Tsan Yuk Hospital and the Nurses Training School and staff quarters associated with the Pamela Youde Hospital.

During the year work commenced on the Queen Elizabeth Hospital refurbishment due for completion in 1996. Piling work was completed on the Wong Chuk Hang complex for the elderly and overall completion is expected in 1994. Other hospital projects under design, construction and refurbishment are the Shum Wan Laundry, Prince of Wales Hospital; General and Children's Cancer Centre, Siu Lam Hospital; and Queen Mary Hospital extension and improvements.

Public clinics under construction and due for completion in 1993 are the Tuen Mun Urban Clinic and the Tin Shui Wai Urban Clinic. The Sha Tin Urban Clinic was completed in January 1992.

For the disciplined services, a number of projects were completed this year. Police projects included a Divisional Police Station at Tin Shui Wai, completed in time to serve the new town with its first population in-take, and Ping Shan Police Dog Unit Headquarters. For the Fire Services Department a new combined Sub-Divisional Fire Station, Ambulance Depot and Ambulance Training School at Ma On Shan, as well as new ambulance training facilities were completed.

Among projects under construction during the year were the Sub-Divisional Fire Station at Tsing Yi, Lai King Division Fire Station at Kwai Chung and foundation work for the New Police Headquarters complex.

The Property Services Branch of Architectural Services Department provided maintenance and alteration works to over 6 000 government, Urban Council, Regional Council, Hospital Authority, subvented schools and British Forces buildings. There was a noticeable increase in the number of major refurbishment and fitting out projects being undertaken, including Stage 3 of the refurbishment of Queen Mary Hospital, Central Government Offices West Wing and refurbishment of a building in Kennedy Road as a meeting venue for the Sino-British Joint Liaison Group.

Government's continued commitment to improving facilities for handicapped persons was reflected by the completion of Phase 2 of a rolling programme to modify existing public buildings to facilitate access for the disabled. In total 94 locations ranging from hospitals and post offices to markets and playgrounds have been provided with access and, where feasible, special toilets.

The Antiquities Group within the branch were again rewarded for their work in restoring and repairing historically important buildings in Hong Kong. The Kun Ting Study Hall in Ping Shan was awarded the Hong Kong Institute of Architects President's Prize. The building is a traditional Chinese Study Hall which was authentically restored by artists and craftsman from China using salvaged materials and historical evidence provided by villagers.

The Subvented Projects Division advises departments providing subvention to private organisations for building and maintenance works. These include subvention provided for tertiary institutions and health facilities.

Since the establishment of the Hospital Authority in December 1991 the department has been responsible for monitoring capital subvention for building and improvement projects at facilities under the auspices of the authority.

Advice is also given on facilities to be provided to the government by private developers as a requirement of condition of land grant.

Land Administration

The Lands Administration Office of the Buildings and Lands Department co-ordinates all aspects of land administration throughout the territory.

The office's main functions are to acquire and make available land for the government's development programmes, to dispose of sufficient land to meet demand and to manage all unallocated government land.

Although most government land available for private sector development is sold by public auction or tender, land is also made available at nominal premium to the Housing Authority for its public rental estates and home ownership schemes and to non-profit-making charitable medical and educational institutions which operate schools, hospitals, social welfare and other community services.

A land sales programme is issued at the beginning of each financial year and updated regularly showing the details of public auctions and tenders which are normally held each month. Land in the New Territories is often sold by way of letter B tender, which means that only holders of letter B entitlements are able to bid. These land exchange entitlements were used in the past for the acquisition of land in the New Territories but have ceased being issued since 1983.

Land usage statistics are at Appendix 35.

Land Acquisition
When private property is needed in the public interest, which in most cases is for the implementation of public works projects, and cannot be acquired by negotiation, the use of compulsory powers becomes necessary. Property may then be acquired under the Crown Lands Resumption Ordinance, the Land Acquisition (Possessory Title) Ordinance, the Mass Transit Railway (Land Resumption and Related Provisions) Ordinance or the Roads (Works, Use and Compensation) Ordinance. These ordinances provide for payment of compensation based on the value of property, and for business loss where appropriate, at the date of acquisition. If agreement cannot be reached on the amount payable, either party can refer the claim to the Lands Tribunal for adjudication.

Where land is acquired in the New Territories, a system of *ex-gratia* payments applies with enhanced rates being paid for land situated within the new town development areas and progressively lower rates for land situated outside these areas. In the case of building land, an *ex-gratia* payment is offered in addition to the statutory compensation available. A system of *ex-gratia* payments also applies in the case of old scheduled lots acquired in the urban area. Additionally an *ex-gratia* allowance, known as a Home Purchase Allowance, is normally paid upon resumption of domestic units within the urban area.

During 1992 about 0.4 million square metres of private land was acquired in the New Territories for various projects at an acquisition and clearance cost of about $0.79 billion. These projects included the Lantau Fixed Crossing, the North Lantau Expressway, Tung Chung New Town Development, pumping stations and aqueducts for water supply from China, the Tin Shui Wai West Access and the North East New Territories Landfill Site and its associated works.

In the urban area Kowloon Walled City was finally cleared and demolition of the buildings started. It previously covered an area of 2.7 hectares with a population of some 28 250. Owners and occupiers of 8 494 premises, including 983 premises used for business purposes, were eligible for compensation payable on an *ex-gratia* basis and expenditure on compensation incurred to date is $3,017 million, of which $546 million was incurred during 1992.

Elsewhere in the urban areas of Hong Kong and Kowloon, acquisition for the implementation of urban renewal projects to be carried out by the Land Development

Corporation and Hong Kong Housing Society, together with other smaller projects involved 538 properties and expenditure of $2,244 million.

Land Disposal

All land in Hong Kong is held by the government which sells or grants leasehold interests. Such grants and leases are made in accordance with the terms set out in Annex III to the Sino-British Joint Declaration. The total amount of new land to be granted is not to exceed 50 hectares a year, excluding land to be granted to the Hong Kong Housing Authority for public rental housing, but the Land Commission may increase this limit and regularly does. The land disposal limit this year is 164.30 hectares with a 5-hectare reserve. Premium income obtained from land transactions is shared equally, after deduction of the average cost of land production, between the Hong Kong Government and the future Hong Kong Special Administrative Region Government.

Normal land grants and leases are now made for terms expiring not later than June 30, 2047. They are made at premium and nominal rental until June 30, 1997, after which date an annual rent equivalent to three per cent of the property's rateable value will apply.

Land Sales

There was a steep increase in residential property prices in 1991 exacerbated by the problem of speculation in new developments. In order to combat this, and in addition to other fiscal measures introduced by the Government, the Lands Administration Office, with the agreement of the Land Commission, disposed of land through the Land Sales Programme that will provide a substantial increase in the number of residential units when compared with previous years.

Major land transactions/negotiations in 1992 included the invitation of expressions of interest for a 60-hectare site on east Tsing Yi for Container Terminal 9 with the granting of the site in early 1993.

Two grants of land in the Central District of Hong Kong Island were made to the Land Development Corporation for redevelopment of inner city areas into new commercial/ residential buildings with provision for markets, bazaars and varying social service facilities.

Three sites with a total area of 3.07 hectares were sold under the Private Sector Participation Scheme which will provide a total of 4 600 flats. A further eight sites were granted to the Hong Kong Housing Authority for the development of home ownership Schemes. These included two large sites comprising 2.66 hectares and 2.77 hectares in Kowloon East.

In the New Territories, nine sites with a total area of 9.98 hectares were sold by tender restricted to holders of Land Exchange Entitlements (Letters A/B), thereby reducing the amount of outstanding Letters B to be redeemed to approximately, 3 500 000 square feet. Commercial/residential sites in Tseung Kwan O comprised a total of three sites in this programme and amounted to an area of 7.05 hectares.

Land Registration

The Land Registration Ordinance provides for registration of all instruments affecting land in the Land Office, one of the two major sections of the Land Division of the Registrar General's Department. Registration is by means of a memorial form containing the essential particulars of the instrument which are then placed on a computerised (except in the New Territories District Land Registries) register relating to the particular piece of land or individual premises affected, such as residential flats, shops, and commercial and industrial premises. The registers provide a complete picture of the title to each property from the grant of the government lease. They are available for search by the public on payment of a small fee. The memorials and a complete copy of each registered instrument are kept and are also available for search in microfilm form (except in the New Territories District Land Registries) by the public on payment of a fee.

The ordinance also provides that all instruments registered under it shall have priority according to their respective dates of registration, unless they are registered within one month of execution, in which case priority relates back to the date of the instrument. For charging orders made by the court and pending court actions, priority runs from the day following the date of registration. The ordinance further provides that unregistered instruments, other than *bona fide* leases at a rack rent for a term not exceeding three years, shall be null and void as against any subsequent *bona fide* purchaser or mortgagee for valuable consideration.

Registration is therefore essential to the protection of title, but does not guarantee it. Approval in principle has been given by the government to investigate the merits of changing the present system of land registration to one of title registration. A working party chaired by the Registrar General and comprising prominent members of the legal profession was set up and has made its report. Legislative amendments based on the report are being put in place.

The records of transactions effecting land on Hong Kong Island, Kowloon, New Kowloon and some of the urban areas of the New Territories are kept at the Land Office, Victoria. Those relating to transactions affecting land in the remainder of the New Territories are kept in the appropriate District Land Registries in the New Territories. Before any land transaction is completed a land search to ascertain property ownership should always be made. During the year, 3 207 280 such public land searches were made and 685 136 instruments registered throughout the territory, compared with 3 168 942 and 823 842 respectively in 1991. At the end of the year, there were 1 505 003 property owners, an increase of 57 612 over the previous year.

On December 1, 1992 the Legal Advisory and Conveyancing Section of the Land Division of the Registrar General's Department was transferred to the Buildings and Lands Department to form a new Legal Advisory and Conveyancing Office within the department. This office provides professional legal services to the government for all government land transactions and associated matters. It is responsible for the issue, renewal, variation and termination of government leases as well as the drafting and completion of conditions of sale, grants and exchanges of government lands, the apportionment of government rents and premia, and the recovery of outstanding rents. It also provides conveyancing services for the Housing Authority in connection with the sale of flats built under the Home Ownership Scheme and for The Financial Secretary Incorporated in connection with the extension of non-renewable government leases, the purchase and sale of government accommodation in private developments, mortgages to secure interest-free loans to private schools, the purchase of properties for government staff quarters and group housing schemes for the elderly. It is also responsible for the processing of the Consent Applications which are governed by the rules of the Land Authority

Consent Scheme. During the year, 21 applications involving 10 124 units in the urban areas were approved and in the New Territories 30 applications involving 15 013 units were approved.

Land registration statistics are at Appendix 34.

Survey and Mapping

The Survey and Mapping Office is responsible for defining and recording land boundaries of all existing and new land developments, providing and maintaining the territory-wide survey control system, mapping the territory at various scales for land administration, engineering and government purposes and managing a computerised land information system.

Geodetic control systems, which are horizontal and vertical control networks covering the whole territory, have been established and maintained to a high degree of accuracy. These systems provide the necessary origin and control points for cadastral (property boundary), topographical mapping, engineering and other surveys.

There is a world-wide trend to use a Global Positioning System (GPS) in place of conventional methods to fix geodetic control points. This method makes use of signals from orbiting satellites to determine the position of any point on earth. The Survey and Mapping Office will use GPS for geodetic work in the near future.

Cadastral surveying is an important function of the office, serving the public and government by defining property boundaries. The office maintains a comprehensive graphical record of all leasehold and government land boundaries in the territory. Landowners may request the office, on payment of a fee, to supply boundary information or to reset-out the private lot boundaries on ground. Legislation will be introduced to administer boundary surveys by authorised persons in order to protect the public interest, regulate private sector practices and strengthen the cadastral survey system. Contracting out of some cadastral surveys covering small house lots in the New Territories continued in 1992.

The wide range of mapping coverage maintained by the office has always provided an important support service in the administration, planning and development of Hong Kong. The most definitive series of maps and the foundation of all other mapping is the large scale (1:1 000) basic topographical series (3 000 sheets). In addition, there are other smaller scale maps such as the monochrome map series at 1:5 000 (157 sheets) and the coloured map series at 1:20 000 (16 sheets); 150 000 (two sheets); 1:100 000 (one sheet) and 1:200 000 (one sheet). Two monochrome street map series at 1:10 000 and 1:15 000 of the urban areas in Hong Kong, Kowloon and parts of the New Territories are produced for special uses and as a base for the popular guide-book *Hong Kong Guide – Streets and Places*. Demand for leisure maps, in the form of the *Countryside Series* (seven sheets) and the *Tourist Guide*, has been strong and the design and contents are continually updated to make subsequent editions more attractive and informative to users.

Maps are obtainable from conveniently located outlets throughout the territory.

The Survey and Mapping Office provides extensive cartographic services for many government departments. These include full-colour mapping for the geological series, base maps for weather forecasting, aeronautical charts, electoral boundary maps and pollution control plans. Its Reprographic Unit also provides services in photo-reproduction and plan copying, and serves as an essential back-up for in-house map reduction and other cartographic activities.

The computerised land information system is being installed in District Survey Offices by phases once the digital map data and land records are available. The system processes and analyses land information and is a useful tool for enquiry on land status and decision making. The system also automates the production of large scale maps and cadastral plans. Up-to-date mapping and boundary information can be made readily available to users. Besides producing standard 1:1 000 survey sheets containing full topographical features, the system can also produce plans according to the user's specifications. The users can choose the features to be shown, such as buildings, roads and contour lines; colours and symbols for different features; and plan scale and plan size. Mapping information in digital form may be supplied to the public on payment of a licence fee and direct on-line access to the central mapping data may also be possible. The data conversion for other districts in the territories will be speeded up by contracting out the work and is scheduled to be completed by 1994.

The Photogrammetric Survey Section provides aerial photographs and photogrammetric mapping as well as data for engineering design work, volumetric calculations for quarry and controlled tipping operations, environmental studies and town planning work. The Air Survey Unit is also on call for quick response photography in emergency operations such as storms, flooding and landslips.

Drainage Services
The Drainage Services Department is responsible for planning, designing, constructing, operating and maintaining sewerage, sewage treatment and stormwater drainage infra-structures.

Treatment and disposal of foul water
The treatment and disposal of foul water, that is domestic sewage and trade and industrial effluent, is based on standards, strategies and programmes drawn up by the Environmental Protection Department. Projects on foul water disposal can be broadly divided into three categories: 'existing schemes' which are sewerage or sewage treatment projects which have been in the public works programme before the new strategy evolved and which are compatible with the new strategy for the treatment and disposal of sewage to satisfy new water quality standards; 'sewerage masterplan schemes' which are sewerage rehabilitation and improvement projects to ensure the proper collection of sewage in foul sewers, and the 'strategic sewage disposal scheme' which is a massive project to collect all the sewage from Hong Kong Island, Kowloon, Tsuen Wan and Tseung Kwan O into a deep tunnel intercepting sewer system that will discharge, after treatment on Stonecutters Island, through a long sea outfall into the Dangan Channel.

Under the 'existing schemes' category the largest project is the North West Kowloon Sewage Treatment and Disposal Scheme. In this scheme, the sewage from Sham Shui Po, Mong Kok and Yau Ma Tei with a total population of about 1.2 million will be collected and treated prior to discharge. All construction works have been completed and the operation of the scheme has been in commission since August 1992. The second largest project in this category is the Tolo Harbour Effluent Export Scheme to export the sewage effluent from the Sha Tin and Tai Po sewage treatment works and discharge it into Victoria Harbour. The works comprise sewage pumping stations, rising mains, submarine pipelines and a sewer tunnel of 3.2-metre diameter and 7.5 kilometres in length under Tsz Wan Shan. The sewer tunnel was broken through in June 1992 and construction for the whole of the works is scheduled for completion in two stages in 1993 and 1995.

Other projects which are being implemented under this first category include the construction of a sewage screening plant to serve a population of 1.2 million in the Tsuen Wan and Kwai Chung area, a secondary sewage treatment plant to serve the rural public housing in Peng Chau and the upgrading and extending of the existing Tseung Kwan O sewage treatment plant. In late 1992, the government completed the construction of the Ha Tsuen sewage pumping station, the San Wai sewage treatment works, and the rising main between them, which together form part of the North West New Territories Sewerage Scheme. The extension of Yuen Long sewage treatment works was also completed in 1992.

Under the second category, projects are being implemented to improve the sewage collection, treatment and disposal facilities in the areas of Tsuen Wan, Kwai Chung, Tsing Yi, Yuen Long, Kam Tin and Port Shelter. Design works are being carried out for these projects and construction works are scheduled for commencement either in 1993 or 1994. In East Kowloon and the southern district of Hong Kong Island, works to improve sewage disposal facilities have already started.

Under the third category, engineering feasibility studies were carried out to study the details for the implementation of the strategic sewage disposal scheme. The studies have provided useful information for the design of this massive sewerage scheme involving a system of deep sewer tunnels.

Stormwater drainage

For stormwater drainage, the Drainage Services Department is responsible for the formulation of strategies, standards, project planning and implementation. Past records indicate that the North and North-West New Territories are particularly vulnerable to flooding. Further to an initial territory-wide study carried out by consultants in 1989 to review rainfall, stream flow and flooding prediction, the department has commissioned another study with the aim of drawing up basin management plans for the main rivers in the North and North-West New Territories and to examine in more detail what local flood mitigation measures can be taken. In addition, pamphlets giving advice on what to do and what not to do in a flooding situation have been widely distributed through District Offices to people living in flood-prone areas.

Among structural measures, which the government has already put in hand, are the construction of main drainage channels in the North-West New Territories flood plains and local works to protect low-lying villages. Construction of 6.5 kilometres of channels for the Tin Shui Wai hinterland has been completed and design has already been put in hand for another 14 kilometres of channels in Yuen Long, Kam Tin and Ngau Tam Mei with a view to starting work on site in 1993. As an associated measure, flood water pumping systems have also been constructed to mitigate the impact of flooding in low lying villages. About a dozen, mainly in the New Territories, are currently in operation and more are planned for construction in the future.

The ground work for the creation of a Land Drainage Ordinance has been completed and a Land Drainage Bill is being prepared. The bill, when enacted, will empower the government to access and maintain important watercourses running through private land, or through government land but surrounded by private land.

Operation and maintenance of drainage system

With the commissioning of each additional item of infrastructure there is a consequential increased commitment in operations and maintenance. At present, the sewage treatment facilities are being operated to provide grit removal and screening for sewage of some 1.3 million cubic metres per day and to provide full biological treatment for sewage of another 350 000 cubic metres per day. Sludges produced from both sewage treatment works and water treatment works at Sha Tin are dumped at sea by the 1 400 cubic metre-capacity purpose-built vessel Sha Tin Prince which commenced operation in March 1991. The environmental effect of such dumping is carefully monitored.

The department also operates an all-the-year-round emergency storm damage organisation. This organisation is run by staff working on a rotational basis and is supported by the department's direct labour force and contractors. Its operation ensures that emergency situations, even outside normal working hours, can be dealt with efficiently.

Effective maintenance of the drainage infrastructures is an essential part of the total effort to reduce the risk of flooding as well as to ensure the proper and effective disposal of foul water. Since the establishment of the department, the approach to operation and maintenance of the public drainage system has progressively shifted from crisis management to preventive maintenance. Resources have been deployed to carry out regular inspection, cleansing, repair and improvement of the drainage system, especially at identified drainage black spots. The results are promising and although the public drainage system has become larger and more complex with urbanisation, the number of drainage complaints, chokage and flooding show steadily declining trends. The department now maintains 2 850 kilometres of watercourses, drains and sewers, increasing at the rate of 50 kilometres per year. Some 90 000 cubic metres of silt are removed from drains and watercourses each year to keep their pollution level low and keep them free-flowing.

Geotechnical Control

The Geotechnical Engineering Office (GEO) of the Civil Engineering Department was established after the landslip disasters of the 1970s, and the control of geotechnical aspects of construction works in the interest of public safety continues to be one of its foremost duties. Checks were made on 6 494 design proposals in 1992.

The GEO also operates the Landslip Warning System and a 24-hour emergency service to provide advice on landslips. An exceptionally heavy rainfall event occurred on May 8, 1992, which resulted in more than 350 landslip incidents, two of which involved fatalities. GEO staff attended all of these incidents giving advice on immediate measures to prevent further danger as well as on permanent remedial measures.

In June 1992 arrangements were made for members of the public to gain access to the government's catalogue of slopes and to obtain information about the results of the squatter area studies undertaken by GEO.

During 1992, landslip preventive works were completed on 33 slopes and retaining walls requiring the expenditure of $62.3 million in the Landslip Preventive Measures Programme and substantial remedial works were carried out to three major landslips. Preliminary studies were carried out on 1 602 slopes and retaining walls and detailed geotechnical investigations were finished on 53 slopes and retaining walls. In addition, the inspection of a number of boulder and rock outcrop features along Seymour Cliffs in the Mid-Levels was undertaken, with preventive stabilisation works completed on 45 features, at a cost of $2.6

Preceding page: *A jade lover with her collection. Both for its value and beauty jade is sought after in Hong Kong.*

Left and below: *Art specialists at an auction preview.*

Above: *Antique and modern art and ornaments go under the auctioneer's hammer.*

Following Pages (left): *Modern Chinese oil paintings command considerable interest and high prices.*
Right (top to bottom): *A dealer discusses the merits of an exhibit; experts examine an antique horse and carry out tests to check its age.*

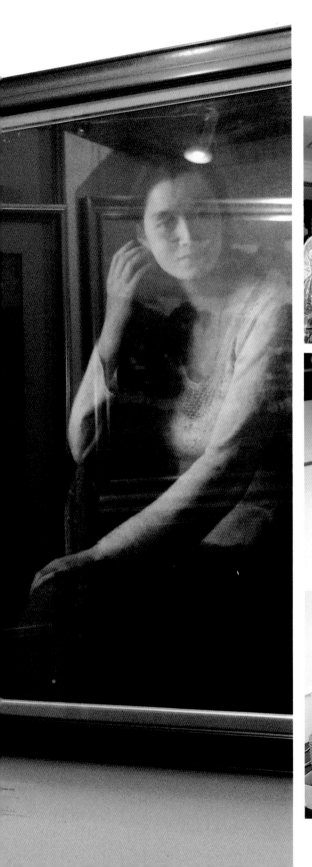

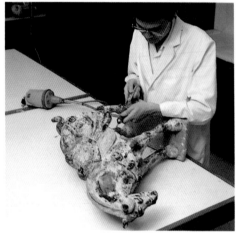

A young buyer studies a fine antique watch at a specialist clock shop.

million. Works also commenced on the extension to the Mid-Levels boulder fence behind Conduit Road together with *in-situ* stabilisation of large boulders in the boulder field behind the fence. Completion of this project will be mid-1993 at an estimated cost of $5.8 million. Stabilisation works were in progress to the slopes of an old landfill borrow area at Fung Shing Street, Ngau Chi Wan, with a contract sum of $6.9 million. Remedial works to four disused air raid precaution tunnels were completed at a cost of $9.2 million.

The Hong Kong Geological Survey continues to publish 1:20 000 scale geological maps and memoirs for the land and marine areas of the territory. During 1992, new geological maps for Silver Mine Bay, Kat O Chau and Cheung Chau were published. Geological maps at 1:20 000 scale are now available for more than 80 per cent of the territory. A seismotectonic study and a gravity survey of the territory were completed during the year. Large-scale (1:5 000) geological survey work is well underway in the development areas of North Lantau. Geophysical survey and borehole data for the mapping are being transferred into a computer database, and computer-aided cartography is being developed for map production. Engineering geology studies have been essentially completed in North Lantau, and have identified the major geotechnical constraints that could significantly affect the costs or timely implementation of the new airport and related projects and the future port-related developments in the area.

The Geotechnical Information Unit (GIU), which houses the largest collection of geotechnical data in Hong Kong, continues to serve as an important reference centre in its premises in the Civil Engineering Building in Ho Man Tin. The GIU served more than 4 000 users during the year.

The office's work on the use of underground space continued in 1992. Geoguide 4: *Guide to Cavern Engineering*, which is aimed at providing guidance on design and construction of caverns, has been published and is now on sale. The office also continued to carry out studies to establish cavern development opportunities on a regional basis, and preliminary engineering geological studies of specific sites for potential cavern projects. In 1992, four preliminary engineering geology studies for various cavern uses were completed. Geotechnical advice was also provided on cavern projects being planned or constructed by other departments.

The Marine Geotechnology Section provided advice and carried out research and development work on the marine geotechnical aspects of Port and Airport Development Strategy (PADS) projects, notably on foundations for marine structures and reclamations.

A comprehensively revised draft edition of Geoguide 1: *Guide to Retaining Wall Design* was circulated to private and public sector practitioners both in Hong Kong and overseas in 1992, and much valuable comment was obtained which assisted in finalising the document for publication.

The GEO manages the Public Works Central Laboratory at Kowloon Bay and five public works regional laboratories in various parts of Hong Kong. The six public works laboratories together employ over 150 staff, of whom 10 are professionals and 140 are of technical and clerical grades. Over 250 000 tests on various construction materials were carried out during 1992. The laboratories are accredited under the Hong Kong Laboratory Accreditation Scheme (HOKLAS) to provide calibration services, as well as to carry out tests on such construction materials as concrete, steel, aggregates, cement and pulverised fuel ash. Application for HOKLAS accreditation of bituminous materials testing is in hand.

The office continues to upgrade the level of services available for land and r
ground investigations and geophysical surveys. A number of major ground investig
were undertaken for PADS, including the terminal building at Chek Lap Kok Ai
Lantau Fixed Crossing, West Kowloon Expressway, Western Harbour Develo
Study, and for studies on the restoration of a number of old landfill sites. N
investigations continued for assessment of marine sources of sand in Hong Kong wate
use in planned reclamation works.

Fill Management

The territory's fill resources are managed by the Fill Management Committee (
whose Secretariat is housed in the Geotechnical Engineering Office (GEO) of the
Engineering Department. Around 350 million cubic metres of fill from marine sourc
a similar quantity from land sources are needed for new reclamations over the n
years. The FMC Secretariat uses a comprehensive computerised database on whi
committee makes decisions on reservation, allocation and efficient utilisation
resources for all government and major private projects. During 1992, some 115 m
cubic metres of marine fill were allocated for the construction of reclamations.

Water Supplies

Water from China

The supply of water from China is now the major single source of supply for Hong
and it is from this source that all future increases in demand will be met. This dates b
1960 when a scheme was first formulated for receiving a piped supply of 22.7 millior
metres a year. Today, the annual supply from China stipulated under the agreeme
increased to 600 million cubic metres and this will continue to increase in stages
million cubic metres by 1995. Apart from the fixed quantities of supply stipulated
agreements, there are provisions to purchase additional supplies from China in years
rainfall in Hong Kong. In view of the very low reservoir storage level in February 19
additional supply of 105 million cubic metres was agreed for the period of March 1
February 1993. Subsequently, abnormally high rainfall was recorded in March to
China agreed to defer the delivery of 38 million cubic metres of the additional quar
the period of March 1993 to February 1994. The concept of seeking a supply from
and steps taken by the Water Supplies Department of Hong Kong to realise such
have brought about radical changes to the history of water supplies in the territory.

Following the agreement reached with the Chinese Authority in December 1
increase the China water supply up to a maximum of 1 100 million cubic metres per
cope with the anticipated demands beyond 1994, a conceptual plan was developed
necessary works to receive and distribute the additional supply. The works v
implemented in stages with the Stage I works to be completed by end-1994. The S
works include some 22 kilometres of large-diameter delivery pipes, new pumping s
at Muk Wu, Tai Po Tau, Au Tau and Sai O and uprating of an existing pumping sta
Tai Mei Tuk. The first contract commenced work in December 1991. Works in pi
included new pumping stations at Muk Wu and Tai Po Tau as well as delivery pi
between the two pumping stations.

Water Works

Full supply was maintained throughout the year. At the beginning of 1992, there were 177 million cubic metres of water in storage, compared with 179 million cubic metres at the start of 1991. The combined storage of Hong Kong's largest reservoirs, High Island and Plover Cove, was 133 million cubic metres. Rainfall for the year was 2 679 millimetres compared with the average of 2 214 millimetres. Water piped from China during the year totalled 668 million cubic metres.

A peak consumption of 2.82 million cubic metres per day was experienced, compared with the 1991 peak of 2.76 million cubic metres. The average daily consumption throughout the year was 2.43 million cubic metres, an increase of 0.6 per cent compared with the 1991 average of 2.42 million cubic metres. The consumption of potable water totalled 889 million cubic metres compared with 884 million cubic metres in 1991. In addition, 127 million cubic metres of salt water for flushing was supplied, compared with 123 cubic metres in 1991.

With reliable supplies available from China, it was decided by the Executive Council in July 1989 to dispose of the Lok On Pai Desalting Plant. The site of the decommissioned plant has been handed over to the Provisional Airport Authority as a trans-shipment centre for the construction of the new airport.

Planning studies were completed during the year for the improvement of water supply to Tseung Kwan O, Tuen Mun, Tai Po, Sheung Shui, Fanling, East Kowloon and West Kowloon including the new reclamation area. These included the provision of salt water supplies to Tseung Kwan O and Tai Po. Planning is in hand for the major new treatment works at Tai Po (formerly at Pak Ngau Shek) and Ngau Tam Mei. Further planning for the improvement of system capacity to meet the demand arising from new developments in Yuen Long, Tin Shui Wai and the metropolitan south-eastern area of Kowloon, the central, western mid level and high level areas of Hong Kong Island and the Northwest New Territories is also in progress. A planning study on the treatment and disposal of sludge generated from the existing treatment works was also completed.

Regarding water supply to the new airport at Chek Lap Kok and other developments in North Lantau associated with the Port and Airport Development Strategy, works for the permanent water supply system will be implemented in stages with the Stage I works to be commissioned by mid-1996 to phase in with the commissioning of the new airport. The Stage I works include submarine and land mains, a water treatment works, pumping stations, a fresh water service reservoir and a raw water aqueduct between Siu Ho Wan and Silvermine Bay. Part of the design work was in an advanced stage. Mainlaying work along the North Lantau Expressway commenced in June 1992. The bulk of the works will commence by the end of 1993. The temporary water supply system providing water supply to construction activities for the new airport and other infrastructural projects was completed.

Consultants have completed the investigation for the Ma On Shan Treatment Works and proceeded with the detailed design. Design work by in-house staff has been completed on the Sham Tseung Treatment Works Stage I and continued on the extension of Sheung Shui Treatment Works. Other major design works in progress included the flushing water supply system in Ma On Shan and Tai Po, additional service reservoirs, pumping stations and water supply networks in Tuen Mun, Yau Kom Tau, Tsuen Wan, Tsing Yi, Tseung Kwan O, Hong Kong west mid level, Ap Lei Chau and Repulse Bay. Design works for the improvement of chlorine storage facilities in Tsuen Wan, Tuen Mun and Tai Po Tau Treatment Works and Tai Lam Chung Pre-Chlorination House were also in progress. Design of the expansion of the distribution network to supply remote villages in the New Territories continued.

Construction for the Au Tau Treatment Works Stage II and a new intake tower in Tai Lam Chung Reservoir commenced. Construction works for the Sham Tseng Treatment Works and extension of Yau Kom Tau Treatment Works were in progress.

Au Tau Treatment Works Stage I and Pak Kong Treatment Works Stage II were put into operation. The distribution system was continuously extended and enlarged to meet urban and rural demands in the territory. Expansion of the distribution network to supply remote villages in the New Territories continued.

The number of consumer accounts continued to rise at a rate of about three per cent per annum and the consumer account base expanded to approximately 1.93 million at the beginning of 1992. Computer systems were widely employed to provide efficient and effective enquiry services; handling applications for new water supply and change of consumer; and issuing water bills, connection fees and deposit demand notes. A project to introduce handheld computers for meter reading in order to further improve efficiency of the billing process was carried out during the year with a target implementation date of early 1993. Efforts to promote the autopay service continued, and the number of consumer accounts using autopay for payment of water charges reached 201 000 or about 10 per cent of all consumers.

A SAVE WATER publicity campaign continued in the early months of the year but was scaled down since May following heavy rainfall which greatly improved the reservoir storage situation. The public was reminded of the importance of following safety guidelines in the installation of electric thermal storage type water heaters for domestic purposes. Consumers' attention was drawn to their responsibility for maintenance of their plumbing installations and carrying out simple checks themselves in the event of supply problems prior to seeking assistance from the Water Authority.

Electricity

Electricity supply is currently provided by two commercial companies – the Hongkong Electric Company Limited (HEC), which supplies Hong Kong Island and the neighbouring islands of Ap Lei Chau and Lamma, and China Light and Power Company Limited (CLP), which supplies the whole of Kowloon and the New Territories, including Lantau and a number of outlying islands.

The two supply companies are investor-owned and do not operate on a franchise basis. The government monitors the financial arrangements of the companies through a mutually agreed scheme of control agreements. The agreements require each company to seek the approval of the government for certain aspects of their financing plans, including projected tariff levels.

The operations of the three generating companies affiliated to CLP, namely, Peninsula Electric Power Company Limited (PEPCO), Kowloon Electricity Supply Company Limited (KESCO) and Castle Peak Power Company Limited (CAPCO) were consolidated under CAPCO in April 1992. CAPCO's present generating facilities include Tsing Yi 'A' (796mw), Tsing Yi 'B' (876mw), Castle Peak 'A' (1 752mw), Castle Peak 'B' (2 708mw) and Penny's Bay (300mw) power stations. The total installed capacity is 6 432mw

The government has also approved the installation by CLP of four 600mw blocks of additional generating capacity, the first two of which will be installed in a new power station at Black Point, Tuen Mun, in 1996 and 1997 respectively. The other two blocks will be commissioned within the periods 1998 to 2000 and 1999 to 2001. All of them will be fuelled by natural gas piped from the Yacheng 13-1 gas field off Hainan Island in China.

CAPCO is 60 per cent owned by Exxon Energy Limited and 40 per cent by CLP, while the associated transmission and distribution systems are wholly owned by CLP. CLP's present scheme of control agreement will expire on September 30, 1993. The government has entered into a new agreement with CLP, Exxon Energy Limited and their generating companies that will commence on October 1, 1993 and last for 15 years.

CLP's transmission system operates at 400kV, 132kV and 66kV, and distribution is effected mainly at 33kV, 11kV and 346 volts. The supply is 50 hertz alternating current, normally at 200 volts single phase or 346 volts three phase.

CLP has more than 170 primary and over 6 903 secondary substations in its transmission and distribution network. An extra high voltage transmission system at 400kV to transmit power from the Castle Peak Stations to the various load centres was completed in 1986. It comprises a double-circuit overhead line system encircling the New Territories, underground cables and seven extra high voltage substations. Construction and planning work for the addition of new extra high voltage substations and for reinforcement of the existing system are in progress.

In HEC's supply areas, electricity is supplied entirely from the Lamma Power Station. At the end of 1992, the total installed capacity at the Lamma Power Station was 2 605mw. There are plans to add a further 350mw unit to Lamma in the mid-1990s.

HEC's transmission system operates at 275kV, 132kV and 66kV and distribution is effected mainly at 11kV and 346 volts. With the exception of a small proportion of 132kV overhead transmission lines, all supplies are transmitted and distributed by underground or by submarine cables. The supply is 50 hertz, 200 volts single phase and 346 volts three phase. Supplies at high voltage are also made available to consumers.

The transmission systems of CLP and HEC are interconnected by a cross-harbour link, thereby achieving cost savings to consumers through economic energy transfers between the two systems and a reduction in the amount of generating capacity that needs to be kept spinning as reserve against the tripping of other units. The interconnection, commissioned in 1981, currently has a capacity of 720mvA.

CLP's system is also interconnected with that of Guangdong General Power Company of China and electricity is exported to Guangdong Province each day. Such sales, which are made from existing generating capacity at off-peak times, are governed by an agreement with the government signed in March 1992 under which CLP's consumers receive priority of supply and 80 per cent of the profit from the sales.

Also, in July 1985, CLP signed a contract with the China Merchants Steam Navigation Company Limited for the supply of electricity starting from late 1986 for a period of ten years to the industrial zone of She Kou and the adjacent Che Wan area, both in Guangdong Province. The arrangements, which afford She Kou a reliable electricity supply without subsidy from Hong Kong consumers, is illustrative of the close co-operation on energy matters which has developed on both sides of the border.

On January 18, 1985, the Hong Kong Nuclear Investment Company (a wholly-owned subsidiary of CLP) and the Guangdong Nuclear Investment Company (wholly owned by the Chinese Ministry of Nuclear Industry) signed the Joint Venture Contract for the formation of the Guangdong Nuclear Power Joint Venture Company, to construct and operate a nuclear power station at Daya Bay in Guangdong Province.

The Guangdong Nuclear Power Station will comprise two 985mw pressurised water reactors which are scheduled for commissioning in 1993 and 1994 respectively. About 70 per cent of the power from the station will be purchased by CLP to meet part of the longer-term demand for electricity in its area of supply.

The new Electricity Ordinance enacted in 1990 provides among other things for the registration of electrical workers and contractors. To ensure that electrical work is carried out by qualified personnel, only registered electrical workers and contractors are allowed to practise with effect from June 1, 1992. To be eligible for registration, they must possess the necessary experience and qualifications. The registration of electrical workers and contractors started in November 1990 and November 1991 respectively. By the end of 1992, 50 706 and 6 118 qualified electrical workers and contractors had been registered.

In May 1990, the government decided that the electricity supply voltage in Hong Kong should be upgraded from 200 volts single phase or 346 volts three phase to 220 volts single phase or 380 volts three phase. A Supply Voltage Advisory Committee was appointed in February 1991 to advise on the implementation of voltage upgrading in the territory. The voltage upgrading is planned to be carried out in two phases and to be completed in about six years. Phase I conversions, covering existing installations inside government buildings, started in August 1990 and was completed in November 1992. Phase II conversions will cover existing installations in Housing Authority and private sector buildings. This phase commenced in January 1993 and will take about four years to complete.

Main electricity statistics and sales figures are at Appendix 36.

Gas

Gas is widely used throughout the territory for domestic, commercial and industrial purposes. Two main types of fuel gas are available: Towngas, distributed by Hong Kong and China Gas Company Limited (HKCG); and Liquefied Petroleum Gas (LPG), supplied by major oil companies based in Hong Kong, namely Shell, Mobil, Esso, Caltex, Hong Kong Oil, China Resources and British Petroleum. Towngas is mainly supplied as a manufactured gas, but for some customers substitute natural gas (SNG) is supplied under the Towngas trademark. The constituents of LPG are butane and propane mixed in approximate proportions of 75 and 25 per cent respectively.

The total number of gas customers in Hong Kong is about 1.86 million. In 1992, Towngas accounted for 63 per cent of the total fuel gas sold in energy terms and LPG for 37 per cent.

HKCG manufactures Towngas at two plants, one at Ma Tau Kok and the other in the Tai Po Industrial Estate. Both use naphtha as a feedstock. They currently have output capacities of 2.2 and 8.4 million cubic metres per day respectively.

Towngas is distributed through an integrated distribution system to about 910 thousand customers for cooking and heating purposes. The mains network extends to the urban areas of Hong Kong Island, including Aberdeen, Repulse Bay, Stanley and Ap Lei Chau; Kowloon; and many new towns in the New Territories, including Sha Tin and Tai Po, Yuen Long and Tsing Yi Island. HKCG is currently constructing a 90km network of 600mm diameter transmission pipeline in the New Territories. The new transmission line is designed to operate at elevated pressure and will provide an additional 0.8 million cubic metres of 'line pack' storage capacity.

SNG is distributed by HKCG under the Towngas trademark from a temporary plant located in Tuen Mun specifically designed and operated to provide the gas requirements of this new town. The plant will need to remain *in-situ* until the new transmission pipeline connecting Tai Po to Tuen Mun has been completed.

LPG is imported into Hong Kong by sea. About 63 per cent of total sales is distributed to customers, via dealer networks, in portable cylinders. The remaining 37 per cent is distributed through piped gas systems from bulk LPG storage and vaporiser installations which are located in or adjacent to the developments being supplied.

Currently there are about 535 LPG dealers operating within the territory. Additionally, 23 LPG site operators manage 475 bulk storage installations under government-monitored arrangements. Altogether there are 950 000 LPG customers.

In 1982, the government introduced a piped gas policy to discourage further growth in the use of gas cylinders in domestic dwellings; and at the same time began a programme of encouraging the upgrading of sub-standard gas water heaters. The percentage of domestic dwellings now using cylinders has fallen to less than 35 per cent in 1992; and the number of upgraded gas water heaters amounts to some 62 250. Apart from suicide cases there were no fatalities arising from fuel gas incidents during 1992.

As further means of safeguarding the general public and gas consumers, the Gas Safety Ordinance was introduced on April 1, 1991. This ordinance and its associated regulations constitute a comprehensive package of safety legislation covering all aspects of fuel gas importation, manufacture, storage, transport, supply and use of gas. The Director of Electrical and Mechanical Services was appointed as the Gas Authority and the Gas Safety Advisory Committee was established for the purpose of advising the authority upon all relevant matters. Since April 1, 1992 it has been necessary for all gas supply companies, gas installers and contractors to be registered with the Gas Authority. In 1992, seven gas supply companies, 2 427 gas installers and 353 gas contractors were registered under the scheme. In addition, the administrative arrangements for controlling safety in the transportation of LPG in tankers and cylinder wagons have been transferred from the Director of Fire Services to the Gas Authority.

The government and the fuel gas supply industry have adopted risk assessment techniques for the detailed examination of all appropriate potentially hazardous gas installations. The risk assessments facilitate the taking of remedial measures where necessary, with the aim of ensuring that residents in the vicinity of these installations are not exposed to unacceptable risk levels.

Professional Registration

The Architects Registration Ordinance and the Engineers Registration Ordinance were enacted in 1990. The registration boards have been set up and there are now 927 registered architects and 993 registered professional engineers. The Surveyors Registration Ordinance and the Planners Registration Ordinance were enacted in July 1991. Their registration boards have been established and the registers will be open to applicants. Registration for all four professions requires, in addition to approved professional qualifications, ordinary residence and at least one year's professional experience in Hong Kong.

15
TRANSPORT

THE first signs of the massive new transport infrastructure to be built under the airport core programme appeared during the year when works commenced on the Lantau Fixed Crossing and reclamations in West Kowloon and North Lantau.

Of the 10 airport core projects, six are related to transport links, the Western Harbour Crossing, the West Kowloon Expressway, the Tsing Yi section of Route 3, the Lantau Fixed Crossing, the North Lantau Expressway and the Airport Railway.

The growth in the number of vehicles on Hong Kong's roads is continuing at a high rate. However, traffic conditions did not deteriorate generally during the year as new roads and improved traffic management techniques enhanced capacity.

The need for the continued expansion of road and rail infrastructure, and the management of vehicle growth in the longer term were confirmed by a study to update the Second Comprehensive Transport Study that was completed by mid-1992. Since road transport accounts for two-thirds of all public transport journeys, the maintenance of bus speeds is an important objective. Greater efficiency in the movement of freight by road, rail and sea will also play a part in alleviating road congestion. In this regard, a Freight Transport Study will report its findings in early 1993. The objective of efficient use of limited road space is complemented by the policy of encouraging the use of railways as a mass carrier. A Railway Development Study has been commissioned to draw up a railway development programme up to 2011. The report on the study will be available in early 1993.

Emphasis continues to be placed on improving the efficiency with which transport and related services are delivered to the public. The Transport Department has continued its programme to contract out the management of certain services which are better provided by the private sector. During the year contracts were awarded for the management of the new Kowloon Bay Vehicle Examination Centre, and the four remaining government-run road tunnels. A contract for the management of a new cross-border coach terminal will be awarded in 1993, and preparatory work is proceeding to contract out the management of parking meters.

Changes were made during the year to the bus franchising arrangements, with the aim of promoting healthy competition. In June, the government invited tenders for a franchise to operate 26 bus routes taken away from China Motor Bus Company (CMB)'s current network. The franchise was awarded to Citybus Limited and the new services will start in September 1993.

Administration

The Transport Branch of the Government Secretariat, headed by the Secretary for Transport, is responsible for overall policy formulation, direction and co-ordination of internal transport matters. He is assisted by the Transport Advisory Committee, which advises the Governor in Council on major transport policies and issues. The committee has 11 appointed members, including the chairman and six government officials. The Secretary for Transport also chairs the Transport Policy Co-ordinating Committee which oversees the implementation of major internal transport policies.

The Transport Department and the Highways Department are responsible for the execution of transport policies and measures, and the highways construction and maintenance programme.

The Commissioner for Transport, the head of the Transport Department, is the authority for administering the Road Traffic Ordinance and legislation regulating public transport operations other than railways. His responsibilities cover strategic transport planning, road traffic management, government road tunnels, car parks and metered parking spaces, and the regulation of internal road and waterborne public transport. He is also the authority for the licensing of drivers and the registration, licensing and inspection of vehicles.

While the Police Force is the principal agency for enforcing traffic legislation and prosecuting offenders, the prosecutions unit of the Transport Department also handles prosecutions involving safety defects found on buses, disqualifications under the Driving Offence Points System and breaches of vehicle safety regulations and government tunnel regulations. In 1992, the unit conducted 14 prosecutions in respect of buses and other vehicles, 4 767 cases for which disqualification was sought under the Driving Offence Points System and 96 prosecutions in respect of breach of tunnel and other regulations.

A Transport Tribunal, set up under the Road Traffic Ordinance and chaired by a non-government official, provides the public with a channel of appeal against decisions made by the Commissioner for Transport in respect of registration and licensing of vehicles, issue of hire car permits and passenger service licences, and designation of car testing centres.

The Director of Highways heads the Highways Department, which is responsible for designing and building all highways, their repair and maintenance, and also for studying new railway networks.

Planning

The Updating of the Second Comprehensive Transport Study has been finalised. It provides a territorial transport infrastructure development strategy up to 2011, taking account of the port and airport projects. Key findings from this exercise have been fed into the Railway Development Study, commissioned to establish a long term railway development programme, and the Freight Transport Study. Apart from these studies, a Travel Characteristics Survey was carried out to obtain trip-making and socio-economic data from households as an aid to forward planning of transport infrastructure and services.

Construction works on some of the airport core programme projects, such as Tsing Ma Bridge and North Lantau Expressway, have commenced and works on other projects are progressing to ensure completion in time for the opening of the new airport. A study is being planned to examine the transport and traffic requirements of the new airport, with the focus on transport links with other parts of the territory. The study will also examine the impact of the westward emphasis of the new airport and the airport-related highways projects on the existing transport patterns.

Cross-Border Traffic

There are three road crossing points between Hong Kong and China at Sha Tau Kok, Man Kam To and Lok Ma Chau. Total capacity of the three crossings is about 30 000 vehicles per day. Starting from July 1, 1992, the opening time of the crossings was advanced by half an hour to 7 am, and the closing time at the Man Kam To Crossing was extended by two hours to 10 pm for goods vehicles. Commencing December 1, 1992, the closing time at Lok Ma Chau was also extended to 10 pm.

Cross-border vehicular traffic increased by about 12 per cent during the year compared with 1991. The increase mainly occurred at Lok Ma Chau. The average daily traffic figures at the three crossing points in 1992 were about 1 800, 9 700 and 6 300 at Sha Tau Kok, Man Kam To and Lok Ma Chau respectively. Goods vehicles accounted for 95 per cent of the traffic reflecting the rapid growth in trade and industrial links with China. At the end of the year, 23 companies operated tourist coach services across the border.

The Kowloon-Canton Railway continued to play an important role in the freight and passenger traffic between Hong Kong and China. Some 2.81 million tonnes (revenue tonnes) of freight (1991: 3.18 million tonnes) and 1.9 million head of livestock (1991: 1.9 million) were brought into Hong Kong by rail. Exports to China by rail accounted for 1.18 million revenue tonnes, an increase of 12 per cent from the 1.05 million tonnes carried in 1991. Cross-border passenger traffic on the railway was 38 million in 1992 (1991: 34 million). A further extension of the terminal building at Lo Wu is being constructed to cope with growth in rail traffic. The project is scheduled for completion in early 1995.

In 1992, ferry services between Hong Kong and China carried 5.1 million passengers (4.3 million in 1991). At the end of the year, there were 26 ferry routes between Hong Kong and China operated by eight companies. The China Ferry Terminal in Canton Road has sufficient capacity to meet demand beyond the turn of the century.

The opening of the Shenzhen Airport in October 1991 provided a further impetus to the growth of cross-border traffic. There are now coach and ferry services between the airport and Hong Kong. These new services are expected to continue to expand and to further utilise the spare capacity at the Lok Ma Chau Crossing and the Hong Kong China Ferry Terminal.

Construction of Phase I of the Guangzhou–Shenzhen–Zhuhai Superhighway linking Guangzhou and Huanggang started in January 1992. When completed, it will further increase cross-border traffic, particularly through Lok Ma Chau.

Road Network

Hong Kong's roads have one of the highest vehicle densities in the world. At the end of 1992, there were 414 638 licensed vehicles and about 1 559 kilometres of roads – 415 on Hong Kong Island, 392 in Kowloon and 752 in the New Territories. This high vehicle density, combined with the difficult terrain and dense building development, poses a constant challenge to transport planning, road construction and maintenance. There are eight major road tunnels, over 762 flyovers and bridges, 426 footbridges and 239 subways to assist the mobility of vehicles and people.

To cope with the ever-increasing transport demands, the Highways Department has continued an extensive construction programme, with about 50 road projects under construction and a similar number being actively planned at any one time.

Expenditure on highway construction was about $2,393 million, while another $613 million was spent on improving and maintaining existing roads.

Strategic Road Network

The spine of the strategic road network is Route 1, which runs from Aberdeen on the southern shore of Hong Kong Island and cuts through Kowloon peninsula and the New Territories to the Lok Ma Chau border crossing point.

On Hong Kong Island, Route 8 runs along the northern shore from the Cross-Harbour Tunnel via the Island Eastern Corridor to Shau Kei Wan and Chai Wan in the east. Route 7 stretches westwards from the Cross-Harbour Tunnel along the northern shore, via Gloucester Road, Harcourt Road and Connaught Road to Hill Road at Kennedy Town.

On the mainland, Route 2 runs from the Kowloon Bay Reclamation, through the Airport Tunnel, via the East and West Kowloon Corridors, Tsuen Wan Road, Tuen Mun Road and Yuen Long Northern Bypass to the junction of Castle Peak Road and Lok Ma Chau Border Link Road. Route 4 runs along the base of the foothills separating Kowloon from the New Territories and connects Lai Chi Kok with Kwun Tong and further with Tseung Kwan O through the Tseung Kwan O Tunnel. Route 5, another strategic road, is a seven-kilometre two-way trunk road connecting Sha Tin with Tsuen Wan via the Shing Mun Tunnels. It forms part of the New Territories Circular Road System.

The Eastern Harbour Crossing, which forms part of Route 6, opened in September 1989. The remaining sections of Route 6 including Kwun Tong Bypass, Tate's Cairn Tunnel and the approach road linking Tate's Cairn Tunnel to Tolo Highway were all completed in June 1991.

Improvements to Major Road Networks

In the north New Territories, remaining sections of the New Territories Circular Road from Pak Shek Au to Au Tau are being constructed in stages. Phase III between Fairview Park and Mai Po was opened in August 1991 and the remaining Phase IV from Fairview Park to Au Tau will be completed in early 1993.

The Yuen Long to Tuen Mun Eastern Corridor is under construction in the north-west New Territories for completion in mid 1993 to provide an eastern continuation of Route 2. This corridor is a dual two lane trunk road along the eastern side of Castle Peak Road to connect with the Yuen Long Southern Bypass, construction of which started in early 1992 and is scheduled for completion in late 1994.

To improve cross-border traffic and relieve access to the north-west New Territories, the Country Park section of Route 3 is under planning for completion by late 1990s. It will be a dual three-lane carriageway connecting Ting Kau with Yuen Long. Consideration is being given to privatising this project.

215

New Airport Access

The relocation of the airport to Chek Lap Kok requires additional road links to serve the new airport and its supporting community. The major highway projects to cater for airport traffic include the Western Harbour Crossing, West Kowloon Expressway, Kwai Chung and Tsing Yi sections of Route 3, the Lantau Fixed Crossing and the North Lantau Expressway.

The Western Harbour Crossing will be a tunnel constructed by a private sector franchisee under a 'build, operate and transfer' arrangement with dual three-lane capacity connecting the western end of Hong Kong Island with the West Kowloon Reclamation. Construction is planned to start in mid-1993. Upon its completion in mid-1997, it will also help to relieve congestion of the existing cross harbour tunnels.

The West Kowloon Expressway will link the northern portal of Western Harbour Crossing to Lai Chi Kok, forming an important part of Route 3. It will be a dual three-lane carriageway which will serve the West Kowloon Reclamation and will substantially relieve the local and distributor roads in central and west Kowloon. Connecting Kwai Chung with the Lantau Fixed Crossing, the Tsing Yi section of Route 3 will be a dual three-lane carriageway extending into a dual four-lane viaduct in Kwai Chung to cope with the high traffic volume. Construction for this section of Route 3 is expected to start in 1993.

The Lantau Fixed Crossing will comprise the Kap Shui Mun Bridge linking north-east Lantau to Ma Wan and the Tsing Ma Bridge across the Ma Wan Channel. The latter, in the form of a suspension bridge with a main span of about 1.4 kilometres, will be one of the longest of its kind in the world and will become a prominent landmark in Hong Kong. The construction of Tsing Ma Bridge commenced in May 1992 for completion in mid-1997. Construction of the Kap Shui Mun Bridge, with a main central span of 430 metres, will be completed at the same time. The crossing will provide a road and rail link with Lantau Island. The North Lantau Expressway will be a 12.5-kilometre dual three-lane carriageway along the northern coast of Lantau linking the Lantau Fixed Crossing to the new airport at Chek Lap Kok. The construction of the expressway is in three sections. Work on the first two sections at Tai Ho and Yam O started in June and October 1992.

The Airport Core Programme also includes a rail link which will provide both a fast and efficient train service to the new airport and a domestic service to bring relief to the Nathan Road Corridor of the Mass Transit Railway, serve new developments on the West Kowloon Reclamation and the Tung Chung New Town, and provide a third cross harbour rail link.

Environmental Impact of Road Construction

The environmental impact of new road projects is carefully appraised at the planning stage by the Highways Department. Where practical, measures such as landscaping works, artificial contouring of surrounding hillsides and installation of noise barriers are considered. Pre-cast decorative concrete panels applied to the retaining wall of the Gascoigne Road Flyover project and the enclosed-type noise barrier for the section of the Tate's Cairn Tunnel approach roads near Richland Gardens in Kowloon Bay are two good examples. Where necessary, consideration is also given to providing air-conditioning units and double glazing in domestic premises where noise levels cannot be brought within the required standard by other means.

Road Opening Works

Besides serving as carriageways for vehicles and pedestrians, the highways also provide space to install various utility services, such as water mains, sewers and electric and telephone cables. To cope with the demand resulting from the rapid development in Hong Kong, utility companies often have to excavate the carriageways and footways to maintain services by renewal, repair, and enlargement of pipes, cables and ducts. On average 160 new road openings are started every working day. These are co-ordinated and controlled by the Highways Department through a permit system, under which utility companies are required to carry out works to a required standard and in a limited period of time. In order to co-ordinate these works and to minimise disruption, the department holds monthly Road Opening Co-ordinating Committee meetings with the utility companies, police and the Transport Department.

Tunnels

The Lion Rock Tunnel, which links Kowloon and Sha Tin, began single tube operation in 1967 with a second tube added in 1978. At a flat toll of $6 per vehicle, it is the most heavily-used government tunnel. It was used by 77 000 vehicles a day in 1992.

The Aberdeen Tunnel was opened in 1982. It links the north and south sides of Hong Kong Island, with a daily traffic volume of 50 000 vehicles. This government owned tunnel is operated and managed by a private tunnel company under a management contract for three years. The toll is $5.

The Shing Mun Tunnels, opened to traffic in 1990, link Sha Tin to Tsuen Wan. The average daily traffic, which has increased steadily since opening, was 40 000 vehicles in 1992. The toll is $5.

The Tseung Kwan O Tunnel was opened in late 1990. Linking Kowloon to Tseung Kwan O New Town, it was used by 14 000 vehicles daily, charging a $3 toll per vehicle. From July 1, 1992, the operation hours of the tunnel were extended to operate between 7 am and midnight. The tunnel opened for 24 hours per day from January 1993.

The toll-free Airport Tunnel provides direct road access from Hung Hom to Hong Kong International Airport, and also passes underneath the airport runway to Kowloon Bay. Opened in 1982, it was used by an average of 53 000 vehicles per day in 1992.

Similar to Aberdeen Tunnel, the management of the Lion Rock Tunnel, Airport Tunnel, Shing Mun Tunnels and Tseung Kwan O Tunnel have been contracted out by the Government to the private sector with effect from January 1993. Toll charges remain under government control.

The Cross Harbour Tunnel, opened in 1972, connects Causeway Bay on Hong Kong Island and Hung Hom in Kowloon. Used by an average of 120 000 vehicles each day in 1992, it is one of the world's busiest four-lane road tunnels. Tolls now range from $4 to $30, including a government passage tax.

The Eastern Harbour Crossing is the second cross-harbour road tunnel. Opened in September 1989, it links Quarry Bay on Hong Kong Island and Cha Kwo Ling in Kowloon. It is connected by an elevated section of Route 6 to the Kowloon portal of Tate's Cairn Tunnel. By the end of 1992, traffic in this tunnel averaged 70 000 vehicles per day. Tolls now range from $5 to $30.

The Tate's Cairn Tunnel was opened to traffic in June 1991, to provide an additional direct road link between the north-east New Territories and Kowloon. The tunnel

217

measures four kilometres from portal to portal and is the longest road tunnel in the territory. The daily throughput at the Tate's Cairn Tunnel has been increasing steadily. I carried 70 000 vehicles a day at the end of 1992. Tolls now range from $4 to $8.

The Cross Harbour Tunnel, the Eastern Harbour Crossing and Tate's Cairn Tunnel were all built by private sector franchisees under 'build, operate and transfer' arrangements.

Traffic Management and Control

At the end of the year, there were about 1 060 signalised junctions in the Territory comprising 430 in Kowloon, 270 on Hong Kong Island and 360 in the New Territories.

In Kowloon, the operation of about 350 signalised junctions was under the control of the existing Kowloon Area Traffic Control (ATC) System, which has been in operation for more than 15 years. Due to its now obsolete technology and limited capacity, it is difficult to maintain and expand the system. Work to replace it with a modern system with adequate capacity commenced in early 1992, and the new system using a traffic responsive control technique will be commissioned in 1995. At that time, all the signalised junctions in the Kowloon peninsula will be controlled by the new system.

On Hong Kong Island, the operation of all the signalised junctions on the northern shore from Kennedy Town to Shau Kei Wan is under the control of the Hong Kong ATC System. The expansion of the system to the Mid-Levels area was substantially completed during the year. In total, about 220 junctions on Hong Kong Island were under ATC control.

Implementation works for the traffic monitoring Closed Circuit Television (CCTV) System for Hong Kong Island were completed during the year at a project cost of $18 million. Under the scheme, 35 roadside cameras were commissioned.

As the first step to extend ATC to the new towns, a contract for the installation of a new ATC System for the Tsuen Wan New Town was awarded together with the Kowloon ATC renewal contract. Initially, an interim system providing basic ATC facilities will be commissioned in 1993 controlling some 85 junctions in Tsuen Wan, Kwai Chung and Tsing Yi. The final system providing traffic responsive control will be completed in 1995. The ATC system will also be supplemented by a traffic monitoring CCTV system. When this system is commissioned in 1995, it will have about 20 roadside cameras.

Following Tsuen Wan New Town, ATC will be extended to Shatin New Town, and planning has already started for implementation of the scheme by 1996.

Parking

The government owns 14 multi-storey car parks which provide 8 200 parking spaces. They are operated and managed by a private company under a management contract. Off-street public parking is also provided by the Civil Aviation Department at Hong Kong International Airport and by the Kowloon-Canton Railway Corporation at its terminus. The private sector also operates multi-storey and open-air public car parks in commercial buildings, housing estates and open-air lots providing over 50 000 parking spaces. On-street parking is usually metered and provided at locations where traffic conditions permit. By the end of the year, there were 13 000 metered spaces throughout the territory, most of which operate between 8 am and midnight from Monday to Saturday. In Causeway Bay, Happy Valley and Tsim Sha Tsui, where parking demand is high, operation has been extended to include Sundays and public holidays to facilitate a better turnover of parking spaces.

Licensing

The number of new private cars registered increased from 31 131 in 1991 to 41 878 in 1992, an increase of 34.52 per cent. Despite the use of financial restraint measures which include increasing the First Registration Tax of new private cars from a range of 80 per cent to 100 per cent to 90 per cent to 120 per cent of the cars' Cost Insurance Freightage values on March 6, 1991, the total number of licensed cars in December 1992 was 237 035, a growth of 11.80 per cent over the figure in December 1991.

The total number of registered goods vehicles in December 1992 was 140 491, an increase of 6 462 or 4.82 per cent compared with the total of 134 029 in December 1991. Included in these were 105 606 light goods vehicles which grew by 2.36 per cent compared with 1991. In line with the policy to restrain the ownership and use of this class of vehicles, the First Registration Tax and annual licensing fees of van-type light goods vehicles were increased by 50 per cent and 90 per cent and $4,140 and $2,115 respectively. This has had the effect of reducing the number of light goods vehicles but slightly increasing the number of medium goods vehicles. By the end of December, the number of licensed light goods vehicles stood at 88 432, a decrease of 1.34 per cent over the same period in 1991. Meanwhile, the number of medium goods vehicles increased by 9.78 per cent to 30 006 by end-1992.

At the end of the year, the total number of licensed vehicles in all classes was 407 858, an increase of 7.42 per cent over 1991.

At the end of 1992, there were 961 235 licensed drivers; an increase of 5.95 per cent over the numbers in 1990. The number of new learner-drivers increased from 5 946 per month in 1991 to 6 164 per month in 1992.

Since the introduction of the Driving Offence Points System in 1984, 16 918 drivers have been disqualified. A total of 201 091 warning notices have been served and 355 020 drivers have incurred penalty points for committing offences scheduled under the Road Traffic (Driving-Offence Points) Ordinance. The figures for 1992 were 4 767, 38 225 and 30 446 respectively.

Vehicle Examination

During 1992 there were major changes to vehicle inspection in the Territory. In June, the management and operation of New Kowloon Bay Centre was taken over by a Government contractor who had been awarded a three-year contract following a competitive tendering exercise.

With effect from August 1, 1992, it became necessary for all light goods vehicles manufactured before 1989 to be inspected annually, while all medium and heavy goods vehicles made before 1987 also required inspection from the same date. This is an important step in ensuring the road worthiness of commercial vehicles.

Private cars over six years old continued to be inspected at the 17 designated car testing centres operated by the private sector, as were goods vehicles with a gross vehicle weight under 1.9 tonnes over three years old. In 1992, 87 913 cars and 6 628 light goods vehicles were inspected at car testing centres, while a further seven centres were added to the scheme during 1992.

All public transport vehicles continued to be inspected annually, while the random inspection of in-service franchised buses was increased slightly.

Changes to the vehicle emission controls came into effect on January 1 and resulted in approval being given for many new models of private car designed to use unleaded petrol only.

Road Safety

Traffic accidents involving injury decreased by 0.1 per cent in 1992. During the year there were 15 310 accidents, of which 3 439 were serious and 316 fatal. This compares with 15 327 in 1991 (3 561 serious, 300 fatal). In-depth investigations were carried out at 114 traffic accident blackspots in order to identify accident causes. Remedial accident prevention measures were recommended at 89 of these locations. These measures, when implemented, have been shown to reduce accidents by 30 per cent on average. Accident statistics are at Appendix 39.

Road safety campaigns continued to play an important role in reducing traffic accidents. The major themes of 1992 campaigns were adult pedestrian safety, particularly for the elderly, and promoting road safety for drivers, especially light goods vehicle drivers and motorcyclists. Posters, television announcements and leaflets were produced and widely distributed. To convey road safety messages to mass audiences, a series of radio and television road safety programmes were broadcast. A set of 'dos' and 'don'ts' which aim to convey simple rules to motorists and pedestrians was publicised through various established channels such as the Road Safety Quarterly and district functions organised by the police. A road safety jingle was composed and broadcast on radio. A road safety campaign targeted at kindergarten children was launched in mid-1992.

The new microcomputer-based traffic accident data system has been in use since 1991. Accident records are updated daily. Accident statistics and map plots for traffic accident blackspot analysis and road safety strategy formulation are retrieved, compiled and analysed as a basis for instituting road safety improvements.

By the end of 1992, the Road Safety Association of Hong Kong operated 640 school road safety patrols and school staff patrols operated at 627 schools, all with the objective of ensuring the safety of school children on their way to and from school. The Road Safety Council, an advisory body, continued to co-ordinate all road safety matters in the territory.

Public Transport

The Hong Kong public transport system is notable for its variety of modes and operators, its intensity of usage, and the absence of Government subsidies. A network of rail, ferry, bus and other road services extends to almost every part of the territory.

Railways

There are five rail systems, comprising a heavily-utilised underground/elevated mass transit system, a busy suburban railway, a modern light railway, a traditional street tramway and the Peak funicular railway. The first three rail systems are operated by public corporations, wholly owned by Government. The other two are owned by the private sector.

Mass Transit Railway

The Mass Transit Railway Corporation (MTRC) operates a three-line metro system comprising 43 route-kilometres with 38 stations served by a fleet of 671 cars operating in eight car trains. The system was opened in stages between October 1979 and August 1989. Trains run at two-minute intervals in the morning peak period on the Tsuen Wan line, and every two and a quarter minutes on the Kwun Tong and Island lines. In the evening peak period, trains run every two and a quarter minutes on the Tsuen Wan line and every two and a half minutes on the other two lines. A four-minute headway prevails on all three lines during the daytime off-peak period.

Patronage increased slightly during the year, and by the year's end the railway was carrying 2.05 million passengers a day. In relation to the length of the system it is the second busiest underground railway in the world. Adult fares range from $3 to $8.5 per trip according to distance travelled.

A plan for the construction and financing the Airport Railway is in hand. This new railway, when built, will consist of two separate rail services: a dedicated express service linking Chek Lap Kok Airport to Central, with stations at the airport, Tsing Yi, West Kowloon and Central and a domestic service between Tung Chung and Central with stations at Tung Chung, Tsing Yi, Lai King, Tai Kok Tsui, West Kowloon and Central. The domestic service will interchange with the Tsuen Wan line of the existing MTR system at Lai King and the Island Line at Central, thus bringing relief to the MTR Nathan Road corridor.

Kowloon-Canton Railway

The Kowloon-Canton Railway was opened in 1910 and was double-tracked and electrified in the early 1980s. Formerly a government department, it was vested in the Kowloon-Canton Railway Corporation (KCRC) in February 1982.

Although the 34-kilometre railway caters for freight trains to and from China, for four daily passenger through trains each way between Kowloon and Guangzhou and since January 8, 1993 two daily passenger through trains each way between Kowloon and Foshan, it principally provides a suburban service to the new towns of the north-eastern New Territories. This traffic has grown substantially throughout the period since the first electric trains were introduced in 1982, and by the end of 1992 the railway handled 561 600 passenger journeys daily. Peak period average headways range from five minutes at the northern end of the line to almost every three minutes between Fo Tan and Kowloon. Passenger traffic is carried in a fleet of 351 cars operated in train formations of 12 cars. There are 13 stations along the railway. A major programme to replace old escalators and install additional ones began in 1991 and continued throughout the year.

Freight is handled by about 12 trains each way daily, which hauled 2.8 million revenue tonnes of inbound freight and 1.2 million tonnes of outbound freight in 1992. There are five goods yards at Hung Hom, Ho Man Tin, Mong Kok, Sha Tin and Fo Tan, and a marshalling yard at Lo Wu. Freight trains are hauled by a fleet of 12 diesel locomotives. In addition, a Hung Hom–Daleng railway container shuffle service was commissioned on December 7, 1992.

Light Rail Transit

In addition to its main line, the KCRC owns and operates the 30.7-kilometre Light Rail Transit (LRT) system in the north-western New Territories which commenced operation in September 1988. An extension was opened on November 3, 1991, between Tuen Mun Ferry Pier and Yau Oi Estate. Two other extensions, to north-east Tuen Mun and San Shing, were commissioned on February 2, 1992. The extensions increased the number of stops served by the system from 41 to 51. Six services are provided on the network by a fleet of 85 cars which operate either singly or in pairs. By the end of the year, 314 100 boardings a day were handled on the LRT and on its feeder bus services, which are also operated by the KCRC within the transit service area extending from Tuen Mun to Yuen Long. The LRT operates with zonal fares providing free transfers from one route to another within the zone and to and from feeder buses. Ordinary adult fares range from $2.7 to $3.9.

An extension to the new town of Tin Shui Wai was commissioned on February 10, 1993. Delivery of an additional batch of 30 cars started in September 1992, and is scheduled for completion before mid-1993.

Tramways

Electric trams have operated on Hong Kong Island since 1904. Today, Hongkong Tramways Limited operates six overlapping services over 13 kilometres of double track along the north shore of Hong Kong Island between Kennedy Town and Shau Kei Wan and along nearly three kilometres of single line around Happy Valley. The 163 trams including two open-balcony trams for tourists and private hire, comprise the only all-double-deck tram fleet in the world. All trams had been re-bodied by 1991. Tramway patronage rose marginally during 1992, with an average of 338 000 boardings daily. Fares remained at $1 for adults and $0.5 for children.

Funicular

Hong Kong's other 'tramway' is actually a cable-hauled funicular railway operated by the Peak Tramways Company from Central (Garden Road) to the Peak (Victoria Gap). The 1.4 kilometre line began operation in 1888 and climbs 373 metres on gradients as steep as one-in-two. The line was modernised in August 1989. The service caters largely for sightseers but also serves Peak district commuters. The line serves an average 8 925 passengers a day. One-way fares for adults and children are $10 and $4 respectively.

Road Passenger Transport

Road passenger transport accounted for two-thirds of all public transport journeys. Of the journeys made by road, over half were on franchised buses, with the remainder handled by non-franchised buses, green minibuses, public light buses and taxis.

Franchised Buses

The standard and capacity of franchised bus services continued to improve through effective planning and co-ordination. There are four franchised bus companies which together carried 3.4 million passenger boardings daily on a network of 434 regular routes.

The largest bus operator is the Kowloon Motor Bus Company (1933) Limited (KMB), which ran 266 bus routes in Kowloon and the New Territories in addition to 33 cross-harbour routes operated jointly with the China Motor Bus Company (CMB) and two cross-harbour routes of its own. During the year, the quality of services provided by KMB was upgraded by introducing 16 air-conditioned bus routes. KMB also operates 'Airbus' services to and from the airport, comprising three routes to Hong Kong Island and one within Kowloon.

The KMB fleet at the end of the year comprised 3 121 registered vehicles, including 2 610 double-deck conventional buses and 241 and 270 air-conditioned double and single deck buses respectively. Their capacities range from 24 to 164 places. In 1992, KMB made 970 million passenger trips and operated 234 million vehicle-kilometres, compared with 973 million passenger trips and 217 million vehicle-kilometres in 1991. KMB's current franchise extends until August 31, 1997. Fares ranged from $0.50 to $8.50 for non air-conditioned and from $1.20 to $15.0 for air-conditioned services.

To attract commuters who might otherwise have used and overloaded the busy section of the Mass Transit Railway (MTR) along Nathan Road, eight new air-conditioned bus routes were introduced in 1992, offering express services from Tsuen Wan, Tsing Yi, Yuen Long and Tai Po to Tsim Sha Tsui in Kowloon. In addition, five new cross harbour routes from Kowloon, Lei Muk Shue, Kwai Tsing and Ma On Shan to Hong Kong Island were put into operation in the summer. The provision of such services helped keep the MTR passenger flows along Nathan Road within acceptable levels.

Bus services on Hong Kong Island are provided by the China Motor Bus Company (CMB), which operated 97 Island routes and, jointly with KMB, 33 cross-harbour routes. At the end of 1992, CMB's fleet comprised 1 004 double-deckers and 23 single-deckers, of which 61 and 22 respectively were are air-conditioned. They made 263 million passenger trips and travelled 52 million vehicle-kilometres during the year compared with 266 million and 52 million respectively in 1991. During the year, CMB purchased 20 air-conditioned double-deckers and four air-conditioned single-deckers for improving services. Fares ranged from $1.60 to $15. The company's franchise extends until August 31, 1995 but 26 of its existing routes are to be withdrawn from its network in 1993.

The New Lantao Bus Company (1973) Limited (NLB) operates six regular and one recreational franchised routes on Lantau Island with a fleet of 61 single-deck and 15 double-deck buses. Most NLB services connect with the ferries at Mui Wo. Operational efficiency was improved in September 1991 by the opening of a new bus depot in Mui Wo. The average weekday ridership on NLB in 1992 was 8 680 passengers. Boosted by recreational traffic, average patronage on Sundays and public holidays was 18 470 passengers. Fares ranged from $1.1 to $19. To better meet peak recreational demand, NLB introduced in June 1991 a special service between Mui Wo and Po Lin Monastery, using air-conditioned coaches ferried to Lantau at weekends. In 1992, average patronage on this special service was 2 070 passengers per day.

The fourth franchised bus operator is Citybus Limited. This company had been running non-franchised bus services since 1979. In August 1991, it was awarded a franchise for a route between Central (Macau Ferry) and MacDonnell Road using nine buses on which a $4.50 fare was charged. This was the first franchised bus route awarded by competitive tender.

To promote healthy competition among transport services providers, 24 Hong Kong Island routes and two cross harbour tunnel routes with a total fleet requirement of 200 buses will be withdrawn from CMB's network upon the expiry of its current franchise on

223

August 31, 1993. Citybus Limited was awarded the franchise in September 1992 for these 26 routes to commence service on September 1, 1993 for a period of three years.

Minibuses

Hong Kong's minibuses are licensed to carry a maximum of 16 seated passengers. There were 6 900 minibuses in 1992. Of these, 4 350 were public light buses (PLB), and 2 550 private light buses. The PLBs are authorised to carry passengers at separate fares. The private light buses are authorised only to carry group passengers and the collection of separate fares is not permitted.

The operation of PLBs is regulated by a passenger service licence. There are two types of PLBs. Those in green livery provide services according to official schedules. In 1992, there were 1 468 of them operating on 214 approved routes, each with fixed fares and timetables. They carried 705 000 passengers a day. Red PLBs operate without a schedule. They do not have fixed routes, timetables and fares. In 1992, there were about 2 868 red PLBs which carried 1 016 000 passengers daily.

In line with government policy to convert more red PLBs to operate on scheduled routes, more new scheduled routes will be identified. In 1992, one green minibus selection exercise was conducted for application by minibus operators.

Taxis

The quota governing the maximum number of taxis that may be licensed in the urban area, the New Territories and Lantau, was reviewed in late 1991. During the year, no new licences for urban taxis were issued. At the end of 1992, there were 14 949 urban taxis, 2 731 New Territories taxis, and 40 Lantau taxis, carrying an average of 1 077 100, 188 500 and 1 050 daily passengers respectively.

The operating boundary of New Territories taxis was revised in 1992 to enable them to ply between the north-east and north-west New Territories via the Shing Mun Tunnels.

During the year, a working group was set up by the Transport Advisory Committee to review the government's policies on taxis. A public consultation exercise was launched by the Transport Advisory Committee in October 1992 to seek public views on various measures identified by the working group for the improvement of taxi services.

Non-Franchised Bus Operators

Residents' services were introduced in 1982 to give commuters an added choice. These services operate primarily during peak hours, supplementing services provided by the franchised bus operators. This helps keep down the number of franchised buses that would otherwise be left idle during off peak hours. Residents' organisations may request a non-franchised bus operator to apply for such a service, which requires a passenger service licence. Residents' services operate in accordance with approved schedules of service, which specify the routing, timetable and stopping places. A licence is normally valid for one year and may be renewed if there is a continuing need for the service.

At the end of the year, there were 79 residents' services running 70 000 passenger trips a day. Vehicles used on these services ranged from small coaches to double-deck buses. Sixteen residents' services were introduced during the year providing bus services from various residential areas mainly in the New Territories, the mid-levels and the southern part of Hong Kong Island.

Apart from residents' services, non-franchised bus operators also serve the needs of factory employees, tourists and students on a group hire basis. At the end of 1992, the licensed fleet of non-franchised buses totalled 4 011 vehicles, of which 288 were double-deckers. An increasing proportion of these vehicles were air-conditioned.

Ferries

Ferries remain a well-used mode for crossing the harbour. They also provide an important transport link to the new towns in north-west New Territories and are essential for travelling to Hong Kong's outlying islands. Existing services are provided largely by two franchised operators – Star Ferry Company Limited (SF) and the Hong Kong and Yaumati Ferry Company Limited (HYF).

SF operates 12 vessels across the harbour and, during the year, carried 35.8 million passengers on its three routes. Fares ranged from $1 to $1.5.

HYF owned 73 licensed vessels and operated 23 ferry routes, including passenger and vehicular services across the harbour, hoverferry services to north-west New Territories, services to the outlying islands and charter services. In 1992, the company carried 112 500 passengers and 6 600 vehicles daily. A cross-harbour trip cost $3.3 for a passenger and $4 for a private car. Fares for passenger services to the new towns range from $5 to $15 and the outlying islands from $4.50 to $23.

Fourteen other ferry services were operated by eight licensed operators, including the service to Discovery Bay, Lantau. These were supplemented by kaitos, or local village ferry services, which were licensed to serve remote coastal settlements. At the end of the year, 109 kaitos were in operation, run by 94 operators.

The Port of Hong Kong

Hong Kong is the largest container port in the world. In 1992 it handled almost eight million TEUs (20-foot equivalent units). It is also one of the busiest world ports in terms of vessel arrivals and cargo and passenger throughput. Some 146 000 ocean-going and river trade vessels arrive in Hong Kong annually, handling over 100 million tonnes of cargo, and 19 million international passengers, the majority of whom are carried on the world's largest fleet of high speed ferries operating to neighbouring China and Macau. Forecast growth in cargo (particularly containers) and passenger throughput have resulted in planning and development of new port facilities to meet a doubling of current demand by 2006.

With limited and diminishing water area to accommodate the current and forecast levels of port activity, marine safety and navigational efficiency are a major concern. To address these matters, the waters of Hong Kong are covered by a modern computer/radar Vessel Traffic System, run by the Marine Department of the Hong Kong Government. Its effectiveness, coupled with a comprehensive system of aids to navigation, fairways, marine traffic separation schemes, and harbour patrols, has contributed to Hong Kong's continuing low level of marine accidents by world standards.

Hong Kong is a prominent centre for ship owning, ship financing and ship management activities, and local ship owners and ship managers control a significant percentage of the world's tonnage. The territory operates the Hong Kong Shipping Register which reflects the government's long-term commitment to the highest international standards of maritime safety while recognising commercial realities.

The port as a whole is administered by the Marine Department, which is responsible for all aspects of Hong Kong's maritime affairs. The principal function of the department in relation to the port is to ensure that conditions exist for ships to enter port, work their cargoes and depart as quickly and safely as possible.

The Director of Marine is the Pilotage Authority and is advised by the Pilotage Advisory Committee. The authority has wide powers to regulate and control the pilotage service although the pilots themselves operate as a private company. Tugs are also privately owned and operated. Ships over 5 000 gross registered tonnes are required to engage pilots when moving within the port and its approaches.

Immigration and quarantine facilities for vessels calling at Hong Kong are available round the clock at the Western Quarantine Anchorage. At the Eastern Quarantine Anchorage, these services are available between 6 am and 6 pm daily and, in the case of the quarantine service, on request through the Vessel Traffic Centre of the Marine Department. These services, including advance clearance, may be applied for by radio.

The Marine Department provides and maintains 76 mooring buoys within the port for ships to work cargo in the stream. There are two classes of buoy suitable for vessels up to 137 and 183 metres in length respectively. The majority of these are typhoon moorings to which vessels may remain secured during tropical storms, thus reducing operational costs.

In 1992, some 146 000 ocean-going and river-trade vessels called at Hong Kong and loaded and discharged more than 100 million tonnes of cargo, of which 55 per cent was containerised. This included 60 million tonnes of general goods from ocean-going vessels.

A variety of harbour craft play a significant role in the efficient running of the port. During the year over 1 800 lighters and 280 motorised cargo boats transported cargo to and from ocean-going ships in the anchorages and at buoys in the harbour, and private or public cargo working areas ashore. These are part of Hong Kong's 20 000 local vessels which include ferries, barges, fishing boats and pleasure vessels.

The port handled 7.97 million TEUs in 1992. Of these, about 67 per cent or 5.08 million TEUs were handled at Terminals 1 to 7 of the Kwai Chung Container Port, and another 33 per cent or 2.54 million TEUs from vessels in the stream. Expansion of container terminal facilities continued apace, with construction of the four berth Terminal 8 well advanced. This new terminal, with a capacity of 1.6 million TEUs, is being formed by reclamation at the north-western part of Stonecutters Island. Its first berth is scheduled to come into operation in 1993. Planning for the construction of Terminal 9 is progressing well with the first berth required in 1995.

The port has served Hong Kong's needs well. But it will not be able to cope in its present form if the growth in traffic volume experienced over the past decade continues as anticipated. Thus, plans are well advanced for major developments which, when completed, will more than double the port's capacity by 2006. The principal features are to develop container terminals together with other marine facilities on Tsing Chau Tsai peninsula on Lantau Island over the next decade. (See Chapter 17)

The government has always taken the view that it generally should not undertake activities which can be done commercially, and often more efficiently, by the private sector. In many ways Hong Kong leads the world in this respect and the port is an excellent example. Most of the port facilities, such as the container terminals and dockyards, are privately built, owned and operated.

Consultation to reach consensus with the users and operators of port facilities has always been an important factor in Hong Kong's economic success. The private sector is fully represented on important committees which advise the government on port policy, operations and land-related issues relevant to container terminals. The massive and diverse development of the port over the next decade will require wide and detailed consultation on all aspects of port planning. A Port Development Board was established in 1990 for this purpose. The Port Operations Committee, which was re-organised in 1992, advises the Director of Marine on the operational needs of the port. Membership of the board and committee is drawn from a cross-section of shipping, government, commercial and port user interests.

Shipping Services

Passenger throughput at the ferry terminals managed by the Marine Department is also on the increase. In 1992, the China Ferry Terminal in Tsim Sha Tsui and the Macau Ferry Terminal in Central handled a total of 19.3 million passengers on routes to China and Macau of which 14.1 million used the Macau service and 5.2 million the China services. This throughput represented an increase of 7.8 per cent over 1991.

The implementation of the computer/radar Vessel Traffic System has been completed. This now plays a vital role in the monitoring of shipping movements in Hong Kong waters with the aims of enhancing safety and navigation efficiency. Participation in the system is compulsory in that vessels are obliged to respond to the Vessel Traffic Centre of the Marine Department for information requested, and to follow the advice or instructions given.

The department's launches patrol the main harbour area and its approaches. They are in continuous radio contact with the Vessel Traffic Centre, thereby enabling them to respond to any emergency and fulfil the centre's executive functions. Well-equipped fleets of fire boats, tugs, oil-pollution control vessels and marine police launches are also available to respond to emergencies in the harbour.

The full fleet of about 375 powered vessels maintained by the Marine Department is a highly visible part of the port. In addition to harbour patrol launches, fire boats and police vessels, the government has launches used for immigration, port health and customs clearance of international shipping and for the survey of international shipping. The fleet also comprises lighters, airport rescue craft, floating clinics and launches for transporting government staff. The department also maintains scavenging craft together with a contracted fleet of other vessels who together collect and scavenge some 5 900 tonnes of refuse annually from ocean-going ships and Hong Kong waters.

All government vessels are specially designed to meet their users' needs. The Marine Department designs and procures new vessels, maintains the whole fleet, and mans and operates about 70 general purpose craft. In 1991, the government awarded a $300-million contract to an Australian shipbuilder for the construction of six police patrol/command launches. The first two were delivered during 1992.

Bunkering facilities within the port are readily available to all vessels at commercial wharves and oil terminals, or from a large fleet of private bunkering barges. Fresh water can also be provided alongside berths, or from a private fleet of fresh-water boats.

The port has extensive facilities for repairing, dry-docking and slipping all types of vessels, including oil rigs. Vessels of up to 150 000 deadweight tonnes can be accommodated. A large number of other shipyards are available to undertake repairs to small vessels and build and maintain sophisticated patrol craft and pleasure vessels.

During the year, the government, through the Marine Department, Customs and Excise Department, and the Marine Police, introduced further measures to combat the increasing number of smuggling incidents involving pleasure vessels exporting goods to China. As a direct result of the measures taken, this illegal activity has been substantially reduced.

Hong Kong's economic success has resulted in constant growth of the territory's international trade. This has led to the large increase in the size and number of ships visiting the port, and the consequential demand for accurate and up-to-date hydrographic surveying and charting services. The Marine Department intends to establish its own hydrographic office to perform these functions in order to satisfy the identified needs of port users.

By international agreement, the Marine Department is the Maritime Search and Rescue Co-ordinator for the area of the South China Sea north of latitude 10°N and west of longitude 120°E, excluding the immediate coastal waters of neighbouring states. The Maritime Rescue Co-ordination Centre is manned continuously and monitors all the various emergency communications channels. A full search and rescue mission can be activated and run by fully-trained staff. Suitably equipped search and rescue vessels and aircraft are available and additional assistance can be obtained from other rescue co-ordination centres in the region. Radio communications equipment costing $20 million has been installed and is operated in the centre to facilitate full implementation of the Global Maritime Distress and Safety System.

Hong Kong is a prominent centre for ship owning, ship financing and ship management activities. Most local ship owners and connected businesses are represented by the Hong Kong Shipowners' Association, whose members control a significant percentage of the world's tonnage. At the end of 1992, the association members' fleet stood at 1 223 ocean-going vessels totalling 71.2 million deadweight tonnes or 40.1 million gross registered tonnage, of which 137 vessels representing 12.2 per cent of the gross registered tonnage, were registered in Hong Kong. The association is either a member of or works closely with all significant international maritime bodies to contribute and share in major developments concerning merchant shipping worldwide.

Statutory surveys of all Hong Kong-registered vessels are undertaken worldwide by Marine Department surveyors or authorised classification societies for the issue of certificates. These accord with international conventions relating to maritime safety, pollution prevention and crew accommodation promulgated by the International Maritime Organisation and the International Labour Organisation. United Kingdom and foreign ships visiting Hong Kong are also surveyed by Marine Department on request by their administrations.

During 1992, a total of 1 176 ships visiting the Port of Hong Kong were subjected to inspection to enforce international conventions. This represented about 25 per cent of ocean-going ships (which exclude river-trade coastal ships) which visited Hong Kong inspected under the International Convention on Standards of Training, Certification and Watchkeeping for Seafarers, and two per cent inspected under the International Convention for the Safety of Life at Sea and the International Convention for the Prevention of Pollution from Ships. Of this second group about 70 per cent required deficiencies to be made good before the ship could sail from Hong Kong.

Hong Kong has one of the world's largest fleets of sophisticated high speed passenger craft, comprising jetfoils, hydrofoils, sidewall hovercraft and catamarans. These dynamically-supported craft operate from Hong Kong to Macau and various ports in China. Safety is enhanced by the adoption of failure-mode effect analysis in analysing/ predicting shipboard system failures as part of the statutory requirements, supported by supervised crew training.

A plan-approval and survey service is also provided for local vessels. Those vessels plying within the waters of Hong Kong need to be licensed under the Shipping and Port Control Ordinance and are inspected and issued with certificates. A major review of the procedures and requirements for the certification of local craft is under way with the intention of developing a rationalised approach to the safety and control of the many disparate types of craft operating in Hong Kong. A free inspection and advice service is operated to promote safe working practices in ship repairing, ship breaking and cargo handling afloat.

The Marine Department conducts a wide range of examinations for persons requiring certificates of competency for service on vessels of all sizes and types operating in international and local waters. The department also monitors all aspects of training at approved establishments for the acquisition of various maritime qualifications recognised by the government and required by international conventions.

A major concern of the government and Hong Kong ship owners is the falling recruitment of local seafarers. Concerted efforts have been made by the Marine Department, Hong Kong Shipowners' Association, Merchant Navy Training Board, training institutions and seafarers' unions to stimulate the recruitment of trainee officers and to enhance the image of seafaring careers. The Hong Kong Shipowners' Association has agreed to sponsor 40 deck cadets at the Seamen's Training Centre and 30 engineering cadets for the three-year course at Hong Kong Polytechnic. By 1993, training courses currently offered by different educational institutes for seafarers will be provided centrally by the Vocational Training Council.

The Marine Department's Seamen's Recruiting Office and the Mercantile Marine Office register supervise the employment of about 2 800 active seafarers on board some 680 ships of various flags. Considerable attention has been given to providing more comprehensive training for Hong Kong seafarers. The Seamen's Training Centre provides training courses for new entrants and in-service training for seamen to comply with the requirements of the International Convention on Standards of Training, Certification and Watchkeeping for Seafarers, 1978.

Details of International Movements of Vessels, Passengers and Cargo are given at Appendix 37.

Hong Kong Shipping Register

The Hong Kong Shipping Register, which came into operation under local legislation in December 1990, reflects the government's commitment to the highest international standards of maritime safety while recognising commercial realities. Its supporting legislation embodies internationally-based standards for vessel construction, equipment and manning and is consistent with Hong Kong's obligations under International Maritime Organisation and International Labour Organisation conventions, including those on safety of life at sea, training and certification of crew, and protection of the marine environment. Administered by the Marine Department, the register had a total fleet amounting to 7.2 million gross registered tonnage at the end of 1992.

Hong Kong is independently represented as an Associate Member of the International Maritime Organisation and, in accordance with the Sino-British Joint Declaration, this status will continue after 1997. During the year Hong Kong played host to an IMO working group involved in revising the Code of Safety for Dynamically Supported Craft. This is one area in which Hong Kong has made a considerable contribution to the IMO's work. Others include the development of the Protocol to the 1997 International Convention for the Safety of Fishing Vessels and initiating work on international eyesight standards.

Civil Aviation
The year saw the resumption of strong growth both in passenger and cargo throughput at the airport, following a moderate growth period in 1991 due to the Gulf War and the worldwide economic slowdown. A total of 22.1 million passengers passed through the terminal, an increase of 15.3 per cent over the total of 19.2 million in the previous year. A total of 956 896 tonnes of cargo, valued at $332 654 million, were handled, compared with 849 786 tonnes of air cargo valued at $282 635 million in 1991. Air transport continued to play an important role in Hong Kong's external trade. Of Hong Kong's total trade in imports, exports and re-exports, air transport took about 18 per cent, 30 per cent and 13 per cent in value terms respectively. The USA remained the major market for exports and re-exports by air, accounting for 37 per cent and 23 per cent respectively.

In 1992, an increase of 10.3 per cent in aircraft movements was recorded, bringing the annual total to 120 999 of which 76 per cent were wide-bodied aircraft.

The programme of improvements at Kai Tak started in 1988 and is expected to be completed by the end of 1993. It is aimed at enabling the airport to meet continuing high growth in passenger and cargo throughput until the commissioning of the new airport at Chek Lap Kok, off the north coast of Lantau Island. (See Chapter 16)

In March, facilities within the passenger terminal were reconfigured and an additional passenger handling facility was brought into operation to cope with the continued growth in passengers transiting through Hong Kong, particularly passengers from Taiwan transferring to flights to the People's Republic of China. Furthermore, a second interline baggage handling facility was commissioned. A mechanised system for the recovery of self-help trolleys was put into operation to increase the efficiency of trolley retrieval from the transport terminus back to the baggage reclaim hall.

In August, the refurbishment of the older part of the passenger terminal building, costing $283 million, was completed. Passengers can now enjoy both a more attractive environment and more efficient facilities on their arrival and departure through the building.

Other improvements made within the passenger terminal building include the installation of two additional flight information display boards and the commissioning of a new Cathay Pacific Airways airside first class lounge. The latter facilitated a reorganisation of the available lounge space to optimise use of its existing area.

Several schemes to improve transport facilities and road access to the airport were also completed in 1992. They included improvements to Sung Wong Toi Road to facilitate traffic flow from the west; the realignment of the Eastern Road and the provision of a new roundabout at the eastern approach to the airport. The transport terminus was expanded to provide more space for waiting taxis and airport buses.

During the year, work also commenced on a number of new improvement projects including the widening of the departure pier area to relieve congestion in the airside departure lounge, and construction of an eight-bus dock to provide additional facilities to serve passengers transferring to aircraft positioned on outer bays. A contract was also signed in August to replace three pairs of passenger boarding bridges. Installation work is expected to start in May 1993 with completion in September.

In October, work started on resurfacing and regrooving the runway and is due to be completed in April 1993.

Efforts to increase aircraft parking capacity continued. Four additional parking bays for B747-sized aircraft, equipped with fixed ground power, refuelling facilities and floodlighting, were put into operation in November. Development of a further 11 parking bays on the Kowloon Bay Reclamation is on schedule. Completion of this new apron will be in phases in 1993 during which two new taxiway bridges will also be commissioned to provide a circular taxiway system linking this apron to the runway.

Installation of a computerised aircraft parking bay allocation system commenced in December. The system, when fully operational in June 1993, will maximise the utilisation of aircraft parking bays so that increased demand from traffic growth can be met.

Aside from physical developments, improvement to air traffic control facilities were also implemented. During the year the precision approach radar was replaced. Equipment installation and staff training took approximately two months to complete and the new radar was put into operation in November. Work on improvements to the existing radar system is continuing, with the approach surveillance radar and terminal area radar scheduled for replacement in mid-1993 and end-1994 respectively.

The Civil Aviation Department will be responsible for the provision of the air traffic control system for the new airport at Chek Lap Kok. Work on drawing up specifications for the various components of the system has already started with a view to calling tenders early in 1993.

To further enhance security arrangements at Kai Tak Airport all airlines have now complied with a requirement that all checked baggage of departing passengers be security screened by X-ray. To this end, all check-in desks at the passenger terminal have been equipped with modern X-ray equipment. Kai Tak Airport is now one of the few airports in the world where all departing passengers' checked baggage is security screened by X-ray.

As part of a continuing process of equipment updating, the Airport Fire Contingent took delivery of a replacement foam tender vehicle during the year. With the airport expanding into the South Apron another motorised inflatable rescue boat has been purchased. A contract for a further fire rescue vessel for delivery in early 1993 has also been concluded. This additional equipment will ensure adequate fire and rescue cover within the water area between the runway promontory and the South Apron.

Hong Kong is home to three airlines. During the year, Cathay Pacific Airways (CPA), the largest of the three, commenced scheduled all-cargo services to Los Angeles in July and scheduled passenger services to Adelaide and Cebu in October and December respectively. To cope with the increasing scale of its operations, CPA acquired three B747-400s and converted one of its B747-200 passenger aircraft into a freighter. At the end of 1992, its fleet comprised 18 L1011s, seven B747-200s, six B747-300s, 14 B747-400s and four B747-200 freighters, a total of 49 aircraft.

Hong Kong Dragon Airlines (Dragonair) continues to operate scheduled services to seven cities in China and four other cities in Asia with its five B737s and one L1011. In addition, the airline commenced scheduled services to Hiroshima in July. It also operates a number of non-scheduled passenger services to other cities in Asia, mostly in China and Japan.

Air Hong Kong (AHK) continues to operate scheduled all-cargo services to Manchester, Brussels, Nagoya and Ho Chi Minh City and non-scheduled cargo services to a number of destinations in Asia with its three B747F and one B707F aircraft. In October, the airline commenced scheduled all-cargo services to Singapore.

The year saw the introduction of scheduled air services to Hong Kong by Vietnam Airlines, Scandinavian Airlines System, Aeroflot and Tower Air. As a result, the number of scheduled airlines serving Hong Kong increased to 50. During the year, these airlines operated about 1 130 direct round trip services weekly between Hong Kong and some 92 other cities. In addition to the scheduled services, an average of 250 non-scheduled flights were operated by both scheduled and non-scheduled airlines each week.

In 1992, the Air Transport Licensing Authority granted five licences to Hong Kong Airlines, one to Cathay Pacific Airways, one to Dragonair and three to Air Hong Kong.

16
AIRPORT

FOR an externally orientated economy like Hong Kong, an efficient international airport plays a vital role. Efficient road and rail transport facilities are also essential, along with land for development. Without such basic ingredients, an economy like Hong Kong's cannot flourish and grow.

The Airport Core Programme (ACP) has been designed to provide these facilities in 10 core projects which will build a base for economic expansion into the next century. Hong Kong's key role as a centre for international and regional aviation will be enhanced by a new modern airport located away from centres of urban population and capable of operating round-the-clock. Associated infrastructure developments will relieve serious traffic congestion, open up new land for urban development and for further expansion of port facilities. New space will be provided for recreational activities, and there will be overall environmental benefits.

The programme comprises: an airport at Chek Lap Kok off north Lantau to replace Kai Tak in 1997; six road and rail projects, including extensive tunnels and bridges, stretching from the central district under the harbour, along the west side of Kowloon, across Tsing Yi and Ma Wan, and along the north Lantau coast; two major land reclamations in West Kowloon and Central; and a new town on north Lantau.

Overall the programme is based on sound financial principles with good returns for government investments and maximum involvement of the private sector. Cost-effective concepts and designs have been drawn up for individual projects. Contracts are being placed on the basis of open and fair tender evaluations, and there are strong and comprehensive financial and project management controls.

The Need to Replace Kai Tak

A new airport is needed because Kai Tak, which has only one runway, is approaching its full capacity of 24 million passengers a year and cannot viably be enlarged beyond a current expansion programme. In terms of international traffic, it is already the world's fourth busiest airport for passengers, and freight. It handles about 80 per cent of Hong Kong's six million visitors a year and 30 per cent of its domestic exports. It also plays an important role in the development of southern China, as well as Hong Kong.

In the past year, throughput of passengers has been growing at about 12 per cent. This means that Kai Tak will be unable to accommodate forecast passenger demand before the new airport at Chek Lap Kok is planned to open in 1997. If this happens, Hong Kong's

233

economy will begin to suffer: for example, the economic disbenefits to Hong Kong of not going ahead with the airport have been estimated to be at least $420 billion over the period 1997–2010. This represents only quantifiable losses: it does not include indirect losses caused for example by declining effectiveness of Hong Kong as an international trading and financial centre, which could double the estimate.

The ACP was conceived in 1991 out of the Port and Airport Development Strategy (PADS) which had been unveiled in 1989 after years of study. PADS had been designed to provide, in the most cost effective way, for the growth of both the port and the airport. It includes major extensions to Hong Kong's container port and other developments, which are going ahead separately, whereas the 10 ACP projects are all associated with the opening of the airport at Chek Lap Kok (with the first of two planned runways) in 1997.

Memorandum of Understanding

In September 1991, the Prime Ministers of Britain and China signed the 'Memorandum of Understanding Concerning the Construction of the New Airport in Hong Kong and Related Questions' (MOU). This memorandum recognises the 'urgent need for a new airport in Hong Kong in order to ensure and develop its prosperity and stability', and the 'need for the airport project to be cost effective'. It requires the Hong Kong Government to complete the ACP projects 'to the maximum extent possible' by June 30, 1997, and says that the Chinese Government will 'support the construction of the new airport and related projects'.

The MOU also provides for a joint Airport Committee which has been set up under the auspices of the Sino-British Joint Liaison Group. This committee has become the primary forum for discussions with China on the ACP. The main topics of discussion during 1992 were overall financing plans for the airport and airport railway.

The Consultative Committee on the New Airport and Related Projects (ACC), established under the MOU, held six plenary meetings and four special meetings in 1992 on various aspects of the ACP. Four sub-committees were formed relating to: the airport and its related land development projects; traffic and transport; financial matters and planning; and the environment and people's livelihood. A total of 18 sub-committee meetings were held in 1992.

Implementing and Financing the ACP

The ACP is being implemented by the government, two statutory corporations wholly owned by the government, and by a franchisee to be appointed for the Western Harbour Crossing (WHC). The government is carrying out direct capital works projects to reclaim land, and to build highways and a new town near the airport. The Airport Authority (AA), which is to replace the existing Provisional Airport Authority, is responsible for building and operating the airport. The Mass Transit Railway Corporation (MTRC) will build and operate the Airport Railway. The WHC will be wholly privatised.

The estimated cost of the 10 ACP projects was announced in April 1992 at $112.2 billion (in March 1991 prices). This equals $163.7 billion in money of the day. (Sometimes known as out-turn prices, money of the day takes into account the impact of inflation on the value of the dollar while projects are designed and built, thus providing a more realistic projection of out-turn prices. This is particularly relevant to the ACP because most contracts are let on a fixed price lump sum basis, meaning that the contract award price is already adjusted to cover inflation over the contract period).

The government's capital expenditure on the ACP works programme is approximately $60 billion. This is expected to amount, between 1992–3 and 1996–7, to 25 per cent of the government's total capital expenditure (which covers public works, and other expenditure from the Loan Fund and non-recurrent account of the General Revenue Account). The remaining 75 per cent of the government's total capital expenditure will be spent on other social services and essential activities.

The ACP provides ample opportunities for private sector participation. These can be in the form of: investment in franchises for the Western Harbour Crossing and facilities at the airport; commercial lending for the airport and the railway; and real estate development associated with the airport and the railway.

Benefits for the Community
The main benefits for the community – in addition to the airport itself – will come from the improved road and rail facilities, an easing of congestion in West Kowloon, and the opening up of North Lantau. The closure of Kai Tak will also have environmental benefits because some 350 000 residents living under the flight path will escape the noise of aircraft. Overall there will be the substantial benefits to Hong Kong's economy that have already been mentioned.

The government's proposed financial contribution would also yield substantial benefits for taxpayers. For example, it is estimated that by the year 2020, the new airport, the Lantau Fixed Crossing, and the Airport Railway would have generated additional revenue for the government totalling over $300 billion comprising: nearly $50 billion from the airport at Chek Lap Kok (over and above the revenues which Kai Tak would generate); over $75 billion from the MTRC; over $190 billion from the Lantau Fixed Crossing. An internal rate of return approaching 12 per cent by 2020, and close to 15 per cent by 2040, has been forecast on the government's proposed investment in those elements of the ACP directly required to support the new airport.

New Reclaimed Land
The ACP involves the creation of 1 828 hectares of new land comprising: a 938-hectare reclamation area, centred around the islands of Chek Lap Kok and Lam Chau off northern Lantau, which will provide a platform of 1 248 hectares (including the islands) for the airport itself; a 540 hectare strip along the northern shore of Lantau for Tung Chung New Town Phase I; a 330 hectare reclamation off West Kowloon; and a 20-hectare section of a larger reclamation adjacent to the Central–Wanchai urban area on Hong Kong Island.

The West Kowloon Reclamation will provide housing for 91 000 people and some five hectares of commercial space, as well as vital road and rail arteries linking Kowloon with the new airport and the north-west New Territories. A 20-hectare portion of the Central–Wanchai Reclamation will provide opportunities for the development of Hong Kong's central business district, plus a site for the Central terminus of the Airport Railway. Both reclamations will include abundant landscaping and areas of open space.

Tung Chung new town, occupying two valleys at Tung Chung and Tai Ho on northern Lantau and a coastal strip of reclamation between them, is planned to house 20 000 people

235

by 1997 and 200 000 by 2011. In addition to providing support services for the new airport it will accommodate commercial and industrial developments and will serve as an impressive gateway to Hong Kong for visitors. There will be a mixture of private, public rental, and home ownership scheme housing, several shopping centres, an office and hotel complex in the town centre, and a peripheral 52-hectare industrial park. Extensive landscaping has been designed to shield the town from the airport to the north-west and to provide generous recreational areas, supplemented by the hilly backdrop of Lantau Country Park to the south. Strong emphasis has been placed on community facilities and both local and long-distance rail and bus transport.

The Airport at Chek Lap Kok
Detailed planning of the airport at Chek Lap Kok progressed rapidly in 1992. The Provisional Airport Authority, a statutory corporation set up in April 1990 with the Hong Kong Government as its sole shareholder, is planning an airport which will be operationally safe and efficient, environmentally friendly, and commercially viable.

Scheduled to open in 1997 with the first of two planned runways on a 1 248-hectare island site, the airport will have an immediate annual capacity of 35 million passengers and 1.5 million tonnes of cargo. There is provision for this to expand incrementally to 87 million passengers and 9.0 million tonnes of cargo by the year 2040. Because of its location off North Lantau, the airport will be able to operate round-the-clock without causing noise problems for Hong Kong residents.

In the first quarter of 1992, the authority completed the airport's master plan, and a draft financial plan was agreed with the government. The master plan sets out comprehensive planning and design criteria for the formation of the airport island and facilities, providing for a phased development into a two-runway airport.

A commercial plan was also drawn up. It aims to enhance the airport's financial viability and operational efficiency by maximising private sector participation. The authority's commercial strategy is aimed at providing quality through competition where practicable, while deriving market-based licence fees. Airport-related commercial activities on the island will cover about 100 hectares of land and will include hotels, offices, and other business activities.

After completion of the master plan, detailed design work has continued. International bids were invited by the authority, and a contract was awarded, for the design of the passenger terminal and concourse complex.

The terminal will occupy an area of over 430 000 square metres and will be 1.4 kilometres in length (equal to the distance from the City Hall in Central across the harbour to the Hong Kong Space Museum). It is being designed as a single, long and sweeping structure with glass cladding.

International tenders were invited during the year for the site preparation contract, which involves reclaiming land and constructing the airport island platform. An international consortium was selected from the tenderers in July, after the design of the platform had been modified with realignment of the southern runway and terminal building at a cost saving of $150 million. The government obtained Finance Committee approval at the end of November for funds to allow the authority to award this contract. This decision enabled the government to take an important step forward on the ACP, and afforded more time to seek an agreement with China on the overall financing plan.

Preceding Page: *A visitor to Ocean Park aviary.*

Opposite page: *Kowloon's best known market for bird fanciers is known as 'Bird Street'.*

Right: *The popularity of bird keeping brings brisk business to dealers.*

Left: *Taking the pets for a walk.*

Below: *Birds are the main talking point when enthusiasts gather during their morning stroll.*

Opposite page: *Birds are part of the family for many people.*

Left: *The new Sir Edward Youde aviary in Hong Kong Park offers a natural habitat for hundreds of exotic birds from many parts of the world.*

Right: *An international population of birds at the aviary attracts both bird lovers and tourists.*

Following page: *A cockatoo swoops down to take its entertainment fee from a spectator at an Ocean Park bird show.*

Work on the contract, which involves moving 331 million cubic metres of material, started in December. On average, eight million cubic metres of material – equivalent to eight times the volume of the Bank of China building in Central Hong Kong – will need to be moved every month for 41 months. The islands of Chek Lap Kok and Lam Chau will be levelled, and the excavated materials will be used for the reclamation, along with marine sand and other fill material. In advance of this contract, 38 hectares of land were formed at Chek Lap Kok under an Advance Works Contract.

The authority also invited expressions of interest during 1992 for a wide range of construction activities and commercial franchises, including infrastructure design, air cargo handling, aircraft maintenance and engineering, catering, and aviation fuel supply.

As an organisation, the authority developed into a recognised corporate entity. Between March 1991 and the end of 1992, it grew from a staff of one (the chief executive officer) to well over 400, with most key positions filled.

New Transport Facilities

The ACP includes five major highway projects designed to cater for the new airport's traffic and to relieve congestion on existing roads. They comprise the Western Harbour Crossing, West Kowloon Expressway, Kwai Chung and Tsing Yi sections of Route 3, the Lantau Fixed Crossing, and the North Lantau Expressway.

Together with the Airport Railway, they will also provide rapid transit between Tung Chung New Town and Central, so stimulating developments on north Lantau in the same way that the Kowloon Canton Railway triggered development in the eastern New Territories when it was double-tracked and electrified.

Congestion will be relieved in West Kowloon, Kwai Chung and Tsing Yi: for example, when the West Kowloon Expressway opens, peak hour traffic volume on the existing West Kowloon Corridor is projected to drop by as much as 40 per cent.

New Highways

The Western Harbour Crossing has been planned as a dual three-lane immersed tube road tunnel linking the West Kowloon Reclamation to the Western District of Hong Kong Island. In addition to providing a key part of the airport highway route, it is also intended to relieve congestion at the two existing cross harbour tunnels. Like these two tunnels, it is intended to be financed, constructed and operated by the private sector under a 30-year franchise. Private sector bids were invited in 1992, and the government subsequently negotiated with a consortium which submitted the single conforming bid. Construction is planned to start in mid-1993, for completion in mid-1997.

The project comprises a two kilometre tunnel, associated approach roads, a major road interchange on Hong Kong Island and a toll plaza. The tunnel will link the new West Kowloon Expressway with a new section of elevated road on Hong Kong Island connecting with Connaught Road Central.

The West Kowloon Expressway will link the northern portal of the Western Harbour Crossing to Lai Chi Kok, forming an important part of Route 3, with a dual three-lane carriageway. It will serve developments on the West Kowloon Reclamation and will also substantially relieve existing local and distributor roads in central and west Kowloon. A further section of Route 3 will connect Kwai Chung with the Lantau Fixed Crossing through Tsing Yi, with a dual four-lane viaduct in Kwai Chung.

The Lantau Fixed Crossing will comprise: the Tsing Ma suspension bridge linking Tsing Yi to Ma Wan; viaducts crossing Ma Wan; and the Kap Shui Mun Bridge, with a cable stayed design, linking Ma Wan to Lantau. The Tsing Ma Bridge will become a prominent Hong Kong landmark: its main span of about 1.4 kilometres will be the world's longest, carrying both road and railway. Construction contracts for the bridges and viaducts were awarded in 1992.

The North Lantau Expressway will be a 12.5-kilometre dual three-lane carriageway along the northern coast of Lantau, linking the Lantau Fixed Crossing to Tung Chung New Town and the airport at Chek Lap Kok. Construction of the expressway is being carried out in three sections and work on the first two sections started in 1992.

Airport Railway

The Airport Railway has been planned to provide two separate rail services, 34-kilometres long, operating mainly on the same tracks but with separate platforms: a fast passenger link to the airport at Chek Lap Kok, called the Airport Express Line, and a domestic service called the Lantau Line. Both will have maximum operating speeds of 135 kilometres per hour, compared to 80 kilometres per hour on existing MTR lines.

The Airport Express Line is designed as an all-seated, business class-type express service providing a 23-minute link between Hong Kong Central and the airport, with only two stops at West Kowloon and Tsing Yi. It is envisaged that five-car trains will be used initially, increasing as required to a maximum of 10-car trains, operating at 4.5 minute frequency.

Serving northern Lantau, western Kowloon, and Central, the Lantau Line is designed as a conventional mass transit commuter service. It has been designed to bring much needed relief to the existing MTR Tsuen Wan Line, particularly the Nathan Road Corridor where the MTR is now carrying its capacity of 72 000 passengers at the morning peak hour. Stations are planned at Hong Kong Central, West Kowloon, Tai Kok Tsui, Lai King, Tsing Yi and Tung Chung New Town, with provision for additional stations later.

Tung Chung New Town, the terminus of the Lantau Line, is targeted to have a population of 200 000 by 2011. Other new town developments along the route of the railway have been planned at Tai Ho, Yam O and Tung Chung West where stations can be added later.

Five sites totalling approximately 62 hectares have been identified along the railway route for residential and commercial property development. They are at Hong Kong Central, West Kowloon, Tai Kok Tsui, Tsing Yi and Tung Chung.

During 1992, the government agreed a draft financial plan for the railway with the Mass Transit Railway Corporation (MTRC) which is to be responsible for building and operating the railway. Following completion of a feasibility study, preliminary design work was started on the railway's eight kilometres of tunnels, six kilometres of elevated structures and 20 kilometres of ground level track.

Government Contracts and Tenders

A total of 18 government construction contracts worth over $18 billion had been awarded by the end of 1992, of which nine contracts worth more than $15 billion were awarded in 1992. All were on time and within budget estimates. They represented about 50 per cent of the total value of the government's ACP contracts.

Two contracts with a total value of $8.78 billion were awarded for the Lantau Fixed Crossing – one for the Tsing Ma Bridge and the other for the Kap Shui Mun Bridge and Ma Wan Viaduct.

On the North Lantau Expressway, contracts for the Tai Ho and Yam O sections, which make up two thirds of the length, were let for a total of $4.4 billion. Tenders for the Tung Chung section were invited in March 1993.

On the West Kowloon Reclamation, seven contracts costing some $4.3 billion were let for a variety of work. Five more are due to be let in 1993. A site formation contract costing $732 million was also let for the Tung Chung development where construction of public housing and government facilities is scheduled to start in 1994.

Tenders for the first phase of the Central and Wanchai Reclamation engineering works were invited in June 1992. They were returned in September 1992.

On Route 3, prequalification exercises for a tunnel and viaduct were completed and tenders were invited in August and September. Tenders for the bridge were invited in November 1992.

Tenders for the north and south sections of the West Kowloon Expressway were scheduled to be invited in the first quarter of 1993.

The government has stressed that it welcomes international participation in the contracts and that it is strictly applying its traditional level playing field approach on tendering procedures and the award of contracts.

A significant number of international companies have won construction and site investigation contracts, often in joint ventures. They have come from a wide range of countries including Japan, the United Kingdom, the United States, the People's Republic of China, Australia, France, the Netherlands, New Zealand and Italy as well as Hong Kong. Firms winning consultancies have come from the UK, USA, the Netherlands and Japan as well as Hong Kong.

The selection of contractors, whether local or multi-national, is strictly based on the extent to which they can meet the government's requirements in terms of completion on time, within the government's required standards and specifications, and at the lowest possible price.

Management and Cost Controls

An overall strategy has been drawn up to establish the scope of the ACP, the critical programme objectives, and the budget. This is the basis for the overall programme and project management. Fixed price lump sum contracts are being used for most projects to minimise risks to the government, especially from inflation and the estimation of quantities.

A cost control system has been introduced for the ACP, laying down procedures for monitoring, scrutinising, and controlling costs during the design and construction of the government-funded projects. Early warnings of cost increases are reported to the New Airport Projects Co-ordination Office (NAPCO) and department heads. Proposed design changes leading to higher costs have to be fully justified and approved before detailed design is started. This system enables trends, which could lead to cost increases, to be identified early. If cost increases are accepted, offsetting savings are sought in the same or other ACP projects.

Government works departments, and non-government participants such as the Provisional Airport Authority, MTRC, and the Western Harbour Crossing franchisee, have full responsibility for their own project-level planning, execution, control, and management. They are required to complete projects on time and within budget and to report progress, and co-ordinate their work, through NAPCO.

Comprising government staff integrated with consultants from International Bechtel, NAPCO's job is to ensure compliance with plans, programmes and budgets, and to act as a focal point for the management of project interfaces and resolution of problems.

Apart from the cost control systems, the highly competitive tendering system has also been effective in controlling expenditure on the ACP.

Protecting the Environment

Environmental impact assessment (EIA) studies have been undertaken for each of the projects, sometimes at both the feasibility and detailed design stages, and as an integral part of project planning and design. These studies have generally shown that, with suitable mitigation measures in place, the projects will be environmentally acceptable when they are built and operating.

The island formed at Chek Lap Kok by the airport reclamation will allow tidal water to flow between the airport and the north Lantau coastline, flushing partially enclosed areas of water to the east. Most of the natural coastline to the west of Tung Chung will be retained. Following ecological studies, a colony of rare Romer's tree frogs has been rescued from Chek Lap Kok. Mangrove communities are also to be re-established, and compensatory new woodlands are to be planted.

An environmental project office has been established by the Environmental Protection Department (EPD) to monitor pollution in the West Kowloon area during work on the reclamation and associated transport projects. The office consists of senior EPD staff and a specialist consultancy team with experience. It will monitor overall environmental quality and handle pollution problems.

Safety at Work

The government continued to promote safety at work, and began to implement a package of safety measures on the ACP construction sites. The Airport Core Programme Construction Safety Manual was published in July 1992, setting out the government's policy and objectives, and safety measures.

These requirements are being incorporated in each contract to ensure there is an effective safety management system on sites, including a special site management committee. Accident prevention and safety management training courses are being organised for site staff.

The government, together with the Provisional Airport Authority and MTRC, started compiling a database to assist with the monitoring of accident rates, analysis of the causes of accidents, and formulation of prevention measures. Safety promotion campaigns and awards are being organised to increase awareness, especially among construction workers. The MTRC and Provisional Airport Authority have agreed to implement similar measures.

17
PORT DEVELOPMENT

HONG KONG's port already handles more containers a year than the whole of Britain. Only the USA and Japan have a bigger container throughput than Hong Kong.

Each year, between now and the year 2011, Hong Kong must increase its handling capacity by one million containers. That is the equivalent of building every year a port the size of Oakland, California, or Felixstowe, Britain's busiest container port.

To handle this huge rise in throughput the territory will build a completely new port on the north-east of Lantau Island. This will involve one of the world's biggest civil engineering projects.

Plans call for the completion of 17 new container berths at Lantau. Hong Kong's present container port at Kwai Chung has 14 berths with another eight to be built by 1995.

Container berths are not the only facilities needed. The new port will need back-up and cargo working areas, ship-repair facilities, a river trade terminal to handle vessels from China and an extensive road network including an expressway. Eventually a link, by tunnel or bridge, will connect Lantau directly with Hong Kong Island. New channels must be dredged to provide marine access and breakwaters constructed to shelter working container vessels from wave action.

Like Kwai Chung, the new port will not just serve Hong Kong which owes its very existence to its position as an entrepôt for China. With the modernisation of China's economy and its opening up to world markets, that entrepôt trade has assumed a renewed importance.

Many of the goods transhipped to and from China through Hong Kong move by river boats down the Pearl River, for generations the gateway to trade with China. To cater specifically for this private companies will build and operate a River Trade Terminal at Tuen Mun on the mainland north of Lantau.

The new port cannot begin to operate until 1997, when the Lantau Fixed Crossing, one of the world's longest suspension bridges, comes into operation. The bridge will provide transport access to both the new port and the new airport at Chek Lap Kok.

Hong Kong may have to wait until 1997 for its new facilities on Lantau, but meanwhile the port must handle ever increasing amounts of cargo. Clearly port operators cannot wait for the new facilities on Lantau to commence work. To cope with increasing demand two new container terminals will come into operation close to the present container port. Lack of space at Kwai Chung means these will be sited at Stonecutters Island (Terminal 8) and at South-East Tsing Yi Island (Terminal 9).

Work is already well underway at Terminal 8, which involves the reclamation of 110 hectares of land to the north of Stonecutters Island.

Of the reclaimed land, 48 hectares will house a four-berth terminal while 62 hectares will be used for back-up facilities.

As with Hong Kong's other seven terminals, private companies are designing, building and will operate Terminal 8. The government has awarded development rights to a consortium formed by Modern Terminals Ltd., Hongkong International Terminals Ltd. (the two major terminal operators at Kwai Chung) and mainland Chinese shipping operators.

Construction of Terminal 8 started in October 1991. The first berth should begin operation in mid-1993 and the whole terminal should be completed by the end of 1994.

The government is expected to execute the grant of Terminal 9 early in 1993. The terminal will comprise 60 hectares containing four berths with a total capacity of 1.6 million 20-foot equivalent units a year, the same start up capacity as Terminal 8. A further 26 hectares will be available for back-up purposes and there will be an additional 39 hectares for industrial and community use.

The first berth at Terminal 9 should be operating by mid 1995.

Port Development Board

Hong Kong has never had a Port Authority as port facilities were built and are operated by private companies. But with a development as massive and extensive as the new port there is a need for a co-ordinating body to keep development plans up to date and to act as a link between the private and government bodies involved.

The Port Development Board (PDB) is filling that role. Set up in April 1990, the board has a non-official chairman and advises the Governor, through the Secretary for Economic Services, on all aspects of port planning and development.

Specifically, the PDB's brief is to assess development needs in the light of changing demand, port capacity, productivity and performance. It considers the competitiveness of Hong Kong compared with other major regional ports.

The board recommends strategies for creating new port facilities and co-ordinates government and private sector involvement in developing them. It acts as a focal point for ideas and opinions expressed by port operators or anyone affected by the port expansion.

Among the board's first tasks was to update the forecasts from which consultants had produced plans.

The PDB found that total port traffic should continue to grow by 6.5 per cent a year between 1990 and 2011 when total throughput will reach 284.2 million tonnes. This will include 179.6 million tonnes of inward cargo and 104.7 million tonnes of outward cargo. More than 90 per cent of the cargo will be carried by ocean-going vessels and the rest by river vessels.

Transhipment traffic will account for 21 per cent of the ocean traffic in 2011, a slight increase on the 20 per cent in 1990.

Analysed by commodity, inward cargo in 2006 will consist mainly of coal (30 per cent), petroleum products (21 per cent) and chemical and related products (10 per cent). About 43 per cent of the cargo will be containerised, 34 per cent dry bulk, 21 per cent liquid bulk and two per cent break-bulk.

Outward cargo will comprise mainly manufactured articles (35 per cent), petroleum products (18 per cent), primary materials (12 per cent) and machinery and transport equipment (nine per cent).

The board estimates that the number of fully containerised ships calling at Hong Kong will increase from 8 390 in 1990 to 21 000 by 2006. The number of conventional general cargo ships will remain constant.

From these figures the PDB has concluded that by 2011 the new port will need 17 additional container berths each with a quay length of 320 metres; about 9 600 metres of cargo working seafrontage; some 300 hectares of land for backup areas at container terminals and about 4 000 hectares of buoy and anchorage area to support port operations.

The board has also concluded that the new port infrastructure must include ship repair facilities to service the growing fleet of ocean-going vessels calling at Hong Kong. Besides servicing these ships such repair facilities will ensure that the port can recover quickly from a major maritime accident or from storm damage.

Ship repairing is among the oldest industries in Hong Kong, and like the port itself, has suffered from a scarcity of waterfront land, particularly land with good deep-water access.

The PDB recommends planning a dockyard industry supporting a minimum of eight floating or dry docks (supported by alongside berths or finger piers) by the mid-1990s with flexibility to increase the number of docks to at least 10 by 2006.

From its early days Hong Kong has been a buoyage port with most cargoes handled over the sides of ships into or out of lighters moored alongside vessels. Even with the growth of containerisation the port still handles much of its cargo in this way. Lighters carry containers to and from ships anchored mid-stream

In 1991, 23 million tonnes of cargo was handled like this of which 44 per cent was containerised. The year under review saw a 62 per cent increase in mid-stream container handling to a total of 2.5 million TEUs.

The Port Development Board has plenty of work ahead as it finalises more detailed plans for port expansion. To help it plan for special needs in the port it originally had three committees, the Ship Repair Facilities Committee, the River Trade Cargo Activities Committee and the Mid-Stream Operations Committee.

In June and July 1991 board members endorsed the setting up of the Port Land and Transport Committee and the Container Handling Committee. A Working Group was established in March 1992 to examine appropriate institutional arrangements for future port development.

The Port Land and Transport Committee advises the government on land required to support port cargo handling facilities. This includes land for ancillary port operations and transport systems required to ensure smooth movement of cargo to and from the port.

The Container Handling Committee provides data, analyses and advice to the government on container handling facilities. It examines world-wide containerisation trends, Hong Kong's position in the Asia Pacific Region and the increased potential for containerisation in China.

Through the work of its various committees the Port Development Board will continue to act as a bridge between the government's strategic planning proposals and the commercial necessities of a successful port.

Development Studies

That Hong Kong would need huge new port facilities to cope with its phenomenal growth became apparent in the early 1980s. It was also obvious that Kai Tak, one of the world's busiest airports, would reach its maximum capacity in the mid 1990s and that a new airport would have to be built.

Just as Hong Kong's phenomenal business success had put pressure on the port it had stretched the facilities at Kai Tak airport. As with the Kwai Chung container port, geography meant that Kai Tak was incapable of expansion. Hong Kong needed a new airport as well as a new port. It made economic and engineering sense to consider both together.

In July 1987 the Executive Council approved the launching of the Port and Airport Development Study. Its acronym, PADS, has since entered the everyday language of Hong Kong.

In October 1989 the Governor, Sir David Wilson, announced that both the airport and new port would be built at Lantau Island.

Although PADS determined the general site of the port, stretching south-east from Penny's Bay on Lantau towards Hong Kong Island, it did not decide its exact pattern.

Since August 1991 APH Consultants, have, on behalf of the government, been carrying out the Lantau Port and Western Harbour Development Studies to decide the best layout for the new port. APH is a joint venture of Acer, Au Posford Consultants Ltd. and Frederick R. Harris (Far East) Ltd.

The consultants examined five options including a peninsula, a series of connected islands with berth entrances to the east and to the west, and east and west facing basins. They evaluated different configurations from port and harbour aspects, marine risk and navigation, environmental impact, transport and traffic links and onshore land planning.

The evaluation showed a strong preference for the west-facing island layout. Its main advantages are:

* Long term development potential is much higher than for other configurations.
* The preferred western approach channel allows for better marine traffic arrangements and manoeuvering into and out of the port basins. Ship/ship and ship/ferry encounter risk is low, typhoon evacuation fast and traffic control needs are small.
* Water quality impacts are similar for all concepts. West facing islands will mean better air quality because the expressway serving the port will be located further from residential areas in Discovery Bay and on Peng Chau.
* While there are no great differences for traffic and transport arrangements, the Island West will give better direct port access.
* From an on-shore and general planning viewpoint, Island West is compatible with developments on Peng Chau and Discovery Bay.
* Island West will mean the lowest cost for Phase One development of the port. Comprising the first four berths of Terminal 10, this will be the most expensive phase. It will include flyovers, road junctions, interchanges and other infrastructure that must be in place before later phases begin.

Strategy Review

Throughout the year the PDB and the government's Planning Department, with the help of consultants, have been carrying out the Port Development Strategy Review.

The review sought to:
* update PADS port cargo and commodity forecasts to 2006 and to extrapolate these to 2011;
* reassess the economics of mid-stream operations;
* re-examine the port-mix scenario recommended by PADS;
* determine long-term requirements for typhoon shelters, shipyards, container back-up and river-trade facilities; and
* include the revised forecasts in a total programme for different types of physical facilities.

The review found that between 1980 and 1990 total port traffic grew by 12.5 per cent a year.

In forecasting future growth the review took into account several key factors, including: developments in Hong Kong; developments in China; the world economic outlook; potential competition from regional ports; containerisation trends; likely impact of port charges on traffic growth; and the outlook for transhipment traffic.

The review forecast that the number of ocean-going vessels calling at Hong Kong would increase from 20 363 in 1990 to 33 000 a year by 2006. The number of fully cellular container ships would rise from 8 390 to 21 000 in the same period.

The port development plan and programme will be reviewed regularly to ensure that it remains relevant to Hong Kong's needs and that it can be achieved within the required time.

Through the refinement of periodic strategy reviews and the regular monitoring of the progress and updating of the port development plan and programme, the competitive advantage of Hong Kong can be assured well into the 21st century.

18
PUBLIC ORDER

THE Hong Kong Government gives high priority to the fight against crime and the maintenance of public order. The Fight Crime Committee, chaired by the Chief Secretary, provides valuable advice and puts forward recommendations on areas of public concern and on measures to improve the maintenance of law and order.

The Royal Hong Kong Police has operational responsibility for crime prevention and detection, the maintenance of public order and, since April, 1992, has fully resumed responsibility for the detection of illegal immigrants on the border.

The Immigration Department, through its control of the entry and exit points and activities directed at discovering illegal immigrants, contributes significantly to the maintenance of law and order.

In anti-narcotics operations the police maintain close liaison with the Customs and Excise Department. The latter also maintains links with overseas customs authorities and plays a major part in combating smuggling and enforcing the Copyright Ordinance.

The Independent Commission Against Corruption enforces the Prevention of Bribery Ordinance and promotes greater community awareness of the evils of corruption.

The Correctional Services Department administers the penal system and runs correctional and rehabilitative programmes. The department also manages six Detention Centres for Vietnamese Migrants.

The Fire Services Department gives advice on fire protection and provides fire-fighting and rescue services. It also operates the major ambulance service.

Fight Crime Committee
In 1992, the Fight Crime Committee continued to provide advice on measures to combat crime. Specific subjects considered included measures to counter organised and serious crimes, triads in schools, crime involving juvenile and young offenders, robberies of goldsmith and jewellery shops, regulation of the security industry and ways to encourage the public to participate actively in the fight crime effort.

The Organised Crime Bill was published in the form of a White Bill for public comment in August 1991. In the light of the comments received, the Fight Crime Committee agreed that the bill should be refined and improved to form the Organised and Serious Crimes Bill. This bill was introduced into the Legislative Council on July 15. The objective of the bill is to tackle organised crime, including triads, and other serious crimes effectively by, among other things, enhanced investigative powers and provisions to enable heavier entences to be imposed. District Boards and District Fight Crime Committees were briefed on the bill after its introduction into the Legislative Council. An *ad hoc* group of the Legislative Council is studying the bill in detail.

The Fight Crime Committee supported in principle in September 1990 the proposal to introduce a statutory post-release supervision scheme for adult offenders. The scheme aims to rehabilitate ex-offenders, reduce the threat posed by some to public safety, reduce the chances of their committing further crimes and turn them into useful members of society. The Fight Crime Committee further examined how the scheme could operate in July 1991. The Post Release Supervision Bill, which sets out the framework for the scheme, is under preparation. It is expected that the bill will be introduced into the Legislative Council in 1993.

The committee has devoted much of its attention to the problem of juvenile crime, in particular, triad activities in schools. There is no indication of an organised triad campaign to enter schools for recruitment. However, more can be done by schools and the government to strengthen liaison and to educate youngsters on the pernicious nature of triad activities. An inter-departmental working group has been set up to consider ways to reinforce support for schools which face triad problems. The police have also stepped up presence near such schools.

Triads are only one aspect of the juvenile delinquency problem. The majority of the youngsters who commit crime are not related to triad societies. The question why these youngsters commit crime is the subject of a research which the research team of the Social Sciences Research Centre of the University of Hong Kong has been commissioned to undertake by a sub-committee of the Fight Crime Committee. The purpose of the research is to find out the social causes of crime committed by offenders aged between seven to 20. The study started in September and is expected to be completed in early 1994.

The Young Offenders Assessment Panel continued to provide advice to the courts on the rehabilitation programmes most likely to reform juveniles and young people. A special Outward Bound course has also been arranged for inmates of the Correctional Services Department.

During the year, the Security and Guarding Services Bill was further refined in preparation for its submission to the Executive Council. The bill aims at regulating the security industry through a licensing system to be run on two levels, namely, the licensing of persons who do security work (including watchmen) and the licensing of the security companies themselves.

In view of the spate of armed robberies on goldsmith and jewellery shops in the early part of 1992, a working group set up by the committee has reviewed the security measures for such premises. The working group recommended that the goldsmith and jewellery trade should regulate its own security measures by setting up a Security Measures Group to promote acceptable standards of security. The group also proposes a set of guidelines on minimum standards of security relating to alarms, safes and access control for goldsmith and jewellery shops to follow. These recommendations were endorsed by the committee.

The District Fight Crime Committees continued to play an important role in the fight against crime. They monitored the crime situation in their districts and helped foster both community awareness of the need to prevent crime and community participation in combating crime.

Members of all 19 District Fight Crime Committees took part in a Fight Crime Conference in October. The conference provided an opportunity to reinforce the link between the committee and the district committees and to exchange views on crime-related matters.

Police Force

Following a comparatively quiet opening to the year, a spate of major armed robberies and associated violence occurred in the three-month period between March and May. Groups of armed criminals, mainly from China, showed callousness and brutality previously unknown to Hong Kong. Firearms were discharged wantonly on crowded streets and hand grenades thrown at pursuing police officers. In one case, two victims were shot dead simply for failing to respond quickly enough.

This outbreak of violence at an unprecedented level, without any actual increase in the number of crimes, naturally attracted headline media coverage and calls from all levels of the community for effective response.

The police responded with a number of initiatives which rapidly brought the situation under control. Police presence on the street was reinforced with the redeployment of all available personnel. Stop and search operations were mounted to identify suspects.

Crime prevention publicity was stepped up. It targeted high risk premises such as jewellery shops.

The Force criminal intelligence system focussed on the identification of local organisers and drivers for the gangs of mainland criminals.

Perhaps most significantly, liaison with China was enhanced to unprecedented levels. The Commissioner of Police, Mr Li Kwan-ha, made a number of widely publicised visits to various parts of China, including Beijing and Guangzhou, and received full co-operation. Regular liaison at all levels between Hong Kong and Chinese police officers quickly developed to become the norm.

Among measures agreed early in the year was the appointment of two Chinese liaison officers to be stationed in Hong Kong to facilitate the flow of criminal investigation intelligence. As at year's end, the arrival date of the liaison officers had not been firmed up.

The problem of illegal immigrants from China was even greater than in 1991, as indicated by 40 per cent more arrests. Illegal immigration is a natural result of Hong Kong's geographical and economic circumstances, including a present shortage of labour but in 1992 it was also fuelled by various rumours of a government amnesty, the arrival of the new Governor, and the impression that illegal work would be possible on the port and airport projects. Such impressions were also deliberately fostered by criminals organising the importation of illegal immigrants from the southern part of China, particularly for unscrupulous sectors of the building industry. This organised employment of illegal immigrants especially on building sites became more common in 1992 and has been tackled by various measures including sanctions on contractors who have allowed employment of illegal immigrants by their sub-contractors, and publicity and recruitment of more help from the legitimate workers, whose livelihood is most threatened, against illegal immigrant employment.

The problem of missing vehicles, particularly high-valued private cars, and their subsequent smuggling into China, remained a cause of concern throughout the year. This phenomenon was high on the agenda in liaison with mainland officials. Six vehicles were eturned from China in the last quarter of the year. Recently, China has also announced measures to ban the registration as well as transfer of ownership of right-hand-drive vehicles in the Guangdong province. These measures, if properly enforced, will effectively educe the theft of high-valued private cars.

The year continued to witness major developments in the Force to meet future needs. Kowloon was split into two regions – Kowloon East and Kowloon West – and three new police stations at Waterfront, Ma On Shan and Tin Shui Wai were opened.

Technological advances also progressed on schedule to modernise the Force. These included the upgrading and enhancement of the computer-based command and control system. This has enabled a more efficient and rapid deployment of resources to incidents.

In May, an inter-departmental study on the recruitment and retention of junior police officers was conducted. A package of recommendations, including those on improved remuneration for junior police officers, was approved by the Executive Council.

In July, a high-profile recruitment campaign was launched. By the end of the year, a total of 1 789 constables was recruited. This represented a 43.6 per cent increase over last year.

Crime

The total number of crimes reported to police in 1992 was 84 056, a decrease of 5.2 per cent compared with 88 659 in 1991. The crime rate, defined in terms of the number of crimes per 100 000 of the population, was 1 446.4. This represented a drop of 6.1 per cent, compared with 1991. The crime rate of Hong Kong has been steady in recent years, ranging from 1 407.1 to 1 547.9.

Violent crime, a category which includes murder, wounding, serious assault, rape, indecent assault, kidnap, blackmail, criminal intimidation, robbery and arson, registered a decline in the year, with a total of 18 567 cases being recorded, compared with 19 558 in 1991. Robbery, wounding and serious assault accounted for 76 per cent of the total number of violent crimes in 1992.

Vehicle theft remained a cause for concern. There were 6 918 motor vehicles reported missing in 1992, compared with 6 475 in 1991.

The number of robberies involving the use of firearms – both genuine and pistol like objects – was 418, compared with 547 in 1991.

A total of 37 953 crimes or 45.2 per cent was detected in 1992, and some 41 780 persons were arrested for various criminal offences. Of the persons arrested, 6 533 were juvenile offenders (aged under 16) and 7 656 were young person offenders (aged between 16 and 20).

Organised Crime and Triads

A general trend towards increased violence and incidents involving the use of genuine firearms was noted in the early months of the year. In 1992, 56 genuine firearms, and 50 grenades were seized, compared with 116 and nine respectively in the previous year.

A series of violent robberies involving the use of powerful firearms occurred in April and May. In some of these incidents, grenades were thrown indiscriminately, resulting in fatal and serious injuries to several members of the public and the police. Prompt action by the police contained the trend effectively. Subsequent investigations also led to the arrests of many key members of the gangs.

249

There was a tendency for criminals to flee to China after committing crimes in Hong Kong. However, continued and improving close co-operation between Hong Kong and the mainland police authorities curbed the trend.

Illegal immigrants' involvement in armed robberies in Hong Kong remained significant. These people were generally unfamiliar with the local situation and often collaborated with local criminals in committing crimes.

There was an increased use of firearms by triad gangs in settling disputes among themselves. The Sun Yee On, which was responsible for over 50 per cent of the triad-related offences in Hong Kong, was the major target of investigation by the police throughout the year. Several successful operations resulted in the arrest of a large number of triad members and office-bearers of the gang. They were charged with triad-related offences, possession of firearms, rape, money laundering, extortion and other offences. Investigation into other triad groups, including the Wo Shing Wo, 14K and Wo On Lok also led to a number of arrests.

Following the occurrence of a number of incidents involving well-known film directors and movie stars, the police also focussed on triad involvement in the Hong Kong film industry. Despite some successes, it remained difficult to collate evidence in triad-related investigations. This can be attributed to the reluctance on the part of members of the public, particularly the victims, to come forward as witnesses. The Organised and Serious Crimes Bill, which was introduced into the Legislative Council in July, requires persons having information relevant to an investigation to answer questions. In preparation for the passage of this bill, the police are giving consideration to how measures for protecting witnesses can be stepped up.

Despite continued efforts to combat the theft of luxury vehicles, the number of such cases increased steadily throughout the year. A total of 1 889 luxury vehicles was stolen in 1992, compared with 802 in 1991. This rise was fuelled by the conveniently located and seemingly insatiable market in China. High-powered speedboats remained a popular means of transport for the smuggling of these vehicles. Some improvements in prevention have been achieved with the introduction of improved anti-theft devices by car manufacturers.

During the year, co-operation with overseas law enforcement agencies was stepped up significantly. Two cases were particularly worthy of note. In the first case, two men were arrested in Hong Kong in connection with the pay-off for a case of kidnap which occurred in Canada. In the second case, a Japanese man was identified in Hong Kong to have been involved in a bomb incident in Japan. Closer liaison with China also resulted in a number of arrests of violent criminals on both sides of the border.

Commercial Crime

During the year, the Commercial Crime Bureau's Fraud Division continued to investigate complaints from the business sector. A noteworthy case of fraudulent trading involved more than 1 400 victims. The Counterfeit and Forgery Division saw more successes in the fight against counterfeit and forgery activities. In one incident, a printing factory was found to be engaged in the production of counterfeit Japanese banknotes, each of 10 000 yen in face value. In another case, 500 forged credit cards and a number of counterfeit passports were seized from a manufacturing centre located in a domestic premises.

On the international front, the Intelligence Section continued to monitor the activities of international fraudsters. A number of attempted deceptions were successfully averted. A one-week seminar was held with Public Security Bureau officials in Guangdong, China. Liaison with overseas law enforcement agencies led to arrests in Hong Kong, the Netherlands and the United States of America.

The year also saw the introduction of the Computer Crimes Bill into the Legislative Council. Upon enactment of the bill, the Commercial Crime Bureau will be able to investigate crimes involving the use of computers.

Narcotics

The repeated bumper harvest of opium in the Golden Triangle meant that more heroin was passed onto world markets. Although significant seizures were made locally throughout the year, the abundance in supply led to a fall in prices.

Continuing the trend of the last few years, No. 4 heroin almost completely replaced the No. 3 product as the main drug abused in Hong Kong. The majority of drug addicts in the territory use heroin, although there was evidence of other psychotropic substances being abused, particularly by the young.

On the enforcement side, major successes against highly organised trafficking groups were achieved both locally and internationally, while the territory's level of co-operation and liaison with overseas law enforcement agencies continued to grow.

Of particular note was the seizure of a shipment of No. 4 heroin (396 kilograms) in June. This was the second largest heroin seizure ever in the territory, with the drugs having a retail value of $171 million. In addition, there were two major seizures of cannabis, one of 1 555 kilograms in May and another of 1 200 kilograms in July.

The Drug Trafficking (Recovery of Proceeds) Ordinance, which provides for the restraint and confiscation of the assets of convicted drug traffickers, continued to be a valuable weapon in the fight against the illicit drug trade. The legislation resulted in the freezing of $175,096,447 of drug-related assets to date.

Some 611.99 kilograms of opiate drugs, comprising opium, No. 3 heroin and No. 4 heroin, were seized, compared with 183.94 kilograms in 1991. There were 8 853 arrests for narcotics offences, compared with 7 688 in the previous year.

Crime Prevention

The Crime Prevention Bureau continued to promote the concept of crime prevention through structured publicity and the provision of professional advice to the community. Vehicle-related crime in particular was accorded a high priority, followed by domestic security.

Liaison between the bureau and the insurance and motor vehicle industries continued. It resulted in the introduction of more measures to reduce the incidence of vehicle theft, including education of the public on the need for better vehicle protection and the pursuit of better security measures in newly manufactured vehicles.

The phased police response to activated intruder alarms worked well. Man-hours were saved and standards of installation and maintenance improved, thereby reducing the number of false alarms.

Juvenile anti-crime education continued through the medium of the 'Robotcop', a computerised robot, which was used in over 200 displays in schools, youth functions, shopping centres and exhibitions throughout the year.

Crime Information

The Criminal Records Bureau is the sole repository for criminal records in Hong Kong. It houses complete records on all persons convicted of crime in the territory.

The records and indices held by the bureau comprise details of persons wanted, suspected offenders, missing persons, stolen property, outstanding warrants and missing vehicles. Currently the indices hold particulars of some 551 612 criminal records, 12 225 wanted persons, 2 551 missing persons, 9 613 outstanding warrants and 602 missing vehicles. During 1992, the Enhanced Police Operational Nominal Index Computer System (EPONICS) dealt with a total of 2 601 141 enquiries.

Ballistics and Firearms Identification

The Ballistics and Firearms Identification Bureau handled 338 cases in 1992, compared with 344 in 1991. A total of 56 commercially-manufactured firearms and three homemade and converted firearms were seized.

Fully-automatic weapons were used by criminals in a number of shooting incidents; a Polish assault rifle and a Polish sub-machine-gun were seized in related successful operations against armed gangs. Examination of these weapons showed that both firearms had been used in previous criminal shooting incidents in the territory.

Identification

The Identification Bureau continued to provide an efficient service to all units in the Force in fingerprint technology and forensic photography.

The Phase I computerisation of fingerprint identification proved effective. A total of 555 fingerprint identifications were achieved in the year. A feasibility study on the Phase II of the project was being carried out.

During the year, officers from the Scenes of Crime Section attended 25 069 crime scenes to examine traces of finger, palm and sole prints, resulting in 1 140 persons being identified as having connection with 1 220 criminal cases.

The Main Fingerprint Collection processed 99 351 arrest fingerprint forms and identified 34 846 persons with previous convictions.

Interpol

The Hong Kong National Central Bureau of the International Criminal Police Organisation, more commonly known as Interpol, is one of the most active members in the South-East Asian region. It handles an average of some 8 000 cases of crimes of various nature every year, including deportations and extraditions.

The bureau acts as a co-ordination centre in dealing with criminal information and associated enquiries between Hong Kong and the rest of the world, and disseminates information on behalf of the formations within the Force to participating countries. It also maintains close liaison with local consulate officials.

Two officers are seconded to the Interpol General Secretariat in Lyons, France, and close liaison with the secretariat is thereby maintained. In recent years, contacts with China have increased markedly, and an additional post, established at superintendent level, was created in October 1991 to cope with the increasing volume of work generated.

Public Order
There was no incident of major public disorder in Hong Kong during 1992.

The Police Tactical Unit (PTU) Companies were, however, again heavily committed to assisting in anti-crime patrols and a wide variety of operations.

In October, the formation of the fourth Field Patrol Detachment (FPD) Company completed the police resumption of border duties from the Army. In the year, a total of 2 210 officers of varying ranks were trained in internal security measures and FPD tactics.

Routine training of District Internal Security (IS) Units continued throughout the year. In addition, public order training for women police commenced in July, with the formation of a women's IS Company. For the first time, CID officers also attended PTU to receive instruction on tactics in dealing with armed suspects.

Illegal Immigration
During 1992, a total of 35 645 illegal immigrants was arrested by the Security Forces. This represented a 40 per cent increase over 1991. There was a particular increase in the numbers arriving by sea, with 42.9 per cent compared to 39.4 per cent in 1991.

A total of 32.6 per cent of those arrested had made previous illegal visits to the territory. Good prospects of employment were considered the main attraction. As a result, police action against employers was stepped up, focussing on construction sites, factories, restaurants and other places which provided employment opportunities.

Vietnamese Migrants
All Vietnamese migrants are held in detention centres to await a screening process to establish their refugee status in accordance with the 1951 United Nations Convention. Those classified as economic migrants are kept in detention centres, pending repatriation to Vietnam.

Due to the large influx of over 20 000 in 1991, it was agreed with the Vietnamese authorities that all new arrivals from October 29, 1992 onwards would be screened immediately and those screened out as non-refugees promptly repatriated. This policy effectively curbed the upward trend, and only 12 arrivals were recorded in 1992.

However, the existing population continued to place a strain on both the police force and Hong Kong in terms of financial commitment, manpower and resources. The Shek Kong Detention Centre incident in February 1992, which claimed 24 lives, vividly demonstrated the underlying tension and the potential dangers in managing a community of this nature.

On the positive side, with the implementation of the Orderly Repatriation Programme, the number of Vietnamese volunteering to return home markedly increased. This, together with the small number of arrivals, gave rise to optimism that an end to this tragic problem could soon be in sight.

As of December 31, the total number of Vietnamese migrants stood at 45 387, of which 2 600 were accorded refugee status, 27 245 were classified as non-refugees, 1 547 were pending screening and 70 were Vietnamese illegal immigrants from China. Resettlement accounted for 3 439, and 421 births were recorded. Two hundred and eighty were repatriated to Vietnam under the Orderly Repatriation Programme. Voluntary repatriation stood at 12 332 and 35 ex-China Vietnamese illegal immigrants from China were returned to China.

Traffic

The year recorded a rise in vehicle registration, resulting in an increase in traffic density hence additional pressure on the limited road space. This increase in density translated into a figure of 270.5 vehicles per kilometre.

Traffic congestion at peak periods continued to increase and the rush hours were extended. This resulted in traffic police becoming more heavily committed to traffic control matters.

The accident rate remained stable, with a marginal decrease of 0.1 per cent. The number of serious traffic accidents, however, decreased by 3.5 per cent.

The most common causes for accidents continued to be speed related. Vigorous enforcement action was taken, resulting in more than 160 000 speeding offences being detected and processed during the year. Technological advances in speed detection systems permitted the deployment of vehicle-borne computerised systems, such as VASCAR, and helped reduce speed-related offences and accidents.

Efforts to improve road safety through education continued, with a resultant downward trend in accident involvement among children and the elderly, despite an increase in these age brackets in the population.

Marine Region

The year 1992 saw a marked increase in the number of arrests of illegal immigrants en route to Hong Kong from China by negotiating the sea boundaries. On average, 97 illegal immigrants were caught each day compared with 70 in 1991. Throughout the year the use of vessels to smuggle illegal immigrants into Hong Kong continued to rise and accounted for almost half of the illegal immigrants intercepted.

Marine Region also played a major role in search and rescue operations within the very busy territorial waters of Hong Kong. As at December 31, the region had responded to 183 incidents as compared to 181 in 1991. These ranged from searching for missing sailboarders to dealing with sinking large ocean-going vessels, both in inshore waters and in and around the international boundary.

Two officers received the Queen's Gallantry Medal from Her Majesty the Queen at an investiture ceremony at Buckingham Palace for their outstanding bravery displayed in the course of rescuing crew members from a sinking ship during the passage of a typhoon. Another two officers received the Queen's Commendation for Brave Conduct for their part in the rescue of a group of fisherfolk from rocks off Lantau Island in adverse weather conditions.

The new base for Marine East Division at Tui Min Hoi, Sai Kung, was opened, as was a police post at Sok Kwu Wan on Lamma Island.

Of the 21 new launches ordered in the latest phase of the launch expansion programme, one command/patrol, six inshore patrol and two logistics vessels were taken into service.

Bomb Disposal

During 1992, the Explosive Ordnance Disposal Unit dealt with a total of 5 745 explosive devices, ranging from improvised bombs made by criminals to unexploded shells, vintage aircraft bombs and pyrotechnics. The year 1992 saw an increase in the use of grenades by criminals, with a resultant seizure and disposal of 50 bombs, a 556 per cent increase over 1991.

Community Relations

It has been the Force's long standing objective to seek more active support from the public in the fight against crime. In this connection, a territory-wide Fight Crime Campaign was conducted throughout the year under a main theme of 'Join Forces Against Crime'. Pivoting on the four sub-themes of 'What to Report', 'How to Report', 'Safe to Report' and 'Duty to Report', the campaign produced a comprehensive package, comprising two TV Announcements of Public Interest (APIs), a mobile exhibition and a series of poster displays in the Mass Transit Railway (MTR) and other prime locations.

The Good Citizen Award Scheme and the Good Citizen of the Year Award Scheme continued to prove effective as a means of promoting public assistance in the fight against crime. These two schemes are jointly administered by the Royal Hong Kong Police and the Hong Kong General Chamber of Commerce. Since the inception of these two schemes in 1972 and 1984 respectively, 2 264 persons have received the Good Citizen Award and 25 persons have been awarded the Good Citizen of the Year Award, in recognition of their outstanding courage, resourcefulness and initiative.

The Police Hotline (527 7177) received a total of 6 254 calls from civic-minded citizens, resulting in 1 602 persons arrested for various crimes. Another method by which the public could supply information to the police was by completing a Crime Information Form (CIF). In 1992, the police received 2 111 completed forms which resulted in 475 arrests.

The Junior Police Call (JPC), enjoyed an active membership of 169 312 members and 14 063 leaders. Since its inception in 1974, the JPC movement has remained an effective tool in harnessing the collective efforts of young people to assist the police in the fight against crime. Members took part in fight crime activities and crime prevention campaigns. In addition, JPC members also participated in a wide range of community services such as flag-selling and fund-raising activities for charitable organisations. The success of the movement has helped to develop its members into healthy youth and responsible citizens of the future.

The Royal Hong Kong Police, in conjunction with Radio Television Hong Kong, produced three television programmes. The objective of these programmes was to convey crime prevention messages and to appeal to viewers for crime information. Reconstructions of crime cases in a dramatised format or in a documentary approach were featured to elicit public response. These programmes, known as Crime Watch, Police Call and Police Report, are broadcast on a regular basis on both the English and Chinese channels of the two local television stations. Audience ratings of these programmes remained high.

During the year, the Force handled 108 visits, receiving a total of 444 overseas and 723 local visitors, whose status ranged from Members of Parliament to college students.

Planning and Development

The beginning of the year saw plans for the split of Kowloon into Kowloon West and Kowloon East Regions reach fruition on January 1. The two Regional Headquarters are based at Kowloon City and Tseung Kwan O respectively.

Plans for the split of the New Territories into New Territories North and South Regions gained momentum, and a target implementation date for April 1, 1993 was set. Once implemented, the two Regional Headquarters will be based at Tai Po and Ma On Shan respectively.

Force-wide planning centred on developments taking place in North Lantau and West Kowloon. A temporary police station at Tung Chung in North Lantau currently under construction will, on completion in late 1993, provide a base for enhanced police coverage until the permanent stations planned for Chek Lap Kok Airport and Tung Chung New Town become operational.

The South East Kowloon Development Study was actively monitored in anticipation that additional police services will be required in that area as a result of flight operations at Kai Tak Airport being moved to Chek Lap Kok.

Tin Shui Wai Divisional Police Station and new facilities for the Police Dog Unit at Ping Shan were completed during the year. The construction of new ranges at the Police Tactical Unit continued and work on the refurbishment or modification of facilities at nine police stations commenced. New quarters for junior police officers on a site in Wong Tai Sin were added to the list of the quarters construction programme underway at Tsing Yi and Fanling.

The construction of a second tower block for the new Police Headquarters at Arsenal Street commenced in mid-1992. On completion in 1996, this building will accommodate most of the headquarters formations presently housed in leased accommodation.

Communications

Last year's programme to replace outdated and inefficient telephone exchanges in police facilities continued. Following the acquisition of a large number of facsimile machines, document transmission throughout the territory was speeded.

The difficult terrain and working conditions experienced by the Field Patrol Detachment and the increased workload arising from its assumption of all anti-illegal immigration duties previously undertaken by the military along the border with Shenzhen placed considerable strain on existing communications. To overcome this problem, a new radio system was introduced. This greatly improved communications and the co-ordination of operations.

Communications also have a role to play in the training of police officers in regard to the use of firearms. The provision of interactive audio/video systems during the year to simulate real life situations added a significant new dimension to the firearms training programme.

The heavy involvement of the Marine Police in combating both smuggling and illegal immigration put stress on existing facilities in the maintenance of communications equipment. The removal of the Marine Radio Workshop to improved facilities in the Canton Road Government Offices and the opening of a new maintenance facility in the new Tui Min Hoi Marine Police Base in Sai Kung provided a much needed additional maintenance capability. The introduction of a computer-based management system for maintenance schedules and management of spare parts further helped to reduce the amount of idle time of equipment caused by technical failure or routine preventive maintenance.

Planning to meet the communications needs of police facilities at the new airport and for the increased policing required by planned development on Lantau Island also commenced during the year. This will remain a single major commitment of the engineering resources for the foreseeable future.

On a continuing basis, as old communications systems enter the second half of their life expectancy, planning has begun to identify suitable replacement equipment, to meet the changing needs of the Force through the application of state-of-the-art technology and to contribute towards the development of a fully integrated force-wide communications system.

Information Technology

The Information Technology Branch continued to plan, develop and implement computer-based information technology systems in accordance with the Force's Information Technology Strategy. The ever-growing workload of operational units, coupled with manpower retention and recruitment difficulties, had resulted in the need for improved efficiency and effectiveness at all levels of the Force – an area in which information technology plays an important role.

Work continued throughout 1992 to upgrade and enhance the computer-based Command and Control System used by the Force to more effectively command, control and deploy resources to incidents. Work was in hand to incorporate several additional sub-systems to expand the system by the provision of remote terminals to all police stations and to provide separate internal security and training and exercise modes. When work is completed in late 1993, all levels of the Force will have direct access to the system, thereby enabling commanders and operational units to have an immediate access to the most up-to-date and wide-ranging information relevant to their particular needs. As an associated development, an additional interface was put into operation during the year, enabling a direct access to other government systems which held motor vehicle, driver and identity card data.

An experimental project to fully computerise Wan Chai District with the objective of producing an essentially paperless station environment moved closer to completion during the year, following the successful incorporation of a personnel and training sub-system. Although this is only a pilot project, the exercise has so far been very successful. It has laid the cornerstone for the eventual full computerisation of all police stations, which is, however, subject to funding approval.

Work continued throughout the year to extend the Criminal Intelligence Computer System to attend to the need of the Narcotics Bureau and Commercial Crime Bureau with a view to enhancing the Force's intelligence gathering and analysis capabilities in these complex and important areas of law enforcement.

The production of an infrastructure which integrates all major computer systems to enhance efficiency by the provision of state-of-the-art technology to support the Force in the discharge of its duties remains the overall direction of the Information Technology Strategy.

Transport

Transport Branch is responsible for the procurement and maintenance of the Force vehicle fleet and the training and management of police drivers. The establishment of the fleet, standing at 2 276 at the end of the year, is reviewed on an annual basis, with additional vehicles purchased to stay in line with operational requirements.

With the increase in the number of roads making up the strategic road network and the problems associated with its policing, consideration was given to upgrading the motor cycles used for patrol purposes. Trials were carried out with a number of motor cycle brands to determine which was the most suitable for police use.

An automatic car washing plant was built at Police Headquarters. It proved to be successful and consideration was given to introducing further plants throughout the Force. Additionally, funds were requested for a computerised fuel dispensing system, which would reduce the number of personnel required to operate petrol pumps and provide greatly enhanced information on vehicle fuel consumption to bring about more effective management of the Force fleet.

Research

Research Branch carries out studies and assessments of Force organisation and also reviews its tactics and special equipment needs. Its objectives are not only to maintain efficiency and cost-effectiveness but also to ensure the Force is properly equipped to carry out its job.

In 1992, following the introduction of computerised information systems for police stations, Research Branch conducted a study of Force nomenclature with an aim to standardising post, rank and departmental titles.

In circumstances whereby possible manpower savings might be identified, studies were undertaken on the most appropriate level of manning for Regional Missing Persons Units and the MTR Police Control Room.

In order that patrol officers might be better protected from criminals armed with high velocity weapons and hand grenades, a study was conducted on the armouring of police vehicles.

Following a series of proposals concerning ways of enhancing recruitment and retention of officers, Research Branch conducted a wide-ranging review of the ratio of male to female officers within the Force with a view to extending the operational role of female officers.

In view of the rapid pace of development in Hong Kong, studies also commenced to find out the factors affecting the size and layout of foot and motor cycle patrol beats. Another study concerning expansion within the Force addressed the potential amalgamation of formation registries in the new Police Headquarters Phase II complex.

Inspection Services Wing

The Management Resources Studies which commenced in 1991 were concluded during the first quarter of 1992, with a total of 29 studies being completed. A wide range of recommendations were made, resulting in savings in manpower and capital and recurrent costs.

Regular Force inspections to ensure the effective and efficient operation and administration of the Force resumed in April 1992. These inspections, now in their fourth cycle, will take five years to complete. Up to the end of 1992, 14 formations had been inspected.

Licensing and Societies Registration

During the first half of the year 32 societies were registered by the Registrar of Societies, who also exempted 118 from the requirement to be registered. Since the enactment of the Societies (Amendment) Ordinance 1992 on July 17, 344 societies have notified the Societies Officer of their establishment. For the whole year, 116 societies were dissolved.

258

An average of 3 000 people applied for registration as watchmen every month. At the end of the year 20 000 watchmen were registered, with 1 000 of them licensed to carry arms.

A total of 1 700 persons were licensed to possess arms for competition or target shooting, and 180 persons applied for arms licences throughout the year.

At the end of the year, 725 notifications of public meetings were processed. 300 licences for public processions, 826 loudspeakers and 959 lion dance permits were issued.

A total of 183 applications for massage establishment licences, 148 applications for auctioneer licences, 270 applications for marine store dealer licences, 159 applications for pawnbroker licences and 46 applications for temporary liquor licences were processed within the year.

Police Dog Unit

The Police Dog Unit was founded in 1949 and its headquarters at the former Ping Shan Police Station in the New Territories established in 1965. Basic, assessment, refresher training courses, breeding and all veterinary support functions are carried out at the headquarters. On completion of their training, handlers and their dogs are posted to various formations. The unit is expanding its areas of expertise to include explosives search capability.

Complaints Against Police

The Complaints Against Police Office investigates all complaints from the public concerning the conduct and behaviour of members of the Force, including civilian staff and auxiliary police officers. The investigation of all complaints against police is monitored by the independent Police Complaints Committee.

In 1992, 3 250 complaints were received, an increase of 96 cases or 3.0 per cent over 1991. Over 98 per cent of the complaints in 1992 were made by persons either involved with or subjected to police action. Complaints of assault, neglect of duty and conduct/manner made up the majority of the complaints, 79 per cent in the total. Investigations into 3 102 cases were completed, of which 64 cases (2.1 per cent) were substantiated, 20 cases (0.6 per cent) classified as false, and 2 116 cases (68.2 per cent) were either withdrawn or not persuable. A total of 391 cases were dealt with by way of the new Informal Resolution Scheme introduced force-wide at the beginning of 1992. These represented 12 per cent of all complaints. A total of 13 police officers were disciplined and five charged with offences as a result of the complaints. In addition, 219 officers were subject to corrective action.

The Complaints Against Police Office is also responsible for advising Force members on how complaints can be prevented. Throughout the year lectures and seminars on complaint prevention continued to be organised for junior police officers with the aim of improving public relations and reducing situations of conflict.

Personnel and Recruitment

At December 31, 1992, the Force establishment totalled 27 206 and 5 820 for disciplined and civilian staff respectively.

With regard to the recruitment of inspectors, 28 local candidates were appointed from 169 applicants, while 20 overseas officers were taken on strength during the same period. In addition, 38 junior police officers were promoted to inspectors.

There was a significant improvement in the recruitment of constables during the year. A total of 9 885 applications for constables were received, with 1 789 subsequently being taken on strength. Compared with 1991, the number of applications increased by 615 (6.8 per cent) while the number appointed to the rank rose by 543 (43.6 per cent).

Conditions of Service

In 1991 the Commissioner made several submissions to the Administration, proposing among other things that a special allowance be given to retain junior officers in particular as well as to attract new entrants. An inter-departmental Study Group on the Recruitmen and Retention of Junior Police Officers was appointed in early 1992. This group published its findings in May. A total of 42 recommendations were made relating to salaries, quarters and conditions of service. All junior police officers subsequently received an average five per cent salary increase.

Training

Training continues to be a vital part of a police officer's career, starting with basic training on recruitment, followed by in-service training, which takes place both locally and overseas and training after promotion.

Training for newly recruited inspectors and constables takes place at the Police Training School at Wong Chuk Hang, a modern 18 hectare campus. The 36-week inspectors' and the 24-week constables' initial training courses cover similar projects: criminal law, social studies, police and court procedures, drill, firearms, first aid, physical fitness, swimming life saving and self defence. Inspectors are trained to higher levels than constables and their course includes training in management and leadership. As part of recruit training expatriate inspectors study colloquial Cantonese while functional English is taught to local inspectors.

In-service training follows at regular intervals throughout an officer's service, mainly to keep officers up-to-date with new legislation and procedures. It also consists of tailor-made courses for officers in more specialised branches such as marine, traffic, catering, financial investigation and instructional work. In addition, language courses of English, Mandarin and Vietnamese are run. During the year, some 50 officers were sent to the United Kingdom, Canada, the United States, New Zealand, Australia and Malaysia for manage ment, specialist and technical training.

The Force encourages officers who, on their own initiative, seek to improve their job-related skills by enrolling in local tertiary institutes on a part-time basis or by undertaking distance learning courses. A prime example was the successful completion by 21 officers of the Hong Kong University Certificate course in criminal justice in the year They are now eligible to proceed to the two year part-time Master of Arts course in public order. Subject to the exigencies of the service, these officers are granted day release to attend lectures.

Promotion training takes place as soon as possible after an officer's promotion, at the Police Training School for non-commissioned officers and at Force Training Wing Head quarters in Hennessy Centre for chief inspectors and superintendents. The instruction is specifically designed to equip officers with the management and decision making skills necessary for their new ranks. It serves to broaden their outlook and provide an effective base for their further development. The syllabi consist of lectures from a wide cross section of the community, including senior police and government officers, academics, executives from commerce and industry and members of the Legislative and Executive Councils.

At the Detective Training School, courses at standard and advanced levels are conducted to improve the standard of criminal investigation throughout the Force.

All officers were trained on the new Rules and Directions for the Questioning of Suspects and the Taking of Statements which came into operation on October 1, replacing the previously used Judges' Rules.

Throughout the year, great emphasis was placed on weapon training. New courses were designed, new indoor revolver ranges brought into use and greater awareness of tactics on the street taught to officers in front-line operational units.

Promotions

Promotion prospects in the Force remained good at most levels. During the year, a total of 39 gazetted officers were promoted to senior superintendent of police and above, 33 chief inspectors to superintendent, 50 senior inspectors to chief inspector, 61 sergeants to station sergeant and 201 constables to sergeant. In addition, nine exceptionally experienced station sergeants also advanced to the rank of inspector.

In 1992, 549 officers retired from the Force, 38 officers were invalided out, 681 resigned, 260 were compulsorily retired and 30 were either dismissed or had their services terminated.

Awards

A total of 1 365 officers were awarded the Colonial Police Long Service Medal after 18 years of continuous police service; 368 officers were awarded the 1st Clasp to the Medal after 25 years service and another 244 officers were awarded the 2nd Clasp after 30 years service. In addition, four officers were awarded the Queen's Police Medal for Distinguished Service (QPM), and 27 officers the Colonial Police Medal for Meritorious Service (CPM). Three officers received the Queen's Commendation for Brave Conduct, and 38 officers were awarded the Governor's Commendation.

Welfare

The origins of the present Force welfare organisation can be traced back to 1948, when a welfare fund was established under the Police Force Ordinance. From this early beginning, the Force Welfare Branch has grown extensively, and it now provides a wide range of services including personal welfare, catering, sports and recreation, psychological consultation and assistance on retirement to all members of the Force and their families.

During the year, staff made 5 280 casework visits and conducted 3 507 casework interviews throughout the territory.

The Family Life Education Programme, which aims to educate parents about their children's emotional and learning difficulties, continued to prove popular among participating officers and their families. A total of 1 888 children of regular and auxiliary police officers were awarded bursaries from the Police Children's Education Trust and the Police Education and Welfare Trust to assist them to pursue education at various levels.

Royal Hong Kong Auxiliary Police

Manned entirely by part-time volunteers from all walks of life, the Royal Hong Kong Auxiliary Police has a proud history dating back to 1914. The traditional role of the Force is to provide the regular police with additional manpower for such emergencies as natural disasters and public disorder.

Day to day, the Auxiliary Police are fully integrated with their regular counterparts to provide a wide variety of constabulary duties in the field of crime prevention, neighbourhood policing, traffic control, special duties and community relations. The Auxiliary Police also provide support in communication duties in police command and control centres.

The present strength of the Force is 5 636 out of a total establishment of 5 746 in all ranks. Approximately 12 per cent of the Force are women officers.

Throughout the year, the average daily turnout of auxiliaries for normal constabulary duty was 850 officers. Until April 6, an additional 50 personnel were called on each day to provide guard duties at refugee camps set up to house the large numbers of Vietnamese migrants. Deployment as a regional reserve of the Force for unexpected contingencies and pre-planned anti-crime operations was subsequently made.

Customs and Excise

The Customs and Excise Department is organised into five major branches – the Headquarters Branch, the Operations Branch, the Investigation Branch, the Trade Controls Branch and the Civil Secretariat. It has an establishment of 3 897 posts and is primarily responsible for the collection and protection of revenue payable under the Dutiable Commodities Ordinance, the suppression of illicit trafficking in narcotics, the prevention and detection of smuggling, and the enforcement of intellectual property protection legislation.

Revenue Protection

The department is responsible for collecting revenue on five groups of dutiable commodities in Hong Kong – liquor, tobacco, hydrocarbon oil, methyl alcohol and cosmetics. In 1992, revenue of $7,277 million was collected on these dutiable commodities, an increase of $1,058 million (or 17 per cent) as compared with $6,219 million in 1991.

Duty on non-alcoholic beverages, which was imposed in 1985, was abolished on March 4, 1992. However, new legislation prohibiting the use of duty-exempt diesel oil by pleasure vessels was introduced on June 1. This was because the exemption of duty on diesel oil was originally intended as an economic incentive to benefit industry and fishing and not intended to subsidise recreational activities.

In a related field, cases involving the illegal use of duty-exempt diesel oil by road vehicles increased significantly. Some 338 persons were arrested and 122 664 litres of industrial diesel oil were seized.

In addition to small quantities of duty-free cigarettes brought in by visitors and returning local residents at the entry points, substantial quantities of dutiable cigarettes continued to be smuggled into Hong Kong from China by vehicles and small vessels. This resulted in a serious proliferation of the illegal sale of dutiable cigarettes in markets and other outlets. Enforcement action was stepped up to prevent these activities and, as a result, 1 842 cases were detected and 15 million cigarettes with a duty potential of $8 million were seized.

Anti-Narcotics Operations

The department plays an important role in the prevention and suppression of illicit trafficking in narcotic drugs. Apart from suppressing the illicit trafficking of drugs locally, the department also exchanges intelligence and co-operates closely with other Customs administrations and law enforcement agencies in the fight against drug traffickers at the international level.

During the year, the department prosecuted 998 persons for drugs offences and seized 303 kilograms of heroin, 25 kilograms of opium and 73 kilograms of cannabis.

Recovery of Drug Trafficking Proceeds

The department has a responsibility for enforcing the Drug Trafficking (Recovery of Proceeds) Ordinance which is an effective tool in confiscating assets derived from drug trafficking.

During 1992, the department successfully obtained four court orders prohibiting dealing with realisable properties amounting to $14.6 million which were suspected to be connected with drug trafficking offences. Three cases were concluded with the confiscation of drug proceeds totalling $0.1 million.

Anti-smuggling and Import and Export Controls

In 1992, the department detected 778 smuggling cases under the Import and Export Ordinance, arrested 1 052 persons and seized $223 million worth of goods.

Smuggling between Hong Kong and China remained prevalent in 1992. Smuggling by sea, especially in Tolo Harbour, was particularly serious in early 1992. In May, in order to stop this, the Joint Police/Customs Anti-smuggling Task Force installed a 1.3 kilometre floating boom across the mouth of Tolo Harbour. Since the erection of the boom, smuggling activities have been contained.

In addition to these measures, two legislative amendments, namely the Import and Export (General) Regulations (Amendment of Schedules) Order 1992 and the Import and Export (Carriage of Articles) Regulations (Amendment of Schedule) Order 1992, were introduced in May 1992 to control the import and export of left hand drive vehicles and of outboard engines exceeding 150 horsepower, and the carriage of outboard engines exceeding 150 horsepower by vessels under 250 tons respectively.

Strategic Commodities

To tighten the control of strategic commodities, the Import and Export (Strategic Commodities) (Amendment) Regulations 1992 came into effect in May 1992. Licensing control on the import and export of strategic commodities was extended to include certain articles capable of being used in connection with chemical, biological or nuclear weapons, in so far as the importer or exporter knows that they will be used, or suspects that they might be used, for those purposes. The list of controlled articles was also expanded by including certain biological agents.

Customs Co-Operation Council

The Customs Co-Operation Council (CCC), of which Hong Kong is a member, was originally established to improve and rationalise international Customs operations and facilitate international trade. The Customs and Excise Department has assisted the CCC to

263

run a regional liaison office established in Hong Kong since December 1987. This is a central body, primarily for the co-ordination, analysis and dissemination of intelligence on Customs fraud and drug-related matters within the Economic and Social Commission for Asia and the Pacific Region.

Enforcement of Intellectual Property Rights Protection Legislation
The Customs and Excise Department investigates complaints relating to infringement of copyright and trade marks as well as false trade descriptions. Apart from maintaining close liaison with overseas enforcement authorities and with the owners of copyright and trade marks in the fight against counterfeiting and piracy, government officers have also been sent to international conferences and seminars on intellectual property rights protection.

The piracy of computer software and video tapes was contained significantly by the department's continued enforcement action. A new type of piracy of TV games emerged in 1992. Large quantities of infringing TV games and printed circuit boards were seized from various retail outlets and TV games centres with a total value of $37.80 million.

In suppressing illicit trade in counterfeit and falsely-labelled goods, seizures amounting to $193.40 million were recorded in 1992. Great attention was paid to the eradication of local manufacturing and distribution centres. Efforts were also made to eliminate retail outlets for fake watches, leatherware and clothing articles.

Police Complaints Committee
The main function of the Police Complaints Committee is to monitor and review investigation by the Complaints Against Police Office (CAPO) of the Royal Hong Kong Police of complaints made against the police by the public. Set up in 1986 to replace the former UMELCO Police Group, the committee is an independent body appointed by the Governor. The chairman and two vice-chairmen are normally drawn from the Office of Members of the Executive and Legislative Councils (OMELCO). Committee members include eight Justices of the Peace, the Attorney General or his representative and the Commissioner for Administrative Complaints.

During the year, the committee endorsed 3 102 complaint cases, after being satisfied that each case had been thoroughly and impartially investigated by CAPO. Arising from the reviewing of these complaint cases, the committee proposed a number of changes to police practices, procedures and instructions, with a view to improving the overall effectiveness of the complaint system and assisting the Commissioner of Police in minimising public complaints against the police.

Independent Commission Against Corruption
The Independent Commission Against Corruption (ICAC) is independent of the Civil Service; its commissioner is directly responsible to the Governor. It fights corruption on three fronts: investigation, prevention and education. It carries out this work through three functional departments – Operations, Corruption Prevention and Community Relations.

The ICAC received a total of 2 276 reports of corruption allegations in 1992. Setting aside those arising from public elections, 1 167 reports concerned the private sector, which was an increase of two per cent over 1991. Another 1 032 reports were made against civil servants, an increase of six per cent compared with 1991. There were 58 reports against employees of public bodies as compared with 64 in 1991.

Apart from reporting suspicions and fears of corruption, some members of the public tend to regard the ICAC as a conduit for general grievances against various government departments. In 1992, the ICAC received 820 non-corruption complaints, 594 of which were subsequently referred to the government departments concerned.

Operations

The Operations Department receives and investigates reports of suspected corruption offences under the Prevention of Bribery Ordinance and the ICAC Ordinance and deals with election malpractices under the Corrupt and Illegal Practices Ordinance.

Of the 2 276 corruption reports in 1992, the majority were lodged by members of the public who either visited or telephoned the department's report centre or one of ICAC's eight regional offices; 68 per cent of them were willing to identify themselves. The year saw an exceptionally high proportion of reports which were pursuable: 1 679 reports contained sufficient information for an investigation to commence.

The department's investigative case load remained at a high level during the year. Investigations resulted in the prosecution of 303 persons; another 167 were cautioned for lesser breaches of the law. At the end of the year 117 cases were awaiting trial and 1 001 investigations were still in progress.

The department has completed 178 investigations arising from the 1991 public elections: 10 persons have been charged, four persons were cautioned on the advice of the Attorney General, and another 76 verbally warned for minor election offences.

Video and audio recording of interviews with suspects are now a standard practice in the department's investigative process. All interview rooms were converted to offer video and audio recording facilities by the end of the year.

After a comprehensive review of the Prevention of Bribery and the Independent Commission Against Corruption Ordinances, legislative changes had been introduced to bring them in line with Hong Kong Bill of Rights Ordinance. These changes have ensured that the law continues its effectiveness and the ICAC maintains its capability to investigate corruption.

Computerisation of the department's manual records in a mainframe computer was completed in the end of the year; it has improved the department's capability to search and co-relate data.

Corruption Prevention

The Corruption Prevention Department is responsible for reviewing the practices and procedures of government departments and public bodies and recommending changes to reduce the likelihood of corruption. The department's Advisory Services Group provides free and confidential advice to private organisations on request.

During 1992, the department carried out 95 studies of specific activities within government departments and public bodies, addressing problems related to the implementation of policies and legislation and the management control of procedures and systems.

The department worked closely with the Immigration Department to plug any loopholes which might exist in the approval of applications for imported labour. This was complemented by a review of the labour legislation and corresponding enforcement measures to ensure compliance by employers. The department also conducted a major study of the inspection and verification procedures of the trade control function of the Customs and Excise Department.

The management of private multi-storey buildings had generated a sizeable proportion of corruption compliants. In conjunction with the City and New Territories Administration, the department introduced standard deeds of mutual covenant and produced a handbook advising owners' corporations on building management. It also assisted in reviewing the legislation in an attempt to improve the management of owners' corporations and to provide a legal framework conducive to effective building management.

The department played a consultative role in the privatisation of certain government functions and activities especially in the transport field. The main concern was to ensure that the selection criteria for tenderers were objective, and the operating procedures of the successful tenderers were free from corruption opportunities.

The department's Advisory Services Group responded to requests for assistance from 188 companies in 1992. It gave advice on ethical guidelines for employees and improvements to system controls to prevent corruption and fraud. Also, as the number of credit card frauds increased, the group recommended measures to companies concerned to prevent the illicit release of credit card information by corrupt employees to counterfeiting syndicates.

Community Relations

The Community Relations Department educates the public against the evils of corruption and enlists their support to fight the problem; it also aims to promote higher social and business ethical standards. It works through the mass media as well as direct personal approaches for different target audiences.

The department's eight regional offices act as focal points for carrying out anti-corruption liaison work and providing preventive education services to the community.

The department continued to place emphasis on the commercial and manufacturing sectors. Corruption prevention packages were produced for companies in the trading, real estate, hotel, property management, advertising, airline, travel and retailing industries. The packages were specially designed to help the chief executive identify corruption-prone areas in his company and to suggest preventive measures. During the year, specially-trained staff of the department established personal contacts with chief executives and senior managers of 1 820 companies to introduce these packages to them.

Using the less labour-intensive method of direct mail, the department put anti-corruption messages across to over 13 000 small trading firms during the year. This method was developed specifically to enhance liaison with the large number of small-sized firms.

A total of 58 organisations from both the private and public sectors took part in the department's Community Participation Programme under which they organised their own anti-corruption activities and received a small ICAC subsidy towards the cost of those activities.

For government departments and public bodies, the department conducted talks and seminars for a total of 18 350 existing staff and new recruits. The objective was to inform them of the law and to enhance their awareness against bribery in the course of their duty.

On the mass media front, in addition to a series of television, radio and press advertisements, advertising on buses and telephone booths was introduced to motivate the public to support ICAC's work and to report corruption offences. A television drama series based on actual ICAC cases was televised during the year. The television series aimed to increase the public's understanding of ICAC's investigation work. A radio drama phone-in programme was produced with the co-operation of Radio Television Hong Kong. It provided a forum for the public to express their views on issues about corruption.

A new package of anti-corruption teaching material has been developed by the department for launching in early 1993: the 'Onward to 21 – Life and Work Guidance Package' is designed to instil a positive attitude and a strong sense of work ethics in would-be school leavers.

International Co-operation

International inter-agency co-operation is essential if effective action is to be taken against corruption which crosses all forms of borders and boundaries. A good example was the great success in the crackdown of syndicated corruption-related crime in credit card fraud in which inter-agency cooperation was an essential element.

In March, the commissioner and heads of the ICAC's three departments delivered key speeches at the Fifth International Anti-Corruption Conference held in Amsterdam. The commissioner led an ICAC delegation to China to visit the Guangdong Provincial People's Procuratorate and the Supreme People's Procuratorate in September, and the Hainan Supervision Bureau in October for a general exchange of views and experience.

In Hong Kong, the ICAC played host to a regional seminar on corruption-related crime in September with a view to creating a multi-agency forum within the Asia-Pacific region for discussion of particular operational problems which have regional or global implications. The seminar was attended by 16 overseas delegates from six countries. During the year, the ICAC also received 65 visitors from law enforcement agencies of various countries, including the United Kingdom, the United States of America, Australia, China, Egypt, Zambia and Tanzania.

On the investigation side, the Operations Department sent its officers overseas on more than 118 occasions for specific enquiries into various cases.

Checks and Balances

To minimise the possibility of any abuse of power, the ICAC is subject to a stringent system of checks and balances. At the policy level the ICAC is guided by an Advisory Committee on Corruption which reviews and advises the commissioner on all aspects of anti-corruption policy, strategy and legislation. It comprises seven prominent citizens and three government officials.

When an investigation is completed, decisions to prosecute are made independently by the Attorney General or his representatives. The courts alone decide on the guilt or innocence of the accused. If the Attorney General's decision is not to prosecute, then the results of the investigation are submitted for advice on what further action is necessary to the Operations Review Committee comprising four civic leaders appointed by the Governor and four senior officials.

Two other committees, the Citizens Advisory Committee on Community Relations and the Corruption Prevention Advisory Committee, review and advise on the work of the Community Relations Department and Corruption Prevention Department respectively.

Members of the public can lodge formal complaints against ICAC officers to an ICAC Complaints Committee comprising eight members, among who are five members of the

267

Executive and Legislative Councils, the Attorney General and the Commissioner for Administrative Complaints. In addition, the Operations Department has an internal investigation group which monitors and investigates corruption and the criminal behaviour of any ICAC officer.

The Way Ahead

The ICAC will be reaching its 20th year of operation in 1994. While corruption is no longer a way of life as it was when the Commission was established in 1974, the community must continue to remain vigilant. Given continued public support, the ICAC is confident that the problem will be kept under control in the run-up to 1997 and beyond.

Government Laboratory

The Forensic Science Division of the Government Laboratory provides a comprehensive scientific forensic service to law enforcement departments in Hong Kong. During the year, it was actively engaged in the scientific investigation of such diverse crimes as armed robbery, homicide, arson, fatal traffic accidents, commercial fraud, manufacture and trafficking of narcotic drugs and possession of controlled pharmaceutical preparations. In line with its commitment for the provision of expert evidence in courts of law, the service not only encompasses a wide range of analytical tasks but also, where necessary, supplements the analytical results with informed scientific opinion on their significance. The scientific evidence can be instrumental, not only in helping law enforcement agencies and the Crown Prosecutor decide whether or not to prosecute but also in assisting the court in criminal trials at all levels. In this way, the division forms an important link between law and order and judiciary services.

The nine specialist sections of the Division are organised into two groups. The Presumptive Evidence Group concentrates on cases involving opinion evidence, whilst the Definitive (Statutory) Evidence Group concentrates on the activities of the sections concerned with drug analysis. In addition, the division provides a 24-hour scene-of-crime service to law enforcement agencies in Hong Kong. During the year 551 crime scenes were attended with scientific evidence collected at the scenes of crime for subsequent examination.

After three years of painstaking development, with over 600 samples profiled to establish a database for the local ethnic community, DNA profiling is now at a stage where limited casework can be undertaken for investigations where body fluid analysis is vital for the police investigation, in particular serious crime against the person, such as serial rape cases and homicide. As a new service, funding for the DNA Section has been restricted by the government austerity drive but it was still possible for more than 1 000 case-related profiles to be performed and that demands for DNA profiling will increase. Increases in both document items received and case numbers were experienced in the Questioned Documents Section and the trend is in line with Hong Kong becoming one of the world's major financial centres. The escalating trend in the number of cases involving vehicle engine or chassis number restorations has reflected the growing menace of vehicle theft in the city.

The Definitive (Statutory) Evidence Group deals with drug analysis and forensic toxicology which are method intensive. During the year, over 5 800 biological samples, 50 000 urine samples for drug monitoring, 50 000 opiate drug samples and 28 000 non-opiate drug samples were examined. Overall the group has encountered increasing numbers

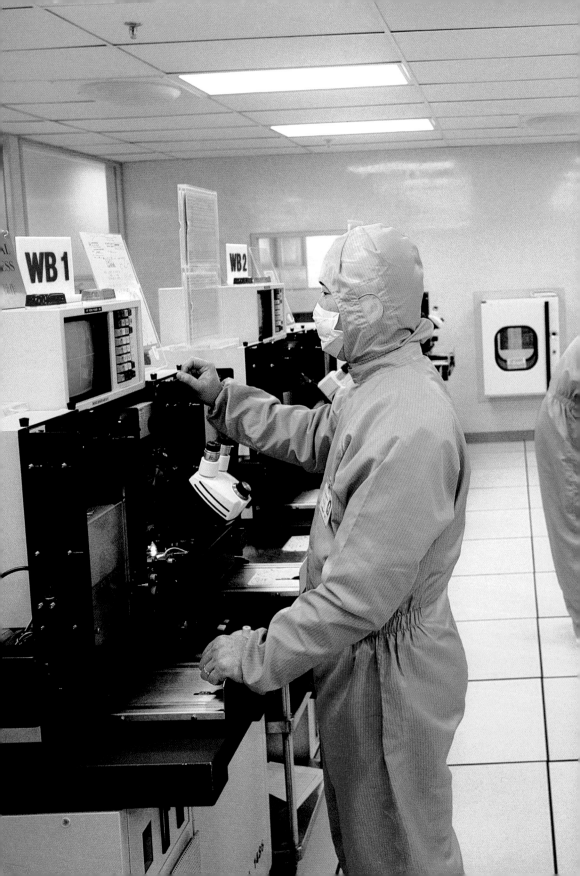

Preceding page: *Precise dimensions and surface quality are the most important considerations in the manufacture of high quality electro-deposited copper foil used in the manufacture of computer circuit boards.*

Left and below: *Technicians at work in the manufacture, checking and testing of semi-conductors, an important electronic component in the manufacture of computers and consumer products.*

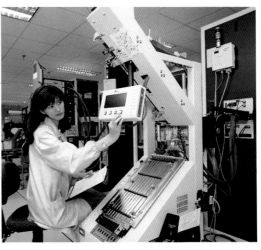

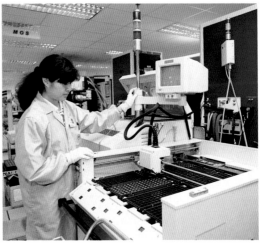

Stages in the production of compact discs: recording **(left),** *duplicating and cutting* **(below).**

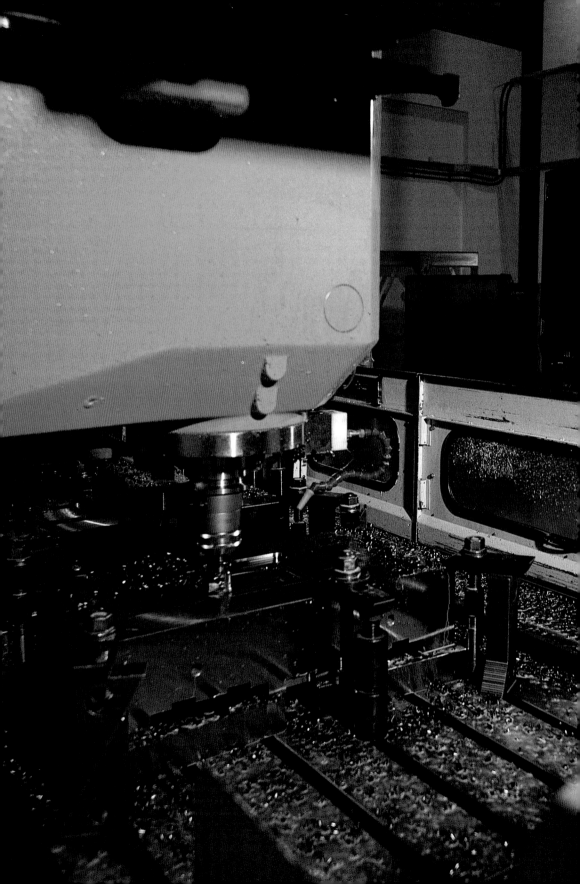

Engineers at work on the production of metal moulds and dies **(left)** for use in the manufacture of plastics products and **(below)** the design of machinery parts by computer.

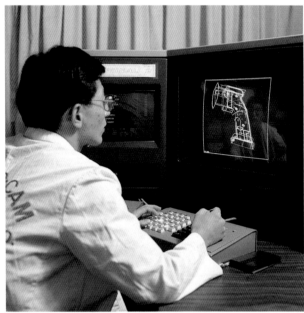

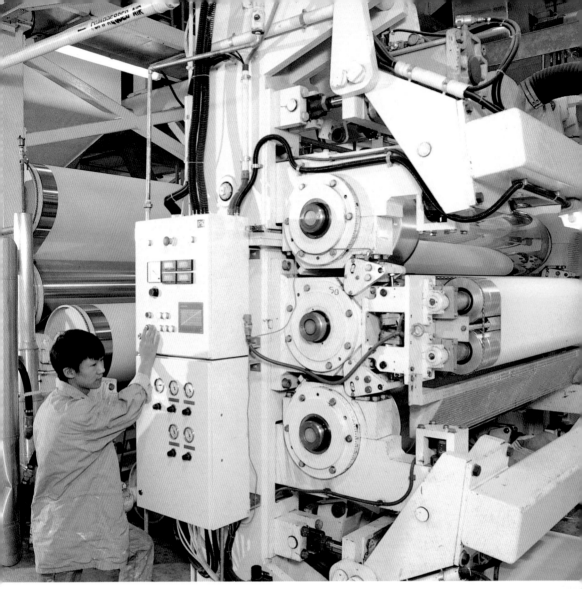

Above: *Chemical coating and drying in the manufacture of facsimile paper.*

Right: *Paper cutting and packing.*

of a wider range of drugs. For example, in late 1991–early 1992 there was an emergence of heroin laced with methylamphetamine, two drugs of opposite physiological effect, one a narcotic analgesic, the other a central nervous stimulant. The advantage of automated analytical systems has been recognised and assay of heroin is now fully automated. In addition, considerable efforts have been directed towards improving work flow and intelligence gathering by the use of computers so that drug trends can be more closely monitored and the relevant authorities more quickly alerted and appropriate legislation eventuated to control any changing drug abuse situation.

In December the Forensic Science Division vacated its dispersed Police Headquarters locations to join its sister division, Analytical and Advisory Services, in a new custom-built Government Laboratory complex, in Ho Man Tin. The co-ordination of resources and vastly improved facilities resulting from the move will herald a new era in the progress of forensic analysis in Hong Kong.

Immigration Department

By controlling entry into Hong Kong, the Immigration Department plays an important role in maintaining law and order.

Through examination at control points and vetting of visa applications, undesirable persons including international criminals and terrorists are detected and refused entry into Hong Kong. In 1992, 21 662 such travellers and persons not in possession of proper documentation were refused permission to land and 2 477 persons were refused visas.

Detection of Forged Travel Documents

During the year, a total of 2 840 forged travel documents were detected, representing an increase of 1.68 per cent on the 2 793 in 1991.

Sustained efforts were required to guard against the upsurge in the use of forged travel documents by illegal immigrants and travellers. Intelligence on forgery was collected and quickly disseminated. There was frequent contact with other local and overseas law enforcement agencies and consulates, and special operations are mounted against forgery syndicates.

Interception of Wanted Persons

During the year, 101 055 persons were intercepted at immigration control points and immigration and registration of persons offices. Of these, 654 were wanted in connection with murder cases, 4 373 were suspected robbers, 52 455 were involved in the trafficking of dangerous drugs and 36 403 were involved in other criminal offences. In addition, 239 known or suspected terrorists were identified at points of entry.

Illegal Immigration

The availability of employment opportunities in Hong Kong continued to attract large numbers of illegal immigrants to the territory. The lower wages accepted by those immigrants encouraged unscrupulous employers to offer them employment. Frequent checks were therefore conducted at target locations, including construction sites, factories, restaurants and other places of employment. Illegal immigrants arrested at these places were prosecuted and sentenced to imprisonment before they were repatriated to their

269

places of origin. Employers of illegal immigrants, including principal contractors in the construction industry, were also prosecuted and fined and, in serious cases, custodial sentences were imposed. In addition, publicity has emphasised that there will be no amnesties.

In 1992, a total of 43 096 illegal immigrants were apprehended and repatriated. This represents an increase of 28.01 per cent on the 33 667 in 1991.

Investigation and Prosecution of Immigration Offences

During the year, a total of 6 639 charges were laid against persons who had committed various immigration offences. Apart from illegal immigration, these offences included illegal remaining, breach of condition of stay, making false statements or representations, and conspiracy in the use and supply of forged documents.

Deportation and Removal

The Immigration Department is responsible for the application, issue and execution of deportation and removal orders. During the year, 6 188 persons who were convicted for possession or trafficking in dangerous drugs, deception, theft and other criminal offences were considered for deportation, and consequently 199 were deported. In addition, 4 746 persons were removed from Hong Kong under removal orders. These included 4 400 illegal immigrants and 346 persons who had breached their condition of stay.

Fire Services

It was again a busy and eventful year for the Fire Services Department which responded to 27 810 fire calls, 17 056 special service calls, 251 058 emergency and 172 924 non-emergency ambulance calls.

The fires caused 43 deaths and 573 people injured, including 32 firemen. A total of 22 347 people were rescued by Fire Services personnel during the year.

Fire Prevention

The department is responsible for formulating and enforcing fire safety regulations. It also advises and assists the community on fire protection measures and abatement of fire hazards. Besides updating and reviewing existing fire safety legislation and Codes of Practice, the Fire Protection Bureau places great emphasis on public education concerning fire prevention. In addition to a major publicity campaign, fire officers gave 409 lectures/ talks during the year to a total audience of 17 965 from different sectors of the community, including students. These were supplemented by exhibitions and demons-trations aimed at educating the public on fire safety. The department is also responsible for research on matters associated with fire safety. A total of 5 018 fire hazard complaints were received from members of the public in 1992. There is a growing public concern about fire hazards and an increasing awareness of the services provided by the department. Fire Services personnel made 74 489 inspections of all types of premises and issued 4 473 abatement notices for the removal of fire hazards. There were 523 prosecutions during the year for non-compliance with abatement notices and for summonses, resulting in fines amounting to about $1.8 million. Furthermore, direct prosecutions on obstruction to means of escape and indiscriminate blocking of fire exits in buildings amounted to 210 convictions with total fines of $0.8 million.

Plans for new buildings are vetted by the department, and during this process requirements for built-in fire protection are specified and advice is given. Some 7 100 submissions of building plans were processed during the year.

Upon the enactment of the Hotel and Guesthouse Accommodation Ordinance and the Clubs (Safety of Premises) Ordinance in 1991, six fire protection officers were deployed to assist the controlling authority, the Secretary for Home Affairs, in the licensing process on fire safety matters. In 1992, a total of 776 and 1 685 inspections were made by fire officers to hotels/guesthouses and club establishments respectively. Requirements to upgrade fire safety measures in these premises to current standards were also issued.

Ambulance Services

The Ambulance Service, staffed by 2 063 uniformed personnel and 153 civilians, operates 281 ambulances and ambulance-aided motorcycles from 29 depots/stations throughout the territory and from many fire stations.

During the year, the service handled a total of 423 982 emergency and non-emergency calls providing assistance to 546 352 people, representing an average of 1 158 calls per day.

Facilities on ambulances are constantly reviewed and all ambulances are equipped with analgesic apparatus, piped oxygen, inflatable splints, special stretchers and incubator-carrying capability.

A radio/telephone patching system was installed in the Fire Services Communication Centre to enable interactive communication between ambulances and major hospitals.

A group of ambulance personnel were trained in the use of automatic advisory defibrillators to handle patients/casualties suffering from heart attacks. Since December 1991, all ambulance-aid motorcycles have been equipped with defibrillators.

Plans have been formulated to enhance the standard of ambulance service to paramedic level. Two ambulance officers have been sent to the Academy, Institute of Justice, British Columbia, Canada, for paramedic training. These officers will be involved in the planning of locally-organised paramedic training courses.

With a view to better utilising ambulance resources, the department is planning to hive off the non-emergency ambulance service to the Hospital Authority in phases.

Appliances and Workshops

The department has some 700 modern operational appliances and vehicles fitted with up-to-date fire-fighting and rescue equipment to ensure that fast and efficient fire-fighting and rescue operations can be carried out. During the year, 50 new or replacement appliances and vehicles of various kinds were put into service.

The department is constantly evaluating new products from different parts of the world to see if they can be used locally. A new type of pumping appliance, which has excellent road holding characteristics and exceptional manoeuvrability, will be introduced to Hong Kong.

To maintain its fleet of fire appliances and rescue equipment in an effective and satisfactory condition, the department operates four workshops – one each on Hong Kong Island, and in the New Territories, and two in Kowloon.

Communications

The computer based mobilising and communication system installed in the Fire Services Communication Centre enables rescue and ambulance resources to be mobilised efficiently

271

and effectively. This system assists the department to respond to about 85 per cent of all fire calls within the prescribed graded response time and to about 91 per cent of all emergency ambulance calls within the target travel time.

Staff Training

The Fire Services Training School at Pat Heung, New Territories, provides initial training for all ranks except senior firemen/firewomen (control) in the Mobilising and Communications Group. In August 1992 a new Ambulance Training School at Ma On Shan in Sha Tin was established and took over the training of ambulance personnel. The various training courses range from three to 26 weeks in duration.

During the year, 272 recruits comprising 48 station officers, five senior firemen (control), seven senior firewomen (control), 167 firemen and 45 ambulancemen successfully completed their initial training.

The Fire Services Training School also provides training to 525 staff of other government departments and private organisations on basic fire-fighting and the use of breathing apparatus. In response to requests from fire services of other countries, the school also provides training for their officers.

To meet operational needs and for career development purposes, 12 officers were sent to the United Kingdom, the United States, Canada and Japan for management and professional training. In-service training is provided for 216 fire and 1 001 ambulance personnel. The Driving Training School conducted appliance driving and operation courses for 1 476 officers and other ranks during the year.

Establishment and Recruitment

As at the end of 1992, the establishment stood at 7 228 and 728 for uniformed and civilian staff respectively. The department continued its recruitment exercises with 65 station officers, 12 senior firemen/firewomen (control) and 310 firemen being appointed. Standards are high and on average only 13.5 per cent are accepted for appointment.

Buildings and Quarters

In line with government policy to provide an emergency response to all areas within minimum set times according to the category of risk, the department continues to plan and build fire stations and ambulance depots at strategic locations to cope with local developments.

During the year, Siu Lek Yuen Fire Station, Ma On Shan Fire Station, Ma On Shan Ambulance Depot and Ho Man Tin Ambulance Depot were completed to improve services in these areas. There are now 63 fire stations, 29 ambulance depots/stations and five fireboat stations in the territory. Planning is in hand for the provision of about 980 additional married quarters for firemen and ambulancemen.

Correctional Services

The Correctional Services Department administers a wide range of programmes for both adult and young offenders, drug addicts and the criminally insane. Broadly, three categories of service are provided – custodial, after-care and industries. In addition, the department also manages detention centres for Vietnamese migrants.

At the end of 1992, the department was managing 19 correctional institutions, three halfway houses, a staff training institute, an escort unit, a custodial ward in Queen Mary Hospital and one in Queen Elizabeth Hospital and six detention centres for Vietnamese migrants. Policy guidance and administrative support is provided from its headquarters. There were 7 070 staff looking after 11 207 inmates, 32 746 Vietnamese migrants, and 3 256 persons under after-care supervision.

During the year, the number of Vietnamese migrants gradually decreased as a consequence of the implementation of the Orderly Return Programme and there was a decline in the number of Chinese illegal immigrants in custody. The workload of the department in managing Vietnamese migrants however remains heavy. This is due to taking over the management of some 6 500 Vietnamese migrants from the police-run Sek Kong Detention Centre.

Male Offenders

Prisoners are assigned to institutions according to their security rating, which takes into account, among other things, the risk they pose to the community and whether or not they are first offenders.

There are 11 prisons for adult male prisoners including:
* four of maximum security: Stanley Prison, Shek Pik Prison, Siu Lam Psychiatric Centre and Lai Chi Kok Reception Centre;
* three of medium security: Ma Po Ping Prison, Tung Tau Correctional Institution and Victoria Prison; and
* four of minimum security: Tai Lam Correctional Institution, Pik Uk Prison, Tong Fuk Centre and Ma Hang Prison.

Stanley Prison and Shek Pik Prison house prisoners serving long sentences or life imprisonment. Siu Lam Psychiatric Centre accommodates the criminally insane and those requiring psychiatric treatment. Adult males awaiting trial or remanded in custody during court hearings are detained at Lai Chi Kok Reception Centre which also has a separate section for male civil debtors. Victoria Prison houses illegal immigrants pending repatriation to China and a special section at Ma Hang Prison has been set aside for geriatric prisoners. Adult prisoners released under the Pre-Release Employment Scheme are provided with accommodation at Phoenix House, a halfway house for adult and young offenders.

Young Male Offenders

The department administers four correctional programmes for young male offenders under the Prisons, Training Centres, Drug Addiction Treatment Centres and Detention Centres Ordinances.

The maximum security Pik Uk Correctional Institution is run as a reception centre and training centre as well as a prison for young offenders under 25 years of age, including those who are remanded for pre-sentence reports on their suitability for admission to the training centre programmes.

Cape Collinson Correctional Institution houses those between the ages of 14 and 17, and Lai King Training Centre, those between 18 and 20 years who have been sentenced to the training centre programme.

Lai Sun Correctional Institution on Hei Ling Chau accommodates young prisoners aged between 14 and 20. To cope with the increased penal population, a portion of Sha Tsui

273

Detention Centre was gazetted in April 1989 to hold young prisoners between 14 and 20 years of age. Since early 1990, sections of Lai Sun Correctional Institution and Sha Tsui Detention Centre have been further utilised to accommodate adult prisoners, under a separate programme, in order to cope with the then increasing number of illegal immigrant prisoners. During 1992, the general overcrowding was slightly eased.

A very effective detention centre programme is carried out at the medium security Sha Tsui Detention Centre. There are two sections, one for young offenders aged between 14 and 20 and the other for young adults aged between 21 and 24. The detention centre programme emphasises strict discipline, strenuous training, hard work and a vigorous routine.

Young male offenders released under supervision from the detention or training centres or from prisons under the Pre-Release Employment Scheme may also be placed in Phoenix House. Residents in this halfway house must go out to work or attend full-time school in the day time. Young offenders identified as having special needs on discharge from a training centre or detention centre are required to stay in the house for up to three months before they are permitted to live at home or in other places while continuing to be under after-care supervision.

Female Offenders

Adult females serve their sentences at Tai Lam Centre for Women which also has sections for remand prisoners and those undergoing drug addiction treatment. Most of the women are employed in an industrial laundry which provides services to government departments and public hospitals.

Female offenders under 21 years of age are held at Tai Tam Gap Correctional Institution where separate sections are provided for training centre inmates, drug addiction treatment centre inmates, young prisoners and remands.

Bauhinia House serves as a halfway house for women and girls released under supervision from the training centre or under the Pre-release Employment Scheme. Residents in this halfway house also go out to work during the day and return in the evening.

Drug Addiction Treatment

Drug addicts found guilty of an offence punishable by imprisonment may be sentenced under the Drug Addiction Treatment Centres Ordinance to a drug addiction treatment centre. They can be detained for two to 12 months depending on their progress. In-centre treatment is followed by 12-months statutory after-care supervision.

Male addicts are treated at Hei Ling Chau Addiction Treatment Centre while female adult addicts receive treatment at Tai Lam Centre for Women and the young at Tai Tam Gap Correctional Institution.

The drug addiction treatment programme aims to detoxify, restore physical health and, through the application of therapeutic and rehabilitative treatment, wean addicts from their dependence on drugs. There is also intensive follow-up after-care supervision during which time supervisees may be recalled for further treatment should supervision conditions be contravened.

Assistance is also given to addiction treatment centre inmates with post-release employment and accommodation. Temporary accommodation is available at the New Life

House, a halfway house for those who are in need of such support immediately following release.

Young Offender Assessment Panel

The Young Offender Assessment Panel, comprising staff from the Correctional Services and Social Welfare Departments, was established in April 1987 to provide magistrates with recommendations on the most appropriate programmes of rehabilitation for young offenders between 14 and 25. The service provided by the panel is available to Juvenile Courts and certain magistracies.

Education and Vocational Training

Offenders under the age of 21 attend educational and vocational training classes conducted by qualified teachers. Textbooks compiled by the department are used to provide inmates with more suitable and practical learning material matching their maturity in personality growth and development.

Adult offenders attend evening classes on a voluntary basis run by part-time teachers recruited by the department. Self-study packages and external correspondence courses are also available for those who are interested in taking part.

Both young and adult offenders are encouraged to take part in public examinations organised by the City and Guilds of London Institute, Pitman Examinations Institute, London Chamber of Commerce and Industry, and the Hong Kong Examinations Authority. Inmates are permitted to sit for the Hong Kong Certificate of Education examinations as school candidates. Some adult offenders have also participated in degree courses offered by the local Open Learning Institute and other academic institutions. In addition, a direct referral system has also been established with the Vocational Training Council, the Construction Industry Training Authority and the Clothing Industry Training Centre to help young inmates further their training upon release.

Skill training programmes have also been introduced on a voluntary basis for adult offenders at Ma Po Ping Prison, Tong Fuk Centre, Tai Lam Correctional Institution, Pik Uk Prison, Tung Tau Correctional Institution and Tai Lam Centre for Women.

Medical Services

All institutions have their own medical units providing basic treatment, health and dental care, including radiodiagnostic and pathological examinations as well as prophylactic inoculations. Inmates requiring specialist treatment are either referred to a visiting consultant or to specialist clinics in public hospitals. Those requiring hospitalisation are usually kept in custodial wards in public hospitals under the charge of correctional services officers.

Siu Lam Psychiatric Centre continues to treat prisoners with mental health problems and offer psychiatric consultations and assessments for inmates referred by other institutions and the courts.

Ante-natal and post-natal care is provided within institutions for female inmates but babies are normally delivered in public hospitals.

In addition to the custodial ward at Queen Mary Hospital, the department took over the security management of the custodial ward at Queen Elizabeth Hospital in June 1992. Although HIV/AIDS is still not a problem among the penal population, the department is committed to a programme of education and prevention.

275

Psychological Services
Clinical psychologists and specially-trained officers provide a wide range of counselling services for inmates with emotional difficulties, behavioural or personality problems. Professional consultation is offered to the courts, relevant review boards and the management of institutions to facilitate their decision making with regard to the disposal, treatment and management of the offenders. Research projects are regularly undertaken in order to improve treatment programmes and to reduce recidivism.

Visiting Justices
Justices of the Peace appointed by the Governor visit penal institutions and the centres for Vietnamese migrants, either fortnightly or monthly, depending on the type of institution. They investigate complaints, inspect diets and report on living and working conditions. They may also advise the Commissioner of Correctional Services on the employment of prisoners and work opportunities after release.

Inspectorate and Management Services
The Department's Inspectorate and Management Services Division provides support to continuously refine and develop departmental strategy and policy on penal management functions. The division consists of three units each tasked with the responsibility to systematically review and streamline procedures, rules and regulations; to conduct inspections and to monitor activities in penal institutions; and to redress grievances and investigate complaints lodged by the prisoners and the public as well as correctional services staff.

After-care Services
After-care services are provided to inmates discharged from training, detention and drug addiction treatment centres, and to young prisoners, also including adult prisoners who participate in the Release Under Supervision and Pre-Release Employment Schemes. The primary objective of after-care is to assist offenders in their rehabilitation and re-integration into the community. It also plays an essential role in enhancing their determination in leading an industrious and law-abiding life upon discharge.

After-care commences immediately after the admission of an inmate into an institution. Each inmate is assigned to the care of an after-care officer who will provide him with adequate support and guidance enabling him to adapt to the institutional programme. A sound relationship between the inmate, his family and the after-care officer is established to help the inmate overcome obstacles to rehabilitation.

Inmates are assisted, through individual and group counselling, to gain a better insight into problems arising from their social inadequacies. They are helped to become better prepared to cope with difficulties upon release.

Regular contacts with the ex-inmates are maintained during their statutory supervision period by the after-care officers to ensure that the supervisees gradually settle down in the community and that the terms of the supervision orders are strictly complied with. Any breach of supervision conditions may result in the person being recalled for a further period of training or treatment.

Under the provisions of the Prisoners (Release Under Supervision) Ordinance, prisoners, other than those serving life sentences or subject to deportation upon discharge, who have served not less than half or 20 months (whichever period is the longer) of a sentence of three years or more may apply to join the Release Under Supervision Scheme for the remaining portion of their sentences; and those who are serving sentences of two years or more and are within six months of completing their sentence after taking into consideration remission, may apply to join the Pre-Release Employment Scheme. Following approval by the Release Under Supervision Board, successful applicants then go out to work and reside in a designated hostel under the supervision of after-care officers for the balance of their sentence. The aim of the scheme is to enable suitable, eligible and motivated prisoners to serve their sentences in an open environment under close supervision. Prisoners who breach supervision conditions may be recalled to serve the remainder of their sentences.

The success of the after-care programmes is measured by the percentage of supervisees who complete supervision without reconviction and, where applicable, remain drug-free. At the end of 1992, the annual success rates were 93 per cent for detention centre inmates, 71 per cent for male training centre inmates, 92 per cent for female training centre inmates, 77 per cent for young male prisoners, 100 per cent for young female prisoners, 64 per cent for male drug addiction treatment centre inmates, 72 per cent for female drug addiction treatment centre inmates, 100 per cent for Release Under Supervision Scheme and 100 per cent for Pre-Release Employment Scheme.

Correctional Services Industries

Correctional Services Industries aim to keep prisoners and inmates gainfully employed, thereby reducing the risk of unrest through boredom and lack of constructive activities. The industries also help to reduce government expenditure by providing products and services to government departments and public organisations.

All convicted prisoners who are medically fit are required by law to work six days per week. Prisoners are paid for their work and they can make use of their earnings to purchase food extras and other canteen items approved by the management. More importantly, they acquire the habit of doing useful work through participation in industrial production, eventually helping them to find a job after release.

The industries run a number of trades, the largest being laundry and garment making. Other trades include silkscreening, printing, envelope making, bookbinding, shoe-making, fibreglass work, metal work, leather work, precast concrete and carpentry. The commercial value of goods and services provided for the year is estimated to be $300 million.

Detention Centres

The award of automatic refugee status to Vietnamese people reaching Hong Kong discontinued following a change in policy on June 16, 1988. In May 1990, the department ceased to be responsible for managing closed centres for refugees, a task first undertaken in July 1982.

Under the existing policy, Vietnamese people arriving in Hong Kong will be screened by immigration officers while being held in detention centres to determine their status. Those screened in as refugees are transferred to open centres, while those screened out will remain in the detention centres until arrangements can be made for their repatriation. Any person who has been screened out may appeal to a Refugee Status Review Board which has the power to overturn that decision.

The department now manages six centres for Vietnamese migrants who are held pending their screening procedure or repatriation arrangement. They include the detention centre at Chi Ma Wan, Hei Ling Chau, Nei Kwu Chau, Whitehead and High Island, and a reception centre at Green Island.

Voluntary agencies, co-ordinated by the United Nations High Commissioner for Refugees (UNHCR), continue to provide valuable services in detention centres, complementing those provided by the department.

Staff Training

The department's Staff Training Institute is responsible for the planning and implementation of training programmes for both new and serving officers. All recruit officers and assistant officers must undergo a Basic Training Course for a period of 2: weeks and 20 weeks respectively. The training syllabus includes the relevant laws of Hong Kong, foot-drill, self-defence, physical training, weaponry, anti-riot drill, first-aid criminology, penology, basic psychology, social work and leadership training. Prior to completion of probation, officers and assistant officers are required to undergo further training in anti-riot techniques for eight weeks and seven weeks respectively.

Development training and job-orientated courses are provided throughout the year for serving officers to update their professional knowledge, to prepare for promotion and to equip selected officers for duties in specialised fields such as counselling, after-care, nursing, psychological services and physical education. Weekly in-service training is carried out within institutions to cater for the needs of individual institutions.

Non-Government Organisations

A number of organisations assist the department in providing services to help ex-prisoners reintegrate into the community. These organisations include the Society for the Rehabilitation of Offenders, Hong Kong Caritas Lok Heep Club and the Christian Kun Sun Association who provide a wide range of services, such as case work, counselling, hostel accommodation, employment guidance, recreational activities as well as care for those who have a history of mental illness.

Civil Aid Services

The Civil Aid Services (CAS) is an auxiliary emergency relief organisation. Its main role is to support other regular government departments tackling emergency situations. The CAS is financed by the government and has an establishment of 3 818 uniformed and disciplined adult volunteers, 3 232 cadets and 126 permanent staff.

Role and Responsibilities

With a heavy emphasis on coping with natural disasters, the tasks of the CAS are numerous and far-reaching. The volunteers are trained to perform counter-disaster duties during tropical cyclones, when landslips and flooding occur; to search for and rescue persons trapped in collapsed buildings; to fight forest fires and to patrol country parks; to manage Vietnamese detention centres; to combat oil pollution at sea; to assist the police in crowd control and incident management; and to perform first-aid, casualty handling and evacuation. They also carry out difficult mountain rescue operations. On any weekend or public holiday it is normal for over 500 volunteers to perform duty.

Civil Duties

The CAS is also very heavily committed in the performance of civic duties in normal times. During the year, adult volunteers help to organise and provide crowd control, communications and marshalling services in charity fund-raising activities, government campaigns and at other public functions.

Vietnamese Migrant Duties

The CAS permanent staff and volunteers are presently required to manage two Vietnamese Centres, namely the New Horizons Vietnamese Refugee Departure Centre for Vietnamese refugees who have been accepted for resettlement overseas and the Kai Tak Vietnamese Migrant Transit Centre for Vietnamese migrants who have volunteered for repatriation to Vietnam, pregnant Vietnamese women pending delivery, together with their accompanying relatives from detention centres elsewhere and other Vietnamese migrants lodged temporarily while seeking medical treatment/advice or other facilities.

The work in the centres is both physically and psychologically exhausting. Duties are performed under demanding and difficult conditions. Much dedication and patience is required of those involved.

The CAS has been capable of meeting all demands encountered in this area thus far. CAS volunteers have been involved in dealing with the Vietnamese migrant problem since 1975 and continuously since 1988. This work will continue for the foreseeable future.

Service Training

Service training is divided into centralised courses and unit training, both of which are designed to promote and maintain the operational efficiency of the services. The centralised courses in 1992–3 embrace a wide variety of subjects. In addition to normal counter-disaster courses, first aid, fire fighting and conventional rescue instruction have been included, the aim being to train adult volunteers in disaster control and management during large-scale emergencies and at civic functions.

Overseas training was organised for both permanent staff and volunteer officers. In 1992, one officer attended the Asian Disaster Preparedness Centre in Bangkok, Thailand, for disaster management training and two officers were attached to the Royal Air Force in the United Kingdom to undergo advanced Mountain Rescue Training. A contingent of senior CAS Officers was invited to visit the Civil Defence establishment in Shanghai in April 1992 to study the disaster management technology in China.

Cadet Corps

The Cadet Corps is divided into three girl units, 24 boy units and five mixed units spread throughout the territory. Cadets enter at the age of 12 to 14 and undertake a series of training courses. Tuition includes training in basic mechanical and electrical engineering, carpentry and fibreglass moulding, printing and book-binding as well as training in photography and interior design. The cadets are also trained in countryside preservation, first-aid, crowd-control psychology, road safety, rock climbing, orienteering, expeditions and trekking. They are encouraged to participate in the Duke of Edinburgh Award Scheme. In 1992, four cadets qualified for the Gold Award, 20 for Silver Awards and 72 for Bronze Awards. At 18, the cadets leave the corps and may join the Adult Services.

Royal Hong Kong Auxiliary Air Force
The Royal Hong Kong Auxiliary Air Force (RHKAAF), based at Kowloon Bay, provides a variety of flying services for the government. It operates a fleet of 15 aircraft: two twin-engined Beech Super King Airs, a Britten-Norman Islander, four Slingsby Firefly trainers and eight Sikorsky helicopters. Two Sikorsky Blackhawk helicopters were delivered in January 1993 to provide specialist flying support to the police. With an establishment of 226 permanent staff and 47 part-time volunteers comprising aircrew, engineers and administrative staff, the RHKAAF can operate round-the-clock for seven days a week during an emergency. Over 6 152 hours were flown during the year.

In 1992, the RHKAAF responded to 898 requests for emergency medical evacuation and rescue. Some of these came from the local fleet of about 5 000 fishing boats, many of which now have high-frequency radios enabling them to call for assistance when necessary. A total of 127 search and rescue operations were carried out, involving helicopters and fixed-wing aircraft. During the dry season, the helicopters assisted in 113 fire-fighting operations and dropped over 1 345 tonnes of water on bush and forest fires in areas inaccessible to conventional fire-fighting appliances.

The Police Force and the Correctional Services made frequent use of helicopters for training and operational purposes. Helicopter flights were routinely provided to transport engineering staff to hilltops to carry out maintenance and repair work at communications repeater stations. During the year, about 6 768 government officers were flown to various areas in the course of their duties. Flying services were also provided to give official overseas visitors an overview of the territory. Helicopter flying services were provided daily to the police for border patrol duty.

The Super King Airs maintained regular offshore patrols in connection with anti-illegal immigration operations and were also heavily employed in support of the Buildings and Lands Department's continuing need for aerial surveys, photography and map-making. The Fireflys and Islander provided pilot training for the squadron's cadet pilots.

The Royal Hong Kong Auxiliary Air Force, one of Her Majesty's Commonwealth Air Forces, disbanded on March 31, 1993 and on April 1, 1993 was re-established as the Hong Kong Government Flying Service and become a full-time civilian disciplined Force providing flying services to the Hong Kong Government under civil aviation legislation.

19
TRAVEL AND TOURISM

HONG KONG's outbound travel business is operated by some 1 000 travel agents who are licensed by the Registrar of Travel Agents under the Travel Agents Ordinance. The ordinance provides the statutory framework for regulation of the outbound travel industry. In order to be licensed, a travel agent must be a member of the Travel Industry Council of Hong Kong.

The council is an approved organisation of travel agents in Hong Kong. It comprises seven association members: Hong Kong Association of Travel Agents Limited; Federation of Hong Kong Travellers Limited; International Chinese Tourist Association Limited; Society of International Air Transport Association Passenger Agents Limited; Hong Kong Taiwan Tourist Operators Association Limited; Hong Kong Association of China Travel Organisers Limited; and Hong Kong Outbound Tour Operators' Association Limited. The council regulates member travel agents by means of codes of practice and occasional directives. Members who breach the rules of self-regulation risk losing their council membership and their licence to operate.

Outbound travellers on tours are covered by a scheme that offers a high degree of protection. Formerly, a one per cent levy was raised on all outbound tour fares to make up the Travel Industry Council Reserve Fund, which was established in 1988. If a licensed travel agent should collapse, outbound travellers might claim compensation from this fund for up to 70 per cent of tour fares paid. A recent review of the regulatory scheme recommended a reform package which included a split of the levy into two: a 0.15 per cent levy for the council in recognition of its self-regulatory efforts and a 0.85 per cent levy for the reserve fund for compensating aggrieved travellers. In addition, the review recommended that when the reserve fund had accumulated $100 million, the compensation rate to eligible outbound travellers would be revised upwards to 80 per cent of tour fares paid and the levy for the reserve fund would be reduced to 0.35 per cent. Whenever the reserve fund fell below $70 million, the levy for the reserve fund would be increased to 0.85 per cent and would stay at this level until the fund reached $100 million again. The review also recommended the reconstitution of the fund into an independent statutory body to enhance its public accountability and transparency. Part of the reform package has been implemented. Full implementation of the package shall await enactment of the Travel Agents (Amendment) Bill 1992 which was introduced into the Legislative Council on October 14, 1992.

In 1992, there was no travel agent failure. The reserve fund increased by $30,723,112 in 1992 and had a balance of $118,248,957 at the end of the year. The fund has paid out $12,709,093 in compensation since its inception.

Tourism

Tourism is one of Hong Kong's largest service industries and the territory's third largest earner of foreign exchange. Recovering from the effects of the Gulf War a new record number of visitors, some 7.0 million, came to Hong Kong in 1992, an increase of 15.5 per cent over the previous year. Tourism earnings registered an increase of 20.0 per cent in 1992, reaching a total of $47.5 billion.

Hong Kong remained Asia's most popular travel destination. The biggest growth in visitors in recent years has been from the neighbouring countries in the Asian region, notably Taiwan and Japan, which accounted for 23.4 per cent and 19.0 per cent respectively in 1992, as well as South-East Asia (17.4 per cent) and South Korea (2.8 per cent). Visitors from Western Europe, the United States/Canada and Australia/New Zealand accounted for 13.6 per cent, 12.5 per cent and 4.4 per cent respectively.

To cater for the accommodation needs of the continuing growth of visitors to Hong Kong, six new hotels opened in 1992, bringing the total number of rooms available in Hong Kong to 33 400.

Hong Kong Tourist Association

The HKTA was established by the Hong Kong Government in 1957 to develop the territory's tourism industry for the benefit of Hong Kong. The association works to increase the number of visitors to Hong Kong; promotes the improvement of visitor facilities; secures overseas publicity for the territory's attractions; co-ordinates the activities of the tourism industry; and advises the government on matters relating to the industry.

The chairman and members of the Board of Management of the HKTA are appointed by the Governor. The association receives an annual subvention from the government to assist it in carrying out its work. It also derives funds from membership dues, the sale of publications and souvenirs, and from its own commercial tours.

At the end of December 1992, the association had 1 778 members, comprising airlines, hotels, travel agents, tour operators and retail, restaurant and other visitor service establishments.

The HKTA maintains two information and gift centres: at the basement of Jardine House and at the Kowloon Star Ferry concourse. In addition, it operates two information counters at Hong Kong International Airport at Kai Tak. Together, these centres assisted 2.2 million visitors in 1992.

The association also operates a general information telephone service in nine languages for visitors in Hong Kong and a special shopping information service. Together, these lines handled enquiries from 59 000 visitors in 1992.

During the year, a new 'Infofax' service was introduced, expanding further HKTA's information service worldwide. The service gave members of the local and overseas travel trade and consumers access to information on sightseeing, shipping, dining, special interest activities and a calendar of events. The association also distributed some 9.5 million pieces of literature in 12 languages to visitors on arrival.

The HKTA has built up a network of 17 overseas offices through which overseas marketing of Hong Kong as a travel destination is primarily undertaken. It also has agreements with Cathay Pacific Airways Ltd. whereby the airline acts as the association's information agent in an additional 42 cities around the world.

The year 1992 continued to be an active year for the HKTA. It headed Hong Kong delegations to 13 major travel trade events overseas, including the World Travel Market in London and International Tourism Bourse in Berlin. It also participated in *Festival Hong Kong '92* in Canada to promote Hong Kong as a travel destination to potential visitors from that market. The association was involved in a travel agency window display contest, a Hong Kong carnival, travel trade seminars, a Hong Kong food festival, dragon boat races and department store promotions.

In conjunction with such other travel industry partners as the Hong Kong Hotels Association and airlines, the HKTA carried out various marketing campaigns overseas. They included: a South-East Asia roadshow to Bangkok, Singapore, Kuala Lumpur, Jakarta and Manila; a Hong Kong/Macau 'update seminar' in five Japanese cities; and a Hong Kong travel mission to Taiwan.

Familiarisation visits to Hong Kong were arranged for 4 160 travel agents and a further 640 visiting travel trade personnel were briefed to encourage them either to include Hong Kong in their itineraries or to extend the Hong Kong portion of their Far East packages. In addition the association assisted 1 430 overseas media representatives with their coverage of Hong Kong. For example 66 food writers and members of television crews were brought in to cover the 1992 *Hong Kong Food Festival*, resulting in extensive overseas publicity for Hong Kong's culinary attractions.

In co-operation with Cathay Pacific Airways Ltd. the HKTA initiated a *Friends of Hong Kong Super City* programme which aims to develop a corps of Hong Kong and Cathay Pacific supporters in travel agencies overseas which have a track record of promoting Hong Kong. The programme enables travel agency staff to give better advice about Hong Kong when discussing holiday plans with their clients.

In the marketing of Hong Kong as a tourist destination, the HKTA organised a series of events to promote the territory as a year-round travel destination, marketing its unique blend of East and West and extensive range of attractions. For example, the *Hong Kong Dragon Boat Festival – International Races 1992*, considered the premier championship of this sport, was organised in June for the 17th consecutive year and again received wide international publicity. A total of 29 overseas and 127 local teams competed in the race programme and the *Row for Charity* events raised HK$1.2 million for the Community Chest. In addition the HKTA marketed other special events such at the *Hong Kong Arts Festival* and the *Cathay Pacific/Hong Kong Bank Invitation Seven-A-Side Rugby Tournament* which highlighted Hong Kong's role as a major venue for performing arts and sports.

The association also actively promoted Hong Kong as a venue for convention and incentive travel business. Efforts made in this area have been rewarded in a 15.0 per cent increase in delegates attending conventions and exhibitions in Hong Kong. Highlights included the *1992 Pacific Area Travel Association Conference*, one of the most prestigious travel trade events, which was held in Hong Kong in March, when some 1 500 travel industry leaders from around the world experienced first-hand Hong Kong's unique blend of East and West as well as its sophisticated facilities. In June, the *75th Lions Clubs*

283

International Convention, the largest meeting to be hosted by Hong Kong, brought 25 000 Lions Clubs members and their spouses to the territory.

To broaden the appeal of Hong Kong, the association continued to operate a number of special interest tours for visitors. HKTA's *The Land Between Tour*, the *Come Horseracing Tour*, and the *Housing Tour and Home Visit* were among the top five nominated by eight journalists from overseas travel trade publications in the *1992 Best Hong Kong Tour Awards* programme. To promote a greater interest in Hong Kong's heritage, new full-day and revised half-day versions of the *Heritage Tour* were launched. In addition, a new *Sai Kung Explorer's Guide* was published to introduce visitors to this lesser-known area of Hong Kong.

To encourage visitors to stay longer in the territory, the association continued to develop the *Hong Kong – Stay an Extra Day* campaign to increase visitors' awareness of Hong Kong's varied attractions. The *Hong Kong a la Carte* promotion, which rewards visitors booking a longer than average holiday in Hong Kong with a booklet of bonuses, was expanded to include more special offers from retail, dining, sightseeing and entertainment establishments.

In co-operation with the Agriculture and Fisheries Department, a 'Green Tourism' project was launched in February. A site near the Tai Mo Shan Country Park Visitor Centre was designated 'Green Dragon Garden' where visitors can plant a tree to commemorate their visit to Hong Kong.

Locally, to highlight the tourism industry's contribution to Hong Kong during the past 35 years and to enhance the community's recognition of and support for the industry the HKTA organised a Tourism Day in December. The programme's activities included a dinner to salute tourism industry veterans, a charity 'walkathon', a tree-planting ceremony, hotel visits for secondary school students and a tourism investment seminar. A new television commercial with the theme *Tourism Works for Hong Kong* was broadcast on all four local channels to highlight the contribution of the industry to the territory's economic well-being.

To maintain Hong Kong's position as a top travel destination, the importance of training in the tourism industry to maintain Hong Kong's high reputation for service remained a priority of the association. Its Industry Training Department runs various programmes for staff in the retail trade, as well as courses designed specifically for tour co-ordinators and restaurant personnel. For school-leavers interested in joining the industry, the association organises the Tourism Employees Preparatory Programme. The complementary *Job Bazaar* enables prospective employers to meet participants in this programme. There is also a free Tourism Employees Recruitment Service.

The HKTA continued to encourage higher levels of courtesy through the on-going *Hong Kong Cares* courtesy campaign. During the year the association organised a Hong Kong Cares Courtesy Awards scheme for retail assistants which received 2 500 nominations from visitors from 30 countries.

For the 25th year, the HKTA organised the Student Ambassador Programme whereby 100 students heading overseas for their tertiary education took part in a month-long briefing programme to increase their awareness of various aspects of Hong Kong which would enable them to talk more knowledgeably about their home. With the co-operation of the Scout Association of Hong Kong, a Tourism Ambassador Badge has been introduced. To earn it, scouts have to attend a workshop which introduces them to the tourism industry in Hong Kong, and then work with the HKTA by helping visitors at the information and gift centres.

The association publishes regular reports on the performance of Hong Kong's tourism industry and conducts a visitor survey which monitors changes in the basic demographics of all visitors, their activities, spending patterns and their attitudes towards Hong Kong's tourism facilities.

20
THE ARMED SERVICES

THE Armed Services in Hong Kong are a unique blend in that the garrison is both tri-national and tri-service. The tri-national element comprises Gurkhas from Nepal, who make up nearly half the garrison strength; locally-recruited Hong Kong Chinese; and service personnel from the United Kingdom. In addition, Hong Kong has its own locally-raised regiment of part-time soldiers – the Royal Hong Kong Regiment (The Volunteers).

The tri-service element is provided by the mix of Royal Navy, Army and Royal Air Force personnel and the picture is completed by the civilian work force, predominantly locally-recruited Hong Kong Chinese, which supports the uniformed services. All these elements combine to produce the garrison's unique identity.

Garrison's Role
The role of the garrison is to provide a tangible demonstration of the United Kingdom's sovereignty and commitment to Hong Kong until 1997, and thus to contribute to security, stability and prosperity in the territory. This role has remained unaltered for many years.

In order to meet this role the garrison must retain a balanced and flexible capability to assist the Hong Kong Government, if and when necessary, in a number of tasks. These include: assistance in the maintenance of stability, security and confidence within the territory; maintenance of territorial integrity of Hong Kong's sea, land and air boundaries; support to Royal Hong Kong Police operations; disaster and emergency relief; and contribution to regional security.

Commander British Forces
The Commander British Forces, with the rank of major-general, is in overall command of the Royal Navy, Army and Royal Air Force elements based in Hong Kong.

The Garrison
The garrison numbers about 9 800 men and women, comprising 7 500 military and some 2 300 civilian support staff.

The Royal Navy has its headquarters in HMS Tamar in Central, but is due to move to a new base on Stonecutters Island in mid 1993 to allow the redevelopment of the east Tamar site.

Moving to Stonecutters will be the Navy's three Peacock-class patrol craft, plus all related operational and support facilities. Headquarters British Forces will continue to operate from the Prince of Wales Building in west Tamar after the move.

During 1992 the Royal Navy was again active in continuing operations at sea to counter smuggling and illegal immigration; and was again called upon in its search and rescue role when maritime disasters struck civilian shipping.

The Army comprises the largest element of the garrison, although its size was reduced with the amalgamation of two Gurkha battalions in the autumn of 1992. This reduction reflected the completion of the handover of responsibility for the Sino-Hong Kong border from the garrison to the Royal Hong Kong Police.

This adjustment resulted in a smaller infantry brigade made up of one United Kingdom battalion (currently The Black Watch, which took over from the 1st Battalion The Royal Regiment of Wales in January 1993) and two Gurkha battalions supported by Gurkha engineer signals and transport regiments. Army units in Hong Kong are completed by an Army Air Corps squadron, equipped with Scout helicopters, and a maritime troop, part of the transport regiment, which operates three landing craft.

The Royal Air Force is based at Sek Kong in the New Territories where it operates a squadron of Wessex helicopters.

Training and Operations

As the garrison is unique in its make-up, so is it in its ability to use its blend of troops and skills in a wide range of training and operations. This involves a busy programme throughout the year with combined exercises involving the three services and the Royal Hong Kong Regiment, as well as Five Power Defence Agreement exercises with the armed forces of Singapore, Malaysia, Australia and New Zealand.

Exercises are held in Hong Kong in locations like Lantau Island and the New Territories, but Hong Kong lacks suitable areas for realistic training with some of the weaponry with which British Forces are normally equipped, which means that some exercises are held overseas in order to maintain a high standard of military skills; for instance the infantry go to ranges in Australia to fire the Milan anti-tank weapon.

During 1992, the garrison was not called upon to send troops to operate outside Hong Kong's boundaries in the same numbers as in the previous year, but a squadron of Queen's Gurkha Engineers was sent to Western Samoa to assist with hurricane relief operations and individuals were called upon to assist with United Nations operations, including in Cambodia.

Vietnamese Migrants

In 1992, despite the small number of Vietnamese migrants arriving in Hong Kong, the garrison continued to provide logistical and technical support in dealing with the problem. The western end of RAF Sek Kong continued to be used as a temporary camp, but the numbers of migrants accommodated there reduced throughout the year as the camp gradually closed down.

The Lo Wu training camp also continued to serve as a departure centre for migrants awaiting voluntary return to Vietnam. During the year the Army's maritime troop moved some 10 000 migrants between locations and the Royal Navy assisted in the transfer of hundreds of returnees under the Orderly Repatriation Programme.

The Garrison and the Community

The garrison contributes to the well-being of the wider community in many ways. Apart from the high-profile events which highlight the garrison's presence, there is much behind-the-scenes activity which goes largely unreported.

When a typhoon threatens, the garrison automatically moves to a higher state of alert. Emergency communications are set up and troops placed on stand-by for any tasks they might be given. The troops are backed up by a wide range of equipment and supplies held in disaster relief stores.

The Royal Navy operates the only recompression chamber in the region to treat divers who may have re-surfaced too quickly. There is also a clearance diving team ready to assist civilian authorities in underwater tasks.

Local people bring a wide variety of skills to the garrison, either in uniform as members of the Hong Kong Military Service Corps or the Chinese Division of the Royal Navy, or as civilians in a wide range of jobs. Apart from supplying essential translation skills, they are to be found working as drivers, medical orderlies, teachers, secretaries, book-keepers, military police, guards, dog handlers, signallers or mechanics.

Just as the community plays an important part in the life of the garrison, the garrison itself takes an active role in the lives of local communities. In addition to participation in displays, band performances and open days enjoyed by thousands of people, smaller groups of servicemen and women support a wide variety of charities and involve themselves in projects concerning the young, the elderly and the disabled.

Every year the Queen's Gurkha Signals provide logistic support for Trailwalker, when hundreds of enthusiasts walk the length of the MacLehose Trail to raise funds for charity. The popularity of this event increases year by year both in terms of the number of teams taking part and in terms of money raised which has risen to over HK$7 million.

The annual Navy Days at HMS Tamar attracted their usual full house and many thousands also flocked to Stonecutters Island for the Hong Kong Military Service Corps open day.

Garrison teams and individuals also play a leading role in the territory's sporting programme. Gurkha military engineers provided the design expertise and manpower for the construction of various youth projects, and several hundred youngsters attended camps run by the garrison to experience activities including physical training and assault courses, shooting, map reading, first-aid, hill-walking, canoeing and sailing.

Royal Hong Kong Regiment (The Volunteers)

The Royal Hong Kong Regiment (The Volunteers) was first formed in May 1854, when the Crimean War led to a reduction of the British military presence in Hong Kong.

The regiment, then known as the Hong Kong Volunteer Defence Corps, was heavily involved in the battle for Hong Kong in December 1941, during which over 2 200 soldiers and officers were mobilised. The Hong Kong Volunteer Defence Corps was awarded 19 decorations and 18 mentions in despatches for gallantry and service during the war.

Today it is a light reconnaissance regiment of part-time volunteers. Its role, though primarily one of internal security, also includes reconnaissance, anti-illegal immigration operations and assistance to other government departments in the event of natural disasters. It is administered and financed by the Hong Kong Government but if called out it is commanded by the Commander British Forces and forms part of 48 Gurkha Infantry

Brigade. The present Honorary Colonel of the regiment is the Chief Secretary, Sir David Ford. The Regiment will be disbanded in September 1995. By then, it will have existed in various forms for 141 years.

The regiment has an establishment of 946 volunteers and 54 permanent staff, including 10 regular soldiers on loan from the British Army, one of whom is the Commanding Officer. The volunteers come from all walks of life and are of various nationalities, although over 97 per cent are Chinese. Last May, a total of 113 recruits, of whom 18 were female, successfully completed their six-month basic training. The regiment's final cadre of recruits started training in late September 1992. This last recruiting drive attracted over 1 000 applicants.

The regiment consists of four Sabre squadrons, a home guard squadron, a training squadron and a headquarters squadron which includes a women's troop with a strength of 80 who provide support in various operational duties as searchers, interpreters and radio operators. The regiment also runs a junior leaders' corps of 300 boys, aged from 14 to 17, which provides training in youth activities and leadership skills.

Each year, selected volunteers are sent for overseas training and on attachments to British Army regiments in the United Kingdom. Officer cadets receive military training at the Royal Military Academy, Sandhurst, before they receive their commissions.

The training commitment for each volunteer is two evenings and one weekend each month. There are also centrally-organised regimental training programmes such as military courses, regimental camps and exercises. The annual camps, which are the highlights of the year's training, take place over eight days each in April/May and October/November. Starting in 1992, for both camps, the Volunteers were deployed to the border for anti-illegal immigration operations. The first border camp of 1992 took place in May. Working alongside the police, the Volunteers captured a total of 104 illegal immigrants and took part in several police operations.

21
COMMUNICATIONS AND THE MEDIA

THE news media in Hong Kong includes nearly 70 daily newspapers (including one in braille), around 600 periodicals, two private television companies, a regional satellite television service, one government radio-television station, two commercial radio stations and a radio service station for the British Forces. A new subscription television service is expected to be operational by late 1993.

The availability in Hong Kong of the latest in telecommunications technology ensures a continuous interflow of information with most parts of the world and this, together with growing interest in Hong Kong affairs, attracts international news media representatives to establish regional bases here.

News agencies, newspapers with international readership and overseas broadcasting corporations have bureaux and offices in Hong Kong. Regional publications produced here have been successful, underlining the territory's strong position as a financial, industrial, trading and communications centre.

The news media also play a significant role in the territory's precautionary measures against sudden climatic threats – alerting, informing and advising the public in the event of typhoons or rainstorms.

Continuing advances and innovations in the communications field have enabled the Hong Kong Government to expand its information services. To promote community participation and civic awareness, it produces and contributes to numerous public affairs programmes on radio and television.

Information Policy
The Information Co-ordinator in the Chief Secretary's Office has overall policy responsibility for the government's public relations strategy, while the Information Services Department is the executive agency for implementing that policy. The main aim is to keep the media fully informed of all the government's plans and policies so that the public are kept aware of the government activities which affect their lives. Apart from formulating policy on information and related matters, the Information Co-ordinator advises the government on the presentation of its policies, and on public relations matters generally, both within Hong Kong and overseas.

Information Services Department
The Information Services Department, also known as the Government Information Services (GIS), provides the link between the administration and the information media

and, through the latter, enhances public understanding of government policies, decisions and activities.

The department is organised into two wings – the Local and Administration Wing and the Overseas Public Relations Wing. It has a staff of 539 of whom 364 are Information Grade and 175 are General Grade officers. Of the 364 Information Grade officers, 220 are deployed in government departments, policy branches in the Government Secretariat and Hong Kong Government overseas offices.

Local and Administration Wing

The wing, made up of four divisions, is responsible for News, Departmental Units and Media Research, Publicity and Administration.

The News Division maintains direct contact with the media on a 24-hour basis. It is linked by teleprinter to over 80 newspapers, news agencies, television and radio stations, government departments and other individual organisations. It also has a facsimile transmission system operating to 29 outlets, which is particularly important for communicating in the Chinese language. The division produces a Daily Information Bulletin (DIB) in both English and Chinese which contains about 20 of the more important press releases on an average day.

The division also runs a Press Enquiry Service that operates round the clock. It has a comprehensive Press Library holding press cuttings and copies of all government press releases and a smaller Reference Library for use by journalists, researchers and students.

The Departmental Units and Media Research Division is divided into two sub-divisions.

The Departmental Units Sub-Division co-ordinates the work of Information Grade officers in the Information and Public Relations Units of 30 government departments and Policy Branches in the Government Secretariat.

The Media Research Sub-Division keeps the government informed of public opinion as expressed in the media by the production of a daily summary by 9 am each day called the *Media Summary*. It also produces special reports on matters of topical and special interest.

The Publicity Division is made up of three sub-divisions. The Promotions Sub-Division plans and implements all government campaigns and publicity programmes to educate the public on major issues of concern and create public awareness of civic responsibilities. Publicity messages are disseminated through films, publications, radio announcements, press advertisements, exhibitions and a host of other promotional activities such as launch ceremonies, float parades, concerts and variety shows. Increased efforts have been made to get the messages across to a wide sector of the community through joint programme production and coverage with the electronic media. In 1992, nine major government campaigns were organised. Some well-established campaigns such as those on environmental protection, fight crime, AIDS prevention and civic education, continued to be matters of priority. Several new campaigns, on building safety, voltage conversion, and energy conservation, were promoted for the first time.

The Publishing Sub-Division produces a wide variety of government publications, including the Hong Kong Annual Report. Every year it distributes around six million copies of publications such as fact sheets, pamphlets and posters, and sells some four million copies of books and miscellaneous printed materials including annual reports and government forms. It arranges and places all government advertising in the media.

The Creative Sub-Division is responsible for all government design and display services and film and photographic work.

The Administration Division provides administrative, personnel and financial support services for the department.

Overseas Public Relations Wing

The Overseas Public Relations Wing was set up during the year by combining the Overseas Public Relations Sub-Division of the department and the Visits Division of the Information Co-Ordinator's Office. The new wing devises government's overseas public relations strategy, co-ordinates all international publicity efforts, monitors Hong Kong's image overseas and handles VIP visits.

Overseas Public Relations Division

The Overseas Public Relations Division co-ordinates the government's publicity efforts overseas and produces and distributes promotional materials worldwide. This includes feature articles, books, pamphlets and television newsclips. The division also runs a sponsored visitors programme under which influential journalists are invited to visit Hong Kong to gain a better understanding of the territory. It provides assistance for other visiting journalists requiring information and interviews with government officials and community leaders, and maintains close liaison with news agencies and foreign correspondents based in Hong Kong.

The division also keeps in very close touch with the information and public relations units of the government's overseas offices, providing them with the necessary information to present an accurate and up-to-date picture of Hong Kong.

Visits Division

The Visits Division sponsors and invites VIP visitors including influential politicians, parliamentarians, government officials and businessmen from countries with close relations with Hong Kong to visit the territory. It plans, organises and co-ordinates their visit programmes and briefings aimed at improving their understanding of Hong Kong.

Like the sponsored visitors programmes, the Visits Section runs the sponsored speakers programme under which arrangements are made for senior government officials and prominent local personalities to address targeted audiences overseas. These programmes are complemented by participation in international seminars, cultural activities, and other events.

Overseas Projects Section

The section mounts, very often in conjunction with the private sector, promotional activities for projecting Hong Kong's image overseas. It also co-ordinates high-level missions to other territories and countries.

In these tasks, it maintains close contact with the Government's Overseas Offices, consuls-general and commissioners of foreign countries in Hong Kong, various non-government agencies involved in the promotion of Hong Kong such as the Hong Kong Trade Development Council, the Hong Kong Tourist Association, chambers of commerce and major Hong Kong companies.

The Press

Hong Kong's flourishing free press consists of 67 newspapers and 608 periodicals, which have a high readership. They include 39 Chinese-language dailies and two English-language dailies. One of the English dailies publishes a daily braille edition, in conjunction with the Hong Kong Society for the Blind. A number of news agency bulletins – Chinese, English and Japanese – are also registered as newspapers.

Of the Chinese-language dailies, 26 cover mainly general news, both local and overseas, while others cover solely entertainment, especially television and cinema news, and two concentrate on finance. The larger papers include Chinese communities overseas in their distribution networks, and some have editions printed outside Hong Kong, in particular in the United States, Canada, Britain and Australia.

Hong Kong is the South-East Asian base for many newspapers, magazines, news agencies and electronic media. Among the international news agencies with offices in Hong Kong are Associated Press, Reuters, United Press International, Agence France-Presse, Kyodo News Service of Japan, Agencia EFE of Spain and LUSA of Portugal. *Newsweek* and *Time* magazines have editions printed in Hong Kong, which is also the base for the regional magazines *Asiaweek* and the *Far Eastern Economic Review*, as well as the *Asian Wall Street Journal* and the *International Herald Tribune*.

Several organisations represent and cater for people working in the news media in Hong Kong. The Newspaper Society of Hong Kong represents Chinese and English newspaper proprietors. It is empowered to act in matters affecting the interests of its members. The Hong Kong Journalists Association, founded in 1968, is the only territory-wide trade union for local journalists. It seeks to recommend better training, pay and conditions in journalism, and advises its members in the event of disputes with employers. As an active member of the International Federation of Journalists, it plays a significant role in the international press freedom movement, particularly in the Asia-Pacific region. The Foreign Correspondents' Club offers its members social facilities and a range of professional activities, including news conferences, briefings and films. The Hong Kong Press Club provides an opportunity for journalists to meet socially.

A sum of $300,000 was allocated by the Vocational Training Council to the Journalism Training Board and Advertising, Public Relations and Publishing Training Board to conduct no less than a dozen up-grading courses for the mass media. The most popular courses were: Newspro-English Oral Skills for Journalists (by the British Council), Putonghua for Journalists (by the City Polytechnic of Hong Kong) and Advertising Management Course (by 4A's.)

Hong Kong's Image Overseas

Overview

One of the main objectives of the government's information policy is to project a proper image of Hong Kong to overseas communities.

As international interest in the major issues confronting Hong Kong has increased, so the government, in co-operation with other members of 'Hong Kong Inc.' has expanded the programme of joint promotional activities mounted overseas.

Overseas Offices

The Hong Kong Government's overseas public relations efforts are concentrated on its major business partners in North America, Europe and the Asia-Pacific region. Its overseas offices in these regions play a leading role in promoting Hong Kong.

London

The News and Public Relations Unit of the Hong Kong Government Office in London works closely with GIS to provide a press service on Hong Kong matters for the British media and for Hong Kong journalists based in the United Kingdom. It also provides enquiry and information services for the public about events and developments in Hong Kong, backed by the most comprehensive library outside Hong Kong. The unit maintains close contact with journalists from both national and regional media, briefs and helps plan programmes for media visiting Hong Kong, and assists visiting journalists from Hong Kong. It organises a panel of speakers of about 100 former government officers and businessmen who have retired or now work in Britain.

The unit monitors British parliamentary proceedings and both national and regional media coverage of Hong Kong affairs, responding where necessary to inaccurate reports. It also publishes a newsletter, *Dateline Hong Kong*, which is distributed among organisations and individuals with a close interest in Hong Kong.

North America

In North America, media relations are conducted through the government's Economic and Trade Offices in Washington, New York, San Francisco and Toronto. These offices provide a general news and information service for the media and work with GIS to produce special news releases, features and articles tailored to the specific requirements of various American and Canadian publications. Close contact is maintained with journalists in all major centres of both countries. The units also provide them with assistance and information for preparing articles on Hong Kong and help journalists visiting Hong Kong with briefings, research material and interviews. Each year the information units of these offices organise in conjuction with GIS a series of sponsored visits to Hong Kong by American and Canadian journalists.

The units also handle numerous public and business enquiries on all types of issues. To supplement this service, a monthly digest of events and happenings in Hong Kong is produced and mailed to contacts throughout North America. The units participate in a variety of exhibitions and seminars as a means of establishing further contact with the electronic and print media and to publicise Hong Kong. The units also monitor the American and Canadian news media producing for Hong Kong daily news and weekly news and economic summaries.

To strengthen these efforts a public relations firm is used to implement a public relations plan and strategy for Hong Kong, and to assist with organising speaking platforms and tours for visiting speakers from Hong Kong and senior officers of the Economic and Trade Offices in North America.

To coincide with the Toronto Office's first anniversary, a month-long *Festival Hong Kong 92* was held in Canada. The festival, with the theme, 'Bridge across the Pacific', has been the largest overseas promotion ever organised by the Hong Kong Government. It presented over 150 cultural, educational, business and sporting events in five major cities –

Vancouver, Calgary, Toronto, Ottawa and Montreal, with fringe activities staged in another six cities: Edmonton, Winnipeg, Regina, Halifax, Saskatoon and London. With the support of volunteers and local communities, the festival scored a tremendous success with massive media coverage and the programmes were well attended by hundreds and thousands of Canadians together with senior government officials, legislators, dignitaries, community leaders and delegations from Hong Kong.

To mark the closing of the festival, to thank Canada for her friendship, and to promote Hong Kong as Canada's bridge to Asia, the Governor, the Rt Hon Christopher Patten, made an official visit to the country. During his four-day visit in November, he met with the Prime Minister, senior Federal and Provincial Ministers, City Mayors and community leaders.

Europe

The Brussels Office is responsible, among other things, for the government's public relations and publicity efforts in the European Community and its member states (except the United Kingdom which is the responsibility of the London Office) and in Switzerland and Austria. The public relations and press team in the office works closely with Hong Kong and the Hong Kong Family in Europe to give information about Hong Kong to contacts in both the public and private sectors and in the media in Europe to develop and sustain their interest in Hong Kong affairs. The Brussels team also monitors and collects information appearing in the European media which is of relevance or importance to Hong Kong.

Under the sponsored visitors programme, the Brussels Office invites opinion leaders and decision makers from the European Commission, member states governments and major European businesses to visit Hong Kong, to enable them to have a better understanding of its needs and importance. Members of the European Parliament and European media are also included in this programme. In addition, the Brussels Office arranges speaking engagements in many EC countries for senior Hong Kong Government officials and leading members of the Hong Kong community, to explain recent developments.

Japan

The Tokyo Office is responsible for the government's public relations efforts in Japan. It liaises with Japanese ministries and other organisations and arranges programmes for Japanese government officials and other VIPs to visit Hong Kong. It also organises speaking engagements for senior government officers in Japan.

Its Information Unit provides enquiry and information services for the local public about events and developments in Hong Kong; maintains close contacts with the local media; briefs and helps plan programmes for those visiting Hong Kong; and monitors the local media coverage of Hong Kong affairs, responding where necessary to reports of relevance to Hong Kong. The office also maintains contacts with other Hong Kong-based organisations and companies in Japan with a view to optimising Hong Kong's overall promotional efforts.

Australia and New Zealand

There are at present no government offices in Australia and New Zealand, but a public relations firm has been appointed to provide public relations coverage in this region.

Printing and Publishing

A reputation for good printing quality, quick and reliable delivery and competitive prices continues to boost the international status of Hong Kong's printing industry. The territory is a leading centre for printing and publishing with 4 394 printing establishments, employing 38 497 people, and more than 200 publishing houses, including many from overseas which have set up offices or regional headquarters in Hong Kong. Hong Kong printers are investing substantially in advanced machinery and equipment and are taking positive steps to develop the United States market.

The industry constitutes 10 per cent of all manufacturing establishments and seven per cent of employment in the manufacturing sector. Most of the printing factories (78 per cent) are engaged in general jobbing work, and most of the remainder deal with related work, such as typesetting and book-binding. There are also 24 newspaper printers.

Use of the latest technology, especially computerised equipment, has enabled the industry to become highly specialised. The local electronics industry contributes to the plant and equipment both of the more sophisticated printing companies and of publishers, who are becoming increasingly involved in the use of data and word-processing systems for editorial production and stock control.

The output data can be converted or interfaced with typesetting equipment at realistic cost to provide publishers with the additional benefits of fast and cost-efficient printing. An increasing number of Chinese language word-processors are being installed to meet demand.

Domestic exports of printed matter increased in value terms by 12 per cent over the previous year. Material printed locally with a total value of $4,414 million was exported, with the United States, China, the United Kingdom, Taiwan and Australia being the main customers. Books, pamphlets, newspapers, journals and periodicals accounted for over 70 per cent of exports of printed products. The biggest customers for this reading material were the United States, the United Kingdom and Australia.

Overall, the printing and publishing industries contributed five per cent of gross output of the manufacturing sector.

Telecommunication Services

The guiding principle underlying Hong Kong's telecommunications policy is that the widest range of services should be available to all at reasonable cost.

Hong Kong now has one of the highest telephone densities in South-East Asia. By the end of 1992, there were an estimated 3.6 million telephones served by 2.8 million exchange lines, representing a telephone density of 63 telephones per 100 population.

Basic public telecommunications services are provided under franchise by the Hong Kong Telephone Company Limited and Hong Kong Telecom International Limited. Under the Telephone Ordinance, the Hong Kong Telephone Company Limited has the exclusive right until June 30, 1995 to provide a public voice telephone service by wire within Hong Kong. Hong Kong Telecom International Limited has been granted an exclusive licence until September 30, 2006, to provide a range of public international telecommunications services, including telephone, telex, telegram and leased circuits for data and facsimile.

In June, the Secretary for Economic Services announced the results of a review of telecommunications policy. From 1993 additional networks will be licensed to provide competition to the Hong Kong Telephone Company, initially in provision of data and fax services and then, beyond June 1995, in voice telephony. The Hong Kong Telephone Company's tariffs will be regulated by a price cap mechanism, which will limit overall increases to four percentage points below the prevailing rate of inflation. Resale of private leased circuits for the provision of value added services will be further liberalised, and in future companies and organisations will be licensed to provide their own external telecommunications links.

Among significant developments on the local telecommunications scene during the year, the programme to modernise the local public switched telephone network continued apace, with modern signalling techniques already implemented in the exchanges and 97 per cent of the network digitised, producing one of the most advanced networks in the world.

New 'permission to connect' procedures were implemented with effect from April 1992. Under the new arrangement, permission from Hong Kong Telephone Company Limited is not required for connection of single line equipment such as telephone sets and facsimile machines to the public switched telephone network. However, consumers have been advised to use only equipment that has passed a voluntary compliance test. This test is designed to ensure that equipment is compatible with the basic operation of the network, to protect both the users and the network operator's personnel from electrical hazards and to avoid damage to network equipment. Compliance test specifications are issued by the Telecommunications Authority.

The popularity of facsimile communication continued to grow at the expense of telex traffic which dropped by 16 per cent to 43 million minutes in 1992. In contrast, the number of facsimile lines reached 184 000 by the end of the year. A public packet-switched data network called Datapak, operated by the Hong Kong Telephone Company Limited, offers a wide range of advanced data communication facilities.

Hong Kong is connected to the world by overland and submarine cables, satellites and terrestrial radio links. The more important cables include the Hong Kong–Guangdong optical fibre cable, the Hong Kong–Shenzhen optical fibre cable, the Singapore–Hong Kong–Taiwan submarine cable, the Hong Kong–Luzon submarine cable, the Hong Kong–Japan–Korea optical fibre submarine cable and the Hong Kong–Taiwan 2 optical fibre submarine cable. There is one optical fibre submarine cable being planned for operation in 1993: the Asia Pacific Cable (APC) linking Malaysia, Singapore, Hong Kong, Taiwan and Japan. Hong Kong Telecom International Limited operates a satellite earth station at Stanley with six Standard-A, one Standard-B and one Standard-G antennae communicating with international satellites over the Indian Ocean and the Pacific Ocean.

The only remaining external terrestrial radio links are with China, Macau and Laos.

In 1992, international telephone traffic grew by 26 per cent to 2 025 million minutes. More than 210 overseas countries and territories, and more than 1 078 cities in China can be called using the International Direct Dialling service.

In addition to the services provided by Hong Kong Telephone Company Limited and Hong Kong Telecom International Limited, a wide variety of competitive public telecommunications services are provided by other companies under Public Non-Exclusive Telecommunications Services (PNETS) and Public Radiocommunications Service (PRS) licences granted by the Telecommunications Authority. Such services include public mobile radio telephone, public mobile data communication, one-way data message, public community repeater, electronic mail (text mail and voice mail), electronic data interchange

(EDI), value added facsimile transmission (for example, text-facsimile conversion), second generation cordless telephone (Telepoint), digital public mobile radio telephone and videotext services. By December 1992, 46 PNETS licences and 10 PRS licences were in force.

Special arrangements have been agreed between Hong Kong and the United Kingdom, the United States, Japan and Australia to facilitate the use of international private leased circuits (IPLCs) for value added data and facsimile services. Under these arrangements operators of international value-added network services (IVANS) may use IPLCs to carry third party traffic at normal flat-rate tariffs.

A Hong Kong registered company, Asia Satellite Telecommunications Company Limited, operates a regional telecommunications satellite, AsiaSat–1. Following its successful launch in April 1990, AsiaSat–1 now offers telecommunications services to the region, from the Middle East to Japan.

Public mobile radio telephone services (PMRS) continue to expand. During the year the number of subscribers increased from 189 500 to 233 500, one of the highest per capita figures in the world. To cater for future growth in demand and to promote competition in this market, the Telecommunications Authority approved in July a new operator to operate digital PMRS using the GSM standard. In addition, approval has been given to the three existing operators to digitise their existing analogue systems increasing both quality and capacity. One digital system, employing the USDC standard, started service in October 1992.

Another very popular service in Hong Kong is the public radio paging service. By December 1992, 1 042 000 pagers had been licensed. On a per capita basis, Hong Kong has one of the highest penetrations in the world for radio paging services (approximately one in 5.6). The pagers in use are mainly tone, numeric and alphanumeric pagers. Paging services conveying messages in Chinese characters are gaining in popularity. In 1991, a licence was awarded to a consortium to operate an international radio paging service using the 931MHz frequency band. The service will be launched in 1993.

During the year, two of the four licensed Telepoint service operators launched their second generation cordless telephone (CT2) services. The third operator is expected to launch the service in 1993. By December 1992, there were 7 900 public base stations installed throughout Hong Kong and 37 300 subscribers.

The Postmaster General, appointed by the Governor as the Telecommunications Authority, administers the Telecommunication Ordinance and the Telephone Ordinance, which govern the establishment and operation of all telecommunications services. The Postmaster General acts as an adviser to the government on matters concerning the development of public telecommunications services, and is a member of the Broadcasting Authority.

The Telecommunications Branch of the Post Office supports the Telecommunications Authority in the execution of his functions. One of the most important functions carried out by the branch is the management of the radio spectrum to ensure that it is utilised efficiently. It also co-ordinates the use of the radio spectrum with the administrations of adjacent territories to minimise radio interference. In May 1992, the Telecommunications Authority signed a frequency co-ordination agreement with the Telecommunications Administration in Guangdong. This agreement provides for compatible technical standards and procedures for the co-ordination of frequencies in the two territories.

Under the Telecommunication Ordinance, the branch issues licences for all forms of radio communication in Hong Kong. It conducts examinations of radio operating personnel and issues certificates to suitably qualified persons in compliance with the Radio Regulations of the International Telecommunication Union. It also inspects ship radio and radar installations.

The branch provides advisory and planning services for the communication requirements of government departments and subvented institutions, co-ordinates and regulates the use of radio communication sites, monitors the technical performance of broadcast services and investigates complaints concerning reception quality.

Postal Services

In 1992, the Hong Kong Post Office joined the United States Postal Service and 30 other postal administrations in co-sponsoring the 1992 Olympic Games held in Albertville, France, and Barcelona, Spain. Under the co-sponsorship arrangement, each postal administration served as the official express courier for the 1992 Olympic Games within its own territory. The Hong Kong Post Office was the official express courier of the Amateur Sports Federation and Olympic Committee of Hong Kong. The objectives of the co-sponsorship were to strengthen the role of postal administrations in the world communications infrastructure and to further the ideals of the Olympic movement. Various philatelic products were issued during the year to to mark the co-sponsorship. These were very popular with collectors.

The Hong Kong Post Office provides an efficient and reliable postal service to the territory. Two mail deliveries are provided each weekday in mainly commercial and industrial areas, with one delivery in residential areas. Most local letters are delivered within one working after the day of posting, although bulk postings and second class mail take slightly longer. Air mail to overseas destinations is usually despatched within 24 hours of posting. Air mail arriving from overseas is normally delivered by the next working day.

In 1992, the Post Office handled 982 million letters and parcels (a daily average of 2.69 million), representing an increase of 3.8 per cent over 1991. Approximately 10 629 tonnes of letter mail and 5 382 tonnes of parcels were despatched abroad by air, an overall increase of 7.5 per cent on 1991.

The Speedpost service, which provides a door-to-door collection and delivery service for customers sending time-sensitive documents, samples or merchandise, continued to grow. The service is now available to 61 countries, including Australia, Canada, China, France, Germany, Japan, Singapore, South Korea, Taiwan, the United Kingdom and the United States of America. During the year 4.0 million items were handled, an increase of 13.9 per cent over 1991. This volume was the world's third highest after the United States and Japan.

In August 1992, the Post Office introduced, for a trial period of six months, a Household Circular Service whereby organisations and businesses could send advertising materials, unstamped, unenveloped and unaddressed, to their target recipients through the post. If successful, the service will be provided on a long-term basis.

To keep pace with the expansion and development of new towns and to cope with the growth in demand for postal facilities, five branch post offices were opened. One post office was closed down because of site redevelopment. The total number of branch post offices in the territory is now 122. Causeway Bay Post Office, Wan Chai Post Office and Tsuen Wan Post Office were relocated to larger premises during the year in order to provide improved services to those districts.

With the aim of lowering operating costs and enhancing efficiency, the Post Office continued its efforts to identify opportunities for automation in its mail handling process. Following the introduction of a Mechanised Letter Sorting System in mid-1990, plans are in hand to install letter sorting machines in delivery offices in the New Territories.

To provide greater convenience to customers, 13 electronically operated stamp vending machines were installed at 10 major post offices during the year. These new machines, which issue stamps of four different denominations, accept all Hong Kong coins and give change. More machines are being ordered for installation at other post offices.

There are also plans to computerise the redirection service and Speedpost acceptance procedures in 1993. Computer terminals will be installed at major sorting offices and Speedpost acceptance offices.

The Post Office issued six sets of special stamps in 1992. The first set was released in January 1992 to mark the Year of the Monkey. The second set was released in February to commemorate the 40th anniversary of the accession to the throne of Her Majesty Queen Elizabeth II. In April a set of four stamps and a souvenir sheet were released to mark the 1992 Olympic Games. Special stamps depicting stamp collecting were issued in July, and a fifth set, released in September, was on the theme of Chinese opera. November saw the release of a set of greetings stamps and a stamp booklet.

A new set of definitive stamps was released on June 16 to replace the definitive stamps issued in 1987. This was the sixth set of Hong Kong definitive stamps issued in the reign of Her Majesty Queen Elizabeth II.

A number of philatelic products were also issued during the year. These included new design labels for the Year of the Monkey in March, and two $10 definitive stamp sheetlets to mark participation in international stamp exhibitions in Chicago, USA, and Kuala Lumpur, Malaysia, by the Hong Kong Post Office in May and September respectively. In August a prestige stamp album containing special stamps issued by 12 postal administrations to mark the 1992 Olympic Games was issued.

Broadcasting Authority

The regulation of television and commercial sound broadcasting is the responsibility of the Broadcasting Authority, a statutory body established in September 1987. The authority has 12 members, nine of whom are appointed non-official members representing a cross-section of the community and three are government officers. Its major function is to secure proper standards in programme and advertising content and technical performance of the two wireless television licensees and the two commercial radio licensees through provisions in the Television Ordinance, Telecommunication Ordinance and the Broadcasting Authority Ordinance. Since January 1992, the authority's jurisdiction has been extended to cover satellite television and sound broadcast.

During the year, the authority assisted the government in a comprehensive review of the television broadcasting industry and made a number of important changes to the television codes of practice. The authority also advised the government in the formulation and evaluation of a proposal for the establishment of a subscription television service in Hong Kong.

Complaints Committee

All complaints relating to wireless and satellite television and sound broadcasting are considered by the Complaints Committee of the Broadcasting Authority. Complaints may be lodged in writing or through a 24-hour hotline provided by the authority. During the year, the authority dealt with 707 complaints concerning quality and standard of television and radio programmes and advertisements. Acting on the recommendations of the Complaints Committee, the authority issued 10 warnings and nine serious warnings to the two wireless television stations and the satellite television station, one warning to a commercial radio station and imposed three fines on the two wireless television stations and one fine on a commercial radio station in the year.

Working Group on Review of Codes of Practice

The Working Group on Review of Codes of Practice of the authority met regularly during the year to review the codes of practice on programme, advertising and technical standards for television and radio. The television broadcasting review conducted during the year has resulted in recommendations by the working group to lift the restrictions on certain types of advertisements. These included advertisements on local property, financial services, educational institutions, matrimonial services, correspondence clubs and condoms. Programming restrictions on advertising breaks, minimum programme segment duration requirements and repetition of children programmes were also relaxed for television to give the stations more flexibility in programme scheduling and presentation. The working group also drew up new codes to regulate programme sponsorship, substantiation of claims made in advertisements, off-shore deposit advertisements, and teloping of advertisements and non-programme material on television during the year.

Wireless Television

Television viewing remained Hong Kong's most popular leisure activity in 1992, with more than 98 per cent of households owning one television set or more. Sixty-eight per cent of them also owned a video cassette recorder. Each of the two franchised stations, Television Broadcasts Limited (TVB) and Asia Television Limited (ATV), provides one Chinese and one English language service and together, on average, transmitted over 560 hours of programming per week, a slight increase of about two per cent compared with 1991.

Competition between the two wireless television stations remained keen. Both tried to strengthen their audience shares through exploration of new grounds in programming. Efforts were made to diversify programme content and to enrich programme scheduling. A variety of programmes like magazine shows, 'infotainment' programmes, game shows and musical programmes were provided during prime time in addition to serialised dramas. Programming in fringe hours was also strengthened. First-run programmes were scheduled in the morning, afternoon and late evening hours in addition to the usual line-up of repeats.

On the Chinese services, locally produced serialised dramas remained the main attraction, with stories revolving around romance, human conflicts, kung fu fantasies and police and gangster confrontation while feature films and telemovies continued to enjoy a steady share of popularity.

301

Significant efforts were made to improve the quality of children programmes. World renowned cartoon series, children drama series, documentaries on family relations and extravaganza activities for children audiences were offered. Youth-orientated programmes were scheduled during the summer vacation.

Beauty pageants, game contests, charity fund-raising events and musical specials constituted standard fare for viewers. There were also programmes covering activities in cities in mainland China and neighbouring countries, giving the programming a regional dimension.

On the English services, films, imported dramas and musical specials remained major attractions. Quality documentaries, arts and cultural programmes were regular parts of the usual programme line-up.

News and information programmes remained an important part of programming on all services. English services continued to carry satellite telecasts of news programmes from the United States.

Coverage of international sports events was given priority in programme scheduling during the year, especially the 25th Olympic Games in Barcelona which were given prominent coverage on all services. Satellite feeds were widely used to provide live coverage. Other major international sports events covered in the year included the European Nations Cup, Wimbledon tennis and the French Open tennis tournaments.

There was an increase in the use of multi-channel sound television broadcasts with the introduction of the Near Instantaneous Compounding and Multiplexing (NICAM) system. Feature films, documentaries and sports programmes were broadcast in bi-lingual format, which proved popular and enabled the English services to attract more Chinese-speaking viewers.

Since 1982, Television Home Viewing Groups, now with a total membership of 570, have been set up in Hong Kong's 19 districts to provide a continuous flow of public opinion on television programming and advertising. Three regional panels, one each for Hong Kong Island, Kowloon and the New Territories, consisting of representatives from the home viewing groups, and special panels for English-speaking viewers and children and youth programmes chaired by members of the Broadcasting Authority keep the authority in close contact with the community.

There was continuous improvement in television transmission coverage during the year. Among the 24 transposer stations completed, 23 had already adopted the combined broad-band antenna system, offering a more standardised control of the quality of transmission signals. Three more transposer stations are being planned and the ultimate aim is to provide satisfactory television signals transmission to all areas with a population of 2 000 within a radius of three kilometres.

Satellite Television
The year marked the first anniversary of STAR TV's satellite television and sound service from Hong Kong to the Pan Asian region. Five channels providing news, sports, music, entertainment and Chinese programmes are receivable in countries as far apart as Japan and Turkey, Indonesia and Mongolia. The service is predominantly in the English language but also includes Putonghua. An additional channel in the Indian language was launched in October 1992. The STAR TV service also carries the BBC World Service radio programmes.

Subscription Television

Following a comprehensive review of the broadcasting environment in Hong Kong, the government drew up a regulatory framework to encourage the development of a subscription television service. Interested parties were invited to forward proposals to establish a subscription television service in Hong Kong. It was expected that a licence would be issued in early 1993.

Radio Television Hong Kong (Television)

During 1992, Radio Television Hong Kong (RTHK) produced 12 hours of public affairs television programmes each week. Of these, five hours of programmes were broadcast in prime time throughout the week on the Chinese channels of the two commercial stations (TVB and ATV). Most of RTHK's programmes focus on promoting civic responsibility and social awareness. They fall basically into six categories: current affairs, drama, information and community services, variety and games shows, children's and youth programmes and general educational programmes. According to a media report the average audience size of RTHK programmes during prime time on the two commercial stations was 1 275 785 and 206 962. RTHK continued to win the viewers' support in an independent survey on qualitative rating.

The year 1992 was an important year historically for Hong Kong. It saw the departure of one Governor, Lord Wilson, and the arrival of the new Governor Mr Chris Patten. RTHK provided live television coverage of both events. As regards current affairs generally, with the *Common Sense, Headliner, City Forum* and *Media Watch* programmes, current issues are explored and analysed through different perspectives which encourage better public understanding of social events. *Today in LegCo*, a weekly production, allows the public to assess the performance of those serving in the Legislative Council.

For drama, the highlight of 1992 was the production of two new feature dramas. *Below the Lion Rock* reflected the social and psychological change in the run-up to 1997 and the *Disabled Drama* series portrayed the disabled and how they integrate into the community.

In collaboration with the Construction Industry Training Authority and the Hong Kong Housing Authority, RTHK produced a very successful variety show promoting the role and work of the two organisations. The annual *Summer Youth Programme* encouraged young people to make use of their leisure time with healthy activities. *Academic Quiz* helped to promote the broadening of knowledge and to spotlight the talented.

Programmes designed for youth and children were another focus of production. *Play School* had special features every week to cater for children of pre-school age; while *Science Time* with a lively presentation introduced various science-related topics. *Community Youth Club Workshop* and the new *Youth Programme* featured various phenomena and viewpoints of young people. The *Parenting Programme* focused on family education and the improvement of understanding between the two generations.

In educational programmes, language continued to be one of the main topics. A new English language series was produced adopting the format of the British Broadcasting Corporation's *The Lost Secret* and adding local teaching materials. A daily *One Minute's English* was also a new programme teaching English words in an easy-to-understand manner. The *Putonghua* series continued to be produced to facilitate the learning of the language.

303

Doctor and You, a programme co-produced with the Hong Kong Medical Association, adopted a new approach by using 'infotainment' format and seeking greater audience participation. The *Sex Education* programme completed its fifth series.

RTHK's Educational Television Division and the Education Department continued to jointly produce curriculum-based and special educational programmes for schools. These programmes, transmitted on the commercial television channels for eight hours every weekday during school time, were watched by about 622 000 school children from Primary 3 to Secondary 3.

Sound Broadcasting

Fifteen radio channels are broadcasting in Hong Kong – seven operated by RTHK, three by the Hong Kong Commercial Broadcasting Company (Commercial Radio), three by Metro Broadcast Corporation Limited (Metro Broadcast), and two by the British Forces Broadcasting Service (BFBS).

Radio Television Hong Kong (Radio)

RTHK, a publicly-funded station, is charged with providing balanced and objective broadcasting services to inform, educate and entertain the people of Hong Kong. Its news and public affairs programmes aim to provide timely, accurate and in-depth news reports. The Director of Broadcasting is its editor-in-chief.

RTHK maintained its international links with overseas radio stations. Apart from co-operating with the BBC, the Chinese Programme Service co-produced programmes with radio stations in China and overseas, and Chinese communities abroad were kept informed of developments in Hong Kong and vice versa.

RTHK now broadcasts 1 148 hours a week. Its main Chinese and English services, Radio 1 and Radio 3 respectively, operate 24 hours a day. The station has developed an individual identity for each of its channels.

Radio 1 is the main news and information channel of the Chinese Programme Service. It provides fast, accurate and in-depth financial, traffic and weather reports. Major political and social events are covered extensively and the public mood of the time is aptly reflected through the channel's phone-in programmes *Talkabout* and *Headliner*.

The three hour public affairs magazine programme *Newsrama* has become a major feature of Radio 1, bringing to listeners up to the minute happenings around the territory to the listeners. *Guangdong on the Line* was relaunched in September for a 20-episode series in co-operation with Guangdong Radio Station to improve understanding of the legal systems in China and Hong Kong. Radio 1 also provides family magazine and sports programmes for the more mature listener. The channel carried comprehensive reports on the 1992 Olympic Games round the clock during the two-week period of the Games.

Radio 2, the most popular station in the territory, is designed as a youth channel and provides programmes ranging from civic education to entertainment. The channel organises a large number of community activities for its audience. Spearheaded by a number of youth organisations, the *Solar Project* campaign was produced to encourage the young generation to play a positive role in community affairs; the *Top Ten Chinese Gold Songs Award Presentation Concert* which was in its 15th year to promote local music talent, raised funds for charitable organisations.

Radio 3 has in recent years adopted a broader, more international profile in response to the needs of the multi-national English speaking community in Hong Kong. The channel is committed to several projects which help promote the use and enjoyment of the English language. *Hong Kong Report* is a programme for young people made by local students. Radio 3 also co-organises an annual short story writing competition and this year launched its first radio drama writing competition. The station broadcasts local, regional and international news, locally made features, music and magazine programmes including its morning current affairs programme *Hong Kong Today*. Radio 3's charity campaign *Operation Santa Claus* continued to raise millions of dollars for children's charities in Hong Kong.

Radio 4, the bilingual channel for fine music and the arts, broadcasts a wide range of fine music and regular relays of concerts held at major cultural venues in the territory. The channel also promotes local musical talent and creative music through programmes such as *Young Music Makers* and *Musicarama '92* respectively. In 1992, Radio 4 launched its *RTHK Singers*, a handpicked chamber choral group of very high standard, providing quality choral programmes on air and in concert halls.

Radio 5 provides cultural and minority interest programmes like Chinese opera, provincial music and features in Putonghua. The channel specialises in producing programmes for the elderly and for children. A special project, *Care for the Elderly*, which included visits to different types of hostels for the elderly was organised in the year.

Radio 6 relays the BBC World Service 24 hours a day. It broadcasts world news and a wide range of programmes from drama and music to science, sport and current affairs.

Radio 7 widened its service to become a news information and traffic channel with effect from May 6, 1991, and extended its broadcasting hours from 0600–2400 hours to 0600–0200 hours from August 1, 1991 onwards. It provides news summaries, financial information, updated traffic information, weather and emergency messages at 15-minute intervals on weekdays and Saturday mornings with middle-of-the-road music in between. Only half-hourly news summaries, traffic and weather reports are provided on Saturday afternoon and all through Sunday in order to meet audience demand at that time for more 'golden oldies'.

Commercial Radio
Commercial Radio operates two Chinese services on FM frequencies and one English service on an AM frequency on a 24-hour basis.

News and current affairs programmes like *Breakfast Show*, *Morning This Minute* and *Hong Kong This Minute* are the main features on CR1. The channel is also simulcast on the English service, CRE, during weekday afternoons.

CR2 continues to appeal to students and young people by promoting local pop music. The channel also demonstrated its commitment to community service by launching concerts with the Friends of the Earth and the Committee on Smoking and Health to arouse wider awareness of environmental protection and hazards of smoking to health.

CRE has broadened its programme format to meet the needs of the English-speaking audience. Its weekday morning programmes adopt a magazine style and feature music, games, 'infotainment' segments like local and overseas stocks reports, 'dos' and 'don'ts' of the day and regular news updates.

305

Joining forces with other print and electronic media, Commercial Radio also devoted considerable efforts in raising funds for the education of children in China, including the launching of *Project Hope*.

Metro Broadcast

Metro Broadcast also operates three channels, one English AM service and two FM services, on a 24-hour basis and has entered its second year of operation.

Metro News is Asia's only 24-hour English news channel. It is designed for news and information seekers and visitors coming through Hong Kong. It broadcasts local and world news at half-hourly intervals. Programmes also include financial and business information, sports news and features on travel, health, science and technology. The channel also operates an open line for the public to phone in during studio discussion programmes on public affairs and financial matters.

Hit Radio is a music channel broadcast mainly in Chinese. The channel's target listenership is the age group between 12 and 25. The disc jockeys call themselves the 'Hit Radio family' and organise outdoor activities for listeners to promote the station. The channel also organised a number of celebrity concerts to mark its first anniversary.

FM Select is a bilingual music channel for adults aged 25 and over. Nostalgic pieces of the thirties, forties and fifties, popular jazz, favourite tunes from the fifties to the eighties and selections of current pops are played non-stop throughout the day on this channel.

As a demonstration of its commitment to community affairs, Metro Broadcast launched a charity auction of gifts donated by show business celebrities on Father's Day with proceeds going to single-parent children. Other activities included visits to children centres and homes for the elderly.

British Forces Broadcasting Service

The British Forces Broadcasting Service (BFBS) is part of the radio division of the Services Sound and Vision Corporation, a worldwide organisation providing entertainment, information and training films, video, television and radio services for the British Forces, under contract to the Ministry of Defence.

BFBS provides two radio services designed for the particular needs of the Gurkhas and British Forces serving in Hong Kong, Brunei and Nepal.

Nepali programmes, broadcast for 90 hours each week from Sek Kong in the New Territories, cater for the interests of the Brigade of Gurkhas, providing music and features reflecting daily life with the brigade in Hong Kong as well as in Nepal and Brunei.

The English-language service broadcasts 24 hours a day with most of the programmes coming from the main studio complex in Sek Kong. News, reviews, sport, quiz programmes and audience participation phone-ins help to complete the service.

The BFBS satellite enables the station to broadcast a regular weekly show live from London and major programmes such as BBC Four's *The World This Weekend* and BBC Radio 5's *Sport on 5* as well as other major sporting and State occasions.

The production centre in London has a brief to keep its overseas listeners in touch with home and provides specialist programmes on a variety of subjects involving many of Britain's premier broadcasting personalities. BFBS London also provides live news every hour on the hour.

Film Industry

Despite the popularity of video clubs and the widespread ownership of video cassette recorders, cinema-going remained a popular leisure activity. Attendance in 1992 totalled 47 million, compared with 51 million in 1991. The number of cinemas increased from 166 in 1991 to 175 in 1992. Mini-cinemas, have replaced large cinemas and have proved popular to cinema-goers.

While imported films continued to be popular, good quality local films were still the favourites. During the year, locally-produced films totalled 376 (including 11 co-productions) compared with 211 (including four co-productions) in 1991. Action films and comedies continued to dominate the market. The biggest box-office hits for the year included Justice My Foot, which grossed $49.9 million. All's Well Ends Well ($49.0 million), Royal Tramp ($40.9 million) and Royal Tramp II ($36.6 million).

Films are classified into three categories: approved for exhibition to persons of any age (Category I); to be advertised as not suitable for children (Category II); and to be exhibited only to people aged 18 years or above (Category III). Classification standards are based on the result of regular surveys of community views. A statutory panel of advisers, comprising about 200 members drawn from a wide cross-section of the community, assists in the classification process.

During the year 1 186 films intended for public exhibition were submitted for classification compared with 1 337 in 1991. Of these, 232 were classified Category I (with no excisions); 485 Category II (36 with excisions); and 469 Category III (322 with excisions). A total of 3 350 items including video tapes, slides and laser discs were exempted from classification.

22
RELIGION AND CUSTOM

IN Hong Kong, every major faith is practised with complete freedom.

Buddhist monasteries and Taoist temples co-exist with Christian churches, mosques, and Hindu and Sikh temples. All major religious bodies have established schools which offer a general education apart from religious instruction. Ancestral worship is also widely practised in Hong Kong since the local people are still greatly influenced by Confucianism which, though not a religion, teaches a moral code based on human relations.

Traditional Festivals

Many customs of the Hong Kong people are observed in their celebration of traditional Chinese festivals, which offer occasions for family union and feasting.

There are five major Chinese festivals, all of which are statutory public holidays. Leading them all is the Lunar New Year which is celebrated in the first few days of the first moon, with visits and gifts being exchanged between friends and relatives and children receiving 'lucky' money. The Ching Ming Festival in the springtime is the traditional occasion for visiting ancestral graves. The Dragon Boat Festival is celebrated on the fifth day of the fifth moon in early summer. This festival, which was originally held in memory of an ancient Chinese poet who had committed suicide by jumping into a river, has developed into a joyous event for dragon boat races and eating cooked rice dumplings wrapped in lotus leaves.

The Mid-Autumn Festival falls on the 15th day of the eighth moon and gifts of mooncakes, fruit and wine are exchanged while adults and children alike carry colourful lanterns to the parks and countryside at night to appreciate the full moon. The Chung Yeung Festival, on the ninth day of the ninth moon, is another occasion for visiting ancestral graves. Many people celebrate the festival by climbing hills in remembrance of an ancient Chinese family which fled to the top of a high mountain to escape from plague and death.

Buddhism and Taoism

Buddhism and Taoism, the leading Chinese religions, maintain a strong hold on the population, especially among older folk.

There are about 360 Chinese temples in Hong Kong. Some temples are centuries old, built by fishermen or early settlers. Because of the short supply of land some temples are established inside multi-storey buildings to cater for the spiritual needs of smaller circles of city dwellers.

All Chinese temples are required to be registered under the Chinese Temples Ordinance. The Chinese Temples Committee manages some 40 public temples and the income, from donations by worshippers, is used for preservation and restoration not only of public temples but also privately-owned temples of historical value. Any surplus is also put towards a charity fund which over the years has been contributing to general charities such as scholarships for needy university students and subsidies to local welfare organisations. Most of the large temples and monasteries are open to the public.

Each temple is dedicated to one or two deities enshrined in the main hall, with side halls housing subsidiary deities. Since Buddhism and Taoism are both accepted as traditional Chinese religions, Buddhist and Taoist deities are often honoured together within one temple. Leading deities include Buddha, Kwun Yum (the Buddhist Goddess of Mercy), and Lui Cho (a Taoist god).

There is also a diversity of deified mortals traditionally worshipped as a result of their performance of actual or mythical feats. Foremost among these is Tin Hau, the Queen of Heaven and Protectress of Seafarers, worshipped originally by the fishing population but now by others in the community as well, reflecting Hong Kong's dependence on fishing and on sea trade. There are at least 24 Tin Hau Temples in Hong Kong, the most famous being in Joss House Bay, which is visited by tens of thousands of worshippers each year at Tin Hau Festival on the 23rd day of the third moon.

Other deified mortals include Kwan Tai, the god of war and righteousness; Pak Tai, lord of the north and patron of Cheung Chau Island; Hung Shing, god of the south seas and a weather prophet; and Wong Tai Sin, a Taoist deity, in whose honour a temple built 71 years ago in north-eastern Kowloon in traditional Chinese architectural style enjoys great popularity. Dedicated to the gods of literary attainment and martial valour, Man Mo Temple in Hollywood Road on Hong Kong Island, run by the Tung Wah Group of Hospitals, a charitable organisation, is also very popular. The Che Kung Temple at Sha Tin in the New Territories, dedicated to a general in the Sung Dynasty, is visited by tens of thousands of worshippers during Lunar New Year.

Protestant Community

The presence of the Protestant community dates back to 1841. In the 150 years since the first Protestant church came into being, the community has grown to 258 000 in 872 congregations that comprise 52 denominations and independent churches. The Baptists form the largest denomination followed by the Lutherans. Other major denominations are Adventists, Anglicans, Christian and Missionary Alliance, Church of Christ in China (representing the Presbyterian and Congregational traditions), Methodists and Pentecostals. With their emphasis on youth work, many congregations have a high proportion of young people. Since the 1970s, the number of independent churches has increased significantly due to the strong evangelical zeal of lay Christians.

The Protestant churches are also deeply involved in education, health care and social welfare. Protestant organisations operate three post-secondary colleges – Chung Chi College at the Chinese University of Hong Kong, Hong Kong Baptist College and Lingnan College. They run 122 secondary schools, 141 primary schools and 146 kindergartens.

309

In addition, they operate 13 theological seminaries and Bible institutes, 16 Christian publishing houses and 57 Christian book shops.

They run seven hospitals with 2 126 beds, 24 clinics and 61 social service organisations that provide a wide range of social services including 108 community and youth centres, 35 day care centres, eight children's homes, 27 homes for the elderly, 78 elderly centres, three schools for the deaf, 10 training centres for the mentally handicapped and 20 camp sites. Five international hotel-type guest houses are managed by the YMCA and YWCA.

Ninety-six para-church agencies and various Christian action groups have been established to minister to the needs of the Protestant community and to respond to current issues and concerns in Hong Kong society at large. The church is involved in overseas aid by supporting emergency relief and development projects in third world countries. The 'Five Loaves and Two Fish' campaign, sponsored by Hong Kong Christian Council, was the first overseas aid project initiated in Hong Kong. Two weekly newspapers, *The Christian Weekly* and *The Christian Times*, bring news and comments from a Christian perspective to the Christian community.

Two ecumenical bodies facilitate co-operative work among the Protestant churches in Hong Kong. The oldest of the two, dating back to 1915, is the Hong Kong Chinese Christian Churches Union with a membership of 259 congregations. The second co-operative body is the Hong Kong Christian Council, formed in 1954. Major mainline denominations and ecumenical services constitute the membership core of the council, which is committed to building closer relationships among all churches in Hong Kong as well as with churches overseas, and to stimulating local Christians to play an active part in the development of Hong Kong society. It seeks to serve the wider community through its auxiliary agencies such as the Hong Kong Christian Service, Christian Industrial Committee, United Christian Medical Service, Alice Ho Miu Ling Nethersole Hospital and the Christian Family Service Centre. The council runs weekly 'Alternative Tours' which give visitors and residents an opportunity to see how the church is serving the community.

In the area of social concern, the Protestant community has played an active role in arousing public interest in Hong Kong's democratic development and in promoting the love of Hong Kong by organising the 'We Love Hong Kong Campaign'. It has supported such issues as labour welfare and the guarantee of human rights in Hong Kong in the future.

Roman Catholic Community

The Roman Catholic Church has been present in Hong Kong since the territory's early days. The church was established as a mission prefecture in 1841 and as an apostolic vicariate in 1874. It became a diocese in 1946.

In 1969, Francis Chen-peng Hsu was installed as the first Chinese Bishop of the Hong Kong diocese, and he was succeeded in 1973 by Peter Wang-kei Lei. The present bishop, John Baptist Cheng-chung Wu, was consecrated in 1975, and was made Cardinal in 1988.

About 254 800 people, or five per cent of the population, are Catholics. They are served by 350 priests, 74 brothers, and 659 sisters. There are 61 parishes and 34 centres for Mass. The majority of the services and other religious activities are conducted in Chinese, with a few churches providing services in English.

The diocese has established its own administrative structure while maintaining traditional links with the Pope and with other Catholic communities around the world.

It uses the same scriptures and has similar ecclesial communions in the universal Church throughout the world, with which it maintains close fellowship. The assistant secretary-general of the Federation of Asian Bishops' Conference has his office in Hong Kong.

Along with its apostolic work, one of the prime concerns of the diocese has been for the well-being of all the people of Hong Kong. In education, there are 275 Catholic schools and kindergartens which have about 290 512 pupils. There is the Catholic Board of Education to assist in this area. The medical and social services include six hospitals, nine clinics, 17 social centres, 11 hostels, 29 homes for the aged, one home for the handicapped and many self-help clubs and associations. Caritas is the official social welfare arm of the church in Hong Kong.

These services are open to all people – indeed, 95 per cent of those who have benefited from the wide range of services provided by the diocese are not Catholics.

To reach people through the media, the diocese publishes two weekly newspapers, *Kung Kao Po* and *The Sunday Examiner*. In addition, the Diocesan Audio-Visual Centre produces tapes and films for use in schools and parishes and the Hong Kong Catholic Social Communications Office acts as an overall information and public relations channel for the diocese.

Muslim Community

There are about 50 000 Muslims in Hong Kong. More than half of them are Chinese with the rest being either locally born non-Chinese or believers from Pakistan, India, Malaysia, Indonesia and Middle Eastern and African countries. Four principal mosques are used daily for prayers. The oldest is the Jamia Mosque in Shelley Street on Hong Kong Island which was built before the turn of the century and rebuilt in 1915. It can accommodate a congregation of 400.

Also on Hong Kong Island is the Masjid Ammar and Osman Ramju Sadick Islamic Centre. Opened in 1981, this eight-storey centre in Wan Chai houses a mosque on two floors, a community hall, a library, a medical clinic, classrooms and offices. The mosque, which is managed by the Islamic Union of Hong Kong, can accommodate 700 people but up to 1 500 if necessary, by using other available space in the centre.

Situated on what is sometimes called the 'Golden Mile' in Nathan Road is the Kowloon Mosque and Islamic Centre which was opened in May 1984. This imposing building, with white marble finishing, is a distinctive landmark in Tsim Sha Tsui. The mosque can accommodate a congregation of about 2 000 and has, in addition to the three prayer halls, a community hall, a medical clinic and a library.

There are two Muslim cemeteries, both on Hong Kong Island – one at Happy Valley and the other at Cape Collinson, Chai Wan. The Cape Collinson cemetery also has a mosque.

The co-ordinating body for all Islamic religious affairs is the Incorporated Trustees of the Islamic Community Fund of Hong Kong. A board of trustees comprising representatives of four Muslim organisations, namely the Islamic Union of Hong Kong, the Pakistan Association, the Indian Muslim Association and the Dawoodi Bohra Association, is responsible for the management and maintenance of mosques and cemeteries. The trustees are also responsible for organising the celebration of Muslim festivals and other religious events. Charitable work among the Muslim community,   311 including financial aid for the needy, medical facilities and assisted education, is conducted through various local Muslim organisations.

Hindu Community

The religious and social activities of the 12 000 members of Hong Kong's Hindu community are centred on the Hindu Temple in Happy Valley. The Hindu Association of Hong Kong is responsible for the upkeep of the temple, which is also used for meditation periods, yoga classes and other community activities. Naming, engagement and marriage ceremonies are performed at the temple according to Hindu custom. Religious music sessions, discourses and recitals are conducted every Sunday morning and Monday evening. The Sunday sessions are regularly attended by members of the community. Every Sunday a free community meal is served at the temple.

The temple is frequently visited by swamis and learned men from overseas who give spiritual lectures to the community. A number of festivals are observed, the more important being the Holi Festival, the Birth of Lord Krishna, Shivaratri, Dussehra and Diwali. Various linguistic groups among the Hindus organise additional festivals and prayer meetings on occasions of special significance to their group.

Other important services rendered by the temple are to administer the last rites and arrange for cremation and related ceremonies. The temple is also responsible for the upkeep of the Hindu crematorium at Cape Collinson.

Sikh Community

The Sikhs – distinguished by their stylised turbans and unshorn hair – first came to Hong Kong from the Punjab in North India as part of the British Armed Forces in the 19th century. Because of their generally strong physique, they also comprised a large segment of the Hong Kong Police Force before World War II.

Today, members of the community are engaged in a variety of occupations. The centre of their religious and cultural activities is the Sikh Temple at 371 Queen's Road East, Wan Chai, Hong Kong. A special feature of the temple, which was established in 1901, is the provision of free meals and short-term accommodation for overseas visitors of any faith. Religious services, which include hymn singing, readings from the Guru Granth (the Sikh Holy Book) and sermons by the priest, are held every Sunday morning. The temple also houses a library which contains a good selection of books on the Sikh religion and culture, and runs a 'starters' school for Indian children aged between four and six to prepare them for English primary schools in Hong Kong.

The main holy days and festivals observed are the birthdays of Guru Nanak (founder of the faith), Guru Gobind Singh (the 10th Guru) and Baisakhi (birthday of all Sikhs).

Jewish Community

Hong Kong's Jewish community – comprising families from various parts of the world – worships on Friday evenings, Saturday mornings and Jewish holidays at the Synagogue *Ohel Leah* in Robinson Road, Hong Kong Island. The synagogue was built in 1901 on land given by Sir Jacob Sassoon and his family. The original site included a Rabbi's residence and school, as well as a recreation club for the 1 000 people in the congregation. There is also a Jewish Cemetery, which is located at Happy Valley.

The site adjoining the synagogue, which once housed the school and club, is currently under reconstruction and the club has been temporarily relocated to Melbourne Plaza, Central. It has two restaurants serving Kosher meals prepared under rabbinical supervision from 8 am to 11 pm daily and a specialist library with information on the history of Judaism in Hong Kong and China.

Other Faiths

As well as the major religions practised in Hong Kong, faiths such as that of the Baha'is and Zoroastrianism have also found their place here.

23
RECREATION, SPORTS AND THE ARTS

LEISURE activities make an important contribution to the quality of life and Hong Kong residents now have access to a wide range of recreational, sporting and cultural facilities. Many of these are provided by the Urban and Regional Councils, which are autonomous bodies empowered to formulate policies for the provision and management of cultural and recreational facilities in their respective areas. They build and operate games halls and pitches, swimming pools and parks, museums, libraries and other recreational facilities, as well as organising and supporting a host of cultural, sporting and recreational activities. The government's policies on recreation, sport, culture and heritage matters are co-ordinated by the Recreation and Culture Branch headed by the Secretary for Recreation and Culture. He is assisted by several expert bodies, including the Council for the Performing Arts and Antiquities Advisory Board. Many other individuals and associations play an essential role in creating and improving opportunities for fulfilling leisure activities in Hong Kong.

Highlights of the year included the launching of the world's largest bilingual public library computerisation project for Regional Council libraries, the opening of the Hong Kong Visual Arts Centre and the Lai Chi Kok Public Library, and the operation of a third mobile library van to provide library services to remote areas. This year also saw the 20th anniversary of the Hong Kong Arts Festival and the setting up of a Heritage Trust in the name of the former Governor Lord Wilson of Tillyorn to mark his governorship. Both councils mounted numerous cultural and entertainment events during the year. Major events included the 16th International Film Festival, the 14th Festival of Asian Arts and the Hong Kong Independent Short Film Competition presented by the Urban Council, and the month-long Regional Council Festival and a *Dance in Residence* project organised by the Regional Council.

The Arts

In world terms, Hong Kong's arts community is still in its youth, with all the characteristics of dynamism, new ideas and rapid growth which that implies. While talent and creativity have always been present, it is only in recent years, that with financial support from both the public and private sectors, the arts community has been able to capitalise on its creativity and increase the number and range of its activities. As a result there are now two professional orchestras, three full-time dance companies, three professional drama groups

314

and hundreds of amateur groups, including orchestras, bands, choirs, dance groups and drama clubs. The Urban and Regional Councils run arts venues throughout Hong Kong, so that access to culture is no longer confined to people living in the main urban areas. The two councils have also become patrons of the arts in their own right, either by funding performing groups directly, or assisting them with presentations.

Council for the Performing Arts
The government's support to the performing arts is co-ordinated by the Secretary for Recreation and Culture, who works closely with the Council for the Performing Arts. The council, which comprises 15 appointed and two official members, is responsible for advising the government on the development of the performing arts and the disbursement of funds on performing arts activities. It has expert committees on specific aspects of the arts, including music, drama, dance, arts services and Chinese opera, and also advises on general issues such as business sponsorship.

The council continued its efforts to promote business sponsorship through the matching grant scheme under which arts groups receive a dollar for each dollar of business sponsorship they secure, up to a maximum of $100,000 for each project, and a reception was held in April to present commemorative certificates to sponsors. With the objective to promote original scriptwriting, the council presented its awards for outstanding original scripts for the second year consecutively. To mark its 10th anniversary, the council published a report covering developments in the performing arts in Hong Kong during the period 1982 to 1992.

On the advice of the Council for the Performing Arts, four performing arts organisations, the Chung Ying Theatre Company, the Hong Kong Ballet, the City Contemporary Dance Company and the Hong Kong Arts Festival, received general support grants totalling about $27.6 million in 1992–3. In addition, $3 million was awarded to the Exploration Theatre, $1 million to the Hong Kong Sinfonietta as seeding grants and about $3.6 million to other local performing arts groups as grants for individual projects. Among these were a music project to promote the understanding and appreciation of contemporary music and music creativity among school pupils and a project to provide training and performance opportunities for emerging Cantonese opera performers.

The survey commissioned by the council to assess the population's attitude to the arts was completed. The results of the survey provide empirical data for planning and resource allocation for performing arts development and will also be useful for audience building and other purposes.

Performing Groups
Hong Kong Philharmonic Orchestra
The Hong Kong Philharmonic Orchestra entered its 17th professional season under its Music Director David Atherton, Principal Guest Conductor Kenneth Jean and Resident Conductor Yip Wing-sie. The 92-strong orchestra is funded by the Urban Council, but it also receives contributions from the business community and individuals.

During 1992, the orchestra gave 121 performances in the Hong Kong Cultural Centre, the City Hall and other places throughout the territory. Thirty per cent of these performances was for students.

The highlight of the year was the appearance of British pianist Peter Donohoe in the Russian Romantic Music Festival in June and July in which he performed the four concertos of Rachmaninov.

Renowned artists, such as pianists Peter Katin, Jon Kimura Parker, Kathryn Scott, Anne Queffelec and Arthur Pizzaro, appeared as soloists with the orchestra. Cellists Steven Isserlis and Misha Maisky, vocalist Philip Langridge and violinist Nobuko Imai, together with the orchestra, brought high-quality programmes.

The Urban Council runs three professional performing companies – the Hong Kong Repertory Theatre, the Hong Kong Chinese Orchestra and the Hong Kong Dance Company.

Hong Kong Repertory Theatre

Hong Kong Repertory Theatre celebrated its 15th anniversary in 1992 by staging George F. Walker's *Nothing Sacred* which was directed jointly by the company's Artistic Director, Dr Daniel Yang, and American director Edward Hastings.

The local audience continued to give enthusiastic support to the company. In 1992 the company staged seven productions – five translated plays and two originals – in 89 performances, attracting 44 042 people. In addition, the company gave 78 performances, including free performances and lecture demonstrations, in schools, community arts centres and the foyer of the Hong Kong Cultural Centre. These performances attracted a total audience of 14 722.

Hong Kong Chinese Orchestra

Hong Kong Chinese Orchestra is Hong Kong's only professional Chinese music orchestra. In 1992 the 85-member orchestra gave 89 performances under the baton of its new Resident Conductor, Xia Feiyun, and various guest conductors, attracting a total audience of 724 000.

Apart from regular concerts, the orchestra also presented ensemble concerts, participated in district arts festivals and organised free outreach performances at community arts centres, community centres and schools. It also participated in the Festival Hong Kong '92 in Toronto and Vancouver, Canada, in October.

Recognised as one of the world's leading Chinese orchestras, it explores new frontiers in Chinese music by experimenting with new techniques and styles. It continues to expand the Chinese orchestral music repertoire by commissioning local and overseas composers to work on new compositions and arrangements.

Hong Kong Dance Company

Hong Kong Dance Company is the only professional Chinese dance company in the territory to present Chinese traditional and folk dances and new dance dramas choreographed on Chinese and Hong Kong themes.

In 1992, the company presented four major productions in 17 performances, attracting 11 453 people. In addition, the company gave free performances and lecture demonstrations in community arts centres, schools and community centres to 48 469 people.

Preceding page: *Crew from Hong Kong-based airline Dragonair enjoy another happy landing.*

Left: *The control tower at Hong Kong International Airport.*

Below: *Hong Kong International Airport cargo terminal is being expanded to deal with growing traffic.*

Bottom: *The cargo terminal control centre.*

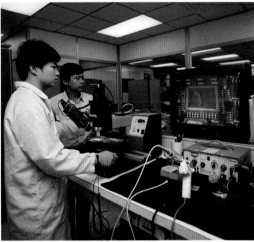

Maintenance work at Hong Kong International Airport.

Left: *The cabin crew training centre operated by Hong Kong's Cathay Pacific Airlines.*

Below: *Chefs meet to ensure the quality of food served aboard aircraft departing from Hong Kong.*

Bottom: *Food being prepared for first class passengers.*

Above: *A training simulator creates on the ground a realistic flying environment.*

Right: *An external view of the training simulator.*

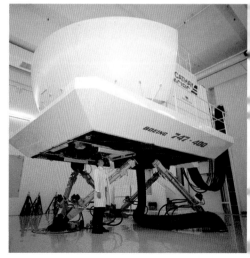

The company went on two overseas tours in 1992. In February, it took part in the Third China Arts Festival in Kunming by staging two performances of a new dance drama, *The Snow is Red*, co-choreographed by the company's Artistic Director, Shu Qiao, and reputed choreographer Hua Chao from China. In October, the company participated in Festival Hong Kong '92 in Canada by staging a newly adapted version of the dance drama *Rouge*.

The Chung Ying Theatre Company

The Chung Ying Theatre Company, which is supported by the Council for the Performing Arts, began the year with *Far Way Home*, the first locally commissioned work ever staged in the annual Hong Kong Arts Festival. Winner of Best Script (Original) and Best Director (Comedy/Farce) in the First Hong Kong Drama Awards (91–92) organised by Hong Kong Federation of Drama Societies, the production returned in June to play to Sha Tin audiences.

A spooky musical *The Dracula Spectacula*, directed by visiting British director Chris Harris, was sold out during July's International Arts Carnival, and made a come back for family audiences at Sheung Wan Civic Centre in December.

British clown Gerry Flanagan re-directed the highly original devised work *Fools, Fools, Fools!*, for a re-run in October in Ngau Chi Wan Civic Centre before taking off to Toronto, Montreal and Vancouver as part of Festival Hong Kong '92.

Artistic Director Chris Johnson directed Rupert Chan's adaptation of Russian playwright Nikolai Erdman's *The Suicide*. Set in Canton in the 1950s the play was part of the City Hall's 30th anniversary celebratory programme. She also directed a commissioned work on an environmental theme in November. The outdoor project, in collaboration with the British Council, was staged both aboard a ferry and on Stonecutters Island.

The company also re-staged the Cantonese version of Willy Russell's *Educating Rita* in March. On the education side, *Fools, Fools, Fools!* toured schools throughout the territory and *Monkey See, Monkey Do* was presented as part of Hong Kong Cultural Centre's education programme, in addition to the ongoing workshop programme.

City Contemporary Dance Company

The City Contemporary Dance Company, Hong Kong's first professional modern dance company, started its dance season by staging its Artistic Director, Willy Tsao's *Wanderings In The Cosmos* in the 1992 Hong Kong Arts Festival. In March a major dance and music production *Rite of Spring and Lam Mot* was specially commissioned by the Urban Council to celebrate its 30th anniversary with choreography by Helen Lai and Willy Tsao staged at the Hong Kong Cultural Centre Concert Hall. Other major productions presented by the company during the year included *Salome Dance For Peace* in April–May at Hong Kong Arts Centre Shouson Theatre; *Stories About Certain Women* in June–July at the City Hall Theatre 30th anniversary celebration of the City Hall; *Invisible Cities* at Hong Kong Arts Centre Shouson Theatre in July, *Made In Hong Kong: Very Good!* in August at the Fringe Club; and *Three Dreams* in November at the Hong Kong Academy For Performing Arts Drama Theatre.

The company also mounted two overseas tours to Dalian, Shenyang, Beijing and Tianjin in North-eastern China, and Ottawa and Montreal as part of Festival Hong Kong '92, in September and October respectively.

The company continued to run its evening dance school, the City Contemporary Theatre and Gallery, and opened a new City Contemporary Club to further encourage innovative arts in Hong Kong. Company members also continued to visit as many as 100 local primary and secondary schools to promote dance education and appreciation among young people.

Hong Kong Ballet

Nineteen ninety two was exciting year for Hong Kong Ballet under the new artistic direction of Bruce Steivel who has focussed on the development of the company at home and abroad. This year the Hong Kong Ballet was invited to open the Singapore Arts Festival, to participate in the Festival Hong Kong '92 in Canada and to visit Shanghai for the company's third tour there. International touring is a gainful experience for the company as it gives critics of other nations the opportunity to measure its performances against the international standards of dance today.

At home Hong Kong Ballet premiered two new full-length ballets *Coppelia* for the Regional Council's International Children's Arts Festival in August, and *A Midsummer Night's Dream* in September, accompanied by the Hong Kong Philharmonic, and commissioned by the Urban Council. Another high point earlier in the year was a triple bill programme which included Jean-Paul Comelin's *Les Nuits d'Ete* and Balanchine's *Who Cares?*. Audiences enjoyed an interesting and entertaining year, which was concluded with the world's most popular ballet *The Nutcracker*.

Through the outreach activities of the ballet's education unit the number of participatory courses, workshops and special theatre performances continued to cater to the growing audiences for ballet throughout the territory.

The Exploration Theatre

The Exploration Theatre was established in 1982. It is the first theatrical company supported by the Council for the Performing Arts under the seeding grant scheme.

The year 1992 marked the 10th anniversary of the Exploration Theatre. To commemorate the occasion, the play, *Moonlight Opera* was staged in July. The play brought about the unprecedented co-operation of top dramatists with renowned playwright Raymond To, director Ng Ka Hai, and a cast of experienced actors.

The Exploration Theatre has an active educational programme and took its original productions – *Dear Papa and Mama* and *It's a Long Road to Freedom* – to 60 colleges and secondary schools.

Hong Kong Sinfonietta

Hong Kong Sinfonietta which comprises young local musicians, was established in 1990. The Sinfonietta has been supported by the Council for the Performing Arts under the seeding grant scheme since 1991. Apart from providing performance opportunities for local musicians, it also offers orchestral support to local performing groups. Its repertoire includes traditional orchestral pieces and works of local composers.

The Sinfonietta has accompanied many local performing groups, such as the Hong Kong Oratorio Society, the Hong Kong Children's Choir and the Hong Kong Baptist College Choir. Its concerts in 1992 included the *Romantic Highlights* series, the *Enchanting*

Romantic Suites series and the *Outstanding Young Local Talent Concert*. In addition, the Sinfonietta also presents student concerts and foyer performances.

Hong Kong Academy for Performing Arts

Hong Kong Academy for Performing Arts is a tertiary institution which was established to foster and provide for training, education and research in the performing and related technical arts. Emphasis is put on both Chinese and western traditions. The academy is divided into four schools – dance, drama, music and technical arts. The School of Dance has three streams – ballet, Chinese dance and modern dance – which now includes musical theatre dance. The School of Music offers courses in Chinese and western music. The School of Technical Arts provides training in theatre and television.

In the 1992–3 academic year, there were 583 students on full-time courses leading to the awards of Bachelor of Fine Arts degrees, professional diploma, advanced diploma, diploma, advanced certificate and certificate. In addition, 828 students were enrolled on junior courses in dance and music which were provided for talented young people of school age. Continuing education in dance for evening part-time students was also offered by the School of Dance.

During the course of the year the academy was accredited by the Hong Kong Council for Academic Accreditation as an institution capable of awarding degrees, and as a result of the validation by teams of international experts of the degree proposals submitted by the four schools, the Schools of Dance and Music admitted students to their Bachelor of Fine Arts courses in September, and the Schools of Drama and Technical Arts will begin their degree courses in September 1993.

This change of status to a degree-awarding institution is a milestone in the short history of the academy, and is a recognition of the importance of the performing arts to the cultural life of Hong Kong.

The School of Dance presented a number of performances during the year, notably the Graduation Dance Concert. There were also opportunities for the students to show their abilities as choreographers in the creative projects evenings. The School of Dance joined forces with the School of Music for *An Evening with Cole Porter*, and the major dance event of the autumn was *Time Travellers* a major new work with particular appeal to young audiences. The School of Dance participated with great success in the International Festival of Dance Academies in Taiwan during the summer.

The School of Drama mounted plays including Ibsen's *An Enemy of the People*, Simon's *Bare Foot in the Park*, Shakespeare's *Macbeth* (set in Tibet), and a new musical, *Autumn City Story*. A new version of Moliere's *Don Juan*, and a play based on a Chinese traditional theme *Nuwa Mends the Sky*, which was toured in France, were produced. A revised version of *Nuwa*, designed for a larger stage and Hong Kong audiences was produced in the drama theatre in October.

The School of Music gave their regular series of concerts during the year, notably the Exxon-sponsored *Young Professional Musicians Platforms* on Tuesday evenings which concentrated on Baroque and 20th century music; Monday lunch-time concerts; and Friday piano recitals. The Opera Department presented Kurt Weill's *Rise and Fall of the City of Mahagonny* in April, conducted by Gordon Kember, directed by Fredric Mao and designed by visiting German designer Jurgen Lancier. The opera performance at the end of the year was the academy's most ambitious project: Bizet's *Carmen*, conducted by Carlo Cillario, directed by Anthony Besch and designed by Peter Rice. During June and July the Summer Music Festival covered a wide repertoire, including performances of Stravinsky's *Soldier's Tale* and *Concerto for Piano and Wind Instruments*, conducted by Denis de Coteau, Academy composers and the Chinese Music Department were featured in the festival.

The School of Technical Arts was involved in all the dance, drama and opera productions, with design and management students contributing significantly to the success of many of them. The school also organised several exhibitions of student work during the year, and participated in a study tour of Italy. Television courses continued to develop, with student crews working on a drama production under the direction of visiting British Broadcasting Corporation producer Ronald Smedley.

All four schools combined to produce *Hong Kong Heartbeat* which was performed in the Barbican Hall as part of a Hong Kong promotion in London in January. Her Royal Highness the Princess of Wales attended one of the performances and met members of the company. A revised version of *Heartbeat* was taken to Canada in October, and performed in Calgary and Ottawa.

The Foundation of Businesses in Support of the Arts

Business for Art is the working name for the Foundation of Businesses in Support of the Arts, a non-profit organisation established in 1990 by a group of prominent business people in Hong Kong. Its main objective is to encourage, assist and promote local arts in all forms and also to encourage the business community to support the arts through supporting art projects which would benefit the local art community, particularly up-and-coming young artists.

Business for Art has succeeded in matching several artists seeking funds to business sponsors wishing to sponsor arts projects. It also assisted local artists in packaging their talents in order to attract sponsorship, at the same time ensuring that the needs of business sponsors were recognised.

Business for Art presented the gala premiere of *42nd Street*, a world-renowned Broadway musical at the Lyric Theatre of the Hong Kong Academy for Performing Arts in March.

Hong Kong Arts Centre

Hong Kong Arts Centre is an independent, non-profit organisation founded in 1977 to promote arts and culture. Its funding derives from rental income, box office, corporate sponsorship and donations from benevolent individuals. It incorporates the 440-seat Shouson Theatre, the 200-seat Lim Por Yen Film Theatre, the 100-seat McAulay Studio, the Pao Sui Loong and Pao Yue Kong Galleries, the Atrium Gallery, rehearsal rooms, art and craft studios, music practice rooms and classrooms.

As a multi-discipline organisation, Hong Kong Arts Centre offers a platform for contemporary work in the performing, visual and cinematic arts as well as featuring new, avant garde and multi-media art forms. It encourages non-established artists of all disciplines and the development of indigenous art forms. Substantial resources are dedicated to outreach work in arts education, with a view to promoting appreciation of all art forms and activities.

In 1992 the centre was visited by over 1.1 million people, many of whom attended the 910 stage and screen performances, 70 exhibitions and 372 arts-related classes and courses held within its venues. Highlights of the year included the exhibitions *Man Ray – The Bazaar Years: A Fashion Retrospective; The Graphic Art of Wilfredo Lam* and the *Manulife Young Artists Series*; and the film programmes *Life as a Magic Lantern: An Ingmar Bergman Restrospective*; and *Whirlwind from the East: An East European Film Festival.*

British Council

One of the aims of the British Council in Hong Kong is to foster cultural understanding between Britain and Hong Kong through a balanced programme of music, drama, dance, exhibitions, film shows and related masterclasses and workshops catering to the interests of local residents. The council works in conjunction with local organisations and supports collaborative projects between British artists and local performing companies.

In 1992 the council co-organised a number of arts events with local organisations including the Theatre de Complicite performing *The Winter's Tale*, the Nash Ensemble and the opera *Tosca* produced by Stephen Lawless during the Hong Kong Arts Festival and several acts in the Hong Kong Festival Fringe. It also co-organised a visit by the London Festival Orchestra, a Beatles retrospective of film shows, an exhibition sponsored by Thorn EMI and an environmental theatre project on Stonecutters Island jointly presented with the Chung Ying Theatre Company, sponsored by the David Shepherd Conservation Foundation.

Cultural Events

Hong Kong Arts Festival

Since its founding in 1973, the Hong Kong Arts Festival has been bringing rich artistic experience to the people of Hong Kong. In 1992, over 90 000 people attended 124 performances in a festival lasting 23 days.

To celebrate its 20th anniversary and salute the achievements of local artists and arts organisations over the years, the festival opened with a Hong Kong Performing Arts Day. Local arts companies performed in various cultural venues while young musicians, dancers and actors provided six hours of non-stop entertainment in the Cultural Centre foyer and piazza.

Highlights of the festival included the renowned Les Ballets de Monte-Carlo, the Berlin Symphony Orchestra, vocalist Grace Bumbry, a special opera production of *Tosca*, and a series of programmes focusing on the arts scene of a rapidly changing Europe.

The New Spirit of Europe was explored in programmes featuring avant-garde companies such as Hungary's Katona Jozsef Theatre, Britain's Theatre de Complicité, Sweden's Cullberg Ballet, and La La La Human Steps from Montreal, North America's European metropolis. The Zurich New Music Ensemble offered an interpretation of the continent's latest music and two new works (including a commissioned piece) by Hong Kong composers. Scotswoman Evelyn Glennie gave the territory its first ever percussion recital, the programme of which included a commissioned work by a local composer.

The festival's programme was also noted for its diversity. *Africa Oye* brought extraordinary sights and sounds to Hong Kong's urban environment. Asian presentations included the Shanghai Kunju Opera Troupe, the Umewaka Noh Theatre Company, and

321

Hong Kong's Chung Ying Theatre Company, which staged an original script by a local playwright.

Hong Kong Festival Fringe
Since its founding 10 years ago, the Festival Fringe has developed from an annual open arts festival into a successful year-round operation that gives the emerging artists of Hong Kong the opportunity to hone their skills and create new works.

Festival Fringe 1992, staged for three weeks in January, was attended by some 300 000 people.

In 1992 the Fringe Club and Sydney Theatre Company produced *Great Expectations* for the Festival of Asian Arts. It was premiered at the Grand Theatre, Hong Kong Cultural Centre, on October 16.

Manned by a small and dedicated staff and open throughout the year, the Fringe Club provides artists with rent-free venues for performances and exhibitions. Its facilities include a 100-seat theatre, several rehearsal studios, a bar with an exhibition area, a pottery workshop with showroom, a restaurant, a gallery and offices. The Fringe Club arranges performances, exhibitions and classes on a year-round basis. It also houses a theatre workshop and a mime and movement laboratory. An active outreach programme chalked up over 300 shows and special projects during the year.

Urban Council Presentations
To popularise the arts among the people of Hong Kong, the Urban Council invited local and overseas artists to present a wide variety of performances in 1992. The performances totalled 325 and attracted 233 260 people.

The varied programmes included orchestral concerts by the Munich Philharmonic Orchestra and the Polish National Radio Symphony Orchestra; instrumental recitals by Bernard Roberts, Frank Peter Zimmermann, John O'Conor, Vadim Repin, Pepe Romero and Mstislav Rostropovich; a vocal recital by Renata Scotto; and performances by the Vienna Chamber Orchestra, the Albert NcNeil Jubilee Singers, the Wallace Collection and the Vienna Virtuosi. On the theatre and dance front, there were opera productions of *Otello* and by the Guangdong and Guangxi Cantonese Opera Troupe; performances by the National Ballet of Canada, Ballet Folklorico de Mexico, Les Ballets Trockadero de Monte Carlo, and the Hong Kong International Ballroom and Latin American Dance Championship. The council also commissioned and presented the Hong Kong Ballet's new production of *A Midsummer Night's Dream*.

To celebrate the 30th anniversary of the City Hall, local talents were engaged for performances from May to December. Among them were pianists including Chiu Yee-ha, Choi Sown-le, Tam Ka-kit, Gabriel Kwok and Nancy Loo; the Chung Ying Theatre Company; the Hong Kong Federation of Drama Societies; the Hong Kong Movie and TV Theatrical Society; the Wang Kwong Chinese Orchestra; the Pan Asia Symphony Orchestra; the Hong Kong Ballet; the City Contemporary Dance Company; 12 local choruses and many others.

Symphony Under the Stars – the first free outdoor light classical concert for family audiences – was presented with Hong Kong Philharmonic Orchestra at Happy Valley Sports Ground in November, attracting 30 000 people.

Hong Kong International Film Festival
Hong Kong International Film Festival presented by the Urban Council is one of the world's major annual non-competitive film festivals.

The 16th festival in 1992 presented a programme of 170 films from 31 countries. The films were divided into four sections, international cinema, Asian cinema, Hong Kong Panorama 1991–92 and Hong Kong Cinema Retrospective.

International Cinema featured *Nitrate Can't Wait (But Films Don't Burn): Archival Treasures* which was a series of masterpieces preserved by overseas archives and private collectors. In this section, the organiser also paid tribute to the late German director R.W. Fassbinder. In the Asian Cinema, special homage was paid to Chinese director Ling Zifeng and Japanese actress Li Xianglan (Yoshiko Yamaguchi). The *Asian Beat Road Movies Series* was chosen as an outstanding selection of latest Asian films. *In Memory of Three Asian Filmmakers* marked the recent deaths of three respected filmmakers, G. Aravindan of India, Lino Brocka of the Philippines and Permpol Cheyaroon of Thailand. The Hong Kong Panorama 1991–92 showed Hong Kong's top-quality productions of 1991, while the Hong Kong Cinema Retrospective featured 36 films under the theme of *Overseas Chinese Figures in Cinema*.

Over 82 000 tickets were sold in the festival.

Hong Kong Independent Short Film Competition
To promote the production of quality non-commercial short films and encourage creative independent film production in the territory, the first Hong Kong Independent Short Film Competition was launched in 1992. It comprised three sections: fiction, non-fiction and animation.

International Arts Carnival
The annual summer festival of the Urban Council entered its 11th year in 1992. It serves to stimulate the interest of children and young people in the performing arts and provide cultural programmes for them during their summer vacation.

The carnival took place in July and August with a total of 25 shows of magic, mime, puppetry, acrobatics, children's musical and drama, music and ballet staged by seven local groups and three overseas groups. In addition, a free fun fair, comprising a marching band, variety show, magic show, cartoon video wall, and games, arts and crafts stalls, was held at the piazza of the Hong Kong Cultural Centre.

The carnival attracted a total audience of 68 913.

Festival of Asian Arts
The 14th Festival of Asian Arts presented by the council was held in October and November, featuring seven local and 10 overseas performing groups.

Performers from Hong Kong, China, India, Indonesia, Iraq, Israel, Japan, Korea, Turkey, Tajikistan and Australia presented various facets of Asian culture, ranging from east-west jazz to folk and modern dance, and from traditional to modern musical theatre. An exhibition of Chinese painting and calligraphy by Guangdong and Hong Kong artists was held at the Hong Kong Museum of Art.

Recitals, free outdoor performances, dance workshops and lecture demonstrations related to the theme of the festival were also held. An Asian food parade featuring Asian epicurean delights was presented during the festival period.

323

Entertainment Programmes

During the year, the Urban Council staged 243 entertainment programmes in parks, playgrounds, community halls, housing estates and community arts centres in the urban areas. Most of these programmes were free. The programmes were attended by over 128 000 people.

Annual territory-wide events organised by the council included a spring lantern festival, a summer fun festival, mid-autumn lantern carnivals, a Christmas carnival, District Cantonese opera parade and a concert in the park. About 650 000 people attended these events.

The council also played a part in the co-ordination of the 1992 lunar new year fireworks display and was one of the organisers of the Hong Kong Dragon Boat Festival international races.

Regional Council Presentations

The Regional Council presented a diverse programme of music, opera, drama, dance, film shows and other performing arts to cater to the tastes of local residents and to build up new audiences.

In presenting established artists of high standing, as well as novel programmes, the council aims to broaden the horizons of concert-goers. In 1992, overseas artists appearing under the council's auspices included Pei Yanling with the Hebei Clapper Opera Troupe, the I Musical de Montreal, Les Ballets Jazz de Montreal, Guitar Virtuoso Paco Pena and his Flamenco Dance Company, the American Symphony Orchestra, the London Festival Orchestra with pianist Pascal Roge, and the I Wan-jen Puppet Troupe under the leadership of Li Tianlu.

To strengthen the cultural content of the 1992 Hong Kong Arts Festival programme, the council co-operated with the festival organisers to present performances by Les Ballets de Monte-Carlo and ethnic songs and dance by Africa Oye.

Co-operation between the Regional Council and the Urban Council continued during the year through the invitation of performing companies such as the Hong Kong Chinese Orchestra and Hong Kong Repertory Theatre to perform at the Regional Council's town halls.

Local professional companies were high on the list of Regional Council presentations. The Hong Kong Ballet, Chung Ying Theatre Company, City Contemporary Dance Company and Hong Kong Philharmonic Orchestra all appeared frequently at the council's venues.

In 1992, the council presented 579 programmes, enjoyed by a total audience of 286 269.

International Children's Arts Festival

The International Children's Arts Festival, into its third year in 1992, is an annual event organised by the Regional Council to bring cultural activities to young audiences. Highlights of the 1992 festival included performances by the Yunnan Youth Arts Troupe from China, the Helsinki Junior Strings Orchestra from Finland, the Bambini di Praga from Czechoslovakia, and the On Stage Entertainment Company from the USA. Contributions by local artists included a summer music gallery by Hong Kong Symphony Orchestra, a children's dance drama by the Children's Arts Association of the New Towns, *Coppélia* by Hong Kong Ballet and Story-Building Time and Story-Telling Time –

children's drama workshops by the Chung Ying Theatre Company. In total, the festival featured three fun days, six drama workshops and 48 stage performances, drawing an attendance of 27 216.

Dance in Residence Project
To stimulate and develop interests in modern dance among residents in the council area, the Regional Council introduced a one-year pilot animateur scheme with the City Contemporary Dance Company. A dance animateur is tasked to provide outreach classes, develop performance groups and encourage amateur choreographic ventures.

A total of 14 schools and voluntary organisations joined the scheme with a total of 300 participants.

Visual Arts
The Regional Council's Best of Visual Arts scheme provides additional opportunities for local visual artists to exhibit their works in major civic centres. Under this scheme, local artists and art organisations are presented in one-person or joint exhibitions of works of painting, calligraphy, sculpture, ceramics and printmaking.

In 1992, a total of 14 exhibitions were held attracting 9 957 people.

Entertainment Programmes
The Regional Council regularly presents free cultural and entertainment programmes in community halls, playgrounds and open spaces to provide community leisure activities for residents in the vicinity. In 1992, 340 programmes were organised, attracting 191 911 people.

These free programmes, including Chinese music, western music, Chinese folk dance, modern dance, Cantonese opera, puppet shows, pop shows and variety shows, brought professional performances to the general public and provided opportunities for budding artists to improve their performing skills. The performances also help preserve Chinese cultural heritage such as puppetry and acrobatic art.

Venues
Most performance venues in Hong Kong are built and operated by the Urban and Regional Councils, ranging from major facilities such as the Hong Kong Cultural Centre to smaller multi-purpose centres used for district-based cultural activities.

Urban Council Venues
Hong Kong Cultural Centre
Hong Kong Cultural Centre continues to play its role as a thriving venue of the performing arts in Hong Kong.

Its 2 085-seat Concert Hall, designed with excellent acoustics, is the resident hall of the Hong Kong Philharmonic Orchestra. Apart from local artists and groups, overseas artists performing in the centre during the year included Mstislav Rostropovich, Anne-Sophie Mutter, Frank Peter Zimmermann, Vadim Repin, Jane Watts, Pepe Romero, Renata Scotto, the Chung Trio, the Don Burrows Quartet, the Munich Philharmonic Orchestra and the Vienna Boys' Choir.

The Grand Theatre is a popular venue for operas, musicals, dance, drama and film shows. During 1992, the venue hosted productions of *Tosca, Otello* and *A Flea in Her Ear*, performances by the National Ballet of Canada, the Cullberg Ballet, Ballet Folklorico de Mexico, Les Ballets Trockadero de Monte Carlo and over 100 other performances.

The Studio Theatre with its variable stage configurations has proven to be a valuable venue for small productions requiring an intimate atmosphere. The extensive rehearsal, practice facilities and exhibition areas of Hong Kong Cultural Centre are patronised by many local cultural organisations.

To promote the centre as well as the arts in Hong Kong, 252 regular free foyer programmes, education programmes and organ recitals were held in the cultural centre. Also, a 'friend' scheme with an annual membership of over 2 000 has been organised for dedicated supporters since 1989.

In 1992, patrons visiting the centre totalled about 3.5 million.

City Hall

Since its opening in 1962, the City Hall has become synonymous with the development of the arts and culture in Hong Kong. It continues to be one of the Urban Council's major cultural venues while retaining its popularity as a centre in the urban areas for the performing and visual arts.

The City Hall celebrated its 30th anniversary in 1992 with a series of programmes encompassing all art forms presented throughout the year.

Other significant events presented in the City Hall during the year included the 1992 Hong Kong Arts Festival, the 16th Hong Kong International Film Festival, the International Arts Carnival and the 14th Festival of Asian Arts.

Important civic functions staged at the City Hall included the departure of the former Governor of Hong Kong, Lord Wilson, and the arrival and swearing-in ceremony of the new Governor, the Rt Hon Christopher Patten.

During the year, 366 000 people attended 770 performances in the concert hall, the theatre and the recital hall. In addition, 114 exhibitions were held in the exhibition hall and exhibition gallery.

Ko Shan Theatre

Ko Shan Theatre is the only semi-open-air theatre in Hong Kong. It has 3 000 seats of which 1 000 are in the open.

The theatre is suitable for a broad range of cultural and entertainment events. Cantonese operas and operatic songs are frequently staged in the theatre. The second most popular events are rock concerts. In 1992, 145 378 people attended 107 performances.

Community Arts Centres

Besides the Ko Shan Theatre, the Urban Council operates three community arts centres to promote district-based cultural activities.

Ngau Chi Wan Civic Centre has a 443-seat theatre, a 350-square-metre exhibition hall, a 90-seat lecture room, two music practice rooms and a dance practice area. In the year, the theatre was used for 164 events, including drama, dance, variety shows as well as ceremonies for a total audience of 42 357.

Sheung Wan Civic Centre is made up of a 511-seat theatre, a 150-seat lecture hall, an exhibition hall, a rehearsal hall, a dance practice room, four music practice rooms and two art studios. The Urban Council's performing companies – Hong Kong Chinese Orchestra, Hong Kong Repertory Theatre and Hong Kong Dance Company – are housed in the centre. During the year, 64 000 people attended 378 performances in the centre's theatre and lecture hall.

Sai Wan Ho Civic Centre comprises a 471-seat theatre, a multi-purpose hall, three art studios and two music practice rooms. In 1992, 58 290 people attended 247 performances in the theatre. The multi-purpose hall was extensively used for a variety of functions, including performances and exhibitions.

Indoor Stadia

Hong Kong Coliseum and Queen Elizabeth Stadium managed by the Urban Council are two of Asia's best equipped multi-purpose indoor stadia.

The 12 000-seat coliseum is a popular venue not only for pop concerts by local and international performers, but also for world-class entertainment spectaculars. In 1992 performances staged at the stadium included the Great Moscow Circus, the Magic of David Copperfield, the world championship for five-a-side football, Diana Ross in concert and Placido Domingo in concert. The 75th Lions Club International Convention was also held at the coliseum.

The giant video screen hanging above the centre of the arena is a unique feature of the coliseum. It enables spectators to watch larger-than-life telecasts in colour, including close-up, replay and slow-motion shots of events.

The compact 3 500-seat Queen Elizabeth Stadium plays host to various medium-sized productions, ranging from sports events to pop concerts, and from cultural programmes to conventions. Highlights in 1992 consisted of the Thomas and Uber Cup badminton championships, the 10th Asian Cup table tennis tournament, the jazz concert *Select Live Under the Sky*, the Carlsberg music festival and Air Supply in concert.

In addition to the arena, the stadium provides facilities for recreational activities, such as badminton, squash, volleyball, basketball, table tennis and gymnastics, and committee rooms for lectures and meetings.

Redevelopment of Hong Kong Stadium

Hong Kong Stadium is being redeveloped to increase its seating capacity to 40 000. The project is funded and built by the Royal Hong Kong Jockey Club at a cost of $850 million. On completion in early 1994, the new stadium will be managed by the Urban Council, and will provide a first-class sporting arena and large-scale centre for world class sports, pop/rock concerts and other spectator events.

With the use of the latest construction method, the rugby sevens and major soccer events can be staged in March and April 1993 at the partially completed stadium while the construction is underway.

Regional Council Venues

The Regional Council manages three major cultural centres in Sha Tin, Tsuen Wan and Tuen Mun plus three smaller ones in Yuen Long, Tai Po and Sheung Shui.

Located in the town centres, each major cultural centre houses a 1 400-seat multi-purpose auditorium designed for staging performances ranging from symphony concerts to ballets. Other facilities include a cultural activities hall, an exhibition gallery, lecture rooms, rehearsal spaces, and music and dance studios. All facilities are offered for public hiring at reasonable charges. The centres are well served by public transport and there are restaurants, shopping centres and carparks in their vicinity.

For the smaller cultural centres, an 800-seat auditorium and ancillary function rooms are provided.

Computerised Ticketing

The Urban Council operates URBTIX (Urban Ticketing System), a computerised system providing a full range of ticketing services primarily in support of culture and entertainment events. URBTIX not only sells tickets for the Urban Council's own presentations, but also acts as a ticketing agent and offers the same quality ticketing services for events presented by the Regional Council, Hong Kong Arts Centre, the Academy for the Performing Arts and other organisations.

URBTIX services include counter and postal bookings as well as telephone reservations. It also handles telephone bookings for its registered patrons.

URBTIX runs a network of 18 outlets throughout Hong Kong Island, Kowloon and the New Territories, all capable of providing 'real time' transactions. During the year, 4.2 million tickets were sold through the system.

Music Office

The Music Office, a part of the Government Secretariat's Recreation and Culture Branch, plays an active role in providing instrumental music training and promoting interest in music among young people.

The Instrumental Music Training Scheme is open to young people between six and 23 years of age. Over 660 training classes in both western and Chinese instruments for about 3 000 trainees were conducted in six music centres. For talented young musicians, special training is provided. To help young people in taking musical training, the Music Office hires out musical instruments to its trainees at a modest charge. The office also encourages the handicapped to enjoy music by holding concerts and training sessions at special schools.

In addition to instrumental training, the trainees are provided with aural and theory training as well as orchestral and band training. Masterclasses and seminars are conducted by local and overseas visiting musicians. The office also manages two symphony orchestras, five string orchestras, six Chinese orchestras, six symphonic bands and two choirs.

To promote interest in music among young people, the office organises an annual music gala and various music festivals. Another major activity is the *Music for the Millions* concerts. Over 290 such concerts were presented in schools, community and welfare facilities all over Hong Kong for a total audience of 123 000.

The office organises international music exchanges to foster mutual understanding among young musicians and to broaden their horizons. In September, an ensemble of the Hong Kong Youth Chinese Orchestra and the Festival Hong Kong Children's Chorus performed in Festival Hong Kong '92 in Toronto and Calgary, Canada. At the same time, the office hosted visits by various youth music groups from Singapore, Australia, the USA and South Africa.

Hong Kong Jockey Club Music Fund

The Hong Kong Jockey Club Music Fund was set up in December 1979 with a donation of $10 million from the jockey club for the promotion and development of music, dance and other related activities. It is a non-statutory trust fund, administered by a board of trustees. The fund awarded 119 grants and eight scholarships totalling $2,240,000 in 1992, enabling young people to study music and dance abroad, and assisting local schools and organisations to acquire musical instruments and dance equipment.

Museums

Hong Kong Museum of Art

Since its opening in November 1991 the new Hong Kong Museum of Art in Tsim Sha Tsui has won popular support. In 1992 the museum attracted 129 071 visitors and 725 school parties with 18 133 students.

The museum's permanent galleries on contemporary Hong Kong art, historical pictures, Chinese antiquities and Chinese fine art continued to display selected items from the museum collection on a rotation basis. The special exhibition gallery was devoted to the staging of local and overseas exhibitions on both Chinese and Western art.

The City Vibrance – Recent Works in Western Media by Hong Kong Artists, The Contemporary Hong Kong Art Biennial Exhibition and The *Hong Kong Artists Series* were organised to promote local art. To celebrate the City Hall's 30th anniversary, *Works by Urban Council Fine Arts Award Winners 1975 to 1992* was organised. *The Splendour of the Qing Dynasty*, a joint presentation by the Urban Council and the Min Chiu Society, and the *Modern Chinese Painting and Calligraphy by Guangdong and Hong Kong Artists from the Taiyilou Collection* presented the best of Chinese art to the public. The *Kagoshima Art* exhibition, jointly presented with Kagoshima Prefectural Government, introduced paintings and prints by artists from this southern Japanese prefecture.

The Xubaizhai Gallery was officially opened in September for the display of the world renowned Xubaizhai collection of ancient Chinese painting and calligraphy donated by Low Chuck-tiew. The inaugural exhibition, *A Gift of Heritage*, was a selection of 80 Chinese paintings and calligraphy works from the collection.

In 1992, the Flagstaff House Museum of Tea Ware organised exhibitions on Chinese tea drinking, Chinese ceramic tea vessels and *The Art of the Yixing Potter* from the K.S. Collection. A tea ware competition was also organised to cultivate interest in pottery-making.

Hong Kong Visual Arts Centre was built to provide studio support for budding artists to practise. The centre provides equipped workshop facilities for ceramics, sculpture and print-making for hire by artists at subsidised rates. To mark its opening in April, an inaugural exhibition, *Hong Kong Graphic Prints*, was jointly organised with the Hong Kong Graphics Society. The exhibition *Modern Art in Glass – Murano, Venice 1992* was also presented in association with the Nuova Marco Polo Glass Gallery of Italy at the centre's exhibition gallery in November. In addition to the hiring of the exhibition gallery, artists studios, seminar rooms and lecture hall, the centre also organised art courses, lectures and art video shows.

329

During the year, the Urban Council continued to acquire important works of art to strengthen the museum collection and received significant donations from generous donors. Donations included a collection of 30 Chinese paintings by Chao Shao-an, eight items of Qing porcelain from Kalam Cheung and his wife, a 17th century huanghuali horseshoe armchair from the Min Chiu Society, an oil painting *The British Naval Detachment Camped at Kowloon* from Gerald Godfrey and a white-glazed 'monk's cap' ewer engraved with Tibetan inscription from Dr K.S. Lo.

To develop the role of the museum as a visual arts education centre, various educational activities were organised. These included art lectures, demonstrations, workshops, guided tours, gallery talks, art video shows and small-scale travelling exhibitions. They attracted a total attendance of 21 430 participants.

Hong Kong Space Museum

Hong Kong Space Museum's Hall of Astronomy and Hall of Space Science displayed over 50 new exhibits, most of which were visitor-participatory, audio-visual or computer-interactive. Around 257 733 people visited the exhibition halls during the year. In addition to permanent exhibitions in the museum's two exhibition halls, a temporary exhibition *Antarctica – The Final Frontier* was also held.

In 1992, major attractions offered by the museum's space theatre included three Omni-max film shows *The Deepest Garden, Ring of Fire* and *Antarctica*; three sky shows *The Enigma of Time, Questions* and *From Fiction to Science*; and two educational programmes for students, – *The New Solar System* and *The Friendly Sky*. The shows attracted a total audience of 0.5 million people.

The museum published a 1993 astro-calendar. Other activities included nine lectures, 10 courses and 24 film shows on astronomy, space science and related topics.

Hong Kong Science Museum

Hong Kong Science Museum was one of the most popular venues in the territory for visitors to explore the world of science and technology. During 1992, a total of 480 000 visitors from all walks of life visited the museum.

The exhibits covered basic scientific principles, mathematics, earth science, life science, the daily application of technology, home technology, energy, communication, transportation, and high-tech exhibits such as computers and robotics. The most prominent exhibit was a 20-metre high energy machine and many were hands-on exhibits which were not only entertaining but also educational.

To supplement the exhibition programmes, the museum also organised special thematic exhibitions. Two special exhibitions were organised in 1992. The *Mount Everest Exhibition* was jointly organised with the Boston Museum of Science and Hong Kong Mountaineering Union, while the *Michael Faraday and the Modern World* exhibition was jointly organised with the Science Museum of London.

In addition to exhibition programmes to arouse public interest in science, the museum also organised a wide range of activities including popular science lectures, workshops, science competitions, fun science experiments for children, and science films shows. The museum also sponsored science and technology activities organised at the museum by other

organisations, such as the 25th Joint Schools Science Exhibition.

The museum continued to receive strong support from the community and the private sector. The IBM China/Hong Kong Corporation donated $4.8 million for setting up a computer classroom while the China Light and Power Company Limited sponsored $1.5 million for the *Michael Faraday and the Modern World* exhibition.

Heritage

Growing awareness of the importance to the community of Hong Kong's cultural and historical heritage is reflected in the activities of the museums run by the Urban and Regional Councils, and the work of the Antiquities Advisory Board as well as the Antiquities and Monuments Office. The Secretary for Recreation and Culture is the antiquities authority and implements the provisions of the Antiquities and Monuments Ordinance. Through exhibitions, guided tours, publications, local studies, and community involvement projects, the museums and Antiquities and Monuments Office seek to achieve their twin objectives of preserving Hong Kong's heritage and increasing public awareness of its importance.

The year also saw the establishment of the Lord Wilson Heritage Trust – a milestone of heritage conservation in the territory. Apart from commemorating the contributions of Lord Wilson of Tillyorn in heritage preservation during his governorship, it provides a venue through which the community at large can actually take part and join hands in the cause. With this additional source of funding, more programmes on the protection and promotion of local heritage will become possible.

Hong Kong Museum of History

During the year Hong Kong Museum of History presented a large-scale thematic exhibition entitled *Gems of Liangzhu Culture from the Shanghai Museum*, in which 93 exquisite artifacts selected from the Liangzhu culture collection in the Shanghai Museum were put on display. Supplemented with photographs, models and other visual aids, the exhibition introduced the characteristics of the Liangzhu culture and threw light on the early development of Chinese civilisation, attracting 60 000 visitors. To complement the exhibition, and to provide a chance for Chinese and Hong Kong scholars to exchange views regarding research on Liangzhu culture, a special seminar on the subject was held and was well received.

In December, an exhibition, *Dress in Hong Kong: A Century of Change and Customs*, was presented to trace the original and stylistic changes in local costume. The exhibition covered about 150 items of local costume of the major ethnic groups and a series of tableaux depicting Hong Kong life and society in the past. A total of 64 000 people visited the exhibition.

A permanent exhibition, *The Story of Hong Kong* illustrating the development of Hong Kong from a small fishing village to a metropolis, remained very popular, attracting a total attendance of 165 000. A related inter-school competition of study projects on the history of Hong Kong education was held.

At the invitation of the Antiquities and Monuments Office, the museum's excavation team conducted a salvage excavation at Sha Lau Tong Wan, Ma Wan. The excavation lasted about a month and a number of pottery ware and shards with stamped patterns estimated to be dated between 4 000 and 5 000 years ago were discovered.

A wide range of educational activities were organised by the museum throughout the year with the attendance of the regular weekend programme remaining very high. Folk craft courses, such as the making of miniature pot plants, Chinese knotting with gems, art of beads-stringing and embroidery, batik and tie dyeing as well as Chinese paper craft, were all fully subscribed. Field trips were organised to study libraries and Hakka villages in the New Territories and other places of interest, including the Lions Nature Education Centre, Mai Po Nature Reserve and Ma Shi Chau. A series of *Experiencing Archaeology* workshops was also offered to secondary students during the summer vacation. Other extension services, such as travelling exhibitions, and the loan of slide packs and videos, were still much sought after.

The Lei Cheng Uk Branch Museum, featuring a new display of *Costume of Han Dynasty*, was visited by 58 600 people whereas the Law Uk Folk Museum, in which an exhibition on Chinese and Japanese folk art was staged, attracted a total of 35 000 visitors.

Sheung Yiu Folk Museum
Situated at a scenic spot in Sai Kung, this museum is housed in a fortified Hakka village built in the late 19th century. The 500-square metre village comprises eight domestic units, pig pens, an open courtyard and an entrance gate tower, and is situated on a raised platform about two metres above ground level. The village, together with a nearby lime kiln, was gazetted as a monument in 1981. Period furniture and local farming implements are displayed. Despite its remoteness, the museum attracted 103 000 visitors in 1992.

The Hong Kong Railway Museum
This open air museum, occupying an area of 6 500 square metres, is located at the town centre of Tai Po Market. It comprises the old Tai Po Market railway station building, six passenger coaches dating from 1911 to 1974 and an educational audio-visual room housed in a mock-up of an electric train. The station building, in unique Chinese decorative style, was built in 1913. Some 233 000 visited the museum in 1992.

Sam Tung Uk Museum
The museum, located in Tsuen Wan, was originally an old Hakka walled village built in 1786 by a Chan family. The layout of the 2 000-square metre village resembles a chequer-board with an entrance hall, an assembly hall and an ancestral hall along the central axis. Because of its historical significance, the village was declared a monument in 1981. After restoration, it was furnished with traditional Hakka furniture and farming implements. As the largest museum of its kind in the territory, it attracted 375 000 local and overseas visitors in 1992.

Three exhibitions were staged at the museum during the year. An exhibition on a journey into Hong Kong's archaeological past introduced recent excavation findings and basic concepts of archaeology. Another exhibition entitled *Dear John, Postcard Images of Hong Kong in the 1920s* was organised to introduce to the public the visual images of the city in the early 20th century. An exhibition featuring the museum's collection of Cantonese opera artefacts gethered and catalogued in the past five years was opened in November.

Antiquities Advisory Board
The Antiquities Advisory Board has 15 appointed members drawn from a variety of backgrounds. They include archaeologists, historians, architects, anthropologists, planners

and curators. The board advises the government on which sites and structures merit protection through declaration as monuments.

Several historical buildings and structures including St Stephen's Girls' College on Hong Kong Island and the Yi Tai Study Hall in Kam Tin were declared as monuments during the year. The latter is the first historical item formally protected under the law in this most historical settlement within the territory. The Antiquities Advisory Board also examined a number of pre-war schools, lighthouses and courts, and graded them in accordance with their historical significance, architectural merits and other factors.

Restoration of Ching Shu Hin in Ping Shan, Yuen Long, began in December, supported by generous sponsorship. Work to consolidate and restore the walls and gate towers of Kun Lung Wai in Fanling also started towards the end of the year. Several other major restoration projects which started in 1991 were all satisfactorily completed in 1992. These included the Hau Kui-shek Ancestral Hall at Ho Sheung Heung, the Yeung Hau Temple at Ha Tsuen, Yuen Long, the Tang Chung-ling Ancestral Hall in Fanling and the Kang Yung Study Hall in Sha Tau Kok.

During the summer university students were employed to survey Chinese temples on Hong Kong Island. Historical and ethnological studies of the Tung Chung valley on Lantau, which is to accommodate the new airport community, were undertaken by the Chinese University.

The year 1992 was a most active and fruitful year for rescue archaeology. With generous support from the Royal Hong Kong Jockey Club, a series of rescue excavations took place to extract archaeological information and material from sites affected by airport projects. The operations included excavations at Taipo on Lantau, Pak Mong and Pa Tau Kwu by the Institute of Chinese Studies, Chinese University of Hong Kong; at Sha Lau Tong Wan, Ma Wan, by the Hong Kong Museum of History and at Penny's Bay by the Hong Kong Archaeological Society.

A major rescue excavation at Yung Long in Tuen Mun was conducted jointly by the Antiquities and Monuments Office and the Hong Kong Archaeological Society. This operation was made possible by a sizeable contribution from the China Light and Power Co. Ltd., which is constructing a power station at the site.

The Antiquities and Monuments Office was keen to encourage an interest in local heritage among the public, particularly the younger generation. Guided tours, talks and workshops were organised for youth groups and school students. A photographic competition on monuments was held, with a hope that through the artistic manoeuvre of cameras, the unique and elegant facets of local heritage could be captured and shared by the community at large. It met with encouraging response and close to 2 000 entries were received. Apart from information pamphlets, a popular full colour publication on heritage was produced. The office also co-operated with Wan Chai District Board to produce a booklet on the district's relics and legends. Another similar publication for Islands District Board was underway. Following the success of the conference *The Future of Hong Kong's Past* on development and heritage conservation in 1991, the office organised another symposium, *In Search of Times Past*, to discuss the principles and techniques of building conservation. Some 120 people participated in the event. The office's permanent home at the former Kowloon British School in Tsim Sha Tsui was also officially opened by Lord Wilson in May. It is now a resource centre for disseminating the message of heritage preservation.

Public Libraries

Urban Council Libraries

The Urban Council Public Libraries continued to grow in 1992 which saw the opening of Lai Chi Kok Public Library, replacing Mei Foo Sun Chuen Public Library on rented premises. Pok Fu Lam Public Library, which opened in 1970, was refurbished. Renovation works to expand the City Hall Public Library also started in September.

The Urban Council operated 29 public libraries, including a specialised library on the arts at Hong Kong Cultural Centre. Under the current library expansion programme, the number of libraries will be increased to 41 in the next few years.

Facilities provided by the libraries include lending services for adults and children, newspapers and periodicals services, audio-visual services, students' study rooms, a wide range of extension activities as well as block loan services to non-profit making organisations and penal institutions. Reading machines for the blind were also available in City Hall Public Library and Kowloon Central Library.

In addition to books, over 70 bibliographical and information databases on Compact Disc Read Only Memory (CD-ROM) were provided in the reference libraries. A computer network was planned during the year to centralise all CD-ROM databases in the City Hall Reference Library and to make available ready information to district libraries through dial access. In addition, on-line search facilities to local and overseas databases were planned to locate up-to-date information for readers.

The installation of book detection systems in the council's libraries continued during the year, bringing the total number of libraries so equipped to 22.

During the year, the council endorsed an action plan to computerise library operations to provide a more efficient library service. It is expected that the computerisation project will be fully implemented by mid-1995.

In 1992, the library collection increased to 2.7 million items, including 2.6 million books and 147 428 items of audio-visual materials. The council libraries will continue to acquire suitable materials to increase the library stock to 3.3 million items, to reach the target of one item per head of the urban population. The libraries also subscribed to 4 283 copies of local and overseas newspapers and periodicals.

Urban Council libraries housed a number of unique collections for public use. These include the British Standards, the Hok Hoi collection of classical Chinese thread-sewn rare books, the Kotewall collection of old Chinese and English books, the Royal Asiatic Society collection on Hong Kong and China studies, the Oriental Ceramic Society collection, the Royal Institution of Naval Architects and the Institute of Marine Engineers collection, the Hong Kong Stock Exchange collection and course materials of the Open Learning Institute of Hong Kong. The City Hall Library is the depository library for Hong Kong, United Nations and World Bank publications.

A total of 8.2 million books and 286 000 audio-cassette tapes were loaned during 1992 while 16.9 million books were read in the libraries. The year saw the registration of 82 400 new members, bringing the total membership to 1 845 000.

The three reference libraries at the City Hall, Kowloon Central Library and the Arts Library were heavily used, with a total of 77 244 reference enquiries handled by the reference library staff and 782 796 reference books consulted.

Two competitions on creative writing in Chinese were organised to cultivate interest in creative Chinese writing. The winning entries were published for sale to encourage wider participation and to provide healthy reading materials. Since the inception of the awards in 1979, 53 titles have been published.

To publicise the high standard of books printed and published locally, a competition on the best produced books in Hong Kong was organised jointly with Hong Kong Trade Development Council. The 20 winning entries were exhibited at the Hong Kong Book Fair in July and the Frankfurt Book Fair in Germany in October.

A reading programme for young people was held to arouse their interest in reading. Since the programme was first launched in 1984, 85 086 young people have enrolled as members and have read a total of 1.2 million books.

A wide range of other extension activities and outreach programmes were organised by the libraries. They included book exhibitions, interest clubs, subject talks, children's hours, computer literacy projects and library visits and attracted a total of 2.9 million people.

Regional Council Libraries
The Regional Council operates 22 public libraries in the nine New Territories districts and three mobile libraries serving 35 regular stops. These libraries, with a membership of 804 000, have a total stock of 1.6 million books and 94 000 items of audio-visual materials.

Public library services are particularly well received in developing new towns. During the year, 5.97 million books and audio cassettes were lent out for home use while 12.25 million books were read in the libraries. Sha Tin Central Library, the council's first central library, remained the most heavily patronised library in Hong Kong.

To promote greater use of library services, extension activities such as book exhibitions, subject talks and interest groups are regularly organised for different age groups. These activities are popular and form an integral part of the public library service. During the year, some 2.15 million people participated in the various activities.

As an ongoing programme, a computer literacy project is organised at Sha Tin Central Library, Tuen Mun Central Library and North Kwai Chung Public Library. In all, 3 020 people attended the computer lectures and interest clubs organised.

Since 1991, the council has annually organised a Shih or T'zu poetry writing competition to promote interest in the basic knowledge of Chinese tones. The 1992 poetry writing competition featuring T'zu attracted immense public interest with more than 600 entries.

Educational kits in the form of discovery boxes are provided in the council's central and district libraries. They are well-liked by children in the story hours and interest clubs and have become a regular form of library extension activity.

In collaboration with the Education Department, study rooms are provided in Sha Tin and Tuen Mun central libraries and in district libraries at Tsuen Wan, South Kwai Chung, North Kwai Chung, Yuen Long, Sai Kung, Cheung Chau and Tai Po providing a total of 1 140 seats. To cater to the needs of students, these study rooms are open seven days a week, from 7.30 am to 9.30 pm daily, from March 16 to June 30 each year. Study rooms will also be provided in central and district libraries under planning.

To further strengthen the council's library services, its third central library, located in Tsuen Wan, is earmarked to start operation in mid-1993.

Computerisation of Library Services
The Regional Council's library services are being computerised to improve service and enhance efficiency. The first computerised library is expected to come into operation in

February 1993 and all other council libraries to be automated in April 1994. This will open a new chapter in public library service as it will be the first major public library system in the world to provide an integrated library automation service for both Chinese and English library materials.

Installation of the mainframe computer at the Regional Council Building was completed in October 1992. It will be connected with some 300 terminals being installed at the council's libraries. The issue of computerised borrower's cards for registered borrowers started in the same month. During the year, work also started on building up a bibliographical database for the council's 1.8 million Chinese and English library materials.

Apart from achieving faster and better processing of library materials, the computerisation project is also expected to help save a net $76 million over the next seven years. This is obtainable from achieving a gross saving of $169 million less the project cost of $93 million.

Books Registration Office

Hong Kong is a major printing centre. Under the Books Registration Ordinance (Chapter 142), all books first published, produced or printed locally are preserved permanently in depository libraries after registration with the Books Registration Office. The office enforces the ordinance and supervises the collection of publications from publishers and printers. A list of registered books is gazetted to provide bibliographic information at quarterly intervals. In 1992, the office registered a total of 7 260 books and 9 100 periodicals.

The office is the local agent for the International Standard Book Numbering System (ISBN), and helps to promote its use among the publishing and book-selling trades. In all, 1 130 publishers' identifiers conforming to ISBN were issued.

Sports and Recreation

Sports and recreation activities and facilities are many and varied in Hong Kong. The Urban and Regional Councils, in addition to developing and managing facilities such as sports grounds, playgrounds, indoor games halls, holiday camps, swimming pools and beaches, organise training courses and sporting competitions for people of all ages and abilities. The councils also encourage passive recreation by providing parks and landscaping services within their respective areas.

The Sir David Trench Fund for Recreation disburses grants for the construction and improvement of recreational and sporting facilities as well as for the purchase of equipment.

Sports Development Board

Hong Kong Sports Development Board is a statutory body responsible for promoting the development of sports and physical recreation in Hong Kong. In the financial year 1991–2, the sum of $50 million was allocated to the Hong Kong Sports Development Board. Of this allocation, a total of $28 million was used for sports development purposes which included funding support to the Amateur Sports Federation and Olympic Committee of Hong Kong for expenses relating to the 1992 Olympic Games, and to sports associations for their staff salaries, office expenses and sports development programmes. The amount was also used for the board's special projects, including its international exchange programmes, community sports programmes, and the organisation, in conjunction with the University of Canberra and Hong Kong Sports Institute, of degree courses in sports administration and coaching in Hong Kong.

The concept of identifying target sports and providing them with increased resources for development has been well received. Four such sports were identified initially: badminton, squash, swimming and windsurfing. Three more sports were added to this category in March 1992: football, rowing and table tennis. Others will be considered on a performance related basis.

Progress has been made in the coach education field since the inception in 1991 of the coach development programme, the major component of which is the Hong Kong Coach Accreditation Programme. The support given to this initiative by sports associations bodes well for future development. In 1991–2, an amount of $2 million was allocated to the programmes.

The Sports Aid Foundation Fund and the Sports Aid for the Disabled Fund, administered by the board, increased substantially its level of support to leading athletes and 47 who satisfied the criteria were grant-aided. The total allocation granted in 1992 was $2.38 million.

Board staff have been active in securing additional funds from the commercial sector in support of sports associations development programmes. The Sports Sponsorship Advisory Services, which was introduced during the year, generated more than $12 million of sponsorship funding for Hong Kong sport in 1992, with a number of agreements running for several years.

Sporting Achievements

Teams from Hong Kong regularly participate in international sporting competitions.

At the First World Wushu Championships, Leung Yat-ho won a gold medal in the men's nanquan. Ng Siu-ching won four silver medals in the women's spear, sword, long boxing and all-round event. Li Fai also won a silver medal in the women's cudgel and three bronze medals in the women's sword, long boxing and all-round event. At the 3rd Asian Wushu Championships, the Hong Kong athletes won a total of twelve medals in twelve events, including a gold medal for Li Fai in the women's cudgel event.

At the fourth Pacific Bowls Championships 1991, Hong Kong bowlers won two gold medals, one silver medal and one bronze medal in the men's triples, women's triples, men's doubles and men's fours respectively. The bowlers included George Souza, David Tso, Mel Stewart, Mark McMahon, Noel Kennedy, Lena Yeung Ching, Linda Smith and Eva Ho.

At the Asian Squash Championships 1992, Abdul Faheem Khan won a gold medal in the men's individual event. At the 17th East Asian Squash Championship, Khan won another gold medal in the men's individual event, and together with Andrew Shum, Tony Choi and Yang Man-sum, were champions of the men's team event. The women's team also won a silver medal in the team event. The players were Dawn Olsen, Angela O'Brien, Catherine Radcliffe and Ann Chan.

In table tennis, Chan Tan-lui, Chai Po-wah and Chan Suk-yuen won the championship in the women's team event at the 11th Asian Table Tennis Championships. Chai Po-wa won a bronze medal in the women's singles at the 9th Asian Cup Table Tennis Championships, and Chan Tan-lui won a silver medal at the China Open Table Tennis Championships.

In badminton, Wong Wai-lap won a bronze medal in the men's singles at the French Open 1992. Chan Siu-kwong and Chung Hoi-yuk won a silver medal in the mixed doubles at the Asian Badminton Championships 1992.

At the 2nd Asian Junior Cycling Championships, Wong Kam-po won the gold medal in the 129.5 kilometres individual road race.

In a yachting event, the 6th Asian Regatta, the Hong Kong team won three gold medals, one silver medal and one bronze medal in the men's Lechner A390, Hobie 16, Flying Fifteen, and women's Laser events respectively. The athletes included Sam Wong, Tong Shing, David Ong, Ronnie Fung, Mike Scantlebury, Eric Lockeyear, Rolf Heemskerk and Lyn Jones.

At the 12th FIQ Asian Tenpin Bowling Championships, Choi Miu-chu, Catherine Che and Rose Chung won the championship in the ladies' trios. Choi also won the silver medal in the ladies' singles event. Franco Lau and Frankie Cheung won the bronze medal in the men's doubles event.

At the 4th Asian Canoeing Championships, Hong Kong canoe polo team won a gold medal while Cheng Mei-po won a bronze medal in the women's 500 metres singles kayak. Kwok Lin-wui and Lee Chun-sai won a bronze medal in the women's 500 metres doubles kayak and Tsang Chak-fai and Sham Wang kit won a bronze medal in the men's 500 metres doubles kayak.

At the 4th Asian Rowing Championships, Ho Kim-fai won a silver medal in the women's lightweight single sculls, and together with Pang Bik-har won a silver medal in the women's lightweight double sculls. Kai Ramming, partnered with Chiang Wing-hung, won a silver medal in the men's lightweight double sculls while Ramming also won a bronze medal in the men's lightweight single sculls.

At the 4th Asian Swimming Championships, Michael Wright won two bronze medals in the men's 50 metres and 100 metres freestyle events.

At the 7th Asian Judo Championships, Law Lai-wah won a bronze medal at the women's −56 kilogram event and, a bronze medal at the 4th Commonwealth Judo Tournament. In the same tournament, Lee Kan won a bronze medal in the men's −60 kilogram event.

At the 2nd Asian Youth and Cadet Fencing Championships, Lee Lea-Anne won the gold medal while Chan Wing-sze won the silver medal in the women's under 17 epee event. Leung Yin-sha won a silver medal in the women's under 17 foil event.

At the World Amateur Snooker Championship 1992, Yao Kam-wai won the second runner-up in the world amateur snooker event.

Hong Kong Sports Institute

The aim of Hong Kong Sports Institute, formerly the Jubilee Sports Centre, is to provide an environment in which athletic talent can be identified, nurtured and developed. This aim implies the pursuit of excellence by athletes and coaches.

The mandate of the institute is sixfold: athlete development and management; coach education and development; sports science, sports medicine and research; resource information; international exchanges, and co-operation with other bodies.

In 1992, the institute offered a sports scholarship scheme for over 180 local high-performance athletes in 16 sports, receiving comprehensive services on coaching, facilities, accommodation, dietary advice, sports science, sports medicine, fitness training, overseas training and support for education and employment. Twenty six scholarship athletes represented Hong Kong in the Barcelona Olympics out of the 38 delegates.

During the year, the institute provided a venue for large scale sports functions. In March, sports medicine professionals and sports scientists from 90 countries gathered at the institute for the International Sports Medicine Conference. The Hong Kong Sports Institute also staged Sports Expo '92 in conjunction with Hong Kong Trade Development Council and Hong Kong Sports Development Board in July.

To encourage public participation in sports the institute formed sports clubs for members of the public. These included tennis, squash, swimming and badminton clubs. Throughout the year, the institute also organised sports courses at different levels for the general public.

Amateur Sports Federation and Olympic Committee of Hong Kong

The Amateur Sports Federation and Olympic Committee of Hong Kong, recognised by the International Olympic Committee in 1951 as the official olympic committee of the territory, controls Hong Kong's participation in the Olympic, Commonwealth, Asian, East Asian and World Games. It plays a major role in promoting sports in Hong Kong by encouraging participation in international competitions by its 60 affiliated sports associations. It is the acknowledged voice of sport in Hong Kong and throughout the sports world.

One of the objectives of the federation is the promotion of sports education. For more than two decades it has sponsored sports leaders, administrators, coaches, technical officials and athletes to attend courses and conferences held locally and overseas.

It organises monthly courses on sports leadership, sports administration, sports medicine, sports science, plus courses on sport management and sport coaching in conjunction with the United States Sports Academy. It sends Hong Kong representatives to the annual International Olympic Academy and sponsors three Olympic solidarity courses each year.

Special sports education activities during the year included a weekend sports camp on commercialisation in sports and the Olympic movement; a seminar, in conjunction with Hong Kong Polytechnic, on biomechanics of sports; a seminar, in conjunction with the Education Department of Hong Kong, on the Olympic movement; and a weekend seminar in conjunction with the University of Oregon on sports leadership.

The federation, together with governing sports bodies and municipal councils, organises an annual event The Hong Kong Festival of Sports. This large-scale community-building event held each year since 1985, attracts wide participation and continues for more than two months.

Urban Council

The Urban Council manages a wide range of sports and recreational facilities, and runs numerous low-cost introductory courses to attract participation by people of all ages. The council also encourages and promotes sporting activities by subsidising competitions organised by various governing bodies.

On Hong Kong Island, seven major projects were completed in 1992, namely the Urban Council Java Road Complex with an indoor games hall; Hollywood Road Park featuring a traditional Chinese garden with pavilions, pai laus, water features and extensive landscaped areas; Sai Wan Ho Playground; Chai Wan Park Extension; Western Park; Harcourt Garden; and Wan Chai Park. They offer a wide range of active and passive recreational facilities for people of different ages.

In Kowloon two major projects were completed in Kwun Tong district: Laguna Park with a traditional Chinese garden providing a pleasant tranquil spot for local residents and Lam Wah Street Playground with a five-a-side soccer pitch. Other completed projects in Kowloon included two children's play areas in Muk Lun Street Playground and Lai Chi Kok Park. The new Lok Fu Recreation Ground comprises a full-size synthetic grass soccer-cum-hockey pitch and a landscaped park.

Apart from providing new facilities the Urban Council also continues to upgrade its existing facilities. During the year, Southorn Playground and the bowling greens of Victoria Park were improved and upgraded, while ball games areas at Tsz Wan Shan service reservoir were resurfaced and extended. Spectator stands providing 10 000 additional seats were also installed at Aberdeen Sports Ground to facilitate the holding of school athletic meets.

Regional Council
Under the auspices of the Regional Council, over 355 500 people took part in 5 300 training courses, competitions and recreation programmes, including water sports, ball games, racquet games, athletics, archery, fencing, cycling, gymnastics, multigym-fitness and dancing. Region-wide activities, such as the International Sand Sculpture Competition, the Kite Flying Carnival and the Sports Carnival for the Elderly were well received with more than 7 500 participants.

Two highly popular schemes were launched in 1992: one aimed at developing ballet skills as a form of recreation and sport activity for youngsters; while the other provided opportunities for participants and school children to watch demonstrations by professional basketball players. About 240 youngsters aged eight to 20 joined a ballet development scheme co-organised with the Hong Kong Ballet and sponsored by Wai Yin Club. They attended a four-phase training programme, comprising a 27-week training course, a five-day training camp and an open performance, which lasted from September 1992 to April 1993.

The council appreciates the special needs of the disabled in sports. In 1992, a total subsidy of $265,000 was granted to voluntary agencies to organise 90 sporting events for the physically and mentally handicapped.

A sports subsidy scheme has been in operation since 1986 to encourage sports associations to organise competitions, training courses and spectator events. During 1992 subsidies of $3 million were allocated to 165 projects, benefiting 139 500 people.

During the year, the council held training courses for some 240 instructors in various sports.

As a catalyst to the promotion of sports and recreational events at the district level, a variety of programmes including basic training courses, camping, excursions, competitions and fun days were mounted in each of the nine districts in the Regional Council area. In 1992, $11 million was allocated to the organisation of 5 140 district programmes which drew 216 000 participants.

The council took part in the Sports Expo '92 organised in July by Hong Kong Trade Development Council and various sports promotion bodies at Hong Kong Sports Institute in Sha Tin. The many water based facilities of the council were presented to visitors.

Sports and Recreation Venues

In 1992, 10 new sports and recreation venues were completed in the Regional Council area. There are now 27 indoor recreation centres, 13 swimming pool complexes, 89 tennis courts, 100 squash courts and 12 sportsgrounds. The newly completed Tai Po complex will be installed with full electronic display equipment in 1993. Furthermore, two fully air-conditioned indoor recreation centres, the first of their kind in the Regional Council area, have been planned for Tsuen Wan and Kwai Tsing districts. They will be completed in 1993 and 1994.

The council has three water sports centres – Tai Mei Tuk, Chong Hing and Wong Shek – and three holiday camps – Lady MacLehose Holiday Village, Sai Kung Outdoor Recreation Centre and Tso Kung Tam Outdoor Recreation Centre. During the year, 70 000 people made use of the water sports centres and 301 000 the holiday camps.

Regional Council Festival '92

The Regional Council organises a month-long festival every two years to provide a wide spectrum of recreation, sport, cultural and environmental hygiene promotional activities. The third such festival, RegCo '92, adopted 'Towards a better life' as its theme to reflect the council's commitment to providing better municipal services, and making the New Territories a better place in which to live and work.

RegCo '92 attracted over two million participants and spectators. Its opening parade and carnival held at Sha Tin Town Centre in the evening of November 14 was watched by 1.6 million viewers on live television and by 50 000 spectators along the parade route. There were over 20 attractive floats and a spectacular dance featuring a pair of 88-metres-long air borne dragons. The performances were led by the Xi'an Folk Art Troupe from Shaanxi province, and there was a demonstration of traditional music and dances by participants of different nationalities in their native costumes.

The festival offered both local and international events. The latter included the First Asian Championship in Sports Acrobatics, International Basketball Championship, International Handicapped Meet, International Kite Flying Festival, International Sand Sculpture Competition, and International Folklore Festival.

Among the highlights were two major exhibitions, the Ice Sculpture Fun Fair which displayed ice-carvings by Harbin master-craftsmen within a huge ice house, and the Lantern Festival which put on show 30 sets of lanterns assembled in Sichuan style. An exhibition of Chinese paintings by Lingnan School master, Kwan Shan-yue, was held at Sha Tin Town Hall.

Local events ranged from sport, cultural and entertainment activities to environmental improvement programmes. There were the Toy Festival, the Corporate Games, the Masters Games, open days of the council's leisure facilities, a photography competition, household and restaurant cleanliness competitions, litter bin design and garden design competitions, a waste reduction campaign, a drawing competition which attracted 3 000 school children, and a tree planting day.

Cultural presentations were staged by a number of well-known overseas groups as well as local artists and performing companies. From overseas were the Ballet National de Marseille Roland Petit from France, the SWF-Symphony Orchestra Baden-Baden from Germany, the China Broadcast Chinese Orchestra, the Chick Corea New Akoustic Band

341

from the USA, the Zhanjiang Cantonese Opera Troupe, the Circus-On-Stage, and the Dance Brazil.

Locally, the council commissioned the High Noon Production Co. to produce a comic drama, *Fools*, while district organisations offered a wide variety of performances including Cantonese opera, children's choir, drama, and dance drama. In total, the cultural programmes of the festival attracted 44 159 people.

The festival ended on December 13 with a variety show at Sha Tsui Road Playground in Tsuen Wan which was also broadcast live on television.

District Festivals Subsidy Scheme
Under the District Festivals Subsidy Scheme, the Regional Council assists local bodies to organise public recreation, sports and cultural activities most suited to their own districts. The types of programme covered include arts and sports festivals, dragon boat races, mid-autumn festival celebrations and lunar new year carnivals.

During the year, some $5 million was allocated to the nine districts under the jurisdiction of the council in support of 53 festive celebrations for the participation of a total of over 600 000 people.

Festival Hong Kong '92 in Canada
As part of the programme of Festival Hong Kong '92 in Canada, the Regional Council's museums section presented its first overseas exhibition on Cantonese opera, *The Art of Chinese Theatre: Made in Hong Kong*, in Toronto from August 15 to September 27, and in Vancouver from October 17 to January 17.

The exhibition introduced to the Canadian public how Hong Kong has given life to this century-old form of theatrical art and the council's policy to preserve and promote the heritage of Cantonese opera as part of the territory's cultural identity.

Through the broadcast of video and audio tapes and display of the council's rich collection on Cantonese opera, which includes photographs, models, props, costumes and musical instruments, the exhibition explored the history, development and transformation of Cantonese opera in the 20th century.

Beaches and Swimming Pools
Swimming is Hong Kong's most popular form of summer recreation. During 1992, some 13.4 million people visited the beaches and another 6.9 million enjoyed using the numerous public swimming pools managed by the municipal councils.

There are at present 42 gazetted bathing beaches, 12 on Hong Kong Island managed by the Urban Council and 30 in the New Territories managed by the Regional Council. Facilities provided at these beaches range from changing rooms, toilets, showers, first-aid posts, lookout towers, light refreshment kiosks to picnic areas and other ancillary facilities. The water quality of these beaches is regularly checked and made known to the public.

The two councils manage 27 public swimming complexes: 14 in the Urban Council area and 13 in the Regional Council area. The competition pools in these complexes have been built to international standards. Three public swimming pool projects are under planning in the urban areas. As a first step to provide leisure pool facilities to the public, the Urban

Council has installed some innovative water equipment in the shallow pools of Chai Wan and Lei Cheng Uk swimming pools.

The Regional Council installed four new swimming pool complexes with coin-operated turnstiles for public use in 1992. They are at Sheung Shui, Sai Kung, Mui Wo and Hin Tin. Sheung Shui and Hin Tin pools are fitted with water slides and splash pools, which are very popular with youngsters.

The councils regularly organise learn-to-swim classes to promote water safety. During the year, over 1 820 swimming classes and training programmes were held for more than 40 500 people in the territory by the councils.

The councils also encourage the formation of life-guard clubs at their swimming venues. These clubs help maintain a steady supply of voluntary life-guards to augment the councils' regular life-guard service. At the end of the year, life-guard clubs operating in the Urban and Regional Council areas were 13 and eight respectively.

To bring the message of safe swimming to a wide spectrum of the public, the Urban Council again launched a water safety campaign in 1992. Major functions of the campaign included a water safety slogan competition which attracted 4 429 entries, a Water Design Competition in which 752 students took part, and a series of activities performed by the 'water safety ambassador' dressed in a dolphin outfit at the council's aquatic venues during the peak swimming season.

A package of safety measures was implemented by the Regional Council to enhance safety on beaches against any threat of shark attack, including distribution of an information leaflet and setting up of an additional lookout post at each Regional Council beach to provide a better view of the beach area and adjacent waters. In order to step up surveillance, the council secured assistance from Royal Hong Kong Auxiliary Air Force in deploying its light aircraft for shark patrol exercises for a period of three months during Saturdays, Sundays and public holidays in the swimming season.

Summer Youth Programme

The territory-wide Summer Youth Programme is organised each year for children and young people aged between six and 25. Social and recreational programmes and community service activities help them to develop their skills, appreciate human relationships, understand the community in which they live and enhance their sense of responsibility to the community.

In 1992 the Summer Youth Programme was officially launched on July 4, bearing the central theme *Share the Fun, Serve the Community*. About 13 684 activities were organised and 1.36 million young people took part between July and September. Over $34 million, of which $12.7 million was donated by the Jockey Club, went into the programme. The balance was made up by the government, district boards, Urban Council, Regional Council, private donations and participants' fees. A total of 22 outstanding volunteers were awarded Summer Youth Programme scholarships and attended training courses organised by the Outward Bound School.

Ocean Park

Located on the southern side of Hong Kong Island, Ocean Park is South East Asia's largest oceanarium and Hong Kong's premier theme park. Built on a site of 87 hectares, Ocean Park includes Middle Kingdom, a Chinese cultural village and Water World.

343

More than 2.5 million people visited Ocean Park in 1992, while total attendance since the park opened in 1977 passed the 30-million mark.

Built on hilly land, the headland and lowland areas of Ocean Park are linked by a cable car system, and from Tai Shue Wan entrance at Middle Kingdom by the world's longest covered outdoor escalator.

In the summer of 1992, Ocean Park celebrated its 15th anniversary with the opening of its $30 million Ocean Park Tower. The tower, part of the park's $600 million five year expansion plan that spans through 1997, is the tallest observation tower in Asia.

Seventy two metres tall and 200 metres above sea level, the tower offers a 360 degree bird's eye view of Hong Kong and the nearby harbours and islands.

In the headland thrills area, there are six exciting thrill rides. Marineland includes a 3 500-seat ocean theatre staging regular shows by the killer whale, dolphins and sealions, the newly renovated wave cove with sealions, seals and penguins, and a $40 million shark aquarium, which is home to more than 80 sharks of 20 species. In addition, a new look atoll reef exhibiting more than 5 000 fish will re-open after its $50 million renovation.

In the lowland gardens are the goldfish pagoda with over 100 species of goldfish; a butterfly house with 1 500 butterflies and a greenhouse complex. The 'kids' world' there will soon feature new rides, a creative play area, game booths, dolphins' pool, and an in-park fun tram for family enjoyment.

Water World is the first and largest water playpark in Asia. It has two main pools, three fun slides and a leisure 'Lazy River'. Water World has attracted nearly three million swimmers since it opened in 1984.

Middle Kingdom recreates 5 000 years of Chinese history in 13 dynasties with temples, shrines, pavilions, pagodas and palaces. Theatrical cultural performances, street demonstrations in Chinese arts and crafts, acrobatic and kung fu shows plus lion dances bring special experiences to visitors.

In addition, the aviaries are homes to more than 2 000 birds of 150 species. There are also a 'birds' theatre', a parrot garden and a new flamingo pond.

Outward Bound School

Hong Kong Outward Bound School is a private registered charity of a worldwide network of 35 such schools, providing land and sea-based training programmes for personal and professional development.

The purpose of each course is to improve the trainees' self-confidence, resourcefulness, leadership, communication skills and personal effectiveness. Trainees include employees of major corporations and smaller businesses, senior government officers, teachers, social workers, students as well as the handicapped, socially deprived and juvenile delinquents.

Training is held on the school's twin-masted training ship, the brigantine *Ji Fung* (Spirit of Resolution), and from the residential base in Tai Mong Tsai, Sai Kung, as well as the Sir Murray MacLehose Training Base, situated at Double Haven in Mirs Bay.

In recent years, there has been a growing recognition by corporations that these courses are an effective team building and training strategy for older adults, resulting in a continuous increase in the demand for 'team building', 'adult challenge', and special 'contract' courses.

In 1992, the school operated a total of over 150 courses for over 3 600 trainees and more than 31 000 trainee programme days.

Financing is provided through tuition income, charitable donations and a government subvention which enables the participation of young people who are unable to afford the full course fee.

Projects have been carried out to upgrade buildings, grounds and facilities at the Tai Mong Tsai and Wong Wan Chau bases and plans are being developed to create an additional 36-bed self-sustaining facility in Ah Kung Wan.

Adventure Ship

Adventure Ship Limited is a registered charitable organisation operating a 27.5 metres long, three-masted Chinese Junk, *Huan*, the biggest sailing junk in the territory, providing sail and nautical training for underprivileged or handicapped young people in Hong Kong since 1977.

The purpose of the training is to improve the self-confidence of the participants. Every year over 5 000 young people from primary schools, secondary schools, hostels, homes, children and youth centres, community centres, multi-disciplinary centres, churches and others have benefited from the programmes. Any non-profit making organisation with an aim of enhancing the development of youth is eligible to apply.

Adventure Ship Limited provides, day and overnight, up to five-day training. Sponsored trips are organised for those groups which otherwise could not afford to sail. Apart from individual sponsors, Adventure Ship Limited is largely subvented by the Community Chest and the Royal Hong Kong Jockey Club (Charities) Limited.

To enhance communication and co-operation with other welfare agencies, Adventure Ship Limited has been trying to put more social work elements into its service provision. Recently, staff with social work qualifications were recruited and it is expected that with the accomplishment of a new clubhouse, the services and facilities of Adventure Ship Limited can be up-graded and better utilised.

Youth Hostels

Hong Kong Youth Hostels Association is a registered charity providing outdoor leisure opportunities for young people, particularly the 18 to 26 age group, although members may be of any age. The association has six operational hostels, mostly away from the urban areas and in scenic places. The association has over 32 000 members, who may make use of the 5 000 hostels throughout the world, thus being able to stay in economical accommodation of a good standard while travelling abroad.

The hostel at Mount Davis was completely refurbished in 1992, dividing the dormitories into smaller rooms and air-conditioning the buildings. The new hostel at Plover Cove which will open in 1993, is a modern three-storey building, fully air-conditioned and adjacent to many recreational facilities.

Urban Council Parks

The Urban Council has an extensive building programme for large modern parks.

The first of these – Kowloon Park – features many special attractions including a sports complex with an ultra-modern Olympic pool, indoor and outdoor leisure pools and an air-conditioned indoor games hall. There is also a history museum, an aviary, a popular bird lake, a sculpture walk, a creative playground and a garden piazza for staging a wide range of culture and entertainment activities.

A second major park located on Hong Kong Island, Hong Kong Park, was opened to the public in May 1991. It was constructed as a joint venture between the Urban Council and the Royal Hong Kong Jockey Club, which donated $170 million of the total cost of $398 million. Among the park's facilities are the 3 000-square-metre walk-in Edward Youde Aviary, the Forsgate Conservatory and spectacular water features. The Flagstaff House Museum of Tea Ware and Hong Kong Squash Centre are also part of the park. Educational activities are organised in the park for schoolchildren, with emphasis on conserving the natural environment and wild life resources.

The third major park development, Lei Yue Mun Park, occupies the historic site of the old Lyemun Barracks. The site was first developed by the Urban Council in 1987 as a holiday camp and activity centre. In view of its high patronage, the council has planned to provide more attractions in the park for visitors. One of the newly added attractions is a horse riding school funded and built by the Royal Hong Kong Jockey Club. In the longer term, other attractions are also under planning, including a museum, an indoor leisure centre, a free-form pool and other facilities suitable for all visitors.

Zoological and Botanical Gardens

Managed by the Urban Council, the Hong Kong Zoological and Botanical Gardens are the oldest and among the most popular public gardens in the territory. Situated on a 5.35-hectare site overlooking Government House, the gardens contain a wide variety of plants and animals, and are notable for their pleasant environment and imaginative use of space.

The gardens were constructed between 1861 and 1871, divided by Albany Road. The old garden, on the east side of the road, houses an extensive bird collection while the new garden, opened in 1871, is home for the mammals. The botanical section is mainly located in the old garden.

The Urban Council puts considerable emphasis on the breeding and conservation of endangered species. The gardens house 19 endangered species of mammals, birds and reptiles and, despite the urban environment, are one of the most successful breeding centres. This has been borne out by the increased breeding loans arranged through the relevant international breeding programmes for endangered species.

The bird collection is one of the most comprehensive in Asia, with over 1 000 birds of 300 different species. Though less comprehensive, the mammal collection is varied and interesting. The mammals include diverse creatures, such as the echidna, an egg-laying mammal, and the world's third largest cat, the jaguar. To further enrich the zoological collection, a reptile enclosure will be developed on the site of the old greenhouse in late 1992. As the sale and transfer of stock among countries is becoming increasingly difficult, in-house breeding is now essential and has resulted in the development of local expertise in husbandry, aided by improved veterinary support for monitoring health and diagnostic laboratory work.

The gardens also feature more than 500 species of trees and shrubs. The fountain terrace features a large central fountain, and the landscaped surrounds include more than 250 species of ornamental shrubs and flowering plants.

The medicinal plant collection, established in 1987, has generated much interest. To update the display facilities, the existing shade house built some 40 years ago is now undergoing redevelopment for completion in 1993.

In recent years, the educational role of the gardens has been further developed, with numerous school and club visits.

Regional Council Parks

Over 394 parks and gardens of various sizes, including four town parks, are managed by the Regional Council.

Tuen Mun Town Park is the largest park in the New Territories. Occupying an area of 12.5 hectares, the park has an ornamental lake for rowing and a 160-metre water cascade, the largest of its kind in Hong Kong. Other main features include an open-air performance arena, children's playground and skating rink.

North District Central Park covers 9.6 hectares and is provided with a sports hall, amphitheatre, artificial lake and children's playground.

The 8.5 hectare Sha Tin Central Park, with its Chinese garden and adventure playground, is the most popular park.

Special features of the 7.5 hectare Yuen Long Town Park include a seven-level pagoda with a built-in aviary which houses more than 210 birds of 50 species. The park also has the first gateball pitch in the Regional Council area.

Country Parks

Despite Hong Kong's largely urban environment, opportunities for outdoor recreation are not lacking in the territory. No place is far from green countryside and there are 21 country parks covering over 40 per cent of the total land area. Over 10 million visits were made to these parks during 1992. They are most popular during the cool, dry months of October to April.

The Director of Agriculture and Fisheries is the Country Parks Authority. With the advice of the Country Parks Board and its various committees, he is responsible for the management of land and provision of the facilities within country parks. These facilities include picnic and barbecue areas, walking trails, rain shelters, toilets, information posts and visitor centres. A new visitor centre was opened at Tai Mo Shan Country Park in January, extending the educational and recreational aspects of the country parks.

Horticulture and Landscape Services

Urban Council

The Urban Council is heavily committed to improving the urban environment with landscaping. It provides a full range of landscaping services, including design and planning, plant production, planting, maintenance and conservation, all undertaken by its own staff. All new projects undertaken by the council are expected to have a landscape element, where possible. The council also plays a key role in preserving trees in the urban areas and in extending planting areas along the highways.

In 1992, the Urban Council planted about 7 500 trees and 815 200 bamboos, creepers and flowering plants. About 90 per cent of the plants were produced in its own plant nurseries with the balance met by commercial stocks.

In addition to over 400 plant species being used in the council's planting projects, horticultural staff are constantly introducing suitable exotic overseas flora to Hong Kong. In 1992, over 130 new species of plants were introduced from the Philippines, South Africa,

Taiwan and the USA for display and educational purposes in the Forsgate Conservatory of Hong Kong Park.

Apart from planting more trees, conservation has never been neglected. The council's horticultural staff have been actively involved in the retention of trees on development sites, or planting replacement vegetation if the removal of the trees is unavoidable.

In view of the slow progress in planting trees on pavements in the urban areas, the council's horticultural staff drew up a comprehensive roadside tree planting programme in early 1992. Working closely with the District Boards, government departments and private organisations, 825 roadside trees were planted to beautify the city environment.

The Urban Council also recognised the need to further 'green' the city. It has designated 1993 as its 'Green Year' to make Hong Kong a garden city. A working group was formed in September to monitor all the relevant activities to be launched in 1993.

Regional Council

The Regional Council maintains 651 hectares of greenery in parks, gardens, sports grounds, soccer pitches, games areas and children's playgrounds in the New Territories. It also manages amenity plots and soft landscape along highways and roads. In 1992, over 367 373 trees, shrubs, palms, creepers, ground covers and seasonal flowers were planted in parks, playgrounds and roadside amenities. The council manages four nurseries in Tsuen Wan, Tuen Mun, Sha Tin and Tai Po. Tung Tze Nursery in Tai Po, which covers four hectares, is the biggest. In 1992, the nurseries together produced 3 273 trees, 180 947 shrubs, 64 668 ground covers, 1 507 creepers and 137 707 seasonal flowers.

To promote interest in gardening and to educate the public on keeping Hong Kong green, the council organised 15 horticultural classes. The nurseries also conducted guided tours and lectures for visitors at open days.

Among the council's amenities features are its theme gardens. At Hing Fong Road Playground in Kwai Tsing, there is a scented garden, while Fanling Recreation Ground in North District has a garden of hibiscus. Residents of Sai Kung can rest in the shade of palms at Sha Tsui Playground Garden. Sheung Chuen Park in Yuen Long is graced with conifers. Roses carpet the garden at Tuen Mun Town Park, while Yuen Long Town Park boasts an azalea garden and Sha Tin Central Park an assorted seasonal flower garden.

Hong Kong Flower Show

Since 1987, the Urban Council and the Regional Council have been jointly organising the annual Hong Kong Flower Show. The show has become a major public event popular with professional horticulturalists and flower lovers.

The 1992 Show held at Victoria Park in March attracted more than 70 horticultural organisations from 12 countries, and was visited by 350 000 people.

Festival Hong Kong '92

Festival Hong Kong '92, under the theme *Bridge across the Pacific*, was the biggest overseas promotion ever launched by the Hong Kong Government in conjunction with the private sector. This festival, reciprocating Festival Canada '91, held in Hong Kong in May 1991, toured five major cities across Canada in September and October 1992 (Toronto, Montreal, Calgary, Ottawa and Vancouver).

A multi-faceted event involving a total budget of HK$40 million with the Hong Kong Government and the private sector contributing on an equal basis, Festival Hong Kong '92 took to Canada cultural performances and exhibitions, sports demonstrations, food and film festivals, trade and economic seminars and academic exchanges. To complement these Hong Kong programmes organising committees in Canada also hosted a variety of events which included street carnivals, store promotions, fashion shows, dragon dances and dragon boat races. A total of over 100 events was staged bringing full Hong Kong colours to Canadian friends across the Pacific.

Seen as a major promotion overseas, Festival Hong Kong '92 was attended by prominent local personalities from Hong Kong and senior government officials, including the Governor and the Chief Secretary. Canadian Prime Minister Mr Brian Mulroney and the Governor of Hong Kong, Mr Christopher Patten, were the festival honorary patrons.

Festival Hong Kong '92 established a stronger relationship with Canada through trade and cultural exchanges and showed friends in Canada a representative picture of Hong Kong's life and culture.

24
THE ENVIRONMENT

WHAT is the environment? Simply, that which surrounds us – the solid earth, the sea, the air, the plants and animals that live on the earth and in the sea – and the things that man has built. Like all species, we depend entirely on our environment for survival.

This chapter is a review of the state of Hong Kong's environment in 1992. Some things change little from year to year. Our topography and geology, for example, and the hydrography of our seas, although our knowledge of these permanent features does develop. Other things change almost from minute to minute, so this chapter records both the climate and the weather we experienced in 1992.

Despite the steady progress of Hong Kong's urbanisation, we still have many species of plant and animal life on the land and in the water. Protection of both habitat and species is an important part of our environmental conservation activities.

Pollution by human activity is potentially one of the greatest threats to the environment. It is in the area of pollution control that Hong Kong's commitment to conservation is at its most active, and there are many highlights to record.

Without doubt, one of the highlights of 1992 was when a group of members of Hong Kong Conservancy Association attended the United Nations conference on the environment in Rio de Janeiro. It will be for future years to judge the global benefits of the conference, but conservation in Hong Kong has taken a clear step forward in maturity as a result of participation.

At home, sound if more prosaic progress continued. Important new laws came into force: controls on the handling and disposal of chemical waste; extension of the Water Pollution Control Ordinance to a new control zone that includes the new airport site at Chek Lap Kok; new regulations on vehicle design standards that impose emission limits comparable to the most stringent standards in the world; new noise regulations that tighten controls on specific construction equipment; and a review of the livestock waste control programme leading to more effective controls on these noxious organic pollutants.

The development of better sewage and solid waste disposal facilities made significant advances. Sewerage master plan studies were completed for Tsuen Wan, Kwai Chung and Tsing Yi, North West Kowloon, Yuen Long and Kam Tin, Central, Western and Wan Chai West. The Drainage Services Department has now begun to implement these plans.

A new refuse transfer station, serving Hong Kong Island East, was commissioned in November 1992. This is an important step in the government's waste disposal strategy.

350

The Environmental Protection Department made its control over all forms of pollution more responsive to local problems when it set up two local control offices in 1991. These offices achieved very encouraging results in 1992 and now deal more effectively with local issues, keeping potential pollution black spots under closer supervision than was possible with centralised control.

Climate

Hong Kong's climate is sub-tropical, tending towards temperate for nearly half the year. During November and December there are pleasant breezes, plenty of sunshine and comfortable temperatures. Many people regard these as the best months of the year. January and February are more cloudy, with occasional cold fronts followed by dry northerly winds. It is not uncommon for temperatures to drop below 10°C in urban areas. The lowest temperature recorded at the Royal Observatory is 0°C, although sub-zero temperatures and frost occur at times on high ground and in the New Territories.

March and April can also be very pleasant although there are occasional spells of high humidity. Fog and drizzle can be particularly troublesome on high ground which is exposed to the south-east, and air traffic and ferry services are occasionally disrupted by reduced visibility.

May to August are hot and humid with occasional showers and thunderstorms, particularly during the mornings. Afternoon temperatures often exceed 31°C whereas at night, temperatures generally remain around 26°C with high humidity. There is usually a fine dry spell in July which may possibly last for one to two weeks, or for even longer in some years.

September is the month during which Hong Kong is most likely to be affected by typhoons, although tropical cyclones of varying strength are not unusual at any time between May and November. On average, about 31 tropical cyclones form in the western North Pacific or China seas every year, and about half of them reach typhoon strength (maximum winds of 118 kilometres per hour or more).

When a tropical cyclone is about 700 to 1 000 kilometres south-east of Hong Kong, the weather is usually fine and exceptionally hot, but isolated thunderstorms sometimes occur in the evenings. If the centre comes closer to Hong Kong, winds will increase and rain can become heavy and widespread. Heavy rain from tropical cyclones may last for a few days and subsequent landslips and flooding sometimes cause more damage than the winds.

The mean annual rainfall ranges from around 1 300 millimetres at Waglan Island to more than 3 000 millimetres in the vicinity of Tai Mo Shan. About 80 per cent of the rain falls between May and September. The wettest month is August, when rain occurs about four days out of seven and the average monthly rainfall at the Royal Observatory is 391.4 millimetres. The driest month is January, when the monthly average is only 23.4 millimetres and rain falls only about six days a month.

Severe weather phenomena that can affect Hong Kong include tropical cyclones, strong winter and summer monsoon winds, monsoon troughs and thunderstorms with associated squalls that are most frequent from April to September. Waterspouts and hailstorms occur infrequently, while snow and tornadoes are rare.

Climatological data are given in Appendix 45.

Topography and Geology

The topography of Hong Kong is characterised by steep granitic and volcanic mountains. Much of the footslope terrain is blanketed by debris flow deposits and other forms of colluvium transported by erosion and mass movement from the hillsides. Some 40 per cent of the landmass is volcanic in origin, about 20 per cent is granitic, 15 per cent is colluvial and almost 10 per cent is alluvial in nature. The highest peak is Tai Mo Shan (957 metres) located in the central New Territories, and there are four peaks which exceed 750 metres, all on Lantau Island. Victoria Peak, the highest on Hong Kong Island and best known as a major tourist attraction, is ranked 18th in the territory with an elevation of 554 metres.

The territory lies on the edge of the ancient Sinian landmass formed more than 600 million years ago, and which now extends from Shandong in northern China to the Gulf of Hainan. The geological strata forming the landmass were deposited beneath the sea but were subsequently folded and faulted in mountain-building earth movements. A second period of mountain building, beginning about 160 million years ago, was accompanied by explosive volcanic activity that resulted in the deposition of thick layers of ash and lava culminating in the intrusion of large granitic bodies between 147 and 136 million years ago. The mountains formed from these deposits were subsequently eroded, with the material washed from the slopes into the valleys, plains and shallow seas.

During the Quaternary period of the last 1.6 million years, sea level has been fluctuating, falling as water was trapped in the expanding polar ice caps and rising as the ice caps melted. While sea level was low, Hong Kong was surrounded by broad plains crossed by distributary channels of the Pearl River delta which deposited large amounts of sand and gravel. During periods of high sea level, such as at present, the sea covers the earlier deltaic plain, and mud is deposited in the waters around Hong Kong. The fluctuations of sea level during the Quaternary have therefore resulted in a sequence of mud, sand and gravel up to 100 m thick in the present offshore area.

The erosion of the hills accelerated following destruction of the natural vegetation during the widespread colonisation of the area in the Song Dynasty (960–1279). Hong Kong's rocks are generally deeply weathered and much of the terrain is prone to landslips. More than 20 per cent of the terrain in the territory shows evidence of instability.

Generally, the granitic and volcanic rocks can be excavated quite easily for use as reclamation material. Sand and gravel dredged from offshore areas are also a valuable resource. Hong Kong has few mineral resources, although deposits of lead, zinc, quartz, kaolin, beryl and graphite have been mined in small quantities, and iron and tungsten were once extracted in significant amounts. Granites in Hong Kong have long been quarried for building purposes, and are now used as aggregates.

The natural landscape in the urban areas has been extensively modified as a result of site formation associated with development. Many of the natural granitic hills have been removed, and the material used as fill for the various reclamations. Almost 4 000 hectares of the developed land is reclamation.

Much of the undeveloped terrain in Hong Kong consists of steeply-sloping ground where soils are thin and nutrient deficient. These soils support only grassland or shrubland, except in protected valleys where small areas of broad leaf woodland survive, or in water catchments and country parks where re-afforestation has succeeded in establishing pines and deciduous trees.

An important agricultural area is the alluvial plain around Yuen Long in the north-west New Territories. These alluvial lowlands were probably formed within the last 33 000 years, and some areas are still prone to flooding. More than 5 000 hectares of floodplain occurs in the territory and much of it is located in the Yuen Long district. The natural deposition of sediment is continuing around the Deep Bay area, where brackish fish ponds have been established successfully in areas that once were mudflats, mangrove swamps or salt-water rice paddies.

As Hong Kong lacks large rivers, lakes or underground water supplies, reservoirs have been constructed in large valleys such as Shek Pik, Tai Lam Chung, and in coastal areas such as Plover Cove and High Island, where embayments and channels have been enclosed by large dams. In most instances, the catchment areas of the reservoirs have been designated as country parks.

New geological maps are being produced at a scale of 1:20 000 by the Geological Survey of Hong Kong, located within the Geotechnical Engineering Office, and maps for more than 80 per cent of the territory have been published. Detailed geological maps at 1:5 000 scale have been published for areas in Yuen Long and are being prepared for Ma On Sha, Northern Lantau and Tsing Yi.

Information about the terrain is also contained in the 55 maps and 12 reports of the Geotechnical Area Studies Programme. Published documents are available through the Government Publications Sales Centre.

Hydrography and Oceanography

Approximately two thirds of the territory of Hong Kong, or almost 1 830 square kilometres, is covered by the sea. Historically, the sea has been very important, as a highway for international shipping and in the form of a large and sheltered anchorage. Hong Kong is now one of the busiest ports in the world. Offshore areas have assumed greater importance in recent years with the increasing number of offshore engineering projects in the marine environment, including reclamations, tunnels, pipelines, cables and especially as a source of fill.

Maximum water depths reach a little over 30 metres in the south-eastern corner of territorial waters to the south of Mirs Bay. More commonly, water depths range between 10–15 metres, with a generally flat and featureless muddy seabed that slopes gently southwards. Several deeper channels occur in constricted tidal pathways, as for example in Urmston Road, the East Lamma Channel, Lei Yue Mun, Sheung Sz Mun and Lo Chau Mun.

During the Quaternary geological period, the last 1.6 million years, world sea level fell and rose several times during each of the four major glaciations when water was taken up to form great ice sheets. In south-east Asia, the sea-level fell to between 120–150 metres below its present level, which would have exposed an area of continental shelf about 130 kilometres wide to the south of Hong Kong. During this low sea-level period the Pearl River deposited alluvial sand and silt as channels over this wide plain.

As the ice began to melt at the end of the last glaciation, sea-levels rose reaching their present level about 6 000 years ago. The returning sea deposited fine clays and silts (marine mud) over the earlier alluvial deposits. Recent boreholes drilled offshore have revealed a sequence of up to 20 metres of marine mud overlying up to 80 metres of predominantly alluvial deposits which in turn overlie bedrock.

Terrestrial Fauna

The physical and climatic environment of Hong Kong provides woody and grassy habitats for a wide variety of native animal and plant life. Under the pressure of urbanisation, larger animal species are rarely seen, but reptiles and amphibians, birds and many kinds of insects are common.

Most of Hong Kong's countryside is protected by the Forests and Countryside Ordinance, the Wild Animals Protection Ordinance, the Country Parks Ordinance, and the Animals and Plants (Protection of Endangered Species) Ordinance.

One of the most important sites in Hong Kong for wildlife is the Mai Po Marshes. A restricted area under the Wild Animals Protection Ordinance and managed jointly by the Agriculture and Fisheries Department and the World Wide Fund for Nature (Hong Kong), it is an internationally significant site for migratory and resident birdlife. Its 380 hectares of mudflats, shrimp ponds and dwarf mangroves provide a rich habitat, particularly for ducks and waders. More than 250 species of birds have been observed in this area, and at least 110 of them are rarely seen elsewhere in the territory. Yim Tso Ha, also a restricted area, is the largest egretry in Hong Kong. Five species, the Chinese pond heron, night heron, cattle egret, little egret, great egret and occasionally the rare Swinhoe's egret as well, nest there regularly. Hundreds of egrets can be found there between April and September, the nesting season. Egretries are also found at Mai Po Village, A Chau, Jim Uk, Tsim Bei Tsui, Lok Ma Chau, Ho Pui Tsuen and Tai Po Market.

Although traditional *fung shui* woods near the old villages and temples are increasingly affected by development, they continue to provide an important habitat for many birds. Sightings in wooded areas include an assortment of warblers, flycatchers and robins.

Areas around the Kowloon reservoirs are inhabited by monkeys that originated either from those which had been released or had escaped from captivity. There are breeding groups of both long-tailed macaques and rhesus monkeys. Smaller mammals are common, with the woodland shrew, house shrew and bats being numerous in some rural areas. The Chinese porcupine, with its strikingly-coloured black and white quills, is still present in parts of the New Territories and Hong Kong Island.

Occasional reports are still received of sightings of less common species such as the leopard cat, civet cat, ferret badger, pangolin and barking deer. However, the increasing obtrusion of human activity into the countryside means an uncertain future for these species. There are wild boars in some remote areas, occasionally causing damage to farm crops.

Snakes, lizards and frogs are plentiful in Hong Kong. There are also various species of terrapins and turtles. Most of the local snakes are not poisonous and death from snakebite is rare. The poisonous land snakes are: the banded krait, with black and yellow bands; the many-banded krait, with black and white bands; Macclelland's coral snake, which is coral red with narrow, black transverse bars; the Chinese cobra and the hamadryad or king cobra, both of which are hooded; the rare mountain pit viper; the red-necked keelback with a red patch on the neck; and the white-lipped pit viper or bamboo snake. The bamboo snake is bright green and less venomous than others, but it is not easily seen and strikes readily if approached. The king cobra, kraits and corals prey almost exclusively on other snakes.

Several species of sea snakes, all of which are venomous, are to be found in Hong Kong waters. However, they have never been known to attack bathers. Two amphibians of special interest are the Hong Kong newt and Romer's tree frog, which have not been recorded elsewhere in the South-East Asian region.

There are more than 200 recorded species and forms of colourful butterflies, several of which, as caterpillars, cause considerable damage to farmers' crops. These include the two commonly found species of cabbage whites, the swallowtails, and the beautiful but less common small blue. Among the many local moths are the giant silkworm moths, including the cynthia, fawn, atlas and moon. The atlas has an average wing span of 23 centimetres and the moon, 18 centimetres.

Of the local plant bugs, two are especially noted for their colour and shape. They are the rare and beautiful spotted tea bug, which has been recorded only on hilltops, and the lantern fly, which has delicately coloured wings and a remarkably long forehead. Dragon and damsel flies are common, as are wasps and metallic-coloured beetles. Of particular interest is the giant red-spotted longhorn beetle which feeds on mountain tallow and wood-oil trees. Many other species of longhorn beetles infest living or weakened trees.

Since its introduction into Hong Kong in 1938, the African giant snail has become a major pest in vegetable crops and gardens. Farmers are also troubled by several types of slug. One of these, veronicella, is a large, black slug sufficiently different from the other slugs to be placed in a separate family.

Aquatic Fauna

Hong Kong lies some 320 kilometres south of the Tropic of Cancer on the southern coast of China. Being at the junction of the vast temperate Palaearctic Japonic zoogeographical regions and the huge Indo-Pacific Province, Hong Kong possesses very diverse varieties of aquatic animals and plants. There are over 150 commercially important species of fish, crustaceans and molluscs.

The waters of Hong Kong can be divided into three sectors. Under the influence of the Zhu Jiang (Pearl River), the biggest river in southern China, the western sector is predominantly brackish. The area to the east is more oceanic while the central sector is transitional between brackish and oceanic. In some localities, notably the Tolo Harbour region, pollution associated with recent rapid urban development has decimated the abundance and diversity of aquatic life. Pollution-sensitive organisms such as coral are now found only in a few clean yet remote oceanic areas in the north east. Nevertheless, various locations still serve as spawning and nursery grounds for many aquatic species, and these in turn attract transient predators such as Spanish mackerel, little tuna, dolphinfish, sailfish and sharks.

Shark sightings have been recorded in Hong Kong waters. Most are small to medium in size and pose little danger to humans. Bigger sharks have occasionally been sighted in Mirs Bay in the north-eastern New Territories.

Four species of whale and eight species of dolphin have hitherto been recorded in Hong Kong waters and strandings occur quite frequently. The black finless porpoise and the Chinese white dolphin are the most common in terms of occurrence. In 1992, seven strandings were reported, three involving black finless porpoise and one pygmy sperm whale. Other sightings included one case each of Chinese white dolphin, striped dolphin and an unidentified whale.

Flora

Situated near the northern limit of the distribution of tropical Asian flora, Hong Kong has an abundant variety of plant life. It is estimated that there are about 2 600 species of vascular plants, both native and introduced.

With the introduction of various conservation measures the hillsides and slopes, which were formerly bare ground, have now been planted with trees of both local and exotic species. In addition to greening and beautifying the countryside, woodlands are also important as an habitat for wild life, in the management of water catchments and in providing recreational opportunities for the public.

Remnants of the original forest cover, either scrub forest or well-developed woodlands, are still found in steep ravines. They have survived the destructive influences of man through their location in precipitous topography and the moist winter micro-climate.

Countryside Conservation and Management

The Agriculture and Fisheries Department is the principal government agency responsible for the conservation and management of Hong Kong's countryside. The Forests and Countryside Ordinance provides for the general protection of vegetation, and special protection is given to certain plants, including native camellias, magnolias, orchids, azaleas and the Chinese New Year flower.

The Wild Animals Protection Ordinance prohibits hunting wild animals or possession, sale or export of protected wild animals and restricts the entry of unauthorised members of the public into important wildlife habitats, the Mai Po Marshes and the Yim Tso Ha Egretry.

The Country Parks Ordinance provides for the designation, control and management of the most important areas of countryside as country parks, and special areas, and enables them to be developed for recreational, conservation and educational purposes. It gives particular protection to vegetation and wildlife. There are now 21 country parks and 14 special areas, covering over 40 per cent of the land area in the territory. There were over 10.5 million visitors to country parks in 1992.

Overall enforcement of the ordinances is carried out by nature wardens and park wardens. These officers also provide information at seven visitor centres and escort groups on guided visits. In addition to general conservation of the countryside, Hong Kong has adopted the concept of identifying and conserving sites of special scientific interest, such as a site where a rare tree or a rare species of butterfly can be found. Fifty sites have so far been identified.

The Agriculture and Fisheries Department is also responsible for the co-ordination and implementation of off-site ecological mitigation measures recommended by consultants to alleviate the adverse impact of the new airport and related projects.

Meteorological Services

Royal Observatory

The Royal Observatory was established in 1883, mainly to provide scientific information for the safe navigation of ships. In the ensuing century, the observatory has evolved in line with the changing needs of the community. The scope of studies it conducts and services it provides now cover the fields of hydrometeorology, climatology, physical oceanography, applied meteorology and radiation monitoring and assessment. The observatory also operates the official time service for Hong Kong, provides basic astronomical information and maintains a seismological monitoring network.

Of all the services, the most visible aspects are undoubtedly weather forecasting and warnings of hazardous weather – responsibilities borne by the Central Forecasting Office. Bulletins and advice are issued to meet the diverse requirements of the public, shipping, aviation, industry, fishing, recreation, off-shore oil-prospecting operations and other special users.

Whenever Hong Kong is threatened by tropical cyclones, frequent warnings with advice on necessary precautions are widely disseminated. The heavy rain episode on May 8, 1992 led to the introduction of a colour-coded rainstorm alert and warning system. A rainstorm warning is now issued whenever Hong Kong is affected by heavy rain which may cause serious road flooding and traffic congestion. Other warnings operated by the Royal Observatory include warnings on thunderstorm, flooding, landslips, storm surges, fire danger, strong monsoon winds and frost.

Particular importance is attached to the effective dissemination of up-to-date weather information to the public, the media and other users. Regular TV weather programmes on current and future weather events are presented by professional meteorologists from Monday to Friday. Live interviews and briefings are also given by forecasters over the radio and television when the situation warrants. Two special bulletins with accompanying weather charts as illustrations are prepared for the Press each day.

For members of the public requiring instant access to weather forecasts or tropical cyclone information, the observatory operates a dial-a-weather service. The demand for this service continues to grow. There are now 17 lines for public weather forecasts and four lines for south China coastal waters bulletins. More than eight million calls were handled in 1992. On average, over 24 000 calls were handled on a typical day with rates exceeding 1 400 calls per hour at times.

Information is also provided to INFOTEX and INFOFAX which are services that make available to telex and telefax terminal holders a large variety of routine weather information, including pictorial information such as the daily weather map. Since 1990, IDD subscribers can also obtain recorded weather information by dialling pre-specified numbers. Weather information is also made available for access by terminals connected to a commercial communication and paging network.

In response to the difficulties experienced by fishermen in receiving the south China coastal waters bulletins through regular radio broadcasts, special arrangements were made with Hongkong Telecom International to broadcast the forecasts three times a day.

Specialised weather services are provided to engineering contractors, public utility companies, public transport operators, operators of oil rigs and other commercial enterprises and special users. Special weather information is supplied through teletype, telex or telefax.

Weather Forecasting, Monitoring and Prediction
To provide a wide range of meteorological services described in the previous section, the Royal Observatory maintains a weather watch round the clock. Weather observers at the Royal Observatory Headquarters and Hong Kong International Airport make regular observations on local weather conditions. Additional observations are made by volunteers and other collaborating agencies at other remote locations.

Apart from manual observation, a network of automatic weather stations telemeters real-time weather data to the Central Forecasting Office at the Observatory Headquarters from Cheung Chau, King's Park, Ta Kwu Ling, Lau Fau Shan, Tsing Yi, Sha Tin, Tuen Mun, Wong Chuk Hang, Tai Po Kau, Sai Kung, Tseung Kwan O, Sha Lo Wan and Waglan Island. These stations provide a comprehensive coverage on regional weather variation. For the safety of aviation, wind conditions at the airport and its vicinity are monitored continuously by a network of anemometers. In collaboration with Guangdong Meteorological Bureau, the observatory also operates an automatic weather station at Huangmao Zhou, an island 40 kilometres south of Lantau Island and strategically located for monitoring tropical cyclones approaching from the south.

Rainfall information has always been important in Hong Kong because of its effects on water resources management and also because of the susceptibility of slopes to landslips in heavy rain. A dense network of 143 raingauge stations provides information on the spatial distribution and intensity of rainfall in various parts of Hong Kong. Sixty-nine of these stations are equipped to provide up to the minute information every five minutes. Rain cloud development, movement and intensity within 512 kilometres of Hong Kong are monitored by a digital radar system which also produces objective short-term rainfall estimates at selected places. A lightning detection system locates cloud-to-ground lightning within a range of about 130 kilometres and a spherics recorder is used to register thunderstorm activity within a range of about 100 kilometres. Assimilation of all information is essential for assessing the likelihood of flooding and landslips.

For the real-time monitoring of floods in north-western New Territories, water-level and rainfall information at Kam Tin is telemetered directly to the Observatory Headquarters. The system was scheduled to include 12 more stations by the end of 1992. Tide data are collected from eight gauges in the territory for operational warning of sea flooding. Wave information for forecasting the sea state of local waters is obtained in real time from a wave recorder at Waglan Island. Numerical models are used to predict the likelihood of storm surges in tropical cyclone situations. Storm surge warnings are issued when a significant rise in sea level is forecast.

Besides surface observations, upper-air conditions are measured by radiosondes carried by balloons launched at King's Park Meteorological Station. For an overview of weather systems, hourly high resolution satellite cloud pictures are received from the Japanese Geostationary Meteorological Satellite. The satellite imageries, which cover east Asia and the western Pacific, greatly facilitate the monitoring of weather systems when they are outside the range of the radar system.

Weather prediction requires constant meteorological data exchange with other countries. This is achieved through telecommunication circuits dedicated to the transmission of meteorological data. The Royal Observatory exchanges meteorological data with overseas centres via three international circuits, the Hong Kong-Beijing circuit, the Hong Kong-Tokyo circuit and the Hong Kong-Bangkok circuit.

In recent years, the vagaries and evolution of weather have become better understood through experience gained in analysing and interpreting the outputs of numerical weather prediction models run at the Royal Observatory and other major meteorological centres abroad. With the continuing advances in the accuracy and reliability of numerical model outputs, useful weather outlooks several days ahead can now be issued with confidence.

The Year's Weather

With an extreme rainfall surplus during the first seven months of the year and a contrasting record dry spell from August to November, the annual rainfall for 1992 amounted to 2 678.8 millimetres, 21 per cent above the annual mean of 2 214.3 millimetres.

Seven consecutive wet months from January to July produced a record-breaking 2 410.6 millimetres of rainfall, more than the normal amount for the whole year. There were several episodes of heavy rain in March, April and May. A disastrous rainstorm on May 8 led to the introduction of the new rainstorm alert/warning system. The Red and Black Rainstorm Warnings were first issued during the heavy rain brought by Tropical Storm Faye on July 18. July was a month of frequent tropical cyclone activity, with tropical cyclone warning signals being raised for three storms over a period of 12 days.

A four-month drought lasted from August to November with a record low total rainfall of 201.8 millimetres during the period. Tropical cyclones were conspicuously absent in the vicinity of Hong Kong and as a result, tropical cyclone rainfall in 1992 was only slightly more than half of normal. The tendency of the tropical cyclones to track northwards east of Taiwan led to some very hot conditions in August and September.

Despite the fact that January was relatively sunny, the monthly rainfall of 40.0 millimetres was 70 per cent above the January normal of 23.4 millimetres. A substantial portion of the month's rain fell on January 5 during a spell of active winter monsoon. The dominance of the winter monsoon was reflected by the unusually high monthly mean pressure of 1 022.2 hectopascals (hPa), the sixth highest on record for January.

February was generally gloomy and damp. The active winter monsoon, alternating between the northerlies and the easterlies, brought a prolonged spell of clouds, rain and mist for most part of the month. The monthly rainfall of 142.8 millimetres was nearly three times the February normal of 48.0 millimetres and produced the sixth wettest February on record. The total duration of sunshine in February was only about two-thirds of normal.

March was still damp and wet. Clouds and mist were prevalent as moisture converged upon the south China coastal areas. The monthly mean relative humidity was as high as 90 per cent, making it the most humid March since 1978. The monthly rainfall of 242.4 millimetres was over three and a half times the March normal of 66.9 millimetres. Half of the month's rain fell on March 3 during the approach of an active cold front. It was the second wettest March day on record. The total rainfall in the first quarter of the year was the second highest on record.

Prolonged heavy downpours affected Hong Kong in April and hail was reported in Causeway Bay and Pokfulam Village on April 4. With a monthly rainfall total of 492.2 millimetres, it was the wettest April since observations began in 1884. Rain was heaviest on April 10 with a daily total of 160.7 millimetres – the second highest for a single day in April. As the wet anomaly persisted, the accumulated rainfall finally exceeded the previous record by the end of April.

May was another wet and unsettled month. Against a background of storm clouds and rain, the duration of bright sunshine for the whole month was a meagre total of 93.8 hours, the fifth lowest ever for May. A very intense and disastrous rainstorm occurred on May 8 due to the effects of an active trough of low pressure in the vicinity of Hong Kong. The hourly rainfall of 109.9 millimetres at the Royal Observatory between 6 and 7 am that day was the highest ever recorded. The daily rainfall of 324.1 millimetres on May 8 rendered it

359

the second wettest May day on record. The deluge was, however, a very localised event with Kowloon Peninsula and the northern part of Hong Kong Island bearing the brunt of the rainstorm. Four people were killed and one was reported missing in accidents brought about by the heavy rain. Most of the mudslips and floods occurred on Hong Kong Island. The worst mudslip was at Baguio Villa where 10 buildings had to be temporarily closed, affecting more than 1 500 residents. Altogether, about 200 cases of mudslips and around 300 cases of flooding were reported. Many roads on steep slopes were turned into torrents and the flood water paralysed road traffic in the urban areas.

June was the sixth consecutive month with above-normal rainfall. The monthly total of 532.8 millimetres was 42 per cent above the June normal of 376.0 millimetres. The first tropical cyclone in the year to affect Hong Kong was Typhoon Chuck which necessitated the hoisting of the No. 3 Strong Wind Signal on June 27 and 28.

July was also wetter than normal. The monthly rainfall of 358.1 millimetres was 11 per cent above the normal of 323.5 millimetres. Rain was mostly associated with active south-west monsoon early in the month and the subsequent passages of three tropical cyclones. The newly introduced Red and Black Rainstorm Warnings were issued for the first time on July 18 for the heavy rain brought by Tropical Storm Faye. On July 22, Severe Tropical Storm Gary prompted the hoisting of the No. 8 Gale or Storm Signal.

In sharp contrast to the wet anomaly which persisted from January to July, August was one of the driest and hottest Augusts on record. The monthly rainfall was only about one-quarter of the normal of 391.4 millimetres, making it the driest August since 1962. One of the hottest days ever experienced in Hong Kong was on August 30 when the daily mean temperature was a record high 32.0 degrees. The minimum temperature of 30.0 degrees that day was the second highest for all months. the monthly relative humidity of 77 per cent and monthly rainfall of 97.7 millimetres were both the third lowest recorded in August.

September was hot and sunny with little rain. The mean daily minimum temperature of 26.8 degrees for the month was the highest on record for September. In respect of the daily mean temperature of 31.1 degrees and the minimum temperature of 29.5 degrees, September 1 was the hottest September day on record. The month's rainfall of 63.1 millimetres was only about 21 per cent of the September normal of 299.7 millimetres. It was the driest September since 1966 and the fourth driest September on record.

October was very much dominated by the north-east monsoon. Temperatures were generally below normal in a month of mainly fine and dry weather. The monthly rainfall of 30.9 millimetres was only about 21 per cent of the October normal of 144.8 millimetres.

The north-east monsoon was even more active in November. The monthly mean pressure of 1 020.1 hPa was the second highest for November. Under the influence of the continental anti-cyclone, the weather was characterised by sunny and clear skies. The relative humidity dropped to a minimum of 19 per cent on the afternoon of November 10, the lowest since 1971 for November. About 70 cases of hill fire were reported on November 9 and 10. With only three days of rain in the month, the monthly rainfall of 10.1 millimetres was only about 29 per cent of the November normal of 35.1 millimetres.

The winter monsoon moderated in December and it was one of the warmest Decembers on record. The monthly mean minimum temperature of 17.4 degrees and the monthly mean temperature of 19.2 degrees were respectively the second and third highest for December. The dry spell came to an end and the month was unusually humid with mist or haze occurring on eight days. Fog was reported inside the harbour on the morning of

December 28 and this was the first time in December since 1955. The monthly rainfall of 66.4 millimetres was nearly two and a half times the December normal of 27.3 millimetres, with most of the rain falling during an unseasonal spell of damp and wet weather after Christmas.

Climate, Oceanographic and Geophysical Services
The Royal Observatory carries out climate, oceanographic and geophysical studies. Its professional advice is often sought by consultants working on government or private projects. When an engineering project demands substantial data collection and analysis over a prolonged period, special studies are conducted.

A climatological information service is provided to meet the needs of the general public and to cater for the specialised interests of shipping, aviation, agriculture, fishery, engineering, industries, judicial proceedings, and recreational planning. In particular, analyses on the probabilities of high winds, heavy rain, waves and surges are undertaken using mathematical models as well as statistics of extremes. Spectral analysis is applied to wave data to derive information useful to engineering design work. Other potential applications include hydrological forecasting, water resources planning, drainage design, water quality control, reservoir design and operation, irrigation and other infra-structural projects.

Climate change is another subject of interest and concern. The Royal Observatory participates actively in international climate programmes and, through the World Meteorological Organisation, liaises with the Intergovernmental Panel on Climate Change to keep abreast of scientific developments in the field.

In line with its responsibilities for emergency response services relating to inclement weather and other natural disasters, the Royal Observatory is to co-ordinate and formulate technical emergency advice should an unlikely accidental release of radioactivity occur at the Guangdong Nuclear Power Station at Daya Bay. In order to fulfil this responsibility, the Royal Observatory has established an Environmental Radiation Monitoring and Assessment Programme to monitor the radiation levels in Hong Kong in the atmospheric, terrestrial, food and aquatic pathways. The programme, which began in 1987, entails the collection and measurement of samples of air, water, soil and food regularly, at a number of locations in the territory. An Early Alerting Network has also been established to continuously monitor the ambient gamma dose rate in the territory and to provide an alert of any deviation of dose rate from the background level. In the event of an emergency, a Monitoring and Assessment Centre at the Observatory Headquarters will be activated to monitor and assess the radiological and meteorological information collected, co-ordinate a multi-departmental food and water monitoring programme to estimate the transport, dispersion and deposition of any radioactivity over the territory, and to provide technical advice to government on any necessary countermeasures.

As a component of the Airport Core Programme, the Royal Observatory has already started work in planning and designing the meteorological facilities required to support the future operation of the new airport at Chek Lap Kok. In addition to the basic aeronautical meteorological observation equipment, state-of-art systems will be acquired and installed for data processing, information distribution and wind shear detection and warning.

To monitor earthquakes and seismicity, three short-period seismometers are operated at Cheung Chau, High Island and Tsim Bei Tsui. Long-period seismographs at the Observatory Headquarters record tremors from all over the world. Strong-motion accelerographs are operated at the Observatory Headquarters and Tate's Cairn. About 130 earth tremors with epicentres within 320 kilometres of Hong Kong are detected annually. Reports of significant tremors are routinely made known to the general public via the media. Seismic data are used by structural engineers in the design of buildings. Such data are also made available to local and overseas scientific institutions for their studies.

The Hong Kong Time Standard is provided by a caesium beam atomic clock at the Observatory Headquarters. Accuracy within fractions of a microsecond a day is maintained. The time service is operated by relaying a six-pip time signal to Radio Television Hong Kong for broadcast.

The State of the Environment

Hong Kong is known above all as one of the world's great cities. It has seen in the past half century a rate of growth in industrial and commercial prosperity that is unrivalled. This growth has brought environmental problems that are common to cities around the world, but may be experienced less in Hong Kong in future because of the government's strong commitment to improving the environment.

One of the ways in which the community has managed to sustain economic growth has been by developing new cities in what were formerly rural areas, on the nuclei of small fishing or market towns. The government's planners and builders have taken some care for the environment in creating these new cities. The 20-year record of marine water pollution, for example, shows that a steep decline in water quality in Victoria Harbour in the seventies, did not continue in the eighties, when the decline was much less steep. On the other hand, areas like Tolo Harbour, with the impact of massive new town growth, showed a steep decline in water quality in the early eighties; this decline has been halted and is expected to reverse soon, as the benefits of pollution control are felt.

Despite the intensity of its urban development, there are still parts of Hong Kong that remain rural, and there are great areas of open water. Some of these areas are badly affected by livestock rearing and cottage industries; others are free from the threat of pollution and offer tremendous opportunities for conservation and recreation.

The following sections consider the environmental problems and opportunities in each of these broad landscape groups in turn. Hong Kong's environmental quality is usually measured in terms of environmental quality objectives. These state in measurable terms the quality of the environment that is just adequate to restore or maintain desired conservation goals, such as the protection of health or the ability of the environment to sustain some beneficial use such as fishing or swimming.

Urban environmental quality

Hong Kong's older urban areas have a dense mix of housing, community facilities, commerce and industry, with an infrastructure that falls short of modern standards. Poor urban landscape, air and water pollution, noise, and waste disposal problems are common. The government has committed a great deal of money and effort to meeting these challenges.

Hong Kong's objectives for air quality are comparable to internationally recognised air quality standards for the protection of general public health. The actual air quality does not always meet the objectives. Total suspended particulates, respirable suspended particulates and nitrogen dioxide are often high. In 1992, the highest annual averages recorded were 155 micrograms per cubic metre of total suspended particulates and 71 micrograms per cubic metre of respirable suspended particulates, both above the objectives. Nitrogen dioxide is near its objective of 80 micrograms per cubic metre. Emissions from motor vehicles are the main source of these pollutants and strict new vehicle emission standards have been imposed to tackle an expected increase.

Transport is also a factor in noise, which is unavoidable in a vibrant metropolitan city like Hong Kong, packed with commercial and industrial activities. The ever increasing demand for transport has led to serious noise problems in areas close to major roads and rail transport corridors. Residents under the flight path and near Kai Tak Airport will be relieved from high levels of aircraft noise when the airport moves to Chek Lap Kok in 1997. The government has imposed new controls on noisy construction equipment to reduce the noise problem.

Urban sewerage in Hong Kong grew as the city did, without an overall strategy and is not adequate for present needs. There are many connections between foul sewerage and storm drains, and the Environmental Protection Department has estimated that only half the city's sewage, a million tonnes a day, gets any treatment before it flows into the sea.

The resulting load of water pollution has a very severe impact in confined areas such as typhoon shelters. In the worst of these, such as Kowloon Bay typhoon shelter beside Kai Tak airport, foul smelling and toxic gases arise from the polluted water. A major resewerage project in east Kowloon is now under construction. With the investment of over $500 million, this will bring substantial relief to the area by 1994.

Even in the open harbour, water quality is not good. The median concentration of dissolved oxygen, a good indicator of water quality, is close to fifty per cent saturation, the minimum level the water quality objectives allow. Phase I of the strategic sewage disposal scheme, for which detailed investigations are now in progress, will reduce harbour pollution.

With the community's growing expectations for a better environment, the need for a cost-effective, secure and environmentally acceptable waste management programme is apparent. Special categories of waste such as chemical and clinical wastes, decomposing carcasses and various types of sludge also need tighter control, not only on disposal but also storage, transport and treatment. The disposal arrangements must not add to air or water pollution.

Many firms produce chemical wastes. Disposal of these wastes to sewers can harm the fabric of sewers and the operation of sewage treatment plants and cause contamination of coastal waters. Controls on chemical waste, introduced in 1992, have already identified and registered some 9 000 chemical waste producers. The Waste Disposal (Chemical Waste) (General) Regulation requires cradle to grave tracking and controlled disposal of chemical waste in an environmentally acceptable manner.

The environment of new towns

To some extent, the territory's new towns face the same environmental problems as the old urban area. However they have been better planned. They tend to be more spacious, and are better provided with sewers and facilities for waste disposal.

One of the important features of new towns is that they intrude into what were rural areas, where water pollution in rivers, streams and the sea has become a problem. With the

363

declaration of the North Western Water Control Zone in 1992, the protection of the Water Pollution Control Ordinance extended to all new towns.

Despite better planning in the new towns, some water pollution still occurs. In Tolo Harbour, a major part of the pollution comes from connections of effluents from industrial and commercial areas to storm water drains. The nutrient rich effluent has contributed to poor water quality in the harbour. A tunnel that will divert reclaimed water from Sha Tin and Tai Po to a less sensitive area, completing the major elements of the Tolo Harbour Action Plan, broke through in May 1992. This will produce immense benefits to Tolo when it is operational in 1993.

Another pollution problem is heavy metal from industrial discharges. High concentrations of heavy metals upset the performance of the government's sewage treatment works, thereby adding to environmental pollution. However, statutory controls have been successful in reducing pollution loading in the various water control zones.

Rural areas and the sea
In the developed parts of the New Territories, water pollution in many rivers and streams is still severe. Some streams have recorded a degree of pollution equivalent to 10 times the strength of raw domestic sewage, and a thick, foul crust on streams is common. This pollution is a serious health risk where it passes through towns such as Yuen Long and Tuen Mun.

The cause of much of this pollution is the territory's livestock industry. Before 1987, the total amount of waste produced annually by about 0.7 million pigs and 1.2 million poultry in Hong Kong was 840 000 tonnes. This was equivalent to the pollution load of the raw sewage from a population of two million people. Most of it ended up in Hong Kong's small streams and rivers and then the sea. By the end of 1992, this load had been reduced to only 360 000 tonnes.

In the sea, away from the urban areas and confined bays, water quality objectives are met most of the time. However, dredging and dumping as part of the process of land formation and construction imposed severe pressure during 1992. Extensive areas of muddy water were visible at times, and fishermen in some areas complained of reduced fish catches. Illegal dumping and short dumping (outside the designated areas) of spoil damage marine life.

Bathing beaches have been an important recreational resource in Hong Kong for many years, and because of their attractive locations they have acted as a magnet for high quality housing. This has caused serious pollution in the past, but most of Hong Kong's beaches are now fit for swimming. The government uses strict standards for bacteria levels at bathing beaches. The Environmental Protection Department devised these standards, which relate to the degree of sewage pollution, in a very thorough study of the health risk that bathers face. The following table shows how beaches were classified in 1990, 1991 and 1992. Unfortunately, complaints occur even at beaches that are free from sewage pollution, usually because of floating litter and occasionally because of slime caused by algae.

Beach grade	Health risk cases per 1 000 swimmers	Number of beaches		
		1990	*1991*	*1992*
Good	Undetectable	22	27	22
Fair	Under 10	26	19	22
Poor	10 to 15	6	7	9
Very poor	Over 15	2	3	3

Protecting the Environment

The administrative framework

The Environmental Protection Department is the government's main store of expertise in the pollution control and planning aspects of conservation. Its tasks include: providing advice on policy, and monitoring progress to the policy goals for all aspects of pollution; undertaking environmental planning and assessment; devising, enforcing and reviewing the effectiveness of environmental legislation, including the livestock waste control scheme, and recommending new or amended legislation; planning and developing facilities for liquid and solid waste disposal.

Other departments play a major role in protecting Hong Kong's environment. The Planning Department takes care of the environment in government urban and rural planning at strategic and local level. The Drainage Services Department designs, builds, operates and maintains sewerage and sewage treatment and disposal facilities throughout the territory. The Territory Development Department carries out sewerage and sewage disposal works in new towns. The Urban Services Department and Regional Services Department provide refuse collection services and maintain environmental hygiene. The Civil Engineering Department oversees and operates landfills for the disposal of waste. The Agriculture and Fisheries Department is responsible for wildlife and countryside conservation, manages agricultural weirs, and operates and maintains departmental farm waste treatment facilities. The Electrical and Mechanical Services Department operates refuse incinerators. The Marine Department clears floating refuse and oil from harbour waters and enforces the law on oil spills.

Planning against Pollution

Environmental planning aims to achieve land uses that are environmentally acceptable and compatible between neighbours. It is carried out at various levels.

At the strategic level, the Metroplan Study, completed in 1990, created a framework. Studies such as the Territorial Development Strategy Review are building on this, to recommend improvements to Hong Kong's existing or proposed land use, environment and transport structure.

The Territorial Development Strategy study recognised at the outset that environmental factors were fundamentally important. It aimed to improve not only the efficiency of the territory but, more importantly, the quality of life.

Environmentally desirable land use changes are being more precisely defined through sub-regional development strategy reviews. In 1992 work continued on the environmental assessments associated with both the North-West and South-West New Territories Development Strategy Reviews.

Environmental assessment work arising from the Metroplan has reached down to district level in the form of environmental planning studies, which are part of the district development statements. In 1992 the West Kowloon Development Statement was finished and work commenced on both the Tsuen Wan and Kwai Tsing Development Statement and the South East Kowloon Study.

Work on defining the cumulative environmental effects of developments in and around Deep Bay continued during 1992. During the year the Hong Kong–Guangdong Environmental Protection Liaison Group considered a joint report on pollution and development

365

of Deep Bay. The two sides have agreed on a joint action plan for controlling development and pollution. This aims to preserve and protect Hong Kong's sites of special scientific interest, including the important ecosystems of Mai Po and Inner Deep Bay, as well as the Fu Tien Nature Reserve on the Shenzhen side.

At the district planning level, the Hong Kong Housing Society and the Land Development Corporation now review major public housing schemes and redevelopment initiatives within the urban areas. Sites with severe environmental problems, such as severe traffic noise, for which there are no practical controls, should be rezoned and appropriately developed. At other less problematic sites proper building designs and layouts will reduce the environmental impacts to acceptable levels.

The government intends to include lease conditions requiring developers to provide suitable windows and air conditioning to protect future residents against aircraft noise under the flight path of the Kai Tak airport. The airport will operate until mid 1997.

Planning applications for major projects that may cause environmental concerns must include documents that show their environmental acceptability. Unacceptable proposals are often rejected, or have stringent environmental requirements imposed as conditions of approval.

The most common reason for rejecting a planning proposal on environmental grounds in the main urban area is the juxtaposition of incompatible land uses. One notable example is a proposal to build two high-rise residential blocks next to Kennedy Town Abattoir. This could cause intractable noise and odour problems to future residents. The government is now looking for a way to move the abattoir as soon as possible to provide for existing and proposed housing in the area.

Other examples, where residential and industrial interfaces have in the most part been overcome, include a cotton mill redevelopment in Tuen Mun and a redevelopment adjacent to a cement plant in Tsing Yi.

Port and airport development
During 1992 the focus for the Port and Airport Development Strategy shifted towards the implementation of the recommendations of environmental impact studies. The strategy includes projects related to the airport and port. The airport related projects comprise a number of project elements: the new airport at Chek Lap Kok; North Lantau new town developments; transport links to Hong Kong Island comprising the North Lantau Expressway, the Lantau Fixed Crossing, Route 3, the West Kowloon Expressway, the Western Harbour Crossing, the Airport Railway; the West Kowloon Reclamation; and the Central and Wanchai Reclamation. The port related projects comprise the South-East Tsing Yi development for a container terminal, Lantau Port and Harbour Developments and the Tuen Mun and Tseung Kwan O Port Development.

This focus on the implementation issues entailed two aspects. First is the difficult process of translating the environmental impact assessments into contract and lease conditions for the construction phase of the projects. Second is incorporating environmental monitoring and auditing into the construction and operating phases of each development.

The construction of the West Kowloon Reclamation and road and rail links to the new airport will have some adverse environmental consequences. Already, the application of environmental planning has set out to redress these impacts through land use plans and pollution mitigation measures, for example by set backs to cut the impact of noise.

During construction such measures include noise barriers and dust suppression. By mid 1993 the interception of polluted flows in storm water drains is expected to be in place. Without this, the water quality in temporary embayments caused by the phasing of the reclamation to allow for the reprovisioning of market, ferry and dockyard services, would be poor.

Due to the sensitivity of West Kowloon, an environmental project office has been set up to monitor and audit the many contracts and projects that interface in the area. The office will be the focal point for advice and guidance on any necessary remedial measures to overcome unacceptable or unanticipated impacts. It will keep the public informed on the environmental performance of the projects.

Power generation

In response to the rising demand for electricity expected in the coming decades, the local power companies have submitted separate proposals to the government for increasing generation capacities. They propose to expand either on their existing sites or on additional land to be granted.

Hong Kong Electric Company Ltd. proposes to build two additional 350 megawatt coal-fired generating units at its Lamma Island site. An impact assessment for the expansion, completed in 1992, identified air quality as the key environmental issue.

Residents on Hong Kong Island would suffer increased air pollution, especially by harmful sulphur dioxide gas emitted when normal coal, containing sulphur, burns. To reduce the cumulative effects of air pollution from the new and existing units the company will install flue gas desulphurisation systems on its new units. It will also limit the sulphur content in the coal it uses.

The chosen flue gas desulphurisation system produces a large amount of solid gypsum as a waste for disposal. The pulverised fuel ash disposal strategy, which the company developed a few years ago in consultation with the government, includes lagoons that have been found to be environmentally acceptable. Subject to further clarification and decisions on the appropriate lagoon size, this part of the strategy will proceed in 1993.

China Light and Power Company Ltd. proposes a 6 000 megawatt facility to be built at a new site in addition to a gas turbine station at Penny's Bay and at its existing coal-fired facility at Castle Peak. An extensive site search study, for the 6 000 megawatt facility, incorporated an environment and planning factor as one of the major criteria for site selection. The study concluded that Black Point, at Tuen Mun, is the best location.

Several issues still needing resolution include adequate measures to reduce air pollutants and to mitigate the effects of the large volume of cooling water to be discharged into Deep Bay.

Rural issues

As a result of rapid developments within the territory, the amount of construction wastes arriving at the existing landfills in rural areas has increased dramatically in the past two or three years. There is an urgent need for a solution to maintain an adequate reserve of landfill capacity for domestic wastes before the commissioning of the new strategic landfills that are still under construction.

Extensions at three existing landfills, namely Pillar Point, Tseung Kwan O Stage I and Shuen Wan, are essential. Assessments have explored all possible means to reduce nuisance to adjacent land users. Studies that aim to restore certain old landfills are in progress.

367

The Rural Planning and Improvement Strategy has moved forward with special efforts to terminate many thousands of polluting short term land uses. Village sewage improvement schemes in the rural parts of the New Territories have also made a contribution.

As a result of the revision of the livestock waste control scheme, it is intended that, anyone wishing to farm livestock should require a licence. This will provide a powerful planning tool to ensure that there will be no new livestock farms where they would not be in keeping with other prevailing land uses.

The government's policy with regard to potentially hazardous installations (PHIs) is to control the risks associated with PHIs within an acceptable level by requiring the installations themselves to be constructed and operated to the highest possible standards and by controlling the land uses within their vicinity. Since 1988, the acceptability of risk associated with a PHI has been evaluated against a set of Interim Risk Guidelines (IRGs). With more than four years of experience in applying the IRGs, the government is now reviewing the problems encountered and considering a set of final guidelines for use in Hong Kong.

Chlorine has been used in Hong Kong for water disinfection at water treatment works and swimming pools for several decades. Since chlorine is highly toxic, there is a growing concern about the potential hazard to people living in the vicinity of chlorine stores and transportation routes in case of accidental releases. An evaluation was completed on the potential hazards associated with the storage and use of liquid chlorine at all major water treatment works. Implementation of the recommended improvement measures will be completed by 1993. The Urban Services Department and Regional Services Department are converting to smaller containers for chlorine than used at present and are considering the use of alternative disinfectants which are safer than chlorine as a long-term measure. Also, measures for mitigating the risks associated with the transportation of chlorine to water treatment works and chlorine stores are being implemented progressively.

Legislation and Pollution Control
Hong Kong has five main laws that control pollution. They are: the Waste Disposal Ordinance; the Water Pollution Control Ordinance; the Air Pollution Control Ordinance; the Noise Control Ordinance; and the Ozone Layer Protection Ordinance. Most of these have various subsidiary regulations and other statutory provisions, such as technical memoranda, that give specific effect to the intentions of the principal laws.

The government has adopted a system of environmental quality objectives as a general principle in its pollution control laws. The objectives are set at levels that will protect conservation goals, such as the protection of public health or the preservation of a natural ecosystem. This system usually gives the required environmental benefit at the least cost, because the limits it imposes on pollutant emissions are no more stringent or costly than is necessary to protect the conservation goal. It also makes the maximum safe use of the environment's capacity to neutralise pollution.

The following sections show how the laws apply to the various sources of pollution and environmental harm that can exist in Hong Kong.

Industrial and commercial emissions
Industry and commerce is Hong Kong's way of life. However, commercial and industrial success has been bought at the expense of severe degradation of the environment. The

penalty is being paid in adverse ecological changes, a heavy but usually hidden financial burden on the community, and great risks to community health.

The government's pollution control strategy aims not to harm industry and commerce, but to work in partnership with firms so that all may benefit from a better environment. There are often direct economic benefits to be gained from activities that benefit the environment, such as recycling and the introduction of pollution prevention in manufacturing. These methods are better than pollution control techniques, that have to be applied after a waste material has become a potential pollutant.

The government would prefer industry and commerce to recognise the benefits of waste minimisation and pollution prevention, but it is inevitable that this cannot be an entirely voluntary process. Nowhere is this more apparent than in the case of the Water Pollution Control Ordinance, which first came into effective operation in 1987, and has been gradually extended to a series of water control zones. These zones do not yet cover the most heavily industrialised areas.

The North Western Water Control Zone came into being in April 1992, bringing the number of zones in operation to seven, covering 92 per cent of the territory. Three zones remain to be declared. The Eastern and Western Buffer Zones should be declared in mid 1993, when polluting discharges from some of the main industrial and developed areas around Victoria Harbour will come under control.

Every trade effluent in a water control zone needs a licence, which will specify the maximum amount of pollutants that may be emitted. The standards vary from place to place in accordance with the conservation goals and water quality objectives for the receiving water body. Licence standards usually follow a set of published guidelines.

Considerable efforts are made to ensure that effluents meet the standards set in licences. In 1992, Environmental Protection Department inspectors took more than 4 500 effluent samples and made over 12 000 laboratory tests.

This activity has had great success. For example, in Tolo Harbour, the first water control zone, more than 100 expedient connections were rectified. The organic pollution load on the harbour has been reduced by 75 per cent. Concentrations of heavy metals in the digested sludge of the Sha Tin sewage treatment works have been reduced to such an extent that the sludge now meets the stringent standards that apply to marine disposal. In the Southern Water Control Zone, over 90 per cent of private sewage treatment plants are now operating satisfactorily and the water quality of many popular bathing beaches has improved as a result.

In the Deep Bay Water Control Zone, the Environmental Protection Department has managed to divert about 7 000 m³/day of industrial effluents from the storm drains to the foul sewerage system. This is equivalent to the organic pollution load from a population of 50 000 people. For those recently declared zones, such as north-western waters, the reduction in pollution is comparatively low as the controls have been in force for a short time only. In the established zones of Port Shelter and Junk Bay, the reduction is as much as 70 and 50 per cent of the organic pollution load respectively. Over all control zones, the department estimates that so far it has achieved an average of about 50 per cent reduction in the target pollution load by enforcing the Water Pollution Control Ordinance. The reduction is expected to increase further when the controls have been fully implemented.

Pollution of the once notorious Ho Chung River, 'the black river of Sai Kung', has improved dramatically due to effective control of the major industrial polluters. An interceptor scheme, diverting further pollution sources away from the river for treatment, is scheduled to be completed in mid-1993 and its benefits will be visible afterwards.

There are also cases where using clean technology rather than conventional pollution control has produced environmental benefits. A good example is the case of a large film processor in the Port Shelter water control zone. It adopted a new processing system to prevent the discharge of a toxic pollutant, rather than building an expensive and wasteful treatment plant. Good results have been achieved.

The Waste Disposal Ordinance is complementary to the Water Pollution Control Ordinance in controlling industrial pollution. It provides the statutory framework for the management of all solid waste in Hong Kong.

The legislature passed new regulations to control chemical waste from industry and commerce in 1992: the Waste Disposal (Chemical Waste) (General) Regulation; the Waste Disposal (Forms and Fees for Licences) Regulation; and the Waste Disposal (Appeal Board) Regulation were enacted.

These regulations empower the government to control chemical waste from its point of production to its point of disposal.

Under the regulations, chemical waste producers must register with the disposal authority, the Director of Environmental Protection, and must send their chemical waste to licensed facilities for treatment and disposal. Only licensed collectors may collect and transport chemical waste. The conditions in each licence demand a safe collection and transport service using skilled, trained staff and proper equipment and vehicles.

The regulations also impose statutory requirements for packaging, labelling and storage of chemical waste, to safeguard public health and minimise risk to the environment.

The regulations take effect in stages. Control of waste containing asbestos, poly-chlorinated biphenyls and tannery offcuts became effective in late 1992. Control on other chemical wastes will be implemented in early 1993 to coincide with the commissioning of the Chemical Waste Treatment Facility Centre.

Registration of existing chemical waste producers was completed in November, 1992, and new waste producers must apply for registration before beginning any activity that generates chemical waste. To assist chemical waste producers in complying with the new regulation, a number of guide books, leaflets and a new code of practice on packaging, labelling and storage of chemical waste were published. The codes of practice on asbestos waste and polychlorinated biphenyl waste were revised in the light of the controls on chemical waste.

Waste disposal licences will be issued under the Waste Disposal Ordinance to chemical waste disposal facilities, which will treat, recycle, or dispose of chemical waste in an environmentally acceptable manner. On its commissioning early in 1993, the Chemical Waste Treatment Centre will become one of the most important licensed disposal facilities in Hong Kong. It will provide also a fleet of licensed collection vehicles.

A system of consignment notes, called trip tickets, helps the cradle to grave control on chemical waste. A tailor-made computer information management system tracks waste movements engraved on the trip tickets. All responsible parties, including the waste producer, the waste collector and the reception manager of the waste disposal site must supply accurate details of each consignment of waste.

In addition to liquid and solid wastes, many factories and commercial enterprises produce emissions to the air. The Environmental Protection Department operates air pollution controls under the Air Pollution Control Ordinance. A number of subsidiary regulations under the ordinance provide specific controls on furnaces and chimneys, dark smoke emissions, fuel composition, and specified processes.

The installation and alteration of furnaces, ovens and chimneys need prior approval from the department. This commonly affects industrial furnaces, restaurant stoves and chimneys serving emergency generators. The requirement for prior approval is to prevent emissions from new installations causing air pollution problems when they come into operation, and to ensure that the district air quality objective will not be violated. During 1992, the department processed 692 applications.

Nuisance and environmental problems caused by dark smoke emissions, which commonly result from poor maintenance or incorrect operation of fuel burners, arouse great public concern, especially when factories are near homes. The Air Pollution Control (Smoke) Regulations provide controls on dark smoke emission, limiting the darkness of smoke to Ringelmann shade number 1 which corresponds to 20 per cent opacity.

In July 1990 the Air Pollution Control (Fuel Restriction) Regulations banned fuel oils with a sulphur content over 0.5 per cent by weight or a viscosity over six centistokes at 40°C. The sulphur content of solid fuels is limited to one per cent by weight. Due to unfavourable topography in the Sha Tin area, which restricts atmospheric dispersion, only gaseous fuels may be used there.

The enforcement of the fuel restriction regulations has successfully reduced emission of sulphur dioxide by 80 per cent. These regulations have brought about some reduction in nitrogen oxides and particulates.

Certain industrial processes, which are liable to cause significant air pollution, are specified for control under the licensing system provided by the Air Pollution Control Ordinance and the specified processes regulations. They include power utilities, incinerators, gas production plants and cement plants.

The ordinance exempts from licensing most of the specified processes, which existed before October 2, 1987. In 1992, there were 97 exempt premises compared with 48 licences in force. As the exempt premises are not obliged to adopt the best practicable means to control the emission of air pollution, they continue to cause problems.

Therefore in the Air Pollution Control (Amendment) Bill that was submitted to the Legislative Council in June 1992, proposal was made to allow cancellation by class of the exemption of existing premises in phases.

The bill also proposed to increase the number of specified processes from 23 to 31. The additional processes are pathological waste incinerators, organic chemical works, petroleum works, zinc galvanising works, rendering works, non-ferrous metallurgical works, glass works and paint works. Together with the proposal to adopt a technical memorandum approach in issuing air pollution abatement notices, this will provide a better control of the air polluting industries in Hong Kong.

Enforcement of the air pollution law involves complaint investigations, providing technical advice, issuing warning notices to require polluters to abate their emissions, and prosecution. In 1992, 1 570 complaint cases were investigated; 8 432 inspections of plant; 1 445 cases were given technical advice; 112 warning notices issued; and 302 successful prosecutions. Fines on offenders ranged from $300 to $25,000.

Noise from industrial or commercial premises is controlled under the Noise Control Ordinance. The Environmental Protection Department responds to complaints and may serve noise abatement notices that require reduction of excessive noise by a given date. Failure to comply with noise abatement notices is an offence, liable to prosecution. During 1992, 2 392 complaints were investigated; 246 noise abatement notices served; and 87 cases prosecuted. Fines on noise offenders ranged from $1,000 to $50,000.

Transport
Transport by road and rail may cause air pollution and noise nuisance. Shipping is less likely to cause these problems, but may cause water pollution through inappropriate waste disposal.

Large diesel vehicles are major contributors to vehicle emissions. The government is developing control strategies that include up to date emission standards for large vehicles and tightened inspection and maintenance requirements on certain classes of vehicles to reduce emissions.

Since April 1991 all petrol stations must sell unleaded petrol, to ensure its availability for cars with catalytic converters. The market share of unleaded petrol averaged about 56 per cent in 1992, even though the price advantage for unleaded petrol of $1.01 was reduced to $0.29 in April.

The Air Pollution Control (Vehicle Design Standards) (Emission) Regulations became effective in January 1992. These regulations require that all new vehicles of 2.5 tonnes or less must meet stringent emission standards. To comply, petrol cars must be fitted with catalytic converter emission control devices and engine management systems. The regulations also require that all petrol driven cars registered after January 1992 must use unleaded petrol.

The existing scheme for reporting 'spotted' smoky vehicles was revised in October 1991. Smoky vehicles that are spotted are now directed to attend a designated testing centre to confirm that the smoke problem has been rectified. There are 20 centres in operation, which examined 44 426 vehicles in 1992.

In some areas, traffic noise is not only causing problems during day-time, it may also disturb sleep at night. A practical way to minimise sleep disturbance is to divert traffic, particularly heavy vehicles, away from noise sensitive receivers. An amendment to the Road Traffic Ordinance made in 1992 enables the authority to regulate traffic on environmental grounds.

Noise from the operation of rail transport is controlled under the Noise Control Ordinance. During 1992, the Mass Transit Railway Corporation completed noise mitigation work on the viaducts near Tsui Wan Estate, Chai Wan. It plans to do the same at Heng Fa Chuen, Chai Wan. Meanwhile the Kowloon-Canton Railway Corporation is preparing a comprehensive noise mitigation programme for various locations along its lines.

Controls on the discharge of oily wastes, noxious liquids and other harmful materials from ships have been introduced under the Merchant Shipping (Prevention and Control of Pollution) Ordinance. Among other things, the law sets minimum requirements aboard ocean-going and local vessels to prevent polluting discharges.

Construction and demolition
The noise and vibration of the percussive pile-driver, once so characteristic of Hong Kong's massive construction programme, is now minimised by restricting its operation during the day. Construction industry is no less active, however, and still generates much

372

noise from its operation. Construction activities still generate smoke and dust as well as producing vast quantities of solid waste that need safe disposal.

The Noise Control Ordinance, its regulations and two technical memoranda, are the major instruments for the control of construction noise. The Environmental Protection Department controls the operation of powered mechanical equipment in general construction work during weekday night-time (7 pm to 7 am) and on Sundays and public holidays by means of a construction permit system. The department assesses permit applications in accordance with noise criteria and procedures contained in a technical memorandum. The permits generally specify the number and type of equipment that may be used.

The department has recognised the need to provide controls on specific types of particularly noisy construction equipment during daytime. Hand held percussive breakers and air compressors, which affect tens of thousands of people when being used for demolition and in road works, are the first equipment to come under control. The regulations came into effect on March 1, 1992 and were implemented in stages through the year. All hand held breakers and air compressors must now satisfy stringent noise requirements and need a 'green' noise emission label before they may be used in Hong Kong. There were 2 915 label applications and 2 763 labels issued.

Whenever practical, the department will require the use of silenced equipment and adoption of noise reduction measures to minimise the noise impact. The EPD and the police respond to complaints relating to night-time construction work, and carry out inspections. In 1992, there were 1 670 permit applications; 1 412 permits issued; and 36 prosecutions.

For the construction of the airport core projects, the department issued a total of 80 permits. The Executive Council granted exemptions for the construction of the new airport and the Lantau fixed crossing subject to the provision of noise mitigation measures and stringent monitoring requirements.

The Noise Control Ordinance bans percussive piling from 7 pm to 7 am on weekdays and any time on Sundays and public holidays. Percussive piling at other times is controlled by a permit system, which confines operations to specific hours in a day. It employs a time restriction mechanism so that those piling operations that most affect noise sensitive receivers will be allowed to work fewer hours. This system encourages contractors to use some of the quieter piling methods currently available and to enable noise sensitive receivers to plan their activities to minimise interruption. During 1992 there were 496 permit applications; 495 permits issued; and six prosecutions.

One of the important air pollution concerns in construction and demolition is the control of asbestos. The Air Pollution Control (Amendment) Bill submitted to the Legislative Council in June 1992, proposed to introduce a full range of measures for the control of materials containing asbestos in buildings and ships, registration of asbestos consultants, contractors, supervisors and laboratories, and banning the import and sale of asbestos (amosite and crocidolite). To pave the way for the effective enforcement of the new regulations, the Environmental Protection Department installed a transmission electron microscope in September 1991. This provides analytical support for the definitive identification of asbestos fibres.

During 1992, the department made 360 inspections, mainly on building demolition and renovation sites, including Kowloon Walled City, temporary housing areas, housing estates and private buildings, to ensure any asbestos materials involved were handled and disposed of properly. Its asbestos laboratory, which is covered by the Hong Kong Laboratory Accreditation Scheme, analysed 250 bulk samples and 310 air samples.

Construction and demolition wastes, including dredged material, that meet a tight quality specification, may be dumped at sea, subject to licensing control under the Dumping at Sea Act 1974 (Overseas Territories) Order 1975. Anyone who intends to dump dredged marine spoil or excavated material that is unsuitable for reclamation purposes must first obtain a licence from the Director of Environmental Protection.

Spoil grounds have been designated for the disposal of dredged marine spoil or excavated material unsuitable for reclamation purposes. All marine dumping activities must be carried out at these designated spoil grounds in an appropriate manner in accordance with the marine dumping licence.

In view of the serious impact of illegal spoil dumping on marine life, the Environmental Protection Department has revised its marine dumping action plan. With effect from January 2, 1993, a vessel must be equipped with an automatic self-monitoring device before it can be listed in the marine dumping licence. The device will track all marine dumping operations by keeping a continuous record of the draft and the position of the vessel, so that the authority can trace any illegal dumping, with more cost-effective deployment of control staff.

The department maintains tighter enforcement through frequent marine patrols, strict licensing conditions and prosecution of offenders. It will revoke the licence and refuse a new licence to repeat offenders. During 1992, the department brought four successful prosecutions upon a repeat offender at the District Court resulting in a total fine of $200,000.

Livestock

Indiscriminate disposal of waste from the livestock industry is one of the main causes of pollution in New Territories streams, and is a hazard to the health of many people in Hong Kong. In 1987 a law was made to prevent pollution by livestock waste. It came into effect in June 1988, when livestock keeping was banned in the old urban areas of Hong Kong Island and Kowloon, and in the new towns. At the same time controls over waste disposal came into effect in the first three of 25 areas to which control would be extended over a period of seven years. They were Tolo Harbour, Anglers Beach and Mui Wo. At the end of 1992 about 75 per cent of the original 18 000 active and inactive farms were in areas where pollution control legislation applies.

Complementing these controls is an administrative scheme to help operators affected by them. If an operator wishes to continue in business he is eligible for a grant and a loan to help him pay for pollution control facilities. Since the start of the scheme about $1.6 million has been paid out in capital grants and loans. If an operator chooses to cease business rather than install pollution control equipment he is eligible for an allowance ex gratia to tide him over until he finds other employment. Since the start of the scheme about $500 million has been paid out in allowances, of which about $160 million was paid out in 1992.

During 1992, the livestock waste control scheme stopped pollution equivalent to the raw sewage from 300 000 people being discharged into the environment. This brought to about 55 per cent the total reduction in livestock waste pollution since the inception of the control scheme.

In 1992 there was a review of the livestock waste control scheme, including the legislative provisions. It is proposed that a revised scheme would be introduced, the main elements of which will be licensing of all livestock farms, subject to compliance with pollution controls; the regulations will be made easier to enforce and maximum fines will be raised; and the ban on livestock keeping will be extended.

Ozone – a global responsibility
To control ozone depleting substances, fulfilling Hong Kong's obligation as a party to the Montreal Protocol on Substances that Deplete the Ozone Layer, the Ozone Layer Protection Ordinance was enacted in 1989. This ordinance prohibits local manufacturing of chlorofluorocarbons (CFCs) and bromofluorocarbons (halons), and it restricts the import and export of these substances through licensing and quota controls. In 1992, there were two prosecutions under the ordinance, with fines ranging from $10,000 to $25,000.

Following the second meeting of the parties to the Montreal Protocol in June 1990, the control of ozone depleting substances has been extended in 1993 to 1,1,1-trichloroethane, carbon tetrachloride and 10 other fully halogenated CFCs and the ordinance will be amended accordingly.

As a requirement of the Montreal Protocol, imports of products containing CFCs and halons, such as air conditioning equipment and portable fire extinguishers, from non-party countries will be prohibited starting from May 1993. Subsidiary legislation will be introduced to effect the controls.

Subsidiary legislation banning the venting of CFCs into the atmosphere during the decommissioning or servicing of air conditioning or refrigeration units is also in preparation. While this set of regulations aims to minimise the emission of CFCs into the atmosphere, reducing demand for virgin materials, it will also encourage recovery and recycling within Hong Kong industries in order to cope with the phasing out programme.

Neighbourhood noise
Noise from domestic premises and public places is commonly known as neighbourhood noise. The police carry out enforcement on noise. During 1992, the police dealt with 352 complaints and prosecuted 12 cases.

Provision of Facilities and Services
Every day, Hong Kong produces two million tonnes of sewage and 7 900 tonnes of municipal solid wastes. The government has adopted detailed strategies to deal with these challenges. The sewage strategy requires improved sewage collection facilities under sewerage master plans and a system of deep tunnels and treatment works to treat and dispose of the sewage from the urban area.

During 1992, detailed site investigation and engineering studies continued for the strategic sewage disposal scheme. This will collect the sewage from urban Kowloon and the north and south-west areas of Hong Kong Island for treatment and final disposal via a deep tunnelled outfall into the oceanic currents south of Hong Kong. Continued work on developing and implementing sewerage master plans made good progress during 1992.

Domestic, commercial and industrial wastes, collectively referred to as municipal solid waste, is forecast to increase by 3.2 per cent annually over the next 14 years. By the year 2006 some 12 300 tonnes of municipal solid waste will require collection and disposal each day. The waste disposal plan setting out the framework for management of all waste types was published in late 1989. The plan specifies the waste disposal strategy for the territory and sets out a programme for phasing out old facilities and the provision of new facilities and services.

Sewerage master plans

The existing provision of sewerage in Hong Kong is inadequate. There is a complete absence of sewerage in many developed areas or villages in the rural areas. In areas with some sewerage there is widespread under capacity, heavy siltation and numerous expedient connections of sewage discharges to the storm drains, particularly in the older industrial areas.

To overcome the problem, the government is preparing a total of 16 comprehensive sewage master plans covering all sewage catchments in Hong Kong. These plans form the basis for providing adequate sewer networks to collect and convey sewage to the local treatment facilities. By the end of 1992, eight sewerage master plan studies had been completed while six were part complete.

During 1992, the 'first aid' measures proposed in the Tolo Harbour catchment study on unsewered developments were completed. Construction of the sewerage facilities proposed in both the East Kowloon and the Hong Kong Island South sewerage master plan studies was under way. Detailed designs of the proposed sewerage facilities for Tolo Harbour, North West Kowloon, Tsuen Wan, Kwai Chung and Tsing Yi, Port Shelter, Yuen Long and Kam Tin were in progress.

Sewage treatment and disposal

Shau Kei Wan screening plant and outfall was commissioned in February 1992, and the north west Kowloon sewage treatment and disposal project was completed late in 1992.

Construction of sewerage improvements proposed in the east Kowloon sewerage master plan began in March 1992 and are scheduled for completion late in 1994. The improvement work includes the provision of a relief sewer, dry weather flow interceptors, two pumping stations and associated sewage pumping mains.

A new sewerage system for South Hong Kong Island, proposed in the sewerage master plan study for that area, is being built. The system includes an underground sewage treatment works for Stanley, a screening plant and sewerage at Shek O and a number of pumping stations, one of which will pump sewage from the Repulse Bay area to an existing treatment facility at Aberdeen.

Tolo Harbour effluent export scheme, which is an important element of the Tolo Harbour Action Plan, is now under construction. It aims to reduce the amount of pollution entering the particularly sensitive waters of Tolo Harbour. Stage 1 of the work between Sha Tin and Kai Tak nullah is scheduled for completion in 1993 and completion of Stage 2 between Tai Po and Sha Tin is expected in 1995. On completion, treated effluent from both Tai Po and Sha Tin sewage treatment works will be removed entirely from the Tolo Harbour catchment and discharged to less sensitive waters.

Landfills

Most municipal solid waste is currently disposed of at three landfills, located at Tseung Kwan O, Shuen Wan and Pillar Point Valley, while the rest is incinerated. The current territorial waste disposal strategy is to develop three large landfills in remote areas of the New Territories to provide the necessary capacity for disposal of waste for the next 20 years.

These landfills will be served by a network of refuse transfer stations located in the urban area. The refuse transfer stations will receive waste collected by small refuse collection vehicles and deliver the waste in bulk to the landfills in sealed containers either by road or marine transport thereby reducing the overall transportation cost and minimising environmental nuisances. The landfills and transfer stations will be designed, constructed and operated to the highest environmental standards by experienced waste management contractors.

Tenders for the design, construction and operation of the three landfills are being invited from pre-qualified international waste management contractors. The expected dates of commissioning are West New Territories Landfill, 1993; South-East New Territories Landfill, 1994; and North-East New Territories Landfill, 1995.

The territory produces large quantities of solid wastes from construction activities, some 12 400 tonnes per day during 1992. The disposal of such large quantities of wastes at existing landfills in recent years has led to a short term critical shortage of waste disposal capacity. To overcome this problem the capacity of the existing landfills is being increased and arrangements were made to advance the programme of some reclamation activities so that suitable construction wastes could be used to create land, rather than using up valuable landfill space.

The decomposition of refuse produces not only large quantities of a highly polluting liquid called leachate, but also produces gases, some of which may be explosive under certain circumstances. Studies on the collection, treatment and disposal of landfill gas and leachate generated from the existing and completed landfill sites are being carried out. These studies will identify solutions to mitigate the landfill gas and leachate problems and finalise the requirements for fitting pollution control systems and landfill restoration works. A gas control system was installed at Sai Tso Wan landfill in 1991 and the system is operating satisfactorily with no sign of gas migration off the site.

The phased restoration works programme developed under a study for the completed urban landfills at Jordan Valley, Ma Yau Tong Centre, Ma Yau Tong West, Gin Drinkers Bay and Ngau Chi Wan will proceed in 1993. Studies on the restoration of Tseung Kwan O landfills, the North-West New Territories landfills and Shuen Wan landfill were commissioned in 1992 and the steps to implement restoration works will commence after completion of the studies in 1993.

Refuse transfer stations

As part of its waste disposal strategy, the government is developing a network of refuse transfer stations. They will centralise the collection of refuse and ensure that its transport to remote landfill sites is effective and economical.

The transfer stations will be built to high environmental standards and their development will enable the government to close the poorly located incinerators currently operating in Hong Kong. This will eliminate a significant source of air pollution in the urban area.

The first transfer station at Kowloon Bay has been in service since April 1991. It is operating satisfactorily, processing an average of 1 600 tonnes of municipal refuse per day.

Construction of the second transfer station at Island East was completed in November 1992. Collected refuse is compacted into sealed containers and then delivered to landfill sites by purpose built vessels. After the commissioning of this transfer station, the incinerator at Kennedy Town will be phased out in early 1993 to improve air quality in the vicinity.

Tenders for the third refuse transfer station at Sha Tin were invited from pre-qualified experienced waste management contractors in 1992. The station is expected to be operational in 1994.

A study into the feasibility of building an underground transfer station inside a rock cavern site on the western side of Hong Kong Island was commissioned in 1992. Detailed planning of this underground transfer station is in progress and tenders will be invited in 1993. Consultancy studies for refuse transfer station projects for the outlying islands, Yuen Long and West Kowloon commenced in 1992, with target commissioning dates in 1995 and 1996.

Chemical and special wastes

There were until recently no central treatment facilities for chemical wastes in Hong Kong and there were practical, technological and financial obstacles to local industries having their own. This led the government, in December 1990, to appoint a specialist contractor to design, build and operate a chemical waste treatment centre on Tsing Yi Island.

The centre is the first integrated facility for chemical waste in the region. It was completed in late 1992, and will be fully commissioned in early 1993. It provides collection, transport, treatment and final disposal of chemical waste, helping the waste producers to comply with the law.

The Chemical Waste Treatment Centre serves also as the regional reception point for oily and noxious liquid wastes from ships. This meets Hong Kong's obligations under the International Convention for the Prevention of Pollution from Ships and its Protocol (the Marpol Convention).

Until the full legislative controls come into force, a permit system regulates the disposal of chemical waste at the Tseung Kwan O and Pillar Point Valley landfills. A screening procedure at the Tseung Kwan O waste reception laboratory checks that the wastes delivered to the landfill match the description in the permits. This system ensures a high standard of safety and will detect the delivery of unacceptable wastes.

The asbestos waste action plan, introduced in 1990, continued to be an effective means of ensuring that waste producers and disposal contractors follow safety guidelines in the code of practice on asbestos waste.

With the implementation of legislative control, the permit system is being replaced by new statutory requirements. Most of the chemical wastes are diverted to the chemical waste treatment centre for proper treatment before final disposal.

All chemical wastes and treated residue delivered to the landfill for disposal are chemically analysed in a standard screening procedure. This system will ensure proper 'cradle to grave' tracking and control on all chemical wastes.

In a five year trial, treated sludges from the waterworks and sewage treatment processes at Sha Tin are disposed of at sea near Waglan Island, using a purpose-built vessel. Approximately 40 000 cubic metres of sludge is disposed of every month at the spoil ground, which has been selected after detailed environmental monitoring. Monitoring of the water and marine sediment quality at the spoil ground is continuing in order to provide an early indication of any adverse effects on the environment.

A study of the long term arrangements for the disposal of waterworks and sewage sludges looked into both new and well established technologies, including energy recovery. It recommended that sludges be dewatered, dried, and buried in landfills.

In view of the unsatisfactory disposal arrangements for clinical waste, animal carcasses and some security wastes, a study was made on the development of a central incinerator to dispose of such wastes. It is planned to have a facility in 1995.

The Environmental Protection Department provided a free livestock waste collection service in certain areas, notably the Tolo Harbour, River Indus, the Upper Shenzhen River catchments, and the Tsuen Wan, Tai Lam Chung and Tuen Mun areas. This was to encourage farmers to remove manure solids from their farms and dispose of them responsibly. The manure was transported to a government-operated composting plant at Sha Ling for conversion to compost and eventual recycling. In 1992 some 2 200 tonnes of solid livestock waste were collected and composted.

Monitoring and investigations

The assessment of progress towards policy goals is one of the key activities of the Environmental Protection Department. Its routine monitoring and special investigations form the basis for all the strategic planning, provision of facilities and statutory controls that aim to improve the environment.

The department operates its own marine pollution investigation vessel, which monitors water quality in all 10 of the existing and proposed water control zones. It has a network of nearly 100 monitoring points in inland waters, and keeps 42 publicly managed bathing beaches under surveillance. The results of this monitoring form a comprehensive record of the chemical, physical and microbiological quality of Hong Kong's waters, which goes back to 1972.

All the data are published regularly, and can be made available to scientists and engineers on computer discs or tapes to contribute to their work. Members of the public are usually most interested in the summary reports of bathing water quality, which are issued to the media and published in newspapers every two weeks during summer.

Standards and objectives for water quality draw heavily on the results of water quality monitoring and a number of special investigations that the department carries out. In 1992, work was carried out in cooperation with the Chinese University of Hong Kong, as the third phase of a long term investigation to quantify the link between pollution of bathing waters and health risks.

Another field of investigation is the impact of toxic chemicals in the environment. This leads to an assessment of the safety of specific materials for use in the local environment and to the refinement of effluent standards.

Mathematical models are used in much of the department's water quality assessment work, and the EPD provides a service to other government departments whose activities might have a major impact on the flow and quality of sea water around Hong Kong.

The department operates an air quality monitoring network consisting of 11 stations. The stations are equipped with continuous ambient monitoring instruments for measuring sulphur dioxide, nitrogen oxides, respirable and total suspended particulates (dusts), photochemical oxidants, carbon monoxide and lead.

The results of measurement at the Kwai Chung, Central and Western, and Mong Kok monitoring stations are reported each month and published in the leading newspapers. These stations broadly represent air quality respectively in districts close to industrial areas, in combined commercial and industrial districts, and near road traffic in built-up urban areas.

The department also operates a mobile air quality monitoring laboratory. In 1992, it was used to conduct an air quality study in Chai Wan, where no fixed station has yet been established.

In view of concerns about high nitrogen dioxide levels adjacent to roads, a territory-wide survey of nitrogen oxides concentration was carried out starting from the end of 1991, to supplement measurements made at the fixed air quality monitoring stations. About 100 passive diffusion tube samplers were used to record nitrogen oxide levels. The results so far confirm that nitrogen oxides levels are generally high throughout Hong Kong's busy road network.

The department measures municipal solid waste arisings twice a year to collect up-to-date information for planning future waste disposal facilities. Compared with the 1991 arisings, total waste quantities deposited at landfills and incinerators dropped by 15 per cent to 20 300 tonnes per day in 1992. The decrease was due to a 24 per cent reduction in the amount of construction waste received at the landfills whereas the quantities of domestic waste, industrial waste and commercial waste increased by seven per cent, one per cent and 11 per cent respectively. The decrease in construction waste disposed of at landfills was due to the increased use of such wastes to create land in reclamations.

Local waste recovery activities continued to play an important role in waste management, resulting in the export of substantial quantities of recovered waste materials for recycling overseas. A total of 1.4 million tonnes of waste materials including waste paper, metals and plastic were exported in 1992, generating export earnings of $2.4 billion. About 550 000 tonnes of waste paper, used lubricating oil, metals, plastic scrap and glass were reprocessed locally in 1992.

The government continued to encourage waste separation at source, which will help recycling activities and reduce the demand for scarce landfill space. A pilot scheme for construction waste recycling, involving sorting and reprocessing different types of construction waste, was carried out in May 1992. The main finding of the trial was that a large proportion of construction waste could be used to create land after limited sorting and removal of undesirable material such as wood. It was concluded that much of this separation of different materials in construction wastes could practically take place at source.

The Environmental Protection Department also carries out noise monitoring and surveys. It is concerned about roads in densely populated and congested metropolitan areas. Resurfacing noisy roads with quiet surfacing material will continue to provide relief for people adversely affected by traffic noise.

The need to protect residents from the impact of future operational noise from major development projects is a continuing preoccupation for the noise specialists in the Environmental Protection Department. For example, in the cases of the Western Harbour Crossing and the development of Container Terminal 9, not only quiet surfacing material, barriers and road covers have been thoroughly considered and acoustic insulation will be offered to some 3 000 homes to reduce the noise.

25
POPULATION AND IMMIGRATION

At the end of 1992, there were 5 902 100 people in Hong Kong, comprising 3 003 900 males and 2 898 200 females. This represents an increase of 11.0 per cent on the 1982 population estimate of 5 319 500.

The annual growth rate of the population averaged 1.0 per cent over the 10-year period. The average annual growth of the population was 1.1 per cent during 1983–7, and 1.0 per cent during 1988–92. The slower growth in population during the second half of the decade was partly due to a decrease in the number of births. There was also a net outflow of local residents in recent years.

The rate of natural increase in the population dropped steadily over the 10-year period from 12 to seven per 1 000. This was the result of a declining birth rate, down from 16 per 1 000 in 1982 to 12 per 1 000 in 1992, and a stable death rate, at about five per 1 000.

With its land area of only 1 076 square kilometres, and 5 902 100 people, Hong Kong is one of the most densely-populated places in the world. The overall population density per square kilometre was 5 590 in 1992. The figure conceals wide variations between different areas in the territory. The density in the areas of Hong Kong Island, Kowloon and New Kowloon was 26 450 people per square kilometre, while that in the New Territories was 2 700 per square kilometre. As a result of the continuing development of the new towns, there has been a substantial redistribution of the population from Kowloon and New Kowloon to the New Territories during the past decade, whereas the share of the population on Hong Kong Island showed no significant change. The proportion of the resident population on Hong Kong Island was 22.2 per cent, that in Kowloon and New Kowloon was 33.8 per cent and that in the New Territories was 43.6 per cent.

The age distribution of the population has changed considerably over the past 10 years. In 1982, 24.3 per cent of the population were under 15; in 1992 the figure was 20.5 per cent. On the other hand, the proportion of people aged 65 and above has risen from 6.8 per cent to 8.9 per cent over the same period. Along with these changes, the population aged between 15 and 64 increased from 68.9 per cent in 1982 to 70.6 per cent in 1992. Meanwhile, the dependency ratio – the ratio of the young and the aged to people in the 15 to 64 age group – has dropped from 453 per 1 000 in 1982 to 418 per 1 000 in 1992.

Compared with 10 years ago, the ratio of males to females in the population has declined. In 1992, there were 1 036 males per 1 000 females; in 1982 the figure was 1 079.

It is estimated that some 60 per cent of the people were born in Hong Kong and some 34 per cent in China.

More statistics are given at Appendix 28.

Immigration Department

The work of the Immigration Department falls into two main streams, controlling people moving into and out of Hong Kong, and providing travel documents and registration facilities for local residents. The work embraces such diverse fields as the issue of travel documents, visas and identity cards, naturalisation, and the registration of births, deaths and marriages. Considerable effort also goes into detecting and prosecuting those who breach the immigration laws and repatriating those who have entered Hong Kong illegally.

Immigration policies are framed to limit permanent population growth, and to control the entry of foreign workers. Every effort is made to streamline immigration procedures for Hong Kong residents, tourists and businessmen. At the same time the department aims to prevent either the entry of undesirable persons or the departure of persons wanted for criminal offences.

To take full advantage of advanced information technology and to improve the efficiency, quality and cost-effectiveness of services provided to the public, the department is implementing a long-term information systems strategy. The new system is likely to take four years to come on line. By that time, the department's productivity is expected to improve by between 10 and 15 per cent.

Much of the department's work requires international co-operation both to facilitate legitimate travel and to stop illegal immigration. Immigration officers make regular visits overseas to maintain and enhance liaison with colleagues in other immigration control enforcement agencies.

Immigration Control

Passenger traffic continued to increase in 1992. During the year, 77.0 million passengers travelled in and out of Hong Kong, up 11.4 per cent on the 69.1 million in 1991. Movements to and from China also increased by 14.0 per cent, from 42.1 million in 1991 to 48.0 million in 1992.

The number of visitors from Taiwan also increased from 1.4 million in 1991 to 1.8 million in 1992, up 28.6 per cent. Multiple visit permits, introduced in June 1990, and the 'Jumbo' multiple visit permits introduced in June 1991 were well received.

During the year, a total of 365 000 residents of China visited Hong Kong: 160 000 individually and 205 000 in groups, up 22.1 per cent on the 299 000 in 1991.

To facilitate passenger traffic between Hong Kong and Shenzhen, opening hours at the Lo Wu Terminal were extended from $14\frac{1}{2}$ hours to 16 hours from July 1.

Vehicular traffic to and from China continued to increase in 1992. To relieve congestion at the border crossing points, opening hours at Man Kam To were extended from $12\frac{1}{2}$ hours to 15 hours from July 1. Since then the crossing points at Lok Ma Chau and Sha Tau Kok have opened half an hour earlier.

Legal Immigration

During the year, the number of new arrivals from the mainland remained at about 28 400. Of these, 11 128 were wives, 12 457 were children and 1 082 were husbands of local residents. Thus, some 87 per cent of all such arrivals entered for the purpose of family reunification.

Illegal Immigration

During the year, the number of illegal immigrants arrested increased. On average, there were 97 arrested each day, compared with 70 in 1991 and 76 in 1990. Most illegals came to Hong Kong looking for jobs, attracted by higher wages. Many were drawn by rumours of opportunities on the new airport project. Frequent checks were conducted on construction sites, factories and other places of employment. Illegal immigrants found at places of work were prosecuted and sentenced to imprisonment before being repatriated. Their employers were also prosecuted. Most were fined but, in serious cases, prison sentences were imposed.

Emigration

Emigration has been a feature of life in Hong Kong for over a hundred years. The number of persons leaving Hong Kong increased from an average of 20 000 a year in the early 1980s to 30 000 in 1987 and 60 000 in 1991. The estimate for 1992 was over 60 000. The reason for the increase was a combination of factors: some people were nervous about Hong Kong's future after the change of sovereignty in 1997, while at the same time there were more immigration opportunities available in the more popular destination countries.

Among those who emigrated in 1992, over 23 000 were in professional, technical, administrative and managerial occupations. To counter the outflow of talent, the government has adopted a three-fold strategy: to be more flexible over proposals for importing skills from neighbouring countries; to facilitate the return of former migrants; and to increase the number of graduates from Hong Kong's tertiary institutions.

The government, with the assistance of other governments, also sought to retain people in Hong Kong through various schemes such as the British Nationality Scheme and the United States Deferred Immigrant Visas Scheme. The first phase of the British Nationality Scheme began on December 1, 1990. At the end of 1992 a total of 66 555 applications had been received. Preparations have been made for the second phase of the scheme to begin in early 1994. This scheme enables up to 50 000 persons and their dependants to acquire British citizenship without leaving Hong Kong. The special provision in the United States Immigration Act of 1990, which allows the deferred take-up of immigrant visas up to the end of 2001, would enable the beneficiaries to have the confidence to stay and work in Hong Kong in the next 10 years or so.

Personal Documentation

During the year, a total of 241 000 passports were issued, up 0.1 per cent on 1991. This total included 150 123 passports issued to persons with the status of British National (Overseas). Demand for Certificates of Identity dropped by five per cent to 127 400. There was also a decrease in the demand for re-entry permits which accounted for 36 per cent of the 580 100 travel documents issued.

From mid-1992, people applying for Hong Kong British passports and Certificates of Identity have been able to do so by post. This removed the need for them to attend in person when submitting their applications. The service has proved popular.

With the completion of the Second Identity Card Re-issue Exercise in December 1991, all identity cards issued before July 1, 1987 were declared invalid. Now, there are two types of new identity cards, namely the Hong Kong Permanent Identity Card, which states that the holder has the right of abode in Hong Kong, and the Hong Kong Identity Card which does not state that right. These cards will remain valid beyond July 1, 1997 until they are replaced by the future Hong Kong Special Administrative Region Government. In 1992, 550 000 new identity cards were issued, 273 500 to new arrivals and persons having reached the age of 11 or 18, and 226 200 to persons who had lost or damaged their identity cards or whose identity cards needed amending.

Naturalisation
After the phenomenal increase in 1990, the number of applications for naturalisation levelled off in 1991 but increased again in 1992. During the year, a total of 5 381 applications for naturalisation were received, up 20 per cent on the 4 499 applications in 1991.

Marriages
The registration of marriages, births and deaths is the responsibility of the Immigration Department.

All marriages in Hong Kong are governed by the Marriage Ordinance and the Marriage Reform Ordinance. Under the Marriage Ordinance, at least 15 days' notice of an intended marriage must be given to the Registrar of Marriages. The registrar has discretionary powers to reduce the period of notice if there are special circumstances or to grant a special licence dispensing with notice altogether. But this is done only in exceptional circumstances.

Marriages may take place at any of the 217 places of public worship licensed for the celebration of marriages, or at any of the 10 full-time marriage registries and three part-time sub-registries. Of the 10 full-time marriage registries, four are also open on Sundays. They are the City Hall Marriage Registry, Cotton Tree Drive Marriage Registry, Sha Tin Marriage Registry and Tsim Sha Tsui Marriage Registry. During the year 43 235 marriages were performed in the registries and 2 467 at licensed places of worship. All records are maintained permanently in the General Register Office.

The Marriage Reform Ordinance provides that all marriages entered into in Hong Kong on or after October 7, 1971, shall imply the voluntary union, for life, of one man and one woman to the exclusion of all others. They may be contracted only in accordance with the Marriage Ordinance. Certain customary marriages and others known as 'modern marriages' remain valid, provided that they were entered into before October 7, 1971. Such marriages may be post-registered or dissolved. During the year, 17 customary and 60 'modern marriages' were post-registered.

Special arrangements are made to enable Vietnamese illegal immigrants in detention centres to register their marriages in Hong Kong. In 1992, 1 028 marriages were contracted under these arrangements.

The Registrar of Marriages is also responsible for issuing Certificates of Absence of Marriage Records to local residents. During the year 33 276 such certificates were issued, down 11.91 per cent on the 37 775 in 1991.

Births and Deaths
The registration of births and deaths is compulsory. The General Register Office keeps all records of births and deaths.

During the year, 72 206 live births and 30 528 deaths were registered, compared with 70 135 and 28 685 respectively in 1991. The figures, when adjusted for under-registration, gave a natural increase in population for 1992 of about 40 600 (0.7 per cent).

A birth which has not been registered within one year may be post-registered with the consent of the Registrar of Births and Deaths and on payment of a fee of $120. During the year, 430 births were post-registered in this manner.

Birth registration services in the urban districts are provided by two main registries, one on Hong Kong Island and one in Kowloon. There are also five birth registries in the rural areas. In the outlying areas and islands, births are normally registered at rural committee offices by visiting district registrars. Visiting services are also provided to register the births of babies born in detention centres to Vietnamese illegal immigrants (1 697 in 1992).

There are two death registries, one on Hong Kong Island and one in Kowloon. Deaths in the rural areas are registered at local police stations except in Tsuen Wan and Kwai Chung where deaths are registered in a death registry. Apart from registration of deaths, the death registries issued 1 388 removal permits in 1992 for the purpose of removing bodies for burial outside Hong Kong.

Establishment and Recruitment

At year end, the department had an establishment of 3 498 disciplined staff, 20 (0.6 per cent) less than in 1991. The number of civilian staff was 2 072. During the year, 114 immigration assistants were recruited.

Staff Training

The department provides training for both new and serving officers. Recruits undergo a 12-week induction training which covers law, immigration policies and procedures, foot-drill, physical training, swimming, first-aid and practical attachments. As part of the career development programme, in-service and specialised training is also provided within the department and in outside organisations.

During the year, 112 recruits completed their induction training. A further 3 283 serving officers received various types of job-related, management, development and other aspects of continuation training. Of these, some 13 officers were selected for overseas attachment and training in the United Kingdom, the United States, and Netherlands, France, and Germany.

Vietnamese Migrants

The year saw a major breakthrough for Hong Kong on the Vietnamese migrant problem. Only 12 Vietnamese migrants arrived in 1992, whereas over 16 000 were either settled overseas or repatriated to Vietnam. The corresponding figures for 1991 were 20 200 and 14 200.

In 1989, the international community endorsed a Comprehensive Plan of Action (CPA) for dealing with the Indo-Chinese refugee problem. While the CPA provides that Vietnamese migrants who are classified as refugees under the terms of the 1951 United Nations Convention and 1967 Protocol are eligible for resettlement, it also states that those who are determined not to be refugees should return to Vietnam. The full implementation of the CPA was finally made possible for Hong Kong with the signing of a Statement of

Understanding with the Vietnamese Government on October 29, 1991, which provided for the orderly repatriation of all Vietnamese migrants found to be non-refugees. A total of 367 have since been returned to Vietnam under this programme. The momentum of the voluntary repatriation programme organised by the United Nations High Commissioner for Refugees (UNHCR) also picked up significantly during the course of 1992 reaching an annual record of 12 300 or an average of 1 025 per month.

It is important that migrants returning to Vietnam should be assured that they may do so safely and without fear of persecution. The Hong Kong Government will not send back to Vietnam anyone whom they or the UNHCR believe is a genuine refugee. The Vietnamese Government has given firm guarantees that no returnees will be persecuted. All returnees are closely monitored on their return by the UNHCR to ensure that the guarantees are fully respected. Since March 1989, over 26 700 Vietnamese migrants have returned to Vietnam from Hong Kong and there has not been a single substantiated case of persecution to date.

At the same time, the Hong Kong Government and the international community recognise that while the economy in Vietnam has been improving gradually, returnees may have difficulties in re-establishing themselves on their return. The UNHCR therefore provides financial assistance to returnees to help them to resume their normal lives in Vietnam. The reintegration assistance programme run by the European Community in Vietnam also offers returnees job creation schemes, training courses, start-up loans for businesses and helps finance local infrastructure and health projects. In September 1992, the United States Government announced its intention of contributing US$2 million to fund programmes for assisting in the reintegration of Vietnamese migrants who have returned home. To complement these international efforts, the Hong Kong Government contributed $10 million in July 1992 to finance small-scale infrastructure projects in the poorer migrant producing areas in Vietnam in order to raise living standards and increase employment opportunities for returnees.

By the end of 1992, there were 42 800 Vietnamese migrants and 2 550 refugees in Hong Kong. Of the 42 800 Vietnamese migrants, over 27 000 had been screened out and 15 800 were awaiting screening. The screening policy was introduced on June 16, 1988. Since that date, all new arrivals have been screened to determine their refugee status. The screening process is carried out by immigration officers working under guidelines drawn up in consultation with the office of the UNHCR. Vietnamese screened in as refugees before April 1991 and still awaiting resettlement reside in the Pillar Point Vietnamese Refugee Centre managed by the Hong Kong Housing Services for Refugees Ltd. on behalf of the UNHCR. Those screened in since April 1991 are transferred to the Regional Refugee Transit Centre in Bataan in the Philippines. All those screened out as non-refugees are held in detention centres pending repatriation to Vietnam. They have the right to have their cases reviewed by an independent Refugee Status Review Board (RSRB). Officials of the UNHCR are involved in monitoring the screening process and in preparing cases for review by the RSRB. To speed the pace of refugee status determination, additional resources were injected into the screening process during the year. Over 200 immigration officers, 125 temporary Vietnamese interpreters and six RSRB panels are now engaged in screening work.

Since the introduction of screening, 5 200 have been screened in as refugees and 38 100 have been screened out. At the review stage, in 14 000 cases involving 29 800 persons, the first instance decision has been upheld and in 720 cases involving 1 800 people it has been reversed. The UNHCR has determined 910 people to be refugees under its own mandate.

The resettlement of refugees continued to go satisfactorily in 1992. During the year, 3 430 refugees were resettled overseas with Canada, Australia, and the United States remaining the three major resettlement countries. A total of 1 270 refugees left Hong Kong for the Regional Refugee Transit Centre in Bataan over the same period.

The cost of looking after the 45 350 Vietnamese migrants and refugees in Hong Kong amounted to $1,290 million in 1992. The Hong Kong Government met $996 million of this cost and the United Kingdom Government contributed $80 million to the UNHCR specifically for UNHCR's programme in Hong Kong. While the UNHCR agreed to meet $225 million of the 1992 cost, at the end of 1992 it had yet to repay the Hong Kong Government an outstanding debt of $670 million accumulated since 1989.

In view of the gradual reduction in the size of the camp population, two detention centres were closed during the year. The Argyle Street Detention Centre managed by the Civil Aid Services was closed in April 1992. The Shek Kong Detention Centre was closed down by phases in the later half of 1992, thus releasing over 200 police officers for normal law enforcement duties.

On the eve of the Vietnamese Tet festival in February 1992, a major tragedy occurred in Shek Kong Detention Centre, when 24 Vietnamese died and over 100 were injured in the course of a disturbance triggered off by an argument between northerners and southerners. Following police investigations, a number of Vietnamese migrants were arrested and charged with rioting and murder. A High Court judge was appointed by the Governor to conduct an independent enquiry into the incident. Various recommendations were subsequently made by him to improve security measures and arrangements for dealing with emergency situations in the camps. These recommendations were accepted by the Hong Kong Government and have been implemented by the departments concerned. The tragic incident underlines the dangers of leaving people in camps indefinitely and the urgency of returning people safely to their homes in Vietnam.

Hong Kong is still faced with a major humanitarian problem in trying to care for over 45 350 people in Vietnamese detention and refugee centres. However, an end to the problem appears to be in sight. Given the existing arrival and departure trends, which are expected to continue, the aim is to close all the camps within the next three years.

26
HISTORY

ON December 19, 1984, the Prime Minister of the United Kingdom of Great Britain and Northern Ireland, Mrs Margaret Thatcher, and the Prime Minister of the People's Republic of China, Mr Zhao Ziyang, acting on behalf of their respective governments, signed the Sino-British Joint Declaration on the Question of Hong Kong.

Negotiations leading to the signing of the Joint Declaration had begun after a visit to Peking (Beijing) by the British Prime Minister in September, 1982.

Under the terms of the Joint Declaration, British administration and jurisdiction over Hong Kong will continue to June 30, 1997, and Hong Kong will from July 1, 1997, become a Special Administrative Region (SAR) of the People's Republic of China.

The Joint Declaration provides that for 50 years after 1997, Hong Kong's lifestyle will remain unchanged, and China's socialist system and policies will not be practised in the SAR.

The SAR will have its own government and legislature composed of local inhabitants and will enjoy a high degree of autonomy, except in foreign and defence affairs, which are the responsibilities of the Central People's Government.

So as to ensure a smooth transition to the SAR, the Joint Declaration also provides for the establishment of the Sino-British Joint Liaison Group and the Land Commission. Both sides now meet regularly to conduct consultation on the implementation of the Joint Declaration. (More details about the implementation of the Sino-British Joint Declaration are given in Chapter 4.)

A Place from Which to Trade

Hong Kong's history has been one of material and social improvement: the expansion of cities and towns by cutting into hillsides, reclaiming the land from the sea, and the building of homes, schools, hospitals and other forms of public facilities to meet the demands of the growing population.

Yet, in its early days, the territory was regarded as an uninviting prospect for settlement. The population of about 3 650 was scattered over 20 villages and hamlets and 2 000 fishermen lived on board their boats in the harbour. Its mountainous terrain deficient in fertile land and water, Hong Kong possessed only one natural asset, a fine and sheltered anchorage. Largely the reason for the British presence that began in the 1840s, Victoria Harbour was strategically located on the trade routes of the Far East, and was soon to become the hub of a burgeoning *entrepôt* trade with China.

Hong Kong's development into a commercial centre began with its founding as a settlement under the British flag in 1841. At the end of the 18th century the British dominated the foreign trade at Canton (Guangzhou) but found conditions unsatisfactory, mainly because of the conflicting viewpoints of two quite dissimilar civilisations.

The Chinese regarded themselves as the only civilised people and foreigners trading at Canton were subject to residential and other restrictions. Confined to the factory area, they were allowed to remain only for the trading season, during which they had to leave their families at Macau. They were forbidden to enter the city and to learn the Chinese language. Shipping dues were arbitrarily varied and generally much bickering resulted between the British and Chinese traders. Yet there was mutual trust and the spoken word alone was sufficient for even the largest transactions.

Trade had been in China's favour and silver flowed in until the growth of the opium trade – from 1800 onwards – reversed this trend. The outflow of silver became more marked from 1834, after the East India Company lost its monopoly of the China trade, and the foreign free traders, hoping to get rich quickly, joined the lucrative opium trade which the Chinese had made illegal in 1799. This led to the appointment of Lin Ze-xu (Lin Tse-hsu) in March 1839 as special Commissioner in Canton with orders to stamp out the opium trade. A week later he surrounded the foreign factories with troops, stopped food supplies and refused to allow anyone to leave until all stocks of opium had been surrendered and dealers and ships' masters had signed a bond not to import opium on pain of execution. Captain Charles Elliot, RN, the British Government's representative as Superintendent of Trade, was shut up with the rest and authorised the surrender of 20 283 chests of opium after a siege of six weeks.

Elliot would not allow normal trade to resume until he had reported fully to the British Government and received instructions. The British community retired to Macau and, when warned by the Portuguese Governor that he could not be responsible for their safety, took refuge on board ships in Hong Kong harbour in the summer of 1839.

Lord Palmerston, the Foreign Secretary, decided that the time had come for a settlement of Sino-British commercial relations. Arguing that, in surrendering the opium, the British in Canton (Guangzhou) had been forced to ransom their lives – though, in fact, their lives had never been in danger – he demanded either a commercial treaty that would put trade relations on a satisfactory footing, or the cession of a small island where the British could live free from threats under their own flag.

An expeditionary force arrived in June 1840 to back these demands, and thus began the so-called First Opium War (1840–2). Hostilities alternated with negotiations until agreement was reached between Elliot and Qishan (Keshen), the Manchu Commissioner. Lin had been replaced by Qishan after his exile in disgrace over the preliminaries of a treaty.

Under the Convention of Chuenpi (Chuanbi), January 20, 1841, Hong Kong Island was ceded to Britain. A naval landing party hoisted the British flag at Possession Point on January 26, 1841, and the island was formally occupied. In June, Elliot began to sell plots of land and settlement began.

Neither side accepted the Chuenpi terms. The cession of a part of China aroused shame and anger among the Chinese, and the unfortunate Qishan was ordered to Peking in chains, Palmerston was equally dissatisfied with Hong Kong, which he contemptuously described as 'a barren island with hardly a house upon it', and refused to accept it as the island station that had been demanded as an alternative to a commercial treaty.

'You have treated my instructions as if they were waste paper,' Palmerston told Elliot in a magisterial rebuke, and replaced him. Elliot's successor, Sir Henry Pottinger, arrived in August 1841 and conducted hostilities with determination. A year later, after pushing up the Yangtze River (Chang Jiang) and threatening to assault Nanking (Nanjing), he brought the hostilities to an end by the Treaty of Nanking, signed on August 29, 1842.

In the meantime, the Whig Government in England had fallen and, in 1841, the new Tory Foreign Secretary, Lord Aberdeen, issued revised instructions to Pottinger, dropping the demand for an island.

Pottinger, who had returned to Hong Kong during the winter lull in the campaign, was pleased with the progress of the new settlement and, in the Treaty of Nanking, deviated from his instructions by demanding both a treaty and an island, thus securing Hong Kong. In addition, five Chinese ports, including Canton, were opened for trade. The commercial treaty was embodied in the supplementary Treaty of the Bogue (Humen), October, 1843, by which the Chinese were allowed free access to Hong Kong Island for trading purposes.

Lease of New Territories

The Second Anglo-Chinese War (1856–8) arose out of disputes over the interpretation of the earlier treaties and over the boarding of a British lorcha, the *Arrow*, by Chinese in search of suspected pirates. The Treaty of Tientsin (Tianjin), 1858, which ended the war, gave the British the privilege of diplomatic representation in China. The first British envoy, Sir Frederick Bruce, who had been the first Colonial Secretary in Hong Kong, was fired on at Taku (Dagu) Bar on his way to Peking to present his credentials, and hostilities were renewed from 1859–60.

The troops serving on this second expedition camped on Kowloon peninsula, as the territory's earliest photographs show. Finding it healthy, they wished to retain it as a military cantonment, with the result that Sir Harry Parkes, Consul at Canton, secured from the Viceroy the perpetual lease of the peninsula as far as Boundary Street, including Stonecutters Island. The Convention of Peking, 1860, which ended the hostilities, provided for its outright cession.

Other European countries and Japan subsequently demanded concessions from China, particularly after Germany, France and Russia rescued China from the worst consequences of its defeat by Japan in 1895. In the ensuing tension, Britain felt that efficient defence of Hong Kong harbour demanded control of the land around it.

By a convention signed in Peking on June 9, 1898, respecting an extension of Hong Kong territory, the New Territories – comprising the area north of Kowloon up to the Shum Chun (Shenzhen) River, and 235 islands – was leased for 99 years. The move was directed against France and Russia, not against China whose warships were allowed to use the wharf at Kowloon City. There, Chinese authority was permitted to continue 'except insofar as may be inconsistent with the military requirements for the defence of Hong Kong'. However, an Order in Council of December 27, 1899, revoked this clause and the British unilaterally took over Kowloon City. There was some desultory opposition when the British took over the New Territories in April 1899, but this soon disappeared. The area was declared to be part of the overall territory of Hong Kong but was administered separately from the urban area.

Initial Growth

The new settlement did not go well at first. It attracted unruly elements, while fever and typhoons threatened life and property. Crime was rife. The Chinese influx was unexpected because it was not anticipated they would choose to live under a foreign flag. The population rose from 32 983 (31 463 Chinese) in 1851 to 878 947 (859 425 Chinese) in 1931.

The Chinese asked only to be left alone and thrived under a liberal British rule. Hong Kong became a centre of Chinese emigration and trade with Chinese communities abroad. Ocean-going shipping using the port increased from 2 889 ships in 1860 to 23 881 in 1939. The dominance of the China trade forced Hong Kong to conform to Chinese usage and to adopt the silver dollar as the currency unit in 1862. In 1935, when China went off silver, Hong Kong had to follow suit with an equivalent 'managed' dollar.

Hong Kong's administration followed the normal pattern for a British territory overseas, with a governor nominated by Whitehall and nominated Executive and Legislative Councils with official majorities. The first non-government members of the Legislative Council were nominated in 1850, and the first Chinese in 1880; the first non-government members of the Executive Council appeared in 1896, and the first Chinese in 1926. In 1972, the long-standing arrangement that two electoral bodies – the Hong Kong General Chamber of Commerce and the Unofficial Justices of the Peace – were each allowed to nominate a member to the Legislative Council, was discontinued.

The British residents pressed strongly for self-government on a number of occasions, but the home government consistently refused to allow the Chinese majority to be subject to the control of a small European minority.

A Sanitary Board was set up in 1883, became partly elected in 1887, and developed into an Urban Council in 1936. The intention, at first, was to govern the Chinese through Chinese magistrates seconded from the mainland. But this system of two parallel administrations was only half-heartedly applied and broke down mainly because of the weight of crime. It was completely abandoned in 1865 in favour of the principle of equality of all races before the law. In that year, the Governor's instructions were significantly amended to forbid him to assent to any ordinance 'whereby persons of African or Asiatic birth may be subjected to any disabilities or restrictions to which persons of European birth or descent are not also subjected'. Government policy was *laissez-faire*, treating Hong Kong as a market place where all were free to come and go and where the government held the scales impartially.

Public and utility services developed – the Hong Kong and China Gas Company in 1861, the Peak Tram in 1885, the Hongkong Electric Company in 1889, China Light and Power in 1903, the electric Tramways in 1904 and the then government-owned Kowloon-Canton Railway, completed in 1910. There were successive reclamations dating from 1851 – notably one completed in 1904 in Central District, which produced Chater Road, Connaught Road and Des Voeux Road, and another in Wan Chai between 1921 and 1929.

A system of public education began in 1847 with grants to the Chinese vernacular schools. Later, the voluntary schools – mainly run by missionaries – were included in a grant scheme, in 1873. The College of Medicine for the Chinese, founded in 1887, developed into the University of Hong Kong in 1911 and offered arts, engineering and medical faculties.

After the Chinese revolution of 1911, which overthrew the Manchu Dynasty, there was a long period of unrest in China and large numbers of people found shelter in Hong Kong. The agitation continued after Chinese participation in World War I brought in its wake strong nationalist and anti-foreign sentiment – inspired both by disappointment over failure at the Versailles peace conference to regain the German concessions in Shantung (Shandong), and by the post-war radicalism of the Kuomintang. The Chinese sought to abolish all foreign treaty privileges in China. Foreign goods were boycotted and the unrest spread to Hong Kong, where a seamen's strike in 1922 was followed by a serious general strike in 1925–6 under pressure from Canton. This petered out, though not before causing considerable disruption in Hong Kong. Britain, with the largest foreign stake in China, was at that time a main target of anti-foreign sentiment, but in this role it was soon to be replaced by Japan.

The 1930s and World War II

During World War I, Japan presented its '21 demands' to China. Then, in 1931, Japan occupied Manchuria and the attempt to detach China's northern provinces led to open war in 1937. Canton fell to the Japanese in 1938, resulting in a mass flight of refugees to Hong Kong. It was estimated that some 100 000 refugees entered in 1937, 500 000 in 1938 and 150 000 in 1939 – bringing the population at the outbreak of World War II to an estimated 1.6 million. It was thought that at the height of the influx about 500 000 people were sleeping in the streets.

Japan entered World War II when, on December 7, 1941, its aircraft bombed United States warships at Pearl Harbour and at approximately the same time Japanese armed forces attacked Hong Kong (December 8, 1941, local time). The Japanese invaded Hong Kong from across the mainland border and, subsequently, the British were forced to withdraw from the New Territories and Kowloon on to Hong Kong Island. After a week of stubborn resistance on the island, the defenders – including the local Volunteer Corps – were overwhelmed and Hong Kong surrendered on Christmas Day. The Japanese occupation lasted for three years and eight months.

Trade virtually disappeared, currency lost its value, the supply of food was disrupted and government services and public utilities were seriously impaired. Many residents moved to Macau – the Portuguese province hospitably opening its doors to them. Towards the latter part of the occupation, the Japanese sought to ease the food problems by organising mass deportations. In the face of increasing oppression, the bulk of the community remained loyal to the allied cause. Chinese guerillas operated in the New Territories and escaping allied personnel were assisted by the rural population.

Soon after news of the Japanese surrender was received on August 14, 1945, a provisional government was set up by the Colonial Secretary, Mr (later Sir) Frank Gimson. On August 30, Rear Admiral Sir Cecil Harcourt arrived with units of the British Pacific Fleet, to establish a temporary military government. Civil government was formally restored on May 1, 1946, when Sir Mark Young resumed his interrupted governorship.

The Post-War Years

Following the Japanese surrender, Chinese civilians – many of whom had moved into China during the war – returned at the rate of almost 100 000 a month. The population, which by August 1945 had been reduced to about 600 000, rose by the end of 1947 to an estimated 1.8 million. Then, in the period 1948–9, as the forces of the Chinese Nationalist Government began to face defeat in civil war at the hands of the communists, Hong Kong received an influx unparalleled in its history. Hundreds of thousands of people – mainly from Kwangtung (Guangdong) Province, Shanghai and other commercial centres – entered the territory during 1949 and the spring of 1950. By mid-1950, the population was estimated to be 2.2 million. Since then it has continued to rise and now totals 5.9 million.

After a period of economic stagnation caused by the United Nations' embargo on trade with China, Hong Kong began to industrialise. No longer could the territory rely solely on its port to provide prosperity for its greatly increased population. From the start, the industrial revolution was based on cotton textiles, gradually adding woollens and, in the late 1960s, man-made fibres and made-up garments. Although the share of total exports held by textiles and clothing has declined over the past 10 years, these still make up around 40 per cent of domestic exports by value. While textiles remain the mainstay of Hong Kong's economy, major contributions are made by electronic products, watches and clocks, plastic goods and other light industries.

Associated with events in China, 1966 saw mounting tension in Hong Kong which during 1967 developed into a series of civil disturbances affecting all aspects of life and temporarily paralysing the economy. But, by year-end, the disturbances were contained and the community continued its tradition of peaceful progress.

In development of the post-war years, Hong Kong has continued to build up its role as an *entrepôt* with its neighbours and trade with China has been no exception. Coupled with tourism, this has led to vast improvements in communications with an increasing number of people entering China from or through Hong Kong, its natural gateway, each year. One of the territory's carriers, Dragonair, and three Chinese airlines, namely China Southern Airline, Air China and China Eastern Airlines, operate scheduled, and a considerable number of charter, services between Hong Kong and cities in China. Additionally, three other Chinese airlines, China Southwest Airlines and China Northern Airlines and China Northwest Airlines, operate only charter services between Hong Kong and destinations in China. The Kowloon-Canton Railway runs, jointly with Guangzhou's railway administration, four daily 'through' trains in each direction between Kowloon and Guangzhou. A number of direct bus services operate different routes into Guangdong and other parts of southern China and there are daily ferry services to Guangzhou and other ports in South China, operating with dynamically supported craft as well as conventional ferries.

To keep pace with the development, strong emphasis is placed by the government on infrastructural improvements. The territory has been completely transformed into a modern city with efficient road and rail links, tunnels and flyovers, as well as multi-lane highways which have opened up many hitherto remote areas.

The development of Hong Kong's economic base has enabled the government to increase spending on education, housing, health and social welfare over the years – from $14,399 million in 1982–3 to an estimated $58,787 million in 1992–3.

Starting with emergency measures to house some 50 000 people made homeless in the Shek Kip Mei squatter fire in 1953, Hong Kong's public housing programme now provides rental and self-owned flats of an increasingly higher standard for nearly three million people.

The programme, given impetus by the Long Term Housing Strategy to provide affordable housing for all those in need by the turn of the century, is being implemented by the Housing Authority.

Expenditure on education facilities and improvements for Hong Kong's young and vibrant population has always been one of the major considerations in budget preparations and there are now free and compulsory primary and junior secondary school places for every student up to the age of 15. In 1992, the government was able to provide subsidised Secondary 4 places for about 82 per cent of the 15-year-olds in a continuing programme.

In the field of social welfare, major advances have been made by both the government and non-government organisations in the past decade, with expenditure increasing from $1,585 million in 1982–3 to $6,384 million during 1992–3.

The medical and health services are also undergoing vigorous development programmes which will provide two more major acute public hospitals and some 15 additional clinics and polyclinics over the next decade.

A comprehensive system of labour legislation has been built up to provide for employees' benefits and protection, work injury compensation, industry safety and occupational health. In 1992, the Employees Retraining Ordinance was enacted and the Employees Retraining Board was established to administer the retraining scheme for local employees. There was a growing need to retrain local workers displaced from declining industries as a result of economic restructuring in recent years.

Archaeological Background

Archaeological studies in Hong Kong, which began in the 1920s, have uncovered ancient artefacts and other evidence of human activity at numerous sites along the winding shoreline, testifying to events which span more than 6 000 years. The interpretation of these events is still a matter of academic discussion. Archaeologically, Hong Kong is but a tiny part of the far greater cultural sphere of South China, itself as yet imperfectly known.

Despite suggestions that local prehistoric cultures had developed out of incursions from North China or from South-East Asia, there is a growing number of scholars who believe that the prehistoric cultures within the South China region evolved locally, independent of any major outside influences. There is little dispute on the other hand that these earliest periods, from the close of the 4th millennium BC, must be seen within the framework of a changing environment which experienced sea levels rising from depths as low as 100 metres below the present inexorably submerging vast tracts of coastal plain and establishing a basically modern shoreline and ecology to which human groups present in the area had to adapt or perish.

The stone tools, pottery and other artefacts upon which we rely for an insight into the lives of Hong Kong's ancient inhabitants are for the most part preserved in coastal deposits. This pattern of coastal settlement points to a strong maritime orientation and an economy geared to the exploitation of marine resources. However, it would be unwise to over-emphasise this point, since the discovery of archaeological remains is influenced by many factors governing their survival. To quote one example: the erosion of the hilly terrain has been severe, and evidence of inland settlement, though scanty, is not totally absent.

Recent excavations have revealed two main neolithic cultures lying in stratified sequence. At the lower, older level there is coarse, cord-marked pottery together with a fine, soft fragile pottery decorated with incised lines, perforations and occasionally painted. Chipped and polished stone tools are also present. Current indications suggest a 4th millennium BC date for this initial phase.

Cord-marked pottery and chipped stone tools continue as long-lived traditions into the higher, later levels in which appears a new ceramic form decorated with a wide range of impressed geometric patterns. In this phase, beginning in the mid-3rd millennium BC, polished stone tools show better workmanship and a proliferation of forms, some with steps and shoulders, features probably connected with improvements in hafting techniques. Ornaments such as rings, some slotted, in a range of sizes were also made, sometimes with exquisite craftsmanship, from quartz and other suitable stones.

The final phase of Hong Kong's prehistory is marked by the appearance of bronze at about the middle of the 2nd millennium BC. Bronze artefacts do not seem to have been in common use, but fine specimens of weapons, swords, arrowheads and halberds, and tools such as socketed axes and fish hooks have been excavated from Hong Kong sites. There is evidence, too, from Kwo Lo Wan on Chek Lap Kok and Tung Wan and Sha Lo Wan on Lantau, in the form of stone moulds, that the metal was actually worked locally.

The pottery of the Bronze Age comprises a continuation of the earlier cord-impressed and geometric traditions and a new ware, fired at much higher temperature leading to vitrification. This so-called hard geometric ware is decorated with designs many of which are reminiscent of the geometric patterns of the late neolithic, but with their own distinctive style including the well-known 'Kui-dragon' or 'double F' pattern, so characteristic of this period.

Archaeology is silent on such questions as to the ethnic and linguistic affinities of the ancient peoples. However, some light is shed on these matters at the beginnings of recorded history, for ancient Chinese literary records speak of maritime peoples occupying China's south-eastern seaboard and known to them as 'Yue'. It is probable, therefore, that some at least of Hong Kong's prehistoric inhabitants belonged to the 'Hundred Yue', as this diverse group of peoples were often called.

Interesting archaeological features, almost certainly made by these people, are the rock carvings, most of which are geometric in style, at Shek Pik, on Kau Sai, Po Toi, Cheung Chau and Tung Lung islands and at Big Wave Bay and Wong Chuk Hang on Hong Kong Island.

The military conquest of South China by the north during the Qin and Han dynasties must have brought increasing numbers of Han settlers into the region and exerted a variety of influences on the indigenous populations. These events are testified by the discovery in excavations of coins of the Qin (221–207 BC) and Han (206 BC–220 AD) periods, but the outstanding monument to this turbulent period must undoubtedly be the fine brick-built tomb uncovered at Lei Cheng Uk in 1955 with its fine array of typical Han tomb furniture dateable from the early to middle Eastern Han period.

Archaeological remains from later historic periods are at present still poorly known. Recent work has thrown a welcome light on one aspect of life in the Hong Kong of the Tang Dynasty (618–907 AD) through a study of the dome-shaped lime kilns which are an almost ubiquitous feature of the territory's beaches. Lime, a valuable commodity useful for caulking and protecting wooden boats against marine organisms, waterproofing containers, dressing the acid soils of agricultural fields, building and many other purposes, clearly played an important role in the economy of the period.

Strong traditions link Hong Kong with the events surrounding the Mongol incursions and the concluding chapters of the Song Dynasty in the 13th century AD. The Sung Wong Toi inscription, now relocated near the entrance to the Hong Kong International Airport, the Song Inscription in the grounds of the Tin Hau Temple at Joss House Bay, caches of Song coins from Shek Pik, Mai Po, and recently on Kellet Island and celadons of Song type from various sites, especially Nim Shue Wan and Shek Pik on Lantau, date from this epoch.

Recent archaeological studies are beginning to throw fresh light on events in Hong Kong during the Ming (1368–1644) and Qing (1644–1911) dynasties. These include an analysis of considerable quantities of Ming blue and white porcelain collected in recent years from a site at Penny's Bay, Lantau. The results suggest that this porcelain is very fine quality export ware of the kind which found its ways to the courts of South-East Asia and the West and dates from the first few decades of the 16th century AD. The excavation of the Qing period fort on Tung Lung Island has already revealed fascinating details of the internal arrangements of the fortification and the everyday utensils of a remote garrison during the final stages of Imperial China.

APPENDICES

APPENDICES

APPENDIX 1

Units of Measurement

The Legislative Council enacted a new Weights and Measures Ordinance on July 8, 1987, to replace the legislation made in 1885.

The new ordinance, which came into operation in January 1989, provides comprehensively for a modern system of units of measurement and defines the weights and measures that are lawful for use for trade in Hong Kong.

The government's long-term policy aim is that ultimately only metric units will be used in Hong Kong. However, given Hong Kong's long usage of traditional Chinese and British Imperial units, it is accepted that it will take many years before this policy aim is achieved. Furthermore, Hong Kong's heavy reliance on international trade requires that its industrialists and manufacturers must supply goods to their customers' specifications. Some of Hong Kong's major overseas markets have yet to fully adopt the metric system.

The definitions of units of measurement, and the units of measurement and permitted symbols or abbreviations of units of measurement lawful for use for trade in Hong Kong are contained in the first and second schedules to the Weights and Measures Ordinance. The Weights and Measures Conversion Table which sets out equivalent units of measurement in the Chinese, Imperial, metric and United States systems of measurement is contained in the Weights and Measures Order 1990 made under Section 7 of the Weights and Measures Ordinance. These are reproduced below.

FIRST SCHEDULE

DEFINITIONS OF UNITS OF MEASUREMENT

PART I

Measurement of Length

(a) *Metric Units*

1 kilometre	= 1 000 metres
1 metre	= the length of the path travelled by light in vacuum during a time interval of $\frac{1}{299\ 792\ 458}$ of a second
1 decimetre	= 0.1 metre
1 centimetre	= 0.01 metre
1 millimetre	= 0.001 metre

(b) *Imperial Units*

1 mile	= 1 760 yards
1 furlong	= 220 yards
1 chain	= 22 yards
1 yard	= 0.914 4 metre exactly
1 foot	= $\frac{1}{3}$ yard
1 inch	= $\frac{1}{36}$ yard

(c) *Chinese Units*

1 chek	= 0.371 475 metre
1 tsun	= 0.1 chek
1 fan	= 0.1 tsun

PART II

Measurement of Area

(a) *Metric Units*

1 hectare	= 100 ares
1 are	= 100 square metres
1 square metre	= an area equal to that of a square each side of which measures one metre
1 square decimetre	= 0.01 square metre
1 square centimetre	= 0.01 square decimetre
1 square millimetre	= 0.01 square centimetre

(b) *Imperial Units*

1 square mile	= 640 acres
1 acre	= 4 840 square yards
1 rood	= 1 210 square yards
1 square yard	= an area equal to that of a square each side of which measures one yard
1 square foot	= $\frac{1}{9}$ square yard
1 square inch	= $\frac{1}{144}$ square foot

PART III

Measurement of Volume

(a) *Metric Units*

1 cubic metre	= a volume equal to that of a cube each edge of which measures one metre
1 cubic decimetre	= 0.001 cubic metre
1 cubic centimetre	= 0.001 cubic decimetre
1 litre	= a volume equal to that of a cubic decimetre
1 decilitre	= 0.1 litre
1 centilitre	= 0.01 litre
1 millilitre	= 0.001 litre

(b) *Imperial Units*

1 cubic yard	= a volume equal to that of a cube each edge of which measures one yard
1 cubic foot	= $\frac{1}{27}$ cubic yard
1 cubic inch	= $\frac{1}{1\,728}$ cubic foot

PART IV

Measurement of Capacity

(a) *Metric Units*

1 hectolitre	= 100 litres
1 litre	= a volume equal to that of a cubic decimetre
1 decilitre	= 0.1 litre
1 centilitre	= 0.01 litre
1 millilitre	= 0.001 litre

(b) *Imperial Units*

1 gallon	= 4.546 09 cubic decimetres
1 quart	= $\frac{1}{4}$ gallon
1 pint	= $\frac{1}{2}$ quart
1 gill	= $\frac{1}{4}$ pint
1 fluid ounce	= $\frac{1}{20}$ pint

PART V

Measurement of Mass or Weight

(a) *Metric Units*

1 tonne	= 1 000 kilograms
1 kilogram	= a unit of mass equal to the international prototype of the kilogram kept by the International Bureau of Weights and Measures
1 gram	= 0.001 kilogram
1 metric carat	= $\frac{1}{5}$ gram
1 milligram	= 0.001 gram

(b) *Imperial Units*

1 ton	= 2 240 pounds
1 hundredweight	= 112 pounds
1 quarter	= 28 pounds
1 stone	= 14 pounds
1 pound	= 0.453 592 37 kilogram exactly
1 ounce	= $\frac{1}{16}$ pound
1 dram	= $\frac{1}{256}$ pound
1 grain	= $\frac{1}{7\,000}$ pound
1 ounce troy	= $\frac{12}{175}$ pound

(c) *Chinese Units*

1 picul (tam)	= 100 catties
1 catty (kan)	= 0.604 789 82 kilogram
1 tael (leung)	= $\frac{1}{16}$ catty
1 mace (tsin)	= $\frac{1}{160}$ catty
1 candareen (fan)	= $\frac{1}{1\,600}$ catty
1 tael troy	= 37.429 grams
1 mace troy	= $\frac{1}{10}$ tael troy
1 candareen troy	= $\frac{1}{10}$ mace troy

401

SECOND SCHEDULE

UNITS OF MEASUREMENT AND PERMITTED SYMBOLS OR ABBREVIATIONS OF UNITS OF MEASUREMENT LAWFUL FOR USE FOR TRADE

PART I

Measurement of Length

Metric Units		Imperial Units		Chinese Units
kilometre	km	mile		chek
metre	m	chain		tsun
centimetre	cm	yard	yd	fan
millimetre	mm	foot	ft	
		inch	in	

PART II

Measurement of Area

Metric Units		Imperial Units	
hectare	ha	square mile	
are	a	acre	
square metre	m²	square yard	yd²
square decimetre	dm²	square foot	ft²
square centimetre	cm²	square inch	in²
square millimetre	mm²		

PART III

Measurement of Volume

Metric Units		Imperial Units	
cubic metre	m³	cubic yard	yd³
cubic decimetre	dm³	cubic foot	ft³
cubic centimetre	cm³	cubic inch	in³
litre	L		

PART IV

Measurement of Capacity

Metric Units		Imperial Units	
cubic metre	m³	gallon	gal
hectolitre	hL	quart	qt
litre	L	pint	pt
millilitre	mL	gill	
		fluid ounce	fl. oz

PART V

Measurement of Mass or Weight

Metric Units		Imperial Units		Chinese Units
tonne	t	ton		picul
kilogram	kg	hundredweight	cwt	catty
gram	g	quarter	qr	tael
carat (metric)	CM	stone		mace
milligram	mg	pound	lb	candareen
		ounce	oz	tael troy
		dram	dr	mace troy
		grain	gr	candareen troy
		ounce, troy	oz tr	

WEIGHTS AND MEASURES ORDER 1990

WEIGHTS AND MEASURES CONVERSION TABLE

1. Measurement of Length (see note 2)

(a)

Metric Units and Symbols		Imperial Units	Chinese Units
1 kilometre	km = 1 000 metres	= 0.621 371 mile	= 2 691.97 cheks
1 metre	m	= 3.280 84 feet	= 2.691 97 cheks
1 centimetre	cm = 0.01 metre	= 0.393 701 inch	= 2.691 97 fans
1 millimetre	mm = 0.001 metre	= 0.039 370 1 inch	= 0.269 197 fan

(b)

Imperial Units and Symbols		Metric Units	Chinese Units
1 mile	= 1 760 yards	= 1.609 344 kilometres exactly	= 4 332.31 cheks
1 chain	= 22 yards	= 20.116 8 metres exactly	= 54.153 8 cheks
1 yard	yd = 1/22 chain	= 0.914 4 metre exactly	= 2.461 54 cheks
1 foot	ft = 1/3 yard	= 30.48 centimetres exactly	= 8.205 13 tsuns
1 inch	in = 1/36 yard	= 25.4 millimetres exactly	= 6.837 61 fans

(c)

Chinese Units		Metric Units	Imperial Units
1 chek		= 0.371 475 metre	= 1.218 75 feet
1 tsun	= 0.1 chek	= 3.714 75 centimetres	= 1.462 50 inches
1 fan	= 0.1 tsun	= 3.714 75 millimetres	= 0.146 250 inch

2. Measurement of Area (see note 3)

(a)

Metric Units and Symbols		Imperial Units
1 hectare	ha = 100 ares	= 2.471 05 acres
1 are	a = 100 square metres	= 119.599 square yards
1 square metre	m²	= 10.763 9 square feet
1 square decimetre	dm² = 0.01 square metre	= 15.500 0 square inches
1 square centimetre	cm² = 0.01 square decimetre	= 0.155 000 square inch
1 square millimetre	mm² = 0.01 square centimetre	= 0.001 550 00 square inch

(b)

Imperial Units and Symbols		Metric Units
1 square mile	= 640 acres	= 258.999 hectares
1 acre	= 4 840 square yards	= 40.468 6 ares
1 square yard	yd²	= 0.836 127 square metre
1 square foot	ft² = 1/9 square yard	= 0.092 903 0 square metre
1 square inch	in² = 1/144 square foot	= 6.451 6 square centimetres exactly

3. Measurement of Volume (see note 4)

(a)

Metric Units and Symbols		Imperial Units
1 cubic metre	m³	= 1.307 95 cubic yards
1 cubic decimetre	dm³ = 0.001 cubic metre	= 0.035 314 7 cubic foot
1 cubic centimetre	cm³ = 0.001 cubic decimetre	= 0.061 023 7 cubic inch
1 litre	L = 1 cubic decimetre	= 61.023 7 cubic inches

(b)

Imperial Units and Symbols		Metric Units
1 cubic yard	yd³	= 0.764 555 cubic metre
1 cubic foot	ft³ = 1/27 cubic yard	= 28.316 8 cubic decimetres or litres
1 cubic inch	in³ = 1/172 8 cubic foot	= 16.387 1 cubic centimetres

4. Measurement of Capacity

(a)

Metric Units and Symbols		Imperial Units	US Units
1 cubic metre	m³ = 1 000 litres	= 219.969 gallons	= 264.172 gallons
1 hectolitre	hL = 100 litres	= 21.996 9 gallons	= 26.417 2 gallons
1 litre	L	= 35.195 1 fluid ounces	= 33.814 0 fluid ounces
		= 1.759 75 pints	= 2.113 38 liquid pints
			= 1.816 17 dry pints
1 millilitre	mL = 0.001 litre	= 0.035 195 1 fluid ounce	= 0.033 814 0 fluid ounce

(b)	Imperial Units and Symbols		Metric Units	US Units
1 gallon	gal = 160 fluid ounces		= 4.546 09 litres	= 1.200 95 gallons
1 quart	qt = 1/4 gallon		= 1.136 52 litres	= 1.200 95 liquid quarts
				= 1.032 06 dry quarts
1 pint	pt = 1/2 quart		= 0.568 261 litre	= 1.200 95 liquid pints
				= 1.032 06 dry pints
1 gill	= 1/4 pint		= 142.065 millilitres	= 1.200 95 gills
1 fluid ounce	fl oz = 1/20 pint		= 28.413 1 millilitres	= 0.960 760 fluid ounce

(c)	US Units		Metric Units	Imperial Units
1 gallon	= 128 fluid ounces		= 3.785 41 litres	= 0.832 674 gallon
1 liquid quart	= 1/4 gallon		= 0.946 353 litre	= 0.832 674 quart
1 liquid pint	= 1/2 liquid quart		= 0.473 176 litre	= 0.832 674 pint
1 gill	= 1/4 liquid pint		= 0.118 294 litre	= 0.832 674 gill
1 fluid ounce	= 1/16 liquid pint		= 29.573 5 millilitres	= 1.040 84 fluid ounces
1 dry quart			= 1.101 22 litres	= 0.968 939 quart
1 dry pint	= 1/2 dry quart		= 0.550 610 litre	= 0.968 939 pint

5. Measurement of Mass or Weight (see note 5)

(a)	Metric Units and Symbols		Imperial Units	Chinese Units	US Units
1 tonne	t = 1 000 kilograms		= 0.984 207 ton	= 16.534 7 piculs	= 1.102 31 short tons
1 kilogram	kg		= 2.204 62 pounds	= 1.653 47 catties	= 2.204 62 pounds
1 gram	g = 0.001 kilogram		= 0.035 274 0 ounce	= 0.026 455 5 tael	= 0.035 274 0 ounce
1 metric carat	CM = 0.2 gram		= 3.086 47 grains	= 0.052 911 0 mace	= 3.086 47 grains
1 gram	g		= 0.032 150 7 ounce troy	= 2.671 73 candareen troy	= 0.032 150 7 ounce troy

(b)	Imperial Units and Symbols		Metric Units	Chinese Units	US Units
1 ton	= 2 240 pounds		= 1.016 05 tonnes	= 16.800 0 piculs	= 1.12 short tons exactly
1 hundredweight	cwt = 112 pounds		= 50.802 3 kilograms	= 84.000 0 catties	= 1.12 short hundredweights exactly
1 quarter	qr = 28 pounds		= 12.700 6 kilograms	= 21.000 0 catties	= 1 quarter
1 stone	= 14 pounds		= 6.350 29 kilograms	= 10.500 0 catties	= 1 stone
1 pound	lb = 16 ounces		= 0.453 592 37 kilogram exactly	= 0.750 000 catty	= 1 pound
	= 256 drams				
	= 7 000 grains			= 0.750 000 tael	
1 ounce	oz = 1/16 pound		= 28.349 5 grams	= 0.750 000 tael	= 1 ounce
1 dram	dr = 1/256 pound		= 1.771 85 grams	= 0.468 750 mace	= 1 dram
1 grain	gr = 1/7 000 pound		= 0.064 798 9 gram	= 0.171 429 candareen	= 1 grain
1 ounce troy	oz tr = 12/175 pound		= 31.103 5 grams	= 0.831 000 tael troy	= 1 ounce troy

(c)	Chinese Units		Metric Units	Imperial Units	US Units
1 picul	= 100 catties		= 60.479 0 kilograms	= 133.333 pounds	= 133.333 pounds
1 catty			= 0.604 789 82 kilogram	= 21.333 3 ounces	= 21.333 3 ounces
1 tael	= 1/16 catty		= 37.799 4 grams	= 1.333 33 ounces	= 1.333 33 ounces
1 mace	= 1/160 catty		= 3.779 94 grams	= 2.133 33 drams	= 2.133 33 drams
1 candareen	= 1/1 600 catty		= 377.994 milligrams	= 5.833 33 grains	= 5.833 33 grains
1 tael troy			= 37.429 grams	= 1.203 37 ounces troy	= 1.203 37 ounces troy
1 mace troy	= 1/10 tael troy		= 3 742.9 milligrams	= 0.120 337 ounce troy	= 0.120 337 ounce troy
1 candareen troy	= 1/10 mace troy		= 374.29 milligrams	= 0.012 033 7 ounce troy	= 0.012 033 7 ounce troy

(d)	US Units		Metric Units	Imperial Units
1 short ton	= 2 000 pounds		= 0.907 185 tonne	= 0.892 857 ton
1 short hundredweight	= 0.05 short ton		= 45.359 2 kilograms	= 0.892 857 hundredweight

Notes

1. 'US' means United States.
2. In item 1, US units of length are the same as those in the Imperial system.
3. In item 2, US units of area are the same as those in the Imperial system.
4. In item 3, US units of volume are the same as those in the Imperial system.
5. In item 5, except short ton and short hundredweight, US units of mass or weight are the same as those in the Imperial system.

APPENDIX 2
(Chapter 2: Constitution and Administration)

The Executive Council

Type of
appointment   *Names of Members on January 2, 1993*

Presided over by His Excellency the Governor
The Right Honourable Christopher Francis PATTEN

Members:

Ex-officio	The Chief Secretary The Honourable Sir David FORD, KBE, LVO, JP
Ex-officio	The Commander British Forces The Honourable Major General J. P. FOLEY, CB, OBE, MC
Ex-officio	The Financial Secretary The Honourable N. W. H. MACLEOD, CBE, JP
Ex-officio	The Attorney General The Honourable J. F. MATHEWS, CMG, JP
Appointed	The Right Honourable The Baroness DUNN, DBE, JP
Appointed	The Honourable Sir William PURVES, CBE, DSO, JP
Appointed	The Honourable Rosanna WONG Yick-ming, OBE, JP
Appointed	The Honourable Mrs Anson CHAN, CBE, JP (Secretary for Economic Services)
Appointed	The Honourable John CHAN Cho-chak, LVO, OBE, JP (Secretary for Education and Manpower)
Appointed	The Honourable Denis CHANG Khen-lee, QC, JP
Appointed	Professor the Honourable Edward CHEN Kwan-yiu
Appointed	Dr the Honourable Raymond CH'IEN Kuo-fung
Appointed	The Honourable Andrew LI Kwok-nang, CBE, QC, JP
Appointed	Professor the Honourable Felice LIEH MAK, OBE, JP
Appointed	The Honourable Michael SZE Cho-cheung, ISO, JP (Secretary for Constitutional Affairs)
Appointed	The Honourable TUNG Chee-hwa

APPENDIX 3
(Chapter 2: Constitution and Administration)

The Legislative Council

Type of appointment	*Names of Members on January 2, 1993*
	President:
Ex-officio	His Excellency the Governor The Right Honourable Christopher Francis PATTEN
	Deputy President:
Appointed	The Honourable J. J. SWAINE, CBE, QC, JP
	Members:
Ex-officio	The Chief Secretary The Honourable Sir David FORD, KBE, LVO, JP
Ex-officio	The Financial Secretary The Honourable N. W. H. MACLEOD, CBE, JP
Ex-officio	The Attorney General The Honourable J. F. MATHEWS, CMG, JP
Appointed	The Honourable Allen LEE Peng-fei, CBE, JP
Elected	The Honourable Stephen CHEONG Kam-chuen, CBE, JP
Appointed	The Honourable Mrs Selina CHOW LIANG Shuk-yee, OBE, JP
Elected	The Honourable HUI Yin-fat, OBE, JP
Elected	The Honourable Martin LEE Chu-ming, QC, JP
Elected	The Honourable David LI Kwok-po, OBE, JP
Elected	The Honourable NGAI Shiu-kit, OBE, JP
Elected	The Honourable PANG Chun-hoi, MBE
Elected	The Honourable SZETO Wah
Elected	The Honourable TAM Yiu-chung
Elected	The Honourable Andrew WONG Wang-fat, OBE, JP
Elected	The Honourable LAU Wong-fat, OBE, JP
Elected	The Honourable Edward HO Sing-tin, OBE, JP
Elected	The Honourable Ronald Joseph ARCULLI, JP
Appointed	The Honourable Martin Gilbert BARROW, OBE, JP
Appointed	The Honourable Mrs Peggy LAM, OBE, JP
Appointed	The Honourable Mrs Miriam LAU Kin-yee, OBE, JP
Appointed	The Honourable LAU Wah-sum, OBE, JP
Elected	Dr the Honourable LEONG Che-hung, OBE

Type of appointment	*Names of Members on January 2, 1993*
Elected	The Honourable James David McGregor, OBE, ISO, JP
Elected	The Honourable Mrs Elsie Tu, CBE
Elected	The Honourable Peter Wong Hong-yuen, OBE, JP
Elected	The Honourable Albert Chan Wai-yip
Appointed	The Honourable Vincent Cheng Hoi-chuen
Appointed	The Honourable Moses Cheng Mo-chi
Appointed	The Honourable Marvin Cheung Kin-tung, JP
Elected	The Honourable Cheung Man-kwong
Elected	The Honourable Chim Pui-chung
Elected	Rev the Honourable Fung Chi-wood
Elected	The Honourable Frederick Fung Kin-kee
Appointed	The Honourable Timothy Ha Wing-ho, MBE, JP
Elected	The Honourable Michael Ho Mun-ka
Elected	Dr the Honourable Huang Chen-ya
Elected	The Honourable Simon Ip Sik-on, JP
Appointed	Dr the Honourable Lam Kui-chun
Elected	Dr the Honourable Conrad Lam Kui-shing
Elected	The Honourable Lau Chin-shek
Elected	The Honourable Emily Lau Wai-hing
Elected	The Honourable Lee Wing-tat
Elected	The Honourable Gilbert Leung Kam-ho
Appointed	The Honourable Eric Li Ka-cheung, JP
Elected	The Honourable Fred Li Wah-ming
Elected	The Honourable Man Sai-cheong
Appointed	The Honourable Steven Poon Kwok-lim
Appointed	The Honourable Henry Tang Ying-yen, JP
Elected	The Honourable Tik Chi-yuen
Elected	The Honourable James To Kun-sun
Elected	Dr the Honourable Samuel Wong Ping-wai, MBE, JP
Elected	Dr the Honourable Philip Wong Yu-hong
Elected	The Honourable Zachery Wong Wai-yin
Elected	Dr the Honourable Yeung Sum
Elected	The Honourable Howard Young, JP
Elected	Dr the Honourable Tang Siu-tong, JP
Appointed	The Honourable Christine Loh Kung-wai
Appointed	The Honourable Roger Luk Koon-hoo
Appointed	The Honourable Anna Wu Hung-yuk

407

APPENDIX 4
(Chapter 2: Constitution and Administration)

Urban Council

Names of Members on January 2, 1993

Chairman:

Elected by Urban Council   Dr Ronald LEUNG Ding-bong, OBE, JP (A)

Vice-Chairman:

Elected by Urban Council   Mr Lo King-man, MBE, JP (A)

Members:
Mr B. A. BERNACCHI, OBE, QC, JP (E)
The Honourable Mrs Elsie TU, CBE (E)
Miss Cecilia YEUNG Lai-yin (E)
Mr Stephen LAU Man-lung, OBE, JP (A)
Mr Joseph CHAN Yuek-sut (E)
Mr PAO Ping-wing, JP (E)
The Honourable Frederick FUNG Kin-kee (E)
Dr the Honourable Samuel WONG Ping-wai, MBE, JP (A)
The Honourable Marvin CHEUNG Kin-tung, JP (A)
The Honourable MAN Sai-cheong (E)
Mr CHAN Kwok-ming (E)
Mr Ronnie WONG Man-chiu, JP (A)
Mrs Eleanor LING Ching-man, JP (A)
Mr Paul YOUNG Tze-kong, JP (A)
Dr Stan CHEUNG Tsang-kay, JP (A)
Mr Jason YUEN King-yuk (A)
Mr MA Lee-wo (E)
Mr MOK Ying-fan (E)
Mr Daniel WONG Kwok-tung (E)
Mr CHAN Tak-chor (E)
Miss Christina TING Yuk-chee, JP (R)
Mr Ambrose CHEUNG Wing-sum (R)
Mr Albert POON Shun-kwok (R)
Mr FUNG Kwong-chung (R)
Mr Thomas KWOK Ping-kwong, JP (A)
Mr Vincent CHOW Wing-shing (A)
Ms Carlye TSUI Wai-ling (A)
Mr Ronald POON Cho-yiu (A)
Dr LEUNG Ping-chung (A)
Mr WONG Shui-lai (E)
Mr San Stephen WONG Hon-ching (E)
Mr CHIANG Sai-cheong (E)
The Honourable Fred LI Wah-ming (E)
Mr WONG Siu-yee (R)
Ms YEUNG Kam-chun (R)
Mr YIM Kwok-on (R)
Ms Anna TANG King-yung (R)
Mr IP Kwok-chung (R)

   Note: (E) = Elected.   (A) = Appointed.   (R) = Representative.

APPENDIX 5
(Chapter 2: Constitution and Administration)

Regional Council

Names of Members on January 2, 1993

Chairman:
Mr CHEUNG Yan-lung, CBE, JP (A)

Vice-Chairman:
Dr PANG Hok-tuen, JP (A)

Members:
The Honourable Albert CHAN Wai-yip (E)
Mr CHAU Chun-wing (A)
Mr CHAU How-chen, MBE, JP (A)
Mr CHEUNG Hon-chung (E)
Mr CHEUNG Hon-kau, MBE (A)
Mr CHEUNG Kan-kwai (A)
Mr CHEUNG Kuen, MBE (R)
Dr Fanny CHEUNG Mui-ching, JP (A)
Mr CHOW Yick-hay (E)
Mr CHOW Yuk-tong (R)
Mr FONG Loi (A)
Rev the Honourable FUNG Chi-wood (E)
Mr FUNG Pak-tai (E)
Dr Ho Man-wui, JP (A)
Mr Ho Sun-kuen, JP (A)
Mr LAI Kwok-iu (R)
Mr Daniel LAM Wai-keung, JP (Ex)
Mr LAU Kong-wah (E)
The Honourable LAU Wong-fat, OBE, JP (Ex)
The Honourable Gilbert LEUNG Kam-ho (E)
Mr LIU Ching-leung, JP (Ex)
Mr NGAN Kam-chuen (E)
Mr POON Chin-hung (A)
Mr SIN Chung-kai (R)
Mr So Shiu-shing (R)
Mr TANG Pui-tat (R)
Mr TING Yin-wah (E)
Mr TSO Shiu-wai (E)
Mr WAN Yuet-kau (R)
Mr Johnston WONG Hong-chung (E)
Mr WONG Luen-kin (R)
Mr WONG Po-ming, JP (A)
Mr David YEUNG Fuk-kwong (R)
Mr YIM Tin-sang (E)

Note: (A) = Appointed. (E) = Elected. (R) = Representative (District Board). (Ex) = Ex-officio (Heung Yee Kuk).

APPENDIX 6

I. Overseas Representation in Hong Kong

(A) Commonwealth Countries

Countries	Represented by	Countries	Represented by
Antigua and Barbuda	Honorary Consul	Mauritius	Honorary Consul
Australia	Consul-General	New Zealand	Commissioner
Bangladesh	Commissioner	Nigeria	Commissioner
Barbados	Honorary Consul	Pakistan	Consul-General
Botswana	Consul-in-Charge	Papua New Guinea	Honorary Consul
Canada	Commissioner	St Lucia	Honorary Consul
Commonwealth of Dominica	Consul-General	Seychelles	Honorary Consul
		Sierra Leone	Honorary Consul
Cyprus	Honorary Consul	Singapore	Commissioner
Grenada	Honorary Consul	Sri Lanka	Honorary Consul
India	Commissioner	Tonga	Honorary Consul
Jamaica	Honorary Consul	Trinidad and Tobago	Honorary Consul
Malaysia	Commissioner	Western Samoa	Honorary Consul
Maldives	Honorary Consul		
Malta	Honorary Consul		

(There also is a Senior British Trade Commissioner)

(B) Foreign Countries

Countries	Represented by	Countries	Represented by
Argentina	Consul-General	Korea	Consul-General
Austria	Consul-General	Liberia	Honorary Consul
Belgium	Consul-General	Luxembourg	Honorary Consul
Benin	Honorary Consul	Mexico	Consul-General
Bhutan	Honorary Consul	Monaco	Honorary Consul
Brazil	Consul-General	Mongolia	Honorary Consul
Central Africa	Honorary Consul	Morocco	Honorary Consul
Chile	Consul-General	Mozambique	Honorary Consul
Colombia	Consul-General	Myanmar	Consul-General
Costa Rica	Consul-General	Netherlands	Consul-General
Cote D'Ivoire	Honorary Consul	Nicaragua	Honorary Consul
Denmark	Consul-General	Norway	Consul-General
Dominican Republic	Consul-General	Oman	Honorary Consul
Egypt	Consul-General	Panama	Consul-General
Fiji	Honorary Consul	Paraguay	Honorary Consul
Finland	Consul-General	Peru	Consul-General
France	Consul-General	Philippines	Consul-General
Gabon	Honorary Consul	Poland	Consul-in-Charge
Germany	Consul-General	Portugal	Consul-General
Greece	Honorary Consul-General	South Africa	Consul-General
		Spain	Consul-General
Guinea	Honorary Consul	Sweden	Consul-General
Honduras	Honorary Consul	Switzerland	Consul-General
Iceland	Honorary Consul	Thailand	Consul-General
Indonesia	Consul-General	Togo	Honorary Consul
Ireland	Honorary Consul	Turkey	Consul-General
Israel	Consul-General	United States of America	Consul-General
Italy	Consul-General		
Japan	Consul-General	Uruguay	Consul-General
Jordan	Honorary Consul	Venezuela	Consul-General

II. Hong Kong Representation Overseas

GOVERNMENT OFFICES

EUROPE

Brussels
Hong Kong Economic and Trade Office,
Avenue Louise, 228, 1050 Brussels, Belgium.
Tel.: (02) 648-38-33   Cable: HONREP BRUSSELS
Fax: (02) 640-66-55

Geneva
Hong Kong Economic and Trade Office,
37–39 rue de Vermont, 1211 Geneva 20, Switzerland.
Tel.: (022) 734-90-40   Telex: 414196 HKGV CH
Fax: (022) 733-99-04

London
Hong Kong Government Office,
6 Grafton Street, London W1X 3LB, England.
Tel.: (071) 499-9821   Cable: HONGAID LONDON
Fax: (071) 495-5033

NORTH AMERICA

New York
Hong Kong Economic and Trade Office,
British Consulate General, 680 Fifth Avenue,
22nd Floor, New York, NY 10019, USA
Tel.: (212) 265-8888   Fax: (212) 974-3209

San Francisco
Hong Kong Economic and Trade Office,
British Consulate General, 222 Kearny Street,
Suite 402, San Francisco, CA 94108, USA
Tel.: (415) 397-2215   Fax: (415) 421-0646

Washington
Hong Kong Economic and Trade Office,
British Embassy, 1150, 18th Street,
NW Suite 475, Washington DC 20036, USA
Tel.: (202) 331-8947
Cable: PRODROME WASHINGTON
Fax: (202) 331-8958

Toronto
Hong Kong Economic and Trade Office,
Suite 5900, One First Canadian Place,
Toronto, Ontario, M5X 1K2 Canada.
Tel.: (416) 777-2209   Fax: (416) 777-2217

ASIA

Tokyo
Hong Kong Economic and Trade Office,
7th Floor, Nishi-Azabu Mitsui Building,
4-17-30, Nishi-Azabu,
Minato-ku, Tokyo 106, Japan.
Tel.: 81-3-3498-8808   Fax: 81-3-3498-8815

Industrial Promotion Units

EUROPE

Brussels
Industrial Promotion Unit,
Hong Kong Economic and Trade Office,
Avenue Louise 228, 1050 Brussels, Belgium.
Tel.: (02) 648-3966   Fax: (02) 640-6655

London
Industrial Promotion Unit,
Hong Kong Government Office,
6 Grafton Street, London W1X 3LB, England.
Fax: (071) 495-5033

NORTH AMERICA

New York
Industrial Promotion Unit,
Hong Kong Economic and Trade Office,
680 Fifth Avenue, 22nd Floor, New York.
NY 10019, USA
Tel.: (212) 265-7232   Fax: 212 974-3209

San Francisco
Industrial Promotion Unit,
Hong Kong Economic and Trade Office,
222 Kearny Street,
Suite 402, San Francisco, CA 94108, USA
Tel.: (415) 956-4560   Fax: (415) 421-0646

ASIA

Tokyo
Industrial Promotion Unit,
Hong Kong Economic and Trade Office,
7th Floor, Nishi-Azabu Mitsui Building,
4-17-30, Nishi-Azabu, Minato-ku,
Tokyo 106, Japan.
Tel.: 81-3-3498-8808   Fax: 81-3-3498-8815

411

OTHER ORGANISATIONS

Hong Kong Trade Development Council

EUROPE

Amsterdam
Prinsengracht 771, Ground Floor,
1017 JZ Amsterdam, The Netherlands.
Tel.: 31-(020)-627-7101
Cable: CONOTRAD AMSTERDAM
Fax: 31-(020)-622-8529

Athens
48, Aegialias Street, Paradissos,
GR 151 25 Amaroussion, Greece.
Tel.: 30-(1)-685-0830   Fax: 30-(1)-685-0832
        30-(1)-685-2610
(Trade enquiries only)

Barcelona
Balmes, 184 Atico,
08006 Barcelona, Spain.
Tel.: 34-(3)-415-8382   Fax: 34-(3)-416-0148
        34-(3)-415-6628
        34-(3)-415-9458

Budapest
1117 Budapest, Kaposvari u. 5–7
Hungary.
Tel.: 36-(1)-181-3398, 166-6476
Fax: 36-(1)-161-2458

Frankfurt
Kreuzerhohl 5–7, D-6000 Frankfurt/Main 50
Germany.
Tel.: 49-(069)-586011
Cable: CONOTRAD FRANKFURT
Fax: 49-(069)-5890752
Postal Address: P.O. Box 500551
D-6000 Frankfurt/Main 50, Germany

Istanbul
Piyalepasa Bulvari, Kastel Is Merkezi,
D. Blok Kat: 5, 80370 Piyalepasa,
Istanbul, Turkey.
Tel.: 90-(1)-237-02-25   Fax: 90-(1)-254-98-67

London
Swire House, Ground Floor, 59 Buckingham Gate,
London SW1E 6AJ, England.
Tel.: (44)-071-828-1661
Cable: CONOTRAD LONDON SW1
Fax: 44-(071)-828-9976

For trade enquiries in the UK
call 0800-282-980

Milan
2 Piazzetta Pattari, 20122 Milan, Italy.
Tel.: 39-(02)-865405, 865715
Cable: KONGTRAD MILAN
Telex: 333508 HKTDC I   Fax: 39-(02)-860304

Paris
18, rue d'Aguesseau,
75008 Paris, France.
Tel.: 33-(01)-47-42-41-50   Telex: 283098 HKTDC F
Fax: 33-(01)-47-42-77-44

Stockholm
Kungsgatan 6, S-111 43 Stockholm, Sweden.
Tel.: 46-(08)-100677, 115690
Cable: CONOTRAD STOCKHOLM
Telex: 11993 TDC S   Fax: 46-(08)-7231630
Postal Address: P.O. Box 7075
103 92 Stockholm, Sweden

Vienna
Rotenturmstrasse 1-3/8/24, A-1010 Vienna, Austria.
Tel.: 43-(01)-533-98-18
Cable: CONOTRADREP WIEN
Telex: 115079 HKTDC A   Fax: 43-(01)-535-31-56

Zurich
Seestrasse 135, Postfach CH-8027 Zurich,
Switzerland
Tel.: 41-(01)-281-31-55   Fax: 41-(01)-281-31-91

NORTH AMERICA

For trade enquiries in the US
call 1-800-TDC-HKTE

Chicago
333 N. Michigan Ave., Suite 2028,
Chicago, IL 60601, USA
Tel.: 1-(312)-726-4515
Cable: CONOTRAD CHICAGO
Fax: 1-(312)-726-2441

Dallas
Suite 120, World Trade Centre,
2050 Stemmons Freeway, Dallas, TX 75207, USA
Tel.: 1-(214)-748-8162
Cable: HONGTRADS DALLAS
Fax: 1-(214)-742-6701
Postal Address: P.O. Box 58329
Dallas, TX 75258, USA

Los Angeles
Los Angeles World Trade Centre,
350 S. Figueroa Street, Suite #282,
Los Angeles, CA 90071–1386, USA
Tel.: 1-(213)-622-3194
Cable: CONOTRAD LOS ANGELES
Fax: 1-(213)-613-1490

Miami
Courvoisier Centre, Suite 402,
501 Brickell Key Drive,
Miami, FL 33131, USA
Tel.: 1-(305)-577-0414   Fax: 1-(305)-372-9142

New York
219 East 46th Street,
New York, NY10017, USA
Tel.: 1-(212)-838-8688   Fax: 1-(212)-838-8441

San Francisco
c/o Hong Kong Economic and Trade Office,
222 Kearny Street, 4th Floor, Suite 402
San Francisco, CA 94108, USA
Tel.: (1)-415-677-9038
Fax: (1)-415-421-0646
(Trade enquiries only)

Toronto
Suite 1100, National Building, 347 Bay Street,
Toronto, Ont. M5H 2R7, Canada.
Tel.: 1-(416)-366-3594
Cable: CONOTRAD TORONTO
Fax: 1-(416)-366-1569

Vancouver
Suite 700, 1550 Alberni Street, Vancouver,
B.C. V6G 1A3, Canada.
Tel.: 1-(604)-685-0883, 669-4444
Fax: 1-(604)-669-3784

CENTRAL AMERICA

Mexico City
Manuel E. Izaguirre #13, 3er piso Ciudad Satelite,
Mexico City 53310, Mexico.
Tel.: 52-(5)-572-41-13, 572-41-31
Fax: 52-(5)-393-59-40

Panama City
Condominio Plaza Internacional
    Primer Alto, Oficina No. 27
Edificio del Banco Nacional de Panama
Via Espana y Calle 55
Panama City, Republic de Panama.
Tel.: (507) 69-5894, 69-5611, 69-5109

Fax: (507) 69-6183
Postal Address: Apartado Postal 6-4510
El Dorado, Panama City, Panama

ASIA

Bangkok
20th Floor, TST Tower, 21 Vibhavadi Rangsit Road,
Bangkok 10900, Thailand.
Tel.: 66-(2)-273-8800
Fax: 66-(2)-273-8880

Beijing
Room 901, 9th Floor, CITIC Building,
19 Jianguomenwai Dajie, Beijing, China 100004.
Tel.: 86-(01)-512-8661
Fax: 86-(01)-500-3285

Nagoya
Sakae-Machi Building, 4th Floor, 3-23-31 Nishiki,
Naka-ku, Nagoya 460, Japan.
Tel.: 81-(052)-971-3626   Fax: 01-(052)-962-0613

Osaka
Osaka Ekimae Dai-San Building, 6th Floor,
1-1-3 Umeda, Kita-ku, Osaka 530, Japan.
Tel.: 81-(06)-344-5211
Cable: CONNOTRADD OSAKA
Fax: 81-(06)-347-0791

Seoul
720–721, KFSB Building, 16–2, Yoidodong,
Youngdeungpoku, Seoul, Korea.
Tel.: 82-(02)-782-6115/7   Fax: 82-(02)-782-6118

Shanghai
Room 1004, 10th Floor, Shanghai Union Building,
100 Yanan Dong Lu, Shanghai 200002, China.
Tel.: 86-(21)-326-4196, 326-5935
Telex: 30175 TDCSH CN   Fax: 86-(21)-328-7478

Singapore
20 Kallang Avenue, 2nd Floor, Pico Creative Centre,
Singapore 1233.
Tel.: 65-293-7977   Fax: 65-292-7577

Taipei
7th Floor, 315 Sung Chiang Road,
Taipei, Taiwan.
Tel.: 886-(02)-516-6085   Fax: 886-(02)-502-2115

Tokyo
Toho Twin Tower Building,
4th Floor, 1-5-2 Yurakucho
Chiyoda-ku, Tokyo 100, Japan.
Tel.: 81-(03)-3502-3251/5   Fax: 81-(03)-3591-6484

413

AUSTRALIA

Sydney
71 York Street, Sydney, NSW 2000, Australia.
Tel.: 61-(02)-299-8343   Fax: 61-(02)-290-1889
Postal Address: G.P.O. Box 3877
Sydney, NSW 2001, Australia

MIDDLE EAST

Dubai
New Juma Al-Majid Building,
Dubai Sharjah Road, Dubai, U.A.E.
Tel.: 971-(4)-625255
Cable: MARKETS DUBAI
Telex: 46361 MARKET EM
Fax: 971-(4)-663764
Postal Address: P.O. Box 7434 Dubai, U.A.E.

Hong Kong Tourist Association

EUROPE

Barcelona
c/o Sergat Espana S.L., Apdo. Correos 30266,
08080 Barcelona, Spain.
Tel.: (93) 280-5838   Fax: (93) 280-4520
Telex: 54687 FGC E

Frankfurt
Wiesenau 1, 6000 Frankfurt am Main 1,
Germany.
Tel.: (069) 722-841   Fax: (069) 721-244

London
4th/5th Floors, 125 Pall Mall,
London SW1Y 5EA UK
Tel.: (071) 930-4775   Fax: (071) 930-4777

Paris
38 Avenue George V
(Entree 53 Rue Francois ler, 7th Floor)
75008 Paris, France.
Tel.: (01) 4720-3954   Fax: (01) 4723-0965
Telex: 042 650055 ANI F

Rome
c/o Sergat Italia, s.r.l. Piazza Dei Cenci 7/A,
00186 Roma, Italy.
Tel.: (06) 686-9112   Fax: (06) 687-3644
Telex: 623033 SERGAT I

NORTH AMERICA

Chicago
333 North Michigan Avenue,
Suite 2400, Chicago, IL 60601-3966, USA
Tel.: (312) 782-3872   Fax: (312) 782-0864

Los Angeles
Suite 1220, 10940 Wilshire Boulevard,
Los Angeles, CA 90024-3915, USA
Tel.: (310) 208-4582   Fax: (310) 208-1869

New York
5th Floor, 590 Fifth Avenue, New York,
NY 10036-4706 USA
Tel.: (212) 869-5008/9   Fax: (212) 730-2605

Toronto
347 Bay Street, Suite 909,
Toronto, Ontario, M5H 2R7, Canada.
Tel.: (416) 366-2389   Fax: (416) 366-1098

ASIA

Tokyo
4th Floor, Toho Twin Tower Building,
1-5-2 Yurakucho, Chiyoda-ku, Tokyo 100, Japan.
Tel.: (03) 3503-0731   Fax: (03) 3503-0736
Telex: 072 2225678 LUYUTO J

Osaka
8th Floor, Osaka Saitama Building,
3-5-13 Awaji-machi, Chuo-ku, Osaka 541
Tel.: (06) 229-2940   Fax: (06) 229-9648

Singapore
13-08 Ocean Building, 10 Collyer Quay,
Singapore 0104, Republic of Singapore.
Tel.: (65) 532-3668   Fax: (65) 534-3592
Telex: 087 28515 LUYUSN RS

Taipei
c/o Taikoo Travel Agency Ltd.,
7th Floor, 18 Chang An East Road,
Sec. 1, Taipei.
Tel.: (02) 581-2967   Fax: (02) 581-6062

Seoul
c/o Universal Communications Inc.,
4th Floor, Sangrok Building, 187-6,
2-ga, Changchoong-dong, Chung-gu,
Seoul 100-392
Tel.: (02) 274-4080   Fax: (02) 274-7214

SOUTH AFRICA

Johannesburg
c/o Development Promotions (Pty.) Ltd.,
4th Floor, Everite House,
20 De Korte Street, Braamfontein 2001.
Tel.: (011) 339-4865   Fax: (011) 339-2474
Telex: 421741/421740

AUSTRALIA

Sydney
Level 5, 55 Harrington Street,
The Rocks, Sydney, NSW 2000, Australia.
Tel.: (02) 251-2855   Fax: (02) 247-8812

NEW ZEALAND

Auckland
P.O. Box 2120, Auckland, New Zealand.
Tel.: (09) 520-3316   Fax: (09) 520-3327

APPENDIX 7
(Chapter 5: The Economy)

Gross Domestic Product by Expenditure Components at Current Market Prices

$ Million

Expenditure Components of GDP	1990	1991*	1992†
Private consumption expenditure	329,192	390,859	452,252
Government consumption expenditure	43,517	51,460	63,955
Gross domestic fixed capital formation	153,046	175,465	206,156
Change in stocks	5,728	4,224	7,445
Total exports of goods (f.o.b.)	639,874	765,886	924,952
Less imports of goods (c.i.f.)	645,200	782,042	958,462
Exports of services	108,556	121,496	142,754
Less imports of services	75,854	86,212	96,470
Total expenditure on gross domestic product at current market prices	**558,859**	**641,136**	**742,582**
Per capita GDP at current market prices ($)	**97,968**	**111,409**	**127,778**

Gross Domestic Product by Expenditure Components at Constant (1980) Market Prices

Expenditure Components of GDP			
Private consumption expenditure	163,786	177,697	191,998
Government consumption expenditure	16,418	17,532	19,961
Gross domestic fixed capital formation	69,712	76,477	85,153
Change in stocks	3,125	2,952	4,519
Total exports of goods (f.o.b.)	375,842	438,139	521,739
Less imports of goods (c.i.f.)	375,700	446,952	546,385
Exports of services	55,058	57,037	62,820
Less imports of services	45,553	49,196	52,406
Total expenditure on gross domestic product at constant (1980) market prices	**262,688**	**273,686**	**287,399**
Per capita GDP at constant (1980) market prices ($)	**46,049**	**47,558**	**49,453**

Note: * The estimates are subject to revisions later on as more data become available.
        † Preliminary estimates.

Gross Domestic Product at Current Prices by Economic Activity

	1989 $ Million	1989 %	1990 $ Million	1990 %	1991* $ Million	1991* %
1. Agriculture and fishing	1,415	0.3	1,432	0.3	1,441	0.2
2. Mining and quarrying	224	@	210	@	222	@
3. Manufacturing	89,645	18.9	92,241	17.2	94,491	15.5
4. Electricity, gas and water	10,860	2.3	12,612	2.3	13,463	2.2
5. Construction	24,937	5.3	29,836	5.6	32,106	5.3
6. Wholesale, retail and import/export trades, restaurants and hotels	113,998	24.0	130,542	24.3	154,423	25.4
7. Transport, storage and communication	42,214	8.9	50,526	9.4	58,970	9.7
8. Financing, insurance, real estate and business services	94,030	19.8	111,825	20.8	140,072	23.0
9. Community, social and personal services	69,224	14.6	80,334	15.0	93,601	15.4
10. Ownership of premises	51,732	10.9	58,141	10.8	64,960	10.7
less imputed bank service charge	23,800	5.0	30,829	5.7	45,189	7.4
Gross domestic product at factor cost (production-based estimate)	474,479	100.0	536,870	100.0	608,560	100.0
Indirect taxes less subsidies	25,390		29,614		36,323	
Gross domestic product at market prices (production-based estimate)	499,869		566,484		644,883	
Gross domestic product at market prices (expenditure-based estimate)	499,157		558,859		641,136	
Statistical discrepancy	0.1%		1.4%		0.6%	

Note: * The estimates are subject to revisions later on as more data become available.
@Less than 0.05.

APPENDIX 8
(Chapter 5: The Economy)

Public Expenditure by Function

$ Million

Item	Actual 1990–91			Actual 1991–92			Revised Estimate 1992–93		
	Recurrent	Capital	Total	Recurrent	Capital	Total	Recurrent	Capital	Total
Economic	4,178	1,073	5,251	4,797	1,072	5,869	5,470	2,152	7,622
Security									
Internal security	10,203	1,295	11,498	10,995	1,289	12,284	12,492	1,163	13,655
Immigration	935	80	1,015	1,051	82	1,133	1,158	65	1,223
Other	967	83	1,050	1,140	20	1,160	1,263	32	1,295
Sub-total	12,105	1,458	13,563	13,186	1,391	14,577	14,913	1,260	16,173
Social Services									
Social welfare	5,360	451	5,811	6,606	307	6,913	7,657	350	8,007
Health	7,724	1,563	9,287	9,785	1,379	11,164	12,420	1,319	13,739
Sub-total	13,084	2,014	15,098	16,391	1,686	18,077	20,077	1,669	21,746
Education	14,464	1,610	16,074	16,235	2,660	18,895	18,803	3,201	22,004
Environment	672	1,353	2,025	752	1,925	2,677	828	2,435	3,263
Community and external affairs									
Recreation, culture and amenities	3,914	1,721	5,635	4,352	1,389	5,741	5,014	1,419	6,433
District and community relations	639	17	656	696	16	712	707	16	723
Other	275	22	297	289	20	309	297	19	316
Sub-total	4,828	1,760	6,588	5,337	1,425	6,762	6,018	1,454	7,472
Infrastructure									
Transport	1,118	3,320	4,438	1,262	2,486	3,748	1,396	4,366	5,762
Land and buildings	1,342	3,074	4,416	1,918	5,169	7,087	2,093	6,719	8,812
Water supply	2,287	759	3,046	2,761	649	3,410	2,503	1,071	3,574
Sub-total	4,747	7,153	11,900	5,941	8,304	14,245	5,992	12,156	18,148
Support	10,390	1,893	12,283	13,129	1,614	14,743	14,666	1,726	16,392
Housing	3,999	8,417	12,416	5,123	7,454	12,577	5,663	8,815	14,478
Total	68,467	26,731	95,198	80,891	27,531	108,422	92,430	34,868	127,298

APPENDIX 8A

Public Expenditure by Function

$ Million

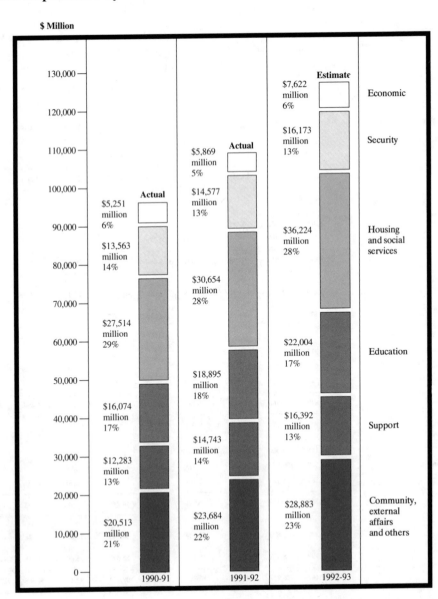

APPENDIX 9
(Chapter 5: The Economy)

Government Expenditure and the Economy

	Actual 1988–89	Actual 1989–90	Actual 1990–91	Actual 1991–92	$ Million Revised Estimate 1992–93
Government Expenditure (see Appendix 10)					
Operating Expenditure	42,035	50,106	61,469	71,677	85,254
Less: Grant to Regional Council	(273)	(273)	(274)	—	—
Transfer to Lotteries Fund	—	—	—	—	(2,300)
	41,762	49,833	61,195	71,677	82,954
Capital Expenditure	11,761	21,260	24,087	20,514	29,846
Less: Debt repayment	—	(1,000)	—	—	—
Equity injections	(157)	(2,287)	(6,214)	(1,794)	(6,072)
	11,604	17,973	17,873	18,720	23,774
Total Government Expenditure	**53,366**	**67,806**	**79,068**	**90,397**	**106,728**
Add: Other public sector bodies	11,433	14,139	16,130	18,025	20,570
Total Public Expenditure§	**64,799**	**81,945**	**95,198**	**108,422**	**127,298**
Gross Domestic Product (GDP) at current market prices (calendar year)	433,657	499,157	558,859	641,136*	742,582†
Growth in GDP:					
Nominal terms	18.0%	15.1%	12.0%	14.7%*	15.8%†
Real terms	8.3%	2.8%	3.2%	4.2%*	5.0%†
Growth in Public Expenditure:					
Nominal terms	20.8%	26.5%	16.2%	13.9%	17.4%
Real terms	7.8%	10.8%	2.3%	2.9%	7.3%
Public Expenditure as percentage of GDP	14.9%	16.4%	17.0%	16.9%	17.1%

Note:

§ The public expenditure comprises expenditure by the Housing Authority, the Urban Council, the Regional Council, expenditure financed by the Government's statutory funds and all expenditure charged to the General Revenue Account. Expenditure by institutions in the private or quasi-private sector is included to the extent of their subventions. The activities of government departments which are partly financed by charges raised on a commercial basis are also included (e.g. airport, waterworks). But not included is expenditure by those organisations, including even statutory organisations, in which the Government has only an equity position, such as the Mass Transit Railway Corporation and, post 1982–83, the Kowloon-Canton Railway Corporation. Similarly, debt repayments and equity payments are excluded as they do not reflect the actual consumption of resources by the Government.

* The estimates are subject to routine revisions later on as more data become available.

† Preliminary estimate.

APPENDIX 10
(Chapter 5: The Economy)

Total Government Revenue and Expenditure and Summary of Financial Position

$ Million

Revenue

	Actual 1990–91	Actual 1991–92	Revised Estimate 1992–93
Operating Revenue			
Direct taxes			
Earnings and profits tax	36,341	44,870	55,831
Indirect taxes			
Duties	5,729	6,844	7,183
General rates	3,039	3,494	4,360
Internal revenue§	13,143	18,406	22,967
Motor vehicle taxes	2,054	3,437	4,956
Royalties and concessions	816	886	1,105
Other revenue			
Fines, forfeitures and penalties	652	885	864
Properties and investments	1,341	1,572	1,715
Reimbursements and contributions	2,172	2,777	3,855
Utilities—			
Airport and air services	1,774	2,106	2,373
Ferry terminals	177	218	245
Government quarries	21	1	—
Postal services	1,777	2,198	2,421
Tunnels	289	302	210
Water	1,579	1,825	1,893
Fees and charges	5,992	7,170	7,993
Interest	4,505	2,982	1,866
Total Operating Revenue	**81,401**	**99,973**	**119,837**
Capital Revenue			
Direct taxes			
Estate duty	656	683	1,000
Indirect taxes			
Taxi concessions	136	302	—
Other revenue			
Land transactions	241	412	245
Miscellaneous	240	86	186
Funds			
Capital Works Reserve Fund (Land sales and interest)	4,002	9,074	9,018
Capital Investment Fund	2,341	2,468	2,358
Loan Fund	506	603	702
Total Capital Revenue	**8,122**	**13,628**	**13,509**
Net borrowing	—	1,098	2,300
Total Government Revenue	**89,523**	**114,699**	**135,646**

Note: § Including bets and sweeps tax, entertainment tax, hotel accommodation tax, air passenger departure tax, Cross Harbour Tunnel passage tax and stamp duties.

			$ Million
Expenditure			*Revised*
	Actual	*Actual*	*Estimate*
	1990–91	*1991–92*	*1992–93*
Operating Expenditure			
Recurrent expenditure			
Personal emoluments	23,443	25,286	25,742
Personnel related expenses	2,396	3,183	3,390
Pensions	2,541	3,401	4,500
Departmental expenses	4,552	4,782	4,661
Other charges	9,712	10,939	11,915
Subventions—			
Education	8,737	9,728	10,851
Medical	2,274	5,452	11,190
Social welfare	1,254	1,587	1,793
University and Polytechnic	3,400	4,357	5,624
Vocational Training Council	706	814	972
Miscellaneous	1,363	1,244	1,394
Other non-recurrent	1,091	904	3,222
Total Operating Expenditure	**61,469**	**71,677**	**85,254**
Capital Expenditure			
General Revenue Account			
Plant, equipment and works	760	746	710
Defence Cost Agreement	16	12	17
Capital subventions	382	416	935
Funds			
Capital Works Reserve Fund	15,641	16,405	20,713
Capital Investment Fund (Equity Investments)	6,214	1,794	6,072
Loan Fund	1,074	1,141	1,399
Total Capital Expenditure and Equity Investments	**24,087**	**20,514**	**29,846**
Total Government Expenditure and Equity Investments	**85,556**	**92,191**	**115,100**

$ Million

Summary of Financial Position

	Actual *1990–91*	*Actual* *1991–92*	*Revised* *Estimate* *1992–93*
Total Government Revenue	**89,523**	**114,699**	**135,646**
Less: Total Government Expenditure and Equity Investments	**85,556**	**92,191**	**115,100**
Consolidated cash surplus	**3,967**	**22,508**	**20,546**
Reserve balance at April 1	**72,577**	**76,544**	**99,052**
Reserve balance at March 31	**76,544**	**99,052**	**119,598**

APPENDIX 10A

Total Government Revenue by Source

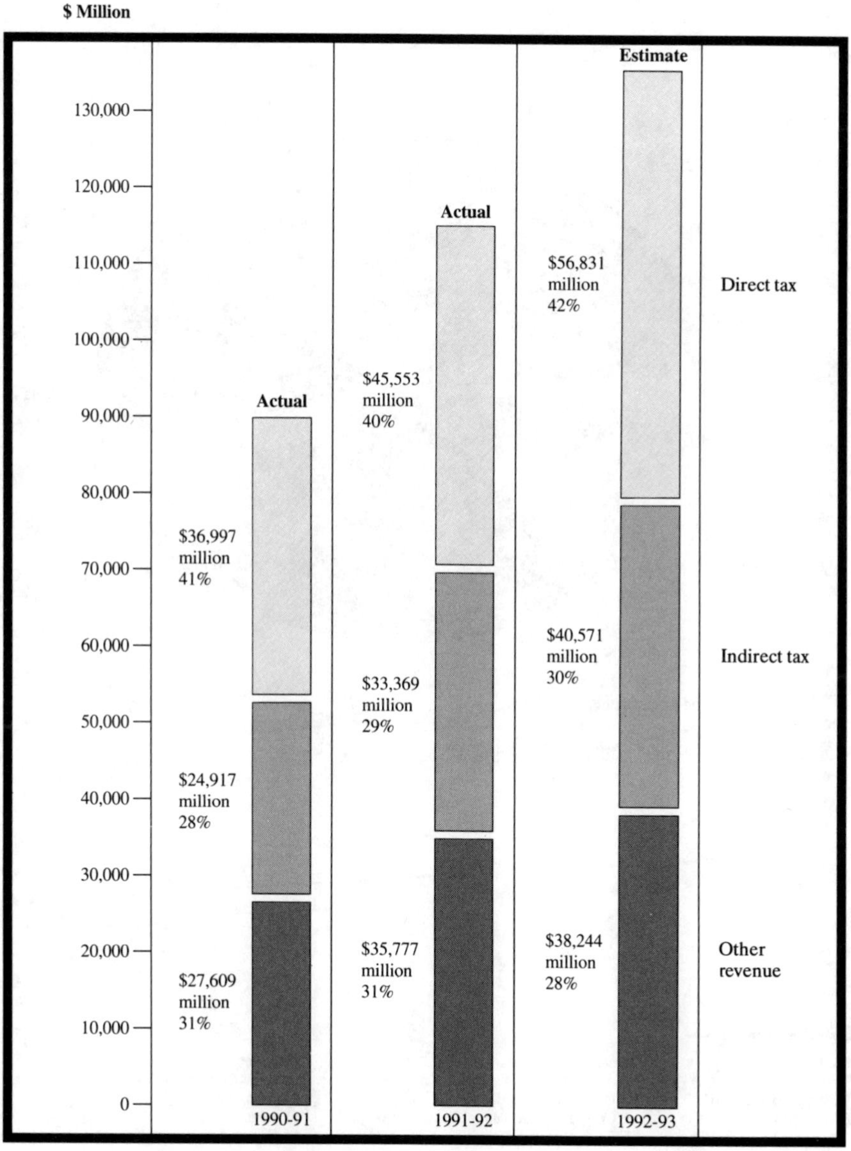

$ Million
130,000
120,000
110,000
100,000
90,000
80,000
70,000
60,000
50,000
40,000
30,000
20,000
10,000
0
Actual
Actual
Estimate
$36,997 million 41%
$24,917 million 28%
$27,609 million 31%
$45,553 million 40%
$33,369 million 29%
$35,777 million 31%
$56,831 million 42%
$40,571 million 30%
$38,244 million 28%
Direct tax
Indirect tax
Other revenue
1990-91
1991-92
1992-93

APPENDIX 11

**Major Sources of Revenue
(1991–92)**

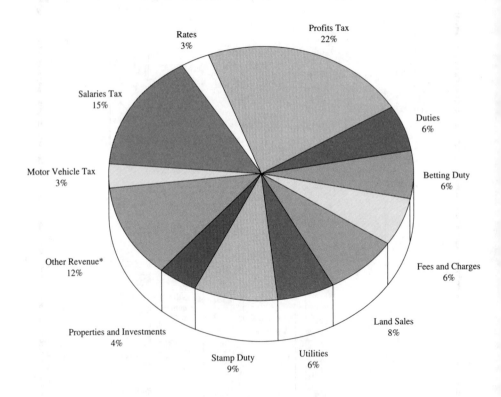

*Other Revenue Includes-

Other Direct Tax:
1. Property Tax
2. Personal Assessment
3. Estate Duties

Other Indirect Tax:
4. Air Passenger Departure Tax
5. Hotel Accommodation Tax
6. Cross Harbour Tunnel Passage Tax
7. Entertainment Tax

Others:
8. Royalties and Concessions
9. Fines
10. Loan Fund
11. Capital Investment Fund

APPENDIX 12
(Chapter 6: Financial and Monetary Affairs)

Exchange Value of the Hong Kong Dollar
(A) Historical changes in the exchange rate system

	Par value of the HK$ in grams of fine gold	£1 = HK$	US$1 = HK$	SDR1 = HK$
December 18, 1946				
IMF parities established; Hong Kong dollar was pegged to sterling	0.223834	16.00	3.970	
September 18, 1949				
Hong Kong dollar devalued *pari passu* with sterling by 30.5%	0.155517	16.00	5.714	
November 20, 1967				
Hong Kong dollar devalued *pari passu* with sterling by 14.3%	0.133300	16.00	6.667	
November 23, 1967				
Hong Kong dollar revalued by 10%, including against sterling, but continues pegged to sterling, at new rate	0.146631	14.55	6.061	
December 18, 1971				
As part of the general currency realignment, Hong Kong dollar and sterling appreciated by 8.57% against US dollar. As a result of USA terminating, in August 1971, the convertibility of US dollar into gold, gold par value no longer had a practical meaning. IMF began to adopt the SDR as its accounting unit		14.55	5.582	6.061
July 6, 1972				
Hong Kong dollar pegged to US dollar following the floating of sterling			5.650	6.134
February 14, 1973				
US dollar devalued; Hong Kong dollar remains pegged, at new rate			5.085	6.134
November 26, 1974				
Hong Kong dollar allowed to float, *ie* the government no longer undertook to maintain a particular rate against any other currency				
October 17, 1983				
Hong Kong dollar was linked to US dollar, through a new arrangement in the note-issue mechanism, at a fixed exchange rate of HK$7.80 = US$1				

(B) Exchange rates of the Hong Kong dollar against several major currencies

End of period	£	US$	DM	¥	SDR	Effective exchange rate* (24–28 Oct 1983 = 100)
		(HK dollars to one unit of foreign currency)				
1974	11.53	4.910	2.03	0.0164	6.012	150.7
1987	14.52	7.760	4.91	0.0637	11.009	100.5
1988	14.17	7.808	4.42	0.0626	10.507	100.6
1989	12.60	7.807	4.63	0.0544	10.261	109.3
1990	14.95	7.801	5.20	0.0576	11.098	109.3
1991	14.53	7.781	5.13	0.0622	11.130	109.2
1992	11.77	7.741	4.80	0.0623	10.644	114.2

Note: * The effective exchange rate index is derived from a weighted average of nominal exchange rates of the Hong Kong dollar against the currencies of 15 principal trading partners.

APPENDIX 13
(Chapter 6: Financial and Monetary Affairs)

Money Supply

$ Million

As at end of year

	1990 HK$	1990 Foreign currency	1990 Total	1991 HK$	1991 Foreign currency	1991 Total	1992 HK$	1992 Foreign currency	1992 Total
Legal tender coins and notes in circulation									
Commercial bank issues (A)	40,886	—	40,886	46,506	—	46,506	58,226	—	58,226
The Hongkong and Shanghai Banking Corporation Limited	34,764	—	34,764	40,194	—	40,194	50,644	—	50,644
Standard Chartered Bank	6,122	—	6,122	6,312	—	6,312	7,582	—	7,582
Government issues (B)	2,375	—	2,375	2,671	—	2,671	2,931	—	2,931
One thousand-dollar gold coins	372	—	372	372	—	372	372	—	372
Five-dollar coins	667	—	667	790	—	790	866	—	866
Two-dollar coins	502	—	502	589	—	589	695	—	695
One-dollar coins	452	—	452	495	—	495	543	—	543
Subsidiary coins	381	—	381	424	—	424	454	—	454
One-cent notes	1	—	1	1	—	1	1	—	1
Authorised institutions' holdings of legal tender coins and notes (C)	5,568	—	5,568	6,569	—	6,569	8,985	—	8,985
Legal tender coins and notes in hands of public (A + B − C) = (D)	37,693	—	37,693	42,608	—	42,608	52,172	—	52,172
Demand deposits with licensed banks (E)	54,132	15,683	69,815	69,161	16,728	85,889	87,307	16,078	103,385
Time deposits with licensed banks (F)§	275,692 (207,959)	577,940 (645,673)	853,632	281,979 (241,744)	629,512 (669,747)	911,491	329,363 (270,673)	662,763 (721,453)	992,126
Negotiable certificates of deposit issued by licensed banks (other than those held by authorised institutions) (G)	12,682	4,557	17,238	13,006	3,944	16,950	13,357	3,859	17,216
Savings deposits with licensed banks (H)	159,468	72,204	231,672	229,287	84,764	314,052	244,792	109,085	353,878
Deposits with restricted licence banks and deposit-taking companies (I)	30,822	45,329	76,152	23,734	39,440	63,174	22,592	31,125	53,718
Negotiable certificates of deposit issued by restricted licence banks and deposit-taking companies (other than those held by authorised institutions) (J)	725	1,101	1,826	341	2,837	3,178	692	1,078	1,770
Money supply									
Definition 1 (D + E)	91,826	15,683	107,509	111,769	16,728	128,497	139,479	16,078	155,557
Definition 2 (D + E + F + G + H)§	539,667 (471,934)	670,383 (738,116)	1,210,050	636,042 (595,808)	734,948 (775,182)	1,370,990	726,992 (668,302)	791,785 (850,475)	1,518,777
Definition 3 (D + E + F + G + H + I + J)§	571,215 (503,482)	716,813 (784,546)	1,288,028	660,117 (619,882)	777,225 (817,460)	1,437,342	750,276 (691,586)	823,989 (882,679)	1,574,265

Note: § Adjusted for foreign currency swap deposits. Unadjusted figures are shown in brackets. Foreign currency swap deposits are deposits involving customers buying foreign currencies in the spot market and placing them as deposits with authorised institutions, while at the same time entering into a forward contract to sell such foreign currencies (principal plus interest) upon maturity of such deposits. For most analytical purposes, they should be regarded as Hong Kong dollar deposits.

APPENDIX 14
(Chapter 6: Financial and Monetary Affairs)

Liabilities and Assets: Licensed Banks

$ Million

As at end of year

	1990 HK$	1990 Foreign currency	1990 Total	1991 HK$	1991 Foreign currency	1991 Total	1992 HK$	1992 Foreign currency	1992 Total
Liabilities									
Amount due to authorised institutions in Hong Kong	194,184	244,802	438,985	228,267	224,906	453,173	210,689	215,352	426,041
Amount due to banks abroad	99,939	2,952,025	3,051,964	124,365	3,113,320	3,237,685	123,341	3,088,241	3,211,582
Deposits from customers§	421,560	733,559	1,155,119	540,193	771,239	1,311,432	602,773	846,616	1,449,390
Negotiable certificates of deposit outstanding	26,344	6,455	32,800	21,284	4,617	25,901	23,617	6,027	29,643
Other liabilities	90,313	89,029	179,342	118,072	103,725	221,797	143,623	93,293	236,916
Total liabilities	**832,340**	**4,025,870**	**4,858,210**	**1,032,181**	**4,217,807**	**5,249,988**	**1,104,043**	**4,249,529**	**5,353,572**
Assets									
Notes and coins	5,561	#	5,561	6,560	1,695	8,255	8,969	1,638	10,606
Amount due from authorised institutions in Hong Kong	210,075	262,931	473,006	265,963	249,829	515,792	263,057	243,870	506,928
Amount due from banks abroad	37,314	2,356,751	2,394,065	42,426	2,214,811	2,257,237	59,976	2,074,946	2,134,922
Loans and advances to customers	542,902	1,136,674	1,679,576	644,149	1,473,077	2,117,226	719,741	1,611,644	2,331,384
Negotiable certificates of deposit (NCD) held:	9,931	9,026	18,957	5,377	8,454	13,831	7,131	10,590	17,721
Issued by licensed banks in Hong Kong	9,239	1,212	10,451	4,550	377	4,927	5,877	1,369	7,247
Issued by restricted licence banks in Hong Kong	261	—	261	426	89	515	555	143	698
Issued by deposit-taking companies in Hong Kong	338	109	448	301	225	526	691	85	776
Issued by banks outside Hong Kong	92	7,705	7,797	100	7,763	7,863	8	8,993	9,001
Negotiable debt instrument held, other than NCDs	N.A.	N.A.	N.A.	25,012	174,816	199,827	33,463	178,950	212,414
Acceptances and bills of exchange held†	1,435	19,275	20,710	2,839	29,655	32,493	3,018	41,515	44,534
Floating rate notes and commercial paper held†	8,634	46,606	55,240	4,937	49,608	54,546	3,528	45,814	49,342
Government bills, notes and bonds*				15,117	52,813	67,929	25,545	45,959	71,505
Other debt instruments held*	43,284	56,809	100,092	2,119	42,740	44,859	1,372	45,662	47,034
Investments in share-holdings*				8,163	1,226	9,389	7,958	1,453	9,411
Interest in land and buildings*				28,812	512	29,324	31,960	445	32,404
Other assets†	26,981	84,020	111,002	27,329	71,778	99,107	29,389	68,392	97,782
Total assets	**886,118**	**3,972,092**	**4,858,210**	**1,053,791**	**4,196,197**	**5,249,988**	**1,161,644**	**4,191,928**	**5,353,572**
Number of licensed banks in operation			**166**			**160**			**161**

Notes: § Unadjusted for foreign currency swap deposits.
N.A. Not available.
Due to re-classification of items in statistical return from 1991:
Foreign currency component available only from 1991, figures before 1991 are included in 'Other assets'.
† Values from 1991 onwards are not strictly comparable to those in the past.
* The nearest equivalent of the total of these four items before 1991 is the item 'Treasury bills, securities, share-holdings and interests in land and buildings'.

Liabilities and Assets: Restricted Licence Banks

$ Million

As at end of year

	1990			1991			1992		
	HK$	Foreign currency	Total	HK$	Foreign currency	Total	HK$	Foreign currency	Total
Liabilities									
Amount due to authorised institutions in Hong Kong	27,924	21,970	49,894	36,963	23,447	60,410	43,187	24,198	67,385
Amount due to banks abroad	684	55,621	56,305	902	56,175	57,076	3,543	65,457	69,000
Deposits from customers§	10,968	32,816	43,784	10,234	29,393	39,627	11,640	22,971	34,611
Negotiable certificates of deposit outstanding	500	589	1,089	733	1,091	1,824	1,232	1,438	2,670
Other liabilities	8,122	26,139	34,260	10,378	25,314	35,692	13,386	29,525	42,910
Total liabilities	**48,198**	**137,134**	**185,332**	**59,210**	**135,419**	**194,629**	**72,988**	**143,589**	**216,576**
Assets									
Notes and coins	@	#	@	@	@	1	@	1	1
Amount due from authorised institutions in Hong Kong	16,999	22,660	39,658	14,229	19,558	33,787	12,760	17,856	30,616
Amount due from banks abroad	526	44,086	44,612	1,078	42,063	43,142	3,303	41,313	44,616
Loans and advances to customers	31,514	15,956	47,470	42,821	19,085	61,906	52,049	21,734	73,782
Negotiable certificates of deposit (NCD) held:	3,419	2,483	5,902	3,399	1,172	4,570	4,700	1,853	6,552
Issued by licensed banks in Hong Kong	2,902	284	3,185	2,641	23	2,664	3,451	438	3,889
Issued by restricted licence banks in Hong Kong	107	—	107	185	—	185	408	225	633
Issued by deposit-taking companies in Hong Kong	401	23	424	565	39	604	754	—	754
Issued by banks outside Hong Kong	10	2,176	2,186	8	1,110	1,118	87	1,190	1,277
Negotiable debt instrument held, other than NCDs	N.A.	N.A.	N.A.	4,720	39,022	43,742	5,911	49,384	55,294
Acceptances and bills of exchange held†	17	201	217	176	1,237	1,414	159	1,686	1,845
Floating rate notes and commercial paper held†	2,357	17,434	19,791	1,666	19,497	21,162	1,583	16,852	18,435
Government bills, notes and bonds*				2,661	7,924	10,585	3,799	19,718	23,517
Other debt instruments held*	1,868	6,521	8,388	217	10,364	10,581	370	11,128	11,498
Investments in share-holdings*				273	739	1,012	132	700	832
Interest in land and buildings*				91	284	375	148	259	407
Other assets†	1,218	18,076	19,294	1,145	4,948	6,093	1,186	3,288	4,474
Total assets	**57,918**	**127,415**	**185,332**	**67,757**	**126,872**	**194,629**	**80,189**	**136,388**	**216,576**
Number of restricted licence banks in operation			**44**			**52**			**55**

Notes: § Unadjusted for foreign currency swap deposits.
@ Less than HK$ 0.5 million.
N.A. Not available.
Due to re-classification of items in statistical return from 1991:
\# Foreign currency component available only from 1991, figures before 1991 are included in 'Other assets'.
† Values from 1991 onwards are not strictly comparable to those in the past.
* The nearest equivalent of the total of these four items before 1991 is the item 'Treasury bills, securities, share-holdings and interests in land and buildings'.

Liabilities and Assets: Deposit-taking Companies

$ Million

As at end of year

	1990 HK$	1990 Foreign currency	1990 Total	1991 HK$	1991 Foreign currency	1991 Total	1992 HK$	1992 Foreign currency	1992 Total
Liabilities									
Amount due to authorised institutions in Hong Kong	22,252	40,230	62,482	26,310	40,207	66,517	28,377	38,154	66,531
Amount due to banks abroad	885	29,529	30,414	429	23,880	24,309	400	22,478	22,879
Deposits from customers§	19,855	12,513	32,368	13,500	10,048	23,547	10,953	8,155	19,107
Negotiable certificates of deposit outstanding	1,508	831	2,339	1,215	2,383	3,598	2,016	388	2,405
Other liabilities	12,397	50,501	62,897	11,572	45,760	57,331	11,992	37,037	49,029
Total liabilities	**56,896**	**133,604**	**190,500**	**53,025**	**122,277**	**175,302**	**53,739**	**106,212**	**159,951**
Assets									
Notes and coins	7	#	7	8	6	14	16	6	22
Amount due from authorised institutions in Hong Kong	18,217	19,921	38,139	11,319	17,319	28,639	9,097	14,363	23,460
Amount due from banks abroad	332	43,552	43,884	211	35,323	35,534	93	30,677	30,770
Loans and advances to customers	32,601	28,962	61,563	36,862	27,778	64,640	40,298	24,094	64,392
Negotiable certificates of deposit (NCD) held:	1,710	2,174	3,884	1,251	2,621	3,871	1,088	1,678	2,765
Issued by licensed banks in Hong Kong	1,522	403	1,925	1,087	272	1,359	931	361	1,292
Issued by restricted licence banks in Hong Kong	63	—	63	56	78	133	79	105	184
Issued by deposit-taking companies in Hong Kong	114	187	301	75	206	282	70	191	261
Issued by banks outside Hong Kong	12	1,584	1,596	33	2,064	2,097	8	1,022	1,030
Negotiable debt instrument held, other than NCDs	N.A.	N.A.	N.A.	897	33,612	34,509	952	30,792	31,745
Acceptances and bills of exchange held†	31	463	494	56	2,207	2,263	63	2,798	2,862
Floating rate notes and commercial paper held†	654	18,484	19,139	585	17,728	18,313	280	14,836	15,117
Government bills, notes and bonds*				109	3,749	3,859	372	4,173	4,545
Other debt instruments held*	872	12,288	13,160	147	9,927	10,074	236	8,985	9,221
Investments in share-holdings*				191	635	826	168	512	681
Interest in land and buildings*				222	150	372	235	87	322
Other assets†	1,432	8,800	10,232	1,347	5,551	6,898	1,024	4,770	5,794
Total assets	**55,855**	**134,644**	**190,500**	**52,308**	**122,995**	**175,302**	**52,971**	**106,980**	**159,951**
Number of deposit-taking companies in operation			**190**			**157**			**146**

Notes: § Unadjusted for foreign currency swap deposits.
      N.A. Not available.
      Due to re-classification of items in statistical return from 1991:
      # Foreign currency component available only from 1991, figures before 1991 are included in 'Other assets'.
      † Values from 1991 onwards are not strictly comparable to those in the past.
      * The nearest equivalent of the total of these four items before 1991 is the item 'Treasury bills, securities, share-holdings and interests in land and buildings'.

APPENDIX 15
(Chapter 7: Industry and Trade)

Hong Kong's External Trade by Major Trading Partners

Imports

	1990		1991		1992		1991–92 Change in per cent
	$ Million	Per cent	$ Million	Per cent	$ Million	Per cent	
Source							
China	236,134	36.8	293,356	37.7	354,348	37.1	+20.8
Japan	103,362	16.1	127,402	16.4	166,191	17.4	+30.4
Taiwan	58,084	9.0	74,591	9.6	87,019	9.1	+16.7
United States	51,788	8.1	58,837	7.6	70,594	7.4	+20.0
Republic of Korea	28,155	4.4	34,944	4.5	44,155	4.6	+26.4
Singapore	26,122	4.1	31,525	4.0	39,087	4.1	+24.0
Federal Republic of Germany*	14,828	2.3	16,641	2.1	21,911	2.3	+31.7
United Kingdom	14,118	2.2	16,545	2.1	19,221	2.0	+16.2
Italy	10,842	1.7	11,729	1.5	14,825	1.6	+26.4
Malaysia	8,200	1.3	9,859	1.3	12,825	1.3	+30.1
Others	90,898	14.1	103,553	13.3	125,118	13.1	+20.8
Merchandise total	**642,530**	**100.0**	**778,982**	**100.0**	**955,295**	**100.0**	**+22.6**

Domestic Exports

	1990		1991		1992		1991–92 Change in per cent
	$ Million	Per cent	$ Million	Per cent	$ Million	Per cent	
Destination							
United States	66,370	29.4	62,870	27.2	64,600	27.6	+2.8
China	47,470	21.0	54,404	23.5	61,959	26.5	+13.9
Federal Republic of Germany*	17,991	8.0	19,318	8.4	15,956	6.8	−17.4
United Kingdom	13,496	6.0	13,706	5.9	12,541	5.4	−8.5
Japan	12,079	5.3	11,666	5.0	10,997	4.7	−5.7
Singapore	7,796	3.5	8,794	3.8	10,360	4.4	+17.8
Taiwan	5,720	2.5	6,066	2.6	6,500	2.8	+7.2
Canada	5,366	2.4	5,014	2.2	5,018	2.1	+0.1
Netherlands	4,964	2.2	5,238	2.3	4,878	2.1	−6.9
France	3,626	1.6	3,710	1.6	3,164	1.4	−14.7
Others	40,998	18.2	40,260	17.4	38,151	16.3	−5.2
Merchandise total	**225,875**	**100.0**	**231,045**	**100.0**	**234,123**	**100.0**	**+1.3**

Re-exports

	1990		1991		1992		1991–92 Change in per cent
	$ Million	Per cent	$ Million	Per cent	$ Million	Per cent	
Destination							
China	110,908	26.8	153,318	28.7	212,105	30.7	+38.3
United States	87,752	21.2	110,802	20.7	148,500	21.5	+34.0
Japan	24,376	5.9	29,574	5.5	37,465	5.4	+26.7
Federal Republic of Germany*	23,406	5.7	32,073	6.0	33,103	4.8	+3.2
Taiwan	21,248	5.1	24,765	4.6	26,156	3.8	+5.6
United Kingdom	12,107	2.9	14,663	2.7	20,591	3.0	+40.4
Singapore	12,572	3.0	12,094	2.3	13,866	2.0	+14.7
Republic of Korea	13,011	3.1	14,631	2.7	13,588	2.0	−7.1
Canada	6,527	1.6	8,498	1.6	11,101	1.6	+30.6
France	6,415	1.5	9,038	1.7	11,039	1.6	+22.1
Others	95,677	23.1	125,385	23.4	163,315	23.6	+30.3
Merchandise total	**413,999**	**100.0**	**534,841**	**100.0**	**690,829**	**100.0**	**+29.2**

Note: * In connection with the unification of Federal Republic of Germany (FRG) and German Democratic Republic (GDR) in October 1990, the trade figures for FRG in 1990 and previous years have been revised by adding those of the previous GDR. This is to ensure comparability of these trade figures with those after the German unification.

APPENDIX 16A
(Chapter 7: Industry and Trade)

Hong Kong's External Trade Analysed by Standard International Trade Classification Revision 3 (SITC Rev. 3)

Imports

			$ Million
Section/division	1990	1991	1992
Food and live animals			
Live animals	2,694	2,924	3,441
Meat and meat preparations	4,546	5,055	5,394
Fish, crustaceans, molluscs and aquatic invertebrates, and preparations thereof	8,507	9,398	10,728
Cereals and cereal preparations	2,307	2,544	3,083
Vegetables and fruit	8,809	10,175	11,040
Others	8,331	9,400	9,783
Sub-total	**35,195**	**39,496**	**43,469**
Beverages and tobacco			
Beverages	4,243	5,050	5,814
Tobacco and tobacco manufactures	9,432	11,102	13,388
Sub-total	**13,675**	**16,152**	**19,203**
Crude materials, inedible, except fuels			
Hides, skins and furskins, raw	1,517	1,659	1,920
Textile fibres (other than wool tops and other combed wool) and their wastes (not manufactured into yarn or fabric)	5,611	7,735	6,898
Metalliferous ores and metal scrap	855	1,076	2,266
Crude animal and vegetable materials, n e s	5,199	5,329	5,472
Others	3,091	3,918	3,894
Sub-total	**16,273**	**19,718**	**20,450**
Mineral fuels, lubricants and related materials			
Petroleum, petroleum products and related materials	12,562	12,966	15,312
Others	3,030	3,366	3,618
Sub-total	**15,593**	**16,331**	**18,930**
Animal and vegetable oils, fats and waxes			
Fixed vegetable fats and oils, crude, refined or fractionated	1,101	1,130	1,026
Others	154	97	107
Sub-total	**1,254**	**1,228**	**1,133**
Chemicals and related products, n e s			
Dyeing, tanning and colouring materials	5,708	6,907	7,844
Medicinal and pharmaceutical products	4,686	6,231	7,577
Plastics in primary forms	13,997	18,629	21,119
Plastics in non-primary forms	5,384	6,842	8,161
Others	18,577	22,198	22,925
Sub-total	**48,351**	**60,806**	**67,627**
Manufactured goods classified chiefly by material			
Paper, paperboard, and articles of paper pulp, of paper or of paperboard	12,403	14,118	16,180
Textile yarn, fabrics, made-up articles, n e s and related products	79,191	93,678	101,322
Non-metallic mineral manufactures, n e s	23,096	24,561	29,335
Iron and steel	11,510	14,226	15,439
Others	29,892	35,861	45,503
Sub-total	**156,091**	**182,443**	**207,778**
Machinery and transport equipment			
Office machines and automatic data processing machines	17,740	23,739	33,921
Telecommunications and sound recording and reproducing apparatus and equipment	49,406	60,094	75,629
Electrical machinery, apparatus and appliances, n e s, and electrical parts thereof	61,969	77,791	95,434
Others	50,552	65,816	102,018
Sub-total	**179,666**	**227,440**	**307,002**
Miscellaneous manufactured articles			
Articles of apparel and clothing accessories	53,506	66,507	80,078
Footwear	14,111	22,338	31,689
Photographic apparatus, equipment and supplies and optical goods, n e s; watches and clocks	35,495	39,233	45,860
Miscellaneous manufactured articles, n e s	46,793	55,694	71,924
Others	23,759	28,696	36,049
Sub-total	**173,666**	**212,468**	**265,599**
Commodities and transactions not classified elsewhere in the SITC	**2,767**	**2,899**	**4,103**
Total merchandise	**642,530**	**778,982**	**955,295**
Gold and specie	18,149	28,692	30,774
Grand total	**660,679**	**807,674**	**986,069**

Note: n e s = not elsewhere specified.

Domestic Exports

Section/division	1990	1991	$ Million 1992
Food and live animals			
Fish, crustaceans, molluscs and aquatic invertebrates, and preparations thereof	737	773	731
Cereals and cereal preparations	221	267	342
Miscellaneous edible products and preparations	772	871	975
Others	588	618	592
Sub-total	**2,318**	**2,530**	**2,640**
Beverages and tobacco			
Beverages	333	377	405
Tobacco and tobacco manufactures	3,017	2,613	2,610
Sub-total	**3,350**	**2,990**	**3,016**
Crude materials, inedible, except fuels			
Pulp and waste paper	396	442	372
Textile fibres (other than wool tops and other combed wool) and their wastes (not manufactured into yarn or fabric)	115	119	105
Metalliferous ores and metal scrap	1,525	1,295	1,341
Others	128	103	101
Sub-total	**2,164**	**1,958**	**1,919**
Mineral fuels, lubricants and related materials	774	1,277	2,091
Animal and vegetable oils, fats and waxes	95	76	113
Chemicals and related products, n e s			
Dyeing, tanning and colouring materials	515	688	942
Essential oils and resinoids and perfume materials; toilet, polishing and cleansing preparations	659	750	882
Plastics in primary forms	3,354	3,576	3,367
Plastics in non-primary forms	1,213	1,352	1,292
Chemical materials and products, n e s	594	731	697
Others	340	384	506
Sub-total	**6,675**	**7,482**	**7,686**
Manufactured goods classified chiefly by material			
Paper, paperboard, and articles of paper pulp, of paper or of paperboard	2,232	2,369	2,841
Textile yarn, fabrics, made-up articles, n e s and related products	16,862	17,595	17,226
Non-ferrous metals	777	1,035	1,237
Manufactures of metals, n e s	4,485	4,902	4,788
Others	2,038	1,957	2,224
Sub-total	**26,394**	**27,859**	**28,316**
Machinery and transport equipment			
Office machines and automatic data processing machines	16,250	18,292	20,530
Telecommunications and sound recording and reproducing apparatus and equipment	16,644	15,168	12,983
Electrical machinery, apparatus and appliances, n e s, and electrical parts thereof	17,161	19,251	20,138
Others	6,074	6,839	7,786
Sub-total	**56,130**	**59,550**	**61,437**
Miscellaneous manufactured articles			
Pre-fabricated buildings; sanitary, plumbing, heating and lighting fixtures and fittings, n e s	1,069	965	861
Travel goods, handbags and similar containers	1,122	1,045	1,020
Articles of apparel and clothing accessories	71,853	75,525	77,156
Footwear	1,097	721	548
Professional, scientific and controlling instruments and apparatus, n e s	1,491	1,332	1,480
Photographic apparatus, equipment and supplies and optical goods, n e s; watches and clocks	22,624	20,259	18,879
Miscellaneous manufactured articles, n e s	25,333	23,576	22,152
Others	498	461	430
Sub-total	**125,086**	**123,883**	**122,526**
Commodities and transactions not classified elsewhere in the SITC	**2,890**	**3,440**	**4,381**
Total merchandise	**225,875**	**231,045**	**234,123**
Gold and specie	—	—	—
Grand total	**225,875**	**231,045**	**234,123**

432   *Note:* n e s = not elsewhere specified.

Re-exports

Section/division	1990	1991	$ Million 1992
Food and live animals			
Meat and meat preparations	762	943	1,038
Fish, crustaceans, molluscs and aquatic invertebrates, and preparations thereof	4,103	3,615	3,565
Vegetables and fruit	3,270	4,040	4,412
Coffee, tea, cocoa, spices and manufactures thereof	748	1,034	1,224
Others	2,242	2,898	3,417
Sub-total	**11,126**	**12,529**	**13,656**
Beverages and tobacco			
Beverages	1,556	2,493	3,000
Tobacco and tobacco manufactures	6,621	8,240	9,999
Sub-total	**8,177**	**10,733**	**12,999**
Crude materials, inedible, except fuels			
Cork and wood	598	743	813
Textile fibres (other than wool tops and other combed wool) and their wastes (not manufactured into yarn or fabric)	3,058	4,654	4,618
Metalliferous ores and metal scrap	757	759	1,308
Crude animal and vegetable materials, n e s	3,851	4,658	4,589
Others	1,871	2,346	2,464
Sub-total	**10,135**	**13,160**	**13,792**
Mineral fuels, lubricants and related materials			
Petroleum, petroleum products and related materials	3,239	4,249	5,261
Others	121	128	181
Sub-total	**3,359**	**4,377**	**5,442**
Animal and vegetable oils, fats and waxes	**557**	**489**	**529**
Chemicals and related products, n e s			
Organic chemicals	3,732	5,761	5,069
Medicinal and pharmaceutical products	3,530	4,824	5,711
Plastics in primary forms	6,705	11,344	14,218
Chemical materials and products, n e s	3,795	4,355	5,249
Others	9,743	11,741	13,613
Sub-total	**27,506**	**38,026**	**43,860**
Manufactured goods classified chiefly by material			
Textile yarn, fabrics, made-up articles, n e s and related products	46,923	58,159	67,744
Non-metallic mineral manufactures, n e s	13,048	13,175	14,440
Iron and steel	4,169	6,073	8,448
Manufactures of metals, n e s	7,236	9,642	12,694
Others	14,787	18,450	25,797
Sub-total	**86,164**	**105,499**	**129,123**
Machinery and transport equipment			
Office machines and automatic data processing machines	11,152	15,588	21,994
Telecommunications and sound recording and reproducing apparatus and equipment	36,366	45,079	55,763
Electrical machinery, apparatus and appliances, n e s, and electrical parts thereof	35,067	41,065	53,746
Road vehicles (including air-cushion vehicles)	4,788	8,468	17,186
Others	21,539	27,055	42,936
Sub-total	**108,910**	**137,255**	**191,624**
Miscellaneous manufactured articles			
Articles of apparel and clothing accessories	47,743	63,577	78,095
Foot wear	14,700	24,951	35,327
Photographic apparatus, equipment and supplies and optical goods, n e s; watches and clocks	15,352	21,765	29,651
Miscellaneous manufactured articles, n e s	56,782	71,918	97,316
Others	22,272	29,118	37,038
Sub-total	**156,848**	**211,329**	**277,427**
Commodities and transactions not classified elsewhere in the SITC	**1,216**	**1,444**	**2,378**
Total merchandise	**413,999**	**534,841**	**690,829**
Gold and specie	**2,042**	**845**	**635**
Grand total	**416,040**	**535,686**	**691,464**

Note: n e s = not elsewhere specified.

APPENDIX 16B
(Chapter 7: Industry and Trade)

Hong Kong's Domestic Exports of Principal Commodity Groups

Commodity groups [1]	1990 $ Million	1991 $ Million	1992 $ Million	Percentage Change 1992 Over 1991
Textiles and clothing	88,715	93,120	94,383	+1
Electronic products [2]	58,566	58,617	60,291	+3
Watches and clocks [2]	19,446	17,037	15,476	−9
Plastic products [2]	8,189	7,027	7,508	+7
Jewellery, goldsmiths' and silversmiths' wares	6,074	5,668	5,047	−11
Manufactures of metals	4,485	4,902	4,788	−2
Toys and dolls [2]	5,031	4,431	3,724	−16
Electrical appliances	3,399	3,231	2,028	−37
Total domestic exports [2] of the above 8 groups	176,621	179,176	178,941	*
As a % of all domestic exports	78%	78%	76%	

Notes: (1) For a breakdown of Hong Kong's external trade by the Standard International Trade Classification (SITC) Revision 3, the table in Appendix 16A should be referred to. The statistics there are presented according to the complete classification of commodities by SITC Section, and within each Section, by major SITC Division. The table presented here is compiled for the convenience of those readers who may be more interested in domestic exports of certain commodity groups which are commonly referred to but which may not be readily derived from Appendix 16A because each of them cuts across two or more SITC Sections, Divisions or sub-classifications within such Sections and Divisions.

(2) There is some overlapping in the commodity coverage of 'electronic products' and 'watches and clocks'. Some commodity items, such as digital electronic watches, are included in both groups. There is also overlapping between 'electronic products' and 'toys and dolls' (items such as radio controlled toys, T.V. games and electronic games), and between 'plastic products' and 'toys and dolls' (item such as plastic toys). However, the values of these items are counted only once in the value of 'total domestic exports of the above 8 groups'.

(3) The correspondence between the commodity groups in the above table and the Sections/Divisions in Appendix 16A is as follows:

(i) The commodity group 'textiles and clothing' shown in the above table corresponds to the total of the divisions 'textile yarn, fabrics, made-up articles, n e s and related products' and 'articles of apparel and clothing accessories' in Appendix 16A.

(ii) The commodity group 'electronic products' in the above table has been obtained by re-grouping some commodity items in the SITC Revision 3. A commodity item is a more refined level of breakdown than the commodity Divisions shown in Appendix 16A. Those items constituting 'electronic products' spread across and are part of several commodity Divisions, namely, 'office machines and automatic data processing machines', 'telecommunications and sound recording and reproducing apparatus and equipment', 'electrical machinery, apparatus and appliances, n e s and electrical parts thereof', 'professional, scientific and controlling instruments and apparatus, n e s', 'photographic apparatus, equipment and supplies and optical goods, n e s; watches and clocks', and 'miscellaneous manufactured articles, n e s'.

(iii) The commodity group 'plastic products' shown in the above table has been obtained by re-grouping some commodity items from several Divisions, namely, 'Miscellaneous manufactured articles, n e s' and a few others which are collectively shown as 'others' under the Section 'Miscellaneous manufactured articles' in Appendix 16A.

(iv) The commodity group 'watches and clocks' shown in the above table includes mainly items from the Division 'Photographic apparatus, equipment and supplies and optical goods, n e s; watches and clocks', plus the item metal watch bands which belongs to 'miscellaneous manufactured articles, n e s' in Appendix 16A.

(v) The commodity group 'electrical appliances' shown in the above table is part of the Division 'Electrical machinery, apparatus and appliances, n e s and electrical parts thereof' in Appendix 16A.

(vi) The commodity group "jewellery, goldsmiths' and silversmiths' wares" shown in the above table refers to the total of group 897 of the same description.

(vii) The commodity group 'manufactures of metal' corresponds to the total of Division 69 of the same description.

(viii) The commodity group 'toys and dolls' shown in the above table corresponds to the Group 'Baby carriages, toys, games and sporting goods' minus some items within the group such as baby carriages, playing cards, games and sporting equipment and apparatus.

* Denotes less than 0.5%.

APPENDIX 17
(Chapter 8: Employment)

Number of Establishments and Employment in Manufacturing Industry Analysed by Hong Kong Standard Industrial Classification (HSIC)

Major group/Group	No. of establishments			No. of persons engaged		
	Sep 1990	Sep 1991	Sep 1992	Sep 1990	Sep 1991	Sep 1992
Food manufacturing	892	856	765	18 522	18 666	19 646
Beverage industries	28	22	18	4 871	4 054	3 776
Tobacco manufactures	5	6	6	1 285	1 288	1 309
Wearing apparel except footwear	8 186	7 336	5 840	212 653	187 554	154 975
Outer garments including infants' wear and garment, except knitwear from yarn and leather garments	6 879	6 146	4 760	187 656	165 501	135 679
Under garments and night garments	375	373	334	10 884	11 056	9 883
Fur clothing	196	141	99	4 088	2 333	1 529
Others	736	676	647	10 025	8 664	7 884
Leather and leather products, except footwear and wearing apparel	740	547	484	6 863	5 102	4 134
Products of leather and leather substitutes, except footwear and wearing apparel	216	164	138	2 019	1 461	1 254
Handbags (excl. rattan handbag, straw handbag, plastic shopping bags)	444	332	299	3 899	3 050	2 463
Others	80	51	47	945	591	417
Footwear, except rubber, plastic and wooden footwear	351	284	210	4 216	3 205	2 417
Textiles	5 341	5 055	4 422	107 264	98 724	84 972
Weaving, cotton	219	191	143	10 813	8 825	6 435
Knit outerwear	1 448	1 397	1 140	37 948	36 115	31 632
Bleaching and dyeing	461	424	398	19 816	18 334	16 075
Others	3 213	3 043	2 741	38 687	35 450	30 830
Wood and cork products, except furniture	675	621	576	3 181	2 817	2 509
Furniture and fixtures, except primarily of metal	891	909	771	5 181	4 569	3 744
Wooden furniture and fixtures	637	642	531	3 705	3 288	2 601
Others	254	267	240	1 476	1 281	1 143
Paper and paper products	1 576	1 460	1 295	15 814	13 866	12 754
Containers and boxes of paper & paperboard	1 129	1 032	900	10 042	9 031	7 850
Others	447	428	395	5 772	4 835	4 904
Printing, publishing and allied industries	4 354	4 569	4 394	37 653	39 118	38 497
Job printing	3 308	3 498	3 410	23 843	25 430	25 846
Others	1 046	1 071	984	13 810	13 688	12 651
Chemicals and chemical products	841	768	736	8 128	8 037	7 771
Products of petroleum and coal	2	4	5	220	254	236
Rubber products	119	162	154	1 299	1 211	1 133
Plastic products	4 976	4 377	4 085	51 315	41 522	35 347
Plastic toys	1 200	1 020	996	18 825	14 198	11 986
Others	3 776	3 357	3 089	32 490	27 324	23 361
Non-metallic mineral products, except products of petroleum and coal	391	385	351	3 873	3 655	3 286
Basic metal industries	246	219	211	2 944	2 620	2 810

435

Major group/Group	No. of establishments			No. of persons engaged		
	Sep 1990	Sep 1991	Sep 1992	Sep 1990	Sep 1991	Sep 1992
Fabricated metal products, except machinery and equipment	**6 447**	**6 092**	**5 621**	**50 784**	**46 000**	**39 881**
Buffing, polishing and electro-plating	863	792	728	7 498	6 979	5 433
Fabricated metal products except machinery and equipment, n.e.c.	2 916	2 723	2 610	17 904	15 481	14 081
Others	2 668	2 577	2 283	25 382	23 540	20 367
Office, accounting and computing machinery	**227**	**220**	**160**	**18 388**	**17 337**	**13 508**
Radio, television and communication equipment and apparatus	**365**	**283**	**284**	**18 046**	**10 129**	**8 487**
Electronic parts and components	**488**	**430**	**368**	**27 763**	**25 702**	**24 141**
Electrical appliances and houseware and electronic toys	**357**	**296**	**302**	**13 266**	**10 318**	**7 963**
Electrical appliances and houseware	294	241	252	10 790	8 303	6 465
Electronic toys	63	55	50	2 476	2 016	1 498
Machinery, equipments, apparatus, parts and components, n.e.c.	**6 128**	**5 922**	**5 831**	**42 794**	**41 028**	**37 548**
Special industrial machinery and equipment, except metal and wood working machinery	1 589	1 550	1 519	9 626	9 623	9 020
Industrial machinery and apparatus for the generation of electricity	175	170	200	3 492	3 272	2 892
Machinery and equipment except electrical, n.e.c.	3 708	3 572	3 448	16 847	16 340	14 807
Electronic products, n.e.c.	138	119	131	4 425	3 482	2 735
Others	518	511	533	8 404	8 311	8 094
Transport equipment	**511**	**589**	**541**	**13 340**	**13 269**	**13 134**
Shipyards	98	113	75	5 807	5 269	4 644
Boatyards	276	316	293	1 806	1 915	1 842
Others	137	160	173	5 727	6 085	6 648
Professional and scientific, measuring and controlling equipment, n.e.c., and photographic & optical goods	**1 690**	**1 624**	**1 479**	**32 724**	**29 120**	**24 188**
Watches and clocks, electronic	512	504	437	13 390	12 125	9 720
Cases and parts for watches and clocks, n.e.c.	964	906	815	11 032	8 552	6 534
Others	214	214	227	8 302	8 443	7 934
Manufacturing industries, n.e.c.	**3 260**	**3 244**	**3 030**	**27 830**	**25 500**	**23 014**
Jewellery and related articles	1 032	1 097	1 039	13 939	13 267	11 552
Others	2 228	2 147	1 991	13 891	12 233	11 462
Total	**49 087**	**46 276**	**41 937**	**730 217**	**654 662**	**571 181**

Notes: (1) Up to 4th quarter 1990, figures are analysed by the International Standard Industrial Classification (ISIC). As from March 1991, the Hong Kong Standard Industrial Classification (HSIC) is adopted for the classification of economic activities in place of ISIC. Figures from 1st quarter 1991 onwards are therefore available only in HSIC and are not strictly comparable to those in the past series which are in ISIC. To facilitate comparison over time, figures for 1990 are adjusted to conform to the classification of HSIC and presented in this table.

(2) n.e.c. denotes not elsewhere classified.

APPENDIX 18
(Chapter 8: Employment)

Number of Establishments and Employment in Principal Manufacturing Industry Groups

	No. of establishments [1]			No. of persons engaged [1]		
Industry group [2][3]	*Sep 1990*	*Sep 1991*	*Sep 1992*	*Sep 1990*	*Sep 1991*	*Sep 1992*
Textiles and clothing	13 527	12 391	10 262	319 917	286 278	239 947
Electronics [4]	1 815	1 635	1 446	85 169	71 466	60 653
Watches and clocks [4]	1 784	1 706	1 524	27 960	23 935	18 995
Plastics [4]	4 976	4 377	4 085	51 315	41 522	35 347
Jewellery	1 496	1 522	1 387	17 426	16 204	13 821
Fabricated metal products [4]	6 447	6 092	5 621	50 784	46 000	39 881
Toys and dolls [4]	1 662	1 449	1 383	24 581	18 836	15 617
Electrical appliances	542	470	497	16 985	14 529	12 500
Total of the above groups [4]	29 944	27 554	24 253	554 713	486 411	410 071
(as a % of the corresponding figure of the whole manufacturing sector)	(61%)	(60%)	(58%)	(76%)	(74%)	(72%)

Notes: (1) Up to 4th quarter 1990, figures are analysed by the International Standard Industrial Classification (ISIC). As from March 1991, the Hong Kong Standard Industrial Classification (HSIC) is adopted for the classification of economic activities in place of ISIC. Figures from 1st quarter 1991 onwards are therefore available only in HSIC and are not strictly comparable to those in the past series which are in ISIC. To facilitate comparison over time, figures for 1990 are adjusted to conform to the classification of HSIC and presented in this table.

(2) For a breakdown of the number of establishments and employment in manufacturing industry by the HSIC, the table in Appendix 17 should be referred to. The statistics presented here are figures for industry groups in the manufacturing sector having more significant domestic export value but they cannot be readily derived from Appendix 17 because some of them may cut across more than one Major Group/Group in the HSIC.

(3) The coverage of the industry groups in the above table is given below:

    (i) The industry group 'textile and clothing' corresponds to the major groups 'wearing apparel except footwear' and 'textiles' in Appendix 17.

    (ii) The industry group 'electronics' includes 'office, accounting and computing machinery', 'radio, television and communication equipment and apparatus', 'electronic parts and components', 'electronic toys', 'electronic industrial apparatus', 'watches and clocks, electronic' and 'electronic products, n.e.c.'.

    (iii) The industry group 'watches and clocks' includes 'watches and clocks, mechanical'; 'watches and clocks, electronic'; 'metal wrist watchbands' and 'cases and parts for watches and clocks, n.e.c.'

    (iv) The industry group 'plastics' corresponds to the major group 'plastics products' in Appendix 17.

    (v) The industry group 'electrical appliances' includes 'electrical appliances and houseware', 'dry batteries (excl. lead accumulators)', 'electric and torch bulbs and tubes' and 'electrical products and accessories, n.e.c.'.

    (vi) The industry group 'jewellery' includes 'jewellery' and 'artificial pearls and imitation jewellery'.

    (vii) The industry group 'toys and dolls' includes 'wooden toys', 'rubber toys', 'plastic toys', 'metal toys', 'electronic toys' and 'toys, n.e.c.'.

    (viii) The industry group 'fabricated metal products' corresponds to the major group 'fabricated metal products, except machinery and equipment' in Appendix 17.

(4) There is some overlapping in industrial coverage in some of the above industrial groups:

    (i) 'Watches and clocks, electronic' is included in both 'electronics' and 'watches and clocks' groups.

    (ii) 'Metal wrist watchbands' is included in both 'fabricated metal products' and 'watches and clocks' groups.

    (iii) 'Electronic toys' is included in both 'electronics' and 'toys and dolls' groups.

    (iv) 'Plastic toys' is included in both 'plastics' and 'toys and dolls' groups.

    (v) 'Metal toys' is included in both 'fabricated metal products' and 'toys and dolls' groups.

However, the figures of 'watches and clocks, electronic', 'metal wrist watchbands', 'electronic toys', 'plastic toys' and 'metal toys' are counted only once in the 'total of the above groups'.

APPENDIX 19
(Chapter 8: Employment)

Reported Occupational Accidents

Cause	1990			1991			1992*		
	Fatal	Non-fatal	Total	Fatal	Non-fatal	Total	Fatal	Non-fatal	Total
Machinery: power driven	24	9 064	9 088	20	6 436	6 456	10	2 987	2 997
Machinery: non power driven	—	123	123	1	114	115	1	52	53
Transport	57	3 713	3 770	56	3 196	3 252	45	1 708	1 753
Explosion or fire	6	590	596	12	482	494	7	350	357
Hot or corrosive substance	1	5 466	5 467	—	5 373	5 373	—	2 973	2 973
Gassing, poisoning and other toxic substances	4	80	84	—	61	61	4	30	34
Electricity	8	164	172	7	117	124	7	41	48
Fall of person	50	10 909	10 959	45	11 155	11 200	33	7 175	7 208
Stepping on, striking against or struck by objects	5	24 116	24 121	10	25 390	25 400	11	12 318	12 329
Falling object	14	4 377	4 391	8	3 603	3 611	3	1 882	1 885
Fall of ground	1	23	24	1	16	17	1	18	19
Handling without machinery	1	14 433	14 434	—	12 376	12 376	1	8 706	8 707
Hand tool	—	9 984	9 984	—	9 223	9 223	—	5 190	5 190
Miscellaneous	88	6 222	6 310	85	5 234	5 319	70	3 448	3 518
Causes not yet ascertained	—	5 430	5 430	—	4 824	4 824	79	28 469	28 548
Total	**259**§	**94 694**	**94 953**	**245**§	**87 600**	**87 845**	**272**§	**75 347**	**75 619**

Note: * Figures for 1992 are subject to amendment.
§ Including 15 (in 1990), 18 (in 1991) and 26 (in 1992) which were subsequently verified to be outside the scope of the Employees' Compensation Ordinance because the employees concerned died of natural causes unrelated to work.

APPENDIX 20
(Chapter 8: Employment)

Consumer Price Index (A)
(October 1989–September 1990 = 100)

Section	Weight	Annual average			Index for December		
		1990 (Oct–Dec)	1991	1992	1990	1991	1992
All items	100.00	106.6	114.5	125.2	107.4	118.1	129.3
Food	41.20	105.3	114.1	124.1	106.0	116.5	124.9
Meals away from home	(20.52)	108.2	117.0	129.4	108.9	121.1	133.0
Food, excluding meals away from home	(20.68)	102.5	111.2	118.9	103.0	112.0	116.8
Housing	20.56	108.3	116.6	131.7	109.5	122.0	141.3
Fuel and light	3.18	111.0	110.0	115.7	112.8	111.1	118.1
Alcoholic drinks and tobacco	2.45	106.7	145.5	159.6	108.2	145.6	166.6
Clothing and footwear	4.56	105.3	108.4	117.6	107.9	114.9	125.1
Durable goods	4.92	102.5	104.6	107.0	103.1	105.4	107.7
Miscellaneous goods	5.88	105.7	108.6	116.0	105.7	113.0	120.0
Transport	7.20	107.7	116.1	124.5	108.3	119.5	126.9
Services	10.05	109.0	116.0	129.7	109.4	122.1	136.6

Note: The CPI(A) covers about 50% of urban households with a monthly expenditure of between $2,500 and $9,999 in the base period 1989–90.

Consumer Price Index (B)
(October 1989–September 1990 = 100)

Section	Weight	Annual average			Index for December		
		1990 (Oct–Dec)	1991	1992	1990	1991	1992
All items	100.00	106.7	114.1	125.1	107.6	118.3	129.8
Food	35.34	105.9	114.7	125.1	106.6	117.7	126.7
Meals away from home	(20.51)	108.2	117.0	129.3	108.9	121.2	133.1
Food, excluding meals away from home	(14.83)	102.7	111.6	119.2	103.5	113.0	117.8
Housing	23.77	108.0	116.2	132.0	108.9	122.5	141.8
Fuel and light	2.36	110.3	109.6	115.0	112.1	110.7	117.3
Alcoholic drinks and tobacco	1.64	107.2	138.0	151.8	108.4	139.4	157.7
Clothing and footwear	7.23	105.8	109.4	118.5	108.8	116.1	126.3
Durable goods	5.12	102.4	104.2	106.6	102.9	105.2	107.4
Miscellaneous goods	5.89	104.9	107.7	114.6	104.9	111.4	117.9
Transport	7.57	108.4	116.1	124.5	109.1	118.9	127.1
Services	11.08	108.2	114.8	127.4	108.7	120.5	133.3

Note: The CPI(B) covers about 30% of urban households with a monthly expenditure of between $10,000 and $17,499 in the base period 1989–90.

Hang Seng Consumer Price Index
(October 1989–September 1990 = 100)

Section	Weight	Annual average			Index for December		
		1990 (Oct–Dec)	1991	1992	1990	1991	1992
All items	**100.00**	**107.5**	**114.0**	**125.1**	**108.1**	**118.5**	**130.0**
Food	25.95	105.5	113.3	123.9	106.0	117.4	126.7
Meals away from home	(16.37)	107.0	113.8	126.0	107.2	119.2	130.8
Food, excluding meals away from home	(9.58)	103.2	112.5	120.4	104.0	114.3	119.6
Housing	29.48	110.1	118.1	132.3	111.3	123.5	140.5
Fuel and light	1.76	109.7	110.0	115.0	111.8	111.2	117.2
Alcoholic drinks and tobacco	0.88	107.5	134.6	148.3	108.6	136.7	153.5
Clothing and footwear	8.81	108.9	110.5	125.0	108.0	117.8	130.5
Durable goods	5.86	102.6	105.1	109.9	102.2	107.1	112.6
Miscellaneous goods	5.64	104.8	107.7	113.8	104.8	111.2	116.7
Transport	7.89	109.4	117.3	125.5	110.3	119.8	128.4
Services	13.73	106.9	112.2	123.0	107.7	117.4	127.6

Note: The Hang Seng CPI covers about 10% of urban households, living in private dwellings or Home Ownership Scheme flats and with a monthly expenditure of between $17,500 and $37,499 in the base period 1989–90.

Composite Consumer Price Index
(October 1989–September 1990 = 100)

Section	Weight	Annual average			Index for December		
		1990 (Oct–Dec)	1991	1992	1990	1991	1992
All items	**100.00**	**106.9**	**114.2**	**125.2**	**107.7**	**118.3**	**129.7**
Food	35.07	105.6	114.2	124.4	106.2	117.2	125.9
Meals away from home	(19.45)	108.0	116.3	128.6	108.6	120.7	132.5
Food, excluding meals away from home	(15.62)	102.7	111.6	119.2	103.3	112.7	117.6
Housing	24.06	108.8	116.9	132.0	109.9	122.6	141.2
Fuel and light	2.51	110.5	109.9	115.3	112.4	111.0	117.7
Alcoholic drinks and tobacco	1.74	107.0	141.3	155.3	108.3	142.1	161.7
Clothing and footwear	6.66	106.7	109.5	120.5	108.3	116.4	127.4
Durable goods	5.24	102.5	104.6	107.7	102.7	105.8	109.0
Miscellaneous goods	5.82	105.2	108.0	114.9	105.2	111.9	118.3
Transport	7.52	108.4	116.4	124.8	109.1	119.3	127.4
Services	11.38	108.1	114.4	126.8	108.7	120.1	132.6

Note: The Composite CPI covers all households of the CPI(A), CPI(B) and the Hang Seng CPI.

APPENDIX 21
(Chapter 9: Primary Production)

Imports of Crops, Livestock, Poultry and Fish

Item	Unit	1990	1991	1992
Crops				
Rice (unhusked)	tonne	374 075	391 644	400 165
Wheat	tonne	129 667	133 250	144 887
Other cereals and cereal preparations	tonne	353 141	378 738	373 006
Other field crops	tonne	91 074	88 760	75 209
Vegetables (fresh, frozen or simply preserved)	tonne	389 953	427 335	414 367
Vegetables (preserved or prepared), fruit and nuts (fresh, dried, preserved or prepared)	tonne	881 222	973 305	1 034 559
Flowers	$ thousand	149,545	156,153	177,821
Sugar and honey	tonne	200 820	216 589	193 169
Coffee	tonne	4 853	5 998	6 760
Cocoa	tonne	477	1 572	536
Tea and mate	tonne	21 627	24 274	31 229
Livestock and poultry				
Cattle	head	172 262	156 731	149 505
Sheep, lambs and goats	head	16 163	16 819	15 441
Swine	thousand head	2 848	2 821	2 792
Chicken	tonne	51 830	48 414	50 988
Other poultry	tonne	23 446	20 499	22 178
Live animals	tonne	4 558	3 572	3 090
Meat and meat preparations	tonne	361 155	404 517	470 841
Dairy products and eggs				
Milk (fresh)	tonne	42 676	42 290	49 344
Cream (fresh)	tonne	556	384	354
Milk and cream (evaporated, condensed, powdered, *etc*)	tonne	60 439	74 754	80 448
Butter, cheese and curd	tonne	10 698	11 203	13 739
Eggs (fresh)	thousand	1 386 215	1 451 307	1 518 307
Eggs (preserved)	thousand	190 712	188 063	207 781
Fish and fish preparations				
Fish (fresh, chilled or frozen)	tonne	123 730	162 621	188 865
Fish (dried, salted or smoked)	tonne	9 927	10 436	13 322
Crustaceans and molluscs (fresh, frozen, dried, salted, *etc*)	tonne	117 962	116 257	114 023
Fish products and preparations	tonne	10 208	10 272	7 103
Crustacean and mollusc products and preparations	tonne	4 124	4 782	5 562
Oil and fats (crude or refined)	tonne	40	90	191
Fish meals (animals feeding stuffs)	tonne	45 002	43 601	23 971

APPENDIX 22
(Chapter 9: Primary Production)

Estimated Local Production of Crops, Livestock, Poultry and Fish

Item	Unit	1990	1991	1992
Crops				
Vegetables (fresh, frozen or simply preserved)	tonne	112 000	105 000	95 000
Fresh fruit and nuts	tonne	4 310	3 950	2 730
Flowers	$ thousand	112,000	134,000	157,000
Other field crops*	tonne	1 540	1 260	540
Livestock and poultry				
Cattle	head	280	820	490
Swine‡	thousand head	413	314	182
Chicken	tonne	25 000	23 500	21 200
Other poultry	tonne	12 200	9 900	5 900
Dairy products and eggs				
Milk (fresh)	tonne	1 800	1 670	1 180
Eggs (fresh)	thousand	111 900	84 500	52 600
Fish and fish preparations				
Fish (fresh, chilled or frozen)				
Marine fish§	tonne	169 070	167 500	160 990
Freshwater fish	tonne	6 130	5 900	5 400
Fish (dried, salted or smoked)				
Marine fish	tonne	1 430	1 140	480
Crustaceans and molluscs (fresh, frozen, dried, salted, *etc*)	tonne	22 340	21 840	27 400
Fish products and preparations	tonne	340	330	370
Crustacean and mollusc products and preparations	tonne	160	240	180
Fish meals (animal feeding stuffs)	tonne	29 010	33 280	30 550

Note: * Other field crops include yam, millet, peanut, soybean, sugar cane, sweet potato and water chestnut.
    ‡ Including local swine not slaughtered in abattoirs.
    § Including cultured marine fish.

APPENDIX 23
(Chapter 9: Primary Production)

Local Production and Imports of Ores and Minerals

Tonnes

Item	Production 1990	Production 1991	Production 1992	Imports 1990	Imports 1991	Imports 1992
Quartz	—	—	—	1 790	1 235	1 937
Feldspar	3 820	—	—	178 243	185 599	205 310
Graphite	—	—	—	1 394	2 546	1 569
Kaolin/feldspar sand	16 587	—	—	401 654	480 678	477 896

APPENDIX 24
(Chapter 10: Education)

Number of Educational Institutions by Type*

	1990	As of September 1991	1992
Kindergarten	785	767	743
Primary Schools	681	671	652
Secondary Schools	485	487	494
Special Schools	71	74	74
Technical Institutes	8	8	7
Colleges of Education	4	4	4
Approved Post Secondary Colleges	2	1	1
Tertiary (UPGC-funded) Institutions	5	7	7
Open Learning Institute	1	1	1
Total	**2 042**	**2 020**	**1 983**

Note: * Including evening schools.

Student Numbers by Type of Educational Institutions§

Schools			
Kindergarten	196 466	193 658	189 730
Primary	526 720	517 137	501 625
Secondary	453 423	454 372	461 460
Special education	7 999	8 224	8 257
Sub-total	**1 184 608**	**1 173 391**	**1 161 072**
Technical Institutes#			
Craft courses	28 983	28 173	23 503
Technician courses	28 542	28 245	27 279
Sub-total	**57 525**	**56 418**	**50 782**
Colleges of Education#	**4 979**	**4 891**	**4 355**
Approved Post Secondary Colleges#	**4 730**	**3 373**	**3 070**
Tertiary (UPGC-funded) Institutions†			
Subdegree	24 165	25 832	23 441
First Degree	28 154	32 138	35 745
Postgraduate	5 345	6 960	9 508
Sub-total	**57 664**	**64 930**	**68 694**
Open Learning Institute‡	**13 009**	**17 535**	**14 462**
Total	**1 322 515**	**1 320 538**	**1 302 435**

Note: § Student numbers refer to students in day and evening schools, and full time and part time students in other educational institutions.
  # Figures are as of October.
  † Figures are as of December and the 1992 figures are provisional.
  ‡ No. of active students for October Semesters.

APPENDIX 25
(Chapter 10: Education)

Overseas Examinations

Examinations conducted by Hong Kong Examinations Authority	Candidate Entries		
	1990	*1991*	*1992*
London Chamber of Commerce and Industry	68 800	66 300	65 900
Test of English as a Foreign Language (TOEFL)	40 600	33 200	27 000
Associated Board of the Royal Schools of Music	39 600	42 800	45 100
Pitman Examinations Institute	27 000	24 200	21 400
Chartered Association of Certified Accountants	15 600	16 400	19 400
University of London – General Certificate of Education	11 200	9 200	6 500
Royal Academy of Dancing	5 700	5 900	6 100
Chartered Institute of Bankers	4 500	3 200	2 500
Associated Examining Board – General Certificate of Education	4 300	3 300	2 100
Institute of Chartered Secretaries and Administrators	3 600	3 700	3 700
Test of Spoken English	2 400	1 400	800
City and Guilds of London Institute	2 400	2 300	2 100
University of London – External Degree	1 500	1 700	1 900
Association of Accounting Technicians	1 500	1 700	1 800
University College of Southern Queensland	1 300	1 700	1 400
Australian Insurance Institute	1 300	1 300	1 300
Trinity College of Music	1 000	800	800
Others	10 500	12 200	9 200
Total	**242 800**	**231 300**	**219 000**

Note: Figures are rounded to the nearest hundred.

Conducted by Hong Kong Polytechnic:			
The Engineering Council Examination	879	804	955
Total	**879**	**804**	**955**

APPENDIX 26
(Chapter 10: Education)

Students Leaving Hong Kong for Overseas Studies §

Country	1990	1991	1992
Britain	4 349 #	4 428 #	4 408 #
United States	5 840	5 866	5 410
Canada	5 681	4 541	3 583
Australia	5 258	3 590	2 866

Note: § Figures are based on the number of student visas issued as supplied by visa-issuing authorities.
     # Excluding returned students, students on short courses and Government servants on training courses.

APPENDIX 27
(Chapter 10: Education)

Expenditure on Education

$ Thousand

| | School year Aug–July | | |
	1989–90	1990–91	1991–92
Recurrent expenditure	1,513,074	1,533,854	1 674 343
Capital expenditure	382,666	436,545	492 993
Grants and subsidies	7,750,317	9,571,778	10 287 429
Grants to Universities and Polytechnic (including rates)	3,613,095	4,228,110	5 991 029
University and Polytechnic Grants Committee (including university student grants)	80,769	115,071	121 464
Total	**13,339,921**	**15,885,358**	**18 567 258**
Education expenditure by other departments	1,036,754	1,442,391	1 835 277

APPENDIX 28
(Chapter 11: Health)

Vital Statistics

	1990	1991	1992
Estimated mid-year population	5 704 500	5 754 800	5 811 500
Births:			
Known live births	67 731	68 281‡	70 954
Crude birth rate (per 1 000 population)	12.0	12.0	12.3
Deaths:			
Known deaths	29 136	28 429‡	30 317
Crude death rate (per 1 000 population)	5.2	5.0‡	5.3
Infant mortality rate* (per 1 000 live births)	5.9	6.5	4.7
Neo-natal mortality rate* (per 1 000 live births)	3.8	4.0	2.9
Maternal mortality rate* (per 1 000 total births)	0.04	0.06	0.04
Life expectancy at birth (years)			
Male	74.6	74.9	75.1
Female	80.3	80.5	80.7

Note: * Based on registered deaths.
     ‡ Revised figures.

445

APPENDIX 29
(Chapter 11: Health)

Causes of Death*

	1990	1991	1992†
Infective and parasitic	**1 030**	**950**	**960**
Tuberculosis, all forms	382	409	410
Neoplasms	**8 686**	**8 861**	**9 026**
Malignant, including neoplasms of lymphatic and haematopoietic tissues	8 669	8 832	8 965
Endocrine, nutritional, metabolic and blood	**307**	**324**	**461**
Diabetes mellitus	270	271	368
Nervous system, sense organs and mental disorders	**234**	**213**	**285**
Circulatory system	**8 313**	**8 132**	**8 875**
Heart diseases, including hypertensive diseases	4 976	4 858	5 389
Cerebrovascular diseases	3 075	3 009	3 166
Respiratory system	**5 046**	**4 746**	**5 575**
Pneumonia, all forms	2 000	1 819	1 979
Bronchitis, emphysema and asthma	555	431	486
Digestive system	**1 219**	**1 201**	**1 225**
Peptic ulcer	31	34	38
Chronic liver disease and cirrhosis	319	375	449
Genito-urinary system	**1 358**	**1 292**	**1 224**
Complications of pregnancy, childbirth and the puerperium	**3**	**4**	**3**
Skin, subcutaneous tissues, musculoskeletal system and connective tissues	**67**	**37**	**45**
Congenital anomalies	**186**	**179**	**153**
Certain conditions originating in the perinatal period	**181**	**218**	**206**
Symptoms, signs and ill-defined conditions	**819**	**715**	**818**
Injury and poisoning	**1 752**	**1 810**	**1 672**
All accidents	894	868	797
Suicide and self-inflicted injuries	679	748	705
Unknown	—	—	—
Total deaths	**29 201**	**28 682**	**30 528**

Note: * Based on registered deaths.
      † Provisional figures.

APPENDIX 30
(Chapter 11: Health)

Hospital Beds

	As at end of year		
Category of hospitals	1990	1991	1992†
Hospital Authority hospitals	21 374	21 684	22 395
Correctional Institutions	759	776	827
Government maternity homes/clinics	315	173	164
Private hospitals	2 790	2 907	2 955
Private nursing/maternity homes	44	44	44
Total	**25 282**	**25 584**	**26 385**

Note: † Provisional figures.

APPENDIX 31
(Chapter 11: Health)

Professional Medical Personnel

	As at end of year							
	In Government service			Under Hospital Authority §		Total registered		
	1990	1991#	1992#	1991	1992	1990	1991	1992
Medical – Doctors	1 846@	456@	447@	2 218@	2 333@	6 260‡	6 545‡	6 818‡
Interns on provisional register	234	—	—	234	254	233	232	272
Externs on provisional register	54	—	—	63	21	54	63	69
Dental – Dentists	173	181	182	5	4	1 532‡	1 526‡	1 565‡
Dental hygienists	4	3	4	—	—	89	98	108
Nursing – Registered nurses (general)	7 879	828	841	10 744	11 113	19 121	20 072	20 884
Registered nurses (psychiatric)	1 052	—	—	1 033	1 037	1 242	1 315	1 367
Registered nurses (mental subnormal)	—	—	—	—	—	11	13	16
Registered nurses (sick children)	—	—	—	—	—	3	4	6
Enrolled nurses (general)	1 616	329	325	3 064	3 219	6 724	7 047	7 451
Enrolled nurses (psychiatric)	589	—	—	640	661	578	611	689
Midwives – Midwives (without nursing qualification)	211	107	98	141	131	981	981	981
Pharmacy and Poisons – Pharmacists	80	28	29	82	87	694	720	784
Medical Laboratory Technologists	593	218	227	303	316	—	1 826	2 158
Occupational Therapist	156	4	3	213	213	—	438	499

Note: Annual re-registration is required for doctors, dentists, pharmacists, medical laboratory technologists and occupational therapists.
Registration for medical laboratory technologists and occupational therapists started in 1991.
§   The management responsibility of all public hospitals was taken over by Hospital Authority on December 1, 1991.
#   Figures for 1991 and 1992 were those working in the Department of Health.
@ Including unregistrable medical officers.
‡   Including the professional medical/dental personnel on both the local and overseas lists.

APPENDIX 32
(Chapter 12: Social Welfare)

(A) The Hong Kong Council of Social Service

Member Agencies

Aberdeen Kaifong Welfare Association Social Service Centre
Action Group for Aid to the Mentally Retarded
Against Child Abuse
Agency for Volunteer Service
American Women's Association of Hong Kong Limited
Arts with Disabled Association Hong Kong
Asbury Village Community Centre of the Methodist Church, Hong Kong
Association for Engineering and Medical Volunteer Services
Association for the Advancement of Feminism
Association of Evangelical Free Churches of Hong Kong

Baptist Assembly
Baptist Oi Kwan Social Service
Barnabas Charitable Service Association Limited
Birthright Society Limited
Board of Studies in Social Work, The Chinese University of Hong Kong
Boys' and Girls' Clubs Association of Hong Kong
Boys' Brigade, Hong Kong
Breakthrough Counselling Centre

Canossian Mission (Welfare Services)
Caritas – Hong Kong
Catholic Women's League
Causeway Bay Kaifong Welfare Advancement Association
Chai Wan Areas Kaifong Welfare Advancement Association (HK) Limited
Chai Wan Baptist Church – Social Service Centre
Chain of Charity Movement
China Coast Community Limited
Chinese Evangelical Zion Church Limited Tze Wan Shan Zion Youth Centre
Chinese Young Men's Christian Association of Hong Kong
Ching Chung Taoist Association of Hong Kong Limited

Christian Family Service Centre
Christian and Missionary Alliance Church Union Hong Kong Limited – C & M A Social
Chung Shek Hei (Cheung Chau) Home for the Aged, Limited
Church of Christ in China, Hong Kong Council, Social Welfare Department
Conservancy Association
Community Drug Advisory Council
Church of United Brethen in Christ Hong Kong Ltd – Social Service Division

DACARS, Limited
Department of Applied Social Studies, City Polytechnic of Hong Kong
Department of Applied Social Studies, Hong Kong Polytechnic
Department of Public and Social Administration, City Polytechnic of Hong Kong
Department of Social Work and Social Administration, University of Hong Kong
Diocesan Youth Committee
Duke of Edinburgh's Award

Ebenezer School and Home for the Blind
Evangel Children's Home
Evangelical Free Church of China Hong Fok Tong Social Centre for the Elderly
Evangelical Lutheran Church Social Service – Hong Kong

Family Planning Association of Hong Kong
Finnish Missionary Society
Five Districts Business Welfare Association
Foreign Mission Board, Southern Baptist Convention, Hong Kong – Macau Baptist Mission
Free Methodist Church, Hong Kong

Girls' Brigade, Hong Kong

Hans Andersen Club
Harmony House Limited
Haven of Hope Christian Service

Heep Hong Society for Handicapped Children
Helping Hand Limited
Heung Hoi Ching Kok Lin Association
Holy Carpenter Church and Community Centre
Hong Kong Association for the Mentally Handicapped
Hong Kong Association of Occupational Therapists
Hong Kong Association of Speech Therapists
Hong Kong Association of the Blind
Hong Kong Association of the Deaf
Hong Kong Association of Workers Serving the Mentally Handicapped
Hong Kong Baptist College, Department of Social Work
Hong Kong Baptist Hospital, Au Shue Hung Health Centre
Hong Kong Baptist Theological Seminary
Hong Kong Cancer Fund – Friends of EORTC
Hong Kong Catholic Marriage Advisory Council
Hong Kong Catholic Youth Council
Hong Kong Children and Youth Services
Hong Kong Chinese Women's Club
Hong Kong Christian Concern for the Homeless Association
Hong Kong Christian Mutual Improvement Society
Hong Kong Christian Service
Hong Kong Confederation of Associations of the Handicapped
Hong Kong Council of Women
Hong Kong Down Syndrome Association
Hong Kong Emotion and Health Association Limited
Hong Kong Eye Bank and Research Foundation
Hong Kong Family Welfare Society
Hong Kong Federation of Handicapped Youth
Hong Kong Federation of Societies for Prevention of Blindness
Hong Kong Federation of the Blind
Hong Kong Federation of Youth Groups
Hong Kong Girl Guides Association
Hong Kong Housing Affairs Association
Hong Kong Housing Society
Hong Kong Joint Council of Parents of the Mentally Handicapped

Hong Kong Juvenile Care Centre
Hong Kong Life Guard Club
Hong Kong Lutheran Handicrafts Society
Hong Kong Lutheran Social Service, Lutheran Church – Hong Kong Synod
Hong Kong Macau Conference of Seventh-Day Adventist Church
Hong Kong People's Council on Public Housing Policy
Hong Kong PHAB Association
Hong Kong Playground Association
Hong Kong Recreation and Sports Association
Hong Kong Red Cross
Hong Kong Red Swastika Society
Hong Kong School for the Deaf
Hong Kong Shue Yan College
Hong Kong Social Workers Association Limited
Hong Kong Society for the Aged
Hong Kong Society for the Blind
Hong Kong Society for the Deaf
Hong Kong Society for the Protection of Children
Hong Kong Society for Rehabilitation
Hong Kong Sports Association for the Mentally Handicapped
Hong Kong Sports Association for the Physically Disabled (SAP)
Hong Kong Student Aid Society
Hong Kong Student Services Association
Hong Kong Tuberculosis, Chest and Heart Diseases Association
Hong Kong Workers' Health Centre
Hong Kong Young Women's Christian Association

Industrial Evangelistic Fellowship
Industrial Relations Institute
Institute of Cultural Affairs Limited
International Baptist Church (HK) Limited
International Church of the Foursquare Gospel – Hong Kong Districts Ltd
International Social Service Hong Kong Branch

Jane Shu Tsao Social Centre for the Elderly, Hong Kong Mutual Encouragement Association

Keswick Foundation Limited
Kowloon Union Church Wai Ji Training
   Centre
Kowloon Women's Welfare Club
Kwai Shing Christian Social Service Centre
Kwai Shing Estate Residents' Association
Kwun Tong Methodist Centre

Lai King Estate Tenants' Association
Lai Tak Youth Centre
Lei Fook Church Social Centre for the Elderly
   of the Hong Kong Chinese Christian and
   Missionary Alliance
Link Association
Lok Sin Tong Chu Ting Cheong Home for the
   Aged
Lutheran School for the Deaf

Mary Rose School
Marycove Centre
Maryknoll Sisters
Matilda Child Development Centre
Mental Health Association of Hong Kong
Methodist Ap Lei Chau Centre
Methodist Centre
Methodist Epworth Village Community Centre
Mission Covenant Church of Norway
   (Hong Kong Field)
Mother's Choice Limited

Neighbourhood Advice-Action Council
New Life Psychiatric Rehabilitation
   Association
New Territories Women and Juvenile Welfare
   Association Limited
New Voice Club of Hong Kong
North Point Kaifong Welfare Advancement
   Association

O.M.S. 'St Simon' Home for Fishermen's and
   Workmen's Children

Parents' Association of the Mentally
   Handicapped Limited
Parents' Association of Pre-School
   Handicapped Children
Pentecostal Holiness Church Ling Kwong
   Bradbury Centre for the Blind
Playright Children's Playground Association
   Limited

Po Leung Kuk
Pok Oi Hospital
Pre-School Playgroups Association
Prisoners' Friends' Association
Project Concern Hong Kong
Pui Hong Self-Help Association

Richmond Fellowship of Hong Kong

Salesian Society
Salvation Army
Samaritan Befrienders Hong Kong
Samaritans (English Speaking Service)
Save the Children Fund – Hong Kong
Scout Association of Hong Kong
Sheng Kung Hui Diocesan Welfare Council
Sheng Kung Hui Kei Oi Social Service Centre
Sheng Kung Hui Lady MacLehose Centre
Sheng Kung Hui St Christopher's Home
Shun Tin Christian Children's and Youth
   Centre
Sik Sik Yuen – Social Services Unit
Sisters of the Good Shepherd – Pelletier Hall
Sisters of the Precious Blood – Precious Blood
   Children Village
Social Service Group, Hong Kong University
   Students' Union
Society for Community Organisation
Society for the Aid and Rehabilitation of Drug
   Abusers
Society for the Rehabilitation of Offenders,
   Hong Kong
Society for the Relief of Disabled Children
Society of Boys' Centres
Society of Homes for the Handicapped
Society of St Vincent de Paul
Spastics Association of Hong Kong
St James' Settlement
St John Ambulance Association and Brigade,
   Hong Kong
St Stephen's Society
Stewards' Company (Hong Kong) Limited
Street Sleepers' Shelter Society Trustees
   Incorporated
Suen Mei Speech and Hearing Centre for the
   Deaf

Tai Hang Tung and Nam Shan Estate
   Residents' Association
Tai Wo Hau Residents' Association

TREATS
Tsuen Wan Ecumenical Social Service Centre
Tsung Tsin Mission Social Service Division
Tung Lum Buddhist Aged Home
Tung Sin Tan Home for the Aged
Tung Wah Group of Hospitals

United Christian Medical Service

Victoria Park School for the Deaf

Watchdog Limited
Wong Tai Sin District Federation of Welfare
  Services for the Aged

World Vision of Hong Kong
Wu Oi Christian Centre

Yan Chai Hospital
Yan Oi Tong Community and Indoor Sports
  Centre
Yang Memorial Social Service Centre
Young Men's Christian Association of Hong
  Kong
Young Workers' Confederation

Zion Youth Service Centre

(B) The Community Chest of Hong Kong

Member Agencies

Aberdeen Kaifong Welfare Association
  Community Centre
Action Group for Aid to the Mentally
  Retarded
Adventure Ship Limited
Against Child Abuse
Agency for Volunteer Service
Asbury Village Community Centre for the
  Methodist Church
Association of Evangelical Free Churches of
  Hong Kong

Baptist Oi Kwan Social Service
Barnabas Charitable Service Association
  Limited
Boys' Brigade, Hong Kong
Buddhist Po Ching Home for the Aged
  Women
Butterfly Bay Baptist Church Social Centre
  for the Elderly

Canossian Missions
Caritas – Hong Kong
Chain of Charity Movement

Cheung Hong Baptist Church Social Centre
  for the Elderly
Chinese Young Men's Christian Association of
  Hong Kong
Christian & Missionary Alliance Church
  Union Hong Kong Ltd
Christian Nationals' Evangelism Commission
  Aged People Centre
Church of God Ltd
Community Drug Advisory Council

Duke of Edinburgh's Award

Ebenezer School and Home for the Blind
Evangel Children's Home
Evangelical Lutheran Church – Hong Kong

Family Planning Association of Hong Kong
Finnish Missionary Society

Girl's Brigade (Hong Kong)

Hans Andersen Club
Harmony House Limited
Haven of Hope Christian Service

451

Heep Hong Society for Handicapped Children
Helping Hand
Hong Kong Anti-Cancer Society
Hong Kong Association of the Deaf
Hong Kong Catholic Marriage Advisory
　　Council
Hong Kong Children and Youth Services
Hong Kong Christian Aid to Refugees
Hong Kong Christian Concern for the
　　Homeless Association
Hong Kong Christian Industrial Committee
Hong Kong Christian Mutual Improvement
　　Society
Hong Kong Christian Service
Hong Kong Council of Social Service
Hong Kong Council of Women – Women's
　　Centre
Hong Kong Down Syndrome Association
Hong Kong Evangelical Church Tai Hing
　　Social Centre for the Elderly
Hong Kong Family Welfare Society
Hong Kong Federation of the Blind
Hong Kong Federation of Youth Groups
Hong Kong Housing Authority, North Point
　　Estate Residents' Association
Hong Kong Life Guard Club
Hong Kong Lutheran Social Service
Hong Kong Red Cross
Hong Kong School for the Deaf
Hong Kong Sea Cadet Corps
Hong Kong Sea School
Hong Kong Society for Rehabilitation
Hong Kong Society for the Aged
Hong Kong Society for the Blind
Hong Kong Society for the Deaf
Hong Kong Sports Association for Physically
　　Disabled (SAP)
Hong Kong Sports Association of the Deaf
Hong Kong Students Aid Society

International Church of the Foursquare
　　Gospel – HK District
International Social Service, Hong Kong
　　Branch

Kowloon Union Church Wai Ji Training
　　Centre
Kwun Tong Community Health Project

Lai King Baptist Church Bradbury Social
　　Centre for the Elderly
Lam Tin Alliance Church Social Centre for the
　　Elderly
Lei Fook Church Social Centre for Elderly
Light and Love Home
Lok Wah Swatow Christian Church Social
　　Centre for the Elderly

Marriage and Personal Counselling Service
Maryknoll Sisters Social Service
Mental Health Association of Hong Kong
Methodist Ap Lei Chau Centre
Methodist Church, Hong Kong – Kwun Tong
　　Methodist Centre
Methodist Epworth Village Community Centre
Mission Covenant Church, Yiu On Tong
　　Social Centre
Mother's Choice Limited

Neighbourhood Advice-Action Council
New Life Psychiatric Rehabilitation
　　Association
New Voice Club of Hong Kong
North Point Kaifong Welfare Advancement
　　Association

Pelletier Hall – Good Shepherd Sisters
Pentecostal Church of HK Ltd – Ngau Tau
　　Kok Social Centre for the Elderly
Pentecostal Holiness Church Ling Kwong
　　Bradbury Centre for the Blind
Pinehill Village
Project Care
Project Concern, Hong Kong

Richmond Fellowship of Hong Kong

Salvation Army
Samaritan Befrienders Hong Kong
Samaritans (English Speaking Service)
Sheng Kung Hui Holy Carpenter Social
　　Service Centre – Social Centre for the
　　Elderly
Sheng Kung Hui Diocesan Welfare Council
Sheng Kung Hui Holy Nativity Church Social
　　Service Centre
Sheng Kung Hui Kei Oi Social Service Centre
Sheng Kung Hui Lady MacLehose Centre

Sheng Kung Hui St Luke's Settlement – Social Centre for the Elderly
Sheng Kung Hui St Matthew's Church Senior Citizen's Club – Social Centre for the Elderly
Sheng Kung Hui Holy Carpenter Church Multi-Service Centre for the Elderly
Shun Tin Christian Children's and Youth Centre
Social Centre for the Elderly
Society for the Aid and Rehabilitation of Drug Abusers (SARDA)
Society for the Rehabilitation of Offenders, Hong Kong
Society of Boys' Centres
Society of St Vincent de Paul Central Council – Hong Kong
Spastics Association of Hong Kong
St Christopher's Home

St James' Settlement and Sheltered Workshop
St John Ambulance Association and Brigade
Steward's Company (Hong Kong) Limited
Street Sleepers' Shelter Society Trustees Inc.
Suen Mei Speech and Hearing Centre for the Deaf

Tai Hang Tung and Namshan Estate Residents' Association Ltd
Tsuen Wan Ecumenical Social Service Centre

Watchdog Limited

Yang Memorial Methodist Social Service Centre
Young Women's Christian Association, Hong Kong

APPENDIX 33
(Chapter 13: Housing)

Number of Quarters and Estimated Persons Accommodated as at March 31, 1992

Number of Quarters

Category	Hong Kong Island	Kowloon and New Kowloon	New Territories	Total
Government quarters	**8 000**	**8 700**	**12 000**	**28 700**
Public housing				
Housing Authority estates	68 600	260 700	312 000	641 300
Housing Authority cottage areas	500	400	1 900	2 800
Housing Society estates	10 700	12 500	9 500	32 700
Home Ownership Scheme Blocks*	12 400	33 700	98 600	144 700
Sub-total	**92 200**	**307 300**	**422 000**	**821 500**
Private housing	**306 100**	**322 000**	**324 800**	**952 900**
Total permanent	**406 300**	**638 000**	**758 800**	**1 803 100**

Estimated Persons Accommodated

Category	Hong Kong Island	Kowloon and New Kowloon	New Territories	Total
Government quarters	**20 300**	**19 900**	**21 800**	**62 000**
Public housing				
Housing Authority estates	243 900	821 900	1 180 000	2 245 800
Housing Authority cottage areas	1 400	700	3 600	5 700
Housing Society estates	41 700	42 500	35 700	119 900
Home Ownership Scheme Blocks*	44 600	117 900	348 200	510 700
Sub-total	**331 600**	**983 000**	**1 567 500**	**2 882 100**
Private housing	**904 600**	**889 500**	**823 500**	**2 617 600**
Total permanent	**1 256 500**	**1 892 400**	**2 412 800**	**5 561 700**
Temporary				**168 500**
Marine				**20 800**
Total population				**5 751 000**

Note: * Includes private sector participation scheme and middle income housing.

APPENDIX 34
(Chapter 14: Land, Public Works and Utilities)

Land Office

Item	1990	1991	1992
Instruments registered			
Assignments of whole buildings or sites	4 986	6 704	10 249
Assignments of flats or other units	166 354	182 997	157 920
Agreements for sale and purchase of flats or other units	130 109	180 964	139 927
Building mortgages/building legal charges	155	156	117
Other mortgages/legal charges	185 883	213 081	168 478
Reassignments/receipts/discharges/releases and certificates of satisfaction	111 306	137 030	123 921
Exclusion orders	10	51	6
Re-development orders	4	3	8
Miscellaneous	74 593	102 856	84 510
Total	**673 400**	**823 842**	**685 136**
Conditions of sale, grant, exchange, *etc* registered	598	588	691
Consents granted to entering into agreements for sale and purchase	64	70	51
Modifications and variations of lease conditions	688	656	711
Government leases issued	22	21	20
Determinations of Government rent and premium	196	84	62
Multi-storey building owners corporations registered	152	163	202
Public searches in Land Office records	2 604 294	3 168 942	3 207 280

Considerations in Instruments Registered in Land Office

			$ Thousand
Assignments of whole buildings or sites	27,370,032	41,071,778	58,225,310
Assignments of flats or other units	159,194,079	227,014,978	296,063,889
Agreements for sale and purchase of flats or other units	159,438,252	318,537,996	385,384,460
Building mortgages/building legal charges	9,421,948	8,955,048	5,791,832
Other mortgages/legal charges	77,830,298	92,107,888	88,538,235
Reassignments/receipts/discharges/releases and certificates of satisfaction	33,153,028	40,473,520	45,163,161
Miscellaneous instruments	728,941	10,769,070	267,949
Total	**467,136,578**	**738,930,278**	**879,434,836**

APPENDIX 35
(Chapter 14: Land, Public Works and Utilities)

Land Usage

Class	Approximate area (km²)	Percentage of whole	Remarks
A. Developed Lands			
i. Commercial	2	0.2	
ii. Residential	40	3.7	Including all residential areas except public rental housing estates, HOS/PSPS and temporary housing areas
iii. Public Rental Housing	10	0.9	Including HOS/PSPS
iv. Industrial	9	0.8	Including warehouse and storage
v. Open Space	15	1.4	
vi. Government, Institution and Community Facilities	16	1.5	
vii. Vacant Development Land	36	3.4	Including land with construction in progress
viii. Roads/Railways	23	2.1	Including flyovers and railway lands
ix. Temporary Housing Areas	1	0.1	
B. Non-built-up Lands*			
i. Woodlands	220	20.5	Natural and established woodlands
ii. Grass and scrub	519	48.2	Natural grass and scrubland
iii. Badlands, swamp and mangrove	44	4.1	Land stripped of cover, or denuded granite country including coastal brackish swamp and mangrove
iv. Arable	66	6.1	Cultivable lands, including orchards and market gardens, under cultivation and fallow
v. Fish ponds	16	1.5	Fresh and brackish water fish farming excluding coastal marine fish farms
vi. Temporary structures/livestock farms	12	1.1	
vii. Reservoir	26	2.4	
viii. Other uses	21	2.0	Including cemetery, crematorium, mine and quarry etc.
Total	**1 076**	**100.0**	

Note: * Within these are 413 km² of country parks and special areas designated under the Country Parks Ordinance for protection of vegetation and wild life and for recreation.

APPENDIX 36
(Chapter 14: Land, Public Works and Utilities)

Electricity Consumption, 1992

	Maximum demand megawatts	Sales million megajoules	Consumers hundreds
China Light and Power Company	5 289	86 042	15 643
	(4 828)	(77 183)	(15 211)
The Hongkong Electric Company	1 819	25 975*	4 562
	(1 680)	(24 976)*	(4 455)
Total		**112 017**	**20 205**

Note: Figures in brackets refer to 1991.
    * Excluding inter-connection sales.

Electricity Distribution

			million megajoules
	1990	1991	1992
Domestic	19 037	20 586	21 716
Industrial	24 934	25 051	24 194
Commercial	41 582	45 245	47 971
Street lighting	248	259	271
Export to China	6 470	11 019	17 866
Total	**92 270**	**102 159**	**112 017**

Gas Consumption and Distribution (Town Gas)

			million megajoules
	1990	1991	1992
Domestic	7 596	8 133	9 152
Industrial	583	701	823
Commercial	6 876	7 404	8 232
Total	**15 055**	**16 238**	**18 207**

Local Sales of Liquefied Petroleum Gas (LPG)

			tonnes
	1990	1991	1992†
Total	**200 642**	**202 580**	**211 533**

Note: † Estimated figure.

Water Consumption

			million cubic metres
	1990	1991	1992
Fresh water	873	884	889
Salt water (flushing purposes)	119	123	127

457

APPENDIX 37
(Chapter 15: Transport)

International Movements of Aircraft and Vessels

	1990	1991	1992
Aircraft			
Arrivals	52 886	54 863	60 477†
Departures	52 896	54 855	60 480†
Total	**105 782**	**109 718**	**120 957†**
Ocean-going vessels			
Arrivals	18 847	21 178	26 022†
Departures	18 824	21 217	25 931†
Total	**37 671**	**42 395**	**51 953†**
River steamers, hydrofoils, hoverferries, catamarans and river trading vessels			
Arrivals	102 443	106 673	120 000†
Departures	102 578	106 267	120 000†
Total	**205 021**	**212 940**	**240 000†**

Note: † Provisional figures.

International Movements of Passengers (Immigration figures)

	1990	1991	Thousands 1992
Arrivals			
Air	7 316	7 412	8 451
Sea	8 501	8 984	9 621
Land	16 018	18 167	20 453
Total	**31 835**	**34 563**	**38 525**
Departures			
Air	7 517	7 602	8 636
Sea	8 718	9 235	9 904
Land	15 597	17 737	19 960
Total	**31 832**	**34 574**	**38 500**

Note: All figures quoted here exclude:
    i. Passengers in transit.
    ii. Passengers refused permission to land.
    iii. Military passengers.

International Movements of Commercial Cargo by Different Means of Transport

	1990	1991	Tonnes 1992
Air			
Discharged	352 887	372 126	422 666†
Loaded	449 052	477 660	534 196†
Total	**801 939**	**849 786**	**956 862†**
Ocean-going vessels #			
Discharged	46 241 967	52 898 899	56 790 000†
Loaded	19 766 000	23 546 272	24 960 000†
Total	**66 007 967**	**76 445 171**	**81 750 000†**
River vessels			
Discharged	6 025 821	6 722 342	11 756 000†
Loaded	3 261 603	4 424 955	7 523 000†
Total	**9 287 424**	**11 147 297**	**19 279 000†**
Rail			
Discharged§	1 849 830	1 742 697	1 542 556
Loaded	366 888	338 735	368 992
Total	**2 216 718**	**2 081 432**	**1 911 548**
Road*			
Discharged	4 564 978	5 503 363	6 417 659
Loaded	4 496 075	5 492 129	5 736 337
Total	**9 061 053**	**10 995 492**	**12 153 996**

Note: # Figures on cargo movement by ocean-going vessels are based on the Shipping Statistics System set up by the Census and Statistics Department and are estimated from a sample of consignments on ocean cargo manifests. Figures on cargo movement by river vessels are provided by the Marine Department. The totals of these figures differ from those provided by the Marine Department and used elsewhere in this publication.
    § Excluding livestock totalling 1 986 007 heads in 1990, 1 875 272 heads in 1991 and 1 907 675 heads in 1992.
    * Road transport refers to cross frontier traffic through Man Kam To, Sha Tau Kok and Lok Ma Chau to and from China.
    † Provisional figures.

APPENDIX 38
(Chapter 15: Transport)

Registered/Licensed Motor Vehicles

| | As at end of year | | | | | |
| | 1990 | | 1991 | | 1992 | |
Public service vehicles	*Registered*	*Licensed*	*Registered*	*Licensed*	*Registered*	*Licensed*
Public buses						
China Motor Bus Company	1 022	961	1 015	948	1 011	999
Kowloon Motor Bus Company	2 912	2 885	3 038	3 022	3 109	3 097
New Lantao Bus Company	64	58	70	65	76	64
Others	3 627	3 405	3 780	3 582	4 011	3 743
Public light buses	4 350	4 336	4 350	4 336	4 349	4 336
Taxis	17 380	17 060	17 529	17 308	17 720	17 537
Private vehicles						
Motor cycles	20 683	16 621	22 961	17 762	24 871	18 667
Motor tricycles	14	7	25	15	19	11
Private cars	215 709	197 852	236 747	212 017	265 755	237 035
Private buses	185	180	201	197	240	231
Private light buses	2 551	2 410	2 561	2 384	2 525	2 348
Goods vehicles	130 270	117 745	134 285	118 061	140 755	119 790
Crown vehicles (excluding vehicles of HM Forces)						
Motor cycles	1 259	1 259	1 287	1 287	1 198	1 198
Other motor vehicles	5 381	5 381	5 920	5 920	5 582	5 582
Total	**405 407**	**370 160**	**433 769**	**386 904**	**471 221**	**414 638**
Tramcars						
Hongkong Tramways	163	163	163	163	163	163
Peak Tramways Company	2	2	2	2	2	2
Light Rail Transit	70	70	70	70	82	82
Total	**235**	**235**	**235**	**235**	**247**	**247**

Public Transport: Passengers Carried by Undertaking

| | | | *Thousand journeys* |
	1990	*1991*	*1992†*
Kowloon Motor Bus Company	965 858	968 082	969 689
China Motor Bus Company	280 884	267 145	261 922
New Lantao Bus Company	4 232	4 286	4 010
City Bus§	—	182	962
Kowloon-Canton Railway Bus	27 972	33 984	33 896
Mass Transit Railway Corporation	719 111	725 966	749 066
Kowloon-Canton Railway Corporation	181 077	190 668	199 962
Light Rail Transit	73 149	82 061	91 718
Hongkong Tramways	127 643	123 247	124 063
Peak Tramways Company	3 211	3 132	3 276
Green Minibus	249 003	250 634	256 861
Residential Coach Services	16 429	23 342	25 272
Hongkong and Yaumati Ferry Company	55 202	50 960	44 479
'Star' Ferry Company	37 907	36 602	35 765
Minor Ferries	6 823	7 517	8 283
Public Light Buses #	387 232	378 746	371 350
Taxi #	451 665	455 825	463 797
Total @	**3 587 400**	**3 602 377**	**3 644 370**

Public Transport: Passengers Carried by Area
(excluding passengers of public light buses and taxis)

			Thousand journeys
	1990	*1991*	*1992†*
Hong Kong Island	500 882	489 575	494 995
Kowloon	788 232	764 478	754 294
Cross Harbour			
Ferry	69 505	63 410	56 284
Tunnels	411 336	415 278	423 919
New Territories	978 547	1 035 065	1 079 730
Total @	**2 748 503**	**2 767 807**	**2 809 223**

Public Transport: Daily Average Number of Passengers
Carried by Different Modes of Transport

			Thousand journeys
	1990	*1991*	*1992†*
Bus	3 504	3 489	3 471
Public light bus # and Green Minibus	1 743	1 724	1 716
Taxi #	1 237	1 249	1 267
Ferry	274	260	242
Tram	359	346	348
Railway*	2 666	2 736	2 844
Residential coach	45	64	69
Total @	**9 828**	**9 870**	**9 957**

Note: † Provisional figures.
§ City Bus Ltd. started operating a franchised bus route No. 12A from September 12, 1991.
# Estimate.
* Includes Mass Transit Railway and Light Rail Transit.
@ Figures may not add up to total due to rounding.

APPENDIX 39
(Chapter 18: Public Order)

Traffic Accidents

	1990	1991	1992†
Hong Kong Island	3 691	3 748	3 641
Kowloon	7 847	7 923	7 773
New Territories	3 416	3 619	3 874
Marine	33	37	31
Total	**14 987**	**15 327**	**15 319**

Traffic Casualties

	1990	1991	1992†
Hong Kong Island			
Fatal	70	51	50
Serious	809	838	786
Slight	3 908	3 936	3 955
Kowloon			
Fatal	155	136	153
Serious	1 798	1 834	2 013
Slight	8 149	8 152	8 176
New Territories			
Fatal	94	127	122
Serious	1 314	1 272	1 298
Slight	3 700	4 226	4 411
Marine			
Fatal	—	1	—
Serious	5	18	22
Slight	46	46	68
Total	**20 048**	**20 637**	**21 054**

Note: † Provisional figures.

APPENDIX 40
(Chapter 18: Public Order)

Crime

Police Cases

Type of offence	Number of cases reported			Number of persons arrested		
	1990	1991	1992	1990	1991	1992
Violent Crime						
Rape	111	114	116	109	86	86
Indecent assault	1 078	1 101	1 099	657	655	611
Murder and manslaughter	137	92	108	175	136	138
Attempted murder	11	12	17	5	14	8
Wounding	1 638	1 398	1 170	1 114	1 166	1 008
Serious assault	5 057	4 983	4 600	3 235	3 389	3 157
Assault on police	842	953	1 018	564	609	707
Kidnapping and child stealing	6	8	12	14	24	29
Cruelty to child	68	73	82	70	69	82
Criminal intimidation	457	410	519	316	343	400
Robbery with firearms	66	46	46	31	33	17
Robbery with pistol like object	356	501	372	71	101	64
Other robberies	7 607	8 591	7 976	2 145	2 378	2 342
Aggravated burglary	5	4	1	4	4	1
Blackmail	814	719	883	887	761	938
Arson	567	553	548	87	92	94
Total	**18 820**	**19 558**	**18 567**	**9 484**	**9 860**	**9 682**
Non-Violent Crime						
Burglary	12 696	13 894	13 595	1 341	1 563	1 626
Snatching	2 024	1 995	1 685	309	277	272
Pickpocketing	932	779	675	416	373	281
Shop theft	5 847	6 008	6 362	5 298	5 462	6 008
Theft from vehicle	4 607	4 007	3 497	888	757	854
Taking conveyance without authority	6 434	6 475	7 046	443	431	454
Other thefts	12 309	12 324	11 810	4 312	4 591	4 535
Handling stolen goods	196	230	235	230	300	312
Deception, fraud and forgery	2 017	2 128	2 080	1 227	1 265	1 266
Sexual offences other than rape and indecent assault	1 223	1 052	948	1 102	989	851
Manufacturing and trafficking of dangerous drugs	3 604	2 998	1 803	4 428	3 720	2 192
Serious immigration offences	3 153	4 042	4 452	3 434	4 113	4 473
Criminal damage	5 141	4 422	4 298	1 620	1 307	1 507
Unlawful society offences	1 084	1 096	1 466	594	699	755
Possession of offensive weapon	1 024	1 007	791	1 331	1 335	916
Other crimes	7 189	6 644	4 746	7 556	7 017	5 796
Total	**69 480**	**69 101**	**65 489**	**34 529**	**34 199**	**32 098**
Grand Total	**88 300**	**88 659**	**84 056**	**44 013**	**44 059**	**41 780**
Overall detection rate	1990 = 45.2 per cent		1991 = 45.2 per cent		1992 = 45.2 per cent	

Narcotic Offence Cases

Type of offence	Number of cases reported			Number of persons arrested		
	1990	*1991*	*1992*	*1990*	*1991*	*1992*
Serious offences						
Manufacturing of dangerous drugs	5	5	10	11	12	17
Trafficking in dangerous drugs	93	171	421	127	228	538
Possession of dangerous drugs (indictable offence)	3 506	2 821	1 372	4 290	3 477	1 637
Other serious narcotic offences	—	1	—	—	3	—
Sub-total	**3 604**	**2 998**	**1 803**	**4 428**	**3 720**	**2 192**
Minor offences – Opium						
Simple possession of opium	64	35	29	41	19	18
Possession of equipment	63	39	10	1	12	—
Keeping a divan	18	9	7	14	4	9
Consuming opium	31	21	12	26	11	2
Other opium offences	1	1	—	1	—	—
Sub-total	**177**	**105**	**58**	**83**	**46**	**29**
Minor offences – Heroin						
Simple possession of heroin	1 887	2 776	5 963	1 791	2 698	5 886
Possession of equipment	649	489	545	196	200	240
Keeping a divan	—	2	1	—	5	1
Consuming heroin	118	196	171	62	101	149
Other heroin offences	15	23	35	5	9	16
Sub-total	**2 669**	**3 486**	**6 715**	**2 054**	**3 013**	**6 292**
Minor offences – Other dangerous drugs						
Simple possession	739	823	1 023	657	760	989
Consuming	—	—	1	—	—	2
Other offences	54	34	40	27	25	22
Sub-total	**793**	**857**	**1 064**	**684**	**785**	**1 013**
Total	**7 243**	**7 446**	**9 640**	**7 249**	**7 564**	**9 526**

Note: Serious narcotics offences include police cases only.

463

ICAC Cases

	1990	1991	1992				Total
			Number of persons prosecuted				
			Pending	Convicted	Acquitted	Nolle Prosequi	
Involving individuals employed in government departments							
Architectural Services	—	—	—	—	1	—	1
Buildings and Lands	3	3	—	—	—	—	—
City & New Territories Administration	1	—	—	—	—	—	—
Correctional Services	2	1	1	3	—	—	4
Customs & Excise	—	8	—	—	—	—	—
Drainage Services	—	1	—	—	—	—	—
Environmental Protection	—	1	—	—	—	—	—
Fire Services	—	1	—	—	—	—	—
Highways	—	—	—	1	—	—	1
Housing	2	—	1	—	—	—	1
Immigration	2	—	—	3	—	—	3
Legal	2	—	—	—	—	—	—
Medical & Health§	—	1	—	—	—	—	—
Post Office	—	1	—	—	1	—	1
Regional Services	1	1	—	—	—	—	—
Royal Hong Kong Police	10	8	4	2	3	—	9
Television & Entertainment Licensing Authority	3	—	—	—	—	—	—
Transport	—	1	—	1	—	—	1
Urban Services	3	6	1	2	1	—	4
Water Supplies	—	—	1	—	—	—	1
Sub-total	29	33	8	12	6	—	26
Others							
Crown servants/private individuals‡	26	48	3	9	1	—	13
Public bodies♯	5	21	3	5	1	—	9
Public bodies/private individuals‡	2	4	—	2	—	—	2
Private sector**	222	208	103	127	23	—	253
Sub-total	255	281	109	143	25	—	277
Total	284	314	117	155	31	—	303

Note: § As from April 1, 1989, the Medical and Health Department was restructed to form the Hospital Services Department and the Department of Health. Figures concerning the two new departments for 1991 continue to be classified under the Medical and Health Department.
‡ These are cases in which Crown/public servants and private individuals were involved.
♯ As defined in the Prevention of Bribery Ordinance, Cap. 201.
**These are cases in which only private individuals were involved.

APPENDIX 41
(Chapter 18: Public Order)

Judiciary Statistics

	1990	1991	1992
Supreme Court			
(i) Court of Appeal			
Civil appeals	198	206	211
Criminal appeals	604	588	548
Total	**802**	**794**	**759**
(ii) High Court			
Criminal jurisdiction			
Criminal cases	356	419	424
Appeals from Magistrates	1 817	1 190	1 112
Total	**2 173**	**1 609**	**1 536**
Civil Jurisdiction			
High Court actions	8 901	10 020	9 305
Commercial cases	174	205	152
Construction cases	17	20	13
Miscellaneous proceedings	4 052	3 997	4 206
Adoptions	4	10	8
Divorce	8	6	1
Admiralty jurisdiction	387	421	335
Bankruptcy	955	859	887
Company winding-up	401	422	423
Appeals from Small Claims and Labour Tribunals	101	98	84
Total	**15 000**	**16 058**	**15 414**
District Court			
Criminal cases	1 407	1 235	1 316
Other cases			
Civil actions	29 782	26 369	34 927
Stamp Appeals	29	55	37
Employee's compensation	780	784	693
Distress for rent	3 781	4 557	4 381
Divorce	6 767	7 287	8 067
Adoptions	290	341	319
Lands	5 182	4 875	5 373
Total	**48 018**	**45 503**	**55 113**
Small Claims Tribunal			
Number of cases filed	**39 194**	**38 756**	**38 930**
Labour Tribunal			
Number of cases filed	**4 551**	**4 964**	**5 199**
Obscene Articles Tribunal			
Number of cases filed	**1 802**	**4 675**	**5 740**
Coroner's Court			
Number of death inquiries made	**292**	**270**	**257**
Magistracies			
Charge sheets issued	130 321	111 834	122 111
Summonses issued	322 679	345 977	360 536
Miscellaneous proceedings issued	16 774	16 753	17 131
Anti-litter notices issued	43 865	40 011	38 459
Total	**513 639**	**514 575**	**538 237**
Defendants charged			
Adults	510 515	520 803	551 113
Juveniles	3 429	2 858	2 541
Total	**513 944**	**523 661**	**553 654**
Defendants convicted			
Adults	483 890	479 607	469 245
Juveniles	2 659	2 135	1 782
Total	**486 549**	**481 742**	**471 027**

APPENDIX 42
(Chapter 18: Public Order)

Correctional Services

	1990	As at end of year 1991	1992
Population of			
Prisons	10 027	8 972‡	9 035
Training centres	806	722	576
Detention centres	318	319	271
Treatment centres	944	1 018	1 067
Vietnamese refugees/Vietnamese migrants			
Illegal immigrants	28 386	34 778‡	33 004
Number Discharged under aftercare	3 331‡	3 121‡	3 256

Note: ‡ Revised figure.

APPENDIX 43
(Chapter 21: Communications and the Media)

Communications

	1990	1991	1992 Estimate
Postal traffic:			
Letter mail (million articles)			
Posted to destinations abroad	136.1	142.1	142.8
Posted for local delivery	639.6	711.2	743.5
Received from abroad for local delivery	88.3	87.5	91.0
In transit	3.9	3.8	3.2
Parcels (thousands)			
Posted to destinations abroad	1 330	1 347	1 259
Posted for local delivery	74	51	48
Received from abroad for local delivery	554	508	506
In transit	38	37	40
Telecommunications traffic:			
Telegrams (thousand messages)			
Accepted for transmission	449	344	280
Received	544	425	361
In transit	139	137	129
Telex calls (thousand minutes)			
Outward	26 711	23 907	20 177
Inward	31 524	27 345	23 014
International telephone calls (thousand minutes)			
Outward (voice)	582 004	731 343	917 889
Outward (fax and data)	112 500	135 255	160 407
Inward (voice, fax and data)	613 651	742 617	946 795
Radio pictures			
Transmitted	4	—	—
Received	244	157	97
Broadcast and reception services (thousand hours)			
Press	10.2	0.6	0.4*
Meteorological	109.3	108.5	106.2
International telephone circuits	12 189	14 732	17 800
International telegraph circuits	3 195	3 070	2 900
Telex trunks	2 389	2 373	2 300
International leased circuits	1 805	1 637	1 575
Telephone exchanges	72	75	76
Exchange capacity (thousand lines)	2 763	2 850	2 995
Keylines and PABX lines (thousands)	339	372	407
Fax lines (thousands)	107	137	184
Telephone lines (thousands)	2 447	2 596	2 777
Telephones (thousands)	3 280†	3 455†	3 651†
Telephones per 100 population	56.5†	60.0†	62.7†
Outgoing international calls (million)	205.28	264.56	335.20
Telecommunications licences (all types)	76 699	80 249	83 983

Note: † Estimate.
　　　* Customer terminated its service with effect from August 1992.

APPENDIX 44
(Chapter 23: Recreation, Sports and the Arts)

Recreational Facilities

Facilities	Urban Council			Regional Council		
	1990	1991	1992	1990	1991	1992
Indoor games halls/Indoor recreation centres	30	33	34	18	25	27
Squash courts	113	121	131	66	86	100
Tennis courts	112	112	118	54	68	89
Fitness centres/Sports centres	10	10	10	4	4	4
Stadia (outdoor)	2	2	2	—	—	—
Grass pitches	38	39	39	12	14	17
Hard surfaced pitches	117	118	123	51	76	78
Athletic grounds	9	9	8	9	10	12
Bowling greens	2	2	2	—	—	—
Obstacle golf courses	2	2	2	—	—	—
Roller skating rinks	18	18	17	22	24	24
Jogging tracks	19	21	24	1	1	1
Cycling tracks	3	3	3	—	2	2
Boating parks	1	1	1	2	1	1
Beaches	12	12	12	30	30	30
Swimming pool complexes	14	14	14	8	10	13
Water sports centres	—	—	—	3	3	3
Holiday camps	1	1	1	2	3	3
Gardens/Sitting-out area	716	728	794	370	430	487
Children's playgrounds	242	244	265	195	224	247
Zoos/aviaries	4	4	4	—	1	1
Total area of public open space administered (hectares)*	**510**	**513**	**518**	**615**	**633**	**651**

Note: * Open space on beaches are excluded.

APPENDIX 45
(Chapter 24: The Environment)

Climatological Summary, 1992

Month	Mean pressure at mean sea level	Maximum air temperature	Mean air temperature	Minimum air temperature	Mean dew point	Mean relative humidity	Mean amount of cloud	Total bright sunshine	Total rainfall	Prevailing wind direction	Mean wind speed
	hectopascals	°C	°C	°C	°C	per cent	per cent	hours	mm	degrees	km/h
January	1022.2	23.1	15.7	8.4	9.8	69	43	197.1	40.0	020	24.3
February	1018.3	23.3	15.4	11.2	12.3	83	80	64.1	142.8	070	27.5
March	1015.8	25.5	18.0	9.7	16.2	90	92	37.6	242.4	040	23.0
April	1011.7	29.6	21.9	17.4	19.5	87	85	75.5	492.2	040	19.9
May	1009.4	31.0	24.8	20.2	22.3	86	80	94.0	602.3	090	18.8
June	1006.6	32.8	27.2	22.5	24.5	86	80	134.5	532.8	100	22.9
July	1007.9	32.4	28.2	23.4	24.6	81	66	209.6	358.1	230	25.5
August	1004.2	35.0	29.4	25.6	24.7	77	62	217.3	97.7	020	19.2
September	1007.5	33.5	28.9	24.7	23.9	75	54	200.5	63.1	100	21.5
October	1015.6	31.2	24.6	19.6	17.5	66	44	239.3	30.9	100	27.7
November	1020.1	26.4	20.4	13.1	12.9	64	31	234.4	10.1	090	27.6
December	1020.4	25.4	19.2	11.7	14.9	77	61	151.6	66.4	090	25.6
Year	**1013.3**	**35.0**	**22.8**	**8.4**	**18.6**	**78**	**65**	**1 855.5**	**2 678.8**	**090**	**23.6**

Climatological Normals (1961–1990)

Month	hectopascals	°C*	°C	°C*	°C	per cent	per cent	hours	mm	degrees	km/h
January	1 020.2	26.9	15.8	0.0	10.2	71	58	152.4	23.4	070	24.0
February	1 018.7	27.8	15.9	2.4	11.8	78	73	97.7	48.0	070	23.8
March	1 016.2	30.1	18.5	4.8	15.0	81	76	96.4	66.9	070	22.1
April	1 013.1	33.4	22.2	9.9	19.0	83	78	108.9	161.5	080	19.7
May	1 009.1	35.5	25.9	15.4	22.6	83	74	153.8	316.7	090	19.2
June	1 006.0	35.6	27.8	19.2	24.4	82	75	161.1	376.0	090	21.6
July	1 005.3	35.7	28.8	21.7	24.9	80	65	231.1	323.5	230	20.0
August	1 005.1	36.1	28.4	21.6	24.8	81	66	207.0	391.4	090	18.5
September	1 008.8	35.2	27.6	18.4	23.3	78	63	181.7	299.7	090	21.9
October	1 014.0	34.3	25.2	13.5	19.8	73	56	195.0	144.8	090	27.6
November	1 017.9	31.8	21.4	6.5	15.2	69	53	181.5	35.1	080	27.2
December	1 020.2	28.7	17.6	4.3	11.2	68	49	181.5	27.3	080	25.5
Year	**1 012.9**	**36.1**	**23.0**	**0.0**	**18.6**	**77**	**65**	**1 948.1**	**2 214.3**	**080**	**22.6**

Note: * These extreme values are for the period 1884–1939; 1947–1992.

APPENDIX 46
(Chapter 26: History)

Governors of Hong Kong

The Right Honourable Sir Henry POTTINGER, Bt, PC, GCB   June 26, 1843

Sir John Francis DAVIS, Bt, KCB   May 8, 1844

Sir Samuel George BONHAM, Bt, KCB   March 21, 1848

Sir John BOWRING   April 13, 1854

The Right Honourable the Lord ROSMEAD, PC, GCMG
    (formerly the Right Honourable Sir Hercules ROBINSON, Bt)   September 9, 1859

Sir Richard Graves MACDONNELL, KCMG, CB   March 11, 1866

Sir Arthur Edward KENNEDY, GCMG, CB   April 16, 1872

Sir John Pope HENNESSY, KCMG   April 22, 1877

The Right Honourable Sir George Ferguson BOWEN, PC,
    GCMG   March 30, 1883

Sir George William DES VOEUX, GCMG   October 6, 1887

Sir William ROBINSON, GCMG   December 10, 1891

Sir Henry Arthur BLAKE, GCMG   November 25, 1898

The Right Honourable Sir Matthew NATHAN, PC, GCMG   July 29, 1904

The Right Honourable the Lord LUGARD, PC, GCMG, CB,
    DSO   July 29, 1907

Sir Francis Henry MAY, GCMG   July 24, 1912

Sir Reginald Edward STUBBS, GCMG   September 30, 1919

Sir Cecil CLEMENTI, GCMG   November 1, 1925

Sir William PEEL, KCMG, KBE   May 9, 1930

Sir Andrew CALDECOTT, GCMG, CBE   December 12, 1935

Sir Geoffry Alexander Stafford NORTHCOTE, KCMG   October 28, 1937

Sir Mark Aitchison YOUNG, GCMG   September 10, 1941

Sir Alexander William George Herder GRANTHAM, GCMG   July 25, 1947

Sir Robert Brown BLACK, GCMG, OBE   January 23, 1958

Sir David Clive Crosbie TRENCH, GCMG, MC   April 14, 1964

Lord MACLEHOSE of Beoch, GBE, KCMG, KCVO
    (formerly Sir Crawford Murray MACLEHOSE)   November 19, 1971

Sir Edward YOUDE, GCMG, MBE   May 20, 1982

Lord WILSON of Tillyorn, GCMG
    (formerly Sir David WILSON, GCMG)   April 9, 1987

The Right Honourable Christopher Francis PATTEN   July 9, 1992

INDEX

470

HONG KONG GOVERNMENT PUBLICATIONS
are obtainable from
THE GOVERNMENT PUBLICATIONS CENTRE
GPO Building, Connaught Place, Hong Kong

Leading bookshops throughout Hong Kong

GOVERNMENT INFORMATION SERVICES
(bulk sales and editorial enquiries)
French Mission Building, 1 Battery Path, Central, Hong Kong

and from

THE HONG KONG GOVERNMENT OFFICE
6 Grafton Street, London, W1X, 3LB

A list of current official publications will be sent on request

Printed and Published by H. Myers, Government Printer
at the Government Printing Department, Hong Kong

The Interdependence of
HONG KONG and CHINA

Map Note:
Data supplied by China Light & Power Co. Ltd.,
Agriculture & Fisheries Department, Census &
Statistics Department, Immigration Department
and Water Supplies Department.
Base map is diagrammatic only.

ZHAOQING SHI

Bei Jiang

Xi Jiang

Zhaoqing
Nan'an

Gaom

JIANGMEN SH

SOURCES & VALUE OF
FRESH FOODSTUFF SUPPLIES IN 1991

values in million HK$

12.4%
87.6%

Live Pigs
2 100

1.2%
98.8%
Live Cattle
200

0.6% 12.6%
86.8%
Fruit
3 900

12.5%
5.7%
81.8%

Fresh Water Fish
700

FROM
LOCAL

16.6%   38.1%
45.3%

FROM
CHINA

FROM OTHER
COUNTRIES

TOTAL SUPPLIES
12 900

15.6%
37.8%
46.6%

Marine Fish
2 600

43.8%
56.2%

Live Poultry
1 200

16.2%   34.4%
49.4%

Fresh Vegetable
1 600

2.2% 32.6%
65.2%

Eggs
600

LEGEND

Railway
Road
Road under Construction
Conduit
City/Town
Airport
Power Plant

REVERSION OF POWER SUPPLY IN 1991

ELECTRICITY TO CHINA
2 540 million kWh

CHINA

COAL TO HONG KONG
1.6 million tonnes
(HK$ 486 million)

HONG
KONG

PASSENGER TRAFFIC

TRANSPORTATION MEANS
for Year 1991

	BY AIR
	BY LAND
	BY SEA

in million persons

in million persons

from CHINA to HONG KONG			Year	from HONG KONG to CHINA		
5.0			1982			4.9
6.0			1983			6.1
8.6			1984			8.6
11.9			1985			11.8
12.9			1986			12.8
15.3			1987			15.2
18.2			1988			18.2
16.7			1989			16.7
18.4			1990			18.4
21.1			1991			21.0

0.9   18.2   2.0

2.4   17.7   0.9

from CHINA to HONG KONG

from HONG KONG to CHINA

8

Series AR/17/IHC Edition 1 1993